GREGORY G. DESS
University of Texas at Dallas

GERRY McNAMARA
Michigan State University

ALAN B. EISNER
Pace University

SEUNG-HYUN (SEAN) LEE
University of Texas at Dallas

ninth edition

STRATEGIC MANAGEMENT

text & cases

Mc
Graw
Hill
Education

STRATEGIC MANAGEMENT: TEXT AND CASES, NINTH EDITION

Published by McGraw-Hill Education, 2 Penn Plaza, New York, NY 10121. Copyright © 2019 by McGraw-Hill Education. All rights reserved. Printed in the United States of America. Previous editions © 2016, 2014, and 2012. No part of this publication may be reproduced or distributed in any form or by any means, or stored in a database or retrieval system, without the prior written consent of McGraw-Hill Education, including, but not limited to, in any network or other electronic storage or transmission, or broadcast for distance learning.

Some ancillaries, including electronic and print components, may not be available to customers outside the United States.

This book is printed on acid-free paper.

4 5 6 7 8 9 LWI 21 20 19

ISBN 978-1-259-81395-5 (bound edition)
MHID 1-259-81395-9 (bound edition)

ISBN 978-1-259-89997-3 (loose-leaf edition)
MHID 1-259-89997-7 (loose-leaf edition)

ISBN 978-1-259-89994-2 (instructor's edition)
MHID 1-259-89994-2 (instructor's edition)

Portfolio Director: *Michael Ablassmeir*
Lead Product Developer: *Kelly Delso*
Product Developer: *Anne Ehrenworth*
Executive Marketing Manager: *Debbie Clare*
Content Project Managers: *Harvey Yep* (Core), *Bruce Gin* (Assessment)
Buyer: *Susan K. Culbertson*
Design: *Matt Diamond*
Content Licensing Specialists: *DeAnna Dausener* (Image and Text)
Cover Image: *©Anatoli Styf/Shutterstock*
Compositor: *SPi Global*

All credits appearing on page or at the end of the book are considered to be an extension of the copyright page.

Library of Congress Cataloging-in-Publication Data

Names: Dess, Gregory G., author. | McNamara, Gerry, author. | Eisner, Alan B., author.
Title: Strategic management : text and cases / Gregory G. Dess, University of
  Texas at Dallas, Gerry McNamara, Michigan State University, Alan B.
  Eisner, Pace University.
Description: Ninth edition. | New York, NY : McGraw-Hill Education, [2019]
Identifiers: LCCN 2017052281 | ISBN 9781259813955 (alk. paper)
Subjects: LCSH: Strategic planning.
Classification: LCC HD30.28 .D4746 2019 | DDC 658.4/012—dc23 LC record available at
https://lccn.loc.gov/2017052281

The Internet addresses listed in the text were accurate at the time of publication. The inclusion of a website does not indicate an endorsement by the authors or McGraw-Hill Education, and McGraw-Hill Education does not guarantee the accuracy of the information presented at these sites.

mheducation.com/highered

dedication

To my family, Margie and Taylor and my parents, the late Bill and Mary Dess; and Michael Wood

—Greg

To my wonderful wife, Gaelen, my children, Megan and AJ; and my parents, Gene and Jane

—Gerry

To my family, Helaine, Rachel, and Jacob

—Alan

To my family, Hannah, Paul and Stephen; and my parents, Kenny and Inkyung.

—Sean

about the
authors

Photo provided by the author

©He Gao

Gregory G. Dess

is the Andrew R. Cecil Endowed Chair in Management at the University of Texas at Dallas. His primary research interests are in strategic management, organization-environment relationships, and knowledge management. He has published numerous articles on these subjects in both academic and practitioner-oriented journals. He also serves on the editorial boards of a wide range of practitioner-oriented and academic journals. In August 2000, he was inducted into the *Academy of Management Journal's* Hall of Fame as one of its charter members. Professor Dess has conducted executive programs in the United States, Europe, Africa, Hong Kong, and Australia. During 1994 he was a Fulbright Scholar in Oporto, Portugal. In 2009, he received an honorary doctorate from the University of Bern (Switzerland). He received his PhD in Business Administration from the University of Washington (Seattle) and a BIE degree from Georgia Tech.

Gerry McNamara

is the Eli Broad Professor of Management at Michigan State University. His research draws on cognitive and behavioral theories to explain strategic phenomena, including strategic decision making, mergers and acquisitions, and environmental assessments. His research has been published in the *Academy of Management Journal,* the *Strategic Management Journal, Organization Science, Organizational Behavior and Human Decision Processes,* the *Journal of Applied Psychology,* the *Journal of Management,* and the *Journal of International Business Studies.* Gerry's research has also been abstracted in the *Wall Street Journal, Harvard Business Review, New York Times, Bloomberg Businessweek,* the *Economist,* and *Financial Week.* He serves as an Associate Editor for the *Strategic Management Journal* and previously served as an Associate Editor for the *Academy of Management Journal.* He received his PhD from the University of Minnesota.

©Alan B. Eisner

Alan B. Eisner

is Professor of Management and Department Chair,
Management and Management Science Department,
at the Lubin School of Business, Pace University.
He received his PhD in management from the Stern
School of Business, New York University. His primary
research interests are in strategic management,
technology management, organizational learning,
and managerial decision making. He has published
research articles and cases in journals such as *Advances
in Strategic Management, International Journal of
Electronic Commerce, International Journal of Technology
Management, American Business Review, Journal of
Behavioral and Applied Management,* and *Journal of the
International Academy for Case Studies.* He is the former
Associate Editor of the Case Association's peer-reviewed
journal, *The CASE Journal.*

©Seung-Hyun Lee

Seung-Hyun Lee

is a Professor of strategic management and international
business and the Area Coordinator of the Organization,
Strategy, and International Management area at the
Jindal School of Business, University of Texas at Dallas.
His primary research interests lie on the intersection
between strategic management and international
business spanning from foreign direct investment to
issues of microfinance and corruption. He has published
in numerous journals including *Academy of Management
Review, Journal of Business Ethics, Journal of International
Business Studies, Journal of Business Venturing, and
Strategic Management Journal.* He received his MBA and
PhD from the Ohio State University.

Welcome to the Ninth Edition of *Strategic Management: Text and Cases!*

As noted on the cover, we are happy to introduce Seung-Hyun Lee to the author team. Greg has known Seung since we both joined the faculty at the University of Texas at Dallas in 2002. Seung has developed a very distinguished publication record in both strategic management and international business/international management and he has made many important contributions in these areas in the present edition. In particular, his international expertise has been particularly valuable in further "globalizing" our book.

We appreciate the constructive and positive feedback that we have received on our work. Here's some of the encouraging feedback we have received from our reviewers:

The Dess book comprehensively covers the fundamentals of strategy and supports concepts with research and managerial insights.

Joshua J. Daspit, Mississippi State University

Very engaging. Students will want to read it and find it hard to put down.

Amy Grescock, University of Michigan, Flint

Very easy for students to understand. Great use of business examples throughout the text.

Debbie Gilliard, Metropolitan State University, Denver

I use *Strategic Management* in a capstone course required of all business majors, and students appreciate the book because it synergizes all their business education into a meaningful and understandable whole. My students enjoy the book's readability and tight organization, as well as the contemporary examples, case studies, discussion questions, and exercises.

William Sannwald, San Diego State University

The Dess book overcomes many of the limitations of the last book I used in many ways: (a) presents content in a very interesting and engrossing manner without compromising the depth and comprehensiveness, (b) inclusion of timely and interesting illustrative examples, and (c) EOC exercises do an excellent job of complementing the chapter content.

Sucheta Nadkami, University of Cambridge

The content is current and my students would find the real-world examples to be extremely interesting. My colleagues would want to know about it and I would make extensive use of the following features: "Learning from Mistakes," "Strategy Spotlights," and "Issues for Debate." I especially like the "Reflecting on Career Implications" feature. Bottom line: the authors do a great job of explaining complex material and at the same time their use of up-to-date examples promotes learning.

Jeffrey Richard Nystrom, University of Colorado at Denver

We always strive to improve our work and we are most appreciative of the extensive and thoughtful feedback that many strategy professionals have graciously given us. We endeavored to incorporate their ideas into the Ninth Edition—and we acknowledge them by name later in the Preface.

We believe we have made valuable improvements throughout our many revised editions of *Strategic Management*. At the same time, we strive to be consistent and "true" to our original overriding objective: a book that satisfies three R's—rigor, relevance, and readable. And we are pleased that we have received feedback (such as the comments on the previous page) that is consistent with what we are trying to accomplish.

What are some of the features in *Strategic Management* that reinforce the 3 R's? First, we build in rigor by drawing on the latest research by management scholars and insights from management consultants to offer a current a current and comprehensive view of strategic issues. We reinforce this rigor with our "Issues for Debate" and "Reflecting on Career Implications. . ." that require students to develop insights on how to address complex issues and understand how strategy concepts can enhance their career success. Second, to enhance relevance, we provide numerous examples from management practice in the text and "Strategy Spotlights" (sidebars). We also increase relevance by relating course topic and examples to current business and societal themes, including environmental sustainability, ethics, globalization, entrepreneurship, and data analytics. Third, we stress readability with an engaging writing style with minimal jargon to ensure an effective learning experience. This is most clearly evident in the conversational presentations of chapter opening "Learning from Mistakes" and chapter ending "Issues for Debate."

Unlike other strategy texts, we provide three separate chapters that address timely topics about which business students should have a solid understanding. These are the role of intellectual assets in value creation (Chapter 4), entrepreneurial strategy and competitive dynamics (Chapter 8), and fostering entrepreneurship in established organizations (Chapter 12). We also provide an excellent and thorough chapter on how to analyze strategic management cases.

In developing *Strategic Management: Text and Cases,* we certainly didn't forget the instructors. As we all know, you have a most challenging (but rewarding) job. We did our best to help you. We provide a variety of supplementary materials that should help you in class preparation and delivery. For example, our chapter notes do not simply summarize the material in the text. Rather (and consistent with the concept of strategy), we ask ourselves: "How can we add value?" Thus, for each chapter, we provide numerous questions to pose to help guide class discussion, at least 12 boxed examples to supplement chapter material, and three detailed "teaching tips" to further engage students. For example, we provide several useful insights on strategic leadership from one of Greg's colleagues, Charles Hazzard (formerly Executive Vice President, Occidental Chemical). Also, we completed the chapter notes—along with the entire test bank—ourselves. That is, unlike many of our rivals, we didn't simply farm the work out to others. Instead, we felt that such efforts help to enhance quality and consistency—as well as demonstrate our personal commitment to provide a top-quality total package to strategy instructors. With the Ninth Edition, we also benefited from valued input by our strategy colleagues to further improve our work.

Let's now address some of the key substantive changes in the Ninth Edition. Then we will cover some of the major features that we have had in previous editions.

WHAT'S NEW? HIGHLIGHTS OF THE NINTH EDITION

We have endeavored to add new material to the chapters that reflects the feedback we have received from our reviewers as well as the challenges today's managers face. Thus, we all invested an extensive amount of time carefully reviewing a wide variety of books, academic and practitioner journals, and the business press.

We also worked hard to develop more concise and tightly written chapters. Based on feedback from some of the reviewers, we have tightened our writing style, tried to eliminate redundant examples, and focused more directly on what we feel is the most important content in each chapter for our audience. The overall result is that we were able to update our material, add valuable new content, and—at the same time—shorten the length of the chapters.

Here are some of the major changes and improvements in the Ninth Edition:

- **Big Data/Data Analysis.** A central theme of the Ninth Edition, it has become a leading and highly visible component of a broader technological phenomena—the emergence of digital technology. Such initiatives have the potential to enable firms to better customize their product and service offerings to customers while more efficiently and fully using the resources of the company. Throughout the text, we provide examples from a wide range of industries and government. This includes discussions of how Coca Cola uses data analytics to produce consistent orange juice, IBM's leveraging of big data to become a healthcare solution firm, Caterpillar's use of data analytics to improve machine reliability and to identify needed service before major machine failures, and Digital Reasoning's efforts to use data analytics to enhance the ability of firms to control employees and avoid illegal and unethical behavior.

- **Greater coverage of international business/international management (IB/IM from new co-author).** As we noted at the beginning of the Preface, we have invited Seung-Hyun Lee, an outstanding IB/IM scholar, to join the author team and we are very pleased that he has accepted! Throughout the book we have included many concepts and examples of IB/IM that reflects the growing role of international operations for a wide range of industries and firms. We discuss how differences in national culture impact the negotiation of contracts and whether or not to adapt human resource practices when organizations cross national boundaries. We also include a discussion of how corporate governance practices differ across countries and discuss in depth how Japan is striving to develop balanced governance practices that incorporate elements of U.S. practices while retaining, at its core, elements of traditional Japanese practices. Additionally, we discuss why conglomerate firms thrive in Asian markets even as this form of organization has gone out of favor in the United States and Europe. Finally, we discuss research that suggests that firms in transition economies can improve their innovative performance by focusing on learning across boundaries within the firm compared to learning from outside partners.

- **"Executive Insights: The Strategic Management Process."** Here, we introduce a nationally recognized leader and explore several key issues related to strategic management. The executive is William H. McRaven, a retired four-star admiral who leads the nation's second largest system of higher education. As chief executive officer of the UT System, he oversees 14 institutions that educate 217,000 students and employ 20,000 faculty and more than 70,000 health care professionals, researchers, and staff. He is perhaps best known for his involvement in Operation Neptune Spear, in which he commanded the U.S. Navy Special Forces who located and killed al Qaeda leader Osama bin Laden. We are very grateful for his valuable contribution!

- **Half of the 12 opening "Learning from Mistakes" vignettes that lead off each chapter are totally new.** Unique to this text, they are all examples of what can go wrong, and they serve as an excellent vehicle for clarifying and reinforcing strategy concepts. After all, what can be learned if one simply admires perfection?

- **Over half of our "Strategy Spotlights" (sidebar examples) are brand new, and many of the others have been thoroughly updated.** Although we have reduced the number of Spotlights from the previous edition to conserve space, we still have a total of 64—by far the most in the strategy market. We focus on bringing the most important strategy concepts to life in a concise and highly readable manner. And we work hard to eliminate unnecessary detail that detracts from the main point we are trying to make. Also, consistent with our previous edition, many of the Spotlights focus on two "hot" issues that are critical in leading today's organizations: ethics and environmental sustainability—as well as data analytics in this edition.

Key content changes for the chapters include:

- **Chapter 1 addresses three challenges for executives who are often faced with similar sets of opposing goals which can polarize their organizations.** These challenges, or paradoxes, are called (1) the innovation paradox, the tension between existing products and new ones—stability and change; (2) the globalization paradox, the tension between global connectedness and local needs; and, (3) the obligation paradox, the tension between maximizing shareholder returns and creating benefits for a wide range of stakeholders—employees, customers, society, etc. We also discuss three theaters of practice that managers need to recognize in order to optimize the positive impact of the corporate social responsibility (CSR) initiatives. These are (1) Focusing on philanthropy, (2) Improving operational effectiveness, and (3) Transforming the business model.

- **Chapter 2 introduces the concept of big data/data analytics—a technology that affects multiple segments of the general environment.** A highly visible component of the digital economy, such technologies are altering the way business is conducted in a wide variety of sectors—government, industry, and commerce. We provide a detailed example of how it has been used to monitor the expenditures of federal, state, and local governments.

- **Chapter 3 includes a discussion on program hiring to build human capital.** With program hiring, firms offer employment to promising graduates without knowing which specific job the employee will fill. Firms employing this tactic believe it allows them to meet changing market conditions by hiring flexible employees who desire a dynamic setting. We also include a discussion of how Coca Cola is leveraging data analytics to produce orange juice that is consistent over time and can be tailored to meet local market tastes.

- **Chapter 4 discusses research that has found that millennials have a different definition of diversity and inclusion than prior generations.** That is, millennials look upon diversity as the blending of different backgrounds, experiences, and perspectives within a team, i.e., cognitive diversity. Earlier generations—the X-Generation and the Boomer Generation—tended to view diversity as a representation of fairness and protection for all regardless of gender, race, religion, etc. An important implication is that while many millennials believe that differences of opinion enable teams to excel, relatively few of them feel that their leaders share this perspective. The chapter also provides a detailed example of how data analytics can increase employee retention.

- **Chapter 5 examines how firms can create strong competitive positions in platform markets.** In platform markets, firms act as intermediaries between buyers and sellers. Success is largely based on the ability of the firm to be the de facto provider of this matching process. We discuss several actions firms can take to stake out a leadership position in these markets. In addition, we include a discussion of research outlining how firms can develop organizational structures and policies to draw on customer interactions to improve their innovativeness. The key finding from this research is that it is critical for firms to empower and incent front line employees to look for and share innovative insights they take away from customer interactions.

- **Chapter 6 includes a section on different forms of strategic alliances and when they are most appropriate.** In discussing the differences between contractual alliances, equity alliances, and joint ventures, students can better understand the range of options they have to build cooperative arrangements with other firms and the factors that influence the choice among these options.

- **Chapter 7 explains two important areas in which culture can play a key role in managing organizations across national boundaries.** First, we discuss situations in which it is best to not adapt one's company culture—even if it conflicts with the culture country in which the firm operates. We provide the example of Google's human resource policy of providing employees with lots of positive feedback during performance reviews. Why? Google feels that this is a key reason for its outstanding success in product innovation. Second, we address some of the challenges that managers encounter when they negotiate contracts across national boundaries. We discuss research that identifies several elements of negotiating behaviors that help to identify cultural differences.

- **Chapter 8 identifies factors investors can examine when evaluating the risk of crowdfunded ventures.** When firms raise funds through crowdfunding, they often have limited business and financial histories and haven't yet built up a clear reputation. This raises the risks investors face. We identify some factors investors can look into to clarify the worthiness and risk of firms who are raising financial resources through crowdfunding.

- **Chapter 9 discusses the increasingly important role that activist investors have in the corporate governance of publicly-traded firms.** Activist investors are investors who take small but significant ownership stakes in large firms, typically 5 to 10 percent ownership, and push for major strategic changes in the firm. These activist investors are often successful, winning 70 percent of the shareholder votes they champion and have forced the exit of leaders of several large firms. Additionally, we discuss a corner of Wall Street where women dominate, as corporate governance heads at major institutional investors. These institutional investors hold large blocks of stock in all major corporations. As a result, these female leaders are in a position to push for governance changes in these corporations to make them more responsive to the concerns of investors, such as increasing opportunities for female corporate leaders.

- **Chapter 10 discusses how firms can organize to improve their innovativeness.** Often managers look to outside partners to learn new skills and access new knowledge to improve their innovative performance. We discuss research that suggests that efforts to look to create novel combinations of knowledge within the firm offer greater potential to generate stronger innovation performance. The key advantage of internal knowledge is that it is proprietary and potentially more applicable to the firm's innovation efforts.

- **Chapter 11 includes discussions of multiple firms that have changed their leadership and control systems to respond to challenges they've faced.** This includes Marvin Ellison's efforts to revive JC Penney after prior bad leadership, Target's efforts to change its supply chain system to meet changing customer demands, and the decision procedures JC Johnson Inc. has put in place to improve its ability to lead its industry in sustainability efforts.

- **Chapter 12 highlights the potential to learn from innovation failures.** Too often, firms become risk averse in their behavior in order to avoid failure. We discuss how this can result in missing truly innovative opportunities. Drawing off research by Julian Birkinshaw, we discuss the need for firms to get their employees to take bold innovation actions and steps firms can take to learn from failed innovation efforts to be more effective in future innovation efforts. We also discuss research on the consequences of losing star innovation employees. Firms worry about the loss of key innovation personnel, but research shows that while there are costs associated with the loss of star innovators, there are also potential benefits. Firms that lose key innovators typically experience a loss in exploitation-oriented innovation, but they also often see an increase in exploration-oriented innovation.

- **Chapter 13 provides an example of how the College of Business Administration at Towson University successfully introduced a "live" business case completion across all of it strategic management sections.** The "description" and the "case completion checklist" includes many of the elements of the analysis-decision-action cycle in case analysis that we address in the chapter.

- **Chapter 13 updates our Appendix: Sources of Company and Industry Information.** Here, we owe a big debt to Ruthie Brock and Carol Byrne, library professionals at the University of Texas at Arlington. These ladies have provided us with comprehensive and updated information for the Ninth Edition that is organized in a range of issues. These include competitive intelligence, annual report collections, company rankings, business websites, and strategic and competitive analysis. Such information is invaluable in analyzing companies and industries. We are always amazed by the diligence, competence—and good cheer—that Ruthie and Carol demonstrate when we impose on them every two years!

- **We have worked hard to further enhance our excellent case package with a major focus on fresh and current cases on familiar firms.**
  - More than half of our cases are author-written (much more than the competition).
  - We have updated our users favorite cases, creating fresh stories about familiar companies to minimize instructor preparation time and "maximize freshness" of he content.
  - We have added several exciting new cases to the lineup including Blackberry and Ascena (the successor company to Ann Talyor).
  - We have also extensively updated 28 familiar cases with the latest news.
  - Our cases are familiar yet fresh with new data and problems to solve.

WHAT REMAINS THE SAME: KEY FEATURES OF EARLIER EDITIONS

Let's now briefly address some of the exciting features that remain from the earlier editions.

- **Traditional organizing framework with three other chapters on timely topics.** Crisply written chapters cover all of the strategy bases and address contemporary topics. First, the chapters are divided logically into the traditional sequence: strategy analysis, strategy formulation, and strategy implementation. Second, we include three chapters on such timely topics as intellectual capital/knowledge management, entrepreneurial strategy and competitive dynamics, and fostering corporate entrepreneurship and new ventures.

- **"Learning from Mistakes" chapter-opening cases.** To enhance student interest, we begin each chapter with a case that depicts an organization that has suffered a dramatic performance drop, or outright failure, by failing to adhere to sound strategic management concepts and principles. We believe that this feature serves to underpin the value of the concepts in the course and that it is a preferred teaching approach to merely providing examples of outstanding companies that always seem to get it right. After all, isn't it better (and more challenging) to diagnose problems than admire perfection? As Dartmouth's Sydney Finkelstein, author of *Why Smart Executives Fail,* notes: "We live in a world where success is revered, and failure is quickly pushed to the side. However, some of the greatest opportunities to learn—for both individuals and organizations—come from studying what goes wrong."* We'll see how, for example, why Frederica Marchionni, the CEO that Land's End hired in 2015, failed to spearhead the revival of the brand. Her initiatives geared toward taking the brand upscale turned out to be too much of a shock to the firm's customer base as well as the firm's family culture and wholesome style. As noted by a former executive, "It doesn't look like Land's End anymore. There was never the implication that if you wore Lands' End you'd be on the beach on Nantucket living the perfect life." We'll also explore the bankruptcy of storied law firm Dewey & LeBoeuf LLP. Their failure can be attributed to three major issues: a reliance on borrowed money, making large promises about compensation to incoming partners (which didn't sit well with their existing partners!), and a lack of transparency about the firm's financials.

- **"Issue for Debate" at the end of each chapter.** We find that students become very engaged (and often animated!) in discussing an issue that has viable alternate points of view. It is an exciting way to drive home key strategy concepts. For example, in Chapter 1, Seventh Generation is faced with a dilemma that confronts their values and they must decide whether or not to provide their products to some of their largest customers. At issue: While they sympathize (and their values are consistent) with the striking workers at the large grocery chains, should they cross the picket lines? In Chapter 4, we discuss an issue that can be quite controversial: Does offering financial incentives to employees to lose weight actually work? We will explain a study by professors and medical professionals who conducted a test to explore this issue. And, in Chapter 7, we address Medtronic's decision to acquire Covidien, an Irish-based medical equipment manufacturer for $43 billion. Its primary motive: Lower its taxes by moving its legal home to Ireland—a country that has lower rates of taxation on corporations. Some critics may see such a move as unethical and unpatriotic. Others would argue that it will help the firm save on taxes and benefit their shareholders.

- **"Insights from Research."** We include six of this feature in the Ninth Edition—and half of them are entirely new. Here, we summarize key research findings on a variety of issues and, more importantly, address their relevance for making organizations (and managers!) more effective. For example, in Chapter 2 we discuss findings from a meta-analysis (research combining many individual studies) to debunk several myths about older workers—a topic of increasing importance, given the changing demographics in many developed countries. In Chapter 4, we address a study that explored the viability of re-hiring employees who had previously left the organizations. Such employees, called "boomerangs" may leave an organization for several reasons and such reasons may strongly influence their willingness to return to the organization. In Chapter 5, we summarize a study that looked at how firms can improve their innovativeness by drawing on interactions with customers but only if the firm empowers front line employees to lead innovative efforts and provides incentives to motivate employees to do so. In Chapter 10, we discuss research on firms in transition economies that found firms which learn from both external partners and by spanning boundaries within the firm can improve their innovation. However, learning between units within the firm produced higher innovation performance.

---

*Personal Communication, June 20, 2005.

- **"Reflecting on Career Implications. . ."** We provide insights that are closely aligned with and directed to three distinct issues faced by our readers: prepare them for a job interview (e.g., industry analysis), help them with current employers or their career in general, or help them find potential employers and decide where to work. We believe this will be very valuable to students' professional development.

- **Consistent chapter format and features to reinforce learning.** We have included several features in each chapter to add value and create an enhanced learning experience. First, each chapter begins with an overview and a list of key learning objectives. Second, as previously noted, the opening case describes a situation in which a company's performance eroded because of a lack of proper application of strategy concepts. Third, at the end of each chapter there are four different types of questions/exercises that should help students assess their understanding and application of material:

    1. Summary review questions.
    2. Experiential exercises.
    3. Application questions and exercises.
    4. Ethics questions.

    Given the centrality of online systems to business today, each chapter contains at least one exercise that allows students to explore the use of the web in implementing a firm's strategy.

- **Key Terms.** Approximately a dozen key terms for each chapter are identified in the margins of the pages. This addition was made in response to reviewer feedback and improves students' understanding of core strategy concepts.

- **Clear articulation and illustration of key concepts.** Key strategy concepts are introduced in a clear and concise manner and are followed by timely and interesting examples from business practice. Such concepts include value-chain analysis, the resource-based view of the firm, Porter's five-forces model, competitive advantage boundaryless organizational designs, digital strategies, corporate governance, ethics, data analytics, and entrepreneurship.

- **Extensive use of sidebars.** We include 64 sidebars (or about five per chapter) called "Strategy Spotlights." The Strategy Spotlights not only illustrate key points but also increase the readability and excitement of new strategy concepts.

- **Integrative themes.** The text provides a solid grounding in ethics, globalization, environmental substainability, and technology. These topics are central themes throughout the book and form the basis for many of the Strategy Spotlights.

- **Implications of concepts for small businesses.** Many of the key concepts are applied to start-up firms and smaller businesses, which is particularly important since many students have professional plans to work in such firms.

- **Not just a textbook but an entire package.** *Strategic Management* features the best chapter teaching notes available today. Rather than merely summarizing the key points in each chapter, we focus on value-added material to enhance the teaching (and learning) experience. Each chapter includes dozens of questions to spur discussion, teaching tips, in-class group exercises, and about a dozen detailed examples from business practice to provide further illustrations of key concepts.

TEACHING RESOURCES

Instructor's Manual (IM)

Prepared by the textbook authors, along with valued input from our strategy colleagues, the accompanying IM contains summary/objectives, lecture/discussion outlines, discussion questions, extra examples not included in the text, teaching tips, reflecting on career implications, experiential exercises, and more.

Test Bank

Revised by Christine Pence of the University of California-Riverside, the test bank contains more than 1,000 true/false, multiple-choice, and essay questions. It is tagged with learning objectives as well as Bloom's Taxonomy and AACSB criteria.

- **Assurance of Learning Ready.** Assurance of Learning is an important element of many accreditation standards. Dess 9e is designed specifically to support your Assurance of Learning initiatives. Each chapter in the book begins with a list of numbered learning objectives that appear throughout the chapter. Every test bank question is also linked to one of these objectives, in addition to level of difficulty, topic area, Bloom's Taxonomy level, and AACSB skill area. *EZ Test,* McGraw-Hill's easy-to-use test bank software, can search the test bank by these and other categories, providing an engine for targeted Assurance of Learning analysis and assessment.

- **AACSB Statement.** The McGraw-Hill Companies is a proud corporate member of AACSB International. Understanding the importance and value of AACSB accreditation, Dess 9e has sought to recognize the curricula guidelines detailed in the AACSB standards for business accreditation by connecting selected questions in Dess 9e and the test bank to the general knowledge and skill guidelines found in the AACSB standards. The statements contained in Dess 9e are provided only as a guide for the users of this text. The AACSB leaves content coverage and assessment within the purview of individual schools, the mission of the school, and the faculty. While Dess 9e and the teaching package make no claim of any specific AACSB qualification or evaluation, we have labeled selected questions within Dess 9e according to the six general knowledge and skills areas.

- **Computerized Test Bank Online.** A comprehensive bank of test questions is provided within a computerized test bank powered by McGraw-Hill's flexible electronic testing program, *EZ Test Online* (www.eztestonline.com). *EZ Test Online* allows you to create paper and online tests or quizzes in this easy-to-use program. Imagine being able to create and access your test or quiz anywhere, at any time, without installing the testing software! Now, with *EZ Test Online,* instructors can select questions from multiple McGraw-Hill test banks or author their own and then either print the test for paper distribution or give it online.

- **Test Creation.**
  - Author/edit questions online using the 14 different question-type templates.
  - Create printed tests or deliver online to get instant scoring and feedback.
  - Create question pools to offer multiple versions online—great for practice.
  - Export your tests for use in *WebCT, Blackboard,* and Apple's *iQuiz.*
  - Compatible with *EZ Test Desktop* tests you've already created.
  - Sharing tests with colleagues, adjuncts, TAs is easy.

- **Online Test Management.**
  - Set availability dates and time limits for your quiz or test.
  - Control how your test will be presented.
  - Assign points by question or question type with drop-down menu.
  - Provide immediate feedback to students or delay until all finish the test.
  - Create practice tests online to enable student mastery.
  - Your roster can be uploaded to enable student self-registration.
- **Online Scoring and Reporting.**
  - Automated scoring for most of *EZ Test's* numerous question types.
  - Allows manual scoring for essay and other open response questions.
  - Manual rescoring and feedback are also available.
  - *EZ Test's* grade book is designed to easily export to your grade book.
  - View basic statistical reports.
- **Support and Help.**
  - User's guide and built-in page-specific help.
  - Flash tutorials for getting started on the support site.
  - Support website: *www.mhhe.com/eztest.*
  - Product specialist available at 1-800-331-5094.
  - Online training: *http://auth.mhhe.com/mpss/workshops/.*

PowerPoint Presentation

Prepared by Pauline Assenza of Western Connecticut State University, it consists of more than 400 slides incorporating an outline for the chapters tied to learning objectives. Also included are instructor notes, multiple-choice questions that can be used as Classroom Performance System (CPS) questions, and additional examples outside the text to promote class discussion.

McGraw-Hill Connect® is a highly reliable, easy-to-use homework and learning management solution that utilizes learning science and award-winning adaptive tools to improve student results.

Homework and Adaptive Learning

- Connect's assignments help students contextualize what they've learned through application, so they can better understand the material and think critically.

- Connect will create a personalized study path customized to individual student needs through SmartBook®.

- SmartBook helps students study more efficiently by delivering an interactive reading experience through adaptive highlighting and review.

Connect's Impact on Retention Rates, Pass Rates, and Average Exam Scores

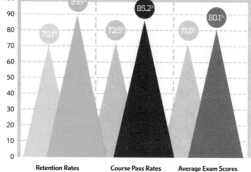

without Connect   with Connect

Over **7 billion questions** have been answered, making McGraw-Hill Education products more intelligent, reliable, and precise.

Using **Connect** improves retention rates by **19.8** percentage points, passing rates by **12.7** percentage points, and exam scores by **9.1** percentage points.

73% of instructors who use **Connect** require it; instructor satisfaction **increases** by 28% when **Connect** is required.

Quality Content and Learning Resources

- Connect content is authored by the world's best subject matter experts, and is available to your class through a simple and intuitive interface.

- The Connect eBook makes it easy for students to access their reading material on smartphones and tablets. They can study on the go and don't need internet access to use the eBook as a reference, with full functionality.

- Multimedia content such as videos, simulations, and games drive student engagement and critical thinking skills.

©McGraw-Hill Education

Robust Analytics and Reporting

©Hero Images/Getty Images

- Connect Insight® generates easy-to-read reports on individual students, the class as a whole, and on specific assignments.
- The Connect Insight dashboard delivers data on performance, study behavior, and effort. Instructors can quickly identify students who struggle and focus on material that the class has yet to master.
- Connect automatically grades assignments and quizzes, providing easy-to-read reports on individual and class performance.

Impact on Final Course Grade Distribution

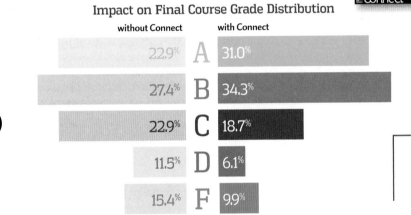

without Connect		with Connect
22.9%	A	31.0%
27.4%	B	34.3%
22.9%	C	18.7%
11.5%	D	6.1%
15.4%	F	9.9%

More students earn **As** and **Bs** when they use **Connect**.

Trusted Service and Support

- Connect integrates with your LMS to provide single sign-on and automatic syncing of grades. Integration with Blackboard®, D2L®, and Canvas also provides automatic syncing of the course calendar and assignment-level linking.
- Connect offers comprehensive service, support, and training throughout every phase of your implementation.
- If you're looking for some guidance on how to use Connect, or want to learn tips and tricks from super users, you can find tutorials as you work. Our Digital Faculty Consultants and Student Ambassadors offer insight into how to achieve the results you want with Connect.

www.mheducation.com/connect

The Business Strategy Game and GLO-BUS Online Simulations

Both allow teams of students to manage companies in a head-to-head contest for global market leadership. These simulations give students the immediate opportunity to experiment with various strategy options and to gain proficiency in applying the concepts and tools they have been reading about in the chapters. To find out more or to register, please visit *www.mhhe.com/thompsonsims.*

ADDITIONAL RESOURCES FOR COURSE DESIGN AND DELIVERY

Create

Craft your teaching resources to match the way you teach! With McGraw-Hill *Create,* *www.mcgrawhillcreate.com,* you can easily rearrange chapters, combine material from other content sources, and quickly upload content you have written, like your course syllabus or teaching notes. Find the content you need in *Create* by searching through thousands of leading McGraw-Hill textbooks. Arrange your book to fit your teaching style. *Create* even allows you to personalize your book's appearance by selecting the cover and adding your name, school, and course information. Order a *Create* book and you'll receive a complimentary print review copy in three to five business days or a complimentary electronic review copy (eComp) via email in about one hour. Go to *www.mcgrawhillcreate.com* today and register. Experience how McGraw-Hill *Create* empowers you to teach *your* students *your* way.

E-Book Options

E-books are an innovative way for students to save money and to "go green." McGraw-Hill's e-books are typically 40 percent of bookstore price. Students have the choice between an online and a downloadable *CourseSmart* e-book.

Through *CourseSmart,* students have the flexibility to access an exact replica of their textbook from any computer that has Internet service, without plug-ins or special software via the version, or create a library of books on their hard drive via the downloadable version. Access to *CourseSmart* e-books is one year.

Features: *CourseSmart* e-books allow students to highlight, take notes, organize notes, and share the notes with other *CourseSmart* users. Students can also search terms across all e-books in their purchased *CourseSmart* library. *CourseSmart* e-books can be printed (5 pages at a time).

More info and purchase: Please visit *www.coursesmart.com* for more information and to purchase access to our e-books. *CourseSmart* allows students to try one chapter of the e-book, free of charge, before purchase.

McGraw-Hill Higher Education and Blackboard

The **Best of Both Worlds**

McGraw-Hill Higher Education and Blackboard have teamed up. What does this mean for you?

1. **Your life, simplified.** Now you and your students can access McGraw-Hill's *Connect* and *Create* right from within your Blackboard course—all with one single sign-on. Say goodbye to the days of logging in to multiple applications.

2. **Deep integration of content and tools.** Not only do you get single sign-on with *Connect* and *Create,* you also get deep integration of McGraw-Hill content and content engines

right in Blackboard. Whether you're choosing a book for your course or building *Connect* assignments, all the tools you need are right where you want them—inside Blackboard.

3. **Seamless gradebooks.** Are you tired of keeping multiple gradebooks and manually synchronizing grades into Blackboard? We thought so. When a student completes an integrated *Connect* assignment, the grade for that assignment automatically (and instantly) feeds into Blackboard grade center.

4. **A solution for everyone.** Whether your institution is already using Blackboard or you just want to try Blackboard on your own, we have a solution for you. McGraw-Hill and Blackboard can now offer you easy access to industry-leading technology and content, whether your campus hosts it or we do. Be sure to ask your local McGraw-Hill representative for details.

McGraw-Hill Customer Care Contact Information

At McGraw-Hill, we understand that getting the most from new technology can be challenging. That's why our services don't stop after you purchase our products. You can email our product specialists 24 hours a day to get product training online. Or you can search our knowledge bank of Frequently Asked Questions on our support website. For customer support, call 800-331-5094, email *hmsupport@mcgraw-hill.com,* or visit *www.mhhe.com/support.* One of our technical support analysts will be able to assist you in a timely fashion.

ACKNOWLEDGMENTS

Strategic Management represents far more than just the joint efforts of the three co-authors. Rather, it is the product of the collaborative input of many people. Some of these individuals are academic colleagues, others are the outstanding team of professionals at McGraw-Hill, and still others are those who are closest to us—our families. It is time to express our sincere gratitude.

First, we'd like to acknowledge the dedicated instructors who have graciously provided their insights since the inception of the text. Their input has been very helpful in both pointing out errors in the manuscript and suggesting areas that needed further development as additional topics. We sincerely believe that the incorporation of their ideas has been critical to improving the final product. These professionals and their affiliations are:

The Reviewer Hall of Fame

Moses Acquaah,
University of North Carolina-Greensboro

Todd Alessandri,
Northeastern University

Larry Alexander,
Virginia Polytechnic Institute

Thomas H. Allison,
Washington State University

Brent B. Allred,
College of William & Mary

Allen C. Amason,
Georgia Southern University

Kathy Anders,
Arizona State University

Jonathan Anderson,
University of West Georgia

Peter H. Antoniou,
California State University-San Marcos

Dave Arnott,
Dallas Baptist University

Marne L. Arthaud-Day,
Kansas State University

Dr. Bindu Arya,
University of Missouri– St. Louis

Jay A. Azriel,
York College of Pennsylvania

Jeffrey J. Bailey,
University of Idaho

David L. Baker, PhD,
John Carroll University

Dennis R. Balch,
University of North Alabama

Bruce Barringer,
University of Central Florida

Barbara R. Bartkus,
Old Dominion University

Barry Bayon,
Bryant University

Brent D. Beal,
Louisiana State University

Dr. Patricia Beckenholdt,
Business and Professional Programs, University of Maryland, University College

Joyce Beggs,
University of North Carolina-Charlotte

Michael Behnam,
Suffolk University

Kristen Bell DeTienne,
Brigham Young University

Eldon Bernstein,
Lynn University

Lyda Bigelow,
University of Utah

David Blair,
University of Nebraska at Omaha

Daniela Blettner,
Tilburg University

Dusty Bodie,
Boise State University

William Bogner,
Georgia State University

David S. Boss, PhD,
Ohio University

Scott Browne,
Chapman University

Jon Bryan,
Bridgewater State College

Charles M. Byles,
Virginia Commonwealth University

Mikelle A. Calhoun,
Valparaiso University

Thomas J. Callahan,
University of Michigan-Dearborn

Samuel D. Cappel,
Southeastern Louisiana State University

Gary Carini,
Baylor University

Shawn M. Carraher,
University of Texas-Dallas

Tim Carroll,
University of South Carolina

Don Caruth,
Amberton University

Maureen Casile,
Bowling Green State University

Gary J. Castrogiovanni,
Florida Atlantic University

Radha Chaganti,
Rider University

Erick PC Chang,
Arkansas State University

Tuhin Chaturvedi,
Joseph M. Katz Graduate School of Business, University of Pittsburgh

Jianhong Chen,
University of New Hampshire

Tianxu Chen,
Oakland University

Andy Y. Chiou,
SUNY Farmingdale State College

Theresa Cho,
Rutgers University

Timothy S. Clark,
Northern Arizona University

Bruce Clemens,
Western New England College

Betty S. Coffey,
Appalachian State University

Wade Coggins,
Webster University-Fort Smith Metro Campus

Susan Cohen,
University of Pittsburgh

George S. Cole,
Shippensburg University

Joseph Coombs,
Virginia Commonwealth University

Christine Cope Pence,
University of California-Riverside

James J. Cordeiro,
SUNY Brockport

Stephen E. Courter,
University of Texas at Austin

Jeffrey Covin,
Indiana University

Keith Credo,
Auburn University

Joshua J. Daspit, PhD,
Mississippi State University

Deepak Datta,
University of Texas at Arlington

James Davis,
Utah State University

Justin L. Davis,
University of West Florida

David Dawley,
West Virginia University

Daniel DeGravel,
California State University Northridge, David Nazarian College of Business and Economics

Helen Deresky,
State University of New York-Plattsburgh

Rocki-Lee DeWitt,
University of Vermont

Jay Dial,
Ohio State University

Michael E. Dobbs,
Arkansas State University

Jonathan Doh,
Villanova University

Dr. John Donnellan,
NJCU School of Business

Tom Douglas,
Clemson University

Jon Down,
Oregon State University

Meredith Downes,
Illinois State University

Alan E. Ellstrand,
University of Arkansas

Dean S. Elmuti,
Eastern Illinois University

Clare Engle,
Concordia University

Mehmet Erdem Genc,
Baruch College, CUNY

Tracy Ethridge,
Tri-County Technical College

William A. Evans,
Troy State University-Dothan

Frances H. Fabian,
University of Memphis

Angelo Fanelli,
Warrington College of Business

Michael Fathi,
Georgia Southwestern University

Carolyn J. Fausnaugh,
Florida Institute of Technology

Tamela D. Ferguson,
University of Louisiana at Lafayette

David Flanagan,
Western Michigan University

Kelly Flis,
The Art Institutes

Karen Ford-Eickhoff,
University of North Carolina Charlotte

Dave Foster,
Montana State University

Isaac Fox,
University of Minnesota

Charla S. Fraley,
Columbus State Community College-Columbus, Ohio

Deborah Francis,
Brevard College

Steven A. Frankforter,
Winthrop University

Vance Fried,
Oklahoma State University

Karen Froelich,
North Dakota State University

Naomi A. Gardberg,
Baruch College, CUNY

Joe Gerard,
Western New England University

J. Michael Geringer,
Ohio University

Diana L. Gilbertson,
California State University-Fresno

Matt Gilley,
St. Mary's University

Debbie Gilliard,
Metropolitan State College-Denver

Yezdi H. Godiwalla,
University of Wisconsin-Whitewater

Sanjay Goel,
University of Minnesota-Duluth

Sandy Gough,
Boise State University

Amy Gresock, PhD
The University of Michigan, Flint

Vishal K. Gupta,
The University of Mississippi

Dr. Susan Hansen,
University of Wisconsin-Platteville

Allen Harmon,
University of Minnesota-Duluth

Niran Harrison,
University of Oregon

Paula Harveston,
Berry College

Ahmad Hassan,
Morehead State University

Donald Hatfield,
Virginia Polytechnic Institute

Kim Hester,
Arkansas State University

Scott Hicks,
Liberty University

John Hironaka,
California State University-Sacramento

Anne Kelly Hoel,
University of Wisconsin-Stout

Alan Hoffman,
Bentley College

Gordon Holbein,
University of Kentucky

Stephen V. Horner,
Pittsburg State University

Jill Hough,
University of Tulsa

John Humphreys,
Eastern New Mexico University

James G. Ibe,
Morris College

Jay J. Janney,
University of Dayton

Lawrence Jauch,
University of Louisiana-Monroe

Dana M. Johnson,
Michigan Technical University

Homer Johnson,
Loyola University, Chicago

Marilyn R. Kaplan,
Naveen Jindal School of Management, University of Texas-Dallas

James Katzenstein,
California State University-Dominguez Hills

Joseph Kavanaugh,
Sam Houston State University

Franz Kellermanns,
University of Tennessee

Craig Kelley,
California State University-Sacramento

Donna Kelley,
Babson College

Dave Ketchen,
Auburn University

John A. Kilpatrick,
Idaho State University

Dr. Jaemin Kim,
Stockton University

Brent H. Kinghorn,
Emporia State University

Helaine J. Korn,
Baruch College, CUNY

Stan Kowalczyk,
San Francisco State University

Daniel Kraska,
North Central State College

Donald E. Kreps,
Kutztown University

Jim Kroeger,
Cleveland State University

Subdoh P. Kulkarni,
Howard University

Ron Lambert,
Faulkner University

Theresa Lant,
New York University

Jai Joon Lee,
California State University Sacramento

Ted Legatski,
Texas Christian University

David J. Lemak,
Washington State University-Tri-Cities

Cynthia Lengnick-Hall,
University of Texas at San Antonio

Donald L. Lester,
Arkansas State University

Wanda Lester,
North Carolina A&T State University

Krista B. Lewellyn,
University of Wyoming

Benyamin Lichtenstein,
University of Massachusetts at Boston

Jun Lin,
SUNY at New Paltz

Zhiang (John) Lin,
University of Texas at Dallas

Dan Lockhart,
University of Kentucky

John Logan,
University of South Carolina

Franz T. Lohrke,
Samford University

Kevin B. Lowe,
Graduate School of Management, University of Auckland

Leyland M. Lucas,
Morgan State University

Doug Lyon,
Fort Lewis College

Rickey Madden, PhD,
Presbyterian College

James Maddox,
Friends University

Ravi Madhavan,
University of Pittsburgh

Paul Mallette,
Colorado State University

Santo D. Marabella,
Moravian College

Catherine Maritan,
Syracuse University

Daniel Marrone,
Farmingdale State College, SUNY

Sarah Marsh,
Northern Illinois University

Jim Martin,
Washburn University

John R. Massaua,
University of Southern Maine

Hao Ma,
Bryant College

Larry McDaniel,
Alabama A&M University

Jean McGuire,
Louisiana State University

Abagail McWilliams,
University of Illinois-Chicago

Ofer Meilich,
California State University-San Marcos

John E. Merchant,
California State University-Sacramento

John M. Mezias,
University of Miami

Michael Michalisin,
Southern Illinois University at Carbondale

Doug Moesel,
University of Missouri-Columbia

Fatma Mohamed,
Morehead State University

Mike Montalbano,
Bentley University

Debra Moody,
University of North Carolina-Charlotte

Gregory A. Moore,
Middle Tennessee State University

James R. Morgan,
Dominican University and UC Berkeley Extension

Ken Morlino,
Wilmington University

Sara A. Morris,
Old Dominion University

Todd W. Moss, PhD,
Syracuse University

Carolyn Mu,
Baylor University

Stephen Mueller,
Northern Kentucky University

John Mullane,
Middle Tennessee State University

Chandran Mylvaganam,
Northwood University

Sucheta Nadkarni,
Cambridge University

Anil Nair,
Old Dominion University

V.K. Narayanan,
Drexel University

Maria L. Nathan,
Lynchburg College

Louise Nemanich,
Arizona State University

Charles Newman,
University of Maryland, University College

Stephanie Newport,
Austin Peay State University

Gerry Nkombo Muuka,
Murray State University

Bill Norton,
University of Louisville

Dr. Jill E. Novak
Texas A&M University

Roman Nowacki,
Northern Illinois University

Yusuf A. Nur,
SUNY Brockport

Jeffrey Richard Nystrom,
University of Colorado-Denver

William Ross O'Brien,
Dallas Baptist University

d.t. ogilvie,
Rutgers University

Floyd Ormsbee,
Clarkson University

Dr. Mine Ozer,
SUNY-Oneonta

Dr. Eren Ozgen,
Troy University-Dothan Campus

Karen L. Page,
University of Wyoming

Jacquelyn W. Palmer,
University of Cincinnati

Julie Palmer,
University of Missouri-Columbia

Daewoo Park,
Xavier University

Gerald Parker,
Saint Louis University

Ralph Parrish,
University of Central Oklahoma

Amy Patrick,
Wilmington University

John Pepper,
The University of Kansas

Douglas K. Peterson,
Indiana State University

Edward Petkus,
Mary Baldwin College

Michael C. Pickett,
National University

Peter Ping Li,
California State University-Stanislaus

Michael W. Pitts,
Virginia Commonwealth University

Laura Poppo,
Virginia Tech

Steve Porth,
Saint Joseph's University

Jodi A. Potter,
Robert Morris University

Scott A. Quatro,
Grand Canyon University

Nandini Rajagopalan,
University of Southern California

Annette L. Ranft,
North Carolina State University

Abdul Rasheed,
University of Texas at Arlington

Devaki Rau,
Northern Illinois University

George Redmond,
Franklin University

Kira Reed,
Syracuse University

Clint Relyea,
Arkansas State University

Barbara Ribbens,
Western Illinois University

Maurice Rice,
University of Washington

Violina P. Rindova,
University of Texas–Austin

Ron Rivas,
Canisius College

David Robinson,
Indiana State University–Terre Haute

Kenneth Robinson,
Kennesaw State University

Simon Rodan,
San Jose State University

Patrick R. Rogers,
North Carolina A&T State University

John K. Ross III,
Texas State University–San Marcos

Robert Rottman,
Kentucky State University

Matthew R. Rutherford,
Gonzaga University

Carol M. Sanchez,
Grand Valley State University

Doug Sanford,
Towson University

William W. Sannwald,
San Diego State University

Yolanda Sarason,
Colorado State University

Marguerite Schneider,
New Jersey Institute of Technology

Roger R. Schnorbus,
University of Richmond

Terry Sebora,
University of Nebraska-Lincoln

John Seeger,
Bentley College

Jamal Shamsie,
Michigan State University

Mark Shanley,
University of Illinois at Chicago

Ali Shahzad,
James Madison University

Lois Shelton,
California State University-Northridge

Herbert Sherman,
Long Island University

Weilei Shi,
Baruch College, CUNY

Chris Shook,
Auburn University

Jeremy Short,
University of Oklahoma

Mark Simon,
Oakland University-Michigan

Rob Singh,
Morgan State University

Bruce Skaggs,
University of Massachusetts

Lise Anne D. Slattern,
University of Louisiana at Lafayette

Wayne Smeltz,
Rider University

Anne Smith,
University of Tennessee

Andrew Spicer,
University of South Carolina

James D. Spina,
University of Maryland

John Stanbury,
George Mason University & Inter-University Institute of Macau, SAR China

Timothy Stearns,
California State University-Fresno

Elton Stephen,
Austin State University

Charles E. Stevens,
University of Wyoming

Alice Stewart,
Ohio State University

Mohan Subramaniam,
Carroll School of Management Boston College

Ram Subramanian,
Grand Valley State University

Roy Suddaby,
University of Iowa

Michael Sullivan,
UC Berkeley Extension

Marta Szabo White,
Georgia State University

Stephen Takach,
University of Texas at San Antonio

Justin Tan,
York University, Canada

Qingjiu Tao, PhD,
James Madison University

Renata A. Tarasievich,
University of Illinois at Chicago

Linda Teagarden,
Virginia Tech

Bing-Sheng Teng,
George Washington University

Alan Theriault,
*University of
California-Riverside*

Tracy Thompson,
*University of
Washington-Tacoma*

Karen Torres,
Angelo State University

Mary Trottier,
*Associate Professor of
Management, Nichols College*

Robert Trumble,
*Virginia Commonwealth
University*

Francis D. (Doug) Tuggle,
Chapman University

K.J. Tullis,
*University of Central
Oklahoma*

Craig A. Turner, PhD,
*East Tennessee State
University*

Beverly Tyler,
*North Carolina State
University*

Rajaram Veliyath,
Kennesaw State University

S. Stephen Vitucci,
*Tarleton State University-
Central Texas*

Jay A. Vora,
St. Cloud State University

Valerie Wallingford, *Ph.D.,*
Bemidji State University

Jorge Walter,
Portland State University

Bruce Walters,
Louisiana Tech University

Edward Ward,
St. Cloud State University

N. Wasilewski,
Pepperdine University

Andrew Watson,
Northeastern University

Larry Watts,
Stephen F. Austin University

Marlene E. Weaver,
*American Public University
System*

Paula S. Weber,
St. Cloud State University

Kenneth E. A. Wendeln,
Indiana University

Robert R. Wharton,
Western Kentucky University

Laura Whitcomb,
*California State University-Los
Angeles*

Scott Williams,
Wright State University

Ross A. Wirth,
Franklin University

Gary Wishniewsky,
*California State University
East Bay*

Diana Wong,
Bowling Green State University

Beth Woodard,
Belmont University

John E. Wroblewski,
*State University of New
York-Fredonia*

Anne York,
*University of Nebraska-
Omaha*

Michael Zhang,
Sacred Heart University

Monica Zimmerman,
Temple University

Second, we would like to thank the people who have made our two important "features" possible. The information found in our six "Insights from Research" was provided courtesy of www.businessminded.com, an organization founded by K. Matthew Gilley, PhD (St. Mary's University) that transforms empirical management research into actionable insights for business leaders. We appreciate Matt's graciousness and kindness in helping us out. And, of course, our "Executive Insights: The Strategic Management Process" would not have been possible without the gracious participation of Admiral William H. McRaven, Retired who is presently Chancellor of the University of Texas System, and Jana Pankratz, Executive Director.

Third, the authors would like to thank several faculty colleagues who were particularly helpful in the review, critique, and development of the book and supplementary materials. Greg's and Sean's colleagues at the University of Texas at Dallas also have been helpful and supportive. These individuals include Mike Peng, Joe Picken, Kumar Nair, John Lin, Larry

Chasteen, Tev Dalgic, and Livia Markoczy. His administrative assistant, Shalonda Hill, has been extremely helpful. Four doctoral students, Brian Pinkham, Steve Sauerwald, Kyun Kim, and Canan Mutlu, have provided many useful inputs and ideas. He also appreciates the support of his dean and associate dean, Hasan Pirkul and Varghese Jacob, respectively. Greg wishes to thank a special colleague, Abdul Rasheed at the University of Texas at Arlington, who certainly has been a valued source of friendship and ideas for us for many years. He provided many valuable contributions to the Ninth Edition. Gerry thanks all of his colleagues at Michigan State University for their help and support over the years. He also thanks his mentor, Phil Bromiley, as well as the students and former students he has had the pleasure of working with, including Cindy Devers, Federico Aime, Mike Mannor, Bernadine Dykes, Mathias Arrfelt, Kalin Kolev, Seungho Choi, Danny Gamache, and Adam Steinbach. Alan thanks his colleagues at Pace University and the Case Association for their support in developing these fine case selections. Special thanks go to Jamal Shamsie at Michigan State University for his support in developing the case selections for this edition.

Fourth, we would like to thank the team at McGraw-Hill for their outstanding support throughout the entire process. As we work on the book through the various editions, we always appreciate their hard work and recognize how so many people "add value" to our final package. This began with John Biernat, formerly publisher, who signed us to our original contract. He was always available to us and provided a great deal of support and valued input throughout several editions. Presently, in editorial, Susan Gouijnstook, managing director, director Mike Ablassmeir, senior product developers Anne Ehrenworth and Katharine Glynn (of Piper Editorial) kept things on track, responded quickly to our seemingly endless needs and requests, and offered insights and encouragement. We appreciate their expertise—as well as their patience! Once the manuscript was completed and revised, content project manager Harvey Yep expertly guided it through the content and assessment production process. Matt Diamond provided excellent design and artwork guidance. We also appreciate executive marketing manager Debbie Clare and marketing coordinator Brittany Berholdt for their energetic, competent, and thorough marketing efforts. Last, but certainly not least, we thank MHE's 70-plus outstanding book reps—who serve on the "front lines"—as well as many in-house sales professionals based in Dubuque, Iowa. Clearly, they deserve a lot of credit (even though not mentioned by name) for our success.

Fifth, we acknowledge the valuable contributions of many of our strategy colleagues for their excellent contributions to our supplementary and digital materials. Such content really adds a lot of value to our entire package! We are grateful to Pauline Assenza at Western Connecticut State University for her superb work on case teaching notes as well as chapter and case PowerPoints. Justin Davis, University of West Florida, along with Noushi Rahman, Pace University, deserve our thanks for their hard work in developing excellent digital materials for *Connect*. Thanks also goes to Noushi Rahman for developing the Connect IM that accompanies this edition of the text. And, finally, we thank Christine Pence, University of California-Riverside, for her important contributions in revising our test bank and chapter quizzes, and Todd Moss, Oregon State University, for his hard work in putting together an excellent set of videos online, along with the video grid that links videos to chapter material.

Finally, we would like to thank our families. For Greg this includes his parents, William and Mary Dess, who have always been there for him. His wife, Margie, and daughter, Taylor, have been a constant source of love and companionship. His father, a career U. S. Air Force pilot took his "final flight" on May 22, 2015. Truly a member of Tom Brokaw's "Greatest Generation," he completed flight school before his 21st birthday and flew nearly 30 missions over Japan in World War II as a B-29 bomber pilot before he turned 23. His wife, five children, and several grandchildren truly miss him. Gerry thanks his wife, Gaelen, for her love, support, and friendship; and his children, Megan and AJ, for their love and the joy they bring to his life. He also thanks his current and former PhD students who regularly inspire and challenge him. Alan thanks his family—his wife, Helaine, and his children, Rachel and Jacob—for their love and support. He also thanks his parents, Gail Eisner and the late Marvin Eisner, for their support and encouragement. Sean thanks his wife, Hannah, and his two boys, Paul and Stephen, for their unceasing love and care. He also thanks his parents, Kenny and Inkyung Lee for being there whenever needed.

a guided tour

Strategic Management
Creating Competitive Advantages

After reading this chapter, you should have a good understanding of the following learning objectives:

LO1-1 The definition of strategic management and its four key attributes.

LO1-2 The strategic management process and its three interrelated and principal activities.

LO1-3 The vital role of corporate governance and stakeholder management, as well as how "symbiosis" can be achieved among an organization's stakeholders.

LO1-4 The importance of social responsibility, including environmental sustainability, and how it can enhance a corporation's innovation strategy.

LO1-5 The need for greater empowerment throughout the organization.

LO1-6 How an awareness of a hierarchy of strategic goals can help an organization achieve coherence in its strategic direction.

©Anatoli Styf/Getty Images

LEARNING OBJECTIVES

Learning Objectives numbered LO5.1, LO5.2, LO5.3, etc., with corresponding icons in the margins to indicate where learning objectives are covered in the text.

LEARNING FROM MISTAKES

What makes the study of strategic management so interesting? Things can change so rapidly! Some start-ups can disrupt industries and become globally recognized names in just a few years. The rankings of the world's most valuable firms can dramatically change in a rather brief period of time. On the other hand, many impressive, high-flying firms can struggle to reclaim past glory or even fail. Recall just four that begin with the letter "b"—Blackberry, Blockbuster, Borders, and Barings. As colorfully (and ironically!) noted by Arthur Martinez, Sears's former Chairman: "Today's peacock is tomorrow's feather duster."[1]

Consider the following:[2]

- At the beginning of 2007, the three firms in the world with the highest market values were Exxon Mobil, General Electric, and Gazprom (a Russian natural gas firm). By early 2017, three high tech firms headed the list—Apple, Alphabet (parent of Google), and Microsoft.
- Only 74 of the original 500 companies in the S&P index were still around 40 years later. And McKinsey notes that the average company tenure on the S&P 500 list has fallen from 61 years in 1958 to about 20 in 2016.
- With the dramatic increase of the digital economy, new entrants are shaking up long-standing industries. Note that Alibaba is the world's most valuable retailer—but holds no inventory; Airbnb is the world's largest provider of accommodations—but owns no real estate; and Uber is the world's largest car service but owns no cars.
- A quarter century ago, how many would have predicted that a South Korean firm would be a global car giant, than an Indian firm would be one of the world's largest technology firms, and a huge Chinese Internet company would list on an American stock exchange?
- *Fortune* magazine's annual list of the 500 biggest companies now features 156 emerging-market firms. This compares with only 18 in 1995!

To remain competitive, companies often must bring in "new blood" and make significant changes in their strategies. But sometimes a new CEO's initiatives makes things worse. Let's take a look at Lands' End, an American clothing retailer.[3]

Lands' End was founded in 1963 as a mail order supplier of sailboat equipment by Gary Comer. As business picked up, he expanded the business into clothing and home furnishings and moved the company to Dodgeville, Wisconsin, in 1978 where he was its CEO until he stepped down in 1990. The firm was acquired by Sears in 2002, but later spun off in 2013. A year later it commenced trading on the NASDAQ stock exchange.

Targeting Middle America, companies like Lands' End, the GAP Inc., and J. C. Penney have had a hard time in recent years positioning themselves in the hotly contested clothing industry. They are squeezed on the high end by brands like Michael Kors Holdings Ltd. and Coach, Inc. On the lower end, fast-fashion retailers including H&M operator Hennes & Mauritz AB are applying pressure by

LEARNING FROM MISTAKES

Learning from Mistakes vignettes are examples of where things went wrong. Failures are not only interesting but also sometimes easier to learn from. And students realize strategy is notjustabout "right or wrong" answers, but requires critical thinking.

4.3 STRATEGY SPOTLIGHT

MILLENNIALS HAVE A DIFFERENT DEFINITION OF DIVERSITY AND INCLUSION THAN PRIOR GENERATIONS

A recent study by Deloitte and the Billie Jean King Leadership Initiative (BJKLI) shows that, in general, Millennials see the concepts of diversity and inclusion through a vastly different lens. The study analyzed the responses of 3,726 individuals who came from a wide variety of backgrounds with representation across gender, race/ethnicity, sexual orientation, national status, veteran status, disabilities, level within an organization, and tenure with an organization. The respondents were asked 62 questions about diversity and inclusion and the findings demonstrated a snapshot of shifting generational mindsets.

Millennials (born between 1977 to 1995) look upon diversity as the blending of different backgrounds, experiences, and perspectives within a team—which is known as cognitive diversity. They use this word to describe the mix of unique traits that help to overcome challenges and attain business objectives. For Millennials, inclusion is the support for a collaborative environ-

These generations view diversity as a representation of fairness and protection for all—regardless of gender, race, religion, ethnicity, or sexual orientation. Here, inclusion is the integration of individuals of all demographics into one workplace. It is the right thing to do, that is, a moral and legal imperative to achieve compliance and equality—regardless of whether it benefits the business. The study found that when asked about the business impact on diversity, Millennials are 71 percent more likely to focus on teamwork. In contrast, 28 percent of non-Millennials are more likely to focus on fairness of opportunity.

The study's authors contend that the disconnect between the traditional definitions of diversity and inclusion and those of Millennials can create problems for businesses. For example, clashes may occur when managers do not permit Millennials to express themselves freely. The study found that while 86 percent of Millennials feel that differences of opinion allow teams to excel, only 59 percent believe that their leaders share this perspective.

The study suggests that a company with an inclusive culture promotes innovation. And it cites research by IBM and Morgan Stanley that shows that companies with high levels of innovation

STRATEGY SPOTLIGHT

These boxes weave themes of ethics, globalization, and technology into every chapter of the text, providing students with a thorough grounding necessary for understanding strategic management. Select boxes incorporate crowdsourcing, environmental sustainability, and ethical themes.

11.2 STRATEGY SPOTLIGHT | ENVIRONMENTAL SUSTAINABILITY, ETHICS

FAMILY LEADERSHIP SUSTAINS THE CULTURE OF SC JOHNSON

SC Johnson, the maker of Windex, Ziploc bags, and Glade Air Fresheners, is known as one of the most environmentally conscious consumer products companies. The family-owned company is run by Fisk Johnson, the fifth generation of the family to serve as firm CEO. It is the 35th largest privately owned firm, with 13,000 employees and nearly $10 billion in sales. Over the decades, the firm has built and reinforced its reputation for environmental consciousness. Being privately owned by the Johnson family is part of it. Fisk Johnson put it this way, "Wall Street rewards that short-termism. . . . We are in a very fortunate situation to not have to worry about those things, and we're very fortunate that we have a family that is principled and has been very principled."

Fisk uses the benefits of dedicated family ownership to work in both substantive and symbolic ways. On the substantive side, he has implemented systems in place to improve its environmental performance. For example, with its Greenlist process, the firm rates the ingredients it uses or is considering using. It then rates each ingredient on several criteria, including biodegradability and human toxicity, and gives the ingredient a score rang-

3 (better or best) from about 20 percent to over 50 percent from 2001 to 2016.

Fisk uses stories from decisions in the past as it acts to sustain its culture of environmental consciousness. In using stories to reinforce the environmental focus within the firm and to explain it to external stakeholders, Fisk Johnson draws on stories relating to decisions his father made as well as ones he's made. Most prominently, he uses a story about a decision his father made to stop using chlorofluorocarbons in the firm's aerosol products. "Our first decision to unilaterally remove a major chemical occurred in 1975, when research began suggesting that chlorofluorocarbons (CFCs) in aerosols might harm Earth's ozone layer. My father was CEO at the time, and he decided to ban them from all the company's aerosol products worldwide. He did so several years before the government played catch-up and banned the use of CFCs from everyone's products." He goes on to say, "You look back on that decision today, in light of the strong laws that came in, and that was a very prescient decision." This story is especially effective since it highlights his father's willingness and ability to take actions that can lead both the government and industry rivals to change. A second story outlines the firm's decision to remove

INSIGHTS

The "Insights" feature is new to this edition. "Insights from Executives" spotlight interviews with executives from worldwide organizations about current issues salient to strategic management. "Insights from Research" summarize key research findings relevant to maintaining the effectiveness of an organization and its management.

1.1 INSIGHTS from executives

THE STRATEGIC MANAGEMENT PROCESS

Admiral William H. McRaven, Retired
Chancellor, University of Texas System

BIOSKETCH

University of Texas Chancellor William H. McRaven, a retired four-star admiral, leads the nation's second largest system of higher education. As chief executive officer of the UT System since January 2015, he oversees 14 institutions that educate 217,000 students and employ 20,000 faculty and more than 70,000 health care professionals, researchers, and staff.

Prior to becoming chancellor, McRaven, a Navy SEAL, was the commander of U.S. Special Operations Command during which time he led a force of 69,000 men and women and was responsible for conducting counter-terrorism operations worldwide. McRaven is also a recognized national authority on U.S. foreign policy and has advised presidents George W. Bush and Barack Obama and other U.S. leaders on defense issues. His acclaimed book, *Spec. Ops: Case Studies in Special Operations Warfare: Theory and Practice,*

SEAL—helps young people move past self-imposed limits of physical and mental endurance and build confidence in themselves to lead others. The result is a person who is capable of leading in an environment of constant stress, chaos, failure and hardships. In fact, to me, basic SEAL training age stereotypes a lifetime sampling of micro-challenges I would later face while leading people and organizations all crammed into six months.

Question 2. In leading Neptune Spear, what were the key leadership decisions you made to build an organization to accomplish this task?

The majority of the key leadership decisions that in past enabled us to accomplish this task began before I took command of the organization—but as a member of the organization and its number 2 leader over a period of years, I had been an engaged student in the trial, error, and the ultimate development of what my old boss, General Stan McChrystal, called a "team of teams." You see, our operational environment was changing at an incredibly rapid pace. Unlike any time in our history the rate of change was—and is—no longer

2.1 INSIGHTS from Research

NEW TRICKS: RESEARCH DEBUNKS MYTHS ABOUT OLDER WORKERS

Overview

People often think that older workers are less motivated and less healthy, resist change and are less trusting, and have more trouble balancing work and family. It turns out these assumptions just aren't true. By challenging these stereotypes in your organization, you can keep your employees working.

What the Research Shows

In a 2012 paper published by *Personnel Psychology,* researchers from the University of Hong Kong and the University of Georgia examined 418 studies of workers' ages and stereotypes. A meta-analysis—a study of studies—was conducted to find out if any of the six following stereotypes about older workers—as compared with younger workers—was actually true:

- They are less motivated.
- They are less willing to participate in training and career development.
- They are more resistant to change.
- They are less trusting.
- They are less healthy.
- They are more vulnerable to work-family imbalance.

retain, and encourage mature employees' continued involvement in workplaces because they have much to offer in the ways of wisdom, experience, and institutional knowledge. The alternative is to miss out on a growing pool of valuable human capital.

How can you deal with age stereotypes to keep older workers engaged? The authors suggest three effective ways:

- Provide more opportunities for younger and older workers to work together.
- Promote positive attributes of older workers, like experience, carefulness, and punctuality.
- Engage employees in open discussions about stereotypes.

Adam Bradshaw of the DeGarmo Group Inc. has summarized research on addressing age stereotypes in the workplace and offers practical advice. For instance, make sure hiring practices identify factors important to the job other than age. Managers can be trained in how to spot age stereotypes and can point out to employees why the stereotypes are often untrue by using examples of effective older workers. Realize that older workers can offer a competitive advantage because of skills they possess that competitors

---

operate mostly on a cash basis, hence a very short collection period. Semiconductor manufacturers sell their output to other manufacturers (e.g., computer makers) on terms such as 2/15 net 45, which means they give a 2 percent discount on bills paid within 15 days and start charging interest after 45 days. Skilled-nursing facilities also have a longer collection period than grocery stores because they typically rely on payments from insurance companies.

The industry norms for return on sales also highlight differences among these industries. Grocers, with very slim margins, have a lower return on sales than either skilled-nursing facilities or semiconductor manufacturers. But how might we explain the differences between

EXHIBIT 3.10
How Financial Ratios Differ across Industries

Financial Ratio	Semiconductors	Grocery Stores	Skilled-Nursing Facilities
Quick ratio (times)	1.9	0.6	1.3
Current ratio (times)	3.6	1.7	1.7
Total liabilities to net worth (%)	35.1	72.7	82.5
Collection period (days)	48.6	3.3	36.5
Assets to sales (%)	131.7	22.1	58.3
Return on sales (%)	24	1.1	3.1

Source: Dun & Bradstreet. *Industry Norms and Key Business Ratios, 2010–2011.* One Year Edition, SIC #3600–3699 (Semiconductors); SIC #5400–5499 (Grocery Stores); SIC #8000–8099 (Skilled-Nursing Facilities). New York: Dun & Bradstreet Credit Services.

EXHIBITS

Both new and improved exhibits in every chapter provide visual presentations of the most complex concepts covered to support student comprehension.

REFLECTING ON CAREER IMPLICATIONS

This section before the summary of every chapter consists of examples on how understanding of key concepts helps business students early in their careers.

Reflecting on Career Implications . . .

This chapter discusses both the long-term focus of strategy and the need for coherence in strategic direction. The following questions extend these themes by asking students to consider their own strategic goals and how they fit with the goals of the firms in which they work or would seek employment.

- **Attributes of Strategic Management:** The attributes of strategic management described in this chapter are applicable to your personal careers as well. What are your overall goals and objectives? Who are the stakeholders you have to consider in making your career decisions (family, community, etc.)? What trade-offs do you see between your long-term and short-term goals?

- **Intended versus Emergent Strategies:** While you may have planned your career trajectory carefully, don't be too tied to it. Strive to take advantage of new opportunities as they arise. Many promising career opportunities may "emerge" that were not part of your intended career strategy or your specific job assignment. Take initiative by pursuing opportunities to get additional training (e.g., learn a software or a statistical package), volunteering for a short-term overseas assignment, etc. You may be in a better position to take advantage of such emergent opportunities if you take the effort to prepare for

them. For example, learning a foreign language may position you better for an overseas opportunity.

- **Ambidexterity:** In Strategy Spotlight 1.1, we discussed the four most important traits of ambidextrous individuals. These include looking for opportunities beyond the description of one's job, seeking out opportunities to collaborate with others, building internal networks, and multitasking. Evaluate yourself along each of these criteria. If you score low, think of ways in which you can improve your ambidexterity.

- **Strategic Coherence:** What is the mission of your organization? What are the strategic objectives of the department or unit you are working for? In what ways does your own role contribute to the mission and objectives? What can you do differently in order to help the organization attain its mission and strategic objectives?

- **Strategic Coherence:** Setting strategic objectives is important in your personal career as well. Identify and write down three or four important strategic objectives you want to accomplish in the next few years (finish your degree, find a better-paying job, etc.). Are you allocating your resources (time, money, etc.) to enable you to achieve these objectives? Are your objectives measurable, timely, realistic, specific, and appropriate?

Cases

Updated case lineup provides nine new cases. The majority of the remaining cases have been revised to "maximize freshness" and minimize instructor preparation time. New cases for this edition include well-known companies such as Tata Starbucks, the Casino Industry, and General Motors.

brief contents

PART 1 STRATEGIC ANALYSIS

PART 2 STRATEGIC FORMULATION

PART 3 STRATEGIC IMPLEMENTATION

PART 4 CASE ANALYSIS

contents

PART 1 STRATEGIC ANALYSIS

PART 2 STRATEGIC FORMULATION

CHAPTER 5

Business-Level Strategy: Creating and Sustaining Competitive Advantages.......... 138

CHAPTER 8

PART 3 STRATEGIC IMPLEMENTATION

CHAPTER 9

cases

21 THE BOSTON BEER COMPANY: POISED FOR GROWTH

Beer

The Boston Beer Company was facing a difficult competitive environment with direct competition from both larger and smaller breweries and from premium imported beers. While further growth would be beneficial in terms of revenue, growing too large could negatively affect the company's status as a craft brewery and the perceptions of its customers.

22 NINTENDO'S SWITCH

Video Games

In 2017 Nintendo launched a new gaming console system named Nintendo Switch. Would the new Joy-Con Controllers and flexible play features be enough to boost consumer numbers and investors' confidence?

23 TATA STARBUCKS: HOW TO BREW A SUSTAINABLE BLEND FOR INDIA

Coffee

Would Starbucks and Tata under new CEO Sumi Ghosh's leadership finally be able to brew a new blend of success in the competitive and complex Indian café market? While management appeared proud of the joint venture's early performance, some critical strategic choices would need to be made to ensure the long-term success of Starbucks in India.

24 WEIGHT WATCHERS INTERNATIONAL INC.

Weight Loss

Weight Watchers was reinventing weight loss for a new generation and hoping profits would jump off the scale. A new "Beyond the Scale" advertising campaign that featured the entrepreneur and talk show host, Oprah Winfrey, claiming that she had lost 40 pounds by using Weight Watchers program.

25 SAMSUNG ELECTRONICS 2017

Consumer Electronics

Samsung rushed the Note 7 to market ahead of Apple's anticipated iPhone 7. The tendency of the Note 7 to burst into flames from a poor battery design subsequently led Samsung to engage in one of its most extensive and costly recalls and to eventually kill the new product.

26 PROCTER & GAMBLE

Consumer Products

Procter & Gamble was the world's largest consumer products conglomerate, with billion-dollar brands such as Tide, Crest, Pampers, Gillette, Right Guard, and Duracell. However, sales were down as consumers were coping with the economic downturn by switching to P&G's lower-priced brands.

27 APPLE INC.: IS THE INNOVATION OVER?

Computers, Consumer Electronics

CEO Tim Cook had driven the stock price up 175% since the death of founder Steve Jobs. Yet Cook was criticized for being too cautious about entering new product categories, pursuing acquisitions, and driving employees to achieve stretch goals. Would Apple be able to innovative without Jobs?

28 JETBLUE AIRLINES: GETTING OVER THE "BLUES"?

Airline

This airline's start-up success story is facing new challenges as operational problems have surfaced and another new pilot is in the CEO's seat.

29 UNITED WAY WORLDWIDE

Nonprofit

As a nonprofit organization, it was imperative for United Way Worldwide to get the necessary support at the local level in order to achieve its stated organizational goals. Would Gallagher's various strategies be successfully implemented, or was the nonprofit's very mission perhaps no longer relevant?

30 EBAY

Internet

The online auction pioneer was entering a critical period. There were questions of what was right for the company to increase shareholder value over the long term, as well as operational issues related to search engine optimization and online security.

31 JAMBA JUICE: MIXING IT UP & STARTING AFRESH

Smoothies/QSR

After years of same-store declines, activist investors were pressuring CEO Dave Pace for a turnaround.

The Strategic Management Process

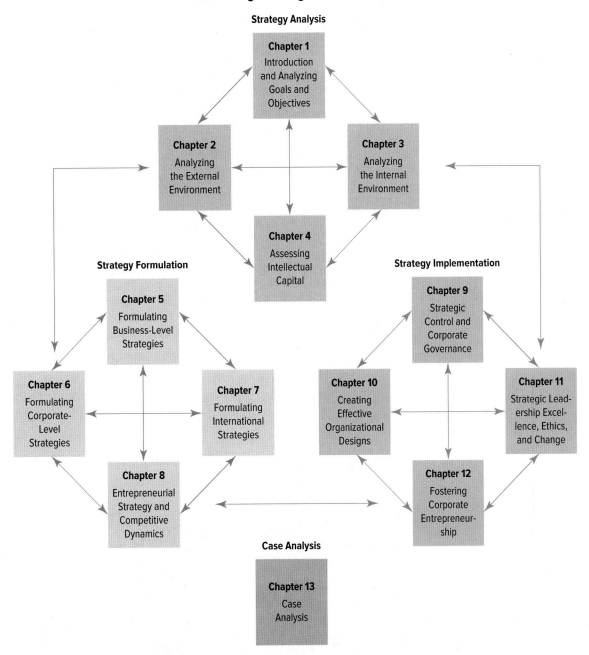

Strategy Analysis

Chapter 1
Introduction and Analyzing Goals and Objectives

Chapter 2
Analyzing the External Environment

Chapter 3
Analyzing the Internal Environment

Chapter 4
Assessing Intellectual Capital

Strategy Formulation

Chapter 5
Formulating Business-Level Strategies

Chapter 6
Formulating Corporate-Level Strategies

Chapter 7
Formulating International Strategies

Chapter 8
Entrepreneurial Strategy and Competitive Dynamics

Strategy Implementation

Chapter 9
Strategic Control and Corporate Governance

Chapter 10
Creating Effective Organizational Designs

Chapter 11
Strategic Leadership Excellence, Ethics, and Change

Chapter 12
Fostering Corporate Entrepreneurship

Case Analysis

Chapter 13
Case Analysis

Strategic Management

Creating Competitive Advantages

After reading this chapter, you should have a good understanding of the following learning objectives:

LO1-1 The definition of strategic management and its four key attributes.

LO1-2 The strategic management process and its three interrelated and principal activities.

LO1-3 The vital role of corporate governance and stakeholder management, as well as how "symbiosis" can be achieved among an organization's stakeholders.

LO1-4 The importance of social responsibility, including environmental sustainability, and how it can enhance a corporation's innovation strategy.

LO1-5 The need for greater empowerment throughout the organization.

LO1-6 How an awareness of a hierarchy of strategic goals can help an organization achieve coherence in its strategic direction.

©Anatoli Styf/Shutterstock

LEARNING FROM MISTAKES

What makes the study of strategic management so interesting? Things can change so rapidly! Some start-ups can disrupt industries and become globally recognized names in just a few years. The rankings of the world's most valuable firms can dramatically change in a rather brief period of time. On the other hand, many impressive, high-flying firms can struggle to reclaim past glory or even fail. Recall just four that begin with the letter "b"—Blackberry, Blockbuster, Borders, and Barings. As colorfully (and ironically!) noted by Arthur Martinez, Sears's former Chairman: "Today's peacock is tomorrow's feather duster."[1]

Consider the following:[2]

- At the beginning of 2007, the three firms in the world with the highest market values were Exxon Mobil, General Electric, and Gazprom (a Russian natural gas firm). By early 2017, three high tech firms headed the list—Apple, Alphabet (parent of Google), and Microsoft.
- Only 74 of the original 500 companies in the S&P index were still around 40 years later. And McKinsey notes that the average company tenure on the S&P 500 list has fallen from 61 years in 1958 to about 20 in 2016.
- With the dramatic increase of the digital economy, new entrants are shaking up long-standing industries. Note that Alibaba is the world's most valuable retailer—but holds no inventory; Airbnb is the world's largest provider of accommodations—but owns no real estate; and Uber is the world's largest car service but owns no cars.
- A quarter century ago, how many would have predicted that a South Korean firm would be a global car giant, than an Indian firm would be one of the world's largest technology firms, and a huge Chinese Internet company would list on an American stock exchange?
- *Fortune* magazine's annual list of the 500 biggest companies now features 156 emerging-market firms. This compares with only 18 in 1995!

To remain competitive, companies often must bring in "new blood" and make significant changes in their strategies. But sometimes a new CEO's initiatives makes things worse. Let's take a look at Lands' End, an American clothing retailer.[3]

Lands' End was founded in 1963 as a mail order supplier of sailboat equipment by Gary Comer. As business picked up, he expanded the business into clothing and home furnishings and moved the company to Dodgeville, Wisconsin, in 1978 where he was its CEO until he stepped down in 1990. The firm was acquired by Sears in 2002, but later spun off in 2013. A year later it commenced trading on the NASDAQ stock exchange.

Targeting Middle America, companies like Lands' End, the GAP Inc., and J. C. Penney have had a hard time in recent years positioning themselves in the hotly contested clothing industry. They are squeezed on the high end by brands like Michael Kors Holdings Ltd. and Coach, Inc. On the lower end, fast-fashion retailers including H&M operator Hennes & Mauritz AB are applying pressure by churning out inexpensive, runway-inspired styles.

To spearhead a revival of the brand, Lands' End hired a new CEO, Frederica Marchionni, in February 2015. However, since her arrival, the firm's stock price has suffered, same store sales declined for all six quarters of her tenure, and the firm kept losing money. It reported a loss of $19.5 million for the year ending January 29, 2016—compared to a $73.8 million profit for the previous year. (And, things didn't get better—it lost another $7.7 million in the first half of 2016.)

So, what went wrong? Lands' End was always known for its wholesome style and corporate culture. Its founder, Gary Comer, who liked to dress casually in jeans and sweaters, had fostered a familial culture. However, things dramatically changed when Ms. Marchionni arrived. Prior to taking the position, she had struck a deal to only spend one week a month in Dodgeville—preferring instead to spend most of her time in an office in New York's garment district. Also, unlike her predecessors, she had private bathrooms in both of her offices—such perks didn't seem to fit well with the firm's culture.

Given Marchionni's background at high-end names like Ferrari and Dolce & Gabbana, she tried to inject more style into the maker of outdoorsy, casual clothes. She added slimmer-fits, stiletto heels and a new line of activewear. In presentations, according to those attending, she derided the company's boxy sweaters and baggy pants as "ugly," asking "Who would wear that?" A photo shoot for a line took place in the Marshall Islands—a very costly location, according to people familiar with the situation. She overhauled the catalog, hired celebrity photographers, and hired a Vogue stylist for input. She also added new price points—including the Canvas line which sells for as much as 30 percent more than the traditional Lands' End collection.

At the end of the day, it appeared that Ms. Marchionni was never able to get Lands' End employees to buy into her vision. And as losses piled up quickly, the board became concerned that she was trying to make too many changes too quickly. Perhaps, she was not given enough time to turn things around—but her approach to re-invent the apparel brand may have been too much of a shock for its customer base as well as the firm's family culture and wholesome style. Maybe Lee Eisenberg, the firm's former creative director, said it best: "It doesn't look like Lands' End anymore. There was never the implication that if you wore Lands' End you'd be on a beach on Nantucket living the perfect life." Marchionni resigned on September 26, 2016—underscoring, as noted by *Fortune.com,* how futile it must be to take such a Middle American brand upscale.

Discussion Questions

1. What actions could Ms. Marchionni have taken to improve Lands' End's prospects for success in the marketplace?
2. Did Lands' End make the right choice in selecting her for the CEO position? Why? Why not?

Today's leaders face a large number of complex challenges in the global marketplace. In considering how much credit (or blame) they deserve, two perspectives of leadership come immediately to mind: the "romantic" and "external control" perspectives.[4] First, let's look at the **romantic view of leadership.** Here, the implicit assumption is that the leader is the key force in determining an organization's success—or lack thereof.[5] This view dominates the popular press in business magazines such as *Fortune, Bloomberg Businessweek,* and *Forbes,* wherein the CEO is either lauded for his or her firm's success or chided for the organization's demise.[6] Consider, for example, the credit that has been bestowed on leaders such as Jack Welch, Andrew Grove, and Herb Kelleher for the tremendous accomplishments when they led their firms, General Electric, Intel, and Southwest Airlines, respectively.

Similarly, Apple's success in the last decade has been attributed almost entirely to the late Steve Jobs, its former CEO, who died on October 5, 2011.[7] Apple's string of hit products, such as iMac computers, iPods, iPhones, and iPads, is a testament to his genius for developing innovative, user-friendly, and aesthetically pleasing products. In addition to being a

romantic view of leadership
situations in which the leader is the key force determining the organization's success—or lack thereof.

perfectionist in product design, Jobs was a master showman with a cult following. During his time as CEO between 1997 and 2011, Apple's market value soared by over $300 billion!

On the other hand, when things don't go well, much of the failure of an organization can also, rightfully, be attributed to the leader.[8] Clearly, actions undertaken by Ms. Marchionni to move Lands' End upscale backfired and hampered its performance. In contrast, Apple fully capitalized on emerging technology trends with a variety of products, including sophisticated smartphones.

The effect—for good or for bad—that top executives can have on a firm's market value can be reflected in what happens when one of them leaves their firm.[9] For example, look what occurred when Kasper Rorsted stepped down as CEO of the German packaged-goods firm Henkel in January, 2016 to become CEO of Adidas: Henkel immediately lost $2 billion in market capitalization, and Adidas gained $1 billion. On the other hand, when Viacom announced that executive chairman Sumner Redstone was stepping down, the firm gained $1.1 billion of market valuation in 30 minutes!

However, such an emphasis on the leader reflects only part of the picture. Consider another perspective, called the **external control view of leadership.** Here, rather than making the implicit assumption that the leader is the most important factor in determining organizational outcomes, the focus is on external factors that may positively (or negatively) affect a firm's success. We don't have to look far to support this perspective. Developments in the general environment, such as economic downturns, new technologies, governmental legislation, or an outbreak of major internal conflict or war, can greatly restrict the choices that are available to a firm's executives. For example, several book retailers, such as Borders and Waldenbooks, found the consumer shift away from brick-and-mortar bookstores to online book buying (e.g., Amazon) and digital books an overwhelming environmental force against which they had few defenses.

> **external control view of leadership** situations in which external forces—where the leader has limited influence—determine the organization's success.

Looking back at the opening Lands' End case, it was clear that Ms. Marchionni faced challenges in the external environment over which she had relatively little control. As noted, chains targeting Middle America such as Lands' End were squeezed on both the higher end by brands such as Coach Inc. and on the lower end by Hennes & Mauritz AB. And as noted by an analyst, her potential for success was adversely affected by "the worst consumer soft goods market in eight years."[10]

Before moving on, it is important to point out that successful executives are often able to navigate around the difficult circumstances that they face. At times it can be refreshing to see the optimistic position they take when they encounter seemingly insurmountable odds. Of course, that's not to say that one should be naive or Pollyannaish. Consider, for example, how one CEO, discussed next, is handling trying times.[11]

Name a general economic woe, and chances are that Charles Needham, CEO of Metorex, is dealing with it.

- Market turmoil has knocked 80 percent off the shares of South Africa's Metorex, the mining company that he heads.
- The plunge in global commodities is slamming prices for the copper, cobalt, and other minerals Metorex unearths across Africa. The credit crisis makes it harder to raise money.
- Fighting has again broken out in the Democratic Republic of Congo, where Metorex has a mine and several projects in development.

Such problems might send many executives to the window ledge. Yet Needham appears unruffled as he sits down at a conference table in the company's modest offices in a Johannesburg suburb. The combat in northeast Congo, he notes, is far from Metorex's mine. Commodity prices are still high, in historical terms. And Needham is confident he can raise enough capital, drawing on relationships with South African banks. "These are the kinds of things you deal with, doing business in Africa," he says.

WHAT IS STRATEGIC MANAGEMENT?

Given the many challenges and opportunities in the global marketplace, today's managers must do more than set long-term strategies and hope for the best.[12] They must go beyond what some have called "incremental management," whereby they view their job as making a series of small, minor changes to improve the efficiency of their firm's operations.[13] Rather than seeing their role as merely custodians of the status quo, today's leaders must be proactive, anticipate change, and continually refine and, when necessary, make dramatic changes to their strategies. The strategic management of the organization must become both a process and a way of thinking throughout the organization.

Defining Strategic Management

LO 1-1

The definition of strategic management and its four key attributes.

strategic management
the analyses, decisions, and actions an organization undertakes in order to create and sustain competitive advantages.

Strategic management consists of the analyses, decisions, and actions an organization undertakes in order to create and sustain competitive advantages. This definition captures two main elements that go to the heart of the field of strategic management.

First, the strategic management of an organization entails three ongoing processes: *analyses, decisions,* and *actions.* Strategic management is concerned with the *analysis* of strategic goals (vision, mission, and strategic objectives) along with the analysis of the internal and external environments of the organization. Next, leaders must make strategic decisions. These *decisions,* broadly speaking, address two basic questions: What industries should we compete in? How should we compete in those industries? These questions also often involve an organization's domestic and international operations. And last are the *actions* that must be taken. Decisions are of little use, of course, unless they are acted on. Firms must take the necessary actions to implement their **strategies.** This requires leaders to allocate the necessary resources and to design the organization to bring the intended strategies to reality.

strategy
the ideas, decisions, and actions that enable a firm to succeed.

Second, the essence of strategic management is the study of why some firms outperform others.[14] Thus, managers need to determine how a firm is to compete so that it can obtain advantages that are sustainable over a lengthy period of time. That means focusing on two fundamental questions:

competitive advantage
a firm's resources and capabilities that enable it to overcome the competitive forces in its industry(ies).

- *How should we compete in order to create* **competitive advantages** *in the marketplace?* Managers need to determine if the firm should position itself as the low-cost producer or develop products and services that are unique and will enable the firm to charge premium prices. Or should they do some combination of both?
- *How can we create competitive advantages in the marketplace that are unique, valuable, and difficult for rivals to copy or substitute?* That is, managers need to make such advantages sustainable, instead of temporary.

Sustainable competitive advantage cannot be achieved through operational effectiveness alone.[15] The popular management innovations of the last two decades—total quality, just-in-time, benchmarking, business process reengineering, outsourcing—are all about operational effectiveness. **Operational effectiveness** means performing similar activities better than rivals. Each of these innovations is important, but none lead to sustainable competitive advantage because everyone is doing them. Strategy is all about being different. Sustainable competitive advantage is possible only by performing different activities from rivals or performing similar activities in different ways. Companies such as Walmart, Southwest Airlines, and IKEA have developed unique, internally consistent, and difficult-to-imitate activity systems that have provided them with sustained competitive advantages. A company with a good strategy must make clear choices about what it wants to accomplish. Trying to do everything that your rivals do eventually leads to mutually destructive price competition, not long-term advantage.

operational effectiveness
performing similar activities better than rivals.

EXHIBIT 1.1

Strategic Management Concepts

Definition: Strategic management consists of the analyses, decisions, and actions an organization undertakes in order to create and sustain competitive advantages.

Key Attributes of Strategic Management
• Directs the organization toward overall goals and objectives.
• Includes multiple stakeholders in decision making.
• Needs to incorporate short-term and long-term perspectives.
• Recognizes trade-offs between efficiency and effectiveness.

The Four Key Attributes of Strategic Management

Before discussing the strategic management process, let's briefly talk about four attributes of strategic management.[16] It should become clear how this course differs from other courses that you have had in functional areas, such as accounting, marketing, operations, and finance. Exhibit 1.1 provides a definition and the four attributes of strategic management.

First, strategic management is *directed toward overall organizational goals and objectives.* That is, effort must be directed at what is best for the total organization, not just a single functional area. Some authors have referred to this perspective as "organizational versus individual rationality."[17] That is, what might look "rational" or ideal for one functional area, such as operations, may not be in the best interest of the overall firm. For example, operations may decide to schedule long production runs of similar products to lower unit costs. However, the standardized output may be counter to what the marketing department needs to appeal to a demanding target market. Similarly, research and development may "overengineer" the product to develop a far superior offering, but the design may make the product so expensive that market demand is minimal.

As noted by David Novak, CEO of Yum Brands:[18]

> I tell people that once you get a job you should act like you run the place. Not in terms of ego, but in terms of how you think about the business. Don't just think about your piece of the business. Think about your piece of the business and the total business. This way, you'll always have a broader perspective.

Second, strategic management *includes multiple stakeholders in decision making.*[19] **Stakeholders** are those individuals, groups, and organizations that have a "stake" in the success of the organization, including owners (shareholders in a publicly held corporation), employees, customers, suppliers, the community at large, and so on. (We'll discuss this in more detail later in this chapter.) Managers will not be successful if they focus on a single stakeholder. For example, if the overwhelming emphasis is on generating profits for the owners, employees may become alienated, customer service may suffer, and the suppliers may resent demands for pricing concessions.

Third, strategic management *requires incorporating both short-term and long-term perspectives.*[20] Peter Senge, a leading strategic management author, has referred to this need as a "creative tension."[21] That is, managers must maintain both a vision for the future of the organization and a focus on its present operating needs. However, financial markets can exert significant pressures on executives to meet short-term performance targets. Studies have shown that corporate leaders often take a short-term approach to the detriment of creating long-term shareholder value.

Andrew Winston addresses this issue in his recent book, *The Big Pivot:*[22]

> Consider the following scenario: You are close to the end of the quarter and you are faced with a project that you are certain will make money. That is, it has a guaranteed positive net present value (NPV). But, it will reduce your earnings for this quarter. Do you invest?

stakeholders individuals, groups, and organizations that have a stake in the success of the organization. These include owners (shareholders in a publicly held corporation), employees, customers, suppliers, and the community at large.

A research study posed this question to 400 CFOs and a majority said they would not do it. Further, 80 percent of the executives would decrease R&D spending, advertising, and general maintenance. So, what occurs when you cut back on these investments to prop up short-term earnings *every* quarter? Logically, you don't invest in projects with favorable paybacks and you underspend on initiatives that build longer-term value. Thus, your earnings targets in the future quarters actually get more difficult to hit.

Fourth, strategic management *involves the recognition of trade-offs between effectiveness and efficiency.* Some authors have referred to this as the difference between "doing the right thing" (**effectiveness**) and "doing things right" (**efficiency**).[23] While managers must allocate and use resources wisely, they must still direct their efforts toward the attainment of overall organizational objectives. As noted by Meg Whitman, Hewlett-Packard's CEO, "Less than perfect strategy execution against the right strategy will probably work. A 100% execution against the wrong strategy won't." [24]

Successful managers must make many trade-offs. It is central to the practice of strategic management. At times, managers must focus on the short term and efficiency; at other times, the emphasis is on the long term and expanding a firm's product-market scope in order to anticipate opportunities in the competitive environment.

To summarize, leaders typically face many difficult and challenging decisions. In a 2016 article in the *Harvard Business Review,* Wendy Smith and her colleagues provide some valuable insights in addressing such situations.[25] The author team studied corporations over many years and found that senior executives are often faced with similar sets of opposing goals, which can polarize their organizations. Such tensions or paradoxes fall into three categories, which may be related to three questions that many leaders view as "either/or" choices.

- Do we manage for today or for tomorrow? A firm's long-term survival requires taking risks and learning from failure in the pursuit of new products and services. However, companies also need consistency in their products and services. This depicts the tension between existing products and new ones, stability and change. This is the *innovation paradox.* For example, in the late 1990s, IBM's senior leaders saw the Internet wave and felt the need to harness the new technology. However, the firm also needed to sustain its traditional strength in client-server markets. Each strategy required different structures, cultures, rewards, and metrics—which could not easily be executed in tandem.

- Do we stick to boundaries or cross them? Global supply chains can be very effective, but they may also lack flexibility. New ideas can emerge from innovation activities that are dispersed throughout the world. However, not having all the talent and brains in one location can be costly. This is the tension between global connectedness and local needs, the *globalization paradox.* In 2009, NASA's director of human health and performance started an initiative geared toward generating new knowledge through collaborative cross-firm and cross-disciplinary work. Not too surprisingly, he faced strong pushback from scientists interested in protecting their turf and their identities as independent experts. Although both collaboration and independent work were required to generate new innovations, they posed organizational and cultural challenges.

- Whom do we focus on, shareholders or stakeholders? Clearly, companies exist to create value. But managers are often faced with the choice between maximizing shareholder gains while trying to create benefits for a wide range of stakeholders— employees, customers, society, etc. However, being socially responsible may bring down a firm's share price, and prioritizing employees may conflict with short-term shareholders' or customers' needs. This is the *obligation paradox.* Paul Polman, Unilever's CEO, launched the Unilever Sustainable Living Plan in 2010. The goal was to double the size of the business over 10 years, improve the health and well-being of more than a billion people, and cut the firm's environmental impact in half. He

effectiveness
tailoring actions to the needs of an organization rather than wasting effort, or "doing the right thing."

efficiency
performing actions at a low cost relative to a benchmark, or "doing things right."

AMBIDEXTROUS BEHAVIORS: COMBINING ALIGNMENT AND ADAPTABILITY

A study involving 41 business units in 10 multinational companies identified four ambidextrous behaviors in individuals. Such behaviors are the essence of ambidexterity, and they illustrate how a dual capacity for alignment and adaptability can be woven into the fabric of an organization at the individual level.

They take time and are alert to opportunities beyond the confines of their own jobs. A large computer company's sales manager became aware of a need for a new software module that nobody currently offered. Instead of selling the customer something else, he worked up a business case for the new module. With management's approval, he began working full time on its development.

They are cooperative and seek out opportunities to combine their efforts with others. A marketing manager for Italy was responsible for supporting a newly acquired subsidiary. When frustrated about the limited amount of contact she had with her peers in other countries, she began discussions with them. This led to the creation of a European marketing forum that meets quarterly to discuss issues, share best practices, and collaborate on marketing plans.

They are brokers, always looking to build internal networks. When visiting the head office in St. Louis, a Canadian plant manager heard about plans for a $10 million investment for a new tape manufacturing plant. After inquiring further about the plans and returning to Canada, he contacted a regional manager in Manitoba, who he knew was looking for ways to build his business. With some generous support from the Manitoba government, the regional manager bid for, and ultimately won, the $10 million investment.

They are multitaskers who are comfortable wearing more than one hat. Although an operations manager for a major coffee and tea distributor was charged with running his plant as efficiently as possible, he took it upon himself to identify value-added services for his clients. By developing a dual role, he was able to manage operations and develop a promising electronic module that automatically reported impending problems inside a coffee vending machine. With corporate funding, he found a subcontractor to develop the software, and he then piloted the module in his own operations. It was so successful that it was eventually adopted by operations managers in several other countries.

A recent *Harvard Business Review* article provides some useful insights on how one can become a more ambidextrous leader. Consider the following questions:

- **Do you meet your numbers?**
- **Do you help others?**
- **What do you do for your peers?** Are you just their in-house competitor?
- **When you manage up, do you bring problems—or problems with possible solutions?**
- **Are you transparent?** Managers who get a reputation for spinning events gradually lose the trust of peers and superiors.
- **Are you developing a group of senior-managers who know you and are willing to back your original ideas with resources?**

Sources: Birkinshaw, J. & Gibson, C. 2004. Building ambidexterity into an organization. *MIT Sloan Management Review,* 45(4): 47–55; and Bower, J. L. 2007. Solve the succession crisis by growing inside-out leaders. *Harvard Business Review,* 85(11): 90–99.

argued that such investments would lead to greater profits over the long term; whereas a singular focus on short-term profits would have adverse effects on society and the environment. His arguments were persuasive to many; however, there have been many challenges in implementing the plan. Not surprisingly, it has caused uncertainty among senior executives that has led to anxiety and fights over resource allocation.

Some authors have developed the concept of **"ambidexterity"** (similar to the aforementioned "innovation paradox"), which refers to a manager's challenge to both align resources to take advantage of existing product markets and proactively explore new opportunities.[26] Strategy Spotlight 1.1 discusses ambidextrous behaviors that are essential for success in today's challenging marketplace.

ambidexterity
the challenge managers face of both aligning resources to take advantage of existing product markets and proactively exploring new opportunities.

THE STRATEGIC MANAGEMENT PROCESS

LO 1-2

The strategic management process and its three interrelated and principal activities.

We've identified three ongoing processes—analyses, decisions, and actions—that are central to strategic management. In practice, these three processes—often referred to as strategy analysis, strategy formulation, and strategy implementation—are highly interdependent and do not take place one after the other in a sequential fashion in most companies.

Intended versus Realized Strategies

strategic management process strategy analysis, strategy formulation, and strategy implementation.

Henry Mintzberg, a management scholar at McGill University, argues that viewing the strategic management process as one in which analysis is followed by optimal decisions and their subsequent meticulous implementation neither describes the strategic management process accurately nor prescribes ideal practice.[27] He sees the business environment as far from predictable, thus limiting our ability for analysis. Further, decisions are seldom based on optimal rationality alone, given the political processes that occur in all organizations.[28]

intended strategy strategy in which organizational decisions are determined only by analysis.

Taking into consideration the limitations discussed above, Mintzberg proposed an alternative model. As depicted in Exhibit 1.2, decisions following from analysis, in this model, constitute the **intended strategy** of the firm. For a variety of reasons, the intended strategy rarely survives in its original form. Unforeseen environmental developments, unanticipated resource constraints, or changes in managerial preferences may result in at least some parts of the intended strategy remaining *unrealized*.

Consider an important trend affecting law firms:

> Many of the leading corporations have reduced their need for outside legal services by increasingly expanding their in-house legal departments.[29] For example, companies and financial institutions spent an estimated $41 billion on their internal lawyers in 2014, a 22 percent increase since 2011. And a survey of 1,200 chief legal officers found that 63 percent of respondents are now "in-sourcing" legal work they used to send out to law firms or other service providers. In response, many large law firms have been forced to move away from commodity practices such as basic commercial contracts to more specialized areas like cross-border transactions and global regulatory issues.

realized strategy strategy in which organizational decisions are determined by both analysis and unforeseen environmental developments, unanticipated resource constraints, and/or changes in managerial preferences.

Thus, the final **realized strategy** of any firm is a combination of deliberate and emergent strategies.

Next, we will address each of the three key strategic management processes—strategy analysis, strategy formulation, and strategy implementation—and provide a brief overview of the chapters.

Exhibit 1.3 depicts the strategic management process and indicates how it ties into the chapters in the book. Consistent with our discussion above, we use two-way arrows to convey the interactive nature of the processes.

EXHIBIT 1.2 Realized Strategy and Intended Strategy: Usually Not the Same

Source: Adapted from Mintzberg, H. & Waters, J. A., "Of Strategies: Deliberate and Emergent," *Strategic Management Journal,* Vol. 6, 1985, pp. 257–272.

EXHIBIT 1.3 The Strategic Management Process

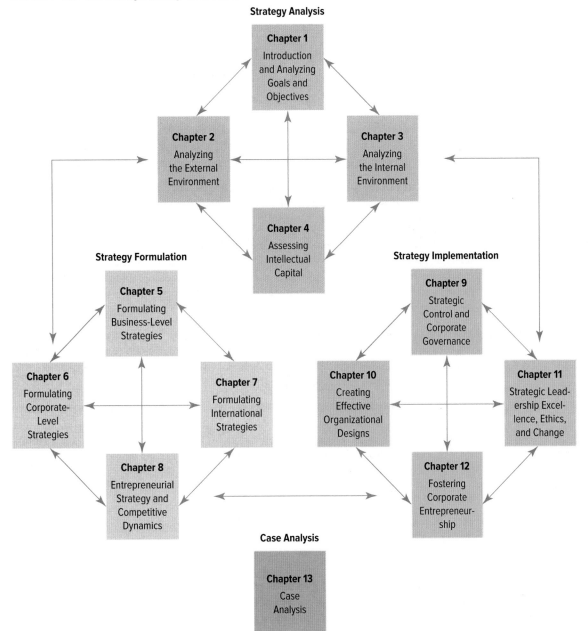

Before moving on, we point out that analyzing the environment and formulating strategies are, of course, important activities in the strategic management process. However, nothing happens until resources are allocated and effective strategies are successfully implemented. Rick Spielman, General Manager of the Minnesota Vikings (of the National Football League), provides valuable insight on this issue.[30] He recalls the many quarterbacks that he has interviewed over the past 25 years and notes that many of them can effectively draw up plays on the whiteboard and "you sit there and it's like listening to an offensive coordinator." However, that is not enough. He points out, "Now can he translate that and make those same decisions and those same type of reads in the two and a half seconds he has to get rid of the ball?"

Strategy Analysis

We measure, study, quantify, analyze every single piece of our business.... But then you've got to be able to take all that data and information and transform it into change in the organization and improvements in the organization and the formalization of the business strategy.

—Richard Anderson, CEO of Delta Air Lines[31]

strategy analysis
study of firms' external and internal environments, and their fit with organizational vision and goals.

Strategy analysis may be looked upon as the starting point of the strategic management process. It consists of the "advance work" that must be done in order to effectively formulate and implement strategies. Many strategies fail because managers may want to formulate and implement strategies without a careful analysis of the overarching goals of the organization and without a thorough analysis of its external and internal environments.

Analyzing Organizational Goals and Objectives (Chapter 1)   A firm's vision, mission, and strategic objectives form a hierarchy of goals that range from broad statements of intent and bases for competitive advantage to specific, measurable strategic objectives.

Analyzing the External Environment of the Firm (Chapter 2)   Managers must monitor and scan the environment as well as analyze competitors. Two frameworks are provided: (1) The general environment consists of several elements, such as demographic and economic segments, and (2) the industry environment consists of competitors and other organizations that may threaten the success of a firm's products and services.

Assessing the Internal Environment of the Firm (Chapter 3)   Analyzing the strengths and relationships among the activities that constitute a firm's value chain (e.g., operations, marketing and sales, and human resource management) can be a means of uncovering potential sources of competitive advantage for the firm.[32]

Assessing a Firm's Intellectual Assets (Chapter 4)   The knowledge worker and a firm's other intellectual assets (e.g., patents) are important drivers of competitive advantages and wealth creation. We also assess how well the organization creates networks and relationships as well as how technology can enhance collaboration among employees and provide a means of accumulating and storing knowledge.[33]

Strategy Formulation

"You can have the best operations. You can be the most adept at whatever it is that you're doing. But, if you have a bad strategy, it's all for naught."

—Fred Smith, CEO of FedEx[34]

strategy formulation
decisions made by firms regarding investments, commitments, and other aspects of operations that create and sustain competitive advantage.

Strategy formulation   is developed at several levels. First, business-level strategy addresses the issue of how to compete in a given business to attain competitive advantage. Second, corporate-level strategy focuses on two issues: (a) what businesses to compete in and (b) how businesses can be managed to achieve synergy; that is, they create more value by working together than by operating as standalone businesses. Third, a firm must develop international strategies as it ventures beyond its national boundaries. Fourth, managers must formulate effective entrepreneurial initiatives.

Formulating Business-Level Strategy (Chapter 5)   The question of how firms compete and outperform their rivals and how they achieve and sustain competitive advantages goes to the heart of strategic management. Successful firms strive to develop bases for competitive advantage, which can be achieved through cost leadership and/or differentiation as well as by focusing on a narrow or industrywide market segment.[35]

Formulating Corporate-Level Strategy (Chapter 6)   Corporate-level strategy addresses a firm's portfolio (or group) of businesses. It asks: (1) What business (or businesses) should we compete in? and (2) How can we manage this portfolio of businesses to create synergies among the businesses?

Formulating International Strategy (Chapter 7)   When firms enter foreign markets, they face both opportunities and pitfalls.[36] Managers must decide not only on the most appropriate entry strategy but also how they will go about attaining competitive advantages in international markets.[37]

Entrepreneurial Strategy and Competitive Dynamics (Chapter 8)   Entrepreneurial activity aimed at new value creation is a major engine for economic growth. For entrepreneurial initiatives to succeed, viable opportunities must be recognized and effective strategies must be formulated.

Strategy Implementation

> *"We could leave our strategic plan on an airplane, and it wouldn't matter. It's all about execution."*

> *—John Stumpf, CEO of Wells Fargo[38]*

Clearly, sound strategies are of no value if they are not properly implemented.[39] **Strategy implementation** involves ensuring proper strategic controls and organizational designs, which includes establishing effective means to coordinate and integrate activities within the firm as well as with its suppliers, customers, and alliance partners.[40] Leadership plays a central role to ensure that the organization is committed to excellence and ethical behavior. It also promotes learning and continuous improvement and acts entrepreneurially in creating new opportunities.

strategy implementation actions made by firms that carry out the formulated strategy, including strategic controls, organizational design, and leadership.

Strategic Control and Corporate Governance (Chapter 9)   Firms must exercise two types of strategic control. First, informational control requires that organizations continually monitor and scan the environment and respond to threats and opportunities. Second, behavioral control involves the proper balance of rewards and incentives as well as cultures and boundaries (or constraints). Further, successful firms (those that are incorporated) practice effective corporate governance.

Creating Effective Organizational Designs (Chapter 10)   Firms must have organizational structures and designs that are consistent with their strategy. In today's rapidly changing competitive environments, firms must ensure that their organizational boundaries—those internal to the firm and external—are more flexible and permeable.[41] Often, organizations develop strategic alliances to capitalize on the capabilities of other organizations.

Creating a Learning Organization and an Ethical Organization (Chapter 11)   Effective leaders set a direction, design the organization, and develop an organization that is committed to excellence and ethical behavior. In addition, given rapid and unpredictable change, leaders must create a "learning organization" so that the entire organization can benefit from individual and collective talents.

Fostering Corporate Entrepreneurship (Chapter 12)   Firms must continually improve and grow as well as find new ways to renew their organizations. Corporate entrepreneurship and innovation provide firms with new opportunities, and strategies should be formulated that enhance a firm's innovative capacity.

Chapter 13, "Analyzing Strategic Management Cases," provides guidelines and suggestions on how to evaluate cases in this course. Thus, the concepts and techniques discussed in the first 12 chapters can be applied to real-world organizations.

In the "Executive Insights: The Strategic Management Process" sidebar we include an interview that the authors conducted with Admiral William H. McRaven, Retired. His distinguished career includes being commander of the U.S. Special Operations Command, and he led Operation Neptune Spear that led to the demise of al Qaeda's leader, Osama bin

THE STRATEGIC MANAGEMENT PROCESS

Admiral William H. McRaven, Retired
Chancellor, University of Texas System

BIOSKETCH

University of Texas Chancellor William H. McRaven, a retired four-star admiral, leads the nation's second largest system of higher education. As chief executive officer of the UT System since January 2015, he oversees 14 institutions that educate 217,000 students and employ 20,000 faculty and more than 70,000 health care professionals, researchers, and staff.

Prior to becoming chancellor, McRaven, a Navy SEAL, was the commander of U.S. Special Operations Command during which time he led a force of 69,000 men and women and was responsible for conducting counter-terrorism operations worldwide. McRaven is also a recognized national authority on U.S. foreign policy and has advised presidents George W. Bush and Barack Obama and other U.S. leaders on defense issues. His acclaimed book, *Spec. Ops: Case Studies in Special Operations Warfare: Theory and Practice,* has been published in several languages. He is noted for his involvement in Operation Neptune Spear, in which he commanded the U.S. Navy Special forces who located and killed al Qaeda leader Osama bin Laden.

McRaven has been recognized for his leadership numerous times by national and international publications and organizations. In 2011, he was the first runner-up for *Time* magazine's Person of the Year. In 2012, *Foreign Policy* magazine named McRaven one of the nation's Top 10 Foreign Policy Experts and one of the Top 100 Global Thinkers. And in 2014, Politico named McRaven one of the Politico 50, citing his leadership as instrumental in cutting through Washington bureaucracy.

McRaven graduated from the University of Texas at Austin in 1977 with a degree in journalism and received his master's degree from the Naval Postgraduate School in Monterey in 1991. In 2012, the Texas Exes honored McRaven with a Distinguished Alumnus Award.

Source: *www.utsystem.edu/chancellor/biography*

Question 1. What leadership lessons did you take away from SEAL training and leadership of SEAL Team 3?

The foundation of effective leadership is being able to lead yourself. This may sound strange, but it is true. Most initial military training—perhaps no more noteworthy than in that training crucible to become a Navy SEAL—helps young people move past self-imposed limits of physical and mental endurance and build confidence in themselves to lead others. The result is a person who is capable of leading in an environment of constant stress, chaos, failure and hardships. In fact, to me, basic SEAL training was a lifetime sampling of micro-challenges I would later face while leading people and organizations all crammed into six months.

Question 2. In leading Neptune Spear, what were the key leadership decisions you made to build an organization to accomplish this task?

The majority of the key leadership decisions that in past enabled us to accomplish this task began before I took command of the organization—but as a member of the organization and its number 2 leader over a period of years, I had been an engaged student in the trial, error, and the ultimate development of what my old boss, General Stan McChrystal, called a "team of teams." You see, our operational environment was changing at an incredibly rapid pace. Unlike any time in our history the rate of change was—and is—no longer linear, it is exponential.

The enemy I faced in Iraq, Afghanistan, Africa, Asia and across the world adapted quickly to our methods of warfare. Using technology, social media and global transportation, they presented tactical and operational problems that today's special operations forces had never seen before. Consequently, our organizations had to adapt to this rapidly changing threat. We had to build a flat chain of command that empowered the leaders below us. We had to reduce our own bureaucracy so we could make timely decisions. We had to constantly communicate so everyone understood the commander's intent and the strategic direction in which we were heading. We had to collaborate in ways that had never been done in the history of special operations warfare. The team of teams we built enabled all of our organizations to derive strength from each other and work together to be successful. It required us to break away from the hierarchical structure—the command structure—that had defined the American military for hundreds of years.

We formed a formal and informal network of subject matter experts bound together by a common mission, using technology to partner in new ways, brought together through operational incentives, and a bottom-up desire with top-down support to solve the most complex problems facing our nation. Essentially, we structured our organization and our processes to use our size, our talent and our operational diversity to achieve an unparalleled level of collaboration in pursuit of common goals.

Though leadership, effective processes, and a trust-based organizational culture had significant parts to play in the success of Neptune Spear, no one should forget it was the actions of well-trained, committed, confident and fiercely determined young Americans who were responsible for the positive outcome of that operation.

Question 3. What lessons have you taken from your military career as you lead a very different type of organization as Chancellor of the University of Texas?

Actually, the duties, responsibilities and organizational relationships are remarkably similar. I am still a servant leader, but instead of serving my country at the national level, I serve the people of Texas. For years as a flag officer I had a frequent and direct relationship with the U.S. Congress; I now have a similar responsibility to inform and respond to the Texas Legislature. Instead of the Secretary of Defense and his staff, and the Chairman of the Joint Chiefs and his staff, providing oversight and guidance, I have the Board of Regents. And the fourteen institutions for which I feel directly responsible are led by very mature professionals who expect a high level of empowerment and autonomy—much like the mature professionals of the large and diverse organizations I commanded over the last decade.

This does not mean, of course, that I approach situations or lead our incredible System the exact same way as I led Special Operations Command—it simply means that I have a comfortable context for the relationships I must build and sustain. The lessons I bring from the military feed off of that—I may have context for these relationships, but I also realize this is a different environment and I must first understand the conditions of the higher education environment before I go about making changes. Understanding the environment—specifically, conducting a strategic assessment—was the focus of my effort for the second half of my first year in office. I knew as the senior leader, I first needed to learn and appreciate the conditions under which we were operating. Another lesson I brought was the importance of establishing relationships early by getting out as much as possible and seeing and listening to others—inside my organization primarily, but also reaching out to stakeholders who lie outside the System. Additionally, I knew from my time in the military that communication and

collaboration—and an organizational culture that reinforces both those things—are critical keys to success.

The aforementioned concept of a "team of teams" was probably the single most valuable organizational change in the history of the modern military, and it continues and matures even today. Navy SEALs work with the Army Special Forces. The Special Forces work with the conventional infantry. The infantry work with the naval aviators. The pilots and crews work with the logisticians. We all work with the intelligence and law enforcement communities and the locals on the ground. And every day we talk. We would look at a problem, and we were finding solutions at a speed unheard of in the past. In other words, everyone has to contribute their ideas—not just listen.

Here at the University of Texas System, I believe we can build our own "team of teams" and we are in the process of doing so. We will use our size, our talent and our diversity to collaborate on difficult issues, and in an environment of competing demands, we will prioritize our objectives so we do not waste effort on inconsequential goals. As the second largest university system in the United States we must apply our resources to those priorities and cut away where we are not effective. And much like my last organization, our rapidly changing environment requires us to constantly innovate to get ahead of our problems while never losing sight of our mission and our objectives.

Question 4. How did you see personal integrity and organizational ethics play out in your military career? Can you provide some examples of actions you took to build or sustain an ethical organization?

You always have to reinforce three main principles of a good organization. That is, all your actions must be moral, legal, and ethical. If you fail to comply with those foundational elements, you and your organization will fail. It all starts with your personal integrity. Maintaining your personal integrity is hard. Being good all the time is difficult. Making the right decisions in the face of temptation is challenging, but you quickly learn that bad decisions have consequences, consequences that are rarely worth the momentary lapse in judgment.

If you do the right thing, particularly when no one is watching, you will be rewarded many times over. The only way to build and sustain an ethical organization is for you, the leader, to demonstrate the qualities you want the organization to uphold. Everyone is watching you—whether you know it or not. The littlest actions and the smallest decisions are all closely observed. The culture begins at the top.

Laden. He recently became Chancellor of the University of Texas System. His experience as an effective leader in both military and university organizations provides valuable insights into the strategic management processes: analysis, formulation, and implementation.

Let's now address two concepts—corporate governance and stakeholder management—that are critical to the strategic management process.

The vital role of corporate governance and stakeholder management, as well as how "symbiosis" can be achieved among an organization's stakeholders.

corporate governance
the relationship among various participants in determining the direction and performance of corporations. The primary participants are (1) the shareholders, (2) the management (led by the chief executive officer), and (3) the board of directors.

THE ROLE OF CORPORATE GOVERNANCE AND STAKEHOLDER MANAGEMENT

Most business enterprises that employ more than a few dozen people are organized as corporations. As you recall from your finance classes, the overall purpose of a corporation is to maximize the long-term return to the owners (shareholders). Thus, we may ask: Who is really responsible for fulfilling this purpose? Robert Monks and Neil Minow provide a useful definition of **corporate governance** as "the relationship among various participants in determining the direction and performance of corporations. The primary participants are (1) the shareholders, (2) the management (led by the chief executive officer), and (3) the board of directors."[42] This relationship is illustrated in Exhibit 1.4.

The board of directors (BOD) are the elected representatives of the shareholders charged with ensuring that the interests and motives of management are aligned with those of the owners (i.e., shareholders). In many cases, the BOD is diligent in fulfilling its purpose. For example, Intel Corporation, the giant $58 billion maker of microprocessor chips, practices sound governance. Its BOD follows guidelines to ensure that its members are independent (i.e., are not members of the executive management team and do not have close personal ties to top executives) so that they can provide proper oversight; it has explicit guidelines on the selection of director candidates (to avoid "cronyism"). It provides detailed procedures for formal evaluations of directors and the firm's top officers.[43] Such guidelines serve to ensure that management is acting in the best interests of shareholders.[44]

Recently, there has been much criticism as well as cynicism by both citizens and the business press about the poor job that management and the BODs of large corporations are doing. We only have to look at the scandals at firms such as Arthur Andersen, Best Buy, Olympus, Enron, Volkswagen, and Wells Fargo.[45] Such malfeasance has led to an erosion of the public's trust in corporations. For example, according to the 2014 CNBC/Burson-Marsteller Corporation Perception Indicator, a global survey of 25,000 individuals, only 52 percent of the public in developed markets has a favorable view of corporations.[46] Forty-five percent felt corporations have "too much influence over the government." More than half of the U.S. public said "strong and influential" corporations are "bad" even if they are promoting innovation and growth, and only 9 percent of the public in the United States says corporate CEOs are "among the most respected" in society.

Perhaps, part of the responsibility—or blame—lies with boards of directors who are often not delivering on their core mission: providing strong oversight and strategic support for management's efforts to create long-term value.[47] In a 2013 study by McKinsey & Co., only

EXHIBIT 1.4 **The Key Elements of Corporate Governance**

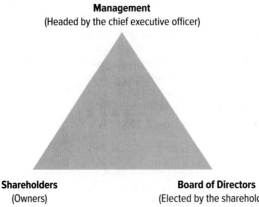

Management
(Headed by the chief executive officer)

Shareholders
(Owners)

Board of Directors
(Elected by the shareholders
to represent their interests)

34 percent of 772 directors agreed that the boards on which they served fully comprehended their firm's strategies. And only 22 percent claimed their boards were completely aware of how their firms created value. Finally, a mere 16 percent claimed their boards had a strong understanding of the dynamics of their firms' industries.

One area in which public anger is most pronounced is the excessive compensation of the top executives of well-known firms. It is now clear that much of the bonus pay awarded to executives on Wall Street in the past was richly undeserved.[48] Case in point, 2011 was a poor year for financial stocks: 35 of the 50 largest financial company stocks fell that year. The sector lost 17 percent—compared to flat performance for the Standard & Poor's 500. However, even as the sector struggled, the average pay of finance company CEOs rose 20.4 percent. For example, JPMorgan CEO Jamie Dimon was the highest-paid banker—with $23.1 million in compensation, an 11 percent increase from the previous year. The firm's shareholders didn't do as well—the stock fell 20 percent.[49]

Of course, executive pay is not restricted to financial institutions. A study released in 2016 entitled "The 100 Most Overpaid CEOs" addressed what it viewed as the "fundamental disconnect between CEO pay and performance."[50] It found that CEO pay grew 997 percent over the most recent 36-year period—a rate that outpaced the growth in the cost of living, the productivity of the economy, and the stock market. The lead author, Rosanna Weaver, argues that the latter point disproves "the claim that the growth in CEO pay reflects the 'performance' of the company, the value of its stock, or the ability of the CEO to do anything but disproportionately raise the amount of his pay." And, a regression analysis conducted by HIP Investor that considered environmental, social, and governance factors came to a similar conclusion: 17 CEOs made at least $20 million more in 2014 than they would have if their pay had been tied to performance.

Clearly, there is a strong need for improved corporate governance, and we will address this topic in Chapter 9.[51] We focus on three important mechanisms to ensure effective corporate governance: an effective and engaged board of directors, shareholder activism, and proper managerial rewards and incentives.[52] In addition to these internal controls, a key role is played by various external control mechanisms.[53] These include the auditors, banks, analysts, an active financial press, and the threat of hostile takeovers.

Alternative Perspectives of Stakeholder Management

stakeholder management
a firm's strategy for recognizing and responding to the interests of all its salient stakeholders.

Generating long-term returns for the shareholders is the primary goal of a publicly held corporation.[54] As noted by former Chrysler vice chairman Robert Lutz, "We are here to serve the shareholder and create shareholder value. I insist that the only person who owns the company is the person who paid good money for it."[55]

Despite the primacy of generating shareholder value, managers who focus solely on the interests of the owners of the business will often make poor decisions that lead to negative, unanticipated outcomes.[56] For example, decisions such as mass layoffs to increase profits, ignoring issues related to conservation of the natural environment to save money, and exerting excessive pressure on suppliers to lower prices can harm the firm in the long run. Such actions would likely lead to negative outcomes such as alienated employees, increased governmental oversight and fines, and disloyal suppliers.

Clearly, in addition to *shareholders,* there are other *stakeholders* (e.g., suppliers, customers) who must be taken into account in the strategic management process.[57] A stakeholder can be defined as an individual or group, inside or outside the company, that has a stake in and can influence an organization's performance. Each stakeholder group makes various claims on the company.[58] Exhibit 1.5 provides a list of major stakeholder groups and the nature of their claims on the company.

Zero Sum or Symbiosis?   There are two opposing ways of looking at the role of stakeholder management.[59] The first one can be termed "zero sum." Here, the various stakeholders

Stakeholder Group	Nature of Claim
Stockholders	Dividends, capital appreciation
Employees	Wages, benefits, safe working environment, job security
Suppliers	Payment on time, assurance of continued relationship
Creditors	Payment of interest, repayment of principal
Customers	Value, warranties
Government	Taxes, compliance with regulations
Communities	Good citizenship behavior such as charities, employment, not polluting the environment

compete for the organization's resources: the gain of one individual or group is the loss of another individual or group. For example, employees want higher wages (which drive down profits), suppliers want higher prices for their inputs and slower, more flexible delivery times (which drive up costs), customers want fast deliveries and higher quality (which drive up costs), the community at large wants charitable contributions (which take money from company goals), and so on. This zero-sum thinking is rooted, in part, in the traditional conflict between workers and management, leading to the formation of unions and sometimes ending in adversarial union–management negotiations and long, bitter strikes.

Consider, for example, the many stakeholder challenges facing Walmart, the world's largest retailer.

> Walmart strives to ramp up growth while many stakeholders are watching nervously: employees and trade unions; shareholders, investors, and creditors; suppliers and joint venture partners; the governments of the United States and other nations where the retailer operates; and customers. In addition many non-governmental organizations (NGOs), particularly in countries where the retailer buys its products, are closely monitoring Walmart. Walmart's stakeholders have different interests, and not all of them share the firm's goals.

There will always be conflicting demands on organizations. However, organizations can achieve mutual benefit through stakeholder symbiosis, which recognizes that stakeholders are dependent upon each other for their success and well-being.[60] Consider Procter & Gamble's "laundry detergent compaction," a technique for compressing even more cleaning power into ever smaller concentrations.

P&G perfected a technique that could compact two or three times as much cleaning powder into a liquid concentration. This remarkable breakthrough has led to not only a change in consumer shopping habits but also a revolution in industry supply chain economics. Here's how several key stakeholders are affected:

> *Consumers* love concentrated liquids because they are easier to carry, pour, and store. *Retailers,* meanwhile, prefer them because they take up less floor and shelf space, which leads to higher sales-per-square-foot—a big deal for Walmart, Target, and other big retailers. *Shipping and wholesalers,* meanwhile, prefer reduced-sized products because smaller bottles translate into reduced fuel consumption and improved warehouse space utilization. And, finally, *environmentalists* favor such products because they use less packaging and produce less waste than conventional products.[61]

Social Responsibility and Environmental Sustainability: Moving beyond the Immediate Stakeholders

Organizations cannot ignore the interests and demands of stakeholders such as citizens and society in general that are beyond its immediate constituencies—customers, owners, suppliers, and employees. The realization that firms have multiple stakeholders and that evaluating their performance must go beyond analyzing their financial results has led to a new way of thinking about businesses and their relationship to society.

First, *social responsibility* recognizes that businesses must respond to society's expectations regarding their obligations to society. Second, the *triple bottom line approach* evaluates a firm's performance. This perspective takes into account financial, social, and environmental performance. Third, *making the case for sustainability initiatives* addresses some of the challenges managers face in obtaining approvals for such projects—and how to overcome them.

Social Responsibility   **Social responsibility** is the expectation that businesses or individuals will strive to improve the overall welfare of society.[62] From the perspective of a business, this means that managers must take active steps to make society better by virtue of the business being in existence.[63] What constitutes socially responsible behavior changes over time. In the 1970s affirmative action was a high priority; during the 1990s and up to the present time, the public has been concerned about environmental quality. Many firms have responded to this by engaging in recycling and reducing waste. And in the wake of terrorist attacks on New York City and the Pentagon, as well as the continuing threat from terrorists worldwide, a new kind of priority has arisen: the need to be vigilant concerning public safety.

> **social responsibility**
> the expectation that businesses or individuals will strive to improve the overall welfare of society.

In order to maximize the positive impact of corporate social responsibility (CSR) initiatives, firms need to create coherent strategies.[64] Research has shown that companies' CSR activities are generally divided across three theaters of practice and assigning the activities accordingly is an important initial step.

- *Theater one: Focusing on philanthropy.* Here, programs are not designed to increase profits or revenues. Examples include financial contributions to civic and charity organizations as well as the participation and engagement of employees in community programs.

- *Theater two: Improving operational effectiveness.* Initiatives in this theater function within existing business models to provide social or environmental benefits and support a company's value creating activities in order to enhance efficiency and effectiveness. They typically can increase revenue or decrease costs—or both. Examples include sustainability initiatives that can reduce the use of resources, waste, or emissions—to cut costs. Or, firms can invest in employee health care and working conditions to enhance retention and productivity—as well as a firm's reputation.

- *Theater three: Transforming the business model.* Improved business performance is a requirement of programs in this theater and is predicated on social and environmental challenges and results. An example would be Hindustan Unilever's Project Shakti in India. Rather than use the typical wholesaler-retailer distribution model to reach remote villages, the firm recruited village women who were provided with training and microfinance loans in order to sell soaps, detergents, and other products door-to-door. More than 65,000 women were recruited and not only were they able to typically double their household's income but it also contributed to public health via access to hygiene products. The project attained more than $100 million in revenues and has led the firm to roll out similar programs in other countries.

A key stakeholder group that appears to be particularly susceptible to corporate social responsibility (CSR) initiatives is customers.[65] Surveys indicate a strong positive relationship between CSR behaviors and consumers' reactions to a firm's products and services.[66] For example:

LO 1-4

The importance of social responsibility, including environmental sustainability, and how it can enhance a corporation's innovation strategy.

- Corporate Citizenship's poll conducted by Cone Communications found that "84 percent of Americans say they would be likely to switch brands to one associated with a good cause, if price and quality are similar."[67]

- Hill & Knowlton/Harris's Interactive poll reveals that "79 percent of Americans take corporate citizenship into account when deciding whether to buy a particular company's product and 37 percent consider corporate citizenship an important factor when making purchasing decisions."[68]

Such findings are consistent with a large body of research that confirms the positive influence of CSR on consumers' company evaluations and product purchase intentions across a broad range of product categories.

The Triple Bottom Line: Incorporating Financial as Well as Environmental and Social Costs
Many companies are now measuring what has been called a **"triple bottom line."** This involves assessing financial, social, and environmental performance. Shell, NEC, Procter & Gamble, and others have recognized that failing to account for the environmental and social costs of doing business poses risks to the company and its community.[69]

> **triple bottom line**
> assessment of a firm's financial, social, and environmental performance.

Social and environmental issues can ultimately become financial issues. According to Lars Sorensen, CEO of Novo Nordisk, a $16 billion global pharmaceutical firm based in Denmark:[70]

> If we keep polluting, stricter regulations will be imposed, and energy consumption will become more costly. The same thing applies to the social side. If we don't treat employees well, if we don't behave as good corporate citizens in our local communities, and if we don't provide inexpensive products for poorer countries, governments will impose regulations on us that will end up being very costly.

The environmental revolution has been almost four decades in the making.[71] In the 1960s and 1970s, companies were in a state of denial regarding their firms' impact on the natural environment. However, a series of visible ecological problems created a groundswell for strict governmental regulation. In the United States, Lake Erie was "dead," and in Japan, people died of mercury poisoning. More recently, Japan's horrific tsunami that took place on March 11, 2011, and Hurricane Sandy's devastation on the East Coast of the United States in late October 2012 have raised alarms.

Environmental sustainability is now a value embraced by the most competitive and successful multinational companies.[72] The McKinsey & Company's survey of more than 400 senior executives of companies around the world found that 92 percent agreed with former Sony president Akio Morita's contention that the environmental challenge will be one of the central issues in the 21st century.[73] Virtually all executives acknowledged their firms' responsibility to control pollution, and 83 percent agreed that corporations have an environmental responsibility for their products even after they are sold.

For many successful firms, environmental values are now becoming a central part of their cultures and management processes.[74] And, as noted earlier, environmental impacts are being audited and accounted for as the "third bottom line." According to a recent corporate report, "If we aren't good corporate citizens as reflected in a Triple Bottom Line that takes into account social and environmental responsibilities along with financial ones—eventually our stock price, our profits, and our entire business could suffer."[75] Also, a CEO survey on sustainability by Accenture debunks the notion that sustainability and profitability are mutually exclusive corporate goals. The study found that sustainability is being increasingly recognized as a source of cost efficiencies and revenue growth. In many companies, sustainability activities have led to increases in revenue and profits. As Jeff Immelt, the CEO of General Electric, puts it, "Green is green."[76] Strategy Spotlight 1.2 shows how Walmart is able to dramatically increase its use of renewable energy—and make money on it, as well.

Many firms have profited by investing in socially responsible behavior, including those activities that enhance environmental sustainability. However, how do such "socially responsible" companies fare in terms of shareholder returns compared to benchmarks such as the Standard & Poor's 500 Index? Let's look at some of the evidence.

> SRI (socially responsible investing) is a broad-based approach to investing that now encompasses an estimated $3.7 trillion, or $1 out of every $9 under professional management in the United States.[77] SRI recognizes that corporate responsibility and societal concerns are considerations in investment decisions. With SRI, investors have the opportunity to put

HOW WALMART DEPLOYS GREEN ENERGY ON AN INDUSTRIAL SCALE—AND MAKES MONEY AT IT.

During a visit to Walmart's store in Mountain View, California, then-President Barack Obama said, "More and more companies like Walmart are realizing that wasting less energy isn't just good for the planet, it's good for business. It's good for the bottom line."

Despite the good public relations that Walmart got from the visit, the $480 billion company is far too savvy to lose money on its renewable energy initiatives. Instead, the retailer has off-loaded its capital investment, along with all of the risk, onto partners such as SolarCity. This minimizes their exposure by benefiting from the federal government's generous subsidies for alternative energy investments.

Walmart has installed 105 megawatts of solar panels on the roofs of 327 stores and distribution centers. That is about 6 percent of their locations and represents enough energy to power 20,000 houses. It has become the nation's largest commercial solar generator and it plans to double its number of panels by 2020.

How has Walmart cut its costs? The way it usually does—by using its tremendous power over its suppliers to risk their own capital in order to get what it wants. For example, it provides access to its roof space to SolarCity, or other installers, who install the panels (at a cost of about $1.2 million for the average store array). The supplier then sells the power generated to Walmart under a long-term deal—at a price that is typically cheaper than what the local electric utility would charge. Claims David Ozment, Walmart's energy chief, "The value proposition is obvious. Why put up our own capital?"

As of 2015, Walmart was getting 26 percent of its worldwide power from green sources—including wind, solar, fuel cells and hydropower. Walmart's longer-term goal is to use a combination of energy-efficient measures to source half of the company's energy needs from renewable sources by 2025. This will also result in an estimated 18 percent emissions reduction from its operations.

Sources: Helman, C. 2015. Everyday renewable energy. *Forbes.* November 23: 66, 68; and Makower, J. 2016. Insider Walmart's 2025 sustainability goals. *www.greenbiz.com.* November 4: np.

their money to work to build a more sustainable world while earning competitive returns both today and over time.

And, as the saying goes, nice guys don't have to finish last. The ING SRI Index Fund, which tracks the stocks of 50 companies, enjoyed a 47.4 percent return in a recent year. That easily beat the 2.65 percent gain of the Standard & Poor's 500 stock index. A review of the 145 socially responsible equity mutual and exchange-traded funds tracked by Morningstar also shows that 65 percent of them outperformed the S&P 500.[78]

Making the Business Case for Sustainability Initiatives We mentioned many financial and nonfinancial benefits associated with sustainability initiatives in the previous section. However, in practice, such initiatives often have difficulty making it through the conventional approval process within corporations. This is primarily because, before companies make investments in projects, managers want to know their return on investment.[79]

The ROIs on sustainability projects are often very difficult to quantify for a number of reasons. Among these are:

1. *The data necessary to calculate ROI accurately are often not available when it comes to sustainability projects.* However, sustainability programs may often find their success beyond company boundaries, so internal systems and process metrics can't capture all the relevant numbers.

2. *Many of the benefits from such projects are intangible.* Traditional financial models are built around relatively easy-to-measure, monetized results. Yet many of the benefits of sustainability projects involve fuzzy intangibles, such as the goodwill that can enhance a firm's brand equity.

3. *The payback period is on a different time frame.* Even when their future benefits can be forecast, sustainability projects often require longer-term payback windows.

Clearly, the case for sustainability projects needs to be made on the basis of a more holistic and comprehensive understanding of all the tangible and intangible benefits rather than whether or not they meet existing hurdle rates for traditional investment projects.

For example, 3M uses a lower hurdle rate for pollution prevention projects. When it comes to environmental projects, IKEA allows a 10- to 15-year payback period, considerably longer than it allows for other types of investment. And Diversey, a cleaning products company, has employed a portfolio approach. It has established two hurdles for projects in its carbon reduction plan: a three-year payback and a cost per megaton of carbon avoided. Out of 120 possible projects ranging from lighting retrofits to solar photovoltaic systems, only 30 cleared both hurdles. Although about 60 of the other ideas could reach *one,* an expanded 90-project portfolio, all added together, met the double hurdle. Subsequently, Diversey was able to increase its carbon reduction goal from 8 to 25 percent and generated a higher net present value.

Such approaches are the result of the recognition that the intangible benefits of sustainability projects—such as reducing risks, staying ahead of regulations, pleasing communities, and enhancing employee morale—are substantial even when they are difficult to quantify. Just as companies spend large fortunes on launching advertising campaigns or initiating R&D projects without a clear quantification of financial returns, sustainability investments are necessary even when it is difficult to calculate the ROI of such investments. The alternative of not making these investments is often no longer feasible.

LO 1-5

The need for greater empowerment throughout the organization.

THE STRATEGIC MANAGEMENT PERSPECTIVE: AN IMPERATIVE THROUGHOUT THE ORGANIZATION

Strategic management requires managers to take an integrative view of the organization and assess how all of the functional areas and activities fit together to help an organization achieve its goals and objectives. This cannot be accomplished if only the top managers in the organization take an integrative, strategic perspective of issues facing the firm and everyone else "fends for themselves" in their independent, isolated functional areas. Instead, people throughout the organization must strive toward overall goals.

The need for such a perspective is accelerating in today's increasingly complex, interconnected, ever-changing, global economy. As noted by Peter Senge of MIT, the days when Henry Ford, Alfred Sloan, and Tom Watson (top executives at Ford, General Motors, and IBM, respectively) "learned for the organization are gone."[80]

To develop and mobilize people and other assets, leaders are needed throughout the organization.[81] No longer can organizations be effective if the top "does the thinking" and the rest of the organization "does the work." Everyone must be involved in the strategic management process. There is a critical need for three types of leaders:

- *Local line leaders* who have significant profit-and-loss responsibility.
- *Executive leaders* who champion and guide ideas, create a learning infrastructure, and establish a domain for taking action.
- *Internal networkers* who, although they have little positional power and formal authority, generate their power through the conviction and clarity of their ideas.[82]

Top-level executives are key in setting the tone for the empowerment of employees. Consider Richard Branson, founder of the Virgin Group, whose core businesses include retail operations, hotels, communications, and an airline. He is well known for creating a culture and an informal structure where anybody in the organization can be involved in generating and acting upon new business ideas. In an interview, he stated: "If someone has an idea, they can pick up the phone and talk to me. I can vote, 'Done, let's do it.' Or, better still, they can just go ahead and do it. They know that they are not going to get a mouthful from me if they make a mistake."[83]

To inculcate a strategic management perspective, managers must create management processes to foster change. This involves planning, leading, and holding people accountable. At Netflix, leading people is not based on one's position in the hierarchy, nor an individual

STRATEGY AND THE VALUE OF INEXPERIENCE

Peter Gruber, chairman of Mandalay Entertainment, discovered that great ideas can come from the least expected sources. During the filming of the movie *Gorillas in the Mist,* his production company faced many problems. Rwanda—the site of the filming—was on the verge of revolution, the film needed to use 200 animals, and the screenplay required the gorillas to follow a script, that is, do what the script called for and "act." If that failed, the fallback position was to use dwarfs in gorilla suits on a soundstage—a strategy that usually failed.

Gruber explains how the "day was saved" by someone with very limited experience:

> We called an emergency meeting to solve these problems. In the middle of it, a young intern asked, "What if you let the gorillas write the story?" Everyone laughed and wondered what she was doing in the meeting with experienced filmmakers. Hours later, someone casually asked her what she had meant. She said, "What if you send a really good cinematographer into the jungle with a ton of film to shoot the gorillas, then you could write a story around what the gorillas did on film." It was a brilliant idea. And we did exactly what she suggested: We sent Alan Root, an Academy Award–nominated cinematographer into the jungle for three weeks. He came back with phenomenal footage that practically wrote the story for us.

The upshot? The film cost $20 million to shoot—half the original budget. And it was nominated for five Academy Awards—including Sigourney Weaver for best actress—and it won two Golden Globe Awards.

Source: Gruber, P. 1998. My greatest lesson. *Fast Company,* 14: 88–90; and *imdb.com.*

---

trait that is taught to people identified as "high potentials."[84] The expectation is that anyone can take initiative, make decisions, and influence others consistent with the firm's strategy. Everyone gets—and receives—feedback from team members, supervisors, managers, and customers. As part of the overall system that emphasizes transparency, there is the shared belief at Netflix that good results depend on people providing their insights and perspectives. Getting alignment, direction, and obtaining results the right way is essential. Those who fail to achieve this are asked to leave the firm.

We'd like to close with our favorite example of how inexperience can be a virtue. It further reinforces the benefits of having broad involvement throughout the organization in the strategic management process (see Strategy Spotlight 1.3).

ENSURING COHERENCE IN STRATEGIC DIRECTION

Employees and managers must strive toward common goals and objectives.[85] By specifying desired results, it becomes much easier to move forward. Otherwise, when no one knows what the firm is striving to accomplish, individuals have no idea of what to work toward. Alan Mulally, former CEO at Ford Motor Company, stressed the importance of perspective in creating a sense of mission: "What are we? What is our real purpose? And then, how do you include everybody so you know where you are on that plan, so you can work on areas that need special attention." [86]

Organizations express priorities best through stated goals and objectives that form a **hierarchy of goals,** which includes the firm's vision, mission, and strategic objectives.[87] What visions may lack in specificity, they make up for in their ability to evoke powerful and compelling mental images. On the other hand, strategic objectives tend to be more specific and provide a more direct means of determining if the organization is moving toward broader, overall goals.[88] Visions, as one would expect, also have longer time horizons than either mission statements or strategic objectives. Exhibit 1.6 depicts the hierarchy of goals and its relationship to two attributes: general versus specific and time horizon.

LO 1-6

How an awareness of a hierarchy of strategic goals can help an organization achieve coherence in its strategic direction.

hierarchy of goals organizational goals ranging from, at the top, those that are less specific yet able to evoke powerful and compelling mental images, to, at the bottom, those that are more specific and measurable.

EXHIBIT 1.6 A Hierarchy of Goals

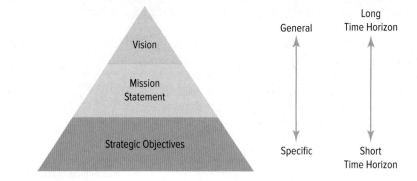

Organizational Vision

A **vision** is a goal that is "massively inspiring, overarching, and long term."[89] It represents a destination that is driven by and evokes passion. For example, Wendy Kopp, founder of Teach for America, notes that her vision for the organization, which strives to improve the quality of inner-city schools, draws many applicants: "We're looking for people who are magnetized to this notion, this vision, that one day all children in our nation should have the opportunity to attain an excellent education." [90]

Leaders must develop and implement a vision. A vision may or may not succeed; it depends on whether or not everything else happens according to an organization's strategy. As Mark Hurd, Hewlett-Packard's former CEO, humorously points out: "Without execution, vision is just another word for hallucination."[91]

In a survey of executives from 20 different countries, respondents were asked what they believed were a leader's key traits.[92] Ninety-eight percent responded that "a strong sense of vision" was the most important. Similarly, when asked about the critical knowledge skills, the leaders cited "strategy formulation to achieve a vision" as the most important skill. In other words, managers need to have not only a vision but also a plan to implement it. Regretfully, 90 percent reported a lack of confidence in their own skills and ability to conceive a vision. For example, T. J. Rogers, CEO of Cypress Semiconductor, an electronic-chip maker that faced some difficulties in 1992, lamented that his own shortsightedness caused the danger: "I did not have the 50,000-foot view, and got caught."[93]

One of the most famous examples of a vision is Disneyland's: "To be the happiest place on earth." Other examples are:

- "Restoring patients to full life." (Medtronic)
- "Our vision is to be the world's best quick service restaurant." (McDonald's)
- "To organize the world's information and make it universally accessible and useful." (Google)
- "To give everyone in the world the power to share and make the world more open and connected" (Facebook)

Although such visions cannot be accurately measured by a specific indicator of how well they are being achieved, they do provide a fundamental statement of an organization's values, aspirations, and goals. Such visions go well beyond narrow financial objectives, of course, and strive to capture both the minds and hearts of employees.

The vision statement may also contain a slogan, diagram, or picture—whatever grabs attention.[94] The aim is to capture the essence of the more formal parts of the vision in a few words that are easily remembered, yet that evoke the spirit of the entire vision statement. In its 20-year battle with Xerox, Canon's slogan, or battle cry, was "Beat Xerox." Motorola's slogan is "Total Customer Satisfaction." Outboard Marine Corporation's slogan is "To Take the World Boating."

Clearly, vision statements are not a cure-all. Sometimes they backfire and erode a company's credibility. Visions fail for many reasons, including the following:[95]

The Walk Doesn't Match the Talk   An idealistic vision can arouse employee enthusiasm. However, that same enthusiasm can be quickly dashed if employees find that senior management's behavior is not consistent with the vision. Often, vision is a sloganeering campaign of new buzzwords and empty platitudes like "devotion to the customer," "teamwork," or "total quality" that aren't consistently backed by management's action.

Irrelevance   Visions created in a vacuum—unrelated to environmental threats or opportunities or an organization's resources and capabilities—often ignore the needs of those who are expected to buy into them. Employees reject visions that are not anchored in reality.

Not the Holy Grail   Managers often search continually for the one elusive solution that will solve their firm's problems—that is, the next "holy grail" of management. They may have tried other management fads only to find that they fell short of their expectations. However, they remain convinced that one exists. A vision simply cannot be viewed as a magic cure for an organization's illness.

Too Much Focus Leads to Missed Opportunities   The downside of too much focus is that in directing people and resources toward a grandiose vision, losses can be significant. It is analogous to focusing your eyes on a small point on a wall. Clearly, you would not have very much peripheral vision. Similarly, organizations must strive to be aware of unfolding events in both their external and internal environment when formulating and implementing strategies.

An Ideal Future Irreconciled with the Present   Although visions are not designed to mirror reality, they must be anchored somehow in it. People have difficulty identifying with a vision that paints a rosy picture of the future but does not account for the often hostile environment in which the firm competes or that ignores some of the firm's weaknesses.

Mission Statements

A company's **mission statement** differs from its vision in that it encompasses both the purpose of the company and the basis of competition and competitive advantage.

Exhibit 1.7 contains the vision statement and mission statement of WellPoint Health Network (renamed Anthem, Inc., in December 2014), a giant $79 billion managed health care organization. Note that while the vision statement is broad-based, the mission statement is more specific and focused on the means by which the firm will compete.

Effective mission statements incorporate the concept of stakeholder management, suggesting that organizations must respond to multiple constituencies. Customers, employees, suppliers, and owners are the primary stakeholders, but others may also play an important role. Mission statements also have the greatest impact when they reflect an organization's enduring,

mission statement
a set of organizational goals that identifies the purpose of the organization, its basis of competition, and competitive advantage.

Vision
WellPoint *will redefine our industry:* Through a new generation of consumer-friendly products that put individuals back in control of their future.

Mission
The WellPoint companies provide health *security* by offering a *choice* of quality branded health and related financial services *designed* to meet the *changing* expectations of individuals, families, and their sponsors throughout a *lifelong* relationship.

Source: WellPoint Health Network company records.

EXHIBIT 1.7
Comparing WellPoint Health Network's Vision and Mission

overarching strategic priorities and competitive positioning. Mission statements also can vary in length and specificity. The three mission statements below illustrate these issues.

- "To produce superior financial returns for our shareholders as we serve our customers with the highest quality transportation, logistics, and e-commerce." (Federal Express)
- "Build the best product, cause no unnecessary harm, use business to inspire and implement solutions to the environmental crisis." (Patagonia)
- "To be the very best in the business. Our game plan is status go . . . we are constantly looking ahead, building on our strengths, and reaching for new goals. In our quest of these goals, we look at the three stars of the Brinker logo and are reminded of the basic values that are the strength of this company . . . People, Quality and Profitability. Everything we do at Brinker must support these core values. We also look at the eight golden flames depicted in our logo, and are reminded of the fire that ignites our mission and makes up the heart and soul of this incredible company. These flames are: Customers, Food, Team, Concepts, Culture, Partners, Community, and Shareholders. As keeper of these flames, we will continue to build on our strengths and work together to be the best in the business." (Brinker International, whose restaurant chains include Chili's and On the Border)[96]

Few mission statements identify profit or any other financial indicator as the sole purpose of the firm. Indeed, many do not even mention profit or shareholder return.[97] Employees of organizations or departments are usually the mission's most important audience. For them, the mission should help to build a common understanding of purpose and commitment to nurture.

A good mission statement, by addressing each principal theme, must communicate why an organization is special and different. Two studies that linked corporate values and mission statements with financial performance found that the most successful firms mentioned values other than profits. The less successful firms focused almost entirely on profitability.[98] In essence, profit is the metaphorical equivalent of oxygen, food, and water that the body requires. They are not the point of life, but without them, there is no life.

Vision statements tend to be quite enduring and seldom change. However, a firm's mission can and should change when competitive conditions dramatically change or the firm is faced with new threats or opportunities.

Sometimes a firm needs to shrink significantly. Such initiatives can enable a firm to regroup, redeploy, and restart profitable growth. Strategy Spotlight 1.4 explains how Perceptual Limited, an Australian investment and trustee group, recovered from financial decline by reducing operating costs, eliminating noncore businesses, and rallying around its founder's original mission.

Strategic Objectives

strategic objectives
a set of organizational goals that are used to put into practice the mission statement and that are specific and cover a well-defined time frame.

Strategic objectives are used to operationalize the mission statement.[99] That is, they help to provide guidance on how the organization can fulfill or move toward the "higher goals" in the goal hierarchy—the mission and vision. Thus, they are more specific and cover a more well-defined time frame. Setting objectives demands a yardstick to measure the fulfillment of the objectives.[100]

Exhibit 1.8 lists several firms' strategic objectives—both financial and nonfinancial. While most of them are directed toward generating greater profits and returns for the owners of the business, others are directed at customers or society at large.

For objectives to be meaningful, they need to satisfy several criteria. An objective must be:

- *Measurable.* There must be at least one indicator (or yardstick) that measures progress against fulfilling the objective.
- *Specific.* This provides a clear message as to what needs to be accomplished.
- *Appropriate.* It must be consistent with the organization's vision and mission.

HOW PERCEPTUAL LIMITED SUCCEEDED BY RALLYING AROUND THE FOUNDER'S ORIGINAL MISSION

Perceptual Limited has enjoyed a long and storied history. It was established in 1886 to manage the trusts and estates of Australia's wealthy families and led the market for most of its history. However, as it grew it lost its focus and began diversifying into several new business areas. By 2011, the firm was struggling—its share price had slid from a high of $84 to $24 in four years and profits were down almost 70 percent. Not surprisingly, shareholders were calling publicly for new leadership and a major repositioning of the firm. Enter Geoff Lloyd, Perceptual's third CEO in twelve months.

Lloyd discovered that the firm had become internally competitive and had grown incredibly complex over time by entering many new businesses—and did not hold leadership positions in most of them. He was convinced that he needed to restore the company to its original core mission: the protection of Australia's wealth. To do this, he realized he would need to make the firm "faster, more confident, and, above all, simpler."

He quickly made many changes. He replaced 10 of 11 members of the management team with people who had no vested interest in the past decisions. He launched Transformation 2015—which included several initiatives directed toward reducing complexity at all levels. These included: (1) reducing the number of businesses from 11 to three—asset management, high net worth advisory and trustee services, and corporate fiduciary services (after all, just two businesses were responsible for 95 percent of the profits!), (2) reducing real estate holdings by half, and (3) reducing headquarters staff by 50 percent. His team also found that Perceptual was using more than 3,000 computer systems and applications.

Along with all of the cutbacks, Lloyd and his management team focused on a plan to gain market share by investing in the firm's core. He led town hall meetings to explain the company's situation and to ignite interest for its core values. Key among his efforts was to get employees to refocus on the founding principles of the company. During the process, Lloyd found something remarkable: Perceptual's original trust business was so strong that it still had its first customer—125 years later.

Efforts by Lloyd and his management team led to a dramatic turnaround. Its stock price more than doubled within four years; employee engagement has significantly increased; the firm is gaining market share in its core markets; and net profits have increased over 16 percent each year from 2011 to 2015.

Sources: Zook, C. & Allen, J. Reigniting growth. *Harvard Business Review.* 94(3): 70-76; *www.perceptual2015. reportonline.com.au*; and, *www.perceptual.com.au.*

- *Realistic.* It must be an achievable target given the organization's capabilities and opportunities in the environment. In essence, it must be challenging but doable.
- *Timely.* There must be a time frame for achieving the objective. As the economist John Maynard Keynes once said, "In the long run, we are all dead!"

When objectives satisfy the above criteria, there are many benefits. First, they help to channel all employees' efforts toward common goals. This helps the organization concentrate and conserve valuable resources and work collectively in a timely manner.

Second, challenging objectives can help to motivate and inspire employees to higher levels of commitment and effort. Much research has supported the notion that people work

EXHIBIT 1.8

Strategic Objectives

Strategic Objectives (Financial)

- Increase sales growth 6 percent to 8 percent and accelerate core net earnings growth from 13 percent to 15 percent per share in each of the next 5 years. (Procter & Gamble)
- Generate Internet-related revenue of $1.5 billion. (AutoNation)
- Increase the contribution of Banking Group earnings from investments, brokerage, and insurance from 16 percent to 25 percent. (Wells Fargo)
- Cut corporate overhead costs by $30 million per year. (Fortune Brands)

Strategic Objectives (Nonfinancial)

- We want a majority of our customers, when surveyed, to say they consider Wells Fargo the best financial institution in the community. (Wells Fargo)
- Reduce volatile air emissions 15 percent by 2015 from 2010 base year, indexed to net sales. (3M)
- Our goal is to help save 100,000 more lives each year. (Varian Medical Systems)
- We want to be the top-ranked supplier to our customers. (PPG)

Sources: Company documents and annual reports.

Seventh Generation's Decision Dilemma

A strike idled 67,300 workers of the United Food and Commercial Workers (UFCW) who worked at Albertsons, Ralphs, and Vons—all large grocery store chains. These stores sold natural home products made by Seventh Generation, a socially conscious company. Interestingly, the inspiration for its name came from the Great Law of the Haudenosaunee. (This Law of Peace of the Iroquois Confederacy in North America has its roots in the 14th century.) The law states that "in our every deliberation we must consider the impact of our decisions on the next seven generations." Accordingly, the company's mission is "To inspire a revolution that nurtures the health of the next seven generations," and its values are to "care wholeheartedly, collaborate deliberately, nurture nature, innovate disruptively, and be a trusted brand."

Clearly, Seventh Generation faced a dilemma: On the one hand, it believed that the strikers had a just cause. However, if it honored the strikers by not crossing the picket lines, the firm would lose the shelf space for its products in the stores it had worked so hard to secure. Honoring the strikers would also erode its trust with the large grocery stores. On the other hand, if Seventh Generation ignored the strikers and proceeded to send its products to the stores, it would be compromising its values and thereby losing trust and credibility with several stakeholders—its customers, distributors, and employees.

Discussion Questions

1. How important should the Seventh Generation values be considered when deciding what to do?
2. How can Seventh Generation solve this dilemma?

Sources: Russo, M. V. 2010. *Companies on a mission: Entrepreneurial strategies for growing sustainably, responsibly, and profitably.* Stanford: Stanford University Press: 94–96; Seventh Generation. 2012. Seventh generation's mission—Corporate social responsibility. *www.seventhgeneration.com,* np; Foster, A. C. 2004. Major work stoppage in 2003. U.S. Bureau of Labor and Statistics. Compensation and Working Conditions. *www.bls.gov,* November 23: np; *Fast Company.* 2008. 45 social entrepreneurs who are changing the world. Profits with purpose: Seventh Generation. *www.fastcompany,* np; and *Ratical.* Undated. The six nations: Oldest living participatory democracy on earth. *www.ratical.org,* np.

harder when they are striving toward specific goals instead of being asked simply to "do their best."

Third, as we noted earlier in the chapter, there is always the potential for different parts of an organization to pursue their own goals rather than overall company goals. Although well intentioned, these may work at cross-purposes to the organization as a whole. Meaningful objectives thus help to resolve conflicts when they arise.

Finally, proper objectives provide a yardstick for rewards and incentives. They will ensure a greater sense of equity or fairness when rewards are allocated.

A caveat: When formulating strategic objectives, managers need to remember that too many objectives can result in a lack of focus and diminished results:

> A few years ago CEO Tony Petrucciani and his team at Single Source Systems, a software firm in Fishers, Indiana, set 15 annual objectives, such as automating some of its software functions. However, the firm, which got distracted by having so many items on its objective list, missed its $8.1 million revenue benchmark by 11 percent. "Nobody focused on any one thing," he says. Going forward, Petrucciani decided to set just a few key priorities. This helped the company to meet its goal of $10 million in sales. Sometimes, less is more![101]

In addition to the above, organizations have lower-level objectives that are more specific than strategic objectives. These are often referred to as short-term objectives—essential components of a firm's "action plan" that are critical in implementing the firm's chosen strategy. We discuss these issues in detail in Chapter 9.

Reflecting on Career Implications . . .

This chapter discusses both the long-term focus of strategy and the need for coherence in strategic direction. The following questions extend these themes by asking students to consider their own strategic goals and how they fit with the goals of the firms in which they work or would seek employment.

- ▣ **Attributes of Strategic Management:** The attributes of strategic management described in this chapter are applicable to your personal careers as well. What are your overall goals and objectives? Who are the stakeholders you have to consider in making your career decisions (family, community, etc.)? What trade-offs do you see between your long-term and short-term goals?

- ▣ **Intended versus Emergent Strategies:** While you may have planned your career trajectory carefully, don't be too tied to it. Strive to take advantage of new opportunities as they arise. Many promising career opportunities may "emerge" that were not part of your intended career strategy or your specific job assignment. Take initiative by pursuing opportunities to get additional training (e.g., learn a software or a statistical package), volunteering for a short-term overseas assignment, etc. You may be in a better position to take advantage of such emergent opportunities if you take the effort to prepare for

them. For example, learning a foreign language may position you better for an overseas opportunity.

- ▣ **Ambidexterity:** In Strategy Spotlight 1.1, we discussed the four most important traits of ambidextrous individuals. These include looking for opportunities beyond the description of one's job, seeking out opportunities to collaborate with others, building internal networks, and multitasking. Evaluate yourself along each of these criteria. If you score low, think of ways in which you can improve your ambidexterity.

- ▣ **Strategic Coherence:** What is the mission of your organization? What are the strategic objectives of the department or unit you are working for? In what ways does your own role contribute to the mission and objectives? What can you do differently in order to help the organization attain its mission and strategic objectives?

- ▣ **Strategic Coherence:** Setting strategic objectives is important in your personal career as well. Identify and write down three or four important strategic objectives you want to accomplish in the next few years (finish your degree, find a better-paying job, etc.). Are you allocating your resources (time, money, etc.) to enable you to achieve these objectives? Are your objectives measurable, timely, realistic, specific, and appropriate?

summary

We began this introductory chapter by defining strategic management and articulating some of its key attributes. Strategic management is defined as "consisting of the analyses, decisions, and actions an organization undertakes to create and sustain competitive advantages." The issue of how and why some firms outperform others in the marketplace is central to the study of strategic management. Strategic management has four key attributes: It is directed at overall organizational goals, includes multiple stakeholders, incorporates both short-term and long-term perspectives, and incorporates trade-offs between efficiency and effectiveness.

The second section discussed the strategic management process. Here, we paralleled the above definition of strategic management and focused on three core activities in the strategic management process—strategy analysis, strategy formulation, and strategy implementation. We noted how each of these activities is highly interrelated to and interdependent on the others. We also discussed how each of the first 12 chapters in this text fits into the three core activities.

Next, we introduced two important concepts—corporate governance and stakeholder management—which must be taken into account throughout the strategic management process. Governance mechanisms can be broadly divided into two groups: internal and external. Internal governance mechanisms include shareholders (owners), management (led by the chief executive officer), and the board of directors. External control is exercised by auditors, banks,

analysts, and an active business press as well as the threat of takeovers. We identified five key stakeholders in all organizations: owners, customers, suppliers, employees, and society at large. Successful firms go beyond an overriding focus on satisfying solely the interests of owners. Rather, they recognize the inherent conflicts that arise among the demands of the various stakeholders as well as the need to endeavor to attain "symbiosis"—that is, interdependence and mutual benefit—among the various stakeholder groups. Managers must also recognize the need to act in a socially responsible manner which, if done effectively, can enhance a firm's innovativeness. The "shared value" approach represents an innovative perspective on creating value for the firm and society at the same time. The managers also should recognize and incorporate issues related to environmental sustainability in their strategic actions.

In the fourth section, we discussed factors that have accelerated the rate of unpredictable change that managers face today. Such factors, and the combination of them, have increased the need for managers and employees throughout the organization to have a strategic management perspective and to become more empowered.

The final section addressed the need for consistency among a firm's vision, mission, and strategic objectives. Collectively, they form an organization's hierarchy of goals. Visions should evoke powerful and compelling mental images. However, they are not very specific. Strategic objectives, on the other hand, are much more specific and are vital to ensuring that the organization is striving toward fulfilling its vision and mission.

1. How is "strategic management" defined in the text, and what are its four key attributes?
2. Briefly discuss the three key activities in the strategic management process. Why is it important for managers to recognize the interdependent nature of these activities?
3. Explain the concept of "stakeholder management." Why shouldn't managers be solely interested in stockholder management, that is, maximizing the returns for owners of the firm—its shareholders?
4. What is "corporate governance"? What are its three key elements, and how can it be improved?
5. How can "symbiosis" (interdependence, mutual benefit) be achieved among a firm's stakeholders?
6. Why do firms need to have a greater strategic management perspective and empowerment in the strategic management process throughout the organization?
7. What is meant by a "hierarchy of goals"? What are the main components of it, and why must consistency be achieved among them?

key terms

romantic view of leadership 4
external control view of leadership 5
strategic management 6
strategy 6
competitive advantage 6
operational effectiveness 6
stakeholders 7
effectiveness 8
efficiency 8

ambidexterity 9
strategic management process 10
intended strategy 10
realized strategy 10
strategy analysis 12
strategy formulation 12
strategy implementation 13
corporate governance 16
stakeholder management 17
social responsibility 19
triple bottom line 20
hierarchy of goals 23
vision 24
mission statement 25
strategic objectives 26

APPLICATION QUESTIONS & EXERCISES

1. Go to the Internet and look up one of these company sites: *www.walmart.com*, *www.ge.com*, or *www.fordmotor.com*. What are some of the key events that would represent the "romantic" perspective of leadership? What are some of the key events that depict the "external control" perspective of leadership?
2. Select a company that competes in an industry in which you are interested. What are some of the recent demands that stakeholders have placed on this company? Can you find examples of how the company is trying to develop "symbiosis" (interdependence and mutual benefit) among its stakeholders? (Use the Internet and library resources.)
3. Provide examples of companies that are actively trying to increase the amount of empowerment in the strategic management process throughout the organization. Do these companies seem to be having positive outcomes? Why? Why not?
4. Look up the vision statements and/or mission statements for a few companies. Do you feel that they are constructive and useful as a means of motivating employees and providing a strong strategic direction? Why? Why not? (*Note:* Annual reports, along with the Internet, may be good sources of information.)

EXPERIENTIAL EXERCISE

Using the Internet or library sources, select four organizations—two in the private sector and two in the public sector. Find their mission statements. Complete the following exhibit by identifying the stakeholders that are mentioned. Evaluate the differences between firms in the private sector and those in the public sector.

Organization Name				
Mission Statement				
Stakeholders (√ = mentioned)				
1. Customers				
2. Suppliers				
3. Managers/employees				
4. Community-at-large				
5. Owners				
6. Others?				
7. Others?				

ETHICS QUESTIONS

1. A company focuses solely on short-term profits to provide the greatest return to the owners of the business (i.e., the shareholders in a publicly held firm). What ethical issues could this raise?

2. A firm has spent some time—with input from managers at all levels—on developing a vision statement and a mission statement. Over time, however, the behavior of some executives is contrary to these statements. Could this raise some ethical issues?

REFERENCES

1. Gunther, M. 2010. Fallen angels. *Fortune,* November 1: 75–78.

2. Colvin, G. 2015. The 21st century corporation. *Fortune,* November 1: 103–112; and, Anonymous. 2016. The rise of superstars. *The Economist,* September 17: 3–16.

3. Kapner, S. & Lublin, J. S. 2016. Lands' end CEO is pushed out after 19 months. *The Wall Street Journal,* September 27: B1; Anonymous. 2016. Lands' End CEO Marchionni out after failing to take brand upscale. *Fortune.com,* September 26: np; and, Kapner, S. 2016. New Lands' End CEO delivers high fashion—and a culture clash. *www. wsj.com,* May 6: np.

4. For a discussion of the "romantic" versus "external control" perspective, refer to Meindl, J. R. 1987. The romance of leadership and the evaluation of organizational performance. *Academy of Management Journal,* 30: 92–109; and Pfeffer, J. & Salancik, G. R. 1978. *The external control of organizations: A resource dependence perspective.* New York: Harper & Row.

5. A recent perspective on the "romantic view" of leadership is provided by Mintzberg, H. 2004. Leadership and management development: An afterword. *Academy of Management Executive,* 18(3): 140–142.

6. For a discussion of the best and worst managers for 2008, read Anonymous. 2009. The best managers. *BusinessWeek,* January 19: 40–41; and The worst managers. On page 42 in the same issue.

7. Burrows, P. 2009. Apple without its core? *BusinessWeek,* January 26/ February 2: 31.

8. For a study on the effects of CEOs on firm performance, refer to Kor, Y. Y. & Misangyi, V. F. 2008. *Strategic Management Journal,* 29(11):1357–1368.

9. Colvin, G. 2016. Developing an internal market for talent. *Fortune.* March 1: 22.

10. Kapner, S. & Lublin, *op. cit.*

11. Ewing, J. 2008. South Africa emerges from the shadows. *BusinessWeek,* December 15: 52–56.

12. For an interesting perspective on the need for strategists to maintain a global mind-set, refer to Begley, T. M. & Boyd, D. P. 2003. The need for a global mind-set. *MIT Sloan Management Review,* 44(2): 25–32.

13. Porter, M. E. 1996. What is strategy? *Harvard Business Review,* 74(6): 61–78.

14. See, for example, Barney, J. B. & Arikan, A. M. 2001. The resource-based view: Origins and implications. In Hitt, M. A., Freeman, R. E., & Harrison, J. S. (Eds.), *Handbook of strategic management:* 124–189. Malden, MA: Blackwell.

15. Porter, M. E. 1996. What is strategy? *Harvard Business Review,* 74(6): 61–78; and Hammonds, K. H. 2001. Michael Porter's big ideas. *Fast Company,* March: 55–56.

16. This section draws upon Dess, G. G. & Miller, A. 1993. *Strategic management.* New York: McGraw-Hill.

17. See, for example, Hrebiniak, L. G. & Joyce, W. F. 1986. The strategic importance of managing myopia. *Sloan Management Review,* 28(1): 5–14.

18. Bryant, A. 2011. *The corner office.* New York: Times Books.

19. For an insightful discussion on how to manage diverse stakeholder groups, refer to Rondinelli, D. A. & London, T. 2003. How corporations and environmental groups cooperate: Assessing cross-sector alliances and collaborations. *Academy of Management Executive,* 17(1): 61–76.

20. Some dangers of a short-term perspective are addressed in Van Buren, M. E. & Safferstone, T. 2009. The quick wins paradox. *Harvard Business Review,* 67(1): 54–61.

21. Senge, P. 1996. Leading learning organizations: The bold, the powerful, and the invisible. In Hesselbein, F., Goldsmith, M., & Beckhard, R. (Eds.), *The leader of the future:* 41–58. San Francisco: Jossey-Bass.

22. Winston, A. S. 2014. *The big pivot.* Boston: Harvard Business Review.

23. Loeb, M. 1994. Where leaders come from. *Fortune,* September 19: 241 (quoting Warren Bennis).

24. Ignatius, A. 2016. The HBR Interview: Hewlett Packard Enterprise CEO Meg Whitman. *Harvard Business Review,* 94(5): 100.

25. This section draws on: Smith, W., Lewis, M., & Tushman, M. 2016. "Both/and" leadership. *Harvard Business Review,* 94(5): 63–70.

26. New perspectives on "management models" are addressed in Birkinshaw, J. & Goddard, J. 2009. What is your management model? *MIT Sloan Management Review,* 50(2): 81–90.

27. Mintzberg, H. 1985. Of strategies: Deliberate and emergent. *Strategic Management Journal,* 6: 257–272.

28. Some interesting insights on decision-making processes are found in Nutt, P. C. 2008. Investigating the success of decision making processes. *Journal of Management Studies,* 45(2): 425–455.

29. Smith, J. 2014. Go-to lawyers are in-house. *The Wall Street Journal,* September 15: B6.

30. Machota, J. 2016. Job description varies for NFL QBs," *The Dallas Morning News.* March 20: 4C.

31. Bryant, A. 2009. The corner office. *nytimes.com,* April 25: np.

32. A study investigating the sustainability of competitive advantage is Newbert, S. L. 2008. Value, rareness, competitive advantages, and performance: A conceptual-level empirical investigation of the resource-based view of the firm. *Strategic Management Journal,* 29(7): 745–768.

33. Good insights on mentoring are addressed in DeLong, T. J., Gabarro, J. J., & Lees, R. J. 2008. Why mentoring matters in a hypercompetitive world. *Harvard Business Review,* 66(1): 115–121.

34. Karlgaard, R. 2014. *The soft edge.* San Francisco: Jossey-Bass.

35. A unique perspective on differentiation strategies is Austin, R. D. 2008. High margins and the quest for aesthetic coherence. *Harvard Business Review,* 86(1): 18-19.

36. Some insights on partnering in the global area are discussed in MacCormack, A. & Forbath, T. 2008. *Harvard Business Review,* 66(1): 24, 26.

37. For insights on how firms can be successful in entering new markets in emerging economies, refer to Eyring, M. J., Johnson, M. W., & Nair, H. 2011. New business models in emerging markets. *Harvard Business Review,* 89(1/2): 88-95.

38. *Fortune.* 2012. December 3: 6.

39. An interesting discussion of the challenges of strategy implementation is Neilson, G. L., Martin, K. L., & Powers, E. 2008. The secrets of strategy execution. *Harvard Business Review,* 86(6): 61-70.

40. Interesting perspectives on strategy execution involving the link between strategy and operations are addressed in Kaplan, R. S. & Norton, D. P. 2008. Mastering the management system. *Harvard Business Review,* 66(1): 62-77.

41. An innovative perspective on organizational design is found in Garvin, D. A. & Levesque, L. C. 2008. The multiunit enterprise. *Harvard Business Review,* 86(6): 106-117.

42. Monks, R. & Minow, N. 2001. *Corporate governance* (2nd ed.). Malden, MA: Blackwell.

43. Intel Corp. 2007. Intel corporation board of directors guidelines on significant corporate governance issues. *www.intel.com*

44. Jones, T. J., Felps, W., & Bigley, G. A. 2007. Ethical theory and stakeholder-related decisions: The role of stakeholder culture. *Academy of Management Review,* 32(1): 137-155.

45. For example, see: The best (& worst) managers of the year, 2003. *BusinessWeek,* January 13: 58-92; and Lavelle, M. 2003. Rogues of the year. *Time,* January 6: 33-45.

46. Baer, D. A. 2014. The West's bruised confidence in capitalism. *The Wall Street Journal,* September 22: A17; and Miller, D. 2014. Greatness is gone. *Dallas Morning News,* October 26: 1 D.

47. Barton, D. & Wiseman, M. 2015. Where boards fall short. *Harvard Business Review,* 93(1/2): 100.

48. Hessel, E. & Woolley, S. 2008. Your money or your life. *Forbes,* October 27: 52.

49. Task, A. 2012. Finance CEO pay rose 20% in 2011, even as stocks stumbled. *www.finance.yahoo.com,* June 5: np.

50. Rosenberg, Y. 2016. This CEO got $142 million more than he deserved. *finance.yahoo.com:* February 17: np.

51. Some interesting insights on the role of activist investors can be found in Greenwood, R. & Schol, M. 2008. When (not) to listen to activist investors. *Harvard Business Review,* 66(1): 23-24.

52. For an interesting perspective on the changing role of boards of directors, refer to Lawler, E. & Finegold, D. 2005. Rethinking governance. *MIT Sloan Management Review,* 46(2): 67-70.

53. Benz, M. & Frey, B. S. 2007. Corporate governance: What can we learn from public governance? *Academy of Management Review,* 32(1): 92-104.

54. The salience of shareholder value is addressed in Carrott, G. T. & Jackson, S. E. 2009. Shareholder value must top the CEO's agenda. *Harvard Business Review,* 67(1): 22-24.

55. Stakeholder symbiosis. 1998. *Fortune,* March 30: S2.

56. An excellent review of stakeholder management theory can be found in Laplume, A. O., Sonpar, K., & Litz, R. A. 2008. Stakeholder theory: Reviewing a theory that moves us. *Journal of Management,* 34(6): 1152-1189.

57. For a definitive, recent discussion of the stakeholder concept, refer to Freeman, R. E. & McVae, J. 2001. A stakeholder approach to strategic management. In Hitt, M. A., Freeman, R. E., & Harrison, J. S. (Eds.), *Handbook of strategic management:* 189-207. Malden, MA: Blackwell.

58. Harrison, J. S., Bosse, D. A., & Phillips, R. A. 2010. Managing for stakeholders, stakeholder utility functions, and competitive advantage. *Strategic Management Journal,* 31(1): 58-74.

59. For an insightful discussion on the role of business in society, refer to Handy, op. cit.

60. Stakeholder symbiosis. op. cit., p. S3. The Walmart example draws on: Camillus, J. 2008. Strategy as a wicked problem. *Harvard Business Review,* 86(5): 100-101.

61. Sidhu, I. 2010. *Doing both.* Upper Saddle River, NJ: FT Press, 7-8.

62. Thomas, J. G. 2000. Macroenvironmetal forces. In Helms, M. M. (Ed.), *Encyclopedia of management* (4th ed.): 516-520. Farmington Hills, MI: Gale Group.

63. For a strong advocacy position on the need for corporate values and social responsibility, read Hollender, J. 2004. What matters most: Corporate values and social responsibility. *California Management Review,* 46(4): 111-119.

64. Rangan, K., Chase, L., & Karim, S. 2015. The truth about CSR. *Harvard Business Review,* 93(1/2): 41-49.

65. Bhattacharya, C. B. & Sen, S. 2004, Doing better at doing good: When, why, and how consumers respond to corporate social initiatives. *California Management Review,* 47(1): 9-24.

66. For some findings on the relationship between corporate social responsibility and firm performance, see Margolis, J. D. & Elfenbein, H. A. 2008. *Harvard Business Review,* 86(1): 19-20.

67. Cone Corporate Citizenship Study, 2002, *www.coneinc.com.*

68. Refer to *www.bsr.org.*

69. For an insightful discussion of the risks and opportunities associated with global warming, refer to Lash, J. & Wellington, F. 2007. Competitive advantage on a warming planet. *Harvard Business Review,* 85(3): 94-102.

70. Ignatius, A. 2015. Leadership with a conscience. *Harvard Business Review,* 93(11): 50-63.

71. This section draws on Hart, S. L. 1997. Beyond greening: Strategies for a sustainable world. *Harvard Business Review,* 75(1): 66-76; and Berry, M. A. & Rondinelli, D. A. 1998. Proactive corporate environmental management: A new industrial revolution. *Academy of Management Executive,* 12(2): 38-50.

72. For a creative perspective on environmental sustainability and competitive advantage as well as ethical implications, read Ehrenfeld, J. R. 2005. The roots of sustainability. *MIT Sloan Management Review,* 46(2): 23-25.

73. McKinsey & Company. 1991. *The corporate response to the environmental challenge.* Summary Report. Amsterdam: McKinsey & Company.

74. Delmas, M. A. & Montes-Sancho, M. J. 2010. Voluntary agreements to improve environmental quality: Symbolic and substantive cooperation. *Strategic Management Journal,* 31(6): 575-601.

75. Vogel, D. J. 2005. Is there a market for virtue? The business case for corporate social responsibility. *California Management Review,* 47(4): 19-36.

76. Esty, D. C. & Charnovitz, S. 2012. Green rules to drive innovation. *Harvard Business Review,* 90(3): 120-123.

77. Chamberlain, M. 2013. Socially responsible investing: What you need to know. *Forbes.com,* April 24: np.

78. Kaahwarski, T. 2010. It pays to be good. *Bloomberg Businessweek,* February 1 to February 8: 69.

79. This discussion draws on Kuehn, K. & McIntire, L. 2014. Sustainability a CFO can love. *Harvard Business Review,* 92(4): 66-74; and Esty, D. C. & Winston, A. S. 2009. *Green to gold.* Hoboken, NJ: Wiley.

80. Senge, P. M. 1990. The leader's new work: Building learning organizations. *Sloan Management Review,* 32(1): 7-23.

81. For an interesting perspective on the role of middle managers in the strategic management process, refer to Huy, Q. H. 2001. In praise of middle managers. *Harvard Business Review,* 79(8): 72-81.

82. Senge, 1996, op. cit., pp. 41-58.

83. Kets de Vries, M. F. R. 1998. Charisma in action: The transformational abilities of Virgin's Richard Branson and ABB's Percy Barnevik. *Organizational Dynamics,* 26(3): 7-21.

84. Worley, C. G., Williams, T. & Lawler, E. E. III. 2016. Creating management processes built for change. *MIT Sloan Management Review,* 58(1): 77-82.

85. An interesting discussion on how to translate top management's goals into concrete actions is found in Bungay, S. 2011. How to make the most of your company's strategy. *Harvard Business Review,* 89(1/2): 132-140.

86. Bryant, A. 2011. *The corner office.* New York: St. Martin's/Griffin, 171.

87. An insightful discussion about the role of vision, mission, and strategic objectives can be found in Collis, D. J. & Rukstad, M. G. 2008. Can you say what your strategy is? *Harvard Business Review,* 66(4): 82-90.

88. Our discussion draws on a variety of sources. These include Lipton, M. 1996. Demystifying the development of an organizational vision. *Sloan Management Review,* 37(4): 83-92; Bart, C. K. 2000. Lasting inspiration. *CA Magazine,* May: 49-50; and Quigley, J. V. 1994. Vision: How leaders develop it, share it, and sustain it. *Business Horizons,* September-October: 37-40.

89. Lipton, op. cit.

90. Bryant, A. 2011. *The corner office.* New York: St. Martin's/Griffin, 34.

91. Hardy, Q. 2007. The uncarly. *Forbes,* March 12: 82-90.

92. Some interesting perspectives on gender differences in organizational vision are discussed in Ibarra, H. & Obodaru, O. 2009. Women and the vision thing. *Harvard Business Review,* 67(1): 62-70.

93. Quigley, op. cit.

94. Ibid.

95. Lipton, op. cit. Additional pitfalls are addressed in this article.

96. Company records.

97. Lipton, op. cit.

98. Sexton, D. A. & Van Aukun, P. M. 1985. A longitudinal study of small business strategic planning. *Journal of Small Business Management,* January: 8-15, cited in Lipton, op. cit.

99. For an insightful perspective on the use of strategic objectives, refer to Chatterjee, S. 2005. Core objectives: Clarity in designing strategy. *California Management Review,* 47(2): 33-49.

100. Ibid.

101. Harnish, V. 2011. Five ways to get your strategy right. *Fortune,* April 11: 42.

Analyzing the External Environment of the Firm

Creating Competitive Advantages

After reading this chapter, you should have a good understanding of the following learning objectives:

LO2-1 The importance of developing forecasts of the business environment.

LO2-2 Why environmental scanning, environmental monitoring, and collecting competitive intelligence are critical inputs to forecasting.

LO2-3 Why scenario planning is a useful technique for firms competing in industries characterized by unpredictability and change.

LO2-4 The impact of the general environment on a firm's strategies and performance.

LO2-5 How forces in the competitive environment can affect profitability, and how a firm can improve its competitive position by increasing its power vis-à-vis these forces.

LO2-6 How the Internet and digitally based capabilities are affecting the five competitive forces and industry profitability.

LO2-7 The concept of strategic groups and their strategy and performance implications.

©Anatoli Styf/Shutterstock

LEARNING FROM MISTAKES

Analyzing the external environment is a critical step in recognizing and understanding the opportunities and threats that organizations face. And here is where some companies fail to do a good job. The fact is that few things really "sell themselves"—especially if they are new to the market. According to Booz & Company, 66 percent of new products fail within two years, and, according to the Doblin Group, an astonishing 96 percent of all innovations fail to deliver any return on a company's investment.[1]

Consider the example of Salemi Industries and the launch of its product, Cell Zone, in 2005. Although it tried to carefully analyze its potential market, it misread the market's demand for the product and paid a steep price for its mistake.[2] Mobile phone usage was sharply increasing, and its founder observed that patrons in places such as restaurants would be annoyed by the chatter of a nearby guest having a private (but loud!) conversation. Salemi Industries interpreted this observation as an opportunity to create the Cell Zone: a "commercial sound resistant cell phone booth that provides a convenient and disturbance-free environment to place and receive phone calls . . . with a design feature to promote product or service on its curvilinear outer shell," according to the firm's website.

Salemi Industries' key error was that it failed to take into consideration an emerging technology—the increasing popularity of text messaging and other nonvoice communication technology applications and how that would affect the sales of its product. In addition to this technology shift, the target locations (restaurants) thought the price ($3,500) was too steep, and they were not interested in or willing to give up productive square footage for patrons to hold private conversations. Not surprisingly, the firm has sold only 300 units (100 of them in college libraries), and Salemi Industries has lost over $650,000 to date.

Discussion Questions

1. What is the biggest stumbling block for Cell Zone?
2. Are there other market segments where Cell Zone might work?

"We built a better mousetrap but there were no mice" (commenting on his firm's development *of blue windshield glass for the automobile industry).*[3]

Gary W. Weber, PPG Industries

Successful managers must recognize opportunities and threats in their firm's external environment. They must be aware of what's going on outside their company. If they focus exclusively on the efficiency of internal operations, the firm may degenerate into the world's most efficient producer of buggy whips, typewriters, or carbon paper. But if they miscalculate the market, opportunities will be lost—hardly an enviable position for their firm. As we saw from the Cell Zone example, misreading the market can lead to negative consequences.

In *Competing for the Future,* Gary Hamel and C. K. Prahalad suggest that "every manager carries around in his or her head a set of biases, assumptions, and presuppositions about the structure of the relevant 'industry,' about how one makes money in the industry, about who the competition is and isn't, about who the customers are and aren't, and so on."[4] Environmental analysis requires you to continually question such assumptions. Peter Drucker, considered the father of modern management, labeled these interrelated sets of assumptions the "theory of the business."[5] One could attribute much of the failure of Ms. Marchionni's tenure at Lands' End to her efforts to re-invent the apparel brand in a way that was in conflict with both its customer base as well as the firm's family culture and wholesome style—as we discussed in in the opening case in Chapter 1.

A firm's strategy may be good at one point in time, but it may go astray when management's frame of reference gets out of touch with the realities of the actual business situation. This results when management's assumptions, premises, or beliefs are incorrect or when internal inconsistencies among them render the overall "theory of the business" invalid. As Warren Buffett, investor extraordinaire, colorfully notes, "Beware of past performance 'proofs.' If history books were the key to riches, the Forbes 400 would consist of librarians."

In the business world, many once-successful firms have fallen. Today we may wonder who will be the next Blockbuster, Borders, Circuit City, or Radio Shack.

ENHANCING AWARENESS OF THE EXTERNAL ENVIRONMENT

LO 2-1

The importance of developing forecasts of the business environment.

perceptual acuity
the ability to sense what is coming before the fog clears.

So how do managers become environmentally aware?[6] Ram Charan, an adviser to many Fortune 500 CEOs, provides some useful insights with his concept of **perceptual acuity**.[7] He defines it as "the ability to sense what is coming before the fog clears." He draws on Ted Turner as an example: Turner saw the potential of 24-hour news before anyone else did. All the ingredients were there, but no others connected them until he created CNN. Like Turner, the best CEOs are compulsively tuned to the external environment and seem to have a sixth sense that picks up anomalies and detects early warning signals which may represent key threats or opportunities.

How can perceptual acuity be improved? Although many CEOs may complain that the top job is a lonely one, they can't do it effectively by sitting alone in their office. Instead, high-performing CEOs are constantly meeting with people and searching out information. Charan provides three examples:

- One CEO gets together with his critical people for half a day every eight weeks to discuss what's new and what's going on in the world. The setting is informal, and outsiders often attend. The participants look beyond the lens of their industry because some trends that affect one industry may impact others later on.
- Another CEO meets four times a year with about four other CEOs of large, but noncompeting, diverse global companies. Examining the world from multiple perspectives, they share their thinking about how different trends may develop. The CEO then goes back to his own weekly management meeting and throws out "a bunch of hand grenades to shake up people's thinking."
- Two companies ask outsiders to critique strategy during their board's strategy sessions. Such input typically leads to spirited discussions that provide valued input on the hinge assumptions and options that are under consideration. Once, the focus was on pinpointing the risk inherent in a certain strategy. Now, discussions have led to finding that the company was missing a valuable opportunity.

We will now address three important processes—scanning, monitoring, and gathering competitive intelligence—used to develop forecasts.[8] Exhibit 2.1 illustrates relationships among these important activities. We also discuss the importance of scenario planning in anticipating major future changes in the external environment and the role of SWOT analysis.[9]

EXHIBIT 2.1 Inputs to Forecasting

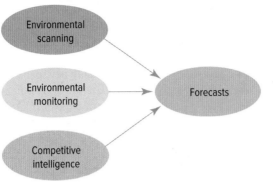

The Role of Scanning, Monitoring, Competitive Intelligence, and Forecasting

Environmental Scanning   **Environmental scanning** involves surveillance of a firm's external environment to predict environmental changes and detect changes already underway.[10,11] This alerts the organization to critical trends and events before changes develop a discernible pattern and before competitors recognize them.[12] Otherwise, the firm may be forced into a reactive mode.[13]

Experts agree that spotting key trends requires a combination of knowing your business and your customer as well as keeping an eye on what's happening around you. Such a big-picture/small-picture view enables you to better identify the emerging trends that will affect your business.

Leading firms in an industry can also be a key indicator of emerging trends.[14] For example, with its wide range of household goods, Procter & Gamble is a barometer for consumer spending. Any sign that it can sell more of its premium products without cutting prices sharply indicates that shoppers may finally be becoming less price-sensitive with everyday purchases. In particular, investors will examine the performance of beauty products like Olay moisturizers and CoverGirl cosmetics for evidence that spending on small, discretionary pick-me-ups is improving.

Environmental Monitoring   **Environmental monitoring** tracks the evolution of environmental trends, sequences of events, or streams of activities. They may be trends that the firm came across by accident or ones that were brought to its attention from outside the organization.[15] Monitoring enables firms to evaluate how dramatically environmental trends are changing the competitive landscape.

One of the authors of this text has conducted on-site interviews with executives from several industries to identify indicators that firms monitor as inputs to their strategy process. Examples of such indicators included:

- *A Motel 6 executive.* The number of rooms in the budget segment of the industry in the United States and the difference between the average daily room rate and the consumer price index (CPI).
- *A Pier 1 Imports executive.* Net disposable income (NDI), consumer confidence index, and housing starts.
- *A Johnson & Johnson medical products executive.* Percentage of gross domestic product (GDP) spent on health care, number of active hospital beds, and the size and power of purchasing agents (indicates the concentration of buyers).

Such indices are critical for managers in determining a firm's strategic direction and resource allocation.

environmental scanning
surveillance of a firm's external environment to predict environmental changes and detect changes already under way.

LO 2-2

Why environmental scanning, environmental monitoring, and collecting competitive intelligence are critical inputs to forecasting.

environmental monitoring
a firm's analysis of the external environment that tracks the evolution of environmental trends, sequences of events, or streams of activities.

Competitive Intelligence   **Competitive intelligence** (CI) helps firms define and understand their industry and identify rivals' strengths and weaknesses.[16] This includes the intelligence gathering associated with collecting data on competitors and interpreting such data. Done properly, competitive intelligence helps a company avoid surprises by anticipating competitors' moves and decreasing response time.[17]

Examples of competitive analysis are evident in daily newspapers and periodicals such as *The Wall Street Journal, Bloomberg Businessweek,* and *Fortune.* For example, banks continually track home loan, auto loan, and certificate of deposit (CD) interest rates charged by rivals. Major airlines change hundreds of fares daily in response to competitors' tactics. Car manufacturers are keenly aware of announced cuts or increases in rivals' production volume, sales, and sales incentives (e.g., rebates and low interest rates on financing). This information is used in their marketing, pricing, and production strategies.

Keeping track of competitors has become easier today with the amount of information that is available on the Internet. The following are examples of some websites that companies routinely use for competitive intelligence gathering.[18]

- *Slideshare.* A website for publicly sharing PowerPoint presentations. Marketing teams have embraced the platform and often post detail-rich presentations about their firms and products.
- *Quora.* A question-and-answer site popular among industry insiders who embrace the free flow of information about technical questions.
- *Ispionage.* A site that reveals the ad words that companies are buying, which can often shed light on new campaigns being launched.
- *YouTube.* Great for finding interviews with executives at trade shows.

At times, a firm's aggressive efforts to gather competitive intelligence may lead to unethical or illegal behaviors.[19] Strategy Spotlight 2.1 provides an example of a company, United Technologies, that has set clear guidelines to help prevent unethical behavior.

A word of caution: Executives must be careful to avoid spending so much time and effort tracking the actions of traditional competitors that they ignore new competitors. Further, broad environmental changes and events may have a dramatic impact on a firm's viability. Peter Drucker, wrote:

> Increasingly, a winning strategy will require information about events and conditions outside the institution: noncustomers, technologies other than those currently used by the company and its present competitors, markets not currently served, and so on.[20]

Consider the failure of specialized medical lab Sleep HealthCenters.[21] Until recently, patients suffering from sleep disorders, such as apnea, were forced to undergo expensive overnight visits to sleep clinics, including Sleep HealthCenters, to diagnose their ailments. The firm was launched in 1997 and quickly expanded to over two dozen locations. Revenue soared from nearly $10 million in 1997 to $30 million in 2010.

However, the rapid improvements in the price and performance of wearable monitoring devices changed the business, gradually at first and then suddenly. For one thing, the more comfortable home setting produced more effective measurements. And the quick declines in the cost of wearable monitoring meant patients could get the same results at one-third the price of an overnight stay at a clinic. By 2011, Sleep HealthCenters' revenue began to decline, and the firm closed 20 percent of its locations. In 2012, its death knells sounded: Insurance companies decided to cover the less expensive option. Sleep HealthCenters abruptly closed its doors.

Environmental Forecasting   Environmental scanning, monitoring, and competitive intelligence are important inputs for analyzing the external environment. **Environmental forecasting** involves the development of plausible projections about the direction, scope,

ETHICAL GUIDELINES ON COMPETITIVE INTELLIGENCE: UNITED TECHNOLOGIES

United Technologies (UT) is a $65 billion global conglomerate composed of world-leading businesses with rich histories of technological pioneering, such as Otis Elevator, Carrier Air Conditioning, and Sikorsky (helicopters). UT believes strongly in a robust code of ethics. One such document is the Code of Ethics Guide on Competitive Intelligence. This encourages managers and workers to ask themselves these five questions whenever they have ethical concerns.

1. Have I done anything that coerced somebody to share this information? Have I, for example, threatened a supplier by indicating that future business opportunities will be influenced by the receipt of information with respect to a competitor?

2. Am I in a place where I should not be? If, for example, I am a field representative with privileges to move around in a customer's facility, have I gone outside the areas permitted? Have I misled anybody in order to gain access?

3. Is the contemplated technique for gathering information evasive, such as sifting through trash or setting up an electronic "snooping" device directed at a competitor's facility from across the street?

4. Have I misled somebody in a way that the person believed sharing information with me was required or would be protected by a confidentiality agreement? Have I, for example, called and misrepresented myself as a government official who was seeking some information for some official purpose?

5. Have I done something to evade or circumvent a system intended to secure or protect information?

Sources: Nelson, B. 2003. The thinker. *Forbes,* March 3: 62–64; The Fuld war room–Survival kit 010. Code of ethics (printed 2/26/01); and *www.yahoo.com.*

---

speed, and intensity of environmental change.[22] Its purpose is to predict change.[23] It asks: How long will it take a new technology to reach the marketplace? Will the present social concern about an issue result in new legislation? Are current lifestyle trends likely to continue?

Some forecasting issues are much more specific to a particular firm and the industry in which it competes. Consider how important it is for Motel 6 to predict future indicators, such as the number of rooms, in the budget segment of the industry. If its predictions are low, it will build too many units, creating a surplus of room capacity that would drive down room rates.

A danger of forecasting is that managers may view uncertainty as black and white and ignore important gray areas.[24] The problem is that underestimating uncertainty can lead to strategies that neither defend against threats nor take advantage of opportunities.

In 1977 one of the colossal underestimations in business history occurred when Kenneth H. Olsen, president of Digital Equipment Corp., announced, "There is no reason for individuals to have a computer in their home." The explosion in the personal computer market was not easy to detect in 1977, but it was clearly within the range of possibilities at the time. And, historically, there have been underestimates of the growth potential of new telecommunication services. The electric telegraph was derided by Ralph Waldo Emerson, and the telephone had its skeptics. More recently, an "infamous" McKinsey study in the early 1980s predicted fewer than 1 million cellular users in the United States by 2000. Actually, there were nearly 100 million.[25]

Obviously, poor predictions about technology change never go out of vogue. Consider some other "gems"–predicted by very knowledgeable people:[26]

- (1981) "Cellular phones will absolutely not replace local wire systems." Inventor Marty Cooper
- (1995) "I predict the Internet will soon go spectacularly supernova and in 1996 catastrophically collapse." Robert Metcalfe, founder of 3Com
- (1997) "Apple is already dead." Former Microsoft CTO Nathan Myhrvold.
- (2005) "There's just not that many videos I want to watch." Steve Chen, CTO and co-founder of YouTube, expressing concerns about the firm's long-term viability.

LO 2-3

Why scenario planning is a useful technique for firms competing in industries characterized by unpredictability and change.

- (2006) "Everyone's always asking me when Apple will come out with a cell phone. My answer is 'Probably never.'" David Pogue, *The New York Times*
- (2007) "There's no chance that the iPhone is going to get significant market share." Steve Ballmer, Microsoft

Jason Zweig, an editor at *The Wall Street Journal,* provides an important cautionary note (and rather colorful example!) regarding the need to question the reliability of forecasts: "Humans don't want accuracy; they want assurance . . . people can't stand ignoring all predictions; admitting that the future is unknowable is just too frightening."[27]

> The Nobel laureate and the late Stanford University economist Kenneth Arrow did a tour of duty as a weather forecaster for the U.S. Air Force during World War II. Ordered to evaluate mathematical models for predicting the weather one month ahead, he found that they were worthless. Informed of that, his superiors sent back another order: "The Commanding General is well aware that the forecasts are no good. However, he needs them for planning purposes."

scenario analysis
an in-depth approach to environmental forecasting that involves experts' detailed assessments of societal trends, economics, politics, technology, or other dimensions of the external environment.

Scenario Analysis **Scenario analysis** is a more in-depth approach to forecasting. It draws on a range of disciplines and interests, among them economics, psychology, sociology, and demographics. It usually begins with a discussion of participants' thoughts on ways in which societal trends, economics, politics, and technology may affect an issue.[28] Scenario analysis involves the projection of future possible events. It does not rely on extrapolation of historical trends. Rather, it seeks to explore possible developments that may only be connected to the past. That is, several scenarios are considered in a scenario analysis in order to envision possible future outcomes.

Consider PPG Industries.[29] The Pittsburgh-based producer of paints, coatings, specialty materials, chemicals, glass, and fiberglass has paid dividends each year since 1899. One of the key tools it uses today in its strategic planning is scenario analysis.

> PPG has developed four alternative futures based on differing assumptions about two key variables: the cost of energy (because its manufacturing operations are energy-intensive) and the extent of opportunity for growth in emerging markets. In the most favorable scenario, cost of energy will stay both moderate and stable and opportunities for growth and differentiation will be fast and strong. In this scenario, PPG determined that its success will depend on having the resources to pursue new opportunities. On the other hand, in the worst case scenario, the cost of energy will be high and opportunities for growth will be weak and slow. Such a scenario would call for a complete change in strategic direction.
>
> Between these two extremes lies the possibility of two mixed scenarios. First, opportunity for growth in emerging markets may be high, but the cost of energy may be volatile. In this scenario, the company's success will depend on coming up with more efficient processes. Second, cost of energy may remain moderate and stable, but opportunities for growth in emerging markets may remain weak and slow. In this situation, the most viable strategy may be one of capturing market share with new products.
>
> Developing strategies based on possible future scenarios seems to be paying off for PPG Industries. For the five years ending in 2016, PPG's stock has enjoyed a compounded growth rate exceeding 17 percent.

SWOT Analysis

To understand the business environment of a particular firm, you need to analyze both the general environment and the firm's industry and competitive environment. Generally, firms compete with other firms in the same industry. An industry is composed of a set of firms that produce similar products or services, sell to similar customers, and use similar methods of production. Gathering industry information and understanding competitive dynamics among the different companies in your industry is key to successful strategic management.

SWOT analysis
a framework for analyzing a company's internal and external environments and that stands for strengths, weaknesses, opportunities, and threats.

One of the most basic techniques for analyzing firm and industry conditions is **SWOT analysis.** SWOT stands for strengths, weaknesses, opportunities, and threats. It provides "raw material"—a basic listing of conditions both inside and surrounding your company.

The <u>S</u>trengths and <u>W</u>eaknesses refer to the internal conditions of the firm—where your firm excels (strengths) and where it may be lacking relative to competitors (weaknesses). <u>O</u>pportunities and <u>T</u>hreats are environmental conditions external to the firm. These could be factors in either the general or the competitive environment. In the general environment, one might experience developments that are beneficial for most companies, such as improving economic conditions that lower borrowing costs, or trends that benefit some companies and harm others. An example is the heightened concern with fitness, which is a threat to some companies (e.g., tobacco) and an opportunity to others (e.g., health clubs). Opportunities and threats are also present in the competitive environment among firms competing for the same customers.

The general idea of SWOT analysis is that a firm's strategy must:

- Build on its strengths.
- Remedy the weaknesses or work around them.
- Take advantage of the opportunities presented by the environment.
- Protect the firm from the threats.

Despite its apparent simplicity, the SWOT approach has been very popular. First, it forces managers to consider both internal and external factors simultaneously. Second, its emphasis on identifying opportunities and threats makes firms act proactively rather than reactively. Third, it raises awareness about the role of strategy in creating a match between the environmental conditions and the firm's internal strengths and weaknesses. Finally, its conceptual simplicity is achieved without sacrificing analytical rigor.

While analysis is necessary, it is also equally important to recognize the role played by intuition and judgment. Steve Jobs, the legendary former chairman of Apple, took a very different approach in determining what customers *really* wanted:[30]

> Steve Jobs was convinced market research and focus groups limited one's ability to innovate. When asked how much research was done to guide Apple when he introduced the iPad, Jobs famously quipped: "None. It isn't the consumers' job to know what they want. It's hard for (consumers) to tell you what they want when they've never seen anything remotely like it."
>
> Jobs relied on his own intuition—his radarlike feel for emerging technologies and how they could be brought together to create, in his words "insanely great products, that ultimately made the difference." For Jobs, who died in 2011 at the age of 56, intuition was no mere gut call. It was, as he put it in his often-quoted commencement speech at Stanford, about "connecting the dots, glimpsing the relationships among wildly disparate life experiences and changes in technologies."

THE GENERAL ENVIRONMENT

The **general environment** is composed of factors that can have dramatic effects on firm strategy.[31] We divide the general environment into six segments: demographic, sociocultural, political/legal, technological, economic, and global. Exhibit 2.2 provides examples of key trends and events in each of the six segments of the general environment.

Before addressing each of the six segments in turn, consider Dominic Barton's insights in response to a question posed to him by an editor of *Fortune* magazine: *What are your client's worries right now?* (Barton is global managing director of McKinsey, the giant consulting firm.)[32]

> "They're pretty consistent around the world. The big one now is geopolitics. Whether you're in Russia, China, anywhere the assumed stability that was there for the past 20 or so years—it's not there. The second is technology, which is moving two to three times faster than management. Most CEOs I talk to are excited and paranoid at the same time. Related to that is cyber security: the amount of time and effort to protect systems and look at vulnerabilities is big.

LO 2-4

The impact of the general environment on a firm's strategies and performance.

general environment
factors external to an industry, and usually beyond a firm's control, that affect a firm's strategy.

EXHIBIT 2.2

**General Environment:
Key Trends and Events**

Demographic

- Aging population
- Rising affluence
- Changes in ethnic composition
- Geographic distribution of population
- Greater disparities in income levels

Sociocultural

- More women in the workforce
- Increase in temporary workers
- Greater concern for fitness
- Greater concern for environment
- Postponement of family formation

Political/Legal

- Tort reform
- Americans with Disabilities Act (ADA) of 1990
- Deregulation of utility and other industries
- Increases in federally mandated minimum wages
- Taxation at local, state, federal levels
- Legislation on corporate governance reforms in bookkeeping, stock options, etc. (Sarbanes-Oxley Act of 2002)
- Affordable Care Act (Obamacare)

Technological

- Genetic engineering
- Three-dimensional (3D) printing
- Computer-aided design/computer-aided manufacturing systems (CAD/CAM)
- Research in synthetic and exotic materials
- Pollution/global warming
- Miniaturization of computing technologies
- Wireless communications
- Nanotechnology
- Big Data/Data Analysis

Economic

- Interest rates
- Unemployment rates
- Consumer price index
- Trends in GDP
- Changes in stock market valuations

Global

- Increasing global trade
- Currency exchange rates
- Emergence of the Indian and Chinese economies
- Trade agreements among regional blocs (e.g., NAFTA, EU, ASEAN)
- Creation of WTO (leading to decreasing tariffs/free trade in services)
- Increased risks associated with terrorism

"A fourth trend is the shift in economic power, with 2.2 billion new middle-class consumers in the next 15 years, and it's moving to Asia and Africa. Do you have the right type of people in your top 100? Are you in those markets? Those are the four big ones we see everywhere."

The Demographic Segment

Demographics are the most easily understood and quantifiable elements of the general environment. They are at the root of many changes in society. Demographics include elements such as the aging population,[33] rising or declining affluence, changes in ethnic composition, geographic distribution of the population, and disparities in income level.[34]

The impact of a demographic trend, like all segments of the general environment, varies across industries. Rising levels of affluence in many developed countries bode well for brokerage services as well as for upscale pets and supplies. However, this trend may adversely affect fast-food restaurants because people can afford to dine at higher-priced restaurants. Fast-food restaurants depend on minimum-wage employees to operate efficiently, but the competition for labor intensifies as more attractive employment opportunities become prevalent, thus threatening the employment base for restaurants. Let's look at the details of one of these trends.

The aging population in the United States and other developed countries has important implications. Although the percentage of those 65 and over in the U.S. workforce bottomed in the 1990s, it has been rising ever since.[35] According to the Bureau of Labor Statistics, 59 percent of workers 65 and older were putting in full-time hours in 2013, a percentage that has increased steadily over the past decade. And, according to a 2014 study by Merrill Lynch and the Age Wave Consulting firm, 72 percent of preretirees aged 50 and over wanted to work during their retirement. "Older workers are to the first half of the 21st century what women were to the last half of the 20th century," says Eugene Steuerle, an economist at the Urban Institute.

There are a number of misconceptions about the quality and value of older workers. The Insights from Research box on pages 44 and 45, however, debunks many of these myths.

> **demographic segment of the general environment** genetic and observable characteristics of a population, including the levels and growth of age, density, sex, race, ethnicity, education, geographic region, and income.

The Sociocultural Segment

Sociocultural forces influence the values, beliefs, and lifestyles of a society. Examples include a higher percentage of women in the workforce, dual-income families, increases in the number of temporary workers, greater concern for healthy diets and physical fitness, greater interest in the environment, and postponement of having children. Such forces enhance sales of products and services in many industries but depress sales in others. The increased number of women in the workforce has increased the need for business clothing merchandise but decreased the demand for baking product staples (since people would have less time to cook from scratch). The health and fitness trend has helped industries that manufacture exercise equipment and healthful foods but harmed industries that produce unhealthful foods.

Increased educational attainment by women in the workplace has led to more women in upper-management positions.[36] Given such educational attainment, it is hardly surprising that companies owned by women have been one of the driving forces of the U.S. economy; these companies (now more than 9 million in number) account for 40 percent of all U.S. businesses and have generated more than $3.6 trillion in annual revenue. In addition, women have a tremendous impact on consumer spending decisions. Not surprisingly, many companies have focused their advertising and promotion efforts on female consumers.

> **sociocultural segment of the general environment** the values, beliefs, and lifestyles of a society.

The Political/Legal Segment

Political processes and legislation influence environmental regulations with which industries must comply.[37,38] Some important elements of the political/legal arena include tort

> **political/legal segment of the general environment** how a society creates and exercises power, including rules, laws, and taxation policies.

NEW TRICKS: RESEARCH DEBUNKS MYTHS ABOUT OLDER WORKERS

Overview

People often think that older workers are less motivated and less healthy, resist change and are less trusting, and have more trouble balancing work and family. It turns out these assumptions just aren't true. By challenging these stereotypes in your organization, you can keep your employees working.

What the Research Shows

In a 2012 paper published by *Personnel Psychology,* researchers from the University of Hong Kong and the University of Georgia examined 418 studies of workers' ages and stereotypes. A meta-analysis—a study of studies—was conducted to find out if any of the six following stereotypes about older workers—as compared with younger workers—was actually true:

- They are less motivated.
- They are less willing to participate in training and career development.
- They are more resistant to change.
- They are less trusting.
- They are less healthy.
- They are more vulnerable to work-family imbalance.

After an exhaustive search of studies dealing with these issues, the investigators' meta-analytic techniques turned up some interesting results. Older workers' motivation and job involvement are actually slightly higher than those of younger workers. Older workers are slightly more willing to implement organizational changes, are not less trusting, and are not less healthy than younger workers. Moreover, they're not more likely to have issues with work-family imbalance. Of the six investigated, the only stereotype supported was that older workers are less willing to participate in training and career development.

Why This Matters

Business leaders must pay attention to the circumstances of older workers. According to the U.S. Bureau of Labor Statistics, 19.5 percent of American workers were 55 and older in 2010, but by 2020 25.2 percent will be 55 and older. Workers aged 25 to 44 should drop from 66.9 to 63.7 percent of the workforce during the same period. These statistics make clear that recruiting and training older workers remain critical.

When the findings of the meta-analysis are considered, the challenge of integrating older workers into the workplace becomes acute. The stereotypes held about older workers don't hold water, but when older workers are subjected to them, they are more likely to retire and experience a lower quality of life. Business leaders should attract, retain, and encourage mature employees' continued involvement in workplaces because they have much to offer in the ways of wisdom, experience, and institutional knowledge. The alternative is to miss out on a growing pool of valuable human capital.

How can you deal with age stereotypes to keep older workers engaged? The authors suggest three effective ways:

- Provide more opportunities for younger and older workers to work together.
- Promote positive attributes of older workers, like experience, carefulness, and punctuality.
- Engage employees in open discussions about stereotypes.

Adam Bradshaw of the DeGarmo Group Inc. has summarized research on addressing age stereotypes in the workplace and offers practical advice. For instance, make sure hiring practices identify factors important to the job other than age. Managers can be trained in how to spot age stereotypes and can point out to employees why the stereotypes are often untrue by using examples of effective older workers. Realize that older workers can offer a competitive advantage because of skills they possess that competitors may overlook.

Professor Tamara Erickson, who was named one of the top 50 global business thinkers in 2011, points out that members of different generations bring different experiences, assumptions, and benefits to the workforce. Companies can gain a great deal from creating a culture that welcomes workers of all ages and in which leaders address biases.

Key Takeaways

- The percentage of American workers 55 years old and older is expected to increase from 19.5 percent in 2010 to 25.2 percent in 2020.
- Many stereotypes exist about older workers. A review of 418 studies reveals these stereotypes are largely unfounded.
- Older workers subjected to negative stereotypes are more likely to retire and more likely to report lower quality of life and poorer health.
- When business leaders accept stereotypes about older workers, they lose out on these workers' wisdom and experience. And by 2020 employers may have a smaller pool of younger workers than they do today.
- Solutions include creating opportunities for younger and older workers to work together and having frank, open discussions about stereotypes.

Research Reviewed

Ng, T. W. H. & Feldman, D. C. 2012. Evaluating six common stereotypes about older workers with meta-analytical data. *Personnel Psychology*, 65: 821–858. We thank Matthew Gilley, PhD, of *businessminded.com* for contributing this research brief.

reform, the Americans with Disabilities Act (ADA) of 1990, the repeal of the Glass-Steagall Act in 1999 (banks may now offer brokerage services), deregulation of utilities and other industries, and increases in the federally mandated minimum wage.[39]

Government legislation can also have a significant impact on the governance of corporations. The U.S. Congress passed the Sarbanes-Oxley Act in 2002, which greatly increases the accountability of auditors, executives, and corporate lawyers. This act responded to the widespread perception that existing governance mechanisms failed to protect the interests of shareholders, employees, and creditors. Clearly, Sarbanes-Oxley has also created a tremendous demand for professional accounting services.

Legislation can also affect firms in the high-tech sector of the economy by expanding the number of temporary visas available for highly skilled foreign professionals.[40] For example, a bill passed by the U.S. Congress in October 2000 allowed 195,000 H-1B visas for each of the following three years—up from a cap of 115,000. However, beginning in 2006 and continuing through 2015, the annual cap on H-1B visas has shrunk to only 65,000—with an additional 20,000 visas available for foreigners with a master's or higher degree from a U.S. institution. Many of the visas are for professionals from India with computer and software expertise. In 2014, companies applied for 172,500 H-1B visas. This means that at least 87,500 engineers, developers, and others couldn't take jobs in the United States.[41] As one would expect, this is a political "hot potato" for industry executives as well as U.S. labor and workers' rights groups. The key arguments against H-1B visas are that H-1B workers drive down wages and take jobs from Americans.

Strategy Spotlight 2.2 discusses recent U.S. legislation that requires companies to disclose metals in their supply chain that are connected to war-torn regions.

The Technological Segment

Developments in technology lead to new products and services and improve how they are produced and delivered to the end user.[42] Innovations can create entirely new industries and alter the boundaries of existing industries.[43] Technological developments and trends include genetic engineering, Internet technology, computer-aided design/computer-aided manufacturing (CAD/CAM), research in artificial and exotic materials, and, on the downside, pollution and global warming.[44] Petroleum and primary metals industries spend significantly to reduce their pollution. Engineering and consulting firms that work with polluting industries derive financial benefits from solving such problems.

Nanotechnology is becoming a very promising area of research with many potentially useful applications.[45] Nanotechnology takes place at industry's tiniest stage: one-billionth of a meter. Remarkably, this is the size of 10 hydrogen atoms in a row. Matter at such a tiny scale behaves very differently. Familiar materials—from gold to carbon soot—display startling and useful new properties. Some transmit light or electricity. Others become harder than diamonds or turn into potent chemical catalysts. What's more, researchers have found that a tiny dose of nanoparticles can transform the chemistry and nature of far bigger things.

technological segment of the general environment innovation and state of knowledge in industrial arts, engineering, applied sciences, and pure science; and their interaction with society.

THE CONFLICT MINERALS LEGISLATION: IMPLICATIONS FOR SUPPLY CHAIN MANAGEMENT

In 2010, the United States Congress enacted Section 1502 of the Dodd-Frank Wall Street Reform and Consumer Protection Act. The law requires companies to disclose whether any tin, tantalum, tungsten, or gold in their supply chain is connected to violent militia groups in the Congo or nine surrounding countries, including Angola, Rwanda, and Sudan.

In a recent year, U.S. companies spent about $700 million and 6 million staff hours in efforts to comply with the rules to disclose "conflict minerals" in their supply chains, according to a study by Tulane University and Assent Compliance, a New York consulting firm. And, as of 2015, companies were required to hire outside auditors to evaluate their results.

With huge financial resources and manpower to conduct thorough examinations of their supply chains, several major technology firms including Microsoft, Apple, and Intel topped the list in terms of compliance with the law and in providing additional information on their processes. But even Microsoft and Apple stated that they were "conflict indeterminable" last year. Intel claimed that its products were "conflict free"—and sent employees to 90 mineral smelters around the world to gather that information.

Consider challenges associated with tracking tantalum—the hard blue-gray metal that is essential to firms' ability to build smaller and lighter cellphones, laptops, hard drives and other devices. According to the U.S. Geological Survey, 12 percent of the world's supply is in the Congo. However, to track the origin of the mineral, companies often have to dig four or five layers deep into their supply chain, as the mineral travels across the globe to various parts manufacturers.

The difficulty in complying with the legislation is further (and colorfully!) depicted by Chris Bayer, a consultant who studied recent reports filed with the SEC. Think about the challenges associated with tracking materials from more than 2 million small-scale or "subsistence" miners in the Eastern Congo who smelt small amounts of metals—and determining their links to guerrilla operations! He asserts, "It's a herculean task [like trying to] apply modern supply-chain logistics to the equivalent of the 1849 California gold rush."

Sources: Chasan, E. 2015. U.S. firms struggle to trace "conflict minerals." *www.wsj.com*, August 3: np; Browning, L. 2015. Companies struggle to comply with rules on conflict materials. *www.nytimes.com*; and Shirodkar, S. M. & Ritter, S. E. 2016. Supply chain management and the conflict materials rules–action items for 2016. *www.dlapiper.com*, February 16: np.

Another emerging technology is physioletics, which is the practice of linking wearable computing devices with data analysis and quantified feedback to improve performance.[46] An example is sensors in shoes (such as Nike+, used by runners to track distance, speed, and other metrics). Another application focuses on people's movements in various work settings. Tesco's employees, for instance, wear armbands at a distribution center in Ireland to track the goods they are gathering. The devices free up time that employees would otherwise spend marking clipboards. The armband also allots tasks to the wearer, forecasts his or her completion time, and quantifies the wearer's precise movements among the facility's 9.6 miles of shelving and 111 loading bays.

The Economic Segment

economic segment of the general environment characteristics of the economy, including national income and monetary conditions.

The economy affects all industries, from suppliers of raw materials to manufacturers of finished goods and services, as well as all organizations in the service, wholesale, retail, government, and nonprofit sectors.[47] Key economic indicators include interest rates, unemployment rates, the consumer price index, the gross domestic product, and net disposable income.[48] Interest rate increases have a negative impact on the residential home construction industry but a negligible (or neutral) effect on industries that produce consumer necessities such as prescription drugs or common grocery items.

Other economic indicators are associated with equity markets. Perhaps the most watched is the Dow Jones Industrial Average (DJIA), which is composed of 30 large industrial firms. When stock market indexes increase, consumers' discretionary income rises and there is often an increased demand for luxury items such as jewelry and automobiles. But when stock valuations decrease, demand for these items shrinks.

The Global Segment

More firms are expanding their operations and market reach beyond the borders of their "home" country. Globalization provides both opportunities to access larger potential markets and a broad base of production factors such as raw materials, labor, skilled managers, and technical professionals. However, such endeavors also carry many political, social, and economic risks.[49]

Examples of key elements include currency exchange rates, increasing global trade, the economic emergence of China, trade agreements among regional blocs (e.g., North American Free Trade Agreement, European Union), and the General Agreement on Tariffs and Trade (GATT) (lowering of tariffs).[50] Increases in trade across national boundaries also provide benefits to air cargo and shipping industries but have a minimal impact on service industries such as bookkeeping and routine medical services.

A key factor in the global economy is the rapid rise of the middle class in emerging countries. The number of consumers in Asia's middle class is rapidly approaching the number in Europe and North America combined. An important implication of this trend is the dramatic change in hiring practices of U.S. multinationals. Consider:

> Thirty-five U.S.-based multinational firms have recently added jobs faster than other U.S. employers, but nearly three-fourths of those jobs were overseas, according to a *Wall Street Journal* analysis. Those companies, which include Wal-Mart Stores Inc., International Paper Co., Honeywell International, Inc., and United Parcel Service, boosted their employment at home by 3.1 percent, or 113,000 jobs, at roughly the same rate of increase as the nation's other employers. However, they also added more than 333,000 jobs in their far-flung—and faster growing—foreign operations.[51]

global segment of the general environment influences from foreign countries, including foreign market opportunities, foreign-based competition, and expanded capital markets.

Relationships among Elements of the General Environment

In our discussion of the general environment, we see many relationships among the various elements.[52] For example, a demographic trend in the United States, the aging of the population, has important implications for the economic segment (in terms of tax policies to provide benefits to increasing numbers of older citizens). Another example is the emergence of information technology as a means to increase the rate of productivity gains in the United States and other developed countries. Such use of IT results in lower inflation (an important element of the economic segment) and helps offset costs associated with higher labor rates.

The effects of a trend or event in the general environment vary across industries. Governmental legislation (political/legal) to permit the importation of prescription drugs from foreign countries is a very positive development for drugstores but a very negative event for U.S. drug manufacturers. Exhibit 2.3 provides other examples of how the impact of trends or events in the general environment can vary across industries.

Data Analytics: A Technology That Affects Multiple Segments of the General Environment

Before moving on, let's consider **Data Analytics** (or, alternatively "Big Data"). Data analytics has been a leading and highly visible component of a broader technological phenomenon—the emergence of digital technology.[53] Such technologies are altering the way business is being conducted in a broad variety of sectors—government, industry, academia, and commerce.

Corporations are increasingly collecting and analyzing data on their customers, including data on customer characteristics, purchasing patterns, employee productivity, and physical asset utilization. These efforts, commonly referred to as "Big Data," have the potential

data analytics The process of examining large data sets to uncover hidden patterns, market trends, and customer preferences.

Segment/Trends and Events	Industry	Positive	Neutral	Negative
Demographic				
Aging population	Health care	✓		
	Baby products			✓
Rising affluence	Brokerage services	✓		
	Fast foods			✓
	Upscale pets and supplies	✓		
Sociocultural				
More women in the workforce	Clothing	✓		
	Baking products (staples)			✓
Greater concern for health and fitness	Home exercise equipment	✓		
	Meat products			✓
Political/legal				
Tort reform	Legal services			✓
	Auto manufacturing	✓		
Americans with Disabilities Act (ADA)	Retail			✓
	Manufacturers of elevators, escalators, and ramps	✓		
Technological				
Genetic engineering	Pharmaceutical	✓		
	Publishing		✓	
Pollution/global warming	Engineering services	✓		
	Petroleum			✓
Economic				
Interest rate decreases	Residential construction	✓		
	Most common grocery products		✓	
Global				
Increasing global trade	Shipping	✓		
	Personal service		✓	
Emergence of China as an economic power	Soft drinks	✓		
	Defense			✓

HOW BIG DATA CAN MONITOR FEDERAL, STATE, AND LOCAL GOVERNMENT EXPENDITURES

Open The Books is a new initiative that uses big data to make the work of city, state, and the federal government more transparent. It was founded in Illinois by Adam Andrzejewski, a big-data expert. He and his team have amassed the computing power to capture a great share of the federal checkbook's vendor spending in the United States, as well as more than 48 states and many local governments.

Open The Books can also trace public salaries, pensions, and donations to political campaigns. Perhaps not too surprisingly, donors and subsidy recipients frequently turn out to be one of the same! Open The Books has created an app that can be quite revealing—the beauty school that receives more than 100 times in grants and student loans what it charges in tuition, and the $1.67 million in federally guaranteed loans received by the brother of a former Illinois director of agriculture.

Let's take a closer look to see what Andrzejewski has uncovered in his study of expenditures by the state of Illinois. He found that it has been two years since Illinois state government had a full-year budget and more than 70,000 vendors are owed $8.2 billion. However, despite a deadlock by the legislature and apparent fiscal insolvency, more than $50 billion has been paid to providers and other entities during the 2016 fiscal year. Who are some of these recipients?

- Comptroller Leslie Munger paid a lobbyist $50,000 out of her budget. The lobbyist, Shea, Paige and Rogal, has garnered more than $370,000 in payments since 2009. A key executive is the chairman emeritus of the Republican Party.
- Since 2005, J. Walter Thompson (JWT), one of the world's largest advertising agencies, has received $178.1 million.
- The Illinois Department of Transportation (IDOT) employs 1,133 civil engineers and 1,155 engineering technicians. Given this bank of talent, one might question why civil engineering firms such as ESI Consultants were paid $3.7 million, as well as other firms at large hourly rates.
- One could claim that IDOT engages in political patronage. On August 31, 2016, Munger paid $4.1 million in "performance bonuses" to 1,230 IDOT employees—members of the Teamsters. However, it may hardly be called a "performance bonus" because one of every two employees qualified for the pay enhancement.

As noted by Andrzejewski, "The Illinois credit ranking is the lowest of all 50 states. But the public patronage machine rolls on."

Sources: Shales, A. 2015. Pulling down state credit ratings. *Forbes,* November 2: 52; and Andrzejewski, A. 2016. The $50 billion Illinois favor factory hums along. *www.forbes.com,* August 31: np.

---

to enable firms to better customize their product and service offerings to customers while more efficiently and fully using the resources of the company. For example, Pepsi used data analytics to develop an algorithm that lowers the rate of inventory stockouts and has shared the algorithm with its partners and retailers. Similarly, Kaiser Permanente collects petabytes of data on the health treatments of its 8 million health care members. This has allowed Kaiser to develop insights on the cost, efficacy, and safety of the treatments provided by doctors and procedures in hospitals.

A recent survey by consultants NewVantage Partners has found that the number of U.S. firms using big data in the past three years has jumped to 63 percent. And 70 percent of firms now say that big data is of critical importance to their firms, a huge increase from 21 percent in 2012. Clearly, this is one of the fastest tech-adoption rates in history. Meanwhile, the title of chief data officer (the C-Suite executive of big data) did not exist until recently. Now, it is found in 54 percent of the firms that were surveyed.

Companies that are taking the lead in the analytics revolution see it as an important source of competitive differentiation. Recently, the MIT Center for Digital Business, along with research sponsor Capgemini Consulting, completed a two-year study. More than 400 companies participated with the goal of determining which companies were attaining a "digital advantage" over industry peers with their use of analytics, social media, and mobile and embedded devices. The study found that companies that do more with digital technologies—and support such investments with leadership and governance mechanisms—are 26 percent more profitable than their industry peers, and outperform average industry performance by 6 to 9 percent.

Spotlight 2.3 is an example of how data analytics can play a key role in monitoring spending in the public sector of the economy.

THE COMPETITIVE ENVIRONMENT

LO 2-5

How forces in the competitive environment can affect profitability, and how a firm can improve its competitive position by increasing its power vis-à-vis these forces.

industry
a group of firms that produce similar goods or services.

competitive environment
factors that pertain to an industry and affect a firm's strategies.

Porter's five forces model of industry competition
a tool for examining the industry-level competitive environment, especially the ability of firms in that industry to set prices and minimize costs.

Managers must consider the competitive environment (also sometimes referred to as the task or industry environment). The nature of competition in an **industry,** as well as the profitability of a firm, is often directly influenced by developments in the competitive environment.

The **competitive environment** consists of many factors that are particularly relevant to a firm's strategy. These include competitors (existing or potential), customers, and suppliers. Potential competitors may include a supplier considering forward integration, such as an automobile manufacturer acquiring a rental car company, or a firm in an entirely new industry introducing a similar product that uses a more efficient technology.

Next, we will discuss key concepts and analytical techniques that managers should use to assess their competitive environments. First, we examine Michael Porter's five-forces model that illustrates how these forces can be used to explain an industry's profitability.[54] Second, we discuss how the five forces are being affected by the capabilities provided by Internet technologies. Third, we address some of the limitations, or "caveats," that managers should be familiar with when conducting industry analysis. Finally, we address the concept of strategic groups, because even within an industry it is often useful to group firms on the basis of similarities of their strategies. As we will see, competition tends to be more intense among firms *within* a strategic group than between strategic groups.

Porter's Five Forces Model of Industry Competition

The **"five forces" model** developed by Michael E. Porter has been the most commonly used analytical tool for examining the competitive environment. It describes the competitive environment in terms of five basic competitive forces:[55]

1. The threat of new entrants.
2. The bargaining power of buyers.
3. The bargaining power of suppliers.
4. The threat of substitute products and services.
5. The intensity of rivalry among competitors in an industry.

Each of these forces affects a firm's ability to compete in a given market. Together, they determine the profit potential for a particular industry. The model is shown in Exhibit 2.4. A manager should be familiar with the five forces model for several reasons. It helps you decide whether your firm should remain in or exit an industry. It provides the rationale for increasing or decreasing resource commitments. The model helps you assess how to improve your firm's competitive position with regard to each of the five forces.[56] For example, you can use insights provided by the five forces model to understand how higher entry barriers discourage new rivals from competing with you.[57] Or you can see how to develop strong relationships with your distribution channels. You may decide to find suppliers who satisfy the price/performance criteria needed to make your product or service a top performer.

Consider, for example, some of the competitive forces affecting the hotel industry.[58] Airbnb, a room-sharing site, offers more rooms than even Marriott. Online travel agencies take a hefty cut of hotel bookings; and price-comparison sites make it difficult to raise room rates. Growing supply may make it harder still. Steven Kent of Goldman Sachs expects that the supply of new rooms in the next two years will outpace the previous five. Already, the previous growth of American occupancy rates has begun to slow.

threat of new entrants
the possibility that the profits of established firms in the industry may be eroded by new competitors.

The Threat of New Entrants   The **threat of new entrants** refers to the possibility that the profits of established firms in the industry may be eroded by new competitors.[59] The extent of the threat depends on existing barriers to entry and the combined reactions from existing

EXHIBIT 2.4 Porter's Five Forces Model of Industry Competition

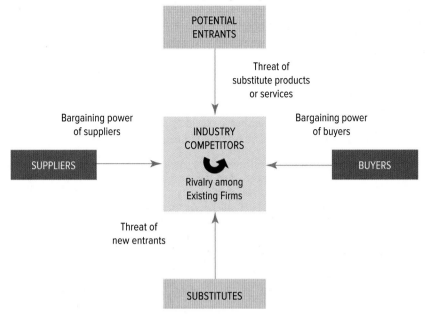

Sources: From Michael E. Porter, "The Five Competitive Forces That Shape Strategy," Special Issue on HBS Centennial. *Harvard Business Review* 86, No. 1 (January 2008), 78–93. Reprinted with permission of Michael E. Porter.

competitors.[60] If entry barriers are high and/or the newcomer can anticipate a sharp retaliation from established competitors, the threat of entry is low. These circumstances discourage new competitors. There are six major sources of entry barriers.

Economies of Scale   **Economies of scale** refers to spreading the costs of production over the number of units produced. The cost of a product per unit declines as the absolute volume per period increases. This deters entry by forcing the entrant to come in at a large scale and risk strong reaction from existing firms or come in at a small scale and accept a cost disadvantage. Both are undesirable options.

economies of scale
decreases in cost per unit as absolute output per period increases.

Product Differentiation   When existing competitors have strong brand identification and customer loyalty, **product differentiation** creates a barrier to entry by forcing entrants to spend heavily to overcome existing customer loyalties.

product differentiation
the degree to which a product has strong brand loyalty or customer loyalty.

Capital Requirements   The need to invest large financial resources to compete creates a barrier to entry, especially if the capital is required for risky or unrecoverable up-front advertising or research and development (R&D).

Switching Costs   A barrier to entry is created by the existence of one-time costs that the buyer faces when switching from one supplier's product or service to another.

switching costs
one-time costs that a buyer/supplier faces when switching from one supplier/buyer to another.

Access to Distribution Channels   The new entrant's need to secure distribution for its product can create a barrier to entry.

Cost Disadvantages Independent of Scale   Some existing competitors may have advantages that are independent of size or economies of scale. These derive from:

- Proprietary products
- Favorable access to raw materials
- Government subsidies
- Favorable government policies

Managers often tend to overestimate the barriers of entry in many industries. There are any number of cases where new entrants found innovative ways to enter industries by cleverly mixing and matching existing technologies. For example, companies, medical researchers, governments, and others are creating breakthrough technology products *without having to create any new technology.*[61] Geoff Colvin, a senior editor at *Fortune,* calls this "the era of Lego Innovation," in which significant and valuable advances in technology can be achieved by imaginatively combining components and software available to everyone. Such a trend serves to reduce entry barriers in many industries because state-of-the-art technology does not have to be developed internally—rather, it is widely available and, Colvin asserts, "we all have access to a really big box of plastic bricks." Consider a few examples:

> MIT's Media Lab has created robots powered by Android smartphones. After all, those devices can see, hear, recognize speech, and talk; they know where they are, how they're oriented, and how fast they're moving. And, through apps and an Internet connection, they can do a nearly infinite number of other tasks, such as recognize faces and translate languages. Similarly, teams at the University of South Carolina combined off-the-shelf eye-tracking technology with simple software they wrote to detect whether a driver was getting drowsy; any modern car has enough computing power to handle this job easily.

bargaining power of buyers
the threat that buyers may force down prices, bargain for higher quality or more services, and play competitors against each other.

The Bargaining Power of Buyers Buyers threaten an industry by forcing down prices, bargaining for higher quality or more services, and playing competitors against each other. These actions erode industry profitability.[62] The power of each large buyer group depends on attributes of the market situation and the importance of purchases from that group compared with the industry's overall business. A buyer group is powerful when:

- *It is concentrated or purchases large volumes relative to seller sales.* If a large percentage of a supplier's sales are purchased by a single buyer, the importance of the buyer's business to the supplier increases. Large-volume buyers also are powerful in industries with high fixed costs (e.g., steel manufacturing).
- *The products it purchases from the industry are standard or undifferentiated.* Confident they can always find alternative suppliers, buyers play one company against the other, as in commodity grain products.
- *The buyer faces few switching costs.* Switching costs lock the buyer to particular sellers. Conversely, the buyer's power is enhanced if the seller faces high switching costs.
- *It earns low profits.* Low profits create incentives to lower purchasing costs. On the other hand, highly profitable buyers are generally less price-sensitive.
- *The buyers pose a credible threat of backward integration.* If buyers either are partially integrated or pose a credible threat of backward integration, they are typically able to secure bargaining concessions.
- *The industry's product is unimportant to the quality of the buyer's products or services.* When the quality of the buyer's products is not affected by the industry's product, the buyer is more price-sensitive.

At times, a firm or set of firms in an industry may increase its buyer power by using the services of a third party. FreeMarkets Online is one such third party.[63] Pittsburgh-based FreeMarkets has developed software enabling large industrial buyers to organize online auctions for qualified suppliers of semistandard parts such as fabricated components, packaging materials, metal stampings, and services. By aggregating buyers, FreeMarkets increases the buyers' bargaining power. The results are impressive. In its first 48 auctions, most participating companies saved over 15 percent; some saved as much as 50 percent.

Strategy Spotlight 2.4 discusses why Apple, Inc., has such powerful bargaining power when they negotiate rental space in malls.

APPLE FLEXES ITS MUSCLE WHEN IT COMES TO NEGOTIATING RENTAL RATES FOR ITS STORES IN MALLS

Not all stores in a mall are created equal. Apple's enormous gravitational pull on mall traffic distorts the market for mall rents and helps win the iPhone maker sweetheart deals. Apple draws in so many shoppers that its stores can single-handedly lift sales by 10 percent at the malls in which they operate, according to Green Street Advisors, a real estate research firm. In fact, Apple accounts for as much as 33 percent of total sales in some of the New England malls in which it operates.

Apple has used its bargaining power to pay no more than 2 percent of its sales a square foot in rent. That compares very favorably with a typical tenant, which pays as much as 15 percent, according to industry executives. In addition to paying a lower percentage of sales for rent, Apple does not pay additional rent if their sales exceed a particular level—a luxury not afforded other retail tenants.

Apple opened its first two retail stores in 2001 at Tysons Corner Center in McClean, Virginia, and in the Glendale Galleria in Glendale, California. As of 2016, it had more than 450 stores in the United States and more than 18 other countries. In addition, it plans to open 25 new stores in China by 2017, bringing its total to 40 in that country. Although the stores account for about only 12 percent of Apple's total revenues, they draw about 1 million visitors a day. Fun fact: That is more than all of the Disney theme parks in the world combined!

Sources: Kapner, S. 2015. Apple stores upend the mall business. *The Wall Street Journal*, March 11: B1 and B4; and Farfan, B. 2016. Apple computer retail stores global locations. *www.the balance.com*, October 12: np.

The Bargaining Power of Suppliers   Suppliers can exert bargaining power by threatening to raise prices or reduce the quality of purchased goods and services. Powerful suppliers can squeeze the profitability of firms so far that they can't recover the costs of raw material inputs.[64] The factors that make suppliers powerful tend to mirror those that make buyers powerful. A supplier group will be powerful when:

> **bargaining power of suppliers**
> the threat that suppliers may raise prices or reduce the quality of purchased goods and services.

- *The supplier group is dominated by a few companies and is more concentrated (few firms dominate the industry) than the industry it sells to.* Suppliers selling to fragmented industries influence prices, quality, and terms.
- *The supplier group is not obliged to contend with substitute products for sale to the industry.* The power of even large, powerful suppliers can be checked if they compete with substitutes.
- *The industry is not an important customer of the supplier group.* When suppliers sell to several industries and a particular industry does not represent a significant fraction of its sales, suppliers are more prone to exert power.
- *The supplier's product is an important input to the buyer's business.* When such inputs are important to the success of the buyer's manufacturing process or product quality, the bargaining power of suppliers is high.
- *The supplier group's products are differentiated, or it has built up switching costs for the buyer.* Differentiation or switching costs facing the buyers cut off their options to play one supplier against another.
- *The supplier group poses a credible threat of forward integration.* This provides a check against the industry's ability to improve the terms by which it purchases.

The formation of Delta Pride Catfish is an example of the power a group of suppliers can attain if they exercise the threat of forward integration.[65] Catfish farmers in Mississippi historically supplied their harvest to processing plants run by large agribusiness firms such as ConAgra and Farm Fresh. When the farmers increased their production of catfish in response to growing demand, they found, much to their chagrin, that processors were holding back on their plans to increase their processing capabilities in hopes of higher retail prices for catfish.

What action did the farmers take? About 120 of them banded together and formed a cooperative, raised $4.5 million, and constructed their own processing plant, which they supplied themselves. ConAgra's market share quickly dropped from 35 percent to 11 percent, and Farm Fresh's market share fell by over 20 percent. Within 10 years, Delta Pride controlled over 40 percent of the U.S. catfish market. Recently, Delta Pride changed its ownership structure and became a closely-held corporation. In 2014, it had revenues of $80 million, employed 600 people, and processed 80 million pounds of catfish.

The Threat of Substitute Products and Services All firms within an industry compete with industries producing **substitute products and services**.[66] Substitutes limit the potential returns of an industry by placing a ceiling on the prices that firms in that industry can profitably charge. The more attractive the price/performance ratio of substitute products, the tighter the lid on an industry's profits.

> **threat of substitute products and services** the threat of limiting the potential returns of an industry by placing a ceiling on the prices that firms in that industry can profitably charge without losing too many customers to substitute products.

Identifying substitute products involves searching for other products or services that can perform the same function as the industry's offerings. This may lead a manager into businesses seemingly far removed from the industry. For example, the airline industry might not consider video cameras much of a threat. But as digital technology has improved and wireless and other forms of telecommunication have become more efficient, teleconferencing has become a viable substitute for business travel. That is, the rate of improvement in the price–performance relationship of the substitute product (or service) is high.

> **substitute products and services** products and services outside the industry that serve the same customer needs as the industry's products and services.

Consider the case of hybrid cars as a substitute for gasoline-powered cars.[67] Hybrid cars, such as the Toyota Prius, have seen tremendous success since the first hybrids were introduced in the late 1990s. Yet the market share of hybrid cars has been consistently low—reaching 2.4 percent in 2009, rising to 3.3 percent (the peak) in 2013, and declining to only 2 percent in 2016. Such results are even more surprising given that the number of models more than doubled between 2009 and 2014—24 to 51. That's more choices, but fewer takers. While some may believe the hybrid car industry feels pressure from other novel car segments such as electric cars (e.g., Nissan Leaf), the primary competition comes from an unusual suspect: plain old gas combustion cars.

The primary reason many environmental and cost-conscious consumers prefer gasoline-powered over hybrid cars is rather simple. Engines of gasoline-powered cars have increasingly challenged the key selling attribute of hybrid cars: fuel economy. While hybrid cars still slightly outcompete modern gasoline cars in terms of fuel economy, consumers increasingly don't see the value of paying as much as $6,000 extra for a hybrid car when they can get around 40 mpg in a gasoline car such as the Chevrolet Cruz or Hyundai Elantra.

The Intensity of Rivalry among Competitors in an Industry Firms use tactics like price competition, advertising battles, product introductions, and increased customer service or warranties. Rivalry occurs when competitors sense the pressure or act on an opportunity to improve their position.[68]

> **intensity of rivalry among competitors in an industry** the threat that customers will switch their business to competitors within the industry.

Some forms of competition, such as price competition, are typically highly destabilizing and are likely to erode the average level of profitability in an industry.[69] Rivals easily match price cuts, an action that lowers profits for all firms. On the other hand, advertising battles expand overall demand or enhance the level of product differentiation for the benefit of all firms in the industry. Rivalry, of course, differs across industries. In some instances it is characterized as warlike, bitter, or cutthroat, whereas in other industries it is referred to as polite and gentlemanly. Intense rivalry is the result of several interacting factors, including the following:

- *Numerous or equally balanced competitors.* When there are many firms in an industry, the likelihood of mavericks is great. Some firms believe they can make moves without being noticed. Even when there are relatively few firms, and they are nearly equal in size and resources, instability results from fighting among companies having the resources for sustained and vigorous retaliation.

- *Slow industry growth.* Slow industry growth turns competition into a fight for market share, since firms seek to expand their sales.
- *High fixed or storage costs.* High fixed costs create strong pressures for all firms to increase capacity. Excess capacity often leads to escalating price cutting.
- *Lack of differentiation or switching costs.* Where the product or service is perceived as a commodity or near commodity, the buyer's choice is typically based on price and service, resulting in pressures for intense price and service competition. Lack of switching costs, described earlier, has the same effect.
- *Capacity augmented in large increments.* Where economies of scale require that capacity must be added in large increments, capacity additions can be very disruptive to the industry supply/demand balance.
- *High exit barriers.* Exit barriers are economic, strategic, and emotional factors that keep firms competing even though they may be earning low or negative returns on their investments. Some exit barriers are specialized assets, fixed costs of exit, strategic interrelationships (e.g., relationships between the business units and others within a company in terms of image, marketing, shared facilities, and so on), emotional barriers, and government and social pressures (e.g., governmental discouragement of exit out of concern for job loss).

Rivalry between firms is often based solely on price, but it can involve other factors. Consider, for example, the intense competition between Uber Technologies Inc. and Lyft Inc., which are engaged in a fierce, ongoing battle in the taxi industry:[70]

> The bitter war between Uber and Lyft has spilled into dozens of cities where they are racing to provide the default app for summoning a ride within minutes. The two rivals are busy undercutting each other's prices, poaching drivers, and co-opting innovations. These actions have increasingly blurred the lines between the two services.
>
> The potential market for these firms may stretch far beyond rides. Investors who have bid up the value of Uber to over $69 billion in August 2016 are betting that it can expand into becoming the backbone of a logistics and delivery network for various services—a type of FedEx for cities.
>
> The recruitment of drivers is the lifeblood for the services as they attempt to build the largest networks with the fastest pickup times. For example, many Uber drivers are motivated to poach Lyft's drivers in order to get a bounty—$500 for referring a Lyft driver and $1,000 for referring a Lyft "mentor," an experienced Lyft contractor who helps train new drivers.
>
> In June 2014, another shot over the bow took place when both companies unveiled similar carpooling services within hours of each other. Lyft Line and Uber Pool let passengers ride with strangers and split the bill—lowering the cost of regular commutes. Lyft claims that it had been developing the carpooling model for several years and acquired a team to lead the effort months ago, according to John Zimmer, Lyft's president. He adds, "I think it's flattering when other companies look at how we're innovating and want to do similar things."

Exhibit 2.5 summarizes our discussion of industry five-forces analysis. It points out how various factors, such as economies of scale and capital requirements, affect each "force."

How the Internet and Digital Technologies Are Affecting the Five Competitive Forces

The Internet is having a significant impact on nearly every industry. Internet-based and digital technologies have fundamentally changed the ways businesses interact with each other and with consumers. In most cases, these changes have affected industry forces in ways that have created many new strategic challenges. In this section, we will evaluate Michael Porter's five-forces model in terms of the actual use of the Internet and the new technological capabilities that it makes possible.

The Threat of New Entrants In most industries, the threat of new entrants has increased because digital and Internet-based technologies lower barriers to entry. For example,

LO 2-6

How the Internet and digitally based capabilities are affecting the five competitive forces and industry profitability.

EXHIBIT 2.5 Competitive Analysis Checklist

Threat of New Entrants Is High When:	High	Low
Economies of scale are		X
Product differentiation is		X
Capital requirements are		X
Switching costs are		X
Incumbent's control of distribution channels is		X
Incumbent's proprietary knowledge is		X
Incumbent's access to raw materials is		X
Incumbent's access to government subsidies is		X

Power of Buyers Is High When:	High	Low
Concentration of buyers relative to suppliers is	X	
Switching costs are		X
Product differentiation of suppliers is		X
Threat of backward integration by buyers is	X	
Extent of buyer's profits is		X
Importance of the supplier's input to quality of buyer's final product is		X

Power of Suppliers Is High When:	High	Low
Concentration relative to buyer industry is	X	
Availability of substitute products is		X
Importance of customer to the supplier is		X
Differentiation of the supplier's products and services is	X	
Switching costs of the buyer are	X	
Threat of forward integration by the supplier is	X	

Threat of Substitute Products Is High When:	High	Low
Differentiation of the substitute product is	X	
Rate of improvement in price–performance relationship of substitute product is	X	

Intensity of Competitive Rivalry Is High When:	High	Low
Number of competitors is	X	
Industry growth rate is		X
Fixed costs are	X	
Storage costs are	X	
Product differentiation is		X
Switching costs are		X
Exit barriers are	X	
Strategic stakes are	X	

businesses that reach customers primarily through the Internet may enjoy savings on other traditional expenses such as office rent, sales-force salaries, printing, and postage. This may encourage more entrants who, because of the lower start-up expenses, see an opportunity to capture market share by offering a product or performing a service more efficiently than existing competitors. Thus, a new cyber entrant can use the savings provided by the Internet to charge lower prices and compete on price despite the incumbent's scale advantages.

Alternatively, because digital technologies often make it possible for young firms to provide services that are equivalent or superior to an incumbent, a new entrant may be able to serve a market more effectively, with more personalized services and greater attention to product details. A new firm may be able to build a reputation in its niche and charge premium prices. By so doing, it can capture part of an incumbent's business and erode profitability.

Another potential benefit of web-based business is access to distribution channels. Manufacturers or distributors that can reach potential outlets for their products more efficiently by means of the Internet may enter markets that were previously closed to them. Access is not guaranteed, however, because strong barriers to entry exist in certain industries.[71]

The Bargaining Power of Buyers   The Internet and wireless technologies may increase buyer power by providing consumers with more information to make buying decisions and by lowering switching costs. But these technologies may also suppress the power of traditional buyer channels that have concentrated buying power in the hands of a few, giving buyers new ways to access sellers. To sort out these differences, let's first distinguish between two types of buyers: end users and buyer channel intermediaries.

End users are the final customers in a distribution channel. Internet sales activity that is labeled "B2C"—that is, business-to-consumer—is concerned with end users. The Internet is likely to increase the power of these buyers for several reasons. First, the Internet provides large amounts of consumer information. This gives end users the information they need to shop for quality merchandise and bargain for price concessions. Second, an end user's switching costs are potentially much lower because of the Internet. Switching may involve only a few clicks of the mouse to find and view a competing product or service online.

In contrast, the bargaining power of distribution channel buyers may decrease because of the Internet. *Buyer channel intermediaries* are the wholesalers, distributors, and retailers who serve as intermediaries between manufacturers and end users. In some industries, they are dominated by powerful players that control who gains access to the latest goods or the best merchandise. The Internet and wireless communications, however, make it much easier and less expensive for businesses to reach customers directly. Thus, the Internet may increase the power of incumbent firms relative to that of traditional buyer channels. Strategy Spotlight 2.5 illustrates some of the changes brought on by the Internet that have affected the legal services industry.

The Bargaining Power of Suppliers   Use of the Internet and digital technologies to speed up and streamline the process of acquiring supplies is already benefiting many sectors of the economy. But the net effect of the Internet on supplier power will depend on the nature of competition in a given industry. As with buyer power, the extent to which the Internet is a benefit or a detriment also hinges on the supplier's position along the supply chain.

The role of suppliers involves providing products or services to other businesses. The term "B2B"—that is, business-to-business—often refers to businesses that supply or sell to other businesses. The effect of the Internet on the bargaining power of suppliers is a double-edged sword. On the one hand, suppliers may find it difficult to hold on to customers because buyers can do comparative shopping and price negotiations so much faster on the Internet.

On the other hand, several factors may also contribute to stronger supplier power. First, the growth of new web-based business may create more downstream outlets for suppliers to sell to. Second, suppliers may be able to create web-based purchasing arrangements that make purchasing easier and discourage their customers from switching. Online procurement systems directly link suppliers and customers, reducing transaction costs and paperwork.[72] Third, the use of proprietary software that links buyers to a supplier's website may create a rapid, low-cost ordering capability that discourages the buyer from seeking other sources of supply. *Amazon.com*, for example, created and patented One-Click purchasing technology that speeds up the ordering process for customers who enroll in the service.[73]

Finally, suppliers will have greater power to the extent that they can reach end users directly without intermediaries. Previously, suppliers often had to work through intermediaries who brought their products or services to market for a fee. But a process known as *disintermediation* is removing the organizations or business process layers responsible for intermediary

BUYER POWER IN LEGAL SERVICES: THE ROLE OF THE INTERNET

The $276 billion U.S. legal services industry, which includes about 180,000 firms, historically was a classic example of an industry that leaves buyers at a bargaining disadvantage. One of the key reasons for the strong bargaining position of law firms is high information asymmetry between lawyers and consumers, meaning that highly trained and experienced legal professionals know more about legal matters than the average consumer of legal services.

The Internet provides an excellent example of how unequal bargaining power can be reduced by decreasing information asymmetry. A new class of Internet legal services providers tries to accomplish just that and is challenging traditional law services along the way. For instance, *LawPivot.com*, a recent start-up backed by Google Ventures and cofounded by a former top Apple Inc. lawyer, allows consumers to interact with lawyers on a social networking site. This service allows customers to get a better picture of a lawyer's legal skills before opening their wallets. As a result, information asymmetry between lawyers and consumers is reduced and customers find themselves in a better bargaining position. Another example is *LegalZoom. com*, a service that helps consumers to create legal documents. Customers familiar with *LegalZoom.com* may use their knowledge of the time and effort required to create legal documents to challenge a lawyer's fees for custom-crafted legal documents.

Sources: Anonymous. 2016. The size of the U.S. legal market: Shrinking piece of a bigger pie: An LEI Graphic. *www.legalexecutiveinstitute.com,* January 11: np; Jacobs, D. L. 2011. Google takes aim at lawyers. *Forbes,* August 8: np; Anonymous. 2011. Alternative law firms: Bargain briefs. *The Economist,* August 13: 64; and Anonymous. 2014. Legal services industry profile. *First Research,* August 25: np.

---

steps in the value chain of many industries.[74] Just as the Internet is eliminating some business functions, it is creating an opening for new functions. These new activities are entering the value chain by a process known as *reintermediation*—the introduction of new types of intermediaries. Many of these new functions are affecting traditional supply chains. For example, delivery services are enjoying a boom because of the Internet. Many more consumers are choosing to have products delivered to their door rather than going out to pick them up.

The Threat of Substitutes Along with traditional marketplaces, the Internet has created a new marketplace and a new channel. In general, therefore, the threat of substitutes is heightened because the Internet introduces new ways to accomplish the same tasks.

Consumers will generally choose to use a product or service until a substitute that meets the same need becomes available at a lower cost. The economies created by Internet technologies have led to the development of numerous substitutes for traditional ways of doing business.

Another example of substitution is in the realm of electronic storage. With expanded desktop computing, the need to store information electronically has increased dramatically. Until recently, the trend has been to create increasingly larger desktop storage capabilities and techniques for compressing information that create storage efficiencies. But a viable substitute has emerged: storing information digitally on the Internet. Companies such as Dropbox and Amazon Web Services are providing web-based storage that firms can access simply by leasing space online. Since these storage places are virtual, they can be accessed anywhere the web can be accessed. Travelers can access important documents and files without transporting them physically from place to place.

The Intensity of Competitive Rivalry Because the Internet creates more tools and means for competing, rivalry among competitors is likely to be more intense. Only those competitors that can use digital technologies and the web to give themselves a distinct image, create unique product offerings, or provide "faster, smarter, cheaper" services are likely to capture greater profitability with the new technology.

Rivalry is more intense when switching costs are low and product or service differentiation is minimized. Because the Internet makes it possible to shop around, it has "commoditized" products that might previously have been regarded as rare or unique. Since the Internet reduces the importance of location, products that previously had to be sought out in geographically distant outlets are now readily available online. This makes competitors in cyberspace seem more equally balanced, thus intensifying rivalry.

The problem is made worse for marketers by the presence of shopping robots ("bots") and infomediaries that search the web for the best possible prices. Consumer websites like mySimon seek out all the web locations that sell similar products and provide price comparisons.[75] Obviously, this focuses the consumer exclusively on price. Some shopping infomediaries, such as CNET, not only search for the lowest prices on many different products but also rank the customer service quality of different sites that sell similarly priced items.[76] Such infomediary services are good for consumers because they give them the chance to compare services as well as price. For businesses, however, they increase rivalry by consolidating the marketing message that consumers use to make a purchase decision into a few key pieces of information over which the selling company has little control.

Using Industry Analysis: A Few Caveats

For industry analysis to be valuable, a company must collect and evaluate a wide variety of information. As the trend toward globalization accelerates, information on foreign markets as well as on a wider variety of competitors, suppliers, customers, substitutes, and potential new entrants becomes more critical. Industry analysis helps a firm not only to evaluate the profit potential of an industry but also to consider various ways to strengthen its position vis-à-vis the five forces. However, we'd like to address a few caveats.

First, *managers must not always avoid low-profit industries (or low-profit segments in profitable industries).*[77] Such industries can still yield high returns for some players who pursue sound strategies. As an example, consider WellPoint Health Network (now Anthem, Inc.), a huge health care insurer:[78]

> In 1986, WellPoint Health Network (when it was known as Blue Cross of California) suffered a loss of $160 million. That year, Leonard Schaeffer became CEO and challenged the conventional wisdom that individuals and small firms were money losers. (This was certainly "heresy" at the time—the firm was losing $5 million a year insuring 65,000 individuals!) However, by the early 1990s, the health insurer was leading the industry in profitability. The firm has continued to grow and outperform its rivals even during economic downturns. By 2016, its revenues and profits were over $80 billion and $2.5 billion, respectively.

Second, five-forces analysis implicitly *assumes a **zero-sum game**, determining how a firm can enhance its position relative to the forces.* Yet such an approach can often be shortsighted; that is, it can overlook the many potential benefits of developing constructive win–win relationships with suppliers and customers. Establishing long-term mutually beneficial relationships with suppliers improves a firm's ability to implement just-in-time (JIT) inventory systems, which let it manage inventories better and respond quickly to market demands. A recent study found that if a company exploits its powerful position against a supplier, that action may come back to haunt the company.[79] Consider, for example, General Motors' heavy-handed dealings with its suppliers:[80]

zero-sum game
a situation in which multiple players interact, and winners win only by taking from other players.

> In 2014, GM was already locked in a public relations nightmare as a deadly ignition defect triggered the recall of over 2.5 million vehicles.[81] At the same time, it was faced with another perception problem: poor supplier relations. GM is now considered the worst big automaker to deal with, according to a new survey of top suppliers in the car industry in the United States.
>
> The annual survey, conducted by the automotive consultant group Planning Perspectives Inc., asks the industry's biggest suppliers to rate the relationships with the six automakers that account for more than 85 percent of all cars and light trucks in the U.S. Those so-called "Tier 1" suppliers say GM is their least favorite big customer—less popular than even Chrysler, the unit of Fiat Chrysler Automobiles that had "earned" the dubious distinction since 2008.
>
> The suppliers gave GM low marks on all kinds of measures, including its overall trustworthiness, its communication skills, and its protection of intellectual property. The suppliers also said that GM was the automaker least likely to allow them to raise prices to

recoup unexpected materials cost increases. In return, parts executives have said they tend to bring hot new technology to other carmakers first—certainly something that makes it more difficult for GM to compete in this hotly contested industry.

Third, the five-forces analysis also has been criticized for *being essentially a static analysis.* External forces as well as strategies of individual firms are continually changing the structure of all industries. The search for a dynamic theory of strategy has led to greater use of game theory in industrial organization economics research and strategy research.

Based on game-theoretic considerations, Brandenburger and Nalebuff recently introduced the concept of the value net,[82] which in many ways is an extension of the five-forces analysis. It is illustrated in Exhibit 2.6. The value net represents all the players in the game and analyzes how their interactions affect a firm's ability to generate and appropriate value. The vertical dimension of the net includes suppliers and customers. The firm has direct transactions with them. On the horizontal dimension are substitutes and complements, players with whom a firm interacts but may not necessarily transact. The concept of complementors is perhaps the single most important contribution of value net analysis and is explained in more detail below.

complements
products or services that have an impact on the value of a firm's products or services.

Complements typically are products or services that have a potential impact on the value of a firm's own products or services. Those who produce complements are usually referred to as complementors.[83] Powerful hardware is of no value to a user unless there is software that runs on it. Similarly, new and better software is possible only if the hardware on which it can be run is available. This is equally true in the video game industry, where the sales of game consoles and video games complement each other. Nintendo's success in the early 1990s was a result of its ability to manage its relationship with its complementors. Nintendo built a security chip into the hardware and then licensed the right to develop games to outside firms. These firms paid a royalty to Nintendo for each copy of the game sold. The royalty revenue enabled Nintendo to sell game consoles at close to their cost, thereby increasing their market share, which, in turn, caused more games to be sold and more royalties to be generated.[84]

We would like to close this section with some recent insights from Michael Porter, the originator of the five-forces analysis.[85] He addresses two critical issues in conducting a good industry analysis, which will yield an improved understanding of the root causes of profitability: (1) choosing the appropriate time frame and (2) a rigorous quantification of the five forces.

EXHIBIT 2.6 **The Value Net**

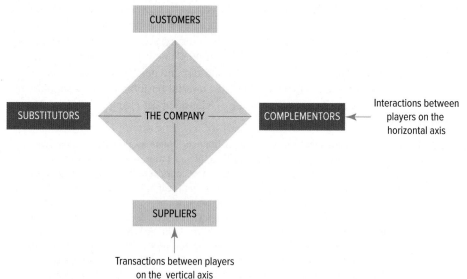

Source: Adapted from "The Right Game: Use Game Theory Shape Strategy," by A. Brandenburger and B. J. Nalebuff, *Harvard Business Review* July–August 1995.

- *Good industry analysis looks rigorously at the structural underpinnings of profitability. A first step is to understand the time horizon.* One of the essential tasks in industry analysis is to distinguish short-term fluctuations from structural changes. A good guideline for the appropriate time horizon is the full business cycle for the particular industry. For most industries, a three- to five-year horizon is appropriate. However, for some industries with long lead times, such as mining, the appropriate horizon may be a decade or more. It is average profitability over this period, not profitability in any particular year, which should be the focus of analysis.

- *The point of industry analysis is not to declare the industry attractive or unattractive but to understand the underpinnings of competition and the root causes of profitability.* As much as possible, analysts should look at industry structure quantitatively, rather than be satisfied with lists of qualitative factors. Many elements of five forces can be quantified: the percentage of the buyer's total cost accounted for by the industry's product (to understand buyer price sensitivity); the percentage of industry sales required to fill a plant or operate a logistical network to efficient scale (to help assess barriers to entry); and the buyer's switching cost (determining the inducement an entrant or rival must offer customers).

Strategic Groups within Industries

In an industry analysis, two assumptions are unassailable: (1) No two firms are totally different, and (2) no two firms are exactly the same. The issue becomes one of identifying groups of firms that are more similar to each other than firms that are not, otherwise known as **strategic groups**.[86] This is important because rivalry tends to be greater among firms that are alike. Strategic groups are clusters of firms that share similar strategies. After all, is Target more concerned about Nordstrom or Walmart? Is Mercedes more concerned about Hyundai or BMW? The answers are straightforward.[87]

These examples are not meant to trivialize the strategic groups concept.[88] Classifying an industry into strategic groups involves judgment. If it is useful as an analytical tool, we must exercise caution in deciding what dimensions to use to map these firms. Dimensions include breadth of product and geographic scope, price/quality, degree of vertical integration, type of distribution (e.g., dealers, mass merchandisers, private label), and so on. Dimensions should also be selected to reflect the variety of strategic combinations in an industry. For example, if all firms in an industry have roughly the same level of product differentiation (or R&D intensity), this would not be a good dimension to select.

What value is the strategic groups concept as an analytical tool? *First, strategic groupings help a firm identify barriers to mobility that protect a group from attacks by other groups.*[89] Mobility barriers are factors that deter the movement of firms from one strategic position to another. For example, in the chainsaw industry, the major barriers protecting the high-quality/dealer-oriented group are technology, brand image, and an established network of servicing dealers.

The second value of strategic grouping is that it *helps a firm identify groups whose competitive position may be marginal or tenuous.* We may anticipate that these competitors may exit the industry or try to move into another group. In recent years in the retail department store industry, firms such as JCPenney and Sears have experienced extremely difficult times because they were stuck in the middle, neither an aggressive discount player like Walmart nor a prestigious upscale player like Neiman Marcus.

Third, strategic groupings *help chart the future directions of firms' strategies.* Arrows emanating from each strategic group can represent the direction in which the group (or a firm within the group) seems to be moving. If all strategic groups are moving in a similar direction, this could indicate a high degree of future volatility and intensity of competition. In the automobile industry, for example, the competition in the minivan and sport utility segments has intensified in recent years as many firms have entered those product segments.

LO 2-7

The concept of strategic groups and their strategy and performance implications.

strategic groups
clusters of firms that share similar strategies.

Fourth, strategic groups are *helpful in thinking through the implications of each industry trend for the strategic group as a whole.* Is the trend decreasing the viability of a group? If so, in what direction should the strategic group move? Is the trend increasing or decreasing entry barriers? Will the trend decrease the ability of one group to separate itself from other groups? Such analysis can help in making predictions about industry evolution. A sharp increase in interest rates, for example, tends to have less impact on providers of higher-priced goods (e.g., Porsches) than on providers of lower-priced goods (e.g., Chevrolet Cobalt), whose customer base is much more price-sensitive.

Exhibit 2.7 provides a strategic grouping of the worldwide automobile industry.[90] The firms in each group are representative; not all firms are included in the mapping. We have identified five strategic groups. In the top left-hand corner are high-end luxury automakers that focus on a very narrow product market. Most of the cars produced by the members of this group cost well over $100,000. Some cost over twice that amount. The 2017 Ferrari California T starts at $210,843, and the 2017 Lamborghini Huracan will set you back $210,000 (in case you were wondering how to spend your employment signing bonus). Players in this market have a very exclusive clientele and face little rivalry from other strategic groups. At the other extreme, in the lower left-hand corner is a strategic group that has low-price/quality attributes and targets a narrow market. These players, Hyundai and Kia, limit competition from other strategic groups by pricing their products very low. The third group (near the middle) consists of firms high in product pricing/quality and average in their product-line breadth. The final group (at the far right) consists of firms with a broad range of products and multiple price points. These firms have entries that compete at both the lower end of the market (e.g., the Ford Focus) and the higher end (e.g., Chevrolet Corvette).

The auto market has been very dynamic and competition has intensified in recent years.[91] For example, some players are going more upscale with their product offerings. In 2009, Hyundai introduced its Genesis, starting at $33,000. This brings Hyundai into direct competition with entries from other strategic groups such as Toyota's Camry and Honda's Accord. And, in 2010, Hyundai introduced the Equus model. It was priced at about $60,000 to compete directly with the Lexus 460 on price. To further intensify competition, some upscale brands are increasingly entering lower-priced segments. In 2014, Audi introduced

EXHIBIT 2.7 **The World Automobile Industry: Strategic Groups**

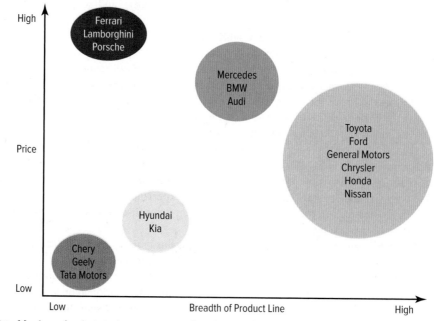

Note: Members of each strategic group are not exhaustive, only illustrative.

Purdue University's Innovative Idea: Income Share Agreements

During the past decade, the cost of higher education in the United States has outpaced growth in personal income as well as cost of living increases. This has resulted in a rapid rise in student indebtedness, which many experts view as a looming crisis. Purdue University has responded to this crisis in an innovative way—allowing students to enroll in return for a fixed percentage of their future income.

Purdue University rolled out the "Back a Boiler" program in 2016, using a concept known as an income-share agreement, or ISA, that is available to rising juniors and seniors. The awards will begin at $5,000 and take into consideration a student's cumulative debt. It is different from a typical loan because students would repay the debt based on a fixed rate linked to their expected income. In a sense, it may be viewed as a gamble that could save them thousands of dollars as compared to traditional loans. But it could also cost them far more if they land high-paying jobs.

To illustrate, a senior majoring in chemical engineering could sign a contract for $10,000 and pay 2.68 percent of her income over seven years, according to Purdue's online calculator. On the other hand, a student planning to work in a less lucrative field such as comparative literature would shell out a larger portion of her paycheck with contracts lasting no longer than nine years. This is shorter than the federal-aid 10-year repayment plan that stretches out much longer if a borrower falls behind. And Purdue caps repayment at 2.5 times the value of the contract with the objective to plow returns into helping future students. As noted by Purdue University's President Mitch Daniels, "Clearly there is an explosion in student debt and the default rate is a concern. That got me seriously thinking about this, not as replacement (for federal loans) but as a new option."

A concern might be that only poor performing students would be more likely to be interested. However, Purdue's plan to offer contracts tailored to individuals will help the school recoup the investment. Another issue is whether ISAs can compete with federal programs such as Pell Grants. One potential positive outcome: If the program takes off, students looking at contracts would see data on predicted earnings—thus, they may be inclined to choose majors that tend to produce more value.

Purdue structured the income shares to be similar to other forms of unsecured consumer debt. However, it has the added protection that has been extremely difficult to obtain with student loans: bankruptcy discharge. The foundation has put protections in place to account for hardship such as not requiring payments for graduates who earn less than $20,000 a year. However, if someone makes about that amount but fails to make payments—they will be pursued through debt collection.

Discussion Questions

1. Would you be interested in taking out an ISA? Why? Why not?
2. In general, what do you see as the main advantage (or disadvantage) of such a program?
3. Do you think it will become successful? And, if so, do you foresee a market for truly private ISAs in the future?

Sources: Anonymous. 2016. The other debt-free college idea. *The Wall Street Journal*, April 17: np; Douglas-Gabriel, D. 2016. At Purdue, student aid based on future earnings could revolutionize college debt. *www.washingtonpost.com*, April: np; Belkin, D. 2015. Seeking options, college students sell their futures. *Dallas Morning News*, August 6: A3; and Anonymous. Income share agreements. *www.purdue.edu* undated.

the Q3 SUV at a base price of only $32,500. And BMW, with its 1-series, is another well-known example. Such cars, priced in the low $30,000s, compete more directly with products from broad-line manufacturers like Ford, General Motors, and Toyota. This suggests that members of a strategic group can overcome mobility barriers and migrate to other groups that they find attractive if they are willing to commit time and resources.

Our discussion would not be complete, of course, without paying some attention to recent entries in the automobile industry that will likely lead to the formation of a new strategic group—placed at the bottom left corner of the grid in Exhibit 2.7. Three firms—China's Zhejiang Geely Holding Company, China's Chery Automobile Company, and India's Tata Motors—have introduced models that bring new meaning to the term "subcompact."[92] Let's take a look at these econoboxes.

Chery's 2013 QQ model sells for between $6,083 and $8,170 in the Chinese market and sports horsepower in the range of only 51 to 74. Geely's best-selling four-door sedan, the Free Cruiser, retails from $5,440 to $7,046. The firm has gone more upscale with some offerings, such as the GX7, a sports utility vehicle with a price starting at $14,910.

For low price-points, India's Tata Motors has everyone beat by the proverbial mile. In January 2008, it introduced the Nano as the "World's Cheapest Car," with an astonishing retail price of only $2,500. It is a four-door, five-seat hatchback that gets 54 miles to the gallon (but this economy originally came with a 30 horsepower motor). Initially, it was a big hit in India. However, after sales peaked at about 80,000 units in 2011–2012, they crashed to only 21,000 units in 2013–2014. As noted by Girish Wagh, the man behind the Nano, "People started looking at Nano not as a low-cost innovation, but as a cheap car. This, among other factors, also hurt the chances." Needless to say, Tata has made many attempts to make the car more upscale, with a correspondingly higher price.

Not surprisingly, some automakers have recently entered the Indian market with more desirable offerings. Several have offerings that are called compact sedans, but they are actually hatchbacks with a tiny trunk tacked on. These models include Suzuki's Dzire, Honda's Amaze, and Hyundai's Xcent. Prices start at around $8,000, and with the added cachet of a sedan silhouette that adds only a few hundred dollars, these models have become very popular with Indian buyers. This niche is one of the few car segments that soared, while the country's overall car market shrunk.

Reflecting on Career Implications . . .

This chapter addresses the importance of the external environment for strategic managers. As a strategic manager, you should strive in your career to benefit from enhancing your awareness of your external environment. The questions below focus on these issues.

- ▣ **Creating the Environmentally Aware Organization:** Advancing your career requires constant scanning, monitoring, and intelligence gathering not only to find future job opportunities but also to understand how employers' expectations are changing. Consider using websites such as LinkedIn to find opportunities. Merely posting your résumé on a site such as LinkedIn may not be enough. Instead, consider in what ways you can use such sites for scanning, monitoring, and intelligence gathering.

- ▣ **SWOT Analysis:** As an analytical method, SWOT analysis is applicable for individuals as it is for firms. It is important for you to periodically evaluate your strengths and weaknesses as well as potential opportunities and threats to your career. Such analysis should be followed by efforts to address your weaknesses by improving your skills and capabilities.

- ▣ **General Environment:** The general environment consists of several segments, such as the demographic, sociocultural, political/legal, technological, economic, and global environments. It would be useful to evaluate how each of these segments can affect your career opportunities. Identify two or three specific trends (e.g., rapid technological change, aging of the population, increase in minimum wages) and their impact on your choice of careers. These also provide possibilities for you to add value for your organization.

- ▣ **Five-Forces Analysis:** Before you go for a job interview, consider the five forces affecting the industry within which the firm competes. This will help you to appear knowledgeable about the industry and increase your odds of landing the job. It also can help you to decide if you want to work for that organization. If the "forces" are unfavorable, the long-term profit potential of the industry may be unattractive, leading to fewer resources available and—all other things being equal— fewer career opportunities.

Managers must analyze the external environment to minimize or eliminate threats and exploit opportunities. This involves a continuous process of environmental scanning and monitoring as well as obtaining competitive intelligence on present and potential rivals. These activities provide valuable inputs for developing forecasts. In addition, many firms use scenario planning to anticipate and respond to volatile and disruptive environmental changes.

We identified two types of environments: the general environment and the competitive environment. The six segments of the general environment are demographic, sociocultural, political/legal, technological, economic, and global. Trends and events occurring in these segments, such as the aging of the population, higher percentages of women in the workplace, governmental legislation, and increasing (or decreasing) interest rates, can have a dramatic effect on a firm. A given trend or event may have a positive impact on some industries and a negative, a neutral, or no impact on others.

The competitive environment consists of industry-related factors and has a more direct impact than the general environment. Porter's five-forces model of industry analysis includes the threat of new entrants, buyer power, supplier power, threat of substitutes, and rivalry among competitors. The intensity of these factors determines, in large part, the average expected level of profitability in an industry. A sound awareness of such factors, both individually and in combination, is beneficial not only for deciding what industries to enter but also for assessing how a firm can improve its competitive position. We discuss how many of the changes brought about by the digital economy can be understood in the context of five-forces analysis. The limitations of five-forces analysis include its static nature and its inability to acknowledge the role of complementors. Although we addressed the general environment and competitive environment in separate sections, they are quite interdependent. A given environmental trend or event, such as changes in the ethnic composition of a population or a technological innovation, typically has a much greater impact on some industries than on others.

The concept of strategic groups is also important to the external environment of a firm. No two organizations are completely different nor are they exactly the same. The question is how to group firms in an industry on the basis of similarities in their resources and strategies. The strategic groups concept is valuable for determining mobility barriers across groups, identifying groups with marginal competitive positions, charting the future directions of firm strategies, and assessing the implications of industry trends for the strategic group as a whole.

SUMMARY REVIEW QUESTIONS

1. Why must managers be aware of a firm's external environment?
2. What is gathering and analyzing competitive intelligence, and why is it important for firms to engage in it?
3. Discuss and describe the six elements of the external environment.
4. Select one of these elements and describe some changes relating to it in an industry that interests you.
5. Describe how the five forces can be used to determine the average expected profitability in an industry.
6. What are some of the limitations (or caveats) in using five-forces analysis?
7. Explain how the general environment and industry environment are highly related. How can such interrelationships affect the profitability of a firm or industry?
8. Explain the concept of strategic groups. What are the performance implications?

key terms

perceptual acuity 36
environmental scanning 37
environmental monitoring 37
competitive intelligence 38
environmental forecasting 38
scenario analysis 40
SWOT analysis 40
general environment 41
demographic segment of the general environment 43
sociocultural segment of the general environment 43
political/legal segment of the general environment 43
technological segment of the general environment 45
economic segment of the general environment 46
global segment of the general environment 47
data analytics 47
industry 50
competitive environment 50
Porter's five-forces model of industry competition 50
threat of new entrants 50
economies of scale 51
product differentiation 51
switching cost 51
bargaining power of buyers 52
bargaining power of suppliers 53
threat of substitute products and services 54
substitute products and services 54
intensity of rivalry among competitors in an industry 54
zero-sum game 59
complements 60
strategic groups 61

EXPERIENTIAL EXERCISE

Select one of the following industries: personal computers, airlines, or automobiles. For this industry, evaluate the strength of each of Porter's five forces as well as complementors.

Industry Force	High? Medium? Low?	Why?
1. Threat of new entrants		
2. Power of buyers		
3. Power of suppliers		
4. Power of substitutes		
5. Rivalry among competitors		
6. Complementors		

APPLICATION QUESTIONS & EXERCISES

1. Imagine yourself as the CEO of a large firm in an industry in which you are interested. Please (1) identify major trends in the general environment, (2) analyze their impact on the firm, and (3) identify major sources of information to monitor these trends. (Use Internet and library resources.)

2. Analyze movements across the strategic groups in the U.S. retail industry. How do these movements within this industry change the nature of competition?

3. What are the major trends in the general environment that have impacted the U.S. pharmaceutical industry?

4. Go to the Internet and look up *www.kroger.com*. What are some of the five forces driving industry competition that are affecting the profitability of this firm?

ETHICS QUESTIONS

1. What are some of the legal and ethical issues involved in collecting competitor intelligence in the following situations?

   a. Hotel A sends an employee posing as a potential client to Hotel B to find out who Hotel B's major corporate customers are.

   b. A firm hires an MBA student to collect information directly from a competitor while claiming the information is for a course project.

   c. A firm advertises a nonexistent position and interviews a rival's employees with the intention of obtaining competitor information.

2. What are some of the ethical implications that arise when a firm tries to exploit its power over a supplier?

REFERENCES

1. Nanton, N. & Dicks, J. W. 2013. Every entrepreneur's biggest mistake (and how to avoid it!). *www.fastcompany.com*. May 21: np.

2. Schneider, J. & Hall, J. 2011. Can you hear me now? *Harvard Business Review,* 89(4): 23; Hornigan, J. 2009. Wireless Internet use—Mobile access to data and information. *www.pewinternet.org,* July 22: np; and Salemi Industries. 2012. Home page. *www.salemiindustries.com,* December 20: np.

3. Weber, G. W. 1995. A new paint job at PPG. *BusinessWeek.* November 13: 74-75.

4. Hamel, G. & Prahalad, C. K. 1994. *Competing for the future.* Boston: Harvard Business School Press.

5. Drucker, P. F. 1994. Theory of the business. *Harvard Business Review,* 72: 95-104.

6. For an insightful discussion on managers' assessment of the external environment, refer to Sutcliffe, K. M. & Weber, K. 2003. The high cost of accurate knowledge. *Harvard Business Review,* 81(5): 74-86.

7. Merino, M. 2013. You can't be a wimp: Making the tough calls. *Harvard Business Review,* 91(11): 73-78.

8. For insights on recognizing and acting on environmental opportunities, refer to Alvarez, S. A. & Barney, J. B. 2008. Opportunities, organizations, and entrepreneurship: Theory and debate. *Strategic Entrepreneurship Journal,* 2(3): entire issue.

9. Charitou, C. D. & Markides, C. C. 2003. Responses to disruptive strategic innovation. *MIT Sloan Management Review,* 44(2): 55-64.

10. Our discussion of scanning, monitoring, competitive intelligence, and forecasting concepts draws on several sources. These include Fahey, L. & Narayanan, V. K. 1983. *Macroenvironmental analysis for strategic management.* St. Paul, MN: West; Lorange, P., Scott, F. S., & Ghoshal, S. 1986. *Strategic control.* St. Paul, MN: West; Ansoff, H. I. 1984. *Implementing strategic management.* Englewood Cliffs, NJ: Prentice Hall; and Schreyogg, G. & Stienmann, H. 1987. Strategic control: A new perspective. *Academy of Management Review,* 12: 91-103.

11. An insightful discussion on how leaders can develop "peripheral vision" in environmental scanning is found in Day, G. S. & Schoemaker, P. J. H. 2008. Are you a "vigilant leader"? *MIT Sloan Management Review,* 49(3): 43-51.

12. Elenkov, D. S. 1997. Strategic uncertainty and environmental scanning: The case for institutional influences on scanning behavior. *Strategic Management Journal,* 18: 287–302.

13. For an interesting perspective on environmental scanning in emerging economies, see May, R. C., Stewart, W. H., & Sweo, R. 2000. Environmental scanning behavior in a transitional economy, Evidence from Russia. *Academy of Management Journal,* 43(3): 403–427.

14. Bryon, E. 2010. For insight into P&G, check Olay numbers. *Wall Street Journal,* October 27: C1.

15. Tang, J. 2010. How entrepreneurs discover opportunities in China: An institutional view. *Asia Pacific Journal of Management,* 27(3): 461–480.

16. Walters, B. A. & Priem, R. L. 1999. Business strategy and CEO intelligence acquisition. *Competitive Intelligence Review,* 10(2): 15–22.

17. Prior, V. 1999. The language of competitive intelligence, Part 4. *Competitive Intelligence Review,* 10(1): 84–87.

18. Hill, K. 2011. The spy who liked me. *Forbes,* November 21: 56–57.

19. Wolfenson, J. 1999. The world in 1999: A battle for corporate honesty. *The Economist,* 38: 13–30.

20. Drucker, P. F. 1997. The future that has already happened. *Harvard Business Review,* 75(6): 22.

21. Downes, L. & Nunes, P. 2014. *Big bang disruption.* New York: Penguin.

22. Fahey & Narayanan, op. cit., p. 41.

23. Insights on how to improve predictions can be found in Cross, R., Thomas, R. J., & Light, D. A. 2009. The prediction lover's handbook. *MIT Sloan Management Review,* 50(2): 32–34.

24. Courtney, H., Kirkland, J., & Viguerie, P. 1997. Strategy under uncertainty. *Harvard Business Review,* 75(6): 66–79.

25. Odlyzko, A. 2003. False hopes. *Red Herring,* March: 31.

26. Szczerba, R. J. 2015. 15 Worst tech predictions of all time. *www.forbes.com.* January 5: np; and, Dunn, M. 2016. Here are 20 of the worst predictions ever made about the future of tech. *www.news.com.au.* March 8: np.

27. Zweig, J. 2014. Lessons Learned from the year of shock. *The Wall Street Journal,* December 31: C1–C2.

28. For an interesting perspective on how Accenture practices and has developed its approach to scenario planning, refer to Ferguson, G., Mathur, S., & Shah, B. 2005. Evolving from information to insight. *MIT Sloan Management Review,* 46(2): 51–58.

29. The PPG example draws on: Camillus, J. C. 2008. Strategy as a wicked problem. *Harvard Business Review,* 86(5): 98-106; *www.ppg.com*; and, *finance.yahoo.com.*

30. Byrne, J. 2012. Great ideas are hard to come by. *Fortune,* April 7: 69 ff.

31. Dean, T. J., Brown, R. L., & Bamford, C. E. 1998. Differences in large and small firm responses to environmental context: Strategic implications from a comparative analysis of business formations. *Strategic Management Journal,* 19: 709–728.

32. Colvin, G. 2014. Four things that worry business. *Fortune,* October 27: 32.

33. Colvin, G. 1997. How to beat the boomer rush. *Fortune,* August 18: 59–63.

34. Porter, M. E. 2010. Discovering—and lowering—the real costs of health care. *Harvard Business Review,* 89(1/2): 49–50.

35. Farrell, C. 2014. Baby boomers' latest revolution: Unretirement. *Dallas Morning News,* October 19: 4P.

36. Challenger, J. 2000. Women's corporate rise has reduced relocations. *Lexington* (KY) *Herald-Leader,* October 29: D1.

37. Watkins, M. D. 2003. Government games. *MIT Sloan Management Review,* 44(2): 91–95.

38. A discussion of the political issues surrounding caloric content on meals is in Orey, M. 2008. A food fight over calorie counts. *BusinessWeek,* February 11: 36.

39. For a discussion of the linkage between copyright law and innovation, read Guterman, J. 2009. Does copyright law hinder innovation? *MIT Sloan Management Review,* 50(2): 14–15.

40. Davies, A. 2000. The welcome mat is out for nerds. *BusinessWeek,* May 21: 17; Broache, A. 2007. Annual H-1B visa cap met—already. *news.cnet.com,* April 3: np; and Anonymous.

Undated. Cap count for H-1B and H-2B workers for fiscal year 2009. *www.uscis.gov:* np.

41. Weise, K. 2014. How to hack the visa limit. *Bloomberg Businessweek,* May 26-June 1: 39–40.

42. Hout, T. M. & Ghemawat, P. 2010. China vs. the world: Whose technology is it? *Harvard Business Review,* 88(12): 94–103.

43. Business ready for Internet revolution. 1999. *Financial Times,* May 21: 17.

44. A discussion of an alternate energy—marine energy—is the topic of Boyle, M. 2008. Scottish power. *Fortune,* March 17: 28.

45. Baker, S. & Aston, A. 2005. The business of nanotech. *BusinessWeek,* February 14: 64–71.

46. Wilson, H. J. 2013. Wearables in the workplace. *Harvard Business Review,* 91(9): 22–25.

47. For an insightful discussion of the causes of the global financial crisis, read Johnson, S. 2009. The global financial crisis—What really precipitated it? *MIT Sloan Management Review,* 50(2): 16–18.

48. Tyson, L. D. 2011. A better stimulus for the U.S. economy. *Harvard Business Review,* 89(1/2): 53.

49. An interesting and balanced discussion on the merits of multinationals to the U.S. economy is found in Mandel, M. 2008. Multinationals: Are they good for America? *BusinessWeek,* March 10: 41–64.

50. Insights on risk perception across countries are addressed in Purda, L. D. 2008. Risk perception and the financial system. *Journal of International Business Studies,* 39(7): 1178–1196.

51. Thurm, S. 2012. U.S. firms add jobs, but mostly overseas. *wsj.com,* April 27: np.

52. Goll, I. & Rasheed, M. A. 1997. Rational decision-making and firm performance: The moderating role of environment. *Strategic Management Journal,* 18: 583–591.

53. Our discussion of data analytics draws on a variety of sources. These include: Kiron, D. 2013. From value to vision: Reimagining the possible with data analytics. *MIT Sloan Management Review (Research Report),* Spring: 3-19; Malone, M. S. 2016. The big-data future has arrived. *The Wall Street Journal,* February 23: A17; and Porter, M. E. &

Heppelmann, J. E. 2015. How smart, connected products are transforming companies. *Harvard Business Review,* 93(10): 96–114.

54. This discussion draws heavily on Porter, M. E. 1980. *Competitive strategy:* chap. 1. New York: Free Press.

55. Ibid.

56. Rivalry in the airline industry is discussed in Foust, D. 2009. Which airlines will disappear in 2009? *BusinessWeek,* January 19: 46–47.

57. Fryer, B. 2001. Leading through rough times: An interview with Novell's Eric Schmidt. *Harvard Business Review,* 78(5): 117–123.

58. Anonymous. 2015. No reservations. *The Economist.* November 21: 63.

59. For a discussion on the importance of barriers to entry within industries, read Greenwald, B. & Kahn, J. 2005. *Competition demystified: A radically simplified approach to business strategy.* East Rutherford, NJ: Portfolio.

60. A discussion of how the medical industry has erected entry barriers that have resulted in lawsuits is found in Whelan, D. 2008. Bad medicine. *BusinessWeek,* March 10: 86–98.

61. Colvin, G. 2014. Welcome to the era of Lego innovations (some assembly required). *Fortune,* April 14: 52.

62. Wise, R. & Baumgarter, P. 1999. Go downstream: The new profit imperative in manufacturing. *Harvard Business Review,* 77(5): 133–141.

63. Salman, W. A. 2000. The new economy is stronger than you think. *Harvard Business Review,* 77(6): 99–106.

64. Mudambi, R. & Helper, S. 1998. The "close but adversarial" model of supplier relations in the U.S. auto industry. *Strategic Management Journal,* 19: 775–792.

65. Stevens, D. (vice president of Delta Pride Catfish Inc.). 2014. *personal communication:* October 16; and Fritz, M. 1988. Agribusiness: Catfish story. *Forbes,* December 12: 37.

66. Trends in the solar industry are discussed in Carey, J. 2009. Solar: The sun will come out tomorrow. *BusinessWeek,* January 12: 51.

67. Edelstein, S. 2014. Could U.S. hybrid car sales be peaking already—and if so, why? *greencarreports.com,* June 16: np; Naughton, K. 2012. Hybrids' unlikely rival: plain old cars. *Bloomberg Businessweek,* February 2: 23–24; Cobb, J. 2016. April 2016 dash board. *www.hybridcars.com,* May 4: np.

68. An interesting analysis of self-regulation in an industry (chemical) is in Barnett, M. L. & King, A. A. 2008. Good fences make good neighbors: A longitudinal analysis of an industry self-regulatory institution. *Academy of Management Journal,* 51(6): 1053–1078.

69. For an interesting perspective on the intensity of competition in the supermarket industry, refer to Anonymous. 2005. Warfare in the aisles. *The Economist,* April 2: 6–8.

70. Macmillan, D. 2014. Tech's fiercest rivalry: Uber vs. Lyft. *online.wsj.com,* August 11: np; Divine, J. 2016. Uber IPO: Losing luster after a $1.2 billion loss. *www.usnews.com,* August 29: np.

71. For an interesting perspective on changing features of firm boundaries, refer to Afuah, A. 2003. Redefining firm boundaries in the face of the Internet: Are firms really shrinking? *Academy of Management Review,* 28(1): 34–53.

72. Time to rebuild. 2001. *The Economist,* May 19: 55–56.

73. *www.amazon.com.*

74. For more on the role of the Internet as an electronic intermediary, refer to Carr, N. G. 2000. Hypermediation: Commerce as clickstream. *Harvard Business Review,* 78(1): 46–48.

75. *www.mysimon.com;* and *www. pricescan.com.*

76. *www.cnet.com;* and *www.bizrate.com.*

77. For insights into strategies in a low-profit industry, refer to Hopkins, M. S. 2008. The management lessons of a beleaguered industry. *MIT Sloan Management Review,* 50(1): 25–31.

78. Foust, D. 2007. The best performers. *BusinessWeek,* March 26: 58–95; Rosenblum, D., Tomlinson, D., & Scott, L. 2003. Bottom-feeding for blockbuster businesses. *Harvard Business Review,* 81(3): 52–59; Paychex 2006 Annual Report; and WellPoint Health Network 2005 Annual Report.

79. Kumar, N. 1996. The power of trust in manufacturer-retailer relationship. *Harvard Business Review,* 74(6): 92–110.

80. Welch, D. 2006. Renault-Nissan: Say hello to Bo. *BusinessWeek,* July 31: 56–57.

81. Kelleher, J. B. 2014. GM ranked worst automaker by U.S. suppliers—survey. *finance.yahoo.com,* May 12: np; and Welch, D. 2006. Renault-Nissan: Say hello to Bo. *BusinessWeek,* July 31: 56–57.

82. Brandenburger, A. & Nalebuff, B. J. 1995. The right game: Use game theory to shape strategy. *Harvard Business Review,* 73(4): 57–71.

83. For a scholarly discussion of complementary assets and their relationship to competitive advantage, refer to Stieglitz, N. & Heine, K. 2007. Innovations and the role of complementarities in a strategic theory of the firm. *Strategic Management Journal,* 28(1): 1–15.

84. A useful framework for the analysis of industry evolution has been proposed by Professor Anita McGahan of Boston University. Her analysis is based on the identification of the core activities and the core assets of an industry and the threats they face. She suggests that an industry may follow one of four possible evolutionary trajectories—radical change, creative change, intermediating change, or progressive change—based on these two types of threats of obsolescence. Refer to McGahan, A. M. 2004. How industries change. *Harvard Business Review,* 82(10): 87–94.

85. Porter, M. I. 2008. The five competitive forces that shape strategy. *Harvard Business Review,* 86(1): 79–93.

86. Peteraf, M. & Shanley, M. 1997. Getting to know you: A theory of strategic group identity. *Strategic Management Journal,* 18 (Special Issue): 165–186.

87. An interesting scholarly perspective on strategic groups may be found in Dranove, D., Peteraf, M., & Shanley, M. 1998. Do strategic groups exist? An economic framework for analysis. *Strategic Management Journal,* 19(11): 1029–1044.

88. For an empirical study on strategic groups and predictors of performance, refer to Short, J. C., Ketchen, D. J., Jr., Palmer, T. B., & Hult, T. M. 2007. Firm, strategic group, and industry influences on performance. *Strategic Management Journal,* 28(2): 147–167.

89. This section draws on several sources, including Kerwin, K. R. & Haughton, K. 1997. Can Detroit make cars that baby boomers like? *BusinessWeek,* December 1: 134–148; and Taylor, A., III. 1994. The new golden age of autos. *Fortune,* April 4: 50–66.

90. Csere, C. 2001. Supercar supermarket. *Car and Driver,* January: 118–127.

91. For a discussion of the extent of overcapacity in the worldwide automobile industry, read Roberts, D., Matlack, C., Busyh, J., & Rowley, I. 2009. A hundred factories too many. *Business Week,* January 19: 42–43.

92. McLain, S. 2014. India's middle class embraces minicars. *The Wall Street Journal,* October 9: B2; Anonymous. 2014. Geely GX7 launched after upgrading: Making versatile and comfortable SUV. *www.globaltimes. ch,* April 18: np; Anonymous. 2014. Adequate Guiyang Geely Free Cruiser higher offer 1,000 yuan now. *www.wantinews.com,* February 20: np; Anonymous. 2013. Restyled Chery QQ hit showrooms with a US$6,083 starting price. *www.chinaautoweb. com,* March 4: np; and Doval, P. 2014. Cheapest car tag hit Tata Nano: Creator. *economictimes.indiatimes. com,* August 21: np.

After reading this chapter, you should have a good understanding of the following learning objectives:

LO3-1 The primary and support activities of a firm's value chain.

LO3-2 How value-chain analysis can help managers create value by investigating relationships among activities within the firm and between the firm and its customers and suppliers.

LO3-3 The resource-based view of the firm and the different types of tangible and intangible resources, as well as organizational capabilities.

LO3-4 The four criteria that a firm's resources must possess to maintain a sustainable advantage and how value created can be appropriated by employees and managers.

LO3-5 The usefulness of financial ratio analysis, its inherent limitations, and how to make meaningful comparisons of performance across firms.

LO3-6 The value of the "balanced scorecard" in recognizing how the interests of a variety of stakeholders can be interrelated.

©Anatoli Styf/Shutterstock

LEARNING FROM MISTAKES

When Twitter first burst upon the scene in 2006, there was almost immediate buzz about the firm and its platform. Having the ability to send out text messages to a circle of friends or followers seemed like a great idea. At the same time, in the words of Evan Williams, one of Twitter's creators, "With Twitter, it wasn't clear what it was. They called it a social network, they called it microblogging, but it was hard to define, because it didn't replace anything. There was this path of discovery with something like that, where over time you figure out what it is." Still, it took off. Growing from only 16,000 users at the end of 2006 to 4 million in 2008 and to 54 million by the end of 2010, it seemed to be on the path to great success.

But the situation has changed since then. Twitter's growth quickly flattened out. The number of users hit 284 million in the third quarter of 2014 but had only grown to 317 million two years later. In fact, the firm experienced a decline in the number of users in the United States in late 2015. Twitter's growth pales in comparison to some of its closest rivals. Over the same two-year period, Snapchat saw its user base grow by 154 percent, while Instagram jumped by a whopping 284 percent. With its flat growth, investors have become quite pessimistic about the firm's value. Its stock price declined by 59 percent from December 2014 to 2016.[1]

Why the quick decline in growth? There just isn't anything terribly unique about Twitter and its core products are not difficult to copy. Facebook created a similar messaging app and has seen its user base grow to 1 billion individuals. WhatsApp, which is owned by Facebook, has also grown to 1 billion users. Instagram has over 500 million users. Twitter also faces strong competition as it tries to expand its global reach since messaging apps that focus on specific geographic regions have also popped up. For example, the Japanese chat app, Line, has 220 million users.

It is unclear whether Twitter can turn it around in this increasingly competitive messaging app market as a standalone firm. The firm appeared to be open to being acquired by a firm that could integrate its messaging app into a larger platform of services. While rumors swirled that Salesforce, Disney, or Alphabet, the parent company of Google, might be interested in buying Twitter in the fall of 2016, no formal offers came. Apparently, these firms just didn't see much value in Twitter. As Marc Benioff, the CEO of Salesforce, stated, "We walked away. It wasn't the right fit for us." Thus, the future for Twitter is unclear.

Discussion Questions

1. Why did Twitter go from an exciting, growing firm to a firm with a flat user base so quickly?
2. What could the firm have done to avoid this situation?
3. What options does the firm have to get back on a path to success?

In this chapter we will place heavy emphasis on the value-chain concept. That is, we focus on the key value-creating activities (e.g., operations, marketing and sales, and procurement) that a firm must effectively manage and integrate in order to attain competitive advantages in the marketplace. However, firms not only must pay close attention to their own value-creating activities but also must maintain close and effective relationships with key organizations outside the firm boundaries, such as suppliers, customers, and alliance partners.

Although Twitter experienced tremendous growth early, it was quickly challenged by other applications that effectively mimicked what Twitter offered. Twitter's resource set and market positioning just was not very difficult to copy.

We will begin our discussion of the firm's internal environment by looking at a value-chain analysis. This analysis gives us insight into a firm's operations and how the firm creates economic value.

VALUE-CHAIN ANALYSIS

value-chain analysis
a strategic analysis of an organization that uses value-creating activities

primary activities
sequential activities of the value chain that refer to the physical creation of the product or service, its sale and transfer to the buyer, and its service after sale, including inbound logistics, operations, outbound logistics, marketing and sales, and service.

support activities
activities of the value chain that either add value by themselves or add value through important relationships with both primary activities and other support activities, including procurement, technology development, human resource management, and general administration.

Value-chain analysis views the organization as a sequential process of value-creating activities. The approach is useful for understanding the building blocks of competitive advantage and was described in Michael Porter's seminal book *Competitive Advantage*.[2] Value is the amount that buyers are willing to pay for what a firm provides them and is measured by total revenue, a reflection of the price a firm's product commands and the quantity it can sell. A firm is profitable when the value it receives exceeds the total costs involved in creating its product or service. Creating value for buyers that exceeds the costs of production (i.e., margin) is a key concept used in analyzing a firm's competitive position.

Porter described two different categories of activities. First, five **primary activities**—inbound logistics, operations, outbound logistics, marketing and sales, and service—contribute to the physical creation of the product or service, its sale and transfer to the buyer, and its service after the sale. Second, **support activities**—procurement, technology development, human resource management, and general administration—either add value by themselves or add value through important relationships with both primary activities and other support activities. Exhibit 3.1 illustrates Porter's value chain.

To get the most out of value-chain analysis, view the concept in its broadest context, without regard to the boundaries of your own organization. That is, place your organization within a more encompassing value chain that includes your firm's suppliers, customers, and alliance partners. Thus, in addition to thoroughly understanding how value is created within the organization, be aware of how value is created for other organizations in the overall supply chain or distribution channel.[3]

Next, we'll describe and provide examples of each of the primary and support activities. Then we'll provide examples of how companies add value by means of relationships among activities within the organization as well as activities outside the organization, such as those activities associated with customers and suppliers.[4]

EXHIBIT 3.1 The Value Chain: Primary and Support Activities

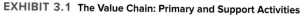

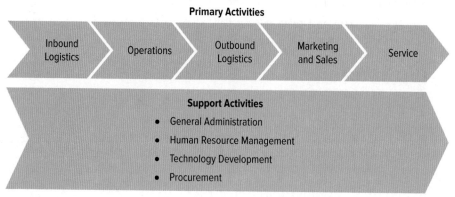

Adapted from *Competitive Advantage: Creating and Sustaining Superior Performance* by Michael E. Porter, 1985, 1998, Free Press.

Primary Activities

Five generic categories of primary activities are involved in competing in any industry, as shown in Exhibit 3.2. Each category is divisible into a number of distinct activities that depend on the particular industry and the firm's strategy.[5]

The primary and support activities of a firm's value chain.

Inbound Logistics Inbound logistics is primarily associated with receiving, storing, and distributing inputs to the product. It includes material handling, warehousing, inventory control, vehicle scheduling, and returns to suppliers.

inbound logistics
receiving, storing, and distributing inputs of a product.

Just-in-time (JIT) inventory systems, for example, were designed to achieve efficient inbound logistics. In essence, Toyota epitomizes JIT inventory systems, in which parts deliveries arrive at the assembly plants only hours before they are needed. JIT systems will play a vital role in fulfilling Toyota's commitment to fill a buyer's new-car order in just five days.[6] This standard is in sharp contrast to most competitors that require approximately 30 days' notice to build vehicles. Toyota's standard is three times faster than even Honda Motors, considered to be the industry's most efficient in order follow-through. The five days represent the time from the company's receipt of an order to the time the car leaves the assembly plant. Actual delivery may take longer, depending on where a customer lives.

Operations Operations include all activities associated with transforming inputs into the final product form, such as machining, packaging, assembly, testing, printing, and facility operations.

operations
all activities associated with transforming inputs into the final product form.

Creating environmentally friendly manufacturing is one way to use operations to achieve competitive advantage. Shaw Industries (now part of Berkshire Hathaway), a world-class competitor in the floor-covering industry, is well known for its concern for the environment.[7] It has been successful in reducing the expenses associated with the disposal of dangerous chemicals and other waste products from its manufacturing operations. Its environmental endeavors have multiple payoffs. Shaw has received many awards for its recycling efforts—awards that enhance its reputation.

Inbound Logistics

- Location of distribution facilities to minimize shipping times.
- Warehouse layout and designs to increase efficiency of operations for incoming materials.

Operations

- Efficient plant operations to minimize costs.
- Efficient plant layout and workflow design.
- Incorporation of appropriate process technology.

Outbound Logistics

- Effective shipping processes to provide quick delivery and minimize damages.
- Shipping of goods in large lot sizes to minimize transportation costs.

Marketing and Sales

- Innovative approaches to promotion and advertising.
- Proper identification of customer segments and needs.

Service

- Quick response to customer needs and emergencies.
- Quality of service personnel and ongoing training.

EXHIBIT 3.2

The Value Chain: Some Factors to Consider in Assessing a Firm's Primary Activities

Source: Adapted from Porter, M. E. 1985. *Competitive Advantage: Creating and Sustaining Superior Performance.* New York: Free Press.

CHIPOTLE'S EFFICIENT OPERATIONS

Peak hours at restaurants create real challenges that must be addressed. Otherwise, business may be lost and, worse yet, customers may never come back. Lines snaking out the doors have long been a bottleneck to growth at U.S. burrito chain Chipotle. However, the company has a plan—actually a four-step plan, to be exact.

The chain managed to accelerate service by six transactions per hour at peak times during a recent quarter (which is a significant increase over the mere two transactions per hour the previous quarter). "We achieved our fastest throughput ever," claims Steve Ells, co-CEO. However, some of Chipotle's fastest restaurants run more than 350 transactions per hour at lunchtime—more than three times the chainwide average.

How are such remarkable increases in productivity attained? By what the company calls "the four pillars of great throughput." These are:

- **Expediters.** An expediter is the extra person between the one who rolls your burrito and the one who rings up your order. The expediter's job? Getting your drink, asking if your order is "to go," and bagging your food.

- **Linebackers.** These are people who patrol the countertops, serving-ware, and bins of food, so the ones who are actually serving customers never turn their backs on them.

- *Mise en place.* In other restaurants, this means setting out ingredients and utensils ready for use. In Chipotle's case, it means zero tolerance for not having absolutely everything in place ahead of lunch and dinner rush hours.

- **Aces in their places.** This refers to a commitment to having what each branch considers its top servers in the most important positions at peak times. Thus, there are no trainees working at burrito rush hour.

Although sales for the firm dropped in late 2015 in response to food safety concerns, its long-term performance has been very impressive. From its founding in 1993, Chipotle has grown to be the largest Mexican quick service restaurant chain in the world.

Sources: Ferdman, R. A. 2014. How Chipotle is going to serve burritos faster, and faster, and faster. *www.qz.com*, January 31: np; Zillman, C. 2014. 2014's top people in business. *Fortune,* December 1: 156; and *statista.com.*

Efficient operations can also provide a firm with many benefits in virtually any industry—including restaurants. Strategy Spotlight 3.1 discusses Chipotle's rather novel approach to improving its operations.

outbound logistics
collecting, storing, and distributing the product or service to buyers.

Outbound Logistics   Outbound logistics is associated with collecting, storing, and distributing the product or service to buyers. These activities include finished goods, warehousing, material handling, delivery vehicle operation, order processing, and scheduling.

Campbell Soup uses an electronic network to facilitate its continuous-replenishment program with its most progressive retailers.[8] Each morning, retailers electronically inform Campbell of their product needs and of the level of inventories in their distribution centers. Campbell uses that information to forecast future demand and to determine which products require replenishment (based on the inventory limits previously established with each retailer). Trucks leave Campbell's shipping plant that afternoon and arrive at the retailers' distribution centers the same day. The program cuts the inventories of participating retailers from about a four- to a two-weeks' supply. Campbell Soup achieved this improvement because it slashed delivery time and because it knows the inventories of key retailers and can deploy supplies when they are most needed.

The Campbell Soup example also illustrates the win–win benefits of exemplary value-chain activities. Both the supplier (Campbell) and its buyers (retailers) come out ahead. Since the retailer makes more money on Campbell products delivered through continuous replenishment, it has an incentive to carry a broader line and give the company greater shelf space. After Campbell introduced the program, sales of its products grew twice as fast through participating retailers as through all other retailers. Not surprisingly, supermarket chains love such programs.

marketing and sales
activities associated with purchases of products and services by end users and the inducements used to get them to make purchases.

Marketing and Sales   Marketing and sales activities are associated with purchases of products and services by end users and the inducements used to get them to make purchases.[9]

They include advertising, promotion, sales force, quoting, channel selection, channel relations, and pricing.[10,11]

Consider product placement. This is a marketing strategy that many firms are increasingly adopting to reach customers who are not swayed by traditional advertising. Mercedes-Benz is a firm that has aggressively pushed for product placement in Hollywood movies. In 2015, Mercedes products appeared in nine of the top 31 blockbuster movies. For example, when the villains in the James Bond movie, *Spectre,* showed up in the desert to pick up Bond, they arrived in a fleet of Mercedes AMGs.[12]

Service   The **service** primary activity includes all actions associated with providing service to enhance or maintain the value of the product, such as installation, repair, training, parts supply, and product adjustment.

Let's see how two retailers are providing exemplary customer service. At *Sephora.com,* a customer service representative taking a phone call from a repeat customer has instant access to what shade of lipstick she likes best. This will help the rep cross-sell by suggesting a matching shade of lip gloss. Such personalization is expected to build loyalty and boost sales per customer. Nordstrom, the Seattle-based department store chain, goes even a step further. It offers a cyber-assist: A service rep can take control of a customer's web browser and literally lead her to just the silk scarf that she is looking for. CEO Dan Nordstrom believes that such a capability will close enough additional purchases to pay for the $1 million investment in software.

service
actions associated with providing service to enhance or maintain the value of the product.

Support Activities

Support activities in the value chain can be divided into four generic categories, as shown in Exhibit 3.3. Each category of the support activity is divisible into a number of distinct value activities that are specific to a particular industry. For example, technology development's discrete activities may include component design, feature design, field testing, process engineering, and technology selection. Similarly, procurement may include activities such as qualifying new suppliers, purchasing different groups of inputs, and monitoring supplier performance.

EXHIBIT 3.3

The Value Chain: Some Factors to Consider in Assessing a Firm's Support Activities

General Administration

- Effective planning systems to attain overall goals and objectives.
- Excellent relationships with diverse stakeholder groups.
- Effective information technology to integrate value-creating activities.

Human Resource Management

- Effective recruiting, development, and retention mechanisms for employees.
- Quality relations with trade unions.
- Reward and incentive programs to motivate all employees.

Technology Development

- Effective R&D activities for process and product initiatives.
- Positive collaborative relationships between R&D and other departments.
- Excellent professional qualifications of personnel.
- Data analytics

Procurement

- Procurement of raw material inputs to optimize quality and speed and to minimize the associated costs.
- Development of collaborative win–win relationships with suppliers.
- Analysis and selection of alternative sources of inputs to minimize dependence on one supplier.

Source: Adapted from Porter, M.E. 1985. *Competitive Advantage: Creating and Sustaining Superior Performance.* New York: Free Press.

Procurement   **Procurement** refers to the function of purchasing inputs used in the firm's value chain, not to the purchased inputs themselves.[13] Purchased inputs include raw materials, supplies, and other consumable items as well as assets such as machinery, laboratory equipment, office equipment, and buildings.[14,15]

Microsoft has improved its procurement process (and the quality of its suppliers) by providing formal reviews of its suppliers. One of Microsoft's divisions has extended the review process used for employees to its outside suppliers.[16] The employee services group, which is responsible for everything from travel to 401(k) programs to the on-site library, outsources more than 60 percent of the services it provides. Unfortunately, the employee services group was not providing suppliers with enough feedback. This was feedback that the suppliers wanted to get and that Microsoft wanted to give.

The evaluation system that Microsoft developed helped clarify its expectations to suppliers. An executive noted: "We had one supplier—this was before the new system—that would have scored a 1.2 out of 5. After we started giving this feedback, and the supplier understood our expectations, its performance improved dramatically. Within six months, it scored a 4. If you'd asked me before we began the feedback system, I would have said that was impossible."[17]

Technology Development   Every value activity embodies technology.[18] The array of technologies employed in most firms is very broad, ranging from technologies used to prepare documents and transport goods to those embodied in processes and equipment or the product itself.[19] **Technology development** related to the product and its features supports the entire value chain, while other technology development is associated with particular primary or support activities.

> Techniq, headquartered in Paris, France, with 40,000 employees in 48 countries, is a world leader in project management, engineering, and construction for the energy industry.[20] Its manufacturing plant in Normandy, France, has developed innovative ways to add value for its customers. This division, Subsea Infrastructure, produces subsea flexible pipes for the oil and gas industry. Its technology innovations have added significant value for its customers and has led to operating margins 50 percent higher than those for the company overall.
>
> Its traditional services include installing, inspecting, maintaining, and repairing pipes in locations around the world, from the Arctic to the Arabian Gulf. However, the company now goes much further. In collaboration with oil services giant Schlumberger, Techniq has developed intelligent pipes that can monitor and regulate the temperature throughout an oil pipeline—important value-added activities for its customers, large oil producers. Fluctuating temperatures pose a major problem—they cause changes in pipe diameter, which makes the flow of oil more variable. This compromises drilling efficiency and is a significant source of costs for Techniq's customers. Using intelligent pipes not only keeps temperatures steadier but also reduces the complexity of subsea drilling layouts and shortens pipe installation times.

Strategy Spotlight 3.2 discusses how Coca-Cola has developed data analytic technologies to produce orange juice that meets the taste demands of a global customer base.

Human Resource Management   **Human resource management** consists of activities involved in the recruiting, hiring, training, development, and compensation of all types of personnel.[21] It supports both individual primary and support activities (e.g., hiring of engineers and scientists) and the entire value chain (e.g., negotiations with labor unions).[22]

Like all great service companies, JetBlue Airways Corporation is obsessed with hiring superior employees.[23] But the company found it difficult to attract college graduates to commit to careers as flight attendants. JetBlue developed a highly innovative recruitment program for flight attendants—a one-year contract that gives them a chance to travel, meet lots of people, and then decide what else they might like to do. It also introduced the idea of training a friend and employee together so that they could share a job. With such employee-friendly initiatives, JetBlue has been very successful in attracting talent.

THE ALGORITHM FOR ORANGE JUICE

Making orange juice sounds simple enough. Squeeze the juice out of some oranges, and there you have it. But making orange juice is not so simple if you are Coca-Cola. The firm is the largest orange juice producer in the world, accounting for 17 percent of the juice sold in the world's top 22 markets, producing under the Minute Maid, Simply Orange, and Del Valle brands. Staying on top is a challenge since the firm has to respond to a range of variables, including weather conditions, differing customer preferences across markets, the flow of product over 12 months when the prime growing season lasts three months, and volatility in demand.

To meet customer expectations on a daily basis and continue to lead the market, Coke has turned to data analytics. As a first step in the process, Coke leverages an algorithm it has developed, called Black Box. Black Box contains detailed data on more than 600 flavors that can be used to make the orange juice customers expect to taste. Coke then matches the characteristics of each batch of raw juice to the algorithm to determine how

to mix together different batches of juice to produce the exact taste it wants to produce. Black Box considers multiple attributes of each batch of juice, including sweetness, acidity, and other taste attributes. Coke also uses the algorithm to evaluate satellite imagery of growing regions. The algorithm allows Coke to consider other factors, such as current demand and prices, weather patterns, and crop yields to maximize the efficiency of the process while producing the quantity and taste of juice to meet the market needs. But if conditions change, such as the emergence of a hurricane or the threat of a freeze in a growing region, Coke can go back to the algorithm and produce a new plan in five to ten minutes. Bob Cross, a consultant who helped Coke develop Black Box, commented that it "is definitely one of the most complex applications of business analytics. It requires analyzing up to one quintillion decision variables to consistently deliver the optimal blend, despite the whims of Mother Nature."

Sources: Sanders, N. 2016. How to use big data to drive your supply chain. *California Management Review.* Spring: 26–48; Stanford, D. 2016. Coke engineers its orange juice–with an algorithm. *bloomberg.com.* January 31: np.

In their efforts to attract high-potential college graduates, some firms have turned to "program hiring." Facebook, Intuit, AB InBev, and others empower their recruiters to make offers on the spot when they interview college students, without knowing what specific position they will fill. These firms search for candidates with attributes such as being a self-starter and a problem-solver, and make quick offers to preempt the market. Later, the new employees have matching interviews with various units in the firm to find the right initial position. The firms may lose out with some candidates who dislike the uncertainty of what their role will be, but they believe the candidates who are open to this type of hiring will be a better fit in a dynamic, creative workplace.[24]

General Administration   **General administration** consists of a number of activities, including general management, planning, finance, accounting, legal and government affairs, quality management, and information systems. Administration (unlike the other support activities) typically supports the entire value chain and not individual activities.[25]

Although general administration is sometimes viewed only as overhead, it can be a powerful source of competitive advantage. In a telephone operating company, for example, negotiating and maintaining ongoing relations with regulatory bodies can be among the most important activities for competitive advantage. Also, in some industries top management plays a vital role in dealing with important buyers.[26]

The strong and effective leadership of top executives can also make a significant contribution to an organization's success. As we discussed in Chapter 1, chief executive officers (CEOs) such as Jack Ma and Mark Zuckerberg have been credited with playing critical roles in the success of Alibaba and Facebook.

Information technology (IT) can also play a key role in enhancing the value that a company can provide its customers and, in turn, increasing its own revenues and profits. Strategy Spotlight 3.3 describes how Schmitz Cargobull, a German truck and trailer manufacturer, uses IT to further its competitive position.

LO 3-2

How value-chain analysis can help managers create value by investigating relationships among activities within the firm and between the firm and its customers and suppliers.

general administration
general management, planning, finance, accounting, legal and government affairs, quality management, and information systems; activities that support the entire value chain and not individual activities.

SCHMITZ CARGOBULL: ADDING VALUE TO CUSTOMERS VIA IT

Germany's truck and trailer manufacturer, Schmitz Cargobull, mainly serves customers that are operators of truck or trailer fleets. Like its rivals, the company derives a growing share of revenue from support services such as financing, full-service contracts for breakdowns and regular maintenance, and spare-parts supplies.

What sets the company apart is its expertise in telematics (the integrated application of telecommunications data) to monitor the current state of any Schmitz Cargobull–produced trailer. Through telematics, key information is continually available to the driver, the freight agent, and the customer. They can track, for instance, when maintenance is done, how much weight has been loaded, the current cargo temperature, and where the vehicle is on its route. Therefore, Schmitz Cargobull customers can better manage their trailer use and minimize the risk of breakdowns. The decision to introduce telematics, not surprisingly, derived from management's belief that real-time sharing of data would bind the company more closely to customers.

In applying its telematic tools in its products, Schmitz Cargobull is providing clear, tangible benefits. It uses information technology only where it makes sense. On the production line, for example, workers implement statistical quality controls manually, rather than rely on an automated system, because the company found manual control improves engagement and job performance.

That strategy has helped Schmitz Cargobull become an industry leader. In 2013, the company controlled 82 percent of the sales of semitrailer reefers (refrigerated trailers) in Germany, and its market share in Europe was about 50 percent. Further, its results for the fiscal year ending March 2014 are most impressive: sales increased by 7.5 percent and pretax profit soared 66 percent.

Sources: Anonymous. 2014. Schmitz Cargobull AG announces earnings and production results for the year ending March 2014. *www.investing.businessweek.com*, July 31: np; Anonymous. 2014. Premiere at the IAA Show 2014: Increased I-beam stability and payload. *www.cargobull.com*, September: np; and Chick, S. E., Huchzermeier, A., & Netessine, S. 2014. Europe's solution factories. *Harvard Business Review,* 92(4): 11–115.

Interrelationships among Value-Chain Activities within and across Organizations

We have defined each of the value-chain activities separately for clarity of presentation. Managers must not ignore, however, the importance of relationships among value-chain activities.[27] There are two levels: (1) **interrelationships** among activities within the firm and (2) relationships among activities within the firm and with other stakeholders (e.g., customers and suppliers) that are part of the firm's expanded value chain.[28]

interrelationships collaborative and strategic exchange relationships between value-chain activities either (a) within firms or (b) between firms. Strategic exchange relationships involve exchange of resources such as information, people, technology, or money that contribute to the success of the firm.

With regard to the first level, Lise Saari, former Director of Global Employee Research at IBM, provided an example by commenting on how human resources needs to be integrated with the other functional areas of the firm. She put it this way: "HR [must be] a true partner of the business, with a deep and up-to-date understanding of business realities and objectives, and, in turn, [must ensure] HR initiatives fully support them at all points of the value chain."

With regard to the second level, Campbell Soup's use of electronic networks enabled it to improve the efficiency of outbound logistics.[29] However, it also helped Campbell manage the ordering of raw materials more effectively, improve its production scheduling, and help its customers better manage their inbound logistics operations.

Integrating Customers into the Value Chain

When addressing the value-chain concept, it is important to focus on the interrelationship between the organization and its most important stakeholder—its customers. Some firms find great value by directly incorporating their customers into the value creation process. Firms can do this in one of two ways.

First, they can employ the "prosumer" concept and directly team up with customers to design and build products to satisfy their particular needs. Working directly with customers in this process provides multiple potential benefits for the firm. As the firm develops individualized products and relationship marketing, it can benefit from greater customer satisfaction and loyalty. Additionally, the interactions with customers can generate insights that lead to cost-saving initiatives and more innovative ideas for the producing firm. In discussing this concept, Hartmut Jenner, CEO of Alfred Karcher, a German manufacturing firm, stated:

> In the future, we will be talking more and more about the "prosumer"—a customer/producer who is even more extensively integrated into the value chain. As a consequence, production processes will be customized more precisely and individually.[30]

Second, firms can leverage the power of crowdsourcing. As introduced in Chapter 2, crowdsourcing occurs when firms tap into the knowledge and ideas of a large number of customers and other stakeholders, typically through online forums. The rise of social media has generated tremendous opportunities for firms to engage with customers.[31] In contrast to prosumer interactions, which allow the firm to gain insights on the needs of a particular customer, crowdsourcing offers the opportunity to leverage the wisdom of a larger crowd. Many companies have encouraged customers to participate in value-creating activities, such as brainstorming advertising taglines or product ideas. These activities not only enable firms to innovate at low cost but also engage customers. Clearly, a marketer's dream! At the same time, crowdsourcing has some significant risks.

Understanding the Perils of Crowdsourcing   While crowdsourcing offers great promise, in practice such programs are difficult to run. At times, customers can "hijack" them. Instead of offering constructive ideas, customers jump at the chance to raise concerns and even ridicule the company. Such hijacking is one of the biggest challenges companies face. Research has shown about half of such campaigns fail. Consider the following marketing-focused crowdsourcing examples:

- In 2006, General Motors tried a "fun" experiment, one of the first attempts to use user-generated advertising. The company asked the public to create commercials for the Chevy Tahoe—ads the company hoped would go viral. Unfortunately, some of the ads did go viral! These include: "Like this snowy wilderness. Better get your fill of it now. Then say hello to global warming. Chevy Tahoe" and "$70 to fill up the tank, which will last less than 400 miles. Chevy Tahoe."
- McDonald's set up a Twitter campaign to promote positive word of mouth. But this initiative became a platform for people looking to bash the chain. Tweets such as the following certainly didn't help the firm's cause: "I lost 50 lbs in 6 months after I quit working and eating at McDonalds" and "The McRib contains the same chemicals used to make yoga mats, mmmmm."

Research has identified three areas of particular concern:

- *Strong brand reputation.* Companies with strong brands need to protect them. After all, they have the most to lose. They must be aware such efforts provide consumers the opportunity to tarnish the brand. Strong brands are typically built through consistent, effective marketing, and companies need to weigh the potential for misbehaving customers to thwart their careful efforts.
- *High demand uncertainty.* Firms are generally more likely to ask for customer input when market conditions are changing. However, this often backfires when demand is highly uncertain, because customers in such markets often don't know what they want or what they will like. For example, Porsche received a lot of negative feedback when it announced plans to release an SUV, but it went ahead anyway, and the Porsche Cayenne was a great success.

- *Too many initiatives.* Firms typically benefit from working repeatedly with the same customers. Often, the quality, quantity, and variety of inputs decrease as the frequency of engagement increases. A study of the Dell IdeaStorm program (in which customers were encouraged to submit product or service ideas) discovered that the same people submitted ideas repeatedly—including submitting ones for things the company already provided. And customers whose ideas were implemented tended to return with additional ideas that were quite similar to their initial suggestions.

Applying the Value Chain to Service Organizations

The concepts of inbound logistics, operations, and outbound logistics suggest managing the raw materials that might be manufactured into finished products and delivered to customers. However, these three steps do not apply only to manufacturing. They correspond to any transformation process in which inputs are converted through a work process into outputs that add value. For example, accounting is a sort of transformation process that converts daily records of individual transactions into monthly financial reports. In this example, the transaction records are the inputs, accounting is the operation that adds value, and financial statements are the outputs.

What are the "operations," or transformation processes, of service organizations? At times, the difference between manufacturing and service is in providing a customized solution rather than mass production as is common in manufacturing. For example, a travel agent adds value by creating an itinerary that includes transportation, accommodations, and activities that are customized to your budget and travel dates. A law firm renders services that are specific to a client's needs and circumstances. In both cases, the work process (operation) involves the application of specialized knowledge based on the specifics of a situation (inputs) and the outcome that the client desires (outputs).

The application of the value chain to service organizations suggests that the value-adding process may be configured differently depending on the type of business a firm is engaged in. As the preceding discussion on support activities suggests, activities such as procurement and legal services are critical for adding value. Indeed, the activities that may provide support only to one company may be critical to the primary value-adding activity of another firm.

Exhibit 3.4 provides two models of how the value chain might look in service industries. In the retail industry, there are no manufacturing operations. A firm such as Nordstrom adds value by developing expertise in the procurement of finished goods and by displaying

EXHIBIT 3.4 Some Examples of Value Chains in Service Industries

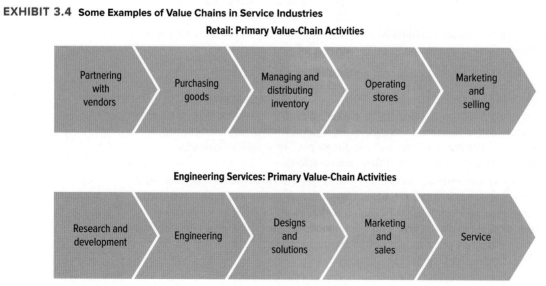

Retail: Primary Value-Chain Activities

Partnering with vendors → Purchasing goods → Managing and distributing inventory → Operating stores → Marketing and selling

Engineering Services: Primary Value-Chain Activities

Research and development → Engineering → Designs and solutions → Marketing and sales → Service

them in its stores in a way that enhances sales. Thus, the value chain makes procurement activities (i.e., partnering with vendors and purchasing goods) a primary rather than a support activity. Operations refer to the task of operating Nordstrom's stores.

For an engineering services firm, research and development provides inputs, the transformation process is the engineering itself, and innovative designs and practical solutions are the outputs. The Beca Group, for example, is a large consulting firm with about 3,000 employees, based in 17 offices throughout the Asia Pacific region. In its technology and innovation management practice, Beca strives to make the best use of the science, technology, and knowledge resources available to create value for a wide range of industries and client sectors. This involves activities associated with research and development, engineering, and creating solutions as well as downstream activities such as marketing, sales, and service. How the primary and support activities of a given firm are configured and deployed will often depend on industry conditions and whether the company is service- and/or manufacturing-oriented.

RESOURCE-BASED VIEW OF THE FIRM

LO 3-3

The resource-based view of the firm and the different types of tangible and intangible resources, as well as organizational capabilities.

The **resource-based view (RBV) of the firm** combines two perspectives: (1) the internal analysis of phenomena within a company and (2) an external analysis of the industry and its competitive environment.[32] It goes beyond the traditional SWOT (strengths, weaknesses, opportunities, threats) analysis by integrating internal and external perspectives. The ability of a firm's resources to confer competitive advantage(s) cannot be determined without taking into consideration the broader competitive context. A firm's resources must be evaluated in terms of how valuable, rare, and hard they are for competitors to duplicate. Otherwise, the firm attains only competitive parity.

A firm's strengths and capabilities—no matter how unique or impressive—do not necessarily lead to competitive advantages in the marketplace. The criteria for whether advantages are created and whether or not they can be sustained over time will be addressed later in this section. Thus, the RBV is a very useful framework for gaining insights as to why some competitors are more profitable than others. As we will see later in the book, the RBV is also helpful in developing strategies for individual businesses and diversified firms by revealing how core competencies embedded in a firm can help it exploit new product and market opportunities.

In the two sections that follow, we will discuss the three key types of resources that firms possess (summarized in Exhibit 3.5): tangible resources, intangible resources, and organizational capabilities. Then we will address the conditions under which such assets and capabilities can enable a firm to attain a sustainable competitive advantage.[33]

resource-based view (RBV) of the firm perspective that firms' competitive advantages are due to their endowment of strategic resources that are valuable, rare, costly to imitate, and costly to substitute.

Types of Firm Resources

Firm resources are all assets, capabilities, organizational processes, information, knowledge, and so forth, controlled by a firm that enable it to develop and implement value-creating strategies.

Tangible Resources   **Tangible resources** are assets that are relatively easy to identify. They include the physical and financial assets that an organization uses to create value for its customers. Among them are financial resource (e.g., a firm's cash, accounts receivable, and its ability to borrow funds); physical resources (e.g., the company's plant, equipment, and machinery as well as its proximity to customers and suppliers); organizational resources (e.g., the company's strategic planning process and its employee development, evaluation, and reward systems); and technological resources (e.g., trade secrets, patents, and copyrights).

tangible resources organizational assets that are relatively easy to identify, including physical assets, financial resources, organizational resources, and technological resources.

Tangible Resources	
Financial	• Firm's cash account and cash equivalents. • Firm's capacity to raise equity. • Firm's borrowing capacity.
Physical	• Modern plant and facilities. • Favorable manufacturing locations. • State-of-the-art machinery and equipment.
Technological	• Trade secrets. • Innovative production processes. • Patents, copyrights, trademarks.
Organizational	• Effective strategic planning processes. • Excellent evaluation and control systems.

Intangible Resources	
Human	• Experience and capabilities of employees. • Trust. • Managerial skills. • Firm-specific practices and procedures.
Innovation and creativity	• Technical and scientific skills. • Innovation capacities.
Reputation	• Brand name. • Reputation with customers for quality and reliability. • Reputation with suppliers for fairness, non–zero-sum relationships.

Organizational Capabilities

• Firm competencies or skills the firm employs to transfer inputs to outputs.
• Capacity to combine tangible and intangible resources, using organizational processes to attain desired end.

EXAMPLES:

• Outstanding customer service.
• Excellent product development capabilities.
• Innovativeness of products and services.
• Ability to hire, motivate, and retain human capital.

Sources: Adapted from Barney, J. B. 1991. Firm Resources and Sustained Competitive Advantage. *Journal of Management,* 17: 101; Grant, R. M. 1991. *Contemporary Strategy Analysis:* 100–102. Cambridge, England: Blackwell Business; and Hitt, M. A., Ireland, R. D., & Hoskisson, R. E. 2001. *Strategic Management: Competitiveness and Globalization* (4th ed.). Cincinnati: South-Western College Publishing.

Many firms are finding that high-tech, computerized training has dual benefits: It develops more-effective employees and reduces costs at the same time. Employees at FedEx take computer-based job competency tests every 6 to 12 months.[34] The 90-minute computer-based tests identify areas of individual weakness and provide input to a computer database of employee skills—information the firm uses in promotion decisions.

intangible resources
organizational assets that are difficult to identify and account for and are typically embedded in unique routines and practices, including human resources, innovation resources, and reputation resources.

Intangible Resources   Much more difficult for competitors (and, for that matter, a firm's own managers) to account for or imitate are **intangible resources,** which are typically embedded in unique routines and practices that have evolved and accumulated over time. These include human resources (e.g., experience and capability of employees, trust, effectiveness of work teams, managerial skills), innovation resources (e.g., technical and scientific expertise, ideas), and reputation resources (e.g., brand name, reputation with suppliers for fairness and with customers for reliability and product quality).[35] A firm's culture may also be a resource that provides competitive advantage.[36]

As an example of how a firm can leverage the value of intangible resources, we turn to Harley-Davidson. You might not think that motorcycles, clothes, toys, and restaurants have much in common. Yet Harley-Davidson has entered all of these product and service markets by capitalizing on its strong brand image—a valuable intangible resource.[37] It has used that image to sell accessories, clothing, and toys, and it has licensed the Harley-Davidson Café in New York City to provide further exposure for its brand name and products.

Social networking sites have the potential to play havoc with a firm's reputation. Consider the unfortunate situation Comcast faced when one of its repairmen fell asleep on the job—and it went viral:

> Ben Finkelstein, a law student, had trouble with the cable modem in his home. A Comcast cable repairman arrived to fix the problem. However, when the technician had to call the home office for a key piece of information, he was put on hold for so long that he fell asleep on Finkelstein's couch. Outraged, Finkelstein made a video of the sleeping technician and posted it on YouTube. The clip became a hit—with more than a million viewings. And, for a long time, it undermined Comcast's efforts to improve its reputation for customer service.[38]

Organizational Capabilities   **Organizational capabilities** are not specific tangible or intangible assets, but rather the competencies or skills that a firm employs to transform inputs into outputs.[39] In short, they refer to an organization's capacity to deploy tangible and intangible resources over time and generally in combination and to leverage those capabilities to bring about a desired end.[40] Examples of organizational capabilities are outstanding customer service, excellent product development capabilities, superb innovation processes, and flexibility in manufacturing processes.[41]

In the case of Apple, the majority of components used in its products can be characterized as proven technology, such as touch-screen and MP3-player functionality.[42] However, Apple combines and packages these in new and innovative ways while also seeking to integrate the value chain. This is the case with iTunes, for example, where suppliers of downloadable music are a vital component of the success Apple has enjoyed with its iPod series of MP3 players. Thus, Apple draws on proven technologies and its ability to offer innovative combinations of them.

> **organizational capabilities**
> the competencies and skills that a firm employs to transform inputs into outputs.

Firm Resources and Sustainable Competitive Advantages

As we have mentioned, resources alone are not a basis for competitive advantages, nor are advantages sustainable over time.[43] In some cases, a resource or capability helps a firm to increase its revenues or to lower costs but the firm derives only a temporary advantage because competitors quickly imitate or substitute for it.[44]

For a resource to provide a firm with the potential for a sustainable competitive advantage, it must have four attributes.[45] First, the resource must be valuable in the sense that it exploits opportunities and/or neutralizes threats in the firm's environment. Second, it must be rare among the firm's current and potential competitors. Third, the resource must be difficult for competitors to imitate. Fourth, the resource must have no strategically equivalent substitutes. These criteria are summarized in Exhibit 3.6. We will now discuss each of these criteria. Then we will examine how Blockbuster's competitive advantage, which seemed secure a decade ago, subsequently eroded, causing the company to file for bankruptcy in 2011.

Is the Resource Valuable?   Organizational resources can be a source of competitive advantage only when they are valuable. Resources are valuable when they enable a firm to formulate and implement strategies that improve its efficiency or effectiveness. The SWOT framework suggests that firms improve their performance only when they exploit opportunities or neutralize (or minimize) threats.

> **LO 3-4**
> The four criteria that a firm's resources must possess to maintain a sustainable advantage and how value created can be appropriated by employees and managers.

Is the resource or capability . . .	Implications
Valuable?	• Neutralize threats and exploit opportunities
Rare?	• Not many firms possess
Difficult to imitate?	• Physically unique • Path dependency (how accumulated over time) • Causal ambiguity (difficult to disentangle what it is or how it could be re-created) • Social complexity (trust, interpersonal relationships, culture, reputation)
Difficult to substitute?	• No equivalent strategic resources or capabilities

The fact that firm attributes must be valuable in order to be considered resources (as well as potential sources of competitive advantage) reveals an important complementary relationship among environmental models (e.g., SWOT and five-forces analyses) and the resource-based model. Environmental models isolate those firm attributes that exploit opportunities and/or neutralize threats. Thus, they specify what firm attributes may be considered as resources. The resource-based model then suggests what additional characteristics these resources must possess if they are to develop a sustained competitive advantage.

Is the Resource Rare?   If competitors or potential competitors also possess the same valuable resource, it is not a source of a competitive advantage because all of these firms have the capability to exploit that resource in the same way. Common strategies based on such a resource would give no one firm an advantage. For a resource to provide competitive advantages, it must be uncommon, that is, rare relative to other competitors.

This argument can apply to bundles of valuable firm resources that are used to formulate and develop strategies. Some strategies require a mix of multiple types of resources—tangible assets, intangible assets, and organizational capabilities. If a particular bundle of firm resources is not rare, then relatively large numbers of firms will be able to conceive of and implement the strategies in question. Thus, such strategies will not be a source of competitive advantage, even if the resource in question is valuable.

Can the Resource Be Imitated Easily?   Inimitability (difficulty in imitating) is a key to value creation because it constrains competition.[46] If a resource is inimitable, then any profits generated are more likely to be sustainable.[47] Having a resource that competitors can easily copy generates only temporary value.[48] This has important implications. Since managers often fail to apply this test, they tend to base long-term strategies on resources that are imitable. IBP (Iowa Beef Processors) became the first meatpacking company in the United States to modernize by building a set of assets (automated plants located in cattle-producing states) and capabilities (low-cost "disassembly" of carcasses) that earned returns on assets of 1.3 percent in the 1970s. By the late 1980s, however, ConAgra and Cargill had imitated these resources, and IBP's profitability fell by nearly 70 percent, to 0.4 percent.

Groupon is a more recent example of a firm that has suffered because rivals have been able to imitate its strategy rather easily:

> Groupon, which offers online coupons for bargains at local shops and restaurants, created a new market.[49] Although it was initially a boon to consumers, it offers no lasting "first-mover" advantage. Its business model is not patentable and is easy to replicate. Not surprisingly, there are many copycats. For example, there was a tremendous amount of churn in the industry in 2012. The number of daily deal sites in the United States rose by almost 8 percent (142 sites), according to Daily Deal Media, which tracks the industry. Meanwhile, globally, 560 daily deal sites closed over the same period!

PRINTED IN TAIWAN: PATH DEPENDENCE IN 3D PRINTING

The world's largest producer of 3D printers for consumers in 2016 wasn't HP, Canon, Brother, or any other widely known printer manufacturer. It was XYZprinting, a Taiwan-based computer component manufacturer. XYZprinting, a subsidiary of the New Kinpo Group, produced 19 percent of the 3D printers sold in 2016. While the 3D printer market is just emerging, Simon Shen, New Kinpo Group's CEO, aims to draw on the firm's infrastructure and experience to build a dominant position as the low-cost leader in the 3D printer market. The firm's da Vinci printer, which can be found in BestBuy, in Toys R Us, and on Amazon.com was honored with the 2016 Editors' Choice Award at the Consumer Electronics Show.

Shen sees three key resources the firm can draw on to build a sustainable advantage. First, the firm has built an efficient supply chain and manufacturing system to produce a range of electronic products that can be leveraged to build 3D printers. Second, it has developed internal control systems to minimize cost in order to thrive in Taiwan's notoriously thin-margin electronics industry. Third, the firm has developed competencies in the R&D of electronic products. Their R&D knowledge and manufacturing skills apply directly to 3D printing since, while the firm is not well known, it is actually one of the world's largest producers of 2D printers, producing them as a contract manufacturer to the world's leading printer companies. With their own manufacturing capabilities and supply chain connections along with their mechanical engineering experience, XYZprinting was able to introduce some of the lowest priced systems on the market. As Wendy Mok, an analyst with IDC, stated, "they have the manufacturing background, they know the difficulty of R&D."

Shen sees all of this providing a set of competencies that later movers will find hard to imitate. In his words, "If you don't have a 2D background, it's difficult to catch up." They are also looking to expand their competencies by extending into more expensive industrial machines to meet specific needs. For example, they are working with a local university to develop the ability to print dental implants. As the market matures, Shen believes they are developing a set of resources and competencies that late movers will find hard to match.

Sources: Einhorn, B. 2016. Made-in-Taiwan used to mean PC, now it's 3D. *bloomberg.com.* April 27: np; Molitch-Hou, M. 2016. How XYZprinting is conquering 3D printing & why you might move to Taiwan. *3dprintingindustry.com.* January 5: np; Anonymous. 2016. XYZprinting forms several new retail partnerships to offer 3D printing solutions to consumers nationwide. *prnewswire.com.* December 6: np; Connery, C. 2016. 3D printers: Desktop market still growing but metal printers prop up struggling industrial segment in 1H. 2016. *tctmagazine.com.* December 6: np.

Clearly, an advantage based on inimitability won't last forever. Competitors will eventually discover a way to copy most valuable resources. However, managers can forestall them and sustain profits for a while by developing strategies around resources that have at least one of the following four characteristics.[50]

Physical Uniqueness   The first source of inimitability is physical uniqueness, which by definition is inherently difficult to copy. A beautiful resort location, mineral rights, or Pfizer's pharmaceutical patents simply cannot be imitated. Many managers believe that several of their resources may fall into this category, but on close inspection, few do.

Path Dependency   A greater number of resources cannot be imitated because of what economists refer to as **path dependency.** This simply means that resources are unique and therefore scarce because of all that has happened along the path followed in their development and/or accumulation. Competitors cannot go out and buy these resources quickly and easily; they must be built up over time in ways that are difficult to accelerate.

path dependency
a characteristic of resources that is developed and/or accumulated through a unique series of events.

The Gerber Products Co. brand name for baby food is an example of a resource that is potentially inimitable. Re-creating Gerber's brand loyalty would be a time-consuming process that competitors could not expedite, even with expensive marketing campaigns. Ashley furniture has found that controlling all steps of its distribution system has allowed it to develop specific competencies that are difficult to match. It has developed specially designed racks in its distribution centers and proprietary inventory management systems that would take time to match. It has also tasked its truck drivers to be "Ashley Ambassadors," building relationships with furniture store managers and employees. Both these operational and relational resources have built up over time and can't be imitated overnight.[51] Also, a crash R&D program generally cannot replicate a successful technology when research findings cumulate. Strategy Spotlight 3.4 outlines how XYZprinting is using its R&D and manufacturing experience to build a path-dependent

AMAZON PRIME: VERY DIFFICULT FOR RIVALS TO COPY

Amazon Prime, introduced in 2004, is a free-shipping service that guarantees delivery of products within two days for an annual fee of $79. According to *Bloomberg Businessweek,* it may be the most ingenious and effective customer loyalty program in all of e-commerce, if not retail in general. It converts casual shoppers into Amazon addicts who gorge on the gratification of having purchases reliably appear two days after they order. Analysts describe Prime as one of the main factors driving Amazon's stock price up nearly 300 percent from 2008 to 2010. Also, it is one of the main reasons why Amazon's sales grew 30 percent during the recession, while other retailers suffered.

By the end of 2015, Amazon had an estimated 60 to 80 million Prime members globally, up from 5 million three years earlier. They are practically addicted to using Amazon—and certainly don't seem to mind the annual membership price boost to $99. Scot Wingo of Channel Advisor, a company that helps online sellers, estimates that people with Prime spend about four times what others do and account for half of all spending at Amazon.

Amazon Prime has proven to be extremely hard for rivals to copy. Why? It enables Amazon to exploit its wide selection, low prices, network of third-party merchants, and finely tuned distribution system. All that while also keying off that faintly irrational human need to maximize the benefits of a club that you have already paid to join. Yet Amazon's success also leads to increased pressure from both public and private entities. For a long time, Amazon was able to avoid collecting local sales taxes because Amazon did not have a local sales presence in many states. This practice distorts competition and strains already tight state coffers. Some states have used a combination of legislation and litigation to convince Amazon to collect sales taxes.

Moreover, rivals—both online and off—have realized the increasing threat posed by Prime and are rushing to respond. For example, in October 2010, a consortium of over 100 retailers, including Staples, Eddie Bauer, and Kay Jewelers, banded together to offer their own copycat $79, two-day shipping program, ShopRunner, which applies to products across their websites. As noted by Fiona Dias, the executive who administers the program, "As Amazon added more merchandising categories to Prime, retailers started feeling the pain. They have finally come to understand that Amazon is an existential threat and that Prime is the fuel of the engine."

Finally, Prime members also gain access to thousands of movies, video games, ebooks, and HBO programming. Prime members may soon also be able to gain access to watch major sports through their Prime membership. As annoying as this might be to Netflix, it is not intended primarily as an assault on Netflix. Rather, CEO Jeff Bezos is willing to lose money on shipping and services in exchange for loyalty.

Sources: Anonymous. 2014. Relentless.com. *The Economist,* June 21: 23–26; McCorvey, J. J. 2013. The race has just begun. *Fast Company,* September: 66–76; Stone, B. 2010. What's in the box? Instant gratification. *Bloomberg Businessweek,* November 29–December 5: 39–40; Kaplan, M. 2011. Amazon Prime: 5 million members, 20 percent growth. *www.practicalcommerce.com,* September 16: np; Fowler, G. A. 2010. Retailers team up against Amazon. *www.wsj.com,* October 6: np; Halkias, M. 2012. Amazon to collect sales tax in Texas. *Dallas Morning News,* April 28: 4A. Kim, E. 2015. These numbers explain why Amazon wants to give so much free stuff to Prime members. *finance.yahoo.com.* October 21: np; and Ramachandran, S. 2016. Amazon explores possible premium sports package with prime membership. *wsj.com.* November 22: np.

---

advantage in the 3D printing market. Clearly, these path-dependent conditions build protection for the original resource. The benefits from experience and learning through trial and error cannot be duplicated overnight.

causal ambiguity
a characteristic of a firm's resources that is costly to imitate because a competitor cannot determine what the resource is and/or how it can be re-created.

Causal Ambiguity   The third source of inimitability is termed **causal ambiguity.** This means that would-be competitors may be thwarted because it is impossible to disentangle the causes (or possible explanations) of either what the valuable resource is or how it can be re-created. What is the root of 3M's innovation process? You can study it and draw up a list of possible factors. But it is a complex, unfolding (or folding) process that is hard to understand and would be hard to imitate.

Often, causally ambiguous resources are organizational capabilities, involving a complex web of social interactions that may even depend on particular individuals. When trying to compete with Google, many competitors, such as Yahoo and Twitter, have found it hard to match Google's ability to innovate and launch new products. Most acknowledge this is tied to Google's ability to hire the best talent and the culture of creativity within the firm, but firms find it very challenging to identify the specific set of actions Google took to build its image and culture or how to match it.

Strategy Spotlight 3.5 describes Amazon's continued success as the world's largest online marketplace. Competitors recently tried to imitate Amazon's free-shipping strategy, but with limited success. The reason is that Amazon has developed an array of interrelated elements of strategy which their rivals find too difficult to imitate.

Social Complexity   A firm's resources may be imperfectly inimitable because they reflect a high level of **social complexity.** Such phenomena are typically beyond the ability of firms to systematically manage or influence. When competitive advantages are based on social complexity, it is difficult for other firms to imitate them.

A wide variety of firm resources may be considered socially complex. Examples include interpersonal relations among the managers in a firm, its culture, and its reputation with its suppliers and customers. In many of these cases, it is easy to specify how these socially complex resources add value to a firm. Hence, there is little or no causal ambiguity surrounding the link between them and competitive advantage.

The Edelman Trust Barometer, a comprehensive survey of public trust, has found that trust and transparency are more critical than ever.[52] For the first time in the survey's history, Edelman found in its 2014 survey that impressions of openness, sincerity, and authenticity were more important to corporate reputation in the United States than the quality of products and services. This means trust affects tangible things such as supply chain partnerships and long-term customer loyalty. People want to partner with you because they have heard you are a credible company built through a culture of trust. In a sense, being a great company to work for also makes you a great company to work with.

Are Substitutes Readily Available?   The fourth requirement for a firm resource to be a source of sustainable competitive advantage is that there must be no strategically equivalent valuable resources that are themselves not rare or inimitable. Two valuable firm resources (or two bundles of resources) are strategically equivalent when each one can be exploited separately to implement the same strategies.

Substitutability may take at least two forms. First, though it may be impossible for a firm to imitate exactly another firm's resource, it may be able to substitute a similar resource that enables it to develop and implement the same strategy. Clearly, a firm seeking to imitate another firm's high-quality top management team would be unable to copy the team exactly. However, it might be able to develop its own unique management team. Though these two teams would have different ages, functional backgrounds, experience, and so on, they could be strategically equivalent and thus substitutes for one another.

Second, very different firm resources can become strategic substitutes. For example, Internet booksellers such as Amazon.com compete as substitutes for brick-and-mortar booksellers such as Barnes & Noble. The result is that resources such as premier retail locations become less valuable. In a similar vein, several pharmaceutical firms have seen the value of patent protection erode in the face of new drugs that are based on different production processes and act in different ways, but can be used in similar treatment regimes. The coming years will likely see even more radical change in the pharmaceutical industry as the substitution of genetic therapies eliminates certain uses of chemotherapy.[53]

To recap this section, recall that resources and capabilities must be rare and valuable as well as difficult to imitate or substitute in order for a firm to attain competitive advantages that are sustainable over time.[54] Exhibit 3.7 illustrates the relationship among the four criteria of sustainability and shows the competitive implications.

In firms represented by the first row of Exhibit 3.7, managers are in a difficult situation. When their resources and capabilities do not meet any of the four criteria, it would be difficult to develop any type of competitive advantage, in the short or long term. The resources and capabilities they possess enable the firm neither to exploit environmental opportunities nor to neutralize environmental threats. In the second and third rows, firms have resources and capabilities that are valuable as well as rare, respectively. However, in both cases the resources and capabilities are not difficult for competitors to imitate or substitute. Here, the

social complexity
a characteristic of a firm's resources that is costly to imitate because the social engineering required is beyond the capability of competitors, including interpersonal relations among managers, organizational culture, and reputation with suppliers and customers.

Is a Resource or Capability . . .				
Valuable?	Rare?	Difficult to Imitate?	Without Substitutes?	Implication for Competitiveness
No	No	No	No	Competitive disadvantage
Yes	No	No	No	Competitive parity
Yes	Yes	No	No	Temporary competitive advantage
Yes	Yes	Yes	Yes	Sustainable competitive advantage

Source: Adapted from Barney, J. B. 1991. Firm Resources and Sustained Competitive Advantage. *Journal of Management,*
17: 99–120.

firms could attain some level of competitive parity. They could perform on par with equally
endowed rivals or attain a temporary competitive advantage. But their advantages would be
easy for competitors to match. It is only in the fourth row, where all four criteria are satisfied, that competitive advantages can be sustained over time. Next, let's look at Blockbuster
and see how its competitive advantage, which seemed to be sustainable for a rather long
period of time, eventually eroded, leading to the company's bankruptcy in 2011.

Blockbuster Inc.: From Sustainable (?) Advantage to Bankruptcy   Blockbuster Video failed
to recognize in time the threat posed to its brick-and-mortar business by virtual services
such as Netflix.[55] At the time, few thought that consumers would trade the convenience of
picking up their videos to waiting for them to arrive in the mail. Interestingly, Blockbuster
had the chance to buy Netflix for $50 million in 2000 but turned down the opportunity.
Barry McCarthy, Netflix's former chief financial officer, recalls the conversation during
a meeting with Blockbuster's top executives: Reed Hastings, Netflix's cofounder, "had the
chutzpah to propose to them that we run their brand online and that they run (our) brand
in the stores and they just about laughed us out of the office. At least initially, they thought
we were a very small niche business."

Users, of course, embraced the automated self-service of Netflix's web-based interface
technology that positioned the start-up to transition from mailing DVDs to streaming content over the Internet. As technologies improved broadband speed, reliability, and adoption,
Netflix transitioned in just a few years to a cloud-based service.

Blockbuster tried to follow each of Netflix's strategic moves. However, it remained a
perennial second in the winner-take-all market for new ways to distribute entertainment
content. Blockbuster continued to lag, weighed down by the high labor costs and real estate
costs of its once-dominant locations—assets that became liabilities. In 2011, after closing
some 900 stores, the company declared bankruptcy.

In the end, Blockbuster's assets were acquired for only $320 million by satellite television
maverick Dish Networks, which was mainly interested in Blockbuster's online channel and
3.3 million customers. Had Blockbuster sold out earlier, or found a way to shed the physical assets
sooner, that price could have been much higher. In 1999, the year Netflix launched its online
subscription service, Blockbuster was valued at nearly $3 billion—nearly 10 times what Dish
ultimately paid. Netflix, on the other hand, had a market cap of $21 billion by the end of 2014.

The Generation and Distribution of a Firm's Profits: Extending the Resource-Based View of the Firm

The resource-based view of the firm is useful in determining when firms will create competitive advantages and enjoy high levels of profitability. However, it has not been developed to

address how a firm's profits (often referred to as "rents" by economists) will be distributed to a firm's management and employees or other stakeholders such as customers, suppliers, or governments.[56] This is an important issue because firms may be successful in creating competitive advantages that can be sustainable for a period of time. However, much of the profits can be retained (or "appropriated") by a firm's employees and managers or other stakeholders instead of flowing to the firm's owners (i.e., the stockholders).*

Consider Viewpoint DataLabs, a subsidiary of software giant Computer Associates, that makes sophisticated three-dimensional models and textures for film production houses, video games, and car manufacturers. This example will help to show how employees are often able to obtain (or "appropriate") a high proportion of a firm's profits:

> Walter Noot, head of production, was having trouble keeping his highly skilled Generation X employees happy with their compensation. Each time one of them was lured away for more money, everyone would want a raise. "We were having to give out raises every six months—30 to 40 percent—then six months later they'd expect the same. It was a big struggle to keep people happy."[57]

Here, much of the profits is being generated by the highly skilled professionals working together. They are able to exercise their power by successfully demanding more financial compensation. In part, management has responded favorably because they are united in their demands and their work involves a certain amount of social complexity and causal ambiguity—given the complex, coordinated efforts that their work entails.

Four factors help explain the extent to which employees and managers will be able to obtain a proportionately high level of the profits that they generate:[58]

- **Employee bargaining power.** If employees are vital to forming a firm's unique capability, they will earn disproportionately high wages. For example, marketing professionals may have access to valuable information that helps them to understand the intricacies of customer demands and expectations, or engineers may understand unique technical aspects of the products or services. Additionally, in some industries such as consulting, advertising, and tax preparation, clients tend to be very loyal to individual professionals employed by the firm, instead of to the firm itself. This enables them to "take the clients with them" if they leave. This enhances their bargaining power.
- **Employee replacement cost.** If employees' skills are idiosyncratic and rare (a source of resource-based advantages), they should have high bargaining power based on the high cost required by the firm to replace them. For example, Raymond Ozzie, the software designer who was critical in the development of Lotus Notes, was able to dictate the terms under which IBM acquired Lotus.
- **Employee exit costs.** This factor may tend to reduce an employee's bargaining power. An individual may face high personal costs when leaving the organization. Thus, that individual's threat of leaving may not be credible. In addition, an employee's expertise may be firm-specific and of limited value to other firms.
- **Manager bargaining power.** Managers' power is based on how well they create resource-based advantages. They are generally charged with creating value through the process of organizing, coordinating, and leveraging employees as well as other forms of capital such as plant, equipment, and financial capital (addressed further in Chapter 4). Such activities provide managers with sources of information that may not be readily available to others.

Chapter 9 addresses the conditions under which top-level managers (such as CEOs) of large corporations have been, at times, able to obtain levels of total compensation that

---

* Economists define rents as profits (or prices) in excess of what is required to provide a normal return.

would appear to be significantly disproportionate to their contributions to wealth generation as well as to top executives in peer organizations. Here, corporate governance becomes a critical control mechanism. Consider shareholders' reaction, in April 2012, to Citigroup's proposed $15 million pay package for then-CEO Vikram Pandit.[59] It was not positive, to say the least. After all, they had suffered a 92 percent decline in the stock's price under Pandit's five-year reign. They rejected the bank's compensation proposal. In October 2012, the board ousted Pandit after the New York–based firm failed to secure Federal Reserve approval to increase its shareholder payouts and Moody's Investors Service cut the bank's credit rating two levels.

Such diversion of profits from the owners of the business to top management is far less likely when the board members are truly independent outsiders (i.e., they do not have close ties to management). In general, given the external market for top talent, the level of compensation that executives receive is based on factors similar to the ones just discussed that determine the level of their bargaining power.[60]

In addition to employees and managers, other stakeholder groups can also appropriate a portion of the rents generated by a firm. If, for example, a critical input is controlled by a monopoly supplier or if a single buyer accounts for most of a firm's sales, this supplier's or buyer's bargaining power can greatly erode the potential profits of a firm. Similarly, excessive taxation by governments can also reduce what is available to a firm's stockholders.

EVALUATING FIRM PERFORMANCE: TWO APPROACHES

This section addresses two approaches to use when evaluating a firm's performance. The first is financial ratio analysis, which, generally speaking, identifies how a firm is performing according to its balance sheet, income statement, and market valuation. As we will discuss, when performing a financial ratio analysis, you must take into account the firm's performance from a historical perspective (not just at one point in time) as well as how it compares with both industry norms and key competitors.[61]

The second perspective takes a broader stakeholder view. Firms must satisfy a broad range of stakeholders, including employees, customers, and owners, to ensure their long-term viability. Central to our discussion will be a well-known approach—the balanced scorecard—that has been popularized by Robert Kaplan and David Norton.[62]

financial ratio analysis
a method of evaluating a company's performance and financial well-being through ratios of accounting values, including short-term solvency, long-term solvency, asset utilization, profitability, and market value ratios.

Financial Ratio Analysis

The beginning point in analyzing the financial position of a firm is to compute and analyze five different types of financial ratios:

- Short-term solvency or liquidity
- Long-term solvency measures
- Asset management (or turnover)
- Profitability
- Market value

Exhibit 3.8 summarizes each of these five ratios.

Appendix 1 to Chapter 13 (the Case Analysis chapter) provides detailed definitions for and discussions of each of these types of ratios as well as examples of how each is calculated. Refer to pages 418 to 427.

A meaningful ratio analysis must go beyond the calculation and interpretation of financial ratios.[63] It must include how ratios change over time as well as how they are interrelated. For example, a firm that takes on too much long-term debt to finance operations will see an immediate impact on its indicators of long-term financial leverage. The additional debt will negatively affect the firm's short-term liquidity ratio (i.e., current and quick ratios) since

The usefulness of financial ratio analysis, its inherent limitations, and how to make meaningful comparisons of performance across firms.

EXHIBIT 3.8 A Summary of Five Types of Financial Ratios

I. Short-term solvency, or liquidity, ratios

$$\text{Current ratio} = \frac{\text{Current assets}}{\text{Current liabilities}}$$

$$\text{Quick ratio} = \frac{\text{Current assets} - \text{Inventory}}{\text{Current liabilities}}$$

$$\text{Cash ratio} = \frac{\text{Cash}}{\text{Current liabilities}}$$

II. Long-term solvency, or financial leverage, ratios

$$\text{Total debt ratio} = \frac{\text{Total assets} - \text{Total equity}}{\text{Total assets}}$$

$$\text{Debt-equity ratio} = \text{Total debt/Total equity}$$

$$\text{Equity multiplier} = \text{Total assets/Total equity}$$

$$\text{Times interest earned ratio} = \frac{\text{EBIT}}{\text{Interest}}$$

$$\text{Cash coverage ratio} = \frac{\text{EBIT} + \text{Depreciation}}{\text{Interest}}$$

III. Asset utilization, or turnover, ratios

$$\text{Inventory turnover} = \frac{\text{Cost of goods sold}}{\text{Inventory}}$$

$$\text{Days' sales in inventory} = \frac{365 \text{ days}}{\text{Inventory turnover}}$$

$$\text{Receivables turnover} = \frac{\text{Sales}}{\text{Accounts receivable}}$$

$$\text{Days' sales in receivables} = \frac{365 \text{ days}}{\text{Receivables turnover}}$$

$$\text{Total asset turnover} = \frac{\text{Sales}}{\text{Total assets}}$$

$$\text{Capital intensity} = \frac{\text{Total assets}}{\text{Sales}}$$

IV. Profitability ratios

$$\text{Profit margin} = \frac{\text{Net income}}{\text{Sales}}$$

$$\text{Return on assets (ROA)} = \frac{\text{Net income}}{\text{Total assets}}$$

$$\text{Return on equity (ROE)} = \frac{\text{Net income}}{\text{Total equity}}$$

$$\text{ROE} = \frac{\text{Net income}}{\text{Sales}} \times \frac{\text{Sales}}{\text{Assets}} \times \frac{\text{Assets}}{\text{Equity}}$$

V. Market value ratios

$$\text{Price-earnings ratio} = \frac{\text{Price per share}}{\text{Earnings per share}}$$

$$\text{Market-to-book ratio} = \frac{\text{Market value per share}}{\text{Book value per share}}$$

the firm must pay interest and principal on the additional debt each year until it is retired. Additionally, the interest expenses deducted from revenues reduce the firm's profitability.

A firm's financial position should not be analyzed in isolation. Important reference points are needed. We will address some issues that must be taken into account to make financial analysis more meaningful: historical comparisons, comparisons with industry norms, and comparisons with key competitors.

Historical Comparisons   When you evaluate a firm's financial performance, it is very useful to compare its financial position over time. This provides a means of evaluating trends. For example, Apple Inc. reported revenues of $234 billion and net income of $53 billion in 2015. Virtually all firms would be very happy with such remarkable financial success. These figures represent a stunning annual growth in revenue and net income of 28 percent and 33 percent, respectively, over Apple's 2014 figures. Had Apple's revenues and net income in 2015 been $150 billion and $30 billion, respectively, it would still be a very large and highly profitable enterprise. However, such performance would have significantly damaged Apple's market valuation and reputation as well as the careers of many of its executives.

Exhibit 3.9 illustrates a 10-year period of return on sales (ROS) for a hypothetical company. As indicated by the dotted trend lines, the rate of growth (or decline) differs substantially over time periods.

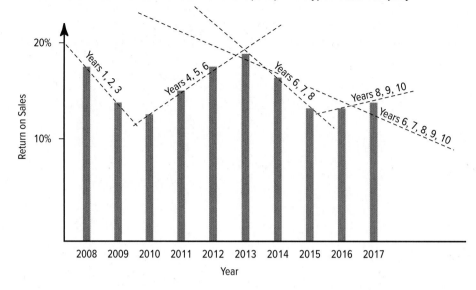

EXHIBIT 3.9 Historical Trends: Return on Sales (ROS) for a Hypothetical Company

Comparison with Industry Norms When you are evaluating a firm's financial performance, remember also to compare it with industry norms. A firm's current ratio or profitability may appear impressive at first glance. However, it may pale when compared with industry standards or norms.

Comparing your firm with all other firms in your industry assesses relative performance. Banks often use such comparisons when evaluating a firm's creditworthiness. Exhibit 3.10 includes a variety of financial ratios for three industries: semiconductors, grocery stores, and skilled-nursing facilities. Why is there such variation among the financial ratios for these three industries? There are several reasons. With regard to the collection period, grocery stores operate mostly on a cash basis, hence a very short collection period. Semiconductor manufacturers sell their output to other manufacturers (e.g., computer makers) on terms such as 2/15 net 45, which means they give a 2 percent discount on bills paid within 15 days and start charging interest after 45 days. Skilled-nursing facilities also have a longer collection period than grocery stores because they typically rely on payments from insurance companies.

The industry norms for return on sales also highlight differences among these industries. Grocers, with very slim margins, have a lower return on sales than either skilled-nursing facilities or semiconductor manufacturers. But how might we explain the differences between

EXHIBIT 3.10
How Financial Ratios
Differ across Industries

Financial Ratio	Semiconductors	Grocery Stores	Skilled-Nursing Facilities
Quick ratio (times)	1.9	0.6	1.3
Current ratio (times)	3.6	1.7	1.7
Total liabilities to net worth (%)	35.1	72.7	82.5
Collection period (days)	48.6	3.3	36.5
Assets to sales (%)	131.7	22.1	58.3
Return on sales (%)	24	1.1	3.1

Source: Dun & Bradstreet. *Industry Norms and Key Business Ratios, 2010–2011.* One Year Edition, SIC #3600–3699 (Semiconductors); SIC #5400–5499 (Grocery Stores); SIC #8000–8099 (Skilled-Nursing Facilities). New York: Dun & Bradstreet Credit Services.

skilled-nursing facilities and semiconductor manufacturers? Health care facilities, in general, are limited in their pricing structures by Medicare/Medicaid regulations and by insurance reimbursement limits, but semiconductor producers have pricing structures determined by the market. If their products have superior performance, semiconductor manufacturers can charge premium prices.

Comparison with Key Competitors   Recall from Chapter 2 that firms with similar strategies are members of a strategic group in an industry. Furthermore, competition is more intense among competitors within groups than across groups. Thus, you can gain valuable insights into a firm's financial and competitive position if you make comparisons between a firm and its most direct rivals. Consider a firm trying to diversify into the highly profitable pharmaceutical industry. Even if it was willing to invest several hundred million dollars, it would be virtually impossible to compete effectively against industry giants such as Pfizer and Merck. These two firms had 2015 revenues of $49 billion and $39 billion, respectively, and both had R&D budgets of over $6.5 billion.[64]

Integrating Financial Analysis and Stakeholder Perspectives: The Balanced Scorecard

LO 3-6

The value of the "balanced scorecard" in recognizing how the interests of a variety of stakeholders can be interrelated.

It is useful to see how a firm performs over time in terms of several ratios. However, such traditional approaches can be a double-edged sword.[65] Many important transactions—investments in research and development, employee training and development, and advertising and promotion of key brands—may greatly expand a firm's market potential and create significant long-term shareholder value. But such critical investments are not reflected positively in short-term financial reports. Financial reports typically measure expenses, not the value created. Thus, managers may be penalized for spending money in the short term to improve their firm's long-term competitive viability!

Now consider the other side of the coin. A manager may destroy the firm's future value by dissatisfying customers, depleting the firm's stock of good products coming out of R&D, or damaging the morale of valued employees. Such budget cuts, however, may lead to very good short-term financials. The manager may look good in the short run and even receive credit for improving the firm's performance. In essence, such a manager has mastered "denominator management," whereby decreasing investments makes the return on investment (ROI) ratio larger, even though the actual return remains constant or shrinks.

The Balanced Scorecard: Description and Benefits   To provide a meaningful integration of the many issues that come into evaluating a firm's performance, Kaplan and Norton developed a **"balanced scorecard."**[66] This provides top managers with a fast but comprehensive view of the business. In a nutshell, it includes financial measures that reflect the results of actions already taken, but it complements these indicators with measures of customer satisfaction, internal processes, and the organization's innovation and improvement activities—operational measures that drive future financial performance.

The balanced scorecard enables managers to consider their business from four key perspectives: customer, internal, innovation and learning, and financial. These are briefly described in Exhibit 3.11.

balanced scorecard
a method of evaluating a firm's performance using performance measures from the customer, internal, innovation and learning, and financial perspectives.

Customer Perspective   Clearly, how a company is performing from its customers' perspective is a top priority for management. The balanced scorecard requires that managers translate their general mission statements on customer service into specific measures that reflect the factors that really matter to customers. For the balanced scorecard to work, managers must articulate goals for four key categories of customer concerns: time, quality, performance and service, and cost.

customer perspective
measures of firm performance that indicate how well firms are satisfying customers' expectations.

EXHIBIT 3.11

The Balanced
Scorecard's Four
Perspectives

- How do customers see us? (customer perspective)
- What must we excel at? (internal business perspective)
- Can we continue to improve and create value? (innovation and learning perspective)
- How do we look to shareholders? (financial perspective)

internal business perspective
measures of firm performance that indicate how well firms' internal processes, decisions, and actions are contributing to customer satisfaction.

Internal Business Perspective   Customer-based measures are important. However, they must be translated into indicators of what the firm must do internally to meet customers' expectations. Excellent customer performance results from processes, decisions, and actions that occur throughout organizations in a coordinated fashion, and managers must focus on those critical internal operations that enable them to satisfy customer needs. The internal measures should reflect business processes that have the greatest impact on customer satisfaction. These include factors that affect cycle time, quality, employee skills, and productivity.

innovation and learning perspective
measures of firm performance that indicate how well firms are changing their product and service offerings to adapt to changes in the internal and external environments.

Innovation and Learning Perspective   Given the rapid rate of markets, technologies, and global competition, the criteria for success are constantly changing. To survive and prosper, managers must make frequent changes to existing products and services as well as introduce entirely new products with expanded capabilities. A firm's ability to do well from an innovation and learning perspective is more dependent on its intangible than tangible assets. Three categories of intangible assets are critically important: human capital (skills, talent, and knowledge), information capital (information systems, networks), and organization capital (culture, leadership).

financial perspective
measures of firms' financial performance that indicate how well strategy, implementation, and execution are contributing to bottom-line improvement.

Financial Perspective   Measures of financial performance indicate whether the company's strategy, implementation, and execution are indeed contributing to bottom-line improvement. Typical financial goals include profitability, growth, and shareholder value. Periodic financial statements remind managers that improved quality, response time, productivity, and innovative products benefit the firm only when they result in improved sales, increased market share, reduced operating expenses, or higher asset turnover.[67]

A key implication is that managers do not need to look at their job as balancing stakeholder demands. They must avoid the following mind-set: "How many units in employee satisfaction do I have to give up to get some additional units of customer satisfaction or profits?" Instead, the balanced scorecard provides a win–win approach—increasing satisfaction among a wide variety of organizational stakeholders, including employees (at all levels), customers, and stockholders.

Limitations and Potential Downsides of the Balanced Scorecard   There is general agreement that there is nothing inherently wrong with the concept of the balanced scorecard.[68] The key limitation is that some executives may view it as a "quick fix" that can be easily installed. If managers do not recognize this from the beginning and fail to commit to it long term, the organization will be disappointed. Poor execution becomes the cause of such performance outcomes. And organizational scorecards must be aligned with individuals' scorecards to turn the balanced scorecards into a powerful tool for sustained performance.

In a study of 50 Canadian medium-size and large organizations, the number of users expressing skepticism about scorecard performance was much greater than the number claiming positive results. A large number of respondents agreed with the statement "Balanced scorecards don't really work." Some representative comments included: "It became just a number-crunching exercise by accountants after the first year," "It is just the latest management fad and is already dropping lower on management's list of priorities as all fads eventually do," and "If scorecards are supposed to be a measurement tool, why is it so hard to measure their results?" There is much work to do before scorecards can become a viable framework to measure sustained strategic performance.

Problems often occur in the balanced scorecard implementation efforts when the commitment to learning is insufficient and employees' personal ambitions are included. Without a set of rules for employees that address continuous process improvement and the personal improvement of individual employees, there will be limited employee buy-in and insufficient cultural change. Thus, many improvements may be temporary and superficial. Often, scorecards that failed to attain alignment and improvements dissipated very quickly. And, in many cases, management's efforts to improve performance were seen as divisive and were viewed by employees as aimed at benefiting senior management compensation. This fostered a "what's in it for me?" attitude.

ISSUE FOR DEBATE

Even as malls around the country see store after store closing, online retailers, both large and small, have started exploring opening brick-and-mortar stores. Amazon has opened a physical bookstore in Seattle's University Village and has plans to open 200 stores. Fabletics, an online athletic clothing retailer, opened six physical stores in the second half of 2016. Birchbox, an online beauty supply store, opened its first brick-and-mortar store in the trendy Soho District of New York City.

There are both potential benefits and pitfalls in opening these physical stores. These online firms are striving to grow the awareness of their brand and build their market position with these stores. They can leverage their customer databases to identify the markets with the greatest potential. Online retailers collect an enormous amount of data about their customers and can base their physical stores in areas where the local demographics suggest there is the greatest density of potential customers. Opening physical stores also offers them the potential to offer a richer experience to their customers. In stores, customers can try on or test the retailer's products and can be brought in for promotional events and seminars related to the firm's products—things that are much more difficult in the online space. Some online retailers, such as Bonobos and Blue Nile, use their stores solely as showrooms where customers try on clothing or jewelry and then order whatever they want online for home delivery. Finally, opening physical stores allows the firm to attract a new set of customers, those who do not regularly shop online.

There are also new challenges in opening physical stores. First, having physical stores requires a significant financial investment. The cost to rent and physically set up store locations can be quite steep, especially in high traffic areas such as New York City and Chicago—the most common targets for initial locations. Second, it can reduce the flexibility of the firm. Store leases typically last several years, leaving firms stuck if the location turns out to be less successful than expected. Also, housing inventory in a range of locations requires longer planning and greater investment than having an online-only model. Third, online store operators have to learn new competencies to compete with physical stores. Online retailers typically have limited experience in predicting consumer demand months ahead of time, a foremost skill needed by brick-and-mortar retailers to be able to stock products in stores. They also don't have experience in staffing, training, and compensating the personnel needed in a physical store. In physical stores, the sales associate is a key asset, but online retailers are more adept at hiring and organizing work for IT, web-marketing, and logistics personnel. Fourth, the legal requirements for running physical stores are more complex. This can include taxation and permitting laws, but the most complex may be the myriad of employment and labor laws that retailers face when they operate in different cities or states.

continued

Discussion Questions

1. Will online retailers, in general, experience a positive outcome in opening physical stores?
2. For what types of online retailers does opening stores make the most sense? Why?
3. Is it more challenging for traditional retailers to build an online space, or for online retailers to build a physical store presence?

Sources: Briggs, F. 2015. Shift of online brands to bricks & mortar stores set to create omni-channel experience for malls. *forbes.com.* August 11: np; Walsh, M. 2016. The future of e-commerce: bricks and mortar. *theguardian.com.* January 30: np; and Bensinger, G. & Kapner, S. 2016. Online stores embrace bricks. *wsj.com.* February 5: np.

Reflecting on Career Implications . . .

▣ **The Value Chain:** It is important that you develop an understanding of your firm's value chain. What activities are most critical for attaining competitive advantage? Think of ways in which you can add value in your firm's value chain. How might your firm's support activities (e.g., information technology, human resource practices) help you accomplish your assigned tasks more effectively? How will you bring your value-added contribution to the attention of your superiors?

▣ **The Value Chain:** Consider the most important linkages between the activities you perform in your organization with other activities both within your firm and between your firm and its suppliers, customers, and alliance partners. Understanding and strengthening these linkages can contribute greatly to your career advancement within your current organization.

▣ **Resource-Based View of the Firm:** Are your skills and talents rare, valuable, and difficult to imitate, and do they have few substitutes? If so, you are in the better position to add value for your firm—and earn rewards and incentives. How can your skills and talents be enhanced to help satisfy these criteria to a greater extent? Get more training? Change positions within the firm? Consider career options at other organizations?

▣ **Balanced Scorecard:** Can you design a balanced scorecard for your life? What perspectives would you include in it? In what ways would such a balanced scorecard help you attain success in life?

summary

In the traditional approaches to assessing a firm's internal environment, the primary goal of managers would be to determine their firm's relative strengths and weaknesses. Such is the role of SWOT analysis, wherein managers analyze their firm's strengths and weaknesses as well as the opportunities and threats in the external environment. In this chapter, we discussed why this may be a good starting point but hardly the best approach to take in performing a sound analysis. There are many limitations to SWOT analysis, including its static perspective, its potential to overemphasize a single dimension of a firm's strategy, and the likelihood that a firm's strengths do not necessarily help the firm create value or competitive advantages.

We identified two frameworks that serve to complement SWOT analysis in assessing a firm's internal environment: value-chain analysis and the resource-based view of the firm. In conducting a value-chain analysis, first divide the firm into a series of value-creating activities. These include primary activities such as inbound logistics, operations, and service as well as support activities such as procurement and human resource management. Then analyze how each activity adds value as well as how *interrelationships* among value activities in the firm and among the firm and its customers and suppliers add value. Thus, instead of merely determining a firm's strengths and weaknesses per se, you analyze them in the overall context of the firm and its relationships with customers and suppliers—the value system.

The resource-based view of the firm considers the firm as a bundle of resources: tangible resources, intangible resources, and organizational capabilities. Competitive advantages that are sustainable over time generally arise from the creation of bundles of resources and capabilities. For advantages to be sustainable, four criteria must be satisfied: value, rarity, difficulty in imitation, and difficulty in substitution. Such an evaluation requires a sound knowledge of the competitive context in which the firm exists. The owners of a business may not capture all of the value created by the firm. The appropriation of value created by a firm between the owners and employees is determined by four factors: employee bargaining power, replacement cost, employee exit costs, and manager bargaining power.

An internal analysis of the firm would not be complete unless you evaluate its performance and make the appropriate comparisons. Determining a firm's performance requires an analysis of its financial situation as well as a review of how well it is satisfying a broad range of stakeholders, including customers, employees, and stockholders. We discussed the concept of the balanced scorecard, in which four perspectives must be addressed: customer, internal business, innovation and learning, and financial. Central to this concept is the idea that the interests of various stakeholders can be interrelated. We provide examples of how indicators of employee satisfaction lead to higher levels of customer satisfaction, which in turn lead to higher levels of financial performance. Thus, improving a firm's performance does not need to involve making trade-offs among different stakeholders. Assessing the firm's performance is also more useful if it is evaluated in terms of how it changes over time, compares with industry norms, and compares with key competitors.

SUMMARY REVIEW QUESTIONS

1. SWOT analysis is a technique to analyze the internal and external environments of a firm. What are its advantages and disadvantages?
2. Briefly describe the primary and support activities in a firm's value chain.
3. How can managers create value by establishing important relationships among the value-chain activities both within their firm and between the firm and its customers and suppliers?
4. Briefly explain the four criteria for sustainability of competitive advantages.
5. Under what conditions are employees and managers able to appropriate some of the value created by their firm?
6. What are the advantages and disadvantages of conducting a financial ratio analysis of a firm?
7. Summarize the concept of the balanced scorecard. What are its main advantages?

EXPERIENTIAL EXERCISE

Caterpillar is a leading firm in the construction and mining equipment industry with extensive global operations. It has approximately 114,000 employees, and its revenues were $47 billion in 2015. In addition to its manufacturing and logistics operations, Caterpillar is well known for its superb service and parts supply, and it provides retail financing for its equipment.

Below, we address several questions that focus on Caterpillar's value-chain activities and the interrelationships among them as well as whether or not the firm is able to attain sustainable competitive advantage(s).

1. Where in Caterpillar's value chain is the firm creating value for its customers?

Value-Chain Activity	Yes/No	How Does Caterpillar Create Value for the Customer?
Primary:		
Inbound logistics		
Operations		
Outbound logistics		
Marketing and sales		
Service		
Support:		
Procurement		
Technology development		
Human resource management		
General administration		

2. What are the important relationships among Caterpillar's value-chain activities? What are the important interdependencies? For each activity, identify the relationships and interdependencies.

	Inbound logistics	Operations	Outbound logistics	Marketing and sales	Service	Procurement	Technology development	Human resource management	General administration
Inbound logistics									
Operations									
Outbound logistics									
Marketing and sales									
Service									
Procurement									
Technology development									
Human resource management									
General administration									

3. What resources, activities, and relationships enable Caterpillar to achieve a sustainable competitive advantage?

Resource/Activity	Is It Valuable?	Is It Rare?	Are There Few Substitutes?	Is It Difficult to Make?
Inbound logistics				
Operations				
Outbound logistics				
Marketing and sales				
Service				
Procurement				
Technology development				
Human resource management				
General administration				

APPLICATION QUESTIONS & EXERCISES

1. Using published reports, select two CEOs who have recently made public statements regarding a major change in their firm's strategy. Discuss how the successful implementation of such strategies requires changes in the firm's primary and support activities.

2. Select a firm that competes in an industry in which you are interested. Drawing upon published financial reports, complete a financial ratio analysis. Based on changes over time and a comparison with industry norms, evaluate the firm's strengths and weaknesses in terms of its financial position.

3. How might exemplary human resource practices enhance and strengthen a firm's value-chain activities?

4. Using the Internet, look up your university or college. What are some of its key value-creating activities that provide competitive advantages? Why?

ETHICS QUESTIONS

1. What are some of the ethical issues that arise when a firm becomes overly zealous in advertising its products?

2. What are some of the ethical issues that may arise from a firm's procurement activities? Are you aware of any of these issues from your personal experience or businesses you are familiar with?

REFERENCES

1. Lapowski, I. 2013. Ev Williams on Twitter's early years, *inc.com.* October 4: np; Shen, L. 2016. Here's why Twitter's stock is plunging. *fortune.com.* October 15: np; Luckerson, V. 2016. This one chart explains why Twitter is in trouble. *time.com.* February 10: np; Covert, J. 2016. Twitter tanks as company struggles to find a buyer. *nypost.com.* October 10: np; Thomas, L. 2016. Twitter struggles to lure advertisers despite user growth. *cnbc.com.* July 26: np; *statista.com.*

2. Our discussion of the value chain will draw on Porter, M. E. 1985. *Competitive advantage:* chap. 2. New York: Free Press.

3. Dyer, J. H. 1996. Specialized supplier networks as a source of competitive advantage: Evidence from the auto industry. *Strategic Management Journal,* 17: 271–291.

4. For an insightful perspective on value-chain analysis, refer to Stabell, C. B. & Fjeldstad, O. D. 1998. Configuring value for competitive advantage: On chains, shops, and networks. *Strategic Management Journal,* 19: 413–437. The authors develop concepts of value chains, value shops, and value networks to extend the value-creation logic across a broad range of industries. Their work builds on the seminal contributions of Porter, 1985, op. cit., and others who have addressed how firms create value through key interrelationships among value-creating activities.

5. Ibid.

6. Maynard, M. 1999. Toyota promises custom order in 5 days. *USA Today,* August 6: B1.

7. Shaw Industries. 1999. Annual report: 14–15.

8. Fisher, M. L. 1997. What is the right supply chain for your product? *Harvard Business Review,* 75(2): 105–116.

9. Jackson, M. 2001. Bringing a dying brand back to life. *Harvard Business Review,* 79(5): 53–61.

10. Anderson, J. C. & Nmarus, J. A. 2003. Selectively pursuing more of your customer's business. *MIT Sloan Management Review,* 44(3): 42–50.

11. Insights on advertising are addressed in Rayport, J. F. 2008. Where is advertising going? Into 'stitials. *Harvard Business Review,* 66(5): 18–20.

12. Sauer, A. 2016. Announcing the 2016 brandcameo product placement awards. *brandchannel.com.* February 24: np.

13. For a scholarly discussion on the procurement of technology components, read Hoetker, G. 2005. How much you know versus how well I know you: Selecting a supplier for a technically innovative component. *Strategic Management Journal,* 26(1): 75–96.

14. For a discussion on criteria to use when screening suppliers for back-office functions, read Feeny, D., Lacity, M., & Willcocks, L. P. 2005. Taking the measure of outsourcing providers. *MIT Sloan Management Review,* 46(3): 41–48.

15. For a study investigating sourcing practices, refer to Safizadeh, M. H., Field, J. M., & Ritzman, L. P. 2008. Sourcing practices and boundaries of the firm in the financial services industry. *Strategic Management Journal,* 29(1): 79–92.

16. Imperato, G. 1998. How to give good feedback. *Fast Company,* September: 144–156.

17. Imperato, G., "How Microsoft Reviews Suppliers," *Fast Company,* September 1998.

18. Bensaou, B. M. & Earl, M. 1998. The right mindset for managing information technology. *Harvard Business Review,* 96(5): 118–128.

19. A discussion of R&D in the pharmaceutical industry is in Garnier, J-P. 2008. Rebuilding the R&D engine in big pharma. *Harvard Business Review,* 66(5): 68–76.

20. Chick, S. E., Huchzermeier, A., & Netessine, S. 2014. Europe's solution factories. *Harvard Business Review,* 92(4): 111–115.

21. Ulrich, D. 1998. A new mandate for human resources. *Harvard Business Review,* 96(1): 124–134.

22. A study of human resource management in China is Li, J., Lam, K., Sun, J. J. M., & Liu, S. X. Y. 2008. Strategic resource management, institutionalization, and employment modes: An empirical study in China. *Strategic Management Journal,* 29(3): 337–342.

23. Wood, J. 2003. Sharing jobs and working from home: The new face of the airline industry. *AviationCareer.net:* February 21.

24. Gellman, L. 2015. When a job offer comes without a job. *Wall Street Journal.* December 2: B1, B7.

25. For insights on the role of information systems integration in fostering innovation, refer to Cash, J. I. Jr., Earl, M. J., & Morison, R.

2008. Teaming up to crack innovation and enterprise integration. *Harvard Business Review,* 66(11): 90–100.

26. For a cautionary note on the use of IT, refer to McAfee, A. 2003. When too much IT knowledge is a dangerous thing. *MIT Sloan Management Review,* 44(2): 83–90.

27. For an interesting perspective on some of the potential downsides of close customer and supplier relationships, refer to Anderson, E. & Jap, S. D. 2005. The dark side of close relationships. *MIT Sloan Management Review,* 46(3): 75–82.

28. Day, G. S. 2003. Creating a superior customer-relating capability. *MIT Sloan Management Review,* 44(3): 77–82.

29. To gain insights on the role of electronic technologies in enhancing a firm's connections to outside suppliers and customers, refer to Lawrence, T. B., Morse, E. A., & Fowler, S. W. 2005. Managing your portfolio of connections. *MIT Sloan Management Review,* 46(2): 59–66.

30. IBM Global CEO Study, p. 27.

31. Verhoef, P. C., Beckers, S. F. M., & van Doorn, J. 2013. Understand the perils of co-creation. *Harvard Business Review,* 91(9): 28; and Winston, A. S. 2014. *The big pivot.* Boston: Harvard Business Review Press.

32. Collis, D. J. & Montgomery, C. A. 1995. Competing on resources: Strategy in the 1990's. *Harvard Business Review,* 73(4): 119–128; and Barney, J. 1991. Firm resources and sustained competitive advantage. *Journal of Management,* 17(1): 99–120.

33. For critiques of the resource-based view of the firm, refer to Sirmon, D. G., Hitt, M. A., & Ireland, R. D. 2007. Managing firm resources in dynamic environments to create value: Looking inside the black box. *Academy of Management Review,* 32(1): 273–292; and Newbert, S. L. 2007. Empirical research on the resource-based view of the firm: An assessment and suggestions for future research. *Strategic Management Journal,* 28(2): 121–146.

34. Henkoff, R. 1993. Companies that train the best. *Fortune,* March 22: 83; and Dess & Picken, *Beyond productivity,* p. 98.

35. Gaines-Ross, L. 2010. Reputation warfare. *Harvard Business Review,* 88(12): 70–76.

36. Barney, J. B. 1986. Types of competition and the theory of

strategy: Towards an integrative framework. *Academy of Management Review,* 11(4): 791-800.

37. Harley-Davidson. 1993. Annual report.

38. Stetler, B. 2008. Griping online? Comcast hears and talks back. *nytimes.com,* July 25: np.

39. For a rigorous, academic treatment of the origin of capabilities, refer to Ethiraj, S. K., Kale, P., Krishnan, M. S., & Singh, J. V. 2005. Where do capabilities come from and how do they matter? A study of the software services industry. *Strategic Management Journal,* 26(1): 25-46.

40. For an academic discussion on methods associated with organizational capabilities, refer to Dutta, S., Narasimhan, O., & Rajiv, S. 2005. Conceptualizing and measuring capabilities: Methodology and empirical application. *Strategic Management Journal,* 26(3): 277-286.

41. Lorenzoni, G. & Lipparini, A. 1999. The leveraging of interfirm relationships as a distinctive organizational capability: A longitudinal study. *Strategic Management Journal,* 20: 317-338.

42. Andersen, M. M. op. cit, p. 209.

43. A study investigating the sustainability of competitive advantage is Newbert, S. L. 2008. Value, rareness, competitive advantages, and performance: A conceptual-level empirical investigation of the resource-based view of the firm. *Strategic Management Journal,* 29(7): 745-768.

44. Arikan, A. M. & McGahan, A. M. 2010. The development of capabilities in new firms. *Strategic Management Journal,* 31(1): 1-18.

45. Barney, J. 1991. Firm resources and sustained competitive advantage. *Journal of Management,* 17(1): 99-120.

46. Barney, 1986, op. cit. Our discussion of inimitability and substitution draws upon this source.

47. A study that investigates the performance implications of imitation is Ethiraj, S. K. & Zhu, D. H. 2008. Performance effects of imitative entry. *Strategic Management Journal,* 29(8): 797-818.

48. Sirmon, D. G., Hitt, M. A., Arregale, J.-L. & Campbell, J. T. 2010. The dynamic interplay of capability strengths and weaknesses: Investigating the bases of temporary competitive advantage. *Strategic Management Journal,* 31(13): 1386-1409.

49. Scherzer, L. 2012. Groupon and deal sites see skepticism replacing promise. *finance.yahoo.com,* November 30: np; The dismal scoop on Groupon. 2011. *The Economist,* October 22: 81; Slater, D. 2012. Are daily deals done? *Fast Company;* and Danna, D. 2012. Groupon & daily deals competition. *beta.fool.com,* June 15: np.

50. Deephouse, D. L. 1999. To be different, or to be the same? It's a question (and theory) of strategic balance. *Strategic Management Journal,* 20: 147-166.

51. Hagerty, J. 2015. A radical idea: Own your supply chain. *Wall Street Journal.* April 30: B1-B2.

52. Karlgaard, R. 2014. *The soft edge.* San Francisco: Jossey-Bass.

53. Yeoh, P. L. & Roth, K. 1999. An empirical analysis of sustained advantage in the U.S. pharmaceutical industry: Impact of firm resources and capabilities. *Strategic Management Journal,* 20: 637-653.

54. Robins, J. A. & Wiersema, M. F. 2000. Strategies for unstructured competitive environments: Using scarce resources to create new markets. In Bresser, R. F., et al. (Eds.), *Winning strategies in a deconstructing world:* 201-220. New York: Wiley.

55. Graser, M. 2013. Blockbuster chiefs lacked the vision to see how the industry was shifting under the video rental chain's feet. *www.variety.com,* November 12: np; Kellmurray, B. 2013. Learning from Blockbuster's failure to adapt. *www.abovethefoldmag.com,* November 13: np; and Downes, L. & Nunes, P. 2014. *Big bang disruption.* New York: Penguin.

56. Amit, R. & Schoemaker, J. H. 1993. Strategic assets and organizational rent. *Strategic Management Journal,* 14(1): 33-46; Collis, D. J. & Montgomery, C. A. 1995. Competing on resources: Strategy in the 1990's. *Harvard Business Review,* 73(4):

118-128; Coff, R. W. 1999. When competitive advantage doesn't lead to performance: The resource-based view and stakeholder bargaining power. *Organization Science,* 10(2): 119-133; and Blyler, M. & Coff, R. W. 2003. Dynamic capabilities, social capital, and rent appropriation: Ties that split pies. *Strategic Management Journal,* 24: 677-686.

57. Munk, N. 1998. The new organization man. *Fortune,* March 16: 62-74.

58. Coff, op. cit.

59. Anonymous. 2013. "All of them are overpaid": Bank CEOs got average 7.7% raise. *www.moneynews.com,* June 3: np.

60. We have focused our discussion on how internal stakeholders (e.g., employees, managers, and top executives) may appropriate a firm's profits (or rents). For an interesting discussion of how a firm's innovations may be appropriated by external stakeholders (e.g., customers, suppliers) as well as competitors, refer to Grant, R. M. 2002. *Contemporary strategy analysis* (4th ed.): 335-340. Malden, MA: Blackwell.

61. Luehrman, T. A. 1997. What's it worth? A general manager's guide to valuation. *Harvard Business Review,* 45(3): 132-142.

62. See, for example, Kaplan, R. S. & Norton, D. P. 1992. The balanced scorecard: Measures that drive performance. *Harvard Business Review,* 69(1): 71-79.

63. Hitt, M. A., Ireland, R. D., & Stadter, G. 1982. Functional importance of company performance: Moderating effects of grand strategy and industry type. *Strategic Management Journal,* 3: 315-330.

64. *finance.yahoo.com.*

65. Kaplan & Norton, op. cit.

66. Ibid.

67. For a discussion of the relative value of growth versus increasing margins, read Mass, N. J. 2005. The relative value of growth. *Harvard Business Review,* 83(4): 102-112.

68. Our discussion draws upon: Angel, R. & Rampersad, H. 2005. Do scorecards add up? *camagazine.com.* May: np.; and Niven, P. 2002. *Balanced scorecard step by step: Maximizing performance and maintaining results.* New York: John Wiley & Sons.

Recognizing a Firm's Intellectual Assets

Moving beyond a Firm's Tangible Resources

After reading this chapter, you should have a good understanding of the following learning objectives:

LO4-1 Why the management of knowledge professionals and knowledge itself are so critical in today's organizations.

LO4-2 The importance of recognizing the interdependence of attracting, developing, and retaining human capital.

LO4-3 The key role of social capital in leveraging human capital within and across the firm.

LO4-4 The importance of social networks in knowledge management and in promoting career success.

LO4-5 The vital role of technology in leveraging knowledge and human capital.

LO4-6 Why "electronic" or "virtual" teams are critical in combining and leveraging knowledge in organizations and how they can be made more effective.

LO4-7 The challenge of protecting intellectual property and the importance of a firm's dynamic capabilities.

©Anatoli Styf/Shutterstock

LEARNING FROM MISTAKES

The 2012 bankruptcy of storied law firm Dewey & LeBoeuf LLP illustrates how even well-established firms can fail because of ineffective management of their talent. The failure of the firm is attributable to three major issues: a reliance on borrowed money, making large promises about compensation to incoming (called "lateral") partners, and a lack of transparency about the firm's financials.

Partnership in a major law firm, considered the brass ring in a legal career, once came with lifetime security, prestige, and entry into the 1 percent—and at times, the one-tenth of the 1 percent. However, the collapse of Dewey & LeBoeuf laid bare the increasingly Darwinian competition for lucrative clients that has afflicted even the highest ranks of the profession. Here was a firm that traced its roots to the 19th century and bore the name of a former Republican presidential candidate and New York governor, Thomas E. Dewey. The New York–based law firm once had 1,300 lawyers but filed for bankruptcy amid a huge exodus of talent and mounting debt. Few firms borrowed as much money as Dewey & LeBoeuf did—its credit line included a private bond placement of $125 million in 2010. And transparency did not seem to be one of Dewey's strengths: Some only learned about this transaction when it surfaced in a news report. One former partner said: "I read about it in the papers. And I certainly didn't sign off on it."

In 2007, Dewey & LeBoeuf was formed in a widely hailed merger of insurance-and-energy-focused LeBoeuf, Lamb, Greene & McRae LLP, and Dewey Ballantine LLP. However, things soured quickly. The newly merged firm grew aggressively by making promises it ultimately couldn't honor—guaranteeing new partners huge salaries, sometimes over $5 million a year. Legacy partners were definitely not happy that new hires were being treated better than they were and, of course, demanded pay pacts of their own. By the fall of 2011, roughly a third of the firm's 300 partners had salary guarantees.

Large law firms sometimes woo big stars by promising to pay them a fixed amount for a year or two—regardless of the firm's or their own financial performance. But most firms use such guarantees very sparingly. By all accounts, Dewey took this practice to an extreme and made compensation guarantees for multiple years. To make matters worse, it offered guarantees to lawyers who did not prove to be rainmakers. News of the widespread guarantees angered the rank-and-file partners at Dewey, many of whom left the firm. Dewey's performance continued to suffer and after a round of failed merger attempts, the firm liquidated. This left thousands of staff and junior lawyers unemployed, and it became the largest law firm failure in U.S. history.

Elizabeth Sharrer, the chairwoman of 500-lawyer Holland and Hart LLP, said, "Leaders hopefully have learned a lesson that if you're making someone a compensation deal you have to hide from our partners, it's not a good deal." Law firms can dissolve within weeks if spooked partners bail. Sharrer notes, "You can circle the drain really, really quickly." Interviews with former partners, consultants, and others in the industry depict Dewey as a firm run by an insular coterie of attorneys and administrators who often withheld critical information from their partners, undermining their own credibility in the process. When the Great Recession of 2008 and 2009 hit and deep problems came to the surface, a sense of shared sacrifice and loyalty was in short supply!

Discussion Questions

1. How could these problems have been avoided at Dewey & LeBoeuf?
2. What practices should firms such as Dewey & LeBoeuf implement to attract and retain top talent?

Sources: Randazzo, S. 2015. Lessons from the Dewey debacle. *The Wall Street Journal.* October 20: B2; Stewart, J. B. 2014. The rise and fall of a rainmaker. *nytimes.com.* December 12: np; Longstreth, A. & Raymond, N. 2012. The Dewey chronicles: The rise and fall of a legal titan, *reuters.com.* May 11: np; and Frank, A. D. 2012. The end of an era. *fortune.com.* May 29: np.

Managers are always looking for stellar professionals who can take their organizations to the next level. However, attracting talent is a necessary but *not* sufficient condition for success. In today's knowledge economy, it does not matter how big your stock of resources is—whether it be top talent, physical resources, or financial capital. Rather, the question becomes: How good is the organization at attracting top talent and leveraging that talent to produce a stream of products and services valued by the marketplace?

Clearly, Dewey & LeBoeuf failed in retaining top talent. The firm lacked transparency and its partners were very resentful when they discovered that newly hired partners were provided with huge guaranteed pay packages. And, as noted, when major problems arose at the firm, there was very little goodwill among the legacy partners. Not surprisingly, many of them bolted and, as is frequently the case, took many of their clients with them.

In this chapter, we also address how human capital can be leveraged in an organization. We point out the important roles of social capital and technology.

THE CENTRAL ROLE OF KNOWLEDGE IN TODAY'S ECONOMY

LO 4-1

Why the management of knowledge professionals and knowledge itself are so critical in today's organizations.

Central to our discussion is an enormous change that has accelerated over the past few decades and its implications for the strategic management of organizations.[1] For most of the 20th century, managers focused on tangible resources such as land, equipment, and money as well as intangibles such as brands, image, and customer loyalty. Efforts were directed more toward the efficient allocation of labor and capital—the two traditional factors of production.

How times have changed. In the last quarter century, employment in the manufacturing sector declined at a significant rate. Today only 9 percent of the U.S. workforce is employed in this sector, compared to 21 percent in 1980.[2] In contrast, the service sector grew from 73 percent of the workforce in 1980 to 86 percent by 2012.

The knowledge-worker segment, in particular, is growing dramatically. Using a broad definition, it is estimated that knowledge workers currently outnumber other types of workers in the United States by at least four to one—they represent between a quarter and a half of all workers in advanced economies. Recent popular press has gone so far as to suggest that, due to the increased speed and competitiveness of modern business, all modern employees are knowledge workers.

knowledge economy
an economy where wealth is created through the effective management of knowledge workers instead of by the efficient control of physical and financial assets.

In the **knowledge economy,** wealth is increasingly created by effective management of knowledge workers instead of by the efficient control of physical and financial assets. The growing importance of knowledge, coupled with the move by labor markets to reward knowledge work, tells us that investing in a company is, in essence, buying a set of talents, capabilities, skills, and ideas—intellectual capital—not physical and financial resources.[3]

EXHIBIT 4.1

Ratio of Market Value
to Book Value for
Selected Companies

Company	Annual Sales ($ billions)	Market Value ($ billions)	Book Value ($ billions)	Ratio of Market to Book Value
Microsoft	85.3	486.8	72.0	6.8
Apple	215.6	627.0	128.3	4.9
Alphabet (parent of Google)	75.0	564.9	120.3	4.7
Oracle	37.0	160.8	47.3	3.4
Intel	55.4	174.0	61.1	2.8
Nucor	16.4	19.3	7.4	2.6
General Motors	152.4	57.2	39.9	1.4

Note: The data on market valuations are as of January 13, 2017. All other financial data are based on the most recently available balance sheets and income statements.

Source: *finance.yahoo.com.*

Human capital is growing more valuable in virtually every business.[4] This trend has been going on for decades as ever fewer workers function as low-maintenance machines—for example, turning a wrench in a factory—and more become thinkers and creators. Intangible assets, mostly derived from human capital, have soared from 17 percent of the S&P 500's market value in 1975 to 84 percent in 2015, according to the advisory firm Ocean Tomo. Even a manufacturer such as Stryker gets 70 percent of its value from intangibles; it makes replacement knees, hips, and other joints that are, in essence, loaded with intellectual capital.

To apply some numbers to our arguments, let's ask, Whats a company worth?[5] Start with the "big three" financial statements: income statement, balance sheet, and statement of cash flow. If these statements tell a story that investors find useful, then a company's market value* should roughly (but not precisely, because the market looks forward and the books look backward) be the same as the value that accountants ascribe to it—the book value of the firm. However, this is not the case. A study compared the market value with the book value of 3,500 U.S. companies over a period of two decades. In 1978 the two were similar: Book was 95 percent of market value. However, market values and book values have diverged significantly. By January 2017, the S&P industrials were—on average—trading at 2.96 times book value.[6] Robert A. Howell, an expert on the changing role of finance and accounting, muses, "The big three financial statements . . . are about as useful as an 80-year-old Los Angeles road map."

The gap between a firms market value and book value is far greater for knowledge-intensive corporations than for firms with strategies based primarily on tangible assets.[7] Exhibit 4.1 shows the ratio of market-to-book value for some well-known companies. In firms where knowledge and the management of knowledge workers are relatively important contributors to developing products and services—and physical resources are less critical—the ratio of market-to-book value tends to be much higher.

As shown in Exhibit 4.1, firms such as Apple, Alphabet (parent of Google), Microsoft, and Oracle have very high market value to book value ratios because of their high investment in knowledge resources and technological expertise. In contrast, firms in more traditional industry sectors such as Nucor and Southwest Airlines have relatively low market-to-book

* The market value of a firm is equal to the value of a share of its common stock times the number of shares outstanding. The book value of a firm is primarily a measure of the value of its tangible assets. It can be calculated by the formula Total assets − Total liabilities.

ratios. This reflects their greater investment in physical resources and lower investment in knowledge resources. A firm like Intel has a market-to-book value ratio that falls between the above two groups of firms. This is because its high level of investment in knowledge resources is matched by a correspondingly huge investment in plant and equipment. For example, Intel invested $3 billion to build a fabrication facility in Chandler, Arizona.[8]

Many writers have defined **intellectual capital** as the difference between a firms market value and book value—that is, a measure of the value of a firm's intangible assets.[9] This broad definition includes assets such as reputation, employee loyalty and commitment, customer relationships, company values, brand names, and the experience and skills of employees.[10] Thus, simplifying, we have:

$$\text{Intellectual capital} = \text{Market value of firm} - \text{Book value of firm}$$

How do companies create value in the knowledge-intensive economy? The general answer is to attract and leverage human capital effectively through mechanisms that create products and services of value over time.

First, **human capital** is the "*individual* capabilities, knowledge, skills, and experience of the company's employees and managers."[11] This knowledge is relevant to the task at hand, as well as the capacity to add to this reservoir of knowledge, skills, and experience through learning.[12]

Second, **social capital** is "the network of relationships that individuals have throughout the organization." Relationships are critical in sharing and leveraging knowledge and in acquiring resources.[13] Social capital can extend beyond the organizational boundaries to include relationships between the firm and its suppliers, customers, and alliance partners.[14]

Third is the concept of "knowledge," which comes in two different forms. First, there is **explicit knowledge** that is codified, documented, easily reproduced, and widely distributed, such as engineering drawings, software code, and patents.[15] The other type of knowledge is **tacit knowledge.** That is in the minds of employees and is based on their experiences and backgrounds.[16] Tacit knowledge is shared only with the consent and participation of the individual.

New knowledge is constantly created through the continual interaction of explicit and tacit knowledge. Consider two software engineers working together on a computer code. The computer code is the explicit knowledge. By sharing ideas based on each individual's experience—that is, their tacit knowledge—they create new knowledge when they modify the code. Another important issue is the role of "socially complex processes," which include leadership, culture, and trust.[17] These processes play a central role in the creation of knowledge.[18] They represent the "glue" that holds the organization together and helps to create a working environment where individuals are more willing to share their ideas, work in teams, and, in the end, create products and services of value.[19]

Numerous books have been written on the subject of knowledge management and the central role that it has played in creating wealth in organizations and countries throughout the developed world.[20] Here, we focus on some of the key issues that organizations must address to compete through knowledge.

We will now turn our discussion to the central resource itself—human capital—and some guidelines on how it can be attracted/selected, developed, and retained.[21] Tom Stewart, former editor of the *Harvard Business Review,* noted that organizations must also undergo significant efforts to protect their human capital. A firm may "diversify the ownership of vital knowledge by emphasizing teamwork, guard against obsolescence by developing learning programs, and shackle key people with golden handcuffs."[22] In addition, people are less likely to leave an organization if there are effective structures to promote teamwork and information sharing, strong leadership that encourages innovation, and cultures that demand excellence and ethical behavior. Such issues are central to this chapter. Although we touch on these issues throughout this chapter, we provide more detail in later chapters. We discuss organizational controls (culture, rewards, and boundaries) in Chapter 9, organization structure and design in Chapter 10, and a variety of leadership and entrepreneurship topics in Chapters 11 and 12.

intellectual capital
the difference between the market value of the firm and the book value of the firm, including assets such as reputation, employee loyalty and commitment, customer relationships, company values, brand names, and the experience and skills of employees.

human capital
the individual capabilities, knowledge, skills, and experience of a company's employees and managers.

social capital
the network of friendships and working relationships between talented people both inside and outside the organization.

explicit knowledge
knowledge that is codified, documented, easily reproduced, and widely distributed.

tacit knowledge
knowledge that is in the minds of employees and is based on their experiences and backgrounds.

HUMAN CAPITAL: THE FOUNDATION OF INTELLECTUAL CAPITAL

LO 4-2

The importance of recognizing the interdependence of attracting, developing, and retaining human capital.

Take away my people, but leave my factories and soon grass will grow on the factory floors. . . . .
Take away my factories, but leave my people and soon we will have a new and better factory.[23]

—*Andrew Carnegie, Steel industry legend*

The importance of talent to organization success is hardly new. Organizations must recruit talented people—employees at all levels with the proper sets of skills and capabilities coupled with the right values and attitudes. Such skills and attitudes must be continually developed, strengthened, and reinforced, and each employee must be motivated and his or her efforts focused on the organization's goals and objectives.[24]

The rise to prominence of knowledge workers as a vital source of competitive advantage is changing the balance of power in today's organization.[25] Knowledge workers place professional development and personal enrichment (financial and otherwise) above company loyalty. Attracting, recruiting, and hiring the "best and the brightest" is a critical first step in the process of building intellectual capital. As noted by law professor Orly Lobel, *talent wants to be free:*[26]

> Companies like Microsoft, Google, and Facebook are so hungry for talent that they acquire (or, as the tech-buzz is now calling it, acq-hire) entire start-ups only to discard the product and keep the teams, founders, and engineers.

Hiring is only the first of three processes in which all successful organizations must engage to build and leverage their human capital. Firms must also *develop* employees to fulfill their full potential to maximize their joint contributions.[27] Finally, the first two processes are for naught if firms can't provide the working environment and intrinsic and extrinsic rewards to *engage* their best and brightest.[28] Interestingly, a recent Gallup study showed that companies whose workers are the most engaged outperform those with the least engaged by a significant amount: 16 percent higher profitability, 18 percent higher productivity, and 25 to 49 percent lower turnover (depending on the industry).[29] The last benefit can really be significant: Software leader SAP calculated that "for each percentage point that our retention rate goes up or down, the impact on our operating profit is approximately $81 million."

These activities are highly interrelated. We would like to suggest the imagery of a three-legged stool (see Exhibit 4.2).[30] If one leg is weak or broken, the stool collapses.

To illustrate such interdependence, poor hiring impedes the effectiveness of development and retention processes. In a similar vein, ineffective retention efforts place additional

EXHIBIT 4.2 Human Capital: Three Interdependent Activities

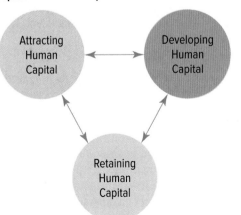

CAN GREEN STRATEGIES ATTRACT AND RETAIN TALENT?

Competing successfully for top talent and retaining high-performing employees are critical factors in an organization's success. Employee recruiting and turnover are, of course, very costly. Losing and replacing a top talent can cost companies up to 200 percent of an employee's annual salary, according to *Engaged! Outbehave Your Competition to Create Customers for Life*.

Today, some 40 percent of job seekers read a company's sustainability report, according to a survey commissioned by the Global Reporting Initiative (GRI). Prospective employees can also riffle through Google in seconds and unearth a myriad of sustainability news and accolades, including an Interbrand "Top 50 Global Green Brand" ranking. Further, a 2014 study by the nonprofit group Net Impact found that business school graduates would take a 15 percent pay cut to:

- Have a job that seeks to make a social or environmental difference in the world (83%)
- Have a job in a company committed to corporate and environmental responsibility (71%)

Below, we discuss an example of a green initiative by a well-known company that helps attract and retain talent:

- Intel's "Green Intel" intranet portal, environmental sustainability network, and environmental excellence awards are beginning to yield benefits for the company. "Intel's employee engagement has resulted in increased employee loyalty, more company pride, and improved morale," according to Carrie Freeman, a sustainability strategist at the firm. Intel managers expect the next organizational health survey will show increased levels of employee pride and satisfaction with their work, which are considered to be good predictors of employee retention.

Sources: Anonymous. 2015. Why a commitment to sustainability can attract and retain the best talent. *grantthornton.com*. April 30: np; Earley, K. 2014. Sustainabilty gives HR teams an edge in attracting and retaining talent. *www.theguardian.com*, February 20: np; Anonymous. 2010. The business case for environmental and sustainability employee education. *National Environmental Education Foundation*, November: np; Mattioli, D. 2007. How going green draws talent, cuts costs. *Wall Street Journal*, November 13: B10; and Lederman, G. 2013. *Engaged! Outbehave your competition to create customers for life*. Ashland, OR: Evolve.

burdens on hiring and development. Consider the following anecdote, provided by Jeffrey Pfeffer of the Stanford University Graduate School of Business:

> Not long ago, I went to a large, fancy San Francisco law firm—where they treat their associates like dog doo and where the turnover is very high. I asked the managing partner about the turnover rate. He said, "A few years ago, it was 25 percent, and now we're up to 30 percent." I asked him how the firm had responded to that trend. He said, "We increased our recruiting." So I asked him, "What kind of doctor would you be if your patient was bleeding faster and faster, and your only response was to increase the speed of the transfusion?"[31]

Clearly, stepped-up recruiting is a poor substitute for weak retention.[32] Although there are no simple, easy-to-apply answers, we can learn from what leading-edge firms are doing to attract, develop, and retain human capital in today's highly competitive marketplace.[33] Before moving on, Strategy Spotlight 4.1 addresses the importance of a firm's "green" or environmental sustainability strategy in attracting young talent.

Attracting Human Capital

> *In today's world, talent is so critical to the success of what you're doing—their core competencies and how well they fit into your office culture. The combination can be, well, extraordinary. But only if you bring in the right people.*[34]
>
> —Mindy Grossman, CEO of HSN (Home Shopping Network)

The first step in the process of building superior human capital is input control: attracting and selecting the right person.[35] Human resource professionals often approach employee selection from a "lock and key" mentality—that is, fit a key (a job candidate) into a lock (the job). Such an approach involves a thorough analysis of the person and the job. Only then can the right decision be made as to how well the two will fit together. How can you fail, the theory goes, if you get a precise match of knowledge, ability, and skill profiles? Frequently, however, the precise matching approach places its emphasis on task-specific skills (e.g., motor skills, specific information processing capabilities, and communication skills) and puts less emphasis on the broad general knowledge and experience, social skills, values, beliefs, and attitudes of employees.[36]

Many have questioned the precise matching approach. They argue that firms can identify top performers by focusing on key employee mind-sets, attitudes, social skills, and general orientations. If they get these elements right, the task-specific skills can be learned quickly. (This does not imply, however, that task-specific skills are unimportant; rather, it suggests that the requisite skill sets must be viewed as a necessary but not sufficient condition.) This leads us to a popular phrase today that serves as the title of the next subsection.

"Hire for Attitude, Train for Skill"   Organizations are increasingly emphasizing general knowledge and experience, social skills, values, beliefs, and attitudes of employees.[37] Consider Southwest Airlines' hiring practices, which focus on employee values and attitudes. Given its strong team orientation, Southwest uses an "indirect" approach. For example, the interviewing team asks a group of employees to prepare a five-minute presentation about themselves. During the presentations, interviewers observe which candidates enthusiastically support their peers and which candidates focus on polishing their own presentations while the others are presenting.[38] The former are, of course, favored.

Alan Cooper, president of Cooper Software, Inc., in Palo Alto, California, goes further. He cleverly *uses technology* to hone in on the problem-solving ability of his applicants and their attitudes before an interview even takes place. He has devised a "Bozo Filter," an online test that can be applied to any industry. Before you spend time on whether job candidates will work out satisfactorily, find out how their minds work. Cooper advised, "Hiring was a black hole. I don't talk to bozos anymore, because 90 percent of them turn away when they see our test. It's a self-administering bozo filter."[39] How does it work?

> The online test asks questions designed to see how prospective employees approach problem-solving tasks. For example, one key question asks software engineer applicants to design a table-creation software program for Microsoft Word. Candidates provide pencil sketches and a description of the new user interface. Another question used for design communicators asks them to develop a marketing strategy for a new touch-tone phone—directed at consumers in the year 1850. Candidates e-mail their answers back to the company, and the answers are circulated around the firm to solicit feedback. Only candidates with the highest marks get interviews.

Sound Recruiting Approaches and Networking   Companies that take hiring seriously must also take recruiting seriously. The number of jobs that successful knowledge-intensive companies must fill is astonishing. Ironically, many companies still have no shortage of applicants. For example, Google, which ranked first on *Fortune*'s 2012 and 2013 "100 Best Companies to Work For," is planning to hire thousands of employees—even though its hiring rate has slowed.[40] The challenge becomes having the right job candidates, not the greatest number of them.

GE Medical Systems, which builds CT scanners and magnetic resonance imaging (MRI) systems, relies extensively on networking. GE has found that current employees are the best source for new ones. Stephen Patscot, VP, human resources, made a few simple changes to double the number of referrals. First, he simplified the process—no complex forms, no bureaucracy, and so on. Second, he increased incentives. Everyone referring a qualified candidate receives a gift certificate from Sears. For referrals who are hired, the "bounty" increases to $2,000. Although this may sound like a lot of money, it is "peanuts" compared to the $15,000 to $20,000 fees that GE typically pays to headhunters for each person hired.[41] Also, when someone refers a former colleague or friend for a job, his or her credibility is on the line. Thus, employees will be careful in recommending people for employment unless they are reasonably confident that these people are good candidates.

Attracting Millennials   The Millennial generation has also been termed "Generation Y" or "Echo Boom" and includes people who were born after 1982. Many call them impatient, demanding, or entitled. However, if employers don't provide incentives to attract and retain young workers, somebody else will. Thus, they will be at a competitive disadvantage.[42]

Why? Demographics are on the Millennials' side—within a few years they will outnumber any other generation. The U.S. Bureau of Labor Statistics projects that by 2020 Millennials will make up 40 percent of the workforce. Baby boomers are retiring, and Millennials will be working for the next several decades. Additionally, they have many of the requisite skills to succeed in the future workplace—tech-savviness and the ability to innovate—and they are more racially diverse than any prior generation. Thus, they are better able to relate rapidly to different customs and cultures.

A study from the Center for Work-Life Policy sums this issue up rather well: Instead of the traditional plums of prestigious title, powerful position, and concomitant compensation, Millennials value challenging and diverse job opportunities, stimulating colleagues, a well-designed communal workspace, and flexible work options. In fact, 89 percent of Millennials say that flexible work options are an important consideration in choosing an employer.

Organizations often miss out on a potential source of talent—former employees! Not everyone who leaves an organization does so because they are unhappy or dissatisfied. Instead, many leave for what they think they believe is a new opportunity. The accompanying "Insights from Research" text box addresses the benefits of hiring former employees (called "boomerangs") who are willing to come back.

Developing Human Capital

It is not enough to hire top-level talent and expect that the skills and capabilities of those employees remain current throughout the duration of their employment. Rather, training and development must take place at all levels of the organization.[43] For example, Solectron assembles printed circuit boards and other components for its Silicon Valley clients.[44] Its employees receive an average of 95 hours of company-provided training each year. Chairman Winston Chen observed, "Technology changes so fast that we estimate 20 percent of an engineer's knowledge becomes obsolete each year. Training is an obligation we owe to our employees. If you want high growth and high quality, then training is a big part of the equation."

Leaders who are committed to developing the people who work for them in order to bring out their strengths and enhance their careers will have committed followers. According to James Rogers, CEO of Duke Energy: "One of the biggest things I find in organizations is that people tend to limit their perceptions of themselves and their capabilities, and one of my challenges is to open them up to the possibilities. I have this belief that anybody can do almost anything in the right context."[45]

In addition to training and developing human capital, firms must encourage widespread involvement, monitor and track employee development, and evaluate human capital.[46]

Encouraging Widespread Involvement   Developing human capital requires the active involvement of leaders at all levels. It won't be successful if it is viewed only as the responsibility of the human resource department. Each year at General Electric, 200 facilitators, 30 officers, 30 human resource executives, and many young managers actively participate in GE's orientation program at Crotonville, its training center outside New York City. Topics include global competition, winning on the global playing field, and personal examination of the new employee's core values vis-à-vis GE's values. As a senior manager once commented, "There is nothing like teaching Sunday school to force you to confront your own values."

WELCOME BACK! RECRUITING BOOMERANG EMPLOYEES

Overview

The common assumption is that turnover creates vacancy problems and expenses to be avoided at all costs. However, sometimes turnover just can't be prevented. Employees who leave an organization aren't always unhappy—some might be willing to come back if given the opportunity. Consider "boomerang" employees as a key recruiting pool to save time and money.

What the Research Shows

Researchers at Texas Christian University, the University of Cincinnati, the University of Illinois, and the University of North Carolina recently published a study in *Personnel Psychology* that examines why employees leave an organization and why they may be willing to return. Using a sample of 452 employees who left and returned for employment, called "boomerangs," and 1,187 who left but had no desire to return, known as "alumni," the authors examined these employees' motives.

Traditional thinking about employment views employee turnover as an end state, where those who leave never want to return. However, this study suggests that this needn't be the case. There may be value in keeping in touch with employees who leave. These findings indicate that employees' willingness to return in the future is influenced by the reasons they left in the first place: Boomerangs were statistically more likely to leave initially for two main reasons. First, they experienced a negative life event, such as taking care of a sick parent that necessitated a change in employment. Second, they received an alternate job offer deemed too good to turn down. The research did find, however, that boomerangs are more likely to accept those alternate jobs in the same industry. Alumni, on the other hand, were statistically more likely to leave because they were dissatisfied with their jobs or because they wanted to change industries.

> *Not all employee turnover is bad. In fact, if business leaders understand the motivations for departures, turnover may create opportunities to bring valued employees back.*

Why This Matters

Employee turnover is expensive. Business leaders appropriate considerable resources trying to minimize employee turnover. Despite best efforts, valued employees still leave the organization. It's an inevitable part of working life. So, what can be done about it? This study indicates that understanding the reasons why employees leave might be beneficial in luring them back.

Boomerang employees are appealing because the training and socialization required for them is quite less than that of other newly hired employees. The implications of this research are that not all employee turnover is bad. In fact, if business leaders understand the motives for departure, turnover may create opportunities to bring valued employees back. This research underscores the essential need for an exit-interview process with all departing employees. Whether conducted in person, online, or on the phone, the interview should assess why an employee is leaving and whether he or she would be willing to return in the future. Ideally, data from the exit interview would connect to a human resource management system with performance information, to allow for easy identification of those high performers leaving for reasons other than dissatisfaction who could be recruited as boomerang employees in the future. Maintaining an active alumni program and asking current managers to identify past employees who would be on their top 10 "hire-back" list are other ways to cultivate a worthy talent pool.

Understanding why employees leave could save your organization money in the long run by broadening the pool of potential hires for future job openings. However, this is not to suggest that you should give up trying to retain valued employees from the start. Maintaining and fostering employee satisfaction remains crucial for reducing turnover caused by dissatisfaction. As a manager, take the initiative to monitor and address employee satisfaction levels so you can prevent your top talent from leaving in the first place.

Key Takeaways

Understanding why employees leave is essential information for company recruiting strategies. Employees are more likely to return and be productive assets if they leave for reasons other than dissatisfaction. Because unhappy employees are more likely to leave and never return, you should monitor and address employee satisfaction levels on an ongoing basis.

Rehiring former employees can save money and time. Make sure your company has exit interviews and alumni programs that track potential boomerang employees.

Apply This Today

Employees are going to leave your organization—that's a fact. Understanding why they leave, though, should be a top priority. By determining the reasons for departure, managers may find that valuable employees are willing to return in the future.

Research Reviewed

Shipp, A. J., Furst-Holloway, S., Harris, T. B., & Rosen, B. 2014. Gone today but here tomorrow: Extending the unfolding model of turnover to consider boomerang employees. *Personnel Psychology,* 67(2): 421–462.

Similarly, A. G. Lafley, Procter & Gamble's former CEO, claimed that he spent 40 percent of his time on personnel.[47] Andy Grove, who was previously Intel's CEO, required all senior people, including himself, to spend at least a week a year teaching high flyers. And Nitin Paranjpe, CEO of Hindustan Unilever, recruits people from campuses and regularly visits high-potential employees in their offices.

Mentoring Mentoring is most often a formal or informal relationship between two people—a senior mentor and a junior protégé.[48] Mentoring can potentially be a valuable influence in professional development in both the public and private sectors. The war for talent is creating challenges within organizations to recruit new talent as well as retain talent.

Mentoring can provide many benefits—to the organization as well as the individual.[49] For the organization, it can help to recruit qualified managers, decrease turnover, fill senior-level positions with qualified professionals, enhance diversity initiatives with senior-level management, and facilitate organizational change efforts. Individuals can also benefit from effective mentoring programs. These benefits include helping newer employees transition into the organization, helping developmental relationships for people who lack access to informal mentoring relationships, and providing support and challenge to people on an organization's "fast track" to positions of higher responsibility.

Mentoring is traditionally viewed as a program to transfer knowledge and experience from more senior managers to up-and-comers. However, many organizations have reinvented it to fit today's highly competitive, knowledge-intensive industries. For example, consider Intel:

> Intel matches people not by job title and years of experience but by specific skills that are in demand. Lory Lanese, Intel's mentor champion at its huge New Mexico plant (with 5,500 employees), states, "This is definitely not a special program for special people." Instead, Intel's program uses an intranet and email to perform the matchmaking, creating relationships that stretch across state lines and national boundaries. Such an approach enables Intel to spread best practices quickly throughout the far-flung organization. Finally, Intel relies on written contracts and tight deadlines to make sure that its mentoring program gets results—and fast.[50]

Intel has also initiated a mentoring program involving its technical assistants (TAs) who work with senior executives. This concept is sometimes referred to as "reverse mentoring" because senior executives benefit from the insights of professionals who have more updated technical skills—but rank lower in the organizational hierarchy. And, not surprisingly, the TAs stand to benefit quite a bit as well. Here are some insights offered by Andy Grove (formerly Intel's CEO):[51]

> In the 1980s I had a marketing manager named Dennis Carter. I probably learned more from him than anyone in my career. He is a genius. He taught me what brands are. I had no idea—I thought a brand was the name on the box. He showed me the connection of brands to strategies. Dennis went on to be Chief Marketing Officer. He was the person responsible for the Pentium name, "Intel Inside"; he came up with all my good ideas.

Monitoring Progress and Tracking Development Whether a firm uses on-site formal training, off-site training (e.g., universities), or on-the-job training, tracking individual progress—and sharing this knowledge with both the employee and key managers—becomes essential. Like many leading-edge firms, GlaxoSmithKline (GSK) places strong emphasis on broader experiences over longer time periods. Dan Phelan, senior vice president and director of human resources, explained, "We ideally follow a two-plus-two-plus-two formula in developing people for top management positions." This reflects the belief that GSK's best people should gain experience in two business units, two functional units (such as finance and marketing), and two countries.

Other companies may take a less formal approach.[52] Alcoa CEO Klaus Kleinfeld says that he brings "the whole executive team into a room for two days to discuss succession planning and the talent that should be developed. We call it Talent Marketplace. In reality it is a fight for great talent." Executives discuss the best employees and candidates for important positions and decide who goes where. "It is not rare that you say, 'Well, that person is ready to develop,' and people are scribbling it down," claims Kleinfeld. "You can bet that when you're not looking, they're already sending notes to the person: 'Hey, we need to talk.'"

Evaluating Human Capital   In today's competitive environment, collaboration and interdependence are vital to organizational success. Individuals must share their knowledge and work constructively to achieve collective, not just individual, goals. However, traditional systems evaluate performance from a single perspective (i.e., "top down") and generally don't address the "softer" dimensions of communications and social skills, values, beliefs, and attitudes.[53]

To address the limitations of the traditional approach, many organizations use **360-degree evaluation and feedback systems.**[54] Here, superiors, direct reports, colleagues, and even internal and external customers rate a person's performance.[55] Managers rate themselves to have a personal benchmark. The 360-degree feedback system complements teamwork, employee involvement, and organizational flattening. As organizations continue to push responsibility downward, traditional top-down appraisal systems become insufficient.[56] For example, a manager who previously managed the performance of three supervisors might now be responsible for 10 and is less likely to have the in-depth knowledge needed to appraise and develop them adequately. Exhibit 4.3 provides a portion of GE's 360-degree leadership assessment chart.

360-degree evaluation and feedback systems superiors, direct reports, colleagues, and even external and internal customers rate a person's performance.

Vision	• Has developed and communicated a clear, simple, customer-focused vision/direction for the organization.
	• Forward-thinking, stretches horizons, challenges imaginations.
	• Inspires and energizes others to commit to Vision. Captures minds. Leads by example.
	• As appropriate, updates Vision to reflect constant and accelerating change affecting the business.
Customer/Quality Focus	
Integrity	
Accountability/Commitment	
Communication/Influence	
Shared Ownership/Boundaryless	
Team Builder/Empowerment	
Knowledge/Expertise/Intellect	
Initiative/Speed	
Global Mind-Set	

EXHIBIT 4.3

An Excerpt from General Electric's 360-Degree Leadership Assessment Chart

Note: This evaluation system consists of 10 "characteristics"—Vision, Customer/Quality Focus, Integrity, and so on. Each of these characteristics has four "performance criteria." For illustrative purposes, the four performance criteria of "Vision" are included.

Source: Adapted from Slater, R. 1994. *Get Better or Get Beaten:* 152–155. Burr Ridge, IL: Irwin Professional Publishing.

At times, a firm's performance assessment methods may get in the way of team success.[57] Microsoft is an example. For many years, the software giant employed a "stack ranking" system as part of its performance evaluation model. With this system, a certain percentage of any team's members would be rated "top performers," "good," "average," "below average," and "poor," regardless of the team's overall performance. Perhaps, in some situations, this type of forced ranking works. However, in Microsoft's case, it had (not too surprisingly!) unintended consequences. Over time, according to inside reports, the stack ranking created a culture in which employees competed with one another rather than against the firm's rivals. And "A" players rarely liked to join groups with other "A" players, because they feared they might be seen as weaker members of the team.

Retaining Human Capital

It has been said that talented employees are like "frogs in a wheelbarrow."[58] They can jump out at any time! By analogy, the organization can either try to force employees to stay in the firm or try to keep them from jumping out by creating incentives.[59] In other words, either today's leaders can provide the challenges, work environment, and incentives to keep productive employees and management from wanting to bail out, or they can use legal means such as employment contracts and noncompete clauses.[60] Firms must prevent the transfer of valuable and sensitive information outside the organization. Failure to do so would be the neglect of a leader's fiduciary responsibility to shareholders. However, greater efforts should be directed at the former (e.g., challenges, good work environment, and incentives), but, as we all know, the latter (e.g., employment contracts and noncompete clauses) have their place.[61]

Gary Burnison, CEO of Korn/Ferry International, the world's largest executive search firm, provides an insight on the importance of employee retention:[62]

> How do you extend the life of an employee? This is not an environment where you work for an organization for 20 years. But if you can extend it from three years to six years, that has an enormous impact. Turnover is a huge hidden cost in a profit-and-loss statement that nobody ever focuses on. If there was a line item that showed that, I guarantee you'd have the attention of a CEO.

Identifying with an Organization's Mission and Values People who identify with and are more committed to the core mission and values of the organization are less likely to stray or bolt to the competition. For example, take the perspective of the late Steve Jobs, Apple's widely admired former CEO:[63]

> When I hire somebody really senior, competence is the ante. They have to be really smart. But the real issue for me is: Are they going to fall in love with Apple? Because if they fall in love with Apple, everything else will take care of itself. They'll want to do what's best for Apple, not what's best for them, what's best for Steve, or anyone else.

"Tribal loyalty" is another key factor that links people to the organization.[64] A tribe is not the organization as a whole (unless it is very small). Rather, it is teams, communities of practice, and other groups within an organization or occupation.

Brian Hall, CEO of Values Technology in Santa Cruz, California, documented a shift in people's emotional expectations from work. From the 1950s on, a "task-first" relationship—"Tell me what the job is, and let's get on with it"—dominated employee attitudes. Emotions and personal life were checked at the door. In the past few years, a "relationship-first" set of values has challenged the task orientation. Hall believes that it will become dominant. Employees want to share attitudes and beliefs as well as workspace.

Challenging Work and a Stimulating Environment Arthur Schawlow, winner of the 1981 Nobel Prize in physics, was asked what made the difference between highly creative and less creative scientists. His reply: "The labor of love aspect is very important. The most success-ful scientists often are not the most talented.[65] But they are the ones impelled by curiosity. They've got to know what the answer is."[66] Such insights highlight the importance of intrin-sic motivation: the motivation to work on something because it is exciting, satisfying, or personally challenging.[67] As noted by Jeff Immelt, former chairman and CEO of General Electric, "You want people with the self-confidence to leave, but you want them to stay. That puts pressure on you to keep work interesting."[68]

Lars Sorensen, CEO of Novo Nordisk, the huge Danish pharmaceutical firm, provides a poignant perspective on how to keep employees engaged: ". . . we bring patients to see employees. We illuminate the big difference we are making. Without our medication, 24 million people would suffer. There is nothing more motivating for people than to go to work and save people's lives."[69]

Firms can also keep highly mobile employees motivated and challenged through oppor-tunities that lower barriers to an employee's mobility within a company. For example, Shell Oil Company has created an "open sourcing" model for talent. Jobs are listed on its intranet, and, with a two-month notice, employees can go to work on anything that interests them.

Financial and Nonfinancial Rewards and Incentives   Financial rewards are a vital organiza-tional control mechanism (as we will discuss in Chapter 9). Money—whether in the form of salary, bonus, stock options, and so forth—can mean many different things to people. It might mean security, recognition, or a sense of freedom and independence.

Paying people more is seldom the most important factor in attracting and retaining human capital.[70] Most surveys show that money is not the most important reason why peo-ple take or leave jobs and that money, in some surveys, is not even in the top 10. Consistent with these findings, Tandem Computers (part of Hewlett-Packard) typically doesn't tell peo-ple being recruited what their salaries would be. People who asked were told that Tandem's salaries were competitive. If they persisted along this line of questioning, they would not be offered a position. Why? Tandem realized a rather simple idea: People who come for money will leave for money.

Another nonfinancial reward is accommodating working families with children. Balancing demands of family and work is a problem at some point for virtually all employees.

Below we discuss how Google attracts and retains talent through financial and nonfi-nancial incentives. Its unique "Google culture," a huge attraction to potential employees, transforms a traditional workspace into a fun, feel-at-home, and flexible place to work.[71]

> Googlers do not merely work but have a great time doing it. The Mountain View, California, headquarters includes on-site medical and dental facilities, oil change and bike repair, foosball, pool tables, volleyball courts, and free breakfast, lunch, and dinner on a daily basis at 11 gourmet restaurants. Googlers have access to training programs and receive tuition reimbursement while they take a leave of absence to pursue higher education. Google states on its website, "Though Google has grown a lot since it opened in 1998, we still maintain a small company feel."

Our discussion of employee retention would not be complete unless we discussed some of the innovations in data analytics that have provided significant benefits to many compa-nies. We address this issue in Strategy Spotlight 4.2.

Enhancing Human Capital: Redefining Jobs and Managing Diversity

Before moving on to our discussion of social capital, it is important to point out that com-panies are increasingly realizing that the payoff from enhancing their human capital can be substantial. Firms have found that redefining jobs and leveraging the benefits of a diverse workforce can go a long way in improving their performance.

WANT TO INCREASE EMPLOYEE RETENTION? TRY DATA ANALYTICS

We have all heard about management by the book. Perhaps, we should consider management by the algorithm. "People analytics" is rapidly emerging as an important tool in the perpetual war to attract and retain talent. Companies have begun hiring data scientists as well as building or buying software that helps predict who will leave and who will make the best vice president.

According to Josh Bersin, principal at Bersin by Deloitte, the HR group at the consulting giant, "It's like *Moneyball* for HR, letting you make better decisions and this year it has really peaked." He states that the percentage of firms using predictive HR analytics has doubled from 4 percent to 8 percent and last year investors poured $2 billion in companies making apps for hiring, performance management, and wellness programs.

Several companies such as Intel Corp., Twitter, and IBM are now using sentiment-analysis software to assess how employees feel about everything from diversity efforts to their prospects for promotion. Such tools enable managers to analyze text such as internal comments on blog posts or responses to open-ended questions on surveys. The goal is to automatically sort through hundreds or thousands of comments to get a feel of where management can make changes that will improve the chances that employees will remain enthusiastic about the company—and ultimately stay there.

McKinsey & Company claims that one company reduced its retention bonuses by $20 million—and employee attrition by half!—because of its use of predictive behavioral analytics. Contrary to expectations, the company discovered that limited investment in management and employee training, and inadequate recognition, were the main drivers of staff defections. In contrast, expensive retention bonuses, which the company had turned to in desperation, turned out to be an ineffective Band-Aid.

A key advantage of the new analytics techniques over traditional approaches (such as exit interviews with departing employees) is that they are predictive, rather than reactive. And they definitely provide more objective information than the more qualitative findings that one would get with a one-on-one discussion.

Sources: Alsever, J. 2016. Is software better at managing people than you are? *Fortune*. March 15: 41-42; King, R. 2015. Companies want to know: How do workers feel? *The Wall Street Journal*. October 14: R3; and, Fecheyr-Lippens, B., Schaninger, B., & Tanner, K. 2015. Power to the new people analytics. *mckinsey.com*. March: np.

Enhancing Human Capital: Redefining Jobs   Recent research by McKinsey Global Institute suggests that by 2020, the worldwide shortage of highly skilled, college-educated workers could reach 38 to 40 million, or about 13 percent of demand.[72] In response, some firms are taking steps to expand their talent pool, for example, by investing in apprenticeships and other training programs. However, some are going further: They are redefining the jobs of their experts and transferring some of their tasks to lower-skilled people inside or outside their companies, as well as outsourcing work that requires less scarce skills and is not as strategically important. Redefining high-value knowledge jobs not only can help organizations address skill shortages but also can lower costs and enhance job satisfaction.

Consider the following examples:

- Orrick, Herrington & Sutcliffe, a San Francisco–based law firm with nine U.S. offices, shifted routine discovery work previously performed by partners and partner-tracked associates to a new service center in West Virginia staffed by lower-paid attorneys.
- In the United Kingdom, a growing number of public schools are relieving head teachers (or principals) of administrative tasks such as budgeting, facilities maintenance, human resources, and community relations so that they can devote more time to developing teachers.
- The Narayana Hrudayalaya Heart Hospital in Bangalore has junior surgeons, nurses, and technicians handle routine tasks such as preparing the patient for surgery and closing the chest after surgery. Senior cardiac surgeons arrive at the operating room only when the patient's chest is open and the heart is ready to be operated on. Such an approach helps the hospital lower the cost to a fraction of the cost of U.S. providers while maintaining U.S.-level mortality and infection rates.

Breaking high-end knowledge work into highly specialized pieces involves several processes. These include identifying the gap between the talent your firm has and what it requires; creating narrower, more-focused job descriptions in areas where talent is scarce; selecting from various options to fill the skills gap; and rewiring processes for talent and knowledge management.

Enhancing Human Capital: Managing Diversity   A combination of demographic trends and accelerating globalization of business have made the management of cultural differences a critical issue.[73] Workforces, which reflect demographic changes in the overall population, will be increasingly heterogeneous along dimensions such as gender, race, ethnicity, and nationality.[74] Demographic trends in the United States indicate a growth in Hispanic Americans from 6.9 million in 1960 to over 35 million in 2000, with an expected increase to over 59 million by 2020 and 102 million by 2050. Similarly, the Asian American population should grow to 20 million in 2020 from 12 million in 2000 and only 1.5 million in 1970. And the African American population is expected to increase from 12.8 percent of the U.S. population in 2000 to 14.2 percent by 2025.[75]

Such demographic changes have implications not only for the labor pool but also for customer bases, which are also becoming more diverse.[76] This creates important organizational challenges and opportunities.

The effective management of diversity can enhance the social responsibility goals of an organization.[77] However, there are many other benefits as well. Six other areas where sound management of diverse workforces can improve an organization's effectiveness and competitive advantages are (1) cost, (2) resource acquisition, (3) marketing, (4) creativity, (5) problem solving, and (6) organizational flexibility.

- *Cost argument.* As organizations become more diverse, firms effective in managing diversity will have a cost advantage over those that are not.
- *Resource acquisition argument.* Firms with excellent reputations as prospective employers for women and ethnic minorities will have an advantage in the competition for top talent. As labor pools shrink and change in composition, such advantages will become even more important.
- *Marketing argument.* For multinational firms, the insight and cultural sensitivity that members with roots in other countries bring to marketing efforts will be very useful. A similar rationale applies to subpopulations within domestic operations.
- *Creativity argument.* Less emphasis on conformity to norms of the past and a diversity of perspectives will improve the level of creativity.
- *Problem-solving argument.* Heterogeneity in decision-making and problem-solving groups typically produces better decisions because of a wider range of perspectives as well as more thorough analysis. Jim Schiro, former CEO of PricewaterhouseCoopers, explains, "When you make a genuine commitment to diversity, you bring a greater diversity of ideas, approaches, and experiences and abilities that can be applied to client problems. After all, six people with different perspectives have a better shot at solving complex problems than sixty people who all think alike."[78]
- *Organizational flexibility argument.* With effective programs to enhance workplace diversity, systems become less determinant, less standardized, and therefore more fluid. Such fluidity should lead to greater flexibility to react to environmental changes. Reactions should be faster and less costly.

Most managers accept that employers benefit from a diverse workforce. However, this notion can often be very difficult to prove or quantify, particularly when it comes to determining how diversity affects a firm's ability to innovate.[79]

New research provides compelling evidence that diversity enhances innovation and drives market growth. This finding should intensify efforts to ensure that organizations both embody and embrace the power of differences.

Strategy Spotlight 4.3 contrasts the views that Millennials have of diversity with those of other generations, and the implications of such differences for organizations.

MILLENNIALS HAVE A DIFFERENT DEFINITION OF DIVERSITY AND INCLUSION THAN PRIOR GENERATIONS

A recent study by Deloitte and the Billie Jean King Leadership Initiative (BJKLI) shows that, in general, Millennials see the concepts of diversity and inclusion through a vastly different lens. The study analyzed the responses of 3,726 individuals who came from a wide variety of backgrounds with representation across gender, race/ethnicity, sexual orientation, national status, veteran status, disabilities, level within an organization, and tenure with an organization. The respondents were asked 62 questions about diversity and inclusion and the findings demonstrated a snapshot of shifting generational mindsets.

Millennials (born between 1977 to 1995) look upon diversity as the blending of different backgrounds, experiences, and perspectives within a team—which is known as cognitive diversity. They use this word to describe the mix of unique traits that help to overcome challenges and attain business objectives. For Millennials, inclusion is the support for a collaborative environment, and leadership at such an organization must be transparent, communicative, and engaging. According to the study, when defining diversity, Millennials are 35 percent more likely to focus on unique experiences, whereas 21 percent of non-Millennials are more likely to focus on representation.

The X-generation (born between 1965 and 1976) and Boomer generation (born between 1946 and 1964) have a different take.

These generations view diversity as a representation of fairness and protection for all—regardless of gender, race, religion, ethnicity, or sexual orientation. Here, inclusion is the integration of individuals of all demographics into one workplace. It is the right thing to do, that is, a moral and legal imperative to achieve compliance and equality—regardless of whether it benefits the business. The study found that when asked about the business impact on diversity, Millennials are 71 percent more likely to focus on teamwork. In contrast, 28 percent of non-Millennials are more likely to focus on fairness of opportunity.

The study's authors contend that the disconnect between the traditional definitions of diversity and inclusion and those of Millennials can create problems for businesses. For example, clashes may occur when managers do not permit Millennials to express themselves freely. The study found that while 86 percent of Millennials feel that differences of opinion allow teams to excel, only 59 percent believe that their leaders share this perspective.

The study suggests that a company with an inclusive culture promotes innovation. And it cites research by IBM and Morgan Stanley that shows that companies with high levels of innovation achieve the quickest growth in profits and that radical innovation outstrips incremental change by generating 10 times more shareholder value.

Sources: Dishman, L. 2015. Millennials have a different definition of diversity and inclusion. *fastcompany*.com, May 18: np; and Anonymous. 2015. For millennials inclusion goes beyond checking traditional boxes, according to a new Deloitte–Billie Jean King Leadership Initiative Study. *prnewswire*.com, May 13: np.

LO 4-3

The key role of social capital in leveraging human capital within and across the firm.

THE VITAL ROLE OF SOCIAL CAPITAL

Successful firms are well aware that the attraction, development, and retention of talent *is a necessary but not sufficient condition* for creating competitive advantages.[80] In the knowledge economy, it is not the stock of human capital that is important, but the extent to which it is combined and leveraged.[81] In a sense, developing and retaining human capital becomes less important as key players (talented professionals, in particular) take the role of "free agents" and bring with them the requisite skill in many cases. Rather, the development of social capital (that is, the friendships and working relationships among talented individuals) gains importance, because it helps tie knowledge workers to a given firm.[82] Knowledge workers often exhibit greater loyalties to their colleagues and their profession than their employing organization, which may be "an amorphous, distant, and sometimes threatening entity."[83] Thus, a firm must find ways to create "ties" among its knowledge workers.

Let's look at a hypothetical example. Two pharmaceutical firms are fortunate enough to hire Nobel Prize–winning scientists.[84] In one case, the scientist is offered a very attractive salary, outstanding facilities and equipment, and told to "go to it!" In the second case, the scientist is offered approximately the same salary, facilities, and equipment plus one additional ingredient: working in a laboratory with 10 highly skilled and enthusiastic scientists. Part of the job is to collaborate with these peers and jointly develop promising drug compounds. There is little doubt as to which scenario will lead to a higher probability of retaining the scientist. The interaction, sharing, and collaboration will create a situation in which the scientist will develop firm-specific ties and be less likely to "bolt" for a higher salary offer. Such ties are critical because knowledge-based resources tend to be more tacit in nature, as we mentioned early in this chapter. Therefore, they are much more difficult to protect against loss (i.e., the individual quitting the organization) than other types of capital, such as equipment, machinery, and land.

Another way to view this situation is in terms of the resource-based view of the firm that we discussed in Chapter 3. That is, competitive advantages tend to be harder for competitors to copy if they are based on "unique bundles" of resources.[85] So, if employees are working effectively in teams and sharing their knowledge and learning from each other, not only will they be more likely to add value to the firm, but they also will be less likely to leave the organization, because of the loyalties and social ties that they develop over time.

How Social Capital Helps Attract and Retain Talent

The importance of social ties among talented professionals creates a significant challenge (and opportunity) for organizations. In *The Wall Street Journal,* Bernard Wysocki described the increase in a type of "Pied Piper effect," in which teams or networks of people are leaving one company for another.[86] The trend is to recruit job candidates at the crux of social relationships in organizations, particularly if they are seen as having the potential to bring with them valuable colleagues.[87] This is a process that is referred to as "hiring via personal networks." Let's look at one instance of this practice.

> Gerald Eickhoff, founder of an electronic commerce company called Third Millennium Communications, tried for 15 years to hire Michael Reene. Why? Mr. Eickhoff says that he has "these Pied Piper skills." Mr. Reene was a star at Andersen Consulting in the 1980s and at IBM in the 1990s. He built his businesses and kept turning down overtures from Mr. Eickhoff.
>
> However, later he joined Third Millennium as chief executive officer, with a salary of just $120,000 but with a 20 percent stake in the firm. Since then, he has brought in a raft of former IBM colleagues and Andersen subordinates. One protégé from his time at Andersen, Mary Goode, was brought on board as executive vice president. She promptly tapped her own network and brought along former colleagues.
>
> Wysocki considers the Pied Piper effect one of the underappreciated factors in the war for talent today. This is because one of the myths of the New Economy is rampant individualism, wherein individuals find jobs on the Internet career sites and go to work for complete strangers. Perhaps, instead of Me Inc., the truth is closer to We Inc.[88]

Another example of social relationships causing human capital mobility is the emigration of talent from an organization to form start-up ventures. Microsoft is perhaps the best-known example of this phenomenon.[89] Professionals frequently leave Microsoft en masse to form venture capital and technology start-ups, called "Baby Bills," built around teams of software developers. For example, Ignition Corporation, of Bellevue, Washington, was formed by Brad Silverberg, a former Microsoft senior vice president. Eight former Microsoft executives, among others, founded the company.

Social Networks: Implications for Knowledge Management and Career Success

Managers face many challenges driven by such factors as rapid changes in globalization and technology. Leading a successful company is more than a one-person job. As Tom Malone put it in *The Future of Work,* "As managers, we need to shift our thinking from command and control to coordinate and cultivate—the best way to gain power is sometimes to give it away."[90] The move away from top-down bureaucratic control to more open, decentralized network models makes it more difficult for managers to understand how work is actually getting done, who is interacting with whom both within and outside the organization, and the consequences of these interactions for the long-term health of the organization.[91]

LO 4-4

The importance of social networks in knowledge management and in promoting career success.

Malcolm Gladwell, in his best-selling book *The Tipping Point*, used the term *connector* to describe people who have *used* many ties to different social worlds.[92] It's not the number of people that connectors know that makes them significant. Rather, it is their ability to link people, ideas, and resources that wouldn't normally bump into one another. In business, connectors are critical facilitators for collaboration and integration. David Kenny, president of Akamai Technologies, believes that being a connector is one of the most important ways in which he adds value:

> Kenny spends much of his time traveling around the world to meet with employees, partners, and customers. He states, "I spend time with media owners to hear what they think about digital platforms, Facebook, and new pricing models, and with Microsoft leaders to get their views on cloud computing. I'm interested in hearing how our clients feel about macroeconomic issues, the G20, and how debt will affect future generations." These conversations lead to new strategic insights and relationships and help Akamai develop critical external partnerships.

Social networks can also help one bring about important change in an organization—or simply get things done! Consider a change initiative undertaken at the United Kingdom's National Health Care Service—a huge, government-run institution that employs about a million people in hundreds of units and divisions with deeply rooted, bureaucratic, hierarchical systems. This is certainly an organization in which you can't rely solely on your "position power":[93]

> John wanted to set up a nurse-led preoperative assessment service intended to free up time for the doctors who previously led the assessments, reduce cancelled operations (and costs), and improve patient care. Sounds easy enough . . . after all, John was a senior doctor and near the top of the hospital's formal hierarchy. However, he had only recently joined the organization and was not well connected internally.
>
> As he began talking to other doctors and to nurses about the change, he was met with a lot of resistance. He was about to give up when Carol, a well-respected nurse, offered to help. She had even less seniority than John, but many colleagues relied on her advice about navigating hospital politics. She knew many of the people whose support John needed and she eventually converted them to the change.

social network analysis
analysis of the pattern of social interactions among individuals.

Social network analysis depicts the pattern of interactions among individuals and helps to diagnose effective and ineffective patterns.[94] It helps identify groups or clusters of individuals that comprise the network, individuals who link the clusters, and other network members. It helps diagnose communication patterns and, consequently, communication effectiveness.[95] Such analysis of communication patterns is helpful because the configuration of group members' social ties within and outside the group affects the extent to which members connect to individuals who:

- Convey needed resources.
- Have the opportunity to exchange information and support.
- Have the motivation to treat each other in positive ways.
- Have the time to develop trusting relationships that might improve the groups' effectiveness.

However, such relationships don't "just happen."[96] Developing social capital requires interdependence among group members. Social capital erodes when people in the network become independent. And increased interactions between members aid in the development and maintenance of mutual obligations in a social network.[97] Social networks such as Facebook may facilitate increased interactions between members in a social network via Internet-based communications.

Let's take a brief look at a simplified network analysis to get a grasp of the key ideas. In Exhibit 4.4, the links depict informal relationships among individuals, such as

EXHIBIT 4.4 A Simplified Social Network

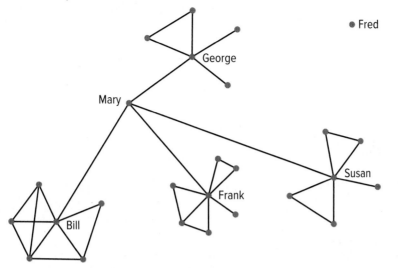

communication flows, personal support, and advice networks. There may be some individuals with literally no linkages, such as Fred. These individuals are typically labeled "isolates." However, most people do have some linkages with others.

To simplify, there are two primary types of mechanisms through which social capital will flow: *closure relationships* (depicted by Bill, Frank, George, and Susan) and *bridging relationships* (depicted by Mary). As we can see, in the former relationships one member is central to the communication flows in a group. In contrast, in the latter relationships, one person "bridges" or brings together groups that would have been otherwise unconnected.

Both closure and bridging relationships have important implications for the effective flow of information in organizations and for the management of knowledge. We will now briefly discuss each of these types of relationships. We will also address some of the implications that understanding social networks has for one's career success.

Closure With **closure,** many members have relationships (or ties) with other members. As indicated in Exhibit 4.4, Bill's group would have a higher level of closure than Frank's Susan's, or George's groups because more group members are connected to each other. Through closure, group members develop strong relationships with each other, high levels of trust, and greater solidarity. High levels of trust help to ensure that informal norms in the group are easily enforced and there is less "free riding." Social pressure will prevent people from withholding effort or shirking their responsibilities. In addition, people in the network are more willing to extend favors and "go the extra mile" on a colleague's behalf because they are confident that their efforts will be reciprocated by another member in their group. Another benefit of a network with closure is the high level of emotional support. This becomes particularly valuable when setbacks occur that may destroy morale or an unexpected tragedy happens that might cause the group to lose its focus. Social support helps the group to rebound from misfortune and get back on track.

But high levels of closure often come with a price. Groups that become too closed can become insular. They cut themselves off from the rest of the organization and fail to share what they are learning from people outside their group. Research shows that while managers need to encourage closure up to a point, if there is too much closure, they need to encourage people to open up their groups and infuse new ideas through bridging relationships.[98]

> **closure**
> the degree to which all members of a social network have relationships (or ties) with other group members.

PICASSO VERSUS VAN GOGH: WHO WAS MORE SUCCESSFUL AND WHY?

Vincent van Gogh and Pablo Picasso are two of the most iconoclastic—and famous—artists of modern times. Paintings by both of them have fetched over $100 million. And both of them were responsible for some of the most iconic images in the art world: Van Gogh's *Self-Portrait* (the one sans the earlobe) and *Starry Night* and Picasso's *The Old Guitarist* and *Guernica.* However, there is an important difference between van Gogh and Picasso. Van Gogh died penniless. Picasso's estate was estimated at $750 million when he died in 1973. What was the difference?

Van Gogh's primary connection to the art world was through his brother. Unfortunately, this connection didn't feed directly into the money that could have turned him into a living success. In contrast, Picasso's myriad connections provided him with access to commercial riches. As noted by Gregory Berns in his book *Iconoclast: A Neuroscientist Reveals How to Think Differently,* "Picasso's wide ranging social network, which

included artists, writers, and politicians, meant that he was never more than a few people away from anyone of importance in the world."*

In effect, van Gogh was a loner, and the charismatic Picasso was an active member of multiple social circles. In social networking terms, van Gogh was a solitary "node" who had few connections. Picasso, on the other hand, was a "hub" who embedded himself in a vast network that stretched across various social lines. Where Picasso smoothly navigated multiple social circles, van Gogh had to struggle just to maintain connections with even those closest to him. Van Gogh inhabited an alien world, whereas Picasso was a social magnet. And because he knew so many people, the world was at Picasso's fingertips. From his perspective, the world was smaller.

* Berns, G., Iconoclast: A Neuroscientist Reveals How to Think Differently. Boston, MA: *Harvard Business Review* Press, 2008.

Sources: Hayashi, A. M. 2008. Why Picasso out earned van Gogh. *MIT Sloan Management Review,* 50(1): 11–12; and Berns, G. 2008. *Icononclast: A Neuroscientist Reveals How to Think Differently.* Boston: Harvard Business Press.

Bridging Relationships   The closure perspective rests on an assumption that there is a high level of similarity among group members. However, members can be quite heterogeneous with regard to their positions in either the formal or informal structures of the group or the organization. Such heterogeneity exists because of, for example, vertical boundaries (different levels in the hierarchy) and horizontal boundaries (different functional areas).

bridging relationships
relationships in a social network that connect otherwise disconnected people.

Bridging relationships, in contrast to closure, stress the importance of ties connecting people. Employees who bridge disconnected people tend to receive timely, diverse information because of their access to a wide range of heterogeneous information flows. Such bridging relationships span a number of different types of boundaries.

structural holes
social gaps between groups in a social network where there are few relationships bridging the groups.

The University of Chicago's Ron Burt originally coined the term **"structural holes"** to refer to the social gap between two groups. Structural holes are common in organizations. When they occur in business, managers typically refer to them as "silos" or "stovepipes." Sales and engineering are a classic example of two groups whose members traditionally interact with their peers rather than across groups.

A study that Burt conducted at Raytheon, a $25 billion U.S. electronics company and military contractor, provides further insight into the benefits of bridging.[99]

> Burt studied several hundred managers in Raytheon's supply chain group and asked them to write down ideas to improve the company's supply chain management. Then he asked two Raytheon executives to rate the ideas. The conclusion: *The best suggestions consistently came from managers who discussed ideas outside their regular work group.*
>
> Burt found that Raytheon managers were good at thinking of ideas but bad at developing them. Too often, Burt said, the managers discussed their ideas with colleagues already in their informal discussion network. Instead, he said, they should have had discussions outside their typical contacts, particularly with an informal boss, or someone with enough power to be an ally but not an actual supervisor.

Implications for Career Success   Let's go back in time in order to illustrate the value of social networks in one's career success. Consider two of the most celebrated artists of all time: Vincent van Gogh and Pablo Picasso. Strategy Spotlight 4.4 points out why these two artists enjoyed sharply contrasting levels of success during their lifetimes.

Effective social networks provide many advantages for the firm.[100] They can play a key role in an individual's career advancement and success. One's social network potentially can provide three unique advantages: private information, access to diverse skill sets, and power.[101] Managers see these advantages at work every day but might not consider how their networks regulate them.

Private Information We make judgments using both public and private information. Today, public information is available from many sources, including the Internet. However, since it is so accessible, public information offers less competitive advantage than it used to.

In contrast, private information from personal contacts can offer something not found in publicly available sources, such as the release date of a new product or knowledge about what a particular interviewer looks for in candidates. Private information can give managers an edge, though it is more subjective than public information since it cannot be easily verified by independent sources, such as Dun & Bradstreet. Consequently the value of your private information to others—and the value of others' private information to you—depends on how much trust exists in the network of relationships.

Access to Diverse Skill Sets Linus Pauling, one of only two people to win a Nobel Prize in two different areas and considered one of the towering geniuses of the 20th century, attributed his creative success not to his immense brainpower or luck but to his diverse contacts. He said, "The best way to have a good idea is to have a lot of ideas."

While expertise has become more specialized during the past few decades, organizational, product, and marketing issues have become more interdisciplinary. This means that success is tied to the ability to transcend natural skill limitations through others. Highly diverse network relationships, therefore, can help you develop more complete, creative, and unbiased perspectives on issues. Trading information or skills with people whose experiences differ from your own provides you with unique, exceptionally valuable resources. It is common for people in relationships to share their problems. If you know enough people, you will begin to see how the problems that another person is struggling with can be solved by the solutions being developed by others. If you can bring together problems and solutions, it will greatly benefit your career.

Power Traditionally, a manager's power was embedded in a firm's hierarchy. But when corporate organizations became flatter, more like pancakes than pyramids, that power was repositioned in the network's brokers (people who bridged multiple networks), who could adapt to changes in the organization, develop clients, and synthesize opposing points of view. Such brokers weren't necessarily at the top of the hierarchy or experts in their fields, but they linked specialists in the firm with trustworthy and informative relationships.[102]

Most personal networks are highly clustered; that is, an individual's friends are likely to be friends with one another as well. Most corporate networks are made up of several clusters that have few links between them. Brokers are especially powerful because they connect separate clusters, thus stimulating collaboration among otherwise independent specialists.

The Potential Downside of Social Capital

We'd like to close our discussion of social capital by addressing some of its limitations. First, some firms have been adversely affected by very high levels of social capital because it may breed **"groupthink"**—a tendency not to question shared beliefs.[103] Such thinking may occur in networks with high levels of closure where there is little input from people outside the network. In effect, too many warm and fuzzy feelings among group members prevent people from rigorously challenging each other. People are discouraged

groupthink
a tendency in an organization for individuals not to question shared beliefs.

from engaging in the "creative abrasion" that Dorothy Leonard of Harvard University describes as a key source of innovation.[104] Two firms that were well known for their collegiality, strong sense of employee membership, and humane treatment—Digital Equipment (now part of Hewlett-Packard) and Polaroid—suffered greatly from market misjudgments and strategic errors. The aforementioned aspects of their culture contributed to their problems.

Second, if there are deep-rooted mind-sets, there would be a tendency to develop dysfunctional human resource practices. That is, the organization (or group) would continue to hire, reward, and promote like-minded people who tend to further intensify organizational inertia and erode innovation. Such homogeneity would increase over time and decrease the effectiveness of decision-making processes.

Third, the socialization processes (orientation, training, etc.) can be expensive in terms of both financial resources and managerial commitment. Such investments can represent a significant opportunity cost that should be evaluated in terms of the intended benefits. If such expenses become excessive, profitability would be adversely affected.

Finally, individuals may use the contacts they develop to pursue their own interests and agendas, which may be inconsistent with the organization's goals and objectives. Thus, they may distort or selectively use information to favor their preferred courses of action or withhold information in their own self-interest to enhance their power to the detriment of the common good. Drawing on our discussion of social networks, this is particularly true in an organization that has too many bridging relationships but not enough closure relationships. In high-closure groups, it is easier to watch each other to ensure that illegal or unethical acts don't occur. By contrast, bridging relationships make it easier for a person to play one group or individual off another, with no one being the wiser.[105] We will discuss some behavioral control mechanisms in Chapter 9 (rewards, control, boundaries) that reduce such dysfunctional behaviors and actions.[106]

LO 4-5

The vital role of technology in leveraging knowledge and human capital.

USING TECHNOLOGY TO LEVERAGE HUMAN CAPITAL AND KNOWLEDGE

Sharing knowledge and information throughout the organization can be a means of conserving resources, developing products and services, and creating new opportunities. In this section we will discuss how technology can be used to leverage human capital and knowledge within organizations as well as with customers and suppliers beyond their boundaries.

Using Networks to Share Information

As we all know, email is an effective means of communicating a wide variety of information. It is quick, easy, and almost costless. Of course, it can become a problem when employees use it extensively for personal reasons. And we all know how fast jokes or rumors can spread within and across organizations!

Email can also cause embarrassment, or worse, if one is not careful. Consider the plight of a potential CEO—as recalled by Marshall Goldsmith, a well-known executive coach:[107]

> I witnessed a series of e-mails between a potential CEO and a friend inside the company. The first e-mail to the friend provided an elaborate description of "why the current CEO is an idiot." The friend sent a reply. Several rounds of e-mails followed. Then the friend sent an e-mail containing a funny joke. The potential CEO decided that the current CEO would love this joke and forwarded it to him. You can guess what happened next. The CEO scrolled down the e-mail chain and found the "idiot" message. The heir apparent was gone in a week.

Email can, however, be a means for top executives to communicate information efficiently. For example, Martin Sorrell, chairman of WPP Group PLC, the huge $15 billion advertising and public relations firm, is a strong believer in the use of email.[108] He emails all of his employees once a month to discuss how the company is doing, address specific issues, and offer his perspectives on hot issues, such as new business models for the Internet. He believes that it keeps people abreast of what he is working on.

Technology can also enable much more sophisticated forms of communication in addition to knowledge sharing. Cisco, for example, launched Integrated Workforce Experience (IWE) in 2010.[109] It is a social business platform designed to facilitate internal and external collaboration and decentralize decision making. It functions much like a Facebook "wall": A real-time news feed provides updates on employees' status and activities as well as information about relevant communities, business projects, and customer and partner interactions. One manager likens it to Amazon. "It makes recommendations based on what you are doing, the role you are in, and the choices of other people like you. We are taking that to the enterprise level and basically allowing appropriate information to find you," he says.

Electronic Teams: Using Technology to Enhance Collaboration

LO 4-6

Why "electronic" or "virtual" teams are critical in combining and leveraging knowledge in organizations and how they can be made more effective.

Technology enables professionals to work as part of electronic, or virtual, teams to enhance the speed and effectiveness with which products are developed. For example, Microsoft has concentrated much of its development on **electronic teams** (or e-teams) that are networked together.[110] This helps to accelerate design and testing of new software modules that use the Windows-based framework as their central architecture. Microsoft is able to foster specialized technical expertise while sharing knowledge rapidly throughout the firm. This helps the firm learn how its new technologies can be applied rapidly to new business ventures such as cable television, broadcasting, travel services, and financial services.

What are electronic teams (or e-teams)? There are two key differences between e-teams and more traditional teams:[111]

electronic teams
a team of individuals that completes tasks primarily through email communication.

- E-team members either work in geographically separated workplaces or may work in the same space but at different times. E-teams may have members working in different spaces and time zones, as is the case with many multinational teams.
- Most of the interactions among members of e-teams occur through electronic communication channels such as fax machines and groupware tools such as email, bulletin boards, chat, and videoconferencing.

E-teams have expanded exponentially in recent years.[112] Organizations face increasingly high levels of complex and dynamic change. E-teams are also effective in helping businesses cope with global challenges. Most e-teams perform very complex tasks and most knowledge-based teams are charged with developing new products, improving organizational processes, and satisfying challenging customer problems. For example, Hewlett-Packard's e-teams solve clients' computing problems, and Sun Microsystems' (part of Oracle) e-teams generate new business models.

Advantages There are multiple advantages of e-teams.[113] In addition to the rather obvious use of technology to facilitate communications, the potential benefits parallel the other two major sections in this chapter—human capital and social capital.

First, e-teams are less restricted by the geographic constraints that are placed on face-to-face teams. Thus, e-teams have the potential to acquire a broader range of "human capital," or the skills and capacities that are necessary to complete complex assignments. So e-team leaders can draw upon a greater pool of talent to address a wider range of problems since they are not constrained by geographic space. Once formed, e-teams can be more flexible in responding to unanticipated work challenges and opportunities because team members can be rotated out of projects when demands and contingencies alter the team's objectives.

Second, e-teams can be very effective in generating "social capital"—the quality of relationships and networks that form. Such capital is a key lubricant in work transactions and operations. Given the broader boundaries associated with e-teams, members and leaders generally have access to a wider range of social contacts than would be typically available in more traditional face-to-face teams. Such contacts are often connected to a broader scope of clients, customers, constituents, and other key stakeholders.

Challenges   However, there are challenges associated with making e-teams effective. Successful action by both traditional teams and e-teams requires that:

- Members *identify* who among them can provide the most appropriate knowledge and resources.
- E-team leaders and key members know how to *combine* individual contributions in the most effective manner for a coordinated and appropriate response.

Group psychologists have termed such activities "identification and combination" activities, and teams that fail to perform them face a "process loss."[114] Process losses prevent teams from reaching high levels of performance because of inefficient interaction dynamics among team members. Such poor dynamics require that some collective energy, time, and effort be devoted to dealing with team inefficiencies, thus diverting the team away from its objectives. For example, if a team member fails to communicate important information at critical phases of a project, other members may waste time and energy. This can lead to conflict and resentment as well as to decreased motivation to work hard to complete tasks.

The potential for process losses tends to be more prevalent in e-teams than in traditional teams because the geographic dispersion of members increases the complexity of establishing effective interaction and exchanges. Generally, teams suffer process loss because of low cohesion, low trust among members, a lack of appropriate norms or standard operating procedures, or a lack of shared understanding among team members about their tasks. With e-teams, members are more geographically or temporally dispersed, and the team becomes more susceptible to the risk factors that can create process loss. Such problems can be exacerbated when team members have less than ideal competencies and social skills. This can erode problem-solving capabilities as well as the effective functioning of the group as a social unit.

A variety of technologies, from email and Internet groups to Skype have facilitated the formation and effective functioning of e-teams as well as a wide range of collaborations within companies. Such technologies greatly enhance the collaborative abilities of employees and managers within a company at a reasonable cost—despite the distances that separate them.

Codifying Knowledge for Competitive Advantage

There are two different kinds of knowledge. Tacit knowledge is embedded in personal experience and shared only with the consent and participation of the individual. Explicit (or codified) knowledge, on the other hand, is knowledge that can be documented, widely distributed, and easily replicated. One of the challenges of knowledge-intensive organizations is to capture and codify the knowledge and experience that, in effect, resides in the heads of its employees. Otherwise, they will have to constantly "reinvent the wheel," which

HOW SAP TAPS KNOWLEDGE WELL BEYOND ITS BOUNDARIES

Traditionally, organizations built and protected their knowledge stocks—proprietary resources that no one else could access. However, the more the business environment changes, the faster the value of what you know at any point in time diminishes. In today's world, success hinges on the ability to access a growing variety of knowledge flows in order to rapidly replenish the firm's knowledge stocks. For example, when an organization tries to improve cycle times in a manufacturing process, it finds far more value in problem solving shaped by the diverse experiences, perspectives, and learning of a tightly knit team (shared through knowledge flows) than in a training manual (knowledge stocks) alone.

Knowledge flows can help companies gain competitive advantage in an age of near-constant disruption. The software company SAP, for example, routinely taps the nearly 3 million participants in its Community Network, which extends well beyond the boundaries of the firm. By providing a virtual platform for customers, developers, system integrators, and service vendors to create and exchange knowledge, SAP has significantly increased the productivity of all the participants in its ecosystem.

According to Mark Yolton, senior vice president of SAP Communications and Social Media, "It's a very robust community with a great deal of activity. We see about 1.2 million unique visitors every month. Hundreds of millions of pages are viewed every year. There are 4,000 discussion forum posts every single day, 365 days a year, and about 115 blogs every day, 365 days a year, from any of the nearly 3 million members."

The site is open to everyone, regardless of whether you are a SAP customer, partner, or newcomer who needs to work with SAP technology. The site offers technical articles, web-based training, code samples, evaluation systems, discussion forums, and excellent blogs for community experts.

Sources: Yolton, M. 2012. SAP: Using social media for building, selling and supporting. *sloanreview.mit.edu*, August 7: np; Hagel, J., III., Brown, J. S., & Davison, L. 2009. The big shift: Measuring the forces of change. *Harvard Business Review*, 87(4): 87; and Anonymous. Undated. SAP developer network. *sap.sys-con.com*: np.

is both expensive and inefficient. Also, the "new wheel" may not necessarily be superior to the "old wheel."[115]

Once a knowledge asset (e.g., a software code or a process) is developed and paid for, it can be reused many times at very low cost, assuming that it doesn't have to be substantially modified each time. For example, Access Health, a call-in medical center, uses technology to capture and share knowledge. When someone calls the center, a registered nurse uses the company's "clinical decision architecture" to assess the caller's symptoms, rule out possible conditions, and recommend a home remedy, doctor's visit, or trip to the emergency room. The company's knowledge repository contains algorithms of the symptoms of more than 500 illnesses. According to CEO Joseph Tallman, "We are not inventing a new way to cure disease. We are taking available knowledge and inventing processes to put it to better use." The software algorithms were very expensive to develop, but the investment has been repaid many times over. The first 300 algorithms that Access Health developed have each been used an average of 8,000 times a year. Further, the company's paying customers— insurance companies and provider groups—save money because many callers would have made expensive trips to the emergency room or the doctor's office had they not been diagnosed over the phone.

The user community can be a major source of knowledge creation for a firm. Strategy Spotlight 4.5 highlights how SAP has been able to leverage the expertise and involvement of its users to develop new knowledge and transmit it to SAP's entire user community.

We close this section with a series of questions managers should consider in determining (1) how effective their organization is in attracting, developing, and retaining human capital and (2) how effective they are in leveraging human capital through social capital and technology. These questions, included in Exhibit 4.5, summarize some of the key issues addressed in this chapter.

EXHIBIT 4.5 Issues to Consider in Creating Value through Human Capital, Social Capital, and Technology

Human Capital

Recruiting "Top-Notch" Human Capital

- Does the organization assess attitude and "general makeup" instead of focusing primarily on skills and background in selecting employees at all levels?
- How important are creativity and problem-solving ability? Are they properly considered in hiring decisions?
- Do people throughout the organization engage in effective networking activities to obtain a broad pool of worthy potential employees? Is the organization creative in such endeavors?

Enhancing Human Capital through Employee Development

- Does the development and training process inculcate an "organizationwide" perspective?
- Is there widespread involvement, including top executives, in the preparation and delivery of training and development programs?
- Is the development of human capital effectively tracked and monitored?
- Are there effective programs for succession at all levels of the organization, especially at the topmost levels?
- Does the firm effectively evaluate its human capital? Is a 360-degree evaluation used? Why? Why not?
- Are mechanisms in place to ensure that a manager's success does not come at the cost of compromising the organization's core values?

Retaining the Best Employees

- Are there appropriate financial rewards to motivate employees at all levels?
- Do people throughout the organization strongly identify with the organization's mission?
- Are employees provided with a stimulating and challenging work environment that fosters professional growth?
- Are valued amenities provided (e.g., flextime, child care facilities, telecommuting) that are appropriate given the organization's mission, its strategy, and how work is accomplished?
- Is the organization continually devising strategies and mechanisms to retain top performers?

Social Capital

- Are there positive personal and professional relationships among employees?
- Is the organization benefiting (or being penalized) by hiring (or by voluntary turnover) en masse?
- Does an environment of caring and encouragement rather than competition enhance team performance?
- Do the social networks within the organization have the appropriate levels of closure and bridging relationships?
- Does the organization minimize the adverse effects of excessive social capital, such as excessive costs and "groupthink"?

Technology

- Has the organization used technologies such as email and networks to develop products and services?
- Does the organization effectively use technology to transfer best practices across the organization?
- Does the organization use technology to leverage human capital and knowledge both within the boundaries of the organization and among its suppliers and customers?
- Has the organization effectively used technology to codify knowledge for competitive advantage?
- Does the organization try to retain some of the knowledge of employees when they decide to leave the firm?

Source: Adapted from Dess, G. G., & Picken, J. C. 1999. *Beyond Productivity:* 63–64. New York: AMACON.

LO 4-7

The challenge of protecting intellectual property and the importance of a firm's dynamic capabilities.

PROTECTING THE INTELLECTUAL ASSETS OF THE ORGANIZATION: INTELLECTUAL PROPERTY AND DYNAMIC CAPABILITIES

In today's dynamic and turbulent world, unpredictability and fast change dominate the business environment. Firms can use technology, attract human capital, or tap into research and design networks to get access to pretty much the same information as their competitors.

So what would give firms a sustainable competitive advantage?[116] Protecting a firm's intellectual property requires a concerted effort on the part of the company. After all, employees become disgruntled and patents expire. The management of intellectual property (IP) involves, besides patents, contracts with confidentiality and noncompete clauses, copyrights, and the development of trademarks. Moreover, developing dynamic capabilities is the only avenue providing firms with the ability to reconfigure their knowledge and activities to achieve a sustainable competitive advantage.

Intellectual Property Rights

Intellectual property rights are more difficult to define and protect than property rights for physical assets (e.g., plant, equipment, and land). However, if intellectual property rights are not reliably protected by the state, there will be no incentive to develop new products and services. Property rights have been enshrined in constitutions and rules of law in many countries. In the information era, though, adjustments need to be made to accommodate the new realities of knowledge. Knowledge and information are fundamentally different assets from the physical ones that property rights have been designed to protect.

> **intellectual property rights**
> intangible property owned by a firm in the forms of patents, copyrights, trademarks, or trade secrets.

The protection of intellectual rights raises unique issues, compared to physical property rights. IP is characterized by significant development costs and very low marginal costs. Indeed, it may take a substantial investment to develop a software program, an idea, or a digital music tune. Once developed, though, its reproduction and distribution cost may be almost zero, especially if the Internet is used. Effective protection of intellectual property is necessary before any investor will finance such an undertaking. Appropriation of investors' returns is harder to police since possession and deployment are not as readily observable. Unlike physical assets, intellectual property can be stolen by simply broadcasting it. Recall Napster and MP3 as well as the debates about counterfeit software, music CDs, and DVDs coming from developing countries such as China. Part of the problem is that using an idea does not prevent others from simultaneously using it for their own benefit, which is typically impossible with physical assets. Moreover, new ideas are frequently built on old ideas and are not easily traceable.

Given these unique challenges in protecting IP, it comes as no surprise that legal battles over patents become commonplace in IP-heavy industries such as telecommunications. Take the recent patent battles Apple has been fighting against smartphone makers running Android, Google's mobile operating system.[117]

> In 2012, Apple and HTC, a Taiwanese smartphone maker, agreed to dismiss a series of lawsuits filed against each other after Apple accused HTC of copying the iPhone. While this settlement may be a sign that Apple's new CEO, Timothy Cook, is eager to end the distractions caused by IP-related litigation, other patent battles continue, including one between Apple and Samsung, the largest maker of Android phones. This legal battle involves much higher stakes, because Samsung shipped almost eight times as many Android smartphones as HTC in the third quarter of 2012. However, Apple's new leadership seems to be more pragmatic about this issue. In Mr. Cook's words, "It is awkward. I hate litigation. I absolutely hate it," suggesting that he is not as enthusiastic a combatant in the patent wars as was his predecessor, Steve Jobs, who famously promised to "destroy Android, because it's a stolen product."

> **dynamic capabilities**
> a firm's capacity to build and protect a competitive advantage, which rests on knowledge, assets, competencies, complementary assets, and technologies. Dynamic capabilities include the ability to sense and seize new opportunities, generate new knowledge, and reconfigure existing assets and capabilities.

Countries are attempting to pass new legislation to cope with developments in new pharmaceutical compounds, stem cell research, and biotechnology. However, a firm that is faced with this challenge today cannot wait for the legislation to catch up. New technological developments, software solutions, electronic games, online services, and other products and services contribute to our economic prosperity and the creation of wealth for those entrepreneurs who have the idea first and risk bringing it to the market.

Dynamic Capabilities

Dynamic capabilities entail the capacity to build and protect a competitive advantage.[118] This rests on knowledge, assets, competencies, and complementary assets and

Does Providing Financial Incentives to Employees to Lose Weight Actually Work?

Assume your employer offered each of its staff $550 to lose weight, an amount that would be subtracted from their health insurance premiums the following year. Do you think it would work? Would it provide enough incentive for some of the employees to shed the pounds?

Approximately four out of five large employers in the United States now offer some type of financial incentive for employees to improve their health. And the Affordable Care Act has encouraged such programs by significantly increasing the amount of money, in the form of a percentage of insurance premiums, that employers can reward (or take away) to improve health factors such as body mass index, blood pressure and cholesterol, as well as for ending the use of tobacco.

Several professors and medical professionals decided to test whether or not incentives actually work. Employees were randomly assigned to two conditions: one group in which employees were offered the $550 incentive and another group—the control group—in which no incentive was offered. After one year the results were reported in the journal *Health Affairs*. The result: Employees assigned to the control group that received no financial incentive had no change in their weight. However, employees who were offered the $550 incentive also didn't lose weight.

Discussion Questions

1. Why do you think the $550 incentive did not result in people losing weight?
2. Can you think of how incentives could have been structured to be more successful?

Source: Patel, M. S., Asch, D. A., & Volpp, K. G. 2016. Does paying employees to lose weight work? *Dallas Morning News*, March 20: 1P, 5P.

---

technologies as well as the ability to sense and seize new opportunities, generate new knowledge, and reconfigure existing assets and capabilities.[119] According to David Teece, an economist at the University of California at Berkeley, dynamic capabilities are related to the entrepreneurial side of the firm and are built within a firm through its environmental and technological "sensing" apparatus, its choices of organizational form, and its collective ability to strategize. Dynamic capabilities are about the ability of an organization to challenge the conventional wisdom within its industry and market, learn and innovate, adapt to the changing world, and continuously adopt new ways to serve the evolving needs of the market.[120]

Examples of dynamic capabilities include product development, strategic decision making, alliances, and acquisitions.[121] Some firms have clearly developed internal processes and routines that make them superior in such activities. For example, 3M and Apple are ahead of their competitors in product development. Cisco Systems has made numerous acquisitions over the years. Cisco seems to have developed the capability to identify and evaluate potential acquisition candidates and seamlessly integrate them once the acquisition is completed. Other organizations can try to copy Cisco's practices. However, Cisco's combination of the resources of the acquired companies and their reconfiguration that Cisco has already achieved places it well ahead of its competitors. As markets become increasingly dynamic, traditional sources of long-term competitive advantage become less relevant. In such markets, all that a firm can strive for are a series of temporary advantages. Dynamic capabilities allow a firm to create this series of temporary advantages through new resource configurations.[122]

Reflecting on Career Implications . . .

This chapter focuses on the growing importance of intellectual assets in the valuation of firms. Since improved organizational performance occurs when firms effectively combine human capital, social capital, and technology, the following questions help students to consider how they can leverage their talents though relationships and technology.

■ **Human Capital:** Identify specific steps taken by your organization to effectively attract, develop, and retain talent. If you cannot identify such steps, you may have fewer career opportunities to develop your human capital at your organization. Do you take advantage of your organization's human resource programs, such as tuition reimbursement, mentoring, and so forth?

■ **Human Capital:** As workplaces become more diverse, it is important to reflect on whether your organization values diversity. What kinds of diversity seem to be encouraged (e.g., age-based or ethnicity-based)? In what ways are your colleagues different from and similar to you? If your firm has a homogeneous workforce, there may be limited perspectives on strategic and operational issues and a career at this organization may be less attractive to you.

■ **Social Capital:** Does your organization have strong social capital? What is the basis of your conclusion that it has strong or weak social capital? What specific programs are in place to build and develop social capital? What is the impact of social capital on employee turnover in your organization? Alternatively, is social capital so strong that you see effects such as "groupthink"? From your perspective, how might you better leverage social capital toward pursuing other career opportunities?

■ **Social Capital:** Are you actively working to build a strong social network at your work organization? To advance your career, strive to build a broad network that gives you access to diverse information.

■ **Technology:** Does your organization provide and effectively use technology (e.g., groupware, knowledge management systems) to help you leverage your talents and expand your knowledge base? If your organization does a poor job in this regard, what can you do on your own to expand your knowledge base using technology available outside the organization?

---

summary

Firms throughout the industrial world are recognizing that the knowledge worker is the key to success in the marketplace. However, they also recognize that human capital, although vital, is still only a necessary, but not a sufficient, condition for creating value. We began the first section of the chapter by addressing the importance of human capital and how it can be attracted, developed, and retained. Then we discussed the role of social capital and technology in leveraging human capital for competitive success. We pointed out that intellectual capital—the difference between a firm's market value and its book value—has increased significantly over the past few decades. This is particularly true for firms in knowledge-intensive industries, especially where there are relatively few tangible assets, such as software development.

The second section of the chapter addressed the attraction, development, and retention of human capital. We viewed these three activities as a "three-legged stool"—that is, it is difficult for firms to be successful if they ignore or are unsuccessful in any one of these activities. Among the issues we discussed in *attracting* human capital were "hiring for attitude, training for skill" and the value of using social networks to attract human capital. In particular, it is important to attract employees who can collaborate with others, given the importance of collective efforts such as teams and task forces. With regard to *developing* human capital, we discussed the need to encourage widespread involvement throughout the organization, monitor progress and track the development of human capital, and evaluate

human capital. Among the issues that are widely practiced in evaluating human capital is the 360-degree evaluation system. Employees are evaluated by their superiors, peers, direct reports, and even internal and external customers. We also addressed the value of maintaining a diverse workforce. Finally, some mechanisms for retaining human capital are employees' identification with the organization's mission and values, providing challenging work and a stimulating environment, the importance of financial and nonfinancial rewards and incentives, and providing flexibility and amenities. A key issue here is that a firm should not overemphasize financial rewards. After all, if individuals join an organization for money, they also are likely to leave for money. With money as the primary motivator, there is little chance that employees will develop firm-specific ties to keep them with the organization.

The third section of the chapter discussed the importance of social capital in leveraging human capital. Social capital refers to the network of relationships that individuals have throughout the organization as well as with customers and suppliers. Such ties can be critical in obtaining both information and resources. With regard to recruiting, for example, we saw how some firms are able to hire en masse groups of individuals who are part of social networks. Social relationships can also be very important in the effective functioning of groups. Finally, we discussed some of the potential downsides of social capital. These include the expenses that firms may bear when promoting social and working relationships among individuals as well as the potential for "groupthink," wherein individuals are reluctant to express divergent (or opposing) views on an issue because of social pressures to conform. We also introduced the concept of social networks. The relative advantages of being central in a network versus bridging multiple networks was discussed. We addressed the key role that social networks can play in both improving knowledge management and promoting career success.

The fourth section addressed the role of technology in leveraging human capital. We discussed relatively simple means of using technology, such as email and networks where individuals can collaborate by way of personal computers. We provided suggestions and guidelines on how electronic teams can be effectively managed. We also addressed more sophisticated uses of technology, such as sophisticated management systems. Here, knowledge can be codified and reused at very low cost, as we saw in the examples of firms in the consulting, health care, and high-technology industries.

In the last section we discussed the increasing importance of protecting a firm's intellectual property. Although traditional approaches such as patents, copyrights, and trademarks are important, the development of dynamic capabilities may be the best protection in the long run.

SUMMARY REVIEW QUESTIONS

1. Explain the role of knowledge in today's competitive environment.
2. Why is it important for managers to recognize the interdependence in the attraction, development, and retention of talented professionals?
3. What are some of the potential downsides for firms that engage in a "war for talent"?
4. Discuss the need for managers to use social capital in leveraging their human capital both within and across their firm.
5. Discuss the key role of technology in leveraging knowledge and human capital.

key terms	
	social capital 106
	explicit knowledge 106
	tacit knowledge 106
	360-degree evaluation and
	feedback systems 113
knowledge economy 104	social network analysis 120
intellectual capital 106	closure 121
human capital 106	bridging relationships 122

structural holes 122
groupthink 123
electronic teams 125

intellectual property
rights 129
dynamic capabilities 129

EXPERIENTIAL EXERCISE

Pfizer, a leading health care firm with $52 billion in revenues, is often rated as one of *Fortune*'s "Most Admired Firms." It is also considered an excellent place to work and has generated high return to shareholders. Clearly, Pfizer values its human capital. Using the Internet and/or library resources, identify some of the actions/strategies Pfizer has taken to attract, develop, and retain human capital. What are their implications? (Fill in the table at bottom of the page.)

APPLICATION QUESTIONS & EXERCISES

1. Look up successful firms in a high-technology industry as well as two successful firms in more traditional industries such as automobile manufacturing and retailing. Compare their market values and book values. What are some implications of these differences?
2. Select a firm for which you believe its social capital—both within the firm and among its suppliers and customers—is vital to its competitive advantage. Support your arguments.
3. Choose a company with which you are familiar. What are some of the ways in which it uses technology to leverage its human capital?
4. Using the Internet, look up a company with which you are familiar. What are some of the policies and procedures that it uses to enhance the firm's human and social capital?

ETHICS QUESTIONS

1. Recall an example of a firm that recently faced an ethical crisis. How do you feel the crisis and management's handling of it affected the firm's human capital and social capital?
2. Based on your experiences or what you have learned in your previous classes, are you familiar with any companies that used unethical practices to attract talented professionals? What do you feel were the short-term and long-term consequences of such practices?

Activity	Actions/Strategies	Implications
Attracting human capital		
Developing human capital		
Retaining human capital		

REFERENCES

1. Parts of this chapter draw upon some of the ideas and examples from Dess, G. G. & Picken, J. C. 1999. *Beyond productivity.* New York: AMACOM.

2. Dekas, K. H., et al. 2013. Organizational citizenship behavior, version 2.0: A review and qualitative investigation of OCBs for knowledge workers at Google and beyond. *Academy of Management Perspectives,* 27(3): 219-237.

3. Stewart, T. A. 1997. *Intellectual capital: The new wealth of organizations.* New York: Doubleday/Currency.

4. Colvin, G. 2015. The 100 best companies to work for. *Fortune.* March 15: 109.

5. Stewart, T. A. 2001. Accounting gets radical. *Fortune,* April 16: 184-194.

6. Adams, S. & Kichen, S. 2008. Ben Graham then and now. *Forbes, www. multpl.com/s-p-500-price-to-book,* November 10: 56.

7. An interesting discussion of Steve Jobs's impact on Apple's valuation is in Lashinsky, A. 2009. Steve's leave— what does it really mean? *Fortune,* February 2: 96-102.

8. Anonymous. 2007. Intel opens first high volume 45 nm microprocessor manufacturing factory. *www.intel.com,* October 25: np.

9. Thomas Stewart has suggested this formula in his book *Intellectual capital.* He provides an insightful discussion on pages 224-225, including some of the limitations of this approach to measuring intellectual capital. We recognize, of course, that during the late 1990s and in early 2000, there were some excessive market valuations of high-technology and Internet firms. For an interesting discussion of the extraordinary market valuation of Yahoo!, an Internet company, refer to Perkins, A. B. 2001. The Internet bubble encapsulated: Yahoo! *Red Herring,* April 15: 17-18.

10. Roberts, P. W. & Dowling, G. R. 2002. Corporate reputation and sustained superior financial performance. *Strategic Management Journal,* 23(12): 1077-1095.

11. For a study on the relationships between human capital, learning, and sustainable competitive advantage, read Hatch, N. W. & Dyer, J. H. 2005. Human capital and learning as a source of sustainable competitive advantage. *Strategic Management Journal,* 25: 1155-1178.

12. One of the seminal contributions on knowledge management is Becker, G. S. 1993. *Human capital: A theoretical and empirical analysis with special reference to education* (3rd ed.). Chicago: University of Chicago Press.

13. For an excellent overview of the topic of social capital, read Baron, R. A. 2005. Social capital. In Hitt, M. A. & Ireland, R. D. (Eds.), *The Blackwell encyclopedia of management* (2nd ed.): 224-226. Malden, MA: Blackwell.

14. For an excellent discussion of social capital and its impact on organizational performance, refer to Nahapiet, J. & Ghoshal, S. 1998. Social capital, intellectual capital, and the organizational advantage. *Academy of Management Review,* 23: 242-266.

15. An interesting discussion of how knowledge management (patents) can enhance organizational performance can be found in Bogner, W. C. & Bansal, P. 2007. Knowledge management as the basis of sustained high performance. *Journal of Management Studies,* 44(1): 165-188.

16. Polanyi, M. 1967. *The tacit dimension.* Garden City, NY: Anchor.

17. Barney, J. B. 1991. Firm resources and sustained competitive advantage. *Journal of Management,* 17: 99-120.

18. For an interesting perspective of empirical research on how knowledge can adversely affect performance, read Haas, M. R. & Hansen, M. T. 2005. When using knowledge can hurt performance: The value of organizational capabilities in a management consulting company. *Strategic Management Journal,* 26(1): 1-24.

19. New insights on managing talent are provided in Cappelli, P. 2008. Talent management for the twenty-first century. *Harvard Business Review,* 66(3): 74-81.

20. Some of the notable books on this topic include Edvisson & Malone, op. cit.; Stewart, op. cit.; and Nonaka, I. & Takeuchi, I. 1995. *The knowledge creating company.* New York: Oxford University Press.

21. Segalla, M. & Felton, N. 2010. Find the real power in your organization. *Harvard Business Review,* 88(5): 34-35.

22. Stewart, T. A. 2000. Taking risk to the marketplace. *Fortune,* March 6: 424.

23. Lobel, O. 2014. *Talent wants to be free.* New Haven, CT: Yale University Press.

24. Insights on Generation X's perspective on the workplace are in Erickson, T. J. 2008. Task, not time: Profile of a Gen Y job. *Harvard Business Review,* 86(2): 19.

25. Pfeffer, J. 2010. Building sustainable organizations: The human factor. *Academy of Management Perspectives,* 24(1): 34-45.

26. Lobel, op. cit.

27. Some workplace implications for the aging workforce are addressed in Strack, R., Baier, J., & Fahlander, A. 2008. Managing demographic risk. *Harvard Business Review,* 66(2): 119-128.

28. For a discussion of attracting, developing, and retaining top talent, refer to Goffee, R. & Jones, G. 2007. Leading clever people. *Harvard Business Review,* 85(3): 72-89.

29. Winston, A. S. 2014. *The big pivot.* Boston: Harvard Business Review Press.

30. Dess & Picken, op. cit., p. 34.

31. Webber, A. M. 1998. Danger: Toxic company. *Fast Company,* November: 152-161.

32. Martin, J. & Schmidt, C. 2010. How to keep your top talent. *Harvard Business Review,* 88(5): 54-61.

33. Some interesting insights on why home-grown American talent is going abroad are found in Saffo, P. 2009. A looming American diaspora. *Harvard Business Review,* 87(2): 27.

34. Grossman, M. 2012. The best advice I ever got. *Fortune,* May 12: 119.

35. Davenport, T. H., Harris, J., & Shapiro, J. 2010. Competing on talent analytics. *Harvard Business Review,* 88(10): 62-69.

36. Ployhart, R. E. & Moliterno, T. P. 2011. Emergence of the human capital resource: A multilevel model. *Academy of Management Review,* 36(1): 127-150.

37. For insights on management development and firm performance in several countries, refer to Mabey, C. 2008. Management development and firm performance in Germany, Norway, Spain, and the UK. *Journal of International Business Studies,* 39(8): 1327-1342.

38. Martin, J. 1998. So, you want to work for the best. . . . *Fortune,* January 12: 77.

39. Cardin, R. 1997. Make your own Bozo Filter. *Fast Company,* October-November: 56.

40. Anonymous. 100 best companies to work for. *money.cnn.com,* undated: np.

41. Martin, op. cit.; Henkoff, R. 1993. Companies that train best. *Fortune,* March 22: 53-60.

42. This section draws on: Garg, V. 2012. Here's why companies should give Millennial workers everything they ask for. *buisnessinsider.com,*

August 23: np; *worklifepolicy.com*; and Gerdes, L. 2006. The top 50 employers for new college grads. *BusinessWeek,* September 18: 64–81.

43. An interesting perspective on developing new talent rapidly when they join an organization can be found in Rollag, K., Parise, S., & Cross, R. 2005. Getting new hires up to speed quickly. *MIT Sloan Management Review,* 46(2): 35–41.

44. Stewart, T. A. 1998. Gray flannel suit? Moi? *Fortune,* March 18: 80–82.

45. Bryant, A. 2011. *The corner office.* New York: St. Martin's Griffin, 227.

46. An interesting perspective on how Cisco Systems develops its talent can be found in Chatman, J., O'Reilly, C., & Chang, V. 2005. Cisco Systems: Developing a human capital strategy. *California Management Review,* 47(2): 137–166.

47. Anonymous. 2011. Schumpeter: The tussle for talent. *The Economist,* January 8: 68.

48. Training and development policy: Mentoring. *opm.gov:* undated, np.

49. Douglas, C. A. 1997. Formal mentoring programs in organizations. *centerforcreativeleadership.org:* np.

50. Warner, F. 2002. Inside Intel's mentoring movement. *fastcompany.com,* March 31: np.

51. Grove, A. 2011. Be a mentor. *Bloomberg Businessweek,* September 21: 80.

52. Colvin, G. 2016. Developing an internal market for talent. *Fortune.* March 1: 22.

53. For an innovative perspective on the appropriateness of alternate approaches to evaluation and rewards, refer to Seijts, G. H. & Lathan, G. P. 2005. Learning versus performance goals: When should each be used? *Academy of Management Executive,* 19(1): 124–132.

54. The discussion of the 360-degree feedback system draws on the article UPS. 1997. 360-degree feedback: Coming from all sides. *Vision* (a UPS Corporation internal company publication), March: 3; Slater, R. 1994. *Get better or get beaten: Thirty-one leadership secrets from Jack Welch.* Burr Ridge, IL: Irwin; Nexon, M. 1997. General Electric: The secrets of the finest company in the world. *L'Expansion,* July 23: 18–30; and Smith, D. 1996. Bold new directions for human resources. *Merck World* (internal company publication), October: 8.

55. Interesting insights on 360-degree evaluation systems are discussed in Barwise, P. & Meehan, Sean. 2008.

So you think you're a good listener. *Harvard Business Review,* 66(4): 22–23.

56. Insights into the use of 360-degree evaluation are in Kaplan, R. E. & Kaiser, R. B. 2009. Stop overdoing your strengths. *Harvard Business Review,* 87(2): 100–103.

57. Mankins, M., Bird, A., & Root, J. 2013. Making star teams out of star players. *Harvard Business Review,* 91(1/2): 74–78.

58. Kets de Vries, M. F. R. 1998. Charisma in action: The transformational abilities of Virgin's Richard Branson and ABB's Percy Barnevik. *Organizational Dynamics,* Winter: 20.

59. For an interesting discussion on how organizational culture has helped Zappos become number one in *Fortune*'s 2009 survey of the best companies to work for, see O'Brien, J. M. 2009. Zappos knows how to kick it. *Fortune,* February 2: 54–58.

60. We have only to consider the most celebrated case of industrial espionage in recent years, wherein José Ignacio Lopez was indicted in a German court for stealing sensitive product planning documents from his former employer, General Motors, and sharing them with his executive colleagues at Volkswagen. The lawsuit was dismissed by the German courts, but Lopez and his colleagues were investigated by the U.S. Justice Department. Also consider the recent litigation involving noncompete employment contracts and confidentiality clauses of *International Paper v. Louisiana-Pacific, Campbell Soup v. H. J. Heinz Co.,* and *PepsiCo v. Quaker Oats's Gatorade.* In addition to retaining valuable human resources and often their valuable network of customers, firms must also protect proprietary information and knowledge. For interesting insights, refer to Carley, W. M. 1998. CEO gets hard lesson in how not to keep his lieutenants. *The Wall Street Journal,* February 11: A1, A10; and Lenzner, R. & Shook, C. 1998. Whose Rolodex is it, anyway? *Forbes,* February 23: 100–103.

61. For an insightful discussion of retention of knowledge workers in today's economy, read Davenport, T. H. 2005. *The care and feeding of the knowledge worker.* Boston, MA: Harvard Business School Press.

62. Weber, L. 2014. Here's what boards want in executives. *The Wall Street Journal,* December 10: B5.

63. Fisher, A. 2008. America's most admired companies. *Fortune,* March 17: 74.

64. Stewart, T. A. 2001. *The wealth of knowledge,* New York: Currency.

65. For insights on fulfilling one's potential, refer to Kaplan, R. S. 2008. Reaching your potential. *Harvard Business Review,* 66(7/8): 45–57.

66. Amabile, T. M. 1997. Motivating creativity in organizations: On doing what you love and loving what you do. *California Management Review,* Fall: 39–58.

67. For an insightful perspective on alternate types of employee–employer relationships, read Erickson, T. J. & Gratton, L. 2007. What it means to work here. *Harvard Business Review,* 85(3): 104–112.

68. Little, L. 2016. Leadership innovation. *Baylor Magazine.* Winter: 31.

69. Ignatius, A. & McGinn, D. 2015. The best performing CEOs in the world. *Harvard Business Review,* 93(11): 63.

70. Pfeffer, J. 2001. Fighting the war for talent is hazardous to your organization's health. *Organizational Dynamics,* 29(4): 248–259.

71. Best companies to work for 2011. 2011. *finance.yahoo.com,* January 20: np.

72. This section draws on Dewhurst, M., Hancock, B., & Ellsworth, D. 2013. Redesigning knowledge work. *Harvard Business Review,* 91 (1/2): 58–64.

73. Cox, T. L. 1991. The multinational organization. *Academy of Management Executive,* 5(2): 34–47. Without doubt, a great deal has been written on the topic of creating and maintaining an effective diverse workforce. Some excellent, recent books include Harvey, C. P. & Allard, M. J. 2005. *Understanding and managing diversity: Readings, cases, and exercises* (3rd ed.). Upper Saddle River, NJ: Pearson Prentice-Hall; Miller, F. A. & Katz, J. H. 2002. *The inclusion breakthrough: Unleashing the real power of diversity.* San Francisco: Berrett Koehler; and Williams, M. A. 2001. *The 10 lenses: Your guide to living and working in a multicultural world.* Sterling, VA: Capital Books.

74. For an interesting perspective on benefits and downsides of diversity in global consulting firms, refer to Mors, M. L. 2010. Innovation in a global consulting firm: When the problem is too much diversity. *Strategic Management Journal,* 31(8): 841–872.

75. Day, J. C. Undated. National population projections. *cps.ipums.org:* np.

76. Hewlett, S. A. & Rashid, R. 2010. The battle for female talent in emerging markets. *Harvard Business Review,* 88(5): 101–107.

77. This section, including the six potential benefits of a diverse workforce, draws on Cox, T. H. & Blake, S. 1991. Managing cultural diversity: Implications for organizational competitiveness. *Academy of Management Executive,* 5(3): 45-56.

78. *www.pwcglobal.com/us/eng/careers/diversity/index.html.*

79. Hewlett, S. A., Marshall, M., & Sherbin, L. 2013. How diversity can drive innovation. *Harvard Business Review,* 91(12): 30.

80. This discussion draws on Dess, G. G. & Lumpkin, G. T. 2001. Emerging issues in strategy process research. In Hitt, M. A., Freeman, R. E., & Harrison, J. S. (Eds.), *Handbook of strategic management:* 3-34. Malden, MA: Blackwell.

81. Wong, S.-S. & Boh, W. F. 2010. Leveraging the ties of others to build a reputation for trustworthiness among peers. *Academy of Management Journal,* 53(1): 129-148.

82. Adler, P. S. & Kwon, S. W. 2002. Social capital: Prospects for a new concept. *Academy of Management Review,* 27(1): 17-40.

83. Capelli, P. 2000. A market-driven approach to retaining talent. *Harvard Business Review,* 78(1): 103-113.

84. This hypothetical example draws on Peteraf, M. 1993. The cornerstones of competitive advantage. *Strategic Management Journal,* 14: 179-191.

85. Wernerfelt, B. 1984. A resource-based view of the firm. *Strategic Management Journal,* 5: 171-180.

86. Wysocki, B., Jr. 2000. Yet another hazard of the new economy: The Pied Piper effect. *The Wall Street Journal,* March 20: A1-A16.

87. Ideas on how managers can more effectively use their social network are addressed in McGrath, C. & Zell, D. 2009. Profiles of trust: Who to turn to, and for what. *MIT Sloan Management Review,* 50(2): 75-80.

88. Ibid.

89. Buckman, R. C. 2000. Tech defectors from Microsoft resettle together. *The Wall Street Journal,* October: B1-B6.

90. Malone, T., The Future of Work. Boston, MA: Harvard Business School Press, April 2004.

91. Aime, F., Johnson, S., Ridge, J. W., & Hill, A. D. 2010. The routine may be stable but the advantage is not: Competitive implications of key employee mobility. *Strategic Management Journal,* 31(1): 75-87.

92. Ibarra, H. & Hansen, M. T. 2011. Are you a collaborative leader? *Harvard Business Review,* 89(7/8): 68-74.

93. Battilana, J. & Casciaro, T. 2013. The network secrets of great change agents. *Harvard Business Review,* 91(7/8): 62-68.

94. There has been a tremendous amount of theory building and empirical research in recent years in the area of social network analysis. Unquestionably, two of the major contributors to this domain have been Ronald Burt and J. S. Coleman. For excellent background discussions, refer to Burt, R. S. 1992. *Structural holes: The social structure of competition.* Cambridge, MA: Harvard University Press; Coleman, J. S. 1990. *Foundations of social theory.* Cambridge, MA: Harvard University Press; and Coleman, J. S. 1988. Social capital in the creation of human capital. *American Journal of Sociology,* 94: S95-S120. For a more recent review and integration of current thought on social network theory, consider Burt, R. S. 2005. *Brokerage & closure: An introduction to social capital.* New York: Oxford Press.

95. Our discussion draws on the concepts developed by Burt, 1992, op. cit.; Coleman, 1990, op. cit.; Coleman, 1988, op. cit.; and Oh, H., Chung, M., & Labianca, G. 2004. Group social capital and group effectiveness: The role of informal socializing ties. *Academy of Management Journal,* 47(6): 860-875. We would like to thank Joe Labianca (University of Kentucky) for his helpful feedback and ideas in our discussion of social networks.

96. Arregle, J. L., Hitt, M. A., Sirmon, D. G., & Very, P. 2007. The development of organizational social capital: Attributes of family firms. *Journal of Management Studies,* 44(1): 73-95.

97. A novel perspective on social networks is in Pentland, A. 2009. How social networks network best. *Harvard Business Review,* 87(2): 37.

98. Oh et al., op. cit.

99. *Hoppe, B. 2004. Good ideas at Raytheon and big holes in our own backyard. connectedness.blogspot.com, July 8: np.*

100. Perspectives on how to use and develop decision networks are discussed in Cross, R., Thomas, R. J., & Light, D. A. 2009. How "who you know" affects what you decide. *MIT Sloan Management Review,* 50(2): 35-42.

101. Our discussion of the three advantages of social networks draws on Uzzi, B. & Dunlap. S. 2005. How to build your network. *Harvard Business Review,* 83(12): 53-60. For an excellent review on the research exploring the relationship between social capital and managerial performance, read Moran, P. 2005. Structural vs. relational embeddedness: Social capital and managerial performance. *Strategic Management Journal,* 26(12): 1129-1151.

102. A perspective on personal influence is in Christakis, N. A. 2009. The dynamics of personal influence. *Harvard Business Review,* 87(2): 31.

103. Prusak, L. & Cohen, D. 2001. How to invest in social capital. *Harvard Business Review,* 79(6): 86-93.

104. Leonard, D. & Straus, S. 1997. Putting your company's whole brain to work. *Harvard Business Review,* 75(4): 110-122.

105. For an excellent discussion of public (i.e., the organization) versus private (i.e., the individual manager) benefits of social capital, refer to Leana, C. R. & Van Buren, H. J. 1999. Organizational social capital and employment practices. *Academy of Management Review,* 24(3): 538-555.

106. The authors would like to thank Joe Labianca, University of Kentucky, and John Lin, University of Texas at Dallas, for their very helpful input in our discussion of social network theory and its practical implications.

107. Goldsmith, M. 2009. How not to lose the top job. *Harvard Business Review,* 87(1): 74.

108. Taylor, W. C. 1999. Whatever happened to globalization? *Fast Company,* December: 228-236.

109. Wilson, H. J., Guinan, P. J., Paris, S., & Weinberg, D. 2011. What's your social media strategy? *Harvard Business Review,* 89(7/8): 23-25.

110. Lei, D., Slocum, J., & Pitts, R. A. 1999. Designing organizations for competitive advantage: The power of unlearning and learning. *Organizational Dynamics,* Winter: 24-38.

111. This section draws upon Zaccaro, S. J. & Bader, P. 2002. E-leadership and the challenges of leading e-teams: Minimizing the bad and maximizing the good. *Organizational Dynamics,* 31(4): 377-387.

112. Kirkman, B. L., Rosen, B., Tesluk, P. E., & Gibson, C. B. 2004. The impact of team empowerment on virtual team performance: The moderating role of face-to-face interaction. *Academy of Management Journal,* 47(2): 175-192.

113. The discussion of the advantages and challenges associated with e-teams draws on Zaccaro & Bader, op. cit.

114. For a study exploring the relationship between team empowerment, face-to-face interaction, and performance in virtual teams, read Kirkman, Rosen, Tesluk, & Gibson, op. cit.

115. For an innovative study on how firms share knowledge with competitors and the performance implications, read Spencer, J. W. 2003. Firms' knowledge sharing strategies in the global innovation system: Empirical evidence from the flat panel display industry. *Strategic Management Journal,* 24(3): 217-235.

116. This discussion draws on Conley, J. G. 2005. *Intellectual capital management.* Kellogg School of Management and Schulich School of Business, York University, Toronto, ON; Conley, J. G. & Szobocsan, J. 2001. Snow White shows the way. *Managing Intellectual P02roperty,* June: 15-25; Greenspan, A. 2004. Intellectual property rights. Federal Reserve Board, Remarks by the chairman, February 27; and Teece, D. J. 1998. Capturing value from knowledge assets. *California Management Review,* 40(3): 54-79. The authors would like to thank Professor Theo Peridis, York University, for his contribution to this section.

117. Wingfield, N. 2012. As Apple and HTC end lawsuits, smartphone patent battles continue. *New York Times, www.nytimes.com,* November 11: 57-63; and Tyrangiel, J. 2012. Tim Cook's freshman year: The Apple CEO speaks. *Bloomberg Businessweek,* December 6: 62-76.

118. E. Danneels. 2011. Trying to become a different type of company: Dynamic capability at Smith Corona. *Strategic Management Journal,* 32(1): 1-31.

119. A study of the relationship between dynamic capabilities and related diversification is Doving, E. & Gooderham, P. N. 2008. *Strategic Management Journal,* 29(8): 841-858.

120. A perspective on strategy in turbulent markets is in Sull, D. 2009. How to thrive in turbulent markets. *Harvard Business Review,* 87(2): 78-88.

121. Lee, G. K. 2008. Relevance of organizational capabilities and its dynamics: What to learn from entrants' product portfolios about the determinants of entry timing. *Strategic Management Journal,* 29(12): 1257-1280.

122. Eisenhardt, K. M. & Martin, J. E. 2000. Dynamic capabilities: What are they? *Strategic Management Journal,* 21: 1105-1121.

5

Business-Level Strategy

Creating and Sustaining Competitive Advantages

After reading this chapter, you should have a good understanding of the following learning objectives:

LO5-1 The central role of competitive advantage in the study of strategic management and the three generic strategies: overall cost leadership, differentiation, and focus.

LO5-2 How the successful attainment of generic strategies can improve a firm's relative power vis-à-vis the five forces that determine an industry's average profitability.

LO5-3 The pitfalls managers must avoid in striving to attain generic strategies.

LO5-4 How firms can effectively combine the generic strategies of overall cost leadership and differentiation.

LO5-5 What factors determine the sustainability of a firm's competitive advantage.

LO5-6 The importance of considering the industry life cycle to determine a firm's **business-level strategy** and its relative emphasis on functional area strategies and value-creating activities.

LO5-7 The need for turnaround strategies that enable a firm to reposition its competitive position in an industry.

©Anatoli Styf/Shutterstock

LEARNING FROM MISTAKES

A&P was the first traditional supermarket operator in the United States, with its roots going back to 1859. In its heyday, the firm operated over 4,200 stores. During the period from 1915 to 1975, A&P was the largest grocery retailer in the country. However it suffered a long, painful decline that led to multiple reorganization efforts as well as bankruptcies. In 2015, the long struggle to revive the firm came to an end when, as part of a bankruptcy filing, A&P sold off or closed its final 256 stores.[1]

What happened to this retailing icon? They were simply stuck in the middle. When it was on top, A&P provided a clear value proposition for its customers. It was one of the most cost-efficient retailers in the market while providing a wide array of products for its customers. As a result, it had both cost and differentiation advantages over its rivals. However, things started to turn in the 1950s. Rather than invest in, expand, and modernize its stores, its controlling owners distributed most of its profits to shareholders through large dividends. At the same time, new and aggressive competitors started to enter the market, and these competitors eroded A&P's distinctive positioning. In the battle to win the business of cost-conscious customers, A&P faced stiff competition from massive general market retailers, most notably Walmart, as well as focused discounters, such as dollar stores and discount grocers, including Aldi. Customers looking for a higher level of service and specialty foods gravitated to grocery retailers that offered a higher level of service in larger stores, such as Wegmans, and newer high-end providers, such as Whole Foods, that offered gourmet foods and wider organic food product lines.

A&P was initially slow to respond to these challenges. When they finally did respond, as Jim Hertel, a grocery industry consultant stated, "They got caught in a downward spiral of sales declines that forced them to cut costs." This resulted in challenges of hiring enough qualified staff and limited funds to update or upgrade stores. Even so, they were still at a cost disadvantage to both Walmart and Aldi. This left A&P with both higher prices than Walmart and other discounters and stores that felt old and dirty. In other words, the firm offered little in terms of value for its customers. After its initial bankruptcy, A&P attempted to modernize its stores and rebrand itself as a more upscale grocery retailer but lacked the financial resources to follow through on the change.

Discussion Questions

1. What decisions did A&P make when it was successful that led to its later failure?
2. How should the firm have responded to the new competitive challenges it faced?
3. What firm do you see today that faces similar challenges? How should this firm respond and act to reinforce its strategic position?

In order to create and sustain a competitive advantage, companies need to stay focused on their customers' evolving wants and needs and not sacrifice their strategic position as they mature and the market around them evolves. Since A&P failed to invest in and reinforce its market position as the grocery industry matured and new entrants came into the market, it is not surprising that its market leadership eroded, and it was forced out of the market.

business-level strategy
a strategy designed for a firm or a division of a firm that competes within a single business.

generic strategies
basic types of business-level strategies based on breadth of target market (industrywide versus narrow market segment) and type of competitive advantage (low cost versus uniqueness).

TYPES OF COMPETITIVE ADVANTAGE AND SUSTAINABILITY

Michael Porter presented three **generic strategies** that a firm can use to overcome the five forces and achieve competitive advantage.[2] Each of Porter's generic strategies has the potential to allow a firm to outperform rivals in their industry. The first, *overall cost leadership,* is based on creating a low-cost position. Here, a firm must manage the relationships throughout the value chain and lower costs throughout the entire chain. Second, *differentiation* requires a firm to create products and/or services that are unique and valued. Here, the primary emphasis is on "nonprice" attributes for which customers will gladly pay a premium.[3] Third, a *focus* strategy directs attention (or "focus") toward narrow product lines, buyer segments, or targeted geographic markets, and they must attain advantages through either differentiation or cost leadership.[4] Whereas the overall cost leadership and differentiation strategies strive to attain advantages industrywide, focusers have a narrow target market in mind. Exhibit 5.1 illustrates these three strategies on two dimensions: competitive advantage and markets served.

Both casual observation and research support the notion that firms that identify with one or more of the forms of competitive advantage outperform those that do not.[5] There has been a rich history of strategic management research addressing this topic. One study analyzed 1,789 strategic business units and found that businesses combining multiple forms of competitive advantage (differentiation and overall cost leadership) outperformed businesses that used only a single form. The lowest performers were those that did not identify with any type of advantage. They were classified as "stuck in the middle." Results of this study are presented in Exhibit 5.2.[6]

For an example of the dangers of being stuck in the middle, consider the traditional supermarket.[7] The major supermarket chains, such as Food Lion and Albertsons, used to be the main source of groceries for consumers. However, they find themselves in a situation today where affluent customers are going upmarket to get their organic and gourmet foods at retailers like Whole Foods Market and budget-conscious consumers are drifting to discount chains such as Walmart, Aldi, and Dollar General.

EXHIBIT 5.1 Three Generic Strategies

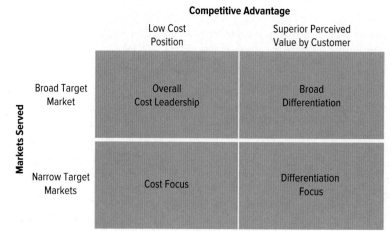

Source: Adapted from *Competitive Strategy: Techniques for Analyzing Industries and Competitors* by Michael E. Porter, 1980, 1998, Free Press.

EXHIBIT 5.2 Competitive Advantage and Business Performance

	Competitive Advantage					
Performance	Differentiation and Cost	Differentiation	Cost	Differentiation and Focus	Cost and Focus	Stuck in the Middle
Return on investment (%)	35.5	32.9	30.2	17.0	23.7	17.8
Sales growth (%)	15.1	13.5	13.5	16.4	17.5	12.2
Gain in market share (%)	5.3	5.3	5.5	6.1	6.3	4.4
Sample size	123	160	100	141	86	105

Overall Cost Leadership

The first generic strategy is **overall cost leadership**. Overall cost leadership requires a tight set of interrelated tactics that include:

- Aggressive construction of efficient-scale facilities.
- Vigorous pursuit of cost reductions from experience.
- Tight cost and overhead control.
- Avoidance of marginal customer accounts.
- Cost minimization in all activities in the firm's value chain, such as R&D, service, sales force, and advertising.

Exhibit 5.3 draws on the value-chain concept (see Chapter 3) to provide examples of how a firm can attain an overall cost leadership strategy in its primary and support activities.

One factor often central to an overall cost leadership strategy is the **experience curve**, which refers to how business "learns" to lower costs as it gains experience with production processes. With experience, unit costs of production decline as output increases in most industries. The experience curve, developed by the Boston Consulting Group in 1968, is a way of looking at efficiency gains that come with experience. For a range of products, as cumulative experience doubles, costs and labor hours needed to produce a unit of product decline by 10 to 30 percent. There are a number of reasons why we find this effect. Among the most common factors are workers getting better at what they do, product designs being simplified as the product matures, and production processes being automated and stream-lined. However, experience curve gains will be the foundation for a cost advantage only if the firm knows the source of the cost reduction and can keep these gains proprietary.

To generate above-average performance, a firm following an overall cost leadership position must attain **competitive parity** on the basis of differentiation relative to competitors.[8] In other words, a firm achieving parity is similar to its competitors, or "on par," with respect to differentiated products.[9] Competitive parity on the basis of differentiation permits a cost leader to translate cost advantages directly into higher profits than competitors. Thus, the cost leader earns above-average returns.[10]

The failure to attain parity on the basis of differentiation can be illustrated with an example from the automobile industry—the Tata Nano. Tata, an Indian conglomerate, developed the Nano to be the cheapest car in the world. At a price of about $2,000, the Nano was expected to draw in middle-class customers in India and developing markets as well as budget conscious customers in Europe and North America. However, it hasn't caught on in either market. The Nano doesn't have some of the basic features expected with cars, such as

overall cost leadership
a firm's generic strategy based on appeal to the industrywide market using a competitive advantage based on low cost.

experience curve
the decline in unit costs of production as cumulative output increases.

competitive parity
a firm's achievement of similarity, or being "on par," with competitors with respect to low cost, differentiation, or other strategic product characteristic.

EXHIBIT 5.3

Value-Chain Activities: Examples of Overall Cost Leadership

Support Activities

Firm Infrastructure

- Few management layers to reduce overhead costs.
- Standardized accounting practices to minimize personnel required.

Human Resource Management

- Minimize costs associated with employee turnover through effective policies.
- Effective orientation and training programs to maximize employee productivity.

Technology Development

- Effective use of automated technology to reduce scrappage rates.
- Expertise in process engineering to reduce manufacturing costs.

Procurement

- Effective policy guidelines to ensure low-cost raw materials (with acceptable quality levels).
- Shared purchasing operations with other business units.

Primary Activities

Inbound Logistics

- Effective layout of receiving dock operations.

Operations

- Effective use of quality control inspectors to minimize rework.

Outbound Logistics

- Effective utilization of delivery fleets.

Marketing and Sales

- Purchase of media in large blocks.
- Sales-force utilization is maximized by territory management.

Service

- Thorough service repair guidelines to minimize repeat maintenance calls.
- Use of single type of vehicle to minimize repair costs.

Source: Adapted from Porter, M. E. 1985. *Competitive Advantage: Creating and Sustaining Superior Performance.* New York: Free Press.

power steering and a passenger side mirror. It also faces concerns about safety. In crash tests, the Nano received zero stars for adult protection and didn't meet basic UN safety requirements. Also, there were numerous reports of Nanos catching fire. Due to all of these factors, the Nano has simply been seen by customers as offering a lousy value proposition.[11]

The lesson is simple. Price is just one component of value. No matter how good the price, the most cost-sensitive consumer won't buy a bad product.

Gordon Bethune, the former CEO of Continental Airlines, summed up the need to provide good products or services when employing a low-cost strategy this way: "You can make a pizza so cheap, nobody will buy it."[12]

Next, we discuss two examples of firms that have built a cost leadership position.

Aldi, a discount supermarket retailer, has grown from its German base to the rest of Europe, Australia, and the United States by replicating a simple business format. Aldi limits the number of products (SKUs in the grocery business) in each category to ensure product turn, to

PRIMARK STRIVES TO BALANCE LOW COSTS WITH ENVIRONMENTAL SUSTAINABILITY

Primark may be the most successful brand most Americans have never heard of. Though it didn't open its first U.S. store until 2015, it has been one of the fastest growing fashion retailers in the world over the last several years—growing by 150 percent between 2008 and 2014. Though its growth slowed to 9 percent in 2016, it continues to expand into new markets and expects its growth to accelerate in 2017. The Irish-based retailer focuses on selling trendy clothes at astonishingly low prices. It emphasizes keeping its cost structure lower than any of its rivals by leveraging streamlined logistics, a very low marketing budget, and its large scale that helps it get bargain prices from its suppliers. It also marks its prices up above cost less than its major rivals. As a result, the average selling price of an article of women's clothing at Primark was 60 percent less than H&M, one of its major rivals, in Britain. It aims to make up for low margins by selling at a higher volume than its rivals. For example, for every square foot, Primark generates 55 percent greater sales annually than H&M. Primark's customers often buy a series of outfits, wear them a few times, and then come back for a fresh set of outfits. Primark appears to be benefiting from the "Instagram effect," where young fashion-conscious consumers feel the need to regularly post selfies of new outfits they just bought.

While it strives for low costs, the firm also tries to balance this with the need for sustainability. Primark developed the Primark Sustainable Cotton Program in partnership with the Self-Employed Women's Association (SEWA) and social business CottonConnect. In this effort, they promote sustainable farming methods to female smallholder cotton farmers in India that provide economic opportunities for women; reduce the use of fertilizer, pesticides and water; and improve cotton yields. As a result of its efforts, Primark has been honored by Greenpeace with a Detox Leader Award and by the Chartered Institute of Procurement with a Best Contribution to Corporate Responsibility Award.

Sources: Anonymous, 2015. Faster, cheaper fashion. *economist.com.* September 5: np; Doshi, V. 2016. Primark tackles fast fashion critics with cotton farmer project in India. *theguardian.com.* September 30: np; McGregor, L. 2016. Can Primark really claim to be sustainable? *sourcingjournalonline.com.* October 17: np; Percival, G. 2016. Irish arm helps to drive 9% sales growth at Primark. *irishexaminer.com.* September 13: np.

ease stocking shelves, and to increase its power over suppliers. It also sells mostly private-label products to minimize cost. It has small, efficient, and simply designed stores. It offers limited services and expects customers to bring their own bags and bag their own groceries. As a result, Aldi can offer its products at prices 40 percent lower than competing supermarkets.[13]

Zulily, an online retailer, has built its business model around lower-cost operations in order to carve out a unique position relative to Amazon and other online retailers. Zulily keeps very little inventory and typically orders products from vendors only when customers purchase the product. It also has developed a bare-bones distribution system. Together, these actions result in deliveries that take an average of 11.5 days to get to customers and can sometimes stretch out to several weeks. Due to its reduced operational costs, Zulily is able to offer attractive prices to customers who are willing to wait.[14]

A business that strives for a low-cost advantage must attain an absolute cost advantage relative to its rivals.[15] This is typically accomplished by offering a no-frills product or service to a broad target market using standardization to derive the greatest benefits from economies of scale and experience. However, such a strategy may fail if a firm is unable to attain parity on important dimensions of differentiation such as quick responses to customer requests for services or design changes. Strategy Spotlight 5.1 discusses how Primark, an Irish clothing retailer, has built a low-cost strategy while also being seen as effectively addressing concerns about environmental sustainability.

LO 5-2

How the successful attainment of generic strategies can improve a firm's relative power vis-à-vis the five forces that determine an industry's average profitability.

Overall Cost Leadership: Improving Competitive Position vis-à-vis the Five Forces An overall low-cost position enables a firm to achieve above-average returns despite strong competition. It protects a firm against rivalry from competitors, because lower costs allow a firm to earn returns even if its competitors eroded their profits through intense rivalry. A low-cost position also protects firms against powerful buyers. Buyers can exert power to drive down prices only to the level of the next most efficient producer. Also, a low-cost position provides more flexibility to cope with demands from powerful suppliers for input cost increases. The factors that lead to a low-cost position also provide a substantial entry barriers position with respect to substitute products introduced by new and existing competitors.[16]

A few examples will illustrate these points. Zulily's close attention to costs helps to protect the company from buyer power and intense rivalry from competitors. Thus, Zulily is able to drive down costs and reduce the bargaining power of its customers. By cutting costs lower than other discount clothing retailers, Primark both lessens the degree of rivalry it faces and increases entry barriers for new entrants. Aldi's extreme focus on minimizing costs across its operations makes it less vulnerable to substitutes, such as discount retailers like Walmart and dollar stores.

Potential Pitfalls of Overall Cost Leadership Strategies Potential pitfalls of an overall cost leadership strategy include:

The pitfalls managers must avoid in striving to attain generic strategies.

- *Too much focus on one or a few value-chain activities.* Would you consider a person to be astute if he canceled his newspaper subscription and quit eating out to save money but then "maxed out" several credit cards, requiring him to pay hundreds of dollars a month in interest charges? Of course not. Similarly, firms need to pay attention to all activities in the value chain.[17] Too often managers make big cuts in operating expenses but don't question year-to-year spending on capital projects. Or managers may decide to cut selling and marketing expenses but ignore manufacturing expenses. Managers should explore *all* value-chain activities, including relationships among them, as candidates for cost reductions.

- *Increase in the cost of the inputs on which the advantage is based.* Firms can be vulnerable to price increases in the factors of production. For example, consider manufacturing firms based in China that rely on low labor costs. Due to demographic factors, the supply of workers 16 to 24 years old has peaked and will drop by a third in the next 12 years, thanks to stringent family-planning policies that have sharply reduced China's population growth.[18] This is leading to upward pressure on labor costs in Chinese factories, undercutting the cost advantage of firms producing there.

- *A strategy that can be imitated too easily.* One of the common pitfalls of a cost leadership strategy is that a firm's strategy may consist of value-creating activities that are easy to imitate.[19] Such has been the case with online brokers in recent years.[20] As of early 2015, there were over 200 online brokers listed on allstocks.com, hardly symbolic of an industry where imitation is extremely difficult. And according to Henry McVey, financial services analyst at Morgan Stanley, "We think you need five to ten" online brokers.

- *A lack of parity on differentiation.* As noted earlier, firms striving to attain cost leadership advantages must obtain a level of parity on differentiation.[21] Firms providing online degree programs may offer low prices. However, they may not be successful unless they can offer instruction that is perceived as comparable to traditional providers. For them, parity can be achieved on differentiation dimensions such as reputation and quality and through signaling mechanisms such as accreditation agencies.

- *Reduced flexibility.* Building up a low-cost advantage often requires significant investments in plant and equipment, distribution systems, and large, economically scaled operations. As a result, firms often find that these investments limit their flexibility, leading to great difficulty responding to changes in the environment. For example, Coors Brewing developed a highly efficient, large-scale brewery in Golden, Colorado. Coors was one of the most efficient brewers in the world, but its plant was designed to mass-produce one or two types of beer. When the craft brewing craze started to grow, the plant was not well equipped to produce smaller batches of craft beer, and Coors found it difficult to meet this opportunity. Ultimately, Coors had to buy its way into this movement by acquiring small craft breweries.[22]

- *Obsolescence of the basis of cost advantage.* Ultimately, the foundation of a firm's cost advantage may become obsolete. In such circumstances, other firms develop new ways of cutting costs, leaving the old cost leaders at a significant disadvantage. The older cost leaders are often locked into their way of competing and are unable to respond to the newer, lower-cost means of competing. This is the position that discount investment advisors now find themselves. Charles Schwab and TD Ameritrade challenged traditional brokers with lower cost business models. Now, they find themselves having to respond to a new class of robo-advisor firms, such as Betterment, that offer even lower cost investment advice using automated data analytic-based computer systems.

Differentiation

As the name implies, a **differentiation strategy** consists of creating differences in the firm's product or service offering by creating something that is perceived *industrywide* as unique and valued by customers.[23] Differentiation can take many forms:

differentiation strategy
a firm's generic strategy based on creating differences in the firm's product or service offering by creating something that is perceived *industrywide* as unique and valued by customers.

- Prestige or brand image (Hotel Monaco, BMW automobiles).[24]
- Quality (Apple, Ruth's Chris steak houses, Michelin tires).
- Technology (Martin guitars, North Face camping equipment).
- Innovation (Medtronic medical equipment, Tesla Motors).
- Features (Cannondale mountain bikes, Ducati motorcycles).
- Customer service (Nordstrom department stores, USAA financial services).
- Dealer network (Lexus automobiles, Caterpillar earthmoving equipment).

Exhibit 5.4 draws on the concept of the value chain as an example of how firms may differentiate themselves in primary and support activities.

Firms may differentiate themselves along several different dimensions at once.[25] For example, the Cheesecake Factory, an upscale casual restaurant, differentiates itself by offering high-quality food, the widest and deepest menu in its class of restaurants, and premium locations.[26]

Firms achieve and sustain differentiation advantages and attain above-average performance when their price premiums exceed the extra costs incurred in being unique.[27] For example, the Cheesecake Factory must increase consumer prices to offset the higher cost of premium real estate and producing such a wide menu. Thus, a differentiator will always seek out ways of distinguishing itself from similar competitors to justify price premiums greater than the costs incurred by differentiating.[28] Clearly, a differentiator cannot ignore costs. After all, its premium prices would be eroded by a markedly inferior cost position. Therefore, it must attain a level of cost *parity* relative to competitors. Differentiators can do this by reducing costs in all areas that do not affect differentiation. Porsche, for example, invests heavily in engine design—an area in which its customers demand excellence—but it is less concerned and spends fewer resources in the design of the instrument panel or the arrangement of switches on the radio.[29] Although a differentiation firm needs to be mindful of costs, it must also regularly and consistently reinforce the foundations of its differentiation advantage. In doing so, the firm builds a stronger reputation for differentiation, and this reputation can be an enduring source of advantage in its market.[30]

Many companies successfully follow a differentiation strategy. For example, Zappos may sell shoes, but it sees the core element of its differentiation advantage as service. Zappos CEO Tony Hsieh puts it this way:[31]

> We hope that 10 years from now people won't even realize that we started out selling shoes online, and that when you say "Zappos," they'll think, "Oh, that's the place with the absolute best customer service." And that doesn't even have to be limited to being an online experience. We've had customers email us and ask us if we would please start an airline, or run the IRS.

EXHIBIT 5.4

Value-Chain Activities:
Examples of
Differentiation

Support Activities

Firm Infrastructure

- Superior MIS—to integrate value-creating activities to improve quality.
- Facilities that promote firm image.
- Widely respected CEO who enhances firm reputation.

Human Resource Management

- Programs to attract talented engineers and scientists.
- Provision of training and incentives to ensure a strong customer service orientation.

Technology Development

- Superior material handling and sorting technology.
- Excellent applications engineering support.

Procurement

- Purchase of high-quality components to enhance product image.
- Use of most-prestigious outlets.

Primary Activities

Inbound Logistics

- Superior material handling operations to minimize damage.
- Quick transfer of inputs to manufacturing process.

Operations

- Flexibility and speed in responding to changes in manufacturing specifications.
- Low defect rates to improve quality.

Outbound Logistics

- Accurate and responsive order processing.
- Effective product replenishment to reduce customer inventory.

Marketing and Sales

- Creative and innovative advertising programs.
- Fostering of personal relationship with key customers.

Service

- Rapid response to customer service requests.
- Complete inventory of replacement parts and supplies.

Source: Adapted from Porter, M. E. 1985. *Competitive Advantage: Creating and Sustaining Superior Performance.* New York: Free Press.

This emphasis on service has led to great success. Growing from an idea to a billion-dollar company in only a dozen years, Zappos is seeing the benefits of providing exemplary service. In Insights from Research, we see that firms are better able to improve their innovativeness when they leverage the value of customer interactions by providing incentives for employees to generate new ideas, build strong networks to share ideas and questions across organizational boundaries, and empower personnel to make bold decisions.

Strategy Spotlight 5.2 discusses how Caterpillar is using data analytics to differentiate the firm and sell new services.

LINKING CUSTOMER INTERACTIONS TO INNOVATION: THE ROLE OF THE ORGANIZATIONAL PRACTICES

Overview

Business leaders have many reasons to want to be innovative. Research has shown customer interactions are important to innovation, but the study discussed below proves that is not enough. Business leaders must organize all employees to leverage customer interaction via particular incentives, communication patterns, and empowerment efforts.

What the Research Shows

Researchers from the Copenhagen Business School published a paper in Organization Science describing ways that companies use customer interactions to improve their innovation performance. The researchers used data from surveys of chief executive officers and other top managers in 169 of the largest Danish companies to determine the factors that improve innovation. The authors argue that merely interacting with customers isn't enough; business leaders must organize employees in certain ways internally to impact innovation performance.

The researchers found that companies whose employees had high customer interaction—those who collaborated with customers on projects and communicated intensely with customers—had better innovation performance and profitability. They found that the more a company's employees interacted with customers, the more its leaders delegated responsibility. As a result, in such companies, employees influenced their own jobs and often worked in teams.

Additionally, the researchers found that the more business leaders delegated responsibility, the more the companies used knowledge incentives. That is, employees' salaries were linked to improvement in skills as well as sharing and upgrading knowledge. This resulted in more communication between functional departments and between management and employees.

The bottom line of this research is this: The link between interaction with customers and innovation performance is indirect, but is related to organizational practices that trigger individual knowledge growth and cross-unit communication.

Why This Matters

It was already known that when employees interact with their users and customers, innovation often increases. But innovation doesn't just happen. Specific organizational practices are necessary to make it happen. The way leaders leverage their employees' customer interactions is through policies about communication, incentives, and empowerment. For example, communication should be encouraged across departments and between managers and employees. Also, rewards for sharing ideas and knowledge should be in place. Finally, employees should be given leeway to make decisions on their own rather than having to deal with red tape.

When these practices are in place, customer interactions are more likely to lead to innovation. But some companies are more equipped than others to receive helpful feedback from their customers. The software company SAP provides an excellent example of how to benefit from customers' ideas. The organization routinely taps more than 1.5 million participants in its Developer Network to post questions and receive quick responses on its virtual platform. Customers, developers, system integrators, and vendors help SAP increase productivity for all participants.

Key Takeaways

- Innovative companies often have higher profits, market values, market share, and credit ratings—and are more likely to survive.

- Interacting with customers can lead to innovation; in fact, many innovations are initiated by customers rather than manufacturers.

- This research also shows that customer interaction is not enough. To have these interactions spur innovative actions requires corporate leaders to enact specific organizational practices.

- Important practices for innovation include incentives to seek and share knowledge, the delegation of responsibility, and internal communication across departments and between managers and employees.

Apply This Today

Employees' interactions with customers have become vital to increasing innovative performance, but it is not enough. Communication between management and employees as well as across departments, incentives to get and share knowledge, and the delegation of responsibility can unleash the creativity of your workforce.

Research Reviewed

Foss, N., Laursen, K., & Pederson, T. 2011. Linking customer interaction and innovation: The mediating role of new organizational practices. *Organization Science,* 22: 980–999.

CATERPILLAR DIGS INTO THE DATA TO DIFFERENTIATE ITSELF

When most people think about the Caterpillar Corporation, they think of big yellow tractors and heavy equipment used in construction and mining. They don't often think of technology and data analytics. But this is an increasing emphasis in the firm. Caterpillar has been adding high-tech tools to its products for years. Cat excavators have been equipped with GPS and laser technology to help the driver set and maintain level digging and grading slopes. Cat has also built in systems to diagnose the ongoing health of the machine.

More recently, Caterpillar has looked to big data to help it grow its business. In an alliance with Uptake, a data analytics firm, they are now building systems to transmit data from machines to the cloud. This will allow Caterpillar to see how its machines are most commonly used, the tasks the machines struggle with, what triggers breakdowns, and when customers are likely to need to replace their machines. Cat itself can use this data to help it develop the next generation of machines—to assess the most common uses for its machines, to build better products, and

to predict customer needs. The plan is to use the data to better differentiate its products. But the company can also use the data to sell differentiated services to its business partners. For example, dealers could use the results of Cat's data collection to predict upcoming repairs and parts needs. End customers would likely value data on machine usage to see if operators are sitting idle too much or if they are improperly using machines. End customers could also benefit from early predictions of possible failures and recommendations for preventative maintenance. For example, in a study of one malfunctioning machine owned by a large mining company, Cat concluded that the firm's new technology would have reduced repair costs from the $650,000 the mining company incurred to $12,000 by identifying an emerging problem before it did serious damage. Thus, Cat sees this technology as allowing it to better serve both its customers and dealers, resulting in new sources of income for Cat as customers see value in buying ongoing data-access and software subscriptions.

Sources: Mehta, S. 2013. Where brains meet brawn. *Fortune*. October 28: 72; Whipp, L. 2016. Caterpillar explores data mining with Uptake. *ft.com*. August 21: np.

Differentiation: Improving Competitive Position vis-à-vis the Five Forces   Differentiation provides protection against rivalry since brand loyalty lowers customer sensitivity to price and raises customer switching costs.[32] By increasing a firm's margins, differentiation also avoids the need for a low-cost position. Higher entry barriers result because of customer loyalty and the firm's ability to provide uniqueness in its products or services.[33] Differentiation also provides higher margins that enable a firm to deal with supplier power. And it reduces buyer power, because buyers lack comparable alternatives and are therefore less price-sensitive.[34] Supplier power is also decreased because there is a certain amount of prestige associated with being the supplier to a producer of highly differentiated products and services. Last, differentiation enhances customer loyalty, thus reducing the threat from substitutes.[35]

Our examples illustrate these points. Porsche has enjoyed enhanced power over buyers because its strong reputation makes buyers more willing to pay a premium price. This lessens rivalry, since buyers become less price-sensitive. The prestige associated with its brand name also lowers supplier power since margins are high. Suppliers would probably desire to be associated with prestige brands, thus lessening their incentives to drive up prices. Finally, the loyalty and "peace of mind" associated with a service provider such as Zappos makes such firms less vulnerable to rivalry or substitute products and services.

Potential Pitfalls of Differentiation Strategies   Potential pitfalls of a differentiation strategy include:

- *Uniqueness that is not valuable.* A differentiation strategy must provide unique bundles of products and/or services that customers value highly. It's not enough just to be "different." An example is Gibson's Dobro bass guitar. Gibson came up with a unique idea: Design and build an acoustic bass guitar with sufficient sound volume so that amplification wasn't necessary. The problem with other acoustic bass guitars was that they did not project enough volume because of the low-frequency bass notes. By adding a resonator plate on the body of the traditional acoustic bass,

Gibson increased the sound volume. Gibson believed this product would serve a particular niche market—bluegrass and folk artists who played in small group "jams" with other acoustic musicians. Unfortunately, Gibson soon discovered that its targeted market was content with the existing options: an upright bass amplified with a microphone or an acoustic electric guitar. Thus, Gibson developed a unique product, but it was not perceived as valuable by its potential customers.[36]

- *Too much differentiation.* Firms may strive for quality or service that is higher than customers desire.[37] Thus, they become vulnerable to competitors that provide an appropriate level of quality at a lower price. For example, consider the expensive Mercedes-Benz S-Class, which ranged in price between $93,650 and $138,000 for the 2011 models.[38] *Consumer Reports* described it as "sumptuous," "quiet and luxurious," and a "delight to drive." The magazine also considered it to be the least reliable sedan available in the United States. According to David Champion, who runs the testing program, the problems are electronic. "The engineers have gone a little wild," he says. "They've put every bell and whistle that they think of, and sometimes they don't have the attention to detail to make these systems work." Some features include a computer-driven suspension that reduces body roll as the vehicle whips around a corner; cruise control that automatically slows the car down if it gets too close to another car; and seats that are adjustable 14 ways and are ventilated by a system that uses eight fans.

- *Too high a price premium.* This pitfall is quite similar to too much differentiation. Customers may desire the product, but they are repelled by the price premium. For example, Duracell was told by the market that it charged too much for batteries.[39] The firm tried to sell consumers on its superior-quality products, but the mass market wasn't convinced. Why? The price differential was simply too high. At one CVS drugstore, a four-pack of Energizer AA batteries was on sale at $2.99 compared with a Duracell four-pack at $4.59. Duracell's market share dropped 2 percent in a recent two-year period, and its profits declined over 30 percent. Clearly, the price/performance proposition Duracell offered customers was not accepted.

- *Differentiation that is easily imitated.* As we noted in Chapter 3, resources that are easily imitated cannot lead to sustainable advantages. Similarly, firms may strive for, and even attain, a differentiation strategy that is successful for a time. However, the advantages are eroded through imitation. Consider Cereality's innovative differentiation strategy of stores that offer a wide variety of cereals and toppings for around $4.[40] As one would expect, once the idea proved successful, competitors entered the market because much of the initial risk had already been taken. These new competitors included stores with the following names: the Cereal Cabinet, The Cereal Bowl, and Bowls: A Cereal Joint. Says David Roth, one of Cereality's founders: "With any good business idea, you're faced with people who see you've cracked the code and who try to cash in on it."

- *Dilution of brand identification through product-line extensions.* Firms may erode their quality brand image by adding products or services with lower prices and less quality. Although this can increase short-term revenues, it may be detrimental in the long run. Consider Gucci.[41] In the 1980s Gucci wanted to capitalize on its prestigious brand name by launching an aggressive strategy of revenue growth. It added a set of lower-priced canvas goods to its product line. It also pushed goods heavily into department stores and duty-free channels and allowed its name to appear on a host of licensed items such as watches, eyeglasses, and perfumes. In the short term, this strategy worked. Sales soared. However, the strategy carried a high price. Gucci's indiscriminate approach to expanding its products and channels tarnished its sterling brand. Sales of its high-end goods (with higher profit margins) fell, causing profits to decline.

Overall Cost Leadership

- Too much focus on one or a few value-chain activities.
- Increase in the cost of the inputs on which the advantage is based.
- A strategy that can be imitated too easily.
- A lack of parity on differentiation.
- Reduced flexibility.
- Obsolescence of the basis of cost advantage.

Differentiation

- Uniqueness that is not valuable.
- Too much differentiation.
- A price premium that is too high.
- Differentiation that is easily imitated.
- Dilution of brand identification through product-line extensions.
- Perceptions of differentiation that vary between buyers and sellers.

EXHIBIT 5.5

Potential Pitfalls of Overall Cost Leadership and Differentiation Strategies

focus strategy
a firm's generic strategy based on appeal to a narrow market segment within an industry.

- *Perceptions of differentiation that vary between buyers and sellers.* The issue here is that "beauty is in the eye of the beholder." Companies must realize that although they may perceive their products and services as differentiated, their customers may view them as commodities. Indeed, in today's marketplace, many products and services have been reduced to commodities.[42] Thus, a firm could overprice its offerings and lose margins altogether if it has to lower prices to reflect market realities.

Exhibit 5.5 summarizes the pitfalls of overall cost leadership and differentiation strategies. In addressing the pitfalls associated with these two generic strategies, there is one common, underlying theme: Managers must be aware of the dangers associated with concentrating so much on one strategy that they fail to attain parity on the other.

Focus

A **focus strategy** is based on the choice of a narrow competitive scope within an industry. A firm following this strategy selects a segment or group of segments and tailors its strategy to serve them. The essence of focus is the exploitation of a particular market niche. As you might expect, narrow focus itself (like merely "being different" as a differentiator) is simply not sufficient for above-average performance.

The focus strategy, as indicated in Exhibit 5.1, has two variants. In a cost focus, a firm strives to create a cost advantage in its target segment. In a differentiation focus, a firm seeks to differentiate in its target market. Both variants of the focus strategy rely on providing better service than broad-based competitors that are trying to serve the focuser's target segment. Cost focus exploits differences in cost behavior in some segments, while differentiation focus exploits the special needs of buyers in other segments.

Let's look at examples of two firms that have successfully implemented focus strategies. LinkedIn has staked out a position as the business social media site of choice. Rather than compete with Facebook head on, LinkedIn created a strategy that focuses on individuals who wish to share their business experience and make connections with individuals with whom they share or could potentially share business ties. In doing so, it has created an extremely strong business model. LinkedIn monetizes its user information in three ways: subscription fees from some users, advertising fees, and recruiter fees. The first two are fairly standard for social media sites, but the advertising fees are higher for LinkedIn since the ads can be more effectively targeted as a result of LinkedIn's focus. The third income source is fairly unique for LinkedIn. Headhunters and human resource departments pay significant user fees, up to $8,200 a year, to have access to LinkedIn's recruiting search engine, which can sift through LinkedIn profiles to identify individuals with desired skills and experiences. The power of this business model can be seen in the difference in user value for LinkedIn when compared to Facebook. For every hour that a user spends on the site, LinkedIn generates $1.30 in income. For Facebook, it is a paltry 6.2 cents.[43]

Marlin Steel Wire Products, a Baltimore-based manufacturing company, has also seen great benefit from developing a niche-differentiator strategy. Marlin, a manufacturer of commodity wire products, faced stiff and ever-increasing competition from rivals based in China and other

LUXURY IN THE E-COMMERCE WORLD

Traditionally, luxury retailers have relied on high levels of personal touch in their stores as well as a sense of exclusivity in order to differentiate themselves from the mass retail markets. As a result, many luxury retailers have looked on the Internet retail market skeptically, thinking it didn't fit their products and the needs of their customers. Rather than offering an indulgent and exclusive retail experience, the Internet promotes accessibility and efficiency. Yoox, an Italian firm, appears to have solved the mystery of how to turn e-commerce into a luxury experience. Yoox designs and manages online stores for nearly 40 luxury brands, including Armani, Diesel, Emilio Pucci, and Brunello Cucinelli. In 2015, the firm booked orders in 100 countries, generating over $1 billion in sales and $19 million in net income.

How has Yoox translated the luxury retail experience to the online world? Its expertise at creating the right experience cuts across the value chain. First, Yoox views itself as a craftsperson, designing each website specifically to the brand. Second, it focuses on the details. This includes training its 60 photographers to create images for each product that match the specific guidelines of each brand. For one clothing retailer, this included using flamenco dancers in its designer images, rather than fashion models. The attention to detail flows through to the packaging. Packers at Yoox's five fulfillment centers are trained on the specific angle of the ribbons for a box containing an Alexander Wang dress versus one containing a Bottega Veneta bag. Third, Yoox has developed innovative algorithms to predict which products will sell at which times and in which geographic regions, allowing effective stocking to meet the needs of customers and providing guidance to retailers on optimal pricing. Finally, Yoox has insisted on exclusive contracts with luxury brands to ensure that it can control the brands' images in the online retail space. These luxury brands have grown reliant on Yoox. About one-third of Yoox's revenue derives from the creation and management of the luxury brands' websites, while the remainder comes from its order-fulfillment services.

Sources: Fairchild, C. 2014. A luxe look for e-commerce. *Fortune,* June 16: 83–84; and Clark, N. 2014. Success draws competition for luxury e-retailer Yoox. *nytimes.com,* December 6: np.

---

emerging markets. These rivals had labor-based cost advantages that Marlin found hard to counter. Marlin responded by changing the game it played. Drew Greenblatt, Marlin's president, decided to go upmarket, automating his production and specializing in high-end products. For example, Marlin produces antimicrobial baskets for restaurant kitchens and exports its products globally. Marlin provides products to customers in 36 countries and, in 2012, was listed as the 162nd fastest-growing private manufacturing company in the United States.[44]

Strategy Spotlight 5.3 illustrates how Yoox has carved out a profitable niche in the online retailing world as a luxury goods provider.

Focus: Improving Competitive Position vis-à-vis the Five Forces   Focus requires that a firm have either a low-cost position with its strategic target, high differentiation, or both. As we discussed with regard to cost and differentiation strategies, these positions provide defenses against each competitive force. Focus is also used to select niches that are least vulnerable to substitutes or where competitors are weakest.

Let's look at our examples to illustrate some of these points. First, by providing a platform for a targeted customer group, businesspeople, to share key work information, LinkedIn insulated itself from rivalrous pressure from existing social networks, such as Facebook. It also felt little threat from new generalist social networks, such as Google +. Similarly, the new focus of Marlin Steel lessened the power of buyers since the company provides specialized products. Also, it is insulated from competitors, which manufacture the commodity products Marlin used to produce.

Potential Pitfalls of Focus Strategies   Potential pitfalls of focus strategies include:

- *Cost advantages may erode within the narrow segment.* The advantages of a cost focus strategy may be fleeting if the cost advantages are eroded over time. For example, early pioneers in online education, such as the University of Phoenix, have faced increasing challenges as traditional universities have entered with their own online programs that allow them to match the cost benefits associated with online delivery systems. Similarly, other firms have seen their profit margins drop as competitors enter their product segment.

- *Even product and service offerings that are highly focused are subject to competition from new entrants and from imitation.* Some firms adopting a focus strategy may enjoy temporary advantages because they select a small niche with few rivals. However, their advantages may be short-lived. A notable example is the multitude of dot-com firms that specialize in very narrow segments such as pet supplies, ethnic foods, and vintage automobile accessories. The entry barriers tend to be low, there is little buyer loyalty, and competition becomes intense. And since the marketing strategies and technologies employed by most rivals are largely nonproprietary, imitation is easy. Over time, revenues fall, profits margins are squeezed, and only the strongest players survive the shakeout.

- *Focusers can become too focused to satisfy buyer needs.* Some firms attempting to attain advantages through a focus strategy may have too narrow a product or service. Consider many retail firms. Hardware chains such as Ace and True Value are losing market share to rivals such as Lowe's and Home Depot that offer a full line of home and garden equipment and accessories. And given the enormous purchasing power of the national chains, it would be difficult for such specialty retailers to attain parity on costs.

LO 5-4

How firms can effectively combine the generic strategies of overall cost leadership and differentiation.

combination strategies
firms' integrations of various strategies to provide multiple types of value to customers.

mass customization
a firm's ability to manufacture unique products in small quantities at low cost.

Combination Strategies: Integrating Overall Low Cost and Differentiation

Perhaps the primary benefit to firms that integrate low-cost and differentiation strategies is the difficulty for rivals to duplicate or imitate.[45] This strategy enables a firm to provide two types of value to customers: differentiated attributes (e.g., high quality, brand identification, reputation) and lower prices (because of the firm's lower costs in value-creating activities). The goal is thus to provide unique value to customers in an efficient manner.[46] Some firms are able to attain both types of advantages simultaneously.[47] For example, superior quality can lead to lower costs because of less need for rework in manufacturing, fewer warranty claims, a reduced need for customer service personnel to resolve customer complaints, and so forth. Thus, the benefits of combining advantages can be additive, instead of merely involving trade-offs. Next, we consider four approaches to combining overall low cost and differentiation.

Adopting Automated and Flexible Manufacturing Systems   Given the advances in manufacturing technologies such as CAD/CAM (computer aided design and computer aided manufacturing) as well as information technologies, many firms have been able to manufacture unique products in relatively small quantities at lower costs—a concept known as **mass customization.**[48]

Let's consider Andersen Windows of Bayport, Minnesota—a $2.3 billion manufacturer of windows for the building industry.[49] Until about 20 years ago, Andersen was a mass producer, in small batches, of a variety of standard windows. However, to meet changing customer needs, Andersen kept adding to its product line. The result was catalogs of ever-increasing size and a bewildering set of choices for both homeowners and contractors. Over a six-year period, the number of products tripled, price quotes took several hours, and the error rate increased. This not only damaged the company's reputation but also added to its manufacturing expenses.

To bring about a major change, Andersen developed an interactive computer version of its paper catalogs that it sold to distributors and retailers. Salespersons can now customize each window to meet the customer's needs, check the design for structural soundness, and provide a price quote. The system is virtually error-free, customers get exactly what they want, and the time to develop the design and furnish a quotation has been cut by 75 percent. Each showroom computer is connected to the factory, and customers are assigned a code number that permits them to track the order. The manufacturing system has been developed to use some common finished parts, but it also allows considerable variation in the final

EXPANDING THE PROFIT POOL IN THE SKY

Commercial airlines find themselves in a very competitive market, facing a number of competitors, having high fixed costs, and experiencing demand that is largely driven by economic conditions. As a result, profits in the airline industry are typically fairly low and often negative. The challenges in this industry are evident in the 23 separate bankruptcies that have occurred in the U.S. airline industry since 2000. However, as anyone who has flown in recent years can attest, airlines have found new sources of profit to augment their income beyond what customers are willing to pay when purchasing a ticket. The fees airlines have added on for ancillary services accounted for $36.7 billion in additional revenue for global airlines in 2015, up from a paltry $2.5 billion in 2008.

The range of revenue sources has expanded in recent years. The most obvious source of service revenue is baggage fees. However, airlines also generate revenue by charging booking fees and by selling premium economy seating, the right to assigned seats, exit-row seating, guarantees that family members can all sit together, earlier boarding of flights, premium meals, pillow and blanket sets, Internet access on board, and the right to hold a reservation before making a purchase commitment. Outside the flight experience itself, airlines are generating revenue by charging fees for credit cards, frequent-flyer programs, and access to airport lounges. The importance of these fees is staggering for some airlines. While Emirates Air relies on these service fees for less than 1 percent of its revenue, 22 percent of Ryanair's revenue and 38 percent of Spirit Airlines' revenue is accounted for by these fees.

By separating the value of the actual flight from the services associated with flying, airlines have greatly expanded the profit pool associated with flying. They have found that flyers may be very price-conscious when purchasing tickets but are willing to shell out more for a range of services. While this does increase their revenue, it may also provide benefits for at least some customers. As Jay Sorensen, CEO of IdeaWorks, notes, "It offers the potential for an airline to better tailor service to the needs of individual customers. They can click and buy the amenities they want rather than the airline deciding what is bundled in the base fare."

Sources: Akasie, J. 2013. With a fee for everything, airlines jet toward a new business model. *minyanville.com,* October 1: np; Perera, J. 2014. Looking at airline fees in 2008 compared to 2014. *chron.com,* November 25: np; and Garcia, M. 2015. Airline fee revenue expected to reach nearly $60 billion in 2015. *skift.com,* November 10: np.

products. Despite its huge investment, Andersen has been able to lower costs, enhance quality and variety, and improve its response time to customers.

Using Data Analytics   As initially discussed in Chapter 2, corporations are increasingly collecting and analyzing data on their customers, including data on customer characteristics, purchasing patterns, employee productivity, and physical asset utilization. These efforts have the potential to allow firms to better customize their product and service offerings to customers while more efficiently and fully using the resources of the company. For example, Caterpillar collects and analyzes large volumes of data about how customers use their tractors. Since this data helps Cat better assess the uses and limitations of their current tractors, the firm can use data analytics to employ more focused and timely product improvement efforts. This allows the firm to simultaneously reduce the cost of new product development efforts and better differentiate their products.[50]

Exploiting the Profit Pool Concept for Competitive Advantage   A **profit pool** is defined as the total profits in an industry at all points along the industry's value chain.[51] Although the concept is relatively straightforward, the structure of the profit pool can be complex.[52] The potential pool of profits will be deeper in some segments of the value chain than in others, and the depths will vary within an individual segment. Segment profitability may vary widely by customer group, product category, geographic market, or distribution channel. Additionally, the pattern of profit concentration in an industry is very often different from the pattern of revenue generation. Strategy Spotlight 5.4 outlines how airlines have expanded the profit pools of their market by adding fees for a variety of services.

profit pool
the total profits in an industry at all points along the industry's value chain.

Coordinating the "Extended" Value Chain by Way of Information Technology   Many firms have achieved success by integrating activities throughout the "extended value chain" by using information technology to link their own value chain with the value chains of their customers and suppliers. As noted in Chapter 3, this approach enables a firm to add value not only through its own value-creating activities but also for its customers and suppliers.

Such a strategy often necessitates redefining the industry's value chain. A number of years ago, Walmart took a close look at its industry's value chain and decided to reframe the competitive challenge. Although its competitors were primarily focused on retailing—merchandising and promotion—Walmart determined that it was not so much in the retailing industry as in the transportation logistics and communications industries. Here, linkages in the extended value chain became central. That became Walmart's chosen battleground. By redefining the rules of competition that played to its strengths, Walmart has attained competitive advantages and dominates its industry.

Integrated Overall Low-Cost and Differentiation Strategies: Improving Competitive Position vis-à-vis the Five Forces Firms that successfully integrate both differentiation and cost advantages create an enviable position. For example, Walmart's integration of information systems, logistics, and transportation helps it to drive down costs and provide outstanding product selection. This dominant competitive position serves to erect high entry barriers to potential competitors that have neither the financial nor physical resources to compete head-to-head. Walmart's size—with over $482 million in sales in 2016—provides the chain with enormous bargaining power over suppliers. Its low pricing and wide selection reduce the power of buyers (its customers), because there are relatively few competitors that can provide a comparable cost/value proposition. This reduces the possibility of intense head-to-head rivalry, such as protracted price wars. Finally, Walmart's overall value proposition makes potential substitute products (e.g., Internet competitors) a less viable threat.

Pitfalls of Integrated Overall Cost Leadership and Differentiation Strategies The pitfalls of integrated overall cost leadership and differentiation include:

- *Failing to attain both strategies and possibly ending up with neither, leaving the firm "stuck in the middle."* A key issue in strategic management is the creation of competitive advantages that enable a firm to enjoy above-average returns. Some firms may become stuck in the middle if they try to attain both cost and differentiation advantages. As mentioned earlier in this chapter, mainline supermarket chains find themselves stuck in the middle as their cost structure is higher than discount retailers offering groceries and their products and services are not seen by consumers as being as valuable as those of high-end grocery chains, such as Whole Foods.
- *Underestimating the challenges and expenses associated with coordinating value-creating activities in the extended value chain.* Integrating activities across a firm's value chain with the value chain of suppliers and customers involves a significant investment in financial and human resources. Firms must consider the expenses linked to technology investment, managerial time and commitment, and the involvement and investment required by the firm's customers and suppliers. The firm must be confident that it can generate a sufficient scale of operations and revenues to justify all associated expenses.
- *Miscalculating sources of revenue and profit pools in the firm's industry.* Firms may fail to accurately assess sources of revenue and profits in their value chain. This can occur for several reasons. For example, a manager may be biased due to his or her functional area background, work experiences, and educational background. If the manager's background is in engineering, he or she might perceive that proportionately greater revenue and margins were being created in manufacturing, product, and process design than a person whose background is in a "downstream" value-chain activity such as marketing and sales. Or politics could make managers "fudge" the numbers to favor their area of operations. This would make them responsible for a greater proportion of the firm's profits, thus improving their bargaining position.

A related problem is directing an overwhelming amount of managerial time, attention, and resources to value-creating activities that produce the greatest margins—to the detriment of other important, albeit less profitable, activities. For example, a car manufacturer may focus too much on downstream activities, such as warranty fulfillment and financing operations, to the detriment of differentiation and cost of the cars themselves.

CAN COMPETITIVE STRATEGIES BE SUSTAINED? INTEGRATING AND APPLYING STRATEGIC MANAGEMENT CONCEPTS

LO 5-5

What factors determine the sustainability of a firm's competitive advantage.

Thus far this chapter has addressed how firms can attain competitive advantages in the marketplace. We discussed the three generic strategies—overall cost leadership, differentiation, and focus—as well as combination strategies. Next we discussed the importance of linking value-chain activities (both those within the firm and those linkages between the firm's suppliers and customers) to attain such advantages. We also showed how successful competitive strategies enable firms to strengthen their position vis-à-vis the five forces of industry competition as well as how to avoid the pitfalls associated with the strategies.

Competitive advantages are, however, often short-lived. As we discussed in the beginning of Chapter 1, the composition of the firms that constitute the Fortune 500 list has experienced significant turnover in its membership over the years—reflecting the temporary nature of competitive advantages. Consider BlackBerry's fall from grace. BlackBerry initially dominated the smartphone market. BlackBerry held 20 percent of the cell phone market in 2009, and its users were addicted to BlackBerry's products, leading some to refer to them as crackberrys. However, the firm's market share quickly eroded with the introduction of touch screen smartphones from Apple, Samsung, and others. BlackBerry was slow to move away from its physical keyboards and saw its market share fall to 0.1 percent by 2016.[53]

Clearly, "nothing is forever" when it comes to competitive advantages. Rapid changes in technology, globalization, and actions by rivals from within—as well as outside—the industry can quickly erode a firm's advantages. It is becoming increasingly important to recognize that the duration of competitive advantages is declining, especially in technology-intensive industries.[54] Even in industries that are normally viewed as "low tech," the increasing use of technology has suddenly made competitive advantages less sustainable.[55] Amazon's success in book retailing at the cost of Barnes & Noble, the former industry leader, as well as cable TV's difficulties in responding to streaming services providers like Netflix and Hulu, serve to illustrate how difficult it has become for industry leaders to sustain competitive advantages that they once thought would last forever.

In this section, we will discuss some factors that help determine whether a strategy is sustainable over a long period of time. We will draw on some strategic management concepts from the first five chapters. To illustrate our points, we will look at a company, Atlas Door, which created an innovative strategy in its industry and enjoyed superior performance for several years. Our discussion of Atlas Door draws on a *Harvard Business Review* article by George Stalk, Jr.[56] It was published some time ago (1988), which provides us the benefit of hindsight to make our points about the sustainability of competitive advantage. After all, the strategic management concepts we have been addressing in the text are quite timeless in their relevance to practice. A brief summary follows.

Atlas Door: A Case Example

Atlas Door, a U.S.-based company, has enjoyed remarkable success. It has grown at an average annual rate of 15 percent in an industry with an overall annual growth rate of less than 5 percent. Recently, its pretax earnings were 20 percent of sales—about five times the industry average. Atlas is debt-free, and by its 10th year, the company had achieved the number-one competitive position in its industry.

Atlas produces industrial doors—a product with almost infinite variety, involving limitless choices of width and height and material. Given the importance of product variety, inventory is almost useless in meeting customer orders. Instead, most doors can be manufactured only after the order has been placed.

How Did Atlas Door Create Its Competitive Advantages in the Marketplace?   *First,* Atlas built just-in-time factories. Although simple in concept, they require extra tooling and machinery to reduce changeover times. Further, the manufacturing process must be organized by product and scheduled to start and complete with all of the parts available at the same time.

Second, Atlas reduced the time to receive and process an order. Traditionally, when customers, distributors, or salespeople called a door manufacturer with a request for price and delivery, they would have to wait more than one week for a response. In contrast, Atlas first streamlined and then automated its entire order-entry, engineering, pricing, and scheduling process. Atlas can price and schedule 95 percent of its incoming orders while the callers are still on the telephone. It can quickly engineer new special orders because it has preserved on computer the design and production data of all previous special orders—which drastically reduces the amount of reengineering necessary.

Third, Atlas tightly controlled logistics so that it always shipped only fully complete orders to construction sites. Orders require many components, and gathering all of them at the factory and making sure that they are with the correct order can be a time-consuming task. Of course, it is even more time-consuming to get the correct parts to the job site after the order has been shipped! Atlas developed a system to track the parts in production and the purchased parts for each order. This helped to ensure the arrival of all necessary parts at the shipping dock in time—a just-in-time logistics operation.

The Result?   When Atlas began operations, distributors had little interest in its product. The established distributors already carried the door line of a much larger competitor and saw little to no reason to switch suppliers except, perhaps, for a major price concession. But as a start-up, Atlas was too small to compete on price alone. Instead, it positioned itself as the door supplier of last resort—the company people came to if the established supplier could not deliver or missed a key date.

Of course, with an average industry order-fulfillment time of almost four months, some calls inevitably came to Atlas. And when it did get the call, Atlas commanded a higher price because of its faster delivery. Atlas not only got a higher price, but its effective integration of value-creating activities saved time and lowered costs. Thus, it enjoyed the best of both worlds.

In 10 short years, the company replaced the leading door suppliers in 80 percent of the distributors in the United States. With its strategic advantage, the company could be selective—becoming the supplier for only the strongest distributors.

Are Atlas Door's Competitive Advantages Sustainable?

We will now take both the "pro" and "con" positions as to whether or not Atlas Door's competitive advantages will be sustainable for a very long time. It is important, of course, to assume that Atlas Door's strategy is unique in the industry, and the central issue becomes whether or not rivals will be able to easily imitate its strategy or create a viable substitute strategy.

"Pro" Position: The Strategy Is Highly Sustainable   Drawing on Chapter 2, it is quite evident that Atlas Door has attained a very favorable position vis-à-vis the five forces of industry competition. For example, it is able to exert power over its customers (distributors) because of its ability to deliver a quality product in a short period of time. Also, its dominance in the industry creates high entry barriers for new entrants. It is also quite evident that Atlas Door has been able to successfully integrate many value-chain activities within the firm—a fact that is integral to its just-in-time strategy. As noted in Chapter 3, such integration of activities provides a strong basis for sustainability, because rivals would have difficulty in imitating this strategy due to causal ambiguity and path dependency (i.e., it is difficult to build up in a short period of time the resources that Atlas Door has accumulated and developed as well as disentangle the causes of what the valuable resources are or how they can be re-created). Further, as noted in Chapter 4, Atlas Door benefits from the social capital that it has developed with a wide range of key stakeholders (Chapter 1). These would include customers, employees, and managers (a reasonable assumption, given how smoothly the internal operations flow and the company's long-term relationships with distributors). It would be very difficult for a rival to replace Atlas Door as the supplier of last resort—given the reputation that it has earned over time for "coming through in the clutch" on time-sensitive orders. Finally, we can conclude that Atlas Door has created competitive advantages in both overall low cost and differentiation (Chapter 5). Its strong linkages among value-chain activities—a requirement for its just-in-time operations—not only lower costs but enable the company to respond quickly to customer orders. As noted in Exhibit 5.4, many of the value-chain activities associated with a differentiation strategy reflect the element of speed or quick response.

"Con" Position: The Strategy Can Be Easily Imitated or Substituted An argument could be made that much of Atlas Door's strategy relies on technologies that are rather well known and nonproprietary. Over time, a well-financed rival could imitate its strategy (via trial and error), achieve a tight integration among its value-creating activities, and implement a just-in-time manufacturing process. Because human capital is highly mobile (Chapter 4), a rival could hire away Atlas Door's talent, and these individuals could aid the rival in transferring Atlas Door's best practices. A new rival could also enter the industry with a large resource base, which might enable it to price its doors well under Atlas Door to build market share (but this would likely involve pricing below cost and would be a risky and nonsustainable strategy). Finally, a rival could potentially "leapfrog" the technologies and processes that Atlas Door has employed and achieve competitive superiority. With the benefit of hindsight, it could use the Internet to further speed up the linkages among its value-creating activities and the order-entry processes with its customers and suppliers. (But even this could prove to be a temporary advantage, since rivals could relatively easily do the same thing.)

What Is the Verdict? Both positions have merit. Over time, it would be rather easy to see how a new rival could achieve parity with Atlas Door—or even create a superior competitive position with new technologies or innovative processes. However, two factors make it extremely difficult for a rival to challenge Atlas Door in the short term: (1) The success that Atlas Door has enjoyed with its just-in-time scheduling and production systems—which involve the successful integration of many value-creating activities—helps the firm not only lower costs but also respond quickly to customer needs, and (2) the strong, positive reputational effects that it has earned with its customers increases their loyalty and would take significant time for rivals to match.

Finally, it is important to also understand that it is Atlas Door's ability to appropriate most of the profits generated by its competitive advantages that make it a highly successful company. As we discussed in Chapter 3, profits generated by resources can be appropriated by a number of stakeholders such as suppliers, customers, employees, or rivals. The structure of the industrial door industry makes such value appropriation difficult: The suppliers provide generic parts, no one buyer is big enough to dictate prices, the tacit nature of the knowledge makes imitation difficult, and individual employees may be easily replaceable. Still, even with the advantages that Atlas Door enjoys, it needs to avoid becoming complacent or it will suffer the same fate as the dominant firm it replaced.

Strategies for Platform Markets

Before moving on to our discussion of industry life-cycle stages and competitive strategy, we introduce and discuss an emerging trend: two-sided or platform markets. In these markets, firms act as intermediaries between two sets of platform users: buyers and sellers. Firms that thrive in these markets often do not produce a product themselves. Instead, successful platform firms create a business that attracts a large range of suppliers and a wide population of customers, becoming the go-to clearinghouse that both suppliers and customers turn to in order to facilitate a transaction. In doing so, they typically successfully combine elements of both cost and differentiation advantages.

These types of markets have been in existence for a long period of time. For example, VISA became the largest credit card company by signing up both the most merchants and the most customers in their card network. Retailers and restaurants now perceive the need to accept VISA credit and debit cards because millions of customers carry them. On the other side, when considering which credit card(s) to carry, most customers feel the need to carry a VISA card since it is accepted by so many merchants. As the VISA example illustrates, the sheer number of buyers and sellers using a given platform provides the platform firm with a differentiated market position while simultaneously allowing it to become a cost leader due to the economies of scale it accrues as it becomes the largest platform.

While these types of markets have existed for decades, they have become increasingly common in the 21st century. Whether it is Amazon in retailing, Facebook in social networks, Airbnb in short-term housing rentals, Uber in driver services, Spotify in streaming services, or Etsy in craft products, platform businesses have taken on increasing prominence in the economy.

But how do firms position themselves to succeed in these two-sided markets? It involves a combination of actions to build a strong position and facilitate optimal interactions between suppliers and users. In doing so, these firms strive to simultaneously limit costs to users and also provide differentiated service. The issues platform businesses need to master to succeed include the following.[57]

- **Draw in users.** The key to success in platform models is to generate the best (and often biggest) base of suppliers and customers. Thus, firms must develop effective pricing and incentives for users to attract and retain them. This typically involves subsidizing early and price-sensitive users. For example, Adobe was able to emerge as the dominant pdf software partly because it allowed users to read and print documents for free. As it established itself as "the" pdf reader software, producers of documents and those who wished to edit documents became increasingly willing to purchase software from Adobe. Thus, Adobe provided the product at no cost to some users while differentiating itself in the eyes of other users. Successful platform providers also find ways to attract and retain "marquee" users. YouTube has done this by allowing users to set up their own channel and compensate them for the volume of traffic they bring in.

- **Create easy and informative customer interfaces.** Platform business providers need to make it easy for users to plug into the platform. For example, Quicken Loans strives to differentiate itself with its Rocket Mortgage product, arguing it is the easiest and quickest system for applying for a home mortgage—typically taking less than 10 minutes to complete the application. By developing an easy to use app that requires no lending officer interaction, Quicken Loans was also able to build a more cost-efficient lending system than traditional loan brokers. Uber similarly worked to differentiate itself with a simple app for users to connect with a driver and by providing updated information on the expected arrival time of the driver. On the supplier side, Apple strives to ease the process for software developers by providing the operating system and underlying library codes needed to develop new software.

- **Facilitate the best connections between suppliers and customers.** Platform businesses can learn a great deal about their suppliers and customers by observing their search and usage patterns. Successful platform firms leverage this data to figure out how to best fill their matchmaking role in bringing together suppliers and users. Google is notable in its ability to tailor advertising to the search patterns of its users in order to increase the success rates for its advertising. Similarly, Airbnb has worked to create systems that increase the likelihood that hosts will agree to offers from potential renters. The firm realizes that renters get frustrated if their rental offers are declined. Additionally, hosts will be dissatisfied if offers come from undesirable renters. Using data analytics, Airbnb analyzed when specific hosts accepted and declined offers and their satisfaction ratings of renters to develop profiles of preferred renter characteristics. Using the resulting algorithm for matching renter characteristics and host preferences, the company saw a 4 percent increase in its rate of converting offers into accepted rental matches.

- **Sequencing the growth of the business.** To maximize the chance of success, platform firms must consciously plan out the sequence of their businesses. This involves thinking in terms of both geographic and product market expansion. In planning out its geographic market expansion, Uber analyzed the supply and demand of the taxi markets in cities across the country and first entered cities with the greatest shortage of taxis. Since it started in markets with unmet demand, Uber was able to expand quickly in these markets to be as cost efficient as possible. It also heavily advertised its business in settings where taxis were likely to be in short supply, such as sporting events and concerts. Once Uber established itself in these markets and developed a brand image, it expanded into other markets. Platform firms also need to consider both the need and opportunity of expanding their product scope. For example, Facebook has looked to continually extend its differentiation by expanding the range of services it offers, and as a result, has been able to put the squeeze on narrow platform providers, such as Twitter. Similarly, Spotify expanded from music to video streaming services in a quest to be a more complete service provider.

If successful, a platform provider becomes the dominant player linking suppliers and customers. This success offers the firm great flexibility in pricing its services as the firm gains a near monopoly in its market.

INDUSTRY LIFE-CYCLE STAGES: STRATEGIC IMPLICATIONS

The **industry life cycle** refers to the stages of introduction, growth, maturity, and decline that occur over the life of an industry. In considering the industry life cycle, it is useful to think in terms of broad product lines such as personal computers, photocopiers, or long-distance telephone service. Yet the industry life-cycle concept can be explored from several levels, from the life cycle of an entire industry to the life cycle of a single variation or model of a specific product or service.

Why are industry life cycles important?[58] The emphasis on various generic strategies, functional areas, value-creating activities, and overall objectives varies over the course of an industry life cycle. Managers must become even more aware of their firm's strengths and weaknesses in many areas to attain competitive advantages. For example, firms depend on their research and development (R&D) activities in the introductory stage. R&D is the source of new products and features that everyone hopes will appeal to customers. Firms develop products and services to stimulate consumer demand. Later, during the maturity phase, the functions of the product have been defined, more competitors have entered the market, and competition is intense. Managers then place greater emphasis on production efficiencies and process (as opposed to the product) engineering

EXHIBIT 5.6 Stages of the Industry Life Cycle

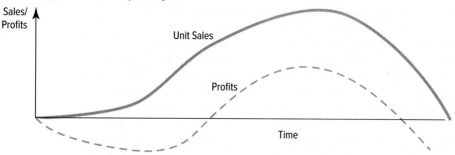

Stage / Factor	Introduction	Growth	Maturity	Decline
Generic strategies	Differentiation	Differentiation	Differentiation Overall cost leadership	Overall cost leadership Focus
Market growth rate	Low	Very large	Low to moderate	Negative
Number of segments	Very few	Some	Many	Few
Intensity of competition	Low	Increasing	Very intense	Changing
Emphasis on product design	Very high	High	Low to moderate	Low
Emphasis on process design	Low	Low to moderate	High	Low
Major functional area(s) of concern	Research and development	Sales and marketing	Production	General management and finance
Overall objective	Increase market awareness	Create consumer demand	Defend market share and extend product life cycles	Consolidate, maintain, harvest, or exit

in order to lower manufacturing costs. This helps to protect the firm's market position and to extend the product life cycle because the firm's lower costs can be passed on to consumers in the form of lower prices, and price-sensitive customers will find the product more appealing.

Exhibit 5.6 illustrates the four stages of the industry life cycle and how factors such as generic strategies, market growth rate, intensity of competition, and overall objectives change over time. Managers must strive to emphasize the key functional areas during each of the four stages and to attain a level of parity in all functional areas and value-creating activities. For example, although controlling production costs may be a primary concern during the maturity stage, managers should not totally ignore other functions such as marketing and R&D. If they do, they can become so focused on lowering costs that they miss market trends or fail to incorporate important product or process designs. Thus, the firm may attain low-cost products that have limited market appeal.

It is important to point out a caveat. While the life-cycle idea is analogous to a living organism (i.e., birth, growth, maturity, and death), the comparison has limitations.[59] Products and services go through many cycles of innovation and renewal. Typically, only fad products have a single life cycle. Maturity stages of an industry can be "transformed" or followed by a stage of rapid growth if consumer tastes change, technological innovations take place, or new developments occur. The cereal industry is a good example. When medical research indicated that oat consumption reduced a person's cholesterol, sales of Quaker Oats increased dramatically.[60]

Strategies in the Introduction Stage

In the **introduction stage,** products are unfamiliar to consumers.[61] Market segments are not well defined, and product features are not clearly specified. The early development of an industry typically involves low sales growth, rapid technological change, operating losses, and the need for strong sources of cash to finance operations. Since there are few players and not much growth, competition tends to be limited.

Success requires an emphasis on research and development and marketing activities to enhance awareness. The challenge becomes one of (1) developing the product and finding a way to get users to try it and (2) generating enough exposure so the product emerges as the "standard" by which all other rivals' products are evaluated.

There's an advantage to being the "first mover" in a market.[62] It led to Coca-Cola's success in becoming the first soft-drink company to build a recognizable global brand and enabled Caterpillar to get a lock on overseas sales channels and service capabilities.

However, there can also be a benefit to being a "late mover." Target carefully considered its decision to delay its Internet strategy. Compared to its competitors Walmart and Kmart, Target was definitely an industry laggard. But things certainly turned out well:[63]

> By waiting, Target gained a late-mover advantage. The store was able to use competitors' mistakes as its own learning curve. This saved money, and customers didn't seem to mind the wait: When Target finally opened its website, it quickly captured market share from both Kmart and Walmart Internet shoppers. Forrester Research Internet analyst Stephen Zrike commented, "There's no question, in our mind, that Target has a far better understanding of how consumers buy online."

Examples of products currently in the introductory stages of the industry life cycle include electric vehicles and space tourism.

Strategies in the Growth Stage

The **growth stage** is characterized by strong increases in sales. Such potential attracts other rivals. In the growth stage, the primary key to success is to build consumer preferences for specific brands. This requires strong brand recognition, differentiated products, and the financial resources to support a variety of value-chain activities such as marketing and sales, and research and development. Whereas marketing and sales initiatives were mainly directed at spurring *aggregate* demand—that is, demand for all such products in the introduction stage—efforts in the growth stage are directed toward stimulating *selective* demand, in which a firm's product offerings are chosen instead of a rival's.

Revenues increase at an accelerating rate because (1) new consumers are trying the product and (2) a growing proportion of satisfied consumers are making repeat purchases.[64] In general, as a product moves through its life cycle, the proportion of repeat buyers to new purchasers increases. Conversely, new products and services often fail if there are relatively few repeat purchases. For example, Alberto-Culver introduced Mr. Culver's Sparklers, which were solid air fresheners that looked like stained glass. Although the product quickly went from the introductory to the growth stage, sales collapsed. Why? Unfortunately, there were few repeat purchasers because buyers treated them as inexpensive window decorations, left them there, and felt little need to purchase new ones. Examples of products currently in the growth stage include cloud computing data storage services and ultra-high-definition television (UHD TV).

introduction stage
the first stage of the industry life cycle, characterized by (1) new products that are not known to customers, (2) poorly defined market segments, (3) unspecified product features, (4) low sales growth, (5) rapid technological change, (6) operating losses, and (7) a need for financial support.

growth stage
the second stage of the product life cycle, characterized by (1) strong increases in sales; (2) growing competition; (3) developing brand recognition; and (4) a need for financing complementary value-chain activities such as marketing, sales, customer service, and research and development.

Strategies in the Maturity Stage

maturity stage
the third stage of the product life cycle, characterized by (1) slowing demand growth, (2) saturated markets, (3) direct competition, (4) price competition, and (5) strategic emphasis on efficient operations.

In the **maturity stage** aggregate industry demand softens. As markets become saturated, there are few new adopters. It's no longer possible to "grow around" the competition, so direct competition becomes predominant.[65] With few attractive prospects, marginal competitors exit the market. At the same time, rivalry among existing rivals intensifies because of fierce price competition at the same time that expenses associated with attracting new buyers are rising. Advantages based on efficient manufacturing operations and process engineering become more important for keeping costs low as customers become more price-sensitive. It also becomes more difficult for firms to differentiate their offerings, because users have a greater understanding of products and services.

An article in *Fortune* magazine that addressed the intensity of rivalry in mature markets was aptly titled "A Game of Inches." It stated, "Battling for market share in a slowing industry can be a mighty dirty business. Just ask laundry soap archrivals Unilever and Procter & Gamble."[66] These two firms have been locked in a battle for market share since 1965. Why is the competition so intense? There is not much territory to gain and industry sales were flat. An analyst noted, "People aren't getting any dirtier." Thus, the only way to win is to take market share from the competition. To increase its share, Procter & Gamble (P&G) spends $100 million a year promoting its Tide brand on television, billboards, buses, magazines, and the Internet. But Unilever isn't standing still. Armed with an $80 million budget, it launched a soap tablet product named Wisk Dual Action Tablets. For example, it delivered samples of this product to 24 million U.S. homes in Sunday newspapers, followed by a series of TV ads. P&G launched a counteroffensive with Tide Rapid Action Tablets ads showed in side-by-side comparisons of the two products dropped into beakers of water. In the promotion, P&G claimed that its product is superior because it dissolves faster than Unilever's product.

Although this is only one example, many product classes and industries, including consumer products such as beer, automobiles, and athletic shoes, are in maturity.

Firms do not need to be "held hostage" to the life-cycle curve. By positioning or repositioning their products in unexpected ways, firms can change how customers mentally categorize them. Thus, firms are able to rescue products floundering in the maturity phase of their life cycles and return them to the growth phase.

Two positioning strategies that managers can use to affect consumers' mental shifts are **reverse positioning,** which strips away "sacred" product attributes while adding new ones, and **breakaway positioning**, which associates the product with a radically different category.[67]

reverse positioning
a break in the industry tendency to continuously augment products, characteristic of the product life cycle, by offering products with fewer product attributes and lower prices.

Reverse Positioning   This strategy assumes that although customers may desire more than the baseline product, they don't necessarily want an endless list of features. With reverse positioning, companies make the creative decision to step off the augmentation treadmill and shed product attributes that the rest of the industry considers sacred. Then, once a product is returned to its baseline state, the stripped-down product adds one or more carefully selected attributes that would usually be found only in a highly augmented product. Such an unconventional combination of attributes allows the product to assume a new competitive position within the category and move backward from maturity into a growth position on the life-cycle curve.

breakaway positioning
a break in the industry tendency to incrementally improve products along specific dimensions, characteristic of the product life cycle, by offering products that are still in the industry but are perceived by customers as being different.

Breakaway Positioning   As noted above, with reverse positioning, a product establishes a unique position in its category but retains a clear category membership. However, with breakaway positioning, a product escapes its category by deliberately associating with a different one. Thus, managers leverage the new category's conventions to change both how products are consumed and with whom they compete. Instead of merely seeing the breakaway product as simply an alternative to others in its category, consumers perceive it as altogether different.

When a breakaway product is successful in leaving its category and joining a new one, it is able to redefine its competition. Similar to reverse positioning, this strategy permits the product to shift backward on the life-cycle curve, moving from the rather dismal maturity phase to a thriving growth opportunity.

Strategies in the Decline Stage

Although all decisions in the phases of an industry life cycle are important, they become particularly difficult in the **decline stage.** Firms must face up to the fundamental strategic choices of either exiting or staying and attempting to consolidate their position in the industry.[68]

The decline stage occurs when industry sales and profits begin to fall. Typically, changes in the business environment are at the root of an industry or product group entering this stage.[69] Changes in consumer tastes or a technological innovation can push a product into decline. For example, the advent of online news services pushed the print newspaper and news magazine businesses into a rapid decline.

Products in the decline stage often consume a large share of management time and financial resources relative to their potential worth. Sales and profits decline. Also, competitors may start drastically cutting their prices to raise cash and remain solvent. The situation is further aggravated by the liquidation of assets, including inventory, of some of the competitors that have failed. This further intensifies price competition.

In the decline stage, a firm's strategic options become dependent on the actions of rivals. If many competitors leave the market, sales and profit opportunities increase. On the other hand, prospects are limited if all competitors remain.[70] If some competitors merge, their increased market power may erode the opportunities for the remaining players. Managers must carefully monitor the actions and intentions of competitors before deciding on a course of action.

Four basic strategies are available in the decline phase: *maintaining, harvesting, exiting, and consolidating.*[71]

- *Maintaining* refers to keeping a product going without significantly reducing marketing support, technological development, or other investments, in the hope that competitors will eventually exit the market. For example, even though most documents are sent digitally, there is still a significant market for fax machines since many legal and investment documents must still be signed and sent using a fax. This mode of transmission is still seen as more secure than other means of transmission. Thus, there may still be the potential for revenues and profits.

- **Harvesting** involves obtaining as much profit as possible and requires that costs be reduced quickly. Managers should consider the firm's value-creating activities and cut associated budgets. Value-chain activities to consider are primary (e.g., operations, sales and marketing) and support (e.g., procurement, technology development). The objective is to wring out as much profit as possible.

- *Exiting the market* involves dropping the product from a firm's portfolio. Since a residual core of consumers exist, eliminating it should be carefully considered. If the firm's exit involves product markets that affect important relationships with other product markets in the corporation's overall portfolio, an exit could have repercussions for the whole corporation. For example, it may involve the loss of valuable brand names or human capital with a broad variety of expertise in many value-creating activities such as marketing, technology, and operations.

- **Consolidation** involves one firm acquiring at a reasonable price the best of the surviving firms in an industry. This enables firms to enhance market power and acquire valuable assets. One example of a consolidation strategy took place in the defense industry in the early 1990s. As the cliché suggests, "peace broke out" at the end of the Cold War and overall U.S. defense spending levels plummeted.[72] Many companies that make up the defense industry saw more than 50 percent of their market disappear. Only one-quarter of the 120,000 companies that once supplied the Department of Defense still serve in that capacity; the others have shut down their defense business or dissolved altogether. But one key player, Lockheed Martin, became a dominant rival by pursuing an aggressive strategy of consolidation. During the 1990s, it purchased 17 independent entities, including General Dynamics'

decline stage
the fourth stage of the product life cycle, characterized by (1) falling sales and profits, (2) increasing price competition, and (3) industry consolidation.

harvesting strategy
a strategy of wringing as much profit as possible out of a business in the short to medium term by reducing costs.

consolidation strategy
a firm's acquiring or merging with other firms in an industry in order to enhance market power and gain valuable assets.

tactical aircraft and space systems divisions, GE Aerospace, Goodyear Aerospace, and Honeywell Electro-Optics. These combinations enabled Lockheed Martin to emerge as the top provider to three governmental customers: the Department of Defense, the Department of Energy, and NASA.

Examples of products currently in the decline stage of the industry life cycle include the video-rental business (being replaced by video on demand), hard disk drives (being replaced by solid-state memory and cloud storage), and desktop computers (being replaced by notebook and tablet computers).

The introduction of new technologies and associated products does not always mean that old technologies quickly fade away. Research shows that in a number of cases, old technologies actually enjoy a very profitable "last gasp."[73] Examples include personal computers (versus tablet computers and other mobile devices), coronary artery bypass graft surgery (versus angioplasty), and vinyl records (versus CDs and digital downloads of music). In each case, the advent of new technology prompted predictions of the demise of the older technology, but each of these has proved to be a resilient survivor. What accounts for their continued profitability and survival?

Retreating to more defensible ground is one strategy that firms specializing in technologies threatened with rapid obsolescence have followed. For example, while angioplasty may be appropriate for relatively healthier patients with blocked arteries, sicker, higher-risk patients seem to benefit more from coronary artery bypass graft surgery. This enabled the surgeons to concentrate on the more difficult cases and improve the technology itself. The advent of television unseated the radio as the major source of entertainment from American homes. However, the radio has survived and even thrived in venues where people are also engaged in other activities, such as driving.

Using the new to improve the old is a second approach. Microsoft has integrated elements of mobile technology into the Windows operating system to address the challenge of Google's Android and Apple's iOS.

Improving the price-performance trade-off is a third approach. IBM continues to make money selling mainframes long after their obituary was written. It retooled the technology using low-cost microprocessors and cut their prices drastically. Further, it invested and updated the software, enabling it to offer clients such as banks better performance and lower costs.

Turnaround Strategies

turnaround strategy
a strategy that reverses a firm's decline in performance and returns it to growth and profitability.

A **turnaround strategy** involves reversing performance decline and reinvigorating growth toward profitability.[74] A need for turnaround may occur at any stage in the life cycle but is more likely to occur during maturity or decline.

Most turnarounds require a firm to carefully analyze the external and internal environments.[75] The external analysis leads to identification of market segments or customer groups that may still find the product attractive.[76] Internal analysis results in actions aimed at reduced costs and higher efficiency. A firm needs to undertake a mix of both internally and externally oriented actions to effect a turnaround.[77] In effect, the cliché "You can't shrink yourself to greatness" applies.

A study of 260 mature businesses in need of a turnaround identified three strategies used by successful companies.[78]

LO 5-7

The need for turnaround strategies that enable a firm to reposition its competitive position in an industry.

- *Asset and cost surgery.* Very often, mature firms tend to have assets that do not produce any returns. These include real estate, buildings, and so on. Outright sales or sale and leaseback free up considerable cash and improve returns. Investment in new plants and equipment can be deferred. Firms in turnaround situations try to aggressively cut administrative expenses and inventories and speed up collection of receivables. Costs also can be reduced by outsourcing production of various inputs for which market prices may be cheaper than in-house production costs.

HOW MINDY GROSSMAN LED HSN'S REMARKABLE TURNAROUND

Mindy Grossman took over the helm of HSN, formerly known as the Home Shopping Network, in 2008, at a very trying time. The Home Shopping Network was falling behind the times as retailing technology changed rapidly in the digital age, and it was saddled with the reputation of being the home for C-list celebrities hawking relatively low-grade jewelry, fashion, and health and beauty products to couch potatoes. The firm had experienced significant leadership turmoil, with seven CEOs in the prior 10 years. It was also facing some of the worst economic conditions since the 1930s. Not surprisingly, the firm experienced a multibillion-dollar loss in 2008.

However, things have changed dramatically since those dark days. HSN generated 169 million in profit on $3.7 billion in sales in 2015. The firm's stock price, which traded as low as $1.42 in 2008, was trading at over $34 a share in late 2016.

At the center of HSN's turnaround is Mindy Grossman, the firm's CEO. She came to HSN after working for a number of clothing manufacturers, including Ralph Lauren, Tommy Hilfiger, and, most recently, Nike. Her recipe for the turnaround reflects a mix of hard business acumen combined with an ability to engage stakeholders in the firm to move the turnaround forward. With her changes, she's moved HSN from being a dowdy cable TV channel to a retailer that meets the needs of busy women by providing them a place to shop wherever they are—at home through their TVs or while traveling for work or at their kids' soccer games through their phones or tablets.

What are Grossman's lessons for managing a turnaround? First, she found value in engaging with employees. Her first day at HSN, she chose to go through the same new-employee orientation that all employees go through. She felt this humanized her in the minds of other employees. On her second day, she held a town-hall meeting so that she could directly introduce herself and set the tone that she was accessible and that all employees were valued and could have a future at HSN. She also set up a policy to regularly have breakfasts and lunches with employees and says, "I learn more from those than from reading any report."

Second, she got the lineup of employees right. She categorizes workers into three categories. "Evangelists" are the employees who are truly enthusiastic about the company and try to rally others. The "Interested" are those who are invested in the firm's success but have something of a wait-and-see attitude. The "Blockers" are toxic and work to limit the firm's ability to change. She saw the need to rid the company of toxicity and pushed out the Blockers quickly. This allowed her to develop a management team, which largely stayed intact for several years, that reflected the strong skills and commitment she desired.

She tailored the company's offerings to meet the changing needs of her customer base. In the deep days of the recession in 2008–2009, this meant shifting from offering high-priced jewelry and fashions to providing products and services that helped HSN's customers save time and money. Later, this meant dramatically growing the company's mobile platforms. Today, over half the new customers come to HSN through their mobile phones. One of the new services attracting them is HSN's online arcade, where customers can play games that allow them to win HSN merchandise, which generated over 100 million plays in its first year.

Key to it all is staying focused on what HSN's strategy is and who its customers are. In the words of Grossman, "We're not trying to be Amazon, all things to all people. We have a highly specialized customer and want to give her the best experience somewhere she can trust."

Sources: Goudreau, J. 2012. How Mindy Grossman is transforming HSN. *forbes.com*, August 29: np; Banjo, S. 2013. HSN enjoys a mobile-shopping rebirth in the digital age. *wsj.com*, July 5: np; and Snyder, B. 2014. How Mindy Grossman turned around HSN. *gsb.stanford.edu/insights*, June 5: np.

- *Selective product and market pruning.* Most mature or declining firms have many product lines that are losing money or are only marginally profitable. One strategy is to discontinue such product lines and focus all resources on a few core profitable areas. For example, in 2014, Procter & Gamble announced that it would sell off or close down up to 100 of its brands, allowing the firm to improve its efficiency and its innovativeness as it focused on its core brands. The remaining 70 to 80 "core" brands accounted for 90 percent of the firm's sales.

- *Piecemeal productivity improvements.* There are many ways in which a firm can eliminate costs and improve productivity. Although individually these are small gains, they cumulate over a period of time to substantial gains. Improving business processes by reengineering them, benchmarking specific activities against industry leaders, encouraging employee input to identify excess costs, increasing capacity utilization, and improving employee productivity lead to a significant overall gain.

Strategy Spotlight 5.5 provides an illustration of a turnaround effort by focusing on the dramatic strategic realignment that Mindy Grossman undertook at HSN (formerly the Home Shopping Network).

Issue for Debate

Shazz Lewis is aiming to shake up the beer business by entering with a brew aimed specifically at women. On its website, Chick beer is described as "the only beer brand designed for women, who drink 25 percent of all beer sold in the U.S." Shazz got the inspiration for Chick beer when she was looking over the more than 400 beers sold in the liquor store that she and her husband owned. She concluded, "there was nothing that shouted out female." Since women consume 700 million cases of beer a year, she saw this as a market that hasn't received enough focus.

To best reach her target market of 21 to 35-year-old women, she crafted it to be low in calories (only 97) and have a "very mellow beer flavor" with a little less carbonation "so it doesn't make you burp." Still, she says this is not a weak beer. "It needed to be a stand-up beer—not fruity-flavored, as full-bodied as a light beer could be." Turning to the look of the product, she designed the packaging to highlight the brand's image. The cardboard carrier is hot pink and black in the image of a purse and includes the tagline "witness the chickness." The bottle labels show the image of a little black dress on a hot pink background. This all has led Megan Gibson, a correspondent for *Time* magazine, to call the brand "patronizing." Jennifer Litz, editor of *Craft Business* daily, commented that some beer drinkers may believe "it's a bit too obviously pandering to create a beer specifically geared toward women." When Lewis was questioned on the brand name and the packaging, she commented, "I happen to think all things chick are terrific. I came up with a slogan that was a little in your face. It was empowering to turn it on its head."

Discussion Questions

1. Is the name and packaging of Chick beer patronizing to women, or is it empowering to turn what has been, at times, a derogatory term on its head?
2. How effectively does Chick beer create differentiation to draw in female beer drinkers? How successful do you think the brand could be?
3. What recommendations would you have for Shazz Lewis to enhance her chances of success in the beer market?

Sources: Shockey, L. 2011. Chick beer founder Shazz Lewis dishes on making girly beer. *villagevoice.com*, September 1: np; Gibson, M. 2011. New 'Chick' beer is a lady-catered brew in a girly, pink package. *newsfeed.time.com*, September 7: np; Snider, M. 2016. Women to get their own beer. *lsj.com*, May 29: np.

Reflecting on Career Implications . . .

This chapter discusses how firms build competitive advantage in the marketplace. The following questions ask you to consider how you can contribute to the competitive advantage of firms you work at as well as how you can develop your own differentiated set of skills and enhance the growth phase of your career.

- **Types of Competitive Advantage:** Are you aware of your organization's business-level strategy? What do you do to help your firm either increase differentiation or lower costs? Can you demonstrate to your superiors how you have contributed to the firm's chosen business-level strategy?

- **Types of Competitive Advantage:** What is your own competitive advantage? What opportunities does your current job provide to enhance your competitive advantage? Are you making the best use of your competitive advantage? If not, what organizations might provide you with better opportunities for doing so? Does your résumé clearly reflect your competitive advantage? Or are you "stuck in the middle"?

- **Understanding *Your* Differentiation:** When looking for a new job or for advancement in your current firm, be conscious of being able to identify what differentiates you from other applicants. Consider the items in Exhibit 5.4 as you work to identify what distinguishes you from others.

- **Industry Life Cycle:** Before you go for a job interview, identify the life-cycle stage of the industry within which your firm is located. You are more likely to have greater opportunities for career advancement in an industry in the growth stage than one in the decline stage.

- **Industry Life Cycle:** If you sense that your career is maturing (or in the decline phase!), what actions can you take to restore career growth and momentum (e.g., training, mentoring, professional networking)? Should you actively consider professional opportunities in other industries?

summary

How and why firms outperform each other goes to the heart of strategic management. In this chapter, we identified three generic strategies and discussed how firms are able not only to attain advantages over competitors but also to sustain such advantages over time. Why do some advantages become long-lasting while others are quickly imitated by competitors?

The three generic strategies—overall cost leadership, differentiation, and focus—form the core of this chapter. We began by providing a brief description of each generic strategy (or competitive advantage) and furnished examples of firms that have successfully implemented these strategies. Successful generic strategies invariably enhance a firm's position vis-à-vis the five forces of that industry—a point that we stressed and illustrated with examples. However, as we pointed out, there are pitfalls to each of the generic strategies. Thus, the sustainability of a firm's advantage is always challenged because of imitation or substitution by new or existing rivals. Such competitor moves erode a firm's advantage over time.

We also discussed the viability of combining (or integrating) overall cost leadership and generic differentiation strategies. If successful, such integration can enable a firm to enjoy superior performance and improve its competitive position. However, this is challenging, and managers must be aware of the potential downside risks associated with such an initiative.

We addressed the challenges inherent in determining the sustainability of competitive advantages. Drawing on an example from a manufacturing industry, we discussed both the "pro" and "con" positions as to why competitive advantages are sustainable over a long period of time.

The concept of the industry life cycle is a critical contingency that managers must take into account in striving to create and sustain competitive advantages. We identified the four stages of the industry life cycle—introduction, growth, maturity, and decline—and suggested how these stages can play a role in decisions that managers must make at the business level. These include overall strategies as well as the relative emphasis on functional areas and value-creating activities.

When a firm's performance severely erodes, turnaround strategies are needed to reverse its situation and enhance its competitive position. We have discussed three approaches—asset cost surgery, selective product and market pruning, and piecemeal productivity improvements.

SUMMARY REVIEW QUESTIONS

1. Explain why the concept of competitive advantage is central to the study of strategic management.
2. Briefly describe the three generic strategies—overall cost leadership, differentiation, and focus.
3. Explain the relationship between the three generic strategies and the five forces that determine the average profitability within an industry.
4. What are some of the ways in which a firm can attain a successful turnaround strategy?
5. Describe some of the pitfalls associated with each of the three generic strategies.
6. Can firms combine the generic strategies of overall cost leadership and differentiation? Why or why not?
7. Explain why the industry life-cycle concept is an important factor in determining a firm's business-level strategy.

key terms

business-level strategy 139
generic strategies 140
overall cost leadership 141
experience curve 141
competitive parity 141
differentiation strategy 145
focus strategy 150
combination strategies 152
mass customization 152
profit pool 153
industry life cycle 159
introduction stage 161
growth stage 161
maturity stage 162
reverse positioning 162
breakaway
    positioning 162
decline stage 163
harvesting strategy 163
consolidation strategy 163
turnaround strategy 164

EXPERIENTIAL EXERCISE

What are some examples of primary and support activities that enable Nucor, a $19 billion steel manufacturer, to achieve a low-cost strategy? (Fill in the following table.)

Value-Chain Activity	Yes/No	How Does Nucor Create Value for the Customer?
Primary:		
Inbound logistics		
Operations		
Outbound logistics		
Marketing and sales		
Service		
Support:		
Procurement		
Technology development		
Human resource management		
General administration		

APPLICATION QUESTIONS & EXERCISES

1. Research Amazon. How has this firm been able to combine overall cost leadership and differentiation strategies?

2. Choose a firm with which you are familiar in your local business community. Is the firm successful in following one (or more) generic strategies? Why or why not? What do you think are some of the challenges it faces in implementing these strategies in an effective manner?

3. Think of a firm that has attained a differentiation focus or cost focus strategy. Are its advantages sustainable? Why? Why not? (*Hint:* Consider its position vis-à-vis Porter's five forces.)

4. Think of a firm that successfully achieved a combination overall cost leadership and differentiation strategy. What can be learned from this example? Are the advantages sustainable? Why? Why not? (*Hint:* Consider its competitive position vis-à-vis Porter's five forces.)

ETHICS QUESTIONS

1. Can you think of a company that suffered ethical consequences as a result of an overemphasis on a cost leadership strategy? What do you think were the financial and nonfinancial implications?

2. In the introductory stage of the product life cycle, what are some of the unethical practices that managers could engage in to enhance their firm's market position? What could be some of the long-term implications of such actions?

REFERENCES

1. Gasparro, A. & Checkler, J. 2015. A&P bankruptcy filing indicates likely demise. *wsj.com.* July 20: np; Bomey, N. & Nguyen, H. 2015. A&P grocery chain files bankruptcy again. *usatoday.com.* July 20: np.

2. For a perspective by Porter on competitive strategy, refer to Porter, M. E. 1996. What is strategy? *Harvard Business Review,* 74(6): 61–78.

3. For insights into how a start-up is using solar technology, see Gimbel, B. 2009. Plastic power. *Fortune,* February 2: 34.

4. Useful insights on strategy in an economic downturn are in Rhodes, D. & Stelter, D. 2009. Seize advantage in a downturn. *Harvard Business Review,* 87(2): 50–58.

5. Some useful ideas on maintaining competitive advantages can be found in Ma, H. & Karri, R. 2005. Leaders beware: Some sure ways to lose your competitive advantage. *Organizational Dynamics,* 343(1): 63–76.

6. Miller, A. & Dess, G. G. 1993. Assessing Porter's model in terms of its generalizability, accuracy, and simplicity. *Journal of Management Studies,* 30(4): 553–585.

7. Gasparro, A. & Martin, T. 2012. What's wrong with America's supermarkets? *wsj.com,* July 12: np.

8. For insights on how discounting can erode a firm's performance, read Stibel, J. M. & Delgrosso, P. 2008. Discounts can be dangerous. *Harvard Business Review,* 66(12): 31.

9. For a scholarly discussion and analysis of the concept of competitive parity, refer to Powell, T. C. 2003. Varieties of competitive parity. *Strategic Management Journal,* 24(1): 61–86.

10. Rao, A. R., Bergen, M. E., & Davis, S. 2000. How to fight a price war. *Harvard Business Review,* 78(2): 107–120.

11. Oltermann, P. & McClanahan, P. 2014. Tata Nano safety under scrutiny after dire crash test results. *guardian.com.* January 31: np.

12. Burrus, D. 2011. *Flash foresight: How to see the invisible and do the impossible.* New York: HarperCollins.

13. Corstjens, M. & Lal, R. 2012. Retail doesn't cross borders. *Harvard Business Review,* April: 104-110.

14. Ng, S. 2014. Zulily customers play the waiting game. *wsj.com,* May 4: np.

15. Interesting insights on Walmart's effective cost leadership strategy are found in Palmeri, C. 2008. Wal-Mart is up for this downturn. *BusinessWeek,* November 6: 34.

16. An interesting perspective on the dangers of price discounting is Mohammed, R. 2011. Ditch the discounts. *Harvard Business Review,* 89(1/2): 23-25.

17. Dholakia, U. M. 2011. Why employees can wreck promotional offers. *Harvard Business Review,* 89(1/2): 28.

18. Jacobs, A. 2010. Workers in China voting with their feet. *International Herald Tribune,* July 13: 1, 14.

19. For a perspective on the sustainability of competitive advantages, refer to Barney, J. 1995. Looking inside for competitive advantage. *Academy of Management Executive,* 9(4): 49-61.

20. Thornton, E. 2001. Why e-brokers are broker and broker. *BusinessWeek,* January 22: 94.

21. Mohammed, R. 2011. Ditch the discounts. *Harvard Business Review,* 89(1/2): 23-25.

22. Wilson, D. 2012. Big Beer dresses up in craft brewers' clothing. *Fortune. com,* November 15: np.

23. For an "ultimate" in differentiated services, consider time-shares in exotic automobiles such as Lamborghinis and Bentleys. Refer to Stead, D. 2008. My Lamborghini—today, anyway. *BusinessWeek,* January 18:17.

24. For an interesting perspective on the value of corporate brands and how they may be leveraged, refer to Aaker, D. A. 2004, *California Management Review,* 46(3): 6-18.

25. A unique perspective on differentiation strategies is Austin, R. D. 2008. High margins and the quest for aesthetic coherence. *Harvard Business Review,* 86(1): 18-19.

26. Eng, D. 2011. Cheesecake Factory's winning formula. *Fortune,* May 2: 19-20.

27. For a discussion on quality in terms of a company's software and information systems, refer to Prahalad, C. K. & Krishnan, M. S. 1999. The new meaning of quality in the information age. *Harvard Business Review,* 77(5): 109-118.

28. The role of design in achieving differentiation is addressed in Brown, T. 2008. Design thinking. *Harvard Business Review,* 86(6): 84-92.

29. Taylor, A., III. 2001. Can you believe Porsche is putting its badge on this car? *Fortune,* February 19: 168-172.

30. Roberts, P. & Dowling, G. 2008. Corporate reputation and sustained superior financial performance. *Strategic Management Journal,* 23: 1077-1093.

31. Mann, J. 2010. The best service in the world. *Networking Times,* January: np.

32. Bonnabeau, E., Bodick, N., & Armstrong, R. W. 2008. A more rational approach to new-product development. *Harvard Business Review,* 66(3): 96-102.

33. Insights on Google's innovation are in Iyer, B. & Davenport, T. H. 2008. Reverse engineering Google's innovation machine. *Harvard Business Review,* 66(4): 58-68.

34. A discussion of how a firm used technology to create product differentiation is in Mehta, S. N. 2009. Under Armour reboots. *Fortune,* February 2: 29-33 (5).

35. Bertini, M. & Wathieu, L. 2010. How to stop customers from fixating on price. *Harvard Business Review,* 88(5): 84-91.

36. The authors would like to thank Scott Droege, a faculty member at Western Kentucky University, for providing this example.

37. Dixon, M., Freeman, K., & Toman, N. 2010. Stop trying to delight your customers. *Harvard Business Review,* 88(7/8).

38. Flint, J. 2004. Stop the nerds. *Forbes,* July 5: 80; and Fahey, E. 2004. Over-engineering 101. *Forbes,* December 13: 62.

39. Symonds, W. C. 2000. Can Gillette regain its voltage? *BusinessWeek,* October 16: 102-104.

40. Caplan, J. 2006. In a real crunch. *Inside Business,* July: A37-A38.

41. Gadiesh, O. & Gilbert, J. L. 1998. Profit pools: A fresh look at strategy. *Harvard Business Review,* 76(3): 139-158.

42. Colvin, G. 2000. Beware: You could soon be selling soybeans. *Fortune,* November 13: 80.

43. Anders, G. 2012. How LinkedIn has turned your resume into a cash machine. *Forbes.com,* July 16: np.

44. Burrus, D. 2011. *Flash foresight: How to see the invisible and do the impossible.* New York: HarperCollins.

45. Hall, W. K. 1980. Survival strategies in a hostile environment, *Harvard Business Review,* 58: 75-87; on

the paint and allied products industry, see Dess, G. G. & Davis, P. S. 1984. Porter's (1980) generic strategies as determinants of strategic group membership and organizational performance. *Academy of Management Journal,* 27: 467-488; for the Korean electronics industry, see Kim, L. & Lim, Y. 1988. Environment, generic strategies, and performance in a rapidly developing country: A taxonomic approach. *Academy of Management Journal,* 31: 802-827; Wright, P., Hotard, D., Kroll, M., Chan, P., & Tanner, J. 1990. Performance and multiple strategies in a firm: Evidence from the apparel industry. In Dean, B. V. & Cassidy, J. C. (Eds.), *Strategic management: Methods and studies:* 93-110. Amsterdam: Elsevier-North Holland; and Wright, P., Kroll, M., Tu, H., & Helms, M. 1991. Generic strategies and business performance: An empirical study of the screw machine products industry. *British Journal of Management,* 2: 1-9.

46. Gilmore, J. H. & Pine, B. J., II. 1997. The four faces of customization. *Harvard Business Review,* 75(1): 91-101.

47. Heracleous, L. & Wirtz, J. 2010. Singapore Airlines' balancing act. *Harvard Business Review,* 88(7/8): 145-149.

48. Gilmore & Pine, op. cit. For interesting insights on mass customization, refer to Cattani, K., Dahan, E., & Schmidt, G. 2005. Offshoring versus "spackling." *MIT Sloan Management Review,* 46(3): 6-7.

49. Goodstein, L. D. & Butz, H. E. 1998. Customer value: The linchpin of organizational change. *Organizational Dynamics,* Summer: 21-34.

50. Kiron, D. 2013. From value to vision: Reimagining the possible with data analytics. *MIT Sloan Management Review Research Report,* Spring: 1-19.

51. Gadiesh & Gilbert, op. cit., pp. 139-158.

52. Insights on the profit pool concept are addressed in Reinartz, W. & Ulaga, W. 2008. How to sell services more profitably. *Harvard Business Review,* 66(5): 90-96.

53. *statista.com/statistics/263439/ global-market-share-held-by-rim-smartphones/.*

54. For an insightful, recent discussion on the difficulties and challenges associated with creating advantages that are sustainable for any reasonable period of time and suggested strategies, refer to D'Aveni, R. A., Dagnino, G. B., & Smith,

K. G. 2010. The age of temporary advantage. *Strategic Management Journal*, 31(13): 1371–1385. This is the lead article in a special issue of this journal that provides many ideas that are useful to both academics and practicing managers. For an additional examination of declining advantage in technologically intensive industries, see Vaaler, P. M. & McNamara, G. 2010. Are technology-intensive industries more dynamically competitive? No and yes. *Organization Science*, 21: 271–289.

55. Rita McGrath provides some interesting ideas on possible strategies for firms facing highly uncertain competitive environments: McGrath, R. G. 2011. When your business model is in trouble. *Harvard Business Review*, 89(1/2): 96–98.

56. The Atlas Door example draws on Stalk, G., Jr. 1988. Time—the next source of competitive advantage. *Harvard Business Review*, 66(4): 41–51.

57. Eisenmann, T., Parker, G., & Van Alstyne, M. 2006. Strategies for two-sided markets. *hbr.org*. October: np; Bonchek, M. & Choudary, S. 2013. Three elements of a successful platform strategy. *hbr.org*. January 31: np; Anonymous. 2016. How Uber, Airbnb and Etsy attracted their first 1,000 customers. *horbes.com*. July 13: np; Ifrach, B. 2015. How Airbnb uses machine learning to detect host preferences. *nerds.airbnb.com*. April 14: np.

58. For an interesting perspective on the influence of the product life cycle and rate of technological change on competitive strategy, refer to Lei, D. & Slocum, J. W., Jr. 2005. Strategic and organizational requirements for competitive advantage. *Academy of Management Executive*, 19(1): 31–45.

59. Dickson, P. R. 1994. *Marketing management*: 293. Fort Worth, TX: Dryden Press; Day, G. S. 1981. The product life cycle: Analysis and application. *Journal of Marketing Research*, 45: 60–67.

60. Bearden, W. O., Ingram, T. N., & LaForge, R. W. 1995. *Marketing principles and practices*. Burr Ridge, IL: Irwin.

61. MacMillan, I. C. 1985. Preemptive strategies. In Guth, W. D. (Ed.), *Handbook of business strategy*: 9-1–9.22. Boston: Warren, Gorham & Lamont; Pearce, J. A. & Robinson, R. B. 2000. *Strategic management* (7th ed.). New York: McGraw-Hill; and Dickson, op. cit., pp. 295–296.

62. Bartlett, C. A. & Ghoshal, S. 2000. Going global: Lessons for late movers. *Harvard Business Review*, 78(2): 132–142.

63. Neuborne, E. 2000. E-tailers hit the relaunch key. *BusinessWeek*, October 17: 62.

64. Berkowitz, E. N., Kerin, R. A., & Hartley, S. W. 2000. *Marketing* (6th ed.). New York: McGraw-Hill.

65. MacMillan, op. cit.

66. Brooker, K. 2001. A game of inches. *Fortune*, February 5: 98–100.

67. Our discussion of reverse and breakaway positioning draws on Moon, Y. 2005. Break free from the product life cycle. *Harvard Business Review*, 83(5): 87–94. This article also discusses stealth positioning as a means of overcoming consumer resistance and advancing a product from the introduction to the growth phase.

68. MacMillan, op. cit.

69. Berkowitz et al., op. cit.

70. Bearden et al., op. cit.

71. The discussion of these four strategies draws on MacMillan, op. cit.; Berkowitz et al., op. cit.; and Bearden et al., op. cit.

72. Augustine, N. R. 1997. Reshaping an industry: Lockheed Martin's survival story. *Harvard Business Review*, 75(3): 83–94.

73. Snow, D. C. 2008. Beware of old technologies' last gasps. *Harvard Business Review*, January: 17–18; Lohr, S. 2008. Why old technologies are still kicking. *New York Times*, March 23: np; and McGrath, R. G. 2008. Innovation and the last gasps of dying technologies. ritamcgrath.com, March 18: np.

74. Coyne, K. P., Coyne, S. T., & Coyne, E. J., Sr. 2010. When you've got to cut costs—now. *Harvard Business Review*, 88(5): 74–83.

75. A study that draws on the resource-based view of the firm to investigate successful turnaround strategies is Morrow, J. S., Sirmon, D. G., Hitt, M. A., & Holcomb, T. R. 2007. Creating value in the face of declining performance: Firm strategies and organizational recovery. *Strategic Management Journal*, 28(3): 271–284.

76. For a study investigating the relationship between organizational restructuring and acquisition performance, refer to Barkema, H. G. & Schijven, M. Toward unlocking the full potential of acquisitions: The role of organizational restructuring. *Academy of Management Journal*, 51(4): 696–722.

77. For some useful ideas on effective turnarounds and handling downsizings, refer to Marks, M. S. & De Meuse, K. P. 2005. Resizing the organization: Maximizing the gain while minimizing the pain of layoffs, divestitures and closings. *Organizational Dynamics*, 34(1): 19–36.

78. Hambrick, D. C. & Schecter, S. M. 1983. Turnaround strategies for mature industrial product business units. *Academy of Management Journal*, 26(2): 231–248.

Corporate-Level Strategy

Creating Value through Diversification

After reading this chapter, you should have a good understanding of the following learning objectives:

LO6-1   The reasons for the failure of many diversification efforts.

LO6-2   How managers can create value through diversification initiatives.

LO6-3   How corporations can use related diversification to achieve synergistic benefits through economies of scope and market power.

LO6-4   How corporations can use unrelated diversification to attain synergistic benefits through corporate restructuring, parenting, and portfolio analysis.

LO6-5   The various means of engaging in diversification—mergers and acquisitions, joint ventures/strategic alliances, and internal development.

LO6-6   Managerial behaviors that can erode the creation of value.

©Anatoli Styf/Shutterstock

LEARNING FROM MISTAKES

For decades, Coca-Cola used independent bottlers to distribute Coke products to stores and restaurants. Coke would manufacture the concentrate used to make its soft drinks, but the actual bottling of the product and distribution to end retailers was handled by about 70 regional bottling firms. In 2010, Coca-Cola undertook a major initiative to buy its bottlers and create a national vertically integrated business operation, where Coke would not only manufacture the concentrate but also own its bottling and distribution system. The firm spent $12.3 billion to acquire Coca-Cola Enterprises, its largest bottling partner. Coke believed it could improve the operations of the bottling network by closing some bottling plants, modernizing others, and creating an integrated national manufacturing system. In doing so, the firm could achieve $350 million in annual cost savings while allowing the firm to nationally roll out new products more quickly. Coke could then also negotiate directly with large, national retailers. In short, the firm would be more efficient and more responsive to customer needs.

However, under pressure from investors, Coca-Cola reversed course in 2015—announcing that it would sell off all of its bottling operations. In the first step of this process, it agreed to sell nine production facilities to three bottling companies for $380 million. Additionally, Coke announced it would complete the process of selling off its remaining bottling plants and distribution facilities by the end of 2017.[1]

What happened to trigger this rapid change? Coke found that being in the bottling business didn't help its financial performance. In the words of Jack Russo, an analyst at Edward Jones Investing, "bottling is a low margin, capital-intensive business." Coke also found upgrading and streamlining its bottling networks was harder and was taking more time than expected. While it initially estimated it could close about one-third of its bottling plants to improve efficiencies, it ended up closing only one-tenth of the plants. As a result, Coke saw its operating margins fall from 20.7 percent in 2009 to 11.4 percent in 2014. Divesting the bottling operations allows Coke to again focus on the more profitable business of selling concentrates and syrups to independent companies that bottle and can drinks and then package and distribute them to stores and restaurants. Analysts expect the firm's operating margins will rise by 50 percent. Returning management of bottling and distribution to local partners will also allow bottling operations to better meet local market needs. Ultimately, Coke's management came to the realization that running a capital-intensive manufacturing business didn't really fit the capabilities of the firm. CEO Muhtar Kent told industry analysts that Coke could now focus on developing and managing brands: "That's what we're best at."

Discussion Questions

1. What are the pros and cons of Coca-Cola owning its bottlers?
2. Why didn't Coca-Cola's acquisition of its bottlers lead to the improvements the firm expected?
3. Will this latest move serve as a clear strategy that will lead to long-term profitability, or is it just a reaction to outside pressures the firm faced?

Coca-Cola's experience with its purchase of its bottlers is more the rule than the exception. Research shows that a majority of acquisitions of public corporations result in value destruction rather than value creation. Many other large multinational firms have also failed to effectively integrate their acquisitions, paid too high a premium for the target's common stock, or were unable to understand how the acquired firm's assets would fit with their own

LO 6-1

The reasons for the failure of many diversification efforts.

EXHIBIT 6.1 Some Well-Known M&A Blunders

Examples of Some Very Expensive Blunders

- Sprint and Nextel merged in 2005. On January 31, 2008, the firm announced a merger-related charge of $31 billion. Its stock had lost 76 percent of its value by late 2012 when it was announced that Sprint Nextel would be purchased by SoftBank, a Japanese telecommunications and Internet firm. SoftBank's stock price dropped 20 percent in the week after announcing it would acquire Sprint.
- AOL paid $114 billion to acquire Time Warner in 2001. Over the next two years, AOL Time Warner lost $150 billion in market valuation.
- In 2012, Hewlett-Packard wrote off $9 billion of the $11 billion it paid for Autonomy, a software company that it purchased one year earlier. After the purchase, HP realized that Autonomy's accounting statements were not accurate, resulting in a nearly 80 percent drop in the value of Autonomy once those accounting irregularities were corrected.
- Similarly, in 2012, Microsoft admitted to a major acquisition mistake when it wrote off essentially the entire $6.2 billion it paid for a digital advertising firm, aQuantive, that it purchased in 2007.
- Yahoo purchased Tumblr for $1.1 billion in 2013 but had written off over 80 percent of this value by the middle of 2016. Commentators have noted that Yahoo's repeated failures to extract value from acquisitions is one of the key reasons it was unable to survive as an independent firm.

Sources: Ante, S. E. 2008. Sprint's wake-up call. *businessweek.com,* February 21: np; Tully, S. 2006. The (second) worst deal ever. *Fortune,* October 16: 102–119; Wakabayashi, D., Troianovski, A., & Ante, S. 2012. Bravado behind Softbank's Sprint deal. *wsj.com,* October 16: np; and Kim, E. 2016.Yahoo just wrote down another $482 million from Tumblr, the company it bought for $1 billion. *businessinsider.com,* July 18: np.

---

corporate-level strategy
a strategy that focuses on gaining long-term revenue, profits, and market value through managing operations in multiple businesses.

lines of business.[2] And, at times, top executives may not have acted in the best interests of shareholders. That is, the motive for the acquisition may have been to enhance the executives' power and prestige rather than to improve shareholder returns. At times, the only other people who may have benefited were the shareholders of the *acquired* firms—or the investment bankers who advise the acquiring firm, because they collect huge fees up front regardless of what happens afterward![3]

Academic research has found that acquisitions, in general, do not lead to benefits for shareholders. A review paper that looked at over 100 studies on mergers and acquisitions concluded that research has found that acquisitions, on average, do not create shareholder value.[4]

Exhibit 6.1 lists some well-known examples of failed acquisitions and mergers.

Many acquisitions ultimately result in divestiture—an admission that things didn't work out as planned. In fact, some years ago, a writer for *Fortune* magazine lamented, "Studies show that 33 percent to 50 percent of acquisitions are later divested, giving corporate marriages a divorce rate roughly comparable to that of men and women."[5]

Admittedly, we have been rather pessimistic so far.[6] Clearly, many diversification efforts have worked out very well—whether through mergers and acquisitions, strategic alliances and joint ventures, or internal development. We will discuss many success stories throughout this chapter. Next, we will discuss the primary rationales for diversification.

MAKING DIVERSIFICATION WORK: AN OVERVIEW

LO 6-2

How managers can create value through diversification initiatives.

diversification
the process of firms expanding their operations by entering new businesses.

Clearly, not all **diversification** moves, including those involving mergers and acquisitions, erode performance. For example, acquisitions in the oil industry, such as British Petroleum's purchases of Amoco and Arco, performed well, as did the Exxon-Mobil merger. MetLife was able to dramatically expand its global footprint by acquiring Alico, a global player in the insurance business, from AIG in 2010 when AIG was in financial distress. Since AIG was desperate to sell assets, MetLife was able to acquire this business at an attractive price. With this acquisition, MetLife expanded its global reach from 17 to 64 countries and increased its non-U.S. revenue from 15 to 40 percent.[7] Many leading high-tech firms such as Google, Apple, and Intel have dramatically enhanced their revenues, profits, and market values through a wide variety of diversification initiatives, including acquisitions, strategic alliances, and joint ventures, as well as internal development.

So the question becomes: Why do some diversification efforts pay off and others produce poor results? This chapter addresses two related issues: (1) What businesses should a corporation compete in? and (2) How should these businesses be managed to jointly create more value than if they were freestanding units?

Diversification initiatives—whether through mergers and acquisitions, strategic alliances and joint ventures, or internal development—must be justified by the creation of value for shareholders.[8] But this is not always the case.[9] Acquiring firms typically pay high premiums when they acquire a target firm. For example, in 2016, Microsoft offered to buy LinkedIn for $26.2 billion, 50 percent higher than LinkedIn's value the day before. In contrast, you and I, as private investors, can diversify our portfolio of stocks very cheaply. With an intensely competitive online brokerage industry, we can acquire hundreds (or thousands) of shares for a transaction fee of as little as $10 or less—a far cry from the 30 to 40 percent (or higher) premiums that corporations typically must pay to acquire companies.

Given the seemingly high inherent downside risks and uncertainties, one might ask: Why should companies even bother with diversification initiatives? The answer, in a word, is *synergy,* derived from the Greek word *synergos,* which means "working together." This can have two different, but not mutually exclusive, meanings.

First, a firm may diversify into *related* businesses. Here, the primary potential benefits to be derived come from *horizontal relationships,* that is, businesses sharing intangible resources (e.g., core competencies such as marketing) and tangible resources (e.g., production facilities, distribution channels).[10] Firms can also enhance their market power via pooled negotiating power and vertical integration. For example, Procter & Gamble enjoys many synergies from having businesses that share distribution resources.

Second, a corporation may diversify into unrelated businesses.[11] Here, the primary potential benefits are derived largely from *hierarchical relationships,* that is, value creation derived from the corporate office. Examples of the latter would include leveraging some of the support activities in the value chain that we discussed in Chapter 3, such as information systems or human resource practices.

Please note that such benefits derived from horizontal (related diversification) and hierarchical (unrelated diversification) relationships are not mutually exclusive. Many firms that diversify into related areas benefit from information technology expertise in the corporate office. Similarly, unrelated diversifiers often benefit from the "best practices" of sister businesses even though their products, markets, and technologies may differ dramatically.

Exhibit 6.2 provides an overview of how we will address the various means by which firms create value through both related and unrelated diversification and also includes a summary of some examples that we will address in this chapter.[12]

RELATED DIVERSIFICATION: ECONOMIES OF SCOPE AND REVENUE ENHANCEMENT

Related diversification enables a firm to benefit from horizontal relationships across different businesses in the diversified corporation by leveraging core competencies and sharing activities (e.g., production and distribution facilities). This enables a corporation to benefit from economies of scope. **Economies of scope** refers to cost savings from leveraging core competencies or sharing related activities among businesses in the corporation. A firm can also enjoy greater revenues if two businesses attain higher levels of sales growth combined than either company could attain independently.

Leveraging Core Competencies

The concept of core competencies can be illustrated by the imagery of the diversified corporation as a tree.[13] The trunk and major limbs represent core products; the smaller branches

LO 6-3

How corporations can use related diversification to achieve synergistic benefits through economies of scope and market power.

related diversification
a firm entering a different business in which it can benefit from leveraging core competencies, sharing activities, or building market power.

economies of scope
cost savings from leveraging core competencies or sharing related activities among businesses in a corporation.

EXHIBIT 6.2

Creating Value through
Related and Unrelated
Diversification

Related Diversification: Economies of Scope

Leveraging core competencies

- 3M leverages its competencies in adhesives technologies to many industries, including automotive, construction, and telecommunications.

Sharing activities

- Polaris, a manufacturer of snowmobiles, motorcycles, watercraft, and off-road vehicles, shares manufacturing operations across its businesses. It also has a corporate R&D facility and staff departments that support all of Polaris's operating divisions.

Related Diversification: Market Power

Pooled negotiating power

- ConAgra, a diversified food producer, increases its power over suppliers by centrally purchasing huge quantities of packaging materials for all of its food divisions.

Vertical integration

- Shaw Industries, a giant carpet manufacturer, increases its control over raw materials by producing much of its own polypropylene fiber, a key input to its manufacturing process.

Unrelated Diversification: Parenting, Restructuring, and Financial Synergies

Corporate restructuring and parenting

- The corporate office of Cooper Industries adds value to its acquired businesses by performing such activities as auditing their manufacturing operations, improving their accounting activities, and centralizing union negotiations.

Portfolio management

- Novartis, formerly Ciba-Geigy, uses portfolio management to improve many key activities, including resource allocation and reward and evaluation systems.

are business units; and the leaves, flowers, and fruit are end products. The core competencies are represented by the root system, which provides nourishment, sustenance, and stability. Managers often misread the strength of competitors by looking only at their end products, just as we can fail to appreciate the strength of a tree by looking only at its leaves. Core competencies may also be viewed as the "glue" that binds existing businesses together or as the engine that fuels new business growth.

core competencies
a firm's strategic
resources that reflect the
collective learning in the
organization.

Core competencies reflect the collective learning in organizations—how to coordinate diverse production skills, integrate multiple streams of technologies, and market diverse products and services.[14] Casio, a giant electronic products producer, synthesizes its abilities in miniaturization, microprocessor design, material science, and ultrathin precision castings to produce digital watches. These are the same skills it applies to design and produce its miniature card calculators, digital cameras, pocket electronic dictionaries, and other small electronics.

For a core competence to create value and provide a viable basis for synergy among the businesses in a corporation, it must meet three criteria:[15]

- ***The core competence must enhance competitive advantage(s) by creating superior customer value.*** Every value-chain activity has the potential to provide a viable basis for building on a core competence.[16] At Gillette, for example, scientists have developed a series of successful new razors, including the Sensor, Fusion, Mach 3, and ProGlide, building on a thorough understanding of several phenomena that underlie shaving. These include the physiology of facial hair and skin, the metallurgy of blade strength and sharpness, the dynamics of a cartridge moving across skin, and the physics of a razor blade severing hair. Such innovations are possible only with an understanding of such phenomena and the ability to combine such technologies

IBM: THE NEW HEALTH CARE EXPERT

Watson, the supercomputer IBM used to win a competition against the best players on the quiz show *Jeopardy!* is now working toward becoming Dr. Watson. Over the decades, IBM has developed strong competencies in raw computing power. With Watson, a computer named after IBM founder Thomas J. Watson, IBM engineers and scientists set out to extend IBM's competencies by building a computing system that can process natural language. Their goal was to build a system that could rival a human's ability to answer questions posed in natural language with speed, accuracy, and confidence. They took four years to develop the system and demonstrated its capabilities in beating two of the greatest champions of *Jeopardy!* in 2011.

Now IBM is aiming to leverage its competencies in the health care arena. In 2013, IBM introduced three applications, one which recommends cancer treatment options and two for reviewing and authorizing treatments and related insurance claims. IBM developed the cancer treatment application with Memorial Sloan-Kettering, one of the world's premier cancer treatment clinics. IBM chose to work on cancer treatment since the volume of research on cancer doubles every five years. As a result, oncologists, the doctors treating cancer, can easily fall behind the cutting edge of research. As Dr. Mark Kris, chief of Memorial Sloan Kettering's Thoracic Oncology Service, stated, "There has been an explosion in medical research, and doctors can't possibly keep up." That is not a problem for Watson. IBM sees this massive volume of research as an opportunity to crowdsource knowledge to develop new, integrated insights. IBM regularly feeds massive amounts of data from medical studies into Watson. In a one-year period, Watson absorbed and analyzed more than 600,000 pieces of medical data and 2 million pages of text from 42 medical journals and clinical trials of cancer treatments. IBM then adds the individual patient's health history and current symptoms to the system. With its natural-language capabilities, Watson can easily process and codify all of the information fed into it. Doctors access the system, using an iPad, enter the patient's symptoms, and within three seconds receive a personalized diagnosis and a prioritized list of recommended tests and treatment options.

While oncology was the first medical specialty for Watson, IBM has expanded the approach and is also providing guidance for the treatment of diabetes, kidney disease, heart disease, and many other areas of medicine. It has even created an entirely new business unit, IBM Watson Health, a cloud-based service selling diagnostic expertise to doctors, hospitals, and insurers.

Sources: Frier, S. 2012. IBM wants to put a Watson in your pocket. *Bloomberg Businessweek,* September 17: 41–42; Groenfeldt, T. 2012. IBM's Watson, Cedars-Sinai and WellPoint take on cancer. *forbes.com,* February 1: np; Henschen, D. 2013. IBM's Watson could be healthcare game changer. *informationweek.com,* February 3: np; *ibm.com;* and Claney, H. 2015. IBM's new health care prescription: A standalone business unit. *fortune.com,* April 13: np..

into innovative products. Customers are willing to pay more for such technologically differentiated products.

- ***Different businesses in the corporation must be similar in at least one important way related to the core competence.*** It is not essential that the products or services themselves be similar. Rather, at least one element in the value chain must require similar skills in creating competitive advantage if the corporation is to capitalize on its core competence. For example, while we might think that film technology and beauty products have little in common, Fujifilm has found a link it could exploit. Fuji took expertise it had developed with collagen, a major component of both photo film and human skin, and used it to develop a new skin care product line, Astalift—a product line that produces over $80 million in sales.[17] Similarly, as discussed in Strategy Spotlight 6.1, IBM is combining its competencies in computing technology with crowdsourced medical research knowledge to provide health care services.

- ***The core competencies must be difficult for competitors to imitate or find substitutes for.*** As we discussed in Chapter 5, competitive advantages will not be sustainable if the competition can easily imitate or substitute them. Similarly, if the skills associated with a firm's core competencies are easily imitated or replicated, they are not a sound basis for sustainable advantages.

Consider Amazon's retailing operations. Amazon developed strong competencies in Internet retailing, website infrastructure, warehousing, and order fulfillment to dominate the online book industry. It used these competencies along with its brand name to expand into a range of online retail businesses. Competitors in these other market areas have had great difficulty imitating Amazon's competencies, and many have simply stopped trying. Instead, they have partnered with Amazon and contracted with Amazon to provide these services for them.[18]

Sharing Activities

As we saw previously, leveraging core competencies involves transferring accumulated skills and expertise across business units in a corporation. Corporations also can achieve synergy by **sharing activities** across their business units. These include value-creating activities such as common manufacturing facilities, distribution channels, and sales forces. As we will see, sharing activities can potentially provide two primary payoffs: cost savings and revenue enhancements.

Deriving Cost Savings   Typically, this is the most common type of synergy and the easiest to estimate. Peter Shaw, head of mergers and acquisitions at the British chemical and pharmaceutical company ICI, refers to cost savings as "hard synergies" and contends that the level of certainty of their achievement is quite high. Cost savings come from many sources, including from the elimination of jobs, facilities, and related expenses that are no longer needed when functions are consolidated and from economies of scale in purchasing. Cost savings are generally highest when one company acquires another from the same industry in the same country. Shaw Industries, a division of Berkshire Hathaway, is the nation's largest carpet producer. Over the years, it has dominated the competition through a strategy of acquisition that has enabled Shaw, among other things, to consolidate its manufacturing operations in a few, highly efficient plants and to lower costs through higher capacity utilization. Honda benefits by sharing small engine development and manufacturing across the more than 15 different types of power equipment it produces. Similarly, General Motors uses a shared engineering group and shared vehicle platforms across its Chevrolet, Buick, and GMC brands.

Sharing activities inevitably involve costs that the benefits must outweigh such as the greater coordination required to manage a shared activity. Even more important is the need to compromise on the design or performance of an activity so that it can be shared. For example, a salesperson handling the products of two business units must operate in a way that is usually not what either unit would choose if it were independent. If the compromise erodes the unit's effectiveness, then sharing may reduce rather than enhance competitive advantage.

ENHANCING REVENUE AND DIFFERENTIATION

Often an acquiring firm and its target may achieve a higher level of sales growth together than either company could on its own. For example, Starbucks has acquired a number of small firms, including La Boulange, a small bakery chain; Teavana, a tea producer; and Evolution Fresh, a juice company. Starbucks can add value to all of these firms by expanding their market exposure as Starbucks offers these products for sale in its national retail chain.[19]

Firms also can enhance the effectiveness of their differentiation strategies by means of sharing activities among business units. A shared order-processing system, for example, may permit new features and services that a buyer will value. As another example, financial service providers strive to provide differentiated bundles of services to customers. By having a single point of contact where customers can manage their checking accounts, investment accounts, insurance policies, bill-payment services, mortgages, and many other services, they create value for their customers.

As a cautionary note, managers must keep in mind that sharing activities among businesses in a corporation can have a negative effect on a given business's differentiation. For example, when Ford owned Jaguar, customers had lower perceived value of Jaguar automobiles when they learned that the entry-level Jaguar shared its basic design with and was manufactured in the same production plant as the Ford Mondeo, a European midsize car. Perhaps it is not too surprising that Jaguar was divested by Ford in 2008.

RELATED DIVERSIFICATION: MARKET POWER

We now discuss how companies achieve related diversification through **market power**. We also address the two principal means by which firms achieve synergy through market power: *pooled negotiating power* and *vertical integration.* Managers do, however, have limits on their ability to use market power for diversification, because government regulations can sometimes restrict the ability of a business to gain very large shares of a particular market. For example, in 2016, in order to approve Anheuser-Busch InBev's planned purchase of SABMiller, the Federal Trade Commission required InBev to divest all of SABMiller's U.S. operations to keep InBev from getting too much market power in the U.S. beer market.

> **market power**
> firms' abilities to profit through restricting or controlling supply to a market or coordinating with other firms to reduce investment.

Pooled Negotiating Power

Similar businesses working together or the affiliation of a business with a strong parent can strengthen an organization's bargaining position relative to suppliers and customers and enhance its position vis-à-vis competitors. Compare, for example, the position of an independent food manufacturer with that of the same business within Nestlé. Being part of Nestlé provides the business with significant clout—greater bargaining power with suppliers and customers—since it is part of a firm that makes large purchases from suppliers and provides a wide variety of products. Access to the parent's deep pockets increases the business's strength, and the Nestlé unit enjoys greater protection from substitutes and new entrants. Not only would rivals perceive the unit as a more formidable opponent, but the unit's association with Nestlé would also provide greater visibility and improved image.

> **pooled negotiating power**
> the improvement in bargaining position relative to suppliers and customers.

When acquiring related businesses, a firm's potential for pooled negotiating power vis-à-vis its customers and suppliers can be very enticing. However, managers must carefully evaluate how the combined businesses may affect relationships with actual and potential customers, suppliers, and competitors. For example, when PepsiCo diversified into the fast-food industry with its acquisitions of Kentucky Fried Chicken, Taco Bell, and Pizza Hut (now part of Yum! Brands), it clearly benefited from its position over these units that served as a captive market for its soft-drink products. However, many competitors, such as McDonald's, refused to consider PepsiCo as a supplier of its own soft-drink needs because of competition with Pepsi's divisions in the fast-food industry. Simply put, McDonald's did not want to subsidize the enemy! Thus, although acquiring related businesses can enhance a corporation's bargaining power, it must be aware of the potential for retaliation.

Vertical Integration

Vertical integration occurs when a firm becomes its own supplier or distributor. That is, it represents an expansion or extension of the firm by integrating preceding or successive production processes.[20] The firm incorporates more processes toward the original source of raw materials (backward integration) or toward the ultimate consumer (forward integration). For example, an oil refinery might secure land leases and develop its own drilling capacity to ensure a constant supply of crude oil. Or it could expand into retail operations by owning or licensing gasoline stations to guarantee customers for its petroleum products.

> **vertical integration**
> an expansion or extension of the firm by integrating preceding or successive production processes.

Vertical integration can be a viable strategy for many firms. Strategy Spotlight 6.2 discusses how Tesla is vertically integrating into battery production to ensure it has an adequate supply of batteries as it expands its production of vehicles.

Benefits and Risks of Vertical Integration Vertical integration is a means for an organization to reduce its dependence on suppliers or its channels of distribution to end users.

TESLA BREAKS INDUSTRY NORMS BY VERTICALLY INTEGRATING

For decades, auto manufacturers vertically integrated and controlled all stages of the manufacturing process. By manufacturing their own components, the auto firms could coordinate design of parts, ensure the quality of components, and also ensure that there was adequate production of the parts they needed. However, in recent decades, auto firms have sold off most of their suppliers. By allowing outside suppliers to compete for contracts, the auto firms found they were able to buy components for lower cost than if they had built them in-house.

In contrast to the direction the major auto firms have gone, Tesla is going all in on building a vertically integrated business model. In 2015, Tesla announced that it was building a "gigafactory" to supply all of the batteries they will need for their cars. Tesla sees at least three benefits from making its own batteries.

First, by taking on the $5 billion cost to build the factory, it is maximizing scale efficiencies in battery manufacturing that could result in a per unit cost reduction of 30 percent. Second, Tesla believes it will be able to better coordinate battery technology development as a vertically integrated firm. Third, if demand for electric vehicles takes off as Tesla expects, it will benefit from having an in-house supplier that can provide a steady supply of batteries rather than having to compete to buy batteries from outside suppliers. There simply isn't enough battery production capacity in the world to provide the batteries needed for Tesla to hit its goal of selling 500,000 vehicles per year. But it is a big bet that will be very costly to Tesla if demand doesn't grow as it expects or if new battery technology makes Tesla's lithium-ion batteries obsolete.

Sources: Gorzelany, J. 2014. Why Tesla's vertical manufacturing move could prove essential to its success. *forbes.com*, February 27: np.; and Randall, T. 2017. Tesla flips the switch on the gigafactory. *bloomberg.com*, January 4.

However, the benefits associated with vertical integration—backward or forward—must be carefully weighed against the risks.[21] The primary benefits and risks of vertical integration are listed in Exhibit 6.3.

Winnebago, the leader in the market for drivable recreational vehicles, with a 33.9 percent market share, illustrates some of vertical integration's benefits.[22] The word *Winnebago* means "big RV" to most Americans. And the firm has a sterling reputation for great quality. The firm's huge northern Iowa factories do everything from extruding aluminum for body parts to molding plastics for water and holding tanks to dashboards. Such vertical integration at the factory may appear to be outdated and expensive, but it guarantees excellent quality. The Recreational Vehicle Dealer Association started giving a quality award in 1996, and Winnebago has won it 20 out of 21 years since.

In making vertical integration decisions, five issues should be considered:[23]

1. *Is the company satisfied with the quality of the value that its present suppliers and distributors are providing?* If the performance of organizations in the vertical chain—both suppliers and distributors—is satisfactory, it may not, in general, be appropriate

EXHIBIT 6.3

Benefits and Risks of
Vertical Integration

Benefits
• A secure source of raw materials or distribution channels.
• Protection of and control over valuable assets.
• Proprietary access to new technologies developed by the unit.
• Simplified procurement and administrative procedures.

Risks
• Costs and expenses associated with increased overhead and capital expenditures.
• Loss of flexibility resulting from large investments.
• Problems associated with unbalanced capacities along the value chain. (For example, the in-house supplier has to be larger than your needs in order to benefit from economies of scale in that market.)
• Additional administrative costs associated with managing a more complex set of activities.

for a company to perform these activities itself. But if firms are not happy with their current suppliers, they may want to backward integrate. For example, Kaiser Permanente, a health provider with 10.6 million subscribers, launched its own medical school to better train physicians to provide the integrated style of care Kaiser is striving to provide.[24]

2. *Are there activities in the industry value chain presently being outsourced or performed independently by others that are a viable source of future profits?* Even if a firm is outsourcing value-chain activities to companies that are doing a credible job, it may be missing out on substantial profit opportunities. Consider Best Buy. When it realized that the profit potential of providing installation and service was substantial, Best Buy forward integrated into this area by acquiring Geek Squad.

3. *Is there a high level of stability in the demand for the organization's products?* High demand or sales volatility is not conducive to vertical integration. With the high level of fixed costs in plant and equipment as well as operating costs that accompany endeavors toward vertical integration, widely fluctuating sales demand can either strain resources (in times of high demand) or result in unused capacity (in times of low demand). The cycles of "boom and bust" in the automobile industry are a key reason why the manufacturers have increased the amount of outsourced inputs.

4. *Does the company have the necessary competencies to execute the vertical integration strategies?* As many companies would attest, successfully executing strategies of vertical integration can be very difficult. For example, Boise Cascade, a lumber firm, once forward integrated into the home-building industry but found that it didn't have the design and marketing competencies needed to compete in this market.

5. *Will the vertical integration initiative have potential negative impacts on the firm's stakeholders?* Managers must carefully consider the impact that vertical integration may have on existing and future customers, suppliers, and competitors. After Lockheed Martin, a dominant defense contractor, acquired Loral Corporation, an electronics supplier, for $9.1 billion, it had an unpleasant and unanticipated surprise. Loral, as a subsidiary of Lockheed, was viewed as a rival by many of its previous customers. Thus, while Lockheed Martin may have seen benefits by being able to coordinate operations with Loral as a captive supplier, it also saw a decline in business for Loral with other defense contractors.

Analyzing Vertical Integration: The Transaction Cost Perspective Another approach that has proved very useful in understanding vertical integration is the **transaction cost perspective**.[25] According to this perspective, every market transaction involves some *transaction costs*. First, a decision to purchase an input from an outside source leads to *search* costs (i.e., the cost to find where it is available, the level of quality, etc.). Second, there are costs associated with *negotiating*. Third, a *contract* needs to be written spelling out future possible contingencies. Fourth, parties in a contract have to *monitor* each other. Finally, if a party does not comply with the terms of the contract, there are *enforcement* costs. Transaction costs are thus the sum of search costs, negotiation costs, contracting costs, monitoring costs, and enforcement costs. These transaction costs can be avoided by internalizing the activity, in other words, by producing the input in-house.

A related problem with purchasing a specialized input from outside is the issue of *transaction-specific investments*. For example, when an automobile company needs an input specifically designed for a particular car model, the supplier may be unwilling to make the investments in plant and machinery necessary to produce that component for two reasons. First, the investment may take many years to recover but there is no guarantee the automobile company will continue to buy from the supplier after the contract expires, typically in one year. Second, once the investment is made, the supplier has no bargaining power. That is, the buyer knows that the supplier has no option but to supply at ever-lower prices because

transaction cost perspective
a perspective that the choice of a transaction's governance structure, such as vertical integration or market transaction, is influenced by transaction costs, including search, negotiating, contracting, monitoring, and enforcement costs, associated with each choice.

the investments were so specific that they cannot be used to produce alternative products. In such circumstances, again, vertical integration may be the only option.

Vertical integration, however, gives rise to a different set of costs. These costs are referred to as *administrative costs*. Coordinating different stages of the value chain now internalized within the firm causes administrative costs to go up. Decisions about vertical integration are, therefore, based on a comparison of transaction costs and administrative costs. If transaction costs are lower than administrative costs, it is best to resort to market transactions and avoid vertical integration. For example, McDonald's may be the world's biggest buyer of beef, but it does not raise cattle. The market for beef has low transaction costs and requires no transaction-specific investments. On the other hand, if transaction costs are higher than administrative costs, vertical integration becomes an attractive strategy. Most automobile manufacturers produce their own engines because the market for engines involves high transaction costs and transaction-specific investments.

LO 6-4

How corporations can use unrelated diversification to attain synergistic benefits through corporate restructuring, parenting, and portfolio analysis.

unrelated diversification
a firm entering a different business that has little horizontal interaction with other businesses of a firm.

parenting advantage
the positive contributions of the corporate office to a new business as a result of expertise and support provided and not as a result of substantial changes in assets, capital structure, or management.

restructuring
the intervention of the corporate office in a new business that substantially changes the assets, capital structure, and/or management, including selling off parts of the business, changing the management, reducing payroll and unnecessary sources of expenses, changing strategies, and infusing the new business with new technologies, processes, and reward systems.

UNRELATED DIVERSIFICATION: FINANCIAL SYNERGIES AND PARENTING

With **unrelated diversification**, unlike related diversification, few benefits are derived from horizontal relationships—that is, the leveraging of core competencies or the sharing of activities across business units within a corporation. Instead, potential benefits can be gained from *vertical (or hierarchical) relationships*—the creation of synergies from the interaction of the corporate office with the individual business units. There are two main sources of such synergies. First, the corporate office can contribute to "parenting" and restructuring of (often acquired) businesses. Second, the corporate office can add value by viewing the entire corporation as a family or "portfolio" of businesses and allocating resources to optimize corporate goals of profitability, cash flow, and growth. Additionally, the corporate office enhances value by establishing appropriate human resource practices and financial controls for each of its business units.

Corporate Parenting and Restructuring

We have discussed how firms can add value through related diversification by exploring sources of synergy *across* business units. Now, we discuss how value can be created *within* business units as a result of the expertise and support provided by the corporate office.

Parenting   The positive contributions of the corporate office are called the **"parenting advantage."**[26] Many firms have successfully diversified their holdings without strong evidence of the more traditional sources of synergy (i.e., horizontally across business units). Diversified public corporations such as Berkshire Hathaway and Virgin Group and leveraged buyout firms such as KKR and Clayton, Dubilier & Rice are a few examples.[27] These parent companies create value through management expertise. How? They improve plans and budgets and provide especially competent central functions such as legal, financial, human resource management, procurement, and the like. They also help subsidiaries make wise choices in their own acquisitions, divestitures, and new internal development decisions. Such contributions often help business units to substantially increase their revenues and profits. For example, KKR, a private equity firm, has a team of parenting experts, called KKR Capstone, that works with newly acquired firms for 12 to 24 months to enhance the acquired firm's value. The team works to improve a range of operating activities, such as new product development processes, sales force activities, quality improvement, and supply chain management.

Restructuring   **Restructuring** is another means by which the corporate office can add value to a business.[28] The central idea can be captured in the real estate phrase "Buy low and sell high." Here, the corporate office tries to find either poorly performing firms with unrealized potential or firms in industries on the threshold of significant, positive change. The parent intervenes, often selling off parts of the business; changing the management; reducing payroll and unnecessary sources of expenses; changing strategies; and infusing the company with new technologies, processes, reward systems, and so forth. When the restructuring is complete, the firm can either "sell high" and capture the added value or keep the business and enjoy financial and competitive benefits.[29]

For the restructuring strategy to work, the corporate management must have the insight to detect undervalued companies (otherwise, the cost of acquisition would be too high) or businesses competing in industries with a high potential for transformation.[30] Additionally, of course, it must have the requisite skills and resources to turn the businesses around, even if they may be in new and unfamiliar industries.

Restructuring can involve changes in assets, capital structure, or management.

- *Asset restructuring* involves the sale of unproductive assets, or even whole lines of businesses, that are peripheral. In some cases, it may even involve acquisitions that strengthen the core business.
- *Capital restructuring* involves changing the debt-equity mix, or the mix between different classes of debt or equity. Although the substitution of equity with debt is more common in buyout situations, occasionally the parent may provide additional equity capital.
- *Management restructuring* typically involves changes in the composition of the top management team, organizational structure, and reporting relationships. Tight financial control, rewards based strictly on meeting short- to medium-term performance goals, and reduction in the number of middle-level managers are common steps in management restructuring. In some cases, parental intervention may even result in changes in strategy as well as infusion of new technologies and processes.

Portfolio Management

During the 1970s and early 1980s, several leading consulting firms developed the concept of **portfolio management** to achieve a better understanding of the competitive position of an overall portfolio (or family) of businesses, to suggest strategic alternatives for each of the businesses, and to identify priorities for the allocation of resources. Several studies have reported widespread use of these techniques among American firms.[31]

While portfolio management tools have been widely used in corporations, research on their use has offered mixed support. However, recent research has suggested that strategically channeling resources to units with the most promising prospects can lead to corporate advantage. Research suggests that many firms do not adjust their capital allocations in response to changes in the performance of units or the attractiveness of the markets in which units of the corporation compete. Instead, allocations are fairly consistent from year to year. However, firms that assess the attractiveness of markets in which the firm competes and the capabilities of each division and then choose allocations of corporate resources based on these assessments exhibit higher levels of corporate survival, overall corporate performance, stock market performance, and the performance of individual business units within the corporation. These effects have also been shown to be stronger when firms compete in more competitive markets and in times of economic distress.[32] These findings have shown that the ability to effectively allocate financial capital is a key competence of high-performance diversified firms.

Description and Potential Benefits The key purpose of portfolio models is to assist a firm in achieving a balanced portfolio of businesses.[33] This consists of businesses whose profitability, growth, and cash flow characteristics complement each other and adds up to a

portfolio management a method of (a) assessing the competitive position of a portfolio of businesses within a corporation, (b) suggesting strategic alternatives for each business, and (c) identifying priorities for the allocation of resources across the businesses.

satisfactory overall corporate performance. Imbalance, for example, could be caused either by excessive cash generation with too few growth opportunities or by insufficient cash generation to fund the growth requirements in the portfolio.

The Boston Consulting Group's (BCG's) growth/share matrix is among the best known of these approaches.[34] In the BCG approach, each of the firm's strategic business units (SBUs) is plotted on a two-dimensional grid in which the axes are relative market share and industry growth rate. The grid is broken into four quadrants. Exhibit 6.4 depicts the BCG matrix. Following are a few clarifications:

1. Each circle represents one of the corporation's business units. The size of the circle represents the relative size of the business unit in terms of revenues.

2. Relative market share, measured by the ratio of the business unit's size to that of its largest competitor, is plotted along the horizontal axis.

3. Market share is central to the BCG matrix. This is because high relative market share leads to unit cost reduction due to experience and learning curve effects and, consequently, superior competitive position.

Each of the four quadrants of the grid has different implications for the SBUs that fall into the category:

- *Stars* are SBUs competing in high-growth industries with relatively high market shares. These firms have long-term growth potential and should continue to receive substantial investment funding.

- *Question marks* are SBUs competing in high-growth industries but having relatively weak market shares. Resources should be invested in them to enhance their competitive positions.

- *Cash cows* are SBUs with high market shares in low-growth industries. These units have limited long-run potential but represent a source of current cash flows to fund investments in "stars" and "question marks."

- *Dogs* are SBUs with weak market shares in low-growth industries. Because they have weak positions and limited potential, most analysts recommend that they be divested.

EXHIBIT 6.4 The Boston Consulting Group (BCG) Portfolio Matrix

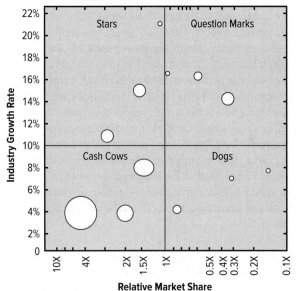

In using portfolio strategy approaches, a corporation tries to create shareholder value in a number of ways.[35] First, portfolio analysis provides a snapshot of the businesses in a corporation's portfolio. Therefore, the corporation is in a better position to allocate resources among the business units according to prescribed criteria (e.g., use cash flows from the cash cows to fund promising stars). Second, the expertise and analytical resources in the corporate office provide guidance in determining what firms may be attractive (or unattractive) acquisitions. Third, the corporate office is able to provide financial resources to the business units on favorable terms that reflect the corporation's overall ability to raise funds. Fourth, the corporate office can provide high-quality review and coaching for the individual businesses. Fifth, portfolio analysis provides a basis for developing strategic goals and reward/evaluation systems for business managers. For example, managers of cash cows would have lower targets for revenue growth than managers of stars, but the former would have higher threshold levels of profit targets on proposed projects than the managers of star businesses. Compensation systems would also reflect such realities. Managers of cash cows understandably would be rewarded more on the basis of cash that their businesses generate than would managers of star businesses. Similarly, managers of star businesses would be held to higher standards for revenue growth than managers of cash cow businesses.

Limitations Despite the potential benefits of portfolio models, there are also some notable downsides. First, they compare SBUs on only two dimensions, making the implicit but erroneous assumption that (1) those are the only factors that really matter and (2) every unit can be accurately compared on that basis. Second, the approach views each SBU as a stand-alone entity, ignoring common core business practices and value-creating activities that may hold promise for synergies across business units. Third, unless care is exercised, the process becomes largely mechanical, substituting an oversimplified graphical model for the important contributions of the CEO's (and other corporate managers') experience and judgment. Fourth, the reliance on "strict rules" regarding resource allocation across SBUs can be detrimental to a firm's long-term viability. Finally, while colorful and easy to comprehend, the imagery of the BCG matrix can lead to some troublesome and overly simplistic prescriptions. For example, division managers are likely to want to jump ship as soon as their division is labeled a "dog."

To see what can go wrong, consider Cabot Corporation.

> Cabot Corporation supplies carbon black for the rubber, electronics, and plastics industries. Following the BCG matrix, Cabot moved away from its cash cow, carbon black, and diversified into stars such as ceramics and semiconductors in a seemingly overaggressive effort to create more revenue growth for the corporation. Predictably, Cabot's return on assets declined as the firm shifted away from its core competence to unrelated areas. The portfolio model failed by pointing the company in the wrong direction in an effort to spur growth—away from its core business. Recognizing its mistake, Cabot Corporation returned to its mainstay carbon black manufacturing and divested unrelated businesses. Today the company is a leader in its field with $2.4 billion in revenues in 2016.[36]

Caveat: Is Risk Reduction a Viable Goal of Diversification?

One of the purposes of diversification is to reduce the risk that is inherent in a firm's variability in revenues and profits over time. That is, if a firm enters new products or markets that are affected differently by seasonal or economic cycles, its performance over time will be more stable. For example, a firm manufacturing lawn mowers may diversify into snowblowers to even out its annual sales. Or a firm manufacturing a luxury line of household furniture may introduce a lower-priced line since affluent and lower-income customers are affected differently by economic cycles.

At first glance the above reasoning may make sense, but there are some problems with it. First, a firm's stockholders can diversify their portfolios at a much lower cost than a corporation, and they don't have to worry about integrating the acquisition into their portfolio. Second, economic cycles as well as their impact on a given industry (or firm) are difficult to predict with any degree of accuracy.

Notwithstanding the above, some firms have benefited from diversification by lowering the variability (or risk) in their performance over time. Consider GE, a firm that manufactures a wide range of products, including aircraft engines, power-generation equipment, locomotive trains, large appliances, healthcare equipment, lighting, water treatment equipment, oil well drilling equipment, and many other products. Offering such a wide range of products has allowed GE to generate stable earnings and a low-risk profile. Due to its earning stability, GE is able to borrow money at favorable rates which it then uses to invest in its own operations and to extend its portfolio even further by acquiring other manufacturers.

Risk reduction in and of itself is rarely viable as a means to create shareholder value. It must be undertaken with a view of a firm's overall diversification strategy.

THE MEANS TO ACHIEVE DIVERSIFICATION

The various means of engaging in diversification—mergers and acquisitions, joint ventures/strategic alliances, and internal development.

acquisitions
the incorporation of one firm into another through purchase.

mergers
the combining of two or more firms into one new legal entity.

We have addressed the types of diversification (e.g., related and unrelated) that a firm may undertake to achieve synergies and create value for its shareholders. Now, we address the means by which a firm can go about achieving these desired benefits.

There are three basic means. First, through acquisitions or mergers, corporations can directly acquire a firm's assets and competencies. Although the terms *mergers* and *acquisitions* are used quite interchangeably, there are some key differences. With **acquisitions**, one firm buys another through a stock purchase, cash, or the issuance of debt.[37] **Mergers**, on the other hand, entail a combination or consolidation of two firms to form a new legal entity. Mergers are relatively rare and entail a transaction among two firms on a relatively equal basis. Despite such differences, we consider both mergers and acquisitions to be quite similar in terms of their implications for a firm's corporate-level strategy.[38]

Second, corporations may agree to pool the resources of other companies with their resource base, commonly known as a joint venture or strategic alliance. Although these two forms of partnerships are similar in many ways, there is an important difference. Joint ventures involve the formation of a third-party legal entity where the two (or more) firms each contribute equity, whereas strategic alliances do not.

Third, corporations may diversify into new products, markets, and technologies through internal development. Called corporate entrepreneurship, it involves the leveraging and combining of a firm's own resources and competencies to create synergies and enhance shareholder value. We address this subject in greater length in Chapter 12.

Mergers and Acquisitions

The most visible and often costly means to diversify is through acquisitions. Over the past several years, several large acquisitions were announced. These include:[39]

- InBev's acquisition of Anheuser-Busch for $52 billion.
- AT&T's acquisition of DirecTV for $67 billion.
- Facebook's acquisition of WhatsApp for $19.4 billion.
- Marriott International's purchase of Starwood Hotels for $13.6 billion.
- Shire Pharmaceutical's $32 billion acquisition of Baxalta.

Exhibit 6.5 illustrates the volatility in worldwide M&A activity over the last several years. Several factors influence M&A activity. Julia Coronado, the chief economist at the investment bank BNP Paribas, highlights two of the key determinants, stating, "When mergers and acquisitions pick up, that's a good sign that businesses are feeling confident enough about the future that they're willing to become aggressive, look for deals, look for ways to

EXHIBIT 6.5 Global Value of Mergers and Acquisitions ($ trillions)

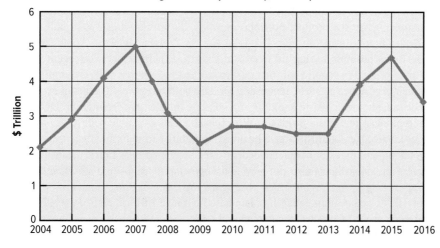

Source: Thomson Financial, Institute of Mergers, Acquisitions, and Alliances (IMAA) analysis.

grow and expand their operations. And it's also an indication that markets are willing to finance these transactions. So it's optimism from the markets and from the businesses themselves."[40] Thus, the general economic conditions and level of optimism about the future influence managers' willingness to take on the risk of acquisitions. Additionally, the availability of financing can influence acquisition activity. During boom periods, financing is typically widely available. In contrast, during recessionary periods, potential acquirers typically find it difficult to borrow money to finance acquisitions.

Governmental policies such as regulatory actions and tax policies can also make the M&A environment more or less favorable. For example, increased antitrust enforcement will decrease the ability of firms to acquire their competitors or possibly firms in closely related markets. In contrast, increased regulatory pressures for good corporate governance may leave boards of directors more open to acquisition offers.

Finally, currency fluctuations can influence the rate of cross-border acquisitions, with firms in countries with stronger currencies being in a stronger position to acquire. For example, the U.S. dollar has increased in value from .72 to .95 euro from early 2014 to late 2016, making it relatively cheaper for U.S. firms to acquire European firms.

Motives and Benefits   Growth through mergers and acquisitions has played a critical role in the success of many corporations in a wide variety of high-technology and knowledge-intensive industries. Here, market and technology changes can occur very quickly and unpredictably.[41] Speed—speed to market, speed to positioning, and speed to becoming a viable company—is critical in such industries. For example, in 2010, Apple acquired Siri Inc. so that it could quickly fully integrate Siri's natural-language voice recognition software into iOS, Apple's operating system.

Mergers and acquisitions also can be a means of *obtaining valuable resources that can help an organization expand its product offerings and services.* Cisco Systems, a computer networking firm, has undertaken over 80 acquisitions in the last decade. Cisco uses these acquisitions to quickly add new technology to its product offerings to meet changing customer needs. Then it uses its excellent sales force to market the new technology to its corporate customers. Cisco also provides strong incentives to the staff of acquired companies to stay on. To realize the greatest value from its acquisitions, Cisco also has learned to integrate acquired companies efficiently and effectively.[42]

Acquiring firms often use acquisitions to acquire critical human capital. These acquisitions have been referred to as acq-hires. In an acq-hire, the acquiring firm believes it needs the specific technical knowledge or the social network contacts of individuals in the target firm. This is especially important in settings where the technology or consumer preferences are highly dynamic. For example, in 2014, Apple purchased Beats Electronics for $3 billion. While Apple valued the product portfolio of Beats, its primary aim was to pull the founders of Beats, Jimmy Iovine and Dr. Dre (aka Andrew Young), into the Apple family. With Apple's iTunes business having hit a wall in growth, experiencing a 1 percent decline in 2013, Apple wanted to acquire new management talent to turn this business around. In addition to their experience at Beats, Iovine and Dr. Dre both have over 20 years of experience in the music industry, with Iovine founding and heading InterScope Records and Dr. Dre being a hip-hop pioneer and music producer. With this acquisition, Apple believes it brought in a wealth of knowledge about the music business, the ability to identify music trends, up-and-coming talent, and industry contacts needed to rejuvenate Apple's music business.[43]

Mergers and acquisitions also can *provide the opportunity for firms to attain the three bases of synergy—leveraging core competencies, sharing activities, and building market power.* Consider some of eBay's acquisitions. eBay has purchased a range of businesses in related product markets, such as GSI Commerce, a company that designs and runs online shopping sites for brick-and-mortar retailers, and StubHub, an online ticket broker. Additionally, it has purchased Korean online auction company Gmarket to expand its geographic scope. Finally, it has purchased firms providing related services, such as Shutl, a rapid-order-fulfillment service provider.

These acquisitions offer the opportunity to leverage eBay's competencies.[44] For example, with the acquisition of GSI, eBay saw opportunities to leverage its core competencies in online systems as well as its reputation to strengthen GSI while also expanding eBay's ability to work with medium to large merchants and brands. eBay can also benefit from these acquisitions by sharing activities. In acquiring firms in related product markets and in new geographic markets, eBay has built a set of businesses that can share in the development of e-commerce and mobile commerce systems. Finally, by expanding into new geographic markets and offering a wider range of services, eBay can build market power as one of the few online retailer systems that provide a full set of services on a global platform. Strategy Spotlight 6.3 highlights how Valeant Pharmaceuticals tried to leverage market power benefits from acquisitions but found the benefits both controversial and short-lived.

Merger and acquisition activity also can *lead to consolidation within an industry and can force other players to merge.*[45] The airline industry has seen a great deal of consolidation in the last several years. With a number of large-scale acquisitions, including Delta's acquisition of Northwest Airlines in 2008, United's acquisition of Continental in 2010, and American's purchase of US Airways in 2013, the U.S. airlines industry has been left with only four major players. In combining, these airlines are both seeking greater efficiencies by combining their networks and hoping that consolidation will dampen the rivalry in the industry.[46]

Corporations can also *enter new market segments by way of acquisitions.* As mentioned above, eBay, a firm that specialized in providing services to individuals and small businesses, moved into providing online retail systems for large merchants with its acquisition of GSI Commerce. Similarly, one of the reasons Fiat acquired Chrysler was to gain access to the U.S. auto market. Exhibit 6.6 summarizes the benefits of mergers and acquisitions.

Potential Limitations   As noted in the previous section, mergers and acquisitions provide a firm with many potential benefits. However, at the same time, there are many potential drawbacks or limitations to such corporate activity.[47]

EXHIBIT 6.6

Benefits of Mergers and Acquisitions

- Obtain valuable resources, such as critical human capital, that can help an organization expand its product offerings.
- Provide the opportunity for firms to attain three bases of synergy: leveraging core competencies, sharing activities, and building market power.
- Lead to consolidation within an industry and force other players to merge.
- Enter new market segments.

VALEANT PHARMACEUTICALS JACKS UP PRICES AFTER ACQUISITIONS BUT LOSES IN THE END

Valeant Pharmaceuticals figured it had found a way to improve its profit margins. Rather than emphasizing drug development, the firm undertook a series of acquisitions where it bought up existing drugs it believed were underpriced and then dramatically raised the prices of those drugs. For example, in February 2015, Valeant announced it was buying the rights to two life-saving heart drugs and immediately increased the list prices for the drugs—one by 212 percent and the other by 525 percent. Similarly, after it purchased Salix Pharmaceuticals, Valeant increased the price of a diabetes drug Salix produced, Glumetza, by about 800 percent. J. Michael Pearson, Valeant's CEO, justified the firm's actions that they were just working to maximize shareholder value when he stated if "products are sort of mispriced and there's an opportunity, we will act appropriately in terms of doing what I assume our shareholders would like us to do." Further, in a statement, Valeant defended its pricing actions, stating it "prices its treatments based on a range of factors, including clinical benefits and the value they bring to patients, payers, and society."

The strategy paid off for Valeant for quite a while. Its stock price rose from $15 a share in early 2010 to over $250 a share in July of 2015, but then it all crashed down. Its price increase triggered a great deal of scrutiny from regulators, and generic manufacturers jumped to create cheaper competitors to Valeant's drugs, many of which either no longer had patent protection or were soon to lose patent protection. Thus, its ability to sustain high drug price revenue appeared questionable. Additionally, the firm had taken on $30 billion in debt to finance its acquisitions and would be unable to meet its debt obligations if it had to cut the prices of its drugs. Coupled with questions about the firm's accounting practices, these concerns led investors to bail out, pushing the stock's price down to $14 a share in December 2016. The turn in events also cost Mr. Pearson his position as firm CEO in April 2016.

Sources: Rockoff, J. & Silverman E. 2015. Pharmaceutical companies buy rivals' drugs, then jack up the prices. *wsj.com*, April 27: np; Pollack, A. & Tavernise, S. 2015. Valeant's drug price strategy enriches it, but infuriates patients and lawmakers. *nytimes.com*, October 4: np; and Vardi, N. 2016. Valeant Pharmaceuticals' prescription for disaster. *forbes.com*, April 13: np.

First, *the takeover premium that is paid for an acquisition typically is very high.* Two times out of three, the stock price of the acquiring company falls once the deal is made public. Since the acquiring firm often pays a 30 percent or higher premium for the target company, the acquirer must create synergies and scale economies that result in sales and market gains exceeding the premium price. Firms paying higher premiums set the performance hurdle even higher. For example, Household International paid an 82 percent premium to buy Beneficial, and Conseco paid an 83 percent premium to acquire Green Tree Financial. Historically, paying a high premium over the stock price has been a poor strategy.

Second, *competing firms often can imitate any advantages realized or copy synergies that result from the M&A.*[48] Thus, a firm can often see its advantages quickly erode. Unless the advantages are sustainable and difficult to copy, investors will not be willing to pay a high premium for the stock. Similarly, the time value of money must be factored into the stock price. M&A costs are paid up front. Conversely, firms pay for R&D, ongoing marketing, and capacity expansion over time. This stretches out the payments needed to gain new competencies. The M&A argument is that a large initial investment is worthwhile because it creates long-term advantages. However, stock analysts want to see immediate results from such a large cash outlay. If the acquired firm does not produce results quickly, investors often divest the stock, driving the price down.

Third, *managers' credibility and ego can sometimes get in the way of sound business decisions.* If the M&A does not perform as planned, managers who pushed for the deal find their reputation tarnished. This can lead them to protect their credibility by funneling more money, or escalating their commitment, into an inevitably doomed operation. Further, when a merger fails and a firm tries to unload the acquisition, the firm often must sell at a huge discount. These problems further compound the costs and erode the stock price.

Fourth, *there can be many cultural issues that may doom the intended benefits from M&A endeavors.* Consider the insights of Joanne Lawrence, who played an important role in the merger between SmithKline and the Beecham Group.[49]

THE WISDOM OF CROWDS: WHEN DO INVESTORS SEE VALUE IN ACQUISITIONS?

By some estimates, 70 to 90 percent of acquisitions destroy shareholder value. But investors do see value in some acquisitions. The question is, When does the wisdom of the investment crowd indicate there is value with acquisitions? Recent research suggests it rests in both the characteristics of the deal and the motivation of the acquiring firm.

The Characteristics of the Deal

Research has identified several deal characteristics that lead to positive investor reactions. Not surprisingly, investors see greater value in acquisitions when the acquiring and the acquired (target) firm are in the same or closely related industries. This is consistent with there being greater potential for synergies when the firms are in similar markets. Second, investors see greater value potential when acquiring managers are seen as responding quickly to new opportunities, such as those provided by the emergence of new technologies or market deregulation. Third, investors have a more positive reaction when the acquiring firm used cash to buy the target, as opposed to giving the target shareholders stock in the combined firm. Acquiring firms often use stock to finance acquisitions when they think their own stock is overvalued. Thus, the use of cash signals that the acquiring firm's managers have confidence in the value of the deal. Fourth, the less the acquiring firm relies on outside advisers, such as investment banks, the more investors see value in the deal. As with the use of cash, managers who rely

primarily on their own knowledge and abilities to manage deals are seen as more confident. Finally, when the target firm tries to avoid the acquisition, investors see less value potential. Defense actions by targets are seen as signals that the target firm will not be open to easy integration with the acquiring firm. Thus, it may be difficult to leverage synergies.

The Motivation of the Acquirer

How much value investors see in the deal is also affected by the motivation of the acquirer. Interestingly, if the acquiring firm is highly profitable, investors see less value in the acquisition. The concern here is that strong performance likely leads managers to become overconfident and more likely to undertake "empire building" acquisitions as opposed to acquisitions that generate shareholder value. Second, if the acquiring firm is highly leveraged, having a high debt-equity ratio, investors see more value in the acquisition. Since the acquiring firm is at a higher risk of bankruptcy, managers of highly leveraged firms are likely to undertake acquisitions only if they are low risk and likely to generate synergistic benefits.

In total, the stock investors look to logical clues about the potential value of the deal and the motives of the acquiring firm managers to assess the value they see. Thus, there appears to be simple but logical wisdom in the crowd.

Sources: McNamara, G., Haleblian, J., & Dykes, B. 2008. Performance implications of participating in an acquisition wave: Early mover advantages, bandwagon effects, and the moderating influence of industry characteristics and acquirer tactics. *Academy of Management Journal,* 51: 113–130; and Schijven, M. & Hitt, M. 2012. The vicarious wisdom of crowds: Toward a behavioral perspective on investor reactions to acquisition announcements. *Strategic Management Journal,* 33: 1247–1268.

The key to a strategic merger is to create a new culture. This was a mammoth challenge during the SmithKline Beecham merger. We were working at so many different cultural levels, it was dizzying. We had two national cultures to blend—American and British—that compounded the challenge of selling the merger in two different markets with two different shareholder bases. There were also two different business cultures: One was very strong, scientific, and academic; the other was much more commercially oriented. And then we had to consider within both companies the individual businesses, each of which has its own little culture.

Exhibit 6.7 summarizes the limitations of mergers and acquisitions.

Strategy Spotlight 6.4 discusses the characteristics of acquisitions that lead investors to see greater value in the combinations.

Divestment: The Other Side of the "M&A Coin" When firms acquire other businesses, it typically generates quite a bit of "press" in business publications such as *The Wall Street Journal, Bloomberg Businessweek,* and *Fortune.* It makes for exciting news, and one thing is for sure—large acquiring firms automatically improve their standing in the Fortune 500 rankings (since it is based solely on total revenues). However, managers must also carefully consider the strategic implications of exiting businesses.

EXHIBIT 6.7

Limitations of Mergers and Acquisitions

- Takeover premiums paid for acquisitions are typically very high.
- Competing firms often can imitate any advantages or copy synergies that result from the merger or acquisition.
- Managers' egos sometimes get in the way of sound business decisions.
- Cultural issues may doom the intended benefits from M&A endeavors.

Divestments, the exit of a business from a firm's portfolio, are quite common. One study found that large, prestigious U.S. companies divested more acquisitions than they kept.[50]

divestment
the exit of a business from
a firm's portfolio.

Divesting a business can accomplish many different objectives.* It can be used to help a firm reverse an earlier acquisition that didn't work out as planned. Often, this is simply to help "cut their losses." Other objectives include (1) enabling managers to focus their efforts more directly on the firm's core businesses,[51] (2) providing the firm with more resources to spend on more attractive alternatives, and (3) raising cash to help fund existing businesses.

Divesting can enhance a firm's competitive position only to the extent that it reduces its tangible (e.g., maintenance, investments, etc.) or intangible (e.g., opportunity costs, managerial attention) costs without sacrificing a current competitive advantage or the seeds of future advantages.[52] To be effective, divesting requires a thorough understanding of a business unit's current ability and future potential to contribute to a firm's value creation. However, since such decisions involve a great deal of uncertainty, it is very difficult to make such evaluations. In addition, because of managerial self-interests and organizational inertia, firms often delay divestments of underperforming businesses.

The Boston Consulting Group has identified seven principles for successful divestiture.[53]

1. *Remove the emotion from the decision.* Managers need to consider objectively the prospects for each unit in the firm and how this unit fits with the firm's overall strategy. Issues related to personal relationships with the managers of the unit, the length of time the unit has been part of the company, and other emotional elements should not be considered in the decision.[54]

2. *Know the value of the business you are selling.* Divesting firms can generate greater interest in and higher bids for units they are divesting if they can clearly articulate the strategic value of the unit.

3. *Time the deal right.* This involves both internal timing, whereby the firm regularly evaluates all its units so that it can divest units when they are no longer highly valued in the firm but will still be of value to the outside market, and external timing, being ready to sell when the market conditions are right.

4. *Maintain a sizable pool of potential buyers.* Divesting firms should not focus on a single potential buyer. Instead, they should discuss possible deals with several hand-picked potential bidders.

5. *Tell a story about the deal.* For each potential bidder it talks with, the divesting firm should develop a narrative about how the unit it is interested in selling will create value for that buyer.

6. *Run divestitures systematically through a project office.* Firms should look at developing the ability to divest units as a distinct form of corporate competencies. While many firms have acquisition units, they often don't have divesting units even though there is significant potential value in divestitures.

7. *Communicate clearly and frequently.* Corporate managers need to clearly communicate to internal stakeholders, such as employees, and external stakeholders, such as customers and stockholders, what their goals are with divestment activity, how it will create value, and how the firm is moving forward strategically with these decisions.

---

* Firms can divest their businesses in a number of ways. Sell-offs, spin-offs, equity carve-outs, asset sales/dissolution, and split-ups are some such modes of divestment. In a sell-off, the divesting firm privately negotiates with a third party to divest a unit/subsidiary for cash/stock. In a spin-off, a parent company distributes shares of the unit/subsidiary being divested pro rata to its existing shareholders and a new company is formed. Equity carve-outs are similar to spin-offs except that shares in the unit/subsidiary being divested are offered to new shareholders. Dissolution involves sale of redundant assets, not necessarily as an entire unit/subsidiary as in sell-offs but a few bits at a time. A split-up, on the other hand, is an instance of divestiture where by the parent company is split into two or more new companies and the parent ceases to exist. Shares in the parent company are exchanged for shares in new companies, and the exact distribution varies case by case.

Strategic Alliances and Joint Ventures

strategic alliance
a cooperative relationship between two or more firms.

A **strategic alliance** is a cooperative relationship between two (or more) firms.[55] Alliances can exist in multiple forms. Contractual alliances are simply based on written contracts between firms. Contractual alliances are typically used for fairly simple alliance agreements, such as supplier, marketing, or distribution relationships that don't require a great deal of integration or technology sharing between firms and have a finite, identifiable end time period. If the terms of the agreement can be clearly laid out in contracts, then contracts can be a complete and effective basis for the agreement. However, when there is uncertainty about how the alliance will proceed and evolve over time or if one firm is much larger than the other, firms will often form equity alliances. In an equity alliance, at least one firm purchases a minority ownership stake in the other. Equity ownership in alliances helps align the interest of the two firms since the firm that buys the ownership stake benefits both from increases in its own value and the value of the partner it now owns a part of. This can reduce concerns that one firm will benefit more from the alliance than the partner firm or take advantage of the partner firm as the alliance evolves. This can be an especially large concern when a very large firm allies with a small firm. By taking an equity stake in the smaller firm, the larger firm signals that it is linking its own money into the success of the smaller firm. **Joint ventures** represent a special case of alliances, wherein two (or more) firms contribute equity to form a new legal entity.

joint ventures
new entities formed within a strategic alliance in which two or more firms, the parents, contribute equity to form the new legal entity.

Strategic alliances and joint ventures are assuming an increasingly prominent role in the strategy of leading firms, both large and small.[56] Such cooperative relationships have many potential advantages.[57] Among these are entering new markets, reducing manufacturing (or other) costs in the value chain, and developing and diffusing new technologies.[58]

Entering New Markets Often a company that has a successful product or service wants to introduce it into a new market. However, it may not have the financial resources or the requisite marketing expertise because it does not understand customer needs, know how to promote the product, or have access to the proper distribution channels.[59]

Zara, a Spanish clothing company, operates stores in over 70 countries. Still, when entering markets very distant from its home markets, Zara often uses local alliance partners to help it negotiate the different cultural and regulatory environments. For example, when Zara expanded into India in 2010, it did it in cooperation with Tata, an Indian conglomerate.[60]

Alliances can also be used to enter new product markets. For example, Lego has expanded its product portfolio by licensing the right to develop products built around characters and brands, such as Star Wars and Harry Potter. It also allied with the digital animation firm Animal Logic Pty Ltd and Warner Bros. to develop the Lego Movie.[61]

Reducing Manufacturing (or Other) Costs in the Value Chain Strategic alliances (or joint ventures) often enable firms to pool capital, value-creating activities, or facilities in order to reduce costs. For example, the PGA and LPGA tours joined together in a strategic alliance that allows them to save costs by jointly marketing golf, develop a shared digital media platform, and jointly negotiate domestic television contracts.[62]

Developing and Diffusing New Technologies Strategic alliances also may be used to build jointly on the technological expertise of two or more companies. This may enable them to develop products technologically beyond the capability of the companies acting independently.[63] The alliance between Ericsson and Cisco discussed in Strategy Spotlight 6.5 aims to allow the two firms to jointly develop new, integrated telecommunication equipment to meet the evolving needs of firms like Verizon and Vodafone.

Potential Downsides Despite their promise, many alliances and joint ventures fail to meet expectations for a variety of reasons.[64] First, without the proper partner, a firm should never consider undertaking an alliance, even for the best of reasons.[65] Each partner should bring the desired complementary strengths to the partnership. Ideally, the strengths contributed

ERICSSON AND CISCO JOIN FORCES TO RESPOND TO THE CHANGING TELECOMMUNICATIONS MARKET

Ericsson AB and Cisco Systems are both giants in providing equipment for the telecommunications and Internet markets. Ericsson, a Swedish firm, is one of the world's leading manufacturers of wireless equipment with $26 billion in sales. Cisco, based in the United States, has revenue of $49 billion and is the world's largest manufacturer of Internet backbone gear. Even with their size and large market presence, they are facing strong challenges. First, they are finding that their telecommunications customers, such as Verizon and AT&T, are looking for complete solutions as they upgrade their technology to launch 5G networks. As part of this, these customers are replacing some special-purpose wireless and network equipment with computers equipped with software. This requires integrating technology that has been sold separately by firms like Ericsson and Cisco. Second, they are facing stronger competition from rivals who can provide these integrated solutions. Chinese system provider Huawei has expertise in both the wireless and Internet equipment arenas and is providing complete solutions for telecom firms. Additionally, Nokia, another leading wireless equipment provider, extended its ability to provide integrated systems when it acquired Alcatel-Lucent, an Internet equipment firm, in early 2016.

Rather than have one of the firms acquire the other, Ericsson and Cisco decided to address these competitive challenges by allying with each other. They initially will work to integrate existing equipment to provide complete solutions to telecom firms. As part of this, they will combine some sales and consulting efforts. As they move forward, they will jointly develop new hardware and services. Since technology is evolving so rapidly, the ultimate scope of the alliance remains somewhat unclear. The complexity of it all took a while to work through—negotiations about the alliance took 13 months, but they have signed a flexible agreement about sharing patented technologies and have a high degree of trust that this is the right course.

Why choose an alliance over the acquisition route that Nokia and Alcatel pursued? Chuck Robbins, Cisco's CEO, made the case for avoiding an acquisition stating that "Neither Ericsson or Cisco really believe that these large mergers typically work." Since the two companies come from different countries and are both large with strong corporate cultures, a full integration would have been a great challenge. Also, an acquisition of firms so large would likely have triggered significant anti-trust concerns and regulatory scrutiny. Hans Vestberg, Ericsson's CEO, made an affirmative case for the alliance, stating, "This is a much more agile and efficient choice. We can start already tomorrow." The firms anticipate that the alliance should increase sales by each firm by at least $1 billion annually.

Sources: Clark, D. & Hansegard, J. 2015. Ericsson, Cisco pool telecom, Internet savvy in wide-reaching alliance. *wsj.com*, November 9: np.; and Higginbotham, S. 2015. Why Cisco and Ericsson are teaming up for future growth. *fortune.com*, November 9: np.

by the partners are unique; thus synergies created can be more easily sustained and defended over the longer term. The goal must be to develop synergies between the contributions of the partners, resulting in a win–win situation. Moreover, the partners must be compatible and willing to trust each other.[66] Unfortunately, often little attention is given to nurturing the close working relationships and interpersonal connections that bring together the partnering organizations.[67]

Internal Development

Firms can also diversify by means of corporate entrepreneurship and new venture development. **In today's economy, internal development is such an important means by which companies expand their businesses that we have devoted a whole chapter to it (see Chapter 12).** Sony and the Minnesota Mining & Manufacturing Co. (3M), for example, are known for their dedication to innovation, R&D, and cutting-edge technologies. For example, 3M has developed its entire corporate culture to support its ongoing policy of generating at least 25 percent of total sales from products created within the most recent four-year period. While 3M exceeded this goal for decades, a push for improved efficiency that began in the early 2000s resulted in a drop to generating only 21 percent of sales from newer products in 2005. By refocusing on innovation, 3M raised that value back up to 33 percent in 2016.

Biocon, the largest Indian biotechnology firm, shows the power of internal development. Kiran Mazumdar-Shaw, the firm's founder, took the knowledge she learned while studying malting and brewing in college to start a small firm that produced enzymes for the beer

> **internal development**
> entering a new business through investment in new facilities, often called corporate enterpreneurship and new venture development.

industry in her Bangalore garage in 1978. The firm first expanded into providing enzymes for other food and textile industries. From there, Biocon expanded on to producing generic drugs and is now the largest producer of insulin in Asia.[68]

Compared to mergers and acquisitions, firms that engage in internal development capture the value created by their own innovative activities without having to "share the wealth" with alliance partners or face the difficulties associated with combining activities across the value chains of several firms or merging corporate cultures.[69] Also, firms can often develop new products or services at a relatively lower cost and thus rely on their own resources rather than turning to external funding.[70]

There are also potential disadvantages. It may be time-consuming; thus, firms may forfeit the benefits of speed that growth through mergers or acquisitions can provide. This may be especially important among high-tech or knowledge-based organizations in fast-paced environments where being an early mover is critical. Thus, firms that choose to diversify through internal development must develop capabilities that allow them to move quickly from initial opportunity recognition to market introduction.

HOW MANAGERIAL MOTIVES CAN ERODE VALUE CREATION

Thus far in the chapter, we have implicitly assumed that CEOs and top executives are "rational beings"; that is, they act in the best interests of shareholders to maximize long-term shareholder value. In the real world, however, they may often act in their own self-interest. We now address some **managerial motives** that can serve to erode, rather than enhance, value creation. These include "growth for growth's sake," excessive egotism, and the creation of a wide variety of antitakeover tactics.

Growth for Growth's Sake

There are huge incentives for executives to increase the size of their firm. And these are not consistent with increasing shareholder wealth. Top managers, including the CEO, of larger firms typically enjoy more prestige, higher rankings for their firms on the Fortune 500 list (based on revenues, *not* profits), greater incomes, more job security, and so on. There is also the excitement and associated recognition of making a major acquisition. As noted by Harvard's Michael Porter, "There's a tremendous allure to mergers and acquisitions. It's the big play, the dramatic gesture. With one stroke of the pen you can add billions to size, get a front-page story, and create excitement in markets."[71]

In recent years many high-tech firms have suffered from the negative impact of their uncontrolled growth. Consider, for example, Priceline.com's ill-fated venture into an online service to offer groceries and gasoline.[72] A myriad of problems—perhaps most importantly, a lack of participation by manufacturers—caused the firm to lose more than $5 million a *week* prior to abandoning these ventures. Such initiatives are often little more than desperate moves by top managers to satisfy investor demands for accelerating revenues. Unfortunately, the increased revenues often fail to materialize into a corresponding hike in earnings.

At times, executives' overemphasis on growth can result in a plethora of ethical lapses, which can have disastrous outcomes for their companies. A good example (of bad practice) is Joseph Berardino's leadership at Andersen Worldwide. Berardino had a chance early on to take a hard line on ethics and quality in the wake of earlier scandals at clients such as Waste Management and Sunbeam. Instead, according to former executives, he put too much emphasis on revenue growth. Consequently, the firm's reputation quickly eroded when it audited and signed off on the highly flawed financial statements of such infamous firms as Enron, Global Crossing, and WorldCom. Berardino ultimately resigned in disgrace in March 2002, and his firm was dissolved later that year.[73]

Egotism

A healthy ego helps make a leader confident, clearheaded, and able to cope with change. CEOs, by their very nature, are intensely competitive people in the office as well as on the tennis court or golf course. But sometimes when pride is at stake, individuals will go to great lengths to win.

Egos can get in the way of a "synergistic" corporate marriage. Few executives (or lower-level managers) are exempt from the potential downside of excessive egos. Consider, for example, the reflections of General Electric's former CEO Jack Welch, considered by many to be the world's most admired executive. He admitted to a regrettable decision: "My hubris got in the way in the Kidder Peabody deal. [He was referring to GE's buyout of the soon-to-be-troubled Wall Street firm.] I got wise advice from Walter Wriston and other directors who said, 'Jack, don't do this.' But I was bully enough and on a run to do it. And I got whacked right in the head."[74] In addition to poor financial results, Kidder Peabody was wracked by a widely publicized trading scandal that tarnished the reputations of both GE and Kidder Peabody. Welch ended up selling Kidder.

The business press has included many stories of how egotism and greed have infiltrated organizations.[75] For example, consider Merrill Lynch's former CEO, John Thain.[76] On January 22, 2009, he was ousted as head of Merrill Lynch by Bank of America's CEO, Ken Lewis:

> Thain embarrassingly doled out $4 billion in discretionary year-end bonuses to favored employees just before Bank of America's rescue purchase of failing Merrill. The bonuses amounted to about 10 percent of Merrill's 2008 losses.
>
> Obviously, John Thain believed that he was entitled. When he took over ailing Merrill in early 2008, he began planning major cuts, but he also ordered that his office be redecorated. He spent $1.22 million of company funds to make it "livable," which, in part, included $87,000 for a rug, $87,000 for a pair of guest chairs, $68,000 for a 19th-century credenza, and (what really got the attention of the press) $35,000 for a "commode with legs."
>
> He later agreed to repay the decorating costs. However, one might still ask: What kind of person treats other people's money like this? And who needs a commode that costs as much as a new Lexus? Finally, a comment by Bob O'Brien, stock editor at Barrons.com, clearly applies: "The sense of entitlement that's been engendered in this group of people has clearly not been beaten out of them by the brutal performance of the financial sector over the course of the last year."

Antitakeover Tactics

Unfriendly or hostile takeovers can occur when a company's stock becomes undervalued. A competing organization can buy the outstanding stock of a takeover candidate in sufficient quantity to become a large shareholder. Then it makes a tender offer to gain full control of the company. If the shareholders accept the offer, the hostile firm buys the target company and either fires the target firm's management team or strips the team members of their power. Thus, **antitakeover tactics** are common, including greenmail, golden parachutes, and poison pills.[77]

The first, **greenmail,** is an effort by the target firm to prevent an impending takeover. When a hostile firm buys a large block of outstanding target company stock and the target firm's management feels that a tender offer is impending, it offers to buy the stock back from the hostile company at a higher price than the unfriendly company paid for it. Although this often prevents a hostile takeover, the same price is not offered to preexisting shareholders. However, it protects the jobs of the target firm's management.

Second, a **golden parachute** is a prearranged contract with managers specifying that, in the event of a hostile takeover, the target firm's managers will be paid a significant severance package. Although top managers lose their jobs, the golden parachute provisions protect their income.

Third, **poison pills** are used by a company to give shareholders certain rights in the event of a takeover by another firm. They are also known as shareholder rights plans.

Clearly, antitakeover tactics can often raise some interesting ethical—and legal—issues.

egotism
managers' actions to shape their firms' strategies to serve their selfish interests rather than to maximize long-term shareholder value.

antitakeover tactics
managers' actions to avoid losing wealth or power as a result of a hostile takeover.

greenmail
a payment by a firm to a hostile party for the firm's stock at a premium, made when the firm's management feels that the hostile party is about to make a tender offer.

golden parachute
a prearranged contract with managers specifying that, in the event of a hostile takeover, the target firm's managers will be paid a significant severance package.

poison pill
used by a company to give shareholders certain rights in the event of takeover by another firm.

Starbucks Moves Far Outside the Coffeehouse

When you say Starbucks, most people instantly think of coffee, specifically coffee prepared by a barista just the way you want it—once you get the Starbucks lingo down. Starbucks is available in over 20,000 coffeehouses in more than 60 countries. Starbucks has experienced amazing growth over the last 30 years as it moved from a small chain of coffeehouses in Seattle to the global powerhouse that it is now. However, the firm faces more limited prospects for growth in its coffee business from this point forward. The coffee market is fairly mature, and Starbucks sees a limited number of new markets in which to expand.

In recent years, Starbucks has diversified into a number of new products and distribution channels to stoke up its growth potential. This has included diversifying into new products to sell through its cafes. Starbucks purchased La Boulange Bakery and now produces baked goods to sell in its cafes. Similarly, it purchased Teavana and is adding tea bars to its cafes. It also purchased Evolution Fresh juice company and now supplies the juices it sells in Starbucks coffeehouses. It is also test marketing additional new products in its cafes—beer and wine in Starbucks Evening concept stores and carbonated beverages in several markets. Starbucks is also making a major push in the grocery aisle. The firm has developed a "signature aisle" which features wood shelving that reflects the appearance of a Starbucks Café. The aisle's desirable end cap (the high-traffic shelf area at the end of an aisle) attracts shoppers' attention to products such as Starbucks' bagged coffee, its single-serve K-cups, and its Via brand instant coffee. But selling coffee in grocery stores is just the first step. Starbucks aims to also distribute its La Boulange bakery products, Teavana teas, and Evolution Fresh juices in grocery stores. It has even been looking further afield as it developed Evolution Harvest snack bars for the grocery aisle and also crafted an alliance with Danone to produce and sell Evolution Fresh yogurt products in grocery stores. The grocery aisle business now accounts for about 7 percent of Starbucks' business, but CEO Howard Schultz envisions the grocery aisle business producing half of the company's sales.

While the growth potential is enticing, there are some potential pitfalls associated with Starbucks' push into new arenas. The perceived differentiation of its coffee products could erode as they become a grocery aisle staple. Also, the growth of grocery sales could cannibalize the sales at cafes as people simply brew their K-cup coffee at home rather than swinging through the Starbucks drive-through on the way to work. In moving into noncoffee products, the question becomes whether or not Starbucks has the competencies to manage other businesses well. While Starbucks has mastered the management of the coffee supply chain and developed a distinctive product, it is not clear that the company has the competencies to produce bakery products, juice, tea, beer, and wine better than outside suppliers. Finally, managing all of these new businesses may distract Starbucks from its core coffee cafe business. The challenge for Starbucks is to know what its core competencies are and to focus on markets that allow it to best exploit those competencies.

Discussion Questions

1. What are Starbucks' core competencies? Do the new businesses allow Starbucks to leverage those competencies?
2. Do Starbucks' diversification efforts appear to be primarily about increasing growth or increasing shareholder value by sharing activities, building market power, and/or leveraging core competencies?
3. Where do you think Starbucks should draw boundaries on what businesses to compete in? Should it keep the new products in the corporate family? Should it continue to move into the grocery retailing space?

Sources: Levine-Weinberg, A. 2014. Starbucks has decades of growth ahead. *money.cnn.com*, November 19: np; Kowitt, B. 2013. Starbucks' grocery gambit. *Fortune*, December 23: np; Strom, S. 2013. Starbucks aims to move beyond beans. *nytimes.com*, October 8: np; and s*tarbucks.com*.

Reflecting on Career Implications . . .

This chapter focuses on how firms can create value through diversification. The following questions lead you to consider how you can develop core competencies that apply in different settings and how you can leverage those skills in different value chain activities or units in your firms.

▣ **Corporate-Level Strategy:** Is your current employer a single business firm or a diversified firm? If it is diversified, does it pursue related or unrelated diversification? Does its diversification provide you with career opportunities, especially lateral moves? What organizational policies are in place to either encourage or discourage you from moving from one business unit to another?

▣ **Core Competencies:** What do you see as your core competencies? How can you leverage them within your business unit as well as across other business units?

▣ **Sharing Infrastructures:** Identify what infrastructure activities and resources (e.g., information systems, legal) are available in the corporate office that are shared by various business units in the firm. How often do you take advantage of these shared resources? Identify ways in which you can enhance your performance by taking advantage of these shared infrastructure resources.

▣ **Diversification:** From your career perspective, what actions can you take to diversify your employment risk (e.g., doing coursework at a local university, obtaining professional certification such as a CPA, networking through professional affiliation, etc.)? In periods of retrenchment, such actions will provide you with a greater number of career options.

summary

A key challenge for today's managers is to create "synergy" when engaging in diversification activities. As we discussed in this chapter, corporate managers do not, in general, have a very good track record in creating value in such endeavors when it comes to mergers and acquisitions. Among the factors that serve to erode shareholder values are paying an excessive premium for the target firm, failing to integrate the activities of the newly acquired businesses into the corporate family, and undertaking diversification initiatives that are too easily imitated by the competition.

We addressed two major types of corporate-level strategy: related and unrelated diversification. With *related diversification* the corporation strives to enter into areas in which key resources and capabilities of the corporation can be shared or leveraged. Synergies come from horizontal relationships between business units. Cost savings and enhanced revenues can be derived from two major sources. First, economies of scope can be achieved from the leveraging of core competencies and the sharing of activities. Second, market power can be attained from greater, or pooled, negotiating power and from vertical integration.

When firms undergo *unrelated diversification,* they enter product markets that are dissimilar to their present businesses. Thus, there is generally little opportunity to either leverage core competencies or share activities across business units. Here, synergies are created from vertical relationships between the corporate office and the individual business units. With unrelated diversification, the primary ways to create value are corporate restructuring and parenting, as well as the use of portfolio analysis techniques.

Corporations have three primary means of diversifying their product markets—mergers and acquisitions, joint ventures/strategic alliances, and internal development. There are key trade-offs associated with each of these. For example, mergers and acquisitions are typically the quickest means to enter new markets and provide the corporation with a high level of control over the acquired business. However, with the expensive premiums that often need to be paid to the shareholders of the target firm and the challenges associated with integrating acquisitions, they can also be quite expensive. Not surprisingly, many poorly performing acquisitions are subsequently divested. At times, however, divestitures can help firms refocus their efforts and generate resources. Strategic alliances and joint ventures between two or more firms, on the other hand, may be a means of reducing risk since they involve the sharing and combining of resources. But such joint initiatives also provide a firm with less control (than it would have with an acquisition) since governance is shared between two independent entities. Also, there is a limit to the potential upside for each partner because returns must be shared as well. Finally, with internal development, a firm is able to capture all of the value from its initiatives (as opposed to sharing it with a merger or alliance partner). However, diversification by means of internal development can be very time-consuming—a disadvantage that becomes even more important in fast-paced competitive environments.

Finally, some managerial behaviors may serve to erode shareholder returns. Among these are "growth for growth's sake," egotism, and antitakeover tactics. As we discussed, some of these issues—particularly antitakeover tactics—raise ethical considerations because the managers of the firm are not acting in the best interests of the shareholders.

SUMMARY REVIEW QUESTIONS

1. Discuss how managers can create value for their firm through diversification efforts.
2. What are some of the reasons that many diversification efforts fail to achieve desired outcomes?
3. How can companies benefit from related diversification? Unrelated diversification? What are some of the key concepts that can explain such success?
4. What are some of the important ways in which a firm can restructure a business?
5. Discuss some of the various means that firms can use to diversify. What are the pros and cons associated with each of these?
6. Discuss some of the actions that managers may engage in to erode shareholder value.

key terms

corporate-level strategy 172
diversification 174
related diversification 175
economies of scope 175
core competencies 176
sharing activities 178
market power 179
pooled negotiating power 179
vertical integration 179
transaction cost perspective 181
unrelated diversification 182
parenting advantage 182
restructuring 182
portfolio management 183
acquisitions 186
mergers 186
divestment 191
strategic alliance 192
joint ventures 192
internal development 193
managerial motives 194
growth for growth's sake 194
egotism 195
antitakeover tactics 195
greenmail 195
golden parachute 195
poison pill 195

APPLICATION QUESTIONS & EXERCISES

1. What were some of the largest mergers and acquisitions over the last two years? What was the rationale for these actions? Do you think they will be successful? Explain.
2. Discuss some examples from business practice in which an executive's actions appear to be in his or her self-interest rather than the corporation's well-being.
3. Discuss some of the challenges that managers must overcome in making strategic alliances successful. What are some strategic alliances with which you are familiar? Were they successful or not? Explain.
4. Use the Internet and select a company that has recently undertaken diversification into new product markets. What do you feel were some of the reasons for this diversification (e.g., leveraging core competencies, sharing infrastructures)?

EXPERIENTIAL EXERCISE

AT&T is a firm that follows a strategy of related diversification. Evaluate its success (or lack thereof) with regard to how well it has (1) built on core competencies, (2) shared infrastructures, and (3) increased market power. (Fill answers in table below.)

Rationale for Related Diversification	Successful/Unsuccessful?	Why?
1. Build on core competencies		
2. Share infrastructures		
3. Increase market power		

ETHICS QUESTIONS

1. It is not uncommon for corporations to undertake downsizing and layoffs. Do you feel that such actions raise ethical considerations? Why or why not?
2. What are some of the ethical issues that arise when managers act in a manner that is counter to their firm's best interests? What are the long-term implications for both the firms and the managers themselves?

REFERENCES

1. Kaplan, J. 2015. Coca-Cola to sell nine U.S. facilities to bottling companies. *bloomberg.com,* September 24: np; Esterl, M. 2016. Coke to step up North American restructuring. *wsj.com,* February 9: np; and Esterl, M. 2016. Coke tweaks its business model again. *wsj.com,* March 23: np.
2. Insights on measuring M&A performance are addressed in Zollo, M. & Meier, D. 2008. What is M&A performance? *BusinessWeek,* 22(3): 55–77.
3. Insights on how and why firms may overpay for acquisitions are addressed in Malhotra, D., Ku, G., & Murnighan, J. K. 2008. When winning is everything. *Harvard Business Review,* 66(5): 78–86.
4. Haleblian, J., Devers, C., McNamara, G., Carpenter, M., & Davison, R. 2009. Taking stock of what we know about mergers and acquisitions: A review and research

agenda. *Journal of Management,* 35: 469-502.

5. Pare, T. P. 1994. The new merger boom. *Fortune,* November 28: 96.

6. A discussion of the effects of director experience and acquisition performance is in McDonald, M. L. & Westphal, J. D. 2008. What do they know? The effects of outside director acquisition experience on firm acquisition performance. *Strategic Management Journal,* 29(11): 1155-1177.

7. Finance and economics: Snoopy sniffs an opportunity; MetLife buys Alico. 2010. *Economist.com,* March 13: np.

8. For a study that investigates several predictors of corporate diversification, read Wiersema, M. F. & Bowen, H. P. 2008. Corporate diversification: The impact of foreign competition, industry globalization, and product diversification. *Strategic Management Journal,* 29(2): 114-132.

9. Kumar, M. V. S. 2011. Are joint ventures positive sum games? The relative effects of cooperative and non-cooperative behavior. *Strategic Management Journal,* 32(1): 32-54.

10. Makri, M., Hitt, M. A., & Lane, P. J. 2010. Complementary technologies, knowledge relatedness, and invention outcomes in high technology mergers and acquisitions. *Strategic Management Journal,* 31(6): 602-628.

11. A discussion of Tyco's unrelated diversification strategy is in Hindo, B. 2008. Solving Tyco's identity crisis. *BusinessWeek,* February 18: 62.

12. Our framework draws upon a variety of sources, including Goold, M. & Campbell, A. 1998. Desperately seeking synergy. *Harvard Business Review,* 76(5): 131-143; Porter, M. E. 1987. From advantage to corporate strategy. *Harvard Business Review,* 65(3): 43-59; and Hitt, M. A., Ireland, R. D., & Hoskisson, R. E. 2001. *Strategic management: Competitiveness and globalization* (4th ed.). Cincinnati, OH: South-Western.

13. This imagery of the corporation as a tree and related discussion draws on Prahalad, C. K. & Hamel, G. 1990. The core competence of the corporation. *Harvard Business Review,* 68(3): 79-91. Parts of this section also draw on Picken, J. C. & Dess, G. G. 1997. *Mission critical:* chap. 5. Burr Ridge, IL: Irwin Professional.

14. Graebner, M. E., Eisenhardt, K. M., & Roundy, P. T. 2010. Success and failure in technology acquisitions: Lessons for buyers and sellers.

Academy of Management Perspectives, 24(3): 73-92.

15. This section draws on Prahalad & Hamel, op. cit.; and Porter, op. cit.

16. A study that investigates the relationship between a firm's technology resources, diversification, and performance can be found in Miller, D. J. 2004. Firms' technological resources and the performance effects of diversification. A longitudinal study. *Strategic Management Journal,* 25: 1097-1119.

17. Khan, N. & Matsuda, K. 2015. Fujifilm shifts focus to stem cells and ebola drugs. *bloomberg.com,* August 17: np.

18. Chesbrough, H. 2011. Bringing open innovation to services. *MIT Sloan Management Review,* 52(2): 85-90.

19. Levine-Weinberg, A. 2014. Starbucks has decades of growth ahead. *money. cnn.com,* November 19: np.

20. This section draws on Hrebiniak, L. G. & Joyce, W. F. 1984. *Implementing strategy.* New York: Macmillan; and Oster, S. M. 1994. *Modern competitive analysis.* New York: Oxford University Press.

21. The discussion of the benefits and costs of vertical integration draws on Hax, A. C. & Majluf, N. S. 1991. *The strategy concept and process: A pragmatic approach:* 139. Englewood Cliffs, NJ: Prentice Hall.

22. Fahey, J. 2005. Gray winds. *Forbes,* January 10: 143.

23. This discussion draws on Oster, op. cit.; and Harrigan, K. 1986. Matching vertical integration strategies to competitive conditions. *Strategic Management Journal,* 7(6): 535-556.

24. Mathews, A. 2015. Kaiser Permanente to launch medical school. *wsj.com,* December 18: np.

25. For a scholarly explanation on how transaction costs determine the boundaries of a firm, see Oliver E. Williamson's pioneering books *Markets and hierarchies: Analysis and antitrust implications* (New York: Free Press, 1975) and *The economic institutions of capitalism* (New York: Free Press, 1985).

26. Campbell, A., Goold, M., & Alexander, M. 1995. Corporate strategy: The quest for parenting advantage. *Harvard Business Review,* 73(2): 120-132; and Picken & Dess, op. cit.

27. Anslinger, P. A. & Copeland, T. E. 1996. Growth through acquisition: A fresh look. *Harvard Business Review,* 74(1): 126-135.

28. This section draws on Porter, op. cit.; and Hambrick, D. C. 1985. Turnaround strategies. In Guth, W. D. (Ed.), *Handbook of business strategy:* 10-1-10-32. Boston: Warren, Gorham & Lamont.

29. There is an important delineation between companies that are operated for a long-term profit and those that are bought and sold for short-term gains. The latter are sometimes referred to as "holding companies" and are generally more concerned about financial issues than strategic issues.

30. Casico, W. F. 2002. Strategies for responsible restructuring. *Academy of Management Executive,* 16(3): 80-91; and Singh, H. 1993. Challenges in researching corporate restructuring. *Journal of Management Studies,* 30(1): 147-172.

31. Hax & Majluf, op. cit. By 1979, 45 percent of Fortune 500 companies employed some form of portfolio analysis, according to Haspelagh, P. 1982. Portfolio planning: Uses and limits. *Harvard Business Review,* 60: 58-73. A later study conducted in 1993 found that over 40 percent of the respondents used portfolio analysis techniques, but the level of usage was expected to increase to more than 60 percent in the near future: Rigby, D. K. 1994. Managing the management tools. *Planning Review,* September-October: 20-24.

32. Fruk, M., Hall, S., & Mittal, D. 2013. Never let a good crisis go to waste. *mckinsey.com,* October: np; and Arrfelt, M., Wiseman, R., McNamara, G., & Hult, T., 2015. Examining a key corporate role: The influence of capital allocation competency on business unit performance. *Strategic Management Journal,* in press.

33. Goold, M. & Luchs, K. 1993. Why diversify? Four decades of management thinking. *Academy of Management Executive,* 7(3): 7-25.

34. Other approaches include the industry attractiveness-business strength matrix developed jointly by General Electric and McKinsey and Company, the life-cycle matrix developed by Arthur D. Little, and the profitability matrix proposed by Marakon. For an extensive review, refer to Hax & Majluf, op. cit.: 182-194.

35. Porter, op. cit.: 49-52.

36. Picken & Dess, op. cit.; Cabot Corporation. 2001. 10-Q filing, Securities and Exchange Commission, May 14.

37. Insights on the performance of serial acquirers is found in Laamanen, T. & Keil, T. 2008. Performance of serial acquirers: Toward an acquisition program perspective. *Strategic Management Journal,* 29(6): 663–672.

38. Some insights from Lazard's CEO on mergers and acquisitions are addressed in Stewart, T. A. & Morse, G. 2008. Giving great advice. *Harvard Business Review,* 66(1): 106–113.

39. Coy, P., Thornton, E., Arndt, M., & Grow, B. 2005. Shake, rattle, and merge. *BusinessWeek,* January 10: 32–35; and Anonymous. 2005. Love is in the air. *The Economist,* February 5: 9.

40. Hill, A. 2011. Mergers indicate market optimism. *www.marketplace. org,* March 21: np.

41. For an interesting study of the relationship between mergers and a firm's product-market strategies, refer to Krishnan, R. A., Joshi, S., & Krishnan, H. 2004. The influence of mergers on firms' product-mix strategies. *Strategic Management Journal,* 25: 587–611.

42. Like many high-tech firms during the economic slump that began in mid-2000, Cisco Systems experienced declining performance. On April 16, 2001, it announced that its revenues for the quarter closing April 30 would drop 5 percent from a year earlier—and a stunning 30 percent from the previous three months—to about $4.7 billion. Furthermore, Cisco announced that it would lay off 8,500 employees and take an enormous $2.5 billion charge to write down inventory. By late October 2002, its stock was trading at around $10, down significantly from its 52-week high of $70. Elstrom, op. cit.: 39.

43. Sisario, B. 2014. Jimmy Iovine, a master of Beats, lends Apple a skilled ear. *nytimes.com,* May 28: np; and Dickey, M. 2014. Meet the executives Apple is paying $3 billion to get. *businessinsider.com,* May 28: np.

44. Ignatius, A. 2011. How eBay developed a culture of experimentation. *Harvard Business Review,* 89(3): 92–97.

45. For a discussion of the trend toward consolidation of the steel industry and how Lakshmi Mittal is becoming a dominant player, read Reed, S. & Arndt, M. 2004. The raja of steel. *BusinessWeek,* December 20: 50–52.

46. Colvin, G. 2011. Airline king. *Fortune,* May 2: 50–57.

47. This discussion draws upon Rappaport, A. & Sirower, M. L.

1999. Stock or cash? The trade-offs for buyers and sellers in mergers and acquisitions. *Harvard Business Review,* 77(6): 147–158; and Lipin, S. & Deogun, N. 2000. Big mergers of 90s prove disappointing to shareholders. *The Wall Street Journal,* October 30: C1.

48. The downside of mergers in the airline industry is found in Gimbel, B. 2008. Why airline mergers don't fly. *BusinessWeek,* March 17: 26.

49. Mouio, A. (Ed.). 1998. Unit of one. *Fast Company,* September: 82.

50. Porter, M. E. 1987. From competitive advantage to corporate strategy. *Harvard Business Review,* 65(3): 43.

51. The divestiture of a business that is undertaken in order to enable managers to better focus on its core business has been termed "downscoping." Refer to Hitt, M. A., Harrison, J. S., & Ireland, R. D. 2001. *Mergers and acquisitions: A guide to creating value for stakeholders.* New York: Oxford University Press.

52. Sirmon, D. G., Hitt, M. A., & Ireland, R. D. 2007. Managing firm resources in dynamic environments to create value: Looking inside the black box. *Academy of Management Review,* 32(1): 273–292.

53. Kengelbach, J., Klemmer, D., & Roos, A. 2012. Plant and prune: How M&A can grow portfolio value. *BCG Report,* September: 1–38.

54. Berry, J., Brigham, B., Bynum, A., Leu, C., & McLaughlin, R. 2012. Creating value through divestitures— Deans Foods: Theory in practice. *Unpublished manuscript.*

55. A study that investigates alliance performance is Lunnan, R. & Haugland, S. A. 2008. Predicting and measuring alliance performance: A multidimensional analysis. *Strategic Management Journal,* 29(5): 545–556.

56. For scholarly perspectives on the role of learning in creating value in strategic alliances, refer to Anard, B. N. & Khanna, T. 2000. Do firms learn to create value? *Strategic Management Journal,* 12(3): 295–317; and Vermeulen, F. & Barkema, H. P. 2001. Learning through acquisitions. *Academy of Management Journal,* 44(3): 457–476.

57. For a detailed discussion of transaction cost economics in strategic alliances, read Reuer, J. J. & Arno, A. 2007. Strategic alliance contracts: Dimensions and determinants of contractual complexity. *Strategic Management Journal,* 28(3): 313–330.

58. This section draws on Hutt, M. D., Stafford, E. R., Walker, B. A., & Reingen, P. H. 2000. Case study: Defining the strategic alliance. *Sloan Management Review,* 41(2): 51–62; and Walters, B. A., Peters, S., & Dess, G. G. 1994. Strategic alliances and joint ventures: Making them work. *Business Horizons,* 4: 5–10.

59. A study that investigates strategic alliances and networks is Tiwana, A. 2008. Do bridging ties complement strong ties? An empirical examination of alliance ambidexterity. *Strategic Management Journal,* 29(3): 251–272.

60. Fashion chain Zara opens its first Indian store. 2010. *bbc.co.uk/news/,* May 31: np.

61. Hoang, H. & Rothaermel, F. 2016. How to manage alliances strategically. *Sloan Management Review,* 76 (Fall): 69–73.

62. Anonymous. 2016. PGA TOUR and LPGA announce strategic alliance agreement. *lpga.com,* March 4: np.

63. Phelps, C. 2010. A longitudinal study of the influence of alliance network structure and composition on firm exploratory innovation. *Academy of Management Journal,* 53(4): 890–913.

64. For an institutional theory perspective on strategic alliances, read Dacin, M. T., Oliver, C., & Roy, J. P. 2007. The legitimacy of strategic alliances: An institutional perspective. *Strategic Management Journal,* 28(2): 169–187.

65. A study investigating factors that determine partner selection in strategic alliances is found in Shah, R. H. & Swaminathan, V. 2008. *Strategic Management Journal,* 29(5): 471–494.

66. Arino, A. & Ring, P. S. 2010. The role of fairness in alliance formation. *Strategic Management Journal,* 31(6): 1054–1087.

67. Greve, H. R., Baum, J. A. C., Mitsuhashi, H. & Rowley, T. J. 2010. Built to last but falling apart: Cohesion, friction, and withdrawal from interfirm alliances. *Academy of Management Journal,* 53(4): 302–322.

68. Narayan, A. 2011. From brewing, an Indian biotech is born. *Bloomberg Businessweek,* February 28: 19–20.

69. For an insightful perspective on how to manage conflict between innovation and ongoing operations in an organization, read Govindarajan, V. & Trimble, C. 2010. *The other side of innovation: Solving the execution*

challenge. Boston: Harvard Business School Press.

70. Dunlap-Hinkler, D., Kotabe, M., & Mudambi, R. 2010. A story of breakthrough versus incremental innovation: Corporate entrepreneurship in the global pharmaceutical industry. *Strategic Entrepreneurship Journal,* 4(2): 106-127.

71. Porter, op. cit.: 43-59.

72. Angwin, J. S. & Wingfield, N. 2000. How Jay Walker built WebHouse on a theory that he couldn't prove. *The Wall Street Journal,* October 16: A1, A8.

73. The fallen. 2003. *BusinessWeek,* January 13: 80-82.

74. The Jack Welch example draws upon Sellers, P. 2001. Get over yourself. *Fortune,* April 30: 76-88.

75. Li, J. & Tang, Y. 2010. CEO hubris and firm risk taking in China: The moderating role of managerial discretion. *Academy of Management Journal,* 53(1): 45-68.

76. John Thain and his golden commode. 2009. Editorial. *Dallasnews.com,* January 26: np; Task, A. 2009. Wall Street's $18.4B bonus: The sense of entitlement has not been beaten out. *finance.yahoo.com,* January 29: np; and Exit Thain. 2009. *Newsfinancialcareers.com,* January 22: np.

77. This section draws on Weston, J. F., Besley, S., & Brigham, E. F. 1996. *Essentials of managerial finance* (11th ed.): 18-20. Fort Worth, TX: Dryden Press, Harcourt Brace.

chapter 7

International Strategy
Creating Value in Global Markets

After reading this chapter, you should have a good understanding of the following learning objectives:

LO7-1 The importance of international expansion as a viable diversification strategy.

LO7-2 The sources of national advantage; that is, why an industry in a given country is more (or less) successful than the same industry in another country.

LO7-3 The motivations (or benefits) and the risks associated with international expansion, including the emerging trend for greater offshoring and outsourcing activity.

LO7-4 The two opposing forces—cost reduction and adaptation to local markets—that firms face when entering international markets.

LO7-5 The advantages and disadvantages associated with each of the four basic strategies: international, global, multidomestic, and transnational.

LO7-6 The difference between regional companies and truly global companies.

LO7-7 The four basic types of entry strategies and the relative benefits and risks associated with each of them.

©Anatoli Styf/Shutterstock

LEARNING FROM MISTAKES

What was supposed to be one of India's hottest new shopping centers didn't turn out that way. Dreams Mall, located in a Mumbai suburb, was built by Housing Development & Infrastructure Ltd. (an Indian real estate development company) to cater to the growing middle class of the world's second-most populous nation. But four years after its grand opening, the "dream" has become, in essence, a retail nightmare. Now, the mall consists of a smattering of struggling stores on the ground floor along with a maze of dark hallways with mostly empty shops. Space that was intended for retailers is used by call centers. And abandoned corridors are rented out for wedding receptions.

Across India, many of the country's more than 300 malls have suffered weak sales and high vacancy rates. This was not anticipated. Developers over the past decade have built more than 250 shopping centers to tap into India's rapidly expanding consumer culture. Some analysts had estimated that India's middle class would grow to more than 400 million people. However, only a sliver of them (less than 10 million by McKinsey & Company's estimates) have sufficient disposable income to make them steady mall customers.

India did not get its first mall until the late 1990s. Developers started building many others after Spencer Plaza in Chennai and a few others were so successful. Some construction companies began building three or more malls right next to each other in some neighborhoods in New Delhi and Mumbai. As noted by Benu Sehgal, vice president at DLF Ltd., a big developer, "Everyone jumped into the mall business with little understanding of who they were actually targeting." Govind Shrikhande, chief executive of one of India's largest retailers, said, "Everyone was opening malls left, right, and center. The consumer was never at the center of the planning process."

Even with high vacancy rates, some Indian malls are doing very well. For example, Select CITYWALK Mall in South Delhi is considered "India's No. 1 mall." Others that are highly successful in India's highly competitive market include DLF Promenade, Ambience Palladium, Phoenix, Inorbit, and Marketcity. What makes these malls successful? They win in the marketplace because they have a sound knowledge of the market and make informed decisions at the right time. For example, Select CITYWALK focused on what is considered "premium" in its positioning in the market: a level lower than affordable luxury. Today the mall is moving toward the affordable luxury category. Also, Select CITYWALK has a nice collection of retailers, such as Zara, Nike, and H&M, a multiplex theater, and great food. As noted by Yogeshwar Sharma, chief executive of Select CITYWALK, "Mall operation is one of the easiest things, given you know the job. Every game has its own rules. If you follow the rules, you are successful, if you don't you fail."

Discussion Questions

1. What lessons can other multinational companies learn from the boom and bust of shopping centers in India?
2. How can foreign retailers be successful in a country in which shopping centers are not attracting enough customers?

Sources: Kulshrestha, A. 2016. India may attract $80 million PE investment in retail real estate, say JLL. *artices. economictimes.indiatimes.com*. April 14: np.; Rana, P. 2015. Empty dream at India's malls. *the Wall Street Journal*. June 17: C1, C8; and, Batra, A. 2015. What makes Select CITYWALK India's successful mall, reveals Yogeshwar Sharma. *retail. economictimes.indiatimes.com*. March 20: np.

In this chapter we discuss how firms create value and achieve competitive advantage in the global marketplace. Multinational firms are constantly faced with many important decisions. These include entry strategies; the dilemma of choosing between local adaptation (in product offerings, locations, advertising, and pricing) and global integration; and others. We will address how firms can avoid pitfalls by developing a better understanding of the business environments of different countries as illustrated by the lukewarm response of Indian consumers to the new malls discussed previously. In addition, we address factors that can influence a nation's success in a particular industry. In our view, this is an important context in determining how well firms eventually do when they compete beyond their nation's boundaries.

THE GLOBAL ECONOMY: A BRIEF OVERVIEW

LO 7-1

The importance of international expansion as a viable diversification strategy.

Managers face many opportunities and risks when they diversify abroad.[1] The trade among nations has increased dramatically in recent years, and it is estimated that recently the trade *across* nations exceeded the trade within nations. In a variety of industries such as semiconductors, automobiles, commercial aircraft, telecommunications, computers, and consumer electronics, it is almost impossible to survive unless firms scan the world for competitors, customers, human resources, suppliers, and technology.[2]

GE's wind energy business benefits by tapping into talent around the world. The firm has built research centers in China, Germany, India, and the United States "We did it," says CEO Jeffrey Immelt, "to access the best brains everywhere in the world." All four centers have played a key role in GE's development of huge 92-ton turbines:[3]

- Chinese researchers in Shanghai designed the microprocessors that control the pitch of the blade.
- Mechanical engineers from India (Bangalore) devised mathematical models to maximize the efficiency of materials in the turbine.
- Power-systems experts in the United States (Niskayuna, New York), which has researchers from 55 countries, do the design work.
- Technicians in Munich, Germany, have created a "smart" turbine that can calculate wind speeds and signal sensors in other turbines to produce maximum electricity.

globalization
a term that has two meanings: (1) the increase in international exchange, including trade in goods and services as well as exchange of money, ideas, and information; (2) the growing similarity of laws, rules, norms, values, and ideas across countries.

The rise of **globalization**—meaning the rise of market capitalism around the world—has undeniably created tremendous business opportunities for multinational corporations. For example, while smartphone sales declined in Western Europe in the third quarter of 2014, they grew at a 50 percent rate in Eastern Europe, the Middle East, and Africa.[4]

This rapid rise in global capitalism has had dramatic effects on the growth in different economic zones. For example, *Fortune* magazine's annual list of the world's 500 biggest companies included 156 firms from emerging markets in 2015, compared to only 18 in 1995.[5] McKinsey & Company predicts that by 2025 about 45 percent of the *Fortune* Global 500 will be based in emerging economies, which are now producing world-class companies with huge domestic markets and a commitment to invest in innovation.

Over half the world's output now comes from emerging markets. This is leading to a convergence of living standards across the globe and is changing the face of business. One example of this is the shift in the global automobile market. China supplanted the United States as the largest market for automobiles in 2009.

One of the challenges with globalization is determining how to meet the needs of customers at very different income levels. In many developing economies, distributions of income remain much wider than they do in the developed world, leaving many impoverished even as the economies grow. The challenge for multinational firms is to tailor their products and services to meet the needs of the "bottom of the pyramid." Global corporations are increasingly changing their product offerings to meet the needs of the nearly 5 billion poor people in the world who inhabit developing countries. Collectively, this represents a very large market with $14 trillion in purchasing power.

Next, we will address in more detail the question of why some nations and their industries are more competitive.[6] This establishes an important context or setting for the remainder of the chapter. After we discuss why some *nations and their industries* outperform others, we will be better able to address the various strategies that *firms* can take to create competitive advantage when they expand internationally.

FACTORS AFFECTING A NATION'S COMPETITIVENESS

Michael Porter of Harvard University conducted a four-year study in which he and a team of 30 researchers looked at the patterns of competitive success in 10 leading trading nations. He concluded that there are four broad attributes of nations that individually, and as a system, constitute what is termed the **diamond of national advantage.** In effect, these attributes jointly determine the playing field that each nation establishes and operates for its industries. These factors are:

- *Factor endowments.* The nation's position in factors of production, such as skilled labor or infrastructure, necessary to compete in a given industry.
- *Demand conditions.* The nature of home-market demand for the industry's product or service.
- *Related and supporting industries.* The presence or absence in the nation of supplier industries and other related industries that are internationally competitive.
- *Firm strategy, structure, and rivalry.* The conditions in the nation governing how companies are created, organized, and managed, as well as the nature of domestic rivalry.

diamond of national advantage
a framework for explaining why countries foster successful multinational corporations; consists of four factors—factor endowments; demand conditions; related and supporting industries; and firm strategy, structure, and rivalry.

factor endowments (national advantage)
a nation's position in factors of production.

Factor Endowments[7,8]

Classical economics suggests that factors of production such as land, labor, and capital are the building blocks that create usable consumer goods and services.[9] However, companies in advanced nations seeking competitive advantage over firms in other nations *create* many of the factors of production. For example, a country or industry dependent on scientific innovation must have a skilled human resource pool to draw upon. This resource pool is not inherited; it is created through investment in industry-specific knowledge and talent. The supporting infrastructure of a country—that is, its transportation and communication systems as well as its banking system—is also critical.

Factors of production must be developed that are industry- and firm-specific. In addition, the pool of resources is less important than the speed and efficiency with which these resources are deployed. Thus, firm-specific knowledge and skills created within a country that are rare, valuable, difficult to imitate, and rapidly and efficiently deployed are the factors of production that ultimately lead to a nation's competitive advantage.

For example, the island nation of Japan has little landmass, making the warehouse space needed to store inventory prohibitively expensive. But by pioneering just-in-time inventory management, Japanese companies managed to create a resource from which they gained advantage over companies in other nations that spent large sums to warehouse inventory.

LO 7-2

The sources of national advantage; that is, why an industry in a given country is more (or less) successful than the same industry in another country.

Demand Conditions

Demand conditions refer to the demands that consumers place on an industry for goods and services. Consumers who demand highly specific, sophisticated products and services force firms to create innovative, advanced products and services to meet the demand. This consumer pressure presents challenges to a country's industries. But in response to these challenges, improvements to existing goods and services often result, creating conditions necessary for competitive advantage over firms in other countries.

demand conditions (national advantage)
the nature of home-market demand for the industry's product or service.

Countries with demanding consumers drive firms in that country to meet high standards, upgrade existing products and services, and create innovative products and services. The conditions of consumer demand influence how firms view a market. This, in turn, helps a nation's industries to better anticipate future global demand conditions and proactively respond to product and service requirements.

Denmark, for instance, is known for its environmental awareness. Demand from consumers for environmentally safe products has spurred Danish manufacturers to become leaders in water pollution control equipment—products it has successfully exported.

Related and Supporting Industries

related and supporting industries (national advantage) the presence, absence, and quality in the nation of supplier industries and other related industries that supply services, support, or technology to firms in the industry value chain.

Related and supporting industries enable firms to manage inputs more effectively. For example, countries with a strong supplier base benefit by adding efficiency to downstream activities. A competitive supplier base helps a firm obtain inputs using cost-effective, timely methods, thus reducing manufacturing costs. Also, close working relationships with suppliers provide the potential to develop competitive advantages through joint research and development and the ongoing exchange of knowledge.

Related industries offer similar opportunities through joint efforts among firms. In addition, related industries create the probability that new companies will enter the market, increasing competition and forcing existing firms to become more competitive through efforts such as cost control, product innovation, and novel approaches to distribution. Combined, these give the home country's industries a source of competitive advantage.

In the Italian footwear industry the supporting industries enhance national competitive advantage. In Italy, shoe manufacturers are geographically located near their suppliers. The manufacturers have ongoing interactions with leather suppliers and learn about new textures, colors, and manufacturing techniques while a shoe is still in the prototype stage. The manufacturers are able to project future demand and gear their factories for new products long before companies in other nations become aware of the new styles.

Firm Strategy, Structure, and Rivalry

firm strategy, structure, and rivalry (national advantage) the conditions in the nation governing how companies are created, organized, and managed, as well as the nature of domestic rivalry.

Rivalry is particularly intense in nations with conditions of strong consumer demand, strong supplier bases, and high new-entrant potential from related industries. This competitive rivalry in turn increases the efficiency with which firms develop, market, and distribute products and services within the home country. Domestic rivalry thus provides a strong impetus for firms to innovate and find new sources of competitive advantage.

This intense rivalry forces firms to look outside their national boundaries for new markets, setting up the conditions necessary for global competitiveness. Among all the points on Porter's diamond of national advantage, domestic rivalry is perhaps the strongest indicator of global competitive success. Firms that have experienced intense domestic competition are more likely to have designed strategies and structures that allow them to successfully compete in world markets.

In the European grocery retail industry, intense rivalry has led firms such as Aldi and Tesco to tighten their supply chains and improve store efficiency. Thus, it is no surprise that these firms are also strong global players.

The Indian software industry offers a clear example of how the attributes in Porter's "diamond" interact to lead to the conditions for a strong industry to grow. Exhibit 7.1 illustrates India's "software diamond," and Strategy Spotlight 7.1 further discusses the mutually reinforcing elements at work in this market.

Concluding Comment on Factors Affecting a Nation's Competitiveness

Porter drew his conclusions based on case histories of firms in more than 100 industries. Despite the differences in strategies employed by successful global competitors, a common

EXHIBIT 7.1 India's Software Diamond

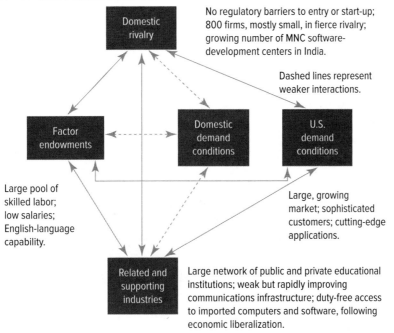

No regulatory barriers to entry or start-up; 800 firms, mostly small, in fierce rivalry; growing number of MNC software-development centers in India.

Dashed lines represent weaker interactions.

Large pool of skilled labor; low salaries; English-language capability.

Large, growing market; sophisticated customers; cutting-edge applications.

Large network of public and private educational institutions; weak but rapidly improving communications infrastructure; duty-free access to imported computers and software, following economic liberalization.

Source: From Kampur D. and Ramamurti R., "India's Emerging Competition Advantage in Services," *Academy of Management Executive: The Thinking Manager's Source.* Copyright © 2001 by Academy of Management.

7.1   STRATEGY **SPOTLIGHT**

INDIA AND THE DIAMOND OF NATIONAL ADVANTAGE

The Indian software industry has become one of the leading global markets for software. The industry has grown to about $110 billion (in export) in 2016 and Indian IT firms provide software and services to over half the Fortune 500 firms. What are the factors driving this success? Porter's diamond of national advantage helps clarify this question. See Exhibit 7.1.

First, *factor endowments* are conducive to the rise of India's software industry. Through investment in human resource development with a focus on industry-specific knowledge, India's universities and software firms have literally created this essential factor of production. For example, India produces the second-largest annual output of scientists and engineers in the world, behind only the United States. In a knowledge-intensive industry such as software, development of human resources is fundamental to both domestic and global success.

Second, *demand conditions* require that software firms stay on the cutting edge of technological innovation. India has already moved toward globalization of its software industry; consumer demand conditions in developed nations such as Germany, Denmark, parts of Southeast Asia, and the United

States created the consumer demand necessary to propel India's software makers toward sophisticated software solutions.*

Third, India has the *supplier base as well as the related industries* needed to drive competitive rivalry and enhance competitiveness. In particular, information technology (IT) hardware prices declined rapidly in the 1990s. Furthermore, rapid technological change in IT hardware meant that latecomers like India were not locked into older-generation technologies. Thus, both the IT hardware and software industries could "leapfrog" older technologies. In addition, relationships among knowledge workers in these IT hardware and software industries offer the social structure for ongoing knowledge exchange, promoting further enhancement of existing products. Further infrastructure improvements are occurring rapidly.

Fourth, with over 800 firms in the software services industry in India, *intense rivalry forces firms to develop competitive strategies and structures.* Although firms like TCS, Infosys, and

*Although India's success cannot be explained in terms of its home-market demand (according to Porter's model), the nature of the industry enables software to be transferred among different locations simultaneously by way of communications links. Thus, competitiveness of markets outside India can be enhanced without a physical presence in those markets.

continued

continued

Wipro have become large, they still face strong competition from dozens of small and midsize companies aspiring to catch them. This intense rivalry is one of the primary factors driving Indian software firms to develop overseas distribution channels, as predicted by Porter's diamond of national advantage.

Sources: Pai M. 2016. No, India's software industry did not die on Friday. *www.ndtv.com.* October 16:np; Sachitanand, R. 2010. The new face of IT. *Business Today,* 19: 62; Anonymous. 2010. Training to lead. *www.Dqindia.com,* October 5:

np; Nagaraju, B. 2011. India's software exports seen up 16–18 pct. in Fy12. *www.reuters.com,* February 2: np; Ghemawat, P. & Hout, T. 2008. Tomorrow's global giants. *Harvard Business Review,* 86(11): 80–88; Mathur, S. K. 2007. Indian IT industry: A performance analysis and a model for possible adoption. *ideas.repec.org,* January 1: np; Kripalani, M. 2002. Calling Bangalore: Multinationals are making it a hub for high-tech research *BusinessWeek,* November 25: 52–54; Kapur, D. & Ramamurti, R. 2001. India's emerging competitive advantage in services. 2001. *Academy of Management Executive,* 15(2): 20–33; World Bank. 2001 *World Development Report:* 6. New York: Oxford University Press; and Reuters. 2001. Oracle in India push, taps software talent. *Washington Post Online,* July 3.

theme emerged: Firms that succeeded in global markets had first succeeded in intensely competitive home markets. We can conclude that competitive advantage for global firms typically grows out of relentless, continuing improvement, and innovation.[10]

INTERNATIONAL EXPANSION: A COMPANY'S MOTIVATIONS AND RISKS

Motivations for International Expansion

LO 7-3

The motivations (or benefits) and the risks associated with international expansion, including the emerging trend for greater offshoring and outsourcing activity.

Increase Market Size There are many motivations for a company to pursue international expansion. The most obvious one is to *increase the size of potential markets* for a firm's products and services.[11] The world's population exceeded 7.6 billion in early 2018, with the U.S. representing less than 5 percent.

Many **multinational firms** are intensifying their efforts to market their products and services to countries such as India and China as the ranks of their middle class have increased over the past decade. The potential is great. An OECD study predicts that consumption by middle-class consumers in Asian markets will grow from $4.9 trillion in 2009 to over $30 trillion by 2020. At that point, Asia will make up 60 percent of global middle-class consumption, up from 20 percent in 2009.[12]

multinational firms
firms that manage operations in more than one country.

Expanding a firm's global presence also automatically increases its scale of operations, providing it with a larger revenue and asset base.[13] As we noted in Chapter 5 in discussing overall cost leadership strategies, such an increase in revenues and asset base potentially enables a firm to *attain economies of scale.* This provides multiple benefits. One advantage is the spreading of fixed costs such as R&D over a larger volume of production. Examples include the sale of Boeing's commercial aircraft and Microsoft's operating systems in many foreign countries.

Filmmaking is another industry in which international sales can help amortize huge developmental costs.[14] For example, 77 percent of the $1.1 billion box-office take for *Transformers: Age of Extinction* came from overseas moviegoers. Similarly, the market for kids' movies is largely outside the U.S., with 70 percent of *Frozen's* $1.3 billion in box-office take coming from overseas.

arbitrage opportunities
an opportunity to profit by buying and selling the same good in different markets.

Take Advantage of Arbitrage *Taking advantage of* **arbitrage opportunities** is a second advantage of international expansion. In its simplest form, arbitrage involves buying something where it is cheap and selling it where it commands a higher price. A big part of Walmart's success can be attributed to the company's expertise in arbitrage. The possibilities for arbitrage are not necessarily confined to simple trading opportunities. It can be applied to virtually any factor of production and every stage of the value chain. For example, a firm may locate its call centers in India, its manufacturing plants in China or Vietnam, and its R&D in Europe, where the specific types of talented personnel may be available at the lowest possible cost. In today's integrated global financial markets, a firm can borrow anywhere in the world where capital is cheap and use it to fund a project in a country where capital is expensive. Such arbitrage opportunities are even more attractive to global corporations because their larger size enables them to buy in huge volume, thus increasing their bargaining power with suppliers.

Enhancing a Product's Growth Potential   *Enhancing the growth rate of a product* that is in its maturity stage in a firm's home country but that has greater demand potential elsewhere is another benefit of international expansion. As we noted in Chapter 5, products (and industries) generally go through a four-stage life cycle of introduction, growth, maturity, and decline. In recent decades, U.S. soft-drink producers such as Coca-Cola and PepsiCo have aggressively pursued international markets to attain levels of growth that simply would not be available in the United States. The differences in market growth potential have even led some firms to restructure their operations. For example, Procter & Gamble relocated its global skin, cosmetics, and personal care unit headquarters from Cincinnati to Singapore to be closer to the fast-growing Asian market.[15]

Optimize the Location of Value-Chain Activities   *Optimizing the physical location for every activity in the firm's value chain* is another benefit. Recall from our discussions in Chapters 3 and 5 that the value chain represents the various activities in which all firms must engage to produce products and services. It includes primary activities, such as inbound logistics, operations, and marketing, as well as support activities, such as procurement, R&D, and human resource management. All firms have to make critical decisions as to where each activity will take place.[16] Optimizing the location for every activity in the value chain can yield one or more of three strategic advantages: performance enhancement, cost reduction, and risk reduction. We will now discuss each of these.

Performance Enhancement   Microsoft's decision to establish a corporate research laboratory in Cambridge, England, is an example of a location decision that was guided mainly by the goal of building and sustaining world-class excellence in selected value-creating activities.[17] This strategic decision provided Microsoft with access to outstanding technical and professional talent. Location decisions can affect the quality with which any activity is performed in terms of the availability of needed talent, speed of learning, and the quality of external and internal coordination.

Strategy&, the consulting unit of PWC, the giant accounting firm, produces an annual survey of the world's 1000 most innovative companies.[18] It found that in 2015, firms that spent 60 percent or more of their R&D budgets overseas enjoyed significantly higher operating margins and return on assets, as well as faster growth in operating income, than their more domestically oriented rivals.

Cost Reduction   Two location decisions founded largely on cost-reduction considerations are (1) Nike's decision to source the manufacture of athletic shoes from Asian countries such as China, Vietnam, and Indonesia and (2) the decision of Volkswagen to locate a new auto production plant in Chattanooga, Tennessee, to leverage the relatively low labor costs in the area as well as low shipping costs due to Chattanooga's close proximity to both rail and river transportation. Such location decisions can affect the cost structure in terms of local manpower and other resources, transportation and logistics, and government incentives and the local tax structure

Performance enhancement and cost-reduction benefits parallel the business-level strategies (discussed in Chapter 5) of differentiation and overall cost leadership. They can at times be attained simultaneously. Consider our example in the previous section on the Indian software industry. When Oracle set up a development operation in that country, the company benefited both from lower labor costs and operational expenses and from performance enhancements realized through the hiring of superbly talented professionals.

Risk Reduction   Given the erratic swings in the exchange ratios between the U.S. dollar and the Japanese yen (in relation to each other and to other major currencies), an important basis for cost competition between Ford and Toyota has been their relative ingenuity at managing currency risks. One way for such rivals to manage currency risks has been to spread the high-cost elements of their manufacturing operations across a few select and carefully chosen locations around the world. Location decisions such as these can affect the overall risk profile of the firm with respect to currency, economic, and political risks.[19]

Learning Opportunities   By expanding into new markets, corporations expose themselves to differing market demands, R&D capabilities, functional skills, organizational processes, and managerial practices. This provides opportunities for managers to transfer the knowledge that results from these exposures back to their home office and to other divisions in the firm. Thus, expansion into new markets provides a range of learning opportunities. For example, when L'Oréal, a French personal care product manufacturer, acquired two U.S. firms that developed and sold hair care products to African-American customers, L'Oréal gained knowledge on what is referred to in the industry as "ethnic hair care." It then took this knowledge and built a new ethnic hair care division in Europe and later began making inroads in African markets. More generally, research suggests that overseas expansion leads to valuable learning at home. One study found that, rather than distracting the firm in its efforts in its home market, overseas acquisitions led to substantial performance improvements, an average of a 12 percent increase, in home markets.[20]

| **reverse innovation** new products developed by developed-country multinational firms for emerging markets that have adequate functionality at a low cost. |

Explore Reverse Innovation   Finally, *exploring possibilities for* **reverse innovation** has become a major motivation for international expansion. Many leading companies are discovering that developing products specifically for emerging markets can pay off in a big way. In the past, multinational companies typically developed products for their rich home markets and then tried to sell them in developing countries with minor adaptations. However, as growth slows in rich nations and demand grows rapidly in developing countries such as India and China, this approach becomes increasingly inadequate. Instead, companies like GE have committed significant resources to developing products that meet the needs of developing nations, products that deliver adequate functionality at a fraction of the cost. Interestingly, these products have subsequently found considerable success in value segments in wealthy countries as well. Hence, this process is referred to as reverse innovation, a new motivation for international expansion.

As $3,000 cars, $300 computers, and $30 mobile phones bring what were previously considered as luxuries within the reach of the middle class of emerging markets, it is important to understand the motivations and implications of reverse innovation. *First,* it is impossible to sell first-world versions of products with minor adaptations in countries where the average annual income per person is between $1,000 and $4,000, as is the case in most developing countries. To sell in these markets, entirely new products must be designed and developed by local technical talent and manufactured with local components. *Second,* although these countries are relatively poor, they are growing rapidly. *Third,* if the innovation does not come from first-world multinationals, there are any number of local firms that are ready to grab the market with low-cost products. *Fourth,* as the consumers and governments of many first-world countries are rediscovering the virtues of frugality and are trying to cut down expenses, these products and services originally developed for the first world may gain significant market shares in developing countries as well.

Potential Risks of International Expansion

When a company expands its international operations, it does so to increase its profits or revenues. As with any other investment, however, there are also potential risks.[21] To help companies assess the risk of entering foreign markets, rating systems have been developed to evaluate political and economic, as well as financial and credit, risks.[22]

EXHIBIT 7.2

A Sample of Country
Risk Ratings,
August 22, 2017

Country Score	Overall Country Rating	Economic Risk	Political Risk	Financial System Risk
Norway	1	2	1	1
Canada	1	1	1	1
United States	1	2	1	1
Singapore	1	2	2	1
Hong Kong	2	2	2	1
South Korea	2	1	2	2
South Africa	4	3	4	3
China	3	2	3	3
Bahrain	4	4	3	3
Kazakhstan	4	3	3	4
Colombia	4	3	4	3
Russia	4	3	4	4
Argentina	5	3	4	5
Libya	5	4	5	5

Source: A.M. Best Company - Used by permission.

Euromoney magazine publishes a semiannual "Country Risk Rating" that evaluates political, economic, and other risks that entrants potentially face.[23] Exhibit 7.2 presents a sample of country risk ratings, published by AM Best. Note that the overall ratings range from 1 to 5, with higher risk receiving the higher score.

Next we will discuss the four main types of risk: political risk, economic risk, currency risk, and management risk.

Political and Economic Risk   Generally speaking, the business climate in the United States is very favorable. However, some countries around the globe may be hazardous to the health of corporate initiatives because of **political risk.**[24] Forces such as social unrest, military turmoil, demonstrations, and even violent conflict and terrorism can pose serious threats.[25] Consider, for example, the ongoing tension and violence in the Middle East associated with the revolutions and civil wars in Egypt, Libya, Syria, and other countries. Such conditions increase the likelihood of destruction of property and disruption of operations as well as nonpayment for goods and services. Thus, countries that are viewed as high risk are less attractive for most types of business.[26]

Another source of political risk in many countries is the absence of the **rule of law.** The absence of rules or the lack of uniform enforcement of existing rules leads to what might often seem to be arbitrary and inconsistent decisions by government officials. This can make it difficult for foreign firms to conduct business.

For example, consider Renault's experience in Russia. Renault paid $1 billion to acquire a 25 percent ownership stake in the Russian automaker AvtoVAZ in 2008. Just one year later, Russian Prime Minister Vladimir Putin threatened to dilute Renault's ownership stake unless it contributed more money to prop up AvtoVAZ, which was then experiencing a significant slide in sales. Renault realized its ownership claim may not have held up in the corrupt Russian court system. Therefore, it was forced to negotiate and eventually agreed to transfer over $300 million in technology and expertise to the Russian firm to ensure its ownership stake would stay at 25 percent.[27]

political risk
potential threat to a firm's operations in a country due to ineffectiveness of the domestic political system.

rule of law
a characteristic of legal systems whereby behavior is governed by rules that are uniformly enforced.

Interestingly, while corporations have historically been concerned about rule-of-law issues in developing markets, such issues have also become a significant concern in developed markets, most critically in the United States. In a 2012 World Economic Forum Global Competitive Report that examined the quality of governmental institutions and the rule of law, the United States fared poorly. Starkly, the United States was ranked among the top 20 countries on only 1 of the 22 measures of institutional quality the survey included. In line with these findings, the International Finance Corporation (IFC) found that governmental hurdles businesses face have become a greater challenge in the United States in recent years. The IFC compiles data annually on the burdens of doing business that are put in place by governments and found that the United States is one of only a few countries surveyed in which doing business has become more burdensome. In nearly 90 percent of countries, governmental burdens have eased since 2006, but the United States has bucked that trend and become a more difficult location in which to operate. As institutions deteriorate, the United States loses its luster as a place to base operations. This sentiment was reflected in a survey of business executives who are alumni of the Harvard Business School. When asked whether they had recently favored basing new operations in the United States or in a foreign location, an overwhelming majority, 84 percent, responded that they had chosen the foreign location. Thus, advanced economies, such as the United States, risk losing out to other countries if they fail to reinforce and strengthen their legal and political institutions.[28]

economic risk
potential threat to a firm's operations in a country due to economic policies and conditions, including property rights laws and enforcement of those laws.

The laws, and the enforcement of laws, associated with the protection of intellectual property rights can be a major potential **economic risk** in entering new countries.[29] Microsoft, for example, has lost billions of dollars in potential revenue through piracy of its software products in many countries, including China. Other areas of the globe, such as the former Soviet Union and some eastern European nations, have piracy problems as well.[30] Firms rich in intellectual property have encountered financial losses as imitations of their products have grown due to a lack of law enforcement of intellectual property rights.[31]

counterfeiting
selling of trademarked goods without the consent of the trademark holder.

Counterfeiting, a direct form of theft of intellectual property rights, is a significant and growing problem. The International Chamber of Commerce estimated that the value of counterfeit goods exceeded $1.7 trillion in 2015, over 2 percent of the world's total economic output. "The whole business has just exploded," said Jeffrey Hardy, head of the anticounterfeiting program at ICC. "And it goes way beyond music and Gucci bags." Counterfeiting has moved well beyond handbags and shoes to include chemicals, pharmaceuticals, and aircraft parts. According to a University of Florida study, 25 percent of the pesticide market in some parts of Europe is estimated to be counterfeit. This is especially troubling since these chemicals are often toxic.[32] In Strategy Spotlight 7.2, we discuss the challenge of fighting counterfeiting in the pharmaceutical business and how Pfizer is attempting to fight this threat to its business.

Currency Risks Currency fluctuations can pose substantial risks. A company with operations in several countries must constantly monitor the exchange rate between its own currency and that of the host country to minimize **currency risks.** Even a small change in the exchange rate can result in a significant difference in the cost of production or net profit when doing business overseas. When the U.S. dollar appreciates against other currencies, for example, U.S. goods can be more expensive to consumers in foreign countries. At the same time, however, appreciation of the U.S. dollar can have negative implications for American companies that have branch operations overseas. The reason for this is that profits from abroad must be exchanged for dollars at a more expensive rate of exchange, reducing the amount of profit when measured in dollars. For example, consider an American firm doing business in Italy. If this firm had a 20 percent profit in euros at its Italian center of operations, this profit would be totally wiped out when converted into U.S. dollars if the euro had depreciated 20 percent against the U.S. dollar. (U.S. multinationals typically

currency risk
potential threat to a firm's operations in a country due to fluctuations in the local currency's exchange rate.

COUNTERFEIT DRUGS: A DANGEROUS AND GROWING PROBLEM

Brian Donnelly has an interesting background. He's both a cop and a pharmacist. He worked as a special agent for the FBI for 21 years, but he also has a PhD in pharmacology. Now he's on the front lines of an important fight: keeping counterfeit drugs from the market. He works as an investigator for Pfizer, one of the world's largest pharmaceutical companies, putting both his pharmacology and law enforcement skills at work to blunt the growing flow of counterfeit drugs. He is one of a small army of former law enforcement officers employed by the pharmaceutical companies working for the same aim.

This is an important fight for two reasons. First, it is of economic consequence for the pharmaceutical companies. Counterfeit drugs are big business. In the United States alone, counterfeit drugs generated around $200 billion in revenue in 2015. They are enticing to customers. For example, while Pfizer's erectile dysfunction pill, Viagra, sells for $15 per tablet, fake versions sold online can be gotten for as little as $1 a pill. The sales of counterfeit drugs cut into the sales and profits of Pfizer and the other pharmaceutical firms. Second and more importantly, these fake drugs are potentially dangerous. The danger comes from both what they contain and what they don't contain. Fake pills have been found to contain chalk, brick dust, paint, and even pesticides. Thus, they may be toxic, and ingesting them may cause significant health problems. On the other side, they may not contain the correct dose or even any of the active ingredients they are supposed to have. This may lead to severe health consequences. For example,

fake Zithromax, an antibiotic, may contain none of the necessary chemical components, leaving the patient unable to fight the infection. According to one estimate, counterfeit drugs contribute to the death of upward of 200,000 people a year globally.

The pharmaceutical firms are fighting back with Donnelly and his colleagues. They use a common law enforcement technique. The fake drugs are sold by local dealers in the United States, who typically sell through websites. These local dealers, called drop dealers, are the easiest to catch. From there, the investigators try to gain information on the major dealers from whom the drop dealers order. If they can get to these folks, they try to take it back to the kingpins manufacturing the drugs. This typically takes them through multiple law enforcement agencies in multiple countries, often back to manufacturing plants in China and India. To find the source, the pharmaceutical companies also use advanced technology. They determine the chemical composition of fake drugs they seize to search for common chemical signatures that point to the possible sourcing plant.

Pfizer is also fighting the fight from another angle. It is now tagging every bottle of Viagra and many other pharmaceuticals with radio-frequency identification (RFID) tags. Pharmacies can read these tags and input the data into Pfizer's system to confirm that these bottles are legitimate Pfizer drugs. This won't stop shady websites from delivering counterfeit drugs, but it will help keep the counterfeits out of legitimate pharmacies.

Sources: McLauglin, J. 2015. The United States isn't immune to counterfeit drugs. *lawstreetmedia.com,* May 8: np; O'Connor, M. 2006. Pfizer using RFID to fight fake Viagra. *RFIDjournal.com,* January 6: np; and Gillette, F. 2013. Inside Pfizer's fight against counterfeit drugs. *Bloomberg Businessweek,* January 17: np.

---

engage in sophisticated "hedging strategies" to minimize currency risk. The discussion of this is beyond the scope of this section.)

Below, we discuss how Israel's strong currency—the shekel—forced a firm to reevaluate its strategy.

> For years O.R.T. Technologies resisted moving any operations outside Israel. However, when faced with a sharp rise in the value of the shekel, the maker of specialized software for managing gas stations froze all local hiring and decided to transfer some developmental work to Eastern Europe. Laments CEO Alex Milner, "I never thought I'd see the day when we would have to move R&D outside of Israel, but the strong shekel has forced us to do so."[33]

Management Risks   **Management risks** may be considered the challenges and risks that managers face when they must respond to the inevitable differences that they encounter in foreign markets. These take a variety of forms: culture, customs, language, income levels, customer preferences, distribution systems, and so on.[34] As we will note later in the chapter, even in the case of apparently standard products, some degree of local adaptation will become necessary.[35]

Differences in cultures across countries can also pose unique challenges for managers.[36] Cultural symbols can evoke deep feelings.[37] For example, in a series of advertisements aimed at Italian vacationers, Coca-Cola executives turned the Eiffel Tower, Empire State Building,

management risk
potential threat to a firm's operations in a country due to the problems that managers have making decisions in the context of foreign markets.

WHEN TO *NOT* ADAPT YOUR COMPANY'S CULTURE—EVEN IF IT CONFLICTS WITH THE LOCAL CULTURE

When companies instill a company culture that includes how people communicate, evaluate each other, and so on, they may often run into problems when they expand internationally. For example, the Dutch shipping company TNT has long emphasized task-oriented efficiency and egalitarian management. However, when it commenced operations in China, neither of those values fit with local norms. As expected, it began to conduct business in a more relationship-oriented and hierarchical manner, as its managers in Asia adapted their styles to attract local clients and motivate their employees.

The problem with such adaptation is that a company's culture can sometimes be a key driver of its success. That is, if you believe that your corporate culture is what made the company great, you should consider maintaining it in all of your offices—even when it conflicts with local practice. This approach becomes particularly relevant for firms with a highly innovative product offering and relatively little local competition. If your culture has led to significant innovation and there is not a strong imperative to understand local consumers, it may be best to ignore the local culture to help maintain the organizational core.

Consider Google. It believes that its culture is a key reason for its outstanding success. Part of this involves providing employees with lots of positive feedback, and the company's performance review begins by instructing managers to "List

the things that this employee did reasonably well." Only then does it state, "List one thing this person could do to have a bigger impact." At Google, products are always considered to be in Beta—and mistakes are praised. For example, before she became COO of Facebook, Sheryl Sandberg was a vice president at Google and her responsibilities included managing their automated advertising system. When she made a mistake that cost Google several million dollars, she admitted her error to co-founder Larry Page. His response was, "I'm so glad that you made this mistake because I want to run a company where we are moving too quickly and doing too much, not being cautious and doing too little. If we don't have any of these mistakes, we're just not taking enough risk."

However, when Google moved into France, it found that positive words were used sparingly and criticism was provided more strongly. A French manager said, "The first time I used the Google form to give a performance review, I was confused. Where was the section to talk about problem areas? 'What did this employee do *really* well?' The positive wording seemed over the top." However, Google's strong corporate culture typically supersedes local preferences. The French manager continued, "After five years at Google France, I can tell you we are now a group of French people who give negative feedback in a very un-French way."

Sources: Meyer, E. 2015. When culture doesn't translate. *Harvard Business Review* 93(10): 66–72; Meyer, E. 2014. Navigating the cultural minefield. *Harvard Business Review* 92(5): 119–123; and Kim, J. 2013. 7 secrets of Google's epic organizational culture. *officevibe.com*, September 30: np.

and Tower of Pisa into the familiar Coke bottle. So far, so good. However, when the white marble columns of the Parthenon that crowns the Acropolis in Athens were turned into Coke bottles, the Greeks became outraged. Why? Greeks refer to the Acropolis as the "holy rock," and a government official said the Parthenon is an "international symbol of excellence" and that "whoever insults the Parthenon insults international culture." Coca-Cola apologized.

An important management challenge involves adapting to different cultures when a firm crosses national boundaries. As we discuss in Strategy Spotlight 7.3, however, if a firm's culture is a key driver of its success, it should maintain and reinforce that corporate culture across different locations—even if it conflicts with local practice.

Global Dispersion of Value Chains: Outsourcing and Offshoring

A major recent trend has been the dispersion of the value chains of multinational corporations across different countries; that is, the various activities that constitute the value chain of a firm are now spread across several countries and continents. Such dispersion of value occurs mainly through increasing offshoring and outsourcing.

A report issued by the World Trade Organization described the production of a particular U.S. car as follows: "30 percent of the car's value goes to Korea for assembly, 17.5 percent to Japan for components and advanced technology, 7.5 percent to Germany for design, 4 percent to Taiwan and Singapore for minor parts, 2.5 percent to U.K. for advertising and marketing services, and 1.5 percent to Ireland and Barbados for data processing. This means that only 37 percent of the production value is generated in the U.S."[38] In today's economy, we are increasingly witnessing two interrelated trends: outsourcing and offshoring.

Outsourcing occurs when a firm decides to utilize other firms to perform value-creating activities that were previously performed in-house.[39] It may be a new activity that the firm is perfectly capable of doing but chooses to have someone else perform for cost or quality reasons. Outsourcing can be to either a domestic or foreign firm.

Offshoring takes place when a firm decides to shift an activity that it was performing in a domestic location to a foreign location.[40] For example, both Microsoft and Intel now have R&D facilities in India, employing a large number of Indian scientists and engineers. Often, offshoring and outsourcing go together; that is, a firm may outsource an activity to a foreign supplier, thereby causing the work to be offshored as well.[41]

The recent explosion in the volume of outsourcing and offshoring is due to a variety of factors. Up until the 1960s, for most companies, the entire value chain was in one location. Further, the production took place close to where the customers were in order to keep transportation costs under control. In the case of service industries, it was generally believed that offshoring was not possible because the producer and consumer had to be present at the same place at the same time. After all, a haircut could not be performed if the barber and the client were separated!

For manufacturing industries, the rapid decline in transportation and coordination costs has enabled firms to disperse their value chains over different locations. For example, Nike's R&D takes place in the United States, raw materials are procured from a multitude of countries, actual manufacturing takes place in China, Indonesia, or Vietnam, advertising is produced in the United States, and sales and service take place in practically all the countries. Each value-creating activity is performed in the location where the cost is the lowest or the quality is the best. Without finding optimal locations for each activity, Nike could not have attained its position as the world's largest shoe company.

The experience of the manufacturing sector was also repeated in the service sector by the mid-1990s. A trend that began with the outsourcing of low-level programming and data entry work to countries such as India and Ireland suddenly grew manyfold, encompassing a variety of white-collar and professional activities ranging from call centers to R&D.

Bangalore, India, in recent years, has emerged as a location where more and more U.S. tax returns are prepared. In India, U.S.-trained and licensed radiologists interpret chest x-rays and CT scans from U.S. hospitals for half the cost. The advantages from offshoring go beyond mere cost savings today. In many specialized occupations in science and engineering, there is a shortage of qualified professionals in developed countries, whereas countries like India, China, and Singapore have what seems like an inexhaustible supply.[42]

While offshoring offers the potential to cut costs in corporations across a wide range of industries, many firms are finding the benefits of offshoring to be more elusive and the costs greater than they anticipated.[43] A study by AMR Research found that 56 percent of companies moving production offshore experienced an increase in total costs, contrary to their expectations of cost savings. In a more focused study, 70 percent of managers said sourcing in China is more costly than they initially estimated.

The cause of this contrary outcome is actually not all that surprising. Common savings from offshoring, such as lower wages, benefits, energy costs, regulatory costs, and taxes, are all easily visible and immediate. In contrast, there are a host of hidden costs that arise over time and often overwhelm the cost savings of offshoring. These hidden costs include:

- *Total wage costs.* Labor cost per hour may be significantly lower in developing markets, but this may not translate into lower overall costs. If workers in these markets are less productive or less skilled, firms end up with a higher number of hours needed to produce the same quantity of product. This necessitates hiring more workers and having employees work longer hours.

outsourcing
using other firms to perform value-creating activities that were previously performed in-house.

offshoring
shifting a value-creating activity from a domestic location to a foreign location.

- *Indirect costs.* In addition to higher labor costs, there are also a number of indirect costs that pop up. If there are problems with the skill level of workers, the firm will find the need for more training and supervision of workers, more raw material and greater scrap due to the lower skill level, and greater rework to fix quality problems. The firm may also experience greater need for security staff in its facilities.
- *Increased inventory.* Due to the longer delivery times, firms often need to tie up more capital in work in progress and inventory.
- *Reduced market responsiveness.* The long supply lines from low-cost countries may leave firms less responsive to shifts in customer demands. This may damage their brand image and also increase product obsolescence costs, as they may have to scrap or sell at a steep discount products that fail to meet quickly changing technology standards or customer tastes.
- *Coordination costs.* Coordinating product development and manufacturing can be difficult with operations undertaking different tasks in different countries. This may hamper innovation. It may also trigger unexpected costs, such as paying overtime in some markets so that staff across multiple time zones can meet to coordinate their activities.
- *Intellectual property rights.* Firms operating in countries with weak IP protection can wind up losing their trade secrets or taking costly measures to protect these secrets.
- *Wage inflation.* In moving overseas, firms often assume some level of wage stability, but wages in developing markets can be volatile and spike dramatically. For example, minimum wages set by provinces in China increased at an average of 18 percent per year in the 2010–2014 period.[44] As Roger Meiners, chairman of the Department of Economics at the University of Texas at Arlington, stated, "The U.S. is more competitive on a wage basis because average wages have come down, especially for entry-level workers, and wages in China have been increasing."

Firms need to take into account all of these costs in determining whether or not to move their operations offshore.

ACHIEVING COMPETITIVE ADVANTAGE IN GLOBAL MARKETS

The two opposing forces—cost reduction and adaptation to local markets—that firms face when entering international markets.

We now discuss the two opposing forces that firms face when they expand into global markets: cost reduction and adaptation to local markets. Then we address the four basic types of international strategies that they may pursue: international, global, multidomestic, and transnational. The selection of one of these four types of strategies is largely dependent on a firm's relative pressure to address each of the two forces.

Two Opposing Pressures: Reducing Costs and Adapting to Local Markets

Many years ago, the famed marketing strategist Theodore Levitt advocated strategies that favored global products and brands. He suggested that firms should standardize all of their products and services for all of their worldwide markets. Such an approach would help a firm lower its overall costs by spreading its investments over as large a market as possible. Levitt's approach rested on three key assumptions:

1. Customer needs and interests are becoming increasingly homogeneous worldwide.
2. People around the world are willing to sacrifice preferences in product features, functions, design, and the like for lower prices at high quality.
3. Substantial economies of scale in production and marketing can be achieved through supplying global markets.[45]

However, there is ample evidence to refute these assumptions.[46] Regarding the first assumption—the increasing worldwide homogeneity of customer needs and interests—consider the number of product markets, ranging from watches and handbags to soft drinks and fast foods. Companies have identified global customer segments and developed global products and brands targeted to those segments. Also, many other companies adapt lines to idiosyncratic country preferences and develop local brands targeted to local market segments. For example, Nestlé's line of pizzas marketed in the United Kingdom includes cheese with ham and pineapple topping on a French bread crust. Similarly, Coca-Cola in Japan markets Georgia (a tonic drink) as well as Classic Coke and Hi-C.

Consider the second assumption—the sacrifice of product attributes for lower prices. While there is invariably a price-sensitive segment in many product markets, there is no indication that this is increasing. In contrast, in many product and service markets—ranging from watches, personal computers, and household appliances to banking and insurance—there is a growing interest in multiple product features, product quality, and service.

Finally, the third assumption is that significant economies of scale in production and marketing could be achieved for global products and services. Although standardization may lower manufacturing costs, such a perspective does not consider three critical and interrelated points. First, as we discussed in Chapter 5, technological developments in flexible factory automation enable economies of scale to be attained at lower levels of output and do not require production of a single standardized product. Second, the cost of production is only one component, and often not the critical one, in determining the total cost of a product. Third, a firm's strategy should not be product-driven. It should also consider other activities in the firm's value chain, such as marketing, sales, and distribution.

Based on the above, we would have a hard time arguing that it is wise to develop the same product or service for all markets throughout the world. While there are some exceptions, such as Boeing airplanes and some of Coca-Cola's soft-drink products, managers must also strive to tailor their products to the culture of the country in which they are attempting to do business. Few would argue that "one size fits all" generally applies.

The opposing pressures that managers face place conflicting demands on firms as they strive to be competitive.[47] On the one hand, competitive pressures require that firms do what they can to *lower unit costs* so that consumers will not perceive their product and service offerings as too expensive. This may lead them to consider locating manufacturing facilities where labor costs are low and developing products that are highly standardized across multiple countries.

In addition to responding to pressures to lower costs, managers must strive to be *responsive to local pressures* in order to tailor their products to the demand of the local market in which they do business. This requires differentiating their offerings and strategies from country to country to reflect consumer tastes and preferences and making changes to reflect differences in distribution channels, human resource practices, and governmental regulations. However, since the strategies and tactics to differentiate products and services to local markets can involve additional expenses, a firm's costs will tend to rise.

The two opposing pressures result in four different basic strategies that companies can use to compete in the global marketplace: international, global, multidomestic, and transnational. The strategy that a firm selects depends on the degree of pressure that it is facing for cost reductions and the importance of adapting to local markets. Exhibit 7.3 shows the conditions under which each of these strategies would be most appropriate.

It is important to note that we consider these four strategies to be "basic" or "pure"; that is, in practice, all firms will tend to have some elements of each strategy.

International Strategy

There are a small number of industries in which pressures for both local adaptation and lowering costs are rather low. An extreme example of such an industry is the "orphan" drug industry. These are medicines for diseases that are severe but affect only a small

LO 7-5

The advantages and disadvantages associated with each of the four basic strategies: international, global, multidomestic, and transnational.

EXHIBIT 7.3 Opposing Pressures and Four Strategies

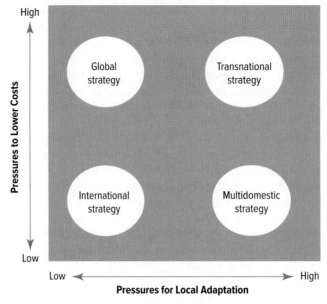

number of people. Diseases such as Gaucher disease and Fabry disease fit into this category. Companies such as Genzyme and Oxford GlycoSciences are active in this segment of the drug industry. There is virtually no need to adapt their products to the local markets. And the pressures to reduce costs are low; even though only a few thousand patients are affected, the revenues and margins are significant, because patients are charged up to $100,000 per year.

An **international strategy** is based on diffusion and adaptation of the parent company's knowledge and expertise to foreign markets. Country units are allowed to make some minor adaptations to products and ideas coming from the head office, but they have far less independence and autonomy compared to multidomestic companies. The primary goal of the strategy is worldwide exploitation of the parent firm's knowledge and capabilities. All sources of core competencies are centralized.

The majority of large U.S. multinationals pursued the international strategy in the decades following World War II. These companies centralized R&D and product development but established manufacturing facilities as well as marketing organizations abroad. Companies such as McDonald's and Kellogg are examples of firms following such a strategy. Although these companies do make some local adaptations, they are of a very limited nature. With increasing pressures to reduce costs due to global competition, especially from low-cost countries, opportunities to successfully employ an international strategy are becoming more limited. This strategy is most suitable in situations where a firm has distinctive competencies that local companies in foreign markets lack.

Risks and Challenges   Below are some of the risks and challenges associated with an international strategy.

- Different activities in the value chain typically have different optimal locations. That is, R&D may be optimally located in a country with an abundant supply of scientists and engineers, whereas assembly may be better conducted in a low-cost location. Nike, for example, designs its shoes in the United States, but all the manufacturing is done in countries like China or Thailand. The international

international strategy
a strategy based on firms' diffusion and adaptation of the parent companies' knowledge and expertise to foreign markets; used in industries where the pressures for both local adaptation and lowering costs are low.

EXHIBIT 7.4 Strengths and Limitations of International Strategies in the Global Marketplace

Strengths	Limitations
• Leverage and diffusion of a parent firm's knowledge and core competencies. • Lower costs because of less need to tailor products and services.	• Limited ability to adapt to local markets. • Inability to take advantage of new ideas and innovations occurring in local markets.

strategy, with its tendency to concentrate most of its activities in one location, fails to take advantage of the benefits of an optimally distributed value chain.

- The lack of local responsiveness may result in the alienation of local customers. Worse still, the firm's inability to be receptive to new ideas and innovation from its foreign subsidiaries may lead to missed opportunities.

Exhibit 7.4 summarizes the strengths and limitations of international strategies in the global marketplace.

Global Strategy

As indicated in Exhibit 7.3, a firm whose emphasis is on lowering costs tends to follow a **global strategy.** Competitive strategy is centralized and controlled to a large extent by the corporate office. Since the primary emphasis is on controlling costs, the corporate office strives to achieve a strong level of coordination and integration across the various businesses.[48] Firms following a global strategy strive to offer standardized products and services as well as to locate manufacturing, R&D, and marketing activities in only a few locations.[49]

A global strategy emphasizes economies of scale due to the standardization of products and services and the centralization of operations in a few locations. As such, one advantage may be that innovations that come about through efforts of either a business unit or the corporate office can be transferred more easily to other locations. Although costs may be lower, the firm following a global strategy may, in general, have to forgo opportunities for revenue growth since it does not invest extensive resources in adapting product offerings from one market to another.

A global strategy is most appropriate when there are strong pressures for reducing costs and comparatively weak pressures for adaptation to local markets. Economies of scale become an important consideration.[50] Advantages to increased volume may come from larger production plants or runs as well as from more efficient logistics and distribution networks. Worldwide volume is also especially important in supporting high levels of investment in research and development. As we would expect, many industries requiring high levels of R&D, such as pharmaceuticals, semiconductors, and jet aircraft, follow global strategies.

Another advantage of a global strategy is that it can enable a firm to create a standard level of quality throughout the world. Let's look at what Tom Siebel, former chairman of Siebel Systems (now part of Oracle), a developer of e-business application software, said about global standardization:

> Our customers—global companies like IBM, Zurich Financial Services, and Citicorp—expect the same high level of service and quality, and the same licensing policies, no matter where we do business with them around the world. Our human resources and legal departments help us create policies that respect local cultures and requirements worldwide, while at the same time maintaining the highest standards.[51]

Risks and Challenges   There are, of course, some risks associated with a global strategy:[52]

- A firm can enjoy scale economies only by concentrating scale-sensitive resources and activities in one or few locations. Such concentration, however, becomes a "double-edged sword." For example, if a firm has only one manufacturing facility, it must export its output (e.g., components, subsystems, or finished products) to other

global strategy
a strategy based on firms' centralization and control by the corporate office, with the primary emphasis on controlling costs; used in industries where the pressure for local adaptation is low and the pressure for lowering costs is high.

markets, some of which may be a great distance from the operation. Thus, decisions about locating facilities must weigh the potential benefits from concentrating operations in a single location against the higher transportation and tariff costs that result from such concentration.

- The geographic concentration of any activity may also tend to isolate that activity from the targeted markets. Such isolation may be risky since it may hamper the facility's ability to quickly respond to changes in market conditions and needs.
- Concentrating an activity in a single location also makes the rest of the firm dependent on that location. Such dependency implies that, unless the location has world-class competencies, the firm's competitive position can be eroded if problems arise. A European Ford executive, reflecting on the firm's concentration of activities during a global integration program in the mid-1990s, lamented, "Now if you misjudge the market, you are wrong in 15 countries rather than only one."

Exhibit 7.5 summarizes the strengths and limitations of global strategies.

Multidomestic Strategy

multidomestic strategy
a strategy based on firms' differentiating their products and services to adapt to local markets; used in industries where the pressure for local adaptation is high and the pressure for lowering costs is low.

According to Exhibit 7.3, a firm whose emphasis is on differentiating its product and service offerings to adapt to local markets follows a **multidomestic strategy**.[53] Decisions evolving from a multidomestic strategy tend to be decentralized to permit the firm to tailor its products and respond rapidly to changes in demand. This enables a firm to expand its market and to charge different prices in different markets. For firms following this strategy, differences in language, culture, income levels, customer preferences, and distribution systems are only a few of the many factors that must be considered. Even in the case of relatively standardized products, at least some level of local adaptation is often necessary.

Consider, for example, the Oreo cookie.[54] Kraft has tailored the iconic cookie to better meet the tastes and preferences in different markets. For example, Kraft has created green tea Oreos in China, chocolate and peanut butter Oreos for Indonesia, and banana and dulce de leche Oreos for Argentina. Kraft has also lowered the sweetness of the cookie for China and reduced the bitterness of the cookie for India. The shape is also on the table for change. Kraft has even created wafer-stick-style Oreos.

Kraft has tailored other products to meet local market needs. For example, with its Tang drink product, it developed local flavors, such as a lime and cinnamon flavor for Mexico and mango Tang for the Philippines. It also looked to the nutritional needs in different countries. True to the heritage of the brand, Kraft has kept the theme that Tang is a good source of vitamin C. But in Brazil, where children often have iron deficiencies, it added iron as well as other vitamins and minerals. The local-focus strategy has worked well, with Tang's sales almost doubling in five years.

To meet the needs of local markets, companies need to go beyond just product designs. One of the simple ways firms have worked to meet market needs is by finding appropriate names for their products. For example, in China, the names of products imbue them with strong meanings and can be significant drivers of their success. As a result, firms have been careful with how they translate their brands. For example, Reebok became *Rui bu,* which

EXHIBIT 7.5 Strengths and Limitations of Global Strategies

Strengths	Limitations
• Strong integration occurs across various businesses.	• Limited ability exists to adapt to local markets.
• Standardization leads to higher economies of scale, which lower costs.	• Concentration of activities may increase dependence on a single facility.
• Creation of uniform standards of quality throughout the world is facilitated.	• Single locations may lead to higher tariffs and transportation costs.

CHALLENGES INVOLVING CULTURAL DIFFERENCES THAT MANAGERS MAY ENCOUNTER WHEN NEGOTIATING CONTRACTS ACROSS NATIONAL BOUNDARIES

When international companies cross borders, they often must deal with cultural differences. And culture has a strong influence on how one thinks, communicates, and acts. It also affects the types of transactions firms make as well as the negotiation process. Cultural differences, for example, between a Chinese public sector plant manager in Shanghai and the head of a Canadian division of a family company in Toronto can create barriers that may impede or completely disrupt the negotiating process.

Let's look at an example that Erin Meyer provided in a recent *Harvard Business Review* article. An American working for a defense company located in the midwestern United States was well trained in basic negotiating techniques such as: Separate people from the process, focus on interests not positions, define your BATNA (best alternative to a negotiated agreement), and so on. He believed that his telephone call to Saudi Arabia was proceeding according to plan. After he had steered his would-be customer to accept the deal, he felt he had reached his goal. But then he made a fatal mistake: He then reviewed the agreement with the client in detail on who had agreed to what. Unfortunately, a soft but firm voice said, "I told you I would do it. You think I don't keep my promises? That I am not good on my word?" Clearly, that was the end of the discussion—and the deal.

Research has shown that there are several elements of negotiating behavior that help to identify cultural differences that often arise during negotiations. The findings are based on a study of 400 people from twelve nationalities. An understanding of such differences can help managers understand their counterparts and anticipate possible misunderstandings. Three of these elements are summarized as follows.

First, negotiators from different cultures tend to view the purpose of the negotiation quite differently. Some look upon the goal as a signed contract, others view it as the development of a relationship. The survey found that 74 percent of Spanish respondents stated that their goal was a contract, while only 33 percent of Indian executives felt this way. Such a cultural difference may explain why Asian negotiators tend to give more time and effort to preliminaries, while North Americans typically want to rush through this first phase of deal making. Although the initial part of a negotiation can be critical in getting to know one another, it would seem less important if the goal is just to get a contract.

Second, based on cultural differences, some people appear to approach deal making with either a process in which both can gain (win-win) or a contest in which one side wins and the other side loses (win-lose). That is, the former sees it as a collaborative process and the other side sees it as confrontational. In the survey, 100 percent of the Japanese respondents stated that they viewed negotiations as a win-win process, whereas only 33 percent of the Spanish executives held that view.

Third, cultural factors can influence the sort of written agreement that is preferred. Americans prefer highly detailed contracts that serve to anticipate many possible circumstances that may arise, no matter how likely they may be. In contrast, Chinese respondents preferred a contract in the form of general principles instead of detailed rules because they believed that if unexpected circumstances arose, the parties should draw on the relationship, not the contract, to resolve differences. Among all the respondents in the survey, 78 percent preferred specific agreements, while only 22 percent desired general agreements. And as expected, there was considerable variation among respondents: While only 11 percent of the English respondents favored general agreements, 45.5 percent of the Japanese and the Germans claimed to do so.

As a cautionary note, one must recognize that cultural differences often arise because when addressing cultural differences, managers frequently rely on stereotypes that can often be pejorative (for example, Portuguese are always running late). Such an attitude can distort expectations about one's counterpart's behavior as well as lead to costly misinterpretations.

Rather than rely on *stereotypes,* one should focus on *prototypes*—cultural averages on various dimensions of values and behaviors. For example, Japanese negotiators typically have more silent periods during negotiations compared to Brazilians. However, there remains a good deal of variation within each culture—meaning that some Brazilians speak less than some Japanese do. Therefore, it would be a mistake to expect a Japanese negotiator who you have never met to be reserved. However, if it turns out a negotiator is very quiet, you should consider her behavior in light of the prototype. Further, such awareness of your own cultural prototypes would aid you in anticipating how your counterpart would interpret your own bargaining behavior.

Sources: Shonk, K. 2016. How to resolve cultural conflict: Overcoming cultural barriers at the negotiation table. *pon.harvard.edu,* August 25: np; Meyer, E. 2015. Getting to Si, Ja, Hai, and Da. *Harvard Business Review,* 93(12): 74–80; Salacuse, J. W. 2004. Negotiating: The top ten ways that culture can affect your negotiation. *iveybusinessjournal.com,* October: np; and Livermore, D. 2015. 10 tips for managing across cultures. *management-issues.com,* May 11: np.

means "quick steps." Lay's snack foods became *Le shi,* which means "happy things." And Coca-Cola's Chinese name, *Ke Kou Ke Le,* translates to "tasty fun."

When companies cross national borders, they typically encounter different cultures. Strategy Spotlight 7.4 addresses some of the challenges that managers may encounter when negotiating contracts and how they may be resolved—or, at least minimized.

Risks and Challenges As you might expect, there are some risks associated with a multido-mestic strategy. Among these are the following:

- Typically, local adaptation of products and services will increase a company's cost structure. In many industries, competition is so intense that most firms can ill afford any competitive disadvantages on the dimension of cost. A key challenge of managers is to determine the trade-off between local adaptation and its cost structure. For example, cost considerations led Procter & Gamble to standardize its diaper design across all European markets. This was done despite research data indicating that Italian mothers, unlike those in other countries, preferred diapers that covered the baby's navel. Later, however, P&G recognized that this feature was critical to these mothers, so the company decided to incorporate this feature for the Italian market despite its adverse cost implications.

- At times, local adaptations, even when well intentioned, may backfire. When the American restaurant chain TGI Fridays entered the South Korean market, it purposely incorporated many local dishes, such as kimchi (hot, spicy cabbage), in its menu. This responsiveness, however, was not well received. Company analysis of the weak market acceptance indicated that Korean customers anticipated a visit to TGI Fridays as a visit to America. Thus, finding Korean dishes was inconsistent with their expectations.

- The optimal degree of local adaptation evolves over time. In many industry segments, a variety of factors, such as the influence of global media, greater international travel, and declining income disparities across countries, may lead to increasing global standardization. On the other hand, in other industry segments, especially where the product or service can be delivered over the Internet (such as music), the need for even greater customization and local adaptation may increase over time. Firms must recalibrate the need for local adaptation on an ongoing basis; excessive adaptation extracts a price as surely as underadaptation.

Exhibit 7.6 summarizes the strengths and limitations of multidomestic strategies.

Transnational Strategy

transnational strategy
a strategy based on firms' optimizing the trade-offs associated with efficiency, local adaptation, and learning; used in industries where the pressures for both local adaptation and lowering costs are high.

A **transnational strategy** strives to optimize the trade-offs associated with efficiency, local adaptation, and learning.[55] It seeks efficiency not for its own sake but as a means to achieve global competitiveness.[56] It recognizes the importance of local responsiveness as a tool for flexibility in international operations.[57] Innovations are regarded as an outcome of a larger process of organizational learning that includes the contributions of everyone in the firm.[58] Also, a core tenet of the transnational model is that a firm's assets and capabilities are dispersed according to the most beneficial location for each activity. Thus, managers avoid the tendency to either concentrate activities in a central location (a global strategy) or disperse them across many locations to enhance adaptation

EXHIBIT 7.6 Strengths and Limitations of Multidomestic Strategies

Strengths	Limitations
• Ability to adapt products and services to local market conditions.	• Decreased ability to realize cost savings through scale economies.
• Ability to detect potential opportunities for attractive niches in a given market, enhancing revenue.	• Greater difficulty in transferring knowledge across countries.
	• Possibility of leading to "overadaptation" as conditions change.

(a multidomestic strategy). Peter Brabeck, former chairman of Nestlé, the giant food company, provides such a perspective:

> The closer we come to the consumer, in branding, pricing, communication, and product adaptation, the more we decentralize. The more we are dealing with production, logistics, and supply-chain management, the more centralized decision making becomes. After all, we want to leverage Nestlé's size, not be hampered by it.[59]

The Nestlé example illustrates a common approach in determining whether or not to centralize or decentralize a value-chain activity. Typically, primary activities that are "downstream" (e.g., marketing and sales, and service), or closer to the customer, tend to require more decentralization in order to adapt to local market conditions. On the other hand, primary activities that are "upstream" (e.g., logistics and operations), or further away from the customer, tend to be centralized. This is because there is less need for adapting these activities to local markets and the firm can benefit from economies of scale. Additionally, many support activities, such as information systems and procurement, tend to be centralized in order to increase the potential for economies of scale.

A central philosophy of the transnational organization is enhanced adaptation to all competitive situations as well as flexibility by capitalizing on communication and knowledge flows throughout the organization.[60] A principal characteristic is the integration of unique contributions of all units into worldwide operations. Thus, a joint innovation by headquarters and by one of the overseas units can lead potentially to the development of relatively standardized and yet flexible products and services that are suitable for multiple markets. Strategy Spotlight 7.5 discusses how Panasonic benefited from moving from a global to a transnational strategy.

Risks and Challenges   As with the other strategies, there are some unique risks and challenges associated with a transnational strategy:

- **The choice of a seemingly optimal location cannot guarantee that the quality and cost of factor inputs (i.e., labor, materials) will be optimal.** Managers must ensure that the relative advantage of a location is actually realized, not squandered because of weaknesses in productivity and the quality of internal operations. Ford Motor Co., for example, has benefited from having some of its manufacturing operations in Mexico. While some have argued that the benefits of lower wage rates will be partly offset by lower productivity, this does not always have to be the case. Since unemployment in Mexico is higher than in the United States, Ford can be more selective in its hiring practices for its Mexican operations. And given the lower turnover among its Mexican employees, Ford can justify a high level of investment in training and development. Thus, the net result can be not only lower wage rates but also higher productivity than in the United States.

- **Although knowledge transfer can be a key source of competitive advantage, it does not take place "automatically."** For knowledge transfer to take place from one subsidiary to another, it is important for the source of the knowledge, the target units, and the corporate headquarters to recognize the potential value of such unique know-how. Given that there can be significant geographic, linguistic, and cultural distances that typically separate subsidiaries, the potential for knowledge transfer can become very difficult to realize. Firms must create mechanisms to systematically and routinely uncover the opportunities for knowledge transfer.

Exhibit 7.7 summarizes the relative advantages and disadvantages of transnational strategies.

PANASONIC'S CHINA EXPERIENCE SHOWS THE BENEFITS OF BEING A TRANSNATIONAL

Panasonic moved into China in the late 1980s, seeing it as a low-cost region in which to manufacture its products. Traditionally, Panasonic had used a global strategy in its operations. It designed standardized products in Japan, manufactured them in low-cost markets, and sold its products primarily in developed markets. China simply served as a manufacturing location.

This worked well until the Chinese economy started to grow and mature. As the Chinese middle class began to emerge, local competitors, such as Haier, quickly jumped in with products designed for the Chinese market and outcompeted Panasonic in the growing market. This led Panasonic to radically change its way of competing in the global market.

Panasonic embraced the need to balance global integration with local adaptation. It set up a Lifestyle Research Center in China. In this center, marketing and product development staff compiled and interpreted data on customer wants and needs. Their charge was to uncover hidden needs in the Chinese market and design products to meet those needs. At the same time, country managers emphasized the need for the center staff to design products that benefited from global integration. For example, staff members were told to regularly work with engineers in Japan to ensure that product designs used standard global parts in the Panasonic system and also leveraged technologies being developed in Japan. Over time, this built trust with the Japanese engineers, who began to discuss how to draw on their knowledge to help design products that could be sold in other markets. Thus, knowledge flowed in both directions: from Japan to China and from China to Japan and, by extension, the rest of the world. The system has worked so well in China that Panasonic has expanded its policies and built lifestyle research centers in Europe and India.

There are five key elements of Panasonic's transnational initiatives. Each allows Panasonic to manage the tension for global integration and local adaptation.

- **Establish a dedicated unit.** One organization should be devoted to embracing the tension. The aim of Panasonic's China Lifestyle Research Center was to both understand Chinese consumers and draw on Panasonic Japan's R&D capabilities.

- **Create an on-the-ground mission.** The unit's mission should state explicitly how local adaptation and cross-border integration support company strategy. The lifestyle center's mission was "data interpretation," not just data collection, to ensure that insights led to viable product proposals that leveraged Panasonic's technology assets.

- **Develop core local staff.** The unit should develop local staff who can engage in both localization and integration activities. At the lifestyle center, each staff member spent a year getting training and extensive coaching in fieldwork and proposal writing for products that leverage Panasonic's technology to meet local needs.

- **Extend the reach.** The unit must constantly push to expand its influence. The lifestyle center's leader ratcheted up communication and interaction between the center and engineers at Panasonic's headquarters to broaden the organization's scope and influence.

- **Strengthen local authority.** Sufficient authority should be given to overseas subsidiaries to enhance their autonomy while ensuring sound global integration. Seeing the early successes of the lifestyle center, Panasonic gave increasing authority to its Chinese operations for deeper local adaptation while also maintaining integrated working relationships between Japan and China.

Sources: Wakayama, T., Shintaku, J., & Amano, T. 2012. What Panasonic learned in China. *Harvard Business Review,* December: 109–113; and Osawa, J. 2012. Panasonic pins hopes on home appliances. *wsj.com,* March 25: np.

LO 7-6

The difference between regional companies and truly global companies.

Global or Regional? A Second Look at Globalization

Thus far, we have suggested four possible strategies from which a firm must choose once it has decided to compete in the global marketplace. In recent years, many writers have asserted that the process of globalization has caused national borders to

EXHIBIT 7.7 Strengths and Limitations of Transnational Strategies

Strengths	Limitations
• Ability to attain economies of scale.	• Unique challenges in determining optimal locations of activities to ensure cost and quality.
• Ability to adapt to local markets.	
• Ability to locate activities in optimal locations.	• Unique managerial challenges in fostering knowledge transfer.
• Ability to increase knowledge flows and learning.	

become increasingly irrelevant.[61] However, some scholars have questioned this perspective, and they have argued that it is unwise for companies to rush into full-scale globalization.[62]

Before answering questions about the extent of firms' globalization, let's try to clarify what "globalization" means. Traditionally, a firm's globalization is measured in terms of its foreign sales as a percentage of total sales. However, this measure can be misleading. For example, consider a U.S. firm that has expanded its activities into Canada. Clearly, this initiative is qualitatively different from achieving the same sales volume in a distant country such as China. Similarly, if a Malaysian firm expands into Singapore or a German firm starts selling its products in Austria, this would represent an expansion into a geographically adjacent country. Such nearby countries would often share many common characteristics in terms of language, culture, infrastructure, and customer preferences. In other words, this is more a case of regionalization than globalization.

Extensive analysis of the distribution data of sales across different countries and regions led Alan Rugman and Alain Verbeke to conclude that there is a stronger case to be made in favor of **regionalization** than globalization. According to their study, a company would have to have at least 20 percent of its sales in each of the three major economic regions—North America, Europe, and Asia—to be considered a global firm. However, they found that only 9 of the world's 500 largest firms met this standard! Even when they relaxed the criterion to 20 percent of sales each in at least two of the three regions, the number only increased to 25. *Thus, most companies are regional or, at best, biregional—not global—even today.*

In a world of instant communication, rapid transportation, and governments that are increasingly willing to open up their markets to trade and investment, why are so few firms "global"? The most obvious answer is that distance still matters. After all, it is easier to do business in a neighboring country than in a faraway country, all else being equal. Distance, in the final analysis, may be viewed as a concept with many dimensions, not just a measure of geographic distance. For example, both Canada and Mexico are the same distance from the United States However, U.S. companies find it easier to expand operations into Canada than into Mexico. Why? Canada and the United States share many commonalities in terms of language, culture, economic development, legal and political systems, and infrastructure development. Thus, if we view distance as having many dimensions, the United States and Canada are very close, whereas there is greater distance between the United States and Mexico. Similarly, when we look at what we might call the "true" distance between the United States and China, the effects of geographic distance are multiplied by distance in terms of culture, language, religion, and legal and political systems between the two countries. On the other hand, although the United States and Australia are geographically distant, the "true" distance is somewhat less when one considers distance along the other dimensions.

Another reason for regional expansion is the rise of **trading blocs** and free trade zones. A number of regional agreements have been created that facilitate the growth of business within these regions by easing trade restrictions and taxes and tariffs. These have included the European Union (EU), North American Free Trade Agreement (NAFTA), Association of Southeast Asian Nations (ASEAN), and MERCOSUR (a South American trading block).

Regional economic integration has progressed at a faster pace than global economic integration, and the trade and investment patterns of the largest companies reflect this reality. After all, regions represent the outcomes of centuries of political and cultural history that results in not only commonalities but also mutual affinity. For example, stretching from Algeria and Morocco in the West to Oman and Yemen in the East, more than 30 countries share the Arabic language and the Muslim religion, making these countries a natural regional bloc. Similarly, the countries of South and Central America share the

regionalization
increasing international exchange of goods, services, money, people, ideas, and information; and the increasing similarity of culture, laws, rules, and norms within a region such as Europe, North America, or Asia.

trading blocs
groups of countries agreeing to increase trade between them by lowering trade barriers.

Spanish language (except Brazil), the Catholic religion, and a history of Spanish colonialism. No wonder firms find it easier and less risky to expand within their region than to other regions.

The four basic types of entry strategies and the relative benefits and risks associated with each of them.

ENTRY MODES OF INTERNATIONAL EXPANSION

A firm has many options available to it when it decides to expand into international markets. Given the challenges associated with such entry, many firms first start on a small scale and then increase their level of investment and risk as they gain greater experience with the overseas market in question.[63]

Exhibit 7.8 illustrates a wide variety of modes of foreign entry, including exporting, licensing, franchising, joint ventures, strategic alliances, and wholly owned subsidiaries.[64] As the exhibit indicates, the various types of entry form a continuum ranging from exporting (low investment and risk, low control) to a wholly owned subsidiary (high investment and risk, high control).[65]

There can be frustrations and setbacks as a firm evolves its international entry strategy from exporting to more expensive types, including wholly owned subsidiaries. For example, according to the CEO of a large U.S. specialty chemical company:

> In the end, we always do a better job with our own subsidiaries; sales improve, and we have greater control over the business. But we still need local distributors for entry, and we are still searching for strategies to get us through the transitions without battles over control and performance.[66]

Exporting

exporting
producing goods in one country to sell to residents of another country.

Exporting consists of producing goods in one country to sell in another.[67] This entry strategy enables a firm to invest the least amount of resources in terms of its product, its organization, and its overall corporate strategy. Many host countries dislike this entry strategy because it provides less local employment than other modes of entry.[68]

Multinationals often stumble onto a stepwise strategy for penetrating markets, beginning with the exporting of products. This often results in a series of unplanned actions to

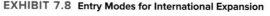

EXHIBIT 7.8 Entry Modes for International Expansion

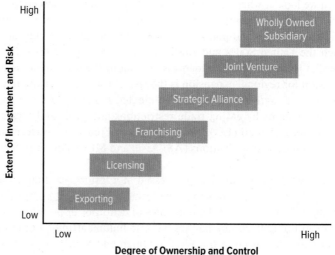

increase sales revenues. As the pattern recurs with entries into subsequent markets, this approach, named a "beachhead strategy," often becomes official policy.[69]

Benefits   Such an approach definitely has its advantages. After all, firms start from scratch in sales and distribution when they enter new markets. Because many foreign markets are nationally regulated and dominated by networks of local intermediaries, firms need to partner with local distributors to benefit from their valuable expertise and knowledge of their own markets. Multinationals, after all, recognize that they cannot master local business practices, meet regulatory requirements, hire and manage local personnel, or gain access to potential customers without some form of local partnership.

Multinationals also want to minimize their own risk. They do this by hiring local distributors and investing very little in the undertaking. In essence, the firm gives up control of strategic marketing decisions to the local partners—much more control than they would be willing to give up in their home market.

Risks and Limitations   Exporting is a relatively inexpensive way to enter foreign markets. However, it can still have significant downsides. Most centrally, the ability to tailor the firm's products to meet local market needs is typically very limited. In a study of 250 instances in which multinational firms used local distributors to implement their exporting entry strategy, the results were dismal. In the vast majority of the cases, the distributors were bought (to increase control) by the multinational firm or were fired. In contrast, successful distributors shared two common characteristics:

- They carried product lines that complemented, rather than competed with, the multinational's products.
- They behaved as if they were business partners with the multinationals. They shared market information with the corporations, they initiated projects with distributors in neighboring countries, and they suggested initiatives in their own or nearby markets. Additionally, these distributors took on risk themselves by investing in areas such as training, information systems, and advertising and promotion in order to increase the business of their multinational partners.

The key point is the importance of developing collaborative, win-win relationships.

To ensure more control over operations without incurring significant risks, many firms have used licensing and franchising as a mode of entry. Let's now discuss these and their relative advantages and disadvantages.

Licensing and Franchising

Licensing and franchising are both forms of contractual arrangements. **Licensing** enables a company to receive a royalty or fee in exchange for the right to use its trademark, patent, trade secret, or other valuable item of intellectual property.[70]

Franchising contracts generally include a broader range of factors in an operation and have a longer time period during which the agreement is in effect. Franchising remains a primary form of American business. According to a survey, more than 400 U.S. franchisers have international exposure.[71] This is greater than the combined totals of the next four largest franchiser home countries—France, the United Kingdom, Mexico, and Austria.

Benefits   In international markets, an advantage of licensing is that the firm granting a license incurs little risk, since it does not have to invest any significant resources into the country itself. In turn, the licensee (the firm receiving the license) gains access to the trademark, patent, and so on, and is able to potentially create competitive advantages. In many cases, the country also benefits from the product being manufactured locally. For example,

licensing
a contractual arrangement in which a company receives a royalty or fee in exchange for the right to use its trademark, patent, trade secret, or other valuable intellectual property.

franchising
a contractual arrangement in which a company receives a royalty or fee in exchange for the right to use its intellectual property; franchising usually involves a longer time period than licensing and includes other factors, such as monitoring of operations, training, and advertising.

Yoplait yogurt is licensed by General Mills from Sodima, a French cooperative, for sale in the United States. The logos of college and professional athletic teams in the United States are another source of trademarks that generate significant royalty income domestically and internationally.

Franchising has the advantage of limiting the risk exposure that a firm has in overseas markets. At the same time, the firm is able to expand the revenue base of the company.

Risks and Limitations   The licensor gives up control of its product and forgoes potential revenues and profits. Furthermore, the licensee may eventually become so familiar with the patent and trade secrets that it may become a competitor; that is, the licensee may make some modifications to the product and manufacture and sell it independently of the licensor without having to pay a royalty fee. This potential situation is aggravated in countries that have relatively weak laws to protect intellectual property. Additionally, if the licensee selected by the multinational firm turns out to be a poor choice, the brand name and reputation of the product may be tarnished.[72]

With franchising, the multinational firm receives only a portion of the revenues, in the form of franchise fees. Had the firm set up the operation itself (e.g., a restaurant through direct investment), it would have had the entire revenue to itself.

Companies often desire a closer collaboration with other firms in order to increase revenue, reduce costs, and enhance their learning—often through the diffusion of technology. To achieve such objectives, they enter into strategic alliances or joint ventures, two entry modes we will discuss next.

Strategic Alliances and Joint Ventures

Joint ventures and strategic alliances have recently become increasingly popular.[73] These two forms of partnership differ in that joint ventures entail the creation of a third-party legal entity, whereas strategic alliances do not. In addition, strategic alliances generally focus on initiatives that are smaller in scope than joint ventures.[74]

Benefits   As we discussed in Chapter 6, these strategies have been effective in helping firms increase revenues and reduce costs as well as enhance learning and diffuse technologies.[75] These partnerships enable firms to share the risks as well as the potential revenues and profits. Also, by gaining exposure to new sources of knowledge and technologies, such partnerships can help firms develop core competencies that can lead to competitive advantages in the marketplace.[76] Finally, entering into partnerships with host-country firms can provide very useful information on local market tastes, competitive conditions, legal matters, and cultural nuances.[77]

Risks and Limitations   Managers must be aware of the risks associated with strategic alliances and joint ventures and how they can be minimized.[78] First, there needs to be a clearly defined strategy that is strongly supported by the organizations that are party to the partnership. Otherwise, the firms may work at cross-purposes and not achieve any of their goals. Second, and closely allied to the first issue, there must be a clear understanding of capabilities and resources that will be central to the partnership. Without such clarification, there will be fewer opportunities for learning and developing competencies that could lead to competitive advantages. Third, trust is a vital element. Phasing in the relationship between alliance partners permits them to get to know each other better and develop trust. Without trust, one party may take advantage of the other by, for example, withholding its fair share of resources and gaining access to privileged information through unethical (or illegal) means. Fourth, cultural issues that can potentially lead to conflict and dysfunctional behaviors need to be addressed. An organization's culture is the set of values, beliefs, and attitudes that influence the behavior and goals of its employees.[79] Thus, recognizing cultural differences, as well as striving to develop elements of a "common culture" for the partnership, is vital. Without a unifying culture, it will become difficult to combine and leverage resources that are increasingly important in knowledge-intensive organizations (discussed in Chapter 4).[80]

Finally, the success of a firm's alliance should not be left to chance.[81] To improve their odds of success, many companies have carefully documented alliance-management knowledge by creating guidelines and manuals to help them manage specific aspects of the entire alliance life cycle (e.g., partner selection and alliance negotiation and contracting). For example, Hewlett-Packard developed 60 different tools and templates, which it placed in a 300-page manual for guiding decision making. The manual included such tools as a template for making the business case for an alliance, a partner evaluation form, a negotiation template outlining the roles and responsibilities of different departments, a list of the ways to measure alliance performance, and an alliance termination checklist.

When a firm desires the highest level of control, it develops wholly owned subsidiaries. Although wholly owned subsidiaries can generate the greatest returns, they also have the highest levels of investment and risk. We will now discuss them.

Wholly Owned Subsidiaries

A **wholly owned subsidiary** is a business in which a multinational company owns 100 percent of the stock. Two ways a firm can establish a wholly owned subsidiary are to (1) acquire an existing company in the home country or (2) develop a totally new operation (often referred to as a "greenfield venture").

wholly owned subsidiary
a business in which a multinational company owns 100 percent of the stock.

Benefits Establishing a wholly owned subsidiary is the most expensive and risky of the various entry modes. However, it can also yield the highest returns. In addition, it provides the multinational company with the greatest degree of control of all activities, including manufacturing, marketing, distribution, and technology development.[82]

Wholly owned subsidiaries are most appropriate where a firm already has the appropriate knowledge and capabilities that it can leverage rather easily through multiple locations. Examples range from restaurants to semiconductor manufacturers. To lower costs, for example, Intel Corporation builds semiconductor plants throughout the world—all of which use virtually the same blueprint. Knowledge can be further leveraged by hiring managers and professionals from the firm's home country, often through hiring talent from competitors.

Risks and Limitations As noted, wholly owned subsidiaries are typically the most expensive and risky entry mode. With franchising, joint ventures, or strategic alliances, the risk is shared with the firm's partners. With wholly owned subsidiaries, the entire risk is assumed by the parent company. The risks associated with doing business in a new country (e.g., political, cultural, and legal) can be lessened by hiring local talent.

For example, Wendy's avoided committing two blunders in Germany by hiring locals to its advertising staff.[83] In one case, the firm wanted to promote its "old-fashioned" qualities. However, a literal translation would have resulted in the company promoting itself as "outdated." In another situation, Wendy's wanted to emphasize that its hamburgers could be prepared 256 ways. The problem? The German word that Wendy's wanted to use for "ways" usually meant "highways" or "roads." Although such errors may sometimes be entertaining to the public, it is certainly preferable to catch these mistakes before they confuse the consumer or embarrass the company.

We have addressed entry strategies as a progression from exporting to the creation of wholly owned subsidiaries. However, we must point out that many firms do not follow such an evolutionary approach.

The Ethicality of Tax Inversions

In June 2014, Medtronic, a Minneapolis-based medical device manufacturer, announced that it would join the tax-inversion acquisition parade. A tax-inversion acquisition occurs when a corporation acquires a target firm based in a lower-tax country and, as part of the transaction, moves its legal headquarters to the target firm's nation. After making this move, the combined corporation's taxes are based on the lower rate of its new home country. This move is perfectly legal according to U.S. law as long as the target firm's shareholders own at least 20 percent of the combined firm. About 50 U.S. corporations have undertaken tax inversions over the last 10 years, but the rate of occurrence appears to be increasing.

Medtronic acquired Covidien, an Irish-based medical equipment manufacturer, in January 2015 for $49.9 billion, and moved its legal home to Ireland. Not much else changed. Medtronic kept its corporate headquarters in Minneapolis. But Medtronic benefits from the move in two primary ways. First, while the tax rate on profits of U.S. corporations is 35 percent, the tax rate on Ireland-based corporate profits is only 12.5 percent. Additionally, the United States is one of only six developed economies that tax the global profits of corporations. If a multinational corporation makes profits in a foreign country, the firm pays taxes on those profits to the foreign government at the rate the foreign country charges. For corporations based in most countries, that is the end of their tax obligations. However, if a U.S.-based firm wants to bring those profits back to its home country either to invest in new facilities or to distribute dividends to its stockholders, it has to pay income tax on the profits earned in foreign markets. The rate the firm pays is the difference in the tax rate in the foreign country and the U.S. rate. For example, if Medtronic earned income in Ireland and then repatriated the profits to the United States, it would face a 22.5 percent additional tax rate, the difference between the U.S. and Irish corporate tax rates. Since Medtronic has accumulated $13 billion in earned profits abroad, it could face $3.5 billion to $4 billion in taxes if it brought those profits home. Thus, corporations, such as Medtronic, undertake tax inversions to save on taxes and, by extension, benefit their shareholders by being able to invest more in the firm to help it grow and/or return higher levels of dividends to shareholders.

Critics, however, point out that these firms are choosing not to pay taxes at the U.S. rates even though they have benefited and will continue to benefit from being American corporations. While inverters change their legal residence, they typically keep their corporate headquarters in the United States and stay listed on a U.S. stock exchange. As a result, they benefit from America's deep financial markets, military might, intellectual property rights and other legal protections, intellectual and physical infrastructure, substantial human capital base, and national research programs. For example, Medtronic won $484 million in contracts with the U.S. government in recent years and plans to complete these contracts even though it will no longer be an American company; it hires students from top-notch American universities; and it files patents for all of its new technologies in the United States. Critics see the decision to move to a lower-tax country as unethical and unpatriotic. Jack Lew, the former U.S. Treasury secretary, echoed this perspective when he stated, "We should prevent companies from effectively renouncing their citizenship to get out of paying taxes. What we need is a new sense of economic patriotism, where we all rise and fall together."

Reflecting on Career Implications . . .

This chapter discusses the challenges and opportunities of international markets. The following questions ask students to consider how the globalization of business can create both opportunities and risks for their careers.

▣ **International Strategy:** Be aware of your organization's international strategy. What percentage of the total firm activity is international? What skills are needed to enhance your company's international efforts? How can you get more involved in your organization's international strategy? For your career, what conditions in your home country might cause you to seek a career abroad?

▣ **Outsourcing and Offshoring:** More and more organizations have resorted to outsourcing and offshoring in recent years. To what extent has your firm engaged in either? What activities in your organization can/should be outsourced or offshored? Be aware that you are competing in the global marketplace for employment and professional advancement. What is the likelihood that your own job may be outsourced or offshored? In what ways can you enhance your talents, skills, and competencies to reduce the odds that your job may be offshored or outsourced?

▣ **International Career Opportunities:** Taking on overseas assignments in other countries can often provide a career boost. There are a number of ways in which you can improve your odds of being selected for an overseas assignment. Studying abroad for a semester or doing an overseas internship are two obvious strategies. Learning a foreign language can also greatly help. Anticipate how such opportunities will advance your short- and long-term career aspirations.

▣ **Management Risks:** Explore ways in which you can develop cultural sensitivity. Interacting with people from other cultures, foreign travel, reading about foreign countries, watching foreign movies, and similar activities can increase your cultural sensitivity. Identify ways in which your perceptions and behaviors have changed as a result of increased cultural sensitivity.

summary

We live in a highly interconnected global community where many of the best opportunities for growth and profitability lie beyond the boundaries of a company's home country. Along with the opportunities, of course, there are many risks associated with diversification into global markets.

The first section of the chapter addressed the factors that determine a nation's competitiveness in a particular industry. The framework was developed by Professor Michael Porter of Harvard University and was based on a four-year study that explored the competitive success of 10 leading trading nations. The four factors, collectively termed the "diamond of national advantage," were factor endowments, demand conditions, related and supporting industries, and firm strategy, structure, and rivalry.

The discussion of Porter's "diamond" helped, in essence, to set the broader context for exploring competitive advantage at the firm level. In the second section, we discussed the primary motivations and the potential risks associated with international expansion. The primary motivations included increasing the size of the potential market for the firm's products and services, achieving economies of scale, extending the life cycle of the firm's products, and optimizing the location for every activity in the value chain. On the other hand, the key risks included political and economic risks, currency risks, and management risks. Management risks are the challenges associated with responding to the inevitable differences that exist across countries such as customs, culture, language, customer preferences, and distribution systems. We also addressed some of the managerial challenges and opportunities associated with offshoring and outsourcing.

Next, we addressed how firms can go about attaining competitive advantage in global markets. We began by discussing the two opposing forces—cost reduction and adaptation to local markets—that managers must contend with when entering global markets. The relative importance of these two factors plays a major part in determining which of the four basic types of strategies to select: international, global, multidomestic, or transnational. The chapter covered the benefits and risks associated with each type of strategy.

The final section discussed the four types of entry strategies that managers may undertake when entering international markets. The key trade-off in each of these strategies is the level of investment or risk versus the level of control. In order of their progressively greater investment/ risk and control, the strategies range from exporting to licensing and franchising, to strategic alliances and joint ventures, to wholly owned subsidiaries. The relative benefits and risks associated with each of these strategies were addressed.

SUMMARY REVIEW QUESTIONS

1. What are some of the advantages and disadvantages associated with a firm's expansion into international markets?

2. What are the four factors described in Porter's diamond of national advantage? How do the four factors explain why some industries in a given country are more successful than others?

3. Explain the two opposing forces—cost reduction and adaptation to local markets—that firms must deal with when they go global.

4. There are four basic strategies—international, global, multidomestic, and transnational. What are the advantages and disadvantages associated with each?

5. What is the basis of Alan Rugman's argument that most multinationals are still more regional than global? What factors inhibit firms from becoming truly global?

6. Describe the basic entry strategies that firms have available when they enter international markets. What are the relative advantages and disadvantages of each?

EXPERIENTIAL EXERCISE

The United States is considered a world leader in the motion picture industry. Using Porter's diamond framework for national competitiveness, explain the success of this industry. (Fill in the chart on page 233.)

APPLICATION QUESTIONS & EXERCISES

1. Data on the "competitiveness of nations" can be found at *www.imd.org/research/publications/wcy/index.cfm*. This website provides a ranking on 4 main factors and 20 subfactors for 61 countries. How might Porter's diamond of national advantage help to explain the rankings for some of these countries for certain industries that interest you?

2. The Internet has lowered the entry barriers for smaller firms that wish to diversify into international markets. Why is this so? Provide an example.

3. Many firms fail when they enter into strategic alliances with firms that link up with companies based in other countries. What are some reasons for this failure? Provide an example.

4. Many large U.S.-based management consulting companies such as McKinsey and Company and the BCG Group have been very successful in the international marketplace. How can Porter's diamond explain their success?

ETHICS QUESTIONS

1. Over the past few decades, many American firms have relocated most or all of their operations from the United States to countries such as Mexico and China that pay lower wages. What are some of the ethical issues that such actions may raise?

2. Business practices and customs vary throughout the world. What are some of the ethical issues concerning payments that must be made in a foreign country to obtain business opportunities?

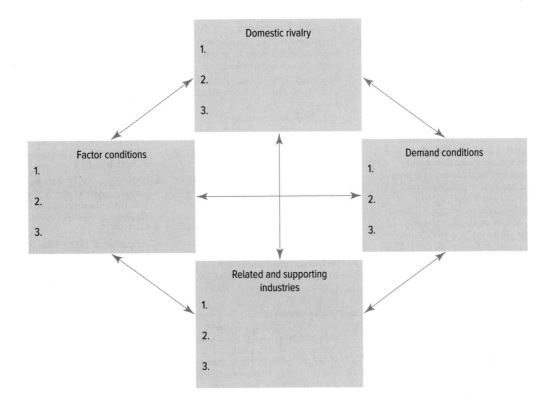

REFERENCES

1. For a discussion on globalization by one of international business's most respected authors, read Ohmae, K. 2005. *The next global stage: Challenges and opportunities in our borderless world.* Philadelphia: Wharton School.

2. Our discussion of globalization draws upon Engardio, P. & Belton, C. 2000. Global capitalism: Can it be made to work better? *Business Week,* November 6: 72–98.

3. Sellers, P. 2005. Blowing in the wind. *Fortune,* July 25: 63.

4. Rivera, J. 2014. Gartner says sales of smartphones grew 20 percent in third quarter of 2014. *gartner.com,* December 15: np.

5. Anonymous. 2016. Why giants thrive. *The Economist.* September 17: 5–7.

6. Some insights into how winners are evolving in emerging markets are addressed in Ghemawat, P. & Hout, T. 2008. Tomorrow's global giants: Not the usual suspects. *Harvard Business Review,* 66(11): 80–88.

7. For another interesting discussion on a country perspective, refer to Makino, S. 1999. MITI Minister

Kaora Yosano on reviving Japan's competitive advantages. *Academy of Management Executive,* 13(4): 8–28.

8. The following discussion draws heavily upon Porter, M. E. 1990. The competitive advantage of nations. *Harvard Business Review,* March–April: 73–93.

9. Landes, D. S. 1998. *The wealth and poverty of nations.* New York: W. W. Norton.

10. A study that investigates the relationship between international diversification and firm performance is Lu, J. W. & Beamish, P. W. 2004. International diversification and firm performance: The s-curve hypothesis. *Academy of Management Journal,* 47(4): 598–609.

11. Part of our discussion of the motivations and risks of international expansion draws upon Gregg, F. M. 1999. International strategy. In Helms, M. M. (Ed.), *Encyclopedia of management:* 434–438. Detroit: Gale Group.

12. Anthony, S. 2012. Singapore sessions. *Harvard Business Review,* 90(4): np.

13. Eyring, M. J., Johnson, M. W., & Nair, H. 2011. New business models in

emerging markets. *Harvard Business Review,* 89 (1/2): 88–98.

14. Cieply, M. & Barnes, B. 2010. After rants, skepticism over Gibson bankability grows in non-U.S. markets. *International Herald Tribune,* July 23: 1.

15. Glazer, E. 2012. P&G unit bids goodbye to Cincinnati, hello to Asia. *wsj.com,* May 10: np.

16. This discussion draws upon Gupta, A. K. & Govindarajan, V. 2001. Converting global presence into global competitive advantage. *Academy of Management Executive,* 15(2): 45–56.

17. Stross, R. E. 1997. Mr. Gates builds his brain trust. *Fortune,* December 8: 84–98.

18. Anonymous. 2016. Why giants thrive. *The Economist.* September 17: 5–7.

19. For a good summary of the benefits and risks of international expansion, refer to Bartlett, C. A. & Ghoshal, S. 1987. Managing across borders: New strategic responses. *Sloan Management Review,* 28(5): 45–53; and Brown, R. H. 1994. *Competing to win in a global economy.* Washington, DC: U.S. Department of Commerce.

20. Capron, L. & Bertrand, O. 2014. Going abroad in search of higher productivity at home. *Harvard Business Review,* 92(6): 26.

21. For an interesting insight into rivalry in global markets, refer to MacMillan, I. C., van Putten, A. B., & McGrath, R. G. 2003. Global gamesmanship. *Harvard Business Review,* 81(5): 62–73.

22. It is important for firms to spread their foreign operations and outsourcing relationships with a broad, well-balanced mix of regions and countries to reduce risk and increase potential reward. For example, refer to Vestring, T., Rouse, T., & Reinert, U. 2005. Hedge your offshoring bets. *MIT Sloan Management Review,* 46(3): 27–29.

23. An interesting discussion of risks faced by Lukoil, Russia's largest oil firm, is in Gimbel, B. 2009. Russia's king of crude. *Fortune,* February 2: 88–92.

24. For a discussion of some of the challenges associated with government corruption regarding entry strategies in foreign markets, read Rodriguez, P., Uhlenbruck, K., & Eden, L. 2005. Government corruption and entry strategies of multinationals. *Academy of Management Review,* 30(2): 383–396.

25. For a discussion of the political risks in China for United States companies, refer to Garten, J. E. 1998. Opening the doors for business in China. *Harvard Business Review,* 76(3): 167–175.

26. Insights on how forensic economics can be used to investigate crimes and wrongdoing are in Fisman, R. 2009. The rise of forensic economics. *Harvard Business Review,* 87(2): 26.

27. Iosebashvili, I. 2012. Renault-Nissan buy into Russia's aged auto giant. *wsj. com,* May 3: np.

28. Ferguson, N. 2013. Is the business of America still business? *Harvard Business Review,* 91(6): 40.

29. For an interesting perspective on the relationship between diversification and the development of a nation's institutional environment, read Chakrabarti, A., Singh, K., & Mahmood, I. 2007. Diversification and performance: Evidence from East Asian firms. *Strategic Management Journal,* 28(2): 101–120.

30. A study looking into corruption and foreign direct investment is Brouthers, L. E., Gao, Y., & McNicol, J. P. 2008. *Strategic Management Journal,* 29(6): 673–680.

31. Gikkas, N. S. 1996. International licensing of intellectual property: The promise and the peril. *Journal of Technology Law & Policy,* 1(1): 1–26.

32. Hargreaves, S. 2012. Counterfeit goods becoming more dangerous. *cnnmoney.com,* September 27: np.

33. Sandler, N. 2008. Israel: Attack of the super-shekel. *BusinessWeek,* February 25: 38.

34. For an excellent theoretical discussion of how cultural factors can affect knowledge transfer across national boundaries, refer to Bhagat, R. S., Kedia, B. L., Harveston, P. D., & Triandis, H. C. 2002. Cultural variations in the cross-border transfer of organizational knowledge: An integrative framework. *Academy of Management Review,* 27(2): 204–221.

35. An interesting discussion on how local companies compete effectively with large multinationals is in Bhatacharya, A. K. & Michael, D. C. 2008. *Harvard Business Review,* 66(3): 84–95.

36. To gain insights on the role of national and regional cultures on knowledge management models and frameworks, read Pauleen, D. J. & Murphy, P. 2005. In praise of cultural bias. *MIT Sloan Management Review,* 46(2): 21–22.

37. Berkowitz, E. N. 2000. *Marketing* (6th ed.). New York: McGraw-Hill.

38. World Trade Organization. *Annual Report 1998.* Geneva: World Trade Organization.

39. Lei, D. 2005. Outsourcing. In Hitt, M. A. & Ireland, R. D. (Eds.), *The Blackwell encyclopedia of management,* Entrepreneurship: 196–199. Malden, MA: Blackwell.

40. Future trends in offshoring are addressed in Manning, S., Massini, S., & Lewin, A. Y. 2008. A dynamic perspective on next-generation offshoring: The global sourcing of science and engineering talent. *Academy of Management Perspectives,* 22(3): 35–54.

41. An interesting perspective on the controversial issue regarding the offshoring of airplane maintenance is in Smith, G. & Bachman, J. 2008. Flying in for a tune-up overseas. *BusinessWeek,* April 21: 26–27.

42. The discussion draws from Colvin, J. 2004. Think your job can't be sent to India? Just watch. *Fortune,* December 13: 80; Schwartz, N. D. 2004. Down and out in white collar America. *Fortune,* June 23: 321–325; and Hagel, J. 2004. Outsourcing is not just about cost cutting. *The Wall Street Journal,* March 18: A3.

43. Porter, M. & Rivkin, J. 2012 Choosing the United States. *Harvard Business Review,* 90(3): 80–93; Bussey, J. 2012. U.S. manufacturing, defying naysayers. *wsj.com,* April 19: np; and Jean, S. & Alcott, K. 2013. Manufacturing jobs have slid steadily as work has moved offshore. *Dallas Morning News,* January 14: 1D.

44. Wong, C. 2014. As China's economy slows, so too does growth in workers' wages. *blogs.wsj.com,* December 17: np.

45. Levitt, T. 1983. The globalization of markets. *Harvard Business Review,* 61(3): 92–102.

46. Our discussion of these assumptions draws upon Douglas, S. P. & Wind, Y. 1987. The myth of globalization. *Columbia Journal of World Business,* Winter: 19–29.

47. Ghoshal, S. 1987. Global strategy: An organizing framework. *Strategic Management Journal,* 8: 425–440.

48. For insights on global branding, refer to Aaker, D. A. & Joachimsthaler, E. 1999. The lure of global branding. *Harvard Business Review,* 77(6): 137–146.

49. Dawar, N. & Frost, T. 1999. Competing with Giants: Survival Strategies for Local Companies in Emerging Markets. *Harvard Business Review ,* 77(3): 119–129.

50. Hout, T., Porter, M. E., & Rudden, E. 1982. How global companies win out. *Harvard Business Review,* 60(5): 98–107.

51. Fryer, B. 2001. Tom Siebel of Siebel Systems: High tech the old-fashioned way. *Harvard Business Review,* 79(3): 118–130.

52. The risks that are discussed for the global, multidomestic, and transnational strategies draw upon Gupta & Govindarajan, op. cit.

53. A discussion on how McDonald's adapts its products to overseas markets is in Gumbel, P. 2008. Big Mac's local flavor. *Fortune,* May 5: 115–121.

54. Einhorn, B. & Winter, C. 2012. Want some milk with your green tea Oreos? *Bloomberg Businessweek,* May 7: 25–26; Khosla, S. & Sawhney, M. 2012. Blank checks: Unleashing the potential of people and business. *Strategy-Business.com,* Autumn: np; and In China, brands more than symbolic. 2012. *Dallas Morning News,* November 27: 3D.

55. Prahalad, C. K. & Doz, Y. L. 1987. *The multinational mission: Balancing local demands and global vision.* New York: Free Press.

56. For an insightful discussion on knowledge flows in multinational corporations, refer to Yang, Q., Mudambi, R., & Meyer, K. E. 2008.

Conventional and reverse knowledge flows in multinational corporations. *Journal of Management,* 34(5): 882-902.

57. Kidd, J. B. & Teramoto, Y. 1995. The learning organization: The case of Japanese RHQs in Europe. *Management International Review,* 35 (Special Issue): 39-56.

58. Gupta, A. K. & Govindarajan, V. 2000. Knowledge flows within multinational corporations. *Strategic Management Journal,* 21(4): 473-496.

59. Wetlaufer, S. 2001. The business case against revolution: An interview with Nestle''s Peter Brabeck. *HarvardBusiness Review,* 79(2): 112-121.

60. Nobel, R. & Birkinshaw, J. 1998. Innovation in multinational corporations: Control and communication patterns in international R&D operations. *Strategic Management Journal,* 19(5): 461-478.

61. Chan, C. M., Makino, S., & Isobe, T. 2010. Does subnational region matter? Foreign affiliate performance in the United States and China. *Strategic Management Journal,* 31(11): 1226-1243.

62. his section draws upon Ghemawat, P. 2005. Regional strategies for global leadership. *Harvard Business Review,* 84(12): 98-108; Ghemawat, P. 2006. Apocalypse now? *Harvard Business Review,* 84(12): 32; Ghemawat, P. 2001. Distance still matters: The hard reality of global expansion. *Harvard Business Review,* 79(8): 137-147; Peng, M. W. 2006. *Global strategy:* 387. Mason, OH: Thomson South-Western; and Rugman, A. M. & Verbeke, A. 2004. A perspective on regional and global strategies of multinational enterprises. *Journal of International Business Studies,* 35: 3-18.

63. For a rigorous analysis of performance implications of entry strategies, refer to Zahra, S. A., Ireland, R. D., & Hitt, M. A. 2000. International expansion by new venture firms: International diversity, modes of entry, technological learning, and performance. *Academy*

of Management Journal, 43(6): 925-950.

64. Li, J. T. 1995. Foreign entry and survival: The effects of strategic choices on performance in international markets. *Strategic Management Journal,* 16: 333-351.

65. For a discussion of how home-country environments can affect diversification strategies, refer to Wan, W. P. & Hoskisson, R. E. 2003. Home country environments, corporate diversification strategies, and firm performance. *Academy of Management Journal,* 46(1): 27-45.

66. Arnold, D. 2000. Seven rules of international distribution. *Harvard Business Review,* 78(6): 131-137.

67. Sharma, A. 1998. Mode of entry and ex-post performance. *Strategic Management Journal,* 19(9): 879-900.

68. This section draws upon Arnold, op. cit., pp. 131-137; and Berkowitz, op. cit.

69. Salomon, R. & Jin, B. 2010. Do leading or lagging firms learn more from exporting? *Strategic Management Journal,* 31(6): 1088-1113.

70. Kline, D. 2003. Strategic licensing. *MIT Sloan Management Review,* 44(3): 89-93.

71. Martin, J. 1999. Franchising in the Middle East. *Management Review,* June: 38-42.

72. Arnold, op. cit.; and Berkowitz, op. cit.

73. An in-depth case study of alliance dynamics is found in Faems, D., Janssens, M., Madhok, A., & Van Looy, B. 2008. Toward an integrative perspective on alliance governance: Connecting contract design, trust dynamics, and contract application. *Academy of Management Journal,* 51(6): 1053-1078.

74. Knowledge transfer in international joint ventures is addressed in Inkpen, A. 2008. Knowledge transfer and international joint ventures. *Strategic Management Journal,* 29(4): 447-453.

75. Wen, S. H. & Chuang, C.-M. 2010. To teach or to compete? A strategic dilemma of knowledge owners in

international alliances. *Asia Pacific Journal of Management,* 27(4): 697-726.

76. Manufacturer-supplier relationships can be very effective in global industries such as automobile manufacturing. Refer to Kotabe, M., Martin, X., & Domoto, H. 2003. Gaining from vertical partnerships: Knowledge transfer, relationship duration, and supplier performance improvement in the U.S. and Japanese automotive industries. *Strategic Management Journal,* 24(4): 293-316.

77. For a good discussion, refer to Merchant, H. & Schendel, D. 2000. How do international joint ventures create shareholder value? *Strategic Management Journal,* 21(7): 723-738.

78. This discussion draws upon Walters, B. A., Peters, S., & Dess, G. G. 1994. Strategic alliances and joint ventures: Making them work. *Business Horizons,* 37(4): 5-11.

79. Some insights on partnering in the global area are discussed in MacCormack, A. & Forbath, T. 2008. *Harvard Business Review,* 66(1): 24, 26.

80. For a rigorous discussion of the importance of information access in international joint ventures, refer to Reuer, J. J. & Koza, M. P. 2000. Asymmetric information and joint venture performance: Theory and evidence for domestic and international joint ventures. *Strategic Management Journal,* 21(1): 81-88.

81. Dyer, J. H., Kale, P., & Singh, H. 2001. How to make strategic alliances work. *MIT Sloan Management Review,* 42(4): 37-43.

82. For a discussion of some of the challenges in managing subsidiaries, refer to O'Donnell, S. W. 2000. Managing foreign subsidiaries: Agents of headquarters, or an independent network? *Strategic Management Journal,* 21(5): 525-548.

83. Ricks, D. 2006. *Blunders in international business* (4th ed.). Malden, MA: Blackwell.

Entrepreneurial Strategy and Competitive Dynamics

After reading this chapter, you should have a good understanding of the following learning objectives:

LO 8-1   The role of opportunities, resources, and entrepreneurs in successfully pursuing new ventures.

LO 8-2   Three types of entry strategies—pioneering, imitative, and adaptive—commonly used to launch a new venture.

LO 8-3   How the generic strategies of overall cost leadership, differentiation, and focus are used by new ventures and small businesses.

LO 8-4   How competitive actions, such as the entry of new competitors into a marketplace, may launch a cycle of actions and reactions among close competitors.

LO 8-5   The components of competitive dynamics analysis—new competitive action, threat analysis, motivation and capability to respond, types of competitive actions, and likelihood of competitive reaction.

©Anatoli Styf/Shutterstock

LEARNING FROM MISTAKES

The disappearing photo app, Snapchat, experienced a meteoric rise. Started by a set of Stanford undergraduate students in 2011, the app had a user base in excess of 150 million and had reached 10 billion daily video views by 2016. As the app grew in popularity, CEO Evan Spiegel and CTO Bobby Murphy found themselves in a long-term battle with Reggie Brown, a Kappa Sigma fraternity brother of theirs who claimed he was the original creator of Snapchat. According to Brown, he shared his idea for an app that would allow users to share photos that would quickly self-destruct with Spiegel. They then recruited Murphy to do computer programming for the app. That first app, Picaboo, evolved into the widely used Snapchat. While the app became a success, the collaboration did not. Spiegel apparently decided that Brown wasn't adding much to the team. He and Murphy locked Brown out of the company's system and disavowed any claims that Brown was one of the firm's founders or had any ownership rights to the company. In 2013, Brown sued, leading to an eventual confidential settlement in 2014. By that time, the overall firm was valued at about $20 billion. While the financial details of the settlement were never made public, Spiegel publicly admitted that Brown was central to the creation of the app, saying, "We acknowledge Reggie's contribution to the creation of Snapchat and appreciate his work in getting the application off the ground."

The Snapchat experience is not at all uncommon. Facebook, Twitter, Tinder, Beats Electronics, and others faced internal drama about who was responsible for the firms' start and who should reap the substantial financial rewards of their success. Why is this so common? Entrepreneurial teams are often composed of friends and family, leading the participants to expect that they can trust their partners and have no need for a written contract or statement of ownership. Luan Tran, the attorney for Brown, put it this way, "You don't think not to trust people you know a lot, and you don't think they are going to screw you. It's good to trust, but it's much better to memorialize your trust in a document." Amir Hassanabadi, another attorney who regularly works with start-up firms, recommends the following for founders on day one of their venture, "Go out to dinner. Settle who's who and what's what. Then put it in writing."[1]

Discussion Questions

1. Why do you think that so many start-up firms have these disputes?
2. Why do founders often fail to work up formal written contracts about ownership and credit?
3. Would you feel comfortable having that conversation early on with a partner in a new business? How would you initiate that conversation?

The Snapchat case illustrates how important it is for start-up firms to formalize the roles of founders and set up formal contracts that lay out responsibilities and ownership rights if they want to avoid later drama.

In this chapter we address entrepreneurial strategies. The previous three chapters have focused primarily on the business-level, corporate-level, and international strategies of incumbent firms. Here we ask: What about the strategies of those entering into a market or industry for the first time? In this chapter, we focus on strategic entrepreneurship—the actions firms take to create new ventures in markets. In Chapter 12, we focus on a related issue—how established firms can build or reinforce an entrepreneurial mindset as they strive to be innovative in markets in which the firm already competes.

Companies wishing to launch new ventures must also be aware that, consistent with the five-forces model in Chapter 2, new entrants are a threat to existing firms in an industry. Entry into a new market arena is intensely competitive from the perspective of incumbents in that arena. Therefore, new entrants can nearly always expect a competitive response from other companies in the industry they are entering. Knowledge of the competitive dynamics that are at work in the business environment is an aspect of entrepreneurial new entry that will be addressed later in this chapter.

Before moving on, it is important to highlight the role that entrepreneurial start-ups and small businesses play in entrepreneurial value creation. Small businesses, those defined as having 500 employees or fewer, create about 65 percent of all new jobs in the United States and also generate 13 times as many new patents per employee as larger firms.[2]

The role of opportunities, resources, and entrepreneurs in successfully pursuing new ventures.

entrepreneurship
the creation of new value by an existing organization or new venture that involves the assumption of risk.

RECOGNIZING ENTREPRENEURIAL OPPORTUNITIES

Defined broadly, **entrepreneurship** refers to new value creation. Even though entrepreneurial activity is usually associated with start-up companies, new value can be created in many different contexts, including:

- Start-up ventures
- Major corporations
- Family-owned businesses
- Nonprofit organizations
- Established institutions

For an entrepreneurial venture to create new value, three factors must be present—an entrepreneurial opportunity, the resources to pursue the opportunity, and an entrepreneur or entrepreneurial team willing and able to undertake the opportunity.[3] The entrepreneurial strategy that an organization uses will depend on these three factors. Thus, beyond merely identifying a venture concept, the opportunity recognition process also involves organizing the key people and resources that are needed to go forward. Exhibit 8.1 depicts the three factors that are needed to successfully proceed—opportunity, resources, and entrepreneur(s). In the sections that follow, we address each of these factors.

EXHIBIT 8.1 Opportunity Analysis Framework

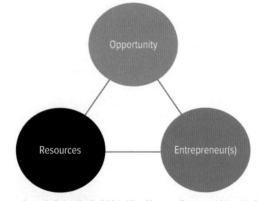

Sources: Based on Timmons, J. A. & Spinelli, S. 2004. *New Venture Creation* (6th ed.). New York: McGraw-Hill/Irwin; and Bygrave, W. D. 1997. The Entrepreneurial Process. In W. D. Bygrave (Ed.), *The Portable MBA in Entrepreneurship* (2nd ed.). New York: Wiley.

Entrepreneurial Opportunities

The starting point for any new venture is the presence of an entrepreneurial opportunity. Where do opportunities come from? For new business start-ups, opportunities come from many sources—current or past work experiences, hobbies that grow into businesses or lead to inventions, suggestions by friends or family, or a chance event that makes an entrepreneur aware of an unmet need. Terry Tietzen, founder and CEO of Edatanetworks, puts it this way, "You get ideas through watching the world and through relationships. You get ideas from looking down the road."[4] For established firms, new business opportunities come from the needs of existing customers, suggestions by suppliers, or technological developments that lead to new advances.[5] For all firms, there is a major, overarching factor behind all viable opportunities that emerge in the business landscape: change. Change creates opportunities. Entrepreneurial firms make the most of changes brought about by new technology, sociocultural trends, and shifts in consumer demand.

How do changes in the external environment lead to new business creation? They spark creative new ideas and innovation. Businesspeople often have ideas for entrepreneurial ventures. However, not all such ideas are good ideas—that is, viable business opportunities. To determine which ideas are strong enough to become new ventures, entrepreneurs must go through a process of identifying, selecting, and developing potential opportunities. This is the process of **opportunity recognition**.[6]

Opportunity recognition refers to more than just the "Eureka!" feeling that people sometimes experience at the moment they identify a new idea. Although such insights are often very important, the opportunity recognition process involves two phases of activity—discovery and evaluation—that lead to viable new venture opportunities.[7]

The discovery phase refers to the process of becoming aware of a new business concept.[8] Many entrepreneurs report that their idea for a new venture occurred to them in an instant, as a sort of "Aha!" experience—that is, they had some insight or epiphany, often based on their prior knowledge, that gave them an idea for a new business. The discovery of new opportunities is often spontaneous and unexpected. For example, Howard Schultz, CEO of Starbucks, was in Milan, Italy, when he suddenly realized that the coffee-and-conversation cafe model that was common in Europe would work in the United States as well. According to Schultz, he didn't need to do research to find out if Americans would pay $3 for a cup of coffee—he just *knew*. Starbucks was just a small business at the time but Schultz began literally shaking with excitement about growing it into a bigger business.[9] Strategy Spotlight 8.1 tells how two brothers took the realization that many people wanted to wear their optimism and turned it into a growing business empire.

Opportunity discovery also may occur as the result of a deliberate search for new venture opportunities or creative solutions to business problems. Viable opportunities often emerge only after a concerted effort. The search process is very similar to a creative process, which may be unstructured and "chaotic" at first but eventually leads to a practical solution or business innovation. To stimulate the discovery of new opportunities, companies often encourage creativity, out-of-the-box thinking, and brainstorming. While a deliberate search can aim to identify truly novel and creative entrepreneurial opportunities, it can also be more focused to look for "obvious" opportunities that others have failed to see. Experienced entrepreneurs discussing ways to look for new entrepreneurial opportunities identify several ways to undertake a structured search for entrepreneurial ideas:[10]

- *Look at what's bugging you.* What are the frustrations you have with current products or processes? Search for ideas on how to address these annoyances to identify entrepreneurial opportunities. For example, Jeannine Fradelizio noticed that at parties she hosted, guests would set down their wine glasses and forget which one was their glass. This would lead them to either abandon that glass and get another or end up drinking from someone else's glass which would sometimes lead to a minor dispute. In an effort to avoid these mix-ups Fradelizio tried having her friends write their names

<div class="margin-note">

opportunity recognition
the process of discovering and evaluating changes in the business environment, such as a new technology, sociocultural trends, or shifts in consumer demand, that can be exploited.

</div>

SEEING OPPORTUNITY IN THE BRIGHT SIDE

People were craving something positive that focused on the good, instead of what is wrong with the world.

—*John Jacobs*

That simple inspiration was the insight that has driven the success of Life is Good T-shirts. Beginning in 1989, John Jacobs and his brother, Bert, had been selling T-shirts out of their van, scraping out a living. They used their own artwork on the shirts and found an audience for their funky designs, especially on college campuses. But after five and a half years in the business, they had a whopping $78 in the bank.

Their business turned with a simple conversation. As John explained, "Then in 1994, we talked about how people seemed worn down by the media's constant focus on the negative side of information." They had a keg party at which they asked friends to comment on drawings they were considering for new shirts. The design that received the most buzz was a simple stick figure that smiled. They paired this design with a simple slogan, "Life is Good," to offer a positive message. They printed up 48 shirts with the new design and sold out within an hour at a street fair. Their inspiration seemed correct. People craved a sense of positivity.

They started working with retailers to sell the shirts. The retailers liked the design but also started asking questions, such as, "Does the smiley guy eat ice cream? Does he roller-skate?" Bert and John responded by starting to draw designs that reflected what made life good. In Bert's words, "Our concept was that optimism is powerful." What they found out was that optimism is a powerful sales slogan. Their sales topped $250,000 within two years.

It's been over 20 years since they had the simple but profound insight that people buy into a positive message. Life is Good now generates nearly $150 million in sales and distributes its clothing through more than 4,500 retail stores in over 30 countries. The firm also has strategic alliances with Hallmark and Smucker's that extend its message to additional products, and John and Bert see further opportunities in publishing and filmmaking with their message that life is good. The brothers have also set up a foundation that hosts festivals to benefit kids overcoming poverty, illness, and violence. Their goal is clear. As Bert stated, "We can be a billion dollar company driving positive social change, teaching, and reinforcing the values we think are most important in the world." The message isn't that life is great or life is perfect but that even in hard times, life is good.

Sources: Buchanan, L. 2006. Life lessons. *inc.com*, October 1: np; Eng, D. 2014. Life is good in the T-shirt business. *Fortune,* May 19: 39–42; and *hoovers.com.*

on their glasses with a marker but found that existing markers either didn't dry quickly enough or wouldn't wash off. She enlisted the help of a chemist and developed the Wine Glass Writer. Sales for the product have risen to over $1.5 million.[11]

- *Talk to the people who know.* If you have a general idea of the market you want to go into, talk to suppliers, customers, and front-line workers in this market. These discussions can lead to insights on how these stakeholders' needs aren't being met and can also open avenues to hear what they would like to see in new products and processes. For example, Precision Hawk, a company using drones to do aerial data analysis, reached out to Hahn Estate Winery so that Precision Hawk could better understand the needs of wineries in analyzing crop health and to develop the capabilities needed to meet those needs.[12]

- *Look to other markets.* One of the most powerful ways of finding new ideas is by borrowing ideas from other markets. This could involve looking at other industries or other geographic markets to identify new ideas. For example, in developing the idea for CarMax, the used-car superstore chain, Richard Sharp drew on his experience leading a major consumer electronics retailer to lay out the logic for his "big box" used-car lots, which allowed him to streamline operations and improve the efficiency of the used-car market. In essence, he decided to build the Best Buy or the Home Depot of the used-car market.

- *Get inspired by history.* Sometimes, the best ideas are not actually new ideas. Opportunities in industries can often be discovered by looking to the past to find good ideas that have slipped out of practice but might now be valued by the market again. For example, Sam Calagione, founder of Ancient Ales, developed an innovative line of craft beers by using ancient brewing techniques and ingredients that differ from modern brews.

mOASIS LEVERAGES TECHNOLOGY TO IMPROVE WATER EFFICIENCY FOR FARMERS

The pervasive drought in California has had dire effects for farmers. At times, water usage restrictions have severely limited the water farmers can use. Even when they don't face difficult water restrictions, farmers have found their water bills go up by as much as 600 percent in recent years. This has led them to look to drought resistant varieties, new fertilizers that reduce water demands, soil sensors that reduce the possibility of overwatering, and other actions to lower water needs.

A startup firm, mOasis, sees further opportunity with an environmentally friendly hydrogel. Farmers apply mOasis's gel polymer to soil when preparing the land for planting.

The hydrogel particles are the size of a grain of sand but can soak up 250 times their weight in water. The hydrogel absorbs water during irrigation and releases it as the soil dries—ensuring the most efficient use of water possible. According to mOasis, farmers using the hydrogel can experience up to 25 percent higher crop yields with 20 percent lower water use. The gel stays effective for about a year but then breaks down into byproducts that are not environmentally damaging in any way.

Sources: Wang, U. 2013. For drought-plagued farmers: A gel that can suck up 250 times its weight in water. *gigaom.com*, October 29: np; Fehrenbacher, K. 2015. How water technology can help farmers survive California's drought. *fortune.com*, June 1: np; and, Vekshin, A. 2014. California water prices soar for farmers as drought grows. *bloomberg.com*, July 24: np.

Opportunity evaluation, which occurs after an opportunity has been identified, involves analyzing an opportunity to determine whether it is viable and strong enough to be developed into a full-fledged new venture. Ideas developed by new product groups or in brainstorming sessions are tested by various methods, including talking to potential target customers and discussing operational requirements with production or logistics managers. A technique known as feasibility analysis is used to evaluate these and other critical success factors. This type of analysis often leads to the decision that a new venture project should be discontinued. If the venture concept continues to seem viable, a more formal business plan may be developed.[13]

Among the most important factors to evaluate is the market potential for the product or service. Established firms tend to operate in established markets. They have to adjust to market trends and to shifts in consumer demand, of course, but they usually have a customer base for which they are already filling a marketplace need. New ventures, in contrast, must first determine whether a market exists for the product or service they are contemplating. Thus, a critical element of opportunity recognition is assessing to what extent the opportunity is viable *in the marketplace.*

For an opportunity to be viable, it needs to have four qualities:[14]

- *Attractive.* The opportunity must be attractive in the marketplace; that is, there must be market demand for the new product or service.
- *Achievable.* The opportunity must be practical and physically possible.
- *Durable.* The opportunity must be attractive long enough for the development and deployment to be successful; that is, the window of opportunity must be open long enough for it to be worthwhile.
- *Value creating.* The opportunity must be potentially profitable; that is, the benefits must surpass the cost of development by a significant margin.

If a new business concept meets these criteria, two other factors must be considered before the opportunity is launched as a business: the resources available to undertake it and the characteristics of the entrepreneur(s) pursuing it. In the next section, we address the issue of entrepreneurial resources; following that, we address the importance of entrepreneurial leaders and teams. But first, consider the opportunities that have been created by the recent surge in interest in environmental sustainability. Strategy Spotlight 8.2 discusses how an entrepreneurial firm is responding to the California drought with an innovative, environmentally sustainable product that helps farmers use water more efficiently.

Entrepreneurial Resources

As Exhibit 8.1 indicates, resources are an essential component of a successful entrepreneurial launch. For start-ups, the most important resource is usually money because a new firm typically has to expend substantial sums just to start the business. However, financial resources are not the only kind of resource a new venture needs. Human capital and social capital are also important. Many firms also rely on government resources to help them thrive.[15]

Financial Resources   Hand-in-hand with the importance of markets (and marketing) to new venture creation, entrepreneurial firms must also have financing. In fact, the level of available financing is often a strong determinant of how the business is launched and its eventual success. Cash finances are, of course, highly important. But access to capital, such as a line of credit or favorable payment terms with a supplier, can also help a new venture succeed.

The types of financial resources that may be needed depend on two factors: the stage of venture development and the scale of the venture.[16] Entrepreneurial firms that are starting from scratch—start-ups—are at the earliest stage of development. Most start-ups also begin on a relatively small scale. The funding available to young and small firms tends to be quite limited. In fact, the majority of new firms are low-budget start-ups launched with personal savings and the contributions of family and friends.[17] Among firms included in the *Entrepreneur* list of the 100 fastest-growing new businesses, 61 percent reported that their start-up funds came from personal savings.[18]

Although bank financing, public financing, and venture capital are important sources of small business finance, these types of financial support are typically available only after a company has started to conduct business and generate sales. Even **angel investors**—private individuals who provide equity investments for seed capital during the early stages of a new venture—favor companies that already have a winning business model and dominance in a market niche.[19] According to Cal Simmons, coauthor of *Every Business Needs an Angel,* "I would much rather talk to an entrepreneur who has already put his money and his effort into proving the concept."[20]

Thus, while the press commonly talks about the role of **venture capitalists** and angel investors in start-up firms, the majority of external funding for young and small firms comes from informal sources such as family and friends. Based on a Kauffman Foundation survey of entrepreneurial firms, Exhibit 8.2 identifies the sources of funding used by start-up businesses and by ongoing firms that are five years old. The survey shows that most start-up funding, about 70 percent, comes from either equity investments by the entrepreneur and the entrepreneur's family and friends or personal loans taken out by the entrepreneur.

---

angel investors
private individuals who provide equity investments for seed capital during the early stages of a new venture.

venture capitalists
companies organized to place their investors' funds in lucrative business opportunities.

EXHIBIT 8.2 Sources of Capital for Start-Up Firms

	Capital Invested in Their First Year	Percentage of Capital Invested in Their First Year	Capital Invested in Their Fifth Year	Percentage of Capital Invested in Their Fifth Year
Insider equity	$33,034	41.1	$13,914	17.9
Investor equity	$ 4,108	5.1	$ 3,108	4.0
Personal debt of owners	$23,353	29.1	$21,754	28.0
Business debt	$19,867	24.7	$39,009	50.1
Total average capital invested	$80,362		$77,785	

Source: From Robb, A., Reedy, E. J., Ballou, J., DesRoches, D., Potter, F., & Zhao, A. 2010. An Overview of the Kauffman Firm Survey. Reproduced with permission from the Ewing Marion Kauffman Foundation.

Once a venture has established itself as a going concern, other sources of financing become readily available. Banks, for example, are more likely to provide later-stage financing to companies with a track record of sales or other cash-generating activity. According to the Kauffman Foundation study, after five years of operation, the largest source of funding is from loans taken out by the business.

At both stages, 5 percent or less of the funding comes from outside investors, such as angel investors or venture capitalists. In fact, few firms ever receive venture capital investments—only 7 of 2,606 firms in the Kauffman study received money from outside investors. But when they do, these firms receive a substantial level of investment—over $1 million on average in the survey—because they tend to be the firms that are the most innovative and have the greatest growth potential. These start-ups typically involve large capital investments or extensive development costs—such as manufacturing or engineering firms trying to commercialize an innovative product—and have high cash requirements soon after they are founded. Since these investments are typically well beyond the capability of the entrepreneur or even a local bank to fund, entrepreneurs running these firms turn to the venture capital market. Other firms turn to venture capitalists when they are on the brink of rapid growth.

Venture capital is a form of private equity financing through which entrepreneurs raise money by selling shares in the new venture. In contrast to angel investors, who invest their own money, venture capital companies are organized to place the funds of private investors into lucrative business opportunities. Venture capitalists nearly always have high performance expectations from the companies they invest in, but they also provide important managerial advice and links to key contacts in an industry.[21]

In recent years, a new source of funding, **crowdfunding,** has emerged as a means for start-ups to amass significant pools of capital.[22] In these peer-to-peer investment systems, individuals striving to grow their business post their business ideas on a crowdfunding website. Potential investors who go to the site evaluate the proposals listed and decide which, if any, to fund. Typically, no individual makes a very sizable funding allotment. Most investors contribute up to a few hundred dollars to any investment, but the power of the crowd is at work. If a few thousand investors sign up for a venture, it can potentially raise over a million dollars. In addition to providing funding, Crowdfunding can also provide entrepreneurs with valuable feedback that can be used to refine or further innovate the firm's products. Investors often comment and offer suggestions. Some entrepreneurs take this further, responding to comments from investors, triggering a new round of feedback.[23]

crowdfunding
funding a venture by pooling small investments from a large number of investors; often raised on the Internet.

The crowdfunding market has taken off since the term was first coined in 2006. The total value of global crowdfunding reached $34 billion in 2015.[24] Some crowdfunding websites allow investors to own actual equity in the firms they fund. Others, such as Kickstarter, don't offer investors equity. Instead, they get a reward from the entrepreneurial firm. For example, Mystery Brewing Company gave its investors logoed bottle openers, tulip-shaped beer glasses, T-shirts, posters, and home-brew recipes.

While crowdfunding offers a new avenue for corporations to raise funding, there are some potential downsides. First, the crowdfunding sites take a slice of the funds raised—typically 4 to 9 percent. Second, while crowdfunding offers a marketplace in which to raise funds, it also puts additional pressure on entrepreneurs. The social network–savvy investors who fund these ventures are quick to comment on their social media websites if the firm misses deadlines or falls short of its revenue projections. Finally, entrepreneurs can struggle with how much information to share about their business ideas. They want to share enough information without releasing critical information that competitors trolling these sites can benefit from. They also may be concerned about posting their financials, since these statements give their suppliers and customers access to sensitive information about margins and earnings.

There are also some concerns that the loose rules in the regulation of crowdfunding could lead to significant fraud by firms soliciting investment. According to Stephen Goodman, an attorney with Pryor Cashman LLP, "The SEC has been extremely skeptical of this [crowdfunding] process." Others have faith in the wisdom of the crowd to catch fraud. They point to the experience with Little Monster Productions, a video game developer. Little Monster was set to raise funds on Kickstarter, but the fund call was closed by Kickstarter when potential investors noticed and commented that Little Monster had stolen some of the images it was using in its game from another game site. Even with potential investors identifying glaring problems with some crowdfunding projects, the likelihood of success with crowdfunded projects is somewhat low. One study found that 75 percent of crowd-funded projects failed to meet their anticipated launch dates.[25] Because the requirements for firms raising funds through crowdfunding are lax, investors need to do their homework. Here are some simple recommendations to keep from getting burned.[26]

- **Financial statements.** Be sure to closely review the corporate tax returns that firms are required to post. Better yet, have your accountant review them to see if anything looks fishy.
- **Licenses and registrations.** You should check to see if the company has current licenses and registrations needed to operate in its chosen industry. This can often be done through online checks with the secretary of state's office or the state's corporation department. Sometimes, it will take a phone call or two. This provides a simple check to see if the company is legitimate.
- **Litigation.** Check to see if the company has been sued. You can search online at the free site justia.com and the law-oriented information sites Westlaw and LexisNexis. Be sure to check under current and former names of the firm and its principals (top managers).
- **Better Business Bureau.** Check the firm's BBB report. Does the firm appear to exist? What is the grade the BBB gives it? Is the firm a BBB member? All of this information gives insight into the firm's current operations and its customer relations.
- **Employment and educational history.** This is a bit tricky because of privacy issues, but you can typically contact colleges listed on the filing forms and inquire if the principals of the firm attended and graduated from the schools they list. You can also search employment histories on the websites of the companies the principals used to work at as well as social network sites, such as LinkedIn and Facebook.
- **Required disclosures.** Read all of the documentation carefully. This includes the shareholder rights statement. This statement will provide information on how much of a stake in the firm you get and how this will be diluted by future offerings. Also, read statements on the company's competition and risks it faces.

Human Capital   Bankers, venture capitalists, and angel investors agree that the most important asset an entrepreneurial firm can have is strong and skilled management.[27] According to Stephen Gaal, founding member of Walnut Venture Associates, venture investors do not invest in businesses; instead, "We invest in people . . . very smart people with very high integrity." Managers need to have a strong base of experience and extensive domain knowledge, as well as an ability to make rapid decisions and change direction as shifting circumstances may require. In the case of start-ups, more is better. New ventures that are started by teams of three, four, or five entrepreneurs are more likely to succeed in the long run than are ventures launched by "lone wolf" entrepreneurs.[28]

The ability of firms to extend their human capital base to outside partners is an especially important skill in the gig economy. Platform firms in this market will only succeed if they can deliver gig workers who deliver a high quality service. Urban professionals who go to Handy to find a contractor to do needed cleaning or painting will only return if the service provider follows through in a timely and professional way. Similarly, customers will only return to Fancy Hands for personal assistance if their first experience with a Fancy Hands assistant is good.[29] Thus, platform firms in these markets need to develop effective systems to recruit and evaluate potential service providers. On the positive side, firms that use a gig economy model greatly reduce the financial resources needed to expand their businesses.

Social Capital   New ventures founded by entrepreneurs who have extensive social contacts are more likely to succeed than are ventures started without the support of a social network.[30] Even though a venture may be new, if the founders have contacts who will vouch for them, they gain exposure and build legitimacy faster.[31] This support can come from several sources: prior jobs, industry organizations, and local business groups such as the chamber of commerce. These contacts can all contribute to a growing network that provides support for the entrepreneurial firm. Janina Pawlowski, cofounder of the online lending company E-Loan, attributed part of her success to the strong advisers she persuaded to serve on her board of directors, including Tim Koogle, former CEO of Yahoo![32]

Strategic alliances represent a type of social capital that can be especially important to young and small firms.[33] Strategic alliances can provide a key avenue for growth by entrepreneurial firms.[34] By partnering with other companies, young or small firms can expand or give the appearance of entering numerous markets or handling a range of operations. According to the National Federation of Independent Business (NFIB), nearly two-thirds of small businesses currently hold or have held some type of alliance. Here are a few types of alliances that have been used to extend or strengthen entrepreneurial firms:

- *Technology alliances.* Tech-savvy entrepreneurial firms often benefit from forming alliances with older incumbents. The alliance allows the larger firm to enhance its technological capabilities and expands the revenue and reach of the smaller firm.
- *Manufacturing alliances.* The use of outsourcing and other manufacturing alliances by small firms has grown dramatically in recent years. Internet-enabled capabilities such as collaborating online about delivery and design specifications have greatly simplified doing business, even with foreign manufacturers.
- *Retail alliances.* Licensing agreements allow one company to sell the products and services of another in different markets, including overseas. Specialty products—the types sometimes made by entrepreneurial firms—often seem more exotic when sold in another country.

Although such alliances often sound good, there are also potential pitfalls. Lack of oversight and control is one danger of partnering with foreign firms. Problems with product quality, timely delivery, and receiving payments can also sour an alliance relationship if it is not carefully managed. With technology alliances, there is a risk that big firms may take advantage of the technological know-how of their entrepreneurial partners. However, even with these potential problems, strategic alliances provide a good means for entrepreneurial firms to develop and grow.

Government Resources   In the United States, the federal government provides support for entrepreneurial firms in two key arenas—financing and government contracting. The Small Business Administration (SBA) has several loan guarantee programs designed to support the growth and development of entrepreneurial firms. The government itself does not typically lend money but underwrites loans made by banks to small businesses, thus reducing the risk associated with lending to firms with unproven records. The SBA also offers training, counseling, and support services through its local offices and Small Business Development Centers.[35] State and local governments also have hundreds of programs to provide funding, contracts, and other support for new ventures and small businesses. These programs are often designed to grow the economy of a region.

Another key area of support is government contracting. Programs sponsored by the SBA and other government agencies ensure that small businesses have the opportunity to bid on contracts to provide goods and services to the government. Although working with the government sometimes has its drawbacks in terms of issues of regulation and time-consuming decision making, programs to support small businesses and entrepreneurial activity constitute an important resource for entrepreneurial firms.

Entrepreneurial Leadership

entrepreneurial leadership
leadership appropriate for new ventures that requires courage, belief in one's convictions, and the energy to work hard even in difficult circumstances; and that embodies vision, dedication and drive, and commitment to excellence.

Whether a venture is launched by an individual entrepreneur or an entrepreneurial team, effective leadership is needed. Launching a new venture requires a special kind of leadership. Research indicates that entrepreneurs tend to have characteristics that distinguish them from corporate managers. Differences include:

- *Higher core self-evaluation.* Successful entrepreneurs evidence higher levels of self-confidence and a higher assessment of the degree to which an individual controls his or her own destiny.[36]
- *Higher conscientiousness.* Entrepreneurs tend to have a higher degree of organization, persistence, hard work, and pursuit of goal accomplishment.
- *Higher openness to experience.* Entrepreneurs also tend to score higher on openness to experience, a personality trait associated with intellectual curiosity and a desire to explore novel ideas.
- *Higher emotional stability.* Entrepreneurs exhibit a higher ability to handle ambiguity and maintain even emotions during stressful periods, and they are less likely to be overcome by anxieties.
- *Lower agreeableness.* Finally, entrepreneurs tend to score lower on agreeableness. This suggests they typically look out primarily for their own self-interest and also are willing to influence or manipulate others for their own advantage.[37]

These personality traits are embodied in the behavioral attributes necessary for successful entrepreneurial leadership—vision, dedication and drive, and commitment to excellence:

- *Vision.* This may be an entrepreneur's most important asset. Entrepreneurs envision realities that do not yet exist. But without a vision, most entrepreneurs would never even get their venture off the ground. With vision, entrepreneurs are able to exercise a kind of transformational leadership that creates something new and, in some way, changes the world. Just having a vision, however, is not enough. To develop support, get financial backing, and attract employees, entrepreneurial leaders must share their vision with others.
- *Dedication and drive.* Dedication and drive are reflected in hard work. Drive involves internal motivation; dedication calls for an intellectual commitment that keeps an entrepreneur going even in the face of bad news or poor luck. They both require patience, stamina, and a willingness to work long hours. However, a business built on the heroic efforts of one person may suffer in the long run. That's why the dedicated entrepreneur's enthusiasm is also important—like a magnet, it attracts others to the business to help with the work.[38]
- *Commitment to excellence.* Excellence requires entrepreneurs to commit to knowing the customer, providing quality goods and services, paying attention to details, and continuously learning. Entrepreneurs who achieve excellence are sensitive to how these factors work together. However, entrepreneurs may flounder if they think they are the only ones who can create excellent results. The most successful, by contrast, often report that they owe their success to hiring people smarter than themselves.

In his book *Good to Great,* Jim Collins makes another important point about entrepreneurial leadership: Ventures built on the charisma of a single person may have trouble growing "from good to great" once that person leaves.[39] Thus, the leadership that is needed to build a great organization is usually exercised by a team of dedicated people working together rather than a single leader. Another aspect of this team approach is attracting team members who fit with the company's culture, goals, and work ethic. Thus, for a venture's leadership to be a valuable resource and not a liability, it must be cohesive in its vision, drive and dedication, and commitment to excellence.

Once an opportunity has been recognized, and an entrepreneurial team and resources have been assembled, a new venture must craft a strategy. Prior chapters have addressed the strategies of incumbent firms. In the next section, we highlight the types of strategies and strategic considerations faced by new entrants.

ENTREPRENEURIAL STRATEGY

Successfully creating new ventures requires several ingredients. As indicated in Exhibit 8.1, three factors are necessary—a viable opportunity, sufficient resources, and a skilled and dedicated entrepreneur or entrepreneurial team. Once these elements are in place, the new venture needs a strategy. In this section, we consider several different strategic factors that are unique to new ventures and also how the generic strategies introduced in Chapter 5 can be applied to entrepreneurial firms. We also indicate how combination strategies might benefit entrepreneurial firms and address the potential pitfalls associated with launching new venture strategies.

To be successful, new ventures must evaluate industry conditions, the competitive environment, and market opportunities in order to position themselves strategically. However, a traditional strategic analysis may have to be altered somewhat to fit the entrepreneurial situation. For example, five-forces analysis (as discussed in Chapter 2) is typically used by established firms. It can also be applied to the analysis of new ventures to assess the impact of industry and competitive forces. But you may ask: How does a new entrant evaluate the threat of other new entrants?

First, the new entrant needs to examine barriers to entry. If the barriers are too high, the potential entrant may decide not to enter or to gather more resources before attempting to do so. Compared to an older firm with an established reputation and available resources, the barriers to entry may be insurmountable for an entrepreneurial start-up. Therefore, understanding the force of these barriers is critical in making a decision to launch.

A second factor that may be especially important to a young venture is the threat of retaliation by incumbents. In many cases, entrepreneurial ventures *are* the new entrants that pose a threat to incumbent firms. Therefore, in applying the five-forces model to new ventures, the threat of retaliation by established firms needs to be considered.

Part of any decision about what opportunity to pursue is a consideration of how a new entrant will actually enter a new market. The concept of entry strategies provides a useful means of addressing the types of choices that new ventures have.

Entry Strategies

One of the most challenging aspects of launching a new venture is finding a way to begin doing business that quickly generates cash flow, builds credibility, attracts good employees, and overcomes the liability of newness. The idea of an entry strategy or "entry wedge" describes several approaches that firms may take to get a foothold in a market.[40] Several factors will affect this decision:

- Is the product/service high-tech or low-tech?
- What resources are available for the initial launch?
- What are the industry and competitive conditions?
- What is the overall market potential?
- Does the venture founder prefer to control the business or to grow it?

entrepreneurial strategy
a strategy that enables a skilled and dedicated entrepreneur, with a viable opportunity and access to sufficient resources, to successfully launch a new venture.

Three types of entry strategies—pioneering, imitative, and adaptive—commonly used to launch a new venture.

In some respects, any type of entry into a market for the first time may be considered entrepreneurial. But the entry strategy will vary depending on how risky and innovative the new business concept is.[41] New-entry strategies typically fall into one of three categories—pioneering new entry, imitative new entry, or adaptive new entry.[42]

Pioneering New Entry   New entrants with a radical new product or highly innovative service may change the way business is conducted in an industry. This kind of breakthrough—creating new ways to solve old problems or meeting customers' needs in a unique new way—is referred to as a **pioneering new entry.** If the product or service is unique enough, a pioneering new entrant may actually have little direct competition. The first personal computer was a pioneering product; there had never been anything quite like it, and it revolutionized computing. The first Internet browser provided a type of pioneering service. These breakthroughs created whole new industries and changed the competitive landscape. And breakthrough innovations continue to inspire pioneering entrepreneurial efforts.

The pitfalls associated with a pioneering new entry are numerous. For one thing, there is a strong risk that the product or service will not be accepted by consumers. The history of entrepreneurship is littered with new ideas that never got off the launching pad. Take, for example, Smell-O-Vision, an invention designed to pump odors into movie theaters from the projection room at preestablished moments in a film. It was tried only once (for the film *Scent of a Mystery*) before it was declared a major flop. Innovative? Definitely. But hardly a good idea at the time.[43]

A pioneering new entry is disruptive to the status quo of an industry. It is likely based on a technological breakthrough. If it is successful, other competitors will rush in to copy it. This can create issues of sustainability for an entrepreneurial firm, especially if a larger company with greater resources introduces a similar product. For a new entrant to sustain its pioneering advantage, it may be necessary to protect its intellectual property, advertise heavily to build brand recognition, form alliances with businesses that will adopt its products or services, and offer exceptional customer service.

Imitative New Entry   Whereas pioneers are often inventors or tinkerers with new technology, imitators usually have a strong marketing orientation. They look for opportunities to capitalize on proven market successes. An **imitative new entry** strategy is used by entrepreneurs who see products or business concepts that have been successful in one market niche or physical locale and introduce the same basic product or service in another segment of the market. Strategy Spotlight 8.3 discusses how Casper Sleep is using an imitative strategy to shake up the mattress market.

Sometimes the key to success with an imitative strategy is to fill a market space where the need had previously been filled inadequately. Entrepreneurs are also prompted to be imitators when they realize that they have the resources or skills to do a job better than an existing competitor. This can actually be a serious problem for entrepreneurial start-ups if the imitator is an established company. Consider the example of Square.[44] Founded in 2010, Square provides a means for small businesses to process credit and debit card sales without signing up for a traditional credit card arrangement that typically includes monthly fees and minimum charges. Square provides a small credit card reader that plugs into a smartphone to users who sign up for its service. Users swipe the card and input the charge amount. Square does the rest for a 2.75 percent transaction fee. As of 2016, Square was processing $46 billion in transactions annually. But success triggers imitation. A host of both upstart and established firms have moved into this new segment. While Square has quickly established itself in the market, it now faces strong competition from major competitors, including Apple, Google, and PayPal. With the strong competition it faces and the thin margins in its business, Square has never been able to turn a profit. As a result, the firm's value when the firm went public in November 2015 was only $2.9 billion, half of its estimated value only a year before.

pioneering new entry
a firm's entry into an industry with a radical new product or highly innovative service that changes the way business is conducted.

imitative new entry
a firm's entry into an industry with products or services that capitalize on proven market successes and that usually have a strong marketing orientation.

CASPER SLEEP AIMS TO BE THE WARBY PARKER OF MATTRESSES

By taking a product that was typically sold in specialty stores with extremely high markups and, instead, allowing customers to order high quality products online at much lower prices, Warby Parker changed the eyeglass business. Casper Sleep aims to do the same thing in the mattress market. For decades, mattresses have been sold in large showrooms at specialty retailers and furniture stores with commissioned sales staff. Prices for a higher end king size mattress set could run up to $5,000. It was hard for anyone to enter this space using an online ordering system since customers had the expectation that they should lie down on a mattress before buying it. Additionally, delivery was a challenge since spring coil mattresses are big and bulky.

Casper Sleep, along with a few other competitors, saw an opportunity as potential customers who had transacted with online retailers for a range of products became more willing to buy furniture online as well. Additionally, latex and foam mattresses are much easier to compress for cost efficient shipping. Casper developed a simple business model and jumped in. It aims to produce the best mattress possible at an attractive price, sell a single model, and offer free delivery. Because the mattress is composed of memory foam and latex, Casper can compress the mattress and deliver it in a box the size of a dorm refrigerator. By all measures, it has been a success. Casper was able to generate $100 million in sales in its first full year of operation and received five star ratings from 81 percent of its customers on Amazon. The benefit for customers is clear. A king mattress on Casper's website is $950, far cheaper than paying for a Temper-Pedic mattress at a local sleep store. Casper also lessens customer concerns about ordering a mattress online by offering a 100-day guarantee and free returns.

Sources: Welch, L. 2016. How Casper Became a $100 Million Company in Less Than Two Years. *inc.com*, March: np; Nassauer, S. 2016. Bed-in-a-box startups challenge traditional mattress makers. *wsj.com*, March 7: np; and Robinson, M. 2015. I just bought a bed from the 'Warby Parker of mattresses' and I will never buy one in stores again. *businessinsider.com*, June 9: np.

Adaptive New Entry   Most new entrants use a strategy somewhere between "pure" imitation and "pure" pioneering. That is, they offer a product or service that is somewhat new and sufficiently different to create new value for customers and capture market share. Such firms are adaptive in the sense that they are aware of marketplace conditions and conceive entry strategies to capitalize on current trends.

According to business creativity coach Tom Monahan, "Every new idea is merely a spin of an old idea. [Knowing that] takes the pressure off from thinking [you] have to be totally creative. You don't. Sometimes it's one slight twist to an old idea that makes all the difference."[45] An **adaptive new entry** approach does not involve "reinventing the wheel," nor is it merely imitative either. It involves taking an existing idea and adapting it to a particular situation. Exhibit 8.3 presents examples of four companies that successfully modified or adapted existing products to create new value.

There are several pitfalls that might limit the success of an adaptive new entrant. First, the value proposition must be perceived as unique. Unless potential customers believe a new product or service does a superior job of meeting their needs, they will have little motivation to try it. Second, there is nothing to prevent a close competitor from mimicking the new firm's adaptation as a way to hold on to its customers. Third, once an adaptive entrant achieves initial success, the challenge is to keep the idea fresh. If the attractive features of the new business are copied, the entrepreneurial firm must find ways to adapt and improve the product or service offering.

Considering these choices, an entrepreneur or entrepreneurial team might ask, Which new entry strategy is best? The choice depends on many competitive, financial, and marketplace considerations. Nevertheless, research indicates that the greatest opportunities may stem from being willing to enter new markets rather than seeking growth only in existing markets. One study found that companies that ventured into arenas that were new to the world or new to the company earned total profits of 61 percent. In contrast, companies that made only incremental improvements, such as extending an existing product line, grew total profits by only 39 percent.[46]

> **adaptive new entry**
> a firm's entry into an industry by offering a product or service that is somewhat new and sufficiently different to create value for customers by capitalizing on current market trends.

EXHIBIT 8.3 Examples of Adaptive New Entrants

Company Name	Product	Adaptation	Result
Under Armour, Inc. Founded in 1995	Undershirts and other athletic gear	Used moisture-wicking fabric to create better gear for sweaty sports.	Under Armour generated over $4.5 billion in 2016 and is now the number-two athletic-clothing firm in the United States after Nike.
Mint.com Founded in 2005	Comprehensive online money management	Created software that tells users what they are spending by aggregating financial information from online bank and credit card accounts.	Mint has over 20 million users and is helping them manage over $3 billion in assets.
Plum Organics Founded in 2005	Organic baby food and snack foods for children	Made convenient line of baby food using organic ingredients.	Plum now has over 20 products, saw sales grow by 44% in 2015, and has over 7% market share in baby food segment.
Spanx Founded in 2000	Footless pantyhose and other undergarments for women	Combined nylon and Lycra to create a new type of undergarment that is comfortable and eliminates panty lines.	Spanx now produces over 200 products generating over $250 million in sales annually.

Sources: Bryan, M. 2007. Spanx Me, Baby! *www.observer.com*, December 10, np.; Carey, J. 2006. Perspiration Inspiration. *BusinessWeek,* June 5: 64; Palanjian, A. 2008. A Planner Plumbs for a Niche. *www.wsj.com*, September 30, np.; Worrell, D. 2008. Making Mint. *Entrepreneur,* September: 55; *www.mint.com*; *www.spanx.com*; *www.underarmour.com*; *plumorganics.com*; *forbes.com/companies/plum-organics/*; Germano, S. 2015. Under Armour Overtakes Adidas in U.S. Sportswear Market. *wsj. com*, January 8: np; Watson, E. 2015. Plum Organics sales surge 44% in 2015 as 'food-forward' formulations tap into needs of millennial shoppers. *foodnavigator-usa. com,* December 16: np; and *blog.mint.com/credit/mint-by-the-numbers-which-user-are-you-040616/*.

However, whether to be pioneering, imitative, or adaptive when entering markets is only one question the entrepreneur faces. A new entrant must also decide what type of strategic positioning will work best as the business goes forward. The strategic choices can be informed by the guidelines suggested for the generic strategies. We turn to that subject next.

Generic Strategies

LO 8-3

How the generic strategies of overall cost leadership, differentiation, and focus are used by new ventures and small businesses.

Typically, a new entrant begins with a single business model that is equivalent in scope to a business-level strategy (Chapter 5). In this section we address how overall low cost, differentiation, and focus strategies can be used to achieve competitive advantages.

Overall Cost Leadership One of the ways entrepreneurial firms achieve success is by doing more with less. By holding down costs or making more efficient use of resources than larger competitors, new ventures are often able to offer lower prices and still be profitable. Thus, under the right circumstances, a low-cost leader strategy is a viable alternative for some new ventures. The way most companies achieve low-cost leadership, however, is typically different for young or small firms.

Recall from Chapter 5 that three of the features of a low-cost approach include operating at a large-enough scale to spread costs over many units of production (economies of scale), making substantial capital investments in order to increase scale economies, and using knowledge gained from experience to make cost-saving improvements. These elements of a cost-leadership strategy may be unavailable to new ventures. Because new ventures are typically small, they usually don't have high economies of scale relative to competitors. Because they are usually cash strapped, they can't make large capital investments to increase their scale advantages. And because many are young, they often don't have a wealth of accumulated experience to draw on to achieve cost reductions.

Given these constraints, how can new ventures successfully deploy cost-leader strategies? Compared to large firms, new ventures often have simple organizational structures that make decision making both easier and faster. The smaller size also helps young firms change more quickly when upgrades in technology or feedback from the marketplace indicate that improvements are needed. They are also able to make decisions at the time they are founded that help them deal with the issue of controlling costs. For example, they may source materials from a supplier that provides them more cheaply or set up manufacturing facilities in another country where labor costs are especially low. Thus, new firms have several avenues for achieving low-cost leadership.

Whatever methods young firms use to achieve a low-cost advantage, this has always been a way that entrepreneurial firms take business away from incumbents—by offering a comparable product or service at a lower price.

Differentiation   Both pioneering and adaptive entry strategies involve some degree of differentiation. That is, the new entry is based on being able to offer a differentiated value proposition. In the case of pioneers, the new venture is attempting to do something strikingly different, either by using a new technology or by deploying resources in a way that radically alters the way business is conducted. Often, entrepreneurs do both.

Amazon founder Jeff Bezos set out to use Internet technology to revolutionize the way books are sold. He garnered the ire of other booksellers and the attention of the public by making bold claims about being the "earth's largest bookseller." As a bookseller, Bezos was not doing anything that had not been done before. But two key differentiating features— doing it on the Internet and offering extraordinary customer service—made Amazon a differentiated success.

There are several factors that make it more difficult for new ventures to be successful as differentiators. For one thing, the strategy is generally thought to be expensive to enact. Differentiation is often associated with strong brand identity, and establishing a brand is usually considered to be expensive because of the cost of advertising and promotion, paid endorsements, exceptional customer service, and so on. Differentiation successes are sometimes built on superior innovation or use of technology. These are also factors that might make it challenging for young firms to excel relative to established competitors.

Nevertheless, all of these areas—innovation, technology, customer service, distinctive branding—are also arenas where new ventures have sometimes made a name for themselves even though they must operate with limited resources and experience. To be successful, according to Garry Ridge, CEO of the WD-40 Company, "You need to have a great product, make the end user aware of it, and make it easy to buy."[47] It sounds simple, but it is a difficult challenge for new ventures with differentiation strategies. Strategy Spotlight 8.4 outlines how the Shakespeare & Co. is attempting to differentiate a new form of local bookstore.

Focus   Focus strategies are often associated with small businesses because there is a natural fit between the narrow scope of the strategy and the small size of the firm. A focus strategy may include elements of differentiation and overall cost leadership, as well as combinations of these approaches. But to be successful within a market niche, the key strategic requirement is to stay focused. Let's consider why that is so.

Despite all the attention given to fast-growing new industries, most start-ups enter industries that are mature.[48] In mature industries, growth in demand tends to be slow and there are often many competitors. Therefore, if a start-up wants to get a piece of the action, it often has to take business away from an existing competitor. If a start-up enters a market with a broad or aggressive strategy, it is likely to evoke retaliation from a more powerful competitor. Young firms can often succeed best by finding a market niche where they can get a foothold and make small advances that erode the position of existing competitors.[49] From this position, they can build a name for themselves and grow.

SHAKESPEARE & CO.: USING TECHNOLOGY TO CREATE A NEW LOCAL BOOKSTORE

With the challenge of discounted books from Amazon and the emergence of digital books, some wondered if there would still be a market for local bookstores. Some of the major chains, including Borders Books, went out of business. Others, like Barnes and Noble and Books-a-Million, faced financial challenges and shrank in size. In spite of these challenges, the number of independent bookstores in the United States actually increased by 34 percent from 2010 to 2015.

Dane Neller saw opportunity in this market. In May 2015, he purchased a historic New York bookstore, Shakespeare & Co., and proceeded to shut the store—so that he could re-imagine the physical bookstore to meet the current needs of the market. "The old ways have to be reinvented. People want to hang out, they want to talk, they want intimacy. But the store has to be productive" said Mr. Neller. His new store dedicates 40 percent less space to displaying books. The focus is on carrying high demand books, leading to faster turn of the inventory on hand

and an overall increase in book sales. In addition to the books on hand, he added an Espresso Book Machine that can print any of seven million published books, including many that are no longer printed by book publishers, in less than five minutes. Customers can also self-publish their own books on the machine. Shakespeare & Co. offers self-publishing packages that range from $149 to $549. To make the store seem more like a destination, he also added a café at the front of the store. He emphasizes a friendly experience for his customers as well. Mr. Neller says, "My customer is here because they care about more than price. They want to be greeted. They want a sense of community, and they have a craving for culture."

By providing a place to find the hottest books, the ability to print more obscure titles, and a service level that is rare in the Big Apple, Shakespeare & Co. is offering a differentiated experience. It seems to be working well. Customer traffic has been robust, and sales per square foot have nearly doubled.

Sources: Trachtenberg, J. 2016. New model for independent bookstores. *wsj. com*, April 19: np; and, Rosen, J. 2015. New Shakespeare & Co. owner envisions a national bookstore chain. *publishersweekly.com*, November 13: np.

Consider, for example, the "Miniature Editions" line of books launched by Running Press, a small Philadelphia publisher. The books are palm-size minibooks positioned at bookstore cash registers as point-of-sale impulse items costing about $4.95. Beginning with just 10 titles in 1993, Running Press grew rapidly and within 10 years had sold over 20 million copies. Even though these books represent just a tiny fraction of total sales in the $23 billion publishing industry, they have been a mainstay for Running Press.[50] As the Running Press example indicates, many new ventures are successful even though their share of the market is quite small.

Combination Strategies

One of the best ways for young and small businesses to achieve success is by pursuing combination strategies. By combining the best features of low-cost, differentiation, and focus strategies, new ventures can often achieve something truly distinctive.

Entrepreneurial firms are often in a strong position to offer a combination strategy because they have the flexibility to approach situations uniquely. For example, holding down expenses can be difficult for big firms because each layer of bureaucracy adds to the cost of doing business across the boundaries of a large organization.[51]

A similar argument could be made about entrepreneurial firms that differentiate. Large firms often find it difficult to offer highly specialized products or superior customer services. Entrepreneurial firms, by contrast, can often create high-value products and services through their unique differentiating efforts.

For nearly all new entrants, one of the major dangers is that a large firm with more resources will copy what they are doing. Well-established incumbents that observe the success of a new entrant's product or service will copy it and use their market power to overwhelm the smaller firm. The threat may be lessened for firms that use combination strategies. Because of the flexibility of entrepreneurial firms, they can often enact combination strategies in ways that the large firms cannot copy. This makes the new entrant's strategies much more sustainable.

Perhaps more threatening than large competitors are close competitors, because they have similar structural features that help them adjust quickly and be flexible in decision making. Here again, a carefully crafted and executed combination strategy may be the best way for an entrepreneurial firm to thrive in a competitive environment. Nevertheless, competition among rivals is a key determinant of new venture success. To address this, we turn next to the topic of competitive dynamics.

COMPETITIVE DYNAMICS

New entry into markets, whether by start-ups or by incumbent firms, nearly always threatens existing competitors. This is true in part because, except in very new markets, nearly every market need is already being met, either directly or indirectly, by existing firms. As a result, the competitive actions of a new entrant are very likely to provoke a competitive response from companies that feel threatened. This, in turn, is likely to evoke a reaction to the response. As a result, a competitive dynamic—action and response—begins among the firms competing for the same customers in a given marketplace.

Competitive dynamics—intense rivalry among similar competitors—has the potential to alter a company's strategy. New entrants may be forced to change their strategies or develop new ones to survive competitive challenges by incumbent rivals. New entry is among the most common reasons why a cycle of competitive actions and reactions gets started. It might also occur because of threatening actions among existing competitors, such as aggressive cost cutting. Thus, studying competitive dynamics helps explain why strategies evolve and reveals how, why, and when to respond to the actions of close competitors. Exhibit 8.4 identifies the factors that competitors need to consider when determining how to respond to a competitive act.

New Competitive Action

Entry into a market by a new competitor is a good starting point to begin describing the cycle of actions and responses characteristic of a competitive dynamic process.[52] However, new entry is only one type of competitive action. Price cutting, imitating successful products, and expanding production capacity are other examples of competitive acts that might provoke competitors to react.

LO 8-4

How competitive actions, such as the entry of new competitors into a marketplace, may launch a cycle of actions and reactions among close competitors.

competitive dynamics intense rivalry, involving actions and responses, among similar competitors vying for the same customers in a marketplace.

LO 8-5

The components of competitive dynamic analysis—new competitive action, threat analysis, motivation and capability to respond, types of competitive actions, and likelihood of competitive reaction.

new competitive action acts that might provoke competitors to react, such as new market entry, price cutting, imitating successful products, and expanding production capacity.

EXHIBIT 8.4 Model of Competitive Dynamics

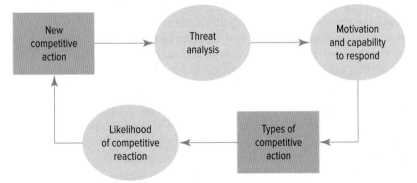

Sources: Adapted from Chen, M. J. 1996. Competitor Analysis and Interfirm Rivalry: Toward a Theoretical Integration. *Academy of Management Review,* 21(1): 100–134; Ketchen, D. J., Snow, C. C., & Hoover, V. L. 2004. Research on Competitive Dynamics: Recent Accomplishments and Future Challenges. *Journal of Management,* 30(6): 779–804; and Smith, K. G., Ferrier, W. J., & Grimm, C. M. 2001. King of the Hill: Dethroning the Industry Leader. *Academy of Management Executive,* 15(2): 59–70.

Why do companies launch new competitive actions? There are several reasons:

- Improve market position
- Capitalize on growing demand
- Expand production capacity
- Provide an innovative new solution
- Obtain first-mover advantages

Underlying all of these reasons is a desire to strengthen financial outcomes, capture some of the extraordinary profits that industry leaders enjoy, and grow the business. Some companies are also motivated to launch competitive challenges because they want to build their reputation for innovativeness or efficiency. For example, Toyota's success with the Prius signaled to its competitors the potential value of high-fuel-economy cars, and these firms have responded with their own hybrids, electric cars, high-efficiency diesel engines, and even more fuel-efficient traditional gasoline engines. This is indicative of the competitive dynamic cycle. As former Intel chairman Andy Grove stated, "Business success contains the seeds of its own destruction. The more successful you are, the more people want a chunk of your business and then another chunk and then another until there is nothing left."[53]

When a company enters into a market for the first time, it is an attack on existing competitors. As indicated earlier in the chapter, any of the entry strategies can be used to take competitive action. But competitive attacks come from many sources besides new entrants. Some of the most intense competition is among incumbent rivals intent on gaining strategic advantages. "Winners in business play rough and don't apologize for it," according to Boston Consulting Group authors George Stalk, Jr., and Rob Lachenauer in their book *Hardball: Are You Playing to Play or Playing to Win?*[54] Exhibit 8.5 outlines their five strategies.

The likelihood that a competitor will launch an attack depends on many factors.[55] In the remaining sections, we discuss factors such as competitor analysis, market conditions, types of strategic actions, and the resource endowments and capabilities companies need to take competitive action.

Threat Analysis

threat analysis
a firm's awareness of its closest competitors and the kinds of competitive actions they might be planning.

Prior to actually observing a competitive action, companies may need to become aware of potential competitive threats. That is, companies need to have a keen sense of who their closest competitors are and the kinds of competitive actions they might be planning.[56] This may require some environmental scanning and monitoring of the sort described in Chapter 2. Awareness of the threats posed by industry rivals allows a firm to understand what type of competitive response, if any, may be necessary.

Being aware of competitors and cognizant of whatever threats they might pose is the first step in assessing the level of competitive threat. Once a new competitive action becomes apparent, companies must determine how threatening it is to their business. Competitive dynamics are likely to be most intense among companies that are competing for the same customers or that have highly similar sets of resources.[57] Two factors are used to assess whether or not companies are close competitors:

market commonality
the extent to which competitors are vying for the same customers in the same markets.

resource similarity
the extent to which rivals draw from the same types of strategic resources.

- **Market commonality.** Whether or not competitors are vying for the same customers and how many markets they share in common. For example, aircraft manufacturers Boeing and Airbus have a high degree of market commonality because they make very similar products and have many buyers in common.
- **Resource similarity.** The degree to which rivals draw on the same types of resources to compete. For example, Huawei and Nokia are telecommunications equipment providers that are based in different continents and have different histories, but they have patent rights to similar technologies, high quality engineering staffs, and global sales forces.

EXHIBIT 8.5 Five Ways to Aggressively Attack Your Rivals

Strategy	Description	Examples
Devastate rivals' profit sanctuaries	Not all business segments generate the same level of profits for a company. Through focused attacks on a rival's most profitable segments, a company can generate maximum leverage with relatively smaller-scale attacks. Recognize, however, that companies closely guard the information needed to determine just what their profit sanctuaries are.	In 2005, Walmart began offering low-priced extended warranties on home electronics after learning that its rivals such as Best Buy derived most of their profits from extended warranties.
Plagiarize with pride	Just because a close competitor comes up with an idea first does not mean it cannot be successfully imitated. Second movers, in fact, can see how customers respond, make improvements, and launch a better version without all the market development costs. Successful imitation is harder than it may appear and requires the imitating firm to keep its ego in check.	In designing its smartphones, Samsung copied the look, feel, and technological attributes of Apple's IPhone. Samsung lost a patent infringement lawsuit to Apple, but by copying Apple, Samsung was able to improve its market position.
Deceive the competition	A good gambit sends the competition off in the wrong direction. This may cause the rivals to miss strategic shifts, spend money pursuing dead ends, or slow their responses. Any of these outcomes support the deceiving firms' competitive advantage. Companies must be sure not to cross ethical lines during these actions.	Max Muir knew that Australian farmers liked to buy from family-firm suppliers but also wanted efficient suppliers. To meet both needs, he quietly bought a number of small firms to build economies of scale but didn't consolidate brands or his sales force so that, to his customers and rivals, they still looked like independent family firms.
Unleash massive and overwhelming force	While many hardball strategies are subtle and indirect, this one is not. This is a full-frontal attack where by a firm commits significant resources to a major campaign to weaken rivals' positions in certain markets. Firms must be sure they have the mass and stamina required to win before they declare war against a rival.	Unilever has taken a dominant position, with 65 percent market share, in the Vietnamese laundry detergent market by employing a massive investment and marketing campaign. In doing so, it decimated the market position of the local, incumbent competitors.
Raise competitors' costs	If a company has superior insight into the complex cost and profit structure of the industry, it can compete in a way that steers its rivals into relatively higher cost/lower profit arenas. This strategy uses deception to make the rivals think they are winning, when in fact they are not. Again, companies using this strategy must be confident that they understand the industry better than their rivals.	Ecolab, a company that sells cleaning supplies to businesses, encouraged a leading competitor, Diversity, to adopt a strategy to go after the low-volume, high-margin customers. What Ecolab knew that Diversity didn't is that the high servicing costs involved with this segment make the segment unprofitable—a situation Ecolab ensured by bidding high enough to lose the contracts to Diversity but low enough to ensure the business lost money for Diversity.

Sources: Berner, R. 2005. Watch Out, Best Buy and Circuit City. *BusinessWeek,* November 10; Stalk, G., Jr. 2006. Curveball Strategies to Fool the Competition. *Harvard Business Review,* 84(9): 114–121; and Stalk, G., Jr., & Lachenauer, R. 2004. *Hardball: Are You Playing to Play or Playing to Win?* Cambridge, MA: Harvard Business School Press. Reprinted by permission of Harvard Business School Press from G. Stalk, Jr., and R. Lachenauer. Copyright 2004 by the Harvard Business School Publishing Corporation; all rights reserved; Lam, Y. 2013. FDI Companies Dominate Vietnam's Detergent Market. *www.saigon-gpdaily.com.vn,* January 22: np; Vascellaro, J. 2012. Apple Wins Big in Patent Case. *www.wsj.com,* August 25: np; and Pech, R. & Stamboulidis, G. 2010. How Strategies of Deception Facilitate Business Growth. *Journal of Business Strategy,* 31(6): 37–45.

When any two firms have both a high degree of market commonality and highly similar resource bases, a stronger competitive threat is present. Such a threat, however, may not lead to competitive action. On the one hand, a market rival may be hesitant to attack a company that it shares a high degree of market commonality with because it could lead to an intense battle. On the other hand, once attacked, rivals with high market commonality will be much more motivated to launch a competitive response. This is especially true in cases where the shared market is an important part of a company's overall business.

How strong a response an attacked rival can mount will be determined by its strategic resource endowments. In general, the same set of conditions holds true with regard to resource similarity. Companies that have highly similar resource bases will be hesitant to launch an initial attack but pose a serious threat if required to mount a competitive response.[58] Greater strategic resources increase a firm's capability to respond.

Motivation and Capability to Respond

Once attacked, competitors are faced with deciding how to respond. Before deciding, however, they need to evaluate not only how they will respond but also their reasons for responding and their capability to respond. Companies need to be clear about what problems a competitive response is expected to address and what types of problems it might create.[59] There are several factors to consider.

First, how serious is the impact of the competitive attack to which they are responding? For example, a large company with a strong reputation that is challenged by a small or unknown company may elect to simply keep an eye on the new competitor rather than quickly react or overreact. Part of the story of online retailer Amazon's early success is attributed to Barnes & Noble's overreaction to Amazon's claim that it was "earth's biggest bookstore." Because Barnes & Noble was already using the phrase "world's largest bookstore," it sued Amazon, but lost. The confrontation made it to the front pages of *The Wall Street Journal,* and Amazon was on its way to becoming a household name.[60]

Companies planning to respond to a competitive challenge must also understand their motivation for responding. What is the intent of the competitive response? Is it merely to blunt the attack of the competitor, or is it an opportunity to enhance its competitive position? Sometimes the most a company can hope for is to minimize the damage caused by a competitive action.

A company that seeks to improve its competitive advantage may be motivated to launch an attack rather than merely respond to one. For example, a number of years ago, *The Wall Street Journal (WSJ)* attacked the *New York Times* by adding a local news section to the New York edition of the *WSJ.* Its aim was to become a more direct competitor of the *Times.* The publishers of the *WSJ* undertook this attack when they realized the *Times* was in a weakened financial condition and would be unable to respond to the attack.[61] A company must also assess its capability to respond. What strategic resources can be deployed to fend off a competitive attack? Does the company have an array of internal strengths it can draw on, or is it operating from a position of weakness?

Consider the role of firm age and size in calculating a company's ability to respond. Most entrepreneurial new ventures start out small. The smaller size makes them more nimble compared to large firms so they can respond quickly to competitive attacks. Because they are not well-known, start-ups also have the advantage of the element of surprise in how and when they attack. Innovative uses of technology, for example, allow small firms to deploy resources in unique ways.

Because they are young, however, start-ups may not have the financial resources needed to follow through with a competitive response.[62] In contrast, older and larger firms may have more resources and a repertoire of competitive techniques they can use in a counterattack. Large firms, however, tend to be slower to respond. Older firms tend to be predictable in their responses because they often lose touch with the competitive environment and rely on strategies and actions that have worked in the past.

Other resources may also play a role in whether a company is equipped to retaliate. For example, one avenue of counterattack may be launching product enhancements or new product/service innovations. For that approach to be successful, it requires a company to have both the intellectual capital to put forward viable innovations and the teamwork skills to prepare a new product or service and get it to market. Resources such as cross-functional teams and the social capital that makes teamwork production effective and efficient represent the type of human capital resources that enhance a company's capability to respond.

Types of Competitive Actions

Once an organization determines whether it is willing and able to launch a competitive action, it must determine what type of action is appropriate. The actions taken will be determined by both its resource capabilities and its motivation for responding. There are also marketplace considerations. What types of actions are likely to be most effective given a company's internal strengths and weaknesses as well as market conditions?

Two broadly defined types of competitive action include strategic actions and tactical actions. **Strategic actions** represent major commitments of distinctive and specific resources. Examples include launching a breakthrough innovation, building a new production facility, or merging with another company. Such actions require significant planning and resources and, once initiated, are difficult to reverse.

Tactical actions include refinements or extensions of strategies. Examples of tactical actions include cutting prices, improving gaps in service, or strengthening marketing efforts. Such actions typically draw on general resources and can be implemented quickly. Exhibit 8.6 identifies several types of strategic and tactical competitive actions that illustrate the range of actions that can occur in a rivalrous relationship.

strategic actions
major commitments of distinctive and specific resources to strategic initiatives.

tactical actions
refinements or extensions of strategies usually involving minor resource commitments.

EXHIBIT 8.6 Strategic and Tactical Competitive Actions

	Actions	Examples
Strategic Actions	• Entering new markets	• Make geographical expansions • Expand into neglected markets • Target rivals' markets • Target new demographics
	• New product introductions	• Imitate rivals' products • Address gaps in quality • Leverage new technologies • Leverage brand name with related products • Protect innovation with patents
	• Changing production capacity	• Create overcapacity • Tie up raw materials sources • Tie up preferred suppliers and distributors • Stimulate demand by limiting capacity
	• Mergers/alliances	• Acquire/partner with competitors to reduce competition • Tie up key suppliers through alliances • Obtain new technology/intellectual property • Facilitate new market entry
Tactical Actions	• Price cutting (or increases)	• Maintain low-price dominance • Offer discounts and rebates • Offer incentives (e.g., frequent flyer miles) • Enhance offering to move upscale
	• Product/service enhancements	• Address gaps in service • Expand warranties • Make incremetal product improvements
	• Increased marketing efforts	• Use guerrilla marketing • Conduct selective attacks • Change product packaging • Use new marketing channels
	• New distribution channels	• Access suppliers directly • Access customers directly • Develop multiple points of contact with customers • Expand Internet presence

Sources: Chen, M. J. & Hambrick, D. 1995. Speed, Stealth, and Selective Attack: How Small Firms Differ from Large Firms in Competitive Behavior. *Academy of Management Journal,* 38: 453–482; Davies, M. 1992. Sales Promotions as a Competitive Strategy. *Management Decision,* 30(7): 5–10; Ferrier, W., Smith, K., & Grimm, C. 1999. The Role of Competitive Action in Market Share Erosion and Industry Dethronement: A Study of Industry Leaders and Challengers. *Academy of Management Journal,* 42(4): 372–388; and Garda, R. A. 1991. Use Tactical Pricing to Uncover Hidden Profits. *Journal of Business Strategy,* 12(5): 17–23.

Some competitive actions take the form of frontal assaults, that is, actions aimed directly at taking business from another company or capitalizing on industry weaknesses. This can be especially effective when firms use a low-cost strategy. The airline industry provides a good example of this head-on approach. When Southwest Airlines began its no-frills, no-meals strategy in the late 1960s, it represented a direct assault on the major carriers of the day. In Europe, Ryanair has similarly directly challenged the traditional carriers with an overall cost leadership strategy.

Guerrilla offensives and selective attacks provide an alternative for firms with fewer resources.[63] These draw attention to products or services by creating buzz or generating enough shock value to get some free publicity. TOMS Shoes has found a way to generate interest in its products without a large advertising budget to match Nike. Its policy of donating one pair of shoes to those in need for every pair of shoes purchased by customers has generated a lot of buzz on the Internet.[64] Over 3 million people have given a "like" rating on TOMS's Facebook page. The policy has a real impact as well, with over 60 million shoes donated as of January 2017.[65]

Some companies limit their competitive response to defensive actions. Such actions rarely improve a company's competitive advantage, but a credible defensive action can lower the risk of being attacked and deter new entry.

Several of the factors discussed earlier in the chapter, such as types of entry strategies and the use of cost leadership versus differentiation strategies, can guide the decision about what types of competitive actions to take. Before launching a given strategy, however, assessing the likely response of competitors is a vital step.[66]

Likelihood of Competitive Reaction

The final step before initiating a competitive response is to evaluate what a competitor's reaction is likely to be. The logic of competitive dynamics suggests that once competitive actions are initiated, it is likely they will be met with competitive responses.[67] The last step before mounting an attack is to evaluate how competitors are likely to respond. Evaluating potential competitive reactions helps companies plan for future counterattacks. It may also lead to a decision to hold off—that is, not to take any competitive action at all because of the possibility that a misguided or poorly planned response will generate a devastating competitive reaction.

How a competitor is likely to respond will depend on three factors: market dependence, competitor's resources, and the reputation of the firm that initiates the action (actor's reputation). The implications of each of these are described briefly as follows.

Market Dependence   If a company has a high concentration of its business in a particular industry, it has more at stake because it must depend on that industry's market for its sales. Single-industry businesses or those where one industry dominates are more likely to mount a competitive response. Young and small firms with a high degree of **market dependence** may be limited in how they respond due to resource constraints.

Competitor's Resources   Previously, we examined the internal resource endowments that a company must evaluate when assessing its capability to respond. Here, it is the competitor's resources that need to be considered. For example, a small firm may be unable to mount a serious attack due to lack of resources. As a result, it is more likely to react to tactical actions such as incentive pricing or enhanced service offerings because they are less costly to attack than large-scale strategic actions. In contrast, a firm with financial "deep pockets" may be able to mount and sustain a costly counterattack.

Actor's Reputation   Whether a company should respond to a competitive challenge will also depend on who launched the attack against it. Compared to relatively smaller firms

CLEANING UP IN THE SOAP BUSINESS

Consumer product companies Colgate-Palmolive, Unilever, Procter & Gamble (P&G), and Henkel compete with each other globally in the soap business. But as regulators found after a long investigation, this wasn't true in France. The firms in this market had colluded to fix prices for nearly a decade. In the words of a Henkel executive, the detergent makers wanted "to limit the intensity of competition between them and clean up the market." The Autorité de la Concurrance, the French antitrust watchdog, hit these four firms with fines totaling $484 million after completing its investigation.

The firms started sharing pricing information in the 1980s, but by the 1990s their cooperation got bolder, morphing into behavior that sounds like something out of a spy novel. In 1996, four brand directors secretly met in a restaurant in a suburb of Paris and agreed to coordinate the pricing of their soap products. They agreed to prearranged prices at which they would sell to retailers and agreed to notify each other of any planned special offers. They gave each firm a secret alias: Pierre for Procter

& Gamble, Laurence for Unilever, Hugues for Henkel, and Christian for Colgate-Palmolive. From that point forward, they allegedly scheduled clandestine meetings four times a year. The meetings, which they called "store checks" in their schedules to limit any questioning they may have received, often lasted an entire afternoon. They would set complex pricing schemes. For example, P&G sold its Ariel brand as an upscale product and coordinated with Unilever to keep Ariel at a 3 percent markup over Unilever's Skip brand. At these meetings, they would also hash out any complaints about whether and how any of the participants had been bending the rules.

The collusion lasted for almost 10 years until it broke down in 2004. Unilever was the first to defect, offering a 10 percent "D-Day" price cut without negotiating it with the three other firms. Other competitors quickly responded with actions that violated the pricing norms they had set.

Sources: Colchester, M. & Passariello, C. 2011. Dirty secrets in soap prices. *wsj.com*, December 9: np; and Smith, H. & White, A. 2011. P&G, Colgate fined by France in $484 million detergent cartel. *Bloomberg.com*, December 11: np.

with less market power, competitors are more likely to respond to competitive moves by market leaders. Another consideration is how successful prior attacks have been. For example, price cutting by the big automakers usually has the desired result—increased sales to price-sensitive buyers—at least in the short run. Given that history, when GM offers discounts or incentives, rivals Ford and Chrysler cannot afford to ignore the challenge and quickly follow suit.

Choosing Not to React: Forbearance and Co-opetition

The above discussion suggests that there may be many circumstances in which the best reaction is no reaction at all. This is known as **forbearance**—refraining from reacting at all as well as holding back from initiating an attack. The decision of whether a firm should respond or show forbearance is not always clear.

Related to forbearance is the concept of **co-opetition.** This is a term that was coined by network software company Novell's founder and former CEO Raymond Noorda to suggest that companies often benefit most from a combination of competing and cooperating.[68] Close competitors that differentiate themselves in the eyes of consumers may work together behind the scenes to achieve industrywide efficiencies.[69] For example, breweries in Sweden cooperate in recycling used bottles but still compete for customers on the basis of taste and variety. Similarly, several competing Hollywood studios came together and agreed to cooperate on buying movie film. They negotiated promises to buy certain quantities of film to keep Kodak from closing down its film manufacturing business.[70] As long as the benefits of cooperating are enjoyed by all participants in a co-opetition system, the practice can aid companies in avoiding intense and damaging competition.[71]

Despite the potential benefits of co-opetition, companies need to guard against cooperating to such a great extent that their actions are perceived as collusion, a practice that has legal ramifications in the United States. In Strategy Spotlight 8.5, we see an example of crossing the line into illegal cooperation.

forbearance
a firm's choice of not reacting to a rival's new competitive action.

co-opetition
a firm's strategy of both cooperating and competing with rival firms.

Once a company has evaluated a competitor's likelihood of responding to a competitive challenge, it can decide what type of action is most appropriate. Competitive actions can take many forms: the entry of a start-up into a market for the first time, an attack by a lower-ranked incumbent on an industry leader, or the launch of a breakthrough innovation that disrupts the industry structure. Such actions forever change the competitive dynamics of a marketplace. Thus, the cycle of actions and reactions that occur in business every day is a vital aspect of entrepreneurial strategy that leads to continual new value creation and the ongoing advancement of economic well-being.

ISSUE FOR DEBATE

Where Have the Entrepreneurs Gone?

The United States has long been seen as the home of a vibrant entrepreneurial economy, but the statistics call this into question. From 1977 to 2011, the number of new start-up firms in the United States declined by 28 percent. More dramatically, relative to the size of the working population, the number of new start-ups has fallen by half. Even Silicon Valley has seen the rate of new business start-ups decline by 50 percent over the last three decades. Entrepreneurial actions have fallen most sharply among younger adults. People age 20 to 34 created only 22.7 percent of all new companies in 2013, down from 34.8 percent in 1996. This is an ironic change given that enrollment in college entrepreneurship programs has been growing.

This declining rate of entrepreneurship is setting off warning bells for many. It leads to less innovation in the economy and slower job opportunity growth. Over the long run, it would lead to lower living standards and stagnant economic growth.

Concerns on this issue have led to a discussion of the underlying causes of this change. The causes of this decline may be emotional or institutional. On the emotional level, it may be that the after-effects of the Great Recession have tilted society toward risk aversion. Additionally, many would-be entrepreneurs are saddled with significant student loan debt, leaving them less willing to take on the risk of entrepreneurship. Consistent with this view, Audrey Baxter, a woman who won a business proposal award as a student at UCLA, opted to take a corporate job when she graduated rather than pushing her small business forward. "Having a secure job with a really good salary was something to be considered carefully," Baxter said.

It may also be that institutional factors are reducing people's willingness or ability to start a business. Weakened antitrust enforcement may be playing a role. Firms have been able to grow and combine in a range of markets, leading to extremely large competitors that dominate markets, increasing the entry barriers for entrepreneurs. Also, lax antitrust enforcement has made it easier for large incumbent firms to respond very aggressively to newcomers, increasing the risk for entrepreneurs. Government red tape is another institutional barrier to entrepreneurs. For example, Celeste Kelly opened a business offering horse massage but had to shut down the business when the Arizona State Veterinary Medical Examining Board ordered her to "cease and desist" because it ruled she was practicing veterinary medicine without a license—even though no veterinarians in the area offered horse massage as a treatment. This may seem like an obscure example, but many businesses, including barbers, bartenders, cosmetologists, and even tour guides, are required to obtain licenses. Less than 5 percent of workers required licenses in the 1950s. That number is now 35 percent. According to economists Morris Kleiner and Alan Krueger, licenses increase the wage costs for a business by 18 percent.

Discussion Questions

1. How concerned are you about the drop in the rate of entrepreneurship?
2. What do you think are the primary causes of the decline?
3. What actions should be taken to increase the rate of new business start-ups? How effective will these actions be?
4. What factors influence your desire to work in an entrepreneurial firm versus an established firm?

Sources: Hamilton, W. 2014. A drop-off in start-ups: Where are all the entrepreneurs? *latimes.com*, September 7: np; Anonymous. 2014. Red tape blues: The best and worst states for small business. *The Economist*, July 5: 23–24; and Anonymous. 2014. Unshackle the entrepreneurs: America's license raj. *The Economist*, July 5: 14.

Reflecting on Career Implications . . .

This chapter focuses on the potential benefits and risks associated with entrepreneurial actions. You can enhance your career by looking for and leveraging entrepreneurial opportunities both in creating a start- up and in firms in which you work. The questions below allow you to explore these possibilities.

▣ **Opportunity Recognition:** What ideas for new business activities are actively discussed in your work environment? Could you apply the four characteristics of an opportunity to determine whether they are viable opportunities? If no one in your organization is excited about or even considering new opportunities, you may want to ask yourself if you want to continue with your current firm.

▣ **Entrepreneurial New Entry:** Are there opportunities to launch new products or services that might add value to the organization? What are the best ways for you to bring these opportunities to the attention of key managers? Or might this provide an opportunity for you to launch your own entrepreneurial venture?

▣ **Entrepreneurial Resources:** Evaluate your resources in terms of financial resources, human capital, and social capital. Are these enough to launch your own venture? If you are deficient in one area, are there ways to compensate for it? Even if you are not interested in starting a new venture, can you use your entrepreneurial resources to advance your career within your firm?

▣ **Competitive Dynamics:** There is always internal competition within organizations: among business units and sometimes even individuals within the same unit. What types of strategic and tactical actions are employed in these internal rivalries? What steps have you taken to strengthen your own position given the "competitive dynamics" within your organization?

summary

New ventures and entrepreneurial firms that capitalize on marketplace opportunities make an important contribution to the U.S. economy. They are leaders in terms of implementing new technologies and introducing innovative products and services. Yet entrepreneurial firms face unique challenges if they are going to survive and grow.

To successfully launch new ventures or implement new technologies, three factors must be present: an entrepreneurial opportunity, the resources to pursue the opportunity, and an entrepreneur or entrepreneurial team willing and able to undertake the venture. Firms must develop a strong ability to recognize viable opportunities. Opportunity recognition is a process of determining which venture ideas are, in fact, promising business opportunities.

In addition to strong opportunities, entrepreneurial firms need resources and entrepreneurial leadership to thrive. The resources that start-ups need include financial resources as well as human and social capital. Many firms also benefit from government programs that support new venture development and growth. New ventures thrive best when they are led by founders or owners who have vision, drive and dedication, and a commitment to excellence.

Once the necessary opportunities, resources, and entrepreneur skills are in place, new ventures still face numerous strategic challenges. Decisions about the strategic positioning of new entrants can benefit from conducting strategic analyses and evaluating the requirements of niche markets. Entry strategies used by new ventures take several forms, including pioneering new entry, imitative new entry, and adaptive new entry. Entrepreneurial firms can benefit from using overall low cost, differentiation, and focus strategies although each of these approaches has pitfalls that are unique to young and small firms. Entrepreneurial firms are also in a strong position to benefit from combination strategies.

The entry of a new company into a competitive arena is like a competitive attack on incumbents in that arena. Such actions often provoke a competitive response, which may, in turn, trigger a reaction to the response. As a result, a competitive dynamic—action and response—begins among close competitors. In deciding whether to attack or counterattack, companies must analyze the seriousness of the competitive threat, their ability to mount a competitive response, and the type of action—strategic or tactical—that the situation requires. At times, competitors find it is better not to respond at all or to find avenues to cooperate with, rather than challenge, close competitors.

SUMMARY REVIEW QUESTIONS

1. Explain how the combination of opportunities, resources, and entrepreneurs helps determine the character and strategic direction of an entrepreneurial firm.
2. What is the difference between discovery and evaluation in the process of opportunity recognition? Give an example of each.
3. Describe the three characteristics of entrepreneurial leadership: vision, dedication and drive, and commitment to excellence.
4. Briefly describe the three types of entrepreneurial entry strategies: pioneering, imitative, and adaptive.
5. Explain why entrepreneurial firms are often in a strong position to use combination strategies.
6. What does the term *competitive dynamics* mean?
7. Explain the difference between strategic actions and tactical actions and provide examples of each.

key terms

entrepreneurship 238
opportunity recognition 239
angel investors 242

venture capitalists 242
crowdfunding 243
entrepreneurial leadership 246
entrepreneurial strategy 247
pioneering new entry 248
imitative new entry 248
adaptive new entry 249
competitive dynamics 253

new competitive action 253
threat analysis 254
market commonality 254
resource similarity 254
strategic actions 257

tactical actions 257
market dependence 258
forbearance 259
co-opetition 259

APPLICATION QUESTIONS & EXERCISES

1. E-Loan and Lending Tree are two entrepreneurial firms that offer lending services over the Internet. Evaluate the features of these two companies. (Fill in the table below.)
   a. Evaluate their characteristics and assess the extent to which they are comparable in terms of market commonality and resource similarity.
   b. Based on your analysis, what strategic and/or tactical actions might these companies take to improve their competitive position? Could E-Loan and Lending Tree improve their performance more through co-opetition than competition? Explain your rationale.
2. Using the Internet, research the Small Business Administration's website (*www.sba.gov*). What different types of financing are available to small firms? Besides financing, what other programs are available to support the growth and development of small businesses?
3. Think of an entrepreneurial firm that has been successfully launched in the last 10 years. What kind of entry strategy did it use—pioneering, imitative, or adaptive? Since the firm's initial entry, how has it used or combined overall low-cost, differentiation, and/or focus strategies?
4. Select an entrepreneurial firm you are familiar with in your local community. Research the company and discuss how it has positioned itself relative to its close competitors. Does it have a unique strategic advantage? Disadvantage? Explain.

Company	Market Commonality	Resource Similarity
E-Loan		
Lending Tree		

Company	Strategic Actions	Tactical Actions
E-Loan		
Lending Tree		

ETHICS QUESTIONS

1. Imitation strategies are based on the idea of copying another firm's idea and using it for your own purposes. Is this unethical or simply a smart business practice? Discuss the ethical implications of this practice (if any).

2. Intense competition such as price wars are an accepted practice in the United States, but cooperation between companies has legal ramifications because of antitrust laws. Should price wars that drive small businesses or new entrants out of business be illegal? What ethical considerations are raised (if any)?

REFERENCES

1. Konrad, A. 2014. Snapchat billionaires protect their stakes by settling with ousted cofounder Reggie Brown. *forbes.com,* September 9: np; Dave, P. 2015. Just getting started? Put it all in writing. *Dallas Morning News,* May 10: 4D; and *statista.com.*

2. *http://web.sba.gov.*

3. Timmons, J. A. & Spinelli, S. 2004. *New venture creation* (6th ed.). New York: McGraw-Hill/Irwin; and Bygrave, W. D. 1997. The entrepreneurial process. In W. D. Bygrave (Ed.), *The portable MBA in entrepreneurship* (2nd ed.). New York: Wiley.

4. Bryant, A. 2012. Want to innovate? Feed a cookie to the monster. *nytimes.com,* March 24: np.

5. Fromartz, S. 1998. How to get your first great idea. *Inc. Magazine,* April 1: 91–94; and Vesper, K. H. 1990. *New venture strategies* (2nd ed.). Englewood Cliffs, NJ: Prentice Hall.

6. For an interesting perspective on the nature of the opportunity recognition process, see Baron, R. A. 2006. Opportunity recognition as pattern recognition: How entrepreneurs "connect the dots" to identify new business opportunities. *Academy of Management Perspectives,* February: 104–119.

7. Gaglio, C. M. 1997. Opportunity identification: Review, critique and suggested research directions. In Katz, J. A. (Ed.), *Advances in entrepreneurship, firm emergence and growth,* vol. 3. Greenwich, CT: JAI Press: 139–202; Lumpkin, G. T., Hills, G. E., & Shrader, R. C. 2004. Opportunity recognition. In Welsch, H. L. (Ed.), *Entrepreneurship: The road ahead:* 73–90. London: Routledge; and Long, W. & McMullan, W. E. 1984. Mapping the new venture opportunity identification process. *Frontiers of entrepreneurship research, 1984:* 567–590. Wellesley, MA: Babson College.

8. For an interesting discussion of different aspects of opportunity discovery, see Shepherd, D. A. & De Tienne, D. R. 2005. Prior knowledge, potential financial reward, and opportunity identification. *Entrepreneurship Theory & Practice,* 29(1): 91–112; and Gaglio, C. M. 2004. The role of mental simulations and counterfactual thinking in the opportunity identification process. *Entrepreneurship Theory & Practice,* 28(6): 533–552.

9. Stewart, T. A. 2002. How to think with your gut. *Business 2.0,* November: 99–104.

10. Anonymous. 2013. How entrepreneurs come up with great ideas. *wsj.com,* April 29: np.

11. Garone, E. 2016. Whose glass is that? A startup has the answer. *wsj.com,* May 1: np.

12. Zaleski, A. 2016. Grapes of math. *fortune.com,* February 1: 28.

13. For more on the opportunity recognition process, see Smith, B. R., Matthews, C. H., & Schenkel, M. T. 2009. Differences in entrepreneurial opportunities: The role of tacitness and codification in opportunity identification. *Journal of Small Business Management,* 47(1): 38–57.

14. Timmons, J. A. 1997. Opportunity recognition. In Bygrave, W. D. (Ed.), *The portable MBA in entrepreneurship* (2nd ed.): 26–54. New York: Wiley.

15. Social networking is also proving to be an increasingly important type of entrepreneurial resource. For an interesting discussion, see Aldrich, H. E. & Kim, P. H. 2007. Small worlds, infinite possibilities? How social networks affect entrepreneurial team formation and search. *Strategic Entrepreneurship Journal,* 1(1): 147–166.

16. Bhide, A. V. 2000. *The origin and evolution of new businesses.* New York: Oxford University Press.

17. Small business 2001: Where are we now? 2001. *Inc.,* May 29: 18–19; and Zacharakis, A. L., Bygrave, W. D., & Shepherd, D. A. 2000. *Global entrepreneurship monitor–National entrepreneurship assessment: United States of America 2000 Executive Report.* Kansas City, MO: Kauffman Center for Entrepreneurial Leadership.

18. Cooper, S. 2003. Cash cows. *Entrepreneur,* June: 36.

19. Seglin, J. L. 1998. What angels want. *Inc.,* 20(7): 43–44.

20. Torres, N. L. 2002. Playing an angel. *Entrepreneur,* May: 130–138.

21. For an interesting discussion of how venture capital practices vary across different sectors of the economy, see Gaba, V. & Meyer, A. D. 2008. Crossing the organizational species barrier: How venture capital practices infiltrated the information technology sector. *Academy of Management Journal,* 51(5): 391–412.

22. Our discussion of crowdfunding draws on Wasik, J. 2012. The brilliance (and madness) of crowdfunding. *Forbes,* June 25: 144–146; Anonymous. 2012. Why crowdfunding may not be path to riches. *Finance.yahoo.com,* October 23: np; and Espinoza, J. 2012. Doing equity crowd funding right. *The Wall Street Journal,* May 21: R3.

23. Stanko, M. & Henard, D. 2016. How crowdfunding influences innovation. *MIT Sloan Management Review,* Spring: 15–17.

24. *crowdexpert.com/crowdfunding-industry-statistics/.*

25. Shchetko, N. 2014. There's no refunding in crowdfunding. *The Wall Street Journal,* November 26: B1, B4.

26. Wasik, J. 2012. The brilliance (and madness) of crowdfunding. *Forbes,* June 25: 144–146; and, Burke, A. 2012. Crowdfunding set to explode with passage of Entrepreneur Access to Capital Act. *forbes.com,* February 29: np.

27. Kroll, M., Walters, B., & Wright, P. 2010. The impact of insider control and environment on post-IPO performance. *Academy of Management Journal,* 53: 693–725.

28. Eisenhardt, K. M. & Schoonhoven, C. B. 1990. Organizational growth: Linking founding team, strategy,

environment, and growth among U.S. semiconductor ventures, 1978–1988. *Administrative Science Quarterly,* 35: 504–529.

29. Anonymous. 2015. There's an app for that. *The Economist,* January 3: 17–20.

30. Dubini, P. & Aldrich, H. 1991. Personal and extended networks are central to the entrepreneurship process. *Journal of Business Venturing,* 6(5): 305–333.

31. For more on the role of social contacts in helping young firms build legitimacy, see Chrisman, J. J. & McMullan, W. E. 2004. Outside assistance as a knowledge resource for new venture survival. *Journal of Small Business Management,* 42(3): 229–244.

32. Vogel, C. 2000. Janina Pawlowski. *Working Woman,* June: 70.

33. For a recent perspective on entrepreneurship and strategic alliances, see Rothaermel, F. T. & Deeds, D. L. 2006. Alliance types, alliance experience and alliance management capability in high-technology ventures. *Journal of Business Venturing,* 21(4): 429–460; and Lu, J. W. & Beamish, P. W. 2006. Partnering strategies and performance of SMEs' international joint ventures. *Journal of Business Venturing,* 21(4): 461–486.

34. Monahan, J. 2005. All systems grow. *Entrepreneur,* March: 78–82; Weaver, K. M. & Dickson, P. 2004. Strategic alliances. In Dennis, W. J., Jr. (Ed.), *NFIB national small business poll.* Washington, DC: National Federation of Independent Business; and Copeland, M. V. & Tilin, A. 2005. Get someone to build it. *Business 2.0,* 6(5): 88.

35. For more information, go to the Small Business Administration website at *www.sba.gov.*

36. Simsek, Z., Heavey, C., & Veiga, J. 2009. The impact of CEO core self-evaluation on entrepreneurial orientation. *Strategic Management Journal,* 31: 110–119.

37. Zhao, H. & Seibert, S. 2006. The big five personality dimensions and entrepreneurial status: A meta-analytic review. *Journal of Applied Psychology,* 91: 259–271.

38. For an interesting study of the role of passion in entrepreneurial success, see Chen, X-P., Yao, X., & Kotha, S. 2009. Entrepreneur passion and preparedness in business plan presentations: A persuasion analysis

of venture capitalists' funding decisions. *Academy of Management Journal,* 52(1): 101–120.

39. Collins, J. 2001. *Good to great.* New York: HarperCollins.

40. The idea of entry wedges was discussed by Vesper, K. 1990. *New venture strategies* (2nd ed.). Englewood Cliffs, NJ: Prentice Hall; and Drucker, P. F. 1985. *Innovation and entrepreneurship.* New York: HarperBusiness.

41. See Dowell, G. & Swaminathan, A. 2006. Entry timing, exploration, and firm survival in the early U.S. bicycle industry. *Strategic Management Journal,* 27: 1159–1182, for a recent study of the timing of entrepreneurial new entry.

42. Dunlap-Hinkler, D., Kotabe, M., & Mudambi, R. 2010. A story of breakthrough vs. incremental innovation: Corporate entrepreneurship in the global pharmaceutical industry. *Strategic Entrepreneurship Journal,* 4: 106–127.

43. Maiello, M. 2002. They almost changed the world. *Forbes,* December 22: 217–220.

44. Pogue, D. 2012. Pay by app: No cash or card needed. *International Herald Tribune,* July 19: 18.

45. Williams, G. 2002. Looks like rain. *Entrepreneur,* September: 104–111.

46. Pedroza, G. M. 2002. Tech tutors. *Entrepreneur,* September: 120.

47. Romanelli, E. 1989. Environments and strategies of organization start-up: Effects on early survival. *Administrative Science Quarterly,* 34(3): 369–387.

48. Wallace, B. 2000. Brothers. *Philadelphia Magazine,* April: 66–75.

49. Buchanan, L. 2003. The innovation factor: A field guide to innovation. *www.forbes.com,* April 21.

50. Kim, W. C. & Mauborgne, R. 2005. *Blue ocean strategy.* Boston: Harvard Business School Press.

51. For more on how unique organizational combinations can contribute to competitive advantages of entrepreneurial firms, see Steffens, P., Davidsson, P., & Fitzsimmons, J. Performance configurations over time: Implications for growth- and profit-oriented strategies. *Entrepreneurship Theory & Practice,* 33(1): 125–148.

52. Smith, K. G., Ferrier, W. J., & Grimm, C. M. 2001. King of the hill: Dethroning the industry leader.

Academy of Management Executive, 15(2): 59–70.

53. Grove, A. 1999. *Only the paranoid survive: How to exploit the crisis points that challenge every company.* New York: Random House.

54. Stalk, G., Jr., & Lachenauer, R. 2004. *Hardball: Are you playing to play or playing to win?* Cambridge, MA: Harvard Business School Press.

55. Chen, M. J., Lin, H. C, & Michel, J. G. 2010. Navigating in a hypercompetitive environment: The roles of action aggressiveness and TMT integration. *Strategic Management Journal,* 31: 1410–1430.

56. Peteraf, M. A. & Bergen, M. A. 2003. Scanning competitive landscapes: A market-based and resource-based framework. *Strategic Management Journal,* 24: 1027–1045.

57. Chen, M. J. 1996. Competitor analysis and interfirm rivalry: Toward a theoretical integration. *Academy of Management Review,* 21(1): 100–134.

58. Chen, 1996, op.cit.

59. Chen, M. J., Su, K. H, & Tsai, W. 2007. Competitive tension: The awareness-motivation-capability perspective. *Academy of Management Journal,* 50(1): 101–118.

60. St. John, W. 1999. Barnes & Noble's epiphany. *www.wired.com,* June.

61. Anonymous. 2010. Is the *Times* ready for a newspaper war? *Bloomberg Businessweek,* April 26: 30–31.

62. Souder, D. & Shaver, J. M. 2010. Constraints and incentives for making long horizon corporate investments. *Strategic Management Journal,* 31: 1316–1336.

63. Chen, M. J. & Hambrick, D. 1995. Speed, stealth, and selective attack: How small firms differ from large firms in competitive behavior. *Academy of Management Journal,* 38: 453–482.

64. Fenner, L. 2009. TOMS Shoes donates one pair of shoes for every pair purchased. *America.gov,* October 19: np.

65. *www.facebook.com/tomsshoes.*

66. For a discussion of how the strategic actions of Apple Computer contribute to changes in the competitive dynamics in both the cellular phone and music industries, see Burgelman, R. A. &

Grove, A. S. 2008. Cross-boundary disruptors: Powerful interindustry entrepreneurial change agents. *Strategic Entrepreneurship Journal,* 1(1): 315–327.

67. Smith, K. G., Ferrier, W. J., & Ndofor, H. 2001. Competitive dynamics research: Critique and future directions. In Hitt, M. A., Freeman, R. E., & Harrison, J. S. (Eds.), *The Blackwell handbook of strategic management:* 315–361. Oxford, UK: Blackwell.

68. Gee, P. 2000. Co-opetition: The new market milieu. *Journal of Healthcare Management,* 45: 359–363.

69. Ketchen, D. J., Snow, C. C., & Hoover, V. L. 2004. Research on competitive dynamics: Recent accomplishments and future challenges. *Journal of Management,* 30(6): 779–804.

70. Fritz, B. 2014. Movie film, at death's door, gets a reprieve. *wsj.com,* July 29: np.

71. Khanna, T., Gulati, R., & Nohria, N. 2000. The economic modeling of strategy process: Clean models and dirty hands. *Strategic Management Journal,* 21: 781–790.

Strategic Control and Corporate Governance

After reading this chapter, you should have a good understanding of the following learning objectives:

LO9-1 The value of effective strategic control systems in strategy implementation.

LO9-2 The key difference between "traditional" and "contemporary" control systems.

LO9-3 The imperative for contemporary control systems in today's complex and rapidly changing competitive and general environments.

LO9-4 The benefits of having the proper balance among the three levers of behavioral control: culture, rewards and incentives, and boundaries.

LO9-5 The three key participants in corporate governance: shareholders, management (led by the CEO), and the board of directors.

LO9-6 The role of corporate governance mechanisms in ensuring that the interests of managers are aligned with those of shareholders from both the United States and international perspectives.

©Anatoli Styf/Shutterstock

LEARNING FROM MISTAKES

Just a few years ago, Tesco was a high-flying global retailer. Throughout the 1990s and early 2000s, Tesco grew to dominate the U.K. retailing market, attaining a 33 percent market share, and successfully expanded into new geographic markets. However, over the last several years, Tesco has faced increasing pressures at home and large struggles outside the U.K. This included a failed entry into the U.S. market and increasing pressure at home from hard-discounting competitors, most notably Lidl and Aldi. In recent years, Tesco has seen its stock price drop by nearly 40 percent, major investors including Warren Buffett bail out, and pressures from investors that forced the ousting of the firm's CEO.

In September 2014, the situation for Tesco got much worse.[1] After an employee alerted the firm's general counsel of accounting irregularities, a full-blown accounting scandal erupted. Senior managers in the U.K. food business had been booking income early and delaying the booking of costs to shore up the financial performance of the firm. The firm was forced to restate its earnings for the first half of 2014, initially to the tune of $408 million, which was later increased to $431 million as the scope of the problem increased. The scandal led to the suspension or dismissal of eight senior executives at Tesco, the suspension of retirement packages for the firm's prior CEO and CFO, and the eventual resignation of the chairman of the board of Tesco. It also triggered an investigation by the U.K.'s accounting watchdog, the Financial Reporting Council, into Tesco's accounting practices for the years 2012, 2013, and 2014.

The scandal has triggered commentators to reassert some long-standing concerns about Tesco's governance and also led them to point out some new concerns. Industry analysts have long been critical of Tesco's board of directors, especially noting that the board lacks retail experience. This likely played a role in the scandal, since the board would have had limited ability to notice the arcane, retail-related accounting practices at the center of the accounting deception. Interestingly, four months before the scandal arose, Tesco's auditor, PricewaterhouseCoopers, warned of the "risk of manipulation" in the accounting of promotional events, the areas that were manipulated, but the board appeared to take no action in its following meeting. The accounting irregularities also arose at a time of limited oversight within the firm. Laurie McIlwee, the firm's chief financial officer, stepped down in April 2014, but her replacement didn't take up the CFO position until December 2014. During that time, Tesco's finances were managed by the CEO's office. Thus, the firm did not have a senior executive whose primary task was to ensure the validity of the firm's financial reporting. Finally, the most senior leadership of the firm was distracted by other tasks. The firm's prior CEO was dismissed in July, and the new CEO took the reins in August 2014. Thus, Dave Lewis, the new CEO, was focusing on learning the business and the firm's operations just as the scandal broke.

The scandal has been quite damaging to the firm, with Tesco's already battered stock price plunging an additional 28 percent during the period the scandal unfolded.

Discussion Questions

1. What changes should Tesco make to avoid future similar scandals?
2. To what degree do you think the scandal at Tesco was related to how the firm had been performing?

strategic control
the process of monitoring and correcting a firm's strategy and performance.

We first explore two central aspects of **strategic control:**[2] (1) *informational control,* which is the ability to respond effectively to environmental change, and (2) *behavioral control,* which is the appropriate balance and alignment among a firm's culture, rewards, and boundaries. In the final section of this chapter, we focus on strategic control from a much broader perspective—what is referred to as *corporate governance.*[3] Here, we direct our attention to the need for a firm's shareholders (the owners) and their elected representatives (the board of directors) to ensure that the firm's executives (the management team) strive to fulfill their fiduciary duty of maximizing long-term shareholder value. As we just saw in the Tesco example, poor governance and control can lead to damaging scandals in firms.

LO 9-1

The value of effective strategic control systems in strategy implementation.

ENSURING INFORMATIONAL CONTROL: RESPONDING EFFECTIVELY TO ENVIRONMENTAL CHANGE

We discuss two broad types of control systems: "traditional" and "contemporary." As both general and competitive environments become more unpredictable and complex, the need for contemporary systems increases.

A Traditional Approach to Strategic Control

traditional approach to strategic control
a sequential method of organizational control in which (1) strategies are formulated and top management sets goals, (2) strategies are implemented, and (3) performance is measured against the predetermined goal set.

The **traditional approach to strategic control** is sequential: (1) strategies are formulated and top management sets goals, (2) strategies are implemented, and (3) performance is measured against the predetermined goal set, as illustrated in Exhibit 9.1.

Control is based on a feedback loop from performance measurement to strategy formulation. This process typically involves lengthy time lags, often tied to a firm's annual planning cycle. Such traditional control systems, termed "single-loop" learning by Harvard's Chris Argyris, simply compare actual performance to a predetermined goal.[4] They are most appropriate when the environment is stable and relatively simple, goals and objectives can be measured with a high level of certainty, and there is little need for complex measures of performance. Sales quotas, operating budgets, production schedules, and similar quantitative control mechanisms are typical. The appropriateness of the business strategy or standards of performance is seldom questioned.[5]

James Brian Quinn of Dartmouth College has argued that grand designs with precise and carefully integrated plans seldom work.[6] Rather, most strategic change proceeds incrementally—one step at a time. Leaders should introduce some sense of direction, some logic in incremental steps.[7] Similarly, McGill University's Henry Mintzberg has written about leaders "crafting" a strategy.[8] Drawing on the parallel between the potter at her wheel and the strategist, Mintzberg pointed out that the potter begins work with some general idea of the artifact she wishes to create, but the details of design—even possibilities for a different design—emerge as the work progresses. For businesses facing complex and turbulent business environments, the craftsperson's method helps us deal with the uncertainty about how a design will work out in practice and allows for a creative element.

Mintzberg's argument, like Quinn's, questions the value of rigid planning and goal-setting processes. Fixed strategic goals also become dysfunctional for firms competing in highly unpredictable competitive environments. Strategies need to change frequently and opportunistically. An inflexible commitment to predetermined goals and milestones can prevent the very adaptability that is required of a good strategy.

LO 9-2

The key difference between "traditional" and "contemporary" control systems.

LO 9-3

The imperative for contemporary control systems in today's complex and rapidly changing competitive and general environments.

EXHIBIT 9.1 Traditional Approach to Strategic Control

Formulate strategies → Implement strategies → Strategic control

A Contemporary Approach to Strategic Control

Adapting to and anticipating both internal and external environmental change is an integral part of strategic control. The relationships between strategy formulation, implementation, and control are highly interactive, as suggested by Exhibit 9.2. The exhibit also illustrates two different types of strategic control: informational control and behavioral control. **Informational control** is primarily concerned with whether or not the organization is "doing the right things." **Behavioral control,** on the other hand, asks if the organization is "doing things right" in the implementation of its strategy. Both the informational and behavioral components of strategic control are necessary, but not sufficient, conditions for success. What good is a well-conceived strategy that cannot be implemented? Or what use is an energetic and committed workforce if it is focused on the wrong strategic target?

Informational control deals with the internal environment as well as the external strategic context. It addresses the assumptions and premises that provide the foundation for an organization's strategy. Do the organization's goals and strategies still "fit" within the context of the current strategic environment? Depending on the type of business, such assumptions may relate to changes in technology, customer tastes, government regulation, and industry competition.

This involves two key issues. First, managers must scan and monitor the external environment, as we discussed in Chapter 2. Also, conditions can change in the internal environment of the firm, as we discussed in Chapter 3, requiring changes in the strategic direction of the firm. These may include, for example, the resignation of key executives or delays in the completion of major production facilities.

In the contemporary approach, information control is part of an ongoing process of organizational learning that continuously updates and challenges the assumptions that underlie the organization's strategy. In such double-loop learning, the organization's assumptions, premises, goals, and strategies are continuously monitored, tested, and reviewed. The benefits of continuous monitoring are evident—time lags are dramatically shortened, changes in the competitive environment are detected earlier, and the organization's ability to respond with speed and flexibility is enhanced.

Contemporary control systems must have four characteristics to be effective:[9]

1. The focus is on constantly changing information that has potential strategic importance.
2. The information is important enough to demand frequent and regular attention from all levels of the organization.
3. The data and information generated are best interpreted and discussed in face-to-face meetings.
4. The control system is a key catalyst for an ongoing debate about underlying data, assumptions, and action plans.

An executive's decision to use the control system interactively—in other words, to invest the time and attention to review and evaluate new information—sends a clear signal to the organization about what is important. The dialogue and debate that emerge from such an interactive process can often lead to new strategies and innovations.

informational control
a method of organizational control in which a firm gathers and analyzes information from the internal and external environment in order to obtain the best fit between the organization's goals and strategies and the strategic environment.

behavioral control
a method of organizational control in which a firm influences the actions of employees through culture, rewards, and boundaries.

EXHIBIT 9.2 Contemporary Approach to Strategic Control

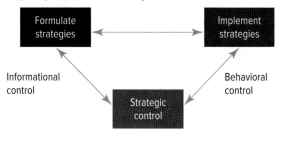

LO 9-4

The benefits of having the proper balance among the three levers of behavioral control: culture, rewards and incentives, and boundaries.

ATTAINING BEHAVIORAL CONTROL: BALANCING CULTURE, REWARDS, AND BOUNDARIES

Behavioral control is focused on implementation—doing things right. Effectively implementing strategy requires manipulating three key control "levers": culture, rewards, and boundaries (see Exhibit 9.3). There are two compelling reasons for an increased emphasis on culture and rewards in a system of behavioral controls.[10]

First, the competitive environment is increasingly complex and unpredictable, demanding both flexibility and quick response to its challenges. As firms simultaneously downsize and face the need for increased coordination across organizational boundaries, a control system based primarily on rigid strategies, rules, and regulations is dysfunctional. The use of rewards and culture to align individual and organizational goals becomes increasingly important.

Second, the implicit long-term contract between the organization and its key employees has been eroded.[11] Today's younger managers have been conditioned to see themselves as "free agents" and view a career as a series of opportunistic challenges. As managers are advised to "specialize, market yourself, and have work, if not a job," the importance of culture and rewards in building organizational loyalty claims greater importance.

Each of the three levers—culture, rewards, and boundaries—must work in a balanced and consistent manner. Let's consider the role of each.

Building a Strong and Effective Culture

organizational culture

a system of shared values and beliefs that shape a company's people, organizational structures, and control systems to produce behavioral norms.

Organizational culture is a system of shared values (what is important) and beliefs (how things work) that shape a company's people, organizational structures, and control systems to produce behavioral norms (the way we do things around here).[12] How important is culture? Very.

Collins and Porras argued in *Built to Last* that the key factor in sustained exceptional performance is a cultlike culture.[13] You can't touch it or write it down, but it's there in every organization; its influence is pervasive; it can work for you or against you.[14] Effective leaders understand its importance and strive to shape and use it as one of their important levers of strategic control.[15]

The Role of Culture   Culture wears many different hats, each woven from the fabric of those values that sustain the organization's primary source of competitive advantage. Some examples are:

- Zappos and Amazon focus on customer service.
- Lexus (a division of Toyota) and Apple emphasize product quality.
- Google and 3M place a high value on innovation.
- Nucor (steel) and Walmart are concerned, above all, with operational efficiency.

EXHIBIT 9.3 Essential Elements of Behavioral Control

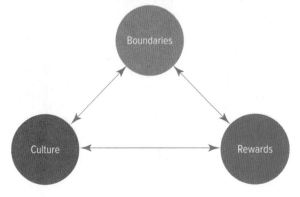

Culture sets implicit boundaries—unwritten standards of acceptable behavior—in dress, ethical matters, and the way an organization conducts its business.[16] By creating a framework of shared values, culture encourages individual identification with the organization and its objectives. Culture acts as a means of reducing monitoring costs.[17]

Strong culture can lead to greater employee engagement and provide a common purpose and identity. Firms have typically relied on economic incentives for workers, using a combination of rewards (carrots) and rules and threats (sticks) to get employees to act in desired ways. But these systems rely on the assumption that individuals are fundamentally self-interested and selfish. However, research suggests that this assumption is overstated.[18] When given a chance to act selfishly or cooperatively with others, over half of employees choose to cooperate, while only 30 percent consistently choose to act selfishly. Thus, cultural systems that build engagement, communication, and a sense of common purpose and identity would allow firms to leverage these collaborative workers.

Sustaining an Effective Culture　Powerful organizational cultures just don't happen overnight, and they don't remain in place without a strong commitment—in terms of both words and deeds—by leaders throughout the organization.[19] A viable and productive organizational culture can be strengthened and sustained. However, it cannot be "built" or "assembled"; instead, it must be cultivated, encouraged, and "fertilized."[20]

Storytelling is one way effective cultures are maintained. 3M is a company that uses powerful stories to reinforce the culture of the firm. One of those is the story of Francis G. Okie.[21] In 1922 Okie came up with the idea of selling sandpaper to men as a replacement for razor blades. The idea obviously didn't pan out, but Okie was allowed to remain at 3M. Interestingly, the technology developed by Okie led 3M to develop its first blockbuster product: a waterproof sandpaper that became a staple of the automobile industry. Such stories foster the importance of risk taking, experimentation, freedom to fail, and innovation—all vital elements of 3M's culture. Strategy Spotlight 9.1 discusses the power of pictures and stories in building a customer-centric culture.

The actions of leaders and culture warriors can also play a critical role in reinforcing a firm's culture.[22] For example, the culture team at Warby Parker, an online eyewear retailer, is responsible for planning company outings and themed luncheons that reinforce company ideals and build a stronger sense of connectedness among workers. The culture team is also involved in screening potential new employees to ensure the firm's culture lives on as it grows. Corporate leaders can actively reinforce culture throughout the organization. Brent Beshore, CEO of adventur.es, a private investment firm, describes how he reinforces culture with personal contact:

> I make a point of walking around the office every day and thanking people for their contributions.
> It could be something as small as, "I really appreciated the email announcement you crafted,"
> or something more substantive like, "Thanks for handling that tough situation a few days ago."
> Thanking them reminds them to thank others and be appreciative of what we have.

Motivating with Rewards and Incentives

Reward and incentive systems represent a powerful means of influencing an organization's culture, focusing efforts on high-priority tasks, and motivating individual and collective task performance.[23] Just as culture deals with influencing beliefs, behaviors, and attitudes of people within an organization, the **reward system**—by specifying who gets rewarded and why—is an effective motivator and control mechanism.[24] The managers at Not Your Average Joe's, a Massachusetts-based restaurant chain, changed their staffing procedures both to let their servers better understand their performance and to better motivate them.[25] The chain uses sophisticated software to track server performance—in both per customer sales and customer satisfaction as seen in tips. Highly rated servers are given more tables and preferred schedules. In shifting more work and better schedules to the best workers, the chain hopes to improve profitability and motivate all workers.

reward system
policies that specify who gets rewarded and why.

USING PICTURES AND STORIES TO BUILD A CUSTOMER-ORIENTED CULTURE

Most firms tout that customers are their most important stakeholders. In firms that have value statements, these statements typically list the firms' responsibilities to their customers first. But it is hard to build and maintain a customer-centric culture. Using visual imagery and stories can help firms put customers at the center of their culture.

The old saying is that "a picture is worth a thousand words." This is certainly true when building a culture. A simple snapshot of a customer or end user can be a powerful motivating tool for workers to care about that customer. For example, radiologists rarely see patients. They look at X-rays from the files of patients, but these patients are typically faceless and anonymous to them. However, when pictures of the patients were added to their files, one study found that radiologists increased the length of their reports on the patients' X-rays by 29 percent and improved the accuracy of their diagnoses by 46 percent. Other firms have found the same effect. Microfinance provider Kiva includes pictures of the entrepreneurs whom it is trying to fund, believing that potential donors feel more of a connection with an entrepreneur when they have seen a picture of him or her.

Stories can also help build a customer-centric culture. Inside the firm, the stories that employees share with each other become imprinted on the organizational mind. Thus, as employees share their positive stories of experiences with customers, they not only provide encouragement for other employees to better meet the needs of customers but also reinforce the storytelling employee's desire to work hard to serve customers. For example, at Ritz-Carlton hotels, employees meet each day for 15 minutes to share stories about how they went the extra yard to meet customers' needs. These stories can even be more significant for new employees, helping them learn about the values of the firm. With outside stories, firms can draw on the accounts of customers to reinvigorate their employees. These can be based on personal statements from customers or even from news stories. To test these effects, one researcher gave lifeguards a few short news stories about swimmers who were saved by lifeguards on other beaches. The lifeguards who heard these stories reported that they found their job more meaningful, volunteered to work more hours, and were rated by their supervisors as being more vigilant in their work one month later.

Managers can help ensure that the stories told support the firm's customer-centric culture by taking the following steps:

- Tell positive stories about employees' interactions with customers.
- Share positive customer feedback with employees.
- Tie employee recognition to positive employee actions.
- Weave stories into the employee handbook and new employee orientation.
- Make sure that mentors in the firm know about the importance of using stories in their mentoring efforts.

The "short story" here is that firms can help build and reinforce a customer-centric culture if they just keep the customer in the center of the stories they tell and make the customer personally relevant to workers.

Sources: Grant, A. 2011. How customers rally your troops. *Harvard Business Review,* 89(6): 96–103; and Heathfield, S. 2014. How stories strengthen your work culture–or not. *humanresources.about.com,* December 29: np.

The Potential Downside   While they can be powerful motivators, reward and incentive policies can also result in undesirable outcomes in organizations. At the individual level, incentives can go wrong for multiple reasons. First, if individual workers don't see how their actions relate to how they are compensated, incentives can be demotivating. For example, if the rewards are related to the firm's stock price, workers may feel that their efforts have little if any impact and won't perceive any benefit from working harder. On the other hand, if the incentives are too closely tied to their individual work, they may lead to dysfunctional outcomes. For example, if a sales representative is rewarded for sales volume, she will be incentivized to sell at all costs. This may lead her to accept unprofitable sales or push sales through distribution channels the firm would rather avoid. Thus, the collective sum of individual behaviors of an organization's employees does not always result in what is best for the organization; individual rationality is no guarantee of organizational rationality.

Reward and incentive systems can also cause problems across organizational units. As corporations grow and evolve, they often develop different business units with multiple reward systems. These systems may differ based on industry contexts, business situations, stage of product life cycles, and so on. Subcultures within organizations may reflect differences among functional areas, products, services, and divisions. To the extent that reward systems reinforce such behavioral norms, attitudes, and belief systems, cohesiveness is reduced; important information is hoarded rather than shared, individuals begin working at cross-purposes, and they lose sight of overall goals.

Such conflicts are commonplace in many organizations. For example, sales and marketing personnel promise unrealistically quick delivery times to bring in business, much to the dismay of operations and logistics; overengineering by R&D creates headaches for manufacturing; and so on. Conflicts also arise across divisions when divisional profits become a key compensation criterion. As ill will and anger escalate, personal relationships and performance may suffer.

Creating Effective Reward and Incentive Programs   To be effective, incentive and reward systems need to reinforce basic core values, enhance cohesion and commitment to goals and objectives, and meet with the organization's overall mission and purpose.[26] For example, Chesapeake Energy set a goal to improve workplace safety. To reinforce this, one year, it gave out over $8 million in "safety bonuses" to over 6,000 employees for following safe work practices.[27]

Effective reward and incentive systems share a number of common characteristics[28] (see Exhibit 9.4). The perception that a plan is "fair and equitable" is critically important. The firm must have the flexibility to respond to changing requirements as its direction and objectives change. In recent years many companies have begun to place more emphasis on growth. To ensure that managers focus on growth, a number of firms have changed their compensation systems to move from a bottom-line focus to one that emphasizes growth, new products, acquisitions, and international expansion.

However, incentive and reward systems don't have to be all about money. Employees respond not only to monetary compensation but also to softer forms of incentives and rewards. In fact, a number of studies have found that for employees who are satisfied with their base salary, nonfinancial motivators are more effective than cash incentives in building long-term employee motivation.[29] Three key reward systems appear to provide the greatest incentives. First, employees respond to managerial praise. This can include formal recognition policies and events. For example, at Mars Central Europe, the company holds an event twice a year at which they celebrate innovative ideas generated by employees. Recognition at the Mars "Make a Difference" event is designed to motivate the winners and also other employees who want to receive the same recognition. Employees also respond well to informal recognition rewards, such as personal praise, written praise, and public praise. This is especially effective when it includes small perks, such as a gift certificate for dinner, some scheduling flexibility, or even an extra day off. Positive words and actions are especially powerful since almost two-thirds of employees in one study said management was much more likely to criticize them for poor performance than praise them for good work. Second, employees feel rewarded when they receive attention from leaders and, as a result, feel valued and involved. One survey found that the number-one factor employees valued was "managerial support and involvement"—having their managers ask for their opinions, involve them in decisions, and give them authority to complete tasks. Third, managers can reward employees by giving them opportunities to lead projects or task forces. In sum, incentives and rewards can go well beyond simple pay to include formal recognition, praise, and the self-esteem that comes from feeling valued.

The Insights from Research box provides further evidence that employees are motivated more when they feel a sense of purpose in their work and feel valued by their employers than when they are only monetarily rewarded for their work.

• Objectives are clear, well understood, and broadly accepted.
• Rewards are clearly linked to performance and desired behaviors.
• Performance measures are clear and highly visible.
• Feedback is prompt, clear, and unambiguous.
• The compensation "system" is perceived as fair and equitable.
• The structure is flexible; it can adapt to changing circumstances.

EXHIBIT 9.4

Characteristics of Effective Reward and Incentive Systems

INSPIRE PASSION—MOTIVATE TOP PERFORMANCE

Overview

Often, managers approach and strive to motivate employees with extrinsic rewards. These produce some results; however, employees tend to perform best when their intrinsic needs are met. Think of ways to highlight the purpose of your employees' work. Allow employees to work on projects that ignite their passions.

What The Research Shows

Employees who are passionate about their jobs are more engaged in their jobs. And employees who are more engaged in their jobs perform them better, according to investigators from the University of Richmond, Nanyang Technological University, and Keppel Offshore and Marine Ltd. in Singapore. Their research, published in the *Journal of Management Studies,* utilized the performance appraisals of 509 headquarters employees of a large insurance company. The employees were given a survey to identify their attitudes toward their jobs. Using structural equations modeling, the researchers found a relationship between the employees' passion for their jobs and their performance of their jobs. However, the effect was significant only when mediated by the employees' absorption in their jobs.

Employees who had job passion identified with their jobs intrinsically and believed their work was meaningful. Therefore, they were able to feel passionate about their jobs while balancing that passion with other aspects of their lives that were also important to them. This resulted in an intensity of focus on and deep immersion in their tasks while they were working. When they were deeply engrossed in work, the employees were not distracted by other activities or roles in their lives. In turn, this job absorption resulted in superior performance on the job.

Why This Matters

While many managers attempt to tap into their employees' passions to motivate them to perform their jobs, external incentives are not the best way to engender internal identification with work. Even positive feedback can become an external incentive if employees work toward receiving that recognition rather than working simply because they identify with and enjoy their jobs. A better way to nurture employees' identification with their work is to provide them with a sense of ownership of their work and, more importantly, to help them see how meaningful their jobs are. For example, to help their employees see the impact of their work on others, Cancer Treatment Centers of America in the Tulsa, Oklahoma, area recruits spouses of employees to form and run a nonprofit organization to raise money for cancer patients' nonmedical expenses.

Kevin Cleary, CEO of Clif Bar and Co., says success is contingent upon an "engaged, inspired and outrageously committed team." He breaks this down into these steps:

1. Engage your employees with the company's mission and vision. If you don't have a mission and vision statement, get employees' contributions to create one you believe in.

2. Once people understand the mission and vision, trust your employees to work. Do not micromanage or assume they need a held hand.

3. Have a business model in which people come first, second, and third.

Cleary says exceptional talent is valuable only when employees believe in the organization's mission.

Key Takeaways

- Employees who are passionate about their jobs will be more engaged and absorbed in them and will perform better.

- When employees like their jobs and view them as important, they will be more passionate about their work.

- Employees whose jobs are significant to their personal identities—relative to the other roles they play in their lives—will be more passionate about their jobs.

- When employees are passionate about their jobs, they become deeply engrossed in their job tasks and aren't easily distracted by other activities.

- Although job passion must be voluntary and driven by employees' internal identities, managers can encourage it by helping employees see the significance of their work.

Apply This Today

Managers can fuel employees' intrinsic motivation by helping them see the meaning in their tasks, the company, and its mission. If employees can find personal meaning and passion in their jobs, the company will be rewarded with significant improvements in performance. To learn more about motivating your employees, visit *businessminded.com.*

RESEARCH REVIEWED

Ho, V. T., Wong, S. S., & Lee, C. H. 2011. A tale of passion: Linking job passion and cognitive engagement to employee work performance. *Journal of Management Studies,* 48(1): 26–47.

Setting Boundaries and Constraints

In an ideal world, a strong culture and effective rewards should be sufficient to ensure that all individuals and subunits work toward the common goals and objectives of the whole organization.[30] However, this is not usually the case. Counterproductive behavior can arise because of motivated self-interest, lack of a clear understanding of goals and objectives, or outright malfeasance. **Boundaries and constraints** can serve many useful purposes for organizations, including:

- Focusing individual efforts on strategic priorities.
- Providing short-term objectives and action plans to channel efforts.
- Improving efficiency and effectiveness.
- Minimizing improper and unethical conduct.

boundaries and constraints
rules that specify behaviors that are acceptable and unacceptable.

Focusing Efforts on Strategic Priorities   Boundaries and constraints play a valuable role in focusing a company's strategic priorities. For example, in 2015, GE sold off its financial services businesses in order to refocus on its manufacturing businesses. Similarly, Pfizer sold its infant formula business as it refocused its attention on core pharmaceutical products.[31] This concentration of effort and resources provides the firm with greater strategic focus and the potential for stronger competitive advantages in the remaining areas.

Steve Jobs would use whiteboards to set priorities and focus attention at Apple. For example, he would take his "top 100" people on a retreat each year. One year, he asked the group what 10 things Apple should do next. The group identified ideas. Ideas went up on the board and then got erased or revised; new ones were added, revised, and erased. The group argued about it for a while and finally identified their list of top 10 initiatives. Jobs proceeded to slash the bottom seven, stating, "We can only do three."[32]

Boundaries also have a place in the nonprofit sector. For example, a British relief organization uses a system to monitor strategic boundaries by maintaining a list of companies whose contributions it will neither solicit nor accept. Such boundaries are essential for maintaining legitimacy with existing and potential benefactors.

Providing Short-Term Objectives and Action Plans   In Chapter 1 we discussed the importance of a firm having a vision, mission, and strategic objectives that are internally consistent and that provide strategic direction. In addition, short-term objectives and action plans provide similar benefits. That is, they represent boundaries that help to allocate resources in an optimal manner and to channel the efforts of employees at all levels throughout the organization.[33] To be effective, short-term objectives must have several attributes. They should:

- Be specific and measurable.
- Include a specific time horizon for their attainment.
- Be achievable, yet challenging enough to motivate managers who must strive to accomplish them.

Research has found that performance is enhanced when individuals are encouraged to attain specific, difficult, yet achievable, goals (as opposed to vague "do your best" goals).[34]

Short-term objectives must provide proper direction and also provide enough flexibility for the firm to keep pace with and anticipate changes in the external environment, new government regulations, a competitor introducing a substitute product, or changes in consumer taste. Unexpected events within a firm may require a firm to make important adjustments in both strategic and short-term objectives. The emergence of new industries can have a drastic effect on the demand for products and services in more traditional industries.

Action plans are critical to the implementation of chosen strategies. Unless action plans are specific, there may be little assurance that managers have thought through all of the resource requirements for implementing their strategies. In addition, unless plans are specific, managers may not understand what needs to be implemented or have a clear time frame for completion.

This is essential for the scheduling of key activities that must be implemented. Finally, individual managers must be held accountable for the implementation. This helps to provide the necessary motivation and "sense of ownership" to implement action plans on a timely basis.

Improving Operational Efficiency and Effectiveness   Rule-based controls are most appropriate in organizations with the following characteristics:

- Environments are stable and predictable.
- Employees are largely unskilled and interchangeable.
- Consistency in product and service is critical.
- The risk of malfeasance is extremely high (e.g., in banking or casino operations).[35]

McDonald's Corp. has extensive rules and regulations that regulate the operation of its franchises.[36] Its policy manual from a number of years ago stated, "Cooks must turn, never flip, hamburgers. If they haven't been purchased, Big Macs must be discarded in 10 minutes after being cooked and French fries in 7 minutes. Cashiers must make eye contact with and smile at every customer."

Guidelines can also be effective in setting spending limits and the range of discretion for employees and managers, such as the $2,500 limit that hotelier Ritz-Carlton uses to empower employees to placate dissatisfied customers.

Minimizing Improper and Unethical Conduct   Guidelines can be useful in specifying proper relationships with a company's customers and suppliers.[37] Many companies have explicit rules regarding commercial practices, including the prohibition of any form of payment, bribe, or kickback. For example, Singapore Airlines has a 17-page policy outlining its anticorruption and antibribery policies.[38]

Behavioral Control in Organizations: Situational Factors

Here, the focus is on ensuring that the behavior of individuals at all levels of an organization is directed toward achieving organizational goals and objectives. The three fundamental types of control are culture, rewards and incentives, and boundaries and constraints. An organization may pursue one or a combination of them on the basis of a variety of internal and external factors.

Not all organizations place the same emphasis on each type of control.[39] In high-technology firms engaged in basic research, members may work under high levels of autonomy. An individual's performance is generally quite difficult to measure accurately because of the long lead times involved in R&D activities. Thus, internalized norms and values become very important.

When the measurement of an individual's output or performance is quite straightforward, control depends primarily on granting or withholding rewards. Frequently, a sales manager's compensation is in the form of a commission and bonus tied directly to his or her sales volume, which is relatively easy to determine. Here, behavior is influenced more strongly by the attractiveness of the compensation than by the norms and values implicit in the organization's culture. The measurability of output precludes the need for an elaborate system of rules to control behavior.[40]

Control in bureaucratic organizations is dependent on members following a highly formalized set of rules and regulations. Most activities are routine, and the desired behavior can be specified in a detailed manner because there is generally little need for innovative or creative activity. Managing an assembly plant requires strict adherence to many rules as well as exacting sequences of assembly operations. In the public sector, the Department of Motor Vehicles in most states must follow clearly prescribed procedures when issuing or renewing driver licenses. Strategy Spotlight 9.2 highlights how Digital Reasoning is using data analytics to strengthen control in major financial firms.

Exhibit 9.5 provides alternative approaches to behavioral control and some of the situational factors associated with them.

USING DATA ANALYTICS TO ENHANCE ORGANIZATIONAL CONTROL

Tim Estes's goal was to develop cognitive computing as a useful business tool. Cognitive computing strives to integrate raw computing power with natural-language processing and pattern recognition to build powerful computer systems that mimic human problem solving and learning. He first found a ready home for his vision in national security. The U.S. Army's Ground Intelligence Center contracted with Digital Reasoning to develop systems to identify potential terrorists on the basis of analyses of large volumes of different sources of data, including emails, travel information, and other data.

More recently, Digital Reasoning has taken its expertise to the financial services industry and, in doing so, is providing a new type of control system to catch potential rogue traders and market manipulators within the firms. Digital Reasoning provides systems Estes refers to as "proactive compliance" to a number of major financial services providers, including Credit Suisse and Goldman Sachs. Digital Reasoning has developed software that looks for information in and patterns across billions of emails, instant messages, media reports, and memos that suggest an employee's intention to engage in illegal or prohibited behavior before the employee crosses the line. Rather than looking for evidence of actions already taken, Digital Reasoning's software looks into ongoing patterns of correspondence to search for evolving personal relationships within the company, putting up red flags when it sees unexpected patterns, such as people in different units of the firm suddenly communicating with unusual frequency or a heightened level of discussion on topics that may be tied to unethical or illegal behavior. Any unusual patterns are then investigated by analysts in each of the financial services' firms. The goal for the firms is to both control employee behavior to stay on the right side of the law and also to send signals to customers and regulators that they are taking steps to stay on the right side of legal and ethical boundaries.

Sources: McGee, J. 2014. When crisis strikes, Digital Reasoning takes action. *tennessean.com*, October 9: np; McGee, J. 2014. Digital reasoning gains $24M from Goldman, Credit Suisse. *tennessean.com*, October 9: np; and Dillow, C. 2014. Nothing to hide, everything to fear. *Fortune*, September 1: 45–48.

Evolving from Boundaries to Rewards and Culture

In most environments, organizations should strive to provide a system of rewards and incentives, coupled with a culture strong enough that boundaries become internalized. This reduces the need for external controls such as rules and regulations.

First, hire the right people—individuals who already identify with the organization's dominant values and have attributes consistent with them. Kroger, a supermarket chain, uses a preemployment test to assess the degree to which potential employees will be friendly and communicate well with customers.[41] Microsoft's David Pritchard is well aware of the consequences of failing to hire properly:

> If I hire a bunch of bozos, it will hurt us, because it takes time to get rid of them. They start infiltrating the organization and then they themselves start hiring people of lower quality. At Microsoft, we are always looking for people who are better than we are.

EXHIBIT 9.5 Organizational Control: Alternative Approaches

Approach	Some Situational Factors
Culture: A system of unwritten rules that forms an internalized influence over behavior.	<ul><li>Often found in professional organizations.</li><li>Associated with high autonomy.</li><li>Norms are the basis for behavior.</li></ul>
Rules: Written and explicit guidelines that provide external constraints on behavior.	<ul><li>Associated with standardized output.</li><li>Most appropriate when tasks are generally repetitive and routine.</li><li>Little need for innovation or creative activity.</li></ul>
Rewards: The use of performance-based incentive systems to motivate.	<ul><li>Measurement of output and performance is rather straightforward.</li><li>Most appropriate in organizations pursuing unrelated diversification strategies.</li><li>Rewards may be used to reinforce other means of control.</li></ul>

Second, training plays a key role. For example, in elite military units such as the Green Berets and Navy SEALs, the training regimen so thoroughly internalizes the culture that individuals, in effect, lose their identity. The group becomes the overriding concern and focal point of their energies.

Third, managerial role models are vital. Andy Grove, former CEO and cofounder of Intel, didn't need (or want) a large number of bureaucratic rules to determine who is responsible for what, who is supposed to talk to whom, and who gets to fly first class (no one does). He encouraged openness by not having many of the trappings of success—he worked in a cubicle like all the other professionals. Can you imagine any new manager asking whether or not he can fly first class? Grove's personal example eliminated such a need.

Fourth, reward systems must be clearly aligned with the organizational goals and objectives. For example, as part of its efforts to drive sustainability efforts down through its suppliers, Marks and Spencer pushes the suppliers to develop employee reward systems that support a living wage and team collaboration.

LO 9-5

The three key participants in corporate governance: shareholders, management (led by the CEO), and the board of directors.

corporate governance
the relationship among various participants in determining the direction and performance of corporations. The primary participants are (1) the shareholders, (2) the management, and (3) the board of directors.

THE ROLE OF CORPORATE GOVERNANCE

We now address the issue of strategic control in a broader perspective, typically referred to as "corporate governance." Here we focus on the need for both shareholders (the owners of the corporation) and their elected representatives, the board of directors, to actively ensure that management fulfills its overriding purpose of increasing long-term shareholder value.[42]

Robert Monks and Nell Minow, two leading scholars in **corporate governance,** define it as "the relationship among various participants in determining the direction and performance of corporations. The primary participants are (1) the shareholders, (2) the management (led by the CEO), and (3) the board of directors."* Our discussion will center on how corporations can succeed (or fail) in aligning managerial motives with the interests of the shareholders and their elected representatives, the board of directors.[43] As you will recall from Chapter 1, we discussed the important role of boards of directors and provided some examples of effective and ineffective boards.[44]

Good corporate governance plays an important role in the investment decisions of major institutions, and a premium is often reflected in the price of securities of companies that practice it. The corporate governance premium is larger for firms in countries with sound corporate governance practices compared to countries with weaker corporate governance standards.[45]

Sound governance practices often lead to superior financial performance. However, this is not always the case. For example, practices such as independent directors (directors who are not part of the firm's management) and stock options are generally assumed to result in better performance. But in many cases, independent directors may not have the necessary expertise or involvement, and the granting of stock options to the CEO may lead to decisions and actions calculated to prop up share price only in the short term.

At the same time, few topics in the business press are generating as much interest (and disdain!) as corporate governance.

Some recent notable examples of flawed corporate governance include:[46]

- In 2016, John Stumpf, CEO of Wells Fargo, was forced to resign after both stakeholder and government scrutiny of the firm's practices. Firm management had instituted very aggressive sales goals for employees, leading employees to create sham accounts using the names and money of the bank's real customers.[47]

---

* Management cannot ignore the demands of other important firm stakeholders such as creditors, suppliers, customers, employees, and government regulators. At times of financial duress, powerful creditors can exert strong and legitimate pressures on managerial decisions. In general, however, the attention to stakeholders other than the owners of the corporation must be addressed in a manner that is still consistent with maximizing long-term shareholder returns. For a seminal discussion on stakeholder management, refer to Freeman, R. E. 1984. *Strategic Management: A Stakeholder Approach.* Boston: Pitman.

- In 2014, three senior executives at Walmart resigned from the firm in the wake of accusations of bribery of government officials in Mexico. In response, Walmart changed both the leadership in this region and its compliance structure.[48]
- In 2012 Japanese camera and medical equipment maker Olympus Corporation and three of its former executives pleaded guilty to charges that they falsified accounting records over a five-year period to inflate the financial performance of the firm. The total value of the accounting irregularities came to $1.7 billion.[49]

Because of the many lapses in corporate governance, we can see the benefits associated with effective practices.[50] However, corporate managers may behave in their own self-interest, often to the detriment of shareholders. Next we address the implications of the separation of ownership and management in the modern corporation, and some mechanisms that can be used to ensure consistency (or alignment) between the interests of shareholders and those of the managers to minimize potential conflicts.

The Modern Corporation: The Separation of Owners (Shareholders) and Management

Some of the proposed definitions for a *corporation* include:

- "The business corporation is an instrument through which capital is assembled for the activities of producing and distributing goods and services and making investments. Accordingly, a basic premise of corporation law is that a business corporation should have as its objective the conduct of such activities with a view to enhancing the corporation's profit and the gains of the corporation's owners, that is, the shareholders." (Melvin Aron Eisenberg, *The Structure of Corporation Law*)
- "An association of individuals, created by law or under authority of law, having a continuous existence independent of the existences of its members, and powers and liabilities distinct from those of its member." (*dictionary.com*)
- "An ingenious device for obtaining individual profit without individual responsibility." (Ambrose Bierce, *The Devil's Dictionary*)[51]

All of these definitions have some validity and each one reflects a key feature of the corporate form of business organization—its ability to draw resources from a variety of groups and establish and maintain its own persona that is separate from all of them. As Henry Ford once said, "A great business is really too big to be human."

Simply put, a **corporation** is a mechanism created to allow different parties to contribute capital, expertise, and labor for the maximum benefit of each party.[52] The shareholders (investors) are able to participate in the profits of the enterprise without taking direct responsibility for the operations. The management can run the company without the responsibility of personally providing the funds. The shareholders have limited liability as well as rather limited involvement in the company's affairs. However, they reserve the right to elect directors who have the fiduciary obligation to protect their interests.

corporation
a mechanism created to allow different parties to contribute capital, expertise, and labor for the maximum benefit of each party.

Over 80 years ago, Columbia University professors Adolf Berle and Gardiner C. Means addressed the divergence of the interests of the owners of the corporation from the professional managers who are hired to run it. They warned that widely dispersed ownership "released management from the overriding requirement that it serve stockholders." The separation of ownership from management has given rise to a set of ideas called "agency theory." Central to agency theory is the relationship between two primary players—the *principals,* who are the owners of the firm (stockholders), and the *agents,* who are the people paid by principals to perform a job on their behalf (management). The stockholders elect and are represented by a board of directors that has a fiduciary responsibility to ensure that management acts in the best interests of stockholders to ensure long-term financial returns for the firm.

Agency theory is concerned with resolving two problems that can occur in agency relationships.[53] *The first is the agency problem that arises (1) when the goals of the principals and agents conflict and (2) when it is difficult or expensive for the principal to verify what the agent is actually doing.*[54] The board of directors would be unable to confirm that the managers were actually acting in the shareholders' interests because managers are "insiders" with regard to the businesses they operate and thus are better informed than the principals. Thus, managers may act "opportunistically" in pursuing their own interests—to the detriment of the corporation.[55] Managers may spend corporate funds on expensive perquisites (e.g., company jets and expensive art), devote time and resources to pet projects (initiatives in which they have a personal interest but that have limited market potential), engage in power struggles (where they may fight over resources for their own betterment and to the detriment of the firm), and negate (or sabotage) attractive merger offers because they may result in increased employment risk.[56]

The second issue is the problem of risk sharing. This arises when the principal and the agent have different attitudes and preferences toward risk. The executives in a firm may favor additional diversification initiatives because, by their very nature, they increase the size of the firm and thus the level of executive compensation.[57] At the same time, such diversification initiatives may erode shareholder value because they fail to achieve some synergies that we discussed in Chapter 6 (e.g., building on core competencies, sharing activities, or enhancing market power). Agents (executives) may have a stronger preference toward diversification than shareholders because it reduces their personal level of risk from potential loss of employment. Executives who have large holdings of stock in their firms are more likely to have diversification strategies that are more consistent with shareholder interests—increasing long-term returns.[58]

At times, top-level managers engage in actions that reflect their self-interest rather than the interests of shareholders. We provide two examples below:

- In addition to an annual base salary of $1.3 million and $10.4 million in stock compensation and bonuses, Heather Bresch, CEO of Mylan Pharmaceuticals, also received $6.4 million in other compensation in 2015. This included $19,200 for the use of a company-provided automobile and $310,000 in personal use of the company jet.[59]
- John Hammergren, the CEO of health care giant McKesson Corporation, has a pretty sweet deal. In 2015, Hammergren took home $25.9 million in salary and stock options. But he's also protected himself well if he's dismissed as CEO. According to the firm's 2015 proxy statement, McKesson would pay Hammergren $141.7 million in unearned compensation if he was terminated. In addition to that, he'd receive a $161 million severance payout that he previously negotiated, resulting in a combined farewell package of $300 million if he was fired.[60]

Governance Mechanisms: Aligning the Interests of Owners and Managers

As noted above, a key characteristic of the modern corporation is the separation of ownership from control. To minimize the potential for managers to act in their own self-interest, or "opportunistically," the owners can implement some governance mechanisms.[61] First, there are two primary means of monitoring the behavior of managers. These include (1) a committed and involved *board of directors* that acts in the best interests of the shareholders to create long-term value and (2) *shareholder activism,* wherein the owners view themselves as share*owners* instead of share*holders* and become actively engaged in the governance of the corporation. Finally, there are managerial incentives, sometimes called "contract-based outcomes," which consist of *reward and compensation agreements.* Here the goal is to carefully craft managerial incentive packages to align the interests of management with those of the stockholders.[62]

We close this section with a brief discussion of one of the most controversial issues in corporate governance—duality. Here, the question becomes: Should the CEO also be chairman of the board of directors? In many Fortune 500 firms, the same individual serves in both roles. However, in recent years, we have seen a trend toward separating these two positions. The key issue is what implications CEO duality has for firm governance and performance.

A Committed and Involved Board of Directors The **board of directors** acts as a fulcrum between the owners and controllers of a corporation. The directors are the intermediaries who provide a balance between a small group of key managers in the firm based at the corporate headquarters and a sometimes vast group of shareholders.[63] In the United States, the law imposes on the board a strict and absolute fiduciary duty to ensure that a company is run consistent with the long-term interests of the owners—the shareholders. The reality, as we have seen, is somewhat more ambiguous.[64]

> **board of directors**
> a group that has a fiduciary duty to ensure that the company is run consistently with the long-term interests of the owners, or shareholders, of a corporation and that acts as an intermediary between the shareholders and management.

The Business Roundtable, representing the largest U.S. corporations, describes the duties of the board as follows:

1. Making decisions regarding the selection, compensation and evaluation of a well-qualified and ethical CEO. The board also appoints or approves other members of the senior management team.
2. Directors monitor management on behalf of the corporation's shareholders. Exercise vigorous and diligent oversight of the corporation's affairs. This includes the following activities.
    a. Plan for senior management development and succession.
    b. Review, understand and monitor the implementation of the corporation's strategic plans.
    c. Review and understand the corporation's risk assessment and oversee the corporation's risk management processes.
    d. Review, understand and oversee annual operating plans and budgets.
    e. Ensure the integrity and clarity of the corporation's financial statements and financial reporting.
    f. Advise management on significant issues facing the corporation.
    g. Review and approve significant corporate actions.
    h. Nominate directors and committee members and oversee effective corporate governance.
    i. Oversee legal and ethical compliance.
3. Represent the interests of all shareholders.[65]

While the roles of the board are fairly clear, following these guidelines does not guarantee that the board will be effective. To be effective, the board needs to allocate its scarce time to the most critical issues to which its members can add value. A survey of several hundred corporate board members revealed dramatic differences in how the most and least effective boards allocated their time. Boards that were seen as being ineffective, meaning they had limited impact on the direction and success of the firm, spent almost all of their time on the basic requirements of ensuring compliance, reviewing financial reports, assessing corporate diversification, and evaluating current performance metrics. Effective boards examined these issues but also expanded the range of issues they discussed to include more forward-looking strategic issues. Effective boards discussed potential performance synergies and the value of strategic alternatives open to the firm, assessed the firm's value drivers, and evaluated potential resource reallocation options. In the end, effective and ineffective boards spent about the same time on their basic board roles, but effective boards spent additional time together to discuss more forward-looking, strategic issues. As a result, board members of effective boards spent twice as many days, about 40 per year, in their role as a board member compared to only about 19 days per year for members of ineffective boards.[66]

Although boards in the past were often dismissed as CEOs' rubber stamps, increasingly they are playing a more active role by forcing out CEOs who cannot deliver on performance.[67] Not only are they dismissing CEOs, but boards are more willing to make strong public statements about CEOs they dismissed. In the past, firms would often announce that a CEO was leaving the position to spend more time with family or pursue new opportunities. More frequently, boards are unambiguously labeling the action a dismissal to signal that they are active and engaged boards. For example, when the Lending Club removed CEO Renaud Laplanche in 2016, Hans Morris, the firm's Executive Chairman, lauded him, saying his "entrepreneurial spirit was critical to the success of the firm." But he also signaled the board was removing Mr. Laplanche since he had failed to build a strong control system and culture, stating "as a public company that provides a financial service, Lending Club must meet the industry's high standards of transparency and disclosure."[68] When Andrew Mason was ousted as head of Groupon, he released a humorous statement saying, "After four and a half intense and wonderful years as CEO of Groupon, I've decided to spend more time with my family. Just kidding—I was fired today."[69]

Another key component of top-ranked boards is director independence.[70] Governance experts believe that a majority of directors should be free of all ties to either the CEO or the company.[71] This means that a minimum of "insiders" (past or present members of the management team) should serve on the board and that directors and their firms should be barred from doing consulting, legal, or other work for the company.[72] Interlocking directorships—in which CEOs and other top managers serve on each other's boards—are not desirable. But perhaps the best guarantee that directors act in the best interests of shareholders is the simplest: Most good companies now insist that directors own significant stock in the company they oversee.[73]

Taking it one step further, research and simple observations of boards indicate that simple prescriptions, such as having a majority of outside directors, are insufficient to lead to effective board operations. Firms need to cultivate engaged and committed boards. There are several actions that can have a positive influence on board dynamics as the board works to both oversee and advise management.[74]

1. *Build in the right expertise on the board.* Outside directors can bring in experience that the management team is missing. For example, corporations that are considering expanding into a new region of the globe may want to add a board member who brings expertise on and connections in that region. Similarly, research suggests that firms that are focusing on improving their operational efficiency benefit from having an external board member whose full-time position is as a chief operating officer, a position that typically focuses on operational activities.

2. *Keep your board size manageable.* Small, focused boards, generally with 5 to 11 members, are preferable to larger ones. As boards grow in size, the ability for them to function as a team declines. The members of the board feel less connected with each other, and decision making can become unwieldy.

3. *Choose directors who can participate fully.* The time demands on directors have increased as their responsibilities have grown to include overseeing management, verifying the firm's financial statements, setting executive compensation, and advising on the strategic direction of the firm. As a result, the average number of hours per year spent on board duties has increased to over 350 hours for directors of large firms. Directors have to dedicate significant time to their roles—not just for scheduled meetings but also to review materials between meetings and to respond to time-sensitive challenges. Thus, firms should strive to include directors who are not currently overburdened by their core occupation or involvement on other boards.

4. ***Balance the need to focus on the past, the present, and the future.*** Boards have a three-tiered role. They need to focus on the recent performance of the firm, how the firm is meeting current milestones and operational targets, and what the strategic direction of the firm will be moving forward. Under current regulations, boards are required to spend a great amount of time on the past as they vet the firm's financials. However, effective boards balance this time and ensure that they give adequate consideration to the present and the future.

5. ***Consider management talent development.*** As part of their future-oriented focus, effective boards develop succession plans for the CEO but also focus on talent development at other upper echelons of the organization. In a range of industries, human capital is an increasingly important driver of firm success, and boards should be involved in evaluating and developing the top management core.

6. ***Get a broad view.*** In order to better understand the firm and make contact with key managers, the meetings of the board should rotate to different operating units and sites of the firm.

7. ***Maintain norms of transparency and trust.*** Highly functioning boards maintain open, team-oriented dialogue wherein information flows freely and questions are asked openly. Directors respect each other and trust that they are all working in the best interests of the corporation.

Because of financial crises and corporate scandals, regulators and investors have pushed for significant changes in the structure and actions of boards. This has resulted in a dramatic rise in the proportion of boards dominated by outsiders (with over 84 percent now being outside board members), a reduction in the size of boards (with most being smaller than 12 members), and a modest increase in the percentage of directors who are female, rising from 12 percent to 15 percent between 2012 and 2016. It has also led to an increase in the amount of time board members spend on their role, which increased from an average of 28 days in 2011 to 33 days in 2015. More specifically, board members reported that they spent significantly more time devoted to discussing firm strategy and evaluating the performance of the firm and its management.[75]

Shareholder Activism As a practical matter, there are so many owners of the largest American corporations that it makes little sense to refer to them as "owners" in the sense of individuals becoming informed and involved in corporate affairs.[76] However, even an individual shareholder has several rights, including (1) the right to sell the stock, (2) the right to vote the proxy (which includes the election of board members), (3) the right to bring suit for damages if the corporation's directors or managers fail to meet their obligations, (4) the right to certain information from the company, and (5) certain residual rights following the company's liquidation (or its filing for reorganization under bankruptcy laws), once creditors and other claimants are paid off.[77]

Collectively, shareholders have the power to direct the course of corporations.[78] This may involve acts such as being party to shareholder action suits and demanding that key issues be brought up for proxy votes at annual board meetings.[79] The power of shareholders has intensified in recent years because of the increasing influence of large institutional investors such as mutual funds (e.g., T. Rowe Price and Fidelity Investments) and retirement systems such as TIAA-CREF (for university faculty members and school administrative staff).[80] Institutional investors hold over 50 percent of all listed corporate stock in the United States.[81]

Shareholder activism refers to actions by large shareholders, both institutions and individuals, to protect their interests when they feel that managerial actions diverge from shareholder value maximization.

Many institutional investors are aggressive in protecting and enhancing their investments. They are shifting from traders to owners. They are assuming the role of permanent shareholders and rigorously analyzing issues of corporate governance. In the process they are reinventing systems of corporate monitoring and accountability.[82]

shareholder activism actions by large shareholders to protect their interests when they feel that managerial actions of a corporation diverge from shareholder value maximization.

HOW WOMEN HAVE COME TO DOMINATE A CORNER OF FINANCE

When you think of a meeting Wall Street leaders and investment bankers, most people would think of a room filled mostly with men. But there is one area of Wall Street that women have come to dominate. The heads of corporate governance at seven of the ten largest institutional investors at the end of 2016 were women. These institutional investors control over $14 trillion in assets. To see the power of institutional investors, consider BlackRock, where Michelle Edkins is the head of corporate governance. BlackRock owns at least 5 percent of the stock of 75 of the largest 100 corporations. It's the single largest shareholder in one out of every five U.S. public firms. State Street and Capital Group, investment firms which also have women corporate governance heads, have at least a 5 percent stake in over 20 of the 100 largest firms.

How does this influence efforts on behalf of shareholders? These female corporate governance heads argue that they work diligently but also quietly as advocates for greater shareholder rights and as change agents in the corporate governance of the firms they have a stake in. Ms. Edkins puts it this way, "We don't meet with CEOs and tell them how to remedy the problem. It's a stylistic difference, and my observation is that this constructive challenge comes more naturally to women."

This doesn't mean these women don't push for important changes. For example, Donna Anderson and her team at the investment firm T. Rowe Price set a policy that they would vote against directors who support dual-class share structures—situations where one class of stock has much stronger voting power (such as 10 votes per share) than other classes of stock (which may even have no voting rights). Ms. Anderson's team is also working on a policy to push for greater gender diversity on boards. As she stated, "We have an interest in seeing more women on boards because there is data that a more diverse board makes better decisions." Anne Sheehan, the corporate governance head at the pension fund CalSTRS, is pushing both for greater gender diversity in boards and a reduction of the pay gap between corporate executives and employees lower in the hierarchy.

Interestingly, while these female corporate governance managers are pushing for greater gender diversity in the leadership of the corporations in which they invest, they face a different struggle in their own business—the lack of men in the field of corporate governance. "It's counterintuitive in finance," Ms. Edkins said, "but when we are hiring, we need to really push that diversity to make sure we have men on the slate."

Sources: Stevenson, A. & Picker, L. 2017. A rare corner of finance where women dominate. *nytimes.com*. January 16: np; and, Craig, S. 2013. The giant of shareholders, quietly stirring. *nytimes.com*. May 18: np.

Consider the proactive behavior of CalPERS, the California Public Employees' Retirement System, which manages nearly $300 billion in assets and is the third-largest pension fund in the world.[83] Every year CalPERS reviews the performance of the 1,000 firms in which it retains a sizable investment.[84] It reviews each firm's short- and long-term performance, governance characteristics, and financial status, as well as market expectations for the firm. CalPERS then meets with selected companies to better understand their governance and business strategy. If needed, CalPERS requests changes in the firm's governance structure and works to ensure shareholders' rights. If CalPERS does not believe that the firm is responsive to its concerns, it considers filing proxy actions at the firm's next shareholders meeting and possibly even court actions. CalPERS's research suggests that these actions lead to superior performance. The portfolio of firms it has included in its review program produced a cumulative return that was 11.59 percent higher than a respective set of benchmark firms over a three-year period. Thus, CalPERS has seen a real benefit of acting as an interested owner, rather than as a passive investor.

More generally, institutional investors have taken an increasingly active role in the corporate governance of firms in which they invest. Strategy Spotlight 9.3 discusses how female executives have taken on key leadership roles in institutional investors and how this has influenced the efforts these firms have undertaken to improve corporate governance.

In addition to traditional institutional investors, a growing set of activist investors aggressively pressure firm managers for major changes.[85] These activist investors include individual investors, such as Carl Icahn, and activist investor funds, such as Pershing Square, ValuAct, and Trian. Activist investors typically purchase a small, but substantial stake in firms, often as little as 5 percent of the firm's stock, and then either pressure the firm to change its leadership or undertake strategic actions, typically a stock buy-back, selling parts of the firm off to focus on core operations, or the initiation of a search for a buyer to acquire the firm. In recent years, activist investors have played a role in the resignations of the CEOs of Procter & Gamble and Microsoft and pushed for the breakup of Motorola and the breakup and sale of Yahoo. Activist investors are often successful since many institutional investors, such as mutual funds, who have little interest in actively overseeing firm management, are willing to support activist investors in their efforts to push management to improve firm profitability and shareholder returns. As a result, when activist investors push for a proxy vote (a vote by firm shareholders), they win over 70 percent of the time. To keep things from coming to a vote, firm management is often willing to negotiate with activist investors to give them part of what they want.

Managerial Rewards and Incentives   As we discussed earlier in the chapter, incentive systems must be designed to help a company achieve its goals.[86] From the perspective of governance, one of the most critical roles of the board of directors is to create incentives that align the interests of the CEO and top executives with the interests of owners of the corporation—long-term shareholder returns.[87] Shareholders rely on CEOs to adopt policies and strategies that maximize the value of their shares.[88] A combination of three basic policies may create the right monetary incentives for CEOs to maximize the value of their companies:[89]

1. Boards can require that the CEOs become substantial owners of company stock.
2. Salaries, bonuses, and stock options can be structured so as to provide rewards for superior performance and penalties for poor performance.
3. Dismissal for poor performance should be a realistic threat.

In recent years the granting of stock options has enabled top executives of publicly held corporations to earn enormous levels of compensation. In 2015, the average CEO in the Standard & Poor's 500 stock index took home 335 times the pay of the average worker—up from 40 times the average in 1980.[90] The counterargument, that the ratio is down from the 514 multiple in 2000, doesn't get much traction.[91]

Many boards have awarded huge option grants despite poor executive performance, and others have made performance goals easier to reach. However, stock options can be a valuable governance mechanism to align the CEO's interests with those of the shareholders. The extraordinarily high level of compensation can, at times, be grounded in sound governance principles.[92] Research by Steven Kaplan at the University of Chicago found that firms with CEOs in the top quintile of pay generated stock returns 60 percent higher than their direct competitors, while firms with CEOs in the bottom quintile of pay saw their stock underperform their rivals by almost 20 percent.[93] For example, Robert Kotik, CEO of video game firm Activision Blizzard, made $64.9 million in 2013, but the firm's stock price rose by over 60 percent that year, producing a strong return for stockholders as well.

CEO Duality: Is It Good or Bad?

CEO duality is one of the most controversial issues in corporate governance. It refers to the dual-leadership structure wherein the CEO acts simultaneously as the chair of the board of directors.[94] Scholars, consultants, and executives who are interested in determining the best way to manage a corporation are divided on the issue of the roles and responsibilities of a CEO. Two schools of thought represent the alternative positions.

Unity of Command   Advocates of the unity-of-command perspective believe that when one person holds both roles, he or she is able to act more efficiently and effectively. CEO duality provides firms with a clear focus on both objectives and operations as well as eliminates confusion and conflict between the CEO and the chairman. Thus, it enables smoother, more effective strategic decision making. Holding dual roles as CEO/chairman creates unity across a company's managers and board of directors and ultimately allows the CEO to serve the shareholders even better. Having leadership focused in a single individual also enhances a firm's responsiveness and ability to secure critical resources. This perspective maintains that separating the two jobs—that of a CEO and that of the chairperson of the board of directors—may produce all types of undesirable consequences. CEOs may find it harder to make quick decisions. Ego-driven chief executives and chairmen may squabble over who is ultimately in charge. The shortage of first-class business talent may mean that bosses find themselves second-guessed by people who know little about the business.[95] Companies like Coca-Cola, JPMorgan, and Time Warner have refused to divide the CEO's and chairman's jobs and support this duality structure.

Agency Theory   Supporters of agency theory argue that the positions of CEO and chairman should be separate. The case for separation is based on the simple principle of the separation of power. How can a board discharge its basic duty—monitoring the boss—if the boss is chairing its meetings and setting its agenda? How can a board act as a safeguard against corruption or incompetence when the possible source of that corruption and incompetence is sitting at the head of the table? CEO duality can create a conflict of interest that could negatively affect the interests of the shareholders.

Duality also complicates the issue of CEO succession. In some cases, a CEO/chairman may choose to retire as CEO but keep his or her role as the chairman. Although this splits up the roles, which appeases an agency perspective, it nonetheless puts the new CEO in a difficult position. The chairman is bound to question some of the new changes put in place, and the board as a whole might take sides with the chairman they trust and with whom they have a history. This conflict of interest would make it difficult for the new CEO to institute any changes, as the power and influence would still remain with the former CEO.[96]

Duality also serves to reinforce popular doubts about the legitimacy of the system as a whole and evokes images of bosses writing their own performance reviews and setting their own salaries. A number of the largest corporations, including Ford Motor Company, General Motors, Citigroup, Oracle, Apple, and Microsoft, have divided the roles between the CEO and chairman and eliminated duality. Finally, more than 90 percent of S&P 500 companies with CEOs who also serve as chairman of the board have appointed "lead" or "presiding" directors to act as a counterweight to a combined chairman and chief executive.

Research suggests that the effects of going from having a joint CEO/chairman to separating the two positions is contingent on how the firm is doing. When the positions are broken apart, there is a clear shift in the firm's performance. If the firm has been performing well, its performance declines after the separation. If the firm has been doing poorly, it experiences improvement after separating the two roles. This research suggests that there is no one correct answer on duality, but that firms should consider their current position and performance trends when deciding whether to keep the CEO and chairman positions in the hands of one person.[97]

External Governance Control Mechanisms

Thus far, we've discussed internal governance mechanisms. Internal controls, however, are not always enough to ensure good governance. The separation of ownership and control that we discussed earlier requires multiple control mechanisms, some internal and some external, to ensure that managerial actions lead to shareholder value maximization. Further, society-at-large wants some assurance that this goal is met without harming other stakeholder groups. Now we discuss several **external governance control mechanisms** that have developed in most modern economies. These include the market for corporate control, auditors, banks and analysts, governmental regulatory bodies, media, and public activists.

external governance control mechanisms methods that ensure that managerial actions lead to shareholder value maximization and do not harm other stakeholder groups that are outside the control of the corporate governance system.

The Market for Corporate Control   Let us assume for a moment that internal control mechanisms in a company are failing. This means that the board is ineffective in monitoring managers and is not exercising the oversight required of it and that shareholders are passive and are not taking any actions to monitor or discipline managers. Under these circumstances managers may behave opportunistically.[98] Opportunistic behavior can take many forms. First, managers can *shirk* their responsibilities. Shirking means that managers fail to exert themselves fully, as is required of them. Second, they can engage in *on-the-job consumption*. Examples of on-the-job consumption include private jets, club memberships, expensive artwork in the offices, and so on. Each of these represents consumption by managers that does not in any way increase shareholder value. Instead, they actually diminish shareholder value. Third, managers may engage in *excessive product-market diversification.*[99] As we discussed in Chapter 6, such diversification serves to reduce only the employment risk of the managers rather than the financial risk of the shareholders, who can more cheaply diversify their risk by owning a portfolio of investments. Is there any external mechanism to stop managers from shirking, consumption on the job, and excessive diversification?

The **market for corporate control** is one external mechanism that provides at least some partial solution to the problems described. If internal control mechanisms fail and the management is behaving opportunistically, the likely response of most shareholders will be to sell their stock rather than engage in activism.[100] As more stockholders vote with their feet, the value of the stock begins to decline. As the decline continues, at some point the market value of the firm becomes less than the book value. A corporate raider can take over the company for a price less than the book value of the assets of the company. The first thing that the raider may do on assuming control over the company is fire the underperforming management. The risk of being acquired by a hostile raider is often referred to as the **takeover constraint.** The takeover constraint deters management from engaging in opportunistic behavior.[101]

Although in theory the takeover constraint is supposed to limit managerial opportunism, in recent years its effectiveness has become diluted as a result of a number of defense tactics adopted by incumbent management (see Chapter 6). Foremost among them are poison pills, greenmail, and golden parachutes. Poison pills are provisions adopted by the company to reduce its worth to the acquirer. An example would be payment of a huge one-time dividend, typically financed by debt. Greenmail involves buying back the stock from the acquirer, usually at an attractive premium. Golden parachutes are employment contracts that cause the company to pay lucrative severance packages to top managers fired as a result of a takeover, often running to several million dollars. Strategy Spotlight 9.4 discusses another way firms can avoid the market for corporate control, and that is to keep or take the firm private.

Auditors   Even when there are stringent disclosure requirements, there is no guarantee that the information disclosed will be accurate. Managers may deliberately disclose false information or withhold negative financial information as well as use accounting methods that distort results based on highly subjective interpretations. Therefore, all accounting statements are required to be audited and certified to be accurate by external auditors. These auditing firms are independent organizations staffed by certified professionals who verify the firm's books of accounts. Audits can unearth financial irregularities and ensure that financial reporting by the firm conforms to standard accounting practices.

However, these audits often fail to catch accounting irregularities. In the past, auditing failures played an important part in the failures of firms such as Enron and WorldCom. A recent study by the Public Company Accounting Oversight Board (PCAOB) found that audits conducted by the Big 4 accounting firms were often deficient. For example, 20 percent of the Ernst & Young audits examined by the PCAOB failed. And this was the best of the Big 4! The PCAOB found fault with 45 percent of the Deloitte audits it examined. Why do these reputable firms fail to find all of the issues in audits they conduct? First, auditors are appointed

---

market for corporate control
an external control mechanism in which shareholders dissatisfied with a firm's management sell their shares.

takeover constraint
the risk to management of the firm being acquired by a hostile raider.

THE RISE OF THE PRIVATELY OWNED FIRM

It used to be that the sign that a firm had made it to the big time was when it would issue an initial public offering and become a publicly traded firm. But times have changed. While there are 20 percent more companies in the United States than the mid-1990s, the number of firms that are publicly traded on a major stock exchange has dropped 45 percent compared to 1995. A number of major firms, including Dell, Safeway, and PetSmart, went from being publicly traded to privately held firms in recent years. Other firms, such as Uber, have simply chosen to stay private for a longer period than successful start-up firms did in the past.

What's driving this change? Firm managers argue that being private gives them the freedom to think longer term and for the benefit of the firm as a whole, rather than simply maximizing the firm's current stock price. It also removes the challenge of activist investors pushing the firm to take actions managers would prefer to avoid, and it lessens the threat of a hostile takeover. One survey found that 77 percent of CEOs of publicly traded firms agree with the statement "It would be easier to manage my company if it were a private company rather than a public company." Another factor driving this change is that many modern technology companies don't need much capital to grow. Platform firms, such as Airbnb and Uber, need little capital since they don't own the hard assets used to serve customers. Other firms outsource capital intensive activities, such as manufacturing, lessening the capital needed to grow. A McKinsey study found that 31 percent of Western companies, those based in the United States, Canada, and Western Europe, now follow an "asset light" business model, compared to 17 percent in 1999. A third factor keeping firms private is that it is expensive to go public. The underwriting and registration costs associated with an initial public offering typically eat up about 14 percent of the funds raised in the offering. A final benefit with staying private is that the firm does not have to submit formal disclosure documents to the SEC and other government agencies. This reduces the risk that key financial or technical information that could benefit rivals or other firm stakeholders leaks out in these documents.

Sources: Colvin, G. 2016. Private desires. *Fortune.* June 1: 51-57; and, Dorward, L. 2017. The advantages of being a privately owned company. *chron.com.* February 11: np.

by the firm being audited. The desire to continue that business relationship sometimes makes them overlook financial irregularities. Second, most auditing firms also do consulting work and often have lucrative consulting contracts with the firms that they audit. Understandably, some of them tend not to ask too many difficult questions, because they fear jeopardizing the consulting business, which is often more profitable than the auditing work.

Banks and Analysts   Commercial and investment banks have lent money to corporations and therefore have to ensure that the borrowing firm's finances are in order and that the loan covenants are being followed. Stock analysts conduct ongoing in-depth studies of the firms that they follow and make recommendations to their clients to buy, hold, or sell. Their rewards and reputation depend on the quality of these recommendations. Their access to information, their knowledge of the industry and the firm, and the insights they gain from interactions with the management of the company enable them to alert the investing community of both positive and negative developments relating to a company.

It is generally observed that analyst recommendations are often more optimistic than warranted by facts. "Sell" recommendations tend to be exceptions rather than the norm. Many analysts failed to grasp the gravity of the problems surrounding failed companies such as Lehman Brothers and Countrywide till the very end. Part of the explanation may lie in the fact that most analysts work for firms that also have investment banking relationships with the companies they follow. Negative recommendations by analysts can displease the management, who may decide to take their investment banking business to a rival firm. Otherwise independent and competent analysts may be pressured to overlook negative information or tone down their criticism.

Governmental Regulatory Bodies   The extent of government regulation is often a function of the type of industry. Banks, utilities, and pharmaceuticals are subject to more regulatory oversight because of their importance to society. Public corporations are subject to more regulatory requirements than private corporations.[102]

JAPANESE GOVERNMENT PUSHES FOR GOVERNANCE REFORM

Corporate governance structures in Japan look very different than those found in the United States. Few members of boards of directors are independent of the firm. Instead, most are also firm managers, meaning they are unlikely to recommend the firm radically change its strategy even if such change may be warranted. Even though many Japanese firms have extensive global operations, only 274 of the approximately 40,000 director positions at Japanese firms were held by foreigners in 2015. Firms within business groups have cross-shareholding, where supplier firms own part of their customer firms and vice versa. Also, banks often own shares in the companies they lend to and, as a result, do not put strong public pressure on client firms to improve their operations or balance sheets. Government regulations do not require that accounting firms that serve as external auditors are independent of the firm. As a result, many firms use closely affiliated "outside" auditors, reducing the pressure the firm faces to accurately report earnings and file financial statements. Finally, top manager compensation is low compared to other countries and not closely tied to firm performance, reducing the incentive for management to take bold actions. These cozy governance systems fit the longstanding Japanese desire for economic stability and lifetime employment.

However, two decades of economic malaise has led Prime Minister Shinzo Abe and his government to push for governance reform. These cozy governance arrangements have resulted in firms that are slow to restructure, not very competitively aggressive, and unable to fully understand the different needs of the global markets in which they compete. One measure of the conservatism of firm management is that, in 2015, Japanese companies were hoarding $1.9 trillion in cash, an amount nearly half the size of the Japanese economy. This is cash firms could use to expand, develop new technologies, or acquire other firms, but these firms were choosing to sit on it instead. Abe and his government are trying to change things with a new corporate governance code. Rather than working up hard and fast rules, Abe's code lays out general principles and relies on social pressure to get firms to change. Companies are advised to improve communication with shareholders, to respond to large shareholder concerns, to focus more on increasing shareholder value, to remove anti-takeover provisions, to increase diversity and the promotion of women, and to use an independent auditor.

There is some evidence these social pressures are working. In 2016, firms distributed a record amount of cash to their stockholders. An increasing number of firms are introducing shareholder friendly measures, such as return on equity targets and regular earnings reports. Corporate boards are also becoming a bit more independent with the average number of outsiders on the boards of large Japanese firms rising from less than one to three members since 2012. Big banks have announced they will reduce their shareholding in customer firms by about 25 percent in the next five years. Cross-shareholdings between firms have reduced to 11 percent of market capitalization in 2016, compared to 34 percent in 1990. Finally, some major firms, such as Hitachi, are divesting unrelated and unprofitable business units and focusing on core, growing business operations.

Japan has no interest in fully incorporating American corporate governance practices. It sees the United States as too short term and shareholder focused. Instead, Abe wants to alter governance practices to push firms to be more aggressive and responsive while also maintaining a degree of stability and a longer term focus.

Sources: Anonymous. 2015. Meet Shinzo Abe, shareholder activist. *economist.com*. June 6: np; Smith, N. 2015. Japan flirts with governance reform. *bloomberg.com*. January 9: np; de Swaan, J. 2016. Abe must double down on Japan's corporate sector reforms. *ft.com*. September 28: np; and, Lewis, L. 2016. Abe's corporate governance reforms show signs of progress. *ft.com*. December 20: np.

All public corporations are required to disclose a substantial amount of financial information by bodies such as the Securities and Exchange Commission. These include quarterly and annual filings of financial performance, stock trading by insiders, and details of executive compensation packages. There are two primary reasons behind such requirements. First, markets can operate efficiently only when the investing public has faith in the market system. In the absence of disclosure requirements, the average investor suffers from a lack of reliable information and therefore may completely stay away from the capital market. This will negatively impact an economy's ability to grow. Second, disclosure of information such as insider trading protects the small investor to some extent from the negative consequences of information asymmetry. The insiders and large investors typically have more information than the small investor and can therefore use that information to buy or sell before the information becomes public knowledge.

Government pressures to improve corporate governance is not only found in the United States. Strategy Spotlight 9.5 discusses how Japanese regulators are pushing for governance reform in a country that has long resisted changes that would lead firms to focus more on shareholders.

Media and Public Activists   The press is not usually recognized as an external control mechanism in the literature on corporate governance. There is no denying that in all developed capitalist economies, the financial press and media play an important indirect role in monitoring the management of public corporations. In the United States, business magazines such as *Bloomberg Businessweek* and *Fortune,* financial newspapers such as *The Wall Street Journal* and *Investor's Business Daily,* as well as television networks like Fox Business Network and CNBC are constantly reporting on companies. Public perceptions about a company's financial prospects and the quality of its management are greatly influenced by the media. For example, the business practices of Turing Pharmaceuticals were called into question in 2015, first on a health care news website, Healio, and then by *USA Today* and the *New York Times.*[103] The ensuing scrutiny resulted in Turing's CEO, Martin Shkreli, being described as "the most hated man in America" in a number of news articles. Shkreli resigned as firm CEO within a few months of the emergence of the scandal.

Similarly, consumer groups and activist individuals often take a crusading role in exposing corporate malfeasance.[104] For example, pressure from activists and consumers led firms that deal in diamonds, gold, and other precious minerals to change their sourcing behavior to ensure that their suppliers are legitimate operators, mines and dealers that provide appropriate wages for workers and safe working conditions as well as refuse to deal in "conflict minerals" (that rebel groups trade so that they can buy arms for military conflicts). This pressure also led to government regulation, part of the Dodd-Frank Act of 2010, that requires dealers in these minerals to disclose the country of origin of minerals they import into the United States.

Corporate Governance: An International Perspective

principal–principal conflicts

conflicts between two classes of principals—controlling shareholders and minority shareholders—within the context of a corporate governance system.

The topic of corporate governance has long been dominated by agency theory and based on the explicit assumption of the separation of ownership and control.[105] The central conflicts are principal–agent conflicts between shareholders and management. However, such an underlying assumption seldom applies outside the United States and the United Kingdom. This is particularly true in emerging economies and continental Europe. Here, there is often concentrated ownership, along with extensive family ownership and control, business group structures, and weak legal protection for minority shareholders. Serious conflicts tend to exist between two classes of principals: controlling shareholders and minority shareholders. Such conflicts can be called **principal–principal (PP) conflicts,** as opposed to *principal-agent* conflicts (see Exhibits 9.6 and 9.7).

EXHIBIT 9.6 Traditional Principal–Agent Conflicts versus Principal–Principal Conflicts: How They Differ along Dimensions

	Principal–Agent Conflicts	Principal–Principal Conflicts
Goal incongruence	Between shareholders and professional managers who own a relatively small portion of the firm's equity.	Between controlling shareholders and minority shareholders.
Ownership pattern	Dispersed—5% to 20% is considered "concentrated ownership."	Concentrated—often greater than 50% of equity is controlled by controlling shareholders.
Manifestations	Strategies that benefit entrenched managers at the expense of shareholders in general (e.g., shirking, pet projects, excessive compensation, and empire building).	Strategies that benefit controlling shareholders at the expense of minority shareholders (e.g., minority shareholder expropriation, nepotism, and cronyism).
Institutional protection of minority shareholders	Formal constraints (e.g., judicial reviews and courts) set an upper boundary on potential expropriation by majority shareholders. Informal norms generally adhere to shareholder wealth maximization.	Formal institutional protection is often lacking, corrupted, or unenforced. Informal norms are typically in favor of the interests of controlling shareholders ahead of those of minority investors.

Source: Adapted from Young, M., Peng, M. W., Ahlstrom, D., & Bruton, G. 2002. Governing the Corporation in Emerging Economies: A Principal–Principal Perspective. *Academy of Management Best Papers Proceedings,* Denver.

EXHIBIT 9.7 Principal–Agent Conflicts and Principal–Principal Conflicts: A Diagram

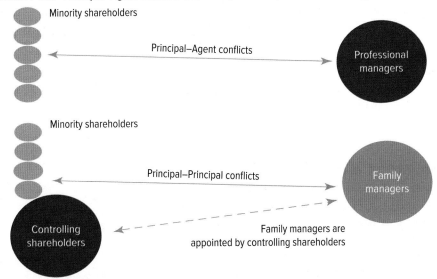

Source: Young, M. N., Peng, M. W., Ahlstrom, D., Bruton, G. D., & Jiang, 2008. Principal–Principal Conflicts in Corporate Governance. *Journal of Management Studies,* 45(1): 196–220; and Peng, M. V. 2006. *Global Strategy.* Cincinnati: Thomson South-Western. We are very appreciative of the helpful comments of Mike Young of Hong Kong Baptist University and Mike Peng of the University of Texas at Dallas.

Strong family control is one of the leading indicators of concentrated ownership. In East Asia (excluding China), approximately 57 percent of the corporations have board chairmen and CEOs from the controlling families. In continental Europe, this number is 68 percent. A very common practice is the appointment of family members as board chairmen, CEOs, and other top executives. This happens because the families are controlling (not necessarily majority) shareholders.

In general, three conditions must be met for PP conflicts to occur:

- A dominant owner or group of owners who have interests that are distinct from minority shareholders.
- Motivation for the controlling shareholders to exercise their dominant positions to their advantage.
- Few formal (such as legislation or regulatory bodies) or informal constraints that would discourage or prevent the controlling shareholders from exploiting their advantageous positions.

The result is often that family managers, who represent (or actually are) the controlling shareholders, engage in **expropriation of minority shareholders,** which is defined as activities that enrich the controlling shareholders at the expense of minority shareholders. What is their motive? After all, controlling shareholders have incentives to maintain firm value. But controlling shareholders may take actions that decrease aggregate firm performance if their personal gains from expropriation exceed their personal losses from their firm's lowered performance.

Another ubiquitous feature of corporate life outside the United States and United Kingdom is *business groups* such as the keiretsus of Japan and the chaebols of South Korea. This is particularly dominant in emerging economies. A **business group** is "a set of firms that, though legally independent, are bound together by a constellation of formal and informal ties and are accustomed to taking coordinated action."[106] Business groups are especially common in emerging economies, and they differ from other organizational forms in that they are communities of firms without clear boundaries.

expropriation of minority shareholders
activities that enrich the controlling shareholders at the expense of the minority shareholders.

business group
a set of firms that, though legally independent, are bound together by a constellation of formal and informal ties and are accustomed to taking coordinated action.

Business groups have many advantages that can enhance the value of a firm. They often facilitate technology transfer or intergroup capital allocation that otherwise might be impossible because of inadequate institutional infrastructure such as excellent financial services firms. On the other hand, informal ties—such as cross-holdings, board interlocks, and coordinated actions—can often result in intragroup activities and transactions, often at very favorable terms to member firms. Expropriation can be legally done through related transactions, which can occur when controlling owners sell firm assets to another firm they own at below-market prices or spin off the most profitable part of a public firm and merge it with another of their private firms.

ISSUE FOR DEBATE

Striking the balance between shareholder rights and the rights of corporate managers to run firms is a challenging issue. Since most shareholders, even institutional investors, own less than 5 percent of the stock in any one firm, there are typically no controlling shareholders who can, on their own, force management to make major changes or address the key concerns of the investors. To address this issue, U.S. regulators have created guidelines that make it easy for shareholders, even small shareholders, to initiate shareholder proposals at annual shareholder meetings. Shareholders who own $2,000 or 1 percent of a firm's stock, whichever is lower, have the right to submit a shareholder proposal. Once submitted, firm management must hold a vote, where all shareholders weigh in on whether they agree that the corporation should address the issues raised in the proposal. If the proposal gets support from at least 3 percent of shareholders, its sponsor can call for a vote on it again at the next shareholder meeting. Proponents of these rules believe that this is corporate democracy in action and keeps management from becoming tone deaf to the concerns of small shareholders.

However, these rules also allow small shareholders with personal concerns, sometimes called "corporate gadflies," to generate shareholder proposals that can potentially create unnecessary and costly work by firms. For example, Choice Hotels had to fight a shareholder proposal from one stockholder, who owned .001 percent of the firm's stock, which called for Choice to measure how much water flowed through every single showerhead in every bathroom in the 6,300 hotels the company owns. Some investors make it something of a career submitting these proposals. Three people, John Chevedden, William Steiner, and James McRitchie and their families, filed 70 percent of all of the shareholder proposals at Fortune 250 firms in 2013. Less than 5 percent of their proposals passed, but the cost to fight them was substantial. According to one estimate, the cost for firms to counter these proposals was $90 million.

Regulators struggle with how to deal with this issue. Making it harder to file shareholder proposals would reduce the cost to corporations, but it would also reduce the voice of shareholders to raise substantive issues.

Discussion Question

1. How would you strike a balance to ensure that shareholders have a voice while limiting the cost of unnecessary proposals? Are the current rules appropriate? If not, how would you change them?

Sources: Engler, J. 2016. How gadfly shareholders keep CEOs distracted. *Wall Street Journal*. May 27: A11; and Soloman, S. 2014. Grappling with the cost of corporate gadflies. *nytimes.com*. August 19: np.

Reflecting on Career Implications . . .

This chapter focuses on the varying means firms can use to control and direct behavior. The following questions ask you how you would respond to different control mechanisms and how you can construct monitoring and control systems to enhance you career.

- **Behavioral Control:** What types of behavioral control does your organization employ? Do you find these behavioral controls helping or hindering you from doing a good job? Some individuals are comfortable with and even desire rules and procedures for everything. Others find that they inhibit creativity and stifle initiative. Evaluate your own level of comfort with the level of behavioral control and then assess the match between your own optimum level of control and the level and type of control used by your organization. If the gap is significant, you might want to consider other career opportunities.

- **Setting Boundaries and Constraints:** Your career success depends to a great extent on you monitoring and regulating your own behavior. Setting boundaries and constraints on yourself can help you focus on strategic priorities, generate short-term objectives and action plans, improve efficiency and effectiveness, and minimize improper conduct. Identify the boundaries and constraints you have placed on yourself and evaluate how each of those contributes to your personal growth and career development. If you do not have boundaries and constraints, consider developing them.

- **Rewards and Incentives:** Is your organization's reward structure fair and equitable? On what criteria do you base your conclusions? How does the firm define outstanding performance and reward it? Are these financial or nonfinancial rewards? The absence of rewards that are seen as fair and equitable can result in the long-term erosion of morale, which may have long-term adverse career implications for you.

- **Culture:** Given your career goals, what type of organizational culture would provide the best work environment? How does your organization's culture deviate from this concept? Does your organization have a strong and effective culture? In the long run, how likely are you to internalize the culture of your organization? If you believe that there is a strong misfit between your values and the organization's culture, you may want to reconsider your relationship with the organization.

summary

For firms to be successful, they must practice effective strategic control and corporate governance. Without such controls, the firm will not be able to achieve competitive advantages and outperform rivals in the marketplace.

We began the chapter with the key role of informational control. We contrasted two types of control systems: what we termed "traditional" and "contemporary" information control systems. Whereas traditional control systems may have their place in placid, simple competitive environments, there are fewer of those in today's economy. Instead, we advocated the contemporary approach wherein the internal and external environment are constantly monitored so that when surprises emerge, the firm can modify its strategies, goals, and objectives.

Behavioral controls are also a vital part of effective control systems. We argued that firms must develop the proper balance between culture, rewards and incentives, and boundaries and constraints. Where there are strong and positive cultures and rewards, employees tend to internalize the organization's strategies and objectives. This permits a firm to spend fewer resources on monitoring behavior, and assures the firm that the efforts and initiatives of employees are more consistent with the overall objectives of the organization.

In the final section of this chapter, we addressed corporate governance, which can be defined as the relationship between various participants in determining the direction and performance of the corporation. The primary participants include shareholders, management (led by the chief executive officer), and the board of directors. We reviewed studies that indicated a consistent relationship between effective corporate governance and financial performance. There are also several internal and external control mechanisms that can serve to align managerial interests and shareholder interests. The internal mechanisms include a committed and involved board of directors, shareholder activism, and effective managerial incentives and rewards. The external mechanisms include the market for corporate control, banks and analysts, regulators, the media, and public activists. We also addressed corporate governance from both a United States and an international perspective.

SUMMARY REVIEW QUESTIONS

1. Why are effective strategic control systems so important in today's economy?
2. What are the main advantages of contemporary control systems over traditional control systems? What are the main differences between these two systems?
3. Why is it important to have a balance between the three elements of behavioral control—culture, rewards and incentives, and boundaries?
4. Discuss the relationship between types of organizations and their primary means of behavioral control.
5. Boundaries become less important as a firm develops a strong culture and reward system. Explain.

6. Why is it important to avoid a "one best way" mentality concerning control systems? What are the consequences of applying the same type of control system to all types of environments?

7. What is the role of effective corporate governance in improving a firm's performance? What are some of the key governance mechanisms that are used to ensure that managerial and shareholder interests are aligned?

8. Define principal–principal (PP) conflicts. What are the implications for corporate governance?

key terms

strategic control 268
traditional approach to
   strategic control 268
informational control 269
behavioral control 269
organizational culture 270
reward system 271
boundaries and
   constraints 275
corporate governance 278

corporation 279
agency theory 280
board of directors 281
shareholder activism 283
external governance control
   mechanisms 286
market for corporate
   control 287
takeover constraint 287
principal–principal
   conflicts 290
expropriation of minority
   shareholders 291
business group 291

EXPERIENTIAL EXERCISE

McDonald's Corporation is the world's largest fast-food restaurant chain. Using the Internet, evaluate the quality of the corporation in terms of management, the board of directors, and shareholder activism. (Fill in the chart below.) Are the issues you list favorable or unfavorable for sound corporate governance?

APPLICATION QUESTIONS & EXERCISES

1. The problems of many firms may be attributed to a traditional control system that failed to continuously monitor the environment and make necessary changes in their strategy and objectives. What companies are you familiar with that responded appropriately (or inappropriately) to environmental change?

2. How can a strong, positive culture enhance a firm's competitive advantage? How can a weak, negative culture erode competitive advantages? Explain and provide examples.

3. Use the Internet to research a firm that has an excellent culture and/or reward and incentive system. What are this firm's main financial and nonfinancial benefits?

4. Using the Internet, go to the website of a large, publicly held corporation in which you are interested. What evidence do you see of effective (or ineffective) corporate governance?

ETHICS QUESTIONS

1. Strong cultures can have powerful effects on employee behavior. How does this create inadvertent control mechanisms? That is, are strong cultures an ethical way to control behavior?

2. Rules and regulations can help reduce unethical behavior in organizations. To be effective, however, what other systems, mechanisms, and processes are necessary?

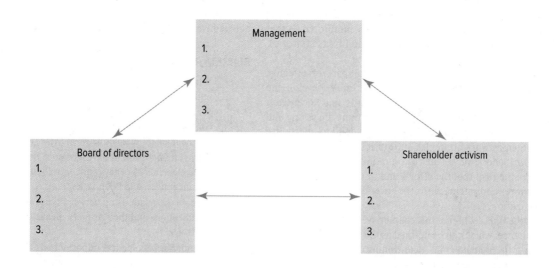

REFERENCES

1. Anonymous. 2014. Not so funny. *economist.com,* September 27: np; Evans, P. & Fleisher, L. 2014. Tesco investigates accounting error. *wsj.com,* September 23: np; Rosenblum, P. 2014. Tesco's accounting irregularities are mind blowing. *forbes.com,* September 22: np; and Davey, J. 2014. UK watchdog to investigate Tesco accounts and auditor PwC. *reuters.com,* December 22: np.

2. This chapter draws upon Picken, J. C. & Dess, G. G. 1997. *Mission critical.* Burr Ridge, IL: Irwin Professional.

3. For a unique perspective on governance, refer to Carmeli, A. & Markman, G. D. 2011. Capture, governance, and resilience: Strategy implications from the history of Rome. *Strategic Management Journal,* 32(3): 332–341.

4. Argyris, C. 1977. Double-loop learning in organizations. *Harvard Business Review,* 55: 115–125.

5. Simons, R. 1995. Control in an age of empowerment. *Harvard Business Review,* 73: 80–88. This chapter draws on this source in the discussion of informational control.

6. Goold, M. & Quinn, J. B. 1990. The paradox of strategic controls. *Strategic Management Journal,* 11: 43–57.

7. Quinn, J. B. 1980. *Strategies for change.* Homewood, IL: Irwin.

8. Mintzberg, H. 1987. Crafting strategy. *Harvard Business Review,* 65: 66–75.

9. This discussion of control systems draws upon Simons, op. cit.

10. Ryan, M. K., Haslam, S. A., & Renneboog, L. D. R. 2011. Who gets the carrot and who gets the stick? Evidence of gender discrimination in executive remuneration. *Strategic Management Journal,* 32(3): 301–321.

11. For an interesting perspective on this issue and how a downturn in the economy can reduce the tendency toward "free agency" by managers and professionals, refer to Morris, B. 2001. White collar blues. *Fortune,* July 23: 98–110.

12. For a colorful example of behavioral control in an organization, see Beller, P. C. 2009. Activision's unlikely hero. *Forbes,* February 2: 52–58.

13. Collins, J. C. & Porras, J. I. 1994. *Built to last: Successful habits of visionary companies.* New York: Harper Business.

14. Lee, J. & Miller, D. 1999. People matter: Commitment to employees, strategy, and performance in Korean firms. *Strategic Management Journal,* 6: 579–594.

15. For an insightful discussion of IKEA's unique culture, see Kling, K. & Goteman, I. 2003. IKEA CEO Anders Dahlvig on international growth and IKEA's unique corporate culture and brand identity. *Academy of Management Executive,* 17(1): 31–37.

16. For a discussion of how professionals inculcate values, refer to Uhl-Bien, M. & Graen, G. B. 1998. Individual self-management: Analysis of professionals' self-managing activities in functional and cross-functional work teams. *Academy of Management Journal,* 41(3): 340–350.

17. A perspective on how antisocial behavior can erode a firm's culture can be found in Robinson, S. L. & O'Leary-Kelly, A. M. 1998. Monkey see, monkey do: The influence of work groups on the antisocial behavior of employees. *Academy of Management Journal,* 41(6): 658–672.

18. Benkler, Y. 2011. The unselfish gene. *Harvard Business Review,* 89(7): 76–85.

19. An interesting perspective on organizational culture is in Mehta, S. N. 2009. Under Armour reboots. *Fortune,* February 2: 29–33.

20. For insights on social pressure as a means for control, refer to Goldstein, N. J. 2009. Harnessing social pressure. *Harvard Business Review,* 87(2): 25.

21. Mitchell, R. 1989. Masters of innovation. *BusinessWeek,* April 10: 58–63.

22. *bigspaceship.com/warby-parker-culture;* and *businesscollective.com/12-ways-to-reinforce-your-company-culture.*

23. Kerr, J. & Slocum, J. W., Jr. 1987. Managing corporate culture through reward systems. *Academy of Management Executive,* 1(2): 99–107.

24. For a unique perspective on leader challenges in managing wealthy professionals, refer to Wetlaufer, S. 2000. Who wants to manage a millionaire? *Harvard Business Review,* 78(4): 53–60.

25. Netessine, S. & Yakubovich, V. 2012. The Darwinian workplace. *Harvard Business Review,* 90(5): 25–28.

26. For a discussion of the benefits of stock options as executive compensation, refer to Hall, B. J. 2000. What you need to know about stock options. *Harvard Business Review,* 78(2): 121–129.

27. Anonymous. 2013. Rewarding your employees: 15 examples of successful incentives in the corporate world. *rrgexec.com.* June 20: np.

28. Carter, N. M. & Silva, C. 2010. Why men still get more promotions than women. *Harvard Business Review,* 88(9): 80–86.

29. Sirota, D., Mischkind, L. & Meltzer, I. 2008. Stop demotivating your employees! *Harvard Management Update,* July: 3–5; Nelson, B. 2003. Five questions about employee recognition and reward. *Harvard Management Update;* Birkinshaw, J., Bouquet, C., & Barsaoux, J. 2011. The 5 myths of innovation. *MIT Sloan Management Review.* Winter, 43–50; and Dewhurst, M. Guthridge, M., & Mohr, E. 2009. Motivating people: Getting beyond money. *mckinsey.com.* November: np.

30. This section draws on Picken & Dess, op. cit., chap. 5.

31. Anonymous. 2012. Nestle set to buy Pfizer unit. *Dallas Morning News,* April 19: 10D.

32. Isaacson, W. 2012. The real leadership lessons of Steve Jobs. *Harvard Business Review,* 90(4): 93–101.

33. This section draws upon Dess, G. G. & Miller, A. 1993. *Strategic management.* New York: McGraw-Hill.

34. For a good review of the goal-setting literature, refer to Locke, E. A. & Latham, G. P. 1990. A *theory of goal setting and task performance.* Englewood Cliffs, NJ: Prentice Hall.

35. For an interesting perspective on the use of rules and regulations that is counter to this industry's (software) norms, refer to Fryer, B. 2001. Tom Siebel of Siebel Systems: High tech the old fashioned way. *Harvard Business Review,* 79(3): 118–130.

36. Thompson, A. A., Jr., & Strickland, A. J., III. 1998. *Strategic management: Concepts and cases* (10th ed.): 313. New York: McGraw-Hill.

37. Weaver, G. R., Trevino, L. K., & Cochran, P. L. 1999. Corporate ethics programs as control systems: Influences of executive commitment and environmental factors. *Academy of Management Journal,* 42(1): 41–57.

38. *www.singaporeair.com/pdf/media-centre/anti-corruption-policy-procedures.pdf.*

39. William Ouchi has written extensively about the use of clan control (which is viewed as an

alternative to bureaucratic or market control). Here, a powerful culture results in people aligning their individual interests with those of the firm. See Ouchi, W. 1981. *Theory Z.* Reading, MA: Addison-Wesley. This section also draws on Hall, R. H. 2002. *Organizations: Structures, processes, and outcomes* (8th ed.). Upper Saddle River, NJ: Prentice Hall.

40. Poundstone, W. 2003. *How would you move Mount Fuji?* New York: Little, Brown: 59.

41. Abby, E. 2012. Woman sues over personality test job rejection. *abcnews.go.com,* October 1: np.

42. Interesting insights on corporate governance are in Kroll, M., Walters, B. A., & Wright, P. 2008. Board vigilance, director experience, and corporate outcomes. *Strategic Management Journal,* 29(4): 363–382.

43. For a brief review of some central issues in corporate governance research, see Hambrick, D. C., Werder, A. V., & Zajac, E. J. 2008. New directions in corporate governance research. *Organization Science,* 19(3): 381–385.

44. Monks, R. & Minow, N. 2001. *Corporate governance* (2nd ed.). Malden, MA: Blackwell.

45. Pound, J. 1995. The promise of the governed corporation. *Harvard Business Review,* 73(2): 89–98.

46. Maurer, H. & Linblad, C. 2009. Scandal at Satyam. *BusinessWeek,* January 19: 8; Scheck, J. & Stecklow, S. 2008. Brocade ex-CEO gets 21 months in prison. *The Wall Street Journal,* January 17: A3; Levine, D. & Graybow, M. 2010. Mozilo to pay millions in Countrywide settlement. *finance. yahoo.com,* October 15: np; Ellis, B. 2010. Countrywide's Mozilo to pay $67.5 million settlement. *cnnmoney. com,* October 15: np; Frank, R., Efrati, A., Lucchetti, A., & Bray, C. 2009. Madoff jailed after admitting epic scam. *The Wall Street Journal,* March 13: A1; and Henriques, D. B. 2009. Madoff is sentenced to 150 years for Ponzi scheme. *www. nytimes.com,* June 29: np.

47. Corkery, M. & Cowley, S. 2016. Wells Fargo CEO John Stumpf quits after scandal. *bostonglobe.com.* October 12: np.

48. Harris, E. 2014. After bribery scandal, high-level departures at Walmart. *nytimes.com,* June 4: np.

49. Anonymous. 2012. Olympus and ex-executives plead guilty in accounting fraud. *nytimes.com,* September 25: np.

50. Corporate governance and social networks are discussed in McDonald, M. L., Khanna, P., & Westphal, J. D. 2008. *Academy of Management Journal,* 51(3): 453–475.

51. This discussion draws upon Monks & Minow, op. cit.

52. For an interesting perspective on the politicization of the corporation, read Palazzo, G. & Scherer, A. G. 2008. Corporate social responsibility, democracy, and the politicization of the corporation. *Academy of Management Review,* 33(3): 773–774.

53. Eisenhardt, K. M. 1989. Agency theory: An assessment and review. *Academy of Management Review,* 14(1): 57–74. Some of the seminal contributions to agency theory include Jensen, M. & Meckling, W. 1976. Theory of the firm: Managerial behavior, agency costs, and ownership structure. *Journal of Financial Economics,* 3: 305–360; Fama, E. & Jensen, M. 1983. Separation of ownership and control. *Journal of Law and Economics,* 26: 301, 325; and Fama, E. 1980. Agency problems and the theory of the firm. *Journal of Political Economy,* 88: 288–307.

54. Nyberg, A. J., Fulmer, I. S., Gerhart, B., & Carpenter, M. 2010. Agency theory revisited: CEO return and shareholder interest alignment. *Academy of Management Journal,* 53(5): 1029–1049.

55. Managers may also engage in "shirking"—that is, reducing or withholding their efforts. See, for example, Kidwell, R. E., Jr. & Bennett, N. 1993. Employee propensity to withhold effort: A conceptual model to intersect three avenues of research. *Academy of Management Review,* 18(3): 429–456.

56. For an interesting perspective on agency and clarification of many related concepts and terms, visit *www. encycogov.com.*

57. The relationship between corporate ownership structure and export intensity in Chinese firms is discussed in Filatotchev, I., Stephan, J., & Jindra, B. 2008. Ownership structure, strategic controls and export intensity of foreign-invested firms in transition economies. *Journal of International Business,* 39(7): 1133–1148.

58. Argawal, A. & Mandelker, G. 1987. Managerial incentives and corporate investment and financing decisions. *Journal of Finance,* 42: 823–837.

59. Woods, L. 2017. The most outrageous CEO salaries and perks. *msn.com.* January 17: np.

60. Swanson, C. 2015. America's 3 most overpaid CEOs. *usatoday.com.* November 10: np.

61. For an insightful, recent discussion of the academic research on corporate governance, and in particular the role of boards of directors, refer to Chatterjee, S. & Harrison, J. S. 2001. Corporate governance. In Hitt, M. A., Freeman, R. E., & Harrison, J. S. (Eds.), *Handbook of strategic management:* 543–563. Malden, MA: Blackwell.

62. For an interesting theoretical discussion on corporate governance in Russia, see McCarthy, D. J. & Puffer, S. M. 2008. Interpreting the ethicality of corporate governance decisions in Russia: Utilizing integrative social contracts theory to evaluate the relevance of agency theory norms. *Academy of Management Review,* 33(1): 11–31.

63. Haynes, K. T. & Hillman, A. 2010. The effect of board capital and CEO power on strategic change. *Strategic Management Journal,* 31(110): 1145–1163.

64. This opening discussion draws on Monks & Minow, op. cit. pp. 164, 169; see also Pound, op. cit.

65. Business Roundtable. 2012. Principles of corporate governance.

66. Bhagat, C. & Kehoe, C. 2014. High performing boards: What's on their agenda? *mckinsey.com,* April: np.

67. The role of outside directors is discussed in Lester, R. H., Hillman, A., Zardkoohi, A., & Cannella, A. A., Jr. 2008. Former government officials as outside directors: The role of human and social capital. *Academy of Management Journal,* 51(5): 999–1013.

68. Rudegeair, P. & Andriotis, A. 2016. Inside the final days of Lending Club CEO Renaud Laplanche. *wsj.com.* May 16: np.

69. Feintzeig, R. 2014. You're fired! And we really mean it. *The Wall Street Journal,* November 5: B1, B6.

70. For an analysis of the effects of outside directors' compensation on acquisition decisions, refer to Deutsch, T., Keil, T., & Laamanen, T. 2007. Decision making in acquisitions: The effect of outside directors' compensation on acquisition patterns. *Journal of Management,* 33(1): 30–56.

71. Director interlocks are addressed in Kang, E. 2008. Director interlocks and spillover effects of reputational penalties from financial reporting fraud. *Academy of Management Journal,* 51(3): 537–556.

72. There are benefits, of course, to having some insiders on the board of directors. Inside directors would be more aware of the firm's strategies. Additionally, outsiders may rely too often on financial performance indicators because of information asymmetries. For an interesting discussion, see Baysinger, B. D. & Hoskisson, R. E. 1990. The composition of boards of directors and strategic control: Effects on corporate strategy. *Academy of Management Review,* 15: 72–87.

73. Hambrick, D. C. & Jackson, E. M. 2000. Outside directors with a stake: The linchpin in improving governance. *California Management Review,* 42(4): 108–127.

74. Corsi, C., Dale, G., Daum, J., Mumm, J., & Schoppen, W. 2010. 5 things board directors should be thinking about. *spencerstuart.com,* December: np; Evans, B. 2007. Six steps to building an effective board. *inc.com* : np; Beatty, D. 2009. New challenges for corporate governance. *Rotman Magazine,* Fall: 58–63; and Krause, R., Semadeni, M., & Cannella, A. 2013. External COO/presidents as expert directors: A new look at the service role of boards. *Strategic Management Journal,* 34(13): 1628–1641.

75. Anonymous. 2011. Corporate boards now and then. *Harvard Business Review* 89(11): 38–39; Choe, S. 2017. Women are, very slowly, getting more seats in the boardroom. *Dallas Morning News,* February 5: 1D, 8D; and Kehoe, C., Lund, F., & Speilman, N. 2016. Toward a value creating board. *mckinsey.com.* February: np.

76. A discussion on the shareholder approval process in executive compensation is presented in Brandes, P., Goranova, M., & Hall, S. 2008. Navigating shareholder influence: Compensation plans and the shareholder approval process. *Academy of Management Perspectives,* 22(1): 41–57.

77. Monks and Minow, op. cit., p. 93.

78. A discussion of the factors that lead to shareholder activism is found in Ryan, L. V. & Schneider, M. 2002. The antecedents of institutional investor activism. *Academy of Management Review,* 27(4): 554–573.

79. For an insightful discussion of investor activism, refer to David, P., Bloom, M., & Hillman, A. 2007. Investor activism, managerial responsiveness, and corporate social performance. *Strategic Management Journal,* 28(1): 91–100.

80. There is strong research support for the idea that the presence of large-block shareholders is associated with value-maximizing decisions. For example, refer to Johnson, R. A., Hoskisson, R. E., & Hitt, M. A. 1993. Board of director involvement in restructuring: The effects of board versus managerial controls and characteristics. *Strategic Management Journal,* 14: 33–50.

81. Anonymous. 2011. Institutional ownership nears all-time highs. Good or bad for alpha-seekers? *allaboutalpha.com,* February 2: np.

82. For an interesting perspective on the impact of institutional ownership on a firm's innovation strategies, see Hoskisson, R. E., Hitt, M. A., Johnson, R. A., & Grossman, W. 2002. *Academy of Management Journal,* 45(4): 697–716.

83. *calpers.ca.gov.*

84. *www.calpers-governance.org.*

85. Anonymous. 2011. Corporate boards now and then. *Harvard Business Review.* 89(11): 38–39.

86. For a study of the relationship between ownership and diversification, refer to Goranova, M., Alessandri, T. M., Brandes, P., & Dharwadkar, R. 2007. Managerial ownership and corporate diversification: A longitudinal view. *Strategic Management Journal,* 28(3): 211–226.

87. Jensen, M. C. & Murphy, K. J. 1990. CEO incentives—It's not how much you pay, but how. *Harvard Business Review,* 68(3): 138–149.

88. For a perspective on the relative advantages and disadvantages of "duality"—that is, one individual serving as both chief executive office and chairman of the board, see Lorsch, J. W. & Zelleke, A. 2005. Should the CEO be the chairman? *MIT Sloan Management Review,* 46(2): 71–74.

89. A discussion of knowledge sharing is addressed in Fey, C. F. & Furu, P. 2008. Top management incentive compensation and knowledge sharing in multinational corporations. *Strategic Management Journal,* 29(12): 1301–1324.

90. Nicks, D. 2016. CEOs make 335 times what workers earn. *time.com.* May 17: np.

91. Sasseen, J. 2007. A better look at the boss's pay. *BusinessWeek,* February 26: 44–45; and Weinberg, N., Maiello, M., & Randall, D. 2008. Paying for failure. *Forbes,* May 19: 114, 116.

92. Research has found that executive compensation is more closely aligned with firm performance in companies with compensation committees and boards dominated by outside directors. See, for example, Conyon, M. J. & Peck, S. I. 1998. Board control, remuneration committees, and top management compensation. *Academy of Management Journal,* 41: 146–157.

93. Anonymous. 2012. American chief executives are not overpaid. *The Economist,* September 8: 67.

94. Chahine, S. & Tohme, N. S. 2009. Is CEO duality always negative? An exploration of CEO duality and ownership structure in the Arab IPO context. *Corporate Governance: An International Review,* 17(2): 123–141; and McGrath, J. 2009. How CEOs work. *HowStuffWorks.com.* January 28: np.

95. Anonymous. 2009. Someone to watch over them. *The Economist,* October 17: 78; Anonymous. 2004. Splitting up the roles of CEO and chairman: Reform or red herring? *Knowledge@Wharton,* June 2: np; and Kim, J. 2010. Shareholders reject split of CEO and chairman jobs at JPMorgan. *FierceFinance.com,* May 18: np.

96. Tuggle, C. S., Sirmon, D. G., Reutzel, C. R., & Bierman, L. 2010. Commanding board of director attention: Investigating how organizational performance and CEO duality affect board members' attention to monitoring. *Strategic Management Journal,* 31: 946–968; Weinberg, N. 2010. No more lapdogs. *Forbes,* May 10: 34–36; and Anonymous. 2010. Corporate constitutions. *The Economist,* October 30: 74.

97. Semadeni, M. & Krause, R. 2012. Splitting the CEO and chairman roles: It's complicated . . . *businessweek.com,* November 1: np.

98. Such opportunistic behavior is common in all principal–agent relationships. For a description of agency problems, especially in the context of the relationship between shareholders and managers, see Jensen, M. C. & Meckling, W. H. 1976. Theory of the firm: Managerial behavior, agency costs, and ownership structure. *Journal of Financial Economics,* 3: 305–360.

99. Hoskisson, R. E. & Turk, T. A. 1990. Corporate restructuring: Governance and control limits of the internal market. *Academy of Management Review,* 15: 459–477.

100. For an insightful perspective on the market for corporate control and how it is influenced by knowledge intensity, see Coff, R. 2003. Bidding wars over R&D-intensive firms: Knowledge, opportunism, and the market for corporate control. *Academy of Management Journal,* 46(1): 74–85.

101. Walsh, J. P. & Kosnik, R. D. 1993. Corporate raiders and their disciplinary role in the market for corporate control. *Academy of Management Journal,* 36: 671–700.

102. The role of regulatory bodies in the banking industry is addressed in Bhide, A. 2009. Why bankers got so reckless. *BusinessWeek,* February 9: 30–31.

103. Timmerman, L. 2015. A timeline of the Turing Pharma controversy. *forbes.com.* September 23: np.

104. Swartz, J. 2010. Timberland's CEO on standing up to 65,000 angry activists. *Harvard Business Review,* 88(9): 39–43.

105. This section draws upon Young, M. N., Peng, M. W., Ahlstrom, D., Bruton, G. D., & Jiang, Y. 2005. Principal-principal conflicts in corporate governance (unpublished manuscript); and, Peng, M. W. 2006. *Global Strategy.* Cincinnati: Thomson South-Western. We appreciate the helpful comments of Mike Young of HongKong Baptist University and Mike Peng of the University of Texas at Dallas.

106. Khanna, T. & Rivkin, J. 2001. Estimating the performance effects of business groups in emerging markets. *Strategic Management Journal,* 22: 45–74.

chapter 10

Creating Effective Organizational Designs

After reading this chapter, you should have a good understanding of the following learning objectives:

LO10-1 The growth patterns of major corporations and the relationship between a firm's strategy and its structure.

LO10-2 Each of the traditional types of organizational structure: simple, functional, divisional, and matrix.

LO10-3 The implications of a firm's international operations for organizational structure.

LO10-4 The different types of boundaryless organizations—barrier-free, modular, and virtual—and their relative advantages and disadvantages.

LO10-5 The need for creating ambidextrous organizational designs that enable firms to explore new opportunities and effectively integrate existing operations.

©Anatoli Styf/Shutterstock

LEARNING FROM MISTAKES

The Boeing 787 Dreamliner is a game changer in the aircraft market.[1] It is the first commercial airliner that doesn't have an aluminum skin. Instead, Boeing designed it to have a composite exterior, which provides a weight savings that allows the plane to use 20 percent less fuel than the 767, the plane it is designed to replace. The increased fuel efficiency and other design advancements made the 787 very popular with airlines. Boeing received orders for over 900 Dreamliners before the first 787 ever took flight.

It was also a game changer for Boeing. In 2003, when Boeing announced the development of the new plane, it also decided to design and manufacture the 787 in a way that was different from what it had ever done before. In the past, Boeing had internally designed and engineered the major components of its planes. Boeing would then provide detailed engineering designs and specifications to its key suppliers. The suppliers would then build the components to Boeing's specifications. To limit the up-front investment it would need to make with the 787, Boeing moved to a modular structure and outsourced much of the engineering of the components to suppliers. Boeing provided them with basic specifications and left it to the suppliers to undertake the detailed design, engineering, and manufacturing of components and subsystems. Boeing's operations in Seattle were then responsible for assembling the pieces into a completed aircraft.

Working with about 50 suppliers on four continents, Boeing found the coordination and integration of the work of suppliers to be very challenging. Some of the contracted suppliers didn't have the engineering expertise needed to do the work and outsourced the engineering to subcontractors. This made it especially difficult to monitor the engineering work for the plane. Jim Albaugh, Boeing's commercial aviation chief, identified a core issue with this change in responsibility and stated, "We gave work to people that had never really done this kind of technology before, and we didn't provide the oversight that was necessary." With the geographic stretch of the supplier set, Boeing also had difficulty monitoring the progress of the supplying firms. Boeing even ended up buying some of the suppliers once it became apparent they couldn't deliver the designs and products on schedule. For example, Boeing spent about $1 billion to acquire the Vought Aircraft Industries unit responsible for the plane's fuselage. When the suppliers finally delivered the parts, Boeing sometimes found they had difficulty assembling or combining the components. With its first 787, it found that the nose section and the fuselage didn't initially fit together, leaving a sizable gap between the two sections. To address these issues, Boeing was forced to co-locate many of its major suppliers together for six months to smooth out design and integration issues.

In the end, the decision to outsource cost Boeing dearly. The plane was three years behind schedule when the first 787 was delivered to a customer. The entire process took billions of dollars more than originally projected and also more than what it would have cost Boeing to design in-house. In early 2013, all 49 of the 787s that had been delivered to customers were grounded because of concerns about onboard fires in the lithium ion batteries used to power the plane—parts that were not designed by Boeing. As Boeing CEO Jim McNerney concluded, "In retrospect, our 787 game plan may have been overly ambitious, incorporating too many firsts all at once—in the application of new technologies, in revolutionary design and build processes, and in increased global sourcing of engineering and manufacturing content."

One of the central concepts in this chapter is the importance of boundaryless organizations. Successful organizations create permeable boundaries among the internal activities as well as between the organization and its external customers, suppliers, and alliance partners. We introduced this idea in Chapter 3 in our discussion of the value-chain concept, which consisted of several primary (e.g., inbound logistics, marketing and sales) and support activities (e.g., procurement, human resource management). There are a number of possible benefits to outsourcing activities as part of becoming an effective boundaryless organization. However, outsourcing can also create challenges. As in the case of Boeing, the firm lost a large amount of control by using independent suppliers to design and manufacture key subsystems of the 787.

Today's managers are faced with two ongoing and vital activities in structuring and designing their organizations.[2] First, they must decide on the most appropriate type of organizational structure. Second, they need to assess what mechanisms, processes, and techniques are most helpful in enhancing the permeability of both internal and external boundaries.

TRADITIONAL FORMS OF ORGANIZATIONAL STRUCTURE

organizational structure
the formalized patterns of interactions that link a firm's tasks, technologies, and people.

Organizational structure refers to the formalized patterns of interactions that link a firm's tasks, technologies, and people.[3] Structures help to ensure that resources are used effectively in accomplishing an organization's mission. Structure provides a means of balancing two conflicting forces: a need for the division of tasks into meaningful groupings and the need to integrate such groupings in order to ensure efficiency and effectiveness.[4] Structure identifies the executive, managerial, and administrative organization of a firm and indicates responsibilities and hierarchical relationships. It also influences the flow of information as well as the context and nature of human interactions.[5]

Most organizations begin very small and either die or remain small. Those that survive and prosper embark on strategies designed to increase the overall scope of operations and enable them to enter new product-market domains. Such growth places additional pressure on executives to control and coordinate the firm's increasing size and diversity. The most appropriate type of structure depends on the nature and magnitude of growth.

Patterns of Growth of Large Corporations: Strategy-Structure Relationships

LO 10-1

The growth patterns of major corporations and the relationship between a firm's strategy and its structure.

A firm's strategy and structure change as it increases in size, diversifies into new product markets, and expands its geographic scope.[6] Exhibit 10.1 illustrates common growth patterns of firms.

A new firm with a *simple structure* typically increases its sales revenue and volume of outputs over time. It may also engage in some vertical integration to secure sources of supply

EXHIBIT 10.1 Dominant Growth Patterns of Large Corporations

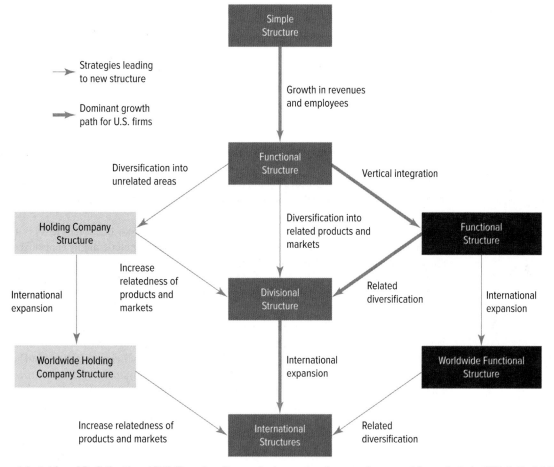

Source: Adapted from J.R. Galbraith and R.K. Kazanjian, *Strategy Implementation: Structure, Systems and Process* 2nd ed., 1986, St. Paul, MN: West Publishing Company.

(backward integration) as well as channels of distribution (forward integration). The simple-structure firm then implements a *functional structure* to concentrate efforts on both increasing efficiency and enhancing its operations and products. This structure enables the firm to group its operations into functions, departments, or geographic areas. As its initial markets mature, a firm looks beyond its present products and markets for possible expansion.

A strategy of related diversification requires a need to reorganize around product lines or geographic markets. This leads to a *divisional structure.* As the business expands in terms of sales revenues, and domestic growth opportunities become somewhat limited, a firm may seek opportunities in international markets. A firm has a wide variety of structures to choose from. These include *international division, geographic area, worldwide product division, worldwide functional,* and *worldwide matrix.* Deciding upon the most appropriate structure when a firm has international operations depends on three primary factors: the extent of international expansion, type of strategy (global, multidomestic, or transnational), and degree of product diversity.[7]

Some firms may find it advantageous to diversify into several product lines rather than focus their efforts on strengthening distributor and supplier relationships through vertical integration. They would organize themselves according to product lines by implementing a divisional structure. Also, some firms may choose to move into unrelated product areas, typically by acquiring existing businesses. Frequently, their rationale is that acquiring assets and competencies is more economical or expedient than developing them internally. Such an unrelated, or conglomerate, strategy requires relatively little integration across businesses and sharing of resources. Thus, a *holding company structure* becomes appropriate. There are many other growth patterns, but these are the most common.*

Now we will discuss some of the most common types of organizational structures—simple, functional, divisional (including two variants: *strategic business unit* and *holding company*), and matrix—and their advantages and disadvantages. We will close the section with a discussion of the structural implications when a firm expands its operations into international markets.[8]

LO 10-2

Each of the traditional types of organizational structure: simple, functional, divisional, and matrix.

simple organizational structure
an organizational form in which the owner-manager makes most of the decisions and controls activities, and the staff serves as an extension of the top executive.

Simple Structure

The **simple organizational structure** is the oldest, and most common, organizational form. Most organizations are very small and have a single or very narrow product line in which the owner-manager (or top executive) makes most of the decisions. The owner-manager controls all activities, and the staff serves as an extension of the top executive.

Advantages   The simple structure is highly informal, and the coordination of tasks is accomplished by direct supervision. Characteristics of this structure include highly centralized decision making, little specialization of tasks, few rules and regulations, and an informal evaluation and reward system. Although the owner-manager is intimately involved in almost all phases of the business, a manager is often employed to oversee day-to-day operations.

Disadvantages   A simple structure may foster creativity and individualism since there are generally few rules and regulations. However, such "informality" may lead to problems. Employees may not clearly understand their responsibilities, which can lead to conflict and confusion. Employees may take advantage of the lack of regulations and act in their own self-interest, which can erode motivation and satisfaction and lead to the possible misuse of organizational resources. Small organizations have flat structures that limit opportunities for upward mobility. Without the potential for future advancement, recruiting and retaining talent may become very difficult.

Functional Structure

When an organization is small (15 or fewer employees), it is not necessary to have a variety of formal arrangements and groupings of activities. However, as firms grow, excessive demands may be placed on the owner-manager in order to obtain and process all of the information necessary to run the business. Chances are the owner will not be skilled in all specialties (e.g., accounting, engineering, production, marketing). Thus, he or she will need to hire specialists in the various functional areas. Such growth in the overall scope and complexity of the business necessitates a **functional organizational structure** wherein the major functions of the firm are grouped internally. The coordination and integration of the functional areas become among the most important responsibilities of the chief executive of the firm (see Exhibit 10.2).

functional organizational structure
an organizational form in which the major functions of the firm, such as production, marketing, R&D, and accounting, are grouped internally.

Functional structures are generally found in organizations in which there is a single or closely related product or service, high production volume, and some vertical integration. Initially, firms tend to expand the overall scope of their operations by penetrating existing markets, introducing similar products in additional markets, or increasing the level of vertical integration. Such expansion activities clearly increase the scope and complexity of the

---

* The lowering of transaction costs and globalization have led to some changes in the common historical patterns that we have discussed. Some firms are, in effect, bypassing the vertical integration stage. Instead, they focus on core competencies and outsource other value-creation activities. Also, even relatively young firms are going global early in their history because of lower communication and transportation costs. For an interesting perspective on global start-ups, see McDougall, P. P. & Oviatt, B. M. 1996. New Venture Internationalization, Strategic Change and Performance: A Follow-Up Study. *Journal of Business Venturing,* 11: 23–40; and McDougall, P. P. & Oviatt, B. M. (Eds.). 2000. The Special Research Forum on International Entrepreneurship. *Academy of Management Journal,* October: 902–1003.

EXHIBIT 10.2 Functional Organizational Structure

Lower-level managers, specialists, and operating personnel

operations. The functional structure provides for a high level of centralization that helps to ensure integration and control over the related product-market activities or multiple primary activities (from inbound logistics to operations to marketing, sales, and service) in the value chain (addressed in Chapters 3 and 4).

Advantages By bringing together specialists into functional departments, a firm is able to enhance its coordination and control within each of the functional areas. Decision making in the firm will be centralized at the top of the organization. This enhances the organizational-level (as opposed to functional area) perspective across the various functions in the organization. In addition, the functional structure provides for a more efficient use of managerial and technical talent since functional area expertise is pooled in a single department (e.g., marketing) instead of being spread across a variety of product-market areas. Finally, career paths and professional development in specialized areas are facilitated.

Disadvantages The differences in values and orientations among functional areas may impede communication and coordination. Edgar Schein of MIT has argued that shared assumptions, often based on similar backgrounds and experiences of members, form around functional units in an organization. This leads to what are often called "stove pipes" or "silos," in which departments view themselves as isolated, self-contained units with little need for interaction and coordination with other departments. This erodes communication because functional groups may have not only different goals but also differing meanings of words and concepts. According to Schein:

> The word "marketing" will mean product development to the engineer, studying customers through market research to the product manager, merchandising to the salesperson, and constant change in design to the manufacturing manager. When they try to work together, they will often attribute disagreements to personalities and fail to notice the deeper, shared assumptions that color how each function thinks.[9]

Such narrow functional orientations also may lead to short-term thinking based largely upon what is best for the functional area, not the entire organization. In a manufacturing firm, sales may want to offer a wide range of customized products to appeal to the firm's customers; R&D may overdesign products and components to achieve technical elegance; and manufacturing may favor no-frills products that can be produced at low cost by means of long production runs. Functional structures may overburden the top executives in the firm because conflicts have a tendency to be "pushed up" to the top of the organization since there are no managers who are responsible for the specific product lines. Functional structures make it difficult to establish uniform performance standards across the entire organization. It may be relatively easy to evaluate production managers on the basis of production volume and cost control, but establishing performance measures for engineering, R&D, and accounting becomes more problematic.

Divisional Structure

divisional organizational structure
an organizational form in which products, projects, or product markets are grouped internally.

The **divisional organizational structure** (sometimes called the multidivisional structure or M-Form) is organized around products, projects, or markets. Each of the divisions, in turn, includes its own functional specialists who are typically organized into departments.[10] A divisional structure encompasses a set of relatively autonomous units governed by a central corporate office. The operating divisions are relatively independent and consist of products and services that are different from those of the other divisions.[11] Operational decision making in a large business places excessive demands on the firm's top management. In order to attend to broader, longer-term organizational issues, top-level managers must delegate decision making to lower-level managers. Divisional executives play a key role: They help to determine the product-market and financial objectives for the division as well as their division's contribution to overall corporate performance.[12] The rewards are based largely on measures of financial performance such as net income and revenue. Exhibit 10.3 illustrates a divisional structure.

General Motors was among the earliest firms to adopt the divisional organizational structure.[13] In the 1920s the company formed five major product divisions (Cadillac, Buick, Oldsmobile, Pontiac, and Chevrolet) as well as several industrial divisions. Since then, many firms have discovered that as they diversified into new product-market activities, functional structures—with their emphasis on single functional departments—were unable to manage the increased complexity of the entire business.

Advantages   By creating separate divisions to manage individual product markets, there is a separation of strategic and operating control. Divisional managers can focus their efforts on improving operations in the product markets for which they are responsible, and corporate officers can devote their time to overall strategic issues for the entire corporation. The focus on a division's products and markets—by the divisional executives—provides the corporation with an enhanced ability to respond quickly to important changes. Since there are functional departments within each division of the corporation, the problems associated with sharing resources across functional departments are minimized. Because there are multiple levels of general managers (executives responsible for integrating and coordinating all functional areas), the development of general management talent is enhanced.

EXHIBIT 10.3 Divisional Organizational Structure

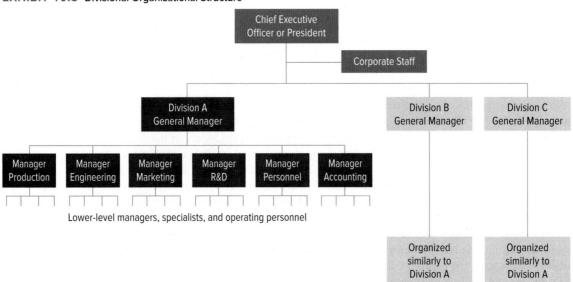

WHOLE FOODS CENTRALIZES TO IMPROVE EFFICIENCY

Whole Foods is making a major change to its structure. Historically, Whole Foods has used a decentralized, regional division structure. This structure, with its 12 semi-autonomous regional divisions, has allowed the firm to be responsive to the needs of customers in each of these regions. Differences across the regions included store layout, the products carried in the stores, and the methods for scheduling workers. However, the firm found this decentralized structure was inefficient and left it vulnerable to competitive attacks by Kroger and Costco, firms that enhanced their organic food portfolio at a lower cost point than Whole Foods. This led to a more than 50 percent drop in Whole Foods' stock price from late 2013 to early 2017.

Whole Foods has responded by centralizing key activities, most notably the firm's purchasing function. This will allow the firm to have one point of purchase with major suppliers, giving it stronger bargaining power since suppliers will be working with one large buyer rather than eleven smaller buyers. It is also developing centralized, automated information systems to simplify and standardize both staff and shelf replenishment scheduling. The firm is also eliminating over 2,000 jobs as part of this restructuring effort.

While this change promises significant efficiency gains, it doesn't come without risks. These changes may harm the firm's reputation as it replaces local products with nationally sourced products. As Jim Hertel, Senior Vice President of the retail consulting firm Willard Bishop stated, "The battle that always gets waged is cost relative to localized consumer preferences. Whole Foods must take care not to damage the reputation for being a top-quality location for regional products." Whole Foods' Global Vice President of Purchasing, Don Clark, is confident the change will not hurt the firm's core identity as "America's Healthiest Grocery Store" or its relationship with its customers.

Source: Brat, I. 2016. Whole Foods works to reduce cost and boost clout with suppliers. *wsj.com*. February 16: np; and, Anonymous. 2016. Whole Foods outlines move from regional to centralized buying. *specialtyfoods.com*. April 6: np.

Disadvantages   It can be very expensive; there can be increased costs due to the duplication of personnel, operations, and investment since each division must staff multiple functional departments. There also can be dysfunctional competition among divisions since each division tends to become concerned solely about its own operations. Divisional managers are often evaluated on common measures such as return on assets and sales growth. If goals are conflicting, there can be a sense of a "zero-sum" game that would discourage sharing ideas and resources among the divisions for the common good of the corporation. In sum, divisional structures, by design, divide people, resources, and knowledge. They insulate divisional managers from other divisional managers, inhibiting their ability to coordinate activities, share resources, and learn from each other.

With many divisions providing different products and services, there is the chance that differences in image and quality may occur across divisions. One division may offer no-frills products of lower quality that may erode the brand reputation of another division that has top-quality, highly differentiated offerings. Since each division is evaluated in terms of financial measures such as return on investment and revenue growth, there is often an urge to focus on short-term performance. If corporate management uses quarterly profits as the key performance indicator, divisional management may tend to put significant emphasis on "making the numbers" and minimizing activities, such as advertising, maintenance, and capital investments, which would detract from short-term performance measures. Strategy Spotlight 10.1 discusses how Whole Foods is trying to overcome some of the limitations of a divisional structure by centralizing key activities.

We'll discuss two variations of the divisional form: the strategic business unit (SBU) and holding company structures.

Strategic Business Unit (SBU) Structure   Highly diversified corporations such as ConAgra, a $13 billion food producer, may consist of dozens of different divisions.[14] If ConAgra were to use a purely divisional structure, it would be nearly impossible for the corporate office to plan and coordinate activities, because the span of control would be too large. To attain synergies, ConAgra has put its diverse businesses into three primary SBUs: food service (restaurants), retail (grocery stores), and agricultural products.

With an **SBU structure,** divisions with similar products, markets, and/or technologies are grouped into homogeneous units to achieve some synergies. These include those discussed in Chapter 6 for related diversification, such as leveraging core competencies, sharing infrastructures, and market power. Generally the more related businesses are within a corporation, the fewer SBUs will be required. Each of the SBUs in the corporation operates as a profit center.

Advantages The SBU structure makes the task of planning and control by the corporate office more manageable. Also, with greater decentralization of authority, individual businesses can react more quickly to important changes in the environment than if all divisions had to report directly to the corporate office.

Disadvantages Since the divisions are grouped into SBUs, it may become difficult to achieve synergies across SBUs. If divisions in different SBUs have potential sources of synergy, it may become difficult for them to be realized. The additional level of management increases the number of personnel and overhead expenses, while the additional hierarchical level removes the corporate office further from the individual divisions. The corporate office may become unaware of key developments that could have a major impact on the corporation.

Holding Company Structure The **holding company structure** (sometimes referred to as a *conglomerate*) is also a variation of the divisional structure. Whereas the SBU structure is often used when similarities exist between the individual businesses (or divisions), the holding company structure is appropriate when the businesses in a corporation's portfolio do not have much in common. Thus, the potential for synergies is limited.

Holding company structures are most appropriate for firms with a strategy of unrelated diversification. Companies such as Berkshire Hathaway and Loews use a holding company structure to implement their unrelated diversification strategies. Since there are few similarities across the businesses, the corporate offices in these companies provide a great deal of autonomy to operating divisions and rely on financial controls and incentive programs to obtain high levels of performance from the individual businesses. Corporate staffs at these firms tend to be small because of their limited involvement in the overall operation of their various businesses.[15]

Advantages The holding company structure has the cost savings associated with fewer personnel and the lower overhead resulting from a small corporate office and fewer hierarchical levels. The autonomy of the holding company structure increases the motivational level of divisional executives and enables them to respond quickly to market opportunities and threats.

Disadvantages There is an inherent lack of control and dependence that corporate-level executives have on divisional executives. Major problems could arise if key divisional executives leave the firm, because the corporate office has very little "bench strength"—additional managerial talent ready to quickly fill key positions. If problems arise in a division, it may become very difficult to turn around individual businesses because of limited staff support in the corporate office.

Strategy Spotlight 10.2 discusses the prominent position of conglomerate firms in Asian countries.

Matrix Structure

One approach that tries to overcome the inadequacies inherent in the other structures is the **matrix organizational structure.** It is a combination of the functional and divisional structures.

WHERE CONGLOMERATES PROSPER

While conglomerates were numerous and well regarded in the United States and Western Europe in the 1960s and 1970s, firms that compete in a wide range of unrelated industries now are seen as being unfocused and unlikely to succeed. As a result, there are only about two dozen conglomerates still in existence in the United States and Europe.

The situation is quite different in much of the rest of the world, especially in Asia. For example, 45 of the largest 50 companies in India belong to a conglomerate business group. In South Korea, it is 40 of the largest 50. Additionally, in India, companies that belong to a conglomerate business group, on average, have outperformed independent companies. They also grow more rapidly than independent firms in their markets. For example, Indian conglomerates grew by more than 20 percent a year in the 2004 to 2013 period. Why is this the case? Some have argued that conglomerate business groups have thrived in developing markets because the social ties within conglomerate business groups serve as a substitute for weak governmental regulation and legal systems. The tightness of the group leads to social pressures that keep companies in line, and the head ownership group can settle disputes between companies. But these conglomerate groups have continued to grow even as the government and legal systems in these countries have modernized and become more westernized.

A second explanation is that the business groups in these countries are structured in a way that offers the benefits of being in a business with a vast range of competencies without some of the costs found in conglomerates in the United States, Canada, and Western Europe. A key difference is that while a conglomerate that is based in the United States, Canada, or Western Europe is a single corporation with a wide set of wholly owned subsidiaries, a conglomerate in Asia is actually made up of a set of legally separate corporations. Each of these corporations has its own board of directors and shareholders, but it is tied to the conglomerate since one of its major owners also owns part of the other corporations in the conglomerate. For example, the Tata group in India is comprised of over 100 separate companies. This type of structure allows the companies to have a degree of independence but also the benefits of size and power. This hybrid structure has a number of benefits.

- **Superior decision making.** The top managers of the affiliated firms have a great deal of autonomy to make decisions—meaning that key strategic decisions are made by managers who are close to the market. Thus, decisions can be quick and based on local market knowledge. In U.S. conglomerates, subsidiary managers typically have much less autonomy and have to get the approval of the corporate office.

- **Access to financial resources.** When affiliated units in business groups need financial capital to fund strategic investments, they can use funds within their own company, look to the central business group to provide funding, or look to outside investors to raise funds. Thus, they have great flexibility in raising capital. In contrast, the corporate offices of U.S. conglomerates typically accumulate financial resources and then allocate these funds to the business units. As a result, there is less funding available since units can't look to outside investors, and the process for allocating capital often becomes very political.

- **More effective managerial incentives.** Since the affiliated units are independent firms, the firm is able to set up evaluation and reward systems for managers that are tailored to the firm's distinctive needs and market position. In contrast, in U.S. conglomerates, the firms typically set up evaluation and rewards systems that are consistent across all of its units.

- **Resources and guidance from the group center.** These affiliated firms also have advantages over independent firms in their own market. These business groups have a center group that can provide strategic insight to the affiliated businesses. The center group will search for long-term business opportunities associated with emerging technologies or market changes and bring promising ideas to the affiliated businesses. This frees up the affiliated businesses to focus on current activities and allow the center group to do the longer term visioning. The center group is also responsible for linking together different businesses when cross-business opportunities arise. Finally, the center group ensures that all of the activities in the businesses align with the identity of the overall group. As a result, each of the businesses benefits from the strong and consistent image associated with the overall business group.

It is unclear if these conglomerates will continue to thrive in these markets, but their ability to sustain their dominance to date and their success in regularly moving into new markets suggest that they will continue to be major players for the foreseeable future.

Source: Hirt, M., Smit, S., and Yoo, W. 2013. Understanding Asia's conglomerates. *mckinsey.com*. February: np; and, Ramachandran, J., Manikandan, K., and Pant, A. 2013. Why conglomerates thrive. *Harvard Business Review*. 91(2): 110-119.

Most commonly, functional departments are combined with product groups on a project basis. For example, a product group may want to develop a new addition to its line; for this project, it obtains personnel from functional departments such as marketing, production, and engineering. These personnel work under the manager of the product group for the duration of the project, which can vary from a few weeks to an open-ended period of time. The individuals

EXHIBIT 10.4 Matrix Organizational Structure

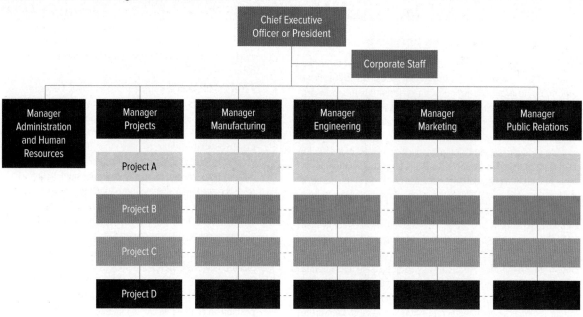

who work in a matrix organization become responsible to two managers: the project manager and the manager of their functional area. Exhibit 10.4 illustrates a matrix structure.

Some large multinational corporations rely on a matrix structure to combine product groups and geographic units. Product managers have global responsibility for the development, manufacturing, and distribution of their own line, while managers of geographic regions have responsibility for the profitability of the businesses in their regions. Vodafone, the wireless service provider, utilizes this type of structure.

Other organizations, such as Cisco, use a matrix structure to try to maintain flexibility. In these firms, individual workers have a permanent functional home but also are assigned to and work within temporary project teams.[16]

Advantages   The matrix structure facilitates the use of specialized personnel, equipment, and facilities. Instead of duplicating functions, as would be the case in a divisional structure based on products, the resources are shared. Individuals with high expertise can divide their time among multiple projects. Such resource sharing and collaboration enable a firm to use resources more efficiently and to respond more quickly and effectively to changes in the competitive environment. The flexibility inherent in a matrix structure provides professionals with a broader range of responsibility. Such experience enables them to develop their skills and competencies.

Disadvantages   The dual-reporting structures can result in uncertainty and lead to intense power struggles and conflict over the allocation of personnel and other resources. Working relationships become more complicated. This may result in excessive reliance on group processes and teamwork, along with a diffusion of responsibility, which in turn may erode timely decision making.

Exhibit 10.5 briefly summarizes the advantages and disadvantages of the functional, divisional, and matrix organizational structures.

LO 10-3

The implications of a firm's international operations for organizational structure.

International Operations: Implications for Organizational Structure

Today's managers must maintain an international outlook on their firm's businesses and competitive strategies. In the global marketplace, managers must ensure consistency between

EXHIBIT 10.5 Functional, Divisional, and Matrix Organizational Structures: Advantages and Disadvantages

Functional Structure	
Advantages	**Disadvantages**
• Pooling of specialists enhances coordination and control.	• Differences in functional area orientation impede communication and coordination.
• Centralized decision making enhances an organizational perspective across functions.	• Tendency for specialists to develop short-term perspective and narrow functional orientation.
• Efficient use of managerial and technical talent.	• Functional area conflicts may overburden top-level decision makers.
• Facilitates career paths and professional development in specialized areas.	• Difficult to establish uniform performance standards.

Divisional Structure	
Advantages	**Disadvantages**
• Increases strategic and operational control, permitting corporate-level executives to address strategic issues.	• Increased costs incurred through duplication of personnel, operations, and investment.
• Quick response to environmental changes.	• Dysfunctional competition among divisions may detract from overall corporate performance.
• Increases focus on products and markets.	• Difficult to maintain uniform corporate image.
• Minimizes problems associated with sharing resources across functional areas.	• Overemphasis on short-term performance.
• Facilitates development of general managers.	

Matrix Structure	
Advantages	**Disadvantages**
• Increases market responsiveness through collaboration and synergies among professional colleagues.	• Dual-reporting relationships can result in uncertainty regarding accountability.
• Allows more efficient utilization of resources.	• Intense power struggles may lead to increased levels of conflict.
• Improves flexibility, coordination, and communication.	• Working relationships may be more complicated and human resources duplicated.
• Increases professional development through a broader range of responsibility.	• Excessive reliance on group processes and teamwork may impede timely decision making.

their strategies (at the business, corporate, and international levels) and the structure of their organization. As firms expand into foreign markets, they generally follow a pattern of change in structure that parallels the changes in their strategies.[17] Three major contingencies that influence the chosen structure are (1) the type of strategy that is driving a firm's foreign operations, (2) product diversity, and (3) the extent to which a firm is dependent on foreign sales.[18]

As international operations become an important part of a firm's overall operations, managers must make changes that are consistent with their firm's structure. The primary types of structures used to manage a firm's international operations are:[19]

- International division
- Geographic-area division
- Worldwide functional
- Worldwide product division
- Worldwide matrix

international division structure
an organizational form in which international operations are in a separate, autonomous division. Most domestic operations are kept in other parts of the organization.

geographic-area division structure
a type of divisional organizational structure in which operations in geographic regions are grouped internally.

worldwide matrix structure
a type of matrix organizational structure that has one line of authority for geographic-area divisions and another line of authority for worldwide product divisions.

worldwide functional structure
a functional structure in which all departments have worldwide reponsibilities.

worldwide product division structure
a product division structure in which all divisions have worldwide responsibilities.

global start-up
a business organization that, from inception, seeks to derive significant advantage from the use of resources and the sale of outputs in multiple countries.

Multidomestic strategies are driven by political and cultural imperatives requiring managers within each country to respond to local conditions. The structures consistent with such a strategic orientation are the **international division** and **geographic-area division structures.** Here, local managers are provided with a high level of autonomy to manage their operations within the constraints and demands of their geographic market. As a firm's foreign sales increase as a percentage of its total sales, it will likely change from an international division to a geographic-area division structure. And, as a firm's product and/or market diversity becomes large, it is likely to benefit from a **worldwide matrix structure.**

Global strategies are driven by economic pressures that require managers to view operations in different geographic areas to be managed for overall efficiency. The structures consistent with the efficiency perspective are the **worldwide functional** and **worldwide product division structures.** Here, division managers view the marketplace as homogeneous and devote relatively little attention to local market, political, and economic factors. The choice between these two types of structures is guided largely by the extent of product diversity. Firms with relatively low levels of product diversity may opt for a worldwide product division structure. However, if significant product-market diversity results from highly unrelated international acquisitions, a worldwide holding company structure should be implemented. Such firms have very little commonality among products, markets, or technologies and have little need for integration.

Global Start-Ups: A Recent Phenomenon

International expansion occurs rather late for most corporations, typically after possibilities of domestic growth are exhausted. Increasingly, we are seeing two interrelated phenomena. First, many firms now expand internationally relatively early in their history. Second, some firms are "born global"—that is, from the very beginning, many start-ups are global in their activities. For example, Logitech International, a leading producer of personal computer accessories, was global from day one. Founded in 1982 by a Swiss national and two Italians, the company was headquartered in both California and Switzerland. R&D and manufacturing were also conducted in both locations and, subsequently, in Taiwan and Ireland.[20]

The success of companies such as Logitech challenges the conventional wisdom that a company must first build up assets, internal processes, and experience before venturing into faraway lands. It also raises a number of questions: What exactly is a global start-up? Under what conditions should a company start out as a global start-up? What does it take to succeed as a global start-up?

A **global start-up** has been defined as a business organization that, from inception, seeks to derive significant competitive advantage from the use of resources and the sale of outputs in multiple countries. Right from the beginning, it uses inputs from around the world and sells its products and services to customers around the world. Geographic boundaries of nation-states are irrelevant for a global start-up.

There is no reason for every start-up to be global. Being global necessarily involves higher communication, coordination, and transportation costs. Therefore, it is important to identify the circumstances under which going global from the beginning is advantageous.[21] First, if the required human resources are globally dispersed, going global may be the best way to access those resources. For example, Italians are masters in fine leather and Swedes in ergonomics. Second, in many cases foreign financing may be easier to obtain and more suitable. Traditionally, U.S. venture capitalists have shown greater willingness to bear risk, but they have shorter time horizons in their expectations for return. If a U.S. start-up is looking for patient capital, it may be better off looking overseas. Third, the target customers in many specialized industries are located in other parts of the world. Fourth, in many industries a gradual move from domestic markets to foreign markets is no longer possible because, if a product is successful, foreign competitors may immediately imitate it. Therefore, preemptive entry into foreign markets may be the only option. Finally, because of high up-front

GLOBAL START-UP, BRCK, WORKS TO BRING RELIABLE INTERNET CONNECTIVITY TO THE WORLD

BRCK is a notable technology pioneer. It's bringing a novel and potentially very valuable product to market, and it is doing so as a truly global start-up. BRCK's first product is a surge-resistant, battery-powered router to provide Internet service, which the firm is simply calling the BRCK. In many parts of the world, power systems are unreliable and offer only intermittent service. Additionally, they are prone to generate power surges that can fry many electronic products, including Internet routers. For example, in 2013, a single power-surge event in Nairobi, Kenya, blew out more than 3,000 routers. BRCK has developed a product to address these issues. Its router has a built-in battery that charges up whenever the power grid is operating and that runs off the battery for up to eight hours when the power grid goes down. It can also handle power surges up to 400 volts. The BRCK is also flexible as to how it connects to the Internet. It can connect directly to an ethernet line, can link up with a Wi-Fi network in its area, and can connect via a wireless phone connection. BRCK is aiming to sell its product to small and medium-size businesses, schools, and medical facilities. Its routers allow up to 20 users to simultaneously connect to the Internet. The technologies it uses are not cutting-edge, but the end product itself is innovative and meets a market need.

What really sets BRCK apart is that it is a global start-up that turns the table on typical global structures. Most tech-oriented global firms design their products in a technology center in the developed world and manufacture the products in a developing country. BRCK has flipped this model. BRCK designs its products in a developing country and manufactures in a developed country. Its corporate headquarters are in Nairobi, Kenya, at a technology center that houses a small group of entrepreneurs. The firm employs a dozen engineers to design its products in its corporate headquarters, and while its offices look a bit like those in Silicon Valley, the building has backup power for times when the Kenyan power grid inevitably goes down. The firm sources most of the components for its routers from Asia and manufactures its products in Austin, Texas. Even its sales are also going global right from the start. As of 2016, the firm had sold BRCKs to customers in 50 countries. The firm has also gotten global acclaim, including winning Fast Company's 2016 Innovation by Design Award, the Global SME Award at the 2016 ITU Global Telecom Conference, and a finalist award at the 2016 African Entrepreneurship Awards.

Sources: Cary, J. 2014. Made in Kenya, assembled in America: This Internet-anywhere company innovates from silicon savannah. *fastcoexist.com,* September 4: np; Vogt, H. 2014. Made in Africa: A gadget startup. *wsj.com,* July 10: np; and Hersman, E. 2017. The year at BRCK. *brck.com.* January 2: np.

development costs, a global market is often necessary to recover the costs. This is particularly true for start-ups from smaller nations that do not have access to large domestic markets.

Successful management of a global start-up presents many challenges. Communication and coordination across time zones and cultures are always problematic. Since most global start-ups have far less resources than well-established corporations, one key for success is to internalize few activities and outsource the rest. Managers of such firms must have considerable prior international experience so that they can successfully handle the inevitable communication problems and cultural conflicts. Another key for success is to keep the communication and coordination costs low. The only way to achieve this is by creating less costly administrative mechanisms. The boundaryless organizational designs that we discuss in the next section are particularly suitable for global start-ups because of their flexibility and low cost.

Strategy Spotlight 10.3 discusses a Kenyan technology start-up with a global vision and scope of operations.

How an Organization's Structure Can Influence Strategy Formulation

Discussions of the relationship between strategy and structure usually strongly imply that structure follows strategy. The strategy that a firm chooses (e.g., related diversification) dictates such structural elements as the division of tasks, the need for integration of activities, and authority relationships within the organization. However, an existing structure can influence strategy formulation. Once a firm's structure is in place, it is very difficult and expensive to change.[22] Executives may not be able to modify their duties and responsibilities greatly or may not welcome the disruption associated with a transfer to a new location. There are costs associated with hiring, training, and replacing executive, managerial, and operating personnel. Strategy cannot be formulated without considering structural elements.

An organization's structure can also have an important influence on how it competes in the marketplace. It can also strongly influence a firm's strategy, day-to-day operations, and performance.[23]

LO 10-4

The different types of boundaryless organizations—barrier-free, modular, and virtual—and their relative advantages and disadvantages.

BOUNDARYLESS ORGANIZATIONAL DESIGNS

The term *boundaryless* may bring to mind a chaotic organizational reality in which "anything goes." This is not the case. As Jack Welch, GE's former CEO, has suggested, boundaryless does not imply that all internal and external boundaries vanish completely, but that they become more open and permeable.[24] We are not suggesting that **boundaryless organizational designs** replace the traditional forms of organizational structure, but they should complement them.

We will discuss three approaches to making boundaries more permeable that help to facilitate the widespread sharing of knowledge and information across both the internal and external boundaries of the organization. The *barrier-free* type involves making all organizational boundaries—internal and external—more permeable. Teams are a central building block for implementing the boundaryless organization. The *modular* and *virtual* types of organizations focus on the need to create seamless relationships with external organizations such as customers or suppliers. While the modular type emphasizes the outsourcing of noncore activities, the virtual (or network) organization focuses on alliances among independent entities formed to exploit specific market opportunities.

boundaryless organizational designs

organizations in which the boundaries, including vertical, horizontal, external, and geographic boundaries, are permeable.

The Barrier-Free Organization

The "boundary" mind-set is ingrained deeply into bureaucracies. It is evidenced by such clichés as "That's not my job" and "I'm here from corporate to help" or by endless battles over transfer pricing. In the traditional company, boundaries are clearly delineated in the design of an organization's structure. Their basic advantage is that the roles of managers and employees are simple, clear, well defined, and long lived. A major shortcoming was pointed out to the authors during an interview with a high-tech executive: "Structure tends to be divisive; it leads to territorial fights."

Such structures are being replaced by fluid, ambiguous, and deliberately ill-defined tasks and roles. Just because work roles are no longer clearly defined, however, does not mean that differences in skills, authority, and talent disappear. A **barrier-free organization** enables a firm to bridge real differences in culture, function, and goals to find common ground that facilitates information sharing and other forms of cooperative behavior. Eliminating the multiple boundaries that stifle productivity and innovation can enhance the potential of the entire organization.

barrier-free organization

an organizational design in which firms bridge real differences in culture, function, and goals to find common ground that facilitates information sharing and other forms of cooperative behavior.

Creating Permeable Internal Boundaries   For barrier-free organizations to work effectively, the level of trust and shared interests among all parts of the organization must be raised.[25] The organization needs to develop among its employees the skill level needed to work in a more democratic organization. Barrier-free organizations also require a shift in the organization's philosophy from executive to organizational development and from investments in high-potential individuals to investments in leveraging the talents of all individuals.

Teams can be an important aspect of barrier-free structures.[26] Jeffrey Pfeffer, author of several insightful books, including *The Human Equation,* suggests that teams have three primary advantages.[27] First, teams substitute peer-based control for hierarchical control of work activities. Employees control themselves, reducing the time and energy management needs to devote to control. Second, teams frequently develop more creative solutions to problems because they encourage the sharing of the tacit knowledge held by individuals.[28] Brainstorming, or group problem solving, involves the pooling of ideas and expertise to enhance the chances that at least one group member will think of a way to solve the problems at hand. Third, by substituting peer control for hierarchical control, teams permit the removal of layers of hierarchy and absorption of administrative tasks previously performed by specialists. This avoids the costs of having people whose sole job is to watch the people who watch other people do the work. Novartis, the Swiss pharmaceutical giant, is leveraging the power of teams by consolidating its R&D activities in four locations. Novartis believes that grouping together and teaming up researchers from different disciplines into self-managed work teams will foster creativity and cooperation.[29]

Some have argued for the need to move more radically to discard formal hierarchical structures and work toward a more democratic team organizational structure.[30] One version of such systems is called a "holacracy." In a holacracy, there is no formal organizational structure in the traditional sense. Instead, employees self-identify into roles, undertaking the types of tasks that they are highly skilled at and interested in. Most employees will have multiple roles. Employees then group together into self-organized teams—or, in the terminology of holacracy, circles—in which they work together to complete tasks, such as circles for service delivery or product development. Since individual employees have multiple roles, they typically belong to multiple circles. This overlapping membership facilitates communication and coordination between circles. The circles within a firm change over time to meet the evolving situation of the firm. Each circle elects a lead, called a "lead link." This lead link guides meetings and sets the general agenda for the circle, although the members of the circle decide democratically on how the circle will complete tasks. The lead link also serves as a member of a higher-level circle. Overseeing it all is the general company circle, a collection of lead links who serve as the leadership team for the firm.

Most firms that have moved to a holacracy way of organizing are small technology firms. These firms see little need for hierarchical authority, and they are attracted to the promises of improved agility and creativity, as well as higher employee morale, with this flexible, autonomous type of structure. However, in 2014, Zappos decided to transition its entire 1,500 employees to a holacracy structure. The new structure initially consisted of 250 circles, and it may grow to 400 circles as the new system gets fully implemented. Tony Hsieh, who was Zappos' CEO and is now lead link of the Experiential SWAT Team, says he wants "Zappos to function more like a city and less like a top-down bureaucratic organization." In making this change, Zappos is serving as a natural experiment to see if a larger firm can operate as a holacracy.

Developing Effective Relationships with External Constituencies   In barrier-free organizations, managers must also create flexible, porous organizational boundaries and establish communication flows and mutually beneficial relationships with internal (e.g., employees) and external (e.g., customers) constituencies.[31] IBM has worked to develop a long-standing cooperative relationship with the Mayo Clinic. The clinic is a customer but more importantly a research partner. IBM has placed staff at the Mayo Clinic, and the two organizations have worked together on technology for the early identification of aneurysms, the mining of data in electronic health records to develop customized treatment plans for patients, and other medical issues.[32]

Barrier-free organizations create successful relationships between both internal and external constituencies, but there is one additional constituency—competitors—with whom some organizations have benefited as they developed cooperative relationships. For example, Coca-Cola and PepsiCo, often argued to be the most intense rivals in business, work together to develop new, environmentally conscious refrigerants for use in their vending machines.[33]

THE BUSINESS ROUNDTABLE: A FORUM FOR SHARING BEST ENVIRONMENTAL SUSTAINABILITY PRACTICES

The Business Roundtable is a group of chief executive officers of major U.S. corporations that was created to promote pro-business public policy. It was formed in 1972 through the merger of three existing organizations: The March Group, the Construction Users Anti-Inflation Roundtable, and the Labor Law Study Committee. The group was called President Obama's "closest ally in the business community."

The Business Roundtable became the first broad-based business group to agree on the need to address climate change through collective action, and it remains committed to limiting greenhouse gas emissions and setting the United States on a more sustainable path. The organization considers that threats to water quality and quantity, rising greenhouse gas emissions, and the risk of climate change—along with increasing energy prices and growing demand—are of great concern.

Its report "Create, Grow, Sustain" provides best practices and metrics from Business Roundtable member companies that represent nearly all sectors of the economy with $6 trillion in annual revenues. CEOs from Walmart, FedEx, PepsiCo, Whirlpool, and Verizon are among the 126 executives from leading U.S. companies that shared some of their best sustainability initiatives in this report. These companies are committed to reducing emissions, increasing energy efficiency, and developing more sustainable business practices.

Let's look, for example, at some of Walmart's initiatives. The firm's CEO, Mike Duke, says it is working with suppliers, partners, and consumers to drive its sustainability program. It has helped establish the Sustainability Consortium to drive metrics for measuring the environmental effects of consumer products across their life cycle. The retailer also helped lead the creation of a Sustainable Product Index to provide product information to consumers about the environmental impact of the products they purchase.

As part of its sustainability efforts, Walmart has completed over 400 renewable energy projects. Combined, these efforts have resulted in more than 1 billion kilowatt-hours of renewable energy production each year, enough power to provide the electrical needs of 78,000 homes.

Walmart's renewable energy efforts have focused on three general initiatives:

- It has invested in developing distributed electrical generation systems on its property. As part of this effort, Walmart has installed 105 megawatts of solar panels—enough to power about 20,000 houses—on the roofs of 327 stores and distribution centers. It plans to double this number by 2020.

- Expanding its contracts with suppliers for renewable energy has also been a focus of Walmart. Thus, Walmart bypasses the local utility to go directly to renewable energy suppliers to sign long-term contracts for renewable energy. With long-term contracts, Walmart has found that providers will give it more favorable terms. Walmart also believes that the long-term contracts give suppliers the incentive to invest in their generation systems, increasing the availability of renewable power for other users.

- In regions where going directly to renewable energy suppliers is difficult or impossible, Walmart has engaged the local utilities to increase their investment in renewable energy.

Sources: Helman, C. 2015. How Walmart became a green energy giant, using other people's money. *forbes.com*. November 4: np; Anonymous. 2010. Leading CEOs share best sustainability practices. *www.environmentalleader.com,* April 26: np; Hopkins, M. No date. Sustainable growth. *www.businessroundtable,* np; Anonymous. 2012. Create, grow, sustain. *www.businessroundtable.org,* April 18: 120; *www.en.wikipedia.org.*

By joining and actively participating in the Business Roundtable—an organization consisting of CEOs of leading U.S. corporations—Walmart has been able to learn about cutting-edge sustainable initiatives of other major firms. This free flow of information has enabled Walmart to undertake a number of steps that have increased the energy efficiency of its operations. These are described in Strategy Spotlight 10.4.

The Insights from Research box offers evidence on how breaking down internal and external boundaries influences learning.

Risks, Challenges, and Potential Downsides   Many firms find that creating and managing a barrier-free organization can be frustrating.[34] Puritan-Bennett Corporation, a manufacturer of respiratory equipment, found that its product development time more than doubled after it adopted team management. Roger J. Dolida, director of R&D, attributed this failure to a lack of top management commitment, high turnover among team members, and infrequent meetings. Often, managers trained in rigid hierarchies find it difficult to make the transition to the more democratic, participative style that teamwork requires.

WHERE EMPLOYEES LEARN AFFECTS FINANCIAL PERFORMANCE

Overview

What company wouldn't want to improve financial performance? Research suggests that when employees of innovative companies engage in learning activities both inside their companies, such as across functional areas, and outside their companies, such as via strategic alliances, they can achieve the best performance. This is particularly true for businesses operating in transitional economies.

What the Research Shows

Businesses are expanding into transitional economies, such as China and India, to capitalize on these large markets. But how can businesses operating in these economies improve their financial performance? Research in *Entrepreneurship, Theory, and Practice* from scholars at Xi'an Jiaotong University and Old Dominion University provides tips to enhance performance. The researchers conducted a study using face-to-face interviews with 607 top managers in manufacturing companies in China. They sought to understand how innovative companies with an "entrepreneurial orientation" could realize better performance when their employees learn about technology, markets, customers, and other important information from a range of sources.

In particular, the researchers examined whether it mattered if companies focused learning activities within their organizations—such as sharing information across functional areas or implementing technology to facilitate internal knowledge sharing—or outside the organization—such as studying competitors, learning from government sources, or engaging in strategic alliances with other companies. The results demonstrated that, in general:

- Companies with a high entrepreneurial orientation engage in more internal learning activities.
- Companies with a moderate entrepreneurial orientation engage in more external learning activities.
- Companies with a low entrepreneurial orientation engage in little external learning.
- When companies with a high entrepreneurial orientation engaged in more internal learning, performance improved.
- Learning from external sources enhanced financial performance but by a lesser amount than learning from internal sources.

Why This Matters

Company leaders have long understood the importance of learning about new markets and entrepreneurial opportunities. This research suggests that where employees learn can have an impact on firm performance. It is useful for companies to engage in multiple learning sources, including developing ways to share knowledge internally and from external sources, such as rivals and government entities. However, the results also suggest that when it comes to being more innovative, entrepreneurial, and financially profitable, managers should emphasize internal learning and knowledge sharing among employees.

Generally, this is because knowledge coming from external sources is more available to all industry competitors, reducing its value and utility toward achieving a competitive advantage. Internal learning, on the other hand, involves members within an organization who combine company-specific knowledge, resources, and intellectual property. This allows the organization to fashion unique and proprietary innovations that are difficult for competitors to replicate.

Overall, to achieve the best performance, innovative companies with entrepreneurial drive should balance external and internal learning activities. Still, relatively more internal learning can generate the best overall performance.

Key Takeaways

- Entrepreneurial businesses operating in transition economies, such as China, can achieve the best performance when engaging in learning activities inside and outside the firm.
- When employees spend more time learning about internal company projects and activities, their companies are more innovative than when they try to learn from competitors in the industry.
- Companies whose employees have an innovative, entrepreneurial spirit and who spend time learning about internal company activities can improve their financial performance.
- Although learning through interactions with competitors or other external sources is valuable, businesses in transition economies can most improve their performance when employee learning is focused on internal company sources.

Research Reviewed

Zhao, Y., Ly, Y., Chen, L. 2011. Entrepreneurial orientation, organizational learning, and performance: Evidence from China. *Entrepreneurship, Theory and Practice* 35: 293–317.

CLOUDFLARE SEES THE NEED FOR STRUCTURE

Like most Internet startup firms, when CloudFlare was formed in 2009, the firm's founders proudly and boldly asserted that the firm would build a boundary-free organization with no hierarchy, no formal titles, and no HR function. CEO Matthew Prince wanted his firm to be flexible and focus on individuals being able to craft their own role and feel rewarded and valued in their chosen role. Bureaucracy and hierarchy would stifle those aims. Prince asserted, "Titles serve to differentiate, often in an arbitrary way, which can lead to perceived or actual unfair treatment. Here, you're judged by your work, not your rank." He also worried that putting people in formal roles would reduce the firm's ability to get the right people in the right roles as conditions changed. For example, the person tabbed to head up a small development team may not be suited to lead a growing venture team that may have 250 people on it. Prince commented that if roles were formalized in this situation, "Either the original person gets demoted, in which case he or she will likely leave, or the new person doesn't get brought in. Neither is a great outcome."

But as the firm succeeded and grew, Prince saw increasing difficulties with the boundaryless structure. In mid-2012, five of the firm's 35 employees quit. Two of the issues at work in these departures were that workers found the lack of a formal reporting structure and the lack of clarity regarding how a mid-level employee would advance frustrating. When problems arose, there was no one to turn to resolve the problem, other than pestering one of the founders. Also, since there were no formal HR policies, there were no policies regarding planning vacations, responding to departures, or developing expectations about work/life balance issues.

Prince knew things would need to change as the firm got larger. "People want feedback. They want direction. When we double our current staff, we will need more hierarchy and managers and processes." By 2015, he had hired a lead product engineer, an HR administrator, and a talent recruiter. CloudFlare still avoided giving people the title of manager, but it put people in key senior roles. As the sales team grew, the firm instituted formal hierarchical levels. Prince quipped that it actually worked, and that the engineering team noticed the sales team appreciated having the hierarchy, commenting, "Hey, they actually look happy and productive. Maybe managers aren't such a bad thing."

CloudFlare's experience shows that too much structure and too much hierarchy can slow things down and constrict information sharing. However, too little structure can also inhibit the ability to get things done and can demotivate workers. The challenge for CloudFlare and other fast growing firms is to find the right balance in providing enough structure but not so much that the firm becomes bureaucratic.

Sources: Gulati, R., & Desantola, A. 2016. Start-ups that last. *hbr.org*. March: np; and, Haden, J. 2013. Why there are no job titles at my company. *inc.com*. October: np.

The pros and cons of barrier-free structures are summarized in Exhibit 10.6. Strategy Spotlight 10.5 discusses how Cloudflare balanced the need for management structure and the desire for a barrier-free organization to facilitate growth.

The Modular Organization

modular organization
an organization in which nonvital functions are outsourced, using the knowledge and expertise of outside suppliers while retaining strategic control.

The **modular organization** outsources nonvital functions, tapping into the knowledge and expertise of "best in class" suppliers, but retains strategic control. Outsiders may be used to manufacture parts, handle logistics, or perform accounting activities.[35] The value chain can be used to identify the key primary and support activities performed by a firm to create value: Which activities do we keep in-house and which activities do we outsource to suppliers?[36] The organization becomes a central hub surrounded by networks of outside suppliers

EXHIBIT 10.6 Pros and Cons of Barrier-Free Structures

Pros	Cons
• Leverages the talents of all employees.	• Difficult to overcome political and authority boundaries inside and outside the organization.
• Enhances cooperation, coordination, and information sharing among functions, divisions, SBUs, and external constituencies.	• Lacks strong leadership and common vision, which can lead to coordination problems.
• Enables a quicker response to market changes through a single-goal focus.	• Time-consuming and difficult-to-manage democratic processes.
• Can lead to coordinated win–win initiatives with key suppliers, customers, and alliance partners.	• Lacks high levels of trust, which can impede performance.

and specialists, and parts can be added or taken away. Both manufacturing and service units may be modular.[37]

Apparel is an industry in which the modular type has been widely adopted. adidas, for example, does little of its own manufacturing. Instead, it contracts with outside suppliers who run over 1,000 manufacturing plants in over 60 different countries. These production facilities are mostly located in low labor cost countries, including Cambodia, China, Egypt, Pakistan, and Turkey.[38] Avoiding large investments in fixed assets helps adidas derive large profits on minor sales increases. Adidas can also keep pace with changing tastes in the marketplace because its suppliers have become expert at rapidly retooling to produce new products.[39]

In a modular company, outsourcing the noncore functions offers three advantages:

1. A firm can decrease overall costs, stimulate new product development by hiring suppliers with talent superior to that of in-house personnel, avoid idle capacity, reduce inventories, and avoid being locked into a particular technology.

2. A company can focus scarce resources on the areas where it holds a competitive advantage. These benefits can translate into more funding for R&D to hire the best engineers and for sales and service to provide continuous training for staff.

3. An organization can tap into the knowledge and expertise of its specialized supply chain partners, adding critical skills and accelerating organizational learning.[40]

The modular type enables a company to leverage relatively small amounts of capital and a small management team to achieve seemingly unattainable strategic objectives.[41] Certain preconditions are necessary before the modular approach can be successful. First, the company must work closely with suppliers to ensure that the interests of each party are being fulfilled. Companies need to find loyal, reliable vendors who can be trusted with trade secrets. They also need assurances that suppliers will dedicate their financial, physical, and human resources to satisfy strategic objectives such as lowering costs or being first to market.

Second, the modular company must be sure that it selects the proper competencies to keep in-house. For adidas, its core competencies are design and marketing, not shoe manufacturing; for Honda, the core competence is engine technology. An organization must avoid outsourcing components that may compromise its long-term competitive advantages.

Strategic Risks of Outsourcing   The main strategic concerns are (1) loss of critical skills or developing the wrong skills, (2) loss of cross-functional skills, and (3) loss of control over a supplier.[42]

Too much outsourcing can result in a firm "giving away" too much skill and control.[43] Outsourcing relieves companies of the requirement to maintain skill levels needed to manufacture essential components.[44] At one time, semiconductor chips seemed like a simple technology to outsource, but they have now become a critical component of a wide variety of products. Companies that have outsourced the manufacture of these chips run the risk of losing the ability to manufacture them as the technology escalates. They become more dependent upon their suppliers.

Cross-functional skills refer to the skills acquired through the interaction of individuals in various departments within a company.[45] Such interaction assists a department in solving problems as employees interface with others across functional units. However, if a firm outsources key functional responsibilities, such as manufacturing, communication across departments can become more difficult. A firm and its employees must now integrate their activities with a new, outside supplier.

The outsourced products may give suppliers too much power over the manufacturer. Suppliers that are key to a manufacturer's success can, in essence, hold the manufacturer "hostage."

Exhibit 10.7 summarizes the pros and cons of modular structures.[46]

EXHIBIT 10.7 Pros and Cons of Modular Structures

Pros	Cons
• Directs a firm's managerial and technical talent to the most critical activities.	• Inhibits common vision through reliance on outsiders.
• Maintains full strategic control over most critical activities—core competencies.	• Diminishes future competitive advantages if critical technologies or other competencies are outsourced.
• Achieves "best in class" performance at each link in the value chain.	• Increases the difficulty of bringing back into the firm activities that now add value due to market shifts.
• Leverages core competencies by outsourcing with smaller capital commitment.	• Leads to an erosion of cross-functional skills.
• Encourages information sharing and accelerates organizational learning.	• Decreases operational control and potential loss of control over a supplier.

The Virtual Organization

In contrast to the "self-reliant" thinking that guided traditional organizational designs, the strategic challenge today has become doing more with less and looking outside the firm for opportunities and solutions to problems. The virtual organization provides a new means of leveraging resources and exploiting opportunities.[47]

virtual organization
a continually evolving network of independent companies that are linked together to share skills, costs, and access to one another's markets.

The **virtual organization** can be viewed as a continually evolving network of independent companies—suppliers, customers, even competitors—linked together to share skills, costs, and access to one another's markets.[48] The members of a virtual organization, by pooling and sharing the knowledge and expertise of each of the component organizations, simultaneously "know" more and can "do" more than any one member of the group could do alone. By working closely together, each gains in the long run from individual and organizational learning.[49] The term *virtual,* meaning "being in effect but not actually so," is commonly used in the computer industry. A computer's ability to appear to have more storage capacity than it really possesses is called virtual memory. Similarly, by assembling resources from a variety of entities, a virtual organization may seem to have more capabilities than it really possesses.[50]

Virtual organizations need not be permanent, and participating firms may be involved in multiple alliances. Virtual organizations may involve different firms performing complementary value activities or different firms involved jointly in the same value activities, such as production, R&D, and distribution. The percentage of activities that are jointly performed with partners may vary significantly from alliance to alliance.[51]

How does the virtual type of structure differ from the modular type? Unlike the modular type, in which the focal firm maintains full strategic control, the virtual organization is characterized by participating firms that give up part of their control and accept interdependent destinies. Participating firms pursue a collective strategy that enables them to cope with uncertainty through cooperative efforts. The benefit is that, just as virtual memory increases storage capacity, the virtual organizations enhance the capacity or competitive advantage of participating firms.

Each company that links up with others to create a virtual organization contributes only what it considers its core competencies. It will mix and match what it does best with the best of other firms by identifying its critical capabilities and the necessary links to other capabilities.[52]

In addition to linking a set of organizations in a virtual organization, firms can create internal virtual organizations, in which individuals who are not located together and may not even be in the same traditional organizational unit are joined together in virtual teams. These teams may be permanent but often are flexible, with changing membership as business needs evolve. For example, advertising agencies often create flexible membership teams for each client to provide the expertise that a firm's advertising program needs.

Challenges and Risks The virtual organization demands that managers build relationships both within the firm and with other companies, negotiate win–win deals for all parties, find the right partners with compatible goals and values, and provide the right balance of freedom and control. Information systems must be designed and integrated to facilitate communication with current and potential partners.

Managers must be clear about the strategic objectives while forming alliances. Some objectives are time-bound, and those alliances need to be dissolved once the objective is fulfilled. Some alliances may have relatively long-term objectives and will need to be clearly monitored and nurtured to produce mutual commitment and avoid bitter fights for control. The highly dynamic personal computer industry is characterized by multiple temporary alliances among hardware, operating system, and software producers.[53] But alliances in the more stable automobile industry have long-term objectives and tend to be relatively stable.

The virtual organization is a logical culmination of joint venture strategies of the past. Shared risks, costs, and rewards are the facts of life in a virtual organization.[54] When virtual organizations are formed, they involve tremendous challenges for strategic planning. As with the modular corporation, it is essential to identify core competencies. However, for virtual structures to be successful, a strategic plan is also needed to determine the effectiveness of combining core competencies.

The strategic plan must address the diminished operational control and overwhelming need for trust and common vision among the partners. This new structure may be appropriate for firms whose strategies require merging technologies (e.g., computing and communication) or for firms exploiting shrinking product life cycles that require simultaneous entry into multiple geographic markets. It may be effective for firms that desire to be quick to the market with a new product or service. The recent profusion of alliances among airlines was primarily motivated by the need to provide seamless travel demanded by the full-fare-paying business traveler. Exhibit 10.8 summarizes the pros and cons of virtual structures.

Boundaryless Organizations: Making Them Work

Designing an organization that simultaneously supports the requirements of an organization's strategy, is consistent with the demands of the environment, and can be effectively implemented by the people around the manager is a tall order for any manager.[55] The most effective solution is usually a combination of organizational types. That is, a firm may outsource many parts of its value chain to reduce costs and increase quality, engage simultaneously in multiple alliances to take advantage of technological developments or penetrate new markets, and break down barriers within the organization to enhance flexibility.

When an organization faces external pressures, resource scarcity, and declining performance, it tends to become more internally focused, rather than directing its efforts toward

EXHIBIT 10.8 Pros and Cons of Virtual Structures

Pros	Cons
• Enables the sharing of costs and skills. • Enhances access to global markets. • Increases market responsiveness. • Creates a "best of everything" organization since each partner brings core competencies to the alliance. • Encourages both individual and organizational knowledge sharing and accelerates organizational learning.	• Harder to determine where one company ends and another begins, due to close interdependencies among players. • Leads to potential loss of operational control among partners. • Results in loss of strategic control over emerging technology. • Requires new and difficult-to-acquire managerial skills.

Source: Miles, R. E., & Snow, C. C. 1986. Organizations: New Concepts for New Forms. *California Management Review,* Spring: 62–73; Miles & Snow. 1999. Causes of Failure in Network Organizations. *California Management Review,* Summer: 53–72; and Bahrami, H. 1991. The Emerging Flexible Organization: Perspectives from Silicon Valley. *California Management Review,* Summer: 33–52.

managing and enhancing relationships with existing and potential external stakeholders. This may be the most opportune time for managers to carefully analyze their value-chain activities and evaluate the potential for adopting elements of modular, virtual, and barrier-free organizational types.

In this section, we will address two issues managers need to be aware of as they work to design an effective boundaryless organization. First, managers need to develop mechanisms to ensure effective coordination and integration. Second, managers need to be aware of the benefits and costs of developing strong and long-term relationships with both internal and external stakeholders.

Facilitating Coordination and Integration   Achieving the coordination and integration necessary to maximize the potential of an organization's human capital involves much more than just creating a new structure. Techniques and processes to ensure the coordination and integration of an organization's key value-chain activities are critical. Teams are key building blocks of the new organizational forms, and teamwork requires new and flexible approaches to coordination and integration.

Managers trained in rigid hierarchies may find it difficult to make the transition to the more democratic, participative style that teamwork requires. As Douglas K. Smith, co-author of *The Wisdom of Teams,* pointed out, "A completely diverse group must agree on a goal, put the notion of individual accountability aside and figure out how to work with each other. Most of all, they must learn that if the team fails, it's everyone's fault."[56] Within the framework of an appropriate organizational design, managers must select a mix and balance of tools and techniques to facilitate the effective coordination and integration of key activities. Some of the factors that must be considered include:

- Common culture and shared values.
- Horizontal organizational structures.
- Communications and information technologies.
- Human resource practices.

Common Culture and Shared Values   Shared goals, mutual objectives, and a high degree of trust are essential to the success of boundaryless organizations. In the fluid and flexible environments of the new organizational architectures, common cultures, shared values, and carefully aligned incentives are often less expensive to implement and are often a more effective means of strategic control than rules, boundaries, and formal procedures. Tony Hsieh, the founder of Zappos, discussed the importance of culture and values this way: "We formalize the definition of our culture into . . . 10 core values at Zappos. And one of the really interesting things I found from the research is that it actually doesn't matter what your values are, what matters is that you have them and that you align the organization around them."[57]

horizontal organizational structures
organizational forms that group similar or related business units under common management control and facilitate sharing resources and infrastructures to exploit synergies among operating units and help to create a sense of common purpose.

Horizontal Organizational Structures   These structures, which group similar or related business units under common management control, facilitate sharing resources and infrastructures to exploit synergies among operating units and help to create a sense of common purpose. Consistency in training and the development of similar structures across business units facilitates job rotation and cross-training and enhances understanding of common problems and opportunities. Cross-functional teams and interdivisional committees and task groups represent important opportunities to improve understanding and foster cooperation among operating units.

Communications and Information Technology (IT)   The effective use of IT can play an important role in bridging gaps and breaking down barriers between organizations. This can include communication systems, such as email and videoconferencing, internal social network systems, knowledge portals, and other technology means to link people within an organization across regions and organizational units. Additionally, firms can leverage point-of-sale inventory systems and RFID technology to facilitate automated communications and coordinated actions with suppliers, distributors, and other firm partners. Thus, information technology should be viewed more as a prime component of an organization's overall strategy than simply in terms of administrative support.

Human Resource Practices   Change always involves and affects the human dimension of organizations. The attraction, development, and retention of human capital are vital to value creation. As boundaryless structures are implemented, processes are reengineered, and organizations become increasingly dependent on sophisticated ITs, the skills of workers and managers alike must be upgraded to realize the full benefits.

The Benefits and Costs of Developing Lasting Internal and External Relationships   Successful boundaryless organizations rely heavily on the relational aspects of organizations. Rather than relying on strict hierarchical and bureaucratic systems, these firms are flexible and coordinate action by leveraging shared social norms and strong social relationships between both internal and external stakeholders.[58] At the same time, it is important to acknowledge that relying on relationships can have both positive and negative effects. To successfully move to a more boundaryless organization, managers need to acknowledge and attend to both the costs and benefits of relying on relationships and social norms to guide behavior.

There are three primary benefits that organizations accrue when relying on relationships:

- *Agency costs within the firm can be dramatically cut through the use of relational systems.* Managers and employees in relationship-oriented firms are guided by social norms and relationships they have with other managers and employees. As a result, the firm can reduce the degree to which it relies on monitoring, rules and regulations, and financial incentives to ensure that workers put in a strong effort and work in the firm's interests. A relational view leads managers and employees to act in a supportive manner and makes them more willing to step out of their formal roles when needed to accomplish tasks for others and for the organization. They are also less likely to shirk their responsibilities.
- *There is also likely to be a reduction in the transaction costs between a firm and its suppliers and customers.* If firms have built strong relationships with partnering firms, they are more likely to work cooperatively with these firms and build trust that their partners will work in the best interests of the alliance. This will reduce the need for the firms to write detailed contracts and set up strict bureaucratic rules to outline the responsibilities and define the behavior of each firm. Additionally, partnering firms with strong relationships are more likely to invest in assets that specifically support the partnership. Finally, they will have much less fear that their partner will try to take advantage of them or seize the bulk of the benefits from the partnership.
- *Since they feel a sense of shared ownership and goals, individuals within the firm as well as partnering firms will be more likely to search for win-win rather than win-lose solutions.* When taking a relational view, individuals are less likely to look out solely for their personal best interests. They will also be considerate of the benefits and costs to other individuals in the firm and to the overall firm. The same is true at the organizational level. Firms with strong relationships with their partners are going to look for solutions that not only benefit themselves but also provide equitable benefits and limited downside for the partnering firms.

While there are a number of benefits with using a relational view, there can also be some substantial costs:

- *As the relationships between individuals and firms strengthen, they are also more likely to fall prey to suboptimal lock-in effects.* The problem here is that as decisions become driven by concerns about relationships, economic factors become less important. As a result, firms become less likely to make decisions that could benefit the firm since those decisions may harm employees or partnering firms. For example, firms may see the economic logic in exiting a market, but the ties they feel with employees that work in that division and partnering firms in that market may reduce their willingness to make the hard decision to exit the market. This can be debilitating to firms in rapidly changing markets where successful firms add, reorganize, and sometimes exit operations and relationships regularly.

- *Since there are no formal guidelines, conflicts between individuals and units within firms, as well as between partnering firms, are typically resolved through ad hoc negotiations and processes.* In these circumstances, there are no legal means or bureaucratic rules to guide decision making. Thus, when firms face a difficult decision where there are differences of opinion about the best course of action, the ultimate choices made are often driven by the inherent power of the individuals or firms involved. This power use may be unintentional and subconscious, but it can result in outcomes that are deemed unfair by one or more of the parties.

- *The social capital of individuals and firms can drive their opportunities.* Thus, rather than identifying the best person to put in a leadership role or the optimal supplier to contract with, these choices are more strongly driven by the level of social connection the person or supplier has. This also increases the entry barriers for potential new suppliers or employees with whom a firm can contract since new firms likely don't have the social connections needed to be chosen as a worthy partner with whom to contract. This also may limit the likelihood that new innovative ideas will enter into the conversations at the firm.

As mentioned earlier in the chapter, the solution may be to effectively integrate elements of formal structure and reward systems with stronger relationships. This may influence specific relationships so that a manager will want employees to build relationships while still maintaining some managerial oversight and reward systems that motivate the desired behavior. This may also result in different emphases with different relationships. For example, there may be some units, such as accounting, where a stronger role for traditional structures and forms of evaluation may be optimal. However, in new product development units, a greater emphasis on relational systems may be more appropriate.

LO 10-5

The need for creating ambidextrous organizational designs that enable firms to explore new opportunities and effectively integrate existing operations.

adaptibility

managers' exploration of new opportunities and adjustment to volatile markets in order to avoid complacency.

CREATING AMBIDEXTROUS ORGANIZATIONAL DESIGNS

In Chapter 1, we introduced the concept of "ambidexterity," which incorporates two contradictory challenges faced by today's managers.[59] First, managers must explore new opportunities and adjust to volatile markets in order to avoid complacency. They must ensure that they maintain **adaptability** and remain proactive in expanding and/or modifying their product-market scope to anticipate and satisfy market conditions. Such competencies are especially challenging when change is rapid and unpredictable.

Second, managers must also effectively exploit the value of their existing assets and competencies. They need to have **alignment,** which is a clear sense of how value is being created in the short term and how activities are integrated and properly coordinated. Firms that achieve both adaptability and alignment are considered *ambidextrous organizations*—aligned and efficient in how they manage today's business but flexible enough to changes in the environment so that they will prosper tomorrow.

Handling such opposing demands is difficult because there will always be some degree of conflict. Firms often suffer when they place too strong a priority on either adaptability or alignment. If it places too much focus on adaptability, the firm will suffer low profitability in the short term. If managers direct their efforts primarily at alignment, they will likely miss out on promising business opportunities.

Ambidextrous Organizations: Key Design Attributes

A study by Charles O'Reilly and Michael Tushman[60] provides some insights into how some firms were able to create successful **ambidextrous organizational designs.** They investigated companies that attempted to simultaneously pursue modest, incremental innovations as well as more dramatic, breakthrough innovations. The team investigated 35 attempts to launch breakthrough innovations undertaken by 15 business units in nine different industries. They studied the organizational designs and the processes, systems, and cultures associated with the breakthrough projects as well as their impact on the operations and performance of the traditional businesses.

Companies structured their breakthrough projects in one of four primary ways:

- Seven were carried out within existing *functional organizational structures.* The projects were completely integrated into the regular organizational and management structure.
- Nine were organized as *cross-functional teams.* The groups operated within the established organization but outside the existing management structure.
- Four were organized as *unsupported teams.* Here, they became independent units set up outside the established organization and management hierarchy.
- Fifteen were conducted within *ambidextrous organizations.* Here, the breakthrough efforts were organized within structurally independent units, each having its own processes, structures, and cultures. However, they were integrated into the existing senior management structure.

The performance results of the 35 initiatives were tracked along two dimensions:

- Their success in creating desired innovations was measured by either the actual commercial results of the new product or the application of practical market or technical learning.
- The performance of the existing business was evaluated.

The study found that the organizational structure and management practices employed had a direct and significant impact on the performance of both the breakthrough initiative and the traditional business. The ambidextrous organizational designs were more effective than the other three designs on both dimensions: launching breakthrough products or services (i.e., adaptation) and improving the performance of the existing business (i.e., alignment).

Why Was the Ambidextrous Organization the Most Effective Structure?

The study found that there were many factors. A clear and compelling vision, consistently communicated by the company's senior management team, was critical in building the ambidextrous designs. The structure enabled cross-fertilization while avoiding cross-contamination. The tight coordination and integration at the managerial levels enabled the newer units to share important resources from the traditional units, such as cash, talent, and expertise. Such sharing was encouraged and facilitated by effective reward systems that emphasized overall company goals. The organizational separation ensured that the new units' distinctive processes, structures, and cultures were not overwhelmed by the forces of "business as usual." The established units were shielded from the distractions of launching new businesses, and they continued to focus all of their attention and energy on refining their operations, enhancing their products, and serving their customers.

alignment
managers' clear sense of how value is being created in the short term and how activities are integrated and properly coordinated.

ambidextrous organizational designs
organizational designs that attempt to simultaneously pursue modest, incremental innovations as well as more dramatic, breakthrough innovations.

In the fall of 2015, Google unveiled a new organizational structure. Google created a holding company, Alphabet Inc., which offers overall oversight for the disparate collection of businesses the firm owns. The parent company is run by firm founders Larry Page and Sergey Brin and its Chief Financial Officer, Ruth Porat. Alphabet is using a hybrid SBU-divisional structure with the main SBU, Google, housing several core businesses, including its search business, YouTube, Android, and the Chrome operating systems. The businesses in the Google SBU accounted for nearly 90 percent of Alphabet's $90 billion of revenue in 2016. Other divisions in the structure include Nest, a smart-home project division; Verily, a group working on health care and disease prevention; and GV, the firm's venture capital arm. The structure also includes an incubator SBU, X, which houses the firm's secretive "moonshot" projects, including Project Loon, a venture to offer Internet service in the developing world with high-altitude balloons; Project Titan, a drone delivery service; and ventures that are not yet publicly known. The hope is that once projects advance inside X and can stand on their own, they can be moved and become their own divisions, an action that took place with Waymo, Google's self-driving car project in 2016.

Larry Page, Alphabet's CEO, says he looked to Warren Buffett's Berskshire Hathaway as a model for running a large, complex organization. His goal is to allow the different units the freedom to focus on their particular areas. Mr. Page wrote in his blog, "Fundamentally, we believe this allows us more management scale, as we can run things independently that aren't very related." The new structure also allows the firm to more effectively control costs in the independent units, resulting in more constrained budgets in these units.

But the transition has not been entirely smooth. From outside, the firm has faced criticism that the new structure simply reinforced the view that it is investing in businesses far from Google's core markets and into markets for which Alphabet's core competencies are not well suited. As Brian Wieser, an analyst with Pivotal Research, stated: "just because they break out the data doesn't mean they'll stop making investments in things that are so far removed from the core business." With the Google[x] businesses losing $3.6 billion in 2016, this criticism is unlikely to wane. The firm has also experienced leadership challenges. In the past, the founders, Larry Page and Sergey Brin, its chairman, Eric Schmidt, and Google's CEO, Sundar Pichal, provided strong leadership to hold it all together. In building all of the operating units, Alphabet needs to develop management talent to run them. This appears to be a work in progress, at best, with one division CEO called "divisive and impulsive" while another has been labeled "mercurial." The structure also makes it harder to coordinate activities across the different business units. For example, while Google was working to develop its home unit Alexa, Alphabet's smart-home division, Nest, had signaled its intention to work with Amazon to link its smart-home products with Amazon's Echo. This raised the potential of Alphabet divisions competing with each other.

Discussion Questions

1. What are the benefits and the costs of making this move? What are the long-run risks of this change? Do the benefits outweigh the costs?

2. Is Alphabet trying to build an ambidextrous organization? Should it be doing so? If yes, what actions can it take to build an ambidextrous firm?

3. Do these issues raise concerns about Alphabet's business portfolio? Should the firm stay the course with the businesses it owns, or should it change? If it should change, how should it change?

Sources: Barr, A., & Winkler, R. 2015. Google creates parent company called Alphabet in restructuring. *wsj.com*. August 11: np; Price, R. & Nudelman, M. 2016. Google's parent company, Alphabet, explained in one chart. *businessinsider.com*. January 12: np; Hempel, J. 2016. Google's Alphabet transition has been tougher than A-B-C. *wired.com*. April 1: np; and Fiegerman, S. 2017. Google's moonshots lost $1 billion last quarter. *money.cnn.com*. January 27: np.

Reflecting on Career Implications . . .

This chapter discusses both organizational structures and the benefits of creating permeable boundaries across structural boundaries. You can enhance your value to your firms and career prospects by developing skills and abilities to span internal and external organizational boundaries. The questions below challenge you to consider ways you can build those skills.

▣ **Boundaryless Organizational Designs:** Does your firm have structural mechanisms (e.g., culture, human resource practices) that facilitate sharing information across boundaries? Regardless of the level of boundarylessness of your organization, a key issue for your career is the extent to which you are able to cut across boundaries within your organization. Such boundaryless behavior on your part will enable you to enhance and leverage your human capital. Evaluate how boundaryless you are within your organizational context. What actions can you take to become even more boundaryless?

▣ **Culture and Shared Values:** Does your firm or department have a strong or weak culture? Consider how your actions can help reinforce or build a strong culture. Also, think of the types of actions leaders in your group can take to strengthen the group's culture. Consider sharing these ideas with your leaders. Do you think they will be receptive to your suggestions? Their response likely gives you further insight into the group's culture.

▣ **Ambidextrous Organizations:** Firms that achieve adaptability and alignment are considered ambidextrous. As an individual, you can also strive to be ambidextrous. Evaluate your own ambidexterity by assessing your adaptability (your ability to change in response to changes around you) and alignment (how good you are at exploiting your existing competencies). What steps can you take to improve your ambidexterity?

summary

Successful organizations must ensure that they have the proper type of organizational structure. Furthermore, they must ensure that their firms incorporate the necessary integration and processes so that the internal and external boundaries of their firms are flexible and permeable. Such a need is increasingly important as the environments of firms become more complex, changing rapidly and unpredictably.

In the first section of the chapter, we discussed the growth patterns of large corporations. Although most organizations remain small or die, some firms continue to grow in terms of revenues, vertical integration, and diversity of products and services. In addition, their geographic scope may increase to include international operations. We traced the dominant pattern of growth, which evolves from a simple structure to a functional structure as a firm grows in terms of size and increases its level of vertical integration. After a firm expands into related products and services, its structure changes from a functional to a divisional form of organization. Finally, when the firm enters international markets, its structure again changes to accommodate the change in strategy.

We also addressed the different types of organizational structure—simple, functional, divisional (including two variations: strategic business unit and holding company), and matrix—as well as their relative advantages and disadvantages. We closed the section with a discussion of the implications for structure that arise when a firm enters international markets. The three primary factors to take into account when determining the appropriate structure are type of international strategy, product diversity, and the extent to which a firm is dependent on foreign sales.

The second section of the chapter introduced the concept of the boundaryless organization. We did not suggest that the concept of the boundaryless organization replaces the traditional forms of organizational structure. Rather, it should complement them. This is necessary to cope with the increasing complexity and change in the competitive environment. We addressed three types of boundaryless organizations. The barrier-free type focuses on the need for the internal and external boundaries of a firm to be more flexible and permeable. The modular type emphasizes the strategic outsourcing of noncore activities. The virtual type centers on the strategic benefits of alliances and the forming of network organizations. We discussed both the advantages and disadvantages of each type of boundaryless organization, and we suggested some techniques and processes that are necessary to successfully implement each type. These are common culture and values, horizontal organizational structures, horizontal systems and processes, communications and information technologies, and human resource practices.

The final section addressed the need for managers to develop ambidextrous organizations. In today's rapidly changing global environment, managers must be responsive and proactive in order to take advantage of new opportunities. At the same time, they must effectively integrate and coordinate existing operations. Such requirements call for organizational designs that establish project teams that are structurally independent units, with each having its own processes, structures, and cultures. But, at the same time, each unit needs to be effectively integrated into the existing management hierarchy.

SUMMARY REVIEW QUESTIONS

1. Why is it important for managers to carefully consider the type of organizational structure that they use to implement their strategies?

2. Briefly trace the dominant growth pattern of major corporations from simple structure to functional structure to divisional structure. Discuss the relationship between a firm's strategy and its structure.

3. What are the relative advantages and disadvantages of the types of organizational structure—simple, functional, divisional, matrix—discussed in the chapter?

4. When a firm expands its operations into foreign markets, what are the three most important factors to take into account in deciding what type of structure is most appropriate? What are the types of international structures discussed in the text, and what are the relationships between strategy and structure?

5. Briefly describe the three different types of boundaryless organizations: barrier-free, modular, and virtual.

6. What are some of the key attributes of effective groups? Ineffective groups?

7. What are the advantages and disadvantages of the three types of boundaryless organizations: barrier-free, modular, and virtual?

8. When are ambidextrous organizational designs necessary? What are some of their key attributes?

EXPERIENTIAL EXERCISE

Many firms have recently moved toward a modular structure. For example, they have increasingly outsourced many of their information technology (IT) activities. Identify three such organizations. Using secondary sources, evaluate (1) the firm's rationale for IT outsourcing and (2) the implications for performance.

Firm	Rationale	Implication(s) for Performance
1.		
2.		
3.		

APPLICATION QUESTIONS & EXERCISES

1. Select an organization that competes in an industry in which you are particularly interested. Go on the Internet and determine what type of organizational structure this organization has. In your view, is it consistent with the strategy that it has chosen to implement? Why? Why not?

2. Choose an article from *Bloomberg Businessweek, Fortune, Forbes, Fast Company,* or any other well-known publication that deals with a corporation that has undergone a significant change in its strategic direction. What are the implications for the structure of this organization?

3. Go on the Internet and look up some of the public statements or speeches of an executive in a major corporation about a significant initiative such as entering into a joint venture or launching a new product line. What do you feel are the implications for making the internal and external barriers of the firm more flexible and permeable? Does the executive discuss processes, procedures, integrating mechanisms, or cultural issues that should serve this purpose? Or are other issues discussed that enable a firm to become more boundaryless?

4. Look up a recent article in the publications listed in question 2 that addresses a firm's involvement in outsourcing (modular organization) or in strategic alliance or network organizations (virtual organization). Was the firm successful or unsuccessful in this endeavor? Why? Why not?

ETHICS QUESTIONS

1. If a firm has a divisional structure and places extreme pressures on its divisional executives to meet short-term profitability goals (e.g., quarterly income), could this raise some ethical considerations? Why? Why not?

2. If a firm enters into a strategic alliance but does not exercise appropriate behavioral control of its employees (in terms of culture, rewards and incentives, and boundaries—as discussed in Chapter 9) who are involved in the alliance, what ethical issues could arise? What could be the potential long-term and short-term downside for the firm?

REFERENCES

1. Wilson, K. & Doz, Y. 2012. 10 rules for managing global innovation. *Harvard Business Review,* 90(10): 84–92; Wallace, J. 2007. Update on problems joining 787 fuselage sections. *Seattlepi.com*, June 7: np; Peterson, K. 2011. Special report: A wing and a prayer: Outsourcing at Boeing. *Reuters.com*, January 20: np; Hiltzik, M. 2011. 787 Dreamliner teaches Boeing costly lesson on outsourcing. *Latimes.com*, February 15: np; Gates, D. 2013. Boeing 787's problems blamed on outsourcing, lack of oversight. *Seattletimes.com*, February 2: np; and Ostrower, J. 2014. Boeing's Key Mission: Cut Dreamliner cost. *wsj.com* . January 7: np.

2. For a unique perspective on organization design, see Rao, R. 2010. What 17th century pirates can teach us about job design. *Harvard Business Review,* 88(10): 44.

3. This introductory discussion draws upon Hall, R. H. 2002. *Organizations: Structures, processes, and outcomes* (8th ed.). Upper Saddle River, NJ: Prentice Hall; and Duncan, R. E. 1979. What is the right organization structure? Decision-tree analysis provides the right answer. *Organizational Dynamics,* 7(3): 59–80. For an insightful discussion of strategy-structure relationships in the organization theory and strategic management literatures, refer to Keats, B. & O'Neill, H. M. 2001. Organization structure: Looking through a strategy lens. In Hitt, M. A., Freeman, R. E., & Harrison, J. S. 2001. *The Blackwell handbook of strategic management:* 520–542. Malden, MA: Blackwell.

4. Gratton, L. 2011. The end of the middle manager. *Harvard Business Review,* 89(1/2): 36.

5. An interesting discussion on the role of organizational design in strategy execution is in Neilson, G. L., Martin, K. L., & Powers, E. 2009. The secrets to successful strategy execution. *Harvard Business Review,* 87(2): 60–70.

6. This discussion draws upon Chandler, A. D. 1962. *Strategy and structure.* Cambridge, MA: MIT Press; Galbraith J. R. & Kazanjian, R. K. 1986. *Strategy implementation: The role of structure and process.* St. Paul, MN: West; and Scott, B. R. 1971. Stages of corporate development. Intercollegiate Case Clearing House, 9-371-294, BP 998. Harvard Business School.

7. Our discussion of the different types of organizational structures draws on a variety of sources, including Galbraith & Kazanjian, op. cit.; Hrebiniak, L. G. & Joyce, W. F. 1984. *Implementing strategy.* New York: Macmillan; Distelzweig, H. 2000. Organizational structure. In Helms, M. M. (Ed.), *Encyclopedia of management:* 692–699. Farmington Hills, MI: Gale; and Dess, G. G. & Miller, A. 1993. *Strategic management.* New York: McGraw-Hill.

8. A discussion of an innovative organizational design is in Garvin, D. A. & Levesque, L. C. 2009. The multiunit enterprise. *Harvard Business Review,* 87(2): 106–117.

9. Schein, E. H. 1996. Three cultures of management: The key to organizational learning. *Sloan Management Review,* 38(1): 9–20.

10. Insights on governance implications for multidivisional forms are in Verbeke, A. & Kenworthy, T. P. 2008. Multidivisional vs. metanational governance. *Journal of International Business,* 39(6): 940–956.

11. Martin, J. A. & Eisenhardt, K. 2010. Rewiring: Cross-business-unit collaborations in multibusiness organizations. *Academy of Management Journal,* 53(2): 265–301.

12. For a discussion of performance implications, refer to Hoskisson, R. E. 1987. Multidivisional structure and performance: The contingency of diversification strategy. *Academy of Management Journal,* 29: 625–644.

13. For a thorough and seminal discussion of the evolution toward the divisional form of organizational structure in the United States, refer to Chandler, op. cit. A rigorous empirical study of the strategy and structure relationship is found in Rumelt, R. P. 1974. *Strategy, structure, and economic performance.* Cambridge, MA: Harvard Business School Press.

14. Koppel, B. 2000. Synergy in ketchup? *Forbes,* February 7: 68–69; and Hitt, M. A., Ireland, R. D., & Hoskisson, R. E. 2001. *Strategic management: Competitiveness and globalization* (4th ed.). Cincinnati, OH: South-Western.

15. Pitts, R. A. 1977. Strategies and structures for diversification. *Academy of Management Journal,* 20(2): 197–208.

16. Silvestri, L. 2012. The evolution of organizational structure. *footnote1. com*, June 6: np.

17. Haas, M. R. 2010. The double-edged swords of autonomy and external knowledge: Analyzing team effectiveness in a multinational organization. *Academy of Management Journal,* 53(5): 989–1008.

18. Daniels, J. D., Pitts, R. A., & Tretter, M. J. 1984. Strategy and structure of U.S. multinationals: An exploratory study. *Academy of Management Journal,* 27(2): 292–307.

19. Habib, M. M. & Victor, B. 1991. Strategy, structure, and performance of U.S. manufacturing and service MNCs: A comparative analysis. *Strategic Management Journal,* 12(8): 589–606.

20. Our discussion of global start-ups draws from Oviatt, B. M. & McDougall, P. P. 2005. The internationalization of entrepreneurship. *Journal of International Business Studies,* 36(1): 2–8; Oviatt, B. M. & McDougall, P. P. 1994. Toward a theory of international new ventures. *Journal of International Business Studies,*

25(1): 45–64; and Oviatt, B. M. & McDougall, P. P. 1995. Global start-ups: Entrepreneurs on a worldwide stage. *Academy of Management Executive,* 9(2): 30–43.

21. Some useful guidelines for global start-ups are provided in Kuemmerle, W. 2005. The entrepreneur's path for global expansion. *MIT Sloan Management Review,* 46(2): 42–50.

22. See, for example, Miller, D. & Friesen, P. H. 1980. Momentum and revolution in organizational structure. *Administrative Science Quarterly,* 13: 65–91.

23. Many authors have argued that a firm's structure can influence its strategy and performance. These include Amburgey, T. L. & Dacin, T. 1995. As the left foot follows the right? The dynamics of strategic and structural change. *Academy of Management Journal,* 37: 1427–1452; Dawn, K. & Amburgey, T. L. 1991. Organizational inertia and momentum: A dynamic model of strategic change. *Academy of Management Journal,* 34: 591–612; Fredrickson, J. W. 1986. The strategic decision process and organization structure. *Academy of Management Review,* 11: 280–297; Hall, D. J. & Saias, M. A. 1980. Strategy follows structure! *Strategic Management Journal,* 1: 149–164; and Burgelman, R. A. 1983. A model of the interaction of strategic behavior, corporate context, and the concept of strategy. *Academy of Management Review,* 8: 61–70.

24. An interesting discussion on how the Internet has affected the boundaries of firms can be found in Afuah, A. 2003. Redefining firm boundaries in the face of the Internet: Are firms really shrinking? *Academy of Management Review,* 28(1): 34–53.

25. Govindarajan, V. G. & Trimble, C. 2010. Stop the innovation wars. *Harvard Business Review,* 88(7/8): 76–83.

26. For a discussion of the role of coaching on developing high-performance teams, refer to Kets de Vries, M. F. R. 2005. Leadership group coaching in action: The zen of creating high performance teams. *Academy of Management Executive,* 19(1): 77–89.

27. Pfeffer, J. 1998. *The human equation: Building profits by putting people first.* Cambridge, MA: Harvard Business School Press.

28. For a discussion on how functional area diversity affects performance, see Bunderson, J. S. & Sutcliffe, K. M. 2002. Comparing alternative conceptualizations of functional diversity in management teams: Process and performance effects. *Academy of Management Journal,* 45(5): 875–893.

29. Falconi, M. 2014. Novartis chairman stresses need for R&D investment. *wsj.com,* March 24: np.

30. Groth, A. 2015. Holacracy at Zappos: It's either the future of management or a social experiment gone awry. *qz.com,* January 14: np; Anonymous. 2014. The holes in holacracy. *economist.com,* July 5: np; and Van De Kamp, P. 2014. Holacracy—A radical approach to organizational design. *medium.com,* August 2: np.

31. Public-private partnerships are addressed in Engardio, P. 2009. State capitalism. *BusinessWeek,* February 9: 38–43.

32. Aller, R., Weiner, H., & Weilart, M. 2005. IBM and Mayo collaborating to customize patient treatment plans. *cap.org,* January: np; and McGee, M. 2010. IBM, Mayo partner on aneurysm diagnostics. *informationweek.com,* January 25: np.

33. Winston, A. 2014: *The big pivot.* Boston: Harvard Business Review Press.

34. Dess, G. G., Rasheed, A. M. A., McLaughlin, K. J., & Priem, R. 1995. The new corporate architecture. *Academy of Management Executive,* 9(3): 7–20.

35. An original discussion on how open sourcing could help the Big 3 automobile companies is in Jarvis, J. 2009. How the Google model could help Detroit. *BusinessWeek,* February 9: 32–36.

36. For a discussion of some of the downsides of outsourcing, refer to Rossetti, C. & Choi, T. Y. 2005. On the dark side of strategic sourcing: Experiences from the aerospace industry. *Academy of Management Executive,* 19(1): 46–60.

37. Tully, S. 1993. The modular corporation. *Fortune,* February 8: 196.

38. *adidas-group.com/en/sustainability/compliance/supply-chain-structure/.*

39. Offshoring in manufacturing firms is addressed in Coucke, K. & Sleuwaegen, L. 2008. Offshoring as a survival strategy: Evidence from manufacturing firms in Belgium. *Journal of International Business Studies,* 39(8): 1261–1277.

40. Quinn, J. B. 1992. *Intelligent enterprise: A knowledge and service based paradigm for industry.* New York: Free Press.

41. For an insightful perspective on outsourcing and its role in developing capabilities, read Gottfredson, M., Puryear, R., & Phillips, C. 2005. Strategic sourcing: From periphery to the core. *Harvard Business Review,* 83(4): 132–139.

42. This discussion draws upon Quinn, J. B. & Hilmer, F. C. 1994. Strategic outsourcing. *Sloan Management Review,* 35(4): 43–55.

43. Reitzig, M. & Wagner, S. 2010. The hidden costs of outsourcing: Evidence from patent data. *Strategic Management Journal,* 31(11): 1183–1201.

44. Insights on outsourcing and private branding can be found in Cehn, S-F. S. 2009. A transaction cost rationale for private branding and its implications for the choice of domestic vs. offshore outsourcing. *Journal of International Business Strategy,* 40(1): 156–175.

45. For an insightful perspective on the use of outsourcing for decision analysis, read Davenport, T. H. & Iyer, B. 2009. Should you outsource your brain? *Harvard Business Review,* 87(2): 38.

46. See also Stuckey, J. & White, D. 1993. When and when not to vertically integrate. *Sloan Management Review,* Spring: 71–81; Harrar, G. 1993. Outsource tales. *Forbes ASAP,* June 7: 37–39, 42; and Davis, E. W. 1992. Global outsourcing: Have U.S. managers thrown the baby out with the bath water? *Business Horizons,* July-August: 58–64.

47. For a discussion of knowledge creation through alliances, refer to Inkpen, A. C. 1996. Creating knowledge through collaboration. *California Management Review,* 39(1): 123–140; and Mowery, D. C., Oxley, J. E., & Silverman, B. S. 1996. Strategic alliances and interfirm knowledge transfer. *Strategic Management Journal,* 17 (Special Issue, Winter): 77–92.

48. Doz, Y. & Hamel, G. 1998. *Alliance advantage: The art of creating value through partnering.* Boston: Harvard Business School Press.

49. DeSanctis, G., Glass, J. T., & Ensing, I. M. 2002. Organizational designs for R&D. *Academy of Management Executive,* 16(3): 55–66.

50. Barringer, B. R. & Harrison, J. S. 2000. Walking a tightrope: Creating value through interorganizational alliances. *Journal of Management,* 26: 367–403.

51. One contemporary example of virtual organizations is R&D consortia. For an insightful discussion, refer to Sakaibara, M. 2002. Formation of R&D consortia: Industry and company effects. *Strategic Management Journal,* 23(11): 1033–1050.

52. Bartness, A. & Cerny, K. 1993. Building competitive advantage through a global network of capabilities. *California Management Review,* Winter: 78–103. For an insightful historical discussion of the usefulness of alliances in the computer industry, see Moore, J. F. 1993. Predators and prey: A new ecology of competition. *Harvard Business Review,* 71(3): 75–86.

53. See Lorange, P. & Roos, J. 1991. Why some strategic alliances succeed and others fail. *Journal of Business Strategy,* January–February: 25–30; and Slowinski, G. 1992. The human touch in strategic alliances. *Mergers and Acquisitions,* July–August: 44–47. A compelling argument for strategic alliances is provided by Ohmae, K. 1989. The global logic of strategic alliances. *Harvard Business Review,* 67(2): 143–154.

54. Some of the downsides of alliances are discussed in Das, T. K. & Teng, B. S. 2000. Instabilities of strategic alliances: An internal tensions perspective. *Organization Science,* 11: 77–106.

55. This section draws upon Dess, G. G. & Picken, J. C. 1997. *Mission critical.* Burr Ridge, IL: Irwin Professional.

56. Katzenbach, J. R. & Smith, D. K. 1994. *The wisdom of teams: Creating the high performance organization.* New York: HarperBusiness.

57. Bulygo, Z. 2013. Tony Hsieh, Zappos, and the art of great company culture. *kissmetrics.com.* February 26: np.

58. Gupta, A. 2011. The relational perspective and east meets west. *Academy of Management Perspectives,* 25(3): 19–27.

59. This section draws on Birkinshaw, J. & Gibson, C. 2004. Building ambidexterity into an organization. *MIT Sloan Management Review,* 45(4): 47–55; and Gibson, C. B. & Birkinshaw, J. 2004. The antecedents, consequences, and mediating role of organizational ambidexterity. *Academy of Management Journal,* 47(2): 209–226. Robert Duncan is generally credited with being the first to coin the term "ambidextrous organizations" in his article entitled: Designing dual structures for innovation. In Kilmann, R. H., Pondy, L. R., & Slevin, D. (Eds.). 1976. *The management of organizations,* vol. 1: 167–188. For a seminal academic discussion of the concept of exploration and exploitation, which parallels adaptation and alignment, refer to March, J. G. 1991. Exploration and exploitation in organizational learning. *Organization Science,* 2: 71–86.

60. This section is based on O'Reilly, C. A. & Tushman, M. L. 2004. The ambidextrous organization. *Harvard Business Review,* 82(4): 74–81.

chapter 11

Strategic Leadership

Creating a Learning Organization and an Ethical Organization

After reading this chapter, you should have a good understanding of the following learning objectives:

LO11-1 The three key interdependent activities in which all successful leaders must be continually engaged.

LO11-2 Two elements of effective leadership: overcoming barriers to change and using power effectively.

LO11-3 The crucial role of emotional intelligence (EI) in successful leadership, as well as its potential drawbacks.

LO11-4 The importance of creating a learning organization.

LO11-5 The leader's role in establishing an ethical organization.

LO11-6 The difference between integrity-based and compliance-based approaches to organizational ethics.

LO11-7 Several key elements that organizations must have to become ethical organizations.

©Anatoli Styf/Shutterstock

LEARNING FROM MISTAKES

It took four generations to build Stroh's Brewing into a major player in the beer industry and just one generation to tear it down. Stroh's was founded in Detroit by Bernard Stroh, who had emigrated from Germany in 1850. Bernard took the $150 he had and a cherished family beer recipe and began selling beer door to door. By 1890, his sons, Julius and Bernard, had grown the family business and were shipping beer around the Great Lakes region. The family business survived prohibition by making ice cream and maple syrup. After World War II ended, the business grew along with the industrial Midwest, seeing its sales surge from 500,000 barrels of beer in 1950 to 2.7 million barrels in 1956. The firm succeeded by following a simple business recipe: catering to the needs of working-class tastes by brewing a simple, drinkable, and affordable beer and treating its employees well. Following this business blueprint, the company found success and growth, resulting in a business that was worth an estimated $700 million in the mid-1980s. A little over a decade later, the firm was out of business.[1]

Its rapid descent from a successful and growing firm to failure is tied to a series of disastrous decisions made by Peter Stroh, representing the fifth generation of the family to lead the firm, who took on the role of CEO in 1980. Rather than stick to the tried-and-true business plan of catering to the needs of the Midwest working class, Peter stepped out to build a larger, national beer empire. He purchased F&M Schaefer, a New York–based brewer, in 1981. He followed this up in 1982 by purchasing Joseph Schlitz Brewing, a firm that was much bigger than Stroh's. To undertake this acquisition, Stroh's borrowed $500 million, five times the value of Stroh's itself. Peter's acquisitions hampered the firm in two key ways. First, working to combine the firms distracted Stroh's from seeing the evolving needs of customers. Most notably, it completely missed the most significant shift in customer tastes in a generation—the emergence of light beer. Also, the heavy debt load taken on to finance the acquisitions left the firm with little money to launch the national advertising campaigns needed to support a company that was now the third-largest brewer in the United States. In the words of Greg Stroh, a cousin of Peter and an employee of the firm, "We made the decision to go national without having the budget. It was like going to a gunfight with a knife. We didn't have a chance."

Stroh's tried various tactics to improve its situation. It tried undercutting the price of its major rivals, Anheuser-Busch and Miller, by offering 15 cans of beer for the price of 12. It laid off hundreds of employees to save on cost. It then changed course, raising prices and nixing the 15-pack containers. Customers rebelled, pushing sales down 40 percent in a single year. The firm was left with 6 million barrels of excess brewing capacity. Finally, the firm took on one last, disastrous acquisition. Stroh's purchased another struggling brewer, G. Heileman, for $300 million, saddling itself with even more debt. While the firm struggled in its core beer business, Peter tried to diversify Stroh's into biotechnology and real estate investing. The almost inevitable end came in 1999 when Stroh's assets were purchased by Pabst Brewing for $350 million—$250 million of which went to the debtholders of the firm.

Discussion Questions

1. Why were the acquisitions so debilitating for Stroh's?
2. What would have been the likely outcome for Stroh's if it hadn't purchased other brands?

Under Peter Stroh's leadership, Stroh's Brewing went from being a successful and growing family business to a failed firm. He took the firm away from its traditional strategy and also missed seeing key shifts in the beer industry. This led him to change the firm's strategy in ways that undercut the value of its brand and its culture, ultimately leading to Stroh's demise and the loss of the family's legacy. In contrast to Peter's ineffective leadership, effective leaders set a clear direction for the firm, create and reinforce valuable strategies, and strengthen firm values and culture.

This chapter provides insights into the role of strategic leadership in managing, adapting, and coping in the face of increased environmental complexity and uncertainty. First, we define leadership and its three interdependent activities—setting a direction, designing the organization, and nurturing a culture dedicated to excellence and ethical behavior. Then, we identify two elements of leadership that contribute to success—overcoming barriers to change and using power effectively. The third section focuses on emotional intelligence, a trait that is increasingly acknowledged to be critical to successful leadership. Next, we emphasize the importance of leaders developing competency companions and creating a learning organization. Here, we focus on empowerment wherein employees and managers throughout an organization develop a sense of self-determination, competence, meaning, and impact that is centrally important to learning. Finally, we address the leader's role in building an ethical organization and the elements of an ethical culture that contribute to firm effectiveness.

LEADERSHIP: THREE INTERDEPENDENT ACTIVITIES

In today's chaotic world, few would argue against the need for leadership, but how do we go about encouraging it? Is it enough to merely keep an organization afloat, or is it essential to make steady progress toward some well-defined objective? We believe custodial management is not leadership. Leadership is proactive, goal-oriented, and focused on the creation and implementation of a creative vision. **Leadership** is the process of transforming organizations from what they are to what the leader would have them become. This definition implies a lot: *dissatisfaction* with the status quo, a *vision* of what should be, and a *process* for bringing about change. An insurance company executive shared the following insight: "I lead by the Noah Principle: It's all right to know when it's going to rain, but, by God, you had better build the ark."

Doing the right thing is becoming increasingly important. Many industries are declining; the global village is becoming increasingly complex, interconnected, and unpredictable; and product and market life cycles are becoming increasingly compressed. When asked to describe the life cycle of his company's products, the CEO of a supplier of computer components replied, "Seven months from cradle to grave—and that includes three months to design the product and get it into production!"

Despite the importance of doing the "right thing," leaders must also be concerned about "doing things right." Charan and Colvin strongly believe that execution, that is, the implementation of strategy, is also essential to success:

> Mastering execution turns out to be the odds-on best way for a CEO to keep his job. So what's the right way to think about that sexier obsession, strategy? It's vitally important—obviously. The problem is that our age's fascination feeds the mistaken belief that developing exactly the right strategy will enable a company to rocket past competitors. In reality, that's less than half the battle.[2]

Thus, leaders are change agents whose success is measured by how effectively they formulate *and* implement a strategic vision and mission.[3]

Many authors contend that successful leaders must recognize three interdependent activities that must be continually reassessed for organizations to succeed. As shown in Exhibit 11.1, these are (1) setting a direction, (2) designing the organization, and (3) nurturing a culture dedicated to excellence and ethical behavior.[4]

leadership
the process of transforming organizations from what they are to what the leader would have them become.

The three key interdependent activities in which all successful leaders must be continually engaged.

EXHIBIT 11.1 Three Interdependent Leadership Activities

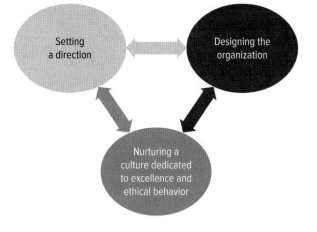

The interdependent nature of these three activities is self-evident. Consider an organization with a great mission and a superb organizational structure but a culture that implicitly encourages shirking and unethical behavior. Or one with a sound direction and strong culture but counterproductive teams and a "zero-sum" reward system that leads to the dysfunctional situation in which one party's gain is viewed as another party's loss and collaboration and sharing are severely hampered. Clearly, such combinations would be ineffective.

Often, failure of today's organizations can be attributed to a lack of equal consideration of these three activities. The imagery of a three-legged stool is instructive: The stool will collapse if one leg is missing or broken. Let's briefly look at each of these activities as well as the value of an ambicultural approach to leadership.

Setting a Direction

A holistic understanding of an organization's stakeholders requires an ability to scan the environment to develop a knowledge of all of the company's stakeholders and other salient environmental trends and events. Managers must integrate this knowledge into a vision of what the organization could become.[5] This necessitates the capacity to solve increasingly complex problems, become proactive in approach, and develop viable strategic options. A strategic vision provides many benefits: a clear future direction; a framework for the organization's mission and goals; and enhanced employee communication, participation, and commitment.

Strategy Spotlight 11.1 discusses how Marvin Ellison exhibits leadership attributes as he tries to bring JC Penney back from the brink.

Designing the Organization

At times, almost all leaders have difficulty implementing their vision and strategies.[6] Such problems may stem from a variety of sources:

- Lack of understanding of responsibility and accountability among managers.
- Reward systems that do not motivate individuals (or collectives such as groups and divisions) toward desired organizational goals.
- Inadequate or inappropriate budgeting and control systems.
- Insufficient mechanisms to integrate activities across the organization.

Successful leaders are actively involved in building structures, teams, systems, and organizational processes that facilitate the implementation of their vision and strategies. Without appropriately structuring organizational activities, a firm would generally be unable to attain an overall low-cost advantage by closely monitoring its costs through detailed and formalized cost and financial control procedures. With regard to corporate-level strategy, a related

setting a direction
a strategic leadership activity of strategy analysis and strategy formulation.

designing the organization
a strategic leadership activity of building structures, teams, systems, and organizational processes that facilitate the implementation of the leader's vision and strategies.

MARVIN ELLISON ATTEMPTS TO TURN JC PENNEY CO. INC. AROUND

JC Penney found a way to generate double-digit growth in the sales of men's shoes in 2015. They simply needed to put the men's footwear displays next to men's clothes. Up until that point, men's shoes were displayed with women's shoes next to women's clothing. The logic for that placement went back to decades ago when women often bought shoes for their husbands. JC Penney just hadn't updated its thinking on this product placement as the world around the firm had changed.

These are the types of challenges facing Marvin Ellison as he tries to turn around the struggling retailer. Ellison is implementing a number of changes in JC Penney stores to stoke up demand and meet the challenge of responding to traditional rivals as well as online retailing. Along with moving men's shoes, Ellison has pushed for other changes to store layouts, such as moving women's fashion jewelry to be near fashion clothing brands. He has also pushed for updates in store décor, especially in areas that pull in store traffic, such as the store's in-house salons. He's also working to extend the store's private-label brands, such as Arizona, St. John's Bay, and a.n.a., to draw in customers who are both price and fashion conscious. He's extended the store's product line to include appliances—a play to pull in former Sears' customers as Sears shrinks its store network. Finally, he's emphasized improving inventory management. In recent years, JC Penney has often found itself out of stock of its hottest items.

He doesn't rely on intuition for any of this. Ellison is a data fanatic. He states "pure intuition without any data gets you in trouble." He previously worked at Home Depot, where he was heavily involved with streamlining the firm's supply chain, integrating store operations, and building an e-commerce platform. At JC Penney, he's emphasizing data-driven decision making. He runs ideas, such as moving men's shoes, through test stores, and if the data shows benefits, he rolls them out across the chain. To manage inventory better, he's implemented a "demand-based logic" system where JC Penney uses real-time sales data to replenish inventory.

But it's not all about data. While he was in college, Ellison worked as a security guard at a Target, and though he saw things and had ideas for improvement, he perceived that management had no interest in hearing from low-level workers. He learned from this early experience that he wants JC Penney to be a company where associates feel they have a voice to offer ideas. To help connect with workers, in his first year at JC Penney, Ellison held town halls with workers at 60 stores and visited over 100 stores. These experiences led him to conclude there was separation between workers and management in the stores. Reflective of this, managers often wore high-priced fashion clothes that were unavailable at JC Penney and out of the reach of most of its workers and customers. To help reduce the barrier between management and associates in stores, he requires all managers to wear JC Penney clothing and the same nametags workers wear.

A big part of Ellison's leadership is to channel everyone at JC Penney to remember what the firm is and to be the best JC Penney it can be. That means being effective in providing a wide range of products to price-conscious consumers in middle-American towns and suburban shopping malls. In executing this turnaround, Ellison says "we're going to start with the foundation: No one can beat us being us." So far, the results are modest but promising. In 2016, JC Penney reported its first profit in six years, and it appears to be stabilizing its sales. But it is a long road for Ellison to turn the firm fully around.

Sources: Wahba, P. 2016. The man who's re-re-re-inventing J.C. Penney. *fortune. com*. March 1: 77–86; and d'Innocenzio, A. 2017. J.C. Penney to shut 130-plus stores, offer early retirements. *finance.yahoo.com*. February 24: np.

diversification strategy would necessitate reward systems that emphasize behavioral measures because interdependence among business units tends to be very important. In contrast, reward systems associated with an unrelated diversification strategy should rely more on financial indicators of performance because business units are relatively autonomous.

These examples illustrate the important role of leadership in creating systems and structures to achieve desired ends. As Jim Collins says about the importance of designing the organization, "Along with figuring out what the company stands for and pushing it to understand what it's really good at, building mechanisms is the CEO's role—the leader as architect."[7]

excellent and ethical organizational culture
an organizational culture focused on core competencies and high ethical standards.

Nurturing a Culture Committed to Excellence and Ethical Behavior

Organizational culture can be an effective means of organizational control.[8] Leaders play a key role in changing, developing, and sustaining an organization's culture. Brian Chesky, cofounder and CEO of Airbnb, clearly understands the role of the leader in building and maintaining an organization's culture. In October 2013, as Airbnb was growing rapidly, Chesky sent out an email to his leadership team imploring the team members to be very conscious to maintain the culture of the firm.[9] He stated, "The culture is what creates the foundation for all future innovation. If you break the culture, you break the machine that creates your products." He then went on to comment that they needed to uphold the firm's values in all they do: who they hire, how they work on a project, how they treat other employees in the hallway, and what they write in emails. Chesky then laid out the power of firm culture in the following words:

> The stronger the culture, the less corporate process a company needs. When the culture is strong, you can trust everyone to do the right thing. People can be independent and autonomous. They can be entrepreneurial. And if we have a company that is entrepreneurial in spirit, we will be able to take our next "(wo)man on the moon" leap. . . . In organizations (or even in a society) where the culture is weak, you need an abundance of heavy, precise rules, and processes.

In sharp contrast, leaders can also have a very detrimental effect on a firm's culture and ethics. Imagine the negative impact that Todd Berman's illegal activities have had on a firm that he cofounded—New York's private equity firm Chartwell Investments.[10] He stole more than $3.6 million from the firm and its investors. Berman pleaded guilty to fraud charges brought by the Justice Department. For 18 months he misled Chartwell's investors concerning the financial condition of one of the firm's portfolio companies by falsely claiming it needed to borrow funds to meet operating expenses. Instead, Berman transferred the money to his personal bank account, along with fees paid by portfolio companies.

Clearly, a leader's behavior and values can make a strong impact on an organization—for good or for bad. Strategy Spotlight 11.2 provides a positive example, with H. Fisk Johnson carrying on a legacy of maintaining a strong ethical culture at his family's firm.

11.2 STRATEGY SPOTLIGHT **ENVIRONMENTAL SUSTAINABILITY, ETHICS**

FAMILY LEADERSHIP SUSTAINS THE CULTURE OF SC JOHNSON

SC Johnson, the maker of Windex, Ziploc bags, and Glade Air Fresheners, is known as one of the most environmentally conscious consumer products companies. The family-owned company is run by Fisk Johnson, the fifth generation of the family to serve as firm CEO. It is the 35th largest privately owned firm, with 13,000 employees and nearly $10 billion in sales. Over the decades, the firm has built and reinforced its reputation for environmental consciousness. Being privately owned by the Johnson family is part of it. Fisk Johnson put it this way, "Wall Street rewards that short-termism. . . . We are in a very fortunate situation to not have to worry about those things, and we're very fortunate that we have a family that is principled and has been very principled."

Fisk uses the benefits of dedicated family ownership to work in both substantive and symbolic ways. On the substantive side, he has implemented systems in place to improve its environmental performance. For example, with its Greenlist process, the firm rates the ingredients it uses or is considering using. It then rates each ingredient on several criteria, including biodegradability and human toxicity, and gives the ingredient a score ranging from 0 to 3, with 3 being the most environmentally friendly. The goal is to increase the percentage of ingredients rated a 2 or a 3 and eliminate those with a score of 0. With this system, the firm has increased the percentage of ingredients rated as a 2 or

3 (better or best) from about 20 percent to over 50 percent from 2001 to 2016.

Fisk uses stories from decisions in the past as it acts to sustain its culture of environmental consciousness. In using stories to reinforce the environmental focus within the firm and to explain it to external stakeholders, Fisk Johnson draws on stories relating to decisions his father made as well as ones he's made. Most prominently, he uses a story about a decision his father made to stop using chlorofluorocarbons in the firm's aerosol products. "Our first decision to unilaterally remove a major chemical occurred in 1975, when research began suggesting that chlorofluorocarbons (CFCs) in aerosols might harm Earth's ozone layer. My father was CEO at the time, and he decided to ban them from all the company's aerosol products worldwide. He did so several years before the government played catch-up and banned the use of CFCs from everyone's products." He goes on to say, "You look back on that decision today, in light of the strong laws that came in, and that was a very prescient decision." This story is especially effective since it highlights his father's willingness and ability to take actions that can lead both the government and industry rivals to change. A second story outlines the firm's decision to remove chlorine as an ingredient in its Saran Wrap. In the late 1990s, regulators and environmentalists were raising concerns that chlorine used in plastic released toxic chemicals when the plastic was burned. As Fisk Johnson explains, this was a difficult situation for

continued

him and the firm. "We set out to figure out an alternative for Saran that didn't contain chlorine, but that's just as good. Bottom line is we couldn't find anything that's just as good. Nothing had those clinging properties. We went out there with an inferior product, and we've been steadily losing business." This story demonstrates that he not only wants to lead the firm to be an agent of change, but he is also willing to sacrifice profits to do the right thing.

The combination of the firm's ownership structure, its strong leader, and its story-driven culture reinforce the firm's willingness to lead the market in environmental awareness. For example, in early 2016, Fisk decided that SC Johnson would be the first firm to list 100 percent of the fragrance ingredients it uses. He saw this decision as a means to push itself and its rivals to use more environmentally friendly fragrance ingredients.

Source: Kaufman, A. 2016. CEO admits that environmentalism does cost him profits. *huffingtonpost.com*. February 18: np; Byron, E. 2016. How Fisk Johnson works to keep the shine on the family business. *wsj.com*. March 11: np; and, Johnson, F. 2015. SC Johnson's CEO on doing the right thing, even when it hurts business. *hbr.org*. March: np.

Managers and top executives must accept personal responsibility for developing and strengthening ethical behavior throughout the organization. They must consistently demonstrate that such behavior is central to the vision and mission of the organization. Several elements must be present and reinforced for a firm to become highly ethical, including role models, corporate credos and codes of conduct, reward and evaluation systems, and policies and procedures. Given the importance of these elements, we address them in detail in the last section of this chapter.

LO 11-2

Two elements of effective leadership: overcoming barriers to change and using power effectively.

GETTING THINGS DONE: OVERCOMING BARRIERS AND USING POWER

The demands on leaders in today's business environment require them to perform a variety of functions. The success of their organizations often depends on how they as individuals meet challenges and deliver on promises. What practices and skills are needed to get the job done effectively? In this section, we focus on two capabilities that are marks of successful leadership—overcoming barriers to change and using power effectively. Then, in the next section, we will examine an important human trait that helps leaders be more effective—emotional intelligence.

Overcoming Barriers to Change

barriers to change
characteristics of individuals and organizations that prevent a leader from transforming an organization.

What are the **barriers to change** that leaders often encounter, and how can leaders best bring about organizational change?[11] After all, people generally have some level of choice about how strongly they support or resist a leader's change initiatives. Why is there often so much resistance? Organizations at all levels are prone to inertia and are slow to learn, adapt, and change because:

vested interest in the status quo
a barrier to change that stems from people's risk aversion.

1. Many people have **vested interests in the status quo.** People tend to be risk-averse and resistant to change. There is a broad stream of research on "escalation," wherein certain individuals continue to throw "good money at bad decisions" despite negative performance feedback.[12]

systemic barriers
barriers to change that stem from an organizational design that impedes the proper flow and evaluation of information.

2. There are **systemic barriers.** The design of the organization's structure, information processing, reporting relationships, and so forth impedes the proper flow and evaluation of information. A bureaucratic structure with multiple layers, onerous requirements for documentation, and rigid rules and procedures will often "inoculate" the organization against change. Strategy Spotlight 11.3 discusses efforts to overcome systemic barriers in the supply chain operations at Target.

behavioral barriers
barriers to change associated with the tendency for managers to look at issues from a biased or limited perspective based on their prior education and experience.

3. **Behavioral barriers** cause managers to look at issues from a biased or limited perspective due to their education, training, work experiences, and so forth. Consider an incident shared by David Lieberman, former marketing director at GVO, an innovation consulting firm:

OVERCOMING SUPPLY CHAIN LIMITATIONS AT TARGET

Arthur Valdez and Benjamin Cook chose to take on a challenging task. Valdez, a longtime Amazon executive, and Cook, a supply chain executive with Apple, signed on to head up Target's chief supply chain and logistics operations in mid-2016. The challenge for Mr. Valdez, Mr. Cook, and Target is to modernize its supply chain system to meet changing market dynamics. Target has developed a very effective supply chain system to meet the needs of a large-scale national retailer, where stores largely stock the same items across the entire chain. But this isn't the market Target competes in anymore. As the chain has added groceries, it aims to stock its stores with fresh, local produce and grocery products. As customers increasingly order online and pick up items in stores, Target needs to develop inventory systems that can stock shelves and also process single orders for customers. As Target CEO, Brian Cornell, stated, "The systems were built to continue to replenish a normal store. Now, we're shipping from stores.

Now, we're trying to localize items. It has added a greater complexity."

To meet these changing demands, Target realized they had to go outside the firm to bring in executives who had experience with fast moving, flexible supply chain operations and who could work to break down traditional barriers in the firm. Mr. Valdez and Mr. Cook will need to restructure a range of operations and reporting relationships. This will include changes in information systems to process single orders, the implementation of technology that allows store staff to search inventory and process orders from the store floor, redesigned warehouses that can handle deliveries from national and local vendors, and different reporting structures to allow local managers to tailor the merchandise they carry. The price tag to change all of these systems is heavy. The changes Mr. Valdez and Mr. Cook will put in place are part of a $7 billion investment Target is making to upgrade its operations.

Sources: Ziobro, P. 2016. Target hires executive to lead supply revamping. *wsj.com*. February 29: np; Gustafson, K. 2017. Target's $7 billion spending plan still leaves some question marks. *cnbc.com*. March 1: np; and Chao, L. 2016. Target hires supply chain executive from Apple. *wsj.com*. July 20: np.

A company's creative type had come up with a great idea for a new product. Nearly everybody loved it. However, it was shot down by a high-ranking manufacturing representative who exploded: "A new color? Do you have any idea of the spare-parts problem that it will create?" This was not a dimwit exasperated at having to build a few storage racks at the warehouse. He'd been hearing for years about cost cutting, lean inventories, and "focus." Lieberman's comment: "Good concepts, but not always good for innovation."

4. **Political barriers** refer to conflicts arising from power relationships. This can be the outcome of a myriad of symptoms such as vested interests, refusal to share information, conflicts over resources, conflicts between departments and divisions, and petty interpersonal differences.

5. **Personal time constraints** bring to mind the old saying about "not having enough time to drain the swamp when you are up to your neck in alligators." Gresham's law of planning states that operational decisions will drive out the time necessary for strategic thinking and reflection. This tendency is accentuated in organizations experiencing severe price competition or retrenchment wherein managers and employees are spread rather thin.

> **political barriers**
> barriers to change related to conflicts arising from power relationships.

> **personal time constraints**
> a barrier to change that stems from people's not having sufficient time for strategic thinking and reflection.

Leaders must draw on a range of personal skills as well as organizational mechanisms to move their organizations forward in the face of such barriers. Two factors mentioned earlier—building a learning organization and building an ethical organization—provide the kind of climate within which a leader can advance the organization's aims and make progress toward its goals.

One of the most important tools a leader has for overcoming barriers to change is his or her personal and organizational power. On the one hand, good leaders must be on guard not to abuse power. On the other hand, successful leadership requires the measured exercise of power. We turn to that topic next.

Using Power Effectively

Successful leadership requires the effective use of power in overcoming barriers to change.[13] As humorously noted by Mark Twain, "I'm all for progress. It's change I object to." **Power**

> **power**
> a leader's ability to get things done in a way he or she wants them to be done.

refers to a leader's ability to get things done in a way he or she wants them to be done. It is the ability to influence other people's behavior, to persuade them to do things that they otherwise would not do, and to overcome resistance and opposition. Effective exercise of power is essential for successful leadership.[14]

A leader derives his or her power from several sources or bases. The simplest way to understand the bases of power is by classifying them as organizational and personal, as shown in Exhibit 11.2.

Organizational bases of power refer to the power that a person wields because of her formal management position.[15] These include legitimate, reward, coercive, and information power. *Legitimate power* is derived from organizationally conferred decision-making authority and is exercised by virtue of a manager's position in the organization. *Reward power* depends on the ability of the leader or manager to confer rewards for positive behaviors or outcomes. *Coercive power* is the power a manager exercises over employees using fear of punishment for errors of omission or commission. *Information power* arises from a manager's access, control, and distribution of information that is not freely available to everyone in an organization.

A leader might also be able to influence subordinates because of his or her personality characteristics and behavior. These would be considered the **personal bases of power**, including referent power and expert power. The source of *referent power* is a subordinate's identification with the leader. A leader's personal attributes or charisma might influence subordinates and make them devoted to that leader. The source of *expert power* is the leader's expertise and knowledge. The leader is the expert on whom subordinates depend for information that they need to do their jobs successfully.

Successful leaders use the different bases of power, and often a combination of them, as appropriate to meet the demands of a situation, such as the nature of the task, the personality characteristics of the subordinates, and the urgency of the issue.[16] Persuasion and developing consensus are often essential, but so is pressing for action. At some point stragglers must be prodded into line.[17] Peter Georgescu, former CEO of Young & Rubicam (an advertising and media subsidiary of the U.K.-based WPP Group), summarized a leader's dilemma brilliantly (and humorously), "I have knee pads and a .45. I get down and beg a lot, but I shoot people too."[18]

Strategy Spotlight 11.4 addresses some of the subtleties of power. Here, the CEO of Siemens successfully brought about organizational change by the effective use of peer pressure.

organizational bases of power
a formal management position that is the basis of a leader's power.

personal bases of power
a leader's personality characteristics and behavior that are the basis of the leader's power.

EXHIBIT 11.2 A Leader's Bases of Power

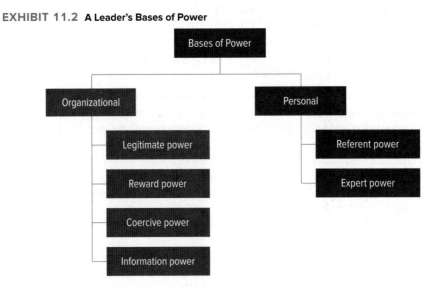

THE USE OF "SOFT" POWER AT SIEMENS

Until 1999, not only was paying bribes in international markets legally allowed in Germany, but German corporations could also deduct bribes from taxable income. However, once those laws changed, German industrial powerhouse Siemens found it hard to break its bribing habit in its sprawling global operations. Eventually a major scandal forced many top executives out of the firm, including CEO Klaus Kleinfeld. As the successor to Kleinfeld, Peter Löscher became the first outside CEO in the more than 160-year history of Siemens in 2007. As an outsider Löscher found it challenging to establish himself as a strong leader inside the bureaucratic Siemens organization. However, he eventually found a way to successfully transition into his new position.

Naturally, in the early stage of his tenure, he lacked internal connections and the bases of power associated with inside knowledge of people and processes. Yet Siemens faced tremendous challenges, such as a lack of customer orientation, and required a strong leader with the ability to change the status quo. Absent a more formal power base, he turned to more informal means to accomplish his mandate of organizational change and increasing customer orientation.

Once a year, all 700 of Siemens top managers come together for a leadership conference in Berlin. Given the historical lack of customer focus, Löscher used peer pressure as an informal (or soft) form of power in order to challenge and eventually change the lack of customer orientation. In preparation for his first leadership conference, Löscher collected the prior year's Outlook calendars from all of his division executives. He calculated how much time they each spent with customers and ranked them. In the meeting, he shared this information, including executives' names.

The results of this exercise were quite remarkable: Löscher spent around 50 percent of his time with customers, more than any other top executive. Clearly, the people who were running the business divisions should rank higher on customer interaction than the CEO. This confirmed the lack of customer orientation in the organization. This ranking has been repeated at every Siemens leadership conference since Löscher took office. Over time, customer orientation has improved because nobody wants to fall short on this metric and endure potential ridicule. Löscher's leadership style and use of soft power during his early time in office seemed to have paid off, as the Siemens board extended his contract as CEO of the German industry icon a year early.

Source: Löscher, P. 2012. The CEO of Siemens on using a scandal to drive change. *Harvard Business Review*, 90(11): 42; and Anonymous. 2011. Löscher soll vorstandschef bleiben. *www.manager-magazin.de*, July 25: np.

EMOTIONAL INTELLIGENCE: A KEY LEADERSHIP TRAIT

> **LO 11-3**
> The crucial role of emotional intelligence (EI) in successful leadership, as well as its potential drawbacks.

In the previous sections, we discussed skills and activities of strategic leadership. The focus was on "what leaders do and how they do it." Now the issue becomes "who leaders *are,*" that is, what leadership traits are the most important. Clearly, these two issues are related, because successful leaders possess the valuable traits that enable them to perform effectively in order to create value for their organization.[19]

There has been a vast amount of literature on the successful traits of leaders.[20] These traits include integrity, maturity, energy, judgment, motivation, intelligence, expertise, and so on. For simplicity, these traits may be grouped into three broad sets of capabilities:

- Purely technical skills (like accounting or operations research).
- Cognitive abilities (like analytical reasoning or quantitative analysis).
- Emotional intelligence (like self-management and managing relationships).

Emotional intelligence (EI) has been defined as the capacity for recognizing one's own emotions and those of others.[21]

Research suggests that effective leaders at all levels of organizations have high levels of EI.[22] After controlling for cognitive abilities and manager personality attributes, EI leads to stronger job performance across a wide range of professions, with stronger effects for professions that require a great deal of human interaction. Interestingly, there is only partial support for the catchy phrase "IQ gets you hired, but EQ (emotional quotient) gets you promoted." Evidence indicates that high levels of EI increase the likelihood of being promoted up to the middle-manager level. However, managers at high levels of the corporate hierarchy tend to evidence lower levels of EI, with the CEOs having, on average, lower levels of EI

> **emotional intelligence (EI)** an individual's capacity for recognizing his or her own emotions and those of others, including the five components of self-awareness, self-regulation, motivation, empathy, and social skills.

than managers at any other level. This is troubling given that firms led by CEOs high in EI outperform firms led by CEOs lower in EI. High-EI CEOs excel in managing relationships, influencing people, and forging alliances both inside and outside the firm. These CEOs can also benefit the firm since their ability to connect with and relate to outside stakeholders helps build the firm's reputation. Thus, firms would benefit from considering more than cognitive ability and easily measured performance metrics when choosing corporate leaders. Including EI as an element to consider would help firms choose superior corporate leaders.

Exhibit 11.3 identifies the five components of EI: self-awareness, self-regulation, motivation, empathy, and social skill.

Self-Awareness

Self-awareness is the first component of EI and brings to mind that Delphic oracle that gave the advice "Know thyself" thousands of years ago. Self-awareness involves a person having a deep understanding of his or her emotions, strengths, weaknesses, and drives. People with strong self-awareness are neither overly critical nor unrealistically optimistic. Instead, they are honest with themselves and others.

People generally admire and respect candor. Leaders are constantly required to make judgment calls that require a candid assessment of capabilities—their own and those of others. People who assess themselves honestly (i.e., self-aware people) are well suited to do the same for the organizations they run.[23]

Self-Regulation

Biological impulses drive our emotions. Although we cannot do away with them, we can strive to manage them. Self-regulation, which is akin to an ongoing inner conversation, frees us from being prisoners of our feelings.[24] People engaged in such conversation feel bad moods and emotional impulses just as everyone else does. However, they find ways to control them and even channel them in useful ways.

Self-regulated people are able to create an environment of trust and fairness where political behavior and infighting are sharply reduced and productivity tends to be high. People who have mastered their emotions are better able to bring about and implement

EXHIBIT 11.3 The Five Components of Emotional Intelligence at Work

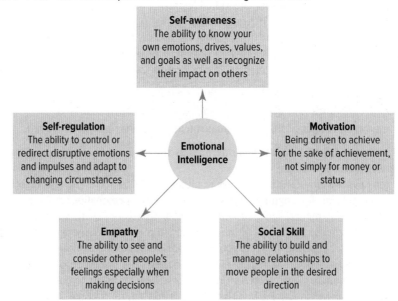

change in an organization. When a new initiative is announced, they are less likely to panic; they are able to suspend judgment, seek out information, and listen to executives explain the new program.

Motivation

Successful executives are driven to achieve beyond expectations—their own and everyone else's. Although many people are driven by external factors, such as money and prestige, those with leadership potential are driven by a deeply embedded desire to achieve for the sake of achievement.

Motivated people show a passion for the work itself, such as seeking out creative challenges, a love of learning, and taking pride in a job well done. They also have a high level of energy to do things better as well as a restlessness with the status quo. They are eager to explore new approaches to their work.

Empathy

Empathy is probably the most easily recognized component of EI. Empathy means thoughtfully considering an employee's feelings, along with other factors, in the process of making intelligent decisions. Empathy is particularly important in today's business environment for at least three reasons: the increasing use of teams, the rapid pace of globalization, and the growing need to retain talent.[25]

When leading a team, a manager is often charged with arriving at a consensus—often in the face of a high level of emotions. Empathy enables a manager to sense and understand the viewpoints of everyone around the table.

Globalization typically involves cross-cultural dialogue that can easily lead to miscues. Empathetic people are attuned to the subtleties of body language; they can hear the message beneath the words being spoken. They have a deep understanding of the existence and importance of cultural and ethnic differences.

Empathy also plays a key role in retaining talent. Human capital is particularly important to a firm in the knowledge economy when it comes to creating advantages that are sustainable. Leaders need empathy to develop and keep top talent, because when high performers leave, they take their tacit knowledge with them.

Social Skill

While the first three components of EI are all self-management skills, the last two—empathy and social skill—concern a person's ability to manage relationships with others. Social skill may be viewed as friendliness with a purpose: moving people in the direction you desire, whether that's agreement on a new marketing strategy or enthusiasm about a new product.

Socially skilled people tend to have a wide circle of acquaintances as well as a knack for finding common ground and building rapport. They recognize that nothing gets done alone, and they have a network in place when the time for action comes.

Social skill can be viewed as the culmination of the other dimensions of EI. People will be effective at managing relationships when they can understand and control their own emotions and empathize with others' feelings. Motivation also contributes to social skill. People who are driven to achieve tend to be optimistic, even when confronted with setbacks. And when people are upbeat, their "glow" is cast upon conversations and other social encounters. They are popular, and for good reason.

A key to developing social skill is to become a good listener—a skill that many executives find to be quite challenging. Deborah Triant, former CEO of Check Point Software Technologies, says, "Debating is easy; listening with an open mind is not. The worst thing that you as a leader can do in the decision-making process is to voice your opinion before anyone else can."[26]

Emotional Intelligence: Some Potential Drawbacks and Cautionary Notes

Many great leaders have great reserves of empathy, interpersonal astuteness, awareness of their own feelings, and an awareness of their impact on others.[27] More importantly, they know how to apply these capabilities judiciously as best benefits the situation. Having some minimum level of EI will help a person be effective as a leader as long as it is channeled appropriately. However, if a person has a high level of these capabilities it may become "too much of a good thing" if he or she is allowed to drive inappropriate behaviors. Some additional potential drawbacks of EI can be gleaned by considering the flip side of its benefits.

Effective Leaders Have Empathy for Others   However, they also must be able to make the "tough decisions." Leaders must be able to appeal to logic and reason and acknowledge others' feelings so that people feel the decisions are correct. However, it is easy to overidentify with others or confuse empathy with sympathy. This can make it more difficult to make the tough decisions.

Effective Leaders Are Astute Judges of People   A danger is that leaders may become judgmental and overly critical about the shortcomings they perceive in others. They are likely to dismiss other people's insights, making them feel undervalued.

Effective Leaders Are Passionate about What They Do, and They Show It   This doesn't mean that they are always cheerleaders. Rather, they may express their passion as persistence in pursuing an objective or a relentless focus on a valued principle. However, there is a fine line between being excited about something and letting your passion close your mind to other possibilities or cause you to ignore realities that others may see.

Effective Leaders Create Personal Connections with Their People   Most effective leaders take time to engage employees individually and in groups, listening to their ideas, suggestions, and concerns and responding in ways that make people feel that their ideas are respected and appreciated. However, if the leader makes too many unannounced visits, it may create a culture of fear and micromanagement. Clearly, striking a correct balance is essential.

From a moral standpoint, emotional leadership is neither good nor bad. On the one hand, emotional leaders can be altruistic, focused on the general welfare of the company and its employees, and highly principled. On the other hand, they can be manipulative, selfish, and dishonest. For example, if a person is using leadership solely to gain power, that is not leadership at all.[28] Rather, that person is using his or her EI to grasp what people want and pander to those desires in order to gain authority and influence. After all, easy answers sell.

CREATING A LEARNING ORGANIZATION

LO 11-4

The importance of creating a learning organization.

To enhance the long-term viability of organizations, leaders also need to build a learning organization. Such an organization is capable of adapting to change, fostering creativity, and succeeding in highly competitive markets.

Successful, innovative organizations recognize the importance of having everyone involved in the process of actively learning and adapting. As noted by a leading expert on learning organizations, MIT's Peter Senge, the days when Henry Ford, Alfred Sloan, and Tom Watson *"learned for the organization"* are gone:

> In an increasingly dynamic, interdependent, and unpredictable world, it is simply no longer possible for anyone to "figure it all out at the top." The old model, "the top thinks and the local acts," must now give way to integrating thinking and acting at all levels. While the challenge is great, so is the potential payoff. "The person who figures out how to harness

the collective genius of the people in his or her organization," according to former Citibank CEO Walter Wriston, "is going to blow the competition away."[29]

Learning and change typically involve the ongoing questioning of an organization's status quo or method of procedure. This means that all individuals throughout the organization must be reflective.[30] Many organizations get so caught up in carrying out their day-to-day work that they rarely, if ever, stop to think objectively about themselves and their businesses. They often fail to ask the probing questions that might lead them to call into question their basic assumptions, to refresh their strategies, or to reengineer their work processes.

To adapt to change, foster creativity, and remain competitive, leaders must build learning organizations. Exhibit 11.4 lists the six key elements of a learning organization.

Inspiring and Motivating People with a Mission or Purpose

Successful **learning organizations** create a proactive, creative approach to the unknown, actively solicit the involvement of employees at all levels, and enable all employees to use their intelligence and apply their imagination. Higher-level skills are required of everyone, not just those at the top.[31] A learning environment involves organizationwide commitment to change, an action orientation, and applicable tools and methods.[32] It must be viewed by everyone as a guiding philosophy and not simply as another change program.

A critical requirement of all learning organizations is that everyone feels and supports a compelling purpose. In the words of William O'Brien, former CEO of Hanover Insurance, "Before there can be meaningful participation, people must share certain values and pictures about where we are trying to go. We discovered that people have a real need to feel that they're part of an enabling mission."[33] Medtronic, a medical products company, does this well. The company's motto is "restoring patients to full life," and it works to bring this to life for its employees. At the company's holiday party, patients, their families, and their doctors come and share their survival and recovery stories. The event inspires employees, who are moved to tears, are able to directly see the results of their work, and are motivated to do even more.

Inspiring and motivating people with a mission or purpose is a necessary but not sufficient condition for developing an organization that can learn and adapt to a rapidly changing, complex, and interconnected environment.

Empowering Employees at All Levels

"The great leader is a great servant," asserted Ken Melrose, former CEO and chairman of Toro Company and author of *Making the Grass Greener on Your Side*.[34] A manager's role becomes one of creating an environment where employees can achieve their potential as they help move the organization toward its goals. Instead of viewing themselves as resource controllers and power brokers, leaders must envision themselves as flexible resources willing to assume numerous roles as coaches, information providers, teachers, decision makers, facilitators, supporters, or listeners, depending on the needs of their employees.[35]

learning organizations organizations that create a proactive, creative approach to the unknown; characterized by (1) inspiring and motivating people with a mission and purpose, (2) empowering employees at all levels, (3) accumulating and sharing internal knowledge, (4) gathering and integrating external information, and (5) challenging the status quo and enabling creativity.

These are the six key elements of a learning organization. Each of these items should be viewed as necessary, *but not sufficient*. That is, successful learning organizations need all six elements.

1. Inspiring and motivating people with a mission or purpose.
2. Developing leaders.
3. Empowering employees at all levels.
4. Accumulating and sharing internal knowledge.
5. Gathering and integrating external information.
6. Challenging the status quo and enabling creativity.

EXHIBIT 11.4

Key Elements of a Learning Organization

The central key to empowerment is effective leadership. Empowerment can't occur in a leadership vacuum. According to Melrose, "You best lead by serving the needs of your people. You don't do their jobs for them; you enable them to learn and progress on the job."

Leading-edge organizations recognize the need for trust, cultural control, and expertise at all levels instead of the extensive and cumbersome rules and regulations inherent in hierarchical control.[36] Some commentators have argued that too often organizations fall prey to the "heroes-and-drones syndrome," wherein the value of those in powerful positions is exalted and the value of those who fail to achieve top rank is diminished. Such an attitude is implicit in phrases such as "Lead, follow, or get out of the way" or, even less appealing, "Unless you're the lead horse, the view never changes." Few will ever reach the top hierarchical positions in organizations, but in the information economy, the strongest organizations are those that effectively use the talents of all the players on the team.

Empowering individuals by soliciting their input helps an organization to enjoy better employee morale. It also helps create a culture in which middle- and lower-level employees feel that their ideas and initiatives will be valued and enhance firm performance.

Accumulating and Sharing Internal Knowledge

Effective organizations must also *redistribute information, knowledge* (skills to act on the information), and *rewards*.[37] To do so, firms need to develop a culture that: (1) encourages employees to offer ideas, ask questions, and express concerns, (2) encourages widespread sharing of information from various sources, (3) identifies opportunities and makes it safe to experiment, (4) encourages collaborative decision making and the sharing of best practices, and (5) utilizes technology to facilitate both the gathering and sharing of information.

Let's take a look at Whole Foods Market, Inc., the largest natural-foods grocer in the United States.[38] An important benefit of the sharing of internal information at Whole Foods becomes the active process of *internal benchmarking*. Competition is intense at Whole Foods. Teams compete against their own goals for sales, growth, and productivity; they compete against different teams in their stores; and they compete against similar teams at different stores and regions. There is an elaborate system of peer reviews through which teams benchmark each other. The "Store Tour" is the most intense. On a periodic schedule, each Whole Foods store is toured by a group of as many as 40 visitors from another region. Lateral learning—discovering what your colleagues are doing right and carrying those practices into your organization—has become a driving force at Whole Foods.

In addition to enhancing the sharing of company information both up and down as well as across the organization, leaders also have to develop means to tap into some of the more informal sources of internal information. In a survey of presidents, CEOs, board members, and top executives in a variety of nonprofit organizations, respondents were asked what differentiated the successful candidates for promotion. The consensus: The executive was seen as a person who listens. According to Peter Meyer, the author of the study, "The value of listening is clear: You cannot succeed in running a company if you do not hear what your people, customers, and suppliers are telling you. . . . Listening and understanding well are key to making good decisions."[39]

Gathering and Integrating External Information

Recognizing opportunities, as well as threats, in the external environment is vital to a firm's success. As organizations *and* environments become more complex and evolve rapidly, it is far more critical for employees and managers to become more aware of environmental trends and events—both general and industry-specific—and more knowledgeable about their firm's competitors and customers. Next, we will discuss some ideas on how to do it.

First, company employees at all levels can use a variety of sources to acquire external information. Firms can tap into knowledge from alliance partners, suppliers, competitors, and the scientific community. For example, in the pharmaceutical and biotechnology industries, participation in networks and alliances is increasingly common and critical to knowledge diffusion and learning. To gain up-to-date information on particular rivals, firms can monitor the direct communications from rival firms and their executives, such as press releases and quarterly-earnings calls. These communications can provide insight on the rival's actions and intended actions. It may also be valuable to follow rival-firm employees' online postings, on Twitter and other platforms, to gain insights on rivals' investments and actions.

Second, **benchmarking** *can be a useful means of employing external information.* Here managers seek out the best examples of a particular practice as part of an ongoing effort to improve the corresponding practice in their own organization.[40] There are two primary types of benchmarking. **Competitive benchmarking** restricts the search for best practices to competitors, while **functional benchmarking** endeavors to determine best practices regardless of industry. Industry-specific standards (e.g., response times required to repair power outages in the electric utility industry) are typically best handled through competitive benchmarking, whereas more generic processes (e.g., answering 1-800 calls) lend themselves to functional benchmarking because the function is essentially the same in any industry.

Ford Motor Company works with its suppliers on benchmarking its competitors' products during product redesigns. At the launch of the redesign, Ford and its suppliers identify a few key components they want to focus on improving. They then do a "tear down" of Ford's components as well as matching components from three or four rivals. The idea is to get early input from suppliers so that Ford can design components that are best in class—lighter, cheaper, and more reliable.[41]

Third, focus directly on customers for information. For example, William McKnight, head of 3M's Chicago sales office, required that salesmen of abrasives products talk directly to the workers in the shop to find out what they needed, instead of calling on only front-office executives.[42] This was very innovative at the time—1909! But it illustrates the need to get to the end user of a product or service. (McKnight went on to become 3M's president from 1929 to 1949 and chairman from 1949 to 1969.)

Challenging the Status Quo and Enabling Creativity

Earlier in this chapter we discussed some of the barriers that leaders face when trying to bring about change in an organization: vested interests in the status quo, systemic barriers, behavioral barriers, political barriers, and time constraints. For a firm to become a learning organization, it must overcome such barriers in order to foster creativity and enable it to permeate the firm. This becomes quite a challenge if the firm is entrenched in a status quo mentality.

Perhaps the best way to challenge the status quo is for the leader to forcefully create a sense of urgency. For example, when Tom Kasten was vice president of Levi Strauss, he had a direct approach to initiating change:

> You create a compelling picture of the risks of *not* changing. We let our people hear directly from customers. We videotaped interviews with customers and played excerpts. One big customer said, "We trust many of your competitors implicitly. We sample their deliveries. We open *all* Levi's deliveries." Another said, "Your lead times are the worst. If you weren't Levi's, you'd be gone." It was powerful. I wish we had done more of it.[43]

Such initiative, if sincere and credible, establishes a shared mission and the need for major transformations. It can channel energies to bring about both change and creative endeavors.

Establishing a "culture of dissent" can be another effective means of questioning the status quo and serving as a spur toward creativity. Here norms are established whereby dissenters can openly question a superior's perspective without fear of retaliation or retribution.

Closely related to the culture of dissent is the fostering of a culture that encourages risk taking. "If you're not making mistakes, you're not taking risks, and that means you're not

benchmarking
managers seeking out best examples of a particular practice as part of an ongoing effort to improve the corresponding practice in their own organization.

competitive benchmarking
benchmarking in which the examples are drawn from competitors in the industry.

functional benchmarking
benchmarking in which the examples are drawn from any organization, even those outside the industry.

going anywhere," claimed John Holt, coauthor of *Celebrate Your Mistakes*.[44] "The key is to make errors faster than the competition, so you have more chances to learn and win."

Companies that cultivate cultures of experimentation and curiosity make sure that *failure* is not, in essence, an obscene word. They encourage mistakes as a key part of their competitive advantage. It has been said that innovation has a great paradox: Success—that is, true breakthroughs—usually come through failure. Below are some approaches to encourage risk taking and learning from mistakes in an organization:[45]

- *Formalize forums for failure.* To keep failures and the important lessons that they offer from getting swept under the rug, carve out time for reflection. GE formalized the sharing of lessons from failure by bringing together managers whose "Imagination Breakthrough" efforts were put on the shelf.
- *Move the goalposts.* Innovation requires flexibility in meeting goals, since early predictions are often little more than educated guesses. Intuit's Scott Cook even goes so far as to suggest that teams developing new products ignore forecasts in the early days. "For every one of our failures, we had spreadsheets that looked awesome," he claims.
- *Bring in outsiders.* Outsiders can help neutralize the emotions and biases that prop up a flop. Customers can be the most valuable. After its DNA chip failed, Corning brought pharmaceutical companies in early to test its new drug-discovery technology, Epic.
- *Prove yourself wrong, not right.* Development teams tend to look for supporting, rather than countervailing, evidence. "You have to reframe what you're seeking in the early days," says Innosight's Scott Anthony. "You're not really seeking proof that you have the right answer. It's more about testing to prove yourself wrong."

Finally, failure can play an important and positive role in one's professional development. Former Utah Governor Scott Matheson had strong views on the benefits of failure.

> You have to suffer failures occasionally in order to have successes. You've got to back up risk-takers in order to encourage people to try out new ideas that might succeed. . . . I never had much patience with the "play it safe" manager who attempted to minimize failures. Those people rarely have successes.[46]

CREATING AN ETHICAL ORGANIZATION

LO 11-5

The leader's role in establishing an ethical organization.

ethics
a system of right and wrong that assists individuals in deciding when an act is moral or immoral and/or socially desirable or not.

organizational ethics
the values, attitudes, and behavioral patterns that define an organization's operating culture and that determine what an organization holds as acceptable behavior.

Ethics may be defined as a system of right and wrong.[47] Ethics assists individuals in deciding when an act is moral or immoral, socially desirable or not. The sources for an individual's ethics include religious beliefs, national and ethnic heritage, family practices, community standards, educational experiences, and friends and neighbors. Business ethics is the application of ethical standards to commercial enterprise.

Individual Ethics versus Organizational Ethics

Many leaders think of ethics as a question of personal scruples, a confidential matter between employees and their consciences. Such leaders are quick to describe any wrongdoing as an isolated incident, the work of a rogue employee. They assume the company should not bear any responsibility for individual misdeeds. In their view, ethics has nothing to do with leadership.

Ethics has everything to do with leadership. Seldom does the character flaw of a lone actor completely explain corporate misconduct. Instead, unethical business practices typically involve the tacit, if not explicit, cooperation of others and reflect the values, attitudes, and behavior patterns that define an organization's operating culture. Ethics is as much an organizational as a personal issue. Leaders who fail to provide proper leadership to institute proper systems and controls that facilitate ethical conduct share responsibility with those who conceive, execute, and knowingly benefit from corporate misdeeds.[48]

GREEN ENERGY: REAL OR JUST A MARKETING PLOY?

Many consumers want to "go green" and are looking for opportunities to do so. Utility companies that provide heat and electricity are one of the most obvious places to turn, because they often use fossil fuels that could be saved through energy conservation or replaced by using alternative energy sources. In fact, some consumers are willing to pay a premium to contribute to environmental sustainability efforts if paying a little more will help curb global warming. Knowing this, many power companies in the United States have developed alternative energy programs and appealed to customers to help pay for them.

Unfortunately, many of the power companies that are offering eco-friendly options are falling short on delivering on them. Some utilities have simply gotten off to a slow start or found it difficult to profitably offer alternative power. Others, however, are suspected of committing a new type of fraud—"greenwashing." This refers to companies that make unsubstantiated claims about how environmentally friendly their products or services really are. In the case of many power companies, their claims of "green power" are empty promises. Instead of actually generating additional renewable energy, most of the premiums are going for marketing costs. "They are preying on people's goodwill," says Stephen Smith, executive director of the Southern Alliance for Clean Energy, an advocacy group in Knoxville, Tennessee.

Consider what two power companies offered and how the money was actually spent:

- Duke Power of Indiana created a program called "GoGreen Power." Customers were told that they could pay a green-energy premium and a specific amount of electricity would be obtained from renewable sources. What actually happened? Less than 18 percent of voluntary customer contributions in one year went to renewable energy development.

- Alliant Energy of Iowa established a program dubbed "Second Nature." Customers were told that they would "support the growth of earth-friendly 'green power' created by wind and biomass." What actually happened? More than 56 percent of expenditures went to marketing and administrative costs, not green-energy development.

Sources: Elgin, B. & Holden, D. 2008. Green power: Buyers beware. *BusinessWeek*, September 29: 68–70; *www.cleanenergy.org*; *duke-energy.com*; and *alliantenergy.com*.

The **ethical orientation** of a leader is a key factor in promoting ethical behavior. Ethical leaders must take personal, ethical responsibility for their actions and decision making. Leaders who exhibit high ethical standards become role models for others and raise an organization's overall level of ethical behavior. Ethical behavior must start with the leader before the employees can be expected to perform accordingly.

There has been a growing interest in corporate ethical performance. Some reasons for this trend may be the increasing lack of confidence regarding corporate activities, the growing emphasis on quality-of-life issues, and a spate of recent corporate scandals. Without a strong ethical culture, the chance of ethical crises occurring is enhanced. Ethical crises can be very expensive—both in terms of financial costs and in the erosion of human capital and overall firm reputation. Merely adhering to the minimum regulatory standards may not be enough to remain competitive in a world that is becoming more socially conscious. Strategy Spotlight 11.5 highlights potential ethical problems at utility companies that were trying to capitalize on consumers' desire to participate in efforts to curb global warming.

The past two decades have been characterized by numerous examples of unethical and illegal behavior by many top-level corporate executives. These include executives of firms such as Enron, Tyco, WorldCom, Adelphia, and HealthSouth, who were all forced to resign and are facing (or have been convicted of) criminal charges. Perhaps the most glaring example is Bernie Madoff, whose Ponzi scheme, which unraveled in 2008, defrauded investors of $50 billion in assets they had set aside for retirement and charitable donations.

The ethical organization is characterized by a conception of ethical values and integrity as a driving force of the enterprise.[49] Ethical values shape the search for opportunities, the design of organizational systems, and the decision-making process used by individuals

> **ethical orientation**
> the practices that firms use to promote an ethical business culture, including ethical role models, corporate credos and codes of conduct, ethically based reward and evaluation systems, and consistently enforced ethical policies and procedures.

and groups. They provide a common frame of reference that serves as a unifying force across different functions, lines of business, and employee groups. Organizational ethics helps to define what a company is and what it stands for.

There are many potential benefits of an ethical organization, but they are often indirect. Research has found somewhat inconsistent results concerning the overall relationship between ethical performance and measures of financial performance.[50] However, positive relationships have generally been found between ethical performance and strong organizational culture, increased employee efforts, lower turnover, higher organizational commitment, and enhanced social responsibility.

The advantages of a strong ethical orientation can have a positive effect on employee commitment and motivation to excel. This is particularly important in today's knowledge-intensive organizations, where human capital is critical in creating value and competitive advantages. Positive, constructive relationships among individuals (i.e., social capital) are vital in leveraging human capital and other resources in an organization. Drawing on the concept of stakeholder management, an ethically sound organization can also strengthen its bonds among its suppliers, customers, and governmental agencies.

LO 11-6

The difference between integrity-based and compliance-based approaches to organizational ethics.

Integrity-Based versus Compliance-Based Approaches to Organizational Ethics

Before discussing the key elements of an ethical organization, one must understand the links between organizational integrity and the personal integrity of an organization's members.[51] There cannot be high-integrity organizations without high-integrity individuals. However, individual integrity is rarely self-sustaining. Even good people can lose their bearings when faced with pressures, temptations, and heightened performance expectations in the absence of organizational support systems and ethical boundaries. Organizational integrity rests on a concept of purpose, responsibility, and ideals for an organization as a whole. An important responsibility of leadership is to create this ethical framework and develop the organizational capabilities to make it operational.[52]

Lynn Paine, an ethics scholar at Harvard, identifies two approaches: the compliance-based approach and the integrity-based approach. (See Exhibit 11.5 for a comparison of compliance-based and integrity-based strategies.) Faced with the prospect of litigation,

EXHIBIT 11.5 Approaches to Ethics Management

Characteristics	Approach	Actions
Ethos	Compliance-based	Conformity with externally imposed standards
	Integrity-based	Self-governance according to chosen standards
Objective	Compliance-based	Prevent criminal misconduct
	Integrity-based	Enable responsible conduct
Leadership	Compliance-based	Driven by legal office
	Integrity-based	Driven by management, with input from functional staff
Methods	Compliance-based	Reduced discretion, training, controls, audits, and penalties
	Integrity-based	Education, leadership, accountability, decision processes, auditing, and penalties
Behavioral Assumptions	Compliance-based	Individualistic, self-interested actors
	Integrity-based	Social actors, guided by a combination of self-interest, ideals, values, and social expectations

several organizations reactively implement **compliance-based ethics programs.** Such programs are typically designed by a corporate counsel with the goal of preventing, detecting, and punishing legal violations. But being ethical is much more than being legal, and an integrity-based approach addresses the issue of ethics in a more comprehensive manner.

An **integrity-based ethics program** combines a concern for law with an emphasis on managerial responsibility for ethical behavior. It is broader, deeper, and more demanding than a legal compliance initiative. It is broader in that it seeks to enable responsible conduct. It is deeper in that it cuts to the ethos and operating systems of an organization and its members—their core guiding values, thoughts, and actions. It is more demanding because it requires an active effort to define the responsibilities that constitute an organization's ethical compass. Most importantly, organizational ethics is seen as the responsibility of management.

A corporate counsel may play a role in designing and implementing integrity strategies, but it is managers at all levels and across all functions who are involved in the process. Once integrated into the day-to-day operations, such strategies can prevent damaging ethical lapses, while tapping into powerful human impulses for moral thought and action. Ethics becomes the governing ethos of an organization and not burdensome constraints. Here is an example of an organization that goes beyond mere compliance to laws in building an ethical organization:

> In teaching ethics to its employees, Texas Instruments, the $13 billion chip and electronics manufacturer, asks them to run an issue through the following steps: Is it legal? Is it consistent with the company's stated values? Will the employee feel bad doing it? What will the public think if the action is reported in the press? Does the employee think it is wrong? If the employees are not sure of the ethicality of the issue, they are encouraged to ask someone until they are cleard about it. In the process, employees can approach high-level personnel and even the company's lawyers. At TI, the question of ethics goes much beyond merely being legal. It is no surprise that this company is a benchmark for corporate ethics and has been honored as one of the World's Most Ethical Companies by the Ethisphere Institute every year since 2007.[53]

Compliance-based approaches are externally motivated—that is, based on the fear of punishment for doing something unlawful. On the other hand, integrity-based approaches are driven by a personal and organizational commitment to ethical behavior.

A firm must have several key elements to become a highly ethical organization:

- Role models.
- Corporate credos and codes of conduct.
- Reward and evaluation systems.
- Policies and procedures.

These elements are highly interrelated. Reward structures and policies will be useless if leaders are not sound role models. That is, leaders who implicitly say, "Do as I say, not as I do," will quickly have their credibility eroded and such actions will sabotage other elements that are essential to building an ethical organization.

Role Models

For good or for bad, leaders are role models in their organizations. Perhaps few executives can share an experience that better illustrates this than Linda Hudson, former president of General Dynamics.[54] Right after she was promoted to become the firm's first female president, she went to Nordstrom and bought some new suits to wear to work. A lady at the store showed her how to tie a scarf in a very unique way. The day after she wore it to work, guess what: No fewer than a dozen women in the organization were wearing scarves tied exactly the same way. She realized that people were watching everything she did and said. She became more aware of the example she offered, the tone she set for the organization,

compliance-based ethics programs
programs for building ethical organizations that have the goal of preventing, detecting, and punishing legal violations.

integrity-based ethics programs
programs for building ethical organizations that combine a concern for law with an emphasis on managerial responsibility for ethical behavior, including (1) enabling ethical conduct; (2) examining the organization's and members' core guiding values, thoughts, and actions; and (3) defining the responsibilities and aspirations that constitute an organization's ethical compass.

LO 11-7

Several key elements that organizations must have to become ethical organizations.

and the way she carried herself. As a leader, she was the role model for many others in the organization, especially for other female managers.

Clearly, leaders must "walk the talk"; they must be consistent in their words and deeds. The values as well as the character of leaders become transparent to an organization's employees through their behaviors. When leaders do not believe in the ethical standards that they are trying to inspire, they will not be effective as good role models. Being an effective leader often includes taking responsibility for ethical lapses within the organization—even though the executives themselves are not directly involved. Consider the actions of the senior executive team at AES, a $14 billion energy company. Several employees of the firm lied to the EPA about water quality at an AES-owned water treatment plant in Oklahoma. Although senior managers had no direct role in the scandal, they agreed to take pay cuts because they saw these employee actions as an indication that they hadn't done enough to communicate AES values.

Such action enhances the loyalty and commitment of employees throughout the organization. By sharing responsibility for misdeeds, top executives—through their highly visible action—make it clear that responsibility and penalties for ethical lapses go well beyond the "guilty" parties. Such courageous behavior by leaders helps to strengthen an organization's ethical environment.

Corporate Credos and Codes of Conduct

corporate credo
a statement of the beliefs typically held by managers in a corporation.

Corporate credos and codes of conduct are mechanisms that provide statements of norms and beliefs as well as guidelines for decision making. They provide employees with a clear understanding of the organization's policies and ethical position. Such guidelines also provide the basis for employees to refuse to commit unethical acts and help to make them aware of issues before they are faced with the situation. For such codes to be truly effective, organization members must be aware of them and what behavioral guidelines they contain.[55]

Large corporations are not the only ones to develop and use codes of conduct. For example, the Baylor College of Medicine, in Houston, has a short code of ethics that sets out basic rules. The code instructs all employees to follow Baylor's Mission Statement, Compliance Program, and Conflict of Interest policy. The code includes basic guidelines for how employees should handle business conduct; financial and medical records; confidentiality; Baylor property; the workplace environment; and contact with the government.[56]

Reward and Evaluation Systems

It is entirely possible for a highly ethical leader to preside over an organization that commits several unethical acts. How? A flaw in the organization's reward structure may inadvertently cause individuals to act in an inappropriate manner if rewards are seen as being distributed on the basis of outcomes rather than the means by which goals and objectives are achieved.[57]

Generally speaking, unethical (or illegal) behaviors are also more likely to take place when competition is intense. Some researchers have called this the "dark side of competition." Consider a couple of examples:[58]

- Competition among educational institutions for the best students is becoming stiffer. A senior admissions officer at Claremont McKenna College resigned after admitting to inflating SAT scores of the incoming classes for six years. The motive, of course, was to boost the school's rankings in the *U.S. News & World Report's* annual listing of top colleges and universities in the United States. Carmen Nobel, who reported the incident in *Working Knowledge* (a Harvard Business School publication), suggested that the scandal "questions the value of competitive rankings."
- A study of 11,000 New York vehicle emission test facilities found that companies with a greater number of local competitors passed cars with considerably high emission rates and lost customers when they failed to pass the tests. The authors of the study concluded, "In contexts when pricing is restricted, firms use illicit quality as a business strategy."

Many companies have developed reward and evaluation systems that evaluate whether a manager is acting in an ethical manner. For example, Raytheon, a $24 billion defense contractor, incorporated the following items in its "Leadership Assessment Instrument":[59]

- Maintains unequivocal commitment to honesty, truth, and ethics in every facet of behavior.
- Conforms with the letter and intent of company policies while working to affect any necessary policy changes.
- Actions are consistent with words; follows through on commitments; readily admits mistakes.
- Is trusted and inspires others to be trusted.

As noted by Dan Burnham, Raytheon's former CEO: "What do we look for in a leadership candidate with respect to integrity? What we're really looking for are people who have developed an inner gyroscope of ethical principles. We look for people for whom ethical thinking is part of what they do—no different from 'strategic thinking' or 'tactical thinking.'"

Policies and Procedures

Many situations that a firm faces have regular, identifiable patterns. Leaders tend to handle such routine by establishing a policy or procedure to be followed that can be applied uniformly to each occurrence. Such guidelines can be useful in specifying the proper relationships with a firm's customers and suppliers. For example, Levi Strauss has developed stringent global sourcing guidelines, and Chemical Bank (part of JPMorgan Chase Bank) has a policy of forbidding any review that would determine if suppliers are Chemical customers when the bank awards contracts.

Carefully developed policies and procedures guide behavior so that all employees will be encouraged to behave in an ethical manner. However, they must be reinforced with effective communication, enforcement, and monitoring, as well as sound corporate governance practices. In addition, the Sarbanes-Oxley Act of 2002 provides considerable legal protection to employees of publicly traded companies who report unethical or illegal practices. Provisions in the act:[60]

- Make it unlawful to "discharge, demote, suspend, threaten, harass, or in any manner discriminate against 'a whistleblower.'"
- Establish criminal penalties of up to 10 years in jail for executives who retaliate against whistleblowers.
- Require board audit committees to establish procedures for hearing whistleblower complaints.
- Allow the secretary of labor to order a company to rehire a terminated whistleblower with no court hearings whatsoever.
- Give a whistleblower the right to a jury trial, bypassing months or years of cumbersome administrative hearings.

ISSUE FOR DEBATE

Is it important that leaders be truthful and transparent with their employees and firm stakeholders? On the one hand, ethical leaders are supposed to show openness and candor with others, and to not deceive investors, partners, and employees. On the other hand, deception and even lying may be important to motivate employees and curry favor with outside stakeholders.

continued

continued

Focusing on employees, research going as far back as the mid-20th century shows that positive feedback, even bogus positive feedback, motivates people to strive to live up with that prior feedback. This has been labeled the Pygmalion Effect. When leaders provide guidance that they believe followers have the potential to be high performers, people strive to meet those expectations. This has been found with students who receive fake test results, sales people who receive strong goals, and military personnel who are given demanding expectations. Additionally, if leaders speak highly about employees to other supervisors, those supervisors treat these employees better. But to do this, leaders must deliver inflated or bogus information to or about their followers. Thus, if leaders want followers to excel beyond their basic capabilities, these leaders will have to say things they may not believe. This may trigger employee growth, but it can also leave employees feeling that leaders are not authentic.

Turning to other firm stakeholders, investors and potential business partners want firms to be open and honest with them. But investors want to invest in and partner firms want to work with firms that are seen as strong and healthy. This creates a tension for corporate managers. If they are truthful, they increase the likelihood that others will trust them, but if leaders successfully convey optimism and confidence, even when it isn't truthful, they can attract support from investors and cooperation from business partners. This support, in turn, can help lead to the success that the leaders try to project. However, if leaders project unwarranted confidence and underdeliver on outcomes, they can erode their legitimacy as leaders.

So, should leaders be truthful or deceptive?

Discussion Questions

1. Is employing deception with employees or firm stakeholders unethical?
2. In what ways can deception pay off for executives? In what ways is it dangerous?
3. Jeffrey Pfeffer, a management scholar, has argued that leaders should be trained to be deceptive. Do you agree or disagree?

Sources: Pfeffer, J. 2016. Why deception is probably the single most important leadership skill. *fortune.com*. June 2: np; and, Kerr, J. 2014. The trickle-down effect of deceptive leadership. *inc.com*. November 12: np.

Reflecting on Career Implications . . .

This chapter examines the skills and activities associated with effective organizational leadership. The questions below challenge you to observe and learn from leaders of firms in which you work and outline issues to consider as you develop your own leadership skills.

▣ **Strategic Leadership:** The chapter identifies three interdependent activities that are central to strategic leadership; namely, setting direction, designing the organization, and nurturing a culture dedicated to excellence and ethical behavior. Both during your life as a student and in organizations at which you have worked, you have often assumed leadership positions. To what extent have you consciously and successfully engaged in each of these activities? Observe the leaders in your organization and assess to what extent you can learn from them the qualities of strategic leadership that you can use to advance your own career.

▣ **Power:** Identify the sources of power used by your superior at work. How do this person's primary source of power and the way he or she uses it affect your own creativity, morale, and willingness to stay with the organization? In addition, identify approaches you will use to enhance your power as you move up your career ladder. Explain why you chose these approaches.

▣ **Emotional Intelligence:** The chapter identifies the five components of emotional intelligence (self-awareness, self-regulation, motivation, empathy, and social skills). How do you rate yourself on each of these components? What steps can you take to improve your emotional intelligence and achieve greater career success?

▣ **Creating an Ethical Organization:** Identify an ethical dilemma that you personally faced in the course of your work. How did you respond to it? Was your response compliance-based, integrity-based, or even unethical? If your behavior was compliance-based, speculate on how it would have been different if it were integrity-based. What have you learned from your experience that would make you a more ethical leader in the future?

Strategic leadership is vital in ensuring that strategies are formulated and implemented in an effective manner. Leaders must play a central role in performing three critical and interdependent activities: setting the direction, designing the organization, and nurturing a culture committed to excellence and ethical behavior. If leaders ignore or are ineffective at performing any one of the three, the organization will not be very successful. We identified two elements of leadership that contribute to success—overcoming barriers to change and using power effectively.

For leaders to effectively fulfill their activities, emotional intelligence (EI) is very important. Five elements that contribute to EI are self-awareness, self-regulation, motivation, empathy, and social skill. The first three elements pertain to self-management skills, whereas the last two are associated with a person's ability to manage relationships with others. We addressed some of the potential drawbacks from the ineffective use of EI. These include the dysfunctional use of power as well as a tendency to become overly empathetic, which may result in unreasonably lowered performance expectations.

Leaders need to play a central role in creating a learning organization. Gone are the days when the top-level managers "think" and everyone else in the organization "does." With rapidly changing, unpredictable, and complex competitive environments, leaders must engage everyone in the ideas and energies of people throughout the organization. Great ideas can come from anywhere in the organization—from the executive suite to the factory floor. The five elements that we discussed as central to a learning organization are inspiring and motivating people with a mission or purpose, empowering people at all levels throughout the organization, accumulating and sharing internal knowledge, gathering external information, and challenging the status quo to stimulate creativity.

In the final section of the chapter, we addressed a leader's central role in instilling ethical behavior in the organization. We discussed the enormous costs that firms face when ethical crises arise—costs in terms of financial and reputational loss as well as the erosion of human capital and relationships with suppliers, customers, society at large, and governmental agencies. And, as we would expect, the benefits of having a strong ethical organization are also numerous. We contrasted compliance-based and integrity-based approaches to organizational ethics. Compliance-based approaches are largely externally motivated; that is, they are motivated by the fear of punishment for doing something that is unlawful. Integrity-based approaches, on the other hand, are driven by a personal and organizational commitment to ethical behavior. We also addressed the four key elements of an ethical organization: role models, corporate credos and codes of conduct, reward and evaluation systems, and policies and procedures.

SUMMARY REVIEW QUESTIONS

1. Three key activities—setting a direction, designing the organization, and nurturing a culture and ethics—are all part of what effective leaders do on a regular basis. Explain how these three activities are interrelated.
2. Define emotional intelligence (EI). What are the key elements of EI? Why is EI so important to successful strategic leadership? Address potential "downsides."
3. The knowledge a firm possesses can be a source of competitive advantage. Describe ways that a firm can continuously learn to maintain its competitive position.
4. How can the five central elements of "learning organizations" be incorporated into global companies?
5. What are the benefits to firms and their shareholders of conducting business in an ethical manner?
6. Firms that fail to behave in an ethical manner can incur high costs. What are these costs, and what is their source?
7. What are the most important differences between an "integrity organization" and a "compliance organization" in a firm's approach to organizational ethics?
8. What are some of the important mechanisms for promoting ethics in a firm?

leadership 334
setting a direction 335
designing the organization 335
excellent and ethical organizational culture 336
barriers to change 338
vested interest in the status quo 338
systemic barriers 338
behavioral barriers 338
political barriers 339
personal time constraints 339
power 339
organizational bases of power 340
personal bases of power 340
emotional intelligence (EI) 341
learning organizations 345
benchmarking 347
competitive benchmarking 347
functional benchmarking 347
ethics 348
organizational ethics 348
ethical orientation 349
compliance-based ethics programs 351
integrity-based ethics programs 351
corporate credo 352

EXPERIENTIAL EXERCISE

Select two well-known business leaders—one you admire and one you do not. Evaluate each of them on the five characteristics of emotional intelligence in the table below.

Emotional Intelligence Characteristics	Admired Leader	Leader Not Admired
Self-awareness		
Self-regulation		
Motivation		
Empathy		
Social skills		

APPLICATION QUESTIONS & EXERCISES

1. Identify two CEOs whose leadership you admire. What is it about their skills, attributes, and effective use of power that causes you to admire them?

2. Founders have an important role in developing their organization's culture and values. At times, their influence persists for many years. Identify and describe two organizations in which the cultures and values established by the founder(s) continue to flourish. You may find research on the Internet helpful in answering this question.

3. Some leaders place a great emphasis on developing superior human capital. In what ways does this help a firm to develop and sustain competitive advantages?

4. In this chapter we discussed the five elements of a "learning organization." Select a firm with which you are familiar and discuss whether or not it epitomizes some (or all) of these elements.

ETHICS QUESTIONS

1. Sometimes organizations must go outside the firm to hire talent, thus bypassing employees already working for the firm. Are there conditions under which this might raise ethical considerations?

2. Ethical crises can occur in virtually any organization. Describe some of the systems, procedures, and processes that can help to prevent such crises.

REFERENCES

1. Dolan, K. 2014. How to blow $9 billion. *Forbes,* July 21: 74–77; Woo, E. 2002. Peter Stroh, 74, head of brewery, philanthropist. *latimes.com*, September 21: np; and Anonymous. 2014. How to lose $700 million: The rise and fall of Stroh's. *finance.yahoo.com*, July 15: np.

2. Charan, R. & Colvin, G. 1999. Why CEOs fail. *Fortune,* June 21: 68–78.

3. Yukl, G. 2008. How leaders influence organizational effectiveness. *Leadership Quarterly,* 19(6): 708–722.

4. These three activities and our discussion draw from Kotter, J. P. 1990. What leaders really do. *Harvard Business Review,* 68(3): 103–111; Pearson, A. E. 1990. Six basics for general managers. *Harvard Business Review,* 67(4): 94–101; and Covey, S. R. 1996. Three roles of the leader in the new paradigm. In Hesselbein, F., Goldsmith, M., & Beckhard, R. (Eds.), *The leader of the future:* 149–160. San Francisco: Jossey-Bass. Some of the discussion of each of the three leadership activity concepts

draws on Dess, G. G. & Miller, A. 1993. *Strategic management:* 320–325. New York: McGraw-Hill.

5. García-Morales, V. J., Lloréns-Montes, F. J., & Verdú-Jover, A. J. 2008. The effects of transformational leadership on organizational performance through knowledge and innovation. *British Journal of Management,* 19(4): 299–319.

6. Martin, R. 2010. The execution trap. *Harvard Business Review,* 88(7/8): 64–71.

7. Collins, J. 1997. What comes next? *Inc.,* October: 34–45.

8. Hsieh, T. 2010. Zappos's CEO on going to extremes for customers. *Harvard Business Review,* 88(7/8): 41–44.

9. Chesky, B. 2014. Don't f*ck up the culture. *linkedin.com*, April 24: np.

10. Anonymous. 2006. Looking out for number one. *BusinessWeek,* October 30: 66.

11. Schaffer, R. H. 2010. Mistakes leaders keep making. *Harvard Business Review,* 88(9): 86–91.

12. For insightful perspectives on escalation, refer to Brockner, J. 1992. The escalation of commitment to a failing course of action. *Academy of Management Review,* 17(1): 39–61; and Staw, B. M. 1976. Knee-deep in the big muddy: A study of commitment to a chosen course of action. *Organizational Behavior and Human Decision Processes,* 16: 27–44. The discussion of systemic, behavioral, and political barriers draws on Lorange, P. & Murphy, D. 1984. Considerations in implementing strategic control. *Journal of Business Strategy,* 5: 27–35. In a similar vein, Noel M. Tichy has addressed three types of resistance to change in the context of General Electric: technical resistance, political resistance, and cultural resistance. See Tichy, N. M. 1993. Revolutionize your company.

Fortune, December 13: 114–118. Examples draw from O'Reilly, B. 1997. The secrets of America's most admired corporations: New ideas and new products. *Fortune,* March 3: 60–64.

13. This section draws on Champoux, J. E. 2000. *Organizational behavior: Essential tenets for a new millennium.* London: South-Western; and The mature use of power in organizations. 2003. *RHR International-Executive Insights,* May 29, *12.19.168.197/ execinsights/8-3.htm.*

14. An insightful perspective on the role of power and politics in organizations is provided in Ciampa, K. 2005. Almost ready: How leaders move up. *Harvard Business Review,* 83(1): 46–53.

15. Pfeffer, J. 2010. Power play. *Harvard Business Review,* 88(7/8): 84–92.

16. Westphal, J. D., & Graebner, M. E. 2010. A matter of appearances: How corporate leaders manage the impressions of financial analysts about the conduct of their boards. *Academy of Management Journal,* 53(4): 15–44.

17. A discussion of the importance of persuasion in bringing about change can be found in Garvin, D. A. & Roberto, M. A. 2005. Change through persuasion. *Harvard Business Review,* 83(4): 104–113.

18. Lorsch, J. W. & Tierney, T. J. 2002. *Aligning the stars: How to succeed when professionals drive results.* Boston: Harvard Business School Press.

19. Some consider EI to be a "trait," that is, an attribute that is stable over time. However, many authors, including Daniel Goleman, have argued that it can be developed through motivation, extended practice, and feedback. For example, in D. Goleman, 1998, What makes a leader? *Harvard Business Review,* 76(5): 97, Goleman addresses this issue in a sidebar: "Can emotional intelligence be learned?"

20. For a review of this literature, see Daft, R. 1999. *Leadership: Theory and practice.* Fort Worth, TX: Dryden Press.

21. EI has its roots in the concept of "social intelligence" that was first identified by E. L. Thorndike in 1920 (Intelligence and its uses. *Harper's Magazine,* 140: 227–235). Psychologists have been uncovering other intelligences for some time now and have grouped them into such clusters as abstract intelligence (the ability to understand and manipulate verbal and mathematical symbols), concrete intelligence (the ability to understand and manipulate objects), and social intelligence (the ability to understand and relate to people). See Ruisel, I. 1992. Social intelligence: Conception and methodological problems. *Studia Psychologica,* 34(4–5): 281–296. Refer to *trochim. human.cornell.edu/gallery.*

22. Joseph, D. & Newman, D. 2010. Emotional intelligence: An integrative meta-analysis and cascading model. *Journal of Applied Psychology,* 95(1): 54–78; Brusman, M. 2013. Leadership effectiveness through emotional intelligence. *workingresourcesblog.com,* September 18: np; and Bradberry, T. 2015. Why your boss lacks emotional intelligence. *forbes.com,* January 6: np.

23. Tate, B. 2008. A longitudinal study of the relationships among self-monitoring, authentic leadership, and perceptions of leadership. *Journal of Leadership & Organizational Studies,* 15(1): 16–29.

24. Moss, S. A., Dowling, N., & Callanan, J. 2009. Towards an integrated model of leadership and self-regulation. *Leadership Quarterly,* 20(2): 162–176.

25. An insightful perspective on leadership, which involves discovering, developing, and celebrating what is unique about each individual, is found in Buckingham, M. 2005. What great managers do. *Harvard Business Review,* 83(3): 70–79.

26. Muoio, A. 1998. Decisions, decisions. *fastcompany.com,* September 30: np.

27. This section draws upon Klemp. G. 2005. *Emotional intelligence and leadership: What really matters.* Cambria Consulting, Inc., *www. cambriaconsulting.com.*

28. Heifetz, R. 2004. Question authority. *Harvard Business Review,* 82(1): 37.

29. Senge, P. M. 1990. The leader's new work: Building learning organizations. *Sloan Management Review,* 32(1): 7–23.

30. Bernoff, J. & Schandler, T. 2010. Empowered. *Harvard Business Review,* 88(7/8): 94–101.

31. Hannah, S. T. & Lester, P. B. 2009. A multilevel approach to building and leading learning organizations. *Leadership Quarterly,* 20(1): 34–48.

32. For some guidance on how to effectively bring about change in organizations, refer to Wall, S. J. 2005. The protean organization: Learning to love change.

Organizational Dynamics, 34(1): 37–46.

33. Covey, S. R. 1989. *The seven habits of highly effective people: Powerful lessons in personal change.* New York: Simon & Schuster.

34. Melrose, K. 1995. *Making the grass greener on your side: A CEO's journey to leading by servicing.* San Francisco: Barrett-Koehler.

35. Tekleab, A. G., Sims, H. P., Jr., Yun, S., Tesluk, P. E., & Cox, J. 2008. Are we on the same page? Effects of self-awareness of empowering and transformational leadership. *Journal of Leadership & Organizational Studies,* 14(3): 185–201.

36. Helgesen, S. 1996. Leading from the grass roots. In Hesselbein et al., The *leader of the future:* 19–24. San Francisco: Jossey-Bass.

37. Bowen, D. E. & Lawler, E. E., III. 1995. Empowering service employees. *Sloan Management Review,* 37: 73–84.

38. Schafer, S. 1997. Battling a labor shortage? It's all in your imagination. *Inc.,* August: 24.

39. Meyer, P. 1998. So you want the president's job . . . *Business Horizons,* January–February: 2–8.

40. The introductory discussion of benchmarking draws on Miller, A. 1998. *Strategic management:* 142–143. New York: McGraw-Hill.

41. Sedgwick, D. 2014. Ford and suppliers jointly benchmark competitors' vehicles. *automotivenews. com,* October 19: np.

42. Main, J. 1992. How to steal the best ideas around. *Fortune,* October 19: 102–106.

43. Sheff, D. 1996. Levi's changes everything. *Fast Company,* June–July: 65–74.

44. Holt, J. W. 1996. *Celebrate your mistakes.* New York: McGraw-Hill.

45. McGregor, J. 2006. How failure breeds success. *Bloomberg Businessweek,* July 10: 42–52.

46. Sitkin, S. 1992. Learning through failure: The strategy of small losses. *Research in Organizational Behavior* 14: 231–266.

47. This opening discussion draws upon Conley, J. H. 2000. Ethics in business. In Helms, M. M. (Ed.), *Encyclopedia of management* (4th ed.): 281–285. Farmington Hills, MI: Gale Group; Paine, L. S. 1994. Managing for organizational integrity. *Harvard Business Review,* 72(2): 106–117; and Carlson, D. S. & Perrewe, P. L. 1995. Institutionalization of organizational ethics through transformational leadership. *Journal of Business Ethics,* 14: 829–838.

48. Pinto, J., Leana, C. R., & Pil, F. K. 2008. Corrupt organizations or organizations of corrupt individuals? Two types of organization-level corruption. *Academy of Management Review,* 33(3): 685-709.

49. Soule, E. 2002. Managerial moral strategies—In search of a few good principles. *Academy of Management Review,* 27(1): 114-124.

50. Carlson & Perrewe, op. cit.

51. This discussion is based upon Paine, Managing for organizational integrity; Paine, L. S. 1997. *Cases in leadership, ethics, and organizational integrity: A Strategic approach.* Burr Ridge, IL: Irwin; and Fontrodona, J. 2002. Business ethics across the Atlantic. Business Ethics Direct, *www.ethicsa. org/BED_art_fontrodone.html.*

52. For more on operationalizing capabilities to sustain an ethical framework, see Largay, J. A., III, & Zhang, R. 2008. Do CEOs worry about being fired when making investment decisions? *Academy of Management Perspectives,* 22(1): 60-61.

53. See *www.ti.com/corp/docs/company/ citizen/ethics/benchmark.shtml*; and *www.ti.com/corp/docs/company/ citizen/ethics/quicktest.shtml.*

54. Bryant, A. 2011. *The corner office:* 91. New York: St. Martin's Griffin.

55. For an insightful, academic perspective on the impact of ethics codes on executive decision making, refer to Stevens, J. M., Steensma, H. K., Harrison, D. A., & Cochran, P. S. 2005. Symbolic or substantive document? The influence of ethics code on financial executives' decisions. *Strategic Management Journal,* 26(2): 181-195.

56. *media.bcm.edu/documents/2015/94/ bcm-code-of-conduct-final-june-2015.pdf.*

57. For a study on the effects of goal setting on unethical behavior, read Schweitzer, M. E., Ordonez, L., & Douma, B. 2004. Goal setting as a motivator of unethical behavior. *Academy of Management Journal,* 47(3): 422-432.

58. Williams, R. 2012. How competition can encourage unethical business practices. *business.financialpost.com,* July 31: np.

59. Fulmer, R. M. 2004. The challenge of ethical leadership. *Organizational Dynamics,* 33(3): 307-317.

60. *www.sarbanes-oxley.com.*

Managing Innovation and Fostering Corporate Entrepreneurship

After reading this chapter, you should have a good understanding of the following learning objectives:

LO12-1 The importance of implementing strategies and practices that foster innovation.

LO12-2 The challenges and pitfalls of managing corporate innovation processes.

LO12-3 How corporations use new venture teams, business incubators, and product champions to create an internal environment and culture that promote entrepreneurial development.

LO12-4 How corporate entrepreneurship achieves both financial goals and strategic goals.

LO12-5 The benefits and potential drawbacks of real options analysis in making resource deployment decisions in corporate entrepreneurship contexts.

LO12-6 How an entrepreneurial orientation can enhance a firm's efforts to develop promising corporate venture initiatives.

©Anatoli Styf/Shutterstock

LEARNING FROM MISTAKES

If you ask a group of students to name a successful company, Google is likely to be one of the first firms mentioned. It dominates online search and advertising, has developed a successful browser, and developed the operating system that powers 82 percent of the smartphones sold in the fourth quarter of 2016.[1] Its success is evident in its stock price, which rose from about $150 in early 2009 to over $525 a share in early 2015. But that doesn't mean that Google has been successful at all it has tried. One of Google's most notable failures occurred when it tried to venture outside the online and wireless markets. In 2006, Google decided to expand its advertising business to radio advertising. After spending several hundred million dollars on its entrepreneurial effort in the radio advertising market, Google pulled the plug on this business in 2009.

Google saw great potential in applying its business model to the radio advertising industry. In the traditional radio advertising model, companies that wished to advertise their products and services contracted with an advertising agency to develop a set of radio spots (commercials). They then bought blocks of advertising time from radio stations. Advertisers paid based on the number of listeners on each station. Google believed that it could develop a stronger model. Its design was to purchase large blocks of advertising time from stations. It would then sell the time in a competitive auction to companies that wished to advertise. Google believed it could sell ad time to advertisers at a higher rate if it could identify what ads on what stations had the greatest impact for advertisers. Thus, rather than charging based on audience size, Google would follow the model it used on the web and charge based on ad effectiveness. To develop the competency to measure ad effectiveness, Google purchased dMarc, a company that developed technology to manage and measure radio ads, for $102 million.

Google's overall vision was even broader. The company also planned to enter print and TV advertising. It could then provide a "dashboard" to marketing executives at firms that would provide information on the effectiveness of advertising on the web, on TV, in print, and on radio. Google would then sell them a range of advertising space among all four to maximize a firm's ad expenditures.

However, Google found that its attempt to innovate the radio market bumped up against two core challenges. First, the radio advertising model was based much more on relationships than online advertising was. Radio stations, advertising firms, and advertising agencies had long-standing relationships that limited Google's ability to break into the market. In fact, few radio stations were willing to sell advertising time to Google. Also, advertising agencies saw Google as a threat to their business model and were unwilling to buy time from Google. Second, Google found that its ability to measure the effectiveness of radio ads was limited. Unlike the case with online markets, where it could measure whether people clicked on ads, the company found it difficult to measure whether listeners responded to ads. Google tried ads that mentioned specific websites that listeners could go to, but it found few people accessed these sites. In the end, Google was able to sell radio time at only a fraction of what radio stations could get from working their traditional advertising deals. This led stations to abandon Google's radio business.

Google found that it had the initiative to innovate the radio market but didn't have the knowledge, experience, or social connections needed to win in this market.

Discussion Questions

1. Why didn't the lessons Google learned in the online advertising market apply to the radio market?
2. Radio is increasingly moving to satellite and streaming systems. Is this a new opportunity for Google, or should it steer clear of radio altogether?

The importance of implementing strategies and practices that foster innovation.

Managing change is one of the most important functions performed by strategic leaders. There are two major avenues through which companies can expand or improve their business—innovation and corporate entrepreneurship. These two activities go hand-in-hand because they both have similar aims. The first is strategic renewal. Innovations help an organization stay fresh and reinvent itself as conditions in the business environment change. This is why managing innovation is such an important strategic implementation issue. The second is the pursuit of venture opportunities. Innovative breakthroughs, as well as new product concepts, evolving technologies, and shifting demand, create opportunities for corporate venturing. In this chapter we will explore these topics—how change and innovation can stimulate strategic renewal and foster corporate entrepreneurship.

MANAGING INNOVATION

innovation
the use of new knowledge to transform organizational processes or create commercially viable products and services.

One of the most important sources of growth opportunities is innovation. **Innovation** involves using new knowledge to transform organizational processes or create commercially viable products and services. The sources of new knowledge may include the latest technology, the results of experiments, creative insights, or competitive information. However it comes about, innovation occurs when new combinations of ideas and information bring about positive change.

The emphasis on newness is a key point. For example, for a patent application to have any chance of success, one of the most important attributes it must possess is novelty. You can't patent an idea that has been copied. This is a central idea. In fact, the root of the word *innovation* is the Latin *novus*, which means "new." Innovation involves introducing or changing to something new.[2]

Among the most important sources of new ideas is new technology. Technology creates new possibilities. Technology provides the raw material that firms use to make innovative products and services. But technology is not the only source of innovations. There can be innovations in human resources, firm infrastructure, marketing, service, or many other value-adding areas that have little to do with anything "high-tech." Strategy Spotlight 12.1 highlights a simple but very successful innovation by Kraft Heinz with its MiO Drops.

Types of Innovation

Although innovations are not always high-tech, changes in technology can be an important source of change and growth. When an innovation is based on a sweeping new technology, it often has a more far-reaching impact. Sometimes even a small innovation can add value and create competitive advantages. Innovation can and should occur throughout an organization—in every department and all aspects of the value chain.

product innovation
efforts to create product designs and applications of technology to develop new products for end users.

One distinction that is often used when discussing innovation is between process innovation and product innovation.[3] **Product innovation** refers to efforts to create product designs and applications of technology to develop new products for end users. Recall from Chapter 5 how generic strategies were typically different depending on the stage of the industry life cycle. Product innovations tend to be more common during the earlier stages of an industry's life cycle. Product innovations are also commonly associated with a differentiation strategy. Firms that differentiate by providing customers with new products or services that offer unique features or quality enhancements often engage in product innovation.

process innovation
efforts to improve the efficiency of organizational processes, especially manufacturing systems and operations.

Process innovation, by contrast, is typically associated with improving the efficiency of an organizational process, especially manufacturing systems and operations. By drawing on new technologies and an organization's accumulated experience (Chapter 5), firms can often improve materials utilization, shorten cycle time, and increase quality. Process innovations are more likely to occur in the later stages of an industry's life cycle as companies seek ways to remain viable in markets where demand has flattened out and competition

MIO DROPS CHANGE THE BEVERAGE GAME

Sometimes relatively small innovations can create significant changes to markets. Kraft Heinz came up with such a change in 2011 when it introduced MiO drops. Kraft Heinz had long had a major stake in the drink mix market with its Crystal Light and Kool Aid powdered beverage brands. Although the MiO product is a relatively incremental innovation, with it Kraft Heinz created an entirely new beverage category, liquid water enhancers. Within three years of its introduction, MiO was a $400 million dollar business for Kraft Heinz and was projected to grow to over $1 billion as Kraft Heinz expanded the product into global markets. Kraft Heinz called MiO "one of the most successful new product introductions" in its history. Kraft Heinz also received a number of innovation awards with MiO, including Walmart's Innovation of the Year Award in 2011 and a Gold Medal Edison Innovation Award in 2012. With MiO's commercial and critical success, it is not surprising to see a number of imitative products, such as Dasani Drops and Powerade Drops by Coke, Hawaiian Punch and Crush Drops from Dr Pepper, and Aquafina Splash from Pepsi. But MiO continues to be the market leader.

What insights led Kraft Heinz to develop this product? Kraft Heinz believed there was an opportunity with Millennial consumers who appeared to be more concerned with health and wellness than prior generations. They were moving away from traditional sweetened drinks and were open to alternative flavored beverages. Additionally, Kraft Heinz thought that a product that allowed customers to tailor the degree of flavoring and sweetening as well as a product that could easily be offered in a wide range of flavors would resonate with what Kraft Heinz saw as Millennials' desire for individual expression. Becky McAnich, MiO's marketing director, puts it this way: "Millennials really personalize every part of their life," and MiO "embraces their individuality, that customization."

Sources: Clements, M. 2013. Kraft's breakthrough innovation with MiO: Marketing to millennials. *chicagonow.com*. February 6: np; and, Latif, R. 2014. Everyone's looking for the big squeeze. *bevnet.com*. March 28: np.

---

is more intense. As a result, process innovations are often associated with overall cost leader strategies, because the aim of many process improvements is to lower the costs of operations.

Another way to view the impact of an innovation is in terms of its degree of innovativeness, which falls somewhere on a continuum that extends from incremental to radical.[4]

- **Radical innovations** produce fundamental changes by evoking major departures from existing practices. These breakthrough innovations usually occur because of technological change. They tend to be highly disruptive and can transform a company or even revolutionize a whole industry. They may lead to products or processes that can be patented, giving a firm a strong competitive advantage. Examples include electricity, the telephone, the transistor, desktop computers, fiber optics, artificial intelligence, and genetically engineered drugs.

radical innovation
an innovation that fundamentally changes existing practices.

- **Incremental innovations** enhance existing practices or make small improvements in products and processes. They may represent evolutionary applications within existing paradigms of earlier, more radical innovations. Because they often sustain a company by extending or expanding its product line or manufacturing skills, incremental innovations can be a source of competitive advantage by providing new capabilities that minimize expenses or speed productivity. Examples include frozen food, sports drinks, steel-belted radial tires, electronic bookkeeping, shatterproof glass, and digital thermometers.

incremental innovation
an innovation that enhances existing practices or makes small improvements in products and processes.

Some innovations are highly radical; others are only slightly incremental. But most innovations fall somewhere between these two extremes (see Exhibit 12.1).

Harvard Business School Professor Clayton M. Christensen identified another useful approach to characterize types of innovations.[5] Christensen draws a distinction between sustaining and disruptive innovations. *Sustaining innovations* are those that extend sales in an existing market, usually by enabling new products or services to be sold at higher margins. Such innovations may include either incremental or radical innovations. For example, smartphone

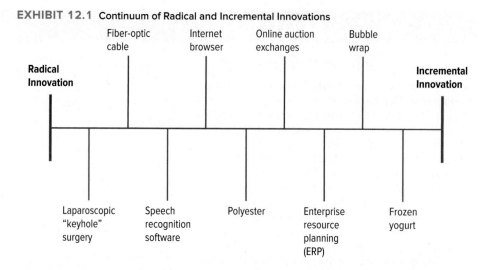

EXHIBIT 12.1 Continuum of Radical and Incremental Innovations

technology was a breakthrough innovation that transformed how people access the Internet. But rather than disrupting the business of Google and Facebook, the rise of the smartphone offered these service providers new opportunities to extend their reach into users' lives.

By contrast, *disruptive innovations* are those that overturn markets by providing an altogether new approach to meeting customer needs. The features of a disruptive innovation make it somewhat counterintuitive. Disruptive innovations:

- Are technologically simpler and less sophisticated than currently available products or services.
- Appeal to less demanding customers who are seeking more convenient, less expensive solutions.
- Take time to take effect and only become disruptive once they have taken root in a new market or low-end part of an existing market.

For example, streaming services, such as Hulu and Amazon Prime Video, have disrupted established cable and satellite systems by providing a more limited but more efficient distribution system for entertainment content. Similarly, sharing services in short-term housing, such as Airbnb, are offering a disruptive innovation that is a strong challenge to the hotel industry. "Instead of sustaining the trajectory of improvement that has been established in a market," says Christensen, a disruptive innovation "disrupts it and redefines it by bringing to the market something that is simpler."[6]

Innovation is both a force in the external environment (technology, competition) and a factor affecting a firm's internal choices (generic strategy, value-adding activities).[7] Nevertheless, innovation can be quite difficult for some firms to manage, especially those that have become comfortable with the status quo.

LO 12-2

The challenges and pitfalls of managing corporate innovation processes.

Challenges of Innovation

Innovation is essential to sustaining competitive advantages. Recall from Chapter 3 that one of the four elements of the balanced scorecard is the innovation and learning perspective. The extent and success of a company's innovation efforts are indicators of its overall performance. As management guru Peter Drucker warned, "An established company which, in an age demanding innovation, is not capable of innovation is doomed to decline and extinction."[8] In today's competitive environment, most firms have only one choice: "Innovate or die."

As with change, however, firms are often resistant to innovation. Only those companies that actively pursue innovation, even though it is often difficult and uncertain, will get a payoff from their innovation efforts. But managing innovation is challenging.[9] As former Pfizer former chairman and CEO William Steere puts it: "In some ways, managing innovation is analogous to breaking in a spirited horse. You are never sure of success until you achieve your goal. In the meantime, everyone takes a few lumps."[10]

What is it that makes innovation so difficult? The uncertainty about outcomes is one factor. Companies are often reluctant to invest time and resources in activities with an unknown future. Another factor is that the innovation process involves so many choices. These choices present five dilemmas that companies must wrestle with when pursuing innovation:[11]

- *Seeds versus weeds.* Most companies have an abundance of innovative ideas. They must decide which of these is most likely to bear fruit—the "seeds"—and which should be cast aside—the "weeds." This is complicated by the fact that some innovation projects require a considerable level of investment before a firm can fully evaluate whether they are worth pursuing. Firms need a mechanism with which they can choose among various innovation projects.

- *Experience versus initiative.* Companies must decide who will lead an innovation project. Senior managers may have experience and credibility but tend to be more risk-averse. Midlevel employees, who may be the innovators themselves, may have more enthusiasm because they can see firsthand how an innovation would address specific problems. Firms need to support and reward organizational members who bring new ideas to light.

- *Internal versus external staffing.* Innovation projects need competent staffs to succeed. People drawn from inside the company may have greater social capital and know the organization's culture and routines. But this knowledge may actually inhibit them from thinking outside the box. Staffing innovation projects with external personnel requires that project managers justify the hiring and spend time recruiting, training, and relationship building. Firms need to streamline and support the process of staffing innovation efforts.

- *Building capabilities versus collaborating.* Innovation projects often require new sets of skills. Firms can seek help from other departments and/or partner with other companies that bring resources and experience as well as share costs of development. However, such arrangements can create dependencies and inhibit internal skills development. Further, struggles over who contributed the most or how the benefits of the project are to be allocated may arise. Firms need a mechanism for forging links with outside parties to the innovation process.

- *Incremental versus preemptive launch.* Companies must manage the timing and scale of new innovation projects. An incremental launch is less risky because it requires fewer resources and serves as a market test. But a launch that is too tentative can undermine the project's credibility. It also opens the door for a competitive response. A large-scale launch requires more resources, but it can effectively preempt a competitive response. Firms need to make funding and management arrangements that allow for projects to hit the ground running, and they need to be responsive to market feedback.

These dilemmas highlight why the innovation process can be daunting even for highly successful firms. Strategy Spotlight 12.2 discusses how Procter & Gamble has been struggling with these challenges to improve its innovativeness. Next, we consider five steps that firms can take to improve the innovation process within the firm.[12]

Cultivating Innovation Skills

Some firms, such as Apple, Google, and Amazon, regularly produce innovative products and services, while other firms struggle to generate new, marketable products. What separates these innovative firms from the rest of the pack? Jeff Dyer, Hal Gregersen, and Clayton Christensen argue it is the innovative DNA of the leaders of these firms.[13] The leaders of these firms have exhibited "discovery skills" that allow them to see the potential

PROCTER & GAMBLE STRIVES TO REMAIN INNOVATIVE

From the development of Ivory Soap in 1879; to Crisco Oil, the first all-vegetable shortening, in 1911; to Crest, the first fluoridated toothpaste in 1955; to the stackable Pringles chips in 1968; to the Swiffer mop in 1998, Procter & Gamble (P&G) has long been known as a successful innovative firm. It led the market with these products and used these innovative products to build up its position as a differentiated consumer products firm. By all measures, P&G is a very successful company and was honored as the Fifth Most Admired Company by *Fortune* magazine in 2012. Still, P&G has found it challenging to remain innovative. The last major innovative blockbuster product P&G launched was Crest Whitestrips, and this product was introduced in 2001. Instead, in recent years, its new products have been extensions of current products, such as adding whitening flecks to Crest toothpaste, or derivatives of current products, such as taking the antihistamine in Nyquil and using it as a sleeping aid, labeled ZzzQuil. With ZzzQuil, P&G is not an innovator in this market, since there were a number of earlier entrants in the sleep market, such as Johnson & Johnson with its Tylenol PM product. One portfolio manager at a mutual fund derided the ZzzQuil product, saying, "It's a sign of what passes for innovation at P&G. It's not enough. It's incremental, derivative."

The factors leading to P&G's struggles to remain innovative should not be surprising. They largely grow out of the success the firm has had. First, with its wide range of products, P&G has a wide range of potential new product extensions and derivatives from which to choose. Though these are unlikely to be blockbusters, they look much safer than truly new innovative ideas. Second, while lower-level managers at P&G may be excited about new, innovative ideas, the division heads of P&G units, who are responsible for developing new products, are likely to shy away from big-bet product launches. These unit heads are also responsible for and rewarded on current division performance, a metric that will be negatively affected by the large costs associated with developing and marketing truly innovative new products. Third, due to its large size, P&G moved R&D responsibilities down to the divisions. While this enhances the divisions' abilities to quickly launch incrementally new products, it doesn't facilitate the collaboration across units often needed to develop boldly new products.

P&G is trying to address these issues by centralizing 20 to 30 percent of its research efforts within a new corporate-level business creation and innovation unit. Having a corporate effort at innovation separates the budget for product development from divisional profit numbers, enhancing the firm's willingness to invest in long-term product development efforts. Also, the corporate unit will be able to foster collaboration between units to develop blockbuster products.

Sources: Coleman-Lochner, L. & Hymowitz, C. 2012. At P&G, the innovation well runs dry. *Bloomberg Businessweek,* September 10: 24–26; and Bussey, J. 2012. The innovator's enigma. *wsj.com,* October 4: np.

in innovations and to move the organization forward in leveraging the value of those innovations.[14] These leaders spend 50 percent more time on these discovery activities than the leaders of less innovative firms. To improve their innovative processes, firms need to cultivate the innovation skills of their managers.

The key attribute that firms need to develop in their managers in order to improve their innovative potential is creative intelligence. Creative intelligence is driven by a core skill of associating—the ability to see patterns in data and integrate different questions, information, and insights—and four patterns of action: questioning, observing, experimenting, and networking. As managers practice the four patterns of action, they will begin to develop the skill of association. To illustrate how the actions of individuals will affect their ability to develop innovative ideas, imagine the following scenario:

> You and a co-worker are both tasked with developing innovative ideas for your firm and then presenting your ideas to firm management in a week. You dedicate each evening to developing innovative ideas and sit at your kitchen table, writing down any ideas that pop into your head. Your co-worker talks with 10 people about the task, including an artist friend, an engineer, a marketing executive, three co-workers from your company, two customers, and two employees from a competing firm. She also visits three local entrepreneurial firms and observes their operations, and tries out four newly introduced product in other product markets. She shares three prototype ideas with four friends, and asks people, "What if I added this capability?" and "What don't you like about the current product?" regularly throughout the week. At the end of the week, who do you think would have developed more innovative and feasible ideas?

The point is that by questioning, observing, experimenting, and networking as part of the innovative process, managers will not only make better innovation decisions now but, more importantly, start to build the innovative DNA needed to be more successful innovators in the future. As they get into the practice of these habits, decision makers will see opportunities and be more creative as they associate information from different parts of their life, different people they come in contact with, and different parts of their organizations. The ability to innovate is not hard-wired into our brains at birth. Research suggests that only one-third of our ability to think creatively is genetic. The other two-thirds is developed over time. Neuroscience research indicates that the brain is "plastic," meaning it changes over time due to experiences. As managers build up the ability to ask creative questions, develop a wealth of experiences from diverse settings, and link together insights from different arenas of their lives, their brains will follow suit and will build the ability to easily see situations creatively and draw upon a wide range of experiences and knowledge to identify creative solutions. The five traits of the effective innovator are described and examples of each trait are presented in Exhibit 12.2.

EXHIBIT 12.2 The Innovator's DNA

Trait	Description	Example
Associating	Innovators have the ability to connect seemingly unrelated questions, problems, and ideas from different fields. This allows them to creatively see opportunities that others miss.	Pierre Omidyar saw the opportunity that led to eBay when he linked three items: (1) a personal fascination with creating more efficient markets, (2) his fiancee's desire to locate hard-to-find collectible Pez dispensers, and (3) the ineffectiveness of local classified ads in locating such items.
Questioning	Innovators constantly ask questions that challenge common wisdom. Rather than accept the status quo, they ask "Why not?" or "What if?" This gets others around them to challenge the assumptions that limit the possible range of actions the firm can take.	After witnessing the emergence of eBay and Amazon, Marc Benioff questioned why computer software was still sold in boxes rather than leased with a subscription and downloaded through the Internet. This was the genesis of Salesforce.com, a firm with over $4.1 billion in sales in 2014.
Observing	Discovery-driven executives produce innovative business ideas by observing regular behavior of individuals, especially customers and potential customers. Such observations often identify challenges customers face and previously unidentified opportunities.	From watching his wife struggle to keep track of the family's finances, Intuit founder Scott Cook identified the need for easy-to-use financial software that provided a single place for managing bills, bank accounts, and investments.
Experimenting	Thomas Edison once said, "I haven't failed. I've simply found 10,000 ways that do not work." Innovators regularly experiment with new possibilities, accepting that many of their ideas will fail. Experimentation can include new jobs, living in different countries, and new ideas for their businesses.	Founders Larry Page and Sergey Brin provide time and resources for Google employees to experiment. Some, such as the Android cell phone platform, have been big winners. Others, such as the Orkut and Buzz social networking systems, have failed. But Google will continue to experiment with new products and services.
Networking	Innovators develop broad personal networks. They use this diverse set of individuals to find and test radical ideas. This can be done by developing a diverse set of friends. It can also be done by attending idea conferences where individuals from a broad set of backgrounds come together to share their perspectives and ideas, such as the Technology, Entertainment, and Design (TED) Conference or the Aspen Ideas Festival.	Michael Lazaridis got the idea for a wireless email device that led him to found Research in Motion, now called BlackBerry, from a conference he attended. At the conference, a speaker was discussing a wireless system Coca-Cola was using that allowed vending machines to send a signal when they needed refilling. Lazaridis saw the opportunity to use the same concept with email communications, and the idea for the BlackBerry was hatched.

Source: Adapted from J.H. Dyer, H.G. Gregerson and C.M. Christensen, "The Innovator's DNA," *Harvard Business Review,* December 2009, pp. 61–67.

FAIR OAKS FARMS SEES THE POWER OF WASTE

Mike McCloskey is a man on a mission. McCloskey owns Fair Oaks Farms, one of the largest dairy farms in the country. With over 36,000 cows, Fair Oaks produces about 430,000 gallons of manure every day. Rather than seeing this simply as waste, Fair Oaks has developed a number of innovations to leverage the power of the waste. To start with, Fair Oaks developed specially designed animal stalls so the manure would be easily collected. The manure is separated from sand and dirt and then put in anaerobic digesters. The manure sits in the digesters for 14 to 21 days and produces gas that is collected and refined into pure methane gas. About half of the methane is used to power the farm and all of its operations. McCloskey looked to sell the rest of the gas but found that it wasn't economical to do so. His answer was to build a fleet of delivery trucks for the dairy that run on compressed natural gas. This allows Fair Oaks to avoid using diesel fuel to deliver its milk; over two million gallons of diesel fuel are saved per year. The next step for Fair Oaks was to turn the remaining manure byproduct into fertilizer. The farm

developed the means to extract much of the water and turn it into a fertilizer paste, some of which is used in the farm's fields. The remainder is used by an outside company that has built a fertilizer plant on Fair Oaks' property. Fair Oaks is now looking for ways to use the remaining water. Mike's plan is to create an artificial wetlands area on the farm that would help clean the water. Mike and his wife, Sue, have also discussed distilling the filtered water and using it to brew beer. What would be the name of their beer? Sue says, "I'm thinking of . . . a Milk Cow Stout." What is the end goal? Mike says, "My dream . . . is to have a zero-carbon-footprint dairy, and I believe we can get there."

But it goes even further. Mike is now developing businesses that can help other dairy farmers to follow his lead. His dairy cooperative owns a part of Newtrient, a firm that is developing digester and methane processing equipment for smaller farms. McCloskey is also partner in a company that is building compressed natural gas filling stations around the country in order to build a market for farm-produced methane gas.

Sources: Donnell, R. 2016. Big agriculture gets its sh*t together. *Fortune.* February 1: 86-92; and Ravve, R. 2013. Could cow manure be the future of green energy? *foxnews.com.* April 9: np.

Defining the Scope of Innovation

Firms must have a means to focus their innovation efforts. By defining the "strategic envelope"—the scope of a firm's innovation efforts—firms ensure that their innovation efforts are not wasted on projects that are outside the firm's domain of interest. Strategic enveloping defines the range of acceptable projects. A **strategic envelope** creates a firm-specific view of innovation that defines how a firm can create new knowledge and learn from an innovation initiative even if the project fails. It also gives direction to a firm's innovation efforts, which helps separate seeds from weeds and builds internal capabilities.

One way to determine which projects to work on is to focus on a common technology. Then innovation efforts across the firm can aim at developing skills and expertise in a given technical area. Another potential focus is on a market theme. Strategy Spotlight 12.3 discusses how Fair Oaks Farms, one of the largest dairy farms in the country, responded to environmental concerns by developing processes to turn animal waste into fuel.

Companies must be clear about not only the kinds of innovation they are looking for but also the expected results. Each company needs to develop a set of questions to ask itself about its innovation efforts:

- How much will the innovation initiative cost?
- How likely is it to actually become commercially viable?
- How much value will it add; that is, what will it be worth if it works?
- What will be learned if it does not pan out?

However a firm envisions its innovation goals, it needs to develop a systematic approach to evaluating its results and learning from its innovation initiatives. Viewing innovation from this perspective helps firms manage the process.[15]

strategic envelope
a firm-specific view of innovation that defines how a firm can create new knowledge and learn from an innovation initiative even if the project fails.

Managing the Pace of Innovation

Along with clarifying the scope of an innovation by defining a strategic envelope, firms also need to regulate the pace of innovation. How long will it take for an innovation initiative to realistically come to fruition? The project timeline of an incremental innovation may be 6 months to 2 years, whereas a more radical innovation is typically long term—10 years or more.[16] Radical innovations often begin with a long period of exploration in which experimentation makes strict timelines unrealistic. In contrast, firms that are innovating incrementally in order to exploit a window of opportunity may use a milestone approach that is more stringently driven by goals and deadlines. This kind of sensitivity to realistic time frames helps companies separate dilemmas temporally so they are easier to manage.

Time pacing can also be a source of competitive advantage because it helps a company manage transitions and develop an internal rhythm.[17] Time pacing does not mean the company ignores the demands of market timing; instead, companies have a sense of their own internal clock in a way that allows them to thwart competitors by controlling the innovation process. With time pacing, the firm works to develop an internal rhythm that matches the buying practices of customers. For example, for years, Intel worked to develop new microprocessor chips every 18 months. The company would have three chips in process at any point in time—one it was producing and selling, one it was currently developing, and one that was just on the drawing board. This pacing also matched the market, because most corporate customers bought new computers about every three years. Thus, customers were then two generations behind in their computing technology, leading them to feel the need to upgrade at the three-year point. In the post-PC era, Apple has developed a similar but faster internal cycle, allowing it to launch a new generation of the iPhone on an annual basis.

This doesn't mean the aim is always to be faster when innovating. Some projects can't be rushed. Companies that hurry their research efforts or go to market before they are ready can damage their ability to innovate—and their reputation. Thus, managing the pace of innovation can be an important factor in long-term success.

Staffing to Capture Value from Innovation

People are central to the processes of identifying, developing, and commercializing innovations effectively. They need broad sets of skills as well as experience—experience working with teams and experience working on successful innovation projects. To capture value from innovation activities, companies must provide strategic decision makers with staff members who make it possible.

This insight led strategy experts Rita Gunther McGrath and Thomas Keil to research the types of human resource management practices that effective firms use to capture value from their innovation efforts.[18] Four practices are especially important:

- Create innovation teams with experienced players who know what it is like to deal with uncertainty and can help new staff members learn venture management skills.
- Require that employees seeking to advance their career with the organization serve in the new venture group as part of their career climb.
- Once people have experience with the new venture group, transfer them to mainstream management positions where they can use their skills and knowledge to revitalize the company's core business.
- Separate the performance of individuals from the performance of the innovation. Otherwise, strong players may feel stigmatized if the innovation effort they worked on fails.

There are other staffing practices that may sound as if they would benefit a firm's innovation activities but may, in fact, be counterproductive:

- Creating a staff that consists only of strong players whose primary experience is related to the company's core business. This provides too few people to deal with the uncertainty of innovation projects and may cause good ideas to be dismissed because they do not appear to fit with the core business.
- Creating a staff that consists only of volunteers who want to work on projects they find interesting. Such players are often overzealous about new technologies or overly attached to product concepts, which can lead to poor decisions about which projects to pursue or drop.
- Creating a climate where innovation team members are considered second-class citizens. In companies where achievements are rewarded, the brightest and most ambitious players may avoid innovation projects with uncertain outcomes.

Unless an organization can align its key players into effective new venture teams, it is unlikely to create any differentiating advantages from its innovation efforts.[19] An enlightened approach to staffing a company's innovation efforts provides one of the best ways to ensure that the challenges of innovation will be effectively met. The nearby Insights from Research box discusses actions a firm can take to use the departure of key employees as a catalyst for new innovative efforts.

Collaborating with Innovation Partners

It is rare for any one organization to have all the information it needs to carry an innovation from concept to commercialization. Even a company that is highly competent with its current operations usually needs new capabilities to achieve new results. Innovation partners provide the skills and insights that are needed to make innovation projects succeed.[20]

Innovation partners may come from many sources, including research universities and the federal government. Each year the federal government issues requests for proposals (RFPs) asking private companies for assistance in improving services or finding solutions to public problems. Universities are another type of innovation partner. Chip-maker Intel, for example, has benefited from underwriting substantial amounts of university research. Rather than hand universities a blank check, Intel bargains for rights to patents that emerge from Intel-sponsored research. The university retains ownership of the patent, but Intel gets royalty-free use of it.[21]

Strategic partnering requires firms to identify their strengths and weaknesses and make choices about which capabilities to leverage, which need further development, and which are outside the firm's current or projected scope of operations.

To choose partners, firms need to ask what competencies they are looking for and what the innovation partner will contribute.[22] These might include knowledge of markets, technology expertise, or contacts with key players in an industry. Innovation partnerships also typically need to specify how the rewards of the innovation will be shared and who will own the intellectual property that is developed.[23]

Innovation efforts that involve multiple partners and the speed and ease with which partners can network and collaborate are changing the way innovation is conducted.[24]

The Value of Unsuccessful Innovation

Companies are often reluctant to pursue innovations due to the high uncertainty associated with innovative efforts. They are torn about whether to invest in emerging technologies, wondering which, if any, will win in the market and offer the best payoff for the firm. Conventional wisdom suggests that firms pay dearly if they bet on the wrong technology or new product direction. However, research by NYU professor J. P. Eggers suggests that

YOU CAN ADAPT TO THE LOSS OF A STAR EMPLOYEE

OVERVIEW

When star employees head for the exit, business leaders surely feel the loss, but research reveals that smart business leaders adapt by looking to fresh talent and formerly unexplored opportunities.

WHAT THE RESEARCH SHOWS

Losing talent may disrupt activity and routines that have served a company well, but it also opens a door to new unexplored opportunities. That is the conclusion reached by researchers from Drexel University and Rutgers University in a recent article in the *Journal of Management*.

Using a sample of 197 U.S. biotechnology companies, the researchers examined the effects of losing a star scientist on his or her company's subsequent innovation efforts. According to the paper, star scientists are innovators who were above the industry average in both the number of patents they produced and the influence of their patents. The researchers included two types of company innovation: exploitation, referring to patent activity related to an organization's existing knowledge, and exploration, patent activity focused on new areas for the company.

During the period studied, 90 stars from 32 organizations left to join other biotechnology firms. The effects of turnover were significant and complex.

- Compared with their peers, companies that lost star scientists saw an average decline of 14 percent in exploitation-related innovation during the next three years.

- At the same time, however, the departure of a star scientist led to a 22 percent average increase in exploration-related innovation during the next three years.

In other words, although the departure of a star scientist was disruptive to existing areas of innovation, companies appeared to adapt by exploring new areas. These effects, moreover, varied from company to company, depending on the characteristics of the star scientist. In general, the more

the scientist was involved in patent activity and collaborated with others in the company, the larger the effects of his or her departure on the organization's subsequent levels of innovation.

WHY THIS MATTERS

Smart managers appreciate the extent to which their organization's competitive performance depends on the talents of its workforce. The majority of academic evidence suggests that the loss of employees hurts corporate performance because it reduces productivity, erodes customer service, and lowers quality. Turnover is particularly worrisome in businesses that require higher education, creativity, or technical skill, because their employees are not easily replaced.

Yet in industries that rely heavily on intellectual capital, such as technology, life sciences, or the arts, the loss of talented employees may have an unexpected benefit for the organization. While turnover of star scientists did disrupt innovation related to the companies' existing lines of research, it also increased the rate of innovation in previously unexplored areas. Companies adapt to the loss of talent by exploring products, brands, and methods they may not have otherwise considered.

KEY TAKEAWAYS

- Employee turnover can both hurt and help an organization.
- The loss of talented employees disrupts innovation related to established products.
- The loss of talented employees allows fresh perspectives and ideas to emerge.
- Companies adapt to star turnover by innovating in formerly unexplored areas.

RESEARCH REVIEWED

Tzabar, D. & Kehoe, R. 2014. Can opportunity emerge from disarray? An examination of exploration and exploitation following star scientist turnover. *Journal of Management*. 40: 449–482.

betting on a losing technology and then switching to the winner can position a company to come out ahead of competitors that were on the right track all along.[25]

His research shows that firms that initially invest in an unsuccessful innovative effort often end up dominating the market in the long run. The key is that the firm remains open to change and to learning from both its mistakes and the experience of the innovators that initially chose to pursue the winning technology. Eggers offers the following insights for companies competing in a dynamic market where it is uncertain which technology will emerge triumphant:

1. *Avoid overcommitting.* This can be difficult as the firm sees the need to build specific expertise and stake out a decisive position to be seen as a leader in the market. However, managers can become entrenched as confirmation bias leads them to focus only on data that suggest they've made the right choice. Eggers suggests firms consider joint ventures and other alliances to avoid overinvestments they may come to regret.

2. *Don't let shame or despair knock you out of the game.* Shame has been shown to be a particularly destructive reaction to failure. Remember that it is very likely no one could have had complete confidence regarding which technology would win. And try to avoid seeing things as worse than they are. Some companies that bet on the wrong technology decide, unnecessarily, to get out of the market entirely, missing out on any future market opportunities.

3. *Pivot quickly.* Once they realized they made a mistake, firms that were ultimately successful changed course and moved quickly. Studies have shown that the ideal moment to enter a high-tech industry is just as the dominant design emerges. So missing the target initially doesn't have to mean that a firm is doomed to failure if the firm moves swiftly as the dominant technology becomes clear.

4. *Transfer knowledge.* Successful firms use the information they gathered in a losing bet to exploit other market opportunities. For example, when flat-panel computer displays were first emerging, it was unclear if plasma or LCD technology would win. IBM initially invested heavily in plasma displays, a bet that turned out to be wrong when LCD technology won out. But IBM took away valuable knowledge from its plasma investments. For example, the heavy glass required by plasma technology forced IBM to become skilled at glass design, which helped it push glass technology in new directions in products such as the original ThinkPad laptop.

5. *Be aware that it can be dangerous to be right at the outset.* Managers in firms that initially select the winning technology have a tendency to interpret their ability to choose the most promising technology as an unconditional endorsement of everything they had been doing. As a result, they fail to recognize the need to rethink some details of their product and the underlying technology. Their complacency can give firms that initially chose the wrong technology the space to catch up and then pull ahead, since the later-moving firms are more open to see the need for improvements and are hungry and aggressive in their actions. The key to who wins typically isn't who is there first. Instead, the winning firm is the one that continuously incrementally innovates on the initial bold innovation to offer the best product at the best price.

Offering additional insight into the potential benefits of unsuccessful innovations, research by Julian Birkinshaw suggests that failure can be a great catalyst for learning.[26] He advises three key steps to ensure that firms can leverage the value of failures. First, firms should study individual projects that did not pan out and gather as many insights as possible from them. This should include what the failure can teach the firm about customers and market dynamics; the organization's culture, strategy, and processes; the decision team and firm leaders; and trends in the market and the larger environment. Second, firms need to crystallize those insights and share them across the organization. This can involve regular meetings where firm leaders share their recent struggles and the lessons learned. It can also involve reports that are shared across the firm. For example, Engineers Without Borders, a global volunteer organization that strives to offer engineering solutions in underdeveloped countries, launched an annual "failure report" that discussed failures and their lessons. Third, he advises that firm leaders take a step back and do overall corporate reviews occasionally to ensure that the overall approach to failure is yielding strong benefits. This can give insight into whether the organization is repeating the same pattern of failure or if it is learning and improving. It can also serve to identify the most widely applicable learning or the most critical areas needed for improvement. Finally, it can also help identify if the firm is being too conservative and failing too infrequently. One key takeaway is that highlighting the value of learning from failures can lessen the fear of failure by showing that it is not the end to an employee's career. Instead, it is the foundation for learning and something to accept as part of the process of innovation. As Sunil Sinha, the head of Tata Quality Management, stated: "We want people to be bold and not be afraid to fail."

CORPORATE ENTREPRENEURSHIP

Corporate entrepreneurship (CE) has two primary aims: the pursuit of new venture opportunities and strategic renewal.[27] The innovation process keeps firms alert by exposing them to new technologies, making them aware of marketplace trends, and helping them evaluate new possibilities. Corporate entrepreneurship uses the fruits of the innovation process to help firms build new sources of competitive advantage and renew their value propositions. Just as the innovation process helps firms to make positive improvements, CE helps firms identify opportunities and launch new ventures.

> **corporate entrepreneurship (CE)**
> the creation of new value for a corporation through investments that create either new sources of competitive advantage or renewal of the value proposition.

Corporate new venture creation was labeled "intrapreneuring" by Gifford Pinchot because it refers to building entrepreneurial businesses within existing corporations.[28] However, to engage in corporate entrepreneurship that yields above-average returns and contributes to sustainable advantages, it must be done effectively. In this section we will examine the sources of entrepreneurial activity within established firms and the methods large corporations use to stimulate entrepreneurial behavior.

In a typical corporation, what determines how entrepreneurial projects will be pursued? The answer depends on many factors, including:

- Corporate culture.
- Leadership.
- Structural features that guide and constrain action.
- Organizational systems that foster learning and manage rewards.

All of the factors that influence the strategy implementation process will also shape how corporations engage in internal venturing.

Other factors will also affect how entrepreneurial ventures will be pursued:

- The use of teams in strategic decision making.
- Whether the company is product- or service-oriented.
- Whether its innovation efforts are aimed at product or process improvements.
- The extent to which it is high-tech or low-tech.

Because these factors are different in every organization, some companies may be more involved than others in identifying and developing new venture opportunities.[29] These factors will also influence the nature of the CE process.

Successful CE typically requires firms to reach beyond their current operations and markets in the pursuit of new opportunities. It is often the breakthrough opportunities that provide the greatest returns. Such strategies are not without risks, however. In the sections that follow, we will address some of the strategic choice and implementation issues that influence the success or failure of CE activities.

Two distinct approaches to corporate venturing are found among firms that pursue entrepreneurial aims. The first is *focused* corporate venturing, in which CE activities are isolated from a firm's existing operations and worked on by independent work units. The second approach is *dispersed,* in which all parts of the organization and every organization member are engaged in intrapreneurial activities.

LO 12-3

How corporations use new venture teams, business incubators, and product champions to create an internal environment and culture that promote entrepreneurial development.

Focused Approaches to Corporate Entrepreneurship

Firms using a **focused approach** typically separate the corporate venturing activity from the other ongoing operations of the firm. CE is usually the domain of autonomous work groups that pursue entrepreneurial aims independent of the rest of the firm. The advantage of this approach is that it frees entrepreneurial team members to think and act without the constraints imposed by existing organizational norms and routines. This independence is often necessary for the kind of open-minded creativity that leads to strategic breakthroughs. The disadvantage is that, because of their isolation from the corporate mainstream, the work groups that concentrate on internal ventures may fail to obtain the resources or support needed to carry an entrepreneurial project through to completion. Two forms—new venture groups (NVGs) and business incubators—are among the most common types of focused approaches.

focused approaches to corporate entrepreneurship corporate entrepreneurship in which the venturing entity is separated from the other ongoing operations of the firm.

new venture group (NVG) a group of individuals, or a division within a corporation, that identifies, evaluates, and cultivates venture opportunities.

New Venture Groups   Corporations often form **new venture groups (NVGs)** whose goal is to identify, evaluate, and cultivate venture opportunities. These groups typically function as semiautonomous units with little formal structure. The NVG may simply be a committee that reports to the president on potential new ventures. Or it may be organized as a corporate division with its own staff and budget. The aims of the NVG may be open-ended in terms of what ventures it may consider. Alternatively, some corporations use an NVG to promote concentrated effort on a specific problem. In both cases, NVGs usually have a substantial amount of freedom to take risks and a supply of resources to do it with.[30]

New venture groups usually have a larger mandate than a typical R&D department. Their involvement extends beyond innovation and experimentation to coordinating with other corporate divisions, identifying potential venture partners, gathering resources, and actually launching the venture.

business incubator a corporate new venture group that supports and nurtures fledgling entrepreneurial ventures until they can thrive on their own as stand-alone businesses.

Business Incubators   The term *incubator* was originally used to describe a device in which eggs are hatched. **Business incubators** are designed to "hatch" new businesses. They are a type of corporate NVG with a somewhat more specialized purpose—to support and nurture fledgling entrepreneurial ventures until they can thrive on their own as stand-alone businesses. Corporations use incubators as a way to grow businesses identified by the NVG. Although they often receive support from many parts of the corporation, they still operate independently until they are strong enough to go it alone. Depending on the type of business, they either are integrated into an existing corporate division or continue to operate as a subsidiary of the parent firm. Strategy Spotlight 12.4 outlines how a number of large firms are using NVGs and business incubators to improve their CE efforts.

Incubators typically provide some or all of the following five functions:[31]

- *Funding.* This includes capital investments as well as in-kind investments and loans.
- *Physical space.* Incubators in which several start-ups share space often provide fertile ground for new ideas and collaboration.
- *Business services.* Along with office space, young ventures need basic services and infrastructure, which may include anything from phone systems and computer networks to public relations and personnel management.
- *Mentoring.* Senior executives and skilled technical personnel often provide coaching and experience-based advice.
- *Networking.* Contact with other parts of the firm and external resources such as suppliers, industry experts, and potential customers facilitates problem solving and knowledge sharing.

BIG FIRMS USE NVGS AND BUSINESS INCUBATORS TO TRIGGER CREATIVITY

Common wisdom is that to be innovative firms need to be small and nimble. Major firms, such as GE, IBM, Coke, Taco Bell, and others, are buying into this wisdom. They have each launched groups within the firm whose expressed purpose is to generate innovations. Here are a few examples of how some large firms across a range of industries are using these focused groups to stoke up the entrepreneurial spirit in the firm.

- **Taco Bell.** Employs a 40 member innovation center team that is tasked with coming up regularly with catchy, innovative food items. Its most notable innovation was Doritos Locos Tacos, which generated over $1 billion in sales in its first year. The group considers dozens of new ideas a week and aims to launch a new menu item every five weeks. These new items typically are only available for a limited time, but they generate 5 percent of sales. Notable products have included Cap'n Crunch Delights (cereal encrusted, icing filled doughnut holes) and DareDevil Loaded Grillers (burritos filled with a collection of hot peppers). This innovative effort has sparked nearly 10 percent annual growth in a mature market.

- **Mondelez.** The food giant created a group called Mobile Futures. The aim of the incubator group is to foster new entrepreneurial efforts that may stay as part of Mondelez but may also be spun off. In a venture that stayed internal, it launched a direct-to-consumer business in the United States with Oreo Colorfilled cookies. The culture of the group facilitated speed with the new product. "We were able to launch it in two-months time instead of two years," said a corporate spokesperson. Another new venture launched through the program, Betabox, was sold off once the business took off.

- **General Electric.** Created a FastWorks program that changes the product development process. Rather than a closed product development cycle that could take up to five years, it created small cross-functional teams that were charged with getting the new product designed and the new business up and running in a matter of months. The first team in the program were thrown into a room together. They became a tight group as they went down to the factory floor and built products together and looked at market research together. Instead of the traditional approach in which salespeople give design requirements and then leave, customers were involved throughout. Having the team hear customer feedback firsthand was a big change, especially for the engineers. They bounced ideas and product prototypes off of retail salespeople who visited GE's training office to learn about GE's products.

- **Tyco.** Launched several Innovation Centers that serve as new venture development groups, and develop new products and services in security, fire protection, and smart connected technologies. The first centers opened were in Silicon Valley and Tel Aviv and employ a few hundred of Tyco's 57,000 employees.

- **MasterCard.** The credit card giant has created dozens of new product design teams to develop new services to meet the technology-driven changes occurring in the e-commerce market. These teams typically have less than two dozen members and operate in a three-floor, open architecture innovation lab in MasterCard's New York office.

The key goal for all of these large and successful firms is to think and act like a small firm to stay on the cutting edge of the market and one step ahead of the entrepreneurial start-ups looking to challenge them if they stumble and fail to innovate.

Sources: Alsever, J. 2015. Startups inside giant companies. *Fortune.* May 1: 33–36; Power, B. 2014. How GE applies lean startup practices. *hbr.org.* April 23: np; and, Ringen, J. 2016. For combining corn, beans, meat, and cheese into genius. *Fast Company.* March: 46–49.

To encourage entrepreneurship, corporations sometimes need to do more than create independent work groups or venture incubators to generate new enterprises. In some firms, the entrepreneurial spirit is spread throughout the organization.

Dispersed Approaches to Corporate Entrepreneurship

The second type of CE is dispersed. For some companies, a dedication to the principles and practices of entrepreneurship is spread throughout the organization. One advantage of this **dispersed approach** is that organizational members don't have to be reminded to think entrepreneurially or be willing to change. The ability to change is considered to be a core capability. This leads to a second advantage: Because of the firm's entrepreneurial reputation, stakeholders such as vendors, customers, or alliance partners can bring new ideas or venture opportunities to anyone in the organization and expect them to be well received. Such opportunities make it possible for the firm to stay ahead of the competition. However, there are disadvantages as well. Firms that are overzealous about CE sometimes feel they

dispersed approaches to corporate entrepreneurship corporate entrepreunership in which a dedication to the principles and policies of entrepreneurship is spread throughout the organization.

must change for the sake of change, causing them to lose vital competencies or spend heavily on R&D and innovation to the detriment of the bottom line. Three related aspects of dispersed entrepreneurship include entrepreneurial cultures that have an overarching commitment to CE activities, resource allotments to support entrepreneurial actions, and the use of product champions in promoting entrepreneurial behaviors.

Entrepreneurial Culture   In some large corporations, the corporate culture embodies the spirit of entrepreneurship. A culture of entrepreneurship is one in which the search for venture opportunities permeates every part of the organization. The key to creating value successfully is viewing every value-chain activity as a source of competitive advantage. The effect of CE on a firm's strategic success is strongest when it animates all parts of an organization. It is found in companies where the strategic leaders and the culture together generate a strong impetus to innovate, take risks, and seek out new venture opportunities.[32]

entrepreneurial culture
corporate culture in which change and renewal are a constant focus of attention.

In companies with an **entrepreneurial culture,** everyone in the organization is attuned to opportunities to help create new businesses. Many such firms use a top-down approach to stimulate entrepreneurial activity. The top leaders of the organization support programs and incentives that foster a climate of entrepreneurship. Many of the best ideas for new corporate ventures, however, come from the bottom up. Catherine Winder, former president of Rainmaker Entertainment, discussed how she welcomed any employee to generate and pitch innovative ideas this way:[33]

> We have an open-door policy for anyone in the company to pitch ideas . . . to describe their ideas in 15 to 30 seconds. If we like the core idea, we'll work with them. If you can be concise and come up with your idea in a really clear way, it means you're on to something.

An entrepreneurial culture is one in which change and renewal are on everybody's mind. Amazon, 3M, Intel, and Cisco are among the corporations best known for their corporate venturing activities. Many fast-growing young corporations also attribute much of their success to an entrepreneurial culture. But other successful firms struggle in their efforts to remain entrepreneurial.

Resource Allotments   Corporate entrepreneurship requires the willingness of the firm to invest in the generation and execution of innovative ideas. On the generation side, employees are much more likely to develop these ideas if they have the time to do so. For decades, 3M allowed its engineers free time, up to 15 percent of their work schedule, to work on developing new products.[34] Intuit follows a similar model, offering employees the opportunity to spend 10 percent of their time on ideas that improve Intuit's processes or on products that address user problems. According to Brad Smith, Intuit's CEO, this time is critical for the future success of Intuit since "innovation is not going to come from me. It's going to come from challenging people to think about new and different ways of solving big, important problems."[35] In addition to time, firms can foster CE by providing monetary investment to fund entrepreneurial ideas. Johnson & Johnson (J&J) uses its Internal Ventures Group to support entrepreneurial ideas developed inside the firm. Entrepreneurs within J&J submit proposals to the group. The review board decides which proposals to fund and then solicits further investments from J&J's operating divisions. Nike's Sustainable Business and Innovation Lab and Google's Ventures Group have a similar charter to review and fund promising corporate entrepreneurship activities. The availability of these time and financing sources can enhance the likelihood of successful entrepreneurial activities within the firm.

Product Champions   Corporate entrepreneurship does not always involve making large investments in start-ups or establishing incubators to spawn new divisions. Often, innovative ideas emerge in the normal course of business and are brought forth and become part of the way of doing business. Entrepreneurial champions are often needed to take charge of internally generated ventures. **Product champions** (or project champions) are those individuals working within a corporation who bring entrepreneurial ideas forward, identify what kind of market exists for the product or service, find resources to support the venture, and promote the venture concept to upper management.[36]

When lower-level employees identify a product idea or novel solution, they will take it to their supervisor or someone in authority. A new idea that is generated in a technology lab may be introduced to others by its inventor. If the idea has merit, it gains support and builds momentum across the organization.[37] Even though the corporation may not be looking for new ideas or have a program for cultivating internal ventures, the independent behaviors of a few organizational members can have important strategic consequences.

No matter how an entrepreneurial idea comes to light, however, a new venture concept must pass through two critical stages or it may never get off the ground:

1. *Project definition.* An opportunity has to be justified in terms of its attractiveness in the marketplace and how well it fits with the corporation's other strategic objectives.

2. *Project impetus.* For a project to gain impetus, its strategic and economic impact must be supported by senior managers who have experience with similar projects. It then becomes an embryonic business with its own organization and budget.

For a project to advance through these stages of definition and impetus, a product champion is often needed to generate support and encouragement. Champions are especially important during the time after a new project has been defined but before it gains momentum. They form a link between the definition and impetus stages of internal development, which they do by procuring resources and stimulating interest for the product among potential customers.[38] Product champions play an important entrepreneurial role in a corporate setting by encouraging others to take a chance on promising new ideas.[39]

Measuring the Success of Corporate Entrepreneurship Activities

At this point in the discussion, it is reasonable to ask whether CE is successful. Corporate venturing, like the innovation process, usually requires a tremendous effort. Is it worth it? We consider factors that corporations need to take into consideration when evaluating the success of CE programs. We also examine techniques that companies can use to limit the expense of venturing or to cut their losses when CE initiatives appear doomed.

Comparing Strategic and Financial CE Goals Not all corporate venturing efforts are financially rewarding. In terms of financial performance, slightly more than 50 percent of corporate venturing efforts reach profitability (measured by ROI) within six years of their launch.[40] If this were the only criterion for success, it would seem to be a rather poor return. On the one hand, these results should be expected, because CE is riskier than other investments such as expanding ongoing operations. On the other hand, corporations expect a higher return from corporate venturing projects than from normal operations. Thus, in terms of the risk–return trade-off, it seems that CE often falls short of expectations.[41]

There are several other important criteria, however, for judging the success of a corporate venture initiative. Most CE programs have strategic goals.[42] The strategic reasons for undertaking a corporate venture include strengthening competitive position, entering into new markets, expanding capabilities by learning and acquiring new knowledge, and building the corporation's base of resources and experience. Three questions should be used to assess the effectiveness of a corporation's venturing initiatives:[43]

1. *Are the products or services offered by the venture accepted in the marketplace?* Is the venture considered to be a market success? If so, the financial returns are likely to be satisfactory. The venture may also open doors into other markets and suggest avenues for other venture projects.

2. ***Are the contributions of the venture to the corporation's internal competencies and experience valuable?*** Does the venture add to the worth of the firm internally? If so, strategic goals such as leveraging existing assets, building new knowledge, and enhancing firm capabilities are likely to be met.[44]

3. ***Is the venture able to sustain its basis of competitive advantage?*** Does the value proposition offered by the venture insulate it from competitive attack? If so, it is likely to place the corporation in a stronger position relative to competitors and provide a base from which to build other advantages.

These criteria include both strategic and financial goals of CE. Another way to evaluate a corporate venture is in terms of the four criteria from the balanced scorecard (Chapter 3). In a successful venture, not only are financial and market acceptance (customer) goals met but so are the internal business and innovation and learning goals. Thus, when assessing the success of corporate venturing, it is important to look beyond simple financial returns and consider a well-rounded set of criteria.[45]

exit champion
an individual working within a corporation who is willing to question the viability of a venture project by demanding hard evidence of venture success and challenging the belief system that carries a venture forward.

Exit Champions   Although a culture of championing venture projects is advantageous for stimulating an ongoing stream of entrepreneurial initiatives, many—in fact, most—of the ideas will not work out. At some point in the process, a majority of initiatives will be abandoned. Sometimes, however, companies wait too long to terminate a new venture and do so only after large sums of resources are used up or, worse, result in a marketplace failure. Motorola's costly global satellite telecom project known as Iridium provides a useful illustration. Even though problems with the project existed during the lengthy development process, Motorola refused to pull the plug. Only after investing $5 billion and years of effort was the project abandoned.[46]

One way to avoid these costly and discouraging defeats is to support a key role in the CE process: **exit champions.** In contrast to product champions and other entrepreneurial enthusiasts within the corporation, exit champions are willing to question the viability of a venture project.[47] By demanding hard evidence and challenging the belief system that is carrying an idea forward, exit champions hold the line on ventures that appear shaky.

Both product champions and exit champions must be willing to energetically stand up for what they believe. Both put their reputations on the line. But they also differ in important ways.[48] Product champions deal in uncertainty and ambiguity. Exit champions reduce ambiguity by gathering hard data and developing a strong case for why a project should be killed. Product champions are often thought to be willing to violate procedures and operate outside normal channels. Exit champions often have to reinstate procedures and reassert the decision-making criteria that are supposed to guide venture decisions. Whereas product champions often emerge as heroes, exit champions run the risk of losing status by opposing popular projects.

The role of exit champion may seem unappealing. But it is one that could save a corporation both financially and in terms of its reputation in the marketplace. It is especially important because one measure of the success of a firm's CE efforts is the extent to which it knows when to cut its losses and move on.

LO 12-5

The benefits and potential drawbacks of real options analysis in making resource deployment decisions in corporate entrepreneurship contexts.

real options analysis (ROA)
an investment analysis tool that looks at an investment or activity as a series of sequential steps, and for each step the investor has the option of (a) investing additional funds to grow or accelerate, (b) delaying, (c) shrinking the scale of, or (d) abandoning the activity.

REAL OPTIONS ANALYSIS: A USEFUL TOOL

One way firms can minimize failure and avoid losses from pursuing faulty ideas is to apply the logic of real options. **Real options analysis (ROA)** is an investment analysis tool from the field of finance. It has been slowly, but increasingly, adopted by consultants and executives to support strategic decision making in firms.

Applied to entrepreneurship, real options suggest a path that companies can use to manage the uncertainty associated with launching new ventures. Some of the most common applications of real options are with property and insurance. A real estate option grants the holder the right to buy or sell a piece of property at an established price some time in the future. The actual market price of the property may rise above the established (or strike) price—or the market value may sink below the strike price. If the price of the property goes up, the owner of the option is likely to buy it. If the market value of the property drops, the option holder is unlikely to execute the purchase. In the latter circumstance, the option holder has limited his or her loss to the cost of the option but during the life of the option retains the right to participate in whatever the upside potential might be.

Applications of Real Options Analysis to Strategic Decisions

The concept of options can also be applied to strategic decisions where management has flexibility. Situations arise where management must decide whether to invest additional funds to grow or accelerate the activity, perhaps delay in order to learn more, shrink the scale of the activity, or even abandon it. Decisions to invest in new ventures or other business activities such as R&D, motion pictures, exploration and production of oil wells, and the opening and closing of copper mines often have this flexibility.[49] Important issues to note are:

- ROA is appropriate to use when investments can be staged; a smaller investment up front can be followed by subsequent investments. Real options can be applied to an investment decision that gives the company the right, but not the obligation, to make follow-on investments.
- Strategic decision makers have "tollgates," or key points at which they can decide whether to continue, delay, or abandon the project. Executives have flexibility. There are opportunities to make other go or no-go decisions associated with each phase.
- It is expected that there will be increased knowledge about outcomes at the time of the next investment and that additional knowledge will help inform the decision makers about whether to make additional investments (i.e., whether the option is in the money or out of the money).

Consider the real options logic that Johnson Controls, a maker of car seats, instrument panels, and interior control systems, uses to advance or eliminate entrepreneurial ideas.[50] Johnson options each new innovative idea by making a small investment in it. To receive additional funding, the idea must continue to prove itself at each stage of development. Here's how Jim Geschke, former vice president and general manager of electronics integration at Johnson, described the process:

> Think of Johnson as an innovation machine. The front end has a robust series of gates that each idea must pass through. Early on, we'll have many ideas and spend a little money on each of them. As they get more fleshed out, the ideas go through a gate where a go or no-go decision is made. A lot of ideas get filtered out, so there are far fewer items, and the spending on each goes up. . . . Several months later each idea will face another gate. If it passes, that means it's a serious idea that we are going to develop. Then the spending goes way up, and the number of ideas goes way down. By the time you reach the final gate, you need to have a credible business case in order to be accepted. At a certain point in the development process, we take our idea to customers and ask them what they think. Sometimes they say, "That's a terrible idea. Forget it." Other times they say, "That's fabulous. I want a million of them."

This process of evaluating ideas by separating winning ideas from losing ones in a way that keeps investments low has helped Johnson Controls grow its revenues to over $38 billion a year. Using real options logic to advance the development process is a key way that firms reduce uncertainty and minimize innovation-related failures.[51] Real options logic can also be used with other types of strategic decisions. Strategy Spotlight 12.5 discusses how Intel uses real options logic in making capacity expansion decisions.

SAVING MILLIONS WITH REAL OPTIONS AT INTEL

The semiconductor business is complex and dynamic. This makes it a difficult one to manage. On the one hand, both the technology in the chips and the consumer demand for chips are highly volatile. This makes it difficult to plan for the future as far as the need for chip designs and production plants is concerned. On the other hand, it is incredibly expensive to build new chip plants, about $5 billion each, and chip manufacturing equipment needs to be ordered well ahead of when it is needed. The lead time for ordering new equipment can be up to three years. This creates a great challenge. Firms have to decide how much and what type of equipment to purchase long before they have a good handle on what the demand for semiconductor chips will be. Guessing wrong leaves the firm with too much or too little capacity.

Intel has figured out a way to limit the risk it faces by using option contracts. Intel pays an up-front fee for the right to purchase key pieces of equipment at a specific future date. At that point, Intel either purchases the equipment or releases the supplier from the contract. In these cases, the supplier is then free to sell the equipment to someone else. This all seems fairly simple. A number of commodities, such as wheat and sugar, have robust option markets. The challenge isn't in setting up the contracts. It is in pricing those contracts. Unlike wheat and sugar, where a large number of suppliers and buyers results in an efficient market that sets the prices of standard commodity products, there are few buyers and suppliers of chip manufacturing equipment. Further,

the equipment is not a standard commodity. As a result, prices for equipment options are the outcome of difficult negotiations.

Karl Kempf, a mathematician with Intel, has figured out how to make this process smoother. Along with a group of mathematicians at Stanford, Kempf has developed a computing logic for calculating the price of options. He and his colleagues create a forecasting model for potential demand. They calculate the likelihood of a range of potential demand levels. They also set up a computer simulation of a production plant. They then use the possible demand levels to predict how many pieces of production equipment they will need in the plant to meet the demand. They run this over and over again, thousands of times, to generate predictions about the likelihood they will need to purchase a specific piece of equipment. They use this information to identify what equipment they definitely need to order. Where there is significant uncertainty about the need for equipment, they use the simulation results to identify the specific equipment for which they need option contracts and the value of those options to Intel. This helps with the pricing.

Intel estimates that in the five years from 2008 to 2012, the use of options in equipment purchases saved the firm in excess of $125 million and provided the firm with at least $2 billion in revenue upside for expansions it could have quickly made using optioned equipment.

Sources: Kempf, K., Erhun, F., Hertzler, E., Rosenberg, T., & Peng, C. 2013. Optimizing capital investment decisions at Intel Corporation. *Interfaces*, 43(1): 62–78; and King, I. 2012. A chipmaker's model mathematician. *Bloomberg Businessweek*, June 4: 35.

Potential Pitfalls of Real Options Analysis

Despite the many benefits that can be gained from using ROA, managers must be aware of its potential limitations or pitfalls. Below we will address three major issues.[52]

back-solver dilemma problem with investment decisions in which managers scheme to have a project meet investment approval criteria, even though the investment may not enhance firm value.

Agency Theory and the Back-Solver Dilemma   Let's assume that companies adopting a real options perspective invest heavily in training and that their people understand how to effectively estimate variance—the amount of dispersion or range that is estimated for potential outcomes. Such training can help them use ROA. However, it does not solve another inherent problem: Managers may have an incentive and the know-how to "game the system." Most electronic spreadsheets permit users to simply back-solve any formula; that is, you can type in the answer you want and ask what values are needed in a formula to get that answer. If managers know that a certain option value must be met in order for the proposal to get approved, they can back-solve the model to find a variance estimate needed to arrive at the answer that upper management desires.

managerial conceit biases, blind spots, and other human frailties that lead to poor managerial decisions.

Managerial Conceit: Overconfidence and the Illusion of Control   Often, poor decisions are the result of such traps as biases, blind spots, and other human frailties. Much of this literature falls under the concept of **managerial conceit**.[53]

First, managerial conceit occurs when decision makers who have made successful choices in the past come to believe that they possess superior expertise for managing uncertainty. They believe that their abilities can reduce the risks inherent in decision making to a much greater extent than they actually can. Such managers are more likely to shift away from analysis to trusting their own judgment. In the case of real options, they can simply declare that any given decision is a real option and proceed as before.

Second, employing the real options perspective can encourage decision makers toward a bias for action. Such a bias may lead to carelessness. The cost to write the first stage of an option is much smaller than the cost of full commitment, and managers pay less attention to small decisions than to large ones. Because real options are designed to minimize potential losses while preserving potential gains, any problems that arise are likely to be smaller at first, causing less concern for the manager. Managerial conceit could suggest that managers will assume that those problems are the easiest to solve and control—a concern referred to as the illusion of control. Managers may fail to respond appropriately because they overlook the problem or believe that since it is small, they can easily resolve it. Thus, managers may approach each real option decision with less care and diligence than if they had made a full commitment to a larger investment.

Managerial Conceit: Irrational Escalation of Commitment   A strength of a real options perspective is also one of its Achilles heels. Both real options and decisions involving **escalation of commitment** require specific environments with sequential decisions.[54]

An option to exit requires reversing an initial decision made by someone in the organization. Organizations typically encourage managers to "own their decisions" in order to motivate them. As managers invest themselves in their decision, it proves harder for them to lose face by reversing course. For managers making the decision, it feels as if they made the wrong decision in the first place, even if it was initially a good decision. Thus, they are likely to continue an existing project even if it should perhaps be ended.[55]

Despite the potential pitfalls of a real options approach, many of the strategic decisions that product champions and top managers must make are enhanced when decision makers have an entrepreneurial mind-set.

escalation of commitment
the tendency for managers to irrationally stick with an investment, even one that is broken down into a sequential series of decisions, when investment criteria are not being met.

ENTREPRENEURIAL ORIENTATION

Firms that want to engage in successful CE need to have an entrepreneurial orientation (EO).[56] **Entrepreneurial orientation** refers to the strategy-making practices that businesses use in identifying and launching corporate ventures. It represents a frame of mind and a perspective toward entrepreneurship that is reflected in a firm's ongoing processes and corporate culture.[57]

An EO has five dimensions that permeate the decision-making styles and practices of the firm's members: autonomy, innovativeness, proactiveness, competitive aggressiveness, and risk taking. These factors work together to enhance a firm's entrepreneurial performance. But even those firms that are strong in only a few aspects of EO can be very successful.[58] Exhibit 12.3 summarizes the dimensions of entrepreneurial orientation. Below, we discuss the five dimensions of EO and how they have been used to enhance internal venture development.

Autonomy

Autonomy refers to a willingness to act independently in order to carry forward an entrepreneurial vision or opportunity. It applies to both individuals and teams that operate outside an organization's existing norms and strategies. In the context of corporate entrepreneurship, autonomous work units are often used to leverage existing strengths in new arenas, identify opportunities that are beyond the organization's current capabilities, and encourage development of new ventures or improved business practices.[59]

The need for autonomy may apply to either dispersed or focused entrepreneurial efforts. Because of the emphasis on venture projects that are being developed outside the normal flow of business, a focused approach suggests a working environment that is relatively autonomous. But autonomy may also be important in an organization where entrepreneurship is part of the

LO 12-6

How an entrepreneurial orientation can enhance a firm's efforts to develop promising corporate venture initiatives.

entrepreneurial orientation
the practices that businesses use in identifying and launching corporate ventures.

autonomy
independent action by an individual or a team aimed at bringing forth a business concept or vision and carrying it through to completion.

EXHIBIT 12.3

Dimensions of
Entrepreneurial
Orientation

Dimension	Definition
Autonomy	Independent action by an individual or team aimed at bringing forth a business concept or vision and carrying it through to completion.
Innovativeness	A willingness to introduce novelty through experimentation and creative processes aimed at developing new products and services as well as new processes.
Proactiveness	A forward-looking perspective characteristic of a marketplace leader that has the foresight to seize opportunities in anticipation of future demand.
Competitive aggressiveness	An intense effort to outperform industry rivals characterized by a combative posture or an aggressive response aimed at improving position or overcoming a threat in a competitive marketplace.
Risk taking	Making decisions and taking action without certain knowledge of probable outcomes; some undertakings may also involve making substantial resource commitments in the process of venturing forward.

Sources: Dess, G. G. & Lumpkin, G. T. 2005. The Role of Entrepreneurial Orientation in Stimulating Effective Corporate Entrepreneurship. *Academy of Management Executive,* 19(1): 147–156; Covin, J. G. & Slevin, D. P. 1991. A Conceptual Model of Entrepreneurship as Firm Behavior. *Entrepreneurship Theory & Practice,* Fall: 7–25; Lumpkin, G. T. and Dess, G. G. 1996. Clarifying the Entrepreneurial Orientation Construct and Linking It to Performance. *Academy of Management Review,* 21: 135–172; and Miller, D. 1983. The Correlates of Entrepreneurship in Three Types of Firms. *Management Science,* 29: 770–791.

corporate culture. Everything from the methods of group interaction to the firm's reward system must make organizational members feel as if they can think freely about venture opportunities, take time to investigate them, and act without fear of condemnation. This implies a respect for the autonomy of each individual and an openness to the independent thinking that goes into championing a corporate venture idea. Thus, autonomy represents a type of empowerment (see Chapter 11) that is directed at identifying and leveraging entrepreneurial opportunities. There are two common techniques firms can use to promote autonomy. First, they can create independent work groups, often called skunkworks, that are tasked with generating new ideas. Second, they can create organizational structures to foster creativity and flexibility, such as breaking large firms into smaller, decentralized entrepreneurial units.

Creating autonomous work units and encouraging independent action may have pitfalls that can jeopardize their effectiveness. Autonomous teams often lack coordination. Excessive decentralization has a strong potential to create inefficiencies, such as duplicating effort and wasting resources on projects with questionable feasibility. For example, Chris Galvin, former CEO of Motorola, scrapped the skunkworks approach the company had been using to develop new wireless phones. Fifteen teams had created 128 different phones, which led to spiraling costs and overly complex operations.[60]

For autonomous work units and independent projects to be effective, such efforts have to be measured and monitored. This requires a delicate balance: Companies must have the patience and budget to tolerate the explorations of autonomous groups and the strength to cut back efforts that are not bearing fruit. Efforts must be undertaken with a clear sense of purpose—namely, to generate new sources of competitive advantage.

Innovativeness

innovativeness
a willingness to introduce novelty through experimentation and creative processes aimed at developing new products and services as well as new processes.

Innovativeness refers to a firm's efforts to find new opportunities and novel solutions. In the beginning of this chapter we discussed innovation; here the focus is on innovativeness—a firm's attitude toward innovation and willingness to innovate. It involves creativity and experimentation that result in new products, new services, or improved technological processes.[61] Innovativeness is one of the major components of an entrepreneurial strategy. As indicated at the beginning of the chapter, however, the job of managing innovativeness can be very challenging.

Innovativeness requires that firms depart from existing technologies and practices and venture beyond the current state of the art. Inventions and new ideas need to be nurtured even when their benefits are unclear. However, in today's climate of rapid change, effectively producing, assimilating, and exploiting innovations can be an important avenue for achieving competitive advantages. Interest in global warming and other ecological concerns has led many corporations to focus their innovativeness efforts on solving environmental problems.

As our earlier discussion of CE indicated, many corporations owe their success to an active program of innovation-based corporate venturing.[62] How firms invest their resources is often a powerful driver for innovativeness. Firms can do this by regularly budgeting significant resources in both product and process R&D to stay ahead of competitors. They can also do it in a more decentralized way by having internal competitions where employees can win funding to start internal new innovative businesses.

Innovativeness can be a source of great progress and strong corporate growth, but there are also major pitfalls for firms that invest in innovation. Expenditures on R&D aimed at identifying new products or processes can be a waste of resources if the effort does not yield results. Another danger is related to the competitive climate. Even if a company innovates a new capability or successfully applies a technological breakthrough, another company may develop a similar innovation or find a use for it that is more profitable. Finally R&D and other innovation efforts are among the first to be cut back during an economic downturn.

Even though innovativeness is an important means of internal corporate venturing, it also involves major risks, because investments in innovations may not pay off. For strategic managers of entrepreneurial firms, successfully developing and adopting innovations can generate competitive advantages and provide a major source of growth for the firm.

Proactiveness

Proactiveness refers to a firm's efforts to seize new opportunities. Proactive organizations monitor trends, identify the future needs of existing customers, and anticipate changes in demand or emerging problems that can lead to new venture opportunities. Proactiveness involves not only recognizing changes but also being willing to act on those insights ahead of the competition.[63] Strategic managers who practice proactiveness have their eye on the future in a search for new possibilities for growth and development. Such a forward-looking perspective is important for companies that seek to be industry leaders. Many proactive firms seek out ways not only to be future-oriented but also to change the very nature of competition in their industry.

proactiveness
a forward-looking perspective characteristic of a marketplace leader that has the foresight to seize opportunities in anticipation of future demand.

Proactiveness puts competitors in the position of having to respond to successful initiatives. The benefit gained by firms that are the first to enter new markets, establish brand identity, implement administrative techniques, or adopt new operating technologies in an industry is called first-mover advantage.[64]

First movers usually have several advantages. First, industry pioneers, especially in new industries, often capture unusually high profits because there are no competitors to drive prices down. Second, first movers that establish brand recognition are usually able to retain their image and hold on to the market share gains they earned by being first. Sometimes these benefits also accrue to other early movers in an industry, but, generally speaking, first movers have an advantage that can be sustained until firms enter the maturity phase of an industry's life cycle.[65]

First movers are not always successful. The customers of companies that introduce novel products or embrace breakthrough technologies may be reluctant to commit to a new way of doing things. In his book *Crossing the Chasm,* Geoffrey A. Moore noted that most firms seek evolution, not revolution, in their operations. This makes it difficult for a first mover to sell promising new technologies.[66]

Careful monitoring and scanning of the environment, as well as extensive feasibility research, are needed for a proactive strategy to lead to competitive advantages. Firms that do it well usually have substantial growth and internal development to show for it. Many of them have been able to sustain the advantages of proactiveness for years.

Competitive Aggressiveness

competitive aggressiveness
an intense effort to outperform industry rivals; characterized by a combative posture or an aggressive response aimed at improving position or overcoming a threat in a competitive marketplace.

Competitive aggressiveness refers to a firm's efforts to outperform its industry rivals. Companies with an aggressive orientation are willing to "do battle" with competitors. They might slash prices and sacrifice profitability to gain market share or spend aggressively to obtain manufacturing capacity. As an avenue of firm development and growth, competitive aggressiveness may involve being very assertive in leveraging the results of other entrepreneurial activities such as innovativeness or proactiveness.

Strategic managers can use competitive aggressiveness to combat industry trends that threaten their survival or market position. Sometimes firms need to be forceful in defending the competitive position that has made them an industry leader. Firms often need to be aggressive to ensure their advantage by capitalizing on new technologies or serving new market needs. An example of competitive aggressiveness would be to dramatically lower prices to take market share from rival firms. Of course, this will only be successful if the attacking firm has a cost advantage over rivals. Another tactic is to regularly imitate rivals by copying new products, marketing messages, or other aspects of their strategy. One advantage of this is that it is generally cheaper to imitate a successful rival.

Another practice companies use to overcome the competition is to make preannouncements of new products or technologies. This type of signaling is aimed not only at potential customers but also at competitors to see how they will react or to discourage them from launching similar initiatives. Sometimes the preannouncements are made just to scare off competitors, an action that has potential ethical implications.

Competitive aggressiveness may not always lead to competitive advantages. Some companies (or their CEOs) have severely damaged their reputations by being overly aggressive. For example, Walmart's aggressive pricing structure has forced smaller, local retailers out of business in many markets. This has led a number of local communities, often at the urging of local retailers, to pass regulations that make it difficult for Walmart to move into or expand operations in these towns and cities.

Competitive aggressiveness is a strategy that is best used in moderation. Companies that aggressively establish their competitive position and vigorously exploit opportunities to achieve profitability may, over the long run, be better able to sustain their competitive advantages if their goal is to defeat, rather than decimate, their competitors.

Risk Taking

risk taking
making decisions and taking action without certain knowledge of probable outcomes. Some undertakings may also involve making substantial resource commitments in the process of venturing forward.

Risk taking refers to a firm's willingness to seize a venture opportunity even though it does not know whether the venture will be successful—to act boldly without knowing the consequences. To be successful through corporate entrepreneurship, firms usually have to take on riskier alternatives, even if it means forgoing the methods or products that have worked in the past. To obtain high financial returns, firms take such risks as assuming high levels of debt, committing large amounts of firm resources, introducing new products into new markets, and investing in unexplored technologies.

All of the approaches to internal development that we have discussed are potentially risky. Whether they are being aggressive, proactive, or innovative, firms on the path of CE must act without knowing how their actions will turn out. Before launching their strategies, corporate entrepreneurs must know their firm's appetite for risk.[67]

Three types of risk that organizations and their executives face are business risk, financial risk, and personal risk:

- *Business risk taking* involves venturing into the unknown without knowing the probability of success. This is the risk associated with entering untested markets or committing to unproven technologies.

- *Financial risk taking* requires that a company borrow heavily or commit a large portion of its resources in order to grow. In this context, risk is used to refer to the risk–return trade-off that is familiar in financial analysis.
- *Personal risk taking* refers to the risks that an executive assumes in taking a stand in favor of a strategic course of action. Executives who take such risks stand to influence the course of their whole company, and their decisions also can have significant implications for their careers.

Even though risk taking involves taking chances, it is not gambling. The best-run companies investigate the consequences of various opportunities and create scenarios of likely outcomes. A key to managing entrepreneurial risks is to evaluate new venture opportunities thoroughly enough to reduce the uncertainty surrounding them.

Risk taking, by its nature, involves potential dangers and pitfalls. Only carefully managed risk is likely to lead to competitive advantages. Actions that are taken without sufficient forethought, research, and planning may prove to be very costly. Therefore, strategic managers must always remain mindful of potential risks. In his book *Innovation and Entrepreneurship*, Peter Drucker argued that successful entrepreneurs are typically not risk takers. Instead, they take steps to minimize risks by carefully understanding them. That is how they avoid focusing on risk and remain focused on opportunity.[68] Risk taking is a good place to close this chapter on corporate entrepreneurship. Companies that choose to grow through internal corporate venturing must remember that entrepreneurship always involves embracing what is new and uncertain.

ISSUE FOR DEBATE

Few would argue with the observation that Tesla is an innovative firm. It has taken out a leading position in developing technology for electric vehicles. It is also building autonomous control systems into its cars. It has taken one seeming step backward and strategically developed its own technology for batteries and manufacturing capacity to produce batteries. It has subtly innovated the design for its cars. Rather than putting the batteries for its cars in what would normally be the engine compartment, it places them under the main compartment of the car, allowing the firm to include a "frunk" (or front trunk) in its cars. It has also innovated on the distribution side of the business by circumventing dealers to sell its cars directly to customers through company-owned showrooms. Thus, it is innovating in ways that change the supply system, the technology of automobile drive trains, the technology of driving, the physical design of cars, and how cars are distributed.

However, it is not clear whether Tesla is offering a disruptive innovation in the automobile market. For this to be the case, Tesla's business model would have to innovate in ways that can significantly undercut the value of the resources of Ford, GM, Toyota, and the other incumbent competitors in the auto industry.

Discussion Questions

1. Do you see Tesla's business model and product as offering a sustaining or a disruptive innovation? Why do you see it this way?
2. In what ways will incumbent firms be able to respond effectively to Tesla? In what ways will it be difficult?
3. Whether or not you see Tesla as offering a disruptive innovation, what would be a different way that an entrepreneurial firm could offer a disruptive innovation in this market?

Reflecting on Career Implications . . .

This chapter focuses on corporate entrepreneurship and innovation. You can provide greater value to your firm and build a higher impact career if you develop innovativeness skills and an entrepreneurial orientation. The questions below identify issues to consider as you build these skills and orientation.

◾ **Innovation:** Identify the types of innovations being pursued by your company. Do they tend to be incremental or radical? Product-related or process-related? Are there ways in which you can add value to such innovations, no matter how minor your contributions are?

◾ **Cultivating Innovation Skills:** Exhibit 12.2 describes the five traits of an effective innovator (associating, questioning, observing, experimenting, and networking). Assess yourself on each of these traits. Practice the skills in your work and professional life to build your skills as an innovator. If you are

interviewing for a job with an organization that is considered high on innovation, it might be in your interest to highlight these traits.

◾ **Real Options Analysis:** Success in your career often depends on creating and exercising career "options." However, creation of options involves costs as well, such as learning new skills, obtaining additional certifications, and so on. Consider what options you can create for yourself. Evaluate the cost of these options.

◾ **Entrepreneurial Orientation:** Consider the five dimensions of entrepreneurial orientation. Evaluate yourself on each of these dimensions (autonomy, innovativeness, proactiveness, competitive aggressiveness, and risk taking). If you are high on entrepreneurial orientation, you may have a future as an entrepreneur. Consider the ways in which you can use the experience and learning from your current job to become a successful entrepreneur in later years.

summary

To remain competitive in today's economy, established firms must find new avenues for development and growth. This chapter has addressed how innovation and corporate entrepreneurship can be a means of internal venture creation and strategic renewal, and how an entrepreneurial orientation can help corporations enhance their competitive position.

Innovation is one of the primary means by which corporations grow and strengthen their strategic position. Innovations can take several forms, ranging from radical breakthrough innovations to incremental improvement innovations. Innovations are often used to update products and services or to improve organizational processes. Managing the innovation process is often challenging, because it involves a great deal of uncertainty and there are many choices to be made about the extent and type of innovations to pursue. By cultivating innovation skills, defining the scope of innovation, managing the pace of innovation, staffing to capture value from innovation, and collaborating with innovation partners, firms can more effectively manage the innovation process.

We also discussed the role of corporate entrepreneurship in venture development and strategic renewal. Corporations usually take either a focused or dispersed approach to corporate venturing. Firms with a focused approach usually separate the corporate venturing activity from the ongoing operations of the firm in order to foster independent thinking and encourage entrepreneurial team members to think and act without the constraints imposed by the corporation. In corporations where venturing activities are dispersed, a culture of entrepreneurship permeates all

parts of the company in order to induce strategic behaviors by all organizational members. In measuring the success of corporate venturing activities, both financial and strategic objectives should be considered. Real options analysis is often used to make better-quality decisions in uncertain entrepreneurial situations. However, a real options approach has potential drawbacks.

Most entrepreneurial firms need to have an entrepreneurial orientation: the methods, practices, and decision-making styles that strategic managers use to act entrepreneurially. Five dimensions of entrepreneurial orientation are found in firms that pursue corporate venture strategies. Autonomy, innovativeness, proactiveness, competitive aggressiveness, and risk taking each make a unique contribution to the pursuit of new opportunities. When deployed effectively, the methods and practices of an entrepreneurial orientation can be used to engage successfully in corporate entrepreneurship and new venture creation. However, strategic managers must remain mindful of the pitfalls associated with each of these approaches.

SUMMARY REVIEW QUESTIONS

1. What is meant by the concept of a continuum of radical and incremental innovations?

2. What are the dilemmas that organizations face when deciding what innovation projects to pursue? What steps can organizations take to effectively manage the innovation process?

3. What is the difference between focused and dispersed approaches to corporate entrepreneurship?

4. How are business incubators used to foster internal corporate venturing?

5. What is the role of the product champion in bringing a new product or service into existence in a corporation? How can companies use product champions to enhance their venture development efforts?

6. Explain the difference between proactiveness and competitive aggressiveness in terms of achieving and sustaining competitive advantage.

7. Describe how the entrepreneurial orientation (EO) dimensions of innovativeness, proactiveness, and risk taking can be combined to create competitive advantages for entrepreneurial firms.

key terms

innovation 362
product innovation 362
process innovation 362
radical innovations 363
incremental innovations 363
strategic envelope 368
corporate entrepreneurship (CE) 373
focused approaches to corporate entrepreneurship 374
new venture groups (NVGs) 374
business incubators 374
dispersed approaches to corporate entrepreneurship 375
entrepreneurial culture 376
product champions 377
exit champions 378
real options analysis (ROA) 378
back-solver dilemma 380
managerial conceit 380
escalation of commitment 381
entrepreneurial orientation 381
autonomy 381
innovativeness 382
proactiveness 383
competitive aggressiveness 384
risk taking 384

EXPERIENTIAL EXERCISE

Select two different major corporations from two different industries (you might use Fortune 500 companies to make your selection). Compare and contrast these organizations in terms of their entrepreneurial orientation. (Fill in the table below.)

Based on your comparison:

1. How is the corporation's entrepreneurial orientation reflected in its strategy?

2. Which corporation would you say has the stronger entrepreneurial orientation?

3. Is the corporation with the stronger entrepreneurial orientation also stronger in terms of financial performance?

APPLICATION QUESTIONS & EXERCISES

1. Select a firm known for its corporate entrepreneurship activities. Research the company and discuss how it has positioned itself relative to its close competitors. Does it have a unique strategic advantage? Disadvantage? Explain.

2. Explain the difference between product innovations and process innovations. Provide examples of firms that have recently introduced each type of innovation. What are the types of innovations related to the strategies of each firm?

3. Using the Internet, select a company that is listed on the NASDAQ or New York Stock Exchange. Research the extent to which the company has an entrepreneurial culture. Does the company use product champions? Does it have a corporate venture capital fund? Do you believe its entrepreneurial efforts are sufficient to generate sustainable advantages?

4. How can an established firm use an entrepreneurial orientation to enhance its overall strategic position? Provide examples.

ETHICS QUESTIONS

1. Innovation activities are often aimed at making a discovery or commercializing a technology ahead of the competition. What are some of the unethical practices that companies could engage in during the innovation process? What are the potential long-term consequences of such actions?

2. Discuss the ethical implications of using entrepreneurial policies and practices to pursue corporate social responsibility goals. Are these efforts authentic and genuine or just an attempt to attract more customers?

Entrepreneurial Orientation	Company A	Company B
Autonomy		
Innovativeness		
Proactiveness		
Competitive aggressiveness		
Risk taking		

REFERENCES

1. Eddy, N. 2014. Android captures 85 percent of smartphone market worldwide. *eweek.com,* August 8: np; Vascellaro, J. 2009. Radio tunes out Google in rare miss for web titan. *wsj.com,* May 12: np; and McGrath, R. 2011. Failing by design. *Harvard Business Review,* 89(4): 76-83; *statista.com.*

2. For an interesting discussion, see Johannessen, J. A., Olsen, B., & Lumpkin, G. T. 2001. Innovation as newness: What is new, how new, and new to whom? *European Journal of Innovation Management,* 4(1): 20-31.

3. The discussion of product and process innovation is based on Roberts, E. B. (Ed.). 2002. *Innovation: Driving product, process, and market change.* San Francisco: Jossey-Bass; Hayes, R. & Wheelwright, S. 1985. Competing through manufacturing. *Harvard Business Review,* 63(1): 99-109; and Hayes, R. & Wheelwright, S. 1979. Dynamics of product-process life cycles. *Harvard Business Review,* 57(2): 127-136.

4. The discussion of radical and incremental innovations draws from Leifer, R., McDermott, C. M., Colarelli, G., O'Connor, G. C., Peters, L. S., Rice, M. P., & Veryzer, R. W. 2000. *Radical innovation: How mature companies can outsmart upstarts.* Boston: Harvard Business School Press; Damanpour, F. 1996. Organizational complexity and innovation: Developing and testing multiple contingency models. *Management Science,* 42(5): 693-716; and Hage, J. 1980. *Theories of organizations.* New York: Wiley.

5. Christensen, C. M. & Raynor, M. E. 2003. *The innovator's solution.* Boston: Harvard Business School Press.

6. Dressner, H. 2004. The Gartner Fellows interview: Clayton M. Christensen. *www.gartner.com,* April 26.

7. For another perspective on how different types of innovation affect organizational choices, see Wolter, C. & Veloso, F. M. 2008. The effects of innovation on vertical structure: Perspectives on transactions costs and competences. *Academy of Management Review,* 33(3): 586-605.

8. Drucker, P. F. 1985. *Innovation and entrepreneurship.* New York: Harper & Row.

9. Birkinshaw, J., Hamel, G., & Mol, M. J. 2008. Management innovation.

Academy of Management Review, 33(4): 825-845.

10. Steere, W. C., Jr. & Niblack, J. 1997. Pfizer, Inc. In Kanter, R. M., Kao, J., & Wiersema, F. (Eds.), *Innovation: Breakthrough thinking at 3M, DuPont, GE, Pfizer, and Rubbermaid:* 123-145. New York: HarperCollins.

11. Morrissey, C. A. 2000. Managing innovation through corporate venturing. *Graziadio Business Report,* Spring, *gbr.pepperdine.edu*; and Sharma, A. 1999. Central dilemmas of managing innovation in large firms. *California Management Review,* 41(3): 147-164.

12. Sharma, op. cit.

13. Dyer, J. H., Gregerson, H. B., & Christensen, C. M. 2009. The innovator's DNA. *Harvard Business Review,* December: 61-67.

14. Eggers, J. P. & Kaplan, S. 2009. Cognition and renewal: Comparing CEO and organizational effects on incumbent adaptation to technical change. *Organization Science,* 20: 461-477.

15. For more on defining the scope of innovation, see Valikangas, L. & Gibbert, M. 2005. Boundary-setting strategies for escaping innovation traps. *MIT Sloan Management Review,* 46(3): 58-65.

16. Leifer et al., op. cit.

17. Bhide, A. V. 2000. *The origin and evolution of new businesses.* New York: Oxford University Press; Brown, S. L. & Eisenhardt, K. M. 1998. *Competing on the edge: Strategy as structured chaos.* Cambridge, MA: Harvard Business School Press.

18. McGrath, R. G. & Keil, T. 2007. The value captor's process: Getting the most out of your new business ventures. *Harvard Business Review,* May: 128-136.

19. For an interesting discussion of how sharing technology knowledge with different divisions in an organization can contribute to innovation processes, see Miller, D. J., Fern, M. J., & Cardinal, L. B. 2007. The use of knowledge for technological innovation within diversified firms. *Academy of Management Journal,* 50(2): 308-326.

20. Ketchen, D. J., Jr., Ireland, R. D., & Snow, C. C. 2007 Strategic entrepreneurship, collaborative innovation, and wealth creation. *Strategic Entrepreneurship Journal,* 1(3-4): 371-385.

21. Chesbrough, H. 2003. *Open innovation: The new imperative for*

creating and profiting from technology. Boston: Harvard Business School Press.

22. For a study of what makes alliance partnerships successful, see Sampson, R. C. 2007. R&D alliances and firm performance: The impact of technological diversity and alliance organization on innovation. *Academy of Management Journal,* 50(2): 364-386.

23. For an interesting perspective on the role of collaboration among multinational corporations, see Hansen, M. T. & Nohria, N. 2004. How to build collaborative advantage. *MIT Sloan Management Review,* 46(1): 22-30.

24. Wells, R. M. J. 2008. The product innovation process: Are managing information flows and cross-functional collaboration key? *Academy of Management Perspectives,* 22(1): 58-60; Dougherty, D. & Dunne, D. D. 2011. Organizing ecologies of complex innovation. *Organization Science,* 22(5): 1214-1223; and Kim, H. E. & Pennings, J. M. 2009. Innovation and strategic renewal in mature markets: A study of the tennis racket industry. *Organization Science,* 20: 368-383.

25. Eggers, J. P. 2014. Get ahead by betting wrong. *Harvard Business Review,* 92(7/8): 26; and Lepore, J. 2014. The disruption machine. *newyorker.com,* June 23: np.

26. Birkinshaw, J. 2016. Increase your return on failure. *Harvard Business Review.* May: 89-93.

27. Guth, W. D. & Ginsberg, A. 1990. Guest editor's introduction: Corporate entrepreneurship. *Strategic Management Journal,* 11: 5-15.

28. Pinchot, G. 1985. *Intrapreneuring.* New York: Harper & Row.

29. For an interesting perspective on the role of context on the discovery and creation of opportunities, see Zahra, S. A. 2008. The virtuous cycle of discovery and creation of entrepreneurial opportunities. *Strategic Entrepreneurship Journal,* 2(3): 243-257.

30. Birkinshaw, J. 1997. Entrepreneurship in multinational corporations: The characteristics of subsidiary initiatives. *Strategic Management Journal,* 18(3): 207-229; and Kanter, R. M. 1985. *The change masters.* New York: Simon & Schuster.

31. Hansen, M. T., Chesbrough, H. W., Nohria, N., & Sull, D. 2000.

Networked incubators: Hothouses of the new economy. *Harvard Business Review,* 78(5): 74–84.

32. For more on the importance of leadership in fostering a climate of entrepreneurship, see Ling, Y., Simsek, Z., Lubatkin, M. H., & Veiga, J. F. 2008. Transformational leadership's role in promoting corporate entrepreneurship: Examining the CEO-TMT interface. *Academy of Management Journal,* 51(3): 557–576.

33. Bryant, A. 2011. Got an idea? Sell it to me in 30 seconds. *nytimes.com,* January 1: np.

34. Gunther, M. 2010. 3M's innovation revival. *cnnmoney.com,* September 24: np; Byrne, J. 2012. The 12 greatest entrepreneurs of our time. *Fortune,* April 9: 76; and Anonymous. 2007. Johnson & Johnson turns to internal venturing. *silico.wordpress.com,* July 16: np.

35. Colvin, G. 2014. Brad Smith: Getting rid of friction. *Fortune,* July 21: 24.

36. For an interesting discussion, see Davenport, T. H., Prusak, L., & Wilson, H. J. 2003. Who's bringing you hot ideas and how are you responding? *Harvard Business Review,* 80(1): 58–64.

37. Howell, J. M. 2005. The right stuff. Identifying and developing effective champions of innovation. *Academy of Management Executive,* 19(2): 108–119. See also Greene, P., Brush, C., & Hart, M. 1999. The corporate venture champion: A resource-based approach to role and process. *Entrepreneurship Theory & Practice,* 23(3): 103–122; and Markham, S. K. & Aiman-Smith, L. 2001. Product champions: Truths, myths and management. *Research Technology Management,* May–June: 44–50.

38. Burgelman, R. A. 1983. A process model of internal corporate venturing in the diversified major firm. *Administrative Science Quarterly,* 28: 223–244.

39. Greene, Brush, & Hart, op. cit.; and Shane, S. 1994. Are champions different from non-champions? *Journal of Business Venturing,* 9(5): 397–421.

40. Block, Z. & MacMillan, I. C. 1993. *Corporate venturing–Creating new businesses with the firm.* Cambridge, MA: Harvard Business School Press.

41. For an interesting discussion of these trade-offs, see Stringer, R. 2000. How to manage radical innovation. *California Management Review,* 42(4): 70–88; and Gompers, P. A. & Lerner, J. 1999. *The venture capital cycle.* Cambridge, MA: MIT Press.

42. Cardinal, L. B., Turner, S. F., Fern, M. J., & Burton, R. M. 2011. Organizing for product development across technological environments: Performance trade-offs and priorities. *Organization Science,* 22: 1000–1025.

43. Albrinck, J., Hornery, J., Kletter, D., & Neilson, G. 2001. Adventures in corporate venturing. *Strategy + Business,* 22: 119–129; and McGrath, R. G. & MacMillan, I. C. 2000. *The entrepreneurial mind-set.* Cambridge, MA: Harvard Business School Press.

44. Kiel, T., McGrath, R. G., & Tukiainen, T. 2009. Gems from the ashes: Capability creation and transforming in internal corporate venturing. *Organization Science,* 20: 601–620.

45. For an interesting discussion of how different outcome goals affect organizational learning and employee motivation, see Seijts, G. H. & Latham, G. P. 2005. Learning versus performance goals: When should each be used? *Academy of Management Executive,* 19(1): 124–131.

46. Crockett, R. O. 2001. Motorola. *BusinessWeek,* July 15: 72–78.

47. The ideas in this section are drawn from Royer, I. 2003. Why bad projects are so hard to kill. *Harvard Business Review,* 80(1): 48–56.

48. For an interesting perspective on the different roles that individuals play in the entrepreneurial process, see Baron, R. A. 2008. The role of affect in the entrepreneurial process. *Academy of Management Review,* 33(2): 328–340.

49. For an interesting discussion on why it is difficult to "kill options," refer to Royer, I. 2003. Why bad projects are so hard to kill. *Harvard Business Review,* 81(2): 48–57.

50. Slywotzky, A. & Wise, R., 2003. *How to Grow When Markets Don't.* New York, NY: Warner Books; Slywotzky, A. & Wise, R. 2003. Double-digit growth in no-growth times. *Fast Company,* April: 66–72; *www.hoovers.com;* and *www.johnsoncontrols.com.*

51. For more on the role of real options in entrepreneurial decision making, see Folta, T. B. & O'Brien, J. P. 2004. Entry in the presence of dueling options. *Strategic Management Journal,* 25: 121–138.

52. This section draws on Janney, J. J. & Dess, G. G. 2004. Can real options analysis improve decision-making? Promises and pitfalls. *Academy of Management Executive,* 18(4): 60–75. For additional insights on pitfalls of real options, consider

McGrath, R. G. 1997. A real options logic for initiating technology positioning investment. *Academy of Management Review,* 22(4): 974–994; Coff, R. W. & Laverty, K. J. 2001. Real options on knowledge assets: Panacea or Pandora's box? *Business Horizons,* 73: 79; McGrath, R. G. 1999. Falling forward: Real options reasoning and entrepreneurial failure. *Academy of Management Review,* 24(1): 13–30; and Zardkoohi, A. 2004. Do real options lead to escalation of commitment? *Academy of Management Review,* 29(1): 111–119.

53. For an understanding of the differences between how managers say they approach decisions and how they actually do, March and Shapira's discussion is perhaps the best. March, J. G. & Shapira, Z. 1987. Managerial perspectives on risk and risk-taking. *Management Science,* 33(11): 1404–1418.

54. A discussion of some factors that may lead to escalation in decision making is included in Choo, C. W. 2005. Information failures and organizational disasters. *MIT Sloan Management Review,* 46(3): 8–10.

55. One very useful solution for reducing the effects of managerial conceit is to incorporate an exit champion into the decision process. Exit champions provide arguments for killing off the firm's commitment to a decision. For a very insightful discussion on exit champions, refer to Royer, I. 2003. Why bad projects are so hard to kill. *Harvard Business Review,* 81(2): 49–56.

56. For more on how entrepreneurial orientation influences organizational performance, see Wang, L. 2008. Entrepreneurial orientation, learning orientation, and firm performance. *Entrepreneurship Theory & Practice,* 32(4): 635–657; and Runyan, R., Droge, C., & Swinney, J. 2008. Entrepreneurial orientation versus small business orientation: What are their relationships to firm performance? *Journal of Small Business Management,* 46(4): 567–588.

57. Covin, J. G. & Slevin, D. P. 1991. A conceptual model of entrepreneurship as firm behavior. *Entrepreneurship Theory and Practice,* 16(1): 7–24; Lumpkin, G. T. & Dess, G. G. 1996. Clarifying the entrepreneurial orientation construct and linking it to performance. *Academy of Management Review,* 21(1): 135–172; and McGrath, R. G. & MacMillan, I. C. 2000. *The entrepreneurial mind-set.* Cambridge, MA: Harvard Business School Press.

58. Lumpkin, G. T. & Dess, G. G. 2001. Linking two dimensions of entrepreneurial orientation to firm performance: The moderating role of environment and life cycle. *Journal of Business Venturing,* 16: 429–451.

59. For an interesting discussion, see Day, J. D., Mang, P. Y., Richter, A., & Roberts, J. 2001. The innovative organization: Why new ventures need more than a room of their own. *McKinsey Quarterly,* 2: 21–31.

60. Crockett, R. O. 2001. Chris Galvin shakes things up—again. *BusinessWeek,* May 28: 38–39.

61. For insights into the role of information technology in innovativeness, see Dibrell, C., Davis, P. S., & Craig, J. 2008. Fueling innovation through information technology in SMEs. *Journal of Small Business Management,* 46(2): 203–218.

62. For an interesting discussion of the impact of innovativeness on organizational outcomes, see Cho, H. J. & Pucik, V. 2005. Relationship between innovativeness, quality, growth, profitability, and market value. *Strategic Management Journal,* 26(6): 555–575.

63. Danneels, E. & Sethi, R. 2011. New product exploration under environmental turbulence. *Organization Science,* 22(4): 1026–1039.

64. Lieberman, M. B. & Montgomery, D. B. 1988. First mover advantages. *Strategic Management Journal,* 9 (Special Issue): 41–58.

65. The discussion of first-mover advantages is based on several articles, including Lambkin, M. 1988. Order of entry and performance in new markets. *Strategic Management Journal,* 9: 127–140; Lieberman & Montgomery, op. cit., pp. 41–58; and Miller, A. & Camp, B. 1985. Exploring determinants of success in corporate ventures. *Journal of Business Venturing,* 1(2): 87–105.

66. Moore, G. A. 1999. *Crossing the chasm* (2nd ed.). New York: HarperBusiness.

67. Miller, K. D. 2007. Risk and rationality in entrepreneurial processes. *Strategic Entrepreneurship Journal,* 1(1–2): 57–74.

68. Drucker, op. cit., pp. 109–110.

Analyzing Strategic Management Cases

After reading this chapter, you should have a good understanding of the following learning objectives:

LO13-1 How strategic case analysis is used to simulate real-world experiences.

LO13-2 How analyzing strategic management cases can help develop the ability to differentiate, speculate, and integrate when evaluating complex business problems.

LO13-3 The steps involved in conducting a strategic management case analysis.

LO13-4 How to get the most out of case analysis.

LO13-5 How integrative thinking and conflict-inducing discussion techniques can lead to better decisions.

LO13-6 How to use the strategic insights and material from each of the 12 previous chapters in the text to analyze issues posed by strategic management cases.

©Anatoli Styf/Shutterstock

Why Analyze Strategic Management Cases?

If you don't ask the right questions, then you're never going to get the right solution. I spent too much of my career feeling like I'd done a really good job answering the wrong question. And that was because I was letting other people give me the question.[1]

—Tim Brown, CEO of IDEO (a leading design consulting firm)

It is often said that the key to finding good answers is to ask good questions. Strategic managers and business leaders are required to evaluate options, make choices, and find solutions to the challenges they face every day. To do so, they must learn to ask the right questions. The study of strategic management poses the same challenge. The process of analyzing, decision making, and implementing strategic actions raises many good questions:

- Why do some firms succeed and others fail?
- Why are some companies higher performers than others?
- What information is needed in the strategic planning process?
- How do competing values and beliefs affect strategic decision making?
- What skills and capabilities are needed to implement a strategy effectively?

How does a student of strategic management answer these questions? By strategic case analysis. **Case analysis** simulates the real-world experience that strategic managers and company leaders face as they try to determine how best to run their companies. It places students in the middle of an actual situation and challenges them to figure out what to do.[2]

Asking the right questions is just the beginning of case analysis. In the previous chapters we have discussed issues and challenges that managers face and provided analytical frameworks for understanding the situation. But once the analysis is complete, decisions have to be made. Case analysis forces you to choose among different options and set forth a plan of action based on your choices. But even then the job is not done. Strategic case analysis also requires that you address how you will implement the plan and the implications of choosing one course of action over another.

A strategic management case is a detailed description of a challenging situation faced by an organization.[3] It usually includes a chronology of events and extensive support materials, such as financial statements, product lists, and transcripts of interviews with employees. Although names or locations are sometimes changed to provide anonymity, cases usually report the facts of a situation as authentically as possible.

One of the main reasons to analyze strategic management cases is to develop an ability to evaluate business situations critically. In case analysis, memorizing key terms and conceptual frameworks is not enough. To analyze a case, it is important that you go beyond textbook prescriptions and quick answers. It requires you to look deeply into the information that is provided and root out the essential issues and causes of a company's problems.

The types of skills that are required to prepare an effective strategic case analysis can benefit you in actual business situations. Case analysis adds to the overall learning experience by helping you acquire or improve skills that may not be taught in a typical lecture course. Three capabilities that can be learned by conducting case analysis are especially useful to strategic managers—the ability to differentiate, speculate, and integrate.[4] Here's how case analysis can enhance those skills:

1. ***Differentiate.*** Effective strategic management requires that many different elements of a situation be evaluated at once. This is also true in case analysis. When analyzing cases, it is important to isolate critical facts, evaluate whether assumptions are useful

LO 13-1

How strategic case analysis is used to simulate real-world experiences.

case analysis
a method of learning complex strategic management concepts—such as environmental analysis, the process of decision making, and implementing strategic actions—through placing students in the middle of an actual situation and challenging them to figure out what to do.

LO 13-2

How analyzing strategic management cases can help develop the ability to differentiate, speculate, and integrate when evaluating complex business problems.

or faulty, and distinguish between good and bad information. Differentiating between the factors that are influencing the situation presented by a case is necessary for making a good analysis. Strategic management also involves understanding that problems are often complex and multilayered. This applies to case analysis as well. Ask whether the case deals with operational, business-level, or corporate issues. Do the problems stem from weaknesses in the internal value chain or threats in the external environment? Dig deep. Being too quick to accept the easiest or least controversial answer will usually fail to get to the heart of the problem.

2. *Speculate.* Strategic managers need to be able to use their imagination to envision an explanation or solution that might not readily be apparent. The same is true with case analysis. Being able to imagine different scenarios or contemplate the outcome of a decision can aid the analysis. Managers also have to deal with uncertainty since most decisions are made without complete knowledge of the circumstances. This is also true in case analysis. Case materials often seem to be missing data or the information provided is contradictory. The ability to speculate about details that are unknown or the consequences of an action can be helpful.

3. *Integrate.* Strategy involves looking at the big picture and having an organizationwide perspective. Strategic case analysis is no different. Even though the chapters in this textbook divide the material into various topics that may apply to different parts of an organization, all of this information must be integrated into one set of recommendations that will affect the whole company. A strategic manager needs to comprehend how all the factors that influence the organization will interact. This also applies to case analysis. Changes made in one part of the organization affect other parts. Thus, a holistic perspective that integrates the impact of various decisions and environmental influences on all parts of the organization is needed.

In business, these three activities sometimes "compete" with each other for your attention. For example, some decision makers may have a natural ability to differentiate among elements of a problem but are not able to integrate them very well. Others have enough innate creativity to imagine solutions or fill in the blanks when information is missing. But they may have a difficult time when faced with hard numbers or cold facts. Even so, each of these skills is important. The mark of a good strategic manager is the ability to simultaneously make distinctions and envision the whole, and to imagine a future scenario while staying focused on the present. Thus, another reason to conduct case analysis is to help you develop and exercise your ability to differentiate, speculate, and integrate. David C. Novak, the chairman and CEO of Yum! Brands, provides a useful insight on this matter:[5]

> I think what we need in our leaders, the people who ultimately run our companies and run our functions, is whole-brained people—people who can be analytical but also have the creativity, the right-brain side of the equation.

Case analysis takes the student through the whole cycle of activity that a manager would face. Beyond the textbook descriptions of concepts and examples, case analysis asks you to "walk a mile in the shoes" of the strategic decision maker and learn to evaluate situations critically. Executives and owners must make decisions every day with limited information and a swirl of business activity going on around them. Consider the example of Sapient Health Network, an Internet start-up that had to undergo some analysis and problem solving just to survive. Strategy Spotlight 13.1 describes how this company transformed itself after a serious self-examination during a time of crisis.

As you can see from the experience of Sapient Health Network, businesses are often faced with immediate challenges that threaten their lives. The Sapient case illustrates how the strategic management process helped it survive. First, the company realistically assessed the environment, evaluated the marketplace, and analyzed its resources. Then it made tough

ANALYSIS, DECISION MAKING, AND CHANGE AT SAPIENT HEALTH NETWORK

Sapient Health Network (SHN) had gotten off to a good start. CEO Jim Kean and his two cofounders had raised $5 million in investor capital to launch their vision: an Internet-based health care information subscription service. The idea was to create an Internet community for people suffering from chronic diseases. It would provide members with expert information, resources, a message board, and chat rooms so that people suffering from the same ailments could provide each other with information and support. "Who would be more voracious consumers of information than people who are faced with life-changing, life-threatening illnesses?" thought Bill Kelly, one of SHN's cofounders. Initial market research and beta tests had supported that view.

During the beta tests, however, the service had been offered for free. The troubles began when SHN tried to convert its trial subscribers into paying ones. Fewer than 5 percent signed on, far less than the 15 percent the company had projected. Sapient hired a vice president of marketing who launched an aggressive promotion, but after three months of campaigning SHN still had only 500 members. SHN was now burning through $400,000 per month, with little revenue to show for it.

At that point, according to SHN board member Susan Clymer, "there was a lot of scrambling around trying to figure out how we could wring value out of what we'd already accomplished." One thing SHN had created was an expert software system that had two components: an "intelligent profile engine" (IPE) and an "intelligent query engine" (IQE). SHN used this system to collect detailed information from its subscribers.

SHN was sure that the expert system was its biggest selling point. But how could the company use it? Then the founders remembered that the original business plan had suggested there might be a market for aggregate data about patient populations gathered from the website. Could they turn the business around by selling patient data? To analyze the possibility, Kean tried out the idea on the market research arm of a huge east coast health care conglomerate. The officials were intrigued. SHN realized that its expert system could become a market research tool.

Once the analysis was completed, the founders made the decision: They would still create Internet communities for chronically ill patients, but the service would be free. And they would transform SHN from a company that processed subscriptions to one that sold market research.

Finally, they enacted the changes. Some of the changes were painful, including laying off 18 employees. However, SHN needed more health care industry expertise. It even hired an interim CEO, Craig Davenport, a 25-year veteran of the industry, to steer the company in its new direction. Finally, SHN had to communicate a new message to its members. It began by reimbursing the $10,000 of subscription fees they had paid.

All of this paid off dramatically in a matter of just two years. Revenues jumped to $1.9 million, and early in the third year SHN was purchased by WebMD. Less than a year after that, WebMD merged with Healtheon. The combined company still operates a thriving office out of SHN's original location in Portland, Oregon.

Sources: Ferguson, S. 2007. Health care gets a better IT prescription. *Baseline,* *www.baselinemag.com,* May 24. Brenneman, K. 2000. Healtheon/WebMD's local office is thriving. *Business Journal of Portland,* June 2; and Raths, D. 1998. Reversal of fortune. *Inc. Technology,* 2: 52–62.

decisions, which included shifting its market focus, hiring and firing, and redeploying its assets. Finally, it took action. The result was not only firm survival but also a quick turnaround leading to rapid success.

HOW TO CONDUCT A CASE ANALYSIS

The steps involved in conducting a strategic management case analysis.

The process of analyzing strategic management cases involves several steps. In this section we will review the mechanics of preparing a case analysis. Before beginning, there are two things to keep in mind that will clarify your understanding of the process and make the results of the process more meaningful.

First, unless you prepare for a case discussion, there is little you can gain from the discussion and even less that you can offer. Effective strategic managers don't enter into problem-solving situations without doing some homework—investigating the situation, analyzing and researching possible solutions, and sometimes gathering the advice of others. Good problem solving often requires that decision makers be immersed in the facts, options, and implications surrounding the problem. In case analysis, this means reading and thoroughly comprehending the case materials before trying to make an analysis.

The second point is related to the first. To get the most out of a case analysis, you must place yourself "inside" the case—that is, think like an actual participant in the case situation. However, there are several positions you can take. These are discussed in the following paragraphs:

- *Strategic decision maker.* This is the position of the senior executive responsible for resolving the situation described in the case. It may be the CEO, the business owner, or a strategic manager in a key executive position.
- *Board of directors.* Since the board of directors represents the owners of a corporation, it has a responsibility to step in when a management crisis threatens the company. As a board member, you may be in a unique position to solve problems.
- *Outside consultant.* Either the board or top management may decide to bring in outsiders. Consultants often have an advantage because they can look at a situation objectively. But they also may be at a disadvantage since they have no power to enforce changes.

Before beginning the analysis, it may be helpful to envision yourself assuming one of these roles. Then, as you study and analyze the case materials, you can make a diagnosis and recommend solutions in a way that is consistent with your position. Try different perspectives. You may find that your view of the situation changes depending on the role you play. As an outside consultant, for example, it may be easy for you to conclude that certain individuals should be replaced in order to solve a problem presented in the case. However, if you take the role of the CEO who knows the individuals and the challenges they have been facing, you may be reluctant to fire them and will seek another solution instead.

The idea of assuming a particular role is similar to the real world in various ways. In your career, you may work in an organization where outside accountants, bankers, lawyers, or other professionals are advising you about how to resolve business situations or improve your practices. Their perspective will be different from yours, but it is useful to understand things from their point of view. Conversely, you may work as a member of the audit team of an accounting firm or the loan committee of a bank. In those situations, it would be helpful if you understood the situation from the perspective of the business leader who must weigh your views against all the other advice that he or she receives. Case analysis can help develop an ability to appreciate such multiple perspectives.

One of the most challenging roles to play in business is as a business founder or owner. For small businesses or entrepreneurial start-ups, the founder may wear all hats at once—key decision maker, primary stockholder, and CEO. Hiring an outside consultant may not be an option. However, the issues faced by young firms and established firms are often not that different, especially when it comes to formulating a plan of action. Business plans that entrepreneurial firms use to raise money or propose a business expansion typically revolve around a few key issues that must be addressed no matter what the size or age of the business. Strategy Spotlight 13.2 reviews business planning issues that are most important to consider when evaluating any case, especially from the perspective of the business founder or owner.

Next we will review five steps to follow when conducting a strategic management case analysis: becoming familiar with the material, identifying the problems, analyzing the strategic issues using the tools and insights of strategic management, proposing alternative solutions, and making recommendations.[6]

Become Familiar with the Material

Written cases often include a lot of material. They may be complex and include detailed financials or long passages. Even so, to understand a case and its implications, you must become familiar with its content. Sometimes key information is not immediately apparent. It may be contained in the footnotes to an exhibit or in an interview with a lower-level employee. In other cases the important points may be difficult to grasp because the subject matter is so unfamiliar. When you approach a strategic case, try the following technique to enhance comprehension:

USING A BUSINESS PLAN FRAMEWORK TO ANALYZE STRATEGIC CASES

Established businesses often have to change what they are doing in order to improve their competitive position or sometimes simply to survive. To make the changes effectively, businesses usually need a plan. Business plans are no longer just for entrepreneurs. The kind of market analysis, decision making, and action planning that is considered standard practice among new ventures can also benefit going concerns that want to make changes, seize an opportunity, or head in a new direction.

The best business plans, however, are not those that are loaded with decades of month-by-month financial projections or that depend on rigid adherence to a schedule of events that is impossible to predict. The good ones are focused on four factors that are critical to new venture success. These same factors are important in case analysis as well because they get to the heart of many of the problems found in strategic cases.

1. **The people.** "When I receive a business plan, I always read the résumé section first," says Harvard Professor William Sahlman. The people questions that are critically important to investors include: What are their skills? How much experience do they have? What is their reputation? Have they worked together as a team? These same questions also may be used in case analysis to evaluate the role of individuals in the strategic case.

2. **The opportunity.** Business opportunities come in many forms. They are not limited to new ventures. The chance to enter new markets, introduce new products, or merge with a competitor provides many of the challenges that are found in strategic management cases. What are the consequences of such actions? Will the proposed changes affect the firm's business concept? What factors might stand in the way of success? The same issues are also present in most strategic cases.

3. **The context.** Things happen in contexts that cannot be controlled by a firm's managers. This is particularly true of the general environment, where social trends, economic changes, or events such as the September 11, 2001, terrorist attacks can change business overnight. When evaluating strategic cases, ask: Is the company aware of the impact of context on the business? What will it do if the context changes? Can it influence the context in a way that favors the company?

4. **Risk and reward.** With a new venture, the entrepreneurs and investors take the risks and get the rewards. In strategic cases, the risks and rewards often extend to many other stakeholders, such as employees, customers, and suppliers. When analyzing a case, ask: Are the managers making choices that will pay off in the future? Are the rewards evenly distributed? Will some stakeholders be put at risk if the situation in the case changes? What if the situation remains the same? Could that be even riskier?

Whether a business is growing or shrinking, large or small, industrial or service-oriented, the issues of people, opportunities, context, and risks and rewards will have a large impact on its performance. Therefore, you should always consider these four factors when evaluating strategic management cases.

Sources: Wasserman, E. 2003. A simple plan. *MBA Jungle,* February: 50–55; DeKluyver, C. A. 2000. *Strategic thinking: An executive perspective.* Upper Saddle River, NJ: Prentice Hall; and Sahlman, W. A. 1997. How to write a great business plan. *Harvard Business Review,* 75(4): 98–108.

- Read quickly through the case one time to get an overall sense of the material.
- Use the initial read-through to assess possible links to strategic concepts.
- Read through the case again, in depth. Make written notes as you read.
- Evaluate how strategic concepts might inform key decisions or suggest alternative solutions.
- After formulating an initial recommendation, thumb through the case again quickly to help assess the consequences of the actions you propose.

Identify Problems

When conducting case analysis, one of your most important tasks is to identify the problem. Earlier we noted that one of the main reasons to conduct case analysis is to find solutions. But you cannot find a solution unless you know the problem. Another saying you may have heard is "A good diagnosis is half the cure." In other words, once you have determined what the problem is, you are well on your way to identifying a reasonable solution.

Some cases have more than one problem. But the problems are usually related. For a hypothetical example, consider the following: Company A was losing customers to a new competitor. Upon analysis, it was determined that the competitor had a 50 percent faster delivery time even though its product was of lower quality. The managers of company A could not understand why customers would settle for an inferior product. It turns out that no one was marketing to company A's customers that its product was superior. A second problem was that falling sales resulted in cuts in company A's sales force. Thus, there were two related problems: inferior delivery technology and insufficient sales effort.

When trying to determine the problem, avoid getting hung up on symptoms. Zero in on the problem. For example, in the company A example, the symptom was losing customers. But the problems were an underfunded, understaffed sales force combined with an outdated delivery technology. Try to see beyond the immediate symptoms to the more fundamental problems.

Another tip when preparing a case analysis is to articulate the problem.[7] Writing down a problem statement gives you a reference point to turn to as you proceed through the case analysis. This is important because the process of formulating strategies or evaluating implementation methods may lead you away from the initial problem. Make sure your recommendation actually addresses the problems you have identified.

One more thing about identifying problems: Sometimes problems are not apparent until *after* you do the analysis. In some cases the problem will be presented plainly, perhaps in the opening paragraph or on the last page of the case. But in other cases the problem does not emerge until after the issues in the case have been analyzed. We turn next to the subject of strategic case analysis.

Conduct Strategic Analyses

This textbook has presented numerous analytical tools (e.g., five-forces analysis and value-chain analysis), contingency frameworks (e.g., when to use related rather than unrelated diversification strategies), and other techniques that can be used to evaluate strategic situations. The previous 12 chapters have addressed practices that are common in strategic management, but only so much can be learned by studying the practices and concepts. The best way to understand these methods is to apply them by conducting analyses of specific cases.

The first step is to determine which strategic issues are involved. Is there a problem in the company's competitive environment? Or is it an internal problem? If it is internal, does it have to do with organizational structure? Strategic controls? Uses of technology? Or perhaps the company has overworked its employees or underutilized its intellectual capital. Has the company mishandled a merger? Chosen the wrong diversification strategy? Botched a new product introduction? Each of these issues is linked to one or more of the concepts discussed earlier in the text. Determine what strategic issues are associated with the problems you have identified. Remember also that most real-life case situations involve issues that are highly interrelated. Even in cases where there is only one major problem, the strategic processes required to solve it may involve several parts of the organization.

Once you have identified the issues that apply to the case, conduct the analysis. For example, you may need to conduct a five-forces analysis or dissect the company's competitive strategy. Perhaps you need to evaluate whether its resources are rare, valuable, difficult to imitate, or difficult to substitute. Financial analysis may be needed to assess the company's economic prospects. Perhaps the international entry mode needs to be reevaluated because of changing conditions in the host country. Employee empowerment techniques may need to be improved to enhance organizational learning. Whatever the case, all the strategic concepts introduced in the text include insights for assessing their effectiveness. Determining how well a company is doing these things is central to the case analysis process.

Financial ratio analysis is one of the primary tools used to conduct case analysis. Appendix 1 to Chapter 13 includes a discussion and examples of the financial ratios that are often used to evaluate a company's performance and financial well-being. Exhibit 13.1 provides a summary of the financial ratios presented in Appendix 1 to this chapter.

financial ratio analysis
a method of evaluating a company's performance and financial well-being through ratios of accounting values, including short-term solvency, long-term solvency, asset utilization, profitability, and market value ratios.

EXHIBIT 13.1 Summary of Financial Ratio Analysis Techniques

Ratio	What It Measures
Short-term solvency, or liquidity, ratios:	
Current ratio	Ability to use assets to pay off liabilities.
Quick ratio	Ability to use liquid assets to pay off liabilities quickly.
Cash ratio	Ability to pay off liabilities with cash on hand.
Long-term solvency, or financial leverage, ratios:	
Total debt ratio	How much of a company's total assets are financed by debt.
Debt-equity ratio	Compares how much a company is financed by debt with how much it is financed by equity.
Equity multiplier	How much debt is being used to finance assets.
Times interest earned ratio	How well a company has its interest obligations covered.
Cash coverage ratio	A company's ability to generate cash from operations.
Asset utilization, or turnover, ratios:	
Inventory turnover	How many times each year a company sells its entire inventory.
Days' sales in inventory	How many days on average inventory is on hand before it is sold.
Receivables turnover	How frequently each year a company collects on its credit sales.
Days' sales in receivables	How many days on average it takes to collect on credit sales (average collection period).
Total asset turnover	How much of sales is generated for every dollar in assets.
Capital intensity	The dollar investment in assets needed to generate $1 in sales.
Profitability ratios:	
Profit margin	How much profit is generated by every dollar of sales.
Return on assets (ROA)	How effectively assets are being used to generate a return.
Return on equity (ROE)	How effectively amounts invested in the business by its owners are being used to generate a return.
Market value ratios:	
Price-earnings ratio	How much investors are willing to pay per dollar of current earnings.
Market-to-book ratio	Compares market value of the company's investments to the cost of those investments.

In this part of the overall strategic analysis process, it is also important to test your own assumptions about the case.[8] First, what assumptions are you making about the case materials? It may be that you have interpreted the case content differently than your team members or classmates. Being clear about these assumptions will be important in determining how to analyze the case. Second, what assumptions have you made about the best way to resolve the problems? Ask yourself why you have chosen one type of analysis over another. This process of assumption checking can also help determine if you have gotten to the heart of the problem or are still just dealing with symptoms.

As mentioned earlier, sometimes the critical diagnosis in a case can be made only after the analysis is conducted. However, by the end of this stage in the process, you should know the problems and have completed a thorough analysis of them. You can now move to the next step: finding solutions.

Propose Alternative Solutions

It is important to remember that in strategic management case analysis, there is rarely one right answer or one best way. Even when members of a class or a team agree on what the problem is, they may not agree upon how to solve the problem. Therefore, it is helpful to consider several different solutions.

After conducting strategic analysis and identifying the problem, develop a list of options. What are the possible solutions? What are the alternatives? First, generate a list of all the options you can think of without prejudging any one of them. Remember that not all cases call for dramatic decisions or sweeping changes. Some companies just need to make small adjustments. In fact, "Do nothing" may be a reasonable alternative in some cases. Although that is rare, it might be useful to consider what will happen if the company does nothing. This point illustrates the purpose of developing alternatives: to evaluate what will happen if a company chooses one solution over another.

Thus, during this step of a case analysis, you will evaluate choices and the implications of those choices. One aspect of any business that is likely to be highlighted in this part of the analysis is strategy implementation. Ask how the choices made will be implemented. It may be that what seems like an obvious choice for solving a problem creates an even bigger problem when implemented. But remember also that no strategy or strategic "fix" is going to work if it cannot be implemented. Once a list of alternatives is generated, ask:

- Can the company afford it? How will it affect the bottom line?
- Is the solution likely to evoke a competitive response?
- Will employees throughout the company accept the changes? What impact will the solution have on morale?
- How will the decision affect other stakeholders? Will customers, suppliers, and others buy into it?
- How does this solution fit with the company's vision, mission, and objectives?
- Will the culture or values of the company be changed by the solution? Is it a positive change?

The point of this step in the case analysis process is to find a solution that both solves the problem and is realistic. A consideration of the implications of various alternative solutions will generally lead you to a final recommendation that is more thoughtful and complete.

Make Recommendations

The basic aim of case analysis is to find solutions. Your analysis is not complete until you have recommended a course of action. In this step the task is to make a set of recommendations that your analysis supports. Describe exactly what needs to be done. Explain why this course of action will solve the problem. The recommendation should also include suggestions for how best to implement the proposed solution because the recommended actions and their implications for the performance and future of the firm are interrelated.

Recall that the solution you propose must solve the problem you identified. This point cannot be overemphasized; too often students make recommendations that treat only symptoms or fail to tackle the central problems in the case. Make a logical argument that shows how the problem led to the analysis and the analysis led to the recommendations you are proposing. Remember, an analysis is not an end in itself; it is useful only if it leads to a solution.

The actions you propose should describe the very next steps that the company needs to take. Don't say, for example, "If the company does more market research, then I would recommend the following course of action. . . ." Instead, make conducting the research part of your recommendation. Taking the example a step further, if you also want to suggest subsequent actions that may be different *depending* on the outcome of the market research,

EXHIBIT 13.2 Preparing an Oral Case Presentation

Rule	Description
Organize your thoughts.	Begin by becoming familiar with the material. If you are working with a team, compare notes about the key points of the case and share insights that other team members may have gleaned from tables and exhibits. Then make an outline. This is one of the best ways to organize the flow and content of the presentation.
Emphasize strategic analysis.	The purpose of case analysis is to diagnose problems and find solutions. In the process, you may need to unravel the case material as presented and reconfigure it in a fashion that can be more effectively analyzed. Present the material in a way that lends itself to analysis—don't simply restate what is in the case. This involves three major categories with the following emphasis:

Background/Problem Statement	10–20%
Strategic Analysis/Options	60–75%
Recommendations/Action Plan	10–20%

Rule	Description
	As you can see, the emphasis of your presentation should be on analysis. This will probably require you to reorganize the material so that the tools of strategic analysis can be applied.
Be logical and consistent.	A presentation that is rambling and hard to follow may confuse the listener and fail to evoke a good discussion. Present your arguments and explanations in a logical sequence. Support your claims with facts. Include financial analysis where appropriate. Be sure that the solutions you recommend address the problems you have identified.
Defend your position.	Usually an oral presentation is followed by a class discussion. Anticipate what others might disagree with, and be prepared to defend your views. This means being aware of the choices you made and the implications of your recommendations. Be clear about your assumptions. Be able to expand on your analysis.
Share presentation responsibilities.	Strategic management case analyses are often conducted by teams. Each member of the team should have a clear role in the oral presentation, preferably a speaking role. It's also important to coordinate the different parts of the presentation into a logical, smooth-flowing whole. How well team members work together is usually very apparent during an oral presentation.

that's OK. But don't make your initial recommendation conditional on actions the company may or may not take.

In summary, case analysis can be a very rewarding process but, as you might imagine, it can also be frustrating and challenging. If you follow the steps described, you will address the different elements of a thorough analysis. This approach can give your analysis a solid footing. Then, even if there are differences of opinion about how to interpret the facts, analyze the situation, or solve the problems, you can feel confident that you have not missed any important steps in finding the best course of action.

Students are often asked to prepare oral presentations of the information in a case and their analysis of the best remedies. This is frequently assigned as a group project. Or you may be called upon in class to present your ideas about the circumstances or solutions for a case the class is discussing. Exhibit 13.2 provides some tips for preparing an oral case presentation.

HOW TO GET THE MOST FROM CASE ANALYSIS

How to get the most out of case analysis.

One of the reasons case analysis is so enriching as a learning tool is that it draws on many resources and skills besides just what is in the textbook. This is especially true in the study of strategy. Why? Because strategic management itself is a highly integrative task that draws on many areas of specialization at several levels, from the individual to the whole of society. Therefore, to get the most out of case analysis, expand your horizons beyond the concepts in this text and seek insights from your own reservoir of knowledge. Here are some tips for how to do that:[9]

- *Keep an open mind.* Like any good discussion, a case analysis discussion often evokes strong opinions and high emotions. But it's the variety of perspectives that makes case analysis so valuable: Many viewpoints usually lead to a more complete analysis. Therefore, avoid letting an emotional response to another person's style or opinion keep you from hearing what he or she has to say. Once you evaluate what is said, you may disagree with it or dismiss it as faulty. But unless you keep an open mind in the first place, you may miss the importance of the other person's contribution. Also, people often place a higher value on the opinions of those they consider to be good listeners.

- *Take a stand for what you believe.* Although it is vital to keep an open mind, it is also important to state your views proactively. Don't try to figure out what your friends or the instructor wants to hear. Analyze the case from the perspective of your own background and belief system. For example, perhaps you feel that a decision is unethical or that the managers in a case have misinterpreted the facts. Don't be afraid to assert that in the discussion. For one thing, when a person takes a strong stand, it often encourages others to evaluate the issues more closely. This can lead to a more thorough investigation and a more meaningful class discussion.

- *Draw on your personal experience.* You may have experiences from work or as a customer that shed light on some of the issues in a case. Even though one of the purposes of case analysis is to apply the analytical tools from this text, you may be able to add to the discussion by drawing on your outside experiences and background. Of course, you need to guard against carrying that to extremes. In other words, don't think that your perspective is the only viewpoint that matters! Simply recognize that firsthand experience usually represents a welcome contribution to the overall quality of case discussions.

- *Participate and persuade.* Have you heard the phrase "Vote early . . . and often"? Among loyal members of certain political parties, it has become rather a joke. Why? Because a democratic system is built on the concept of one person, one vote. Even though some voters may want to vote often enough to get their candidate elected, doing so is against the law. Not so in a case discussion. People who are persuasive and speak their mind can often influence the views of others. But to do so, you have to be prepared and convincing. Being persuasive is more than being loud or long-winded. It involves understanding all sides of an argument and being able to overcome objections to your own point of view. These efforts can make a case discussion more lively. And they parallel what happens in the real world; in business, people frequently share their opinions and attempt to persuade others to see things their way.

- *Be concise and to the point.* In the previous point, we encouraged you to speak up and "sell" your ideas to others in a case discussion. But you must be clear about what you are selling. Make your arguments in a way that is explicit and direct. Zero in on the most important points. Be brief. Don't try to make a lot of points at once by jumping around between topics. Avoid trying to explain the whole case situation at once. Remember, other students usually resent classmates who go on and on, take up a lot of "airtime," or repeat themselves unnecessarily. The best way to avoid this is to stay focused and be specific.

- *Think out of the box.* It's OK to be a little provocative; sometimes that is the consequence of taking a stand on issues. But it may be equally important to be imaginative and creative when making a recommendation or determining how to implement a solution. Albert Einstein once stated, "Imagination is more important than knowledge." The reason is that managing strategically requires more than memorizing concepts. Strategic management insights must be applied to each case differently—just knowing the principles is not enough. Imagination and out-of-the-box thinking help to apply strategic knowledge in novel and unique ways.

- *Learn from the insights of others.* Before you make up your mind about a case, hear what other students have to say. Get a second opinion, and a third, and so forth. Of course, in a situation where you have to put your analysis in writing, you may not be able to learn from others ahead of time. But in a case discussion, observe how various students attack the issues and engage in problem solving. Such observation skills also may be a key to finding answers within the case. For example, people tend to believe authority figures, so they would place a higher value on what a company president says. In some cases, however, the statements of middle managers may represent a point of view that is even more helpful for finding a solution to the problems presented by the case.

- *Apply insights from other case analyses.* Throughout the text, we have used examples of actual businesses to illustrate strategy concepts. The aim has been to show you how firms think about and deal with business problems. During the course, you may be asked to conduct several case analyses as part of the learning experience. Once you have performed a few case analyses, you will see how the concepts from the text apply in real-life business situations. Incorporate the insights learned from the text examples and your own previous case discussions into each new case that you analyze.

- *Critically analyze your own performance.* Performance appraisals are a standard part of many workplace situations. They are used to determine promotions, raises, and work assignments. In some organizations, everyone from the top executive down is subject to such reviews. Even in situations where the owner or CEO is not evaluated by others, top executives often find it useful to ask themselves regularly, Am I being effective? The same can be applied to your performance in a case analysis situation. Ask yourself, Were my comments insightful? Did I make a good contribution? How might I improve next time? Use the same criteria on yourself that you use to evaluate others. What grade would you give yourself? This technique not only will make you more fair in your assessment of others but also will indicate how your own performance can improve.

- *Conduct outside research.* Many times, you can enhance your understanding of a case situation by investigating sources outside the case materials. For example, you may want to study an industry more closely or research a company's close competitors. Recent moves such as mergers and acquisitions or product introductions may be reported in the business press. The company itself may provide useful information on its website or in its annual reports. Such information can usually spur additional discussion and enrich the case analysis. (*Caution:* It is best to check with your instructor in advance to be sure this kind of additional research is encouraged. Bringing in outside research may conflict with the instructor's learning objectives.)

Several of the points suggested for how to get the most out of case analysis apply only to an open discussion of a case, like that in a classroom setting. Exhibit 13.3 provides some additional guidelines for preparing a written case analysis.

EXHIBIT 13.3 Preparing a Written Case Analysis

Rule	Description
Be thorough.	Many of the ideas presented in Exhibit 13.2 about oral presentations also apply to written case analysis. However, a written analysis typically has to be more complete. This means writing out the problem statement and articulating assumptions. It is also important to provide support for your arguments and reference case materials or other facts more specifically.
Coordinate team efforts.	Written cases are often prepared by small groups. Within a group, just as in a class discussion, you may disagree about the diagnosis or the recommended plan of action. This can be healthy if it leads to a richer understanding of the case material. But before committing your ideas to writing, make sure you have coordinated your responses. Don't prepare a written analysis that appears contradictory or looks like a patchwork of disconnected thoughts.
Avoid restating the obvious.	There is no reason to restate material that everyone is familiar with already, namely, the case content. It is too easy for students to use up space in a written analysis with a recapitulation of the details of the case—this accomplishes very little. Stay focused on the key points. Restate only the information that is most central to your analysis.
Present information graphically.	Tables, graphs, and other exhibits are usually one of the best ways to present factual material that supports your arguments. For example, financial calculations such as break-even analysis, sensitivity analysis, or return on investment are best presented graphically. Even qualitative information such as product lists or rosters of employees can be summarized effectively and viewed quickly by using a table or graph.
Exercise quality control.	When presenting a case analysis in writing, it is especially important to use good grammar, avoid misspelling words, and eliminate typos and other visual distractions. Mistakes that can be glossed over in an oral presentation or class discussion are often highlighted when they appear in writing. Make your written presentation appear as professional as possible. Don't let the appearance of your written case keep the reader from recognizing the importance and quality of your analysis.

LO 13-5

How integrative thinking and conflict-inducing discussion techniques can lead to better decisions.

USEFUL DECISION-MAKING TECHNIQUES IN CASE ANALYSIS

The demands on today's business leaders require them to perform a wide variety of functions. The success of their organizations often depends on how they as individuals—and as part of groups—meet the challenges and deliver on promises. In this section we address three different techniques that can help managers make better decisions and, in turn, enable their organizations to achieve higher performance.

First, we discuss integrative thinking, a technique that helps managers make better decisions through the resolution of competing demands on resources, multiple contingencies, and diverse opportunities. Second, we address the concept of "asking heretical questions." These are questions that challenge conventional wisdom and may even seem odd or unusual—but they can often lead to valuable innovations. Third, we introduce two approaches to decision making that involve the effective use of conflict in the decision-making process. These are devil's advocacy and dialectical inquiry.

Integrative Thinking

How does a leader make good strategic decisions in the face of multiple contingencies and diverse opportunities? A study by Roger L. Martin reveals that executives who have a capability known as **integrative thinking** are among the most effective leaders. In his book *The Opposable Mind,* Martin contends that people who can consider two conflicting ideas simultaneously, without dismissing one of the ideas or becoming discouraged about reconciling them, often make the best problem solvers because of their ability to creatively synthesize the opposing thoughts. In explaining the source of his title, Martin quotes F. Scott Fitzgerald, who observed, "The test of a first-rate intelligence is the ability to hold two opposing ideas

integrative thinking
a process of reconciling opposing thoughts by generating new alternatives and creative solutions rather than rejecting one thought in favor of another.

in mind at the same time and still retain the ability to function. One should, for example, be able to see that things are hopeless yet be determined to make them otherwise."[10]

In contrast to conventional thinking, which tends to focus on making choices between competing ideas from a limited set of alternatives, integrative thinking is the process by which people reconcile opposing thoughts to identify creative solutions that provide them with more options and new alternatives. Exhibit 13.4 outlines the four stages of the integrative thinking and deciding process. Martin uses the admittedly simple example of deciding where to go on vacation to illustrate the stages:

- *Salience.* Take stock of what features of the decision you consider relevant and important. For example: Where will you go? What will you see? Where will you stay? What will it cost? Is it safe? Other features may be less important, but try to think of everything that may matter.
- *Causality.* Make a mental map of the causal relationships between the features, that is, how the various features are related to one another. For example, is it worth it to invite friends to share expenses? Will an exotic destination be less safe?
- *Architecture.* Use the mental map to arrange a sequence of decisions that will lead to a specific outcome. For example, will you make the hotel and flight arrangements first, or focus on which sightseeing tours are available? No particular decision path is right or wrong, but considering multiple options simultaneously may lead to a better decision.
- *Resolution.* Make your selection. For example, choose which destination, which flight, and so forth. Your final resolution is linked to how you evaluated the first three stages; if you are dissatisfied with your choices, the dotted arrows in the diagram (Exhibit 13.4) suggest you can go back through the process and revisit your assumptions.

EXHIBIT 13.4 Integrative Thinking: The Process of Thinking and Deciding

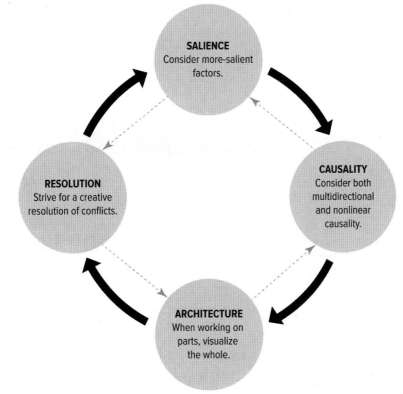

Source: Adaption from Harvard Business School Press from R. L. Martin. *The Opposable Mind,* 2007.

Applied to business, an integrative thinking approach enables decision makers to consider situations not as forced trade-offs—either decrease costs or invest more; either satisfy shareholders or please the community—but as a method for synthesizing opposing ideas into a creative solution. The key is to think in terms of "both-and" rather than "either-or." "Integrative thinking," says Martin, "shows us that there's a way to integrate the advantages of one solution without canceling out the advantages of an alternative solution."

Although Martin found that integrative thinking comes naturally to some people, he also believes it can be taught. But it may be difficult to learn, in part because it requires people to *un*learn old patterns and become aware of how they think. For executives willing to take a deep look at their habits of thought, integrative thinking can be developed into a valuable skill. Strategy Spotlight 13.3 tells how Red Hat Inc. cofounder Bob Young made his company a market leader by using integrative thinking to resolve a major problem in the domain of open-source software.

Asking Heretical Questions

In his recent book *The Big Pivot,* Andrew Winston introduced the concept of heretical innovation to help address the challenges associated with environmental sustainability in today's world.[11] He describes the need to pursue a deeper level of innovation that challenges long-held beliefs about how things work. Central to addressing these challenges

---

13.3   STRATEGY **SPOTLIGHT**

INTEGRATIVE THINKING AT RED HAT, INC.

How can a software developer make money giving away free software? That was the dilemma Red Hat founder Bob Young was facing during the early days of the open-source software movement. A Finnish developer named Linus Torvalds, using freely available UNIX software, had developed an operating system dubbed "Linux" that was being widely circulated in the freeware community. The software was intended specifically as an alternative to the pricey proprietary systems sold by Microsoft and Oracle. To use proprietary software, corporations had to pay hefty installation fees and were required to call Microsoft or Oracle engineers to fix it when anything went wrong. In Young's view it was a flawed and unsustainable business model.

But the free model was flawed as well. Although several companies had sprung up to help companies use Linux, there were few opportunities to profit from using it. As Young said, "You couldn't make any money selling [the Linux] operating system because all this stuff was free, and if you started to charge money for it, someone else would come in and price it lower. It was a commodity in the truest sense of the word." To complicate matters, hundreds of developers were part of the software community that was constantly modifying and debugging Linux—at a rate equivalent to three updates per day. As a result, systems administrators at corporations that tried to adopt the software spent so much time keeping track of updates that they didn't enjoy the savings they expected from using free software.

Young saw the appeal of both approaches but also realized a new model was needed. While contemplating the dilemma, he realized a salient feature that others had overlooked—because

most major corporations have to live with software decisions for at least 10 years, they will nearly always choose to do business with the industry leader. Young realized he had to position Red Hat as the top provider of Linux software. To do that, he proposed a radical solution: provide the authoritative version of Linux and deliver it in a new way—as a download rather than on CD. He hired programmers to create a downloadable version—still free—and promised, in essence, to maintain its quality (for a fee, of course) by dealing with all the open-source programmers who were continually suggesting changes. In the process, he created a product companies could trust and then profited by establishing ongoing service relationships with customers. Red Hat's version of Linux became the de facto standard. By 2000, Linux was installed in 25 percent of server operating systems worldwide and Red Hat had captured over 50 percent of the global market for Linux systems.

By recognizing that a synthesis of two flawed business models could provide the best of both worlds, Young exhibited the traits of integrative thinking. He pinpointed the causal relationships between the salient features of the marketplace and Red Hat's path to prosperity. He then crafted an approach that integrated aspects of the two existing approaches into a new alternative. By resolving to provide a free downloadable version, Young also took responsibility for creating his own path to success. The payoff was substantial: When Red Hat went public in 1999, Young became a billionaire on the first day of trading. And by 2015 Red Hat had over $1.5 billion in annual revenues and a market capitalization of nearly $13 billion.

Sources: Martin, R. L. 2007. *The opposable mind.* Boston: Harvard Business School Press; and *finance.yahoo.com.*

---

is the need to pose "heretical questions"—those that challenge conventional wisdom. Typically, they may make us uncomfortable or may seem odd (or even impossible)—but they often become the means of coming up with major innovations. Although the context of Winston's discussion was environmental sustainability, we believe that his ideas have useful implications for major challenges faced by today's managers in a wide range of firms and industries.

Heretical questions can address issues that are both small and large—from redesigning a single process or product to rethinking the whole business model. One must not discount the value of the approach in considering small matters. After all, the vast majority of people in a company don't have the mandate to rethink strategy. However, anyone in an organization can ask disruptive questions that profoundly change one aspect of a business. What makes this heretical is how deeply it challenges the conventional wisdom.

Consider the fascinating story of UPS's "no left turns," a classic tale in the sustainability world that has become rather well known. The catchy phrase became a rallying cry for mapping out new delivery routes that avoided crossing traffic and idling at stoplights. UPS is saving time, money, and energy—about 85 million miles and 8 million gallons of fuel annually.

Also, take the example of dyeing clothing—a tremendously water-intensive process. Somebody at adidas asked a heretical question: Could we dye clothes with no water? The answer was yes. However, the company needed to partner with a small Thailand-based company, Yeh Group. The DreDye process Adidas is now piloting uses heat and pressure to force pigment into the fibers. The process uses no water and also cuts energy and chemical use by 50 percent!

Finally, in 2010, Kimberly-Clark, the $21 billion firm that is behind such brands as Kleenex and Scott, questioned the simple assumption that toilet paper rolls must have cardboard tubes to hold their shape. It created the Scott Naturals Tube-Free line, which offers this household staple in the familiar cylindrical shape. But it comes with no cardboard core—just a hole the same size. It's been very successful—a key part of the now $100 million Scott Naturals brand. While this product may not save the world, if it became the industry standard, we could eliminate 17 billion tubes that are used in the United States every year and save fuel by shipping lighter rolls. This is a good example of heretical thinking. After all, the product doesn't incrementally use less cardboard—it uses none.

The concept of accepting failure and aiming for deep, heretical innovation is difficult for most organizations to embrace. Ed Catmull, the president and cofounder of animation pioneer Pixar, claims that when you are doing something new, you are by definition doing something you don't know very well, and that means mistakes. However, if you don't encourage mistakes, he says, you won't encourage anything new: "We're very conscientious about making it so that mistakes really aren't thought of as bad . . . they're just learning."

Conflict-Inducing Techniques

Next we address some techniques often used to improve case analyses that involve the constructive use of conflict. In the classroom—as well as in the business world—you will frequently be analyzing cases or solving problems in groups. While the word *conflict* often has a negative connotation (e.g., rude behavior, personal affronts), it can be very helpful in arriving at better solutions to cases. It can provide an effective means for new insights as well as for rigorously questioning and analyzing assumptions and strategic alternatives. In fact, if you don't have constructive conflict, you may get only consensus. When this happens, decisions tend to be based on compromise rather than collaboration.

In your organizational behavior classes, you probably learned the concept of "groupthink."[12] *Groupthink,* a term coined by Irving Janis after he conducted numerous studies on executive decision making, is a condition in which group members strive to reach agreement or consensus without realistically considering other viable alternatives. In effect, group norms bolster morale at the expense of critical thinking, and decision making is impaired.[13]

Many of us have probably been "victims" of groupthink at one time or another in our life. We may be confronted with situations when social pressure, politics, or "not wanting to stand out" may prevent us from voicing our concerns about a chosen course of action. Nevertheless, decision making in groups is a common practice in the management of many businesses. Most companies, especially large ones, rely on input from various top managers to provide valuable information and experience from their specialty area as well as their unique perspectives. Organizations need to develop cultures and reward systems that encourage people to express their perspectives and create open dialogues. Constructive conflict can be very helpful in that it emphasizes the need for managers to consider other people's perspectives and not simply become a strong advocate for positions that they may prefer.

Chapter 11 emphasized the importance of empowering individuals at all levels to participate in decision-making processes. After all, many of us have experienced situations where there is not a perfect correlation between one's rank and the viability of one's ideas! In terms of this course, case analysis involves a type of decision making that is often conducted in groups. Strategy Spotlight 13.4 provides guidelines for making team-based approaches to case analysis more effective.

13.4 STRATEGY SPOTLIGHT

MAKING CASE ANALYSIS TEAMS MORE EFFECTIVE

Working in teams can be very challenging. Not all team members have the same skills, interests, or motivations. Some team members just want to get the work done. Others see teams as an opportunity to socialize. Occasionally, there are team members who think they should be in charge and make all the decisions; other teams have freeloaders—team members who don't want to do anything except get credit for the team's work.

One consequence of these various styles is that team meetings can become time wasters. Disagreements about how to proceed, how to share the work, or what to do at the next meeting tend to slow down teams and impede progress toward the goal. While the dynamics of case analysis teams are likely to always be challenging depending on the personalities involved, one thing nearly all members realize is that, ultimately, the team's work must be completed. Most team members also aim to do the highest-quality work possible. The following guidelines provide some useful insights about how to get the work of a team done more effectively.

Spend More Time Together

One of the factors that prevents teams from doing a good job with case analysis is their failure to put in the necessary time. Unless teams really tackle the issues surrounding case analysis—both the issues in the case itself and organizing how the work is to be conducted—the end result will probably be lacking because decisions that are made too quickly are unlikely to get to the heart of the problem(s) in the case. "Meetings should be a precious resource, but they're treated like a necessary evil," says Kenneth Sole, a consultant who specializes in organizational behavior. As a result, teams that care more about finishing the analysis than getting the analysis right often make poor decisions.

Therefore, expect to have a few meetings that run long, especially at the beginning of the project, when the work is being organized and the issues in the case are being sorted out, and again at the end, when the team must coordinate the components of the case analysis that will be presented. Without spending this kind of time together, it is doubtful that the analysis will be comprehensive and the presentation is likely to be choppy and incomplete.

Make a Focused and Disciplined Agenda

To complete tasks and avoid wasting time, meetings need to have a clear purpose. To accomplish this at Roche, the Swiss drug and diagnostic product maker, CEO Franz Humer implemented a "decision agenda." The agenda focuses only on Roche's highest-value issues, and discussions are limited to these major topics. In terms of case analysis, the major topics include sorting out the issues of the case, linking elements of the case to the strategic issues presented in class or the text, and assigning roles to various team members. Such objectives help keep team members on track.

Agendas also can be used to address issues such as the timeline for accomplishing work. Otherwise, the purpose of meetings may only be to manage the "crisis" of getting the case analysis finished on time. One solution is to assign a team member to manage the agenda. That person could make sure the team stays focused on the tasks at hand and remains mindful of time constraints. Another role could be to link the team's efforts to the steps presented in Exhibit 13.2 and Exhibit 13.3 on how to prepare a case analysis.

Pay More Attention to Strategy

Teams often waste time by focusing on unimportant aspects of a case. These may include details that are interesting but irrelevant or operational issues rather than strategic issues. It is true that useful clues to the issues in the case are sometimes embedded in the conversations of key managers or the trends evident in a financial statement. But once such insights are discovered, teams need to focus on the underlying strategic problems in the case. To solve such problems, major corporations such as Cadbury Schweppes and Boeing hold meetings just to generate strategic alternatives for solving their problems. This gives managers time to consider the implications of various courses of action. Separate meetings are held to evaluate alternatives, make strategic decisions, and approve an action plan.

Once the strategic solutions or "course corrections" are identified—as is common in most cases assigned—the operational implications and details of implementation will flow from the strategic decisions that companies make. Therefore, focusing primarily on strategic issues will provide teams with insights for making recommendations that are based on a deeper understanding of the issues in the case.

Produce Real Decisions

Too often, meetings are about discussing rather than deciding. Teams often spend a lot of time talking without reaching any conclusions. As Raymond Sanchez, CEO of Florida-based Security Mortgage Group, says, meetings are often used to "rehash the hash that's already been hashed." To be efficient and productive, team meetings need to be about more than just information sharing and group input. For example, an initial meeting may result in the team realizing that it needs to study the case in greater depth and examine links to strategic issues more carefully. Once more analysis is conducted, the team needs to reach a consensus so that the decisions that are made will last once the meeting is over. Lasting decisions are more actionable because they free team members to take the next steps.

One technique for making progress in this way is recapping each meeting with a five-minute synthesis report. According to Pamela Schindler, director of the Center for Applied Management at Wittenberg University, it's important to think through the implications of the meeting before ending it. "The real joy of synthesis," says Schindler, "is realizing how many meetings you won't need."

Not only are these guidelines useful for helping teams finish their work, but they can also help resolve some of the difficulties that teams often face. By involving every team member, using a meeting agenda, and focusing on the strategic issues that are critical to nearly every case, the discussion is limited and the criteria for making decisions become clearer. This allows the task to dominate rather than any one personality. And if the team finishes its work faster, this frees up time to focus on other projects or put the finishing touches on a case analysis presentation.

Sources: Mankins, M. C. 2004. Stop wasting valuable time. *Harvard Business Review,* September: 58–65; and Sauer, P. J. 2004. Escape from meeting hell. *Inc.,* May, www.inc.com.

Clearly, understanding how to work in groups and the potential problems associated with group decision processes can benefit the case analysis process. Therefore, let's first look at some of the symptoms of groupthink and suggest ways of preventing it. Then we will suggest some conflict-inducing decision-making techniques—devil's advocacy and dialectical inquiry—that can help to prevent groupthink and lead to better decisions.

Symptoms of Groupthink and How to Prevent It   Irving Janis identified several symptoms of groupthink, including:

- *An illusion of invulnerability.* This reassures people about possible dangers and leads to overoptimism and failure to heed warnings of danger.
- *A belief in the inherent morality of the group.* Because individuals think that what they are doing is right, they tend to ignore ethical or moral consequences of their decisions.
- *Stereotyped views of members of opposing groups.* Members of other groups are viewed as weak or not intelligent.
- *The application of pressure to members who express doubts about the group's shared illusions or question the validity of arguments proposed.*
- *The practice of self-censorship.* Members keep silent about their opposing views and downplay to themselves the value of their perspectives.
- *An illusion of unanimity.* People assume that judgments expressed by members are shared by all.
- *The appointment of mindguards.* People sometimes appoint themselves as mindguards to protect the group from adverse information that might break the climate of consensus (or agreement).

Clearly, groupthink is an undesirable and negative phenomenon that can lead to poor decisions. Irving Janis considers it to be a key contributor to such faulty decisions as the failure to prepare for the attack on Pearl Harbor, the escalation of the Vietnam conflict, and the failure to prepare for the consequences of the Iraqi invasion. Many of the same sorts of flawed decision making occur in business organizations. Janis has provided several suggestions for preventing groupthink that can be used as valuable guides in decision making and problem solving:

- Leaders must encourage group members to address their concerns and objectives.
- When higher-level managers assign a problem for a group to solve, they should adopt an impartial stance and not mention their preferences.
- Before a group reaches its final decision, the leader should encourage members to discuss their deliberations with trusted associates and then report the perspectives back to the group.
- The group should invite outside experts and encourage them to challenge the group's viewpoints and positions.
- The group should divide into subgroups, meet at various times under different chairpersons, and then get together to resolve differences.
- After reaching a preliminary agreement, the group should hold a "second chance" meeting that provides members a forum to express any remaining concerns and rethink the issue prior to making a final decision.

Using Conflict to Improve Decision Making   In addition to the above suggestions, the effective use of conflict can be a means of improving decision making. Although conflict can have negative outcomes, such as ill will, anger, tension, and lowered motivation, both leaders and group members must strive to ensure that it is managed properly and used in a constructive manner.

Two conflict-inducing decision-making approaches that have become quite popular are *devil's advocacy* and *dialectical inquiry*. Both approaches incorporate conflict into the decision-making process through formalized debate. A group charged with making a decision or solving a problem is divided into two subgroups, and each will be involved in the analysis and solution.

devil's advocacy
a method of introducing conflict into a decision-making process by having specific individuals or groups act as a critic to an analysis or planned solution.

With **devil's advocacy,** one of the groups (or individuals) acts as a critic to the plan. The devil's advocate tries to come up with problems with the proposed alternative and suggest reasons why it should not be adopted. The role of the devil's advocate is to create dissonance. This ensures that the group will take a hard look at its original proposal or alternative. By having a group (or individual) assigned the role of devil's advocate, it becomes clear that such an adversarial stance is legitimized. It brings out criticisms that might otherwise not be made.

Some authors have suggested that the use of a devil's advocate can help boards of directors to ensure that decisions are addressed comprehensively and to avoid groupthink.[14] And Charles Elson, a director of Sunbeam Corporation, has argued:

> Devil's advocates are terrific in any situation because they help you to figure a decision's numerous implications. . . . The better you think out the implications prior to making the decision, the better the decision ultimately turns out to be. That's why a devil's advocate is always a great person, irritating sometimes, but a great person.

As one might expect, there can be some potential problems with using the devil's advocate approach. If one's views are constantly criticized, one may become demoralized. Thus, that person may come up with "safe solutions" in order to minimize embarrassment or personal risk and become less subject to criticism. Additionally, even if the devil's advocate is successful with finding problems with the proposed course of action, there may be no new ideas or counterproposals to take its place. Thus, the approach sometimes may simply focus on what is wrong without suggesting other ideas.

EXHIBIT 13.5 Two Conflict-Inducing Decision-Making Processes

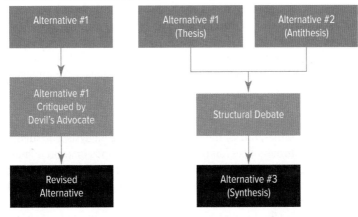

Dialectical inquiry attempts to accomplish the goals of the devil's advocate in a more constructive manner. It is a technique whereby a problem is approached from two alternative points of view. The idea is that out of a critique of the opposing perspectives—a thesis and an antithesis—a creative synthesis will occur. Dialectical inquiry involves the following steps:

1. Identify a proposal and the information that was used to derive it.
2. State the underlying assumptions of the proposal.
3. Identify a counterplan (antithesis) that is believed to be feasible, politically viable, and generally credible. However, it rests on assumptions that are opposite to the original proposal.
4. Engage in a debate in which individuals favoring each plan provide their arguments and support.
5. Identify a synthesis which, hopefully, includes the best components of each alternative.

There are some potential downsides associated with dialectical inquiry. It can be quite time-consuming and involve a good deal of training. Further, it may result in a series of compromises between the initial proposal and the counterplan. In cases where the original proposal was the best approach, this would be unfortunate.

Despite some possible limitations associated with these conflict-inducing decision-making techniques, they have many benefits. Both techniques force debate about underlying assumptions, data, and recommendations between subgroups. Such debate tends to prevent the uncritical acceptance of a plan that may seem to be satisfactory after a cursory analysis. The approach serves to tap the knowledge and perspectives of group members and continues until group members agree on both assumptions and recommended actions. Given that both approaches serve to use, rather than minimize or suppress, conflict, higher-quality decisions should result. Exhibit 13.5 briefly summarizes these techniques.

dialectical inquiry
a method of introducing conflict into a decision-making process by devising different proposals that are feasible, politically viable, and credible but rely on different assumptions and then debating the merits of each.

FOLLOWING THE ANALYSIS-DECISION-ACTION CYCLE IN CASE ANALYSIS

LO 13-6

How to use the strategic insights and material from each of the 12 previous chapters in the text to analyze issues posed by strategic management cases.

In Chapter 1 we defined strategic management as the analysis, decisions, and actions that organizations undertake to create and sustain competitive advantages. It is no accident that we chose that sequence of words because it corresponds to the sequence of events that typically occurs in the strategic management process. In case analysis, as in the real world, this cycle of events can provide a useful framework. First, an analysis of the case in terms of the business environment and current events is needed. To make such an analysis, the case background must be considered. Next, based on that analysis, decisions must be made. This may involve formulating a strategy, choosing between difficult options, moving forward aggressively, or retreating from a bad situation. There are many possible decisions, depending on the case situation. Finally, action is required. Once decisions are made and plans are set, the action begins. The recommended action steps and the consequences of implementing these actions are the final stage.

Each of the previous 12 chapters of this book includes techniques and information that may be useful in a case analysis. However, not all of the issues presented will be important in every case. As noted earlier, one of the challenges of case analysis is to identify the most critical points and sort through material that may be ambiguous or seem unimportant.

In this section we draw on the material presented in each of the 12 chapters to show how it informs the case analysis process. The ideas are linked sequentially and in terms of an overarching strategic perspective. One of your jobs when conducting case analysis is to see how the parts of a case fit together and how the insights from the study of strategy can help you understand the case situation.

1. ***Analyzing organizational goals and objectives.*** A company's vision, mission, and objectives keep organization members focused on a common purpose. They also influence how an organization deploys its resources, relates to its stakeholders, and matches its short-term objectives with its long-term goals. The goals may even impact how a company formulates and implements strategies. When exploring issues of goals and objectives, you might ask:

   - Has the company developed short-term objectives that are inconsistent with its long-term mission? If so, how can management realign its vision, mission, and objectives?
   - Has the company considered all of its stakeholders equally in making critical decisions? If not, should the views of all stakeholders be treated the same or are some stakeholders more important than others?
   - Is the company being faced with an issue that conflicts with one of its long-standing policies? If so, how should it compare its existing policies to the potential new situation?

2. ***Analyzing the external environment.*** The business environment has two components. The general environment consists of demographic, sociocultural, political/legal, technological, economic, and global conditions. The competitive environment includes rivals, suppliers, customers, and other factors that may directly affect a company's success. Strategic managers must monitor the environment to identify opportunities and threats that may have an impact on performance. When investigating a firm's external environment, you might ask:

   - Does the company follow trends and events in the general environment? If not, how can these influences be made part of the company's strategic analysis process?
   - Is the company effectively scanning and monitoring the competitive environment? If so, how is it using the competitive intelligence it is gathering to enhance its competitive advantage?
   - Has the company correctly analyzed the impact of the competitive forces in its industry on profitability? If so, how can it improve its competitive position relative to these forces?

3. ***Analyzing the internal environment.*** A firm's internal environment consists of its resources and other value-adding capabilities. Value-chain analysis and a resource-based approach to analysis can be used to identify a company's strengths and

weaknesses and determine how they are contributing to its competitive advantages. Evaluating firm performance can also help make meaningful comparisons with competitors. When researching a company's internal analysis, you might ask:

- Does the company know how the various components of its value chain are adding value to the firm? If not, what internal analysis is needed to determine its strengths and weakness?
- Has the company accurately analyzed the source and vitality of its resources? If so, is it deploying its resources in a way that contributes to competitive advantages?
- Is the company's financial performance as good as or better than that of its close competitors? If so, has it balanced its financial success with the performance criteria of other stakeholders such as customers and employees?

4. *Assessing a firm's intellectual assets.* Human capital is a major resource in today's knowledge economy. As a result, attracting, developing, and retaining talented workers is a key strategic challenge. Other assets such as patents and trademarks are also critical. How companies leverage their intellectual assets through social networks and strategic alliances, and how technology is used to manage knowledge, may be a major influence on a firm's competitive advantage. When analyzing a firm's intellectual assets, you might ask:

- Does the company have underutilized human capital? If so, what steps are needed to develop and leverage its intellectual assets?
- Is the company missing opportunities to forge strategic alliances? If so, how can it use its social capital to network more effectively?
- Has the company developed knowledge-management systems that capture what it learns? If not, what technologies can it employ to retain new knowledge?

5. *Formulating business-level strategies.* Firms use the competitive strategies of differentiation, focus, and overall cost leadership as a basis for overcoming the five competitive forces and developing sustainable competitive advantages. Combinations of these strategies may work best in some competitive environments. Additionally, an industry's life cycle is an important contingency that may affect a company's choice of business-level strategies. When assessing business-level strategies, you might ask:

- Has the company chosen the correct competitive strategy given its industry environment and competitive situation? If not, how should it use its strengths and resources to improve its performance?
- Does the company use combination strategies effectively? If so, what capabilities can it cultivate to further enhance profitability?
- Is the company using a strategy that is appropriate for the industry life cycle in which it is competing? If not, how can it realign itself to match its efforts to the current stage of industry growth?

6. *Formulating corporate-level strategies.* Large firms often own and manage portfolios of businesses. Corporate strategies address methods for achieving synergies among these businesses. Related and unrelated diversification techniques are alternative approaches to deciding which business should be added to or removed from a portfolio. Companies can diversify by means of mergers, acquisitions, joint ventures, strategic alliances, and internal development. When analyzing corporate-level strategies, you might ask:

- Is the company competing in the right businesses given the opportunities and threats that are present in the environment? If not, how can it realign its diversification strategy to achieve competitive advantages?

- Is the corporation managing its portfolio of businesses in a way that creates synergies among the businesses? If so, what additional business should it consider adding to its portfolio?
- Are the motives of the top corporate executives who are pushing diversification strategies appropriate? If not, what action can be taken to curb their activities or align them with the best interests of all stakeholders?

7. *Formulating international-level strategies.* Foreign markets provide both opportunities and potential dangers for companies that want to expand globally. To decide which entry strategy is most appropriate, companies have to evaluate the trade-offs between two factors that firms face when entering foreign markets: cost reduction and local adaptation. To achieve competitive advantages, firms will typically choose one of three strategies: global, multidomestic, or transnational. When evaluating international-level strategies, you might ask:

- Is the company's entry into an international marketplace threatened by the actions of local competitors? If so, how can cultural differences be minimized to give the firm a better chance of succeeding?
- Has the company made the appropriate choices between cost reduction and local adaptation to foreign markets? If not, how can it adjust its strategy to achieve competitive advantages?
- Can the company improve its effectiveness by embracing one international strategy over another? If so, how should it choose between a global, multidomestic, or transnational strategy?

8. *Formulating entrepreneurial strategies.* New ventures add jobs and create new wealth. To do so, they must identify opportunities that will be viable in the marketplace as well as gather resources and assemble an entrepreneurial team to enact the opportunity. New entrants often evoke a strong competitive response from incumbent firms in a given marketplace. When examining the role of strategic thinking on the success of entrepreneurial ventures and the role of competitive dynamics, you might ask:

- Is the company engaged in an ongoing process of opportunity recognition? If not, how can it enhance its ability to recognize opportunities?
- Do the entrepreneurs who are launching new ventures have vision, dedication and drive, and a commitment to excellence? If so, how have these affected the performance and dedication of other employees involved in the venture?
- Have strategic principles been used in the process of developing strategies to pursue the entrepreneurial opportunity? If not, how can the venture apply tools such as five-forces analysis and value-chain analysis to improve its competitive position and performance?

9. *Achieving effective strategic control.* Strategic controls enable a firm to implement strategies effectively. Informational controls involve comparing performance to stated goals and scanning, monitoring, and being responsive to the environment. Behavioral controls emerge from a company's culture, reward systems, and organizational boundaries. When assessing the impact of strategic controls on implementation, you might ask:

- Is the company employing the appropriate informational control systems? If not, how can it implement a more interactive approach to enhance learning and minimize response times?
- Does the company have a strong and effective culture? If not, what steps can it take to align its values and rewards system with its goals and objectives?

- Has the company implemented control systems that match its strategies? If so, what additional steps can be taken to improve performance?

10. *Creating effective organizational designs.* Organizational designs that align with competitive strategies can enhance performance. As companies grow and change, their structures must also evolve to meet new demands. In today's economy, firm boundaries must be flexible and permeable to facilitate smoother interactions with external parties such as customers, suppliers, and alliance partners. New forms of organizing are becoming more common. When evaluating the role of organizational structure on strategy implementation, you might ask:

- Has the company implemented organizational structures that are suited to the type of business it is in? If not, how can it alter the design in ways that enhance its competitiveness?
- Is the company employing boundaryless organizational designs where appropriate? If so, how are senior managers maintaining control of lower-level employees?
- Does the company use outsourcing to achieve the best possible results? If not, what criteria should it use to decide which functions can be outsourced?

11. *Creating a learning organization and an ethical organization.* Strong leadership is essential for achieving competitive advantages. Two leadership roles are especially important. The first is creating a learning organization by harnessing talent and encouraging the development of new knowledge. Second, leaders play a vital role in motivating employees to excellence and inspiring ethical behavior. When exploring the impact of effective strategic leadership, you might ask:

- Do company leaders promote excellence as part of the overall culture? If so, how has this influenced the performance of the firm and the individuals in it?
- Is the company committed to being a learning organization? If not, what can it do to capitalize on the individual and collective talents of organizational members?
- Have company leaders exhibited an ethical attitude in their own behavior? If not, how has their behavior influenced the actions of other employees?

12. *Fostering corporate entrepreneurship.* Many firms continually seek new growth opportunities and avenues for strategic renewal. In some corporations, autonomous work units such as business incubators and new venture groups are used to focus corporate venturing activities. In other corporate settings, product champions and other firm members provide companies with the impetus to expand into new areas. When investigating the impact of entrepreneurship on strategic effectiveness, you might ask:

- Has the company resolved the dilemmas associated with managing innovation? If so, is it effectively defining and pacing its innovation efforts?
- Has the company developed autonomous work units that have the freedom to bring forth new product ideas? If so, has it used product champions to implement new venture initiatives?
- Does the company have an entrepreneurial orientation? If not, what can it do to encourage entrepreneurial attitudes in the strategic behavior of its organizational members?

We close this chapter with Strategy Spotlight 13.5—an example of how the College of Business and Economics at Towson University went about conducting a "live" business case competition across all of the strategic management sections. The "Description" and "Case Competition Checklist" includes many of the elements of the analysis-decision-action cycle in case analysis that we have discussed.

13.5 STRATEGY SPOTLIGHT

CASE COMPETITION ASSIGNMENT

Brief Description

The purpose of this assignment is to apply theory to a real life strategic management case on Cintas Corporation (Baltimore). Your role is to analyze the case and recommend practical, innovative, and theoretically sound solutions. Participation in the competition will provide invaluable experience and the opportunity to interact with business executives in a meaningful activity. The executives will select the winning teams and identify Gold, Silver, and Bronze Team winners.

The case competition within each section will represent 25 percent of the grade for the course. The rubric for judging the winning team in each section will be standardized across all sections of the strategic management course to address conceptual skills in strategic analysis, strategy formulation, strategy implementation, and strategic control.

The case will be disseminated on the case competition Blackboard site. Each team must give a presentation as described below, turn in a hardcopy of its multimedia presentation and any updated supplementary materials, and upload all relevant materials as specified by the instructor (presentation, supplements).

The team presentation may not exceed fifteen minutes and will be graded based on coverage of all elements in the grading rubric. Approximately five additional minutes will be devoted to responding to questions and comments from the judges.

Case Competition Checklist

Be sure to address all of the following statements in order for your presentation to earn a positive evaluation.

To what extent do you agree with the following statements?

External Analysis

- Effectively uses an analysis of the general business environment to address all key general environment trends.
- Effectively uses Porter's Five Forces model to assess industry attractiveness.

Internal Analysis

- Identifies all key organization resources and capabilities.
- Appropriately discusses all key organization resources and capabilities and identifies the degree to which they serve as the foundation for a competitive advantage.
- Appropriately discusses Cintas Baltimore's strengths and weaknesses.
- Explains in depth all important implications for Cintas Baltimore.

Corporate Alignment

- Evaluates areas of alignment/misalignment (strategic fit) between the catalog line of business in the

restaurant industry and the organization's overall corporate strategy.

Proposed Strategy and Resource Requirements

- Provides a comprehensive strategy for the catalog line of business that spans three years. This should include milestones that you hope to accomplish over that time period. Supplementary materials fully complement and support the presentation.
- Your plan's resource requirements are fully identified and explained.
- Your plan's resource needs are feasible with realistic costs.
- The total cost of your plan does not exceed $45,000 ($15,000 per year).
- All assumptions are clearly explained and logical.
- Strategic alternatives are fully explained in supporting supplementary materials.
- Recommendations address all major issues.
- Recommendations are explained in-depth.

Barriers to Imitation

- Obstacles for competitors to imitate the strategy are fully identified.
- Obstacles for competitors to imitate the strategy are justified with clear logic.

Tactics

- An appropriate number of milestones for the next three years is proposed.
- For each milestone, at least three tactics are proposed. All milestones and tactics clearly pertain to the strategy.

Writing and Presentation Criteria

- Written materials contain no technical/grammar/spelling errors.
- Writing is completely clear and well-organized.
- Writing uses appropriate word choice.
- All ideas not your own are appropriately referenced.
- Arguments are logically compelling.
- All exhibits are referenced.
- All exhibits' relevance is explained.
- Basic information that the business audience would know is not rehashed.
- The presentation is limited to 15 minutes.
- All members of the team present for at least one minute.
- All members are dressed professionally.

- All presenters are enthusiastic (eye contact, no filler words, posture).
- All presenters use proper diction and voice.
- All presenters clearly present the intended content (arguments are convincing).
- All presenters follow a group theme and structure.
- All presenters respond well to questions during the Q&A.

- All presenters show deep understanding of the analyses.
- All presenters are respectful and professional.

Note: We thank a team of contributors at Towson University for sharing this information with us, including Lori Kiyatkin, Doug Sanford, David Brannon, Shana Gass, Shohreh Kaynama, Don Kopka, Mariana Lebron, Jimmy Lien, Wayne Paul, Doug Ross, and Precha Thavikulwat. The information provided here is an abridged version of the materials actually used for the assignment, which would also include the grading rubric, etc.

summary

Strategic management case analysis provides an effective method of learning how companies analyze problems, make decisions, and resolve challenges. Strategic cases include detailed accounts of actual business situations. The purpose of analyzing such cases is to gain exposure to a wide variety of organizational and managerial situations. By putting yourself in the place of a strategic decision maker, you can gain an appreciation of the difficulty and complexity of many strategic situations. In the process you can learn how to ask good strategic questions and enhance your analytical skills. Presenting case analyses can also help develop oral and written communication skills.

In this chapter we have discussed the importance of strategic case analysis and described the five steps involved in conducting a case analysis: becoming familiar with the material, identifying problems, analyzing strategic issues, proposing alternative solutions, and making recommendations. We have also discussed how to get the most from case analysis. Finally, we have described how the case analysis process follows the analysis-decision-action cycle of strategic management and outlined issues and questions that are associated with each of the previous 12 chapters of the text.

key terms

case analysis 393
financial ratio analysis 398
integrative thinking 404
devil's advocacy 410
dialectical inquiry 411

REFERENCES

1. Bryant, A. 2011. *The corner office:* 15. New York: St. Martin's.

2. The material in this chapter is based on several sources, including Barnes, L. A., Nelson, A. J., & Christensen, C. R. 1994. *Teaching and the case method: Text, cases and readings.* Boston: Harvard Business School Press; Guth, W. D. 1985. Central concepts of business unit and corporate strategy. In Guth, W. D. (Ed.), *Handbook of business strategy:* 1–9. Boston: Warren, Gorham & Lamont; Lundberg, C. C., & Enz, C. 1993. A framework for student case preparation. *Case Research Journal,* 13 (Summer): 129–140; and Ronstadt, R. 1980. *The art of case analysis: A guide to the diagnosis of business situations.* Dover, MA: Lord.

3. Edge, A. G. & Coleman, D. R. 1986. *The guide to case analysis and reporting* (3rd ed.). Honolulu, HI: System Logistics.

4. Morris, E. 1987. Vision and strategy: A focus for the future. *Journal of Business Strategy,* 8: 51–58.

5. Bryant, A. 2011. *The corner office:* 15. New York: St. Martin's.

6. This section is based on Lundberg & Enz, op. cit., and Ronstadt, op. cit.

7. The importance of problem definition was emphasized in Mintzberg, H., Raisinghani, D., & Theoret, A. 1976. The structure of "unstructured" decision processes. *Administrative Science Quarterly,* 21(2): 246–275.

8. Drucker, P. F. 1994. The theory of the business. *Harvard Business Review,* 72(5): 95–104.

9. This section draws on Edge & Coleman, op. cit.

10. Evans, R. 2007. The either/or dilemma, *www.ft.com,* December 19: np; and Martin, R. L. 2007. *The opposable mind.* Boston: Harvard Business School Press.

11. This section draws on Winston, A. S. 2014. *The big pivot.* Boston: Harvard Business Review Press.

12. Irving Janis is credited with coining the term *groupthink,* and he applied it primarily to fiascos in government (such as the Bay of Pigs incident in 1961). Refer to Janis, I. L. 1982. *Victims of groupthink* (2nd ed.). Boston: Houghton Mifflin.

13. Much of our discussion is based upon Finkelstein, S. & Mooney, A. C. 2003. Not the usual suspects: How to use board process to make boards better. *Academy of Management Executive,* 17(2): 101–113; Schweiger, D. M., Sandberg, W. R., & Rechner, P. L. 1989. Experiential effects of dialectical inquiry, devil's advocacy, and consensus approaches to strategic decision making. *Academy of Management Journal,* 32(4): 745–772; and Aldag, R J. & Stearns, T. M. 1987. *Management.* Cincinnati: South-Western.

14. Finkelstein and Mooney, op. cit.

FINANCIAL RATIO ANALYSIS*

Standard Financial Statements

One obvious thing we might want to do with a company's financial statements is to compare them to those of other, similar companies. We would immediately have a problem, however. It's almost impossible to directly compare the financial statements of two companies because of differences in size.

For example, Oracle and IBM are obviously serious rivals in the computer software market, but IBM is much larger (in terms of assets), so it is difficult to compare them directly. For that matter, it's difficult to even compare financial statements from different points in time for the same company if the company's size has changed. The size problem is compounded if we try to compare IBM and, say, SAP (of Germany). If SAP's financial statements are denominated in euros, then we have a size *and* a currency difference.

To start making comparisons, one obvious thing we might try to do is to somehow standardize the financial statements. One very common and useful way of doing this is to work with percentages instead of total dollars. The resulting financial statements are called *common-size statements*. We consider these next.

Common-Size Balance Sheets

For easy reference, Prufrock Corporation's 2016 and 2017 balance sheets are provided in Exhibit 13A.1. Using these, we construct common-size balance sheets by expressing each item as a percentage of total assets. Prufrock's 2016 and 2017 common-size balance sheets are shown in Exhibit 13A.2.

Notice that some of the totals don't check exactly because of rounding errors. Also notice that the total change has to be zero since the beginning and ending numbers must add up to 100 percent.

In this form, financial statements are relatively easy to read and compare. For example, just looking at the two balance sheets for Prufrock, we see that current assets were 19.7 percent of total assets in 2017, up from 19.1 percent in 2016. Current liabilities declined from 16 percent to 15.1 percent of total liabilities and equity over that same time. Similarly, total equity rose from 68.1 percent of total liabilities and equity to 72.2 percent.

Overall, Prufrock's liquidity, as measured by current assets compared to current liabilities, increased over the year. Simultaneously, Prufrock's indebtedness diminished as a percentage of total assets. We might be tempted to conclude that the balance sheet has grown "stronger."

Common-Size Income Statements

A useful way of standardizing the income statement, shown in Exhibit 13A.3, is to express each item as a percentage of total sales, as illustrated for Prufrock in Exhibit 13A.4.

This income statement tells us what happens to each dollar in sales. For Prufrock, interest expense eats up $.061 out of every sales dollar and taxes take another $.081. When all is said and done, $.157 of each dollar flows through to the bottom line (net income), and that amount is split into $.105 retained in the business and $.052 paid out in dividends.

These percentages are very useful in comparisons. For example, a relevant figure is the cost percentage. For Prufrock, $.582 of each $1 in sales goes to pay for goods sold. It would be interesting to compute the same percentage for Prufrock's main competitors to see how Prufrock stacks up in terms of cost control.

Ratio Analysis

Another way of avoiding the problems involved in comparing companies of different sizes is to calculate and compare *financial ratios*. Such ratios are ways of comparing and investigating the

---

*This entire appendix is adapted from Rows, S. A., Westerfield, R. W., & Jordan, B. D. 1999. *Essentials of Corporate Finance* (2nd ed.), chap. 3. New York: McGraw-Hill.

	2016	2017
Assets		
Current assets		
Cash	$ 84	$ 98
Accounts receivable	165	188
Inventory	393	422
Total	$ 642	$ 708
Fixed assets		
Net plant and equipment	$2,731	$2,880
Total assets	$3,373	$3,588
Liabilities and Owners' Equity		
Current liabilities		
Accounts payable	$ 312	$ 344
Notes payable	231	196
Total	$ 543	$ 540
Long-term debt	$ 531	$ 457
Owners' equity		
Common stock and paid-in surplus	$ 500	$ 550
Retained earnings	1,799	2,041
Total	$2,299	$2,591
Total liabilities and owners' equity	$3,373	$3,588

Balance sheets as of December 31, 2016 and 2017 ($ millions).

relationships between different pieces of financial information. We cover some of the more common ratios next, but there are many others that we don't touch on.

One problem with ratios is that different people and different sources frequently don't compute them in exactly the same way, and this leads to much confusion. The specific definitions we use here may or may not be the same as others you have seen or will see elsewhere. If you ever use ratios as a tool for analysis, you should be careful to document how you calculate each one, and, if you are comparing your numbers to those of another source, be sure you know how its numbers are computed.

For each of the ratios we discuss, several questions come to mind:

1. How is it computed?
2. What is it intended to measure, and why might we be interested?
3. What is the unit of measurement?
4. What might a high or low value be telling us? How might such values be misleading?
5. How could this measure be improved?

Financial ratios are traditionally grouped into the following categories:

1. Short-term solvency, or liquidity, ratios.
2. Long-term solvency, or financial leverage, ratios.
3. Asset management, or turnover, ratios.
4. Profitability ratios.
5. Market value ratios.

	2016	2017	Change
Assets			
Current assets			
Cash	2.5%	2.7%	+ .2%
Accounts receivable	4.9	5.2	+ .3
Inventory	11.7	11.8	+ .1
Total	19.1	19.7	+ .6
Fixed assets			
Net plant and equipment	80.9	80.3	− .6
Total assets	100.0%	100.0%	.0%
Liabilities and Owners' Equity			
Current liabilities			
Accounts payable	9.2%	9.6%	+ .4%
Notes payable	6.8	5.5	−1.3
Total	16.0	15.1	− .9
Long-term debt	15.7	12.7	−3.0
Owners' equity			
Common stock and paid-in surplus	14.8	15.3	+ .5
Retained earnings	53.3	56.9	+3.6
Total	68.1	72.2	+4.1
Total liabilities and owners' equities	100.0%	100.0%	.0%

Common-size balance sheets as of December 31, 2016 and 2017 (%).

Note: Numbers may not add up to 100.0% due to rounding.

Sales	$2,311
Cost of goods sold	1,344
Depreciation	276
Earnings before interest and taxes	$ 691
Interest paid	141
Taxable income	$ 550
Taxes (34%)	187
Net income	$ 363
Dividends	$121
Addition to retained earnings	242

2017 income statement ($ millions).

Sales	100.0%
Cost of goods sold	58.2
Depreciation	11.9
Earnings before interest and taxes	29.9
Interest paid	6.1
Taxable income	23.8
Taxes (34%)	8.1
Net income	15.7%
Dividends	5.2%
Addition to retained earnings	10.5

2017 Common-size income statement (%).

We will consider each of these in turn. In calculating these numbers for Prufrock, we will use the ending balance sheet (2017) figures unless we explicitly say otherwise. The numbers for the various ratios come from the income statement and the balance sheet.

Short-Term Solvency, or Liquidity, Measures

As the name suggests, short-term solvency ratios as a group are intended to provide information about a firm's liquidity, and these ratios are sometimes called *liquidity measures.* The primary concern is the firm's ability to pay its bills over the short run without undue stress. Consequently, these ratios focus on current assets and current liabilities.

For obvious reasons, liquidity ratios are particularly interesting to short-term creditors. Since financial managers are constantly working with banks and other short-term lenders, an understanding of these ratios is essential.

One advantage of looking at current assets and liabilities is that their book values and market values are likely to be similar. Often (though not always), these assets and liabilities just don't live long enough for the two to get seriously out of step. On the other hand, like any type of near cash, current assets and liabilities can and do change fairly rapidly, so today's amounts may not be a reliable guide to the future.

Current Ratio   One of the best-known and most widely used ratios is the current ratio. As you might guess, the current ratio is defined as:

$$\text{Current ratio} = \frac{\text{Current assets}}{\text{Current liabilities}}$$

For Prufrock, the 2017 current ratio is:

$$\text{Current ratio} = \frac{\$708}{\$540} = 1.31 \text{ times}$$

Because current assets and liabilities are, in principle, converted to cash over the following 12 months, the current ratio is a measure of short-term liquidity. The unit of measurement is either dollars or times. So we could say Prufrock has $1.31 in current assets for every $1 in current liabilities, or we could say Prufrock has its current liabilities covered 1.31 times over.

To a creditor, particularly a short-term creditor such as a supplier, the higher the current ratio, the better. To the firm, a high current ratio indicates liquidity, but it also may indicate an inefficient use of cash and other short-term assets. Absent some extraordinary circumstances, we would expect to see a current ratio of at least 1, because a current ratio of less than 1 would mean that net working capital (current assets less current liabilities) is negative. This would be unusual in a healthy firm, at least for most types of businesses.

The current ratio, like any ratio, is affected by various types of transactions. For example, suppose the firm borrows over the long term to raise money. The short-run effect would be an increase in cash from the issue proceeds and an increase in long-term debt. Current liabilities would not be affected, so the current ratio would rise.

Finally, note that an apparently low current ratio may not be a bad sign for a company with a large reserve of untapped borrowing power.

Quick (or Acid-Test) Ratio Inventory is often the least liquid current asset. It's also the one for which the book values are least reliable as measures of market value, since the quality of the inventory isn't considered. Some of the inventory may later turn out to be damaged, obsolete, or lost.

More to the point, relatively large inventories are often a sign of short-term trouble. The firm may have overestimated sales and overbought or overproduced as a result. In this case, the firm may have a substantial portion of its liquidity tied up in slow-moving inventory.

To further evaluate liquidity, the *quick,* or *acid-test, ratio* is computed just like the current ratio, except inventory is omitted:

$$\text{Quick ratio} = \frac{\text{Current assets} - \text{Inventory}}{\text{Current liabilities}}$$

Notice that using cash to buy inventory does not affect the current ratio, but it reduces the quick ratio. Again, the idea is that inventory is relatively illiquid compared to cash.

For Prufrock, this ratio in 2017 was:

$$\text{Quick ratio} = \frac{\$708 - 422}{\$540} = .53 \text{ times}$$

The quick ratio here tells a somewhat different story than the current ratio, because inventory accounts for more than half of Prufrock's current assets. To exaggerate the point, if this inventory consisted of, say, unsold nuclear power plants, then this would be a cause for concern.

Cash Ratio A very short-term creditor might be interested in the *cash ratio:*

$$\text{Cash ratio} = \frac{\text{Cash}}{\text{Current liabilities}}$$

You can verify that this works out to be .18 times for Prufrock.

Long-Term Solvency Measures

Long-term solvency ratios are intended to address the firm's long-run ability to meet its obligations, or, more generally, its financial leverage. These ratios are sometimes called *financial leverage ratios* or just *leverage ratios.* We consider three commonly used measures and some variations.

Total Debt Ratio The *total debt ratio* takes into account all debts of all maturities to all creditors. It can be defined in several ways, the easiest of which is:

$$\text{Total debt ratio} = \frac{\text{Total assets} - \text{Total equity}}{\text{Total assets}}$$

$$= \frac{\$3,588 - 2,591}{\$3,588} = .28 \text{ times}$$

In this case, an analyst might say that Prufrock uses 28 percent debt.[1] Whether this is high or low or whether it even makes any difference depends on whether or not capital structure matters.

---

[1]Total equity here includes preferred stock, if there is any. An equivalent numerator in this ratio would be (Current liabilities + Long-term debt).

Prufrock has $.28 in debt for every $1 in assets. Therefore, there is $.72 in equity ($1 − .28) for every $.28 in debt. With this in mind, we can define two useful variations on the total debt ratio, the *debt-equity ratio* and the *equity multiplier:*

$$\text{Debt−equity ratio} = \text{Total debt/Total equity}$$
$$= \$.28/\$.72 = .39 \text{ times}$$
$$\text{Equity multiplier} = \text{Total assets/Total equity}$$
$$= \$1/\$.72 = 1.39 \text{ times}$$

The fact that the equity multiplier is 1 plus the debt-equity ratio is not a coincidence:

$$\text{Equity multiplier} = \text{Total assets/Total equity} = \$1/\$.72 = 1.39$$
$$= (\text{Total equity} + \text{Total debt})/\text{Total equity}$$
$$= 1 + \text{Debt−equity ratio} = 1.39 \text{ times}$$

The thing to notice here is that given any one of these three ratios, you can immediately calculate the other two, so they all say exactly the same thing.

Times Interest Earned   Another common measure of long-term solvency is the *times interest earned* (TIE) *ratio.* Once again, there are several possible (and common) definitions, but we'll stick with the most traditional:

$$\text{Times interest earned ratio} = \frac{\text{EBIT}}{\text{Interest paid}}$$
$$= \frac{\$691}{\$141} = 4.9 \text{ times}$$

As the name suggests, this ratio measures how well a company has its interest obligations covered, and it is often called the *interest coverage ratio.* For Prufrock, the interest bill is covered 4.9 times over.

Cash Coverage   A problem with the TIE ratio is that it is based on earnings before interest and taxes (EBIT), which is not really a measure of cash available to pay interest. The reason is that depreciation, a noncash expense, has been deducted. Since interest is most definitely a cash outflow (to creditors), one way to define the *cash coverage ratio* is:

$$\text{Cash coverage ratio} = \frac{\text{EBIT} + \text{Depreciation}}{\text{Interest paid}}$$
$$= \frac{\$691 + 276}{\$141} = \frac{\$967}{\$141} = 6.9 \text{ times}$$

The numerator here, EBIT plus depreciation, is often abbreviated EBDIT (earnings before depreciation, interest, and taxes). It is a basic measure of the firm's ability to generate cash from operations, and it is frequently used as a measure of cash flow available to meet financial obligations.

Asset Management, or Turnover, Measures

We next turn our attention to the efficiency with which Prufrock uses its assets. The measures in this section are sometimes called *asset utilization ratios.* The specific ratios we discuss can all be interpreted as measures of turnover. What they are intended to describe is how efficiently, or intensively, a firm uses its assets to generate sales. We first look at two important current assets: inventory and receivables.

Inventory Turnover and Days' Sales in Inventory   During the year, Prufrock had a cost of goods sold of $1,344. Inventory at the end of the year was $422. With these numbers, *inventory turnover* can be calculated as:

$$\text{Inventory turnover} = \frac{\text{Cost of goods sold}}{\text{Inventory}}$$

$$= \frac{\$1,344}{\$422} = 3.2 \text{ times}$$

In a sense, we sold off, or turned over, the entire inventory 3.2 times. As long as we are not running out of stock and thereby forgoing sales, the higher this ratio is, the more efficiently we are managing inventory.

If we know that we turned our inventory over 3.2 times during the year, then we can immediately figure out how long it took us to turn it over on average. The result is the average *days' sales in inventory:*

$$\text{Day's sales in inventory} = \frac{365 \text{ days}}{\text{Inventory turnover}}$$

$$= \frac{365}{3.2} = 114 \text{ days}$$

This tells us that, on average, inventory sits 114 days before it is sold. Alternatively, assuming we used the most recent inventory and cost figures, it will take about 114 days to work off our current inventory.

For example, we frequently hear things like "Majestic Motors has a 60 days' supply of cars." This means that, at current daily sales, it would take 60 days to deplete the available inventory. We could also say that Majestic has 60 days of sales in inventory.

Receivables Turnover and Days' Sales in Receivables   Our inventory measures give some indication of how fast we can sell products. We now look at how fast we collect on those sales. The *receivables turnover* is defined in the same way as inventory turnover:

$$\text{Receivables turnover} = \frac{\text{Sales}}{\text{Accounts receivable}}$$

$$= \frac{\$2,311}{\$188} = 12.3 \text{ times}$$

Loosely speaking, we collected our outstanding credit accounts and reloaned the money 12.3 times during the year.[2]

This ratio makes more sense if we convert it to days, so the *days' sales in receivables* is:

$$\text{Day's sales in receivables} = \frac{365 \text{ days}}{\text{Receivables turnover}}$$

$$= \frac{365}{12.3} = 30 \text{ days}$$

Therefore, on average, we collect on our credit sales in 30 days. For obvious reasons, this ratio is very frequently called the *average collection period* (ACP).

Also note that if we are using the most recent figures, we can also say that we have 30 days' worth of sales currently uncollected.

Total Asset Turnover   Moving away from specific accounts like inventory or receivables, we can consider an important "big picture" ratio, the *total asset turnover ratio*. As the name suggests, total asset turnover is:

---

[2]Here we have implicitly assumed that all sales are credit sales. If they were not, then we would simply use total credit sales in these calculations, not total sales.

$$\text{Total asset turnover} = \frac{\text{Sales}}{\text{Total assets}}$$

$$= \frac{\$2,311}{\$3,588} = .64 \text{ times}$$

In other words, for every dollar in assets, we generated $.64 in sales.

A closely related ratio, the *capital intensity ratio,* is simply the reciprocal of (i.e., 1 divided by) total asset turnover. It can be interpreted as the dollar investment in assets needed to generate $1 in sales. High values correspond to capital-intensive industries (e.g., public utilities). For Prufrock, total asset turnover is .64, so, if we flip this over, we get that capital intensity is $1/.64 = $1.56. That is, it takes Prufrock $1.56 in assets to create $1 in sales.

Profitability Measures

The three measures we discuss in this section are probably the best known and most widely used of all financial ratios. In one form or another, they are intended to measure how efficiently the firm uses its assets and how efficiently the firm manages its operations. The focus in this group is on the bottom line, net income.

Profit Margin Companies pay a great deal of attention to their *profit margin:*

$$\text{Profit margin} = \frac{\text{Net income}}{\text{Sales}}$$

$$= \frac{\$363}{\$2,311} = 15.7\%$$

This tells us that Prufrock, in an accounting sense, generates a little less than 16 cents in profit for every dollar in sales.

All other things being equal, a relatively high profit margin is obviously desirable. This situation corresponds to low expense ratios relative to sales. However, we hasten to add that other things are often not equal.

For example, lowering our sales price will usually increase unit volume, but will normally cause profit margins to shrink. Total profit (or, more importantly, operating cash flow) may go up or down; so the fact that margins are smaller isn't necessarily bad. After all, isn't it possible that, as the saying goes, "Our prices are so low that we lose money on everything we sell, but we make it up in volume!"[3]

Return on Assets *Return on assets* (ROA) is a measure of profit per dollar of assets. It can be defined several ways, but the most common is:

$$\text{Return on assets} = \frac{\text{Net income}}{\text{Total assets}}$$

$$= \frac{\$363}{\$3,588} = 10.12\%$$

Return on Equity *Return on equity* (ROE) is a measure of how the stockholders fared during the year. Since benefiting shareholders is our goal, ROE is, in an accounting sense, the true bottom-line measure of performance. ROE is usually measured as:

$$\text{Return on enquiry} = \frac{\text{Net income}}{\text{Total enquiry}}$$

$$= \frac{\$363}{\$2,591} = 14\%$$

---

[3]No, it's not; margins can be small, but they do need to be positive!

For every dollar in equity, therefore, Prufrock generated 14 cents in profit, but, again, this is only correct in accounting terms.

Because ROA and ROE are such commonly cited numbers, we stress that it is important to remember they are accounting rates of return. For this reason, these measures should properly be called *return on book assets* and *return on book equity*. In addition, ROE is sometimes called *return on net worth*. Whatever it's called, it would be inappropriate to compare the results to, for example, an interest rate observed in the financial markets.

The fact that ROE exceeds ROA reflects Prufrock's use of financial leverage. We will examine the relationship between these two measures in more detail below.

Market Value Measures

Our final group of measures is based, in part, on information not necessarily contained in financial statements—the market price per share of the stock. Obviously, these measures can be calculated directly only for publicly traded companies.

We assume that Prufrock has 33 million shares outstanding and the stock sold for $88 per share at the end of the year. If we recall that Prufrock's net income was $363 million, then we can calculate that its earnings per share were:

$$\text{EPS} = \frac{\text{Net income}}{\text{Shares outstanding}} = \frac{\$363}{33} = \$11$$

Price-Earnings Ratio   The first of our market value measures, the *price-earnings,* or PE, *ratio* (or multiple), is defined as:

$$\text{PE ratio} = \frac{\text{Price per share}}{\text{Earning per share}}$$
$$= \frac{\$88}{\$11} = 8 \text{ times}$$

In the vernacular, we would say that Prufrock shares sell for eight times earnings, or we might say that Prufrock shares have, or "carry," a PE multiple of 8.

Since the PE ratio measures how much investors are willing to pay per dollar of current earnings, higher PEs are often taken to mean that the firm has significant prospects for future growth. Of course, if a firm had no or almost no earnings, its PE would probably be quite large; so, as always, be careful when interpreting this ratio.

Market-to-Book Ratio   A second commonly quoted measure is the *market-to-book ratio:*

$$\text{Market-to-book ratio} = \frac{\text{Market value per share}}{\text{Book value per share}}$$
$$= \frac{\$88}{(\$2,591/33)} = \frac{\$88}{\$78.5} = 1.12 \text{ times}$$

Notice that book value per share is total equity (not just common stock) divided by the number of shares outstanding.

Since book value per share is an accounting number, it reflects historical costs. In a loose sense, the market-to-book ratio therefore compares the market value of the firm's investments to their cost. A value less than 1 could mean that the firm has not been successful overall in creating value for its stockholders.

Conclusion

This completes our definition of some common ratios. Exhibit 13A.5 summarizes the ratios we've discussed.

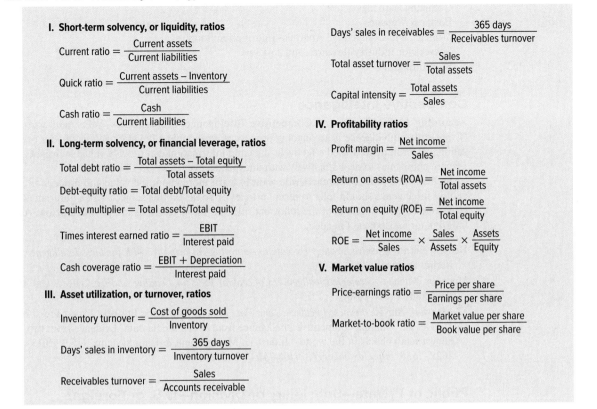

I. Short-term solvency, or liquidity, ratios

$$\text{Current ratio} = \frac{\text{Current assets}}{\text{Current liabilities}}$$

$$\text{Quick ratio} = \frac{\text{Current assets} - \text{Inventory}}{\text{Current liabilities}}$$

$$\text{Cash ratio} = \frac{\text{Cash}}{\text{Current liabilities}}$$

II. Long-term solvency, or financial leverage, ratios

$$\text{Total debt ratio} = \frac{\text{Total assets} - \text{Total equity}}{\text{Total assets}}$$

$$\text{Debt-equity ratio} = \text{Total debt/Total equity}$$

$$\text{Equity multiplier} = \text{Total assets/Total equity}$$

$$\text{Times interest earned ratio} = \frac{\text{EBIT}}{\text{Interest paid}}$$

$$\text{Cash coverage ratio} = \frac{\text{EBIT} + \text{Depreciation}}{\text{Interest paid}}$$

III. Asset utilization, or turnover, ratios

$$\text{Inventory turnover} = \frac{\text{Cost of goods sold}}{\text{Inventory}}$$

$$\text{Days' sales in inventory} = \frac{365 \text{ days}}{\text{Inventory turnover}}$$

$$\text{Receivables turnover} = \frac{\text{Sales}}{\text{Accounts receivable}}$$

$$\text{Days' sales in receivables} = \frac{365 \text{ days}}{\text{Receivables turnover}}$$

$$\text{Total asset turnover} = \frac{\text{Sales}}{\text{Total assets}}$$

$$\text{Capital intensity} = \frac{\text{Total assets}}{\text{Sales}}$$

IV. Profitability ratios

$$\text{Profit margin} = \frac{\text{Net income}}{\text{Sales}}$$

$$\text{Return on assets (ROA)} = \frac{\text{Net income}}{\text{Total assets}}$$

$$\text{Return on equity (ROE)} = \frac{\text{Net income}}{\text{Total equity}}$$

$$\text{ROE} = \frac{\text{Net income}}{\text{Sales}} \times \frac{\text{Sales}}{\text{Assets}} \times \frac{\text{Assets}}{\text{Equity}}$$

V. Market value ratios

$$\text{Price-earnings ratio} = \frac{\text{Price per share}}{\text{Earnings per share}}$$

$$\text{Market-to-book ratio} = \frac{\text{Market value per share}}{\text{Book value per share}}$$

APPENDIX 2 TO CHAPTER 13

SOURCES OF COMPANY AND INDUSTRY INFORMATION*

In order for business executives to make the best decisions when developing corporate strategy, it is critical for them to be knowledgeable about their competitors and about the industries in which they compete. The process used by corporations to learn as much as possible about competitors is often called "competitive intelligence." This appendix provides an overview of important and widely available sources of information that may be useful in conducting basic competitive intelligence. Much information of this nature is available in libraries in article databases and business reference books and on websites. This appendix will recommend a variety of them. Ask a librarian for assistance, because library collections and resources vary.

The information sources are organized into 10 categories:

Competitive Intelligence

Public or Private—Subsidiary or Division—U.S. or Foreign?

Finding Public-Company Information

Guides and Tutorials

*This information was compiled by Ruthie Brock and Carol Byrne, business librarians at The University of Texas at Arlington. We greatly appreciate their valuable contribution.

SEC Filings/EDGAR—Company Disclosure Reports
Company Rankings
Business Websites
Strategic and Competitive Analysis—Information Sources
Sources for Industry Research and Analysis
Search Engines

Competitive Intelligence

According to the Society of Competitive Intelligence Professionals (*http://www.scip.org*), "Competitive Intelligence is an ongoing process of developing a holistic analysis of your organizational environment. If used effectively, data and information can provide valuable insights and prepare companies to deal effectively with unexpected events."

Students and other researchers who want to learn more about the value and process of competitive intelligence should refer to recent articles or books on this subject. Ask a librarian about electronic (ebook) versions of the following titles. A few suggestions are provided below. Ask a librarian for assistance, if needed.

Heesen, Bernd. *Effective Strategy Execution: Improving Performance with Business Intelligence.* Berlin: Springer, 2015.

Maccoby, Michael. *Strategic Intelligence: Conceptual Tools for Leading Change.* Oxford: Oxford University Press, 2015.

Maheshwari, Anil K. *Business Intelligence and Data Mining.* New York: Business Expert Press, 2015.

He, Wu, et al. "Gaining competitive intelligence from social media data: Evidence from two largest retail chains in the world." Industrial Management & Data Systems, 115.9 (2015): 1622–1636. *http://dx.doi.org/10.1108/IMDS-03-2015-0098*

Public or Private—Subsidiary or Division—U.S. or Foreign?

Companies traded on stock exchanges in the United States are required to file a variety of reports that disclose information about the company. This begins the process that produces a wealth of data on public companies and, at the same time, distinguishes them from private companies, which often lack available data. Similarly, financial data of subsidiaries and divisions are typically filed in a consolidated financial statement by the parent company, rather than treated independently, thus limiting the kind of data available on them. On the other hand, foreign companies that trade on U.S. stock exchanges are required to file 20F reports, similar to the 10-K for U.S. companies, the most comprehensive of the required reports. The following directories provide brief facts about companies, including whether they are public or private, subsidiary or division, U.S. or foreign.

Corporate Affiliations. New York, NY: RELX, Inc. (formerly Reed Elsevier), 2017.
   This database of nearly 2 million corporate family relationships identifies ownership between entities such as ultimate parent, parent, subsidiary, joint venture, affiliate, division, factory or plant, branch, group, holding, and non-operating entities (shells). The database content includes both public and private companies, primarily large with U.S.-located headquarters. Detailed executive and board member profiles are provided. Mergers and acquisitions are tracked from announcement to post-merger organizational changes. Corporate Affiliations data is compiled by the LexisNexis Enterprise Entity Management Group. Downloading from multiple searches to one customized spreadsheet is a new feature. Some historical data is also available. Hard copy volumes can be purchased.

ReferenceUSA. Omaha, NE: Infogroup.Inc.
   ReferenceUSA is an online directory of more than 15 million verified businesses located in the United States plus 30 million unverified. New businesses and closed businesses are searchable separately. This resource includes both public and private companies regardless of how small or large, as well as educational, medical, and nonprofit organizations. Job opportunities are provided by *Indeed.com* in search results when available. Specialized

modules include consumer lifestyles, historical records, and health care. Check with a librarian regarding availability of specialized modules at your location.

Finding Public-Company Information

Most companies provide their annual report to shareholders and other financial reports are available on their corporate website usually listed under "Investor Relations" or similar headings. Searching Google with the company's name and annual report or 10K report finds most companies financials. Be aware that all company documents are by default told in the most positive language and images; therefore serious research should include analysts' assessments, SWOT analyses, and newspaper or magazine articles to get a complete and less biased view of the company's strengths and weaknesses.

Mergent Online. Fort Mill, SC: Mergent, Inc.

Mergent Online is a database that provides company reports and financial statements for both U.S. and foreign public companies. Mergent's database has up to 25 years of quarterly and annual financial data that can be downloaded into a spreadsheet for analysis across time or across companies. Tabs lead to other features for further analysis. Students should check with a librarian to determine the availability of this database at their college or university library.

http://mergentonline.com

Guides & Tutorials for Researching Companies and Industries

Researching Public Companies through EDGAR: A Guide for Investors. Washington DC: U.S. Securities and Exchange Commission.

This guide informs EDGAR database users about two different search interfaces: the EDGAR Full-Text Search which searches the full-text filings from the last four years only and the Historical EDGAR Archives Search which searches the headings information only (not full text) for a longer period, from 1994 to 2017 (up to yesterday's filings). Each version has some advantages and disadvantages for the user, depending on how exhaustive their research is.

https://www.sec.gov/investor/pubs/edgarguide.htm

Ten Steps to Industry Intelligence Research. Industry Tutorial. George A. Smathers Libraries, University of Florida, Gainesville, FL.

This tutorial provides a step-by-step approach for finding information about industries, with embedded links to recommended sources.

http://businesslibrary.uflib.ufl.edu/industryresearch

Conducting Business Research. University of Texas at Austin Libraries, Austin, TX.

This tutorial provides a step-by-step process for business research.

www.lib.utexas.edu/services/instruction/learningmodules/businessresearch/intro.html

Guide to Financial Statements. Armonk, NY: IBM.

International Business Machines (IBM) created an educational guide for beginners to learn how to understand and interpret a typical financial statement in a company's annual report.

http://www.ibm.com/investor/help/guide/introduction.wss

How to Read Annual Reports. Armonk, NY: IBM.

An annual report is one of the most important documents a company produces and is often the first document someone consults when researching a company. Created by IBM, this guide explains the purpose of each of the elements that are included in annual reports or 10-K reports, so that novices who are not familiar with business terminology and financials are able to understand.

http://www.ibm.com/investor/help/reports/introduction.wss

Ten Steps to Company Intelligence. Company Research Tutorial. William and Joan Schreyer Business Library, Penn State University, University Park, PA.

This tutorial provides a step-by-step approach to finding company intelligence information.

http://businesslibrary.uflib.ufl.edu/companyresearch

SEC Filings/EDGAR—Company Disclosure Reports

SEC Filings are the various reports that publicly traded companies must file with the Securities and Exchange Commission to disclose information about their corporation. These are often referred to as "EDGAR" filings, an acronym for the Electronic Data Gathering, Analysis and Retrieval System. Some websites and commercial databases improve access to these reports by offering additional retrieval features not available on the official *(www.sec.gov)* website.

EDGAR Database. U.S. Securities and Exchange Commission (SEC), Washington, DC.

Public companies are required to disclose financial information for the benefit of shareholders and other interested researchers and investors. The SEC is the agency which oversees the process and provides free access to more than 21 million filings in their EDGAR database. See also the guide described previously called: *Researching Public Companies through EDGAR. www.sec.gov/edgar/searchedgar/companysearch.html*

LexisNexis Nexis Uni. SEC Filings & Reports. Bethesda, MD: LexisNexis.

SEC filings are available in *Nexis Uni* by selecting "Search by Subject or Topic." Under the Companies category, select SEC Filings. A company-name search or an advanced search can be conducted at that point.

Mergent Online—Government Filings Search.

This database also provides an alternative search interface for SEC filings. *Mergent's Government Filings* search allows searching by company name, ticker, CIK (Central Index Key) number, or industry SIC number. The search can be limited by date and by type of SEC file. Ask a librarian whether your library subscribes to *Mergent Online* for this feature.

Company Rankings

Fortune 500. New York: Time Inc.

The *Fortune 500* list and other company rankings are published in the printed edition of *Fortune* magazine and are also available online.

http://beta.fortune.com/fortune500

Forbes Global 2000. Forbes, Inc.

The companies listed on the Forbes Global 2000 are the biggest and most powerful in the world.

www.forbes.com/global2000/

Business Websites

Big Charts. San Francisco: MarketWatch, Inc.

BigCharts is an easy-to-use investment research website operated by and linked to *MarketWatch.com*. Research tools such as interactive charts, current and historical quotes, industry analysis, and intraday stock screeners, as well as market news and commentary are provided. Supported by site sponsors, it is free to self-directed investors.

http://bigcharts.marketwatch.com/

GlobalEdge. East Lansing, MI: Michigan State University.

GlobalEdge is a web portal providing a significant amount of information about international business, countries around the globe, the U.S. states, industries, and news.

http://globaledge.msu.edu/

Yahoo Finance. Sunnyvale, CA: Yahoo! Inc.

The finance section of Yahoo's website on U.S. world markets, financial news, and other information useful to investors.

http://finance.yahoo.com

Strategic and Competitive Analysis—Information Sources

Analyzing a company can take the form of examining its internal and external environments. In the process, it is useful to identify the company's strengths, weaknesses, opportunities, and threats (SWOT). Sources for this kind of analysis are varied, but perhaps the best would be articles from *The Wall Street Journal,* business magazines, and industry trade publications.

Publications such as these can be found in the following databases available at many public and academic libraries. When using a database that is structured to allow it, try searching the company name combined with one or more keywords, such as "IBM and competition" or "Microsoft and lawsuits" or "AMR and fuel costs" to retrieve articles relating to the external environment.

ABI/INFORM Complete. Ann Arbor, MI: ProQuest LLC.

ABI/INFORM Complete provides abstracts and full-text articles covering disciplines such as management, law, taxation, economics, health care, and information technology from more than 6,800 scholarly, business, and trade publications. Other types of resources include company and industry reports, case studies, market research reports, and a variety of downloadable economic data.

Business Insights: Essentials. Farmington Hills, MI: Gale CENGAGE Learning.

Business Insights provides company and industry intelligence for a selection of public and private companies. Company profiles include parent-subsidiary relationships, industry rankings, products and brands, industry statistics, and financial ratios. Selections of SWOT analysis reports are also available. The Company and Industry comparison tool allows a researcher to compare up to six companies' revenues, employees, and sales data over time. Results are available as an image, chart, or spreadsheet.

Business Source Complete. Ipswich, MA: EBSCO Industries.

Business Source Complete is a full-text database with over 3,800 scholarly business journals covering management, economics, finance, accounting, international business, and more. The database also includes detailed company profiles for more than one million public and private companies, as well as selected country economic reports provided by the Economist Intelligence Unit (EIU). The database includes case studies, investment and market research reports, SWOT analyses, and more. *Business Source Complete* contains over 2,400 peer-reviewed business journals.

Hoover's Academic. Short Hills, NJ: Dun & Bradstreet.

Hoover's provides company and industry information for over 85 million public and private U.S. and international companies. The company profiles include the company's history, key financials, and executive information, as well as access to the latest news stories and SEC filings. Over 900 industries are covered in *Hoover's*.

IBISWorld. Los Angeles, CA: IBISWorld.

The database provides access to detailed industry reports for over 700-plus United States industries. Each report includes industry structure, market characteristics, product and customer segments, cost structure, industry conditions, major players, market share, supply chain structure, and 5-year revenue forecasts. Separate subscriptions are required for the Global and China industry reports.

OneSource. Short Hills, NJ: Dun & Bradstreet.

OneSource provides a wealth of information about U.S. and international public and private companies. The profiles include key executives, a financial report, and the corporate family structure. Also available are recent analyst reports, company SWOT analyses, industry reports, news and SEC filings information. Custom reports can be created and downloaded.

Thomson ONE Research.

Thomson ONE Research offers full-text analytical reports on more than 65,000 companies worldwide. The research reports are excellent sources for strategic and financial profiles of a company and its competitors and of industry trends. Developed by a global roster of brokerage, investment banking, and research firms, these full-text investment reports include a wealth of current and historical information useful for evaluating a company or industry over time.

International Directory of Company Histories. Detroit, MI: St. James Press, 1988–present. 187 volumes to date.

This directory covers more than 11,000 multinational companies, and the series is still adding volumes. Each company history is approximately three to five pages in length and provides a summary of the company's mission, goals, and ideals, followed by company milestones, principal subsidiaries, and competitors. Strategic decisions made during the company's period of existence are usually noted. This series covers public and private companies and nonprofit entities. Entry information includes a company's legal name, headquarters information, URL, incorporation date, ticker symbol, stock exchange listing, sales figures, and the primary North American Industry Classification System (NAICS) code. Further reading selections complete the entry information. Volumes 59 to the most recent are available electronically in the Gale Virtual Reference Library database from Gale CENGAGE Learning.

LexisNexis Academic. Bethesda, MD: LexisNexis.

LexisNexis Academic provides access to legal, company, and industry information, news sources, and public records. Industry information is available through the Company Info tab or the "Search by content type" selection. The Company Dossier tool allows a researcher to compare up to five companies' financial statements at one time with download capabilities.

The Wall Street Journal. New York: Dow Jones & Co.

This respected business newspaper is available in searchable full text from 1984 to the present in the *Factiva* database. The "News Pages" link provides access to current articles and issues of *The Wall Street Journal.* Dow Jones, publisher of the print version of the *Wall Street Journal,* also has an online subscription available at *wsj.com.* Some libraries provide access to *The Wall Street Journal* through the ProQuest Newspapers database.

Sources for Industry Research and Analysis

Factiva. New York: Dow Jones & Co.

The *Factiva* database has several options for researching an industry. One would be to search the database for articles in the business magazines and industry trade publications. A second option in *Factiva* would be to search in the Companies/Markets category for company/industry comparison reports.

Mergent Online. New York: Mergent Inc.

Mergent Online is a searchable database of over 60,000 global public companies. The database offers worldwide industry reports, U.S. and global competitors, and executive biographical information. *Mergent's* Basic Search option permits searching by primary industry codes (either SIC or NAICS). Once the search is executed, companies in that industry should be listed. A comparison or standard peer-group analysis can be created to analyze companies in the same industry on various criteria. The Advanced Search allows the user to search a wider range of financial and textual information. Results, including ratios for a company and its competitors, can be downloaded to a spreadsheet.

North American Industry Classification System (NAICS)

The North American Industry Classification System has officially replaced the Standard Industrial Classification (SIC) as the numerical structure used to define and analyze industries, although some publications and databases offer both classification systems. The NAICS codes are used in Canada, the United States, and Mexico. In the United States, the NAICS codes are used to conduct an Economic Census every five years providing a snapshot of the U.S. economy at a given moment in time.

NAICS: *www.census.gov/eos/www/naics/*

Economic Census: *www.census.gov/programs-surveys/economic-census/year.html*

NetAdvantage. New York: S & P Capital IQ.

The database includes company, financial, and investment information as well as the well-known publication called *Industry Surveys.* Each industry report includes information on the current environment, industry trends, key industry ratios and statistics, and comparative company financial analysis. Available in HTML, PDF, or Excel formats.

Business Insights: Essentials. Farmington Hills, MI: Gale CENGAGE Learning.

Business Insights provides company and industry intelligence for a selection of public and private companies. Company profiles include parent-subsidiary relationships, industry rankings, products and brands, industry statistics, and financial ratios. Selections of SWOT analysis reports are also available. The Company and Industry comparison tool allows a researcher to compare up to six companies' revenues, employees, and sales data over time. Results are available as an image, chart, or spreadsheet.

Plunkett Research Online. Houston, TX: Plunkett Research, Ltd.

Plunkett's provides industry-specific market research, trends analysis, and business intelligence for 34 industries.

Search Engines

Google. Mountain View, CA: Google, Inc.

Recognized for its advanced technology, quality of results, and simplicity, the search engine Google is highly recommended by librarians and other expert web surfers.

www.google.com

Dogpile. Bellevue, WA: InfoSpace, Inc.

Dogpile is a metasearch engine that searches and compiles the most relevant results from more than 12 individual search engines.

http://www.dogpile.com/

CASE 1

ROBIN HOOD*

It was in the spring of the second year of his insurrection against the High Sheriff of Nottingham that Robin Hood took a walk in Sherwood Forest. As he walked he pondered the progress of the campaign, the disposition of his forces, the Sheriff's recent moves, and the options that confronted him.

The revolt against the Sheriff had begun as a personal crusade, erupting out of Robin's conflict with the Sheriff and his administration. Alone, however, Robin Hood could do little. He therefore sought allies, men with grievances and a deep sense of justice. Later he welcomed all who came, asking few questions, and only demanding a willingness to serve. Strength, he believed, lay in numbers.

He spent the first year forging the group into a disciplined band, united in enmity against the Sheriff, and willing to live outside the law. The band's organization was simple. Robin ruled supreme, making all important decisions. He delegated specific tasks to his lieutenants. Will Scarlett was in charge of intelligence and scouting. His main job was to shadow the Sheriff and his men, always alert to their next move. He also collected information on the travel plans of rich merchants and tax collectors. Little John kept discipline among the men, and saw to it that their archery was at the high peak that their profession demanded. Scarlock took care of the finances, converting loot into cash, paying shares of the take, and finding suitable hiding places for the surplus. Finally, Much the Miller's son had the difficult task of provisioning the ever-increasing band of Merrymen.

The increasing size of the band was a source of satisfaction for Robin, but also a source of concern. The fame of his Merrymen was spreading, and new recruits poured in from every corner of England. As the band grew larger, their small bivouac became a major encampment. Between raids the men milled about, talking and playing games. Vigilance was in decline, and discipline was becoming harder to enforce. "Why," Robin reflected, "I don't know half the men I run into these days."

The growing band was also beginning to exceed the food capacity of the forest. Game was becoming scarce, and supplies had to be obtained from outlying villages. The cost of buying food was beginning to drain the band's financial reserves at the very moment when revenues were in decline. Travelers, especially those with the most to lose, were now giving the forest a wide berth. This was costly and inconvenient to them, but it was preferable to having all their goods confiscated.

Robin believed that the time had come for the Merrymen to change their policy of outright confiscation of goods to one of a fixed transit tax. His lieutenants strongly resisted this idea. They were proud of the Merrymen's famous motto: "Rob the rich and give to the poor." "The farmers and the townspeople," they argued, "are our most important allies. How can we tax them, and still hope for their help in our fight against the Sheriff?"

Robin wondered how long the Merrymen could keep to the ways and methods of their early days. The Sheriff was growing stronger and better organized. He now had the money and the men, and was beginning to harass the band, probing for its weaknesses.

The tide of events was beginning to turn against the Merrymen. Robin felt that the campaign must be decisively concluded before the Sheriff had a chance to deliver a mortal blow. "But how," he wondered, "could this be done?"

Robin had often entertained the possibility of killing the Sheriff, but the chances for this seemed increasingly remote. Besides, while killing the Sheriff might satisfy his personal thirst for revenge, it would not improve the situation. Robin had hoped that the perpetual state of unrest, and the Sheriff's failure to collect taxes, would lead to his removal from office. Instead, the Sheriff used his political connections to obtain reinforcement. He had powerful friends at court, and was well regarded by the regent, Prince John.

Prince John was vicious and volatile. He was consumed by his unpopularity among the people, who wanted the imprisoned King Richard back. He also lived in constant fear of the barons, who had first given him the regency, but were now beginning to dispute his claim to the throne. Several of these barons had set out to collect the ransom that would release King Richard the Lionheart from his jail in Austria. Robin was invited to join the conspiracy in return for future amnesty. It was a dangerous proposition. Provincial banditry was one thing, court intrigue another. Prince John's spies were everywhere. If the plan failed, the pursuit would be relentless and retribution swift.

The sound of the supper horn startled Robin from his thoughts. There was the smell of roasting venison in the air. Nothing was resolved or settled. Robin headed for camp promising himself that he would give these problems his utmost attention after tomorrow's raid.

---

* Prepared by Joseph Lampel, City University, London. Copyright Joseph Lampel © 1985, revised 1991. Reprinted with permission.

CASE 2

THE GLOBAL CASINO INDUSTRY IN 2017*

For well over fifty years, the casino business has been on a roll, on its way to becoming a $150 billion a year global industry. For much of that period, the U.S. has been leading the charge, accounting for nearly half the global gambling revenues as recently as 2010. Most of these revenues have come from Las Vegas and Atlantic City, magnets for gamblers from around the world. Over the last couple of decades, these two locations have accounted for a large portion of the total revenues generated by all forms of casinos throughout the United States.

Over the past decade, however, Las Vegas and Atlantic City have had to deal with increased competition from other locales, as casinos have opened all across the U.S. as other states have legalized gambling in order to generate more tax revenues and to promote tourism. Over a dozen states now generate substantial revenue from their casinos, many of which have opened on waterfronts such as rivers and lakes. When combined with Native American casinos, gambling revenues in other parts of the U.S. now exceed those generated by casinos in Las Vegas and Atlantic City.

Casinos in Las Vegas and Atlantic City are able to rely upon gamblers who come from all over the world, as far away as China. Although casinos have operated for a long time in Europe and the Caribbean, no single location was ever able to compete with Las Vegas or Atlantic City. Las Vegas offers more than two dozen large casinos on its strip that have spent lavishly to differentiate themselves from all others. Luxor's pyramids and columns evoke ancient Egypt; Mandalay Bay borrows looks from the Pacific Rim; and the Venetian's plaza and canals re-create the Italian destination.

But more recently, the dominance of Las Vegas and Atlantic City in the global market has been challenged by the development of several casinos along a strip in the former Portuguese colony of Macau. Casinos have existed in Macau for decades, but basically served a local population. Since a monopoly on casinos by a single local tycoon was terminated in 2002, there has been a proliferation of mega-sized high-end casinos there, developed and managed by some of the world's largest casino operators, including those from Las Vegas. This has allowed Macau to grow from a tiny backwater territory to a booming center of gambling, with casinos generating over $40 billion, more than six times that of the Las Vegas strip (see Exhibit 1).

Casinos have spread to other locations across the Asia-Pacific region. Singapore already has two casinos, while the Philippines is opening new ones and Japan is planning to legalize them. Yet even as casinos are expanding into new locations, there are concerns about the potential for gaming revenues. Revenues from gaming have dipped considerably in locations like Macau and Atlantic City over the last three years, while they are still recovering in Las Vegas. Casino owners are trying to figure out how to draw in more gamblers by creating more interest among the younger generation.

Riding an American Wave

Although gambling has existed in the U.S. since colonial times, the recent advent of casinos can be traced back to the legalization of gaming in Nevada in 1931. For many years, this was the only state in which casinos were allowed. After New Jersey passed laws in 1976 to allow gambling in Atlantic City, the large population on the east coast acquired easier access to casinos. Since 1988, more and more states have begun to legalize the operation of casinos because of the tax revenues that they can generate.

As casinos have spread across the U.S., there has been a growing tendency to regard casino gambling as an acceptable form of entertainment for a night out. A large part of the growth in casino revenues has come from slot machines. These coin-operated devices typically account for almost two-thirds of all casino gaming revenues (see Exhibit 2). A major reason for their popularity is that it is easier for prospective gamblers to feed a slot machine than to master the nuances of various table games.

EXHIBIT 1 Top Casino Revenue Locations, 2016 ($ billions)

Location	Revenue
Macau	$32.0
United States	30.0[1]
Singapore	6.0
Australia	4.0
South Korea	2.5
Malaysia	2.0
Philippines	2.0

[1]$6.0 billion comes from Las Vegas.

Source: Morgan Stanley.

* Case prepared by Jamal Shamsie, Michigan State University, with the assistance of Professor Alan B. Eisner, Pace University. Material has been drawn from published sources to be used for purposes of class discussion. Copyright © 2017 Jamal Shamsie and Alan B. Eisner.

EXHIBIT 2 Favorite U.S. Casino Games, 2016

Slot machines	61%
Blackjack	19
Roulette	8
Poker	4
Craps	4

Source: American Gaming Association; author estimates.

EXHIBIT 3 Financials of Macau Casinos, 2016

	Share of Revenues	Share of Profits
High rollers	63%	35%
Low rollers	34	52

Source: Deutsche Bank; author estimates.

Over the years casinos in Las Vegas and Atlantic City have tried to draw gamblers by developing extravagant new properties. The most ambitious recent development in Las Vegas was the opening by MGM Mirage of its City Center, an $8.5 billion mini-city spread over 67 acres that includes luxury hotels, condominium units, restaurants, and shops. Even some of the older properties have undergone extensive renovation, such as Caesars Palace adding a new Colosseum and a new Roman Plaza. Atlantic City welcomed the much-ballyhooed opening of the $2.4 billion Revel Hotel built on 20 acres of beachfront, following the opening several years earlier of another lavish resort, the Borgota Hotel, which offered amenities such as penthouse spas and tropical indoor pools.

Aside from ramping up the appeal of their particular properties, most casinos have also offered incentives to keep their customers from moving over to competitors. These incentives can be particularly helpful in retaining those high rollers who come often and spend large amounts of money. Casinos try to maintain their business by providing complimentary rooms, food, beverages, shows, and other perks each year that are worth billions of dollars. Gamblers can also earn various types of rewards through the loyalty programs offered by the casinos, with the specific rewards being tied to the amount bet on the slot machines and at the tables.

Some of the larger casinos in the U.S. have also tried to fend off competition by growing through mergers and acquisitions. In 2004, Harrah's announced that it was buying casino rival Caesers, allowing it to become the nation's leading operator of casinos, with several properties in both Las Vegas and Atlantic City. This deal came just a month after MGM Mirage had stated that it was buying the Mandalay Resort Group, allowing it to double the number of casinos it held on the Las Vegas strip. Firms that own several casinos can pitch each of their properties to a different market and allow their customers to earn rewards on the firm's loyalty program by gambling at any of these properties.

Exploiting the Chinese Market

Though gambling has been legal for over a century in Macau, which was a former Portuguese territory, its casinos were typically small and seedy. In part, this was because of the monopoly on gambling in the territory that was held by Stanley Ho, a local tycoon. However, this began to change in 2002, as the liberalization of casino licensing led to the development of new casinos by some of the world's largest casino operators, including many of the U.S. firms that wanted to find markets outside of Las Vegas. "The Las Vegas of the Far East" is how Sheldon Adelson, head of Las Vegas Sands, has described the recent development of Macau.

Macau has grown explosively with a tripling of casinos from the dozen or so that existed before 2002. Many are situated on the Cotai strip land that was once a stretch of water between the islands of Coloane and Taipa. Las Vegas–based firms such as Sands and Wynn have been plowing billions of dollars into new casinos there. Sands, which already has a supersized version of the Venetian with a Grand Canal and a Rialto Bridge, has added a complex called the Parisian with an Eiffel Tower. Even locally based Sociedade de Jogos de Macau is opening a $3.9 billion complex that will feature three hotels, one modeled on the Palace of Versailles.

Macau's dramatic rise in the casino business owes much to a collision of geography and history. The Chinese love to gamble, but the leaders in Beijing have long forbidden casinos on the mainland. They did, however, let them continue to operate in Macau after the Portuguese handed over sovereignty in 1999. Like Hong Kong, Macau has retained a degree of legal autonomy and is also a few hours or less flying time from a billion potential gamblers in China. "We sit next to the biggest market in the world," said Edward M. Tracy, chief executive of the Hong Kong–based subsidiary of Las Vegas Sands. "It's one billion more people than the U.S."[1]

Macau has been attracting a growing number of visitors from mainland China. Nearly 20 million people, or one in five Chinese who ventured outside mainland China last year, came to Macau to gamble. Many come from neighboring Guangdong province, usually on day trips. But bigger betters from as far away as Beijing have clearly played an important role in fueling Macau's growth. These high rollers will spend as much as $10 million on gambling in a single trip. They account for up to 65 percent of the revenues for the larger casinos (see Exhibit 3).

Even as Macau has shown remarkable growth over the last decade, its prospects for the future remain quite bright. Analysts at securities firms forecast that gambling revenue from Macau casinos could easily reach $80 billion by 2018. In part, this rise would be driven by an increase in visitors from mainland China because of rising affluence and improved transportation. China had increased the capacity of roads and high-speed trains to the territory, providing access for more visitors. Visitors from all over the world would also have better access because of a series of bridges that would connect Macau with Hong Kong's huge international airport.

Spreading across Asia

The growth of gambling revenues in Macau has led countries across the Asia-Pacific to abandon their hostilities to gambling and to encourage the development of casinos. Casinos have been opening in several countries, including Singapore, Philippines, Malaysia, South Korea, and Australia, and are likely to take off soon in other places such as Japan, Vietnam, Taiwan, and Sri Lanka. A group of investors have even made a deal to open a casino near Vladivostok in Russia's Far East. They claim that it takes less time for a high roller in Beijing to fly there than to steamy Macau.

Singapore, in particular, has been extremely successful with its two new upmarket casinos. In 2010, the island state issued permits to two large casino operators. The Marina Bay Sands is part of Las Vegas–based Sands casino operations and Resorts World Sentosa is run by Malaysia's Genting group. Even though Singapore has limited the size of its casinos and discourages locals from visiting them, they earn more than $6 billion annually, almost as much as all of the casinos on the Las Vegas strip.

Among the other contenders, the Philippines looks like it is poised to claim a substantial share of global casino revenues. Malaysia-based casino giant Genting kickstarted Manila's casino craze when it opened Resorts World Manila opposite the capital's main airport in 2009. The opening of the new casino represented a departure from the older smoke-filled gambling dens and its success has lured other casinos. As many as four new casinos have been developed on a large plot overlooking Manila Bay. The first of these, Solaire Resort and Casino, is a sleek plate-glass building with a suitably flashy interior created by Paul Steelman, a casino designer from Las Vegas.

Efforts are also underway to boost gambling in Japan by getting the government to lift its ban on casinos. At present, gambling is confined to seedy areas such as Kabukicho, a sleazy one-kilometer block of Tokyo. The prime minister, Shinzo Abe, is likely to approve legalization of casinos as a way to boost Japan's sluggish growth. Proponents of casinos argue that casinos will boost the country's earnings from foreign tourists and deliver a tax windfall to the heavily indebted government. A Japanese business magazine has argued that the country is being left behind as neighboring countries are rushing to build upscale casinos with luxury hotels, designer shops, and cultural attractions.

The casino operators that are developing casinos all over the region are hoping that they can lure Chinese high rollers away from Macau. A Chinese businessman who visits Macau's casinos stated that the new Chinese leadership's crackdown on official corruption and flaunting of wealth will drive clients to other locations. "Beijing has too many cameras watching us in Macau," he explained.[2] Solaire, recently opened in Manila, is willing to send a private jet to pick up big spenders from all across China. "If we can get 7 percent of Macau business to come here," said the casino's chief operating officer, "then we all achieve our goals for the market."[3]

Moving beyond Gambling

Over the last couple of decades, Las Vegas has moved beyond gambling to offer visitors many choices for fine dining, great shopping, and top-notch entertainment. This has allowed most of its higher end casinos to generate revenues from offering a wide selection of activities apart from gambling. At MGM Mirage, for example, revenue from non-gaming activities has typically accounted for almost 60 percent of net revenue in recent years. During the 1990s, Las Vegas had tried to become more receptive to families, with attractions such as circus performances, animal reserves, and pirate battles. But the city has been very successful with its recent return to its sinful roots with a stronger focus on topless shows, hot night clubs, and other adult offerings that have been highlighted by the new advertising slogan "What happens in Vegas, stays in Vegas."

By comparison, visitors are drawn to Atlantic City mostly because of gambling. Although it does offer a beach and a boardwalk, along which its dozen large casino hotels are lined, the city has never been able to develop itself as a beach resort. The opening of the much-ballyhooed Revel a few years ago was part of a drive to make Atlantic City much more competitive with Las Vegas. But it failed to replicate the success of the Borgota Hotel, the major new resort to open there in 2003. The failure to develop other forms of entertainment has led to the closing of several big casinos, including the Revel, as casinos that have opened in several neighboring states have drawn gamblers away from Atlantic City.

Macau has also been trying to reduce its dependence on gaming. By 2017, gambling revenues at its casinos were generating revenues that accounted for almost four-fifths of the territory's economy. But these revenues have begun to decline, in part because of the China's economic slowdown. Another factor has been that country's sweeping crackdown on corruption. Many of the high rollers from the mainland were gambling with the proceeds of shady deals, which are now subject to greater scrutiny. This is forcing the casinos to shift their focus away from the older, hardcore gamblers who come primarily to gamble toward younger, fun-loving gamblers who see gambling as only one part of their Macau experience.

The newer casinos are trying to offer more non-gambling activities by including restaurants, shops, cinemas, spas, and even concert arenas. The shops inside Sands casinos in Macau, for example, have been generating as much as $2 billion of revenues. Edward Tracy, the head of Sands China, is also bringing in shows ranging from boxing matches to Bollywood award ceremonies. One of the newly opened casinos has an enormous "fortune diamond" that emerges from a fountain every half-hour to the delight of photo-snapping onlookers. "There's an opportunity for Macau to attract a new breed of customer, one that is looking for a more holistic experience," said Aaron Fischer, a gambling analyst at a brokerage firm.[4]

Macau is now trying to overcome one of its most serious limitations—its small land area, just under 30 square kilometers—by expanding business on the thinly populated island of Hengqin. Three times the size of Macau, the island has been declared a special economic zone by Chinese officials. The idea is for it to develop accommodations and entertainments that can support Macau's aspirations for mass-market tourism. "Hengqin is the game changer for Macau," insists Sands China head Tracy.[5]

Gambling on the Future

In spite of growing competition from the many other U.S. and world locations, Las Vegas and Atlantic City continue fighting for visitors to come for various forms of entertainment as well as gambling—the clubs, stores, and concerts and shows. "I think we're seeing a shift away from Las Vegas as the only gaming destination," said Stephen P. A. Brown from U.N.L.V. "But it is holding up as a tourist destination."[6] Genting, the Malaysian gaming group, has recently taken over the site of the Echelon, which was abandoned because of lack of funds during the recent recession. They intend to develop a stronger presence in the U.S. market by building one of the biggest new resorts in Las Vegas with a 3,500-room hotel and 175,000 feet of gambling space.

Casino operators in Macau are also continuing to make new bets, even as competition grows in neighboring countries. Eight new casino complexes, all of which will offer many forms of entertainment, are being added, promising to almost double the supply of hotel rooms on the strip. Galaxy Entertainment, a local casino firm, claims that with its $7.7 billion expansion its already huge Macau casino will be bigger even than the Pentagon. Another local operator, SJM, has developed a huge new resort on the Cotai strip to include a hotel designed by Versace, an Italian luxury fashion house.

As casinos' emphasis shifts from older high-stakes gamblers to younger customers who enjoy gambling but are interested in dining, drinking, shopping, and taking in shows, casinos are also eager to embrace new types of gaming experiences that will attract Millennials who have grown up playing video and mobile phone games. "Gambling won't go out of fashion. It will just become part of a wider offering," says Ian M. Coughlan, president of Wynn Macau. "We've not really tapped all the demand that exists—we're far from it."[7]

ENDNOTES

1. Bettina Wassener. A hot streak for Macau. *New York Times,* March 26, 2014, p. B7.
2. The rise of the low rollers. *The Economist,* September 7, 2013, p. 63.
3. Ibid., p. 64.
4. Chris Horton. All in on gambling? Not for Macau. *International New York Times,* December 20–21, 2014, p. 1.
5. *The Economist,* p. 64.
6. Adam Nagourney. Las Vegas bounces back, with caveats. *International New York Times,* August 2, 2013.
7. *New York Times,* March 26, 2014, p. B7.

CASE 3

MCDONALD'S IN 2017*

On January 18, 2017, McDonald's announced that it was introducing two new versions of the Big Mac on a limited basis. Although such changes are necessary for the world's largest restaurant chain, the new offerings will be similar to the original version because they will use frozen beef patties and a secret sauce. This is unlikely to address the shift in tastes among consumers for fresher beef and a variety of toppings. In fact, a recent survey indicated a serious cause for concern for the firm, finding that only 20 percent of Millennials had even tried a Big Mac (see Exhibits 1, 2, and 3).

Nevertheless, Steve Easterbrook, who took the helm of McDonald's in March 2015, has continued to push for changes to several of the ingredients that the firm has been using in its products. It has removed high fructose corn syrup from its buns, changed from the use of liquid

margarine to real butter, decided to use chicken that has been raised without antibiotics, and to make use of cage-free eggs. Mike Andres, president of McDonald's USA, explained why the firm has decided to make these changes: "Why take a position to defend them if consumers are saying they don't want them?"[1]

These changes are expected to address some of challenges that McDonald's has been facing in many markets, including the U.S., where it has over 14,000 of its 35,000 mostly franchised restaurants. It has lost a lot of ground with consumers, especially Millennials, who are defecting to traditional competitors like Burger King and Wendy's as well as to new designer burger outlets such as Five Guys and Shake Shack. Changing tastes are also responsible for the loss of customers that are lining up at fast-casual chains such as Chipotle Mexican Grill and Panera Bread, which offer customized ordering and fresh ingredients (see Exhibit 4).

Over the years, McDonald's response to this growing competition was to expand its menu with snacks, salads and new drinks. From 33 basic items that the chain offered in 1990, the menu had grown by 2014 to 121 items. The greatly expanded menu led to a significant increase in

---

* Case prepared by Jamal Shamsie, Michigan State University, with the assistance of Professor Alan B. Eisner, Pace University. Material has been drawn from published sources to be used for purposes of class discussion. Copyright © 2017 Jamal Shamsie and Alan B. Eisner.

EXHIBIT 1
Income Statement
($ millions)

	Year Ending		
	Dec. 31, 2016	Dec. 31, 2015	Dec. 31, 2014
Total Revenue	$24,622	$25,413	$27,441
Operating Income	7,744	7,145	7,949
Net Income	4,686	4,529	4,758

Source: McDonald's.

EXHIBIT 2
Balance Sheet
($ millions)

	Year Ending		
	Dec. 31, 2016	Dec. 31, 2015	Dec. 31, 2014
Current Assets	$ 4,849	$ 9,643	$ 4,186
Total Assets	31,024	37,939	34,281
Current Liabilities	3,468	2,950	2,748
Total Liabilities	33,228	30,851	21,428
Stockholder Equity	(2,204)	7,088	12,853

Source: McDonalds.

EXHIBIT 3
Breakdown of
Revenues ($ millions)

	2016	2015	2014
U.S.	$8,253	$8,559	$8,651
International Lead Markets	7,223	7,615	8,544
High Growth Markets	6,161	6,173	6,845
Foundational Markets & Corporate	2,985	3,066	3,401

Source: McDonald's.

EXHIBIT 4
U.S. Market Share
of Fast-Food Burger
Chains

McDonald's	2016	17.0%
	2014	49.6%
	2012	50.0%
	2010	49.2%
Wendy's	2016	4.4%
	2014	12.3%
	2012	12.2%
	2010	12.7%
Burger King	2016	15.4%
	2014	11.9%
	2012	12.1%
	2010	13.2%
Five Guys	2016	1.8%
	2014	1.7%
	2012	1.5%
	2010	1.1%

Source: *USA Today,* December 8, 2014; and author estimates.

costs and longer preparation times. This forced the firm to increase the prices of many of its items and to take more time to serve customers, moving it away from the attributes that it had built its reputation upon. "McDonald's stands for value, consistency and convenience," said Darren Tristano, a restaurant industry consultant.[2]

The fast food chain has been through a similar crisis before. Back in 2002–2003, McDonald's had experienced a decline in performance because of quality problems as the result of rapid expansion. At that time, the firm had brought James R. Cantalupo back out of retirement to turn things around. He formulated a "Plan to Win," which has been the basis of McDonald's strategy over the last decade. The core of the plan was to increase sales at existing locations by improving the menu, refurbishing the outlets, and extending hours. This time, however, such incremental steps might not be enough.

Pulling out of a Downward Spiral

Since it was founded more than fifty years ago, McDonald's has been defining the fast food business. It provided millions of Americans their first jobs even as it changed their eating habits. It rose from a single outlet in a nondescript Chicago suburb to become one of the largest chains of outlets spread around the globe. But it gradually began to run into various problems which began to slow down its sales growth (see Exhibit 5).

This decline could be attributed in large part to a drop in McDonald's once-vaunted service and quality since its expansion in the 1990s, when headquarters stopped grading franchises for cleanliness, speed, and service. By the end of the decade, the chain ran into more problems because of the tighter labor market. McDonald's began to cut back on

EXHIBIT 5 McDonald's Milestones

1948	Brothers Richard and Maurice McDonald open the first restaurant in San Bernadino, California, that sells hamburgers, fries, and milkshakes.
1955	Ray A. Kroc, 52, opens his first McDonald's in Des Plaines, Illinois. Kroc, a distributor of milkshake mixers, figures he can sell a bundle of them if he franchises the McDonalds' business and install his mixers in the new stores.
1961	Six years later, Kroc buys out the McDonald brothers for $2.7 million.
1963	Ronald McDonald makes his debut as corporate spokesclown using future NBC-TV weatherman Willard Scott. During the year, the company also sells its 1 billionth burger.
1965	McDonald's stock goes public at $22.50 a share. It will split 12 times in the next 35 years.
1967	The first McDonald's restaurant outside the U.S. opens in Richmond, British Columbia. Today there are 31,108 McDonald's in 118 countries.
1968	The Big Mac, the first extension of McDonald's basic burger, makes its debut and is an immediate hit.
1972	McDonald's switches to the frozen variety for its successful French fries.
1974	Fred L. Turner succeeds Kroc as CEO. In the midst of a recession, the minimum wage rises to $2 per hour, a big cost increase for McDonald's, which is built around a model of young, low-wage workers.
1975	The first drive-through window is opened in Sierra Vista, Arizona.
1979	McDonald's responds to the needs of working women by introducing Happy Meals. A burger, some fries, a soda, and a toy give working moms a break.
1987	Michael R. Quinlan becomes chief executive.
1991	Responding to the public's desire for healthier foods, McDonald's introduces the low-fat McLean Deluxe burger. It flops and is withdrawn from the market. Over the next few years, the chain will stumble several times trying to spruce up its menu.
1992	The company sells its 90 billionth burger, and stops counting.
1996	In order to attract more adult customers, the company launches its Arch Deluxe, a "grownup" burger with an idiosyncratic taste. Like the low-fat burger, it also falls flat.
1997	McDonald's launches Campaign 55, which cuts the cost of a Big Mac to $0.55. It is a response to discounting by Burger King and Taco Bell. The move, which prefigures similar price wars in 2002, is widely considered a failure.
1998	Jack M. Greenberg becomes McDonald's fourth chief executive. A 16-year company veteran, he vows to spruce up the restaurants and their menu.
1999	For the first time, sales from international operations outstrip domestic revenues. In search of other concepts, the company acquires Aroma Cafe, Chipotle, Donatos, and, later, Boston Market.
2000	McDonald's sales in the U.S. peak at an average of $1.6 million annually per restaurant. It is, however, still more than at any other fast-food chain.
2001	Subway surpasses McDonald's as the fast-food chain with the most U.S. outlets. At the end of the year it had 13,247 stores, 148 more than McDonald's.
2002	McDonald's posts its first-ever quarterly loss, of $343.8 million. The stock drops to around $13.50, down 40% from five years ago.
2003	James R. Cantalupo returns to McDonald's in January as CEO. He immediately pulls back from the company's 10–15% forecast for per-share earnings growth.
2004	Charles H. Bell takes over the firm after the sudden death of Cantalupo. He states he will continue with the strategies that have been developed by his predecessor.
2005	Jim Skinner takes over as CEO after Bell announces retirement for health reasons.
2006	McDonald's launches specialty beverages, including coffee-based drinks.
2008	McDonald's plans to add McCafes to each of its outlets.
2012	Don Thompson succeeds Skinner as CEO of the chain.
2015	Thompson resigns because of declining performance and is replaced by Steve Easterbrook, the firm's chief branding officer.
2016	McDonald's opens restaurant in the 120th country; the first McDonald's restaurant opens in Astana, Kazakhstan, on March 8, 2016.

Source: McDonald's.

training as it struggled hard to find new recruits, leading to a dramatic falloff in the skills of its employees. According to a 2002 survey by market researcher Global Growth Group, McDonald's came in third in average service time behind Wendy's and sandwich shop Chick-fil-A Inc.

By the beginning of 2003, consumer surveys were indicating that McDonald's was headed for serious trouble. Measures for the service and quality of the chain were continuing to fall, dropping far behind those of its rivals. In order to deal with its deteriorating performance, the firm decided to bring back retired Vice-Chairman James R. Cantalupo, 59, who had overseen McDonald's successful international expansion in the 1980s and 1990s. Cantalupo, who had retired only a year earlier, was perceived to be the only candidate with the necessary qualifications, despite shareholder sentiment for an outsider. The board had felt that it needed someone who knew the company well and could move quickly to turn things around.

Cantalupo realized that McDonald's often tended to miss the mark on delivering the critical aspects of consistent, fast, and friendly service and an all-around enjoyable experience for the whole family. He understood that its franchisees and employees alike needed to be inspired as well as retrained on their role in putting the smile back into the McDonald's experience. When Cantalupo and his team laid out their turnaround plan in 2003, they stressed getting the basics of service and quality right, in part by reinstituting a tough "up or out" grading system that would kick out underperforming franchisees. "We have to rebuild the foundation. It's fruitless to add growth if the foundation is weak," said Cantalupo.[3]

In his effort to focus on the core business, Cantalupo sold off the non-burger chains that the firm had recently acquired. He also cut back on the opening of new outlets, focusing instead on generating more sales from existing outlets. Cantalupo pushed McDonald's to try to draw more customers through the introduction of new products. The chain had a positive response to its increased emphasis on healthier foods, led by a revamped line of fancier salads. The revamped menu was promoted through a new worldwide ad slogan, "I'm loving it," which was delivered by pop idol Justin Timberlake through a set of MTV style commercials.

Striving for a Healthier Image

When Jim Skinner took over from Cantalupo in 2004, he continued to push for McDonald's to change its image. Skinner felt that one of his top priorities was to deal with the growing concerns about the unhealthy image of McDonald's, given the rise of obesity in the U.S. These concerns were highlighted in the popular documentary *Super Size Me*, made by Morgan Spurlock. Spurlock vividly displayed the health risks that were posed by a steady diet of food from the fast food chain. With a rise in awareness of the high fat content of most of the products offered by McDonald's, the firm was also beginning to face lawsuits from some of its loyal customers.

In response to the growing health concerns, one of the first steps taken by McDonald's was to phase out supersizing by the end of 2004. The supersizing option allowed customers to get a larger order of French fries and a bigger soft drink by paying a little extra. McDonald's also announced that it intended to start providing nutrition information on the packaging of its products. The information will be easy to read and will tell customers about the calories, fat, protein, carbohydrates and sodium that are in each product. Finally, McDonald's has also begun to remove the artery-clogging trans fatty acids from the oil that it uses to make its French fries and has recently announced plans to reduce the sodium content in all of its products by 15 percent.

But Skinner was also trying to push out more offerings that are likely to be perceived by customers to be healthier. McDonald's has continued to build upon its chicken offerings using white meat with products such as Chicken Selects. It has also placed a great deal of emphasis upon its new salad offerings. McDonald's has carried out extensive experiments and tests with these, deciding to use higher quality ingredients, from a variety of lettuces and tasty cherry tomatoes to sharper cheeses and better cuts of meat. It offered a choice of Newman's Own dressings, a well-known higher-end brand. "Salads have changed the way people think of our brand," said Wade Thoma, vice president for menu development in the U.S. "It tells people that we are very serious about offering things people feel comfortable eating."[4]

McDonald's has also been trying to include more fruits and vegetables in its well-known and popular Happy Meals. It announced in 2011 that it would reduce the amount of French fries and phase out the caramel dipping sauce that accompanied the apple slices in these meals. The addition of fruits and vegetables has raised the firm's operating costs, because these are more expensive to ship and store because of their more perishable nature. "We are doing what we can," said Danya Proud, a spokesperson for the firm. "We have to evolve with the times."[5]

The rollout of new beverages, highlighted by new coffee-based drinks, represents the chain's biggest menu expansion in almost three decades. Under a plan to add a McCafe section to all of its nearly 14,000 U.S. outlets, McDonald's has been offering lattes, cappuccinos, ice-blended frappes and fruit-based smoothies to its customers. "In many cases, they're now coming for the beverage, whereas before they were coming for the meal," said Lee Renz, an executive who was responsible for the rollout.[6]

Refurbishing the Outlets

As part of its turnaround strategy, McDonald's has also been selling off the outlets that it owned. More than 80 percent of its outlets are now in the hands of franchisees and other affiliates. Skinner is working with the franchisees to address the look and feel of many of the chain's aging stores. Without any changes to their décor, the firm is likely to be left behind by other more savvy fast food and drink retailers. The firm is in the midst of pushing harder to refurbish—or re-image—all of its outlets around the world. "People eat with their eyes first," said Thompson. "If you have a restaurant that is appealing, contemporary, and relevant both from the street and interior, the food tastes better."[7]

The re-imaging concept was first tried in France in 1996 by Dennis Hennequin, an executive in charge of the chain's European operations, who felt that the effort was essential to revive the firm's sagging sales. "We were hip 15 years ago, but I think we lost that," he said.[8] McDonald's has been applying the re-imaging concept to its outlets around the world, with a budget of more than half its total annual capital expenditures. In the U.S., the changes cost as much as $650,000 per restaurant, a cost that is shared with the franchisees when the outlet is not company owned.

One of the prototype interiors being tested out by McDonald's has curved counters with surfaces painted in bright colors. In one corner, a touch-activated screen allows customers to punch in orders without queuing. The interiors can feature armchairs and sofas, modern lighting, large television screens and even wireless Internet access. The firm is also trying to develop new features for its drive-through customers, which account for 65 percent of all transactions in the U.S. They include music aimed at queuing vehicles and a wall of windows on the drive-through side of the restaurant allowing customers to see meals being prepared from their cars.

The chain has even been developing McCafes inside its outlets next to the usual fast food counter. The McCafe concept originated in Australia in 1993 and has been rolled out in many restaurants around the world. McDonald's has been introducing the concept to the U.S. as part of the refurbishment of its outlets. In fact, part of the refurbishment has focused on the installation of a specialty beverage platform across all U.S. outlets. The cost of installing this equipment is running at about $100,000 per outlet, with McDonald's subsidizing part of this expense.

The firm has planned for all McCafes to offer espresso-based coffee, gourmet coffee blends, fresh baked muffins and high-end desserts. Customers will be able to consume these while they relax in soft leather chairs listening to jazz, big band, or blues music. Commenting on this significant expansion of offerings, Marty Brochstein, executive editor of *The Licensing Letter,* said: "McDonald's wants to be seen as a lifestyle brand, not just a place to go to have a burger."[9]

Rethinking the Business Model

In response to the decline in performance, McDonald's is testing other new concepts, including a kiosk in some locations that allows customers to skip the counter and head to tabletlike kiosks where they can customize everything about their burger, from the type of bun to the variety of cheese to the many glossy toppings and sauces that can go on it. Dubbed the "Create Your Taste" platform, McDonald's is hoping the kiosks will attract more younger customers who may be moving away from frozen processed food that is loaded with preservatives. The firm has plans to gradually expand the concept to more locations, but there are risks involved with making such a change. Franchises are concerned about the costs, which can run up to $125,000 per restaurant to make the required changes. The burgers are priced higher at $5.49, can take seven minutes to prepare, can only be ordered from inside the store, and eventually are brought to your table. Franchises have complained the concept cannot be offered to drive-through customers that make up such a large portion of the chain's business. "Customization is not McDonald's historic strength," said Mark Kalinowski, an analyst at Janney Montgomery Scott.[10]

Further, such a change runs counter to the image of inexpensive and fast food that McDonald's has worked hard to build over the years. Easterbrook has acknowledged that its customized menu is a work in progress. He stated that the firm is also testing a downsized version that would allow both in-store and drive-through customers to choose a bun and one of four sandwich types. At the same time, McDonald's is hoping that this will bring more customers inside their outlets, bringing the U.S. counter/drive-thru customer ratio closer to 50/50, up from the current 30/70.

McDonald's has also been working to simplify its menu, reducing the number of "value meal" promotions, groups of items that together cost less than ordering items individually. It has tweaked its "dollar menu" replacing it with "dollar value and more," raising the prices for many items as part of a bid to get each customer to spend more. But McDonald's first introduced these bargain menus because its prices had risen over the years, driving away customers to cheaper outlets. Consequently, as much as 15 percent of the chain's sales have been coming from its "dollar menu" where everything costs a dollar.

McDonald's saw a slight jump in U.S. sales after launching an all-day breakfast at almost half of its locations. The franchises had to be convinced to invest about $5,000 to add food preparation space in order to offer breakfast along with the regular lunch or dinner items. However, sales from the all-day breakfast had begun to flatten out by the end of 2016, as no additional sales were coming from customers who were ordering breakfast.

More Gold in these Arches?

In spite of all the changes that have been made by Easterbrook, sales growth for McDonald's has continued to be sluggish. The firm does, however, believe that sales will rebound in the U.S. as well as in foreign markets. In order to provide a boost to its operations in China and Hong Kong, McDonald's announced a deal with Citic, a state-owned conglomerate, and the Caryle Group, a private equity firm. They plan to open more outlets and to expand to many smaller cities that show potential for growth. "China and Hong Kong represent an enormous growth opportunity for McDonald's," Easterbrook said in a recent news release. "The new partnership will combine one of the world's most powerful brands and our unparalleled quality standards with partners who have an unmatched understanding of the local markets."[11]

McDonald's has also been trying to grow by reaching out to different customer segments with different products at different times of the day. It has tried to target young adults for breakfast with its gourmet coffee, egg sandwiches, and fat-free muffins. It attracts working adults for lunch, particularly those who are squeezed for time, with its burgers and fries. And its introduction of wraps has drawn in teenagers late in the evening after they have been partying.

Restaurant analyst Bryan Elliott commented: "They've tried to be all things to all people who walk in their door."[12] The current marketing campaign, anchored around the catchy phase "I'm loving it," takes on different forms in order to target each of the groups that it is seeking. Larry Light, who was the head of global marketing at McDonald's and pushed for this new campaign, insists that the firm has to exploit its brand through pushing it in many different directions. In spite of these efforts, 30 percent of sales come from just five items: Big Macs, hamburgers, cheeseburgers, McNuggets, and fries.

The expansion of the menu beyond the staple of burgers and fries raises some fundamental questions. Most significantly, it is not clear just how far McDonald's can stretch its brand while keeping all of its outlets under the traditional symbol of its golden arches. In fact, industry experts believe that the long-term success of the firm may well depend on its ability to compete with rival burger chains. "The burger category has great strength," says David C. Novak, chairman and CEO of Yum! Brands, parent of KFC and Taco Bell. "That's America's food. People love hamburgers."[13]

ENDNOTES

1. Stephanie Strom. In a shift, McMuffins with real butter. *New York Times,* August 3, 2016, p. B2.
2. *The Economist.* When the chips are down. January 10, 2015, p. 53.
3. Pallavi Gogoi and Michael Arndt. Hamburger hell. *BusinessWeek,* March 3, 2003, p. 105.
4. Melanie Warner. You want any fruit with that Big Mac? *New York Times,* February 20, 2005, p. 8.
5. Stephanie Strom. McDonald's trims its Happy Meal. *New York Times,* July 27, 2011, p. B7.
6. Janet Adamy. McDonald's coffee strategy is tough sell. *Wall Street Journal,* October 27, 2008, p. B3.
7. Ben Paynter. Super style me. *Fast Company,* October 2010, p. 107.
8. Jeremy Grant. McDonald's to revamp UK outlets. *Financial Times,* February 2, 2006, p. 14.
9. Bruce Horovitz. McDonald's ventures beyond burgers to duds, toys. *USA Today,* November 14, 2003, p. 6B.
10. Hiroko Tabuchi. Faced with sagging sales, McDonald's chief announces a reorganization. *New York Times,* May 5, 2015, p. B3.
11. Amie Tsang and Wee Sui-Lee. McDonald's China operations to be sold to locally led consortium. *New York Times,* January 9, 2017, p. B1.
12. *Fortune,* December 1, 2014, p. 110.
13. Julie Jargon. McDonald's is feeling fried. *Wall Street Journal,* November 9, 2012, p. B2.

CASE 4

ZYNGA: IS THE GAME OVER?*

In 2017, Zynga not only struggled to remain relevant in the gaming industry but fought to seem attractive to investors. During the previous four years, the company had a new CEO almost every year. In 2013, the founder Mark Pincus stepped down and handed the charge to Don Mattrick, a 15-year employee of Electronic Arts expecting to turn the company around. In April 2015, Don Mattrick left the position, and Pincus returned as CEO for the second time. Just a year later

in March 2016, Zynga announced the replacement of Pincus by the new CEO Frank Gibeau, another 20-year employee of Electronic Arts, again expecting to turn around the company.

Zynga's lack of consistent leadership has been critical to not formulating an effective turnaround strategy that might have led to progress. Throughout the revolving door of CEO replacements, Zynga has not developed a substantially successful new game. Consequently, its revenues have been falling over the past years accompanied by consistent net losses. Though Zynga's revenue rose by $53 million by the end of 2015, it still posted a net loss of $121 million for the year (see Exhibits 1 and 2). The primary reason for the increase in 2015 revenue was a surge in the number of

* This case was developed by graduate students Eric S. Engelson, Dev Das, Saad Nazir, and Professor Alan B. Eisner, Pace University. Material has been drawn from published sources to be used for class discussion. Copyright © 2017 Alan B. Eisner.

EXHIBIT 1 Zynga Consolidated Income Statements ($ thousands, except per-share, user, and ABPU data)

	Year Ended December 31:		
	2016	2015	2014
Revenue:			
Online game	$ 547,291	$ 590,755	$ 537,619
Advertising and other	194,129	173,962	152,791
Total revenue	741,420	764,717	690,410
Costs and expenses:			
Cost of revenue	238,546	235,985	213,570
Research and development	320,300	361,931	396,553
Sales and marketing	183,637	169,573	157,364
General and administrative	92,509	143,284	167,664
Impairment of intangible assets	20,677	–	–
Total costs and expenses	855,669	910,773	935,151
Income (loss) from operations	(114,249)	(146,056)	(244,741)
Interest income	3,057	2,568	3,266
Other income (expense), net	6,461	13,306	8,248
Income (loss) before income taxes	(104,731)	(130,182)	(233,227)
Provision for (benefit from) income taxes	3,442	(8,672)	(7,327)
Net income (loss)	$(108,173)	$(121,510)	$(225,900)
Net income (loss) per share attributable to common stockholders			
Basic	$ (0.12)	$ (0.13)	$ (0.26)
Diluted	$ (0.12)	$ (0.13)	$ (0.26)
Weighted average common shares used to compute net income (loss) per share attributable to common stockholders:			
Basic	878,827	913,511	874,509
Diluted	878,827	913,511	874,509

EXHIBIT 2 Zynga Balance Sheets ($ thousands, except par value)

	December 31, 2016	December 31, 2015
Assets		
Current assets:		
Cash and cash equivalents	$ 852,467	$ 742,217
Marketable securities	–	245,033
Accounts receivable	77,260	79,610
Income tax receivable	296	5,233
Restricted cash	6,199	209
Other current assets	29,254	39,988
Total current assets	965,476	1,112,290
Goodwill	613,335	657,671
Other intangible assets, net	25,430	64,016
Property and equipment, net	269,439	273,221
Restricted cash	3,050	986
Other long-term assets	29,119	16,446
Total assets	$ 1,905,849	$ 2,124,630
Liabilities and stockholders' equity		
Current liabilities:		
Accounts payable	$ 23,999	$ 29,676
Income tax payable	1,889	–
Other current liabilities	75,754	77,691
Deferred revenue	141,998	128,839
Total current liabilities	243,640	236,206
Deferred revenue	158	204
Deferred tax liabilities	5,791	6,026
Other non-current liabilities	75,596	95,293
Total liabilities	325,185	337,729
Stockholders' equity:		
Common stock,	3,349,714	3,234,551
$0.00000625 par value, and additional paid in capital - authorized shares: 2,020,517; shares outstanding: 886,850 shares (Class A, 770,269, Class B, 96,064, Class C, 20,517) as of December 31, 2016 and 903,617 (Class A, 769,533, Class B, 113,567, Class C, 20,517) as of December 31, 2015		
Treasury stock	–	(98,942)
Accumulated other comprehensive income (loss)	(128,694)	(52,388)
Accumulated deficit	(1,640,356)	(1,296,320)
Total stockholders' equity	1,580,664	1,786,901
Total liabilities and stockholders' equity	$ 1,905,849	$ 2,124,630

mobile users, accounting for 73 percent of the company's revenue in 2015.[1] However, year-over-year decline in revenues has been primarily attributable to the innovative product pipeline, which Mr. Gibeau has tried to turn around by focusing on development of high-quality mobile applications that had helped to shrink the net losses in 2015.

In response to the wildly successful Clash of Clans by SuperCell, Zynga released a new mobile game, Dawn of Titans, at the end of 2016. Dawn of Titans features high-quality graphics and options to play with other users in real time. The 3D strategy game also allows users to create their own fantasy kingdoms and develop strategy to stay ahead of the other players. Prior to the introduction of Dawn of Titans, the company had launched a new version of Zynga Poker, which includes a sophisticated design and feature set that inspires more competition, authenticity, and social connections between players. Zynga also launched NFL Showdown at the beginning of the NFL season with the intention of adding new features based on customer feedback and play patterns. However, the new product-driven growth was not able to reverse declines in the existing online games.[2]

Zynga's Background

At the time it incorporated in October 2007, Zynga had become a dominant player in the online gaming field, almost entirely through the use of social media platforms. Located in San Francisco, the company was named by CEO Mark Pincus to pay tribute to his deceased beloved pet bulldog Zynga. Although this might have seemed whimsical, Zynga was actually a quite powerful company. Exemplifying Zynga's prominence, Facebook was reported to have earned roughly 12 percent of its revenue from the operations of Zynga's virtual merchandise sales.[3]

No other direct competitor was close to this revenue. Zynga's collection of games continued to expand, with more and more success stories emerging. A relative newcomer to the market, its quick success was astonishing. However, Zynga's impressive financials were possibly at risk because of what some considered questionable decision making. Many of Zynga's competitors, and even some partners, were displeased with the company's actions and began to show it in the form of litigation. Agincourt, a plaintiff in a lawsuit brought against Zynga, stated, "Zynga's remarkable growth has not been driven by its own ingenuity. Rather it has been widely reported that Zynga's business model is to copy creative ideas and game designs from other game developers and then use its market power to bulldoze the games' originators."[4] If lawsuits and ethical issues continued to arise for Zynga, its powerful bulldog could start looking more like a poodle.

The Products

With an abundance of software developers, the ability to create and distribute online games increases by the day, and the demand to play them is equally high. However, while many people find these online games fun and, better yet, therapeutic, others can't understand the hype. The best way to understand the sudden infatuation is to view online gaming as simply a means of relaxation.

In the movies, at least, large executive offices are often shown with putting greens, dartboards, or even a bar full of alcoholic beverages. These amenities are all meant to serve the same purpose: to relieve stress during a hard day's work. We've all been there and looked for a way to cope. However, few of us have the opportunity to use such things as putting greens to unwind at the workplace. And even if we did, how long could we afford to engage in such an activity before being pulled back to our desks?

Stress reduction at work is one of the many purposes that virtual games fulfill: no need to leave our desks; no need to make others around us aware of our relaxation periods; and, better yet, no need to separate the task of relaxation from sitting at our computers while we work. The ability to play these games on office computers and "relax" now and then as the day goes by makes online gaming enticing. This, of course, is just one of many uses for the games. Some people play them after work or at the end of a long day. With the onset of smartphones, people of all ages play these games on the go throughout the day—sitting on the bus, in the waiting room of a doctor's office, or at the Department of Motor Vehicles. Diverting game play is readily available with the click of a button.

Market Size

Compared to other game developers with games present on the Facebook platform, Zynga had once been a dominant force, but by 2016 it failed to surface in the top 5 virtual-gaming rankings (see Exhibits 3 and 4). The King Company appeared to rule with its numerous popular games, including the billion-dollar Candy Crush Saga.

Zynga's virtual games provided the opportunity for constant buildup and improvements, offering users virtual goods and services to increase their gaming experience. These items could be purchased using a credit card and were often needed to accomplish fast progressions in the games. These goods were advertised throughout the games and the user was enticed by price cuts for larger purchases.

Zynga's virtual games could be played both remotely and through social media platforms, most commonly Facebook. Five of Zynga's games, FarmVille, CityVille, Empire and Allies, CastleVille, and Texas HoldEm Poker, were among the most popular games on Facebook. CityVille had over 100 million active monthly users within months of its release in late 2010.[5] On July 1, 2011, Zynga filed with the Securities and Exchange Commission with intention of raising up to $1 billion in its IPO, and its stock began trading on NASDAQ December 16, 2011.[6]

Of course, Zynga was not the only virtual-gaming company striving for this degree of success. There were and are many others, in what seems to be one of the fastest-growing industries. The capability to create online games

EXHIBIT 3 Monthly Users of Facebook Gaming, as of October 2016

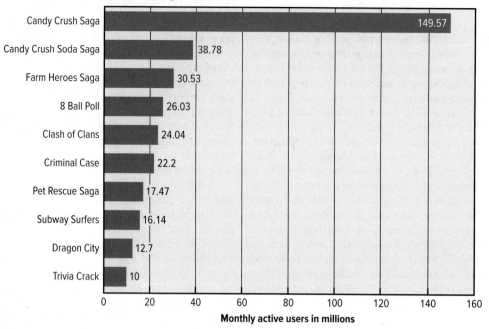

Game	Monthly active users in millions
Candy Crush Saga	149.57
Candy Crush Soda Saga	38.78
Farm Heroes Saga	30.53
8 Ball Poll	26.03
Clash of Clans	24.04
Criminal Case	22.2
Pet Rescue Saga	17.47
Subway Surfers	16.14
Dragon City	12.7
Trivia Crack	10

Source: Statista 2016.

EXHIBIT 4 Top 5 Virtual-Gaming Developers of 2016

Rank	Company	2015 Revenue ($ millions)	Key Games
1	Machine Zone	$1,000	Game of War, Mobile Strike
2	Supercell	2,300	Clash of Clans, Clash Royale, Boom Beach Hay Day
3	EA Mobile	504	Star Wars Galaxy of Heroes, NFL Madden Mobile, The Simpsons: Tapped Out
4	Mixi	2,000	Monster Strike
5	Com2uS	369	Summoners War

Source: www.pocketgamer.biz, 2016 top developers list.

is widespread. Creativity and innovation are accepted to be the grounds on which competing companies challenge each other. With all competitors after the same audience, the industry is prone to a significant amount of head-butting rivalry.

Background of Competitors

RockYou was founded by Lance Tokuda and Jia Shen. Their first product was a slide-show service, crafted to work as an application widget. RockYou was one of the companies invited by Facebook to participate in the F8 event, in which Facebook announced the start of an open platform that would allow third parties to develop and run their own applications on Facebook. RockYou then shifted toward producing more in-depth social application games, such as

Toyland, Zoo World, Hero World, and MyCasino. Its most played game, Zoo World, was a free social media application whereby users tried to build the best zoo they could. The company underwent a phase of major layoffs but continued to work on new and improved games.[7]

GameHouse, based in Seattle, Washington, was a developer, publisher, and distributor of casual games. GameHouse was acquired by RealNetworks for $14.6 million cash and about 3.3 million shares of RNWK common stock, which had an estimated value of $21 million at the time.[8] Prior to its acquisition, GameHouse generated an impressive amount of revenue through the sale of games on its own website, www.gamehouse.com, and through third-party affiliates and other distributors. GameHouse and RealArcade merged their websites into one portal in an effort to create one massive distribution center. RealArcade delivered its games on a downloadable demo basis, with a 60-minute trial time for most games. When the trial expired, the user needed to purchase the full version to continue playing. Users also had the option of purchasing a membership package for a monthly fee. GameHouse later began offering the full version of many of its games, supported by the sale of in-game advertising.[9]

EA Playfish, a subsidiary of Electronic Arts, began as Playfish Ltd., a developer of social network games that were free to play. Who Has the Biggest Brain? was the first success of Playfish Ltd. and was the gateway to the company's ability to raise funding. The company, like many of its competitors, generated revenue by selling virtual goods inside its games. Electronic Arts later acquired Playfish for $400 million. Soon after, Playfish drew approximately 55 million users a month, with over 37 million of those users coming from Facebook.[10] Users could purchase "Playfish Cards" at Walmart, Walgreens, and Toys 'R' Us stores, at which point they could register on the Playfish website to begin earning "Playfish Cash" that could be used to purchase virtual goods within the games. Playfish announced the change from Playfish Cash to individual cash for all games (except Crazy Planets at that time) and allowed users to trade for the new cash.[11]

CrowdStar, based in Burlingame, California, was another developer of social games. Founded by Suren Markosian and Jeff Tseng, it ranked fourth for most monthly active users among Facebook applications.[12] Its most popular titles were Happy Aquarium and Happy Pets. CrowdStar turned down an offer from Microsoft to acquire the company for more than $200 million.[13] The company subsequently raised an additional $23 million and planned on using the money to double its workforce and increase expansion on a global scale. CrowdStar also planned to add about 100 employees, including game developers, server developers, artists, producers, business analysts, and content managers. Peter Relan, CrowdStar's CEO, said the company needed to raise money to exploit opportunities for global expansion in Japan, China, Eastern Europe, and Brazil.[14]

Supercell Oy operated as a subsidiary of Tencent Holdings Limited. Supercell Oy, based in Helsinki, Finland, was another successful developer of mobile games with additional office locations in United States, Japan, South Korea, and China.[15] The initial hit for the company was its browser game called Gunshine.net. In 2011, the company started developing games for tablets and smartphones, gaining worldwide popularity over just a few years. The most popular mobile games developed by Supercell included Clash of Clans, Clash Royale, Boom Beach, and Hay Day, free to download and play. The company had annual revenue of about $2 billion, and its strategy game Clash of Clans was a leading competitor of Zynga's Dawn of Titans. Supercell's flagship game, Clash of Clans, had approximately 100 million daily users, which posed a big competitive challenge for Zynga's Dawn of Titans.[16]

Background of the CEO

Mark Jonathan Pincus was the entrepreneur behind Zynga. He was also the founder of Freeloader, Inc., Tribe Networks, and Support.com.[17] In prior years, Mark was named CEO of the Year in the Crunchies awards,[18] as well as Founder of the Year.[19] Prior to his entrepreneurial endeavors, Pincus worked in venture capital and financial services for several years. After graduating from Wharton, he went on to obtain his master's degree from Harvard Business School. Soon after graduating, Pincus launched his first start-up, Freeloader, Inc., a web-based push technology service. Individual, Inc., acquired the company only seven months later for $38 million.[20] Pincus later founded his third start-up, Tribe.net, one of the first social networks. Tribe.net focused on partnerships with major, yet local, newspapers and was supported by *The Washington Post,* Knight Ridder Digital, and Mayfield Fund.[21] Unfortunately for him, Pincus's resume did not impress his competitors, irritated by what they viewed as his questionable business tactics, nor did it dissuade them from making their feelings known via a lengthening laundry list of threats and lawsuits.

Intellectual Property and Ethical Issues

Nissan has claimed that its trademarks were used without consent in Zynga's game Street Racing. Zynga consequently changed the thumbnail images and renamed all the cars that were branded Nissan and Infiniti to "Sindats" and "Fujis."[22] Zynga was criticized on *Hacker News* as well as other social media sites for filing a patent application involving the ability to obtain virtual currency for cash on gambling and other gaming websites. Many said that the concept was not new and that in fact significant prior art for the concept already existed.[23] The unveiling of the game Mafia Wars generated a lawsuit from the creators of Mob Wars. An attorney of the parent company of Mob Wars said that by making Mafia Wars, Zynga "copied virtually every important aspect of the game."[24] The lawsuit was later settled out of court for an amount between $7 million and $9 million.[25]

California-based web developer SocialApps brought Zynga to court seeking damages for alleged "copyright infringement, violation of trade secrets, breach of written contract, breach of implied-in-fact contract, and breach of confidence." SocialApps claimed to have entered into an agreement with Zynga, allowing Zynga access to the source code for SocialApps' Facebook game MyFarm in exchange for an undisclosed compensation. According to the suit, Zynga was given the code, but failed to pay SocialApps. SocialApps claimed that MyFarm's source code was the foundation of Farmville, as well as many of Zynga's similar games.[26] Following Zynga's release of the game Hidden Chronicles, *Forbes'* Paul Tassi wrote that Zynga "refuses to innovate in any way, and is merely a follower when it comes to ideas and game design."[27]

Ethical issues, though less tangible and definable than intellectual property, were equally troubling in assessments of Zynga's operations. A former employee of the company revealed firsthand quotes from CEO Mark Pincus, such as: "You're not smarter than your competitor. Just copy what they do and do it until you get their numbers." One contractor said he was presented with freelance work from Zynga related to imitating a competitor's application and was given precise instructions to "copy that game."[28] Other past employees, even those at the senior level, spoke out about the corrupt ways that Pincus had apparently decided to operate the business. One quoted the banter of employees in the office, "Do Evil," a twist on the Google motto, "Don't Be Evil."[29]

A former high-level Zynga employee provided an insight into the company's culture, as regarding any emphasis on creativity and originality. According to the employee, a group of designers brought a new and innovative idea to the table, only to have it turned down by Pincus because of his wariness toward a new idea that didn't fit the "tried-and-true" mold of other successes.[30]

Zynga was accused of taking advantage of its end customers, pertaining to a lack of security and safekeeping of consumer information. The Norwegian Consumer Council filed a complaint against Zynga to the Data Inspectorate concerning breaches of the Data Protection Act. According to the Consumer Council, Zynga's terms of use "do not offer a clear description of what is being collected in terms of information or what this information is being used for. Nor do they state how long the information is stored for or how it is protected against unauthorized access." The Consumer Council went even further with its forewarning: "Many of the gravest examples of unreasonable and one-sided terms of use can be found in games providers such as Zynga."[31]

Zynga Going Forward

Although Zynga game users tend to be pleased with Zynga's games, many note there seem to be recurring obstacles that limit that pleasure. Many Zynga users complain of lag time while playing the games. Even more complain that when problems arise, Zynga support staff are nowhere to be found. The company has no customer service initiative and forces users to resort to sending their claims through e-mail—which many believed is ignored, or never read. Further, many believe that the company makes it too difficult for users to make real strides in the games without spending ridiculous sums of money. Based on their experiences, many users believe that Zynga is all about revenue generation and that everything else comes second.

As Zynga looks to the future, where might its next big hit come from? With all the criticism aimed at Zynga's past behavior, will the company continue on the path it has become notorious for and reap further accusations of imitating its competitors' games? Or will Zynga change its approach, gain a reputation for intellectual integrity, and

begin creating true one-of-a-kind games—showing its capabilities as a leader in the industry rather than a follower? With all eyes on the company, it is certain that it won't be easy for Zynga to get away with some of its earlier stunts, especially now as a public company. As a public company, Zynga needs to watch its step or prepare to feel the wrath of its shareholders.

ENDNOTES

1. http://www.pocketgamer.biz/list/62773/top-50-mobile-game-developers-of-2016/entry/48/.
2. Zynga Q4 2014 earnings call transcripts.
3. www.vanityfair.com/business/features/2011/06/mark-pincus-farmville-201106.
4. http://news.cnet.com/8301-31001_3-20093473-261/zynga-targeted-in-patent-infringement-lawsuit/.
5. www.appdata.com/apps/facebook/291549705119-cityville.
6. www.reuters.com/article/2011/11/30/us-zynga-ipo-idUSTRE7AT2FJ20111130.
7. http://techcrunch.com/2010/10/15/rockyou-rocked-by-layoffs-as-it-switches-focus-to-social-games/.
8. http://investor.realnetworks.com/faq.cfm?faqid=2.
9. www.gamehouse.com/.
10. www.gamasutra.com/view/news/32496/Playfish_Social_Games_Reaching_55_Million_Monthly_Players.php.
11. www.insidesocialgames.com/2011/04/19/exclusive-playfish-ending-playfish-cash-going-almost-all-in-on-facebook-credits/.
12. www.appdata.com/devs/30679-crowdstar.
13. www.businessweek.com/news/2010-03-31/crowdstar-said-to-break-off-talks-to-be-bought-by-microsoft.html.
14. http://venturebeat.com/2011/05/23/social-game-leader-crowdstar-raises-23m-from-intel-and-time-warner/.
15. http://www.bloomberg.com/research/stocks/private/snapshot.asp?privcapId=127260687
16. http://www.gamespot.com/articles/100-million-people-play-clash-of-clans-devs-games-/1100-6435433/
17. http://company.zynga.com/about/leadership-team/zynga-management.
18. http://venturebeat.com/2010/01/11/crunchies-winners-facebook-bing/.
19. http://techcrunch.com/2011/01/21/congratulations-crunchies-winners-twitter-takes-best-startup-of-2010/.
20. http://startup2startup.com/2009/06/24/june29-markpincus-zynga/.
21. www.nytimes.com/2007/03/03/technology/03social.html?pagewanted=1&_r=1&ei=5088&en=f718f182170673a4&ex=1330578000.
22. http://mafiawars.wikia.com/wiki/Zynga.
23. http://allfacebook.com/zynga-patent-currency_b20985.
24. www.bizjournals.com/sanfrancisco/stories/2009/07/13/story7.html.
25. http://techcrunch.com/2009/09/13/zynga-settles-mob-wars-litigation-as-it-settles-in-to-playdom-war/.
26. www.joystiq.com/2011/07/18/lawsuit-filed-against-zynga-over-farmville-source-code/.
27. www.forbes.com/sites/insertcoin/2012/01/06/zynga-stock-falls-as-second-post-ipo-game-fails-to-impress/.
28. http://blog.games.com/2010/09/08/zynga-ceo-to-employees-i-dont-f-ing-want-innovation/.
29. http://blogs.sfweekly.com/thesnitch/2011/11/zynga_corporate_culture.php.
30. www.sfweekly.com/2010-09-08/news/farmvillains/4/.
31. http://forbrukerportalen.no/Artikler/2010/Facebook_and_Zynga_reported_to_the_Data_Inspectorate.

CASE 5

QVC*

After years of shrugging off competition from traditional and online retailers, home shopping TV channel QVC is finally seeing cracks in a business model that has relied on impulse purchases by television viewers. QVC's U.S. sales fell 6 percent during the last part of 2016, the first drop in seven years on its home turf. It was especially troubling that this decline extended into the crucial year-end holiday period. The slip raises questions about the resilience of QVC as it faces growing competition from e-commerce along with the drop in cable television subscribers.

Launched in 1986, QVC rapidly grew to become the largest television shopping network. Although it entered the market a couple of years after rival Home Shopping Network, the channel soon built a leading position. By 2016, its reach had extended to almost 350 million households all over the world. It regularly features about 1000 products on its sites each week, leading to almost $9 million in sales (see Exhibits 1 and 2). Beyond the United States, its presence has grown to the U.K., Germany, France, Italy, Japan, and through a 49 percent interest in a joint venture, to China (see Exhibit 3).

The success of QVC is driven by its popular television shows that feature a wide variety of eye-catching products, many of which are unique to the channel. It organizes product searches in cities all over the U.S. in order to continuously find new offerings from entrepreneurs that can be pitched to customers. During any of these search events, the firm has to screen hundreds of products. In one of its recent searches, QVC had to evaluate the appeal of such products as nail clippers that catch clippings, bicycle seats built for bigger bottoms, and novelty items shaped like coffins.

QVC battles a perception that direct-response TV retailers just sell hokey, flimsy, or kitschy goods. Its jewelry selection features prestigious brands such as Tacori, worn by TV stars. It offers clothing from couture designers such as Marc Bouwer, who has made clothing for Angelina Jolie and Halle Berry. And it has recently added exclusive products from reality stars such as Kim Kardashian and Rachel Zoe, who have introduced thousands to QVC, often through social media like Facebook and Twitter. "Rachel Zoe brings so many new customers it's staggering," said CEO Michael George.[1]

QVC has expanded its shopping experience to the Internet, attracting more than 7 million unique monthly visitors by early 2015. It attracts customers from its television channel to its website, making it one of the leading multimedia retailers. Building on this, the firm has been creating a family of mobile shopping applications for smartphones and tablets. Although QVC is still developing this segment, mobile applications already account for almost a third of its sales.

Pursuing a Leading Position

QVC was founded by Joseph Segel in June 1986 and began broadcasting in November that year. Earlier in 1986, Segel had tuned in to the Home Shopping Network, which had been launched two years earlier. He had not been impressed with the crude programming and the down-market products that he saw. But he was convinced that an enhanced

EXHIBIT 1 ANNUAL SALES (In Billions of dollars)

2016	$8.7
2015	8.7
2014	8.8
2013	8.6
2012	8.5
2011	8.3
2010	7.8
2009	7.4
2008	7.3
2007	7.4
2006	7.1
2004	5.7
2001	3.8
1998	2.4
1995	1.6
1992	0.9
1989	0.2

Source: QVC, Liberty Media.

---

* Case prepared by Jamal Shamsie, Michigan State University, with the assistance of Professor Alan B. Eisner, Pace University. Material has been drawn from published sources to be used for purposes of class discussion. Copyright © 2017 Jamal Shamsie and Alan B. Eisner.

EXHIBIT 2 Consolidated Statement of Operations ($ millions)

	Year Ended December 31		
	2016	**2015**	**2014**
Net revenue	$8,682	8,743	8,801
Cost of goods sold	5,540	5,528	5,547
Gross profit	3,142	3,215	3,254
Operating expenses:			
Operating	606	607	618
Selling, general and administrative, including stock-based compensation	728	745	770
Depreciation	142	134	135
Amortization	463	454	452
	1,939	1,940	1,975
Operating income	1,203	1,275	1,279
Other (expense) income:			
Equity in losses of investee	(6)	(9)	(8)
Gains on financial instruments	2	—	—
Interest expense, net	(210)	(208)	(239)
Foreign currency gain	38	14	3
Loss on extinguishment of debt	—	(21)	(48)
	(176)	(224)	(292)
Income before income taxes	1,027	1,051	987
Income tax expense	(385)	(389)	(354)
Net income	642	662	633
Less net income attributable to the noncontrolling interest	(38)	(34)	(39)
Net income attributable to QVC, Inc. stockholder	$ 604	628	594

Source: QVC, Inc.

EXHIBIT 3 Geographic Breakdown of Revenue ($ millions)

	Year Ended December 31,		
(in millions)	**2016**	**2015**	**2014**
United States	$6,120	6,257	6,055
Japan	897	808	908
Germany	865	837	970
United Kingdom	654	718	730
Other countries	146	123	138
Consolidated QVC	$8,682	8,743	8,801

Source: Liberty Media, QVC.

TV shopping network would have the potential to attract a large client base and produce significant profits. He envisioned superior resources he could bring to his network, while the operating expenses for a shopping network could still be kept relatively low.

Over the next few months, Segel raised $30 million in start-up capital, hired several seasoned television executives, and launched QVC. Operating out of headquarters in West Chester, Pennsylvania, QVC offered 24-hour, seven-day television home shopping to viewers. By the end of its first year of operation, QVC reached 13 million homes by satellite and cable systems; 700,000 viewers had become customers, resulting in shipping 3 million orders. Sales had already topped $100 million and the firm was able to show a small profit.

Segel attributed the instant success of his company to the potential offered by television shopping. "Television's combination of sight, sound and motion is the best way to sell a product. It is more effective than presenting a product in print or just putting the product on a store shelf," he stated. "The cost-efficiency comes from the cable distribution system. It is far more economical than direct mail, print advertising, or traditional retail store distribution."[2]

In fall 1988, Segel acquired the manufacturing facilities, proprietary technology, and trademark rights of the Diamonique Corporation, which produced a wide range of simulated gemstones and jewelry that could be sold on QVC shows. Over the next couple of years, Segel expanded QVC by acquiring competitors such as the Cable Value Network Shopping channel (see Exhibit 4).

By 1993, QVC had overtaken Home Shopping Network to become the leading TV shopping channel in sales and profits. Its reach extended to over 80 percent of all cable homes and to 3 million satellite dishes. Segel retired the same year, passing control of the company to Barry Diller. Since then, QVC's sales have continued to grow substantially, widening the gap between it and Home Shopping Network, its closest competitor.

Striving for Retailing Excellence

QVC has established itself as the world's preeminent virtual shopping mall that never closes. Its customers around the world can, and do, shop at any hour at the rate of more than five customers per second. It sells a wide variety of products, using a combination of description and demonstration by live program hosts. QVC is extremely selective in choosing its hosts, screening as many as 3,000 applicants annually in order to pick three. New hosts are trained for at least six months before they are allowed on air. Regularly scheduled shows are each focused on a particular type of product and a well-defined market. Shows typically lasts for one hour and are based on a theme such as *Now You're Cooking* or *Cleaning Solutions.*

QVC frequently entices celebrities such as clothing designers or book authors to appear live on special program segments to sell their own products. In order to prepare them to succeed, celebrities are given training on how to best pitch their offerings. On some occasions, customers are able to call in and have on-air conversations with program hosts and visiting celebrities. Celebrities are schooled in QVC's "backyard-fence" style, which means conversing with viewers the way they would chat with a friendly neighbor. "They're just so down-home, so it's like they're right in your living room demonstrating," said a long time QVC customer.[3]

In spite of the folksy presentation, the sales are minutely managed. Behind the scenes, a producer scans nine television and computer screens to track sales of featured items. "We track new orders per minute in increments of six seconds; we can look backward in time and see what it was that drove that spike," said Doug Rose, who oversees programming and marketing.[4] Hosts and guests are prompted to make adjustments in their pitch that might increase sales. A beauty designer was asked to rub an eyeliner onto her hand, which immediately led to a surge of new orders.

QVC transmits its programming live from its central production facilities in Pennsylvania through uplinks to a satellite. The representatives who staff QVC's four call centers, which handle 180 million or more calls a year, are well trained to take orders. More than 90 percent of orders are shipped within 48 hours from one of QVC's distribution centers. The distribution centers have a combined floor space equivalent to the size of over 100 football fields. An effort is made to see that every item works as it should before it is shipped and that its packaging will protect it during the shipping process. "Nothing ships unless it is quality-inspected first," said one of the logistics managers for QVC. "Since our product is going business-to-consumer, there's no way to fix or change a product-related problem."[5]

All new products must pass through stringent tests that are carried out by QVC's in-house Quality Assurance Lab. Only 15 percent of the products pass the firm's rigorous quality inspection on first try and as many as a third are never offered to the public because they fail altogether.

Searching for Profitable Products

More than 100 experienced, informed buyers comb the world on a regular basis to search for new products to launch on QVC. The shopping channel concentrates on unique products that can be demonstrated on live television. Jeffrey Rayport, author of a book on customer service, states, "QVC staff look for a product that is complex enough—or interesting enough—that the host can talk about it on air."[6] Furthermore, the price of these products must be high enough for viewers to justify the additional shipping and handling charge. Over the course of a typical year, QVC carries more than 60,000 products. As many as 1,000 items are typically offered in any given week, of which about 20 percent are new products for the network. QVC's suppliers range from some of the world's biggest companies to small entrepreneurial enterprises.

About a third of QVC's sales come from broadly available national brands. The firm has been able to build trust

EXHIBIT 4 QVC MILESTONES

1986	Launched by Joseph Segel, broadcasting from studios in West Chester, PA
1987	Expands programming to 24 hours a day
1988	Acquires *Diamonique*, manufacturer of simulated gemstone jewelry
1993	Segel retires and Barry Diller is named Chairman & CEO Launches channel in U.K.
1995	Acquired by Comcast and Doug Briggs takes over as President & CEO
1996	Launches Internet site
2001	Launches channel in Japan
2003	Sold off to Liberty Media
2005	Michael George is named President
2006	George takes over as CEO with retirement of Briggs
2007	Ships its billionth package in the U.S.
2008	Launches QVCHD, a high definition simulcast in the U.S.
2009	Rolls out several mobile services
2010	Launches channel in Italy
2012	Acquires e-commerce shopping site Send the Trend Launches joint venture in China
2013	Launches QVC PLUS as a second channel in the U.S.
2015	Launches channel in France
2016	Launches operations unit in Krakow, Poland, to streamline European business operation.

Source: QVC.

among its customers in large part through offering these well-known brands. QVC relies on promotional campaigns with a variety of existing firms for another third of its sales. It has made deals with Dell, Target, and Bath & Body Works for special limited-time promotional offerings. But QVC has been most successful with products sold exclusively on QVC or not readily available through other distribution channels. Although such products account for only about a third of its sales, the firm has been able to earn higher margins with these proprietary products, many of which come from firms that are either start-ups or new entrants into the U.S. market.

Most vendors are attracted to QVC because they reap higher profits selling through the channel than they would by selling through physical stores. Stores typically require vendors to help to train or pay the sales force and to participate in periodic sales where prices are discounted. QVC rarely sells products at discount prices. Maureen Kelly, founder of Tarte Cosmetics, said she typically makes more from an eight-minute segment on QVC than she used to make in a month at a high-end department store.

QVC has been moving away from some product categories, such as home appliances and electronic gadgets, which offer lower margins. It has been gradually expanding into new product categories that have higher margins, such as cosmetics, apparel, food, and toys. Several of these new categories have displayed the strongest rates of growth in sales for the shopping channel over the past couple of years.

Expanding the Customer Base

QVC reaches almost all the cable television and broadcast satellite homes in the U.S. But only about 10 percent of these households have actually bought anything from the network. Still, QVC has developed a remarkably large customer base, many of whom make as many as 10 purchases (around 24 items) in a year. QVC devotees readily call in to the live segments to offer product testimonials, are up to date on the personal lives of their favorite program hosts, and generally view the channel as entertaining. "As weird as it may sound, for people who love the network, it's good company," says Rayport.[7]

QVC promises to deliver Quality, Value, and Convenience to its viewers. QVC hopes to attract new customers on the basis of the strong reputation that surveys indicate it has established among its current buyers. More than three-quarters of the shopping channel's customers have given it a score of 7 out of 7 for trustworthiness. Once viewers start buying from QVC, they tend to be loyal to the firm. This has led most of its customers to recommend it to their friends.

QVC has benefited from the growing percentage of women entering the workforce, resulting in a significant increase in dual-income families. Although the firm's current customer base spans several socioeconomic groups, it is led by young professional families who have above average disposable income, and enjoy various forms of "thrill-seeking" activities, including ranking shopping relatively high as a leisure activity when compared to the typical consumer.

The firm is exploring an interactive service which would allow viewers to purchase offerings with the single click of a remote. QVC also provides a credit program to allow customers to pay for goods over a period of several months. Everything it sells is backed by a 30-day unconditional money-back guarantee. Furthermore, QVC does not impose any hidden charges, such as a "restocking fee," for any returned merchandise. These policies help the home shopping channel to attract customers for products that they can view but are not able to either touch or feel.

In 2012, QVC built on its existing customer base by acquiring Send the Trend, Inc., an e-commerce destination known for trendy fashion and beauty products. It uses proprietary technology to deliver monthly personalized recommendations that can easily be shared by customers over their social networks for an assortment of prestigious brands in jewelry, beauty and fashion accessories. "The teams at QVC and Send the Trend share a passion for bringing the customer what she wants, in the way she wants it," said Claire Watts, the U.S.–based CEO of QVC.[8]

Positioning for Future Growth

In spite of its success on television, QVC has not ignored opportunities that are emerging in online shopping. Since 1996, the firm has offered a website to complement its television channel which has provided it with another form of access to customers. Initially, the site offered more detailed information about QVC offerings. Since then, it has branched out to develop its own customer base by featuring many products that have not been recently shown on its television channel. Over the last few years, QVC has been fine-tuning its website by offering mobile phone, interactive-television, and iPad apps.

By 2012, QVC.com, a once-negligible part of the QVC empire, accounted for about a third of the firm's domestic revenue. CEO Michael George recently stated that 60 percent of QVC's new customers in the United States buy on the Internet or on mobile devices. "The online business is becoming such a crucial part of the business for QVC," remarked Douglas Anmuth, an analyst at Barclay's Capital.[9] Furthermore, QVC.com is now more profitable than QVC's television operation. It needs fewer call-center workers, and while QVC must share profits with cable companies on TV orders, it does not have to pay them on online orders for products which have not been featured on the air for 24 hours.

The falloff in cable television subscribers may affect QVC. QVC is not immune from shifts in technology usage and people's entertainment choices and information gathering habits. But for many of QVC's loyal consumers, nothing will ever replace shopping via television. Michael George insists that QVC shoppers are less likely to drop cable services because they tend to be slightly older and more affluent. These customers tune in at different times of the day or night and are drawn to the offerings. "We're going to try and find 120 to 140 items every day where we think we can tell compelling stories and inspire you to consider it," he says.[10]

The website does not offer the hybrid of talk show and sales pitch that attracts audiences to the QVC shopping television channel. Online shoppers also miss out on the interaction between hosts and shoppers and the continuous urgent feedback about the time that they may have to place an order before an item is sold out. "You know, on Sundays I might find a program on Lifetime Movie Network, but whatever I'm watching, if it's not QVC, when the commercial comes on I'll flip it back to QVC," said one loyal QVC fan. "I'm just stuck on them."[11]

ENDNOTES

1. Stephanie Clifford. Can QVC translate its pitch online? *New York Times,* November 21, 2010, p. B7.
2. QVC Annual Report, 1987–1988.
3. *New York Times,* November 21, 2010, p. B7.
4. Ibid.
5. Eugene Gilligan. The show must go on. *Journal of Commerce,* April 12, 2004, p. 1.
6. *USA Today,* May 5, 2008, p. 2B.
7. Ibid.
8. Send the Trend relaunches with QVC to bring shoppers a more personalized e-commerce experience. *PR Newswire,* October 2, 2012.
9. *New York Times,* November 21, 2010, p. B7.
10. Paul Ziobro. QVC's strength ebbs as web retail booms. *Wall Street Journal,* January 12, 2017, p. B6.
11. *New York Times,* November 21, 2010, p. B7.

CASE 6

MICROFINANCE: GOING GLOBAL . . . AND GOING PUBLIC?*

In the world of development, if one mixes the poor and nonpoor in a program, the nonpoor will always drive out the poor, and the less poor will drive out the more poor, unless protective measures are instituted right at the beginning.

—Dr. Muhammad Yunus, founder of Grameen Bank[1]

More than 2.5 billion people in the world earn less than $2.50 a day. None of the developmental economics theories have helped change this situation. Less than $2.50 a day means that these unfortunate people have been living without clean water, sanitation, sufficient food to eat, or a proper place to sleep. In Southeast Asia alone, more than 500 million people live under these circumstances. In the past, almost every effort to help the very poor has been either a complete failure or at best partially successful. As Dr. Yunus argues, in every one of these instances, the poor will push the very poor out!

In 1972 Dr. Muhammad Yunus, a young economics professor trained at Vanderbilt, returned home to Bangladesh to take a position at Chittagong University. Upon his arrival, he was struck by the stark contrast between the developmental economics he taught in the classroom and the abject poverty of the villages surrounding the university. Dr. Yunus witnessed more suffering of the poor when, in 1974, inclement weather wiped out food crops and resulted in a widespread and prolonged famine. The theories of developmental economics and the traditional banking institutions, he concluded, were completely ineffectual for lessening the hunger and homelessness among the very poor of that region.

In 1976 Dr. Yunus and his students were visiting the poorest people in the village of Jobra to see whether they could directly help them in any way. They met a group of craftswomen making simple bamboo stools. After paying for their raw materials and financing, the women were left with a profit of just two cents per day. From his own pocket, Dr. Yunus gave $27 to be distributed among 42 craftswomen and *rickshaw* (human-driven transport) drivers. Little did he know that this simple act of generosity was the beginning of a global revolution in microfinance that would eventually help millions of impoverished and poor begin a transition from destitution to economic self-sufficiency. Dr. Yunus was convinced that a nontraditional approach to financing is the only way to help the very poor to help themselves.

The Grameen Project would soon follow—it officially became a bank under the law in 1983. The poor borrowers own 95 percent of the bank, and the rest is owned by the Bangladeshi government. Loans are financed through deposits only, and there are 8.35 million borrowers, of which 97 percent are women. There are over 2,500 branches serving around 81,000 villages in Bangladesh with a staff of more than 22,000 people. Since its inception, the bank has dispersed more than $10 billion, with a cumulative loan recovery rate of 97.38 percent. The Grameen Bank has been profitable every year since 1976 except three years and pays returns on deposits up to 100 percent to its members.[2] In 2006 Dr. Yunus and the Grameen Bank shared the Nobel Peace Prize for the concept and methodology of microfinance, also known as micro-credit or microloans.[3]

What Is Microfinance?

Microfinance involves a small loan (US$20–$750) with a high rate of interest (0 to 200 percent), typically provided to poor or destitute entrepreneurs without collateral.[4] A traditional loan has two basic components captured by interest rates: (1) risk of future payment, and (2) present value (given the time value of money). Risk of future payments is particularly high when dealing with the poor, who are unlikely to have familiarity with credit. To reduce this uncertainty, many microfinance banks refuse to lend to individuals and only lend to groups. Groups have proven to be an effective source of "social collateral" in the microloan process.

In addition to the risk and time value of money, the value of a loan must also include the transaction costs associated with administering the loan. A transaction cost is the cost associated with an economic exchange and is often considered the cost of doing business. For banks like the Grameen Bank, the cost of administering ($125) a small loan may exceed the amount of the small loan itself ($120). These transaction costs have been one of the major deterrents for traditional banks.

Consider a bank with $10,000 to lend. If broken into small loans ($120), the available $10,000 can provide about 83 transactions. If the cost to administer a small loan ($120) is $125, its cost per unit is about 104 percent (!), while the cost of one $10,000 loan is only 1.25 percent.

* This case was developed by Brian C. Pinkham, LL.M., and Dr. Padmakumar Nair, both from the University of Texas at Dallas. Material has been drawn from published sources to be used for class discussion. Copyright © 2011 Brian C. Pinkham and Padmakumar Nair.

Because of the high cost per unit and the high risk of future payment, the rate of interest assigned to the smaller loan is much higher than the rate on the larger loan.

Finally, after these costs are accounted for, there must be some margin (or profit). In the case of microfinance banks, the margins are split between funding the growth of the bank (adding extra branches) and returns on deposits for bank members. This provides even the poorest bank member a feeling of "ownership."

Microfinance and Initial Public Offerings

With the global success of the microfinance concept, the number of private microfinance institutions exploded. Today there are more than 7,000 microfinance institutions, and their profitability has led many of the larger institutions to consider whether or not to "go public." Many microfinance banks redistribute profits to bank members (the poor) through returns on deposits. Once the bank goes public through an initial public offering (IPO), however, there is a transfer of control to public buyers (typically investors from developed economies). This transfer creates a fiduciary duty of the bank's management to maximize value for the shareholders.[5]

For example, Compartamos Banco (Banco) of Mexico raised $467 million in its IPO in 2007. The majority of buyers were leading investment companies from the United States and United Kingdom—the geographic breakdown of the investors was 52 percent U.S., 33 percent Europe, 5 percent Mexico, and 10 percent other Latin American countries. Similarly, Bank Rakyat Indonesia (BRI) raised $480 million in its IPO by listing on multiple stock exchanges in 2003; the majority of investors who purchased the available 30 percent interest in the bank were from the United States and United Kingdom. The Indonesian government controls the remaining 70 percent stake in BRI. In Kenya, Equity Bank raised $88 million in its IPO in late 2006. Because of the small scale of Equity Bank's initial listing on the Nairobi Stock Exchange, the majority of the investors were from eastern Africa.[6] About one-third of the investors were from the European Union and United States."[7]

Compartamos Banco[8]

Banco started in 1990 as a nongovernmental organization (NGO). At the time, population growth in Latin America and Mexico outpaced job growth. This left few job opportunities within the largest population group in Mexico—the low-income. Banco recognized that the payoffs for high-income opportunities were much larger (dollars a day), relative to low-income opportunities that may return only pennies a day. Over the next 10 years, Banco offered larger loans to groups and individuals to help bridge the gap between these low-income and high-income opportunities. However, its focus is to serve low-income individuals and groups, particularly the women who make up 98 percent of Banco's members.

The bank offers two microfinance options available to women only. The first is the *crédito mujer* (women's credit).

This loan ranges from $115 to $2,075, available to groups (12–50) of women. Maturity is four months, and payments are weekly or biweekly.

If a group of women demonstrates the ability to manage credit through the *crédito mujer,* they have access to *crédito mejora tu casa* (home-improvement loans). This loan ranges from $230 to $2,300 with a 6- to 24-month maturity. Payments are either biweekly or monthly.

The average interest rate on these loans is 80 percent. Banco focuses on loans to *groups* of women and requires the guarantee of the group—*every* individual in the group is held liable for the payment of the loan. This provides a social reinforcement mechanism for loan payments typically absent in traditional loans. The bank also prefers groups because they are more likely to take larger loans. This has proven effective even in times of economic downturn, when banks typically expect higher demand for loans and lower recovery of loans.

In 2009, with Mexico still reeling from the economic recession of 2008, Banco provided financing to 1.5 million Mexican households. This represented a growth of 30 percent from 2008. The core of the financing was *crédito mujer,* emphasizing the bank's focus on providing services for the low-income groups. The average loan was 4.6 percent of GDP per capita ($440), compared with an average loan of 54 percent of GDP per capita ($347) at the Grameen Bank in Bangladesh.[9] With pressure from the economic downturn, Banco also reduced its cost per client by more than 5 percent, and it continues (in late 2010) to have a cost per client under $125.

Consider two examples of how these microloans are used. Julia González Cueto, who started selling candy door-to-door in 1983, used her first loan to purchase accessories to broaden the image of her business. This provided a stepping-stone for her decision to cultivate mushrooms and nopales (prickly pear leaves) to supplement her candy business. She now exports wild mushrooms to an Italian restaurant chain. Leocadia Cruz Gómez has had 16 loans, the first in April 2006. She invested in looms and thread to expand her textile business. Today, her workshop has grown, she is able to travel and give classes, and her work is widely recognized.

Beyond the Grameen Bank

These are just a few examples of how capitalistic free-market enterprises have helped the world to progress. It is generally accepted that charitable contributions and government programs alone cannot alleviate poverty. More resources and professional management are essential for microfinance institutions to grow further and sustain their mission. An IPO is one way to achieve this goal when deposits alone cannot sustain the demand for loans. At the same time, investors expect a decent return on their investment, and this expectation might work against the most important goal of microfinancing, namely, to help the very poor. Dr. Yunus has recently reemphasized his concern of the nonpoor driving out the poor, and he talks about microfinance institutions seeking investments from "social-objective-driven" investors with a need to create a separate "social stock market."[10]

The Grameen Bank story, and that of microfinancing, and the current enthusiasm in going public raise several concerns. Institutions like the Grameen Bank have to grow and sustain a long-run perspective. The Grameen Bank has not accepted donor money since 1998 and does not foresee a need for donor money or other sources of external capital. The Grameen Bank charges four interest rates, depending on who is borrowing and for what purpose the money is being used: 20 percent for income-generating loans, 8 percent for housing loans, 5 percent for student loans, and interest-free loans for struggling members (unsympathetically called beggars). (Although these rates would appear to be close to what U.S. banks charge, we must point out that the terms of these loans are typically three or four months. Thus, the annualized interest rates would be four or five times the aforementioned rates.)

The Grameen Bank's "Beggars-As-Members" program is a stark contrast to what has been theorized and practiced in contemporary financial markets—traditional banking would assign high-risk borrowers (like beggars) the highest interest rate compared to more reliable borrowers who are using the borrowed money for generating income. Interestingly, the loan recovery rate is 79 percent from the "Beggars-As-Members" program, and about 20,000 members (out of 110,000) have left begging completely.[11] However, it is difficult to predict the future, and it is possible that the Grameen Bank might consider expanding its capital base by going public just like its Mexican counterpart.

Most developmental economists question the wisdom of going public, because publicly traded enterprises are likely to struggle to find a balance between fiduciary responsibilities and social good.[12] The three large IPOs mentioned above (Banco, BRI, and Equity First) all resulted in improved transparency and reporting for stockholders. However, the profits, which were originally distributed to bank members as returns on deposits, are now split between bank members (poor) and stockholders (made up of mostly EU and U.S. investors). Many of these microfinance banks are feeling the pressure of NGOs and bank members requesting lower interest rates.[13] This trend could potentially erode the large profit margins these banks currently enjoy. When faced with falling profits, publicly traded microfinance institutions will have to decide how best to provide financial services for the very poor and struggling members of the society without undermining their fiduciary duties to stockholders.

ENDNOTES

1. Yunus, M. 2007. *Banker to the poor: Micro-lending and the battle against world poverty.* New York: PublicAffairs.

2. The Grameen Bank removes funding for administration and branch growth from the initial profits and redistributes the remaining profits to bank members. This means that a poor bank member who deposits $1 in January may receive up to $1 on December 31! Grameen Bank, www.grameen-info.org.

3. Grameen Bank, www.grameen-info.org.

4. Microfinance banks vary to the extent that the rates of interest are annualized or specified to the term. Grameen Bank, for instance, annualizes the interest on its microloans. However, many other banks set a periodic rate whereby, in extreme cases, interest may accrue daily. Grameen Bank, www.grameen-info.org.

5. Khavul, S. 2010. Microfinance: Creating opportunities for the poor? *Academy of Management Perspectives,* 24(3): 58–72.

6. Equity Bank, www.equitybank.co.ke.

7. Rhyne, E., & Guimon, A. 2007. The Banco Compartamos initial public offering. *Accion: InSight,* no. 23: 1–17, resources.centerforfinancialinclusion.org.

8. Unless otherwise noted, this section uses information from Banco Compartamos, www.compartamos.com.

9. We calculated all GDP per capita information as normalized to current (as of 2010) U.S. dollars using the International Monetary Fund (IMF) website, www.imf.org. The estimated percentages are from Banco Compartamos, www.compartamos.com.

10. Yunus. 2007. *Banker to the poor.*

11. Grameen Bank, www.grameen-info.org.

12. Khavul. 2010. Microfinance.

13. Rhyne & Guimon. 2007. The Banco Compartamos initial public offering.

CASE 7

WORLD WRESTLING ENTERTAINMENT*

World Wrestling Entertainment was planning to crown its first ever WWE United Kingdom Champion live on the WWE Network during a special, two-night tournament on January 14 and January 15, 2017. "Our passionate U.K. fans deserve their own Champion," said WWE's Vice President Paul Levesque.[1]

Pushing a strategy to cater to local markets is one way WWE is trying to deal with the growing competition from different forms of mixed martial arts, which present a free-for-all of boxing, ju-jitsu, and wrestling, among other disciplines. Ultimate Fighting Championship, for instance, has been expanding around the world, while ONE Championship has been stealing markets in Asia by building up local fighters in each market.

WWE does not have much to worry about in the short run (see Exhibit 1). Its strategy of coupling its live wrestling matches with programming on television, on the web, and on mobile devices has made it one of the world's most social brands. The firm recently added to its presence on the Internet with an exclusive, multi-year agreement to bring WWE programming to Hulu Plus, offering next-day access to its television programs and other exclusive shows. "We continue to see the distribution of our creative content through various emerging channels," Linda McMahon stated in 2009 when she was the firm's president and CEO.[2] Clearly, WWE has moved out of the slump that it endured between 2001 and 2005.

During the 1990s, Vince McMahon used a potent mix of shaved, pierced, and pumped-up muscled hunks; buxom, scantily-clad, and sometimes cosmetically enhanced beauties; and body-bashing clashes of good versus evil to build an empire that claimed over 35 million fans. The vast majority of these fans were males between the ages of 12 and 34, the demographic segment that makes most advertisers drool.

Just when it looked like everything was going well, WWE hit a rough patch. Its attempt to move beyond wrestling to other sports and entertainment was not successful. It failed with its launch of a football league during 2001, which folded after just one season. WWE has not done much better with its foray into movies that use some of its wrestlers. The firm was also struggling with its efforts to build new wrestling stars and to introduce new characters

into its shows. Some of its most valuable younger viewers were turning to new reality-based shows on television such as *Survivor, Fear Factor,* and *Jackass.*

Since 2005, however, WWE has been turning pro wrestling into a perpetual road show that makes millions of fans pass through turnstiles in a growing number of locations around the globe. Its flagship television programs, *Raw* and *Smackdown!* are broadcast in 30 languages in 145 countries reaching 600 million homes around the world. WWE has also been signing pacts with dozens of licensees, including one with toymaker Mattel, to sell DVDs, video games, toys, and trading cards.

Developing a Wrestling Empire

Most of the success of the WWE can be attributed to the persistent efforts of Vince McMahon. A self-described juvenile delinquent who went to military school as a teenager to avoid being sent to a reformatory institution, around 1970 Vince joined his father's wrestling company which operated in northeastern cities such as New York, Philadelphia, and Washington, D.C. He did on-air commentary, developed scripts, and otherwise promoted the wrestling matches.

Vince bought the wrestling firm from his father in 1982, eventually renaming it World Wrestling Federation. At that time, wrestling was managed by regional fiefdoms where everyone avoided encroaching on anyone else's territory. Vince began to change all that by paying local television stations around the country to broadcast his matches. His aggressive pursuit of audiences across the country gradually squeezed out most of the other rivals. "I banked on the fact that they were behind the times, and they were," said Vince.[3]

Vince broke another taboo by admitting to the public that wrestling matches were scripted. Although he made this admission to avoid the scrutiny of state athletic commissions, wrestling fans appreciated the honesty. The WWF began to draw in more fans through the elaborate

EXHIBIT 1 Income Statement ($ millions)

	2016	2015	2014
Net Revenues	$729.2	$658.8	$542.6
Operating Income	55.6	38.8	(42.5)
Net Income	33.8	24.1	(30.1)

Source: WWE Annual Report 2017.

* Case prepared by Jamal Shamsie, Michigan State University, with the assistance of Professor Alan B. Eisner, Pace University. Material has been drawn from published sources to be used for purposes of class discussion. Copyright © 2017 Jamal Shamsie and Alan B. Eisner.

story lines and captivating characters of its wrestling matches. The firm turned wrestlers such as Hulk Hogan and Andre the Giant into mainstream icons of pop culture. By the late 1980s, the WWF's *Raw Is War* had become a top-rated show on cable, and the firm had also begun to offer pay-per-view shows.

Vince faced his most formidable competition after 1988, when Ted Turner bought out World Championship Wrestling, one of the few major rivals that was still operating. Turner spent millions luring away WWF stars such as Hulk Hogan and Macho Man Randy Savage. He used these stars to launch a show on his own TNT channel to go up against WWF's major show, *Raw Is War.* Although Turner's new show caused a temporary dip in the ratings for WWF's shows, Vince fought back with pumped-up scripts, mouthy muscle-men, and Lycra-clad women. "Ted Turner decided to come after me and all of my talent," growled Vince, "and now he's where he should be."[4] In 2001, Vince acquired WCW from Turner's parent firm AOL Time Warner for a bargain price of $5 million.

Because of the manner in which he has eliminated most of his rivals, Vince has earned a reputation for being as aggressive and ambitious as any character in the ring. Paul MacArthur, publisher of *Wrestling Perspective,* an industry newsletter, praised his accomplishments: "McMahon understands the wrestling business better than anyone else. He's considered by most in the business to be brilliant."[5]

Then in 2002, WWF was hit by a ruling from a British court that their original WWF acronym belonged to the World Wildlife Fund. The firm had to undergo a major branding transition, changing its well-known name and triple logo from WWF to WWE.

Although the change in name has been costly, it is not clear that this will hurt the firm in the long run. "Their product is really the entertainment. It's the stars. It's the bodies," said Larry McNaughton, managing director and principal of CoreBrand, a branding consultancy.[6] Vince's wife Linda stated that the new name might actually be beneficial for the firm. "Our new name puts the emphasis on the 'E' for entertainment," she commented.[7]

Creating a Script for Success

It is appropriate to call WWE's entertainments wrestling shows, rather than matches. The wrestlers are characters in ongoing dramatic plots and adventure stories as much as athletes. The content of WWE's live events is akin to television soap operas and Hollywood melodramas. From the start Vince McMahon reduced the amount of actual wrestling in favor of mesmerizing characters and compelling story lines, relying on "good versus evil" and "settling the score" themes. The plots and subplots provide viewers with a mix of action, comedy, violence, sex, and even romance, against a backdrop of pyrotechnics.

Over time, the "matches," or shows, have become ever more heavily scripted, with increasingly intricate plots and dialog. All the details of every match are worked out well in advance, leaving the wrestlers to decide only the manner in which the hero dispatches a villain to the mat. Vince refers to his wrestlers as "athletic performers." They are selected on the basis of their acting ability in addition to their physical stamina.

The firm owns the rights to the characters played by its wrestlers. This allows WWE to continue to exploit the characters developed for the television shows, even after a wrestler that played a character has left the firm. By now Vince holds the rights to many characters that have become familiar to audiences around the world.

By the late 1990s Vince had two weekly shows on television. Besides the original flagship program on the USA cable channel, WWE had added a *Smackdown!* show on the UPN broadcast channel. A continuous story line featured the same characters so that the audience was driven to both the shows. The acquisition of the WCW resulted in a significant increase in the number of wrestling stars under contract. Trying to incorporate almost 150 characters into the story lines for WWE's shows proved to be a challenging task, perhaps resulting in some loss of energy in the plots. At the same time, the move of *Raw* to the Spike TV channel resulted in a loss of viewers.

However, in October 2005, WWE signed a new agreement with NBC that moved *Raw* back to its USA channel. *Smackdown!* is now carried by the Syfy channel, which has been climbing in the charts. WWE's newest show, *Total Divas,* has recently been launched on the E! network. All of these programs have done well in ratings, particularly for male viewers, because of the growth in popularity of a new breed of characters such as John Cena, Chris Benoit, Ray Mysterio, and Triple H. The visibility of these characters is enhanced through profiles on the WWE website and mobile apps.

Managing a Road Show

A typical work week for the WWE can be grueling for the McMahons, for the talent, and for the crew. The organization is now putting on almost 330 live shows a year requiring everyone to be on the road most days of the week. The touring crew includes over 200 members, including stage hands. All of WWE's live events, including those that are used for its two longstanding weekly shows *Raw* and *Smackdown!* as well as the newer ones, are held in different cities. Consequently, the crew is always packing up a dozen 18-wheelers and driving hundreds of miles to get from one performance to another. Since there are no repeats of any WWE shows, the live performances must be held all year round.

The live shows form the core of all of WWE's businesses (see Exhibit 2). They give the firm a big advantage in the entertainment world. Most of the crowd show up wearing WWE merchandise and scream throughout the show. Vince and his crew pay special attention to the response of the audience to different parts of the show. The script for each performance is not set until the day of the show, and

EXHIBIT 2 Principal Activities

Media

Network: Subscriptions to WWE Network, fees for pay-per-view, video-on-demand

Television: Fees for television rights

Home entertainment: Sales of WWE programs on various platforms, including DVDs and Blu Rays

Digital media: Revenues from advertising on websites

Live Events

Live events: Revenues from ticket sales and travel packages for live events

Consumer Products

Licensing: Revenues from royalties or license fees from video games, toys, or apparel

Venue merchandise: Revenues from merchandise at live events

WWE Shop: Revenues from merchandise sales on websites

WWE Studios

WWE Studios: Revenues from investing in producing and distributing films

Source: WWE Annual Report 2017.

sometimes changes are made in the middle of a show. This allows the crew some flexibility to respond to the emotions of the crowd as they witness the unfolding action. Vince boasts: "We're in contact with the public more than any entertainment company in the world."[8]

The shows usually fill up. Tickets and the merchandise sold at the shows cover the cost of production. Sales of merchandise also represent a significant and growing portion of the revenues from each of the live shows. The performances are the source for all the other revenue streams. They provide content for six hours of original television programming as well as for the growing list of pay-per-view and video-on-demand programming. They create strong demand for WWF merchandise purchased apart from the shows ranging from video games and toys to magazines and home videos.

Much of the footage from the live shows is used on the WWE website, which is the growth engine for its new digital media business (see Exhibits 3 and 4). The firm produces a show, *WWE NXT,* exclusively for the website. WWE also offers content on the apps that it has launched for smartphones and tablets. Fans can also follow programming on Hulu Plus, with which the firm signed an exclusive multi-year contract in 2012. All of these channels serve to promote the various offerings of the firm and carry selections from its various other television programs.

The entire operations of WWE are overseen by Vince McMahon, along with some help from other members of his family. While the slick and highly toned Vince can be regarded as the creative muscle behind the growing entertainment empire, his wife Linda has for many years been quietly managing its day-to-day operations. Throughout its existence, she has helped to balance the books, do the deals, and handle the details necessary for the growth and development of the WWF and WWE franchise. Their son and daughter have also been involved with various activities of the enterprise, with Stephanie McMahon holding an executive position in charge of creative development.

Searching for Growth

In 1999, shortly after going public, WWF launched an eight-team football league called the XFL. Promising full competitive sport unlike the heavily scripted wrestling matches, Vince tried to make the XFL a faster-paced, more fan-friendly form of football than the NFL's brand. Vince was able to partner with NBC, which was looking for a lower-priced alternative to the NFL televised games. The XFL kicked off with great fanfare in February 2001. Although the games drew good attendance, television ratings dropped steeply after the first week. The football venture folded after just one season, resulting in a $57 million loss for WWF. Both Vince and Linda insist that the venture could have paid off if it had been given enough time. Vince commented: "I think our pals at the NFL went out of their way to make sure this was not a successful venture."[9]

WWE has also tried to become involved with movie production using its wrestling stars, releasing a few films over the past decade such as Steve Austin's *The Condemned* and John Cena's *Legendary,* and smaller films designed for release in a few theatres and on television. Besides

EXHIBIT 3 Breakdown of Revenues ($ millions)

	2016	2015	2014
Network	$180.9	$159.4	$115.0
Television	241.7	231.1	176.7
Home Entertainment	13.1	13.4	27.3
Digital Media	26.9	21.5	20.9
Live Events	144.4	124.7	108.5
Licensing	49.1	48.9	38.6
Venue Merchandise	24.2	22.4	19.3
WWE Shop	34.6	27.1	20.2
WWE Studios	10.1	7.1	10.9

Source: WWE Annual Report 2017.

EXHIBIT 4 Breakdown of Operating Income ($ millions)

	2016	2015	2014
Network	$43.0	$48.4	$(1.8)
Television	119.8	97.0	61.9
Home Entertainment	5.3	4.6	15.0
Digital Media	4.6	4.4	0.3
Live Events	40.1	36.9	27.8
Licensing	27.4	28.8	20.9
Venue Merchandise	9.8	8.9	7.7
WWE Shop	7.3	5.1	3.5
WWE Studios	(0.2)	(1.5)	0.5

Source: WWE Annual Report 2017.

generating some box office revenues, these movies provide revenues from home video markets, distribution on premium channels, and offerings on pay-per-view.

The firm has all along sought growth opportunities that are driven by its core wrestling business. With more characters at their disposal and different characters being used in each of their shows, WWE has been ramping up the number of live shows, including more in overseas markets. By 2014, the firm was staging almost 70 shows in locations around the world. WWE has been expanding its live performances, introducing them in six new countries, such as UAE and Egypt. The company has opened offices in six cities around the world to manage its overseas operations.

"While it is based in America, the themes are worldwide: sibling rivalry, jealousy. We have had no pushback on the fact it was an American product," said Linda.[10]

Considerable excitement was generated by the launch of WWE 24/7, a subscriber video-on-demand service. The new service allows the firm to distribute for a fee thousands of content hours consisting of highlights from old shows as well as exclusive new programming. Much of the firm's programming, both old and new, is also offered on its website, which has continued to show strong growth. By enabling audiences to watch WWE programming whenever they may want to, these new forms of distribution have allowed the firm to reach out to new audiences.

The new push on mobile devices and also through the Hulu channel has provided ever more opportunities for WWE to expand into digital media. The firm believes that offering their programming on smartphones and tablets will lead to a significant growth in revenues, in part from additional sales of their merchandise. "Our fans have proven that they want to consume WWE content day and night and now, through our new mobile app, they can stay completely connected to the action wherever they are," said Jason Hoch, WWE's recently appointed senior vice president of digital operations.[11]

Staying the Champ

Although WWE may find it challenging to keep building on its already formidable fan base, there is no question that it continues to generate excitement. Most of the excitement is driven by the live shows, which fill up the arenas. "They have the most excited fans that have come through our doors," said the director of sales and marketing at one of the arenas that holds WWE matches. "They make signs, dress up, and cheer constantly."[12] The interest in the live matches is most evident each year with the frenzy that is created by WrestleMania, the annual pop culture extravaganza that has become an almost weeklong celebration of "everything wrestling." No wrestlers become true stars until their performance is featured at WrestleMania, and any true fan must make the pilgrimage at least once in his or her life.

WWE has begun to expand its audience by toning down the sex and violence to make their shows more family friendly. They no longer use fake blood and have toned down the use of abusive language in order to get a rating of TV-PG for their television programming. The new media, such as the launch of shows through streaming video, is expected to bring in younger viewers. "I think any good entertainment product has to change with the times," said McMahon. "You have to have your fingers on the pulse of the marketplace."[13]

Vince McMahon is aware of the growing threat of mixed martial arts, which started in Japan and Brazil, but is spreading. Because of its similarity to wrestling, this new combat sport is likely to pull away some of WWE's fans. However, everyone at WWE is convinced that these "real sports" cannot match the drama and passion of the story lines and characters that enliven their stage and draw audiences to their matches. As Dana White, president of Ultimate Fighting Championship, said: "People have been trying to count the WWE out for years. They are a powerhouse."[14]

Nevertheless, there are questions about the future of WWE after McMahon, who single-handedly built his wrestling empire from his father's small regional business. Although he has involved his wife and children in the firm, Vince has always been the brain behind the strategic moves over the years. The launch of the WWE Network, which represents a significant new step, could be his final act, according to industry observers. "If he has changed how pro wrestling and sports entertainment will reach audiences in the future, I don't think there's a better way to go out," said Brandon Stroud, a wrestling commentator and editor at the sports site *With Leather*.[15]

As for the enduring appeal of pro wrestling, Marty, a 19-year-old wrestling fan quoted in *Fortune* (October 6, 2000), may have expressed it best: "Those who understand don't need an explanation. Those who need an explanation will never understand."

ENDNOTES

1. WWE to crown U.K. champion. *Entertainment Newsweekly,* December 30, 2016.
2. WWE. World Wrestling Entertainment, Inc., reports Q3 results. Press release, February 23, 2005.
3. Bethany McLean. Inside the world's weirdest family business. *Fortune,* October 16, 2000, p. 298.
4. Diane Bradley. Wrestling's real grudge match. *BusinessWeek,* January 24, 2000, p. 164.
5. Don Mooradian. WWF gets a grip after acquisition. *Amusement Business,* June 4, 2001, p. 20.
6. Dwight Oestricher and Brian Steinberg. WW . . . E it is, after fight for F nets new name. *Wall Street Journal,* May 7, 2002, p. B2.
7. David Finnegan. Down but not out, WWE is using a rebranding effort to gain strength. *Brandweek,* June 3, 2002, p. 12.
8. *Fortune,* October 16, 2000, p. 304.
9. Diane Bradley. Rousing itself off the mat? *BusinessWeek,* February 2, 2004, p. 73.
10. Brooke Masters. Wrestling's bottom line is no soap opera. *Financial Times,* August 25, 2008, p. 15.
11. *Business Wire.* WWE launches free mobile second screen app. August 17, 2012.
12. Brandi Ball. The face of the WWE. *McClatchy-Tribune Business News,* January 13, 2011.
13. Seth Berkman. The body slam is buffering. *The New York Times,* March 31, 2014, p. B7.
14. R. M. Schneiderman. Better days, and even the candidates, are coming to WWE. *New York Times,* April 28, 2008, p. B3.
15. *New York Times,* March 31, 2014, p. B1.

CASE 8

GREENWOOD RESOURCES: A GLOBAL SUSTAINABLE VENTURE IN THE MAKING*

"Money still grows on trees."

—**Larry Light, Deputy Editor for Personal Finance,** *Wall Street Journal*[1]

"The answer to some of the world's most pressing concerns (global warming, alternative energy, sustainable forestry) lies in one of the earth's most renewable resources—trees."

—**GreenWood Resources, Inc.**[2]

Jeff Nuss and other senior managers of GreenWood Resources, Inc., emerged after a long deliberation from the conference room in their headquarters in Portland, Oregon, in June 2010. On the one hand, they were inspired by their global vision to build "a resource that lasts forever" and their belief the company, with nearly 70 employees, was finally taking off after almost 10 years of persistent efforts in building the key elements (opportunity, people, resources, and business networks) for a successful tree plantation venture. On the other hand, they had just finished a grueling meeting during which they found it hard to reach a consensus on how to proceed with two strategic investment alternatives in rural China.

Since 2000, Jeff and several other senior managers had traveled to China on numerous occasions. The process of making a deal in the Chinese forest industry had proven to be more time-consuming than anticipated. Complex ownership structures, underdeveloped farming systems, and emerging, sometimes equivocal and unpredictable, government policies characterized the forest industry in China. Chinese farmers who embraced business models and management styles far different than those in the United States posed additional complications.

By March 2009, GreenWood had assessed some 20 potential investment projects in China. The Luxi and Dongji projects passed the initial phase of screening and became the company's top priorities. The due diligence on

these two projects had been extensive, lasting over a year, but both projects still faced considerable obstacles and even potential deadlock. In June 2010, Jeff and his senior management team were still weighing the pros and cons of the two projects, which had been the subject of their last management meeting. They felt that GreenWood needed to proceed carefully to ensure the company's sustainable business criteria (rather than its financial return per se) were met in China but also realized the company needed to show some progress to its major investor in China, Oriental Timber Fund Limited. Jeff needed to bring a recommendation from his senior management team to the investment committee comprising himself and two representatives from Oriental. The decision deadline was approaching. Jeff anticipated that the next senior management meeting would result in a recommendation. Should GreenWood choose one of the two projects?

GreenWood Resources, Inc.

Founding of the Venture

In 1998, after 12 years of experience with CH2M Hill[3] as a bioresources engineer, Jeff Nuss, a native Oregonian, decided to start his own venture, GreenWood Resources, Inc., specializing in the development and management of high-yield, fast-growing tree plantations. Having looked into other potential businesses such as a golf course and a winery, he was eventually convinced, based on his education and years of experience working with poplar tree farms, that investments in tree plantations held great promise for the future (see Appendix 1 for background industry information).

Jeff's plan was to help institutional investors (pension funds, endowments, insurance companies, etc.) and wealthy individuals invest in professionally managed high-yield, short-rotation tree farms (Exhibit 1 illustrates tree rotation length and yield of several representative tree species). He wanted to operate farms in accordance with Forest Stewardship Council (FSC) certification. FSC's objective was to conserve biological diversity and enhance the long-term social and economic well-being of forest workers and local communities (see Exhibit 2).

Firms with FSC certificates were rare because the standards were stringent, often leading to higher operating costs. For example, FSC required the use of less toxic pesticides and herbicides, which were more expensive. It prohibited the use of genetically modified trees. It also demanded

* Copyright © 2014 by the *Case Research Journal* and by Lei Li, Nottingham University Business School China; Howard Feldman, University of Portland; and Alan Eisner, Pace University. This case is developed solely as the basis for class discussion. It is not intended to serve as endorsements, sources of primary data, or illustrations of effective or ineffective management. The authors acknowledge the able assistance of Wendy Ye and Pratik Rachh in the process of developing the case.

EXHIBIT 1 Tree Rotation Length and Yield

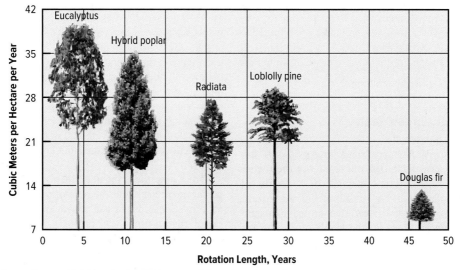

The figure shows that eucalyptus and hybrid poplar ripen for harvest much faster than other species.

Source: GreenWood's brochure.

EXHIBIT 2 Forest Stewardship Council (FSC) Principles and Criteria for Forest Management

1. **Compliance with laws and FSC principles and criteria.** Forest management shall respect all applicable laws of the country in which they occur, and international treaties and agreements to which the country is a signatory, and comply with all FSC principles and criteria.

2. **Tenure and use rights and responsibilities.** Long-term tenure and use rights to the land and forest resources shall be clearly defined, documented, and legally established.

3. **Indigenous people's rights.** The legal and customary rights of indigenous people to own, use, and manage their lands, territories, and resources shall be recognized and respected.

4. **Community relations and workers' rights.** Forest management operations shall maintain or enhance the long-term social and economic well-being of forest workers and local communities.

5. **Benefits from the forest.** Forest management operations shall encourage the efficient use of the forest's multiple products and services to ensure economic viability and a wide range of environmental and social benefits.

6. **Environmental impact.** Forest management shall conserve biological diversity and its associated value, water resources, soil, and unique and fragile ecosystems and landscapes, and, by so doing, maintain the ecological functions and the integrity of the forest.

7. **Management plan.** A management plan—appropriate to the scale and intensity of the operations—shall be written, implemented, and kept up to date. The long-term objectives of management, and the means of achieving them, shall be clearly stated.

8. **Monitoring and assessment.** Monitoring shall be conducted—appropriate to the scale and intensity of forest management—to assess the condition of the forest, yields of forest products, chain of custody, management activities, and their social and environmental impact.

9. **Maintenance of high-conservation-value forests.** Management activities in high-conservation-value forests shall maintain or enhance the attributes which define such forests. Decisions regarding high-conservation-value forests shall always be considered in the context of a precautionary approach.

10. **Plantations.** Plantations shall be planned and managed in accordance with Principles and Criteria 1–9, and Principle 10 and its Criteria. While plantations can provide an array of social and economic benefits, and can contribute to satisfying the world's needs for forest products, they should complement the management of, reduce pressures on, and promote the restoration and conservation of natural forests.

Source: Austin and Reficco 2006.[4]

that 10 percent of tree farms be reserved for native habitats. At the same time, however, the economic benefits were uncertain because most end users of wood products were not necessarily willing to pay a premium price for FSC-certified products. Nevertheless, Jeff felt it was the right thing to do. "At the end of the day, we do what we believe (is right)."

Key Milestones: Building Research Expertise and the Management Team

Looking back, Jeff recalled several key milestones for GreenWood. Having founded GreenWood with his limited personal wealth, Jeff's first milestone occurred when he convinced a large Oregon family office[5] to acquire an existing poplar plantation. As a result of this acquisition, GreenWood not only earned a steady fee through managing the poplar plantation assets for the family office but also inherited a group of staff experienced in plantation management. The head of this group was Dr. Brian Stanton, a renowned expert in poplar hybridization and genetic improvement. Over the years, Dr. Stanton's research team had developed dozens of poplar varieties characterized by high growth rate, strong pest resistance, high wood density, and broad site adaptability.

The second milestone came in 2002. On behalf of the family office, GreenWood helped sell the poplar plantation to GMO Renewable Resources, a large timber investment management organization (TIMO). Despite the ownership change, GreenWood remained the management company, taking care of the plantation assets. This enhanced the company's credibility and stature and helped initiate a business model which integrated tree improvement, nurseries, tree farm operations, product (i.e., log, lumber, chips) sales, and trading and ecosystem services (i.e., monetizing carbon credits, biodiversity credits, water quality, and renewable energy credits and managing land for total ecosystem value).

Other milestones included the formation of a seasoned management team and the development of a series of strategic relationships. In the course of formulating a viable global business plan and raising capital, Jeff was able to successfully put together what he believed was a highly competent management team (see Exhibit 3 for management team biographies and Exhibit 4 for the organizational structure). For example, Hunter Brown, a veteran operational manager with experience in Asia, joined GreenWood as the chief operating officer. Brian Liu, a Chinese American with years of experience working for the Oregon

EXHIBIT 3 Executive Management Team Biographies, 2010

Jeff Nuss is the founder, chairman, and CEO of GreenWood Resources, Inc., and its subsidiaries and is directly responsible for the leadership and strategic direction of the company. He is a leading industry spokesman and advocate for novel methods of sustainable timber production and serves on the boards of the World Forestry Center, Agribusiness Council, and Western Hardwood Council. He received a BS in bioresource engineering and an MS in resource management and policy within the Civil Engineering Department of Oregon State University.

Hunter Brown is chief operating officer of GreenWood Resources, Inc. Prior to joining GreenWood, he was executive vice president for PACCESS, a global supply chain services management firm. He has extensive business experience in Asia. Hunter received a BS in forestry from the University of the South and an MS in forestry from Duke University, and he completed the Executive Program at the Darden School of Business at the University of Virginia.

Lincoln Bach is corporate controller of GreenWood Resources, Inc. Prior to joining GreenWood, he was corporate controller for an international family-wealth-management firm. He had previously served as an audit manager at Deloitte & Touche. He received a BS in accounting from Linfield College and is a CPA and CFP professional.

Brian Stanton is managing director of Tree Improvement Group & Nurseries at GreenWood Resources, Inc. For 20 years, he has overseen the technological developments for poplar on commercial tree farms in the U.S. where he has produced over 40,000 varieties of hybrid poplar that have been tested throughout Chile, China, Europe, and the United States. Brian is the chair of the Poplar and Willow Working Party for the International Union of Forest Research Organizations. He received a BS in biology from West Chester State College, an MS in forestry from the University of Maine, and a PhD in forest resources from Pennsylvania State University.

Don Rice is managing director of Resource Management Group at GreenWood Resources, Inc. Previously, Don was the Oregon poplar resource and manufacturing manager for Potlatch Corporation. Don has a degree in agricultural engineering from Washington State University.

Jake Eaton is managing director of resource planning and acquisitions at GreenWood Resources. He worked for 21 years with Potlatch Corporation. Jake has extensive global experience in short-rotation tree farm silviculture. He holds a BS in forest management from Oregon State University and an MS in silviculture and genetics from University of Montana.

Brian Liu is vice president and general manager of GreenWood Resources, Inc.'s China Operations. Previously, as an international trade representative for the State of Oregon Department of Agriculture, he successfully led the U.S. negotiation teams in opening the Chinese market for Oregon agricultural products. Brian was born and raised in Guangdong, China, and moved to the U.S. at the age of 14. He holds a BS in finance and an MBA in international management from Portland State University. He is fluent in English, Mandarin, and Cantonese.

Source: GreenWood Resources, Inc.

EXHIBIT 4 GreenWood Resources, Inc., Topline Organization Chart, 2010*

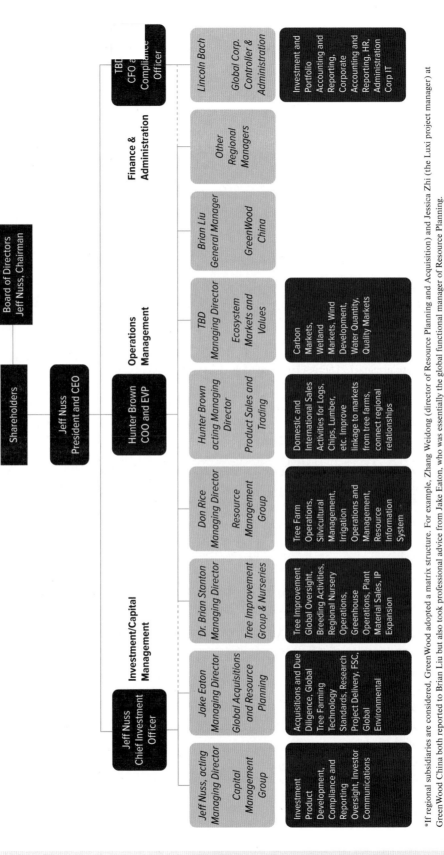

*If regional subsidiaries are considered, GreenWood adopted a matrix structure. For example, Zhang Weidong (director of Resource Planning and Acquisition) and Jessica Zhi (the Luxi project manager) at GreenWood China both reported to Brian Liu but also took professional advice from Jake Eaton, who was essentially the global functional manager of Resource Planning.

Source: GreenWood Resources, Inc.

State Department of Agriculture (responsible for the forest industry), was recruited to lead the company's China operations. Brian had supported GreenWood's endeavors while visiting China as a state government official, and he had been convinced to leave his stable government position to join GreenWood in 2005. In reflecting on his success in recruiting people, Jeff said:

> I am good at connecting to people. In that process, I am getting people around an idea and a vision and motivating (them). . . . I tried to first understand what is really their passion. If that passion can be aligned with (the vision of the company), it makes it really easy to get people on the same page and aboard.

Thanks to the dedication of its people as well as its growing business network, GreenWood looked to expand its operations to China and South America and launched two investment fund-raising campaigns to support its initiatives (see Exhibit 5).

Entering the Chinese Poplar Plantation Industry

Perhaps the most important entrepreneurial initiative for GreenWood was the decision to commit itself to the Chinese poplar plantation market. The poplar plantation industry in the United States was of limited scale. From the very beginning Jeff believed that GreenWood needed to consider opportunities in other regions of the world.

In China, the potential of high-yield, fast-growing plantations in general, and poplar tree farming in particular, was projected to be significant. Furthermore, the concept of "sustainably managing" tree farms was attractive to many people given that growing demand for wood products had resulted in years of excessive logging and, ultimately, significant desertification and deforestation. The country's loss of forestland was almost ignored until the 1990s. In response, China launched a project in 2000 to plant trees and grass in an effort to slow desertification in northern China, including the Beijing region. Nationwide, China set a goal of raising its afforestation (i.e., establishing forestland by planting seeds or trees in open land) rate to 26 percent of its land area by 2050, which would require an increase of forestland in excess of 65 million hectares.[6] To achieve this ambitious goal, high-yield, fast-growing plantations would have to play an important role.

GreenWood's Experience in China

In 2000, Jeff was invited to join a Mercy Corps task force visiting China. Mercy Corps was a Portland, Oregon–based charity whose mission was to alleviate suffering, poverty, and oppression by helping people worldwide to build just, secure, and productive communities. Its cofounder, Ells

EXHIBIT 5 A Chronicle of GreenWood Resources, Inc.

Year	Event
1998	Jeff Nuss founded GreenWood with dedication to the innovative development and management of sustainable tree farms and their products.
1999	GreenWood started to manage poplar plantation assets on behalf of a large Oregonian family office.
2000	Jeff Nuss made the initial visit to China.
2001	Dr. Brian Stanton joined GreenWood.
2002	GreenWood helped sell the poplar plantation assets to GMO Renewable Resources on behalf of the Oregonian family office and consequently became a specialized poplar assets manager for GMO Renewable Resources.
2005	Hunter Brown and Brian Liu joined GreenWood.
2005	GreenWood established its Beijing office in China.
2006	GreenWood established its representative office in Chile.
2007	GreenWood raised $175 million through GreenWood Tree Farm Fund and acquired Potlatch's poplar plantation assets in Oregon.
2008	Oriental Timber Fund Limited made a capital commitment of $200 million for GreenWood to invest in tree plantation assets in China.
2009	Preliminary assessment of 20 potential investment projects was completed by March; the Luxi and Dongji projects became priorities.
2010	GreenWood was due to make an investment decision in China together with Oriental Timber Fund Limited.

Source: Interviews.

Culver, had grown up in China as a missionary's son in the 1940s and firmly believed tree farming could help Chinese rural communities develop and flourish. He convinced Jeff, who had never thought about visiting China, to travel with him to explore the potential opportunities.

GreenWood's entry into China took part in two stages. The first took place in the five years following Jeff's initial trip, from 2000 to 2005. During this period, Jeff and his colleagues visited China three or four times every year with the express purpose of establishing relationships with academics, government agencies, and various businesses in the Chinese forest industry. Greenwood learned the market and local business practices. It also brought plant materials for site adaptability tests to one of the local tree-growing companies with which it planned to partner.

Establishing GreenWood Resources China, Ltd. (GreenWood China), a wholly owned subsidiary of GreenWood, based on greenfield investment,[7] and opening its Beijing office in 2005 highlighted the second stage of GreenWood's entry into China. Brian Liu, vice president and general manager in charge of GreenWood China, explained why it took the company five years before setting up its operating facility:

> Since the No. 9 state council decree was promulgated to encourage Chinese people to go out and grow trees in 2003, a lot of entrepreneurs jumped in. The market was overwhelmed. Some entrepreneurs were doing the wrong thing. For example, "Wanli Afforestation Group" and "Yilin Wood Industry Co., Ltd.," two large local private forestry companies, were involved in some sort of financial scheme. . . . I personally felt something was going wrong, but we didn't know what. It's not the correct way. It's not the Western way. It's just too chaotic for a Western company. In addition, we had financial and personnel constraints.

Jeff recalled the decision to enter China:

> We collectively looked at what we had been doing in China. We came to the conclusion that if we were going to do anything, we couldn't do it from afar . . . we knew that we wanted to go and put a nursery there. . . . China had two main hybrid varietals of poplar trees imported from Europe. We have many new hybrid varietals. We felt the best opportunity for us was that (China) needed more (plant) materials, better materials. . . . The (Chinese) government was issuing policies in the forestry sector that were all laser-driven to industry-based plantations, of which 45 percent were represented by poplar plantations.

Despite the potentially immense opportunities in the Chinese tree plantation market and Jeff's experience, passion, and business connections, raising institutional capital proved to be very challenging. Investors looked to historical performance and operating scale, which made it difficult for a relatively young venture like GreenWood to attract investment funds. GreenWood wanted to raise US$5 million (in the form of equity) to fund its entry but was able to raise only about US$1 million. Regardless, Jeff believed

GreenWood's global vision, entrepreneurial spirit, and relationships with the right people at the right places would eventually lead the company to success.

Brian remembered the process involved in setting up GreenWood's subsidiary in China:

> Jeff got a vision. It's critical that a leader has that vision because a lot of times, people are uncertain when it's a good time to do that. At that time, the company was small with a very limited budget. But his vision was he could get more money. . . . We came to China pretty much with that US$1 million. We didn't know how long it would last. It was very scary. It was a classic example of entrepreneurship. Let's just do it and don't look back.

Fund-Raising Success!

While GreenWood was grappling with funding difficulties in China, an acquisition opportunity arose in the Pacific Northwest region in the United States. Potlatch, a large timber company, changed ownership and decided to sell its poplar plantation assets located in Oregon. Jeff had consulted with Potlatch while working with CH2M Hill. He knew that an acquisition of Potlatch's tree farms would expand GreenWood's scale to a point where the company would be really attractive to capital investors. With the help of his business connections, Jeff established GreenWood Tree Farm Fund L.P. (GTFF) and raised US$175 million of private equity funding. GTFF used the money to purchase 18,000 acres of poplar trees from Potlatch, Inc., as well as three other poplar tree farms totaling an additional 17,000 acres. According to Jeff, this was a breakthrough for the firm that was almost serendipitous in the way it happened.

The expanded scale and personnel resulting from the US$175 million investment in GTFF enabled GreenWood to become a much more visible player in the tree plantation industry. In February 2008, Oriental, a GTFF investor interested in emerging markets, made a commitment of US$200 million to GreenWood for use in the Chinese market.[8]

Brian relished the experience:

> We changed our strategy. A lesson we learned is that you should be able to change. You should have an entrepreneurial spirit. We wanted to raise US$5 million (of equity) but ended up raising US$200 million (of capital commitment.)[9]

Risks and Challenges

China was an exploding timber market. The tree plantation industry, still in its nascent stage, was fragmented and lacked serious competition. GreenWood believed that abundant opportunities were available to it. For example, the company could use its elite plant materials and its sophisticated silvicultural (i.e., forest cultivation) management approach to substantially increase the annual growth of trees (quantity) in China as well as their quality.

GreenWood, however, faced a range of risks and challenges unique to China. First, there was a serious concern with the relatively weak intellectual property protection in the Chinese institutional system. Since plant materials existed in both tree nurseries and farms, it was hard to prevent people from "stealing" them. Elite plant materials were one of GreenWood's most valuable resources and were critical for developing its competitive advantages in China. GreenWood was confident, however, that it could capitalize on its years of experience to create increasingly better plant materials faster than any imitators could possibly copy them.

Second, there were political and social risks everywhere they turned. Chinese forestlands were owned either by the state or collectively. In practice, all kinds of government entities at different administrative levels (including small towns and villages) owned the lands, resulting in a very complex ownership structure. Many farmers worked small, government-allocated plots based on a lease contract of typically 20 to 30 years. GreenWood could negotiate long-term leases only with the local government, which either owned the lands and/or could represent farmers in striking a deal with foreign companies. A thorny issue was that "China's weak contract laws carried a risk for leaseholders. . . . In several instances, unhappy farmers waged protests against foreign companies when they felt they didn't get a fair share on the lease."[10] Thus, there was still a concern of potential expropriation for foreign investors.

Third, GreenWood needed to know where to find the most cost-effective tree farms and learn with whom to partner in acquiring and managing tree assets. The lack of proper documentation of plantation assets complicated this effort.

GreenWood also dealt with several other unique challenges. For example, the Chinese approach to silviculture was rudimentary compared to Western standards. There was a lack of knowledge in tree farm investment, plant materials development, and efficient irrigation, according to Zhang Weidong, director of the Resource Planning and Acquisition Group at GreenWood China.

The differences in silvicultural approaches presented the biggest challenge to Brian. In Western countries, long-term internal rate of return (IRR) was a prevalent business concept. This was at odds, however, with the mind-set of Chinese farmers, who had a short-term focus and wanted to know only the "value" of their timber assets per *mu* (0.067 hectare),[11] which was either a historical price based on the booming market of previous years or a price determined by cumulative capital expenditures plus a desired surplus. Brian noted that his team often used both the Western method and the Chinese method to conduct side-by-side comparisons:

> I call myself a translator, translating Western concepts and applying them to China. . . . It's easier said than done. It took us two years to figure it out.

Another big challenge was cultural, especially the differences in business cultures. GreenWood followed a strict Western procedure when conducting environmental and tree asset evaluations (preliminary investigation, survey, inventory analysis, comprehensive due diligence, etc.), which its potential Chinese partners perceived as inefficient (because the procedure was time-consuming) or even inappropriate (because certain tree plantation data were not available in China). Hunter Brown, the COO of GreenWood, pointed out the key difference:

> The Chinese approach is an informal management style (as opposed to) the much more structured and organized contract-driven style in the U.S.

Furthermore, during the global economic downturn of 2008–2009, there was a growing perception that GreenWood's market-based assessment and pricing were unfair to local farmers and communities.[12] Jake Eaton, director of GreenWood's Global Acquisitions and Resource Planning, acknowledged the disagreement with the company's potential Chinese partners regarding the valuation of existing tree plantation assets. For GreenWood, the valuation was based on current market prices, whereas its Chinese counterparts believed the market would quickly rebound and therefore the valuation should take into account the prices that prevailed prior to the economic downturn.

Business challenges in China notwithstanding, GreenWood grew its business steadily. In 2009, it had about 10 employees in China (out of 70 companywide) and operated five tree nurseries which were used to test GreenWood's elite plant materials for site adaptability.

Investment Opportunities in China

With the capital commitment of US$200 million for the Chinese market, GreenWood, in conjunction with Oriental, established Green China Forestry Company, Ltd. (GCFC). GCFC was essentially responsible for making investment decisions in China. An investment committee, comprising Jeff and two representatives from Oriental, made investment decisions while GreenWood China provided daily management services for a fee (see Exhibit 6 for an illustration of the management and investment relationship). The investment decision-making process consisted of two phases. First, GreenWood China conducted preliminary investigations to identify potential projects.[13] Some 20 potential investment projects had been reviewed by March 2009 (see Exhibit 7).

Marc Hiller, a specialist in Forest Stewardship Council (FSC) at GreenWood, commented on the phase one evaluation:

> In every project, we look at the quality of the (assets), the ability to sell the timber to the markets. . . . Can the tree farms (potentially) meet the FSC requirements? . . . Do the current owners have a lot of conflicts with the local communities? . . . Does the local company have problems with its employees? . . . Were the local farmers coerced to turn in their tree assets for the consolidation purpose?[14] . . . Can we acquire the assets at an attractive rate? . . . What are the financial and legal risks in acquiring the land?

Jeff also stressed the dual significance of financial viability and social responsibility:

> (The process) addresses the environmental and social issues. . . . The model (of sustainability) we hold ourselves to is FSC certification. . . . Of course, we've got to figure out how to become profitable. . . . Sustainability is not achieved unless you are economically sustainable.

Among the 20 potential projects, Luxi and Dongji were the most desirable based on preliminary analyses and thus entered phase two, which consisted of a more comprehensive due diligence analysis including economic, social, and environmental elements. The economic element was mainly reflected in the estimation of internal rate of return (IRR), net present value (NPV), and initial cash outlay. According to GreenWood, the investor's expected IRR was approximately 15 percent. The discount rate for NPV calculation was 10 percent.[15] The social and environmental due diligence analysis largely followed the FSC principles and criteria for forest management such as indigenous people's rights, community relations and workers' rights, compliance with laws and FSC principles, environmental impact, and so on, as described in Exhibit 2.

Both the Luxi and Dongji investments, if executed successfully, could achieve the investor's expected IRR, which was much higher than the approximate average return of 6 percent generated by timber investment in the United States. Moreover, it was anticipated that the investments would help improve the ecological environment in China and contribute to economic and social development in their respective local communities.

However, the two projects differed vastly in terms of physical locations, natural conditions, and partnership opportunities. The difference, as highlighted in GreenWood's detailed due diligence review, led to considerable discussion of the various pros and cons of the two projects.

Luxi Project[16]

Luxi County was located in Shandong, in east China. The county had fertile soil, sophisticated river and water irrigation networks, and other highly favorable natural conditions (ample sunlight, rain, and gentle slopes) for fast-growth, high-yield poplar plantations. Luxi had been making tremendous efforts in afforestation and sustainable economic development since 2002. A plan was executed to build a forestry park where tree plantation, landscaping, and tourism would be integrated to create an ecological system.

GreenWood explored investment opportunities in Luxi starting in late 2005. Since then, company personnel had visited Luxi many times surveying and analyzing tree farms and building *guanxi* (personal connections for mutual benefits)[17] with local government officials. The county government's support and coordination were critical for going forward with an investment since various local government agencies owned large parcels of poplar tree farms.

GreenWood was negotiating with the Luxi Forestry Bureau, a government agency with a mandate to implement government policies, regulate environmental construction, protect forest resources, and organize forestry development within Luxi County. Mr. Jiao, director of Luxi Forestry Bureau, indicated that he hoped GreenWood would help local farmers improve forestry management and facilitate local economic development by contributing capital and tree plantation know-how.

It was not, however, until December 2008 that GreenWood signed a nonbinding letter of intent (LOI) with the Luxi County government specifying the scope of the project. While commending GreenWood's meticulous style in dealing with the project, Jiao speculated that GreenWood's Portland headquarters had limited knowledge of the local situation and was not willing to delegate its responsibilities to the Beijing office. Consequently, the responses from GreenWood tended to be slow during the negotiation.

EXHIBIT 6 Relationships between GreenWood's Management and Investment Organizations

Source: GreenWood internal documents.

EXHIBIT 7 China Potential Investment Projects

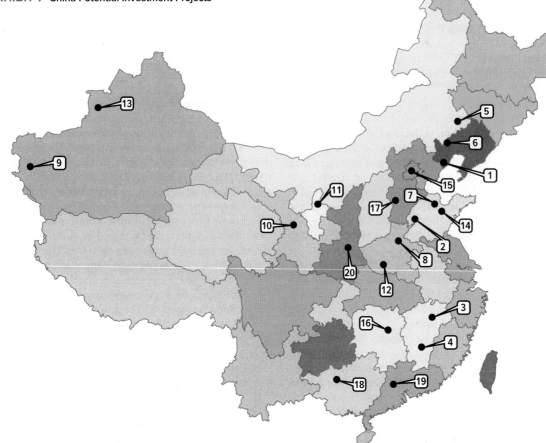

ID	Location	Province (area)
1	BSY	Hebei
2	**Luxi**	**Shandong**
3	Gengmin	Jiangxi
4	Zuheng	Jiangxi
5	**Dongji**	**Inner Mongolia**
6	Chaoyang	Liaoning
7	Dong Ying	Shandong
8	Kaifeng	Henan
9	Kashi	Xinjiang
10	Lanzhou	Gansu
11	Meili	NingXia
12	Nanyang	Henan
13	Yili	Xinjiang
14	Weifang	Shandong
15	Daxing	Beijing
16	AIC	Hunan
17	Jilin	Hebei
18	Nanning	Guangxi
19	Shaoguan	Guangdong
20	Zhongfu	Shaanxi

Source: GreenWood's internal documents.

Jake Eaton agreed the process could have been faster. He pointed out that a major factor slowing down the negotiations was that GreenWood was often not talking to the real decision makers. Jessica Zhi, the Luxi project manager at GreenWood China, also mentioned the complexity of the Luxi project, in part because many local government bureaus were involved and at times leadership changes occurred.

If this project were selected, GreenWood planned to establish a wholly owned foreign enterprise in Luxi for acquiring and developing approximately 100,000 mu (6,667 hectares) of poplar tree plantations. The Luxi Forestry Bureau had been managing these tree plantations since 2002. It was expected to be a primary contractor for GreenWood, providing crop care activities at low labor costs and helping maintain the local relationships. The lease documents for the land were held by several government bureaus and were transferable. The land lease price was 300 to 400 renminbi (RMB), or US$43.90–58.60, per mu per year.[18] Typical lease length was 20 to 30 years, with some leases up to 70 years. GreenWood estimated that an investment of US$30–40 million was required in the first five years.

The high up-front fixed costs required by the Luxi project were a serious concern for the main investor, Oriental, as Jeff noted:

> If you look at the land (lease) pricing in China today, it would make more sense (for the investors) to buy (or lease) the land in another country (such as Australia, New Zealand, Poland and Romania).

As part of the negotiation process, the Luxi Forestry Bureau asked GreenWood to help set up a small wood-processing mill with an estimated investment of US$750,000. The mill, associated with high value-added activities, would provide employment opportunities to local residents. GreenWood, however, gave only a lukewarm response as the mill was not its essential business.

GreenWood planned to adopt a seven-year rotation strategy in Luxi (i.e., trees would be harvested at the age of seven for veneer log and pulpwood). It believed the locally tested GreenWood elite plant materials, coupled with favorable natural conditions and intensive management (e.g., site preparation, planting, spacing and thinning, weed and pest control, and fertilization) could readily enhance tree growth rate by 50 percent from 1.2 cubic meters (m^3) to 1.8m^3 per mu per year.

According to the data provided by the Luxi Forestry Bureau, GreenWood estimated the annual local timber demand within 100 kilometers (62 miles) of the project site was about 2.2 million m^3, which greatly exceeded the existing annual supply of 1 million m^3. As a result, local buyers looked to supplement their supply with imported timber. However, buyers found it increasingly difficult to depend on large volumes of imported timber because of high tariffs (e.g., for Russian logs) and high transportation costs required to bring logs into the area.

In addition to meeting the substantial demand in Luxi and its neighboring county, GreenWood was aiming at Linyi, a timber-processing hub and wood market about 300 kilometers (186.4 miles) from Luxi. There were about 2,600 mills in Linyi, and the largest 200 mills each needed more than 15,000 m^3 of timber annually. However, many of these mills were closing because their export-oriented businesses were seriously affected by the global financial crisis.

GreenWood tried to make an offer to the Luxi County government based on the local market prices of logs and its estimate of standing inventory volume. However, the county government argued that the assessment and subsequent offer would take unfair advantage of local entities and farmers, given the current economic meltdown in China due to the global financial crisis. Moreover, some government officials complained about GreenWood's slow pace in negotiating an agreement, which had resulted in the loss of seasonal planting and harvesting opportunities.

Dongji Project[19]

Dongji was located in the eastern part of the Inner Mongolia Autonomous Region in northeast China. The area suffered not only from a severe timber shortage but also from continued desertification. Although the area was semiarid and subject to windy weather all year, it was suitable for poplar cultivation due to its appropriate soil texture and access to the local river systems. The Dongji land was marginally fertile. It was estimated that the annual tree growth rate would not be much beyond 0.7 m^3 per mu even with GreenWood's elite plant materials and silvicultural management practices. One GreenWood analyst suggested that an annual rate of 0.9 m^3 per mu would be optimistic. Still, Dr. Stanton felt excited about the project because of the challenges it would bring to his research.

To combat desertification, the government of Dongji set up an ambitious goal of raising forest coverage from 22 to 30 percent from 2006 to 2010, resulting in a net increase of forestland by 10 million mu, of which 1.5 million mu was targeted for planting poplar trees.

Unlike the case in Luxi, private firms were essential in developing poplar tree plantations in Dongji. For example, Dongji Lideng Forestry Development Co., Ltd. (Lideng), a potential partner of GreenWood, held a 30-year lease on land totaling 126,600 mu planted with hybrid poplar, whereas 55 state-owned forest farms together had approximately 60,000 mu.

Lideng was a private forestry development company with activities in poplar plantation establishment, poplar nurseries, poplar stumpage, timber harvest rights transfer, and so on. To take advantage of the extensive land resources with large contiguous blocks and low land lease rates ranging from RMB15 to RMB25 per mu per year, the company planned to establish an additional 300,000 mu of poplar plantation within 3 to 5 years. This plan had already been

EXHIBIT 8 Estimated Investment Costs and Yields: Luxi versus Dongji[a]

	Total Existing Area[b] (mu)	Current Standing Inventory Volume (m³)	Stumpage Price (2008) (weighted average, RMB/m³)	Investment in Existing Plantation Assets (RMB)
Luxi	92,073	530,529	559	296,548,734
Dongji	202,650	225,391	445	100,298,995

	Land Lease and Related Expenses[c] (RMB/mu/year)	Crop Care Expenses (RMB/mu/year)	Planting Expenses (RMB/mu, 1st year)	Stumpage Volume at End of Each Rotation (m³/mu)
Luxi	367	110	632	12.6 (year 7)
Dongji	87	45	255	7.0 (year 10)[d]

[a] 1 hectare = 15 mu; 1 U.S. dollar = 6.83 renminbi; the numbers are rounded.

[b] These total existing areas were used in GreenWood's investment feasibility reports.

[c] The related expenses include management fee, security fee, etc.

[d] The growth rate of 0.7 m³ per mu per year for Dongji was deemed to be realistic, whereas the rate of 0.9 m³ per mu per year was mentioned as an optimistic scenario.

Source: Adapted from GreenWood's investment feasibility reports.

approved by the State Forestry Administration, the central government agency for the forestry industry.

Lideng had a trained professional poplar tree planting team equipped with a patented deep planting technique suited to the harsh environment of northern China. The planting technique and its accompanying machinery were the result of a 13-year forestry development research project, led by the United Nations Food and Agriculture Organization (FAO). The company had an annual planting capacity of 200,000 mu. Lideng also told GreenWood that it had the sole right to propagate commercially superior plant materials developed by the FAO project.

In response to GreenWood's interest in its poplar tree farm assets, Lideng offered 82,644 mu out of its existing total for GreenWood's purchase. The remaining 43,000-plus mu had already been bought by individual investors through a government-approved Dongji Stumpage Trading Center, in which Huang Jingbao, the CEO and president of Lideng, was a senior consultant.

GreenWood planned what it considered a prudent strategy for Dongji. First, it would focus on deploying local hybrid varietals while testing the suitability of its home-grown elite plant materials. Second, it would adopt a 10-year rotation scheme due to the low annual growth rate in Dongji. Third, it would capitalize on Lideng's expertise in planting and crop care activities.

In Dongji, timber was mainly consumed in the local market. A potential capacity of 2 million m³ of annual wood consumption existed across 698 wood-processing mills. Though the local market experienced a limited impact from the economic meltdown, there was a concern that Russian timber could potentially flood the market due to Dongji's proximity to the Russian border. Moreover, the export market appeared to be relatively inaccessible for Dongji-based companies due to their inland locations.[20] Jeff and his senior management team also wondered whether there would be any reputational risks if GreenWood collaborated with Lideng. The latter had provided extensive silvicultural management services for Wanli Afforestation Group and Yilin Wood Industry Co., Ltd., the two large private forestry companies noted earlier that were currently under litigation for illegal fund-raising and the use of a pyramid scheme.

Huang believed Lideng and GreenWood would make a great partnership given the potential synergy between his company's local expertise and cost efficiency and GreenWood's sophisticated silvicultural management and leading poplar hybridization technology. However, he also believed his tree plantation assets had been undervalued by at least 20 percent based on GreenWood's assessment. Moreover, he had serious grievances with GreenWood's lengthy decision-making process. He considered dropping the deal if the negotiations continued to drag on for much longer.

What to Do?

Jeff and his senior management team knew expansion in China would help them achieve their vision of maximizing long-term returns for their investors and fulfilling the company's social and environmental responsibilities. They were also aware of potential business challenges as well as economic and political risks in an institutionally unique environment. After reading the two comprehensive due diligence reports, Jeff turned his attention to the financial data (see Exhibit 8) and a summarized assessment of

EXHIBIT 9 Assessment of Economic, Social, and Environmental Viability[a]

	Manager 1 (Beijing Office)[b]		Manager 2 (Beijing Office)		One Executive (Portland HQ)	
	Luxi	Dongji	Luxi	Dongji	Luxi	Dongji
Economic value	5	3–4	5	3	5	3
Social value	5	3–4	4	4	5	3
Environmental stewardship	1	5	3	5	3	5

[a] The scale is 1–5. (1 = very low potential value; 5 = very high potential value.)

[b] The manager pointed out that the ecological system had been considerably improved in Luxi in recent years. Thus, the potential value creation of environmental stewardship by GreenWood had declined.

Source: Interviews.

economic, social, and environmental viability of the two projects prepared by GreenWood staff (see Exhibit 9). Over a year had passed since the announcement of Oriental's capital commitment. Jeff understood that GreenWood needed to proceed with the investment with some sense of urgency, but he wanted to make sure that his team provided the best recommendations possible to the investment committee.

ENDNOTES

1. Light, L. (2009, May 6). "For Some, Sound of Profit Is 'Timber.'" *Wall Street Journal.*
2. See the company's website: www.greenwoodresources.com.
3. CH2M HILL provided a wide range of engineering and land development services including consulting, design, construction, procurement, operations and maintenance, and project management to federal, state, municipal, and local government entities as well as private industries in the U.S. and internationally.
4. Austin, J. and Reficco, E. (2006). Forest Stewardship Council. *Harvard Business School Case* (9-303-047).
5. A family office is a private company that manages investments and trusts for a single wealthy family.
6. Reporter (2009, May). "China to Fully Open Its Forestry Industry." *People's Daily* Online, http://english.peopledaily.com.cn/200111/23/eng20011123_85194.html, accessed on May 14, 2009.
7. Greenfield investment is direct investment to build a new manufacturing, marketing, or administrative facility, as opposed to acquiring existing facilities.
8. The name of this investor was disguised as requested by GreenWood Resources, Inc.

9. GreenWood planned to recruit shareholders (i.e., equity owners) for its business expansion but ended up playing the role of investment (and assets) manager for large investors such as Oriental Timber Fund, Ltd.
10. Hsuan, A. (2009, Feb. 23). "See a Forest through the Trees." *The Oregonian.*
11. *Mu* is a common metric for land in China. 1 hectare = 15 mu, or 2.47 acres.
12. Interviews with GreenWood's two potential partners.
13. Although GreenWood China was responsible for the investigations, the parent company was supervising the relevant activities and controlling the process.
14. When business developers needed to lease a large piece of land for commercial purposes in China, they often tried to incentivize and/or at times coerce through the government agencies the current land users (e.g., farmers) to transfer their land lease contracts.
15. In the broadly defined forest industry, investors prefer long-term hold, good cash flows, and net value appreciation of tree assets resulting from biological growth. Tree plantation assets are also perceived as insurance against economic/financial crisis.
16. This section draws heavily upon Luxi Investment Feasibility Report by GreenWood Resources China, Ltd.
17. "Guanxi, as compared to social capital in the West, tends to be more personal and enduring, and involves more exchanges of favors. In general, relationships tend to precede business in China, whereas in the west it is usually the reverse, i.e., relationships follow as a result of the business." Tung, Worm, and Fang, 2008, *Organizational Dynamics,* 37(1): 69.
18. 1 U.S. dollar = 6.83 renminbi (the Chinese currency) in 2009; the land lease price does not include the price for the trees.
19. This section draws heavily upon Dongji Investment Feasibility Report by GreenWood Resources China, Ltd.
20. Interview with an industry expert on May 11, 2009.

APPENDIX 1

BACKGROUND—TIMBER INVESTMENTS AND TREE PLANTATION MANAGEMENT

Timber Investments

The U.S. had some of the most productive timberland (i.e., tree-growing land) in the world. Traditionally, timber investment was dominated by such large integrated forest product companies as Weyerhaeuser, International Paper Company, Plum Creek Timber Company, and James River Corporation, to name a few.

Since the mid-1990s, however, there had been a significant trend toward institutional ownership of timberlands. Institutional investors such as timber investment management organizations (TIMOs) and real estate investment trusts (REITs) purchased large tracts of land from the traditional forest product companies because of the potential to generate attractive long-term capital returns.[1] "Timber often is likened to high-grade bonds, meant to be held for ten years or more. The average annual timber appreciation for the past decade was 4.1 percent versus minus 3.8 percent for the S&P-500 stock index."[2] Moreover, timber was not closely correlated with other asset classes. "Trees keep growing 4 percent per year, no matter what happens to inflation, interest rates or market trends."[3] In addition, potential federal and state tax benefits could be accrued from timber acquisitions.

Unfortunately, the downside of a timber investment was significant. It required a substantial amount of capital to be invested in a very illiquid asset with no quick payoff. For example, a minimum of $100,000 was required to participate in a TIMO.

Tree Plantations

U.S. commercial timberland was concentrated in the Northwest, Southeast, and Northeast regions of the country. The Northwest and Southeast were managed like farms, with landowners planting trees, allowing them to grow for a number of years, clear cutting the stand, and then planting again. Each cycle was a rotation. The Pacific Northwest contained 90 percent Western hemlock and Douglas fir with normal rotations of 45 to 60 years. In contrast, the Southeast United States was dominated by the Southern yellow pine species, with a typical rotation of 20 to 40 years. The Northeast United States had a diverse mix of trees, which were managed differently.

Plantation forests (as opposed to natural forests) were assuming a rapidly increasing role in commercial timber production. By 2005, the share of global timber production sourced from plantations was estimated as "approaching 50 percent." The largest plantation areas were located in Asia (China, India, and Japan), Europe (Russia, Scandinavia, and Eastern Europe), and the United States.[4]

The increasing importance of tree plantations was attributed to the fact that "less than half of the world's original forests remain, and ongoing deforestation is potentially devastating to the environment. Yet population growth and the increasing standard of living in many countries continue to drive the demand for timber products."[5]

High-yield, fast-growing tree farms lessen the pressure of deforestation by providing the type of timber products demanded by world markets. At the same time, tree farms are a sustainable environmental solution that can improve air and water quality, reclaim deforested land, and produce renewable energy in the form of biomass.[6]

Two popular, high-yield, and fast-growing tree species grown in plantation farms were eucalyptus and poplar. Eucalyptus was concentrated in tropical and subtropical regions of the world, while poplar was grown mainly in more temperate regions.

Hybrid Poplar Plantation Development[7]

Poplar was an important fiber resource for the global pulp and paper industry. In the United States, a number of prominent North American paper companies managed poplar plantations. Hybrid varieties, formed by crossing poplars, cottonwoods, and aspens, were among the first trees domesticated in North America by the pulp and paper industry. Several of these hybrid varieties were used to expand plantation development in the Pacific Northwest in the 1980s and 1990s.

As of 2009, hybrid poplars remained the best choice for hardwood plantation management for the manufacture of premium grades of communication papers throughout all of North America. There was also a growing trend to use hybrid poplars as a source for biomass feedstock for the emerging biofuels and composite-products industries and for hardwood lumber markets.

Key success factors for hybrid poplar plantations included (1) favorable natural site conditions (e.g., flat plain, river bottom), (2) elite plant materials (with high growth rate and strong pest resistance), and (3) sound silvicultural (forest cultivation) management, among others.[8]

Hybrid poplar plantations were tended throughout North America using cultivation methods that included mechanical and chemical methods of weed control, integrated pest management techniques, fertilization, and, in some cases, irrigation. Under competent management, hybrid poplar was the fastest-growing tree in the temperate zone.

APPENDIX ENDNOTES

1. Draffan, G. (2006, April). Notes on Institutional Ownership of Timber. www.endgame.org/timo.html, accessed on May 6, 2009.
2. Light, L. (2009, May 6). "For Some, Sound of Profit Is 'Timber.'" *Wall Street Journal.*
3. Ibid.
4. The Campbell Group. (2009, May 14). Global Supply. www.campbell-group.com/timberland/primer/global-supply.aspx, accessed on May 14, 2009.
5. GreenWood Resources, Inc., brochure.
6. Ibid.
7. This section draws heavily on an internal document of GreenWood Resources titled "Hybrid Poplar and the Pulp and Paper Industry in North America: Implications for a Secured Supply of Quality Fiber for Papermakers Worldwide."
8. *Silvicultural management* refers to integrated management of forestry, which includes land preparation, spacing and thinning, pruning, weed control, pest and disease control, fertilization, irrigation, and harvesting, among others.

CASE 9

FRESHDIRECT: HOW FRESH IS IT?*

On its website, FreshDirect boldly proclaimed, "Our food is fresh, our customers are spoiled. Order on the web today and get next-day delivery of the best food at the best price, exactly the way you want it, with 100 percent satisfaction guaranteed."[1] Recently, however, many consumers questioned the freshness of the food delivered by FreshDirect. Since online shopping did not give customers the chance to feel and choose the products themselves, they had to rely completely on FreshDirect to select the food for them.

Since 2001, operating out of its production center in Long Island City, Queens, FreshDirect had offered online grocery shopping and delivery service in Manhattan, Queens, Brooklyn, Nassau County, Riverdale, Westchester, select areas of Staten Island, the Bronx, the Hamptons, New Jersey including Jersey Shore, Philadelphia, Delaware, and parts of Connecticut. FreshDirect also offered pickup service at its Long Island City facility, as well as corporate service to select delivery zones in Manhattan and summer delivery service to the Hamptons on Long Island.

In 2012, the company decided to move its facility from Long Island City, Queens, to a new 800,000-square-foot property in the Bronx, and received court clearance to do so. FreshDirect had threatened to relocate its operational hub and headquarters to New Jersey, but New York City and the State of New York offered close to a $130 million subsidy package, including tax breaks and abatements, to keep the online grocer in New York City. A petition by the community group South Bronx United had earlier challenged the move arguing that the city had failed to properly analyze the potential environmental impact (e.g., air and noise pollution) that would result from a "truck-intensive" business. However, the court ruled in FreshDirect's favor in 2013.[2]

FreshDirect's new headquarters was slated to open by 2016 (this would be slightly delayed), and CEO Jason Ackerman was delighted with the court's decision. "We are eager to move forward with our plans to bring thousands of jobs to the Bronx and make it easier for people to get fresh food," he declared.[3]

During the early years of the company, FreshDirect had pronounced to the New York City market that it was "the new way to shop for food." This was a bold statement

given that the previous decade had witnessed the demise of numerous online grocery ventures. However, the creators of FreshDirect were confident in the prospects for success of their business. Their entire operation had been designed to deliver on one simple promise to grocery shoppers: "higher quality at lower prices."

While this promise was an extremely common tagline used within and outside the grocery business, FreshDirect had integrated numerous components into its system to give real meaning to their words. Without a retail location, FreshDirect didn't have to pay expensive rent for a retail space. To offer the highest-quality products to its customers, FreshDirect had designed a state-of-the-art production center and staffed it with expert personnel. The 800,000-square-foot production facility newly located in the Bronx would employ about 700 workers when it opened in 2018. The current facility in Long Island City, Queens, would operate until the new building came online. In each FreshDirect warehouse, twelve separate temperature zones ensured that each piece of produce, meat, and other food was kept at its optimal temperature for ripening and/or preservation. The company claimed the entire facility was kept colder and cleaner than any other retail environment.[4]

Further quality management was achieved by an SAP manufacturing software system that controlled every detail of the facility's operations. All of the thermometers, scales, and conveyor belts within the facility were connected to a central command center. Each specific setting was programmed into the system by an expert from the corresponding department—everything from the ideal temperature for ripening a cantaloupe to the amount of flour that went into the French bread. The system was equipped with a monitoring alarm that alerted staff to any deviation from the programmed settings.

FreshDirect maintained extremely high standards for cleanliness, health, and safety. The floor was immaculate. All food-preparation areas and equipment were bathed in antiseptic foam at the end of each day. Incoming and outgoing food was tested in FreshDirect's in-house laboratory, which ensured adherence to USDA guidelines and the Hazard Analysis and Critical Control Point food safety system. In all respects, food passing through the FreshDirect facility met the company's high health and safety standards.[5]

System efficiency was the key to FreshDirect's ability to offer its high-quality products at low prices. The middleman was completely eliminated. Instead of going through an intermediary, both fresh and dry products were ordered

---

* This case was prepared by Professor Alan B. Eisner of Pace University as a basis for class discussion rather than to illustrate either effective or ineffective handling of an administrative situation. Thanks to graduate students Saad Nazir, Dev Das, Rohit R. Phadtare, and Shruti Shrestha for research assistance. Copyright © 2017 Alan B. Eisner.

from individual growers and producers and shipped directly to FreshDirect's production center, where its expert staff prepared them for purchase. In addition, FreshDirect did not accept any slotting allowances.[6] This unique relationship with growers and producers allowed FreshDirect to enjoy reduced purchase prices from its suppliers, passing the savings on to its customers.

Each department of the facility, including the coffee roaster, butcher, and bakery, was staffed by carefully selected experts. FreshDirect offered premium fresh coffees (roasted on site), pastries and breads (baked on site), deli, cheese, meats (roast beef dry-aged on site), and seafood. Perishable produce was FreshDirect's specialty—by buying locally as much as possible and using the best sources of the season, it was able to bring food the shortest distance from farms, dairies, and fisheries to the customer's table.

FreshDirect catered to the tastes of its busy Manhattan clientele by offering a full line of heat-and-serve meals prepared in the FreshDirect kitchen by New York executive chef Michael Stark (formerly of Tribeca Grill) and his team. Another celebrity chef, Terrance Brennan of New York's French-Mediterranean restaurant Picholine, oversaw creation of "restaurant-worthy" four-minute meals. Made from raw ingredients delivered in a "steam valve system" package, these complete meals were not frozen but were delivered ready to cook in a microwave.

The proximity of FreshDirect's processing facility to its Manhattan customer base was a critical factor in its cost-effective operational design. The processing center's location in the South Bronx put approximately 4 million people within a 10-mile radius of FreshDirect, enabling the firm to quickly deliver a large volume of orders.[7] Further, cost controls had been implemented through FreshDirect's order and delivery protocols. Products in each individual order were packed in boxes, separated by type of item (meat, seafood, and produce packed together; dairy, deli, cheese, coffee, and tea packed together; grocery, specialty, and nonrefrigerated products packed together), and placed on a computerized conveyor system to be sorted, assembled, and loaded into a refrigerated truck for delivery.

Orders had to be a minimum of $40, with a delivery charge between $6.99 and $7.99 per order, depending on the order dollar amount and delivery location. Delivery was made by one of FreshDirect's own trucks and was available only during a prearranged two-hour window from 6:30 a.m. to 10 p.m. every day of the week. To attract more customers and to encourage repeat purchases, FreshDirect also offered DeliveryPass that enabled customers to get unlimited free deliveries by purchasing a free delivery subscription for 6 or 12 months. The DeliveryPass price for 6 months was $79 and for 12 months was $129.

Competing with other online grocers like AmazonFresh, specialty gourmet/gourmand stores in Manhattan, and high-end chain supermarkets like Whole Foods, Trader Joe's, and Fairway, FreshDirect was trying to woo the sophisticated grocery shopper with an offer of quality, delivered to the customer's door, at a price more attractive than others in the neighborhood. Operating in the black for the first time in 2005,[8] by choosing to remain a private company and expanding gradually, FreshDirect's owners hoped to turn a daily profit, steadily recovering the estimated $60 million start-up costs, silencing critics, and winning converts.[9]

An interesting idea for expansion was to cater to home cooks who liked to cook from scratch. FreshDirect teamed up with online recipe website Foodily to launch a new service called Popcart. Users could order deliveries of food ingredients directly applicable to online recipes. The Internet was a popular recipe source for home cooks, but shopping for ingredients was widely seen as an unpleasant chore. The new Popcart technology alleviated this burden by linking with the FreshDirect portal and providing next-day deliveries of whatever a recipe called for. "This is really at the heart and soul of making food shopping easier for consumers. About 70% of New Yorkers cook from scratch multiple times a week, and 30% cook multiple times a day. Think about that opportunity," said Jodi Kahn, chief consumer officer for FreshDirect.[10]

In January 2016, aiming a direct attack on the heated competition in online food delivery services, FreshDirect introduced a new service called FoodKick, which promised to deliver food and liquor within an hour of a customer placing an order. FoodKick was initially available in particular areas of Brooklyn and Queens; however, the company planned to expand this service nationwide.[11]

Founding Partners

Cofounder and its first chief executive officer Joseph Fedele was able to bring a wealth of experience in New York City's food industry to FreshDirect. In 1993 he had cofounded Fairway Uptown, a 35,000-square-foot supermarket on West 133 Street in Harlem. Many critics originally questioned the success of a store in that location, but Fairway's low prices and quality selection of produce and meats made it a hit with neighborhood residents, as well as many downtown and suburban commuters.

Cofounder Jason Ackerman, FreshDirect's vice chairman and chief financial officer, had gained exposure to the grocery industry as an investment banker with Donaldson Lufkin & Jenrette, where he specialized in supermarket mergers and acquisitions.

Fedele and Ackerman first explored the idea of starting a large chain of fresh-food stores, but they realized maintaining a high degree of quality would be impossible with a large enterprise. As an alternative, they elected to pursue a business that incorporated online shopping with central distribution. Using the failure of Webvan, the dot-com delivery service that ran through $830 million in five years of rapid expansion, as their example of what not to do, Fedele and Ackerman planned to start slowly, use off-the-shelf software and an automated delivery system, and pay attention to essentials such as forming relationships with key suppliers and micromanaging quality control.[12]

FreshDirect acquired the bulk of its $100 million investment from several private sources, along with the contribution that was expected to come from the State of New York in tax breaks. By locating FreshDirect's distribution center within the state border and promising to create at least 300 permanent, full-time, private-sector jobs in the state, FreshDirect became eligible for a $500,000 training grant from the Empire State Development Jobs Now Program. As its name implied, the purpose of the Jobs Now program was to create new, immediate job opportunities for New Yorkers.

CEO Successions

Although the press was mostly positive about FreshDirect's opportunities, growth and operational challenges remained. In the words of an ex–senior executive of FreshDirect, "The major problem seems to be constant change in Senior Management. I think they are now on their 4th CEO."[13] At the time, the company was actually on its fifth CEO, and it later named its sixth. FreshDirect cofounder Joseph Fedele had remained CEO until January 2004, when cofounder Jason Ackerman succeeded him. Ackerman served as CEO of FreshDirect for a little over seven months; Dean Furbush succeeded him in September 2004. Ackerman remained vice chairman and chief financial officer. The tenure of Dean Furbush lasted a little over two years. Steve Michaelson, president since 2004, replaced Furbush as CEO of FreshDirect in early 2007.[14] In 2008 Michaelson left for another firm, and FreshDirect's chairman of the board, Richard Braddock, expanded his role in the firm and took over as CEO. Braddock said, "I chose to increase my involvement with the company because I love the business and I think it has great growth potential." Braddock had previously worked at private equity firm MidOcean Partners and travel services retailer Priceline.com, where he'd also served as chairman and CEO.[15] Braddock wound up leaving the company in March 2011. Jason Ackerman returned to the role of CEO for a second time.

Business Plan

While business started out relatively slowly, FreshDirect hoped to capture around 5 percent of the New York City grocery market. Availability citywide was originally slated for the end of 2002. However, to maintain its superior service and product quality, FreshDirect chose to expand its service area slowly. This business model seemed to be working well for FreshDirect, as the company continued to gradually expand successfully into new areas surrounding its Long Island City facility. With the success of its business model and its steady growth strategy, by the spring of 2011, FreshDirect had delivery available to select zip codes and neighborhoods throughout Manhattan and as far away as Westchester, Connecticut, New Jersey, and the Hamptons on Long Island (in the summer only).

By early 2017 FreshDirect was serving the Delaware, Jersey Shore, Hamptons, and Philadelphia area, particularly in and around Center City, with plans to eventually expand the service region to the greater Philadelphia area suburbs depending on customer response. The company had a cross dock on Richmond Street, Philadelphia, where orders were sorted after arriving from New York.

The company employed a relatively low-cost marketing approach, which originally consisted mainly of billboards, public relations, and word of mouth to promote its products and services. FreshDirect hired Trumpet, an ad agency that promoted FreshDirect as a better way to shop by emphasizing the problems associated with traditional grocery shopping. For example, one commercial stressed the unsanitary conditions in a supermarket by showing a shopper bending over a barrel of olives as she sneezed, getting an olive stuck in her nose, and then blowing it back into the barrel. The advertisement ended with the question, "Where's your food been?" Another ad showed a checkout clerk morph into an armed robber, demand money from the customer, and then morph back into a friendly checkout clerk once the money was received. The ad urged viewers to "stop getting robbed at the grocery store."[16] FreshDirect enlisted celebrity endorsements from New York City personalities such as film director Spike Lee, actress Cynthia Nixon, former mayor Ed Koch, supermodel Paulina Porizkova, and chef Bobby Flay.[17] The company planned to change its marketing strategy by launching a new testimonial-based campaign using actual customers, rather than celebrities. FreshDirect was number 73 in the Internet Retailer Top 500 Guide of 2016.

Operating Strategy

Building on its efficient low-cost supply chain that eliminated the middleman and sourced direct from farms and fisheries, FreshDirect was able to pursue a make-to-order philosophy.[18] By focusing on providing produce, meat, seafood, baked goods, and coffees that were selected or made to the customer's specific order, FreshDirect offered its customers an alternative to the standardized cuts and choices available at most brick-and-mortar grocery stores. This strategy created a business model that was unique within the grocery business community.

A typical grocery store carried about 25,000 packaged goods, which accounted for approximately 50 percent of its sales, and about 2,200 perishable products, which accounted for the other 50 percent of sales. In contrast, FreshDirect offered about 5,000 perishable products, accounting for approximately 75 percent of its sales, but only about 3,000 packaged goods, which made up the remaining 25 percent of sales.[19]

While this stocking strategy enabled a greater array of fresh foods, it limited the brands and available sizes of packaged goods such as cereals, crackers, and laundry detergents. However, FreshDirect believed that customers would accept a more limited packaged-good selection in order to get lower prices, as evidenced in the success of wholesale grocery stores, which offered bulk sales of limited items.

Jason Ackerman identified the ideal FreshDirect customers as those who bought their bulk staples from Costco on a monthly basis and bought everything else from FreshDirect on a weekly basis.[20]

FreshDirect's Website

FreshDirect's website not only offered an abundance of products to choose from but also provided a broad spectrum of information on the food that was sold and the manner in which it was sold (see Exhibit 1). Web surfers could take a pictorial tour of the FreshDirect facility; get background information on the experts who managed each department; get nutritional information on food items; compare produce or cheese on the basis of taste, price, and usage; specify the thickness of meat or seafood orders and opt for one of several marinades or rubs (see Exhibit 2); search for the right roast and variety of coffee according to taste preferences; and read nutritional information for fully prepared meals. A large selection of recipes was available depending on the items chosen.

For example, if you wanted to purchase chicken, you were first asked to choose from breasts and cutlets, cubes and strips, ground, legs and thighs, specialty parts, split and quartered, whole, or wings. Once your selection was made—let's say you chose breasts and cutlets—you were given further options based on your preference for skin, bone, and thickness. The final selection step offered you a choice of rubs and marinades, including teriyaki, sweet and sour, garlic rosemary, poultry seasoning, lemon herb rub, and salt-and-pepper rub. Throughout, the pages offered nutritional profiles of each cut of meat as well as tips for preparation and storage.

As for FreshDirect's several delivery models, customers within the city were attracted to the FreshDirect service (prearranged two-hour delivery window) because it eliminated the need to carry groceries or park a car near their apartments to unload their purchases. Suburban customers were served in a slightly different manner. Many suburban customers worked at corporations in the tristate area that could arrange for depot drop-off in the office parking lot, creating a central delivery station. FreshDirect sent a refrigerated truck, large enough to hold 500 orders, to these key spots during designated times. Suburbanites, leaving their office building to go to their cars, swung by the FreshDirect truck, picked up their orders, and headed home. FreshDirect could also provide delivery to the parking lot of football or concert events for tailgate parties or picnics. Customers could also pick up their orders directly from the processing center. Orders were ready at the pickup desk 5 to 10 minutes after they were called in.

For business customers in Manhattan, chef-prepared breakfast and luncheon platters and restaurant-quality individual meals were delivered right to the office. FreshDirect offered catering for business meetings and upscale events. FreshDirect provided dedicated corporate account managers and customer service representatives for corporate clients; however, FreshDirect provided only delivery, not setup and platter-arrangement services. The corporate delivery minimum order was $50, and delivery costs were $14.99 (see Exhibit 3).

EXHIBIT 2 Example of FreshDirect Seafood Selection

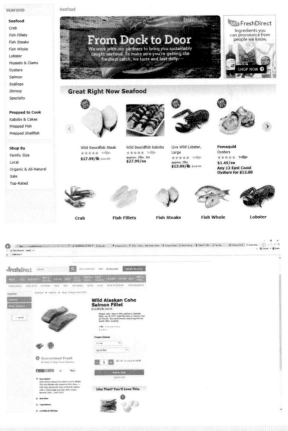

EXHIBIT 1 FreshDirect Website

The Retail Grocery Industry

In the United States, supermarket chains make over $649 billion in sales annually. The typical supermarket carries 39,500 items, averages about 42,800 square feet, and enjoys over $18 million in sales annually.[21] The top 10 supermarket chains in the United States command a large share of the total grocery industry business (see Exhibit 4).

The supermarket business is a low-margin business with net profits of only 1 to 2 percent of revenues. Store profits depend heavily on high customer traffic and rapid inventory turnover, especially for perishables such as produce and meat. Competitors must operate efficiently to make money, so tight control of labor costs and product spoilage is essential. Because of modest capital investment—mainly construction of distribution centers and stores—supermarket chains realize 15 to 20 percent returns on invested capital. Online grocery retailers, like FreshDirect—because of the flexibility of information control, automated order fulfillment, and reduced real estate costs—could potentially have operating margins up to 10 percent, rather than the 3 to 4 percent of traditional supermarkets.[22]

The Online Grocery Segment

Total online grocery shopping sales were estimated to be about $27 billion for the 12 months ending June 2016.[23] This accounted for about 4.4 percent of total grocery sales.

Online grocery shopping was slow to catch on in the 1990s, and industry newcomers had encountered high start-up and operating costs. Sales volumes and profit margins remained too small to cover the high start-up costs. The problem, according to industry analysts, was that consumers had been disappointed in online service, selection, and prices. Coupled with the extensive investment needed in warehousing, fulfillment, and inventory control, this meant the "pure play" e-grocery models were risky. There was a belief then that better success would

EXHIBIT 3 FreshDirect at the Office

EXHIBIT 4 Top 10 North American Food Retailers, 2016

Supermarket Chain	Stores	2016 Sales ($ billions)	Comments
Wal-Mart Stores	5,708	$355.2	Includes Sam's Clubs
Kroger	2,796	109.8	Includes jewelry sales
Costco Wholesale Corp.	602	118.72	Groceries were 72% of total sales
Albertsons	2,230	45.8	Headquartered in Boise, Idaho
Ahold Delhaize	769	26.4	Delhaize Group & Ahold USA
Loblaw Cos.	1,250	34.3	Based in Brampton, Canada
Target Corp.	1,672	69.8	Based in Minneapolis
C&S Wholesale Grocers	50	30	Based in the New Hampshire
Sobeys	1,500	18.8	Headquartered in Nova Scotia, Canada
Supervalu Inc.	1,370	17.53	Headquartered in Minnesota

Source: *Supermarket News* 2017. http://supermarketnews.com/2017-top-75-clickable-list. (Estimated sales and stores count.)

come from traditional grocery retailers that chose to venture online.[24]

However, some analysts expected online grocery sales to grow at a rapid pace as companies improved their service and selection, computer penetration of households rose, and consumers became more accustomed to making purchases online.[25] An article in *Computer Bits* examined the customer base for online grocers, looking specifically at the types of consumers who would be likely to shop online and the kinds of home computer systems that were required for online shopping. An Andersen Consulting report identified six major types of online shoppers (see Exhibit 5), and FreshDirect's Richard Braddock predicted that online grocery sales could account for as much as 20 percent or more of total grocery sales within the next 10 years.[26] A MARC Group study concluded, "Consumers who buy groceries online are likely to be more loyal to their electronic supermarkets, spend more per store 'visit,' and take greater advantage of coupons and premiums than traditional customers."[27]

A problem with online grocery shopping was that consumers were extremely price-sensitive when it came to buying groceries, and the prices of many online grocers at the outset were above those at supermarkets. Shoppers also were unwilling to pay extra to online grocers for home delivery. Consumer price sensitivity meant that online grocers had to achieve a cost structure that would allow them to (1) price competitively, (2) cover the cost of selecting items in the store and delivering individual grocery orders, and (3) have sufficient margins to earn attractive returns on their investment. Some analysts estimated that to be successful, online grocers had to do 10 times the volume of a traditional grocer.[28]

Potential Competitors in the Online Grocery Segment

When online grocers started appearing within the industry, many established brick-and-mortar grocers began offering online shopping in an attempt to maintain and expand their customer base. Two basic models were used for online order fulfillment: (1) pick items from the shelves of existing stores within the grocer's chain, and (2) build special warehouses dedicated to online orders. The demand for home delivery of groceries had been increasing, but in many market areas the demand had not reached a level that would justify the high cost of warehouses dedicated to fulfilling online orders.[29]

Safeway began an ambitious online grocery venture, GroceryWorks, a shopping system that included warehouses dedicated to filling online orders. Unfavorable returns forced Safeway to reevaluate its system, and it eventually chose to form a partnership with Tesco, a U.K.-based grocer. Tesco filled its online orders from the shelves of local stores in close proximity to the customer's home. Safeway and Tesco worked together on GroceryWorks in Portland, Oregon, where they received a positive initial response from customers.[30]

The craze over health food had created room in the grocery industry for organic-food suppliers to enter as an attractive substitute to traditional groceries. When asked what kept him up at night, FreshDirect's former CEO Dean Furbush said that Whole Foods or Trader Joe's moving into a FreshDirect neighborhood was his biggest threat, as that hurt FreshDirect the most.

Whole Foods, the Austin, Texas–based supermarket chain with the organic-health-food focus, had already threatened FreshDirect's sales in Manhattan. Trader Joe's, another specialty food retailer, was opening a store in downtown Union Square, prime territory for FreshDirect.[31] Although commentators believed there was enough room for all, including even street farmers' markets, FreshDirect focused on organic foods to respond to the threats of Whole Foods and other specialty food stores.[32] With the shift among some customers to paying attention to local, sometimes organic, suppliers, FreshDirect highlighted its support of and partnership

EXHIBIT 5 Types of Online Shoppers and Their Propensity to Be Attracted to Online Grocery Shopping

Types of Online Shoppers	Comments
Traditional	Might be older technology-avoiders or simply shoppers who like to sniff-test their own produce and eyeball the meat selection.
Responsible	Feed off the satisfaction of accomplishing this persistent to-do item.
Time-starved	Find the extra costs associated with delivery fees or other markups a small price to pay for saving time.
New technologists	Use the latest technology for any and every activity they can, because they can.
Necessity users	Have physical or circumstantial challenges that make grocery shopping difficult; likely to be the most loyal group of shoppers.
Avoiders	Dislike the grocery shopping experience for a variety of reasons.

Source: Andersen Consulting.

with the local companies that provided their produce, poultry, fish, cheese, milk, eggs, and specialties such as wine (see Exhibit 6). However, its efforts were inconsistent in this area. For example, to help shoppers and checkout operators distinguish between organic and nonorganic produce, FreshDirect wrapped organics in plastic, which in itself is not organic. FreshDirect chairman Jeff Turner recognized the incongruity.[33]

EXHIBIT 6 FreshDirect Local Market Offerings

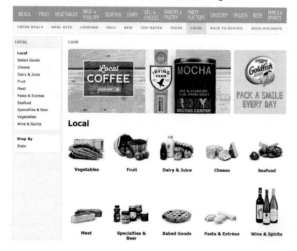

Rivals in the NYC Online Grocery Segment

YourGrocer.com

FreshDirect's most geographically significant competitor in the online grocery industry was YourGrocer.com (see Exhibits 7 to 10). YourGrocer.com was launched in New York City in 1998 with the goal of being the leading online grocery service for the New York metropolitan area. By November 2001 the company ran out of money and was forced to shut down, but in spring 2002, new capital resources were found and the company reopened for business. The second time around, YourGrocer's approach was a little different.

YourGrocer was created with a bulk-buying strategy, believing that customers would order large, economical quantities of goods from the website and the company would make home deliveries in company trucks. During YourGrocer's first life, the ambitious business plan covered a large service area and included the acquisition of another online grocery company, NYCGrocery.com.[34] This business plan was modified in its second life. The company reduced the size of its staff, got rid of warehouses, decided to rent instead of owning its delivery vans, and scaled down its delivery routes.[35] Nassau County and New Jersey were eliminated from the service area, leaving only Manhattan, the Bronx, Brooklyn, Queens, Rockland, Westchester County, and Fairfield County (Connecticut).

EXHIBIT 7 Profiles of Select Online Grocers

Name	Minimum Area Covered	Delivery Order Minimum	Delivery Charge	Method	Specialization
FreshDirect	Manhattan, Queens, Brooklyn, Staten Island, the Bronx, Nassau County, Westchester County, Fairfield County, Hoboken, Philadelphia, Jersey City	$40	$6.99–$7.99, depending on order size and destination; tipping optional	Trucks; delivers every day 6:30 a.m.– 10 p.m. depending on location	• Mostly perishables: fresh produce, meats, baked goods. • Low prices because there is no middleman.
YourGrocer	Manhattan, the Bronx, Westchester, Greenwich, Brooklyn, Queens, Rockland	None	$9.95 for orders > $75; $14.95 for orders < $75	Rented vans; delivers 9 a.m.–9 p.m. depending on location	• Bulk orders of packaged goods.
Peapod	Chicago, Boston, D.C., Long Island, Connecticut, New Jersey, Rhode Island, Milwaukee, Wisconsin, Indiana, New Hampshire, Maryland, Virginia, Pennsylvania	$60	$6.95	Trucks; delivery available 6 a.m. to 1 p.m. on Saturday and 6 a.m.–10 p.m. every other day; *pickup available as well*	• Partner with Giant Foods and Stop & Shop; items picked from shelves of local warehouses near customer's home.
AmazonFresh	Select Cities of New York, Massachusetts, Maryland, Philadelphia and California	None	$9.99 for orders under $40, in addition to 14.99 monthly membership	Order by 10 a.m. for delivery by 6 p.m. & Order by 10 p.m. for delivery by 6 a.m.	• Nonperishables as well as packaged goods.

Source: Company websites.

YourGrocer continued to offer a limited selection of items that could be purchased only in bulk. Deliveries were made in varied time slots, depending on the customer's location in the New York area. There was a $9.95 delivery charge for orders over $75, and $14.95 for orders below $75.

Peapod

Founded in 1989 by brothers Andrew and Thomas Parkinson, Peapod (see Exhibits 11 and 12) was an early pioneer in e-commerce, inventing an online home-shopping service for grocery items years ahead of the commercial emergence of the Internet. With its tagline "Smart Shopping for Busy People," the company began providing consumers with a home-shopping experience in the early 1990s, going so far as to install modems in customer homes to provide an online connection.

From its founding in 1989 until 1998, the company's business model involved filling customer orders by forming alliances with traditional grocery retailers. The company chose a retail partner in each geographic area where it operated and used the partner's local network of retail stores to pick and pack orders for delivery to customers. Peapod personnel would cruise the aisles of a partner's stores, selecting the items each customer ordered, pack and load them into Peapod vehicles, and then deliver them to customers at prearranged times. Peapod charged customers a fee for its service and collected fees from its retail supply partners for using their products in its online service.

In 1997, faced with mounting losses despite growing revenues, Peapod management shifted to a new order-fulfillment business model utilizing a local company-owned central distribution warehouse to store, pick, and pack customer orders for delivery. By mid-1999 the company had opened new distribution centers in three of the eight markets it served—Chicago, Long Island, and Boston—and a fourth distribution center was under construction in San Francisco.

In late spring 2000, Peapod created a partnership with Royal Ahold, an international food provider based in the Netherlands. At the time, Ahold operated five supermarket companies in the United States: Stop & Shop, Tops Market, Giant-Landover, Giant-Carlisle, and BI-LO. In September

---

EXHIBIT 8 Comparison of Prices for Selected Online Grocers

Grocery Item	Prices			
	FreshDirect	YourGrocer	Peapod	AmazonFresh
Tide laundry detergent	$15.99/100 oz.	$27.89/156 oz. ($16.39/100 oz.)	$12.99/100 oz.	$11.99/100 oz.
Wish-Bone Italian dressing	$2.29/8 oz.	$4.48/20 oz.	$3.69/16 oz.	$2.92/16 oz.
Cheerios	$4.49/18 oz.	$4.30/20.3 oz	$4.59/12 oz.	$3.68/18 oz.
Ragu spaghetti sauce	$2.99/24 oz.	$3.30/45 oz.	$2.69/24 oz.	$1.79/24 oz.
Granny Smith apples	$3.99/4 pack (no per-lb. price)	$11.89/6 lb. bag ($1.98/lb.)	$1.49/each	$1.66/lb.

Source: Company websites.

EXHIBIT 9 YourGrocer.com Website

EXHIBIT 10 YourGrocer's Service Focus

New YourGrocer focuses on providing *three benefits* that families in the area most value:

1. Easy ordering over the Internet or on the phone to save hours of thankless shopping. You can use your last order as a starting point to save even more time.

2. Delivery right to the home or office, which eliminates the burden of lifting and transporting heavy and bulky items each month.

3. Significant savings with everyday low prices—not short-duration specials—which reduce what you pay for stock-up groceries and household supplies on average by 25% to 30% below local supermarkets.

Source: www.yourgrocer.com.

EXHIBIT 11 Peapod Website

EXHIBIT 13 AmazonFresh Website

EXHIBIT 12 Peapod Product Selection

EXHIBIT 14 AmazonFresh Product Selection

2000 Peapod acquired Streamline.com Inc.'s operations in Chicago and the Washington, D.C., markets and announced that it planned to exit its markets in Columbus, Ohio, and in Houston, Dallas, and Austin, Texas. All of these moves were made as part of Peapod's strategic plan for growth and future profitability. Under Peapod's initial partnership agreement with Ahold, Peapod was to continue as a stand-alone company, with Ahold supplying Peapod's goods, services, and fast-pick fulfillment centers. However, in July 2001 Ahold acquired all the outstanding shares of Peapod and merged Peapod into one of Ahold's subsidiaries.

By 2017, Peapod offered delivery services from its own warehouses to many areas, including Chicagoland, Milwaukee and southeast Wisconsin, and Indianapolis. Peapod by Stop & Shop provided delivery services in southern New Hampshire, Massachusetts, Rhode Island, Connecticut, New York, and New Jersey. And Peapod by Giant provided delivery services to Maryland, Washington D.C., Virginia, and Philadelphia and southeastern Pennsylvania.[36]

In large markets, orders were picked, packed, loaded, and delivered from a freestanding centralized fulfillment center; in smaller markets, Peapod established fast-pick centralized fulfillment centers adjacent to the facilities of retail partners.[37] Peapod's proprietary transportation routing system ensured on-time delivery and efficient truck and driver utilization.

AmazonFresh

AmazonFresh entered the grocery market in recent years by offering a wide range of dry goods. Amazon was always

a threat to other online retailers because of its existing loyal customer base and legendary customer service. The selection of dry goods rather than perishables meant that Amazon, unlike FreshDirect and Peapod, didn't have to worry about delivery costs on time- and climate-sensitive items.

By mid-2016, AmazonFresh service was available in Boston, and rapidly expanding in select areas of California, New York, New Jersey, Philadelphia, Connecticut, and Maryland. AmazonFresh offered over 95,000 different items available for same day delivery if ordered before 10 a.m. and next day early morning delivery for items ordered between 10 a.m. and 10 p.m. The company had difficulty managing the economics of the grocery delivery business, and it kept membership prices considerably higher than competitors. To become an AmazonFresh member, a customer had to subscribe to Prime Fresh in addition to the subscription of Amazon Prime with a total annual cost of about $299. In contrast, FreshDirect and Peapod charged customers for delivery of the goods purchased, without requiring customers to pay subscription charges.

Still, AmazonFresh remains a vigorous competitor in the online grocery sector with a proven history of success in online retail. All the existing and rising competition amid growth in online grocery stores threatens FreshDirect's future profitability.

Current Challenges

As the online grocery retailing business has matured, all players realize they must pay close attention to customer perception. Online grocery retailers need to "serve their online customers just like they would serve the customers who come into their physical stores."[38] Even mighty Amazon has suffered grocery delivery failures, from out-of-stock problems to delivery glitches and website crashes. Unique challenges confront the business model. Even though FreshDirect has been able to woo local New Yorkers, gaining a *Fast Company* "Local Hero" award, the company has had to absorb "hundreds of thousands of dollars in parking tickets to get its customers its orders within the delivery window."[39]

Some investors have shown confidence in FreshDirect's brand and its strategic approach to expanding outside the New York metro area. J.P. Morgan Asset Management group invested $189 million through its PEG Digital Growth Fund. However, expanding national operations is a challenge for FreshDirect's business model because most people residing outside metro areas own cars and prefer handpicked grocery shopping at nearby stores. According to research published by Morgan Stanley in 2016, about 67 percent of the consumers surveyed stated that they did not buy groceries online because they liked to select the fresh products themselves.[40] The study suggests that buying fresh products online remains an unwelcoming idea for most consumers.

Environmental concerns have started to creep in as a major issue for FreshDirect. First, because of the conveyor packing system at the processing facility, FreshDirect is forced to use lots of cardboard boxes to deliver groceries: Produce comes in one box, dry goods in another, and a single tube of toothpaste in its separate cardboard delivery container. Although FreshDirect has transitioned to the use of 100 percent postconsumer recycled paper,[41] the reusability of the cardboard boxes is limited and the general public is aware that its tax dollars are used to "collect and dispose of the huge stacks of cardboards that FreshDirect's customers leave in the trash."[42] As one environmentally conscious consumer observed, "I was baffled by the number of boxes they used to pack things. Groceries worth $40 came in five boxes. And after I unpacked, I had to discard the boxes. There was no system of returning them to FreshDirect to be recycled."[43]

A second environmental issue is the additional exhaust fumes FreshDirect trucks contribute to the urban atmosphere.[44] Issues of this nature were at the forefront of citizens' concerns regarding the environmental impact that FreshDirect's move into the South Bronx would have on their neighborhood. Third, FreshDirect trucks double-parking on busy city streets only makes traffic congestion worse. As one commentator stated, "It's probably no exaggeration to say that FreshDirect has built its financial success on its ability to fob off its social and environmental costs on the city as a whole."[45]

Some city dwellers even express concern about FreshDirect's adverse effect on the overall makeup of their neighborhoods: "It is not just the impact they have on congestion, pollution, space, etc., but their very adverse impact on the best of businesses in neighborhoods that they can undersell because of their externalized costs. It is these small businesses, farmers markets and local grocery stores, that FreshDirect undercuts, that are some of the best businesses for supporting and preserving our walkable, diverse and safe neighborhoods."[46]

In 2015, a New York federal court decided that FreshDirect must pay $1.2 million in response to a class action lawsuit against the company that it withheld $23 million in tips and wages.[47] A group of FreshDirect's delivery workers claimed that the company charged delivery fees in excess of their fuel and delivery costs. FreshDirect's customers were under the impression that the additional charge was going into the pockets of delivery drivers. FreshDirect had violated regulations under the Fair Labor Standards Act by not paying overtime wages to its workers. As a result, FreshDirect has increased wages for its employees and claims that the average wages for the company's hourly employees are now $12.52 per hour as compared to the federal minimum wage of $8 per hour.[48]

A another major issue for FreshDirect is its customers' concerns about how fresh the produce and meats really are. One of the biggest obstacles to the growth of online ordering of groceries is the inability to view and touch food, particularly fresh produce and meat. Online customers cannot pick up and thump a melon or peel back the leaves on a head of romaine lettuce to check for freshness the same way they could in the grocery store. FreshDirect has received numerous comments from consumers which basically state, "I can't see, touch, and smell the products. I have to rely on you." This lack of control over identifying the freshness of the food is a major concern for customers. The company has recognized the problem and spun this negative aspect of online shopping into a positive one by creating a food-quality rating system. Consumer feedback has jump-started a new way of doing business for FreshDirect.[49]

The company's Daily Produce Rating System ranks the quality of fruits and vegetables available for delivery the next day. The five-star rating system gives shoppers "a foolproof way to ensure that the ripest fruits and crunchiest veggies are consistently delivered to their doorsteps," as advertised at the company's website. The Daily Produce Rating System is based on a daily inspection of all produce in stock by a quality assurance team. Rating criteria include taste, color, firmness, and ripeness. Rankings are based on an easy ratings scale:[50]

- Five stars: "never better, the best we've seen."
- Four stars: "great/delicious."
- Three stars: "good/reliably decent."
- Two stars: "average/inconsistent quality/generally OK."
- One star: "below average/expect wide inconsistency in quality/probably out of season."

Results are updated each morning on FreshDirect's website to let customers know which fruits and veggies are the best bets for the following day. FreshDirect also offers the same five-star rating service for seafood; some 50 to 70 percent of its customers use this feature.[51] The system aims to simulate the in-store shopping experience, allowing the grocers to showcase their best stuff and customers to decide what looks good. "Not everyone is an expert on the seasonality of a fruit or vegetable, so this system takes the guesswork out of choosing the best available items," says FreshDirect's former chief marketing officer Steve Druckman. "Each of the buyers and managers who rate the produce have years on the job, so they have great expertise. I am not aware of any other online or conventional grocer that's developing a system such as this."[52]

However, the strategy comes with a big risk: To gain customers' trust, FreshDirect has had to acknowledge that not every item it stocks is picture-perfect every day. Before implementation not everyone at the company was enthusiastic about the idea. Many feared backlash from consumers about FreshDirect's products' not always being top quality. "Was it scary? Yeah!" recalls Glenn Walsh, the produce manager. "I thought it was insane in the beginning."[53]

Despite the risk, the company claims that the rating system has changed consumer buying patterns. Around 70 percent of customers say they have purchased something they wouldn't have if it weren't for the rating system. Druckman asserts, "One hundred percent of customers changed buying patterns. The rating system works. If we put something out like black seedless grapes or golden pineapples with four stars, we'll sell twice as many of those because of their rating than otherwise."[54]

FreshDirect has upgraded the company's website, using an internal database to profile customers and serve a customized online experience. For example, the site's software analyzes order patterns, reminding customers of their favorite products and suggesting other items they might like, a marketing tool that works well for Netflix and Amazon. The database recognizes whether a visiting customer is a new, infrequent, lapsed, or loyal customer—and provides appropriate messages and ads.

A final major issue for FreshDirect is its new second distribution center in Prince Georges County, Maryland. In the second quarter of 2017, FreshDirect started offering service in Washington, D.C., Virginia, and Maryland as part of a business expansion plan.[55] It is yet to be seen whether FreshDirect will achieve success from the expansion, as Peapod has a strong foothold in the Washington, D.C., market as well as in the nearby cities. Relay Foods, a Charlottesville-based online grocer, has been operating in the Washington, D.C., market since 2008.[56] FreshDirect also faces competition in the area from large supermarket chains, including Giant and Safeway, offering delivery service. FreshDirect's second distribution center appears to face more competitors from the start, offering yet another challenge for FreshDirect managers.

According to research conducted by Morgan Stanley, comparing the year ending 2015 to the year ending 2016, "In the U.S., online grocery penetration [is] expected to increase from 8% to 26% for fresh foods, and 16% to 28% for packaged foods."[57] But despite all the innovations in e-commerce and service offerings, given the rising competition in online grocery services and the persistent preferences of most consumers to handpick fresh food, FreshDirect may still have a long way to go.

ENDNOTES

1. www.freshdirect.com/site_access/site_access.jsp.
2. Wall, Patrick. Undated. Judge tosses lawsuit meant to stop FreshDirect from moving to the Bronx. https://www.dnainfo.com/new-york/20130603/port-morris/judge-tosses-lawsuit-meant-stop-freshdirect-from-moving-bronx.
3. Karni, A. 2013. FreshDirect foes lose in court. *Crains New York,* June 3.
4. http://www.ny1.com/nyc/all-boroughs/news/2016/05/31/exclusive--a-first-look-at-freshdirect-s-new-bronx-home.html.
5. Dubbs, D. 2003. Catch of the day. *Multichannel Merchant,* July 1, multichannelmerchant.com/opsandfulfillment/orders/fulfillment_catch_day.
6. A "slotting allowance" is defined by the American Marketing Association as "1. (retailing definition) A fee paid by a vendor for space in a retail store. 2. (sales promotion definition) The fee a manufacturer pays to a retailer in order to get distribution for a new product. It covers the costs of making room for the product in the warehouse and on the store shelf, reprogramming the computer system to recognize the product's UPC code, and including the product in the retailer's inventory system." www.marketingpower.com/mg-dictionary-view2910.php.
7. Laseter, T. et al. 2003. What FreshDirect learned from Dell. *Strategy Business,* 30 (Spring), www.strategy-business.com/article/8202.
8. Schoenberger, C. R. 2006. Will work with food. *Forbes,* September 18, members.forbes.com/global/2006/0918/041.html.
9. Smith, C. 2004. Splat: The supermarket battle between Fairway, FreshDirect and Whole Foods. *New York: The Magazine,* May 24, nymag.com/nymetro/food/industry/n_10421.
10. Fahey, M. 2014. Foodily, FreshDirect start recipe delivery service. *Crains New York,* August 5.
11. https://www.wsj.com/articles/freshdirect-updates-delivery-service-1452646806.
12. Dignan, L. 2004. FreshDirect: Ready to deliver. *Baseline: The Project Management Center,* February 17, www. baselinemag.com/print_article2/0,1217,a5119342,00.asp.
13. *Chelsea-Wide Blogs.* 2006. chelsea.clickyourblock.com/bb/-archive/index.php?t-128.html.
14. *Supermarket News.* 2007. Michaelson named CEO at FreshDirect; Furbush resigns. January 9, supermarketnews.com/retail_financial/-michaelson_named_ceo_at_freshdirect_furbush_resigns_337/index.html.
15. *InternetRetailer.com.* 2008. FreshDirect's chairman hopes to deliver the goods in bigger role. July 14.
16. Elliot, S. 2003. A "fresh" and "direct" approach. *New York Times,* February 11.
17. Bosman, J. 2006. FreshDirect emphasizes its New York flavor. *New York Times,* January 31, www.nytimes.com/2006/01/31/business/media/31adco.html.
18. Laseter et al., op. cit.
19. Ibid.
20. Ibid.
21. Food Market Institute. Undated. Supermarket facts: Industry overview. www.fmi.org/facts_figs/superfact.htm.

22. Leonhardt, D. 2006. Filling pantries without a middleman. *New York Times,* November 22, www.nytimes.com/2006/11/22/business/22leonhardt.html?pagewanted51&_r52&adxnnlx51164556801-6ScpsMek8edyTRh8S2BWyA.

23. https://www.internetretailer.com/2016/10/06/online-grocery-sales-top-48-billion-worldwide.

24. Kempiak, M., & Fox, M. A. 2002. Online grocery shopping: Consumer motives, concerns and business models. *First Monday,* vol. 7, no. 9, www.firstmonday.org/issues/issue7_9/kempiak. and author estimates.

25. Machlis, S. 1998. Filling up grocery carts online. *Computerworld,* July 27: 4.

26. Hamstra, M. 2010. FreshDirect CEO predicts online gains in next decade. *Supermarket News,* March 1, supermarketnews.com/retail_financial/freshdirect-ceo-projects-online-gains-0301.

27. Woods, B. 1998. America Online goes grocery shopping for e-commerce bargains. *Computer News,* August 10: 42.

28. Fisher, L. M. 1999. Online grocer is setting up delivery system for $1 billion. *New York Times,* July 10: 1.

29. *Frontline Solutions.* 2002. Online supermarkets keep it simple. Vol. 3, no. 2: 46–49.

30. Ibid.

31. Smerd, J. 2005. Specialty foods stores will go head-to-head at Union Square. *New York Sun,* March 4, www.nysun.com/article/10058?page_no51.

32. *Progressive Grocer.* 2005. NYC's FreshDirect launches street fight against Whole Foods. March 3, www.allbusiness.com/retail-trade/food-stores/4258105-1.html.

33. *New Zealand Herald.* 2007. We don't have time to waste. February 3.

34. Joyce, E. 2002. YourGrocer.com wants to come back. *ECommerce,* May 15, ecommerce.internet.com/news/news/-article/0,10375_1122671,00.html.

35. Fickenscher, L. 2002. Bouncing back from cyber limbo: Resurgence of failed dot coms after downsizing. *Crain's New York Business,* June 24.

36. https://www.peapod.com/site/gateway/deliveryAreas.jsp.

37. Peapod Inc. Undated. Corporate fact sheet. www.peapod.com/corpinfo/peapodFacts.pdf.

38. Hamstra, M. 2007. Online stores may need to bone up on their execution. *Supermarket News,* January 29, supermarketnews.com/viewpoints/-online-stores-bone-up-execution/index.html.

39. Danigelis, A. 2006. Customers' first local hero: FreshDirect. *Fast Company,* September, www.fastcompany.com/customer/-2006/articles/local-fresh-direct.html.

40. http://www.morganstanley.com/ideas/online-groceries-could-be-next-big-ecommerce-driver.

41. *Supermarket News.* 2007. FreshDirect transitions to eco-friendly boxes. May 11, supermarketnews.com/fresh_market/-freshdirect_eco_friendly/index.html.

42. *StreetsBlog.* 2006. FreshDirect builds a grocery empire on free street space. November 22, www.streetsblog.org/2006/11/22/fresh-direct-builds-a-grocery-empire-on-free-street-space.

43. Wadia, A. S. 2007. Is FreshDirect good for you? *Metroblogging NYC,* January 30, http://nyc.metblogs.com/2007/01/30/is-freshdirect-good-for-you/.

44. *StreetsBlog,* op. cit.

45. Ibid.

46. Ibid.

47. http://www.workingsolutionsnyc.com/delivery-drivers-face-misclassification-wage-violations/.

48. http://freshdirectfacts.com/jobs/.

49. McConnon, Aili. 2009. The issue: FreshDirect focuses on customer service. *Bloomberg Businessweek,* July 1, www.businessweek.com/managing/content/jun2009/ca20090630_154481.htm.

50. FreshDirect. Undated. About our daily produce rating system. www.freshdirect.com/brandpop.jsp?brandId.5fd_ratings.

51. Cohan, P. 2010. Growth matters: FreshDirect nudges its way to profits. *Dailyfinance,* March 23, www.dailyfinance.com/story/company-news/growth-matters-freshdirect-nudges-its-way-to-profits/19372267/.

52. Briggs, Bill. 2009. FreshDirect takes a new approach to customer service. *Internetretailer.com,* January 7, www.internetretailer.com/mobile/2009/01/07/freshdirect-takes-a-new-approach-to-customer-service.

53. Bruder, J. 2010. At FreshDirect, reinvention after a crisis. *New York Times,* August 12: B9.

54. *Perishable Pundit.* 2009. New York's FreshDirect succeeds when most online grocers have failed. May 22, www.perishablepundit.com/index.php?date505/22/09&pundit52.

55. FreshDirect. Undated. FreshDirect announces expansion to Washington, D.C. http://www.prnewswire.com/news-releases/freshdirect-announces-expansion-to-washington-dc-300424391.htm.

56. Bhattarai, Abha. 2017. FreshDirect is coming to Washington. *The Washington Post,* March 16, https://www.washingtonpost.com/news/business/wp/2017/03/16/freshdirect-is-coming-to-washington/.

57. http://www.morganstanley.com/ideas/online-groceries-could-be-next-big-ecommerce-driver.

CASE 10

DIPPIN' DOTS: IS THE FUTURE FROZEN?*

Dippin' Dots has produced and distributed its tiny flash-frozen beads of ice cream, yogurt, sherbet, and flavored-ice products since microbiologist Curt Jones invented the cryogenic process in 1988. Available in many tastes and types—Original Dots, Dots 'n Cream, Coffee, and Dot Treats—Dippin' Dots' innovative take on frozen food has changed some portion of the public's way of looking at ice cream. Made at the company's production facility in Paducah, Kentucky, Dippin' Dots' unique frozen products are distributed in all 50 states and 11 countries.

At the beginning of 2017, Dippin' Dots had experienced a steep increase in total sales and was involved in numerous lucrative developments. Since being acquired by Fischer Enterprises in 2012, Dippin' Dots had pursued a multi-pronged distribution strategy of establishing partnerships with other renowned amusement destinations such as Philadelphia Zoo, Chuck E Cheese, and several premier parks. The new distribution strategy also included a partnership that involved co-branding between Dippin' Dots and Doc Popcorn, which increased the product presence in nearly 7,000 convenience stores around the U.S.[1] Many challenges remained, however, for the company to expand internationally and achieve organic growth instead of structuring partnership and co-branding contracts.

The company was bailed out of bankruptcy in 2012. There seemed a lot of potential to grow Dippin' Dots at that time. The vision and creativity of the company founder and CEO, Curt Jones, appeared to be complemented perfectly by the business acumen and experience of its president, Scott Fischer.[2]

Recently, Dippin' Dots had added five new franchises within the U.S., increasing the total number of franchises from 130 in 2015 to 135 in 2016.[3] However, the number of Dippin' Dots U.S. franchises was not growing steadily, and the number of international franchises remained stagnant.

A year earlier, Dippin' Dots had celebrated the 30th anniversary of National Ice Cream Month** by attempting to set a new world record in the world of ice cream. Dippin' Dots, the maker of the iconic flash-frozen ice cream and frozen treats, achieved a Guinness World Record title for the number of ice cream cups prepared by a team of five in three minutes. Curt Jones, Dippin' Dots' founder and CEO, was part of the record-setting team. "Our record attempt was a fun and unique way to commemorate the 30th anniversary of National Ice Cream Month," said Jones.

The company had launched the Monster Munch, Kettle Corn Dippin' Dots, and Dinner Dots ice cream lines in 2014. The Monster Munch line included eight monster-themed flavors with what the company called "crazy flavors, crazy names and some crazy ingredients," while the Dinner Dots line included dot-size portions of five savory meals.

The company promoted the low cost of entry and flexibility of its franchising options. In an interview with *CNN Money*, Steve Rothenstein, Dippin' Dots' director of franchising, said the company had a lot of opportunities to suit a variety of business models. With a franchise start-up fee of only $15,000, the company offered an economic option for budding entrepreneurs.

Dippin' Dots was flexible with alternative delivery models in addition to its more traditional brick-and-mortar locations. These included kiosks at malls and carts at community events (e.g., fairs and festivals).

What remained to be seen was whether all these advantages, innovations, and fixes would have a lasting impact on reversing the softness in company revenues and give the financials a much needed boost. Were these enhancements to the product portfolio, promotions, and business expansion efforts clever ways of growing the business, or just a last-ditch effort before the end? Despite the introduction of innovative new products, record-setting promotional events, and enticing franchise expansion opportunities, the future of the company remained uncertain.

Company Overview

In May 2012, Dippin' Dots LLC, a newly formed company based in Oklahoma and funded by private capital, acquired the Paducah, Kentucky–based Dippin' Dots Inc. A motion to approve the proposed sale was filed in April 2012 in the U.S. Bankruptcy Court in Louisville, Kentucky. In November 2011, Dippin' Dots Inc. had filed for Chapter 11 bankruptcy protection in federal court in Kentucky for a combination of reasons, including owing millions to lenders from costly patent litigation, as well as having increased operating costs and plummeting sales. Despite its unique twist on the classic frozen novelty, prior to the acquisition, Dippin' Dots had been encountering abysmal revenues and having trouble maintaining attention in the market. Feeling

---

* This case was prepared by Professor Alan B. Eisner of Pace University and graduate student Brian R. Callahan and Saad Nazir of Pace University as a basis for class discussion rather than to illustrate either effective or ineffective handling of an administrative situation. Copyright © 2017 Alan B. Eisner.

** July was designated National Ice Cream Month by the U.S. government in 1984.

the pressure, the company had looked to innovative new products, promotions, and business-expansion efforts as the hope for a turnaround. In the bankruptcy filing, the company listed about $20.2 million in assets and more than $12 million in liabilities.[4] The acquisition was approved shortly after.

Dippin' Dots employed approximately 170 workers at its facility in Paducah, Kentucky, and Scott Fischer, president of Dippin' Dots LLC, had no particular plan to move the facility or let go any existing employees. Dippin' Dots LLC was unaffiliated with the existing Dippin' Dots Inc. entity. Fischer said:

> We are looking forward to working with the Dippin' Dots management team and employees to maximize the opportunity of the business and realize the company's growth potential in a global market. We are committed to ensuring that Dippin' Dots reclaims its status, not as a novelty of the past, but as the ice cream of the future. This transaction has become a very equitable solution to the parties involved, and we expect a very smooth transition.[5]

Fischer said they had taken the opportunity to acquire Dippin' Dots Inc. in order to rescue the frozen novelty and keep it afloat. Fischer added:

> We are looking forward to rolling up our sleeves and personally meeting with all of the employees, franchisees, and business associates of the company and moving forward in a very stable and productive manner. We see substantial value in the Dippin' Dots brand, one of the most well-known brand names in the retail market.[6]

Showing their enthusiasm for growth, in January 2013 Fischer and the new executive team decided to invest over $3.1 million in the company's home facility in Kentucky, expanding operations and creating 30 new full-time jobs. Prior to the expansion, of Dippin' Dots' 170 workers, 60 lived in the Paducah area. Fischer stated, "This investment underscores our long-term commitment to market the wonderful Dippin' Dots brand, introduce new products to complement existing ones, and maintain the historic ties to Kentucky."[7] Other improvements were to include purchasing energy-efficient equipment, upgrading processes, and renovating the facility.

Earlier, Dippin' Dots had expanded its product line from ice creams to uniquely brewed coffees. Founder Curt Jones took a colder-than-cold instant-freezing process, similar to the one that made Dippin' Dots ice creams so delectable, and redirected that technology to fresh-brewed coffee. Just as he had dubbed Dippin' Dots the "Ice Cream of the Future" two decades earlier, he said the new "coffee dots" would adopt the slogan "Coffee of the Future." Real espresso was made from fresh, high-quality arabica beans and then flash-frozen into dots immediately, capturing the flavor and aroma. Named "Forty Below Joe edible coffee," the coffee dots could be eaten with a spoon, heated with water and milk to make a hot "fresh-brewed" coffee without

brewing, or blended with Frappé beads to make a Dippin' Dots Frappé. Jones's once kid-targeted dots now had a very adult twist.

Jones was thinking about more kid-friendly treats, too. For years Jones had been thinking of coming out with low-calorie, low-fat Dippin' Dots that could meet the nutrition requirements and regulations set by public schools and thus be sold at the schools. The result was "Chillz," a lower-calorie alternative to ice cream. Dippin' Dots Chillz was a low-fat frozen-beaded dessert made with Truvia, an all-natural sweetener. This healthier alternative to ice cream was also an excellent source of vitamin C. It was available in three flavors: Sour Blue Razz, Wango Rainbo, and Chocolate.[8] In the words of Dippin' Dots' vice president of sales, Michael Barrette:

> We're starting to distribute Chillz through the vending channel. We already have two contracts under way and expect to get more. Vending companies know and love the Dippin' Dots brand. With Chillz and other products, it's a great opportunity for them. Schools need that revenue. They've thrown out a lot of products in recent times that have no nutritional value. So we feel bullish about Chillz.[9]

An Innovative Product

The company's chief operation was the sale of BB-sized pellets of flash-frozen ice cream in some two-dozen flavors to franchisees and national accounts throughout the world. As a Six Flags customer commented, "I gotta say, man, they're pretty darn good. . . . Starts off like a rock candy but ends up like ice cream."[10]

Dippin' Dots was the product of a marriage between old-fashioned handmade ice cream and space-age technology. Dippin' Dots were tiny round beads of ice cream made at super-cold temperatures, served at subzero temperatures in a soufflé cup, and eaten with a spoon. The super-cold freezing of Dippin' Dots ice cream, done by liquid nitrogen, cryogenically locked in both flavor and freshness in a way that no other manufactured ice cream could offer. The process virtually eliminated the presence of trapped ice and air, giving the ice cream a fresh flavor and a hard texture. Not only had Jones discovered a new way of making ice cream, but many felt his product was more flavorful and richer than regular ice cream. According to Jones, "I created a way . . . [to] get a quicker freeze so the ice cream wouldn't get large ice crystals. . . . About six months later, I decided to quit my job and go into business."

Jones was a microbiologist by trade, with an area of expertise in cryogenics. His first job was researching and engineering as a microbiologist for ALLtech Inc., a bioengineering company based in Lexington, Kentucky. During his days at ALLtech, Jones worked with different types of bacteria to find new ways of preserving them so that they could be transported throughout the world. He applied a method of freezing using super-cold temperatures with substances such as liquid CO_2 and liquid nitrogen—the same method he later used to create Dippin' Dots.

One process Jones developed was "microencapsulating" the bacteria by freezing their medium with liquid nitrogen. Other scientists thought he was crazy, because nothing like that had ever been done before. Jones, however, was convinced his idea would work. He spent months trying to perfect the process and continued to make progress. While Jones was working over 80 hours a week in ALLtech's labs to perfect the microencapsulating process, he made the most influential decision of his life. He took a weekend off and attended a family barbeque at his parents' house. It just so happened that his mother was making ice cream the day of the barbeque. Jones began to reminisce about homemade ice cream prepared the slow, old-fashioned way. Then Jones wondered if it was possible to flash-freeze ice cream. Instead of using a bacteria medium, was it possible to microencapsulate ice cream?

The answer was yes. After virtually reinventing a frozen dessert that had been around since the second century BC,[11] Jones patented his idea to flash-freeze liquid cream, and he opened the first Dippin' Dots store.[12] Once franchising was offered in 2000, the "Ice Cream of the Future" could be found at thousands of shopping malls, amusement parks, water parks, fairs, and festivals worldwide. Dippin' Dots ice cream was transported coast to coast and around the world by truck, train, plane, and ship. In addition to being transported in specially designed cryogenic transport containers, the product was transported in refrigerated boxes known as pallet reefers. Both types of containers ensured fast and efficient delivery to franchisees around the world. The product was served in 4-, 5-, and 8-ounce cups and in 5-ounce vending prepacks.

Product Specifics

Dippin' Dots flash-frozen beads of ice cream typically are served in a cup or vending package. The ice cream averages 90 calories per serving, depending on the flavor, and has 9 grams of fat. The ice cream is produced by a patented process that introduces flavored liquid cream into a vat of negative 320 degree liquid nitrogen, where it is flash-frozen to produce the bead or dot shape. Once frozen, the dots are collected and either mixed with other flavors or packaged separately for delivery to retail locations. The product has to be stored at subzero temperatures to maintain the consistency of the dots. Subzero storage temperatures are achieved by utilizing special equipment and freezers supplemented with dry ice. Although storage is a challenge for international shipping, the beads can maintain their shape for up to 15 days in their special containers. To maintain product integrity and consistency, the ice cream has to be served at 10 to 20 degrees below zero. A retail location has to have special storage and serving freezers. Because the product has to be stored and served at such low temperatures, it is unavailable in regular frozen-food cases and cannot be stored in a typical household freezer. Therefore, it can be consumed only at or near a retail location, unless stored with dry ice to maintain the necessary storage temperature.

Industry Overview

The frozen dairy industry has traditionally been occupied by family-owned businesses such as Dippin' Dots, full-line dairies, and a couple of large international companies that focus on only a single sales region. The year 2016 was a relatively flat year for the production and sale of ice cream, as volume in traditional varieties remained flat and new types of ice cream emerged. Despite higher ingredient costs, manufacturers were continually churning out new products, though at a slower rate than in the previous year. New products and varieties range from super-premium selections to good-for-you varieties to cobranded packages and novelties. Most novelty ice creams can be found together in supermarket freezer cases, in small freezers in convenience stores, and in carts, kiosks, or trucks at popular summertime events. Ice cream makers have been touched by consolidation trends affecting the overall food and beverage industry that extend beyond their products, as even the big names have been folded into global conglomerates.

The ice cream segment in the United States is a battleground for two huge international consumer-product companies seeking to corner the ice cream market. Those two industry giants are Nestlé SA of Switzerland, the world's largest food company, with more than $88 billion in annual sales, and Unilever PLC of London and Rotterdam, with over $53 billion in annual revenues.[13] Both have been buying into U.S. firms for quite a while, but Nestlé, which already owned the Häagen-Dazs product line, upped the ante with its June 2003 merger with Dreyer's Grand/Edy's Ice Cream Inc. of Oakland, California. But even as the two giants dominate the U.S. ice cream industry, about 500 small businesses continue to produce and distribute frozen treats. As one commentator has said, "Like microbrewers and small-scale chocolate makers, entrepreneurs are drawn to ice cream as a labor of love."[14] Some of the better-known brands are regional ones, such as Blue Bell, based in Brenham, Texas (see Exhibit 1).

Approximately $54 billion was spent on ice cream in 2016.[15] Ice cream and related frozen desserts are consumed by more than 90 percent of households in the United States.[16] Harry Balzar, of the market research firm NPD Group, said about ice cream in general, "It's not a small category, but one that has remained flat for more than a decade, and is not likely to grow."[17] The challenge for producers is to woo customers away from competitors and sustain a loyal fan base by continuing to innovate. The trend toward more healthy treats has spurred the major players, Nestlé and Unilever, to develop reduced-fat product lines that still have the taste and texture of full-fat ice cream. Edy's/Dreyer's, Breyers, and Häagen-Dazs have all continued to experiment, and the "slow churned," "double-churn," and "light" products are seeing increased sales.[18]

A novelty product delivery system in the independent scoop shop is the "slab" concept. Employees at franchises such as Marble Slab Creamery and Cold Stone Creamery work ingredients on a cold granite or marble slab to blend

EXHIBIT 1 Top 10 Ice Cream Brands, 2016

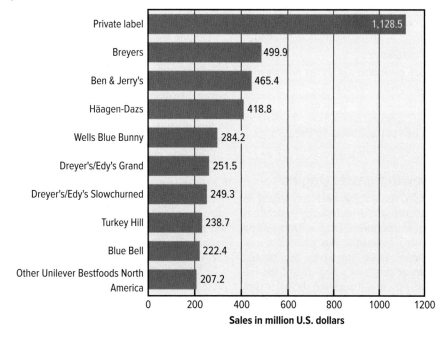

Sales in million U.S. dollars

Source: Statistica 2017.

premium ice cream with the customer's choice of tasty additives, such as crumbled cookies, fruits, and nuts, before serving it in a cup or cone. The novelty is the entertainment of watching the preparation. Both chains rank in *Entrepreneur*'s list of the top 500 franchise opportunities, but commentators are skeptical of their sustainability once the novelty wears off, especially since the average price is $5 for a medium serving.[19]

Kona Ice, shaved ice with a wide range of flavors, was among the popular ice cream brands of 2017. The company's primary selling points are 814 decorated shaved ice cream trucks that entertain customers with colorful characters and tropical music while serving ice cream. Kona Ice franchisees own trucks that they bring to social events, schools, sports events and other community groups. Interestingly, Kona Ice experienced steady growth from the start of the company in 2008 and ranked 127th on *Entrepreneur*'s Franchise 500 list of 2017.[20]

Another prominent participant in the ice cream industry is Yogurtland Franchising Inc. Started in 2006, the California-based company offers 16 flavors of frozen yogurt along with 33 toppings. Customers are charged the price of frozen yogurt by the ounce. Yogurtland has been growing at a significant rate by expanding the number of franchises in the U.S. as well as Venezuela, Australia, Thailand and Dubai. By 2017, the company had 326 franchises and ranked 184th on *Entrepreneur*'s Franchise 500 list.[21]

Industry Segmentation

Frozen desserts come in many forms. Each of the following foods has its own definition, and many are standardized by federal regulations.[22]

- **Ice cream** consists of a mixture of dairy ingredients, such as cream, milk, and nonfat milk, and ingredients for sweetening and flavoring, such as fruits, nuts, and chocolate chips. Functional ingredients, such as stabilizers and emulsifiers, are often included in the product to promote proper texture and enhance the eating experience. By federal law, ice cream must contain at least 10 percent butterfat before the addition of bulky ingredients, and it must weigh a minimum of 4.5 pounds to the gallon.

- **Novelties** are separately packaged single servings of a frozen dessert, such as ice cream sandwiches, fudge sticks, and juice bars, which may or may not contain dairy ingredients.

- **Frozen custard** or **French ice cream** must also contain a minimum of 10 percent butterfat as well as at least 1.4 percent egg yolk solids.

- **Sherbets** have a butterfat content of between 1 and 2 percent and have a slightly higher sweetener content than ice cream. Sherbet weighs a minimum of 6 pounds to the gallon and is flavored with either fruit or other characterizing ingredients.

- **Gelato** is characterized by an intense flavor and is served in a semifrozen state. Gelato contains sweeteners, milk, cream, egg yolks, and flavoring.
- **Sorbet** and **water ices** are similar to sherbets, but they contain no dairy ingredients.
- A **quiescently frozen confection** is a frozen novelty such as a water-ice novelty on a stick.
- **Frozen yogurt** consists of a mixture of dairy ingredients, such as milk and nonfat milk, that have been cultured, as well as ingredients for sweetening and flavoring.

Dippin' Dots' Growth from Its Origins[23]

The growth of Dippin' Dots Inc. has been recognized in the United States and the world by industry watchdogs such as *Inc.* magazine, which ranked Dippin' Dots as one of the 500 fastest-growing companies two years in a row, in 1996 and 1997. Dippin' Dots Franchising Inc. ranked number 4 on *Entrepreneur* magazine's 2004 list of the top 50 new franchise companies, and it achieved the 101st spot on *Entrepreneur*'s Franchise 500 for 2004. In 2005 Dippin' Dots ranked number 2 as a top new franchise opportunity and climbed to number 93 on the Franchise 500 list. By the end of 2009, Dippin' Dots had slid to the 175th position on *Entrepreneur*'s Franchise 500 list.[24] And by 2017 Dippin' Dots had fallen to the 382nd position.[25] Exhibit 2

shows the growth of franchises for Dippin' Dots. Exhibit 3 shows the growth trajectory of revenue and productivity, and Exhibit 4 lists key corporate milestones.

Despite the company's initial success, the achievements of Curt Jones and Dippin' Dots did not come without obstacles. Once Jones had perfected his idea, needing to start a company for the new process of flash-freezing ice cream, like many new entrepreneurs he enlisted the help of his family to support his endeavor. It was essential to start selling his product, and he had no protection for his idea from competitors.

The first obstacle confronting Jones was the need to locate funding to accomplish his goals. He needed money for the patent to protect his intellectual property, and he needed seed money to start manufacturing the ice cream once the patent was granted. At the same time that Jones was perfecting the flash-freezing process for his ice cream, he was also working on a Small Business Administration (SBA) loan to convert the family farm into one that would manufacture ethanol. However, instead of using the farm to produce the alternative fuel, Jones's parents took out a first, and then a second, mortgage to help fund Jones's endeavor. Thus, Jones initiated the entire venture by self-funding his company with personal and family assets.

Unfortunately, the money from Jones's parents was enough to pay for only the patent and some crude manufacturing facilities (a liquid nitrogen tank in his parents' garage).

EXHIBIT 2 Dippin' Dots Franchise Growth

Year	U.S. Franchises	Canadian Franchises	Foreign Franchises	Company Owned
2016	120	1	13	1
2015	115	1	13	1
2014	116	1	13	1

Source: www.entrepreneur.com.

EXHIBIT 3 Dippin' Dots Revenue and Productivity Growth

Year	Revenues (in millions)	Productivity (Revenue/Employee)	Total Employees
2015	$34.80	$185,000	170
2014	$32.85	$185,000	170
2013	$31.26	$180,000	170
2012	$29.87	$175,706	165
2011	$27.70	$167,879	170
2010	$26.70	$157,059	180
2009	$33.90	$188,333	190
2008	$36.00	$189,474	190

Source: www.privco.com/company/dippin-dots-inc, author estimates.

EXHIBIT 4 Dippin' Dots Milestones

1988	Dippin' Dots is established as a company in Grand Chain, Illinois.
1989	First amusement park account debuts at Opryland USA in Nashville.
1990	Production facility moves to Paducah, Kentucky.
1991	Dealer network is established for fair, festival, and commercial retail locations.
1994	First international licensee is set up (Japan).
1995	New 32,000-square-foot production facility opens in Paducah.
1997	Production facility expands by 20,000 square feet; company earns spot on *Inc.* 500 list of fastest-growing private companies in the United States.
2000	Dippin' Dots Franchising Inc. is established, and first franchise is offered; litigation against competitors is initiated to protect patent.
2001	Dippin' Dots enlists 30 new franchisees. *Franchise Times* magazine lists Dippin' Dots third in the United States in number of ice cream franchise locations, behind Baskin-Robbins and Dairy Queen.
2002	Dippin' Dots Franchising Inc. achieves 112th spot on *Entrepreneur* magazine's Franchise 500 list, ranks 69th on its list of the fastest-growing franchise companies, and is named the number 1 new franchise company. Dippin' Dots becomes a regular menu offering at McDonald's restaurants in the San Francisco Bay area.
2003	Dippin' Dots Franchising Inc. achieves 144th spot on *Entrepreneur* magazine's Franchise 500 list and number 4 on *Entrepreneur's* list of the top 50 new franchise companies. Dippin' Dots opens the Ansong manufacturing plant, 80 miles south of Seoul, South Korea.
2004	Dippin' Dots Franchising Inc. ranks number 4 on *Entrepreneur's* Top 50 New Franchise Companies list and achieves 101st spot on *Entrepreneur* magazine's Franchise 500 list. Curt Jones and Dippin' Dots are featured on a segment of the *Oprah Winfrey Show,* appearing in 110 countries. Dippin' Dots is featured among the top 10 ice cream palaces on the Travel Channel. Curt Jones is quoted in Donald Trump's best-selling *The Way to the Top* (p. 131).
2005	International Dairy Foods Association names Dippin' Dots Best in Show for Dot Delicacies. Dippin' Dots also wins three awards for package design. Dippin' Dots Franchising Inc. ranks number 1 on *Franchise Times* magazine's Fast 55 list of the fastest-growing young franchises in the nation. Ice cream cake and ice cream sandwiches (Dotwiches) are introduced to launch the Dot Delicacies program.
2006	Company leadership is restructured. Curt Jones becomes chairman of the board. Tom Leonard becomes president of Dippin' Dots Inc. Dots 'n Cream, conventional ice cream enhanced by beads of Dippin' Dots, is introduced for market testing in Kroger stores in the Midwest. The 200th franchisee begins operations.
2007	Dippin' Dots is available in Colombia, and *www.dippindots.com* V.5 is launched.
2008	Dippin' Dots Franchising Inc. ranks 112th on *Entrepreneur's* Franchise 500 list.
2009	Curt Jones returns to running the day-to-day operations of the firm. Dippin' Dots slides to 175th on *Entrepreneur's* Franchise 500 list.
2010	Dippin' Dots has 3 million Facebook fans.
2011	On November 4, 2011, Dippin' Dots files for chapter 11 bankruptcy.
2012	On May 18, 2012, the purchase of Dippin' Dots by Scott Fischer, president of Dippin' Dots LLC, is approved by U.S. Bankruptcy Court; Scott Fischer joins the team as president.
2013	Dippin' Dots begins distribution to pharmacies and convenience stores to increase access.
2014	Dippin' Dots enters *Guinness World Records* book for producing the largest number of ice cream cups with a team of five in 3 minutes.
2016	Dippin' Dots teams up with the singer/songwriter Dawin for exclusive remix dessert.

Source: Dippin' Dots Inc. Undated. History. www.dippindots.com/more-info/history.html.

He next had to open a store, and doing so required even more money—money that Jones and his family did not have. They were unable to get the SBA loan because, while the product was novel and looked promising, there was no proof that it would sell. So Jones and his newly appointed CFO (his sister) went to an alternative lender who lent them cash at an exorbitant interest rate that was tacked on to the principal weekly if unpaid.

Now in possession of the seed money they needed, Jones and his family opened their first store. Its summertime opening created a buzz in the community. The store was mobbed every night, and Dippin' Dots was legitimized by public demand. With the influx of cash, Jones was able to move his manufacturing operation from his family's garage into a vacant warehouse. There he set up shop and personally made flash-frozen ice cream for 12 hours every day to supply the store.

After the store had been operating for a few months, the Joneses were able to secure small business loans from local banks to cover the expenses of a modest manufacturing plant and office. At the same time, Jones's sister made calls to fairs and other events to learn whether Dippin' Dots products could be sold at them. Luckily for the Joneses, the amusement park at Opryland in Nashville, Tennessee, was willing to have Dippin' Dots as a vendor. Unfortunately, the first Dippin' Dots stand was placed in front of a roller coaster, and people generally did not want ice cream before they went on a ride. After a few unsuccessful weeks, Jones moved the stand and business picked up considerably. Eventually, the Joneses were able to move to an inline location, which was similar to a store, where Dippin' Dots had its own personnel and sitting area to serve customers.

Through word of mouth, interest in Curt Jones and Dippin' Dots spread. Soon other entrepreneurs contacted Jones about opening up stores to sell Dippin' Dots. A dealership network was developed to sell ice cream to authorized vendors and provide support with equipment and marketing. During that time, Jones employed friends in corporate jobs. Dippin' Dots grew into a multimillion-dollar company with authorized dealers operating in all 50 states and internationally.

The result was a cash inflow for Dippin' Dots franchising. A franchise location was any mall, fair, national account, or large family entertainment center. According to the franchising information in 2016, the initial franchise fee was $15,000, with an estimated initial investment ranging from $112,204 to $376,950. In addition, franchisees are required to pay a variable royalty fee.

The Ice Cream of the Future

Dippin' Dots is counting on youthful exuberance to expand growth. "Our core demographic was pretty much 8- to 18-year-olds," said Terry Reeves, former corporate communications director. "On top of that, we're starting to see a generation of parents who grew up on Dippin' Dots and are starting to introduce the products to their kids." Although Dippin' Dots seems to appeal more to youngsters, the product still has to have staying power as customers grow older. As one individual commented, "How can this stuff keep continuing to call itself the 'ice cream of the future'? Well the future is now, folks, and they have been pushing this sorry excuse for ice cream off on me at amusement parks and zoos since I was a little kid."[26]

In 2002 McDonald's reportedly spent $1.2 million on advertising to roll out Dippin' Dots in about 250 restaurants in the San Francisco area. Jones called the deal "open-ended" if it worked favorably for both firms. However, by 2007 Dippin' Dots was available only at a few McDonald's franchises in southern California. Storage and transportation issues were problematic, and the price of the product, 5 ounces for $5, was too steep for all but the die-hard Dippin' Dots fans.

In other marketing efforts, Dippin' Dots ads were running in issues of *Seventeen* and *Nickelodeon* magazines. Additionally, Dippin' Dots hired a Hollywood firm to place its ice cream in the background of television and movie scenes, including the 2003 *Cheaper by the Dozen.* In 2002 the Food Network's *Summer Foods: Unwrapped* showcased Dippin' Dots as one of the most unique and coolest ice cream treats. 'N Sync member Joey Fatone ordered a Dippin' Dots freezer for his home after seeing a Dots vending machine at a theater the band rented in Orlando. Caterers also sought Dippin' Dots for their star clients. A birthday party at the home of NBA star Shaquille O'Neal featured Dippin' Dots ice cream. Dippin' Dots continues to pursue the celebrity word-of-mouth route by serving its products at events such as the MTV awards and celebrity charity functions.

Dippin' Dots' sales come from approximately 131 franchisees, 90 percent of which have multiple locations.[27] Dippin' Dots has met with increased competition in the out-of-home ice cream market. The major threats to Dippin' Dots are other franchise operations, such as Ben & Jerry's, Häagen-Dazs, Baskin-Robbins, Carvel, Dairy Queen, and newcomers such as Cold Stone Creamery, Maggie Moo's, and Marble Slab Creamery (see Exhibit 5).

Although one dealer commented that Dippin' Dots used incoming franchise fees from royalties on sales for its own corporate means rather than for improvements in franchise support, most dealers converted to the new franchise system. Dippin' Dots Franchising Inc. grandfathered existing dealers' locations by issuing a franchise and waiving the franchise fee for the first contract period of five years. Many dealers had to renew their contracts in 2004. While many were initially apprehensive of converting to a franchise system, fewer than 2 percent left the system, and the firm has shown franchise growth.

Meltdown?

In an attempt to counteract the copycat threats from Frosty Bites and Mini Melts, Dippin' Dots brought a patent infringement lawsuit against them in 2005. However,

EXHIBIT 5 Ice Cream Franchises, 2016

Franchise	Start-Up Costs	Number of Franchises
Baskin-Robbins Ice cream, frozen yogurt, frozen beverages	$943–402K	7,728
Ben & Jerry's Ice cream, frozen yogurt, sorbet, smoothies	$156K–486K	582
Bruster's Real Ice Cream Ice cream, frozen yogurt, ices, sherbets	$264K–1.32M	192
Camille's Ice Cream Bars Ice cream, shakes, frozen yogurt	$152K–553K	2
Carvel Ice cream, ice cream cakes	$250K–383K	417
Cold Stone Creamery Ice cream, sorbet	$52K–467K	1,263
Culver Franchising System Inc. Frozen custard, specialty burgers	$1.84M–4.15M	574
Dairy Queen Ice cream, burgers, chicken	$361K–1.83M	6,711
Dippin' Dots Franchising LLC Specialty ice cream, frozen yogurt, ices, sorbet	$112K–377K	135
Freddy's Frozen Custard LLC Frozen custard, steakburgers, hot dogs	$606K–1.18M	234
Fro.Zen.Yo Frozen yogurt	$354K–588K	9
The Haagen-Dazs Shoppe Co. Inc. Ice cream, frozen yogurt	$154K–542K	205
Happy Joe's Pizza, pasta, sandwiches, salads, frozen yogurt	$310K–1M	54
Kona Ice Shaved-ice truck	$117K–136K	814
Marble Slab Creamery Ice cream, frozen yogurt, baked goods	$293K–381K	343
Menchie's Self-serve frozen yogurt	$218K–385K	496
Milani Gelateria Gelato	$176K–242K	1
Paciugo Gelato Caffé Gelato, beverages	$101K–455K	37
Popbar Gelato, sorbetto and frozen yogurt on a stick	$217K–457K	23
Red Mango - Yogurt Cafe & Juice Bar Frozen yogurt, smoothies, juices, wraps	$297K–415K	314
Repicci's Italian Ice Italian ice and gelato	$152K–176K	47

Continued

EXHIBIT 5 *Continued*

Franchise	Start-Up Costs	Number of Franchises
Rita's Italian Ice Italian ice, frozen custard, gelato	$150K–439K	621
Ritter's Frozen Custard Frozen custard	$365K–1.10K	20
Sloan's Ice Cream Ice cream, candy, toys, novelty items	$588K–596K	9
Stricklands Frozen Custard Frozen custard, ice cream, yogurt, sorbet	$188K–315K	4
Sub Zero Ice Cream Ice cream, yogurt, custard, smoothies	$161K–386K	53
Tasti D-Lite Frozen desserts	$234K–423K	60
Yogurtland Franchising Inc. Self-serve frozen yogurt	$310K–702K	326

Source: *Entrepreneur.* Ice cream franchises. As of January 30, 2017, www.entrepreneur.com/franchises/categories/ffqicecr.html.

during the jury trial, Dippin' Dots' testimony in support of the original patent revealed that Jones had made sales of the beaded ice cream product to over 800 customers more than a year before submitting the patent application. Even though Jones argued that these sales were for the purpose of market testing and that the production method had subsequently been further refined, and therefore was deserving of a patent, the court rendered the patent non-enforceable because these sales were not disclosed to the Patent Office. An appeal by Dippin' Dots was denied in 2007, and the patent was declared invalid.[28]

Mini Melts, released from the lawsuit, continued to expand its manufacturing facilities throughout the world; it has plants in South Korea, the Philippines, the United Arab Emirates, Hong Kong, and China as well as the United Kingdom and the United States. Instead of having franchises, Mini Melts sells dealerships for vending machines and kiosks carrying its products. One year Mini Melts CEO Tom Mosey was nominated by Ernst and Young as Entrepreneur of the Year and Mini Melts has been listed in the *Inc.* 500 for two separate ventures over the years.

By 2009 Dippin' Dots had billed itself as the "Ice Cream of the Future" for over 20 years. However, Dippin' Dots was close to a meltdown. Founder Curt Jones said that Dippin' Dots "just got hit by a perfect storm" of soaring operating costs and plummeting sales. Jones resumed daily control over the troubled Dippin' Dots after a three-year break from operations. He let go President Tom Leonard, who had run Samsonite before joining Dippin' Dots in August 2006, and Operations Vice President Dominic Fontana, who had earlier spent about 17 years with Häagen-Dazs. Jones described the separations as amicable and regrettable.

In spite of these challenges, Jones, always the inventor, invested in R&D to create a conventional ice cream product that has super-frozen dots embedded in it and withstands conventional freezers while preserving the super-frozen dots in the ice cream. Called Dots 'n Cream and available in berry creme, caramel cappuccino, mint chocolate, orange creme de la creme, vanilla bean, vanilla over the rainbow, wild about chocolate, and banana split, this product was introduced for market testing in Kroger stores in the Midwest in 2006. Thus, Dippin' Dots was finally on the verge of having a take-home ice cream option. As of April 2011, the Dots 'n Cream product was still available only in a few locations but could be bought online.

By 2010, Dippin' Dots had started an online venture by selling some of its products through its website. Customers could order ice creams, yogurts, and sherbets online, and the items would be delivered to their doors.

A new product line introduced by Dippin' Dots was Dot Delicacies. A new product in this category was Dot Treats. As of April 2011, there were seven different Dot Treats: Solar Freeze, sundaes, floats, shakes, Clusterz, Quakes, and LOL (lots of layers). These products were available at most of the retail locations where Dippin' Dots ice cream was sold.

As mentioned earlier in this case, the company branched out and released a series of coffee-based products. The "coffee dots" were new concepts in coffee—frappé and espresso that could be eaten by spoon or could be made into hot coffee drinks by just adding water and milk. Again, another untapped market Jones and his team tried to enter was the market of healthy ice cream. The new low-fat frozen beaded dessert named "Chillz," made with an all-natural sweetener, was introduced by Dippin' Dots as a healthier alternative to ice cream.

This product was developed with public schools in mind and was being distributed in schools through vending channels.

Despite the development of all the new products, the company's experience and resource base are clearly in the ice cream manufacturing and scoop-shop retailing businesses. Dealing with supermarket chains and vending distribution firms is an ongoing challenge for this relatively small firm. However, with a penchant for innovation (from Curt Jones) and an infusion of business acumen and capital (from Scott Fischer), Dippin' Dots is optimistic about the future, focusing on what it is good at, and looking to recapture attention in the frozen novelty industry.

ENDNOTES

1. Dippin' Dots sales up 60 percent in 2013–15, company expects additional 25 percent increase in 2016, http://www.franchising.com/news/20160524_dippinrsquo_dots_sales_up_60_percent_in_201315_com.html.

2. Saving the ice cream of the future. *Profile Magazine,* http://profilemagazine.com/2013/dippin-dots/.

3. Dippin' Dots Franchising LLC, Franchise information. Jason Daley, entrepreneur staff, Punita Sabharwal. https://www.entrepreneur.com/franchises/dippindotsfranchisingllc/289468.

4. www.nydailynews.com/life-style/eats/dippin-dots-maker-declares-bankruptcy-ice-cream-future-files-chapter-11-reorganization-article-1.973683.

5. www.dippindots.com/news/2012/04/Purchase-Agreement.html.

6. Ibid.

7. www.dippindots.com/news/2013/01/Expand-Manufacturing.html.

8. Dippin' Dots Inc. 2010. Dippin' Dots Chillz frozen treat. *VendingMarketWatch.com,* January 7, www.vendingmarketwatch.com/product/10110602/dippin-dots-chillz-frozen-treat.

9. Perna, G., & Fairbanks, B. 2010. From the future to the present. *Food and Drink Digital,* March 24, www.foodanddrinkdigital.com/reports/dippin'-dots-future-present.

10. Associated Press. 2006. Business blazing for supercold Dippin' Dots. July 23, www.msnbc.msn.com/id/14001806.

11. Ice cream's origins are known to reach back as far as the second century BC, although no specific date of origin is known and no inventor has been indisputably credited with its discovery. We know that Alexander the Great enjoyed snow and ice flavored with honey and nectar. Biblical references also show that King Solomon was fond of iced drinks during harvesting. During the Roman Empire, Nero (AD 54–86) frequently sent runners into the mountains for snow, which was then flavored with fruits and juices. Information from International Dairy Foods Association, Ice Cream Media Kit.

12. The idea of using liquid nitrogen to make ice cream has been around in scientific circles for some time. To learn how to make ice cream this way at home, see www.polsci.wvu.edu/henry/icecream/icecream.html. See also Kurti, N., & This-Benckhard, H. Chemistry and physics in the kitchen. 1994. *Scientific American,* April: 66–71; and www.subzeroicecream.com/press/coldfacts2006.pdf.

13. www.quotes.wsj.com.

14. Anderson, G. 2005. America's favorite ice cream. *CNN/Money.com,* July 29, money.cnn.com/2005/07/25/pf/goodlife/summer_ice_cream.

15. https://www.statista.com/statistics/326315/global-ice-cream-market-size/.

16. Author estimates; and Dairy Facts, International Ice Cream Association, www.idfa.org.

17. Murphy, K. 2006. Slabs are joining scoops in ice cream retailing. *New York Times,* October 26, www.nytimes.com/2006/10/26/business/26sbiz.html.

18. Moskin, J. 2006. Creamy, healthier ice cream? What's the catch? *New York Times,* July 26, www.nytimes.com/2006/07/26/dining/26cream.html. Note: *Slow churned* and *double churned* refer to a process called low-temperature extrusion, which significantly reduces the size of the fat globules and ice crystals in ice cream.

19. Murphy. 2006. Slabs are joining scoops in ice cream retailing.

20. https://www.entrepreneur.com/franchises/konaice/334197.

21. https://www.entrepreneur.com/franchises/yogurtlandfranchisinginc/333815.

22. All definitions are taken from International Dairy Foods Organization (IDFA). Undated. What's in the ice cream aisle? www.idfa.org/news—views/media-kits/ice-cream/whats-in-the-ice-cream-aisle/.

23. Dippin' Dots 10th anniversary promotional video.

24. *Entrepreneur.* 2015. 2015 Franchise 500 rankings, www.entrepreneur.com/franchises/rankings/franchise500-115608/2009,-4.html.

25. Dippin' Dots Franchising LLC, Franchise information.

26. Michelle, S. 2006. Review. Yelp Reviews–Chicago, November 17, www.yelp.com/biz/qnA4ml7Lu-9W4SDJOF1YPA.

27. www.entrepreneur.com.

28. Jones, L. 2010. Dippin' Dots spends millions on patent invalidity. *Noro IP,* November 15, www.noroip.com/news-blog/dippin-dots-spends-millions-on-patent-invalidity/.

CASE 11

KICKSTARTER AND CROWDFUNDING*

On March 1, 2017, Kickstarter released its first annual benefits statement after reincorporating as a Public Benefit Corporation. By becoming a Public Benefit Corporation, Kickstarter renewed its image as a socially responsible corporation and announced that it would donate 5 percent of the company's annual after-tax profit to promote the arts, music, education, and systemic equality.

As a result of advancements in technology and worldwide adoption of media paltforms, the concept of "crowdfunding" had become a norm. According to Wharton School researcher Ethan Mollick, crowdfunding allowed "founders of for-profit, artistic, and cultural ventures to fund their efforts by drawing on relatively small contributions from a relatively large number of individuals using the Internet, without standard financial intermediaries." It was considered "a novel method for funding a variety of new ventures," but it was not without its problems. Although billions of dollars had been raised for projects ranging from something as small as an artist's video diary to large endeavors such as the development of a new product for accessing e-mail or an award-winning film documentary, very little was known about the kinds of mechanisms that made funding efforts successful or whether "existing projects ultimately deliver the products they promise."

One example of this "new phenomenon in entrepreneurship"[1] was the story of Kickstarter. As of February 2017, according to ConsumerAffairs.com, Kickstarter ranked in 3rd position among the top 10 best crowdfunding sites, with over 119,273 successfully funded projects, over 12 million backers, and over $2.86 billion in pledged dollars; 217 projects had raised over $1 million each. Kickstarter also had a success rate of nearly 36 percent—meaning, however, that 64 percent of the time the backers got nothing in return for their donations.[2] What was this crowdfunding thing all about, and was Kickstarter truly a boon for entrepreneurs, or a bust for backers?

"Kickstarter = Dumb people giving money to anonymous people in hope of some goodies in an unspecified amount of time."[3] So read a comment posted in response to a story about one nine-year-old girl's Kickstarter campaign.

Mackenzie Wilson wanted to raise $829 so that she could go to computer camp and create her own video game. (She said her older brothers were making fun of her, and she wanted to prove that girls could do "tech stuff" too.) The trouble was that Kickstarter rules said someone had to be at least 18 years old in order to list a project, so Mackenzie's mom, Susan Wilson, created the information listing. Susan Wilson was a Harvard graduate, a known entrepreneur, and had allegedly promoted her daughter's Kickstarter campaign by tweeting celebrities like Lady Gaga and Ellen DeGeneres to elicit support.

The project launched on March 20, 2013, and within 24 hours it not only had reached its $829 goal but was on its way to getting 1,247 backers and $22,562 in pledges.[4] Despite the success of a campaign that raised a lot of money, Wilson and her family received negative responses. The majority of the negative responses seemed to come from those who believed that Susan Wilson had misrepresented the nature of the project, that she had acted in bad faith—intending to profit from her daughter's story—and thereby had violated Kickstarter's project guidelines. It also received headlines because of the extreme public response—accusations of a scam and death threats against Wilson and her family.

Kickstarter clearly stated that its crowdfunding service could not be used for "charity or cause funding" such as an awareness campaign or scholarship; nor could a project be used to "fund my life"—things like going on vacation, buying a new camera, or paying for tuition. And a project had to have a clear goal, "like making an album, a book, or a work of art. . . . A project is not open-ended. Starting a business, for example, does not qualify as a project." In addition, for Kickstarter to maintain its reputation as one of the top crowdfunding services, it had to make sure it kept control of how the projects were promoted: "Sharing your project with friends, fans, and followers is one thing, but invading inboxes and social networks is another."[5]

Kickstarter responded to comments on the Wilson project by affirming its support, saying, "Kickstarter is a funding platform for creative projects. The goal of this project is to create a video game, which backers are offered for a $10 pledge. On Kickstarter backers ultimately decide the validity and worthiness of a project by whether they decide to fund it."[6] However, backers and Kickstarter fans were concerned, with one user commenting, "It's all of our jobs to be on the lookout for shady Kickstarters and personally I don't want to see it devolve into a make a wish foundation for already privileged kids to learn how to sidestep rules of a website to profit."[7] And therein lay Kickstarter's

---

* This case was prepared by graduate student Eric Engelson of Pace University, Professor Alan B. Eisner of Pace University, Professor Dan Baugher of Pace University, Associate Professor Pauline Assenza, Western Connecticut State University, and graduate student Saad Nazir of Pace University. This case was solely based on library research and was developed for class discussion rather than to illustrate either effective or ineffective handling of an administrative situation. Copyright © 2017 Alan B. Eisner.

dilemma—how to provide a service that allowed funding for obvious commercial ventures while also providing safeguards for backers.

Kickstarter remained a service business, collecting 5 percent of successfully funded projects as a fee for this service, and had kept itself hands-off otherwise. However, in addition to getting comments such as the ones in response to the Wilsons' project, Kickstarter came under fire for providing no guarantees that funded projects would actually produce promised items or deliver on the project's goals. In September 2012, Kickstarter's three founders had even had to create a specific blog post titled "Kickstarter Is Not a Store"—reminding backers that the ventures were *projects* and, as such, would be subject to delays, sometimes long ones, while in development.[8] Kickstarter made it clear that it was the project *creators'* responsibility to complete projects and that it would pull projects from its web pages if project promises were obviously unrealistic or violated copyright or patent law, but otherwise it gave no other protection to backers. And even if a project couldn't fully deliver, Kickstarter collected its fee. By keeping its business model as a fee-for-service commercial venture, was it in danger of losing its reputation and therefore its future business stream?

More competitors were entering the crowdfunding, crowdinvesting, or peer-to-peer lending space, partly because of the Jumpstart Our Business Startups (JOBS) Act passed by Congress in April 2012. The JOBS Act was designed to encourage small business and start-up funding by easing federal regulations, allowing individuals to become investors; and crowdfunding by the likes of Kickstarter was a "major catalyst in shifting the way small businesses" operated and found start-up capital.[9] Crowdsourcing had already changed the way businesses interacted with consumers; crowdfunding needed to figure out "how to build a community of supporters before, during, and after" a business launched.[10] But Kickstarter's founders seemed to believe "a big part of the value backers enjoy throughout the Kickstarter experience" was to get "a closer look at the creative process as the project comes to life."[11] Kickstarter seemed to want to be a place where people could "participate in something"—something they "held dear"—and ultimately become a "cultural institution" that would outlive its founders.[12] Was that the vision of a commercial venture, or was it a wish to eventually become a not-for-profit legitimate cause-funding organization? What did Kickstarter want to be when it ultimately grew up?

The Kickstarter Business Model

By 2017 Kickstarter had become a popular "middleman"—acting as a go-between, connecting the entrepreneur and the capital needed to turn an idea into a reality. The Kickstarter platform had launched on April 28, 2009, created by Perry Chen, Yancey Strickler, and Charles Adler, and was one of the first to introduce the new concept of crowdfunding: raising capital from the general public in small denominations. In a social media–filled world, an opportunity had been recognized—you could count on your peers to help you fund your big idea. Many creators, who were young, inexperienced, low on capital, or any combination of the above, turned to websites such as Kickstarter for financial support for their projects. The site acted as a channel, enabling them to call on their friends, family, and other intrigued peers to help them raise money.

When establishing a listing on Kickstarter, the creator could place his or her project offering in one of 15 different categories: art, comics, crafts, dance, design, fashion, film & video, food, journalism, games, music, photography, publishing, technology, and theater. The project "owner" filled out some basic information, and the listing was on its way. However, certain standards had to be met before the listing could go live. If the project met those requirements, it was approved by the Kickstarter team and listed.

The guidelines were surprisingly basic and straightforward. First and foremost, the listing had to be for a project. As mentioned previously, it could not be for a charity or involve cause funding, nor could it be a "fund my life" kind of a project. The guidelines also disallowed prohibited content. Other than that, the project simply had to fit into one of the 15 designated categories. More recently, however, a few more cautious measures were added to ensure that only real and recognizable listings were created (see the section on rules and regulations later in this case). The project creator now had to set a deadline for the fund-raising, as well as a monetary goal, stating how much money he or she hoped to raise for the project. If that goal was met, the funds were then transferred to the project creator/owner. If the goal was not met, however, all donating parties were given refunds and the project was not funded. Additionally, the project owner could create rewards as incentives for different levels of donations, to be received by the donor if the project met its goal and was therefore funded. The more a donor pledged, the better the reward, which was usually related in some way to the project at hand, such as being the first backer to receive the finished product.

If the project succeeded in reaching its goal, payment was collected through Amazon. The project creator had to have an active Amazon Payments account when setting up his or her project. If a project was successfully funded, the money was transferred from the backers' credit cards to the creator's Amazon Payments account. If the project was not successfully funded, Amazon released the funds back to the backers' credit cards and no charges were issued; Kickstarter never actually possessed the funds at all. Once a project was successfully funded, Kickstarter took 5 percent of the total funds raised, while Amazon took around 3 to 5 percent for its services. After both parties deducted their commissions, the project creator/owner could still expect a payout of about 90 percent of the total money that was raised.[13] On January 6, 2015, Amazon decided to discontinue its payment service with Kickstarter. Kickstarter replaced Amazon with Stripe Payment, a service similar to PayPal.[14] For project creators, Stripe made it easier to collect the funds as it did not require setting up a separate account like Amazon did, and backers could check out faster using Stripe to pay directly via bank accounts or credit cards. It allowed Kickstarter to have a complete control on backers' checkout experience and access to raise funds anywhere in the world.

Kickstarter History

As previously mentioned, the company was launched in April 2009 by its three cofounders: Perry Chen, Yancey Strickler, and Charles Adler. Originally based in New York City, Kickstarter initially raised $10 million from Union Square Ventures and angel investors, including Jack Dorsey of Twitter, Zach Klein of Vimeo, Scott Heiferman of Meetup, and Caterina Fake of Flickr.[15] It all started with the hope of a musical success—a $20,000 late-night concert that Perry Chen was trying to organize at the 2002 New Orleans Jazz Fest. Chen had hopes of bringing a pair of DJs into town to perform. He had found a perfect venue for the concert and even gotten in touch with the DJs' management, yet the show never happened. The problem was the lack of capital, and, even if he had found willing backers, Chen had wondered what he would do if the show was unable to attract sufficient interest to pay back any investment.

This dilemma brought Chen to the realization that the world needed a better way to fund the arts. He thought to himself, "What if people could go to a site and pledge to buy tickets for a show? And if enough money was pledged they would be charged and the show would happen. If not, it wouldn't."[16] Although Chen loved this initial idea, he put it on the back burner at the time, being more focused on making music and not on starting an Internet company. Three years later, in 2005, Chen moved back to New York and began to reconsider the potential for his business idea, but he was unsure how to go about building it. That fall, Chen met Yancey Strickler, the editor-in-chief of *eMusic*, through a mutual friend and approached him with the idea of Kickstarter. Strickler was intrigued, and the two began brainstorming. Then, about a year later, Chen was introduced to Charles Adler. Adler was also intrigued and began working with Chen and Strickler.[17] After months of work, the team had created specifications for an Internet site, yet one major problem remained: None of them knew HTML coding, so the project was put on hold. Adler moved to San Francisco to do some freelance work, and Strickler remained at his day job.

Finally, in the summer of 2008, Chen was introduced to Andy Baio, who joined the team remotely as an adviser, since he was living in Portland, Oregon, at the time. Soon after, Baio and Adler contacted some developers, including Lance Ivy in Walla Walla, Washington, and the site started to take shape. Although the team was scattered throughout the country, they were well connected through Skype and e-mail and finally began building the web portal. By April 28, 2009, Kickstarter had been created and was launched to the public. The idea for creating a new channel for artistic entrepreneurs of all kinds to explore their creativity was finally realized.[18]

Crowdfunding Competition

Although by 2017, Kickstarter had become a well-known name in crowdfunding, many other companies had had the same idea. Not all of them had attracted as much media attention, but this meant that they had also avoided some of the negative press. Being a market follower rather than leader gave Kickstarter a prime opportunity to maintain a clean track record with the media because the company was able to avoid the mistakes made by other similar businesses.

One of the better-known Kickstarter competitors was Indiegogo, founded in January 2008 in San Francisco. Indiegogo was initially funded with $1.5 million from investors such as Zynga cofounder Steve Schoettler. By June 2012, the company had attracted over 100,000 projects from 196 countries. Aiming to "make an even bigger impact," in 2012 Indiegogo raised an additional $15 million in a "Series A" private equity stock offering.[19] CEO Slava Rubin said that the money was needed mostly to hire, build out, and increase resources to take on other crowdsourcing competitors such as Kickstarter. However, while Kickstarter focused on individuals' creative projects, Indiegogo was much more business oriented. Projects on Indiegogo were not regulated as they were on Kickstarter. Indiegogo used an algorithm that decided which projects to promote on the basis of activity and engagement metrics like "funding velocity."[20]

Additionally, Indiegogo projects followed the "keep it all" model—all funds collected were handed over to the project creator, regardless of any goal achievement. If the project fund-raising goal was never met, or the project's objectives were never achieved, it was up to the project creator to refund collected funds to the contributors. Indiegogo was also available for use internationally, while Kickstarter required backers to have either a U.S. or U.K. bank account.[21]

Other online crowdfunding companies, which raised funds for either charitable or creative projects, included ArtistShare for musicians[22] and Fundly for charitable projects and political campaigns—Meg Whitman used Fundly to raise $20 million for her 2010 campaign for governor of California.[23] Illustrating the degree of competition, ArtistShare and Kickstarter had been in a patent dispute since 2011 over ownership of the "methods and apparatuses for financing and marketing a creative work," with ArtistShare claiming Kickstarter infringement.[24] Meanwhile, similar companies that created some buzz in the area of business investment were Crowdfunder and Grow VC. While only in start-up mode, Crowdfunder had made enough noise to grab some attention. This platform enabled funders to participate in three different ways: They could simply donate to a project, lend to a project and receive a return, or purchase equity. However, the third option, purchasing equity through crowdfunding, was still not allowed in the U.S. as of 2013.[25]

Grow VC, similar to Kickstarter, made funds accessible to the company or entrepreneur only when the goal had been reached. One important difference between the two was that Grow VC enabled companies to collect monthly installments from investors, allowing a growing business to collect a continuous influx of funds rather than just a one-time investment. The cap for funding was set at $1 million.[26] Other recognizable competitors were Rockethub, EarlyShares, and Bolstr in the United States, CrowdCube in the United Kingdom, and Symbid, based in the Netherlands. These were only a few of the more publicized newcomers to the industry—there were at least 50 legitimate crowdfunding platforms operating worldwide.[27]

Kickstarter Successes

By January 2017, Kickstarter had launched 338,479 projects, raising $2.86 billion, of which $2.51 billion was successfully collected by project owners, $329 million was unsuccessful, and $27 million was currently in "live" donation status on the site.[28] On February 8, 2012, the first project to ever get a million dollars funded from the site was a project in the design category, an iPod dock created by ElevationLab. Its goal was set at $75,000, and backers reached this goal almost instantly, raising a total of $1,464,706. However, as impressive as this feat was, its top-funding status was short-lived. Six hours later, in the game category, Double Fine beat that goal, receiving $3,336,371 to fund its new adventure game, far exceeding the initial request for $400,000.[29] On March 27, 2015, a California based smartwatch company, Pebble Time, ran a record-breaking Kickstarter campaign by raising a total of $20,338,986.[30] The initial goal was to raise $500,000 yet Pebble Time was able to raise the first million dollars in less than an hour. Pebble Time was founded in 2012, and since then the company had been working to perfect its smartwatch that offered battery time of about 10 days and more than 6,500 applications via an open platform app store. However, one of the pioneers in the fitness tracker and smartwatch industry, Fitbit, acquired the intellectual property and hired key personnel from Pebble Technology Corp. in December 2016.

Other notable projects with over $1 million in funding included the TikTok and LunaTik multitouch watch kits and the Coolest Cooler in the design category; the OUYA TV console and Project Eternity in the games category; the FORM1 3-D printer and the Oculus Rift virtual reality headset in the technology category; and a new Amanda Palmer record, art book, and tour in the music category. Gustin premium men's wear and Ministry of Supply men's dress shirts, in the fashion category, were notably successful offerings, with over $400,000 in pledges.[31] In the movie category, in 2013, *Inocente* became the first Kickstarter crowdfunded film to win an Oscar—for Best Documentary (Short Subject)[32]—and Kickstarter backers donated over $2 million in 12 hours to fund a movie based on the popular *Veronica Mars* franchise.[33] Kickstarter was becoming a source of major support for independent films. According to the company, as of 2013 it had facilitated over $100 million in donations to various "indie" films and had funded 10 percent of all the films shown at the 2013 Sundance Film Festival.[34]

These projects made contributions to Kickstarter's business model. Even with an office in New York City, large amounts of capital raised, and about 125 employees, Kickstarter had to have been profitable. Based on the Januray 2017 statistics, at an average 3 percent cut, Kickstarter should have grossed just over $75 million since the beginning of its business operations.

Kickstarter Failures

However, as in all sectors of capital investment, some Kickstarter projects did not work out as planned. In the world of start-ups, many venture capitalists or angel investors made investments in projects that were inherently risky. Some were lucky and achieved their intended goals or did even better. Others fell short. There were many possible reasons for the failures, including lack of industry knowledge, unrealistic projections of cost, lack of managerial experience, manufacturing capabilities, or simply a lack of competence for the task at hand. These possibilities existed for Kickstarter projects as well, but in the Kickstarter model, investors/backers/donators didn't "own" anything—project creators kept ownership of their work. As Kickstarter pointed out, "Backers are supporting projects to help them come to life, not to profit financially."[35]

This disclaimer didn't stop backers or the media from highlighting Kickstarter's risks. Eyez was one of the better-known project failures on Kickstarter. More than 2,000 backers collectively contributed more than $300,000 to the entrepreneurs developing the high-tech glasses, meant for recording live video. Eyez's product creators promised delivery of the glasses ahead of the fall 2011 goal, yet by 2013 Eyez glasses still weren't being produced and none of the individual backers had received a pair. Meanwhile, the entrepreneurs had stopped providing online updates on the project and wouldn't answer questions from backers.[36] Another prominent failed project was the Skarp campaign in 2015, which raised about $4 million. The project promised to develop and offer a razor that used a laser beam instead of a traditional blade. The Skarp campaign also showed a video demonstrating the procedure of laser razor to cut hair. However, in reality the prototype of the laser razor was far from a properly functioning product.[37] Others, such as the group behind MYTHIC, a nonexistent game from an imaginary team, continued to try to scam the crowdfunding scene.[38]

A major challenge to Kickstarter's business model was related to intellectual property rights. It was probable that anyone with a good idea trying to raise capital through Kickstarter would discover that his or her idea was already stolen by merchants in China. Yekutiel Sherman, an Israeli entrepreneur, spent years developing an innovative smartphone case that unfolded into a selfie stick. In December 2015, Sherman started a Kickstarter campaign, hoping to raise funds to capitalize on the new product. A week later, Sherman found that his designed selfie stick was already on sale by vendors across China. People around the world could buy the new selfie stick using online sites including eBay.

Ongoing Issues—Backers' Concerns; Rules and Regulations

Despite the success Kickstarter had achieved, the company was under fire for many things, particularly regarding false projects, the collection of funds with no end product, and the failure of backers to receive the stated rewards set by project creators. Kickstarter followed the "all or nothing" approach to funding—pledged dollars were collected only if the fund-raising goal was met. In the beginning, Kickstarter tried to explain that the company had no control over the donated funds once these funds were in the hands of the developer—there was no guarantee of product or project "delivery." Additionally, if the fund-raising goal was met but the project never made it to fruition, Kickstarter had no ability to issue refunds. These explanations didn't keep backers from complaining of "delays, deception, and broken promises."[39]

In 2012 the Kickstarter founders felt it was necessary to reiterate "Kickstarter Is Not a Store" and point out, yet again, that "in addition to rewards, a big part of the value backers enjoy throughout the Kickstarter experience is getting a closer look at the creative process as the project comes to life."[40] Kickstarter then implemented a new set of rules, designed to prevent creators from promising a product they couldn't deliver. The goal, Kickstarter said, was to help prevent entrepreneurs from overpromising and disappointing backers by not delivering. By forcing creators to be transparent about their progress, Kickstarter hoped to discourage unrealistic projects and encourage the participation of more creative individuals who had the skills to ship products as promised.

These new rules required Kickstarter's project creators to list all potential problems involved in seeing their projects through to completion; to submit proper supporting materials—no simulations or "renderings," just technical drawings or photos of the actual current prototype; and to create a "reasonable" reward system in which backers received a reward based on their level of participation, which in most cases included a working version of the project in question. Kickstarter prohibited the use of multiple quantities at any reward level: Kickstarter was not a store, but an opportunity to invest in good ideas. The company also included the use of investors' funds in the project creator agreement. The regulations stated that if funds were collected, the creator was required to use those funds toward the creation of the project. If the funds were used for any other purpose, legal repercussions would follow.[41] In 2013 Kickstarter did a "major overhaul" on the set of tools project creators used to communicate with backers, including a "rewards sent" checklist, a tool to survey backers regarding rewards, and a project "dashboard" so that creators could track their progress.[42]

Even if Kickstarter was able to sustain its success with the implementation of tougher approval policies on its end, the future of the size and success of projects was also to be determined by the government and its ability to police the crowdfunding world through its own set of regulations. Recent federal legislation showed the government's intentions to do just that.

The JOBS Act

Signed into law in April 2012 by President Obama, the Jumpstart Our Business Startups (JOBS) Act supported entrepreneurship and the growth of small businesses in the United States and emphasized the new phenomenon of crowdfunding. The act eased federal regulations in regard to crowdfunding by allowing individuals to become investors in new business efforts. However, it also set out specific provisions to regulate just how much funding was acceptable, in order to ensure the financial safety and security of the investors. The new act stated that, as of January 2013, an equity-based company could raise no more than $1 million a year. Additionally, a company could sell to investors only through a middleman—a broker or website—that was registered with the Securities and Exchange Commission (SEC). The middleman could sell only shares that had originated from the company.

The JOBS Act did not yet apply to Kickstarter, because there were no equity sales under its current business model—on its platform, the project creator maintained 100 percent ownership of the product or service.[43] With no cap to investments and minimal federal regulations, people could be more inclined to contribute to a Kickstarter project than invest in projects from an equity investment–based competitor.

The Future for Kickstarter

Perry Chen, the cofounder and person responsible for the idea behind Kickstarter, was interviewed in May 2012 and spoke about Kickstarter's future. Chen talked about funding business start-ups and stated that Kickstarter was not interested in that model: "We're going to keep funding creative projects in the way we currently do it. We're not gearing up for the equity wave if it comes. The real disruption is doing it without equity."[44] Regarding one of the more basic details of Kickstarter's business model, Chen commented on expanding beyond 13 categories, which by 2017 had increased to 15 catagories. Particularly, he spoke about focusing on more public-service projects: "We're also looking at . . . expanding a little bit into urban design and things like bike lanes and bike racks and community gardens.

A lot of cities have approached us, talking to us about projects in that space."[45]

As *Time* magazine said when it voted Kickstarter one of the 50 best inventions of 2010: "Think of Kickstarter as crowdsourced philanthropy."[46] Chen said, back when Kickstarter was founded, that the concept was "not an investment, lending or a charity. . . . It's something else in the middle: a sustainable marketplace where people exchange goods for services or some other benefit and receive some value."[47] Cofounder Yancey Strickler pointed out that "everyday people" had pledged over half a billion dollars to Kickstarter projects in the five years since its founding and said that this "shows the power and passion of the human spirit." As Strickler explained it, "We want to become part of things bigger than ourselves."[48] In an interview with the *Financial Times,* Strickler summed up the idea of Kickstarter, "The aim is to have a sense of purpose but not feel the need to control it much beyond that. This is a canvas that everyone can plug into."[49]

What *would* Kickstarter become? While it seemed to have a clear mission and was certainly profitable, as Wharton School researcher Mollick warned, "Crowdfunding represents a potentially disruptive change in the way that new ventures are funded."[50] Going forward, the Kickstarter founders needed to consider whether they had the right business model for the future.

ENDNOTES

1. Mollick, E. R. 2013. The dynamics of crowdfunding: Determinants of success and failure. University of Pennsylvania–Wharton School. March 25. Available at SSRN: http://ssrn.com/abstract=2088298 *or* http://dx.doi.org/10.2139/ssrn.2088298; from the abstract.

2. Statistics gathered on February 11, 2017, 3:40 p.m. EDT, from www.kickstarter.com/help/stats.

3. Reader comment by Devlin1776, attached to news story: Bindley, K. 2013. 9-year-old's $20,000 Kickstarter campaign draws scam accusations. *Huffington Post,* March 26, www.huffingtonpost.com/2013/03/26/9-year-old-kickstarter-campaign_n_2949294.html#slide=1240691.

4. See the full Kickstarter project listing, plus current status, and both backer and general comments at www.kickstarter.com/projects/susanwilson/9-year-old-building-an-rpg-to-prove-her-brothers-w.

5. See Kickstarter funding guidelines at www.kickstarter.com/help/guidelines. See also comments on the Wilson project as a scam: Multi-millionaire scams Kickstarter for over $22,000—"Sending daughter to game dev camp," http://imgur.com/zwyRWCa.

6. Bindley. 2013. 9-year-old's $20,000 Kickstarter campaign.

7. Ibid.

8. See Chen, P., Strickler, Y., & Adler, C. 2012. Kickstarter is not a store. September 20, www.kickstarter.com/blog/kickstarter-is-not-a-store.

9. Farrell, J. 2012. The JOBS Act: What startups and small businesses need to know. *Forbes,* September 9, www.forbes.com/sites/work-in-progress/2012/09/21/the-jobs-act-what-startups-and-small-businesses-need-to-know-infographic/.

10. Ibid.

11. An, J. 2013. Dude, where's my Kickstarter stuff? Dealing with delays, deception and broken promises. *Digital Trends,* March 20, www.digitaltrends.com/social-media/dude-wheres-my-kickstarter-stuff/#ixzz2OmMqQ4dq.

12. From Strickler, Y. 2013. Talk given at Expand Engadget Conference, March 16, www.youtube.com/watch?v=thlaPwpobMk. Also see the conversation liveblog at www.engadget.com/2013/03/16/kickstarter-yancey-strickler-expand-liveblog/; and the interview with Myriam Joire, Engadget editor, linked at the *Huffington Post* story at www.huffingtonpost.com/2013/03/26/9-year-old-kickstarter-campaign_n_2949294.html#slide=1240691.

13. Nick, D. 2012. The history of Kickstarter: "Crowdfunding" at its best. *1Up.com,* May 14, www.1up.com/do/blogEntry?publicUserId=6111503&bId=9097349.

14. https://www.kickstarter.com/blog/making-payments-easier-for-creators-and-backers.

15. Kafka, P. 2011. Kickstarter fesses up: The crowdsourcing funding start-up has funding, too. *All Things D,* March 17, allthingsd.com/20110317/kickstarter-fesses-up-the-crowd-sourced-funding-startup-had-funding-too/.

16. See Kickstarter Pressroom at www.kickstarter.com/press.

17. Vinh, K. 2012. An interview with Charles Adler of Kickstarter. *Subtraction,* June 28, www.subtraction.com/2012/06/28/an-interview-with-charles-adler-of-kickstarter.

18. *Details.* 2010. 2010 mavericks: Yancey Strickler, Perry Chen, John Auerback & Chris Wong. October, www.details.com/culture-trends/critical-eye/201010/strickler-chen-kickstarter-auerbach-wong-gilt-man.

19. Taylor, C. 2012. Indiegogo raises $15 million series A to make crowdfunding go mainstream. *TechCrunch.com,* June 6, techcrunch.com/2012/06/06/indiegogo-funding-15-million-crowdfunding/.

20. Jeffries, A. 2012. Kickstarter competitor Indiegogo raises $15M, staffing up in New York. *BetaBeat,* June 6, betabeat.com/2012/06/kickstarter-competitor-indiegogo-raises-15-m-staffing-up-in-new-york/.

21. Taylor, C. 2011. Indiegogo wants to give Kickstarter a run for its money. *Gigaom.com,* August 5, gigaom.com/2011/08/05/indiegogo/.

22. See the *Wikipedia* entry at en.wikipedia.org/wiki/ArtistShare.

23. See the *Wikipedia* entry at en.wikipedia.org/wiki/Fundly.

24. Jeffries, A. 2012. Kickstarter wins small victory in patent lawsuit with 2000-era crowdfunding site. *BetaBeat,* May 14, betabeat.com/2012/05/kickstarter-artistshare-fan-funded-patent-lawsuit/.

25. See Crowdfunder: How it works, www.crowdfunder.com/how-it-works#a-1.

26. See Loikkanen, V. 2011. What is Grow VC? *GrowVC.com,* September 8, www.growvc.com/help/2011/09/08/what-is-grow-vc/.

27. See the list of crowdfunding services as of April 1, 2013, on *Wikipedia* at en.wikipedia.org/wiki/Comparison_of_crowd_funding_services; see also Fiegerman, S. 2012. 8 Kickstarter alternatives you should know about. *Mashable.com,* December 6, mashable.com/2012/12/06/kickstarter-alternatives/.

28. See current Kickstarter stats at www.kickstarter.com/help/stats.

29. See Strickler, Y. 2012. The history of #1. *Kickstarter Blog,* April 18, www.kickstarter.com/blog/the-history-of-1-0.

30. https://www.entrepreneur.com/article/235313.

31. See, The most funded projects in Kickstarter history (since 2009!), www.kickstarter.com/discover/most-funded.

32. Watercutter, A. 2013. The first Kickstarter film to win an Oscar takes home crowdsourced gold. *Wired,* February 15, www.wired.com/underwire/2013/02/kickstarter-first-oscar/.

33. McMillan, G. 2013. *Veronica Mars.* Kickstarter breaks records, raises over $2M in 12 hours. *Wired,* March 14, www.wired.com/underwire/2013/03/veronica-mars-kickstarter-record/.

34. Watercutter. 2013. The first Kickstarter film.

35. See, What is Kickstarter? at www.kickstarter.com/hello.

36. Krantz, M. 2012. Crowd-funding dark side: Sometimes investments go down drain. *USA Today,* August 14, usatoday30.usatoday.com/money/markets/story/2012-08-14/crowd-funding-raising-money/57058678/1.

37. https://www.bloomberg.com/view/articles/2015-10-15/failed-inventions-aren-t-scams.

38. Koetsler, J. 2012. Kickstarter dodges responsibility for failed projects. *Venture Beat,* September 4, venturebeat.com/2012/09/04/kickstarter-co-founder-failed-projects/.

39. An. 2013. Dude, where's my Kickstarter stuff?

40. Ibid.

41. Boris, C. 2012. Kickstarter's new rules for entrepreneurs. *Entrepreneur,* September 28, www.entrepreneur.com/blog/224524.

42. See Better tools for project creators, www.kickstarter.com/blog/better-tools-for-project-creators.

43. Farrell. 2012. The JOBS Act.

44. Malik, O. 2012. Kickstarted: My conversation with Kickstarter co-founder Perry Chen. *Gigaom.com,* May 22, gigaom.com/2012/05/22/kickstarter-founder-perry-chen-intervie/#3.

45. Ibid.

46. Snyder, S. J. 2010. Kickstarter one of 50 best inventions of 2010. *Time,* November 11, www.time.com/time/specials/packages/article/0,28804,2029497_2030652_2029823,00.html #ixzz2P9t9PunP.

47. Worthan, J. 2009. A few dollars at a time, patrons support artists on the web. *New York Times,* August 24, www.nytimes.com/2009/08/25/technology/start-ups/25kick.html?_r=1&em.

48. Strickler. 2013. Talk given at Expand Engadget Conference.

49. https://www.ft.com/content/1978854c-d4b5-11e3-bf4e-00144feabdc0.

50. Mollick. 2013. The dynamics of crowdfunding.

CASE 12

EMIRATES AIRLINE IN 2017*

Within three decades, Emirates Airline went from a small start-up to one of the world's biggest carriers measured by international passenger mileage. Started in 1985, the airline deviated from the strategy of most other airlines to use its position between the U.S., Europe, Africa, and Asia to connect flights between distant pairs of cities such as New York and Shanghai or London and Nairobi. Tim Clark, the firm's president, referred to these as "strange city pairs." No airline has grown like Emirates, whose expansion qualifies it to claim the crown of the freewheeling sultan of the skies.

Its strategy of flying large number of passengers all around the world would have been difficult without the

* Case prepared by Jamal Shamsie, Michigan State University, with the assistance of Professor Alan B. Eisner, Pace University. Material has been drawn from published sources to be used for purposes of class discussion. Copyright © 2017 Jamal Shamsie and Alan B. Eisner.

introduction of Boeing 777 long-range planes and Airbus 380 superjumbos. In particular, Emirates has managed over the years to radically redraw the map of the world, transferring the hub of international travel from Europe to the Middle East. Dubai, the hub of Emirates, which currently handles over 80 million passengers each year, has become the world's busiest airport for international passengers. A new terminal, the largest in the world, was recently built at a cost of $4.5 billion just to accommodate the almost 240 Emirates aircraft that fly out to 145 destinations around the world (see Exhibit 1).

Recent developments, however, such as the drop in oil prices and the growth in terrorist attacks have led to a decline in demand. Many companies, particularly in the Middle East, have been cutting back on travel for their employees, reducing the premium revenue that Emirates has been generating from first and business

EXHIBIT 1 Top Global Airlines

There are several rankings of the world's airlines, but a few have consistently been rated highest in service over the last five years. These are listed below in no particular order.

	Started	Main Hub	Fleet	Destinations
SINGAPORE	1972	Singapore	108	63
CATHAY PACIFIC	1946	Hongkong	161	102
EMIRATES	1985	Dubai	221	142
THAI	1960	Bangkok	91	78
ASIANA	1988	Seoul	85	108
ETIHAD	2003	Abu Dhabi	102	109
EVA	1989	Taipei	68	73
AIR NEW ZEALAND	1940	Auckland	106	58
GARUDA	1949	Jakarta	119	102
QATAR	1994	Doha	146	146
ANA	1952	Tokyo	211	73
SOUTH AFRICAN	1934	Johannesburg	60	42
VIRGIN ATLANTIC	1984	London	40	30
QANTAS	1920	Sydney	118	42
LUFTHANSA	1953	Frankfurt	273	190

Source: Skytrax.

class passengers. Growing fears about terrorism have led passengers to cut back on international travel and to reduce connecting through the Middle East. This has led Emirates to switch from the A380 to the smaller Boeing 777 on some routes.

The largest U.S. airlines have alleged that Emirates, like others such as Etihad and Qatar, have received subsidies from their government. These subsidies have, according to these claims, provided Emirates with an unfair advantage. Tim Clark, the president, has responded to such charges by insisting that his carrier has never received government subsidies or obtained free or cheap fuel. The airline has always disclosed its finances, used international auditors, and posted regular quarterly profits (see Exhibits 2 to 5). In fact, according to its financial statements, Emirates has shown profits for the last 27 years. "We are confident that any allegation that Emirates has been subsidized is totally without grounds," Clark declared.[1]

In fact, Emirates claims that it has worked hard to achieve its leading position by offering onboard amenities, like bars and showers on its aircraft, which other carriers find frivolous (see Exhibit 6). Beyond this, it points to the high standards of service from its crew that speak many languages and come from many countries. Emirates' service manager, Terry Daly, employs an inspiring quote: "I may not remember exactly what you said. I may not remember exactly what you did. I will always remember exactly how you made me feel."

EXHIBIT 2 Performance Highlights

Year Ended, 31 March	Passengers Flown (thousands)	Profit or Loss (AEDm)
2005	12,529	2,619
2006	14,498	2,652
2007	17,544	3,339
2008	21,229	4.451
2009	22,731	2,278
2010	27,454	3,565
2011	31,422	5,443
2012	33,981	1,813
2013	39,391	2,839
2014	44,537	3,254
2015	49,292	5,893
2016	51,853	8,330

Source: Emirates Airline.

EXHIBIT 3 Income Statement (United Arab Emirates Dirham)

Consolidated Income Statement for the year ended 31 March		
	2016	2015
Revenue	83,500	86,728
Other operating income	1,544	2,091
Operating costs	(76,714)	(82,926)
Operating profit	**8,330**	**5,893**
Finance income	220	175
Finance costs	(1,329)	(1,449)
Share of results of investments accounted for using the equity method	142	152
Profit before income tax	**7,363**	**4,771**
Income tax expense	(45)	(43)
Profit for the year	**7,318**	**4,728**
Profit attributable to non-controlling interests	193	173
Profit attributable to Emirates' Owner	**7,125**	**4,555**

Source: Emirates Airline.

EXHIBIT 4 Balance Sheet (United Arab Emirates Dirham)

	2016	2015
ASSETS		
Non-current assets		
Property, plant and equipment	82,836	80,554
Intangible assets	1,317	975
Investments accounted for using the equity method	522	544
Advance lease rentals	2,580	920
Loans and other receivables	494	619
Derivative financial instruments	-	21
Deferred income tax asset	3	4
	87,752	**83,627**
Current assets		
Inventories	2,106	1,919
Trade and other receivables	9,321	8,589
Derivative financial Instruments	12	342
Short term bank deposits	7,823	8,488
Cash and cash equivalents	12,165	8,397
	31,427	**27,735**
Total assets	**119,179**	**111,362**
EQUITY AND LIABILITIES		
Capital and reserves		
Capital	801	801
Other reserves	(1,179)	(168)
Retained earnings	32,287	27,253
Attributable to Emirates' Owner	**31,909**	**27,886**
Non-controlling interests	**496**	**400**
Total equity	**32,405**	**28,286**
Non-current liabilities		
Trade and other payables	513	202
Borrowings and lease liabilities	40,845	42,426
Deferred revenue	1,596	1,650
Deferred credits	1,090	207
Derivative financial instruments	440	521
Provisions	3,762	3,589
Deferred income tax liability	4	-
	48,250	**48,595**

continued

EXHIBIT 4 *Continued*

	2016	2015
Current liabilities		
Trade and other payables	27,037	27,770
Income tax liabilities	35	34
Borrowings and lease liabilities	9,260	5,382
Deferred revenue	1,316	1,244
Deferred credits	139	49
Derivative financial instruments	737	2
	38,524	**34,481**
Total liabilities	**86,774**	**83,076**
Total equity and liabilities	**119,179**	**111,362**

Source: Emirates Airline.

EXHIBIT 5 Cash Flow Statement (United Arab Emirates Dirham)

	2016	2015
Operating activities		
Profit before income tax	7,363	4,771
Adjustments for:		
Depreciation and amortisation	8,000	7,446
Finance costs - net	1,109	1,274
(Gain) / loss on sale of property, plant and equipment	(367)	(132)
Share of results of investments accounted for using the equity method	(142)	(152)
Net provision for impairment of trade receivables	21	32
Provision for employee benefits	733	669
Net movement on derivative financial instruments	(5)	(17)
Gain on sale of investments accounted for using the equity method	(12)	-
Employee benefit payments	(585)	(534)
Income tax paid	(62)	(68)
Change in inventories	(168)	(213)
Change in receivables and advance lease rentals	(2,234)	194
Change in provisions, payables, deferred credits and deferred revenue	454	(5)
Net cash generated from operating activities	**14,105**	**13,265**
Investing activities		
Proceeds from sale of property, plant and equipment	6,535	3,478

	2016	2015
Additions to intangible assets	(374)	(157)
Additions to property, plant and equipment	(9,504)	(10,269)
Investments in associates and joint ventures	(19)	(12)
Acquisition of a subsidiary, net of cash acquired	(23)	-
Movement in short term bank deposits	665	266
Finance income	231	168
Dividends from investments accounted for using the equity method	128	115
Net cash used in investing activities	**(2,361)**	**(6,411)**
Financing activities		
Proceeds from loans	1,213	2,215
Repayment of bonds and loans	(1,703)	(622)
Aircraft finance lease costs	(918)	(951)
Other finance costs	(294)	(341)
Repayment of lease liabilities	(4,055)	(5,628)
Dividend paid to Emirates' Owner	(2,100)	(869)
Dividend paid to non-controlling interests	(118)	(68)
Net cash used in financing activities	**(7,975)**	**(6,264)**
Net change in cash and cash equivalents	**3,7696**	**590**
Cash and cash equivalents at beginning of year	8,393	7,800
Effects of exchange rate changes	3	3
Cash and cash equivalents at end of year	**12,165**	**8,393**

Source: Emirates Airline.

EXHIBIT 6 Service For Premium Passengers On Emirates A380

- Offer 1,600 channels of in-seat entertainment
- Serve Cuvee Dom Perignon, 2000 champagne
- Serve Iranian caviar
- Serve gourmet cuisine prepared by chefs of 47 nationalities
- Offer largest selection of premium wines
- Use bone china by Royal Doulton
- Use specially made cutlery by British design house Robert Welch
- Provide Bulgari-designed amenity kits
- Feature a stand-up bar
- Offer two on-board walnut and marble design showers *

* Only for first-class passengers.

Source: Emirates Airline.

Launching a Dream

The roots of Emirates can be traced back to Gulf Air, which was a formidable airline owned by the governments of Bahrain, Abu Dhabi, Qatar, and Oman. In the early 1980s, the young sheikh of Dubai, Sheikh Mohammed bin Rashid al Maktoum, was upset by the decision of Gulf Air to cut flights into and out of Dubai. He responded by resolving to start his own airline that would help build Dubai into a center of business and tourism, given the emirates lack of significant oil resources.

The sheikh recruited British Airways veteran Sir Maurice Flanagan to lay the groundwork for the new airline, which he bankrolled with $10 million in royal funding. He placed a member of his royal family, Sheikh Ahmed bin Saeed al Maktoum, to the top post. At 26 years old, Ahmed bin Saeed had just graduated from the University of Denver in the U.S. Since he had not held a job before, the young sheikh looked to Flanagan in order to figure out how to run the airline.

However, the speculator growth of Emirates can be attributed to Sir Tim Clark, who was handed the critical task of route planning. He recognized that about two-thirds of the world's population was within eight hours of Dubai, but the firm lacked the aircraft to take advantage of its location. This began to change with the arrival of more advanced aircraft, beginning with the introduction of the Boeing 777 in 1996, on to the Airbus A380 in 2008. The long range of these aircraft allowed Emirates to develop routes that could link any two points in the world with one stop in Dubai.

From serving 12 destinations in 1988, Emirates was able to expand at an amazing rate, particularly after it started adding Boeing 777s to its fleet after 1996. The carrier continued to grow even through the recession that started in 2008, taking possession of more new aircraft than any other competitor. "We operated normally. We put on more aircraft. We carried more passengers," said Mohammed H. Mattar, senior vice president of the carrier's airport services.[2]

Providing the Ultimate Experience

Emirates strives to provide the best possible experience to its passengers in all sections of its aircraft. It was the first airline to offer in-flight viewing in the back of every seat. "That seems pretty normal for long haul airlines now, but it wasn't then," said Terry Daly.[3] A caravan of flight attendants, who are fluent in a dozen languages, pass up and down the aisles, providing service with a smile. Daly, who maintains the highest standards for all in-flight services, is known for having once fired eight service supervisors on a single day when he discovered that the flight attendants that they had supervised had deviated from his precise instructions on how to respond to requests from passengers.

From its start, Emirates has also been known for the quality and selection of food that the airline provides, even to passengers in the back of the aircraft. The catering division is one of the world's biggest, a multi-floor maze of monorails, cameras, vast warehouses of wines and liquors, multinational chefs slaving over steaming pans, kettles, grills, stretching as far as the eye can see, along with the latest in robotics, all of which deliver 115,000 meal trays to Emirates planes each day. "It's about making sure the culinary offering is absolutely first class across the airplane," said Daly.[4]

But Emirates has always tried to push further and further on the service and amenities that it provides to its premium-class passengers. Included with a Business Class ticket is a limousine ride to and from the airport, personal assistance with the check-in process, and use of one of its 30 worldwide lounges. One of 600 multinational and multilingual members of a welcome team called *Marhaba,* Arabic for "welcome," help all first- and business-class passengers clear all formalities upon departure and arrival.

Over the years, as Emirates has moved to larger and larger aircraft, it has found ways to enhance the experience of its premium passengers during flight. The airline pioneered the concept of a suite in first class with its launch of the A340 back in 2003. With its 50 A380s, the world's biggest jetliner, Emirates is able to offer 14 first-class suites, each with a vanity table, closet, 23-inch TV screen and electronic doors that seal shut for total seclusion.

First-class passengers also have access to two enormous spa showers, a first in the industry. An event planner who flew first class said, "To walk onto the A380, to have an average size bathroom, a seven minute shower, full size bath towels and your own attendant is pretty amazing."[5] All premium-class passengers—both in first and business class—have access to a big, circular lounge, with a horseshoe-shaped stand-up bar in the center, for which Emirates forfeited a number of business-class seats.

Grooming a Special Employee

Each year, Emirates holds Open Days in more than 140 cities across 70 countries for the purpose of attracting new recruits to join its elite force of 18,000 flight attendants from 140 nationalities who speak more than 50 languages. They are not attracted by the starting salary, which is only about $30,000 per year, or to the free room and board that comes with it. They are excited about the possibility of joining an iconic brand which encompasses people around the world.

The airline offers a vast no-expenses-spared crew training program, where for seven weeks, each new recruit moves through different departments with specialists in various areas. Emirates carefully trains all its employees, from those who check in passengers to those who serve them on their planes. Only about 5 percent of the applicants make it through the selection process. The low acceptance rate pushes people with diverse backgrounds to compete in an American Idol style brains-and-beauty contest for a chance to travel around the world as a member of an Emirates cabin crew.

The exterior of the Emirates' state-of-the-art training facility resembles the fuselage of a jetliner. Inside, everyone pays particular attention to the flight attendants, who must make sure that everyone on the aircraft receives the highest level of service on every single flight. This is particularly important for a carrier whose flights are of long duration because they serve destinations across all continents.

By the end of their training, the newcomers have been instructed in aspects of posture, etiquette, safety, and evacuation. There are strict standards for the color of the lipstick, the shade of the hair, and even the style of the lingerie. According to a recent report, the crew, who are 75 percent women, have an average age of 26 years, compared with an age of over 40 at U.S. airlines. Their weight is carefully monitored, their makeup mandatorily reapplied regularly, and unwed pregnancy is not allowed. Everything must go well with the pinstripe khaki uniform, the color of sand, with white scarfs billowing like exotic sails. Women must adhere to certain hairstyles that the crowning blood-red hat will work with. "When walking through an airport terminal, it's usually a *Catch Me If You Can* movie moment, with passengers all turning their heads," said one of the new recruits.[6]

Like everything else, Emirates goes over the top in what it calls *Nujoum,* the Arabic word for stars, by including motivational team-building exercises in its training program. Travel writer Christine Negroni, who participated in one of these, described the experience that the new recruits typically go through. "It is a combination of a customer service experience and a come-to-Jesus rally, highly produced like a Hollywood spectacular. If you had told me that Disney produced it, I wouldn't doubt it. By the end of the day, they are whipped into a frenzy of feeling *What can I do for Emirates?*"[7]

Communicating to the Masses

In spite of the extra touches and amenities that Emirates can provide for its passengers, the carrier discovered from focus groups that their name was not well known in many parts of the world where they were expanding. They realized that they needed to create a message they could use to develop their brand among consumers that would inform them what to expect from Emirates. This message could also be used to motivate existing and potential employees to rally behind the airline and work to deliver on its promise.

In its usual style of pushing for the best, Emirates summoned the world's top 10 advertising agencies to Dubai to compete for a massive international advertising campaign contract. StrawberryFrog, an advertising agency that had recently started operations in New York City, was one of the firms vying for the contract. Its founder, Scott Goodson, had read an interview with Tim Clark, the president of Emirates, shortly before this gathering of the advertising agencies. "And in that article, he was talking about his vision, that he wanted Emirates to be a global company and wanted to make the world a smaller place by bringing people together," said Goodson.[8]

These comments inspired Goodson to come up with the idea of "Hello Tomorrow," which allowed his firm to clinch the contract with Emirates. These words became not just the theme for an ad campaign but a new way to think about the airline. Through the use of powerful storytelling, images, and music, the message portrayed Emirates not just as a carrier that delivered a superior experience but as a catalyst for connecting a new global culture of shared aspirations, values, enthusiasm, and dreams. In his conversation with Tim Clark, Goodson said: "Ad campaigns are fleeting. The power of a movement is that it can change habits and rally millions."[9]

The StrawberryFrog team spent 18 month at Emirates headquarters educating employees, making them foot soldiers in this "movement" or campaign. In the early spring of 2012, the "Hello Tomorrow" brand was launched, a universal message in myriad languages in 150 countries. In television ads, an Emirates steward pushes his drink cart as a mammoth A380 airplane seems to be literally built around him, its various parts and personnel coming from countries spanning the globe, providing proof that the airline is a truly global enterprise.

Chasing Tomorrow?

Even as Emirates has been trying to set itself apart from other carriers by enhancing the customer experience, it is facing new challenges. It is trying to attract tourists to Dubai to replace some of the connecting passengers that it is losing because of the wars in the Middle East and terrorism there and elsewhere. It is cutting back on its additional orders for the Airbus 380 at least until passenger levels rise again.

At the same time, many of its competitors have been trying to improve on their offerings, particularly for passengers who are willing to pay a little more. Airlines are fighting with each other to attract this more upscale segment as the higher fares allow them to increase their profits without having to add capacity. Singapore Airlines, for example, is trying to beat all competitors by providing a truly enhanced premium economy section. It will offer wider seats with more recline, a cocktail table, more storage space, and a sleek 13.3-inch high-definition screen, the largest in its class. Passengers will be offered state-of-the-art noise canceling headsets and hundreds of channels of entertainment, and they will be offered more options on a menu that will be designed specifically for the premium economy class.

Emirates faces its biggest challenge from its other U.A.E.-based rival, Etihad, which announced an improvement to the first-class suite that Emirates pioneered 12 years ago. Etihad introduced, with grand bravado, a three-room, $21,000 one-way Residence and nine $16,000 one-way one-room First Apartments, complete with Savoy Academy-trained butler and private chefs, on its A380 flights. First offered on flights between Dubai and London, the service is to be expanded to flights between Dubai and New York and Dubai and Sydney.

Some industry analysts have questioned the ability of Emirates to deal with these challenges. Joe Brancatelli, a business travel writer, recently stated: "I could make the case that Emirates' moment has passed. Emirates was the trendy airline three or four years ago."[10] In a recent meeting to announce the latest performance figures for the airline, Emirates Chairman and CEO His Highness Sheikh Ahmed bin Saeed Al Maktoum brushed away these concerns. "Over the years, we have always managed to come up with new products," the young chairman responded.[11]

ENDNOTES

1. Mark Seal. Fly me to the moon . . . with a stop in Dubai. *Departures.com,* Summer 2014, p. 276.
2. Susan Carey. U.S. carriers claim unfair practices. *The Wall Street Journal,* March 6, 2015, p. B 3.
3. *Departures.com.,* Summer 2014, p. 276.
4. Ibid., p. 277.
5. Ibid., p. 277.
6. Ibid., p. 278.
7. Ibid., p. 277.
8. Ibid., p. 310.
9. Ibid., p. 278.
10. Ibid., p. 278.
11. Ibid., p. 275.

CASE 13

CIRQUE DU SOLEIL*

For over three decades, Cirque du Soleil, led by the fire-eater-turned-billionaire Guy Laliberte, has reinvented and revolutionized the circus. From its beginning in 1984, the world's leading producer of high-quality live artistic entertainment has thrilled over 160 million spectators with a novel show concept that is an astonishing theatrical blend of circus acts and street entertainment, featuring spectacular costumes, fairyland sets, spellbinding music, and magical lighting. Cirque manages to run as many as 20 shows at a time and has played in 330 cities across 48 countries.

Cirque du Soleil's business triumphs have mirrored its high-flying aerial stunts, and it is a case study for business journal articles on carving out unique markets. But following a recent bleak outlook report from a consultant, a spate of poorly received shows over the last few years, and a decline in profits, executives at Cirque say they are now restructuring and refocusing their business—shifting some of the attention away from their string of successful shows toward several other potential business ventures.

For the first time in its recent history, Cirque du Soleil failed to generate a profit in 2013. Its market dropped 20 percent from $2.7 billion in 2008. In interviews with *The Wall Street Journal* at Cirque du Soleil's sleek headquarters in Montreal, top executives including founder and 90 percent owner Laliberte talked about the firm's deteriorating finances and their desire to expand into new areas. In 2015, they announced an agreement under which TPG, a global private investment firm, would acquire a majority stake in Cirque du Soleil to fuel its future growth. Cirque has also sold a minority stake to a Chinese investment group that will help launch shows in China.

Debate has swirled over whether Cirque du Soleil should return to its roots or aim for constant reinvention. At the end of 2011, Bain & Co., contracted by Cirque, reported that its market had hit saturation and the company needed to be careful with how many new shows it added. Bain suggested Cirque seek growth by moving their concept to movies, television, and nightclubs. "Guy Laliberté always said we are a rarity—but the rarity was gone," said Marc Gagnon, a former top executive in charge of operations for Cirque du Soleil who left in 2012.[1]

Nevertheless, Cirque du Soleil had finally been successful in establishing a long-running production in

New York City, a combination of theater and acrobatics called *Paramour* that had been running on Broadway since May 25, 2016. The show was distinguished from most other Cirque productions by the use of a script with dialogue along with original songs. While two previous efforts had failed, the firm claimed that its first Broadway venture which had cost $25 million to launch had managed to draw large enough audiences each week to make a profit. *Paramour* managed to achieve this success even though the show received mostly tepid reviews from the critics.

Starting a New Concept

Cirque du Soleil developed out of early efforts of Guy Laliberte, who left his Montreal home at the age of 14 with little more than an accordion. He traveled around, trying out different acts such as fire-eating for spare change in front of Centre Pompidou in Paris. When he returned home, he hooked up with another visionary street performer from Quebec, a stilt-walker named Gilles Ste-Croix. In 1982, Laliberte and Ste-Croix organized a street performance festival in the sleepy town of Baie St. Paul along the St. Lawrence valley.

In 1984, Cirque du Soleil was formed with financial support from the government of Quebec, as banks were reluctant to support the band of fire-eaters, stilt-walkers and clowns. Its breakthrough 1987 show *We Reinvent the Circus* burst on the art scene in Montreal as an entirely new art form. No one had seen anything like it before. Laliberte and Ste-Croix had turned the whole concept of circus on its head. Using story lines, identifiable characters, and an emotional trajectory in the show, Cirque du Soleil embodied far more than a mere collection of disparate acts and feats.

Despite its early success, Cirque du Soleil struggled financially. They took a gamble on making their debut in the U.S. as the opening act of the 1987 Los Angeles Festival. They managed to sell out all of their performances, which were run in a tent on a lot adjacent to downtown's Little Tokyo. Its success in Los Angeles led to the troupe to open shows across the U.S. in cities such as Washington, DC, San Francisco, Miami, and Chicago. Soon after, Cirque du Soleil performed in Japan and Switzerland, introducing their concept to audiences outside North America.

In 1992, Cirque du Soleil took a show called *Nouvelle Experience* to Las Vegas for the first time. It was performed under the big top in the parking lot of the Mirage. The success of this show led to building a permanent theater at

---

* Case prepared by Jamal Shamsie, Michigan State University, with the assistance of Professor Alan B. Eisner, Pace University. Material has been drawn from published sources to be used for purposes of class discussion. Copyright © 2017 Jamal Shamsie and Alan B. Eisner.

Treasure Island for a show called *Mystere,* a nonstop perpetual motion kaleidoscope of athleticism and raw emotion that thrilled audiences. It became the first of the troupe's permanent shows and led to several others that opened in other hotels along the Las Vegas strip. The most spectacular of these was *O* that included acts that are performed in a 25-foot-deep, 1.5 million gallon pool of crystal clear water in a custom built theater at Bellagio.

By the end of 2011, Cirque du Soleil had 22 shows—seven of them in Las Vegas. It had become an international entertainment conglomerate with 4,000 employees in offices all around the world. It had established its headquarters in a $40 million building in Montreal, where all of Cirque's shows are created and produced. Much of the building is devoted to practice studios for various types of performers and a costume department that outfits performers in fantastical hand-painted clothing. Cirque du Soleil recruits many types of talent, among them acrobats, athletes, dances, musicians, clowns, actors, and singers.

Growing with the Concept

Cirque du Soleil hired key people from the National Circus School in its formative years in order to develop its concept of the contemporary circus. Its first recruit was Guy Caron, the head of this school, to be the Cirque's artistic director. Shortly after, the troupe recruited Franco Dragone, another instructor from the National Circus School, who had been working in Belgium. Dragone brought with him his experience in commedia dell'arte techniques, which he imparted to the Cirque performers.

Together, Caron and Dragone were behind the creation of all of the Cirque du Soleil shows during their formative years, including *Saltimbanco, Mystere, Algeria, Quidam* and the extravagant *O.* Under the watchful eye of Laliberte, Cirque developed its unique formula that defined their shows. From the beginning, they promoted the whole show, rather than specific acts or performers. They eliminated spoken dialogue so that their show would not be culture bound, replacing this with a strong emotional sound track that was played from the beginning to the end by live musicians. Performers, rather than a technical crew, moved equipment and props on and off stage so that it did not disrupt the momentum as the show transitioned from one act to the next. Most important, the idea was to create a circus without a ring or animals, as Laliberte believed that the lack of these two elements would draw the audience more into the performance.

Even though Laliberte and his creative team were clearly innovative in their approach, they were not reluctant to obtain inspiration from outside sources. They drew on the tradition of pantomime and masks from circuses in Europe. They learned about blending presentational, musical, and choreographic elements from the Chinese. Caron readily admitted that Cirque took everything that had existed in the past and pulled it into the present, so that it would strike a chord with present day audiences.

All of Cirque du Soleil shows were originally developed to be performed under a Grand Chapiteau, or "big top," for an extended period of time, before they were modified, if necessary, for touring in arenas and other venues. The troupe's grand chapiteaux were easily recognizable by their blue and yellow coloring. The facilities could seat more than 2,600 spectators, and were accompanied by smaller structures that were necessary to accommodate practice sessions, food preparation, and administrative services. However, after the contract to develop *Mystere* for Treasure Island in Las Vegas, Cirque also began to develop shows that were to be performed on a more permanent basis in specially designed auditoriums.

Losing its Touch

Cirque du Soleil continued to expand even as the recent recession cut into demand. It had launched 20 shows in the 23 years from 1984 through 2006, none of which closed during that time, other than a couple of early failures. Over the next six years, however, Cirque opened 14 more shows, five of which flopped and closed early. The reasons for the failures differed. One show, *Zarkana,* couldn't make enough money to cover its production costs playing in New York City's 6,000-seat Radio City Music Hall. *Iris,* in Los Angeles, played in Hollywood, in a seedy neighborhood that despite heavy tourist traffic was commercially marginal. *Zaia,* in Macau, simply didn't appeal to local audiences. Perhaps more troubling, the company's nearly perfect record of producing artistic successes began to waver. *Viva Elvis* and *Banana Shpeel* were among several Cirque shows that garnered terrible reviews. Both shows closed quickly. "Shows like that diluted the brand," said Patrick Leroux, a professor at Montreal's Concordia University who has closely studied Cirque du Soleil.[2]

One problem, say Cirque du Soleil executives, was that audiences didn't understand the differences among various shows carrying the Cirque brand. As a result many people would dismiss the opportunity to see, for instance, the show *Totem* thinking they had already seen something similar in the older *Varekai.* On the other hand, Cirque tried to move in different directions with each of the new shows that it developed. "We're constantly challenging ourselves," Laliberte said.[3] Audiences, however, complained that some newer shows were not as focused on the acrobatic feats that they had come to expect and enjoy from Cirque.

By August 2012, Laliberte had become concerned and convened a five-day summit for executives at his estate outside Montreal. There, he and others drew up plans to lay off hundreds of executives and performers and pare the number of big new touring circus shows Cirque produced. The cuts began soon after and continued through 2013 and amounted to around $100 million of savings, according to Laliberte. The savings included everything from giving out fewer suede anniversary jackets to employees to cutting out child performers and tutors.

Laliberte also reexamined core production costs. The payroll for Cirque's show *O,* in Las Vegas, for instance, had ballooned thanks to a surge in contortionists. "I said, 'Why do we need six contortionists?'" Laliberté, 55, recalled while chain smoking inside his office.[4] In addition to the layoffs, Cirque also suffered a blow to morale when acrobat Sarah Guyard-Guillot was killed during a performance. The company overhauled the show's finale, a "battle" staged on a vertical wall, with performers suspended from motorized wire harnesses. Since the performer's death, Cirque has continued to stage the show, replacing the live finale with a videotape of the scene from a past performance.

A New Direction?

Cirque du Soleil has managed to generate profits out of a business model that is quite challenging. Kenneth Feld, of Ringling Bros. and Barnum and Bailey circus, commented: "If you think about spending $165 million on a show that seats 1,900 people, the economics are just staggering."[5] But Laliberté's stroke of genius was to realize that no Cirque show ever had to close. They could either keep touring or play in locations such as Las Vegas and Orlando that draw a lot of tourists. The troupe managed to build a repertory of shows that could all be running at the same time (see Exhibit 1).

EXHIBIT 1 Cirque du Soleil Shows

Grand Chapiteau & Arena Shows		Resident Shows	
1990	Nouvelle Experience	1993	Mystere* Treasure Island, Las Vegas
1992	Saltimbanco	1998	O* Bellagio, Las Vegas
1994	Alegria	1998	La Nouba* Downtown Disney, Lake Buena Vista
1996	Quidam*	2003	Zumanity* New York New York, Las Vegas
1999	Dralion	2005	Ka* MGM Grand, Las Vegas
2002	Varekai*	2006	Love* The Mirage, Las Vegas
2005	Corteo*	2008	Zaia The Venetian Macao
2006	Delirium	2008	Zed Tokyo Disney Resort, Tokyo
2007	Kooza*	2008	Criss Angel Believe* Luxor, Las Vegas
2007	Wintuk	2009	Viva Elvis Aria Resort & Casino, Las Vegas
2009	Ovo*	2011	Iris Dolby Theatre, Los Angeles
2009	Banana Shpeel	2013	Michael Jackson: One* Mandalay Bay & Resort, Las Vegas
2010	Totem*	2014	JOYA* Riviera Maya, Mexico
2011	Michael Jackson: The Immortal World Tour	2016	PARAMOUR* Lyric Theatre, Broadway, New York
2012	Amaluna*			
2014	Kurios: Cabinet of Curiosities*			
2015	Toruk*			
2016	Luzia*			
2017	Volta*			

*Still in performance.

Source: Cirque du Soleil.

However, the rising costs of new shows and the increase in the number of early flops had cut into the firm's revenues and profits. Yet although revenues dropped to around $850 million in 2015 from $1 billion in 2012, Cirque still managed to return to profitability because of stringent cost controls.

Laliberte has been working with his executive team to come up with a business restructuring plan to manage diversification through the creation of discrete business units under a central corporate entity to try to beef up the noncircus side of the business. *Paramour* was the first show to be launched by a new subsidiary for musical-theater production that is based in New York City.

Another subsidiary of the firm that is operating under the name of 45Degrees is starting work on producing special events. Other new areas that Cirque is venturing into include small cabaret shows at hotels, children's television programs, and theme parks. Executives say that currently the company's biggest growth area isn't a show at all. It is an expanding deal to provide ticketing services to the arena company AEG.

Circus experts say Cirque du Soleil is walking a fine line as it seeks to expand into new ventures without damaging its central brand as a creative entity. But Laliberte is convinced that Cirque can apply its unique talents to other businesses. "We'll be more about intelligent analysis of each project," he remarked to critics who have questioned the new directions.[6] For Laliberte, the stakes are high. He now has new investors that he must satisfy with the future success of his endeavors.

ENDNOTES

1. Alexandra Berzon. Cirque's next act: Rebalancing the business. *The Wall Street Journal,* December 2, 2014, p. B1.
2. Ibid., p. B4.
3. Ibid.
4. Christopher Palmeri. The $600 million circus maximus. *BusinessWeek,* December 13, 2004, p. 82.
5. Berzon, p. B4.
6. Ibid.

CASE 14

PIXAR

Since Pixar launched *Toy Story* in 1995, it has released 17 other films, each of which has debuted at the top of the box office charts (see Exhibit 1). Its films have received critical acclaim, with 10 Academy Award nominations and eight wins for Best Animated Film. This is far more than any other studio since the category was added in 2001.

The only exception to its stellar record was *The Good Dinosaur*, which was released in late 2015, after Pixar had yanked it from release the previous year. The firm had

* Case prepared by Jamal Shamsie, Michigan State University, with the assistance of Professor Alan B. Eisner, Pace University. Material has been drawn from published sources to be used for purposes of class discussion. Copyright © 2017 Jamal Shamsie and Alan B. Eisner.

pulled the film away from its director as it began to search for new ways to rework the story. Pixar had done this before, and insists that rethinking an animated film is not uncommon, especially when you are working with fresh, untested ideas. In the end, although *The Good Dinosaur* worked well as family entertainment, it did not quite meet the lofty standards for originality and creativity set by Pixar's other films.

The continued success of its films has put aside doubts about the ability of Pixar to maintain its creativity after being acquired by the Walt Disney Company in 2006 for the hefty sum of $7.4 billon. The deal was finalized by the late Steve Jobs, the Apple Computer chief executive, who then served as the head of the computer

EXHIBIT 1

Pixar Films

All of Pixar's films released to date have ended up among the top animated films of all time based on worldwide box office revenues in millions of U.S. dollars.

Rank	Title	Year	Revenue ($US millions)
1	Toy Story 3	2010	$1065
2	Finding Nemo	2003	$940
3	Monsters University	2013	$745
4	Up	2009	$735
5	The Incredibles	2005	$630
6	Ratoutille	2007	$620
7	Monsters, Inc	2002	$575
8	Cars 2	2011	$560
9	Brave	2012	$555
10	Wall-E	2009	$535
11	Toy Story 2	1999	$515
12	Finding Dory	2016	$485
13	Cars	2006	$460
14	Toy Story	1995	$390
15	A Bug's Life	1998	$365
16	Inside Out	2015	$356
17	The Good Dinosaur	2015	$123

Source: *IMDB, Variety.*

animation firm Pixar. Disney CEO Bob Iger worked hard to acquire Pixar, whose track record made it one of the world's most successful animation companies. Both Jobs and Iger were aware, however, that they must protect Pixar's creative culture while they carried it over to Disney's environment.

Jobs and Iger were convinced that Pixar's link with Disney would be mutually beneficial for both firms. In Jobs's words: "Disney is the only company with animation in their DNA."[1] John Lasseter, who oversees all story development at Pixar, denied any negative effects from Disney's acquisition of his firm and insisted that Pixar's films were increasingly being subjected to higher standards by critics because of its string of successes. If some of the studio's films had fallen a bit short, this could be attributed to some growing pains rather than compromising on its standards under Disney.

Ed Catmull, president of Pixar, reiterated his firm's commitment to take whatever steps were necessary to put out the best possible films. "Nobody ever remembers the fact that you slipped [up in] a film, but they will remember a bad film," he said.[2] Catmull's remarks indicated that Pixar was dedicated to its lengthy process of playfully crafting a film to replace the standard production line approach traditionally pursued by Disney. This contrast in culture was best reflected in the Oscars that employees at Pixar proudly display, but which someone dressed in Barbie doll clothing.

After having won another Academy Award for Best Animated Film for *Inside Out* the previous year, Pixar failed to receive a nomination in January 2017 for *Finding Dory*. The sequel was heralded by critics, however, and went on to become one of the biggest box office hits of 2016.

Pushing for Computer Animated Films

The roots of Pixar stretch back to 1975 with the founding of a vocational school in Old Westbury, NY, called the New York Institute of Technology. It was there that Edwin E. Catmull, a strait-laced Mormon from Salt Lake City who loved animation but couldn't draw, teamed up with the people who would later form the core of Pixar. "It was artists and technologists from the very start," recalled Alvy Ray Smith, who worked with Catmull during those years. "It was like a fairy tale."[3]

By 1979, Catmull and his team decided to join forces with famous Hollywood director George W. Lucas, Jr. They were hopeful that this would allow them to pursue their dream of making animated films. As part of Lucas's filmmaking facility in San Rafael, California, Catmull's group of aspiring animators was able to make substantial progress in the art of computer animation. But the unit was not able to generate any profits and Lucas was not willing to let it grow beyond using computer animation for special effects.

In 1985 Catmull finally turned to Jobs, who had just been ousted from Apple. Jobs was reluctant to invest in a firm that wanted to make full-length feature films using computer animation. But a year later, Jobs did decide to buy Catmull's unit for just $10 million, which represented a third of Lucas's asking price. While the newly named Pixar Animation Studios tried to push the boundaries of computer animation over the next five years, Jobs ended up having to invest an additional $50 million—more than 25 percent of his total wealth at the time. "There were times that we all despaired, but fortunately not all at the same time," said Jobs.[4]

Still, Catmull's team did continue to make substantial breakthroughs in the development of computer-generated full-length feature films (see Exhibit 2). In 1991, Disney ended up giving Pixar a three-film contract that started with *Toy Story*. When the movie was finally released in 1995, its success surprised everyone in the film industry. Rather than the nice little film Disney had expected, *Toy Story* became the sensation of 1995. It rose to the rank of the third highest grossing animated film of all time, earning $362 million in worldwide box office revenues.

Within days, Jobs had decided to take Pixar public. When the shares, priced at $22, shot past $33, Jobs called his best friend, Oracle CEO Lawrence J. Ellison, to tell him he had company in the billionaire's club. With Pixar's sudden success, Jobs returned to strike a new deal with Disney. Early in 1996, at a lunch with Walt Disney chief Michael D. Eisner, Jobs made his demands: an equal share of the profits, equal billing on merchandise and on-screen credits, and guarantees that Disney would market Pixar films as they did their own.

Boosting the Creative Component

With the success of *Toy Story*, Jobs realized that he had hit something big. He had obviously tapped into his Silicon Valley roots and turned to computers to forge a unique style of creative moviemaking. In each of its subsequent films, Pixar continued to develop computer animation that allowed for more lifelike backgrounds, texture, and movement than ever before. For example, since real leaves are translucent, Pixar's engineers developed special software algorithms that both reflect and absorb light, creating luminous scenes among jungles of clover.

In spite of the significance of these advancements in computer animation, Jobs was well aware that successful feature films would require a strong creative spark. He understood that it would be the marriage of technology with creativity that would allow Pixar to rise above most of its competition. To get that, Jobs fostered a campus-like environment within the newly formed outfit similar to the freewheeling, charged atmosphere in the early days of his beloved Apple, where he also returned as acting CEO. "It's not simply the technology that makes Pixar," said Dick Cook, former President of Walt Disney studios.[5]

Even though Jobs played a crucial supportive role, it was Catmull who was most responsible for ensuring that the firm's technological achievements created synergies with its creative efforts. He has been the keeper of the company's unique innovative culture, which has blended Silicon Valley

EXHIBIT 2 Milestones

1986	Steve Jobs buys Lucas's computer group and christens it Pixar. The firm completes a short film, *Luxo Jr.,* which is nominated for an Oscar.
1988	Pixar adds computer-animated ads to its repertoire, making spots for Listerine, Lifesavers, and Tropicana. Another short, *Tin Toy,* wins an Oscar.
1991	Pixar signs a production agreement with Disney. Disney is to invest $26 million; Pixar is to deliver at least three full-length, computer-animated feature films.
1995	Pixar releases *Toy Story,* the first fully digital feature film, which becomes the top-grossing movie of the year and wins an Oscar. A week after release, the company goes public.
1997	Pixar and Disney negotiate a new agreement: a 50-50 split of the development costs and profits of five feature-length movies. Short *Geri's Game* wins an Oscar.
1998–99	*A Bug's Life* and *Toy Story 2* are released, together pulling in $1.3 billion through box office and video.
2001–04	A string of hits from Pixar: *Monsters Inc., Finding Nemo,* and *The Incredibles.*
2006	Disney acquires Pixar and assigns responsibilities for its own animation unit to Pixar's creative brass. *Cars* is released and becomes another box office hit.
2008	*Wall-E* becomes the fourth film from Pixar to receive the Oscar for a feature-length animated film.
2009	*Up* becomes the Fifth film from Pixar to receive the Oscar for a feature-length animated film.
2011	*Toy Story 3* receives five Oscar nominations and wins two, including one for Best Animated Film.
2011	Steve Jobs dies, leaving Ed Catmull in charge.
2013	*Brave* becomes the seventh film from Pixar to receive an Oscar for Best Animated Film.
2015	*Inside Out* becomes the eighth film from Pixar to receive an Oscar for Best Animated Film.
2016	*Piper* received a nomination for an Oscar for best animated short film

Source: Pixar.

techies, Hollywood production honchos, and artsy animation experts. In the pursuit of Catmull's vision, this eclectic group transformed their office cubicles into tiki huts, circus tents, and cardboard castles with bookshelves stuffed with toys and desks adorned with colorful iMac computers.

One of Catmull's biggest achievements has been the creation of what is called the Pixar Braintrust (see Exhibit 3). This creative group of employees, which includes directors, meets on a regular basis to assess each movie that the firm is developing and offer their ideas for improvement. It is such emphasis on creativity that has kept Pixar on the cutting edge. Each of their films has been innovative in many respects, including of course making the best possible use of computer animation. "They're absolute geniuses," gushed Jules Roman, co-founder and CEO of rival Tippett Studio. "They're the people who created computer animation really."[6]

Catmull has worked hard to build creative innovation into programs to develop all the employees, who are encouraged to devote up to four hours a week, every week, to further their education at Pixar University. The in-house training program offers 110 different courses that cover subjects such as live improvisation, creative writing, painting, drawing, sculpting, and cinematography. For many years,

the school's dean was Randall E. Nelson, a former juggler known to perform his act using chain saws so students in animation classes had something compelling to draw.

Becoming Accomplished Storytellers

A considerable part of the creative energy at Pixar always goes into story development. Jobs understood that a film works only if its story can move the hearts and minds of families round the world. His goal was to develop Pixar into an animated movie studio known for the quality of its storytelling above everything else. "We want to create some great stories and characters that endure with each generation," Jobs stated.[7]

For story development, Pixar relies on 43-year-old John Lasseter, who goes by the title of "vice president of the creative." Known for his collection of 358 Hawaiian shirts and his irrepressible playfulness with toys, Lasseter has been the key to the appeal of all of Pixar's films. Lasseter gets very passionate about developing great stories and then harnessing computers to tell these stories. Most of Pixar's employees believe it is this passion that has ensured the string of commercial hits. Lasseter is widely regarded as the Walt Disney for the 21st century.

EXHIBIT 3

Sample of Roles

Ed Catmull	President, producer
John Lasseter	Chief creative officer, producer, director, writer
Jim Morris	Business manager
Brad Bird	Director, writer
Pete Doctor	Director, writer
Harley Jessup	Production designer
Bill Cone	Production designer
Ricky Nierva	Production designer, art director, character designer
Ralph Eggleston	Art director
Randy Barrett	Character designer, set designer, matte painter
Tia Kratter	Shading art director, digital painter
Bob Pauley	Character designer, sketch artist
Jay Shuster	Character and environment designer

Source: Pixar.

When it's time to start a project, Lasseter isolates a group of eight or so writers and directs them to forget about the constraints of technology. The group bounces ideas off each other, taking collective responsibility for developing a story. While many studios try to rush from script to production, Lasseter takes up to two years just to work out all the details. Once the script has been developed, artists create storyboards that connect the various characters to the developing plot. "No amount of great animation is going to save a bad story," he said. "That's why we go so far to make it right.[8]

Only after the basic story has been set does Lasseter begin to think about what he'll need from Pixar's technologists. And it's always more than the computer animators expect. Lasseter, for example, demanded that the crowds of ants in *A Bug's Life* not be a single mass of look-alike faces. To solve the problem, computer expert William T. Reeves developed software that randomly applied physical and emotional characteristics to each ant. In another instance, writers brought a model of a butterfly named Gypsy to researchers, asking them to write code so that when she rubbed her antennas, you could see the hairs press down and pop back up.

At any stage during the process, Lasseter may go back to potential problems that he may see with the story. In *A Bug's Life,* for example, the story was totally revamped after more than a year of work had been completed. Originally, it was about a troupe of circus bugs run by P.T. Flea that tries to rescue a colony of ants from marauding grasshoppers. But because of a flaw in the story—why would the circus bugs risk their lives to save stranger ants?—co-director Andrew

Stanton recast the story to be about Flik, the heroic ant who recruits Flea's troupe to fight the grasshoppers. "You have to rework and rework it," explained Lasseter. "It is not rare for a scene to be rewritten as much as 30 times."[9]

Pumping Out the Hits

In spite of its formidable string of hits, Pixar has had difficulty in stepping up its pace of production. Although they may cost 30 percent less, computer-generated animated films take considerable time to develop. Because of the desired emphasis on detail, Pixar completed most of the work on a film before moving to the next one, until Catmull and Lasseter decided to work on several projects at the same time. Still, the firm has not been able to release more than one movie a year.

To push for increased production, Pixar has built up its workforce to well over 1,000 employees and turned to a stable of directors to oversee its movies. Lasseter, who directed Pixar's first three films, supervises other directors who are taking the helm. *Monsters Inc., Finding Nemo, The Incredibles, Ratatouille,* and *Brave* were directed by some of this new talent. But there are concerns about the quality of directors that Pixar can rely upon to turn out high-quality animated films. Michael Savner of Bank of America Securities commented: "You can't simply double production. There is a finite amount of talent."[10]

To meet the faster production pace, Catmull has added new divisions, including one for development of new movies and one to oversee movie development shot by shot. The eight-person new-movie development team has helped to generate more ideas for new films. "Once more ideas are percolating, we have more options to choose from so no one artist is feeling the weight of the world on their shoulders," said Sarah McArthur, who served as Pixar's vice president of production.[11]

Catmull keeps pushing technology to improve the quality of the animation. During the production of *Brave,* for example, the animators had to make the curly hair of the main character appear to be natural. Claudia Chung, who worked on the film, talked about their reaction to various methods they kept trying: "We'd kind of roll our eyes and say, 'I guess we can do that,' but inside we were all excited, because it's one more stretch we can do."[12] At the same time, new animation software, Luxo, has allowed the use of fewer people, with no more than 100 animators working on each film.

The high standards of the firm cannot be compromised for the sake of a steady flow of films. This was evident in their decision to delay the launch of *The Good Dinosaur* because they felt that they had to rethink the film. Everyone at Pixar remains committed to the philosophy that every one of Pixar's films should grow out of the very best efforts of the firm's animators, storytellers, and technologists. "Quality is more important than quantity," Jobs had emphasized. "One home run is better than two doubles."[13]

Catmull works hard to retain Pixar's commitment to quality even as it grows. He uses Pixar University to encourage collaboration among employees, and to instill the key values that are tied to Pixar's success. And he has helped devise ways to avoid collective burnout. A masseuse and a doctor now come by Pixar's campus each week, and animators must get permission from their supervisors if they want to work more than 50 hours a week.

To Infinity and Beyond?

Over time the individuals behind the success of Pixar have only become more instrumental. After it acquired Pixar, Disney placed Catmull and Lasseter in charge of the combined animation business of both Pixar and Disney. Two of the films that were nominated in January 2017 for Best Animated Film, *Moana* and *Zootopia,* were both made at Disney under the supervision of these Pixar heads. For Lasseter, the new responsibilities for Disney represent a return to his roots. He had been inspired by Disney films as a kid and he started his career at Disney before being lured away to Pixar by Catmull. "For many of us at Pixar, it was the magic of Disney that influenced us to pursue our dreams of becoming animators, artists, storytellers and filmmakers," Lasseter remarked.[14]

Something that had to be adjusted to was the loss of Jobs, who passed away in 2011. At the same time, everyone at Pixar understands that their success can be attributed to the new talent the firm is able to recruit and train to work together. This recognition leads to a culture of continuous exchange of ideas and fosters a collective sense of responsibility on all their films. "We created the studio we want to work in," Lasseter remarked. "We have an environment that's wacky. It's a creative brain trust: It's not a place where I make my movies—it's a place where a group of people make movies."[15]

Pixar's string of successful films is particularly striking, given that there has been a considerable increase in the number of animated films released each year. Over the past decade, there have been years when as many as 16 films have been offered, as more and more studios have grabbed for a share of this lucrative market. The growth in competition has led to a string of losses at Dreamworks Animation, Pixar's largest competitor. Lasseter welcomes the competition because it forces Pixar to stick to its commitment to quality. "I like healthy competition," he says. "I'd rather be in a healthy industry than be the only player in a dead industry."[16]

> Think about how off-putting a movie about rats preparing food could be, or how risky it must've seemed to start a movie about robots with 39 dialogue-free minutes. We dare to attempt these stories, but we don't get them right on the first pass. This is as it should be.
>
> —*Ed Catmull from his book, Creativity, Inc,*
> *published in 2014*

ENDNOTES

1. Charles Solomon. Pixar Creative Chief to Seek to Restore the Disney Magic. *New York Times,* January 25, 2006, p. C6.
2. Daniel Miller. Pixar Film Delay Leads to Layoffs. *Los Angeles Times,* November 23, 2013, p. B 3.
3. Peter Burrows and Ronald Grover. Steve Jobs: Movie Mogul. *BusinessWeek,* November 23, 1998, p. 150.
4. Ibid.
5. Ibid., p. 146.
6. Ibid.
7. Marc Graser. Pixar Run by Focused Group. *Variety,* December 20, 1999, p. 74.
8. *New York Times,* October 18, 2011, p. C4.
9. Burrows and Grover. *BusinessWeek,* November 23, 1998, p. 146.
10. Andrew Bary. Coy Story. *Barron's,* October 13, 2003, p. 21.
11. Daniel Terdiman. Bravely Going Where Pixar Animation Tech Has Never Gone. *CNET News,* June 16, 2012.
12. Pui-Wing Tam. Will Quantity Hurt Pixar's Quality? *Wall Street Journal,* February 15, 2001, p. B4.
13. Peter Burrows and Ronald Grover. Steve Jobs' Magic Kingdom. *BusinessWeek,* February 6, 2006, p. 66.
14. Solomon. *New York Times,* January 25, 2006.
15. Bary. *Barron's,* October 13, 2003, p. 21.
16. Richard Verrier. Animation Boom May Become Glut. *Los Angeles Times,* August 20, 2013, p. B 3.

CASE 15

CAMPBELL: HOW TO KEEP THE SOUP SIMMERING*

In 2017, Campbell Soup neared the boiling point with numerous challenges. The most important challenge related to its intention of being attractive to health-conscious consumers, although there were others. The company had tried to turn its focus toward fresh food categories, in response to a shift in consumer tastes and preferences for fresh food, by capitalizing on its fresh food division "Campbell Fresh." The company also acquired Garden Fresh Gourmet, one of the most popular refrigerated salsa brands in the U.S. Under the umbrella of its fresh food division, the company started selling fresh carrots, hummus, and salad dressings, but the sales did not meet the expectations of management. The company attributed Campbell Fresh's lack of success to the shortage of carrots amid unsuitable weather conditions in California for carrot crops. The company's CEO, Denise Morrison, said, "I am not pleased with the results of our fourth quarter, 2016. The performance of our Campbell Fresh business, driven predominantly by execution issues, is disappointing. However, we remain confident in our Campbell Fresh strategy and its ability to deliver long-term growth consistent with its portfolio role, as the business remains well-positioned to capitalize on the health and well-being consumer trend."[1]

Denise Morrison, who formerly headed the company's North American soup business, had taken over as CEO several years ago. The change at the top of the company received a lukewarm response from investors, who were watching to see what drastic changes Morrison might have in store. Analysts suggested that Campbell might have missed an opportunity by picking insider Denise Morrison to lead

the world's largest soup maker instead of bringing in outside talent to revive sales.[2]

By 2017, with Morrison at the helm, the Campbell Soup Company had launched more than 50 new products, including 32 new soups. This number was way up from prior years. Morrison also shocked experts with the $1.55 billion buyout of California juice-and-carrot seller Bolthouse Farms, the largest acquisition in Campbell's history.[3] Despite the revitalization of its product line, however, the company failed to accomplish an impressive comeback.

Company Background

Known for its red-and-white soup cans, the Campbell Soup Company was founded in 1869 by Abram Anderson and Joseph Campbell as a canning and preserving business. Over 140 years later, Campbell offered a whole lot more than just soup in a can.

In 2016 the company, headquartered in Camden, New Jersey, implemented a new product category structure by reducing from five categories to three: America's Simple Meals and Beverages, Global Biscuits and Snacks, and Campbell Fresh (see Exhibit 1).

In 2017 Campbell's products were sold in over 100 countries around the world. The company had operations in the United States, Canada, Mexico, Australia, Belgium, China, France, Germany, Indonesia, Malaysia, and Sweden (see Exhibit 2).[4]

The company had for a long time been pursuing strategies designed to expand the availability of its products in existing markets and to capitalize on opportunities in emerging channels and markets around the globe. As an early step, in 1994, Campbell Soup Company, synonymous with the all-American kitchen for 125 years, had acquired Pace Foods Ltd., the world's largest producer of Mexican sauces. Frank Weise, CFO at that time, said that a major motivation for the purchase was to diversify Campbell and

---

* This case study was prepared by Professors Alan B. Eisner and Dan Baugher of Pace University, Professor Helaine J. Korn of Baruch College, City University of New York and graduate student Saad Nazir of Pace University. The purpose of the case is to stimulate class discussion rather than to illustrate effective or ineffective handling of a business situation. Copyright © 2017 Alan B. Eisner.

EXHIBIT 1
Sales by Segment ($ millions)

Go to library tab in Connect to access Case Financials.

	2016	2015	2014	% Change 2016/2015	% Change 2015/2014
Americas Simple Meals and Beverages	**$4,380**	$4,483	$4,588	(2)%	(2)%
Global Biscuits and Snacks	**2,564**	2,631	2,725	(3)	(3)
Campbell Fresh	**1,017**	968	955	5	1
	$7,961	$8,082	$8,268	(1)%	(2)%

Source: The Campbell Soup Company, annual report, 2016.

EXHIBIT 2 Campbell's Principal Manufacturing Facilities

Inside the U.S.		
California	*Michigan*	*Texas*
Bakersfield (CF)	Femdale (CF)	Paris (ASMB)
Dixon (ASMB)	Grand Rapids (CF)	*Utah*
Stockton (ASMB)	*New Jersey*	Richmond (GBS)
Connecticut	East Brunswick (GBS)	*Washington*
Bloomfield (GBS)	*North Carolina*	Everett (CF)
Florida	Maxton (ASMB)	Prosser (CF)
Lakeland (GBS)	*Ohio*	*Wisconsin*
Illinois	Napoleon (ASMB)	Milwaukee (ASMB)
Downers Grove (GBS)	Willard (GBS)	
	Pennsylvania	
	Denver (GBS)	
	Downingtown (GBS)	
Outside the U.S.		
Australia	*Canada*	*Indonesia*
Huntingwood (GBS)	Toronto (ASMB)	Jawa Barat (GBS)
Marleston (GBS)	*Denmark*	*Malaysia*
Shepparton (GBS)	Nørre Snede (GBS)	Selangor Darul Ehsan (GBS)
Virginia (GBS)	Ribe (GBS)	

ASMB–Americas Simple Meals and Beverages
GBS–Global Biscuits and Snacks
CF–Campbell Fresh

Source: The Campbell Soup Company, annual report, 2016.

to extend the Pace brand to other products. In addition, he said, the company saw a strong potential for Pace products internationally. Campbell also saw an overlap with its raw material purchasing operations, since peppers, onions, and tomatoes were already used in the company's soups, V8 juice, barbecue sauce, and pasta sauces.[5] To help reduce some of the price volatility for ingredients, the company used various commodity risk management tools for a number of its ingredients and commodities, such as natural gas, heating oil, wheat, soybean oil, cocoa, aluminum, and corn.[6]

A leading food producer in the United States, Campbell Soup had some presence in approximately 9 out of 10 U.S. households. However, in recent years, the company faced a slowdown in its soup sales, as consumers were seeking more convenient meal options, such as ready meals and dining out. To compete more effectively, especially against General Mills' Progresso brand, Campbell had undertaken various efforts to improve the quality and convenience of its products.

China and Russia

Historically, consumption of soup in Russia and China has far exceeded that in the United States, but in both countries nearly all of the soup is homemade. With their launch of products tailored to local tastes, trends, and eating habits, nevertheless, Campbell presumed that it had a chance to lead in soup commercialization in Russia and China. According to Campbell, "We have an unrivaled understanding of consumers' soup consumption behavior and innovative technology capabilities within the Simple Meals category. The products we developed are designed to serve as a base for the soups and other meals Russian and Chinese consumers prepare at home."[7] For about three years, in both Russia and China, Campbell sent its marketing teams to study the local markets. The main focus was on how Russians and Chinese ate soup and how Campbell could offer something new. As a result, Campbell came up with a production line specifically created for the local

Russian market. Called "Domashnaya Klassika," the line was a stock base for soups that contains pieces of mushrooms, beef, or chicken. Based on this broth, the main traditional Russian soup recipes could be prepared.

But after just four short years, Campbell pulled out of the Russian market that it had thought would be a simmering new location for its products. Campbell's chief operating officer and newly elected CEO Denise Morrison said results in Russia fell below what the company had expected. "We believe that opportunities currently under exploration in other emerging markets, notably China, offer stronger prospects for driving profitable growth within an acceptable time frame," Morrison said.

When the company entered Russia, Campbell knew that it would be challenging to persuade a country of homemade-soup eaters to adopt ready-made soups. When Campbell initially researched the overseas markets, it learned that Russians eat soup more than five times a week, on average, compared with once a week among Americans.[8] This indicated that both the quality and sentiment of the soup meant a great deal to Russian consumers—something that, despite its research, Campbell may have underestimated.

As for China, a few years after Campbell infiltrated the market, CEO Denise Morrison was quoted by *Global Entrepreneur* as saying, "The Chinese market consumes roughly 300 billion servings of soup a year, compared with only 14 billion servings in the U.S."[9] When entering the Chinese market, Campbell had determined that if the company could capture at least 3 percent of the at-home consumption, the size of the business would equal that of its U.S. market share. "The numbers blow your hair back," said Larry S. McWilliams, president of Campbell's international group.[10] While the company did successfully enter the market, it remained to be seen whether Campbell had the right offerings in place to capture such a market share or whether China's homemade-soup culture would be as disinclined to change as Russia's was.

U.S. Soup Revitalization

In September 2010, Campbell launched its first-ever umbrella advertising campaign to support all of its U.S. soup brands with the slogan "It's Amazing What Soup Can Do," highlighting the convenience and health benefits of canned soup. The new campaign supported Campbell's condensed soups, Campbell's Chunky soups, Campbell's Healthy Request soups, and Campbell's Select Harvest soups, as well as soups sold in microwaveable bowls and cups under these brands.[11] Despite other departments flourishing, the soup division continued to struggle, however.

Campbell Soup was one of the first large U.S. packaged-food makers to focus heavily on decreasing sodium across its product line. The salt-reduction push was one of the company's biggest initiatives in acknowledgement of the health-conscious market. "The company had pursued reducing sodium levels and other nutritional health initiatives partly to prepare for expected nutritional labeling changes in the U.S.

But amid the attention on salt-cutting, management focused less on other consumer needs, such as better tastes and exciting varieties," said former CEO Douglas Conant. "I think we've addressed the sodium issue in a very satisfactory way. The challenge for us now is to create some taste adventure."[12] Campbell Soup Company began moving away from reducing salt in its products and focusing more on "taste adventure" as its U.S. soup business was turning cold.

With Campbell reinventing its product offerings and revitalizing its soup line, Conant had decided that his work was done and it was time to retire. He stepped down as CEO in July 2011 at the age of 60. Denise Morrison, formerly president of the North America Soup division, took the reins as chief executive. At the time of her promotion, many were hesitant to accept her as the best candidate for the position. After all, the soup division, which had been her responsibility, had been losing steam and encountering declining sales under her tenure. Yet the company asserted confidence in her to do the job, and Morrison assured everyone that changes were on the way and a shift in focus was in the works. Morrison said that Campbell would bring both the "taste and adventure" back to its soups, with a new expanded product line offering unique flavors and "adding the taste back" by doing away with sodium reduction.

Firm Structure and Management

Campbell Soup was controlled by the descendants of John T. Dorrance, the chemist who invented condensed soup more than a century ago. In struggling times, the Dorrance family had faced agonizing decisions: Should they sell the Campbell Soup Company, which had been in the family's hands for three generations? Should they hire new management to revive flagging sales of its chicken noodle and tomato soups and Pepperidge Farm cookies? Or should Campbell perhaps become an acquirer itself? The company went public in 1954, when William Murphy was the president and CEO. Dorrance family members continued to hold a large portion of the shares. After CEO David Johnson left Campbell in 1998, the company weakened and lost customers,[13] until Douglas Conant became CEO and transformed Campbell into one of the food industry's best performers.

Conant became CEO and director of Campbell Soup Company in January 2001. He joined the Campbell's team with an extensive background in the processed-and packaged-food industry. He had spent 10 years with General Mills, filled top management positions in marketing and strategy at Kraft Foods, and served as president of Nabisco Foods. Conant worked toward the goal of implementing the Campbell's mission of "building the world's most extraordinary food company by nourishing people's lives everywhere, every day."[14] He was confident that the company had the people, the products, the capabilities, and the plans in place to actualize that mission.

Under Conant's direction, Campbell made many reforms through investments in improving product quality, packaging, and marketing. He worked to create a company characterized by innovation. During his tenure, the company improved its financial profile, upgraded its supply chain system, developed a more positive relationship with its customers, and enhanced employee engagement. Conant focused on winning in both the marketplace and the workplace. His efforts produced an increase in net sales from $7.1 billion in fiscal 2005 to $7.67 billion in fiscal 2010.[15]

For Conant, the main targets for investment, following the divestiture of many brands, included simple meals, baked snacks, and vegetable-based beverages. In 2010, the baking and snacking segments sales increased 7 percent, primarily due to currency conditions. Pepperidge Farm sales were comparable to those a year earlier, as the additional sales from the acquisition of Ecce Panis, Inc., and volume gains were offset by increased promotional spending. Some of the reasons for this growth were the brand's positioning, advertising investments, and improvements and additions in the distribution system. Conant also secured an agreement with Coca-Cola North America and Coca-Cola Enterprises Inc. for distribution of Campbell's refrigerated single-serve beverages in the United States and Canada through the Coca-Cola bottler network.[16]

In fiscal year 2010, the company continued its focus on delivering superior long-term total shareowner returns by executing the following seven key strategies:[17]

- Grow its icon brands within simple meals, baked snacks, and healthy beverages.
- Deliver higher levels of consumer satisfaction through superior innovation focused on wellness while providing good value, quality, and convenience.
- Make its products more broadly available and relevant in existing and new markets, consumer segments, and eating occasions.
- Strengthen its business through outside partnerships and acquisitions.
- Increase margins by improving price realization and companywide total cost management.
- Improve overall organizational excellence, diversity, and engagement.
- Advance a powerful commitment to sustainability and corporate social responsibility.

Other major focuses for Conant and Campbell Soup were care for their customers' wellness needs, overall product quality, and product convenience. Some of the main considerations regarding wellness in the U.S. market were obesity and high blood pressure. For example, building on the success of the V8 V-Fusion juice offerings, the company planned to introduce a number of new V8 V-Fusion Plus Tea products. In the baked snacks category, the company planned to continue upgrading the health credentials of its cracker (or savory biscuit) offerings. Responding to consumers' value-oriented focus, Campbell's condensed soups were relaunched with a new contemporary packaging design and an upgrade to the company's gravity-fed shelving system.[18]

In 2011, after 10 years leading the company, Conant retired. His successor, Denise Morrison, had worked for Conant for quite some time, not just at Campbell but at Nabisco as well earlier in their careers. In August 2011, on her first day as CEO, she was set on employing a new vision for the company: "Stabilize the soup and simple meals businesses, expand internationally, grow faster in healthy beverages and baked snacks—and add back the salt."[19] With the younger generation now making up an increasingly large percentage of the population, Morrison knew that the company had to change in order to increase the appeal of its products. At that time, the U.S. population included 80 million people between the ages of 18 and 34, approximately 25 percent of the population. Early on in her role as chief executive, Morrison dispatched Campbell's employees to hipster hubs—including Austin, Texas; Portland, Oregon; London; and Paris—to find out what these potential customers wanted.[20]

To build employee engagement, Campbell provided manager training across the organization. This training was just one part of the curriculum at Campbell University, the company's internal employee learning and development program. Exemplary managers built strong engagement among their teams through consistent action planning. The company emphasized employees' innovation capabilities, leadership behavior, workplace flexibility, and wellness.

Challenges Ahead

In her new role, Morrison said she planned to "accelerate the rate of innovation" at the company. Morrison planned to grow the company's brands through a combination of healthier food and beverage offerings, global expansion, and the use of technology to woo younger consumers. While *innovation* isn't a term typically associated with the food-processing industry, Morrison said that innovation was a key to the company's future success. As an example, she cited Campbell's development of an iPhone application that provided consumers with Campbell's Kitchen recipes. The company's marketing team devised the plan as a way to appeal to technologically savvy, millennial-generation consumers, Morrison said.[21]

In fiscal year 2017, under the ongoing leadership of Morrison, the company continued its focus on unleashing the power of its overall potential and performance. The future plan was to focus on four key strategies to enhance the company's growth:[22]

1. Elevate Trust Through Real Food, Transparency and Sustainability
2. Increase Engagement and Drive Sales Through Digital and E-Commerce
3. Continue to Diversify the Product Portfolio in Health and Well-Being
4. Expand the Company's Presence in Developing Markets

Yet more than a few years into her governance, analysts still had a lukewarm response about Morrison taking over. They still expressed their doubt about whether Morrison was the right choice, rather than some new blood as a CEO replacement.

Industry Overview

The U.S. packaged-food industry had recorded faster current-value growth in recent years mainly due to a rise in commodity prices. In retail volume, however, many categories saw slower growth rates because Americans began to eat out more often again. This dynamic changed for a couple of years when cooking at home became a more popular alternative in response to the recession and the sharp rise in commodity prices in 2008.[23]

After years of expansions and acquisitions, U.S. packaged-food companies were beginning to downsize. In August 2011, Kraft Foods announced that it would split into two companies: a globally focused biscuits and confectionery enterprise and a domestically focused cheese, chilled processed-meats, and ready-meals firm. After purchasing Post cereals from Kraft in 2008, Ralcorp Holdings spun off its Post cereals business (Post Holdings Inc.) in February 2012.[24]

Though supermarkets were the main retail channel for buying packaged food, other competitors were gaining traction by offering lower prices or more convenience. The recession forced shoppers to consider alternative retail channels as they looked for ways to save money. A big beneficiary of this consumer trend was the discounters, which carried fewer items and national brands than supermarkets but offered lower prices in return. For example, dollar store chains Dollar General and Family Dollar expanded their food selections to increase their appeal. Drugstore chains CVS and Walgreens expanded their food selections as well, especially in urban areas, to leverage their locations as a factor of convenience. Mass merchandiser Target continued to expand its PFresh initiative, featuring fresh produce, frozen food, dairy products, and dry groceries.[25]

The increasing availability of refrigeration and other kinds of storage space in homes influenced the demand for packaged goods in emerging markets. However, for consumers who lacked the ability to preserve and keep larger quantities, U.S. companies began selling smaller packages, with portions that could be consumed more quickly (see Exhibit 3).[26]

EXHIBIT 3 Leading U.S. Agricultural Export Destinations, by Value ($US)

Top 15 U.S. agricultural export destinations, by fiscal year, $U.S. value					
FY 2016		**FY 2015**		**FY 2014**	
World Total	129,726,142,939	World Total	139,742,129,299	World Total	152,321,615,876
Canada	20,338,201,356	China	22,610,826,845	China	25,694,818,817
China	19,170,564,522	Canada	21,422,125,064	Canada	21,783,496,415
Mexico	17,656,109,699	Mexico	18,005,115,309	Mexico	19,489,884,901
European Union—28	11,645,339,464	European Union—28	12,309,001,795	Japan	13,363,172,381
Japan	10,614,410,394	Japan	11,691,008,030	European Unoin—28	12,694,931,484
South Korea	5,708,473,736	South Korea	6,421,506,394	South Korea	6,869,115,885
Hong Kong	3,504,972,386	Hong Kong	3,932,441,222	Hong Kong	4,052,103,438
Taiwan	3,080,164,670	Taiwan	3,932,441,222	Taiwan	3,491,316,446
Philippines	2,461,280,059	Colombia	2,583,239,620	Indonesia	2,963,928,886
Indonesia	2,386,390,705	Indonesia	2,441,427,114	Philippines	2,774,280,054
Vietnam	2,354,728,383	Philippines	2,417,382,646	Colombia	2,310,665,909
Colombia	2,251,154,942	Vietnam	2,404,677,258	Vietnam	2,229,935,830
Thailand	1,470,071,504	Thailand	1,713,215,105	Turkey	2,089,835,119
Turkey	1,365,728,465	Turkey	1,572,644,817	Egypt	1,858,177,130
Australia	1,304,071,600	Australia	1,452,910,628	Brazil	1,642,408,763

European Union–27 history revised 12/11/07 to include Romania and Bulgaria who accede in January 2007.
European Union–28 includes Croatia, who acceded in July 2003.
Economic Research Service, USDA.
Updated 12/16/2016.

Source: U.S. Economic Research Service, U.S. Department of Agriculture, 2016, https://www.ers.usda.gov/data-products/foreign-agricultural-trade-of-the-united-states-fatus/fiscal-year/.

Competition

Campbell operated in the highly competitive global food industry and experienced worldwide competition for all of its principal products. The principal areas of competition were brand recognition, quality, price, advertising, promotion, convenience, and service. (See Exhibits 4 and 5.)

Nestlé

Nestlé was the world's number-one food company in terms of sales, the world leader in coffee (Nescafé), one of the world's largest bottled-water (Perrier) makers, and a top player in the pet food business (Ralston Purina). Its most well-known global brands included Buitoni, Friskies, Maggi, Nescafé, Nestea, and Nestlé. The company owned Gerber Products, Jenny Craig, about 75 percent of Alcon Inc. (ophthalmic drugs, contact-lens solutions, and equipment for ocular surgery), and almost 28 percent of L'Oréal.[27] In July 2007 it purchased Novartis Medical Nutrition, and in August 2007 it purchased the Gerber business from Sandoz Ltd., with the goal of becoming a nutritional powerhouse. Furthermore, by adding Gerber baby foods to its baby formula business, Nestlé became a major player in the U.S. baby food sector.

General Mills

General Mills was the U.S. number-one cereal maker, behind Kellogg, fighting for the top spot on a consistent basis. Its brands included Cheerios, Chex, Total, Kix, and Wheaties. General Mills was also a brand leader in flour (Gold Medal), baking mixes (Betty Crocker, Bisquick), dinner mixes (Hamburger Helper), fruit snacks (Fruit Roll-Ups), grain snacks (Chex Mix, Pop Secret), and yogurt (Colombo, Go-Gurt, and Yoplait). In 2001 it acquired Pillsbury from Diageo and doubled the company's size, making General Mills one of the world's largest food companies. Although most of its sales came from the United States, General Mills was trying to grow the reach and position of its brands around the world.[28]

The Kraft Heinz Company

The Kraft Foods Group and H. J. Heinz Company closed a merger deal in July 2015. The combined company was called The Kraft Heinz Company, and became the third largest food company in North America and fifth largest in the world. Its most popular brands included Kraft cheeses, beverages (Maxwell House coffee, Kool-Aid drinks), convenient meals (Oscar Mayer meats and Kraft mac'n cheese), grocery fare (Cool Whip, Shake N' Bake), and nuts (Planters). Kraft Foods Group was looking to resuscitate its business in North America.[29] H. J. Heinz had thousands of products. Even prior to the merger, Heinz products enjoyed first or second place by market share in more than 50 countries. One of the world's largest food producers, Heinz produced ketchup, condiments, sauces, frozen foods, beans, pasta meals, infant food, and other processed-food products. Its flagship product was ketchup, and the company dominated the U.S. ketchup market. Its leading brands included Heinz ketchup, Lea & Perrins sauces, Ore-Ida frozen potatoes, Boston Market, T.G.I. Friday's, and Weight Watchers foods. In 2013 Heinz agreed to be acquired by Berkshire Hathaway and 3G Capital.[30] The post-merger Kraft Heinz Company was also dedicated to offering healthy food products to its customers by adapting to changing tastes and consumer preferences.

Financials

In the 2016 fiscal year, Campbell's earnings from continuing operations decreased from $666 million to $563 million, due to disruptions in product availability for a period of time. Organic sales declined 1 percent, while adjusted earnings per share (EPS) from continuing operations decreased from $2.13 to $1.82. The larger pie of the sales came from the U.S. market, whereas about 19 percent of the company's total sales were from international markets outside the U.S.

(See Exhibits 6, 7, and 8.)

With regard to financials, Morrison stated:

> For fiscal year 2017, the company's sales for year ending 2016 declined by approximately 1 percent to $7.961 amid the negative impact of exchange rate volatility and decrease in organic sales. However, most of the adverse impacts were offset by the benefits achieved by acquiring Garden Fresh Gourmet. The decline in sales could be larger if company had not increased the selling prices in 2016 to offset the loss of sales by decrease in sales volume.[31]

Similarly, for America's Simple Meals and Beverage division, Campbell's sales decreased 2 percent amid the decline in V8 beverages and soup, but increased costs were up, wearing away margins. Also, the Global Biscuits and Snacks division sales decreased 3 percent but for the Campbell Fresh division sales increased 1 percent, which could be better if the company had not gone through the trouble of execution issues and crop destruction.[32]

Sustainability

Campbell Soup Company was named to the Dow Jones Sustainability Indexes (DJSI) repeatedly and to the DJSI World Index. This independent ranking recognized the company's strategic and management approach to delivering economic, environmental, and social performance. Launched in 1999, the DJSI tracked the financial performance of leading sustainability-driven companies worldwide. In selecting the top performers in each business sector, DJSI reviewed companies on several general and industry-specific topics related to economic, environmental, and social dimensions. These included corporate governance, environmental policy, climate strategy, human capital development, and labor practices. Campbell included sustainability and corporate social responsibility as one of its seven core business strategies.[33] Campbell's Napoleon, Ohio, plant had implemented a new renewable

EXHIBIT 4 Campbell's Competitors, by Market Capitalization and Financials

	Industry Peers CPB										
	Morningstar Rating	Market Cap Mil ▼	Net Income Mil	P/S	P/B	P/E	Dividend Yield%	5-Yr Rev CAGR%	Med Oper. Margin%	Interest Coverage	D/E
Campbell Soup Co	★★	**17,483**	**497**	**2.2**	**11.9**	**35.7**	**2.3**	**2.2**	**14.4**	**8.4**	**1.6**
Nestle SA (USD,CHF)	★★★	241,300	8,531	2.7	3.7	28.1	3.0	1.3	14.2	24.1	0.2
Nestle SA (USD,CHF)		240,928	8,531	2.7	3.7	28.1	3.0	1.3	14.2	24.1	0.2
The Kraft Heinz Co (USD)	★★	111,587	3,632	4.2	1.9	32.6	2.6	7.4	14.6	5.4	0.5
Danone SA (USD,EUR)		42,510	1,720	1.8	3.0	22.9	2.6	2.6	10.2	10.5	1.4
Danone SA (USD,EUR)	★★★★	42,325	1,720	1.8	3.0	22.9	2.6	2.6	10.2	10.5	1.4
General Mills Inc (USD)	★★★	34,084	1,628	2.3	8.4	21.9	3.2	2.2	16.0	8.7	1.8
Associated British Foods PLC (USD,GBP)		26,152	818	1.6	3.0	25.6	1.4	3.9	8.2	19.9	0.1
Associated British Foods PLC (USD,GBP)		25,689	818	1.5	2.9	25.2	1.4	3.9	8.2	19.9	0.1
Kellogg Co (USD)	★★★	25,553	694	2.0	13.4	37.2	2.8	-0.3	10.7	3.3	3.5
Hormel Foods Corp (USD)	★★★	18,258	890	2.0	4.0	20.9	1.8	3.8	10.0	103.3	0.1
Conagra Brands Inc (USD)	★	17,613	630	1.6	4.0	34.6	2.4	-1.2	9.6	3.0	0.7
Mead Johnson Nutrition Co (USD)	★★★	16,219	544	4.4	-	30.3	1.9	0.4	22.4	7.0.	–
JM Smucker Co (USD)	★★★	15,493	673	2.1	2.1	23.2	2.2	10.1	14.7	13.3	0.7
Kerry Group PLC (USD,EUR)		14,670	510	2.2	4.7	26.7	0.7	4.2	9.0	12.5	0.6
Kerry Group PLC (USD,EUR)		14,295	510	2.2	4.7	26.0	0.7	4.2	9.0	12.5	0.6
Saputo Inc (USD,CAO)		13,435	704	1.6	4.2	26.0	1.2	12.9	9.5	19.0	0.3
McCormick & Co Inc (USD)	★★	12,645	471	2.9	7.8	29.7	1.7	3.6	14.2	11.5	0.6
McCormick & Co Inc (USD)		12,644	471	2.9	7.8	29.7	1.7	3.6	14.2	11.5	0.6
Meiji Holdings Co Ltd (USD,JPY)		12,466	57,640	1.1	3.2	24.1	1.2	2.0	3.2	97.9	0.1
WH Group Ltd (USD)		12,363	1,034	0.6	2.0	11.7	2.7	–	7.8	7.2	0.4
Grupo Bimbo SAB de CV (USD,MXN)		11,899	6,008	0.9	3.2	37.9	–	13.3	6.0	3.2	1.1
Meiji Holdings Co Ltd (USD,JPY)		11,866	57,640	1.1	3.0	22.9	1.2	2.0	3.2	97.9	0.1
Grupo Bimbo SAB de CV (USD,MXN)		11,805	6,008	0.9	3.2	37.6	0.6	13.3	6.0	3.2	1.1
Ajinomoto Co Inc (USD,JPY)		11,610	28,887	1.2	2.0	44.0	1.4	-0.4	7.2	45.2	0.4
WH Group Ltd (USD)		11,271	1,034	0.5	1.9	10.6	2.9	–	7.8	7.2	0.4
Industry Average		**8,110**	**63,030**	**2.0**	**3.1**	**29.1**	**2.0**	**7.3**	**-61791.9**	**66.5**	**0.8**

Source: Morningstar Inc., http://financials.morningstar.com/competitors/industry-peer.action?t=CPB.

EXHIBIT 5 Campbell Soup Top Competitors' Stock Prices

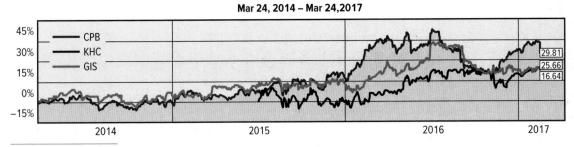

Mar 24, 2014 – Mar 24, 2017

Legend: CPB, KHC, GIS

Values shown: 29.81, 25.66, 16.64

Source: finance.yahoo.com/, retrieved on March 24, 2017.

EXHIBIT 6 Campbell Income Statement

CAMPBELL SOUP COMPANY Consolidated Statements of Earnings (millions, except per share amounts)			
	2016 52 weeks	2015 52 weeks	2014 53 weeks
Net sales	$ 7,961	$ 8.082	$ 8,268
Costs and expenses			
Cost of products sold	5,181	5,300	5,297
Marketing and selling expenses	893	884	929
Administrative expenses	641	601	576
Research and development expenses	124	117	122
Other expenses / (income)	131	24	22
Restructuring charges	31	102	55
Total costs and expenses	7,001	7,028	7,001
Earnings before interest and taxes	960	1,054	1,267
Interest expense	115	108	122
Interest income	4	3	3
Earnings before taxes	849	949	1,148
Taxes on earnings	286	283	374
Earnings from continuing operations	563	666	774
Earnings from discontinued operations	—	—	81
Net earnings	563	666	855
Less: Net earnings (loss) attributable to noncontrolling interests	—	—	(11)
Net earnings attributable to Campbell Soup Company	$ 563	$ 666	$ 866
Per Share — Basic			
Earnings from continuing operations attributable to Campbell Soup Company	$ 1.82	$ 2.13	$ 2.50

Go to library tab in Connect to access Case Financials.

Source: Campbell Soup Company Annual Report, 2016.

EXHIBIT 7 Campbell Balance Sheet

CAMPBELL SOUP COMPANY
Consolidated Statements of Earnings
(millions, except per share amounts)

	July 31, 2016	August 2, 2015
Current assets		
Cash and cash equivalents	$ 296	$ 253
Accounts receivable, net	626	647
Inventories	940	995
Other current assets.	46	198
Total current assets	1,908	2,093
Plant assets, net of depreciation	2,407	2,347
Goodwill	2,263	2,344
Other intangible assets, net of amortization	1,152	1,205
Other assets ($34 and $0 attributable to variable interest entity)	107	88
Total assets	$ 7,837	$ 8,077
Current liabilities		
Short-term borrowings	$ 1,219	$ 1,543
Payable to suppliers and others	610	544
Accrued liabilities	604	589
Dividend payable	100	101
Accrued income taxes	22	29
Total current liabilities	2,555	2,806
Long-term debt	2,314	2,539
Deferred taxes	396	505
Other liabilities	1,039	850
Total liabilities	6,304	6,700
Commitments and contingencies		
Campbell Soup Company shareholders' equity		
Capital stock, $.0373 par value; authorized 560 shares; issued 323 shares	12	12
Additional paid-in capital	354	339
Earnings retained in the business	1,927	1,754
Capital stock in treasury, at cost	(664)	(556)
Accumulated other comprehensive loss	(104)	(168)
Total Campbell Soup Company shareholders' equity	1,525	1,381
Noncontrolling interests	8	(4)
Total equity	1,533	1,377
Total liabilities and equity	$ 7,837	$ 8,077

Go to library tab in Connect to access Case Financials.

Source: Campbell Soup Company Annual Report, 2016.

EXHIBIT 8 Campbell's Key Ratios

Valuation	
P/E Current	31.73
P/E Ratio (with extraordinary items)	35.71
P/E Ratio (without extraordinary items)	34.40
Price to Sales Ratio	2.43
Price to Book Ratio	12.58
Price to Cash Flow Ratio	13.24
Enterprise Value to EBITDA	14.32
Enterprise Value to Sales	2.61
Total Debt to Enterprise Value	0.16
Efficiency	
Revenue/Employee	482,485.00
Income Per Employee	34,121.00
Receivables Turnover	12.51
Total Asset Turnover	1.00
Liquidity	
Current Ratio	0.75
Quick Ratio	0.38
Cash Ratio	0.12
Profitability	
Gross Margin	34.61
Operating Margin	14.29
Pretax Margin	10.66
Net Margin	7.07
Return on Assets	7.07
Return on Equity	38.76
Return on Total Capital	10.69
Return on Invested Capital	14.49
Capital Structure	
Total Debt to Total Equity	231.67
Total Debt to Total Capital	69.85
Total Debt to Total Assets	45.08
Long-Term Debt to Equity	151.74
Long-Term Debt to Total Capital	45.75

Source: MarketWatch Inc. 2017, http://www.marketwatch.com/investing/stock/cpb/profile.

energy initiative, anchored by 24,000 new solar panels. The 60-acre, 9.8-megawatt solar power system was expected to supply 15 percent of the plant's electricity while reducing CO_2 emissions by 250,000 metric tons over 20 years.[34]

Additionally, Campbell employees volunteered an average of 20,000 hours annually at more than 200 nonprofit organizations. Supported by local farmers and Campbell, the Food Bank of South Jersey was earning revenue for hunger relief from sales of *Just Peachy* salsa. The salsa was created from excess peaches from New Jersey and was manufactured and labeled by employee volunteers at Campbell's plant in Camden.[35]

What's Next?

Campbell's advertising campaign failed to assist the company much in gaining the expected traction in the ready-to-serve soup business. Campbell was trying to correct this by introducing new products offering unique flavors into what many considered a rather ordinary product line. If the economy continued to improve would Campbell be successful in its international expansion, especially in lucrative emerging markets such as China? As the recession became a distant memory, would Campbell's name still resonate with American consumers or would consumers venture back to restaurants? Would Campbell Fresh become a success or would it spoil? Would Campbell's soup simmer to perfection, or would the company be in hot water?

ENDNOTES

1. https://www.forbes.com/sites/maggiemcgrath/2016/09/01/campbell-soup-ceo-i-am-disappointed-by-lackluster-campbell-fresh-business/\#290fc1103830.
2. Boyle, M. 2010. Campbell CEO pick may be lost chance, analysts say. *BusinessWeek,* September 29, www.businessweek.com/news/2010-09-29/campbell-ceo-pick-may-be-lost-chance-analysts-say.html.
3. Goudreau, Jenna. 2012. Kicking the can: Campbell's CEO bets on soup-in-a-bag for 20-somethings. *Forbes.com,* December 6, www.forbes.com/sites/jennagoudreau/2012/12/06/kicking-the-can-campbells-ceo-bets-on-soup-in-a-bag-for-20-somethings.
4. Campbells. 2013. Our company. www.campbellsoupcompany.com/around_the_world.asp.
5. Collins, G. 1994. Campbell Soup takes the big plunge into salsa. *New York Times,* November 29: D1.
6. Campbell Soup Co. 2010. 2009 annual report.
7. Campbell Soup Co. 2008. 2007 annual report.
8. *Wall Street Journal.* 2011. Campbell Soup to exit Russia. June 29, online.wsj.com/article/SB10001424052702304447804576414202460491210.html.
9. *Want China Times.* 2013. Campbell Soup aims to break into Chinese market through chef endorsements. March 6, www.wantchinatimes.com/news-subclass-cnt.aspx?id520130306000016&cid51102.
10. Boyle, M. 2009. Campbell's: Not about to let the soup cool. *BusinessWeek,* September 17.
11. News release. 2010. Campbell launches "It's Amazing What Soup Can Do" ad campaign to promote Campbell's U.S. soup brands. September 7, investor.campbellsoupcompany.com/phoenix.zhtml?c588650&p5irol-newsArticle&ID51467644.
12. Brat, I., and Ziobro, P. 2010. Campbell to put new focus on taste. *Wall Street Journal,* November 24, online.wsj.com/article/0,,SB10001424052748704369304575632342839464532,00.html.

13. Abelson, Reed. 2000. The first family of soup, feeling the squeeze; Should it sell or try to go it alone? *New York Times,* July 30, www.nytimes.com/2000/07/30/business/first-family-soup-feeling-squeeze-should-it-sell-try-go-it-alone.html?pagewanted5all&src5pm.

14. Campbell Soup Co. 2008. 2007 annual report.

15. Campbell Soup Co. 2011. 2010 annual report.

16. Press release. 2007. The Coca-Cola Company, Campbell Soup Company and Coca-Cola Enterprises sign agreement for distribution of Campbell's beverage portfolio. investor.shareholder.com/campbell/releasedetail.cfm?ReleaseID5247903.

17. Campbell Soup Co. 2011. 2010 annual report.

18. Ibid.

19. Goudreau, op. cit.

20. Ibid.

21. Katz, Jonathan. 2010. Campbell Soup cooking up a new recipe? *Industry Week,* December 15, www.industryweek.com/companies-amp-executives/iw-50-profile-campbell-soup-cooking-new-recipe.

22. Campbell Soup Co. 2017 annual report.

23. PRNewswire. 2012. U.S. Packaged Food Market—Consumers seek out ethnic & bold flavours—new industry report. *PRNewswire,* March 12, www.prnewswire.com/news-releases/us-packaged-food-market—consumers-seek-out-ethnic–bold-flavours—new-industry-report-142292805.html.

24. ReportsnReports. 2013. Packaged food in the US. April, www.reportsnreports.com/reports/150486-packaged-food-in-the-us.html.

25. Ibid.

26. Graves, T., and Kwon, E. Y. 2009. Standard and Poor's foods and nonalcoholic beverages industry report. July.

27. Hoovers. Undated. Company profiles: Nestlé. www.hoovers.com/company-information/cs/company-profile.Nestlé_SA.6a719827106be6ff.html, accessed April 2013.

28. Hoovers. Undated. Company profiles: General Mills. www.hoovers.com/company-information/cs/company-profile.General_Mills_Inc.a90ba57dc8f51a65.html, accessed April 2013.

29. Hoovers. Undated. Company profiles: Kraft Foods. www.hoovers.com/company-information/cs/company-profile.Kraft_Foods_Group_Inc.43af8ed4b4ae51f2.html, accessed April 2013.

30. Hoovers. Undated. Company profiles: H. J. Heinz Company. www.hoovers.com/company-information/cs/company-profile.H_J_Heinz_Company.1696a42275f81d38.html, accessed April 2013.

31. Campbell Soup Co. 2016 annual report.

32. Ibid.

33. News release. 2010. Campbell Soup company named to Dow Jones Sustainability Indexes. investor.campbellsoupcompany.com/phoenix.zhtml?c588650&p5irol-newsArticle&ID51471159.

34. Campbell Soup Co. 2013. 2012 annual report.

35. Ibid.

CASE 16

HEINEKEN*

Dutch brewer Heineken was expanding its presence around the globe in response to the merger of Anheuser-Busch InBev with SAB Miller giving the combined firm a commanding 30 percent of global beer sales. Heineken was in talks to buy the Brazilian unit of Kirin, which the Japanese parent was planning to sell. The addition of Kirin beer would double Heineken's share in Brazil to 20 percent. The firm was also planning to launch Bintang, its biggest selling beer brand in Indonesia, into the UK and select European markets. An industry spokesman was positive about the move: "There is clearly significant demand for premium world beers. We believe Bintang is perfectly suited to meet this demand."[1]

These moves came on the heels of acquisitions and capacity investments that Heineken had been making in other developing markets. In 2013, the firm had strengthened its position as the world's third largest brewer by taking full ownership of Asian Pacific Breweries, the owner of Tiger, Bintang, and other popular Asian beer brands. With this deal, Heineken added 30 breweries across several countries in the Asia Pacific region. A few years earlier, the firm had acquired Mexican brewer FEMSA Cervesa, producer of Dos Equis, Sol, and Tecate beers, to become a stronger, more competitive player in Latin America.

_____

* Case prepared by Jamal Shamsie, Michigan State University, with the assistance of Professor Alan B. Eisner, Pace University. Material has been drawn from published sources to be used for purposes of class discussion. Copyright © 2017 Jamal Shamsie and Alan B. Eisner.

At the same time, Heineken maintained its leading position across Europe. It had made a high profile acquisition in 2008 of Scottish-based brewer Scottish & Newcastle, the brewer of well-known brands such as Newcastle Brown Ale and Kronenbourg 1664. Although the purchase had been made in partnership with Carlsberg, Heineken was able to gain control of Scottish & Newcastle's operations in several crucial European markets such as the United Kingdom, Ireland, Portugal, Finland, and Belgium.

These decisions to acquire brewers that operate in different parts of the world have been a part of a series of changes that the Dutch brewer has been making to raise its stature in the various markets and to respond to growing consolidation within the industry and changes that are occurring in the global market for beer. Even as sales of beer have stagnated in the U.S. and Europe, demand has been growing elsewhere, especially in developing countries. This has led the largest brewers to expand across the globe through acquisitions of smaller regional and national players (see Exhibits 1 and 2).

The need for change was clearly reflected in the appointment in October 2005 of Jean-Francois van Boxmeer as Heineken's first non-Dutch CEO. He was brought in to replace Thorny Ruys, who had decided to resign because of his failure to show much improvement in performance. Prior to the appointment of Ruys in 2002, Heineken had been run by three generations of Heineken ancestors, whose portraits still adorn the dark paneled office of the CEO in its Amsterdam headquarters. Like Ruys, van Boxmeer

EXHIBIT 1 Income Statement (millions of euros)

	2016	2015	2014	2013
Revenue	20,792	20,511	19,257	19,203
EBIT	2,993	2,785	2,814	2,484
Net profit	1,540	1,892	1,516	1,364

Source: Heineken.

EXHIBIT 2 Balance Sheet (millions of euros)

	2016	2015	2014	2013	2012
Assets	39,321	40,122	34,830	33,337	35,979
Liabilities	24,748	25,052	17,869	17,797	9,260
Equity	14,573	15,070	13,452	12,356	12,805

Source: Heineken.

faced the challenge of preserving the firm's family-driven traditions, while trying to deal with threats Heineken had never faced before.

Confronting a Globalizing Industry

Heineken was one of the pioneers of an international strategy, using cross-border deals to expand its distribution of its Heineken, Amstel, and about 175 other beer brands in more than 100 countries around the globe. For years, it had been picking up small brewers from various countries to add more brands and to get better access to new markets. From its roots on the outskirts of Amsterdam, the firm had evolved into one of the world's largest brewers, operating more than 190 breweries in over 70 countries, claiming about 10 percent of the global market for beer (see Exhibits 3 and 4).

The firm's flagship Heineken brand ranked second only to Budweiser in a global brand survey jointly undertaken by *BusinessWeek* and Interbrand. The premier brand has achieved worldwide recognition according to Kevin Baker, director of alcoholic beverages at British market researcher Canadean Ltd. When a U.S. wholesaler asked a group of marketing students to identify an assortment of beer bottles that had been stripped of their labels, the stubby green Heineken bottle was the only one instantly recognized.

The beer industry has been undergoing significant change in a furious wave of consolidation. Most of the

	2016	2015
Western Europe	10,112	10,227
Americas	5,203	5,159
Africa, Middle East, & Eastern Europe	3,203	3,263
Asia Pacific	2,894	2,483

EXHIBIT 3
Geographical Breakdown of Sales (*millions of euros*)

Source: Heineken.

Markets	Brands
U.S.	Heineken, Amstel Light, Paulaner,[1] Moretti
Netherlands	Heineken, Amstel, Lingen's Blond, Murphy's Irish Red
France	Heineken, Amstel, Buckler,[2] Desperados[3]
Italy	Heineken, Amstel, Birra Moretti
Spain	Heineken, Amstel, Cruzcampo, Buckler
Poland	Heineken, Krolewskie, Kujawiak, Zywiec
China	Heineken, Tiger, Reeb[*]
Singapore	Heineken, Tiger, Anchor, Baron's
India	Heineken, Arlem, Kingfisher
Indonesia	Heineken, Bintang, Guinness
Kazakhstan	Heineken, Amstel, Tian Shan
Egypt	Heineken, Birell, Meister, Fayrouz[2]
Israel	Heineken, Maccabee, Gold Star[*]
Nigeria	Heineken, Star, Maltina, Gulder
South Africa	Heineken, Amstel, Windhoek. Strongbow
Panama	Heineken, Soberana, Crystal, Panama
Chile	Heineken, Cristal, Escudo, Royal

EXHIBIT 4
Significant Heineken Brands In Various Markets

[*]Minority interest
[1]Wheat beer
[2]Nonalcoholic beer
[3]Tequila-flavored beer

Source: Heineken

EXHIBIT 5 Leading Global Brewers (2016 market share based on annual sales, millions of US dollars)

Brewers	Market Share
1. Anheuser-Busch InBev, Leuven, Belgium,	21%
2. SAB Miller, London, UK,*	11
3. Heineken, Amsterdam, Netherlands,	10
4. Carlsberg, Copenhagen, Denmark,	6
5. China Resources Enterprise, China,	4

*To be merged with Anhesuser-Busch InBev.

Source: Beverage World.

bigger brewers have been acquiring or merging with their competitors in foreign markets in order to become global players. Ownership of local brands has propelled them into dominant positions in various markets around the world. Beyond this, they hope acquisitions of foreign brewers can provide them with the manufacturing and distribution capabilities to develop a few global brands. "The era of global brands is coming," said Alan Clark, Budapest-based managing director of SABMiller Europe (see Exhibit 5).[2]

Over the past decade, South African Breweries Plc has acquired U.S.-based Miller Brewing to become a major global brewer. They have acquired Fosters, the largest Australian brewer. U.S.-based Coors linked with Canadian-based Molson in 2005, with their combined operations giving them a leading position among the world's biggest brewers. In 2008, Belgium's Interbrew, Brazil's AmBev, and U.S.-based Anheuser Busch merged to become the largest global brewer with operations across most of the continents. Finally, Anheuser-Busch InBev acquired SAB Miller to become an even more dominant player in the industry.

Since its acquisition of Anheuser Busch, InBev has been attempting to develop not only Budweiser but also Stella Artois, Brahma, and Becks as global flagship brands. Each of these brands originated in different locations, with Budweiser coming from the U.S., Stella Artois coming from Belgium, Brahma from Brazil, and Becks from Germany. Similarly, SAB Miller has been attempting to develop the Czech brand Pilsner Urquell into a global brand. Exports of this pilsner doubled shortly after SAB acquired it in 1999, but sales have since plateaued. John Brock, the CEO of InBev, commented: "Global brands sell at significantly higher prices, and the margins are much better than with local beers."[3]

Wrestling with Change

Although the management of Heineken has moved away from the family for the first time, they have been well aware of the longstanding and well-established family traditions that are difficult to change. Even with the appointment of nonfamily members to manage the firm, a little over half of the shares of Heineken are still owned by a holding company which is controlled by the family. With the death of Freddy Heineken in 2002, the last family member to head the Dutch brewer, control has passed to his only child and

heir, Charlene de Carvalho, who has insisted on having a say in all of the major decisions.

Family members, however, were behind some of changes that were announced at the time of van Boxmeer's appointment to support the firm's next phase of growth as a global organization. As part of the plan, dubbed Fit 2 Fight, the Executive Board was cut down from five members to just CEO van Boxmeer and Chief Financial Officer Rene Hooft Graafland. The change was made to centralize control at the top of the firm to better enable a global strategy. The idea behind the global strategy is to win over younger customers across different markets whose tastes are still developing.

Heineken has created management positions responsible for five different operating regions and several different functional areas. These positions were created to more clearly define different spheres of responsibility. Van Boxmeer has argued that the new structure provides incentives for people to be accountable for their performance: "There is more pressure for results, for achievement."[4] He claims the new structure has already encouraged more risk taking and boosted the level of energy within the firm.

The Executive Committee of Heineken was cut down from 36 to 12 members in order to speed up the decision-making process. Besides the two members of the Executive Board, this management group consists of the managers who are responsible for the different operating regions and several of the key functional areas. Van Boxmeer hopes that the reduction in the size of this group will allow the firm to combat the cumbersome consensus culture that has made it difficult for Heineken to respond swiftly to various challenges even as its industry has been experiencing considerable change.

Finally, all of the activities of Heineken are overseen by a Supervisory Board, which currently consists of 10 members. Individuals that make up this board are drawn from different countries and own a wide range of expertise and experience. The Board sets policies for making major decisions in the firm's overall operations. Members of the Supervisory Board are rotated on a regular basis.

Developing a Global Presence

Van Boxmeer is well aware of the need for Heineken to use its brands to build upon its existing stature across global markets. Yet in spite of its formidable presence in markets around the world with its flagship Heineken brand, the firm has been reluctant to match the recent moves of formidable competitors such as Belgium's InBev and UK's SABMiller, which have grown significantly through mega-acquisitions.

For many years, Heineken limited itself to snapping up small national brewers such as Italy's Moretti and Spain's Cruzcampo that have provided it with small, but profitable avenues for growth. In 1996, Heineken acquired Fischer, a small French brewer, whose Desperados brand has been quite successful in niche markets. Similarly, Paulaner, a wheat beer that the firm picked up in Germany a few years ago, has been making inroads into the U.S. market.

But as other brewers reached out to make acquisitions all over the globe, Heineken risked falling behind its more aggressive rivals. To deal with this growing challenge, the firm broke out of its play-it-safe corporate culture to make a few big deals. In 2003, Heineken spent $2.1 billion to acquire BBAG, a family-owned company based in Linz, Austria. Because of BBAG's extensive presence in Central Europe, Heineken has become the biggest beer maker in seven countries across Eastern Europe. The acquisition of Scottish & Newcastle in 2008 similarly reinforced the firm's dominance in Western Europe.

Heineken's acquisitions in Ethiopia, Singapore, and Mexico have allowed it to build its position in these growing markets. The firm has made an aggressive push into Russia with the acquisition of mid-sized brewing concerns. Through several acquisitions since 2002, Russia has become one of Heineken's largest markets by volume. Heineken now ranks as the third-largest brewer in Russia, behind Sweden's Baltic Beverages Holding and InBev. The firm has also pounced on brewers in far-flung places like Belarus, Panama, Egypt, and Kazakhstan. In Egypt, Ruys bought a majority stake in Al Ahram Beverages Co. and has been using the Cairo-based brewer's fruit-flavored, nonalcoholic malts as an avenue into other Muslim countries. Rene Hooft Graafland, the company's Chief Financial Officer, has stated that Heineken will continue to participate in the consolidation of the $460 billion global retail beer industry by targeting many different markets around the world.

Maintaining a Premium Position

For decades, Heineken was able to rely on the success of its flagship Heineken brand, which enjoyed a leading position among premium beers in many markets around the world. It was the best-selling imported beer in the U.S. for several decades, giving it a steady source of revenues and profits from the world's biggest market. But by the late 1990s, Heineken had lost its 65-year-old leadership among imported beers in the U.S. to Grupo Modelo's Corona. The Mexican beer appeals to a certain segment of younger American beer drinkers, and more importantly, to the growing number of Hispanic Americans who represent one of the fastest growing segments of beer drinkers in the U.S.

The firm was concerned that Heineken was perceived as a stodgy or even an obsolete brand by many young drinkers.

John A. Quelch, a professor at Harvard Business School who has studied the beer industry, said of Heineken: "It's in danger of becoming a tired, reliable, but unexciting brand."[5] The firm has therefore worked hard to increase awareness of their flagship brand among younger drinkers. Heineken also introduced a light beer, Heineken Premium Light, to target the growing market for such beers in the U.S. The firm has managed to reduce the average age of the Heineken drinker from about 40 years old to about 30 years old.

At the same time, Heineken has pushed its other brands to reduce its reliance on its core Heineken brand. It has achieved considerable success with Amstel Light, which has become the leading imported light beer in the U.S. and has been selling well in many other countries. Owing to its acquisitions of smaller breweries around the globe, it has managed to develop a relatively small but loyal base of consumers for its strong local brands—specialty brands such as Murphy's Irish Red and Moretti.

For Hispanics, who account for one-quarter of U.S. sales, Heineken developed specific marketing campaigns, and added popular Mexican beers Tecate, Dos Equis, and others. For years, these had been marketed and distributed by Heineken in the U.S. under a license from FEMSA Cervesa. In 2010, they acquired the firm, giving them full control over all of their brands. Benj Steinman, publisher and editor of newsletter *Beer Marketer's Insight* believed their relationship with FEMSA had been quite beneficial: "This gives Heineken a commanding share of the U.S. import business and . . . gives them a bigger presence in the Southwest . . . and better access to Hispanic consumers," he stated.[6]

Above all, Heineken wants to maintain its leadership in the premium beer industry, which represents the most profitable segment of the beer business. In this category, the firm's brands face competition in the U.S. from domestic beers such as Anheuser's Budweiser Select and imported beers such as InBev's Stella Artois. Premium brews often have slightly higher alcohol content than standard beers, and they are developed through a more exclusive positioning of the brand. This allows a firm to charge a higher price for their premium brands. The flagship Heineken brand remains positioned as a premium beer. A six-pack of Heineken, for example, costs $9, versus around $6 for a six-pack of Budweiser. Just-drinks.com, a London-based online research service, estimates that the market for premium beer will continue to expand over the next decade.

Building on Its Past

The acquisitions in different parts of the world—Asia, Africa, Latin America and Europe—represent an important step in Heineken's quest to build on its global stature. Most analysts expect that van Boxmeer and his team will continue to build Heineken into a powerful global competitor. Without providing any specific details, Graafland, the firm's CFO, makes it clear that the firm's management will take initiatives to drive long-term growth. In his words: "We are positive that the momentum in the company and trends will continue."[7]

Since taking over the helm at Heineken, van Boxmeer has committed himself to accelerating the speed of decision making. There has been some expectation both inside and outside the firm that the new management would try to break loose from the conservative style of the family. Instead, the affable 46-year-old Belgian has indicated that he is trying to streamline the firm's decision-making process rather than to make any drastic shifts in the company's existing culture.

Van Boxmeer's devotion to the firm is evident. Heineken's first non-Dutch CEO spent 20 years working his way up within the firm. He sports cufflinks that are silver miniatures of a Heineken bottle top and opener. "We are in the logical flow of history," he explained. "Every time you have a new leader you have a new kind of vision. It is not radically different, because you are defined by what your company is and what your brands are."[8]

Furthermore, van Boxmeer seems comfortable working within the family-controlled structure. "Since 1952 history has proved it is the right concept," he stated about the current ownership structure. "The whole business about family restraint on us is absolutely untrue. Without its spirit and guidance, the company would not have been able to build a world leader."[9]

ENDNOTES

1. Olly Wehring. Heineken Readies Europe-wide Launch of Indonesia's Bintang Beer. *Just-drinks global news,* January 17, 2017.
2. Jack Ewing & Gerry Khermouch. Waking Up Heineken. *BusinessWeek,* September 8, 2003, p. 68.
3. Richard Tomlinson. The New King of Beers. *Fortune,* October 18, 2004, p. 238.
4. Ian Bickerton & Jenny Wiggins. Change Is Brewing at Heineken. *Financial Times,* May 9, 2006, p. 12.
5. *BusinessWeek,* September 8, 2003, p. 69.
6. Andrew Kaplan. Border Crossings. *Beverage World,* July 15, 2004, p. 6.
7. Christopher C. Williams. Heineken Seeing Green. *Barron's,* September 18, 2006, p. 19.
8. *Financial Times,* May 9, 2006, p. 12.
9. Ibid.

CASE 17

FORD: NO LONGER JUST AN AUTO COMPANY?*

In January 2017 Ford Motor Company celebrated a major milestone as the F-Series became the top-selling truck in the U.S. for the 40th consecutive year—all told, 26 million trucks sold since January 1977. The F-Series had also been the best-selling vehicle in the U.S. for 35 years straight.[1] In February 2017, the F-Series, which included the Super Duty and the all-new F-150 Raptor, hit an all-time annual sales record of 65,956 vehicles.[2] The F-150 was named 2017's Autobytel buyer's choice full-size truck, Edmunds most wanted full-size truck, Cars.com best pickup truck, U.S. News & World Report best truck brand, Kelley BlueBook Best Buy truck, and the Motor Trend Truck of the Year. Commenting on these results, Todd Eckert, Ford truck group marketing manager said, "what's made the F-Series so successful is the Ford truck team's ability to anticipate the needs of our customers better than anyone else—how those needs change, what's most important, and what they need to do to move forward. Their insights help us design, engineer and build America's best-selling trucks."[3]

The ability to anticipate customers' needs is crucial to any company's long-term success, but especially in the capital-intensive, consumer-driven, globally competitive automobile industry. As the major players from Asia, Europe, and the U.S. jockey for position in the sales of traditional trucks and cars, smaller, more innovative companies such as Tesla, Elio Motors, and start-up Faraday Futures are creating concept cars that address consumers' interests in alternative fuels, low operational costs, and self-driving autonomous designs that leave the passenger free to use in-transit time for other more productive pursuits.

Self-driving cars are reported to be coming as early as 2018 to the global roadways; and in 2017 Ford Motor Company was in this business big-time, testing its fleet of 30 autonomous cars in Arizona, California, and Michigan.[4]

Ford Motor Company CEO Mark Fields announced in January 2015 that Ford would be using innovation "not only to create advanced new vehicles but also to help change the way the world moves by solving today's growing global transportation challenges."[5] Given the increasing disruption in the industry, and the obligation to return value to

understandably concerned investors, Mark Fields had some significant decisions to make in the coming years.

Fields had been promoted to CEO in July 2014 on the retirement of Alan Mulally, widely hailed as one of the "five most significant corporate leaders of the last decade," and architect of Ford's eight-year turnaround from the brink of bankruptcy in 2006.[6] It was Mulally who created the vision that drove Ford's revitalization: "ONE Ford." The ONE Ford message was intended to communicate consistency across all departments, all segments of the company, requiring people to work together as one team, with one plan, and one goal: "an exciting viable Ford delivering profitable growth for all."[7] Mulally worked to create a culture of accountability and collaboration across the company. His vision was to leverage Ford's unique automotive knowledge and assets to build cars and trucks that people wanted and valued, and he managed to arrange the financing necessary to pay for it all. The 2009 economic downturn that caused a financial catastrophe for U.S. automakers trapped General Motors and Chrysler in emergency government loans, but Ford was able to avoid bankruptcy because of Mulally's actions.

Mulally had groomed Mark Fields as his successor since 2012, instilling confidence among the company's stakeholders that Ford would be able to continue to be profitable once Mulally stepped down. Even with this preparation, CEO Fields was still facing an industry affected by general economic conditions over which he had little control and a changing technological and sociocultural environment where consumer preferences were difficult to predict. And rivals were coming from unexpected directions. Fields would have to anticipate and address numerous challenges as he positioned the company for continued success.

Attempts at repositioning Ford had been under way for many years. In the 1990s, former CEO Jacques Nasser had emphasized acquisitions to reshape Ford, but day-to-day business activities were ignored in the process. When Nasser left in October 2001, Bill Ford, great-grandson of company founder Henry Ford, took over and emphasized innovation as a core strategy to reshape Ford. In an attempt to stem the downward slide at Ford, and perhaps to jumpstart a turnaround, Bill Ford recruited industry outsider Alan Mulally, who was elected president and chief executive officer of Ford on September 5, 2006. Mulally, former head of commercial airplanes at Boeing, was expected to steer the struggling automaker out of the problems of falling market share and serious financial losses. Mulally created his vision of "ONE Ford" to reshape the company and in 2009

This case study was prepared by Associate Professor Pauline Assenza of Western Connecticut State University; Professor Helaine J. Korn of Baruch College, City University of New York; Professor Naga Lakshmi Damaraju of the Indian School of Business; and Professor Alan B. Eisner of Pace University. The purpose of the case is to stimulate class discussion rather than to illustrate effective or ineffective handling of a business situation. Copyright © 2017 Alan B. Eisner.

finally achieved profitability. He committed Ford to remaining "on track for both [Ford's] overall and North American Automotive pre-tax results to be breakeven or profitable"[8] in the coming years. Mulally was able to sustain this success past the initial stages of his tenure, and maintained profitability up until his retirement in June 2014.

In 2014, as CEO Mark Fields took over, challenging global conditions meant 2014 year-end profit saw a 56 percent drop from 2013—meaning Fields had work to do. In 2015, Fields continued the focus on ONE Ford, highlighting the idea that ONE team, working with ONE plan, could achieve ONE goal, profitable growth for all. By successfully launching 16 new global products, opening the last of ten new plants to support growth in Asia Pacific, and seeing profitable global business unit performance in every region except South America, Ford had the most profitable year ever in 2015, and 2016 was just slightly lower, and the second best ever. The 2016 full year net income of $4.6 billion was down from 2015 due to a one-time pre-tax pension re-measurement. Adjusted pre-tax profit would have been $10.4 billion, on par with 2015. (See income statement in Exhibit 1.)

But in 2016 CEO Mark Fields decided to restructure, creating a new focus, expanding the company's scope from

EXHIBIT 1 Ford Motor Company and Subsidiaries: Income Statement

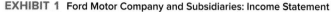

	For the Years Ended December 31,		
	2014	2015	2016
Revenues			
Automotive	$ 135,782	$ 140,566	$ 141,546
Financial Services	8,295	8,992	10,253
Other	—	—	1
Total revenues	144,077	149,558	151,800
Costs and expenses			
Cost of sales	125,025	124,041	126,584
Selling, administrative, and other expenses	11,842	10,502	12,196
Financial Services interest, operating, and other expenses	6,878	7,368	8,904
Total costs and expenses	143,745	141,911	147,684
Interest expense on Automotive debt	797	773	894
Non-Financial Services interest income and other income/(loss), net	76	1,188	1,356
Financial Services other income/(loss), net	348	372	438
Equity in net income of affiliated companies	1,275	1,818	1,780
Income before income taxes	1,234	10,252	6,796
Provision for/(Benefit from) income taxes	4	2,881	2,189
Net income	1,230	7,371	4,607
Less: Income/(Loss) attributable to noncontrolling interests	(1)	(2)	11
Net income attributable to Ford Motor Company	$ 1,231	$ 7,373	$ 4,596
EARNINGS PER SHARE ATTRIBUTABLE TO FORD MOTOR COMPANY COMMON AND CLASS B STOCK			
Basic income	$ 0.31	$ 1.86	$ 1.16
Diluted income	0.31	1.84	1.15
Cash dividends declared	0.50	0.60	0.85

Note: Figures in millions, except per-share amounts; year-end December 31.

Source: Ford Motor Company 10K filings.

vehicles to "mobility," through business model innovation. Of interest in the income statement shown in Exhibit 1 is the presence, for the first time, of an "Other" revenue item, representing the newly operational Ford Smart Mobility LLC, a subsidiary formed to design, build, grow, and invest in emerging mobility services. Designed to compete like a start-up company, Ford Smart Mobility LLC was planning to design and build mobility services on its own, and collaborate with start-ups and tech companies as needed to pursue opportunities.

Going into 2017, Ford was guiding profits lower, primarily because of this intent to invest in the emerging mobility services opportunities. The ONE Ford legacy of Mulally was being adapted. In 2015, the plan had identified the following objectives:

- Aggressively restructure to operate profitably at the current demand and changing model mix.
- Accelerate development of new products, service, and experiences customers want and value.
- Finance our plan and maintain a strong balance sheet.
- Work together effectively as one team.

The new vision was to make "people's lives better by changing the way the world moves," and the strategy was to deliver top quartile shareholder returns through automotive and high-growth mobility businesses.[9] Ford intended to do this by focusing on those strategic priorities in both the core business and emerging opportunities that would fortify, transform, and grow business:

- Fortifying the automotive "profit pillars" of trucks, vans, commercial and utility vehicles; delivering updated performance vehicles such as the Ford GT and Mustang.
- Transforming the underperforming Lincoln, Continental and Navigator luxury products, and repositioning small vehicles in developed markets through redesign; focusing on the needs of emerging markets.
- Growing investments in emerging opportunities, especially in electrification, autonomous vehicles, and mobility services.

In 2017, reminding investors of the company's long-term legacy, Fields pointed out a history going back to founder Henry Ford of "democratizing technology," not just making products for people who could afford luxury vehicles, but using technology to solve problems of mobility and access, providing not only products but also transportation services that made people's lives better.[10] So, although Ford would always sell cars, CEO Fields was making big bets in autonomous technology (self-driving cars), electric vehicles, and other transportation services such as urban mobility solutions via ride-sharing, bike-sharing, and customized interior vehicle experiences serving multiple customer needs.

This vision of a seismic shift in personal transportation was fully supported and even driven by Ford's executive chairman Bill Ford, who had championed the concept of increased mobility back in 2009 when the only things to invest in were "parking and municipal ticketing solutions"[11] Now, in 2017, Bill Ford was supporting the company's movement beyond selling vehicles to investing heavily in mobility services. As the initial architect of this shift, Bill Ford predicted the company could make profit margins of up to 20 percent on new services, more than double what it had traditionally made selling cars and trucks, but the ultimate goal, beyond making money, was to improve people's lives. In doing so, Bill Ford would be protecting his great-grandfather's legacy.[12]

History of the Ford Motor Company

In 2017, Ford Motor Company, based in Dearborn, Michigan, had about 201,000 employees and 62 plants worldwide. It manufactured or distributed the automotive brands Ford and Lincoln across six continents, and provided financial services via Ford Motor Credit. In 2017, it was also aggressively pursuing emerging opportunities with investments in electrification, autonomous vehicles, and consumer mobility. It was the only company in the industry where the company name still honored the vision and innovative legacy of its founder, Henry Ford.

American engineer and industrial icon Henry Ford had been a true innovator. He didn't invent the automobile or the assembly line, but through his ability to recognize opportunities, articulate a vision, and inspire others to join him in fulfilling that vision, he was responsible for making significant changes in the trajectory of the automobile industry and even in the history of manufacturing in America. Starting with the invention of the self-propelled Quadricycle in 1896, Ford had developed other vehicles, primarily racing cars, which attracted a series of interested investors. In 1903, twelve investors backed him in the creation of a company to build and sell horseless carriages, and Ford Motor Company was born.

Starting with the Model A, the company had produced a series of successful vehicles, but in 1908 Henry Ford wanted to create a better, cheaper "motorcar for the great multitude."[13] Working with a group of hand-picked employees, he designed the Model T. The design was so successful, and demand so great, that Ford decided to investigate methods for increasing production and lowering costs. Borrowing concepts from other industries, by 1913 Ford had developed a moving assembly line for automobile manufacture. Although the work was so demanding that it created high employee turnover, the production process was significantly more efficient, reducing chassis assembly time from 12 ½ hours to 2 hours 40 minutes. In 1904, Ford expanded into Canada, and by 1925 Ford had assembly plants in Europe, Argentina, South Africa, and Australia. By the end of 1919, Ford was producing 50 percent of all the cars in the U.S., and the assembly line disruption in the industry had led to the demise of most of Ford's rivals.[14]

The Automotive Industry and Ford Leadership Changes

The automotive industry in the United States has always been a highly competitive, cyclical business. In 2017 there were a wide and growing variety of product offerings from a growing number of manufacturers, including the electric car lineup from Tesla Motors, self-styled as "not just an automaker, but also a technology and design company with a focus on energy innovation."[15] The total number of cars and trucks sold to retail buyers, or "industry demand," varied substantially from year to year depending on general economic situations, the cost of purchasing and operating cars and trucks, and the availability of credit and fuel. Because cars and trucks were durable items, consumers could wait to replace them, and, starting in 2016, the average age of light vehicles on U.S. roads was over 11 years. Partly due to this, replacement demand was forecasted to stay fairly flat for 2017 and beyond. Any increase in sales would be aided by an improvement in the general economic situation, reduced gasoline prices, and lower interest rates for car loans. However, sales in U.S. markets had not belonged only to U.S. manufacturers for some time.

In the U.S., Ford's market share had dropped over time—from almost 25 percent in 1999 to 15.5 percent in 2011,[16] with major blows to market share in the light-vehicle segment. Going into 2017, although still losing ground at 14.9 percent, Ford claimed the second spot in the U.S. market, just behind GM and ahead of Toyota. (See Exhibit 2.)

Originally dominated by the "Big 3" Detroit-based car companies, Ford, General Motors, and Fiat/Chrysler, competition in the United States had intensified since the 1980s, when Japanese carmakers began gaining a foothold in the market. To counter the problem of being viewed as foreign, Japanese companies Nissan, Toyota, and Honda had set up production facilities in the United States and thus gained acceptance from American consumers. Production quality and lean production were judged to be the major weapons that Japanese carmakers used to gain an advantage over American carmakers. Starting in 2003, because of innovative production processes that yielded better quality for American consumers, Toyota vehicles had unquestionably become "a better value proposition" than Detroit's products.[17]

Back in 1999, Ford Motor Company had been in good shape, having attained a U.S. market share of 24.8 percent, and had seen profits reach a remarkable $7.2 billion ($5.86 per share) with pre-tax income of $11 billion. At that time people even speculated that Ford would soon overtake General Motors as the world's number-one automobile manufacturer.[18] But soon Toyota, through its innovative technology, management philosophy of continuous improvement, and cost arbitrage due to its presence in multiple geographic locations, was threatening to overtake GM and Ford.

In addition, unfortunately, the profits at Ford in 1999 had come at the expense of not investing in Ford's future. Jacques Nasser, the CEO at that time, had focused on

EXHIBIT 2 Sales and Share of U.S. Total Market by Manufacturer, 2016

Automaker	Units Sold	% Change	Market Share
General Motors	2,723,667	−2.5%	17.2%
Ford Motor Company	2,361,426	−0.2%	14.9%
Toyota Motor Corporation	2,206,359	−2.4%	13.9%
FCA/Chrysler Group	2,051,796	−0.6%	12.9%
Honda Motor Company	1,477,465	2.9%	9.3%
Nissan Motor Company	1,411,680	4.9%	8.9%
Hyundai-Kia	1,305,945	2.8%	8.2%
Volkswagen Group*	525,176	−4.6%	3.3%
Daimler	343,695	0.6%	2.2%
BMW-Mini	327,711	−10.2%	2.1%
Jaguar-Land Rover	92,531	22.7%	0.6%
Total	**15,850,640**	**0.04%**	—

* Does not include Lamborghini, Alfa Romeo, Chrysler, Dodge, Fiat, Jeep, Ram.
Red font indicates declining year-over-year volume.

Source: Automakers & Autonews.com as of 12/1/2016.

corporate acquisition and diversification rather than new vehicle development. By the time Chairman Bill Ford had stepped in and fired Nasser in 2001, Ford was seeing decline in both market share and profitability. By 2005, market share had dropped to 18.6 percent and Ford had skidded out of control, losing $1.6 billion, pre-tax, in North American profits. It was obvious Ford needed a change in order to adapt and survive. Observers believed the Ford family would take action to prevent further losses: "Ford may need a strongman . . . a Ford characteristic—the 'prime minister' who actually runs the company under the 'constitutional monarch,' a member of the Ford family." It was speculated that Mark Fields, named head of Ford's North American operations in 2005, might be tapped to take that job.[19]

The Ford empire had been around for over a century, and the company had not gone outside its ranks for a top executive since hiring Ernest Breech away from General Motors Corporation in 1946.[20] Since taking the CEO position in 2001, Bill Ford had tried several times to find a qualified successor, "going after such industry luminaries as Renault-Nissan CEO Carlos Ghosn and DaimlerChrysler chairman Dieter Zetsche."[21]

Among large corporations, it had become fairly common to hire a CEO from outside the family or board. According to Joseph Bower from Harvard Business School, around one-third of the time at S&P 500 firms, and around 40 percent of the time at companies that were struggling with problems in operations or financial distress, an outsider was appointed as CEO. The reason might be to get a fresh point of view or to get the support of the board. "Results suggest that forced turnover followed by outsider succession, on average, improves firm performance."[22] Bill Ford claimed that to undertake major changes in Ford's dysfunctional culture, an outsider might be more qualified than even the most proficient auto industry insider.[23]

In 2006, Alan Mulally was selected as the new CEO and was expected to accomplish "nothing less than undoing a strongly entrenched management system put into place by Henry Ford II almost 40 years ago"—a system of regional fiefdoms around the world that had sapped the company's ability to compete in a global industry, a system that Chairman Bill Ford couldn't or wouldn't unwind by himself.[24]

Mulally set his own priorities for fixing Ford: Ford needed to pay more attention to cutting costs and transforming the way it did business than to traditional measurements such as market share.[25] The vision was to have a smaller and more profitable Ford. The overall strategy was to use restructuring as a tool to obtain operating profitability at lower volume and create a mix of products that better appealed to the market.

By 2011, Ford had closed or sold a quarter of its plants and cut its global workforce by more than a third. It also slashed labor and health-care costs, plowing the money back into the design of some well-received new products, like the Ford Fusion sedan and Ford Edge crossover. This put Ford in a better position to compete, especially taking into consideration that General Motors and Chrysler had filed for bankruptcy in 2009, and Toyota had recently announced a major recall of its vehicles for "unintended acceleration" problems.[26] Ford's sales grew at double the rate of the rest of the industry in 2010, but entering 2011 its rivals' problems seemed to be in the rearview mirror, and General Motors, especially, was on the rebound.

Mulally set three priorities: first, to determine the brands Ford would offer, second to be "best in class for all its vehicles," and third to make sure that those vehicles would be accepted and adapt[able] by consumers around the globe: "if a model was developed for the U.S. market, it needed to be adaptable to car buyers in other countries."[27] Mulally said that the "real opportunity going forward is to integrate and leverage our Ford assets around the world" and decide on the best mix of brands in the company's portfolio.[28] The "best mix of brands" appeared to have been established going into 2011, after brands such as Jaguar, Land Rover, Aston Martin, and Volvo were all sold off, and the Mercury brand was discontinued. Ford also had an equity interest in Mazda Motor Corporation, which it reduced substantially in 2010, retaining only a 3.5 percent share of ownership. This left the company with only the Ford and Lincoln brands, but the Lincoln offerings struggled against Cadillac and other rivals for the luxury car market. Mulally acknowledged that this needed fixing, and forecast a date of 2013 for real changes in the Lincoln lineup.[29]

In 2014, thanks to Mulally's vision and perseverance, Ford maintained its position. Ford had introduced 24 vehicles around the world, including the new Mondeo in Europe, but although still profitable, net income was down $4 billion from 2013. Even though Ford maintained its number two position in Europe, behind Volkswagen, major losses had occurred in that sector, primarily due to Russian economic instabilities. South America had also seen losses due to currency devaluation and changing government rules. In addition, Ford's push into Asia-Pacific, specifically China, was behind schedule. North American sales, while still strong, had resulted in operating margin reductions due to recalls and costs associated with the relaunch of the F-150. The one real bright spot was in financial services. Ford Motor Credit, the financing company that loans people money to buy new cars, saw its best results since 2011.[30]

As Mark Fields took over as CEO in 2014, he pointed to the ONE Ford plan as essential to Ford's future: "our ONE Ford plan is build on compelling vision, comprehensive strategy, and relentless implementation, all leading to profitable growth around the world."[31] The actions of Mulally and now Fields, in enacting the ONE Ford plan, had attracted many long-term investors who believed in the strategy. Going into 2015 the financials, especially the balance sheet, appeared strong, and because of this, the company was able to reinstate and subsequently boost the dividend to shareholders, rewarding those investors who had stayed the course. Through 2016, going into 2017, the balance sheet stayed strong. (See Exhibit 3.)

EXHIBIT 3 Ford Motor Company and Subsidiaries: Sector Balance Sheets

	December 31, 2015	December 31, 2016
ASSETS		
Cash and cash equivalents	$ 14,272	$ 15,905
Marketable securities	20,904	22,922
Financial Services finance receivables, net	45,137	46,266
Trade and other receivables, less allowances of $372 and $392	11,042	11,102
Inventories	8,319	8,898
Other assets	2,913	3,368
Total current assets	102,587	108,461
Financial Services finance receivables, net	45,554	49,924
Net investment in operating leases	27,093	28,829
Net property	30,163	32,072
Equity in net assets of affiliated companies	3,224	3,304
Deferred income taxes	11,509	9,705
Other assets	4,795	5,656
Total assets	$ 224,925	$ 237,951
LIABILITIES		
Payables	$ 20,272	$ 21,296
Other liabilities and deferred revenue	19,089	19,316
Automotive debt payable within one year	1,779	2,685
Financial Services debt payable within one year	41,196	46,984
Total current liabilities	82,336	90,281
Other liabilities and deferred revenue	23,457	24,395
Automotive long-term debt	11,060	13,222
Financial Services long-term debt	78,819	80,079
Deferred income taxes	502	691
Total liabilities	196,174	208,668
Redeemable noncontrolling interest	94	96
EQUITY		
Capital stock		
Common Stock, par value $.01 per share (3,976 million shares issued of 6 billion authorized)	40	40
Class B Stock, par value $.01 per share (71 million shares issued of 530 million authorized)	1	1
Capital in excess of par value of stock	21,421	21,630
Retained earnings	14,414	15,634
Accumulated other comprehensive income/(loss)	(6,257)	(7,013)
Treasury stock	(977)	(1,122)
Total equity attributable to Ford Motor Company	28,642	29,170
Equity attributable to noncontrolling interests	15	17
Total equity	28,657	29,187
Total liabilities and equity	$ 224,925	$ 237,951

Note: Figures in millions.

Source: Ford Motor Company 10K filings.

Starting in 2016, CEO Fields began restructuring, and the cash flow reflected this. (See Exhibit 4.) Fields kept watch over an increasingly volatile landscape while strategizing for investments in areas of emerging opportunities. Going into 2017, Fields stated that Ford needed to be "very, very prudent, disciplined" in how cash was used to transform the business.[32] The forecast for 2017 showed total automotive operating cash flow remaining positive through 2018, with the overall cash balance expected to stay at or above the company's minimum target of $20 billion.[33]

EXHIBIT 4 Ford Motor Company and Subsidiaries: Sector Statements of Cash Flows

	For the Years Ended December 31,		
	2014	2015	2016
Cash flows from operating activities			
Net income	$ 1,230	$ 7,371	$ 4,607
Depreciation and tooling amortization	7,385	7,993	9,023
Other amortization	38	(27)	(306)
Provision for credit and insurance losses	305	418	672
Pension and other postretirement employee benefits ("OPEB") expense	4,429	512	2,667
Equity investment (earnings)/losses in excess of dividends received	189	(333)	(178)
Foreign currency adjustments	825	710	283
Net (gain)/loss on changes in investments in affiliates	798	(42)	(139)
Stock compensation	180	199	210
Net change in wholesale and other receivables	(2,208)	(5,090)	(1,449)
Provision for deferred income taxes	(94)	2,120	1,478
Decrease/(Increase) in accounts receivable and other assets	(2,896)	(3,563)	(2,855)
Decrease/(Increase) in inventory	(936)	(1,155)	(815)
Increase/(Decrease) in accounts payable and accrued and other liabilities	5,729	7,758	6,595
Other	(467)	(701)	(1)
Net cash provided by/(used in) operating activities	14,507	16,170	19,792
Cash flows from investing activities			
Capital spending	(7,463)	(7,196)	(6,992)
Acquisitions of finance receivables and operating leases	(51,673)	(57,217)	(56,007)
Collections of finance receivables and operating leases	36,497	38,130	38,834
Purchases of equity and debt securities	(48,694)	(41,279)	(31,428)
Sales and maturities of equity and debt securities	50,264	40,766	29,354
Change related to Venezuelan operations	(477)	—	—
Settlements of derivatives	281	134	825
Other	141	500	62
Net cash provided by/(used in) investing activities	(21,124)	(26,162)	(25,352)

continued

EXHIBIT 4 *continued*

	For the Years Ended December 31,		
	2014	2015	2016
Cash flows from financing activities			
Cash dividends	(1,952)	(2,380)	(3,376)
Purchases of Common Stock	(1,964)	(129)	(145)
Net changes in short-term debt	(3,870)	1,646	3,864
Proceeds from issuance of other debt	40,043	48,860	45,961
Principal payments on other debt	(28,859)	(33,358)	(38,797)
Other	25	(317)	(49)
Net cash provided by/(used in) financing activities	3,423	14,322	7,458
Effect of exchange rate changes on cash and cash equivalents	(517)	(815)	(265)
Net increase/(decrease) in cash and cash equivalents	$ (3,711)	$ 3,515	$ 1,633
Cash and cash equivalents at January 1	$ 14,468	$ 10,757	$ 14,272
Net increase/(decrease) in cash and cash equivalents	(3,711)	3,515	1,633
Cash and cash equivalents at December 31	$ 10,757	$ 14,272	$ 15,905

Note: Figures in millions; year-end December 31.

Source: Ford Motor Company 10K filings.

Ford and the Automobile Industry Changing Product Mix

Going into 2017, the entire automobile industry was facing disruption, but this wasn't unusual. For instance, the 2009 global economic downturn and financial crisis had a significant impact on global sales volumes in the auto industry. The once-profitable business of manufacturing and selling trucks and SUVs had changed. Especially in the U.S., oil prices had been fluctuating, making it difficult to anticipate consumer demand. In 2010, this had caused a shift in consumers' car-buying habits, reducing the demand for large vehicles.

The core strategy at Ford had centered on a change in products, shifting to smaller and more fuel-efficient cars. Ford had imported European-made small vehicles, the European Focus and Fiesta, into North America. It also converted three truck-manufacturing plants to small-car production.[34] The Ford and Lincoln lines were upgraded, emphasizing fuel-economy improvement and the introduction of hybrid cars. In 2012 Ford launched six new Ford hybrid cars in North America and sold more hybrids in the fourth quarter of 2012 than during any quarter in their history. In 2014 Ford began producing its first hybrid electric car in Europe, the Mondeo Hybrid. This car was well-known to those in the U.S., being based on the North American Fusion model hybrid vehicle. By 2014, Ford was the world's second largest manufacturer of hybrids, after Toyota.[35]

By late 2015 gas prices had reduced enough to spur interest in SUVs once again. This trend should have been good for Ford, given their branding emphasis on the F-150, Edge, Escape, and Explorer, but by 2013 Ford and other U.S. manufacturers had shifted production to the small and midsized cars, and in 2014 this positioning hurt Ford. With large inventories of smaller vehicles on dealer lots, U.S. auto manufacturers, including Ford, had to adjust once again to meet the demand for the newly designed cross-over vehicles. The smaller crossovers and SUVs now had greatly improved fuel economy, and were attractive to consumers due to their versatility, while the smaller sedan and compact owners were an older demographic, and less likely to be impulse buyers. These kinds of fluctuations in the industry meant automobile executives had to keep close track of trends and maximize their ability to adjust to demand.[36] Ford, specifically, reconfigured plants to flex back and forth between cars and light trucks. See Exhibit 5 for shifting vehicle sales figures in the U.S. market.

In 2015, Ford relaunched the F-150, as well as further developing 15 other global products. 2016 saw the launch of the F-150 Raptor high-performance off-road pickup truck, and the next-generation Fusion Hybrid Autonomous Development Vehicle, bringing Ford's test fleet of these innovative designs up to 30 vehicles, making it one of the

EXHIBIT 5 U.S. Vehicle Sales by Segment YTD 2017

	Feb 2017	%Chg from Feb '16	YTD 2017	%Chg from YTD 2016
Cars	502,300	−12.1	929,896	−12.1
Midsize	229,280	−14.9	410,951	−17.5
Small	205,740	−9.9	391,868	−7.4
Luxury	67,255	−8.4	126,992	−7.2
Large	25	−64.8	85	−7.6
Light-duty trucks	831,337	6.9	1,547,290	6.4
Pickup	216,100	10.1	394,064	7.2
Cross-over	396,037	11.7	747,375	11.4
Minivan	42,080	−20.3	76,859	−20.6
Small Van	5,435	−26.8	10,510	−26.7
Large Van	27,680	2.6	50,533	2.8
Midsize SUV	79,657	−3.9	147,175	−2.3
Large SUV	27,292	27.5	51,083	27.9
Small SUV	19,473	10.5	34,780	8.2
Luxury SUV	17,583	0.8	34,911	5.0
Total SUV/Cross-over	540,042	9.3	1,015,324	9.6
Total SUV	144,005	3.3	267,949	4.7
Total Cross-over	396,037	11.7	747,375	11.4

Source: http://online.wsj.com/mdc/public/page/2_3022-autosales.html#autosalesB.

largest in the automobile industry. In 2017, the company planned to triple the size of this hybrid fleet to a total of about 90 vehicles.[37] By 2017 Ford had become the top-selling plug-in hybrid brand in the U.S., and was second in overall U.S. electrified vehicle sales. To support this growth, Ford had invested $700 million and projected 700 new jobs in its Flat Rock Assembly Plant in Michigan to build autonomous and electric vehicles.[38]

Ford's most successful vehicles were still the F-series pickup trucks (see Exhibit 6). In 2017, for the 40th consecutive year, the Ford F-series was ranked as America's top-selling vehicle.[39] Ford's vehicles had proven dependable, overall. However, it appeared consumer perceptions had not kept pace with actual performance. J.D. Power and Associates found that the Ford and Lincoln brands still had large lags between actual dependability performance and consumer perception. "Producing vehicles with world-class quality is just part of the battle for automakers; convincing consumers to believe in their quality is equally important," said David Sargent, vice president of global vehicle research at J.D. Power and Associates. "It takes considerable time to positively change consumer perceptions of quality and dependability—sometimes a decade or more—so it is vital for manufacturers to continually improve quality and also

to convince consumers of these gains."[40] For 2016, the highest scoring American-branded cars in the Consumer Reports road test, reliability, owner satisfaction, and safety ratings included the Ford Fusion SE–midsized car, Ford Escape Titanium–compact SUV, and the Ford Edge SEL–midsized SUV. Models with declining reliability included the Lincoln MKX.[41]

Globalizing the Ford Brand

Under the ONE Ford vision, Mulally globalized the Ford brand, meaning that all Ford vehicles competing in global segments would be the same in North America, Europe, and Asia.[42] The company was looking for a reduction of complexity, and thus costs, in the purchasing and manufacturing processes. The idea was to deliver more vehicles worldwide from fewer platforms and to maximize the use of common parts and systems. Mulally felt he had positioned Ford to take advantage of its scale, global products, and brand to respond to the changing marketplace.[43] However, each year posed new challenges.

In 2016 the U.S. auto industry had its best year ever, selling 17.55 million vehicles, breaking the annual sales record set in 2015. Going into 2017, the global marketplace for automobiles was stable, with pockets of strength, but each

EXHIBIT 6 Best-Selling Vehicles in America, 2016

Rank	Vehicle Make	# Sold	% Change Over 2015
1	Ford F-Series Truck	820,799	+5.2%
2	Chevrolet Silverado Truck	574,876	−4.3%
3	RAM Truck	489,418	+8.7%
4	Toyota Camry	388,616	−9.5%
5	Honda Civic	366,927	+9.4%
6	Toyota Corolla	360,483	−0.8%
7	Honda CR-V	357,335	+3.4%
8	Toyota RAV4	352,139	+11.6%
9	Honda Accord	345,225	−2.9%
10	Nissan Rogue	329,904	+14.9%
11	Nissan Altima	307,380	−7.8%
12	Ford Escape	307,069	+0.2%
13	Ford Fusion	265,840	−11.4%
14	Ford Explorer	248,507	−0.3%
15	Chevrolet Equinox	242,195	−12.8%

Source: http://www.businessinsider.com/best-selling-cars-trucks-vehicle-america-2016-2017-1/#3-ram-trucks-489418-87-18.

geographical segment had its issues. Both North American and European auto sales were subject to political uncertainty, due to policy shifts in government. The Chinese and larger Asian market was still growing, although starting to slow. Eastern European economic concerns, especially in Russia, made this a difficult area to manage. South American government regulations and currency fluctuations impacted growth there.[44]

The need for a global strategy was driving all major auto manufacturers to reduce the number of vehicle platforms, while simultaneously adding models in response to consumer preferences. Although the increased complexity raised costs, this more flexible approach allowed for improved product commonality and increased volume. As components could be shared between cars and platforms, this also reduced the number of suppliers. Ford had reduced its supplier base from 1,150 to 750.[45] Although seemingly a positive, this could also prove costly if a major supplier had a problem, as had occurred with Japanese air bag manufacturer Takata in 2014.[46] Ford had to recall 850,000 vehicles for airbag problems in 2014, at a cost of $500 million.[47] Likewise, in 2016 a door latch recall cost Ford nearly $600 million.

For Ford, 2016 saw a record profit in Europe and the second-best profit in Asia-Pacific. For operations outside North America, on a combined basis, Ford generated

a profit of $421 million, nearly double the previous year, and the best result since 2011. CEO Fields attributed this to strengthening brands and adjusting the mix of vehicles in each market, "focusing on the higher margin segments where consumer interest is particularly strong."[48] In Europe, especially, Ford saw double digit growth in sales of its commercial vehicles, specifically the Transit cargo van. (See Exhibit 7.)

Regarding global growth, in Asia, Ford had developed two car plants in India, while also increasing its commitment in China, having invested $5 billion in factories there since 2012.[49] Although the Chinese market was slowing, profit margins were strong, and 2016 was the best sales year ever in China, up 14 percent over 2015, with the luxury or premium and SUV sectors seeing the most expansion. In 2016, Ford Lincoln became the fastest growing luxury brand in China.[50] Ford was betting on this momentum to spur Lincoln sales, having introduced the Lincoln lineup to China in April 2014. Sales growth in this region was critical, given that Ford was late to the China market, with a 2014 share of less than 5 percent, while General Motors controlled 15 percent. Although Ford collaborated with Chinese manufacturer Changan to produce light vehicles such as the Focus, the Lincoln would be imported from America, leaving Ford to "deal with the added cost of import duties that would leave their premium vehicles in a difficult position

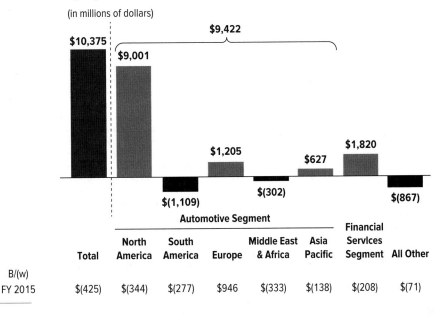

EXHIBIT 7 Ford Performance by Region

(in millions of dollars)

Chart values:
- Total: $10,375
- North America: $9,001
- (bracket): $9,422
- South America: $(1,109)
- Europe: $1,205
- Middle East & Africa: $(302)
- Asia Pacific: $627
- Financial Services Segment: $1,820
- All Other: $(867)

	Total	Automotive Segment					Financial Services Segment	All Other
		North America	South America	Europe	Middle East & Africa	Asia Pacific		
B/(w) FY 2015	$(425)	$(344)	$(277)	$946	$(333)	$(138)	$(208)	$(71)

Source: Ford 10-K.

against rivals who are already well positioned in China."[51] Offsetting this, Ford introduced the Mustang and Taurus in China during 2016, and saw strong sales of these performance vehicles. In 2017, Ford began exporting the all-new F-150 Raptor to China, making it the first high-performance off-road pickup truck to be offered there.

Going into 2017, Ford was taking a new look at how to grow in select emerging markets. Russia and South America (except for Brazil) seemed positioned for recovery, and profitable growth was possible in the Middle East and Africa. Ford was also re-evaluating its strategy and business model for India.

Looking Ahead

Although Fields was clear that he would continue Mulally's ONE Ford legacy, with the support and ongoing vision of chairman Bill Ford, he would do this by "tailoring aspects of the company to his preferences."[52]

Going into 2017, Ford Motor Company was the seventh-largest automobile manufacturer in the world, but like all others who produced a multi-vehicle lineup, Ford was facing considerable uncertainty. Global markets were hard to predict and countries were increasing regulatory requirements for safety and environmental impact. All vehicles were seeing an increase in the amount of onboard technology that required a shift in both engineering and manufacturing priorities. Worldwide manufacturers were making design changes that allowed more lean production and consolidation of suppliers, and consumers were changing how they purchased vehicles and rethinking what they wanted from the transportation experience overall.[53]

Several marked shifts in the overall landscape were occurring: the interest, worldwide, in electric or alternative-fueled vehicles; the development of autonomously controlled cars that were also personally connected to a user who might not be the driver; the reduction in demand for actual automobile ownership in favor of rental or on-demand transportation options. These shifts created opportunities but also challenges for entrenched car manufacturers. Twenty companies were actively pursuing the development of self-driving cars in 2017, and although some of the big auto manufacturers were among them, including BMW, Toyota, Volvo, Nissan, Daimler, Audi, Honda, Hyundai, PSA Groupe, General Motors, and Ford, other technology giants such as Apple, Google, Baidu, Nvidia, and Bosch were entering the race.[54]

Partnerships were inevitable: GM was partnering with Lyft, Ford with Uber, which was trying out the Ford Fusion autonomous vehicle. Ford had put Amazon's virtual digital assistant Alexa in its cars. Ford had invested in Velodyne, a company that developed lidar remote-sensing technology for self-driving cars, and in artificial intelligence software firm Argo AI. Ford had acquired an app-based, crowd-sourced, ride-sharing service, Chariot. Ford had teamed up with Motivate, the global leader in bike-sharing to include the FordPass mobility network in the Ford GoBike commuting transportation option. Through its innovation and research centers, Ford was also developing strategies in fleet and data management, route and journey planning, and telematics, all in an effort to help solve congestion and help move people more efficiently in urban environments.[55]

These fundamental changes in the industry required leadership that could anticipate trends and allocate resources wisely, all while crafting a vision for the future that could inspire all relevant stakeholders to support and promote the company's success. Alan Mulally's "ONE Ford" slogan had helped the automaker avoid bankruptcy and return to a position of financial strength in the industry. Mark Fields's shift seemed to be toward TWO Fords, refocusing the company into both an automaker and a transportation services provider. In October 2016, Fields had said the ONE Ford strategy was "foundational" but that the company had to "evolve." This evolution included plans to offer 13 new electric vehicles by 2020 and a self-driving car ready for commercial use by 2021, and to experiment with ways to provide innovative solutions to transportation and mobility problems in cities across the globe.[56] To do this, Ford had "amped up" innovation efforts inside the company, encouraging its employees to file over 3,200 patents in 2016, more than any other automaker.[57]

Unfortunately, investors were not buying this vision: Ford's stock had fallen by about 30 percent since Mulally's departure in 2014. Despite record earnings in 2016, investors were not sure how the new strategy would play out. One analyst pointed out what others were saying: "They have a lot of the right initiatives; they're doing something in every box. The difference from the Mulally days is there isn't a single message that is more than just public-relations, tying it all together."[58] Mulally's message had been clear, focusing all efforts around a common goal and returning the company to the "basics of auto making." Fields appeared to be positioning the company to take on rivals from other industries, and investors wondered what bike-sharing and artificial intelligence had to do with the car business. Even though the new ventures developed as part of the new Ford Smart Mobility LLC were expected to deliver margins of 20 percent or more, this financial result was not projected to occur until 2020 at least. Some thought Fields needed to "take bolder action," expressing a more "cohesive narrative or game plan."[59]

Could CEO Mark Fields guide Ford to success given these challenges? Henry Ford had the initial vision of disruption in personal transportation. Would the 21st century version of Ford Motor Company be as successful?

ENDNOTES

1. Ford Media. 2017. Unprecedented: Ford F-Series Achieves 40 Consecutive Years as America's Best Selling Truck. January 4. https://media.ford.com/content/fordmedia/fna/us/en/news/2017/01/04/ford-f-series-40-years-best-selling-truck.html.

2. Ford Media. 2017. Ford F-Series, SUVs, Lincoln Post Gains in February. March 1. https://media.ford.com/content/dam/fordmedia/North%20America/US/2017/03/001/Sales-Release-February-2017-with_tables.pdf.

3. Ford Media. 2017. Unprecedented: Ford F-Series Achieves 40 Consecutive Years As America's Best Selling Truck. January 4. https://media.ford.com/content/fordmedia/fna/us/en/news/2017/01/04/ford-f-series-40-years-best-selling-truck.html.

4. Muoio, D. 2017. These 19 Companies Are Racing to Build Self-Driving Cars in the Next 5 Years. BusinessInsider, January 12. http://www.businessinsider.com/companies-making-driverless-cars-by-2020-2017-1/#tesla-recently-made-a-big-move-to-meet-its-goal-of-having-a-fully-self-driving-car-ready-by-2018-1.

5. Ford Media. 2015. Ford at CES Announces Smart Mobility Plan and 25 Global Experiments Designed to Change the Way the World Moves. January 6. https://media.ford.com/content/fordmedia/fna/us/en/news/2015/01/06/ford-at-ces-announces-smart-mobility-plan.html.

6. Caldicott, S. M. 2014. Why Ford's Alan Mulally Is an Innovation CEO for the Record Books. Forbes, June 25. http://www.forbes.com/sites/sarahcaldicott/2014/06/25/why-fords-alan-mulally-is-an-innovation-ceo-for-the-record-books/2/.

7. Ford Motor Company 2014 10K filing.

8. Ford Motor Company. 2009. Ford Reports 4th Quarter 2008 Net Loss of $5.9 Billion; Gained Market Share in U.S., Europe, Achieved Cost Target. January 29. media.ford.com/images/10031/4Qfinancials.pdf.

9. Ford Media. 2016. Amidst Unprecedented Change and Uncertainty, Ford Trend Report Has Consumers at a Crossroads, Reassessing World. December 7. https://media.ford.com/content/fordmedia/fna/us/en/news/2016/12/07/2017-ford-trend-report.html.

10. Thompson. C. 2017. Ford's CEO Reveals His Plan for the Company's Biggest Transformation in History. BusinessInsider, January 15. http://www.businessinsider.com/ford-ceo-mark-fields-interview-2017-1.

11. Newcomb, D. 2016. Bill Ford on Why the Family Business Is Betting on Mobility. Forbes, September 15. https://www.forbes.com/sites/dougnewcomb/2016/09/15/bill-ford-on-why-the-family-business-is-betting-on-mobility/#321209bb659b.

12. Martinez, M. 2017. Bill Ford: Mobility Can Lift Margins. AutoNews, January 16. http://www.autonews.com/article/20170116/OEM02/301169995/bill-ford%3A-mobility-can-lift-margins.

13. The Innovator and Ford Motor Company, The Henry Ford Museum, http://www.thehenryford.org/exhibits/hf/The_Innovator_and_Ford_Motor_Company.asp.

14. http://en.wikipedia.org/wiki/History_of_Ford_Motor_Company.

15. http://www.teslamotors.com/about.

16. MotorIntelligence.com. www.motorintelligence.com.

17. Maynard, M. & Fackler, M. 2006. Toyota Is Poised to Supplant G.M. as World's Largest Carmaker. New York Times, December 23. http://www.nytimes.com/2006/12/23/business/worldbusiness/23toyota.html?_r=0.

18. Flint, J. 2006. Ford: Overhaul Time–Again. Forbes, January 23. http://www.forbes.com/2006/01/23/ford-restructuring-autos-cz_jf_0123flint.html.

19. Ibid.

20. Knowles, F. 2006. Boeing Exec Flies the Coop: Ford Hires Mulally to Turn Things. Chicago Sun-Times, September 6.

21. Welch, D., Kiley, D., & Holmes, S. 2006. Alan Mulally: A Plan to Make Ford Fly. BusinessWeek.

22. Khurana, Rakesh, 2002. Searching for the Corporate Savior: The Irrational Quest for Charismatic CEOs. Princeton, NJ: Princeton University Press.

23. Berfield, S. 2006. The Best Leaders. BusinessWeek Online, December 18.

24. Kiley, D. 2007. Mulally: Ford's Most Important New Model. BusinessWeek Online, January 9. www.businessweek.com.

25. Maynard, M. 2006. Ford Expects to Fall Soon to No. 3 Spot. New York Times, December 21. www.nytimes.com.

26. Durbin, D.-A., & Krisher, T. 2011. Ford Stock Falls after Company Misses Expectations. Associated Press, January 28. www.businessweek.com/ap/financialnews/archives/March2011/D9L1JHCO1.htm.

27. LaRocco, L. A. 2014. For Mulally, Ford's Culture Is Job One. The Street, March 3. http://www.thestreet.com/story/1543980/1/for-mulally-fords-culture-is-job-one.html.

28. Bunkley, N., & Maynard, M. 2007. Ford Breaks String of Losing Quarters, But Says Respite Will Be Brief. New York Times, July 27: C3.

29. Durbin & Krisher. 2011. Ford Stock Falls.

30. Geier, B. 2015. Ford's Profit Beats Estimates, But Its European Outlook Dims. Fortune, January 29. http://fortune.com/2015/01/29/fords-profit-beats-estimates-but-its-european-outlook-dims/.

31. Salerno, C. 2015. What Major Changes in Ford's Management Mean. SeekingAlpha, January 16. http://seekingalpha.com/article/2825536-what-major-changes-in-fords-management-mean.

32. Ford Q4 2016 Results–Earnings Call Transcript. 2017. *Seeking Alpha,* January 26. http://seekingalpha.com/article/4039912-ford-motors-f-ceo-mark-fields-q4-2016-results-earnings-call-transcript?part=single.

33. Media Ford. 2016. Ford Outlines Growth Plan. September 14. https://media.ford.com/content/fordmedia/fna/us/en/news/2016/09/14/ford-outlines-growth-plan.html.

34. Praet, N. V. 2008. US$8.7B Loss Turns Ford. *Financial Post,* July 25.

35. Crowe, P. 2014. Ford Mondeo Hybrid Now in EU Production. *Hybridcars,* November 28. http://www.hybridcars.com/ford-mondeo-hybrid-now-in-eu-production/.

36. DeBord, M. 2016. The US Auto Industry May Surprise Everyone in 2017. *BusinessInsider.* December 21. http://www.businessinsider.com/us-auto-industry-growth-in-2017-2016-12.

37. Ford Media. 2016. Ford Finishes 2016 Strong; Fourth Quarter and Full-Year Profits in Line with Expectations. https://corporate.ford.com/content/dam/corporate/en/investors/investor-events/Quarterly%20Earnings/2017/4Q16-FINAL-Press-Release.pdf.

38. Ford Media. 2017. Ford Adding Electrified F-150, Mustang, Transit by 2020 in Major EV Push. January 3. https://media.ford.com/content/fordmedia/fna/us/en/news/2017/01/03/ford-adding-electrified-f-150-mustang-transit-by-2020.html.

39. Ford Media. 2017. F-150 Dependability Award Underscores Built Ford Tough. February 22. https://media.ford.com/content/fordmedia/fna/us/en/news/2017/02/22/f-150-dependability-award-underscores-built-ford-tough.html.

40. J.D. Power and Associates. 2010. 2010 U.S. Vehicle Dependability Study. March 18. www.jdpower.com/news/pressrelease.aspx?ID52010034; and 2012 U.S.; and 2012 Vehicle Dependability Study. February 14. http://www.jdpower.com/content/press-release-auto/Q5wPftR/2012-u-s-vehicle-dependability-study.htm.

41. Bartlett, J. 2016. Highest-Scoring American Cars, SUVs, and Trucks. *Consumer Reports,* October 14. http://www.consumerreports.org/cars-highest-scoring-american-cars-suvs-trucks/.

42. Ford Motor Company. 2009. Ford Reports 4th Quarter 2008. media.ford.com/images/10031/4Qfinancials.pdf.

43. Ford Motor Company. 2008. Ford Accelerates Transformation Plan. media.ford.com/article_display.cfm?article_id528660.

44. *Business Wire.* 2017. Global Auto Sales Set to Reach 93.5 Million in 2017, but Risk Is Greater than Ever, IHS Markit Says. *Business Wire.* February 21. http://finance.yahoo.com/news/global-auto-sales-set-reach-130000753.html.

45. Hirsh, E., Kakkar, A., Singh, A., Wilk, R. 2015. Auto Trends. *Strategy + business,* January. http://www.strategyand.pwc.com/perspectives/2015-auto-trends.

46. Ma, J., Trudell, C. 2014. Air-Bag Crisis Seen Spurring Shift from Japan's Takata. *BloombergBusiness,* October 24. http://www.bloomberg.com/news/articles/2014-10-23/air-bag-crisis-seen-spurring-shift-from-japan-s-takata.

47. Shepardson, D. 2014. New Ford Recall to Cost $500M, Stock Falls 7.5%. *The Detroit News,* September 29. http://www.detroitnews.com/story/business/autos/ford/2014/09/29/ford-recall-will-cost-million/16441255/.

48. Ford Q4 2016 Results–Earnings Call Transcript. 2017. *Seeking Alpha,* January 26. http://seekingalpha.com/article/4039912-ford-motors-f-ceo-mark-fields-q4-2016-results-earnings-call-transcript?part=single.

49. Ramsey, M. & Stoll, J. D. 2014. Ford Sharply Cuts Full-Year Forecast. *Wall Street Journal,* September 29. http://www.wsj.com/articles/fords-next-super-duty-pickup-to-be-aluminum-1412015106.

50. Ford Media. 2017. Ford Motor Company Posts Record Annual Sales in China. January 6. https://media.ford.com/content/fordmedia/fna/us/en/news/2017/01/06/ford-motor-company-posts-record-annual-sales-in-china–sales-ris.html.

51. Zahid, M. 2014. Ford's Future in the World's Largest Economy. *SeekingAlpha,* December 3. http://seekingalpha.com/article/2727035-fords-future-in-the-worlds-largest-economy.

52. Salerno, C. 2015. What Major Changes in Ford's Management Mean. *SeekingAlpha,* January 16. http://seekingalpha.com/article/2825536-what-major-changes-in-fords-management-mean.

53. Hirsh, E., Kakkar, A., Singh, A., & Wilk, R. 2015. 2015 Auto Industry Trends. *Strategy + business,* January. http://www.strategyand.pwc.com/perspectives/2015-auto-trends.

54. Muoio, D. 2017. These 19 Companies Are Racing to Build Self-Driving Cars in the Next 5 Years. *BusinessInsider,* January 12. http://www.businessinsider.com/companies-making-driverless-cars-by-2020-2017-1/#tesla-recently-made-a-big-move-to-meet-its-goal-of-having-a-fully-self-driving-car-ready-by-2018-1.

55. Ford Media. 2016. Ford Outlines Growth Plan. September 14. https://media.ford.com/content/fordmedia/fna/us/en/news/2016/09/14/ford-outlines-growth-plan.html.

56. Rogers, C. 2016. CEO Mark Fields Sets Ford on a Dual Track: Alongside Core Auto Business, Company Eyes Role as Transportation-Services Provider. *Wall Street Journal (Online),* October 17.

57. Ford Media. 2016. Ford Tops Industry for U.S. Patents Granted in 2016. December 9. https://media.ford.com/content/fordmedia/fna/us/en/news/2016/12/09/ford-tops-industry-for-us-patents-granted-in-2016.html.

58. Rogers, 2016. op. cit.

59. Rogers, 2016. op. cit.

CASE 18

GENERAL MOTORS IN 2017*

On February 14, 2017, Mary T. Barra, the CEO of General Motors, floated the possibility that the company could exit the large but troubled European market by selling its chronically unprofitable Opel unit to the French maker of Peugeot and Citroen cars. The sale would free the firm from persistent losses in Europe and fulfill pledges by Barra to improve overall profit margins and increase returns to shareholders. Shedding Opel would reduce GM's volume by 10 percent and knock the leading U.S. automaker out of the chase to be the top seller globally, a spot it had owned until recently. Under Barra, the firm had been dismantling unprofitable operations, which included abandoning Russia and certain Asian markets.

Industry analysts expected that Barra, who had worked for GM her entire career, would let the firm relapse into the arrogance, complacency, and denial that plunged it into bankruptcy in 2009. Soon after she assumed the helm of GM in January 2014, Barra had to deal with a devastating ignition switch flaw that was tied to 139 deaths and that eventually resulted in $2.1 billion in fines, lawsuit settlements, and recall costs. Barra has managed to avoid any significant effect on the firm's reputation from the bankruptcy and the safety issues. Over the past three years, GM has shown considerable growth in its net income, although its stock has been stuck below the IPO price of $33 per share of 2010 (see Exhibits 1 to 3).

Barra has been preparing GM to be a formidable player in the future. She has pushed the firm to be more involved in new developments, such as electric vehicles, ride sharing, and driverless cars. When the firm launched its first hybrid car, the Volt, in 2010, it was significantly lagging behind all other competitors in terms of investing into emerging technologies. Nevertheless, Barra claims that it was an important first step in acknowledging where GM needed to go.

Since then, GM has launched the new all-electric Bolt, which promises an almost 240-mile range between charges for a price of $30,000 after federal tax credits. It has moved quickly to beat Tesla's new budget-priced Model 3 to market. In January 2016, GM announced a $500 million investment in Lyft, the country's second largest ride-share service. It has subsequently worked with Lyft to develop a program which allows Lyft drivers in seven big cities to rent GM cars at a discount. The firm has acquired Cruise Automation which has built a complex array of software and hardware that uses artificial intelligence to pilot a car.

By making these moves, GM is constructing a portfolio of assets that are dedicated to disrupting its own core business from within. Barra is keenly aware that GM's 223,000 employees will have to behave differently for its future plans to succeed. She must replace a culture of blame and bureaucracy with one driven by accountability and speed. "In this area of rapid transformation, you have to have a culture that's agile," she said. "We still have a lot of work to do."[1]

Moving through Bankruptcy

GM has fallen from its dominant position when it held almost 50 percent of the U.S. market for automobiles. A succession of CEOs over the years failed to halt its decline in spite of their resolve to turn things around. When Richard Wagoner took over in 2000, he carried out three major restructurings, eliminating dozens of plants, tens of thousands of jobs, and jettisoning hundreds of dealers. In spite of these efforts, GM announced a loss of $30.9 billion dollars for 2008, amounting to a staggering $50 a share. The firm had not managed to post a profit since 2004, running up cumulative losses of over $82 billion between 2005 and 2009. Wagoner eventually began to run short of funds and turned to the U.S. government for loans in order to survive. The Obama administration demanded his resignation for its support.

Wagoner was replaced on an interim basis by Frederick A. Henderson, who had been president and chief operating officer of the firm since 2008. Under Henderson, the firm was asked to negotiate with bondholders and the union for further concessions in order to reduce its bloated cost structure. Unable to reach any agreement, the firm announced in late July 2009 that it must seek Chapter 11 bankruptcy protection. Under the terms of the bankruptcy protection, GM was able to wipe out a big chunk of its debt, reducing it from over $46 billion before the filing to around $17 billion afterward, saving about $1 billion a year in interest payments. The U.S. government agreed to invest another $30 billion into the firm, in addition to the $20 billion it had already contributed, in exchange for 61 percent of stock in the new GM.

Shortly after the bankruptcy filing, changes were made to the board of directors and there was a shake-up of the ranks of GM's senior management. The new board was determined to address problems that had been laid bare by the task force that had been assigned by the government to investigate GM in early 2009. They were particularly

---

* Case prepared by Jamal Shamsie, Michigan State University, with the assistance of Professor Alan B. Eisner, Pace University. Material has been drawn from published sources to be used for purposes of class discussion. Copyright © 2017 Jamal Shamsie and Alan B. Eisner.

EXHIBIT 1 Consolidated Income Statements (in millions of dollars)

	Years Ended December 31,		
	2016	2015	2014
Net sales and revenue			
Automotive	$ 156,849	$ 145,922	$ 151,092
GM Financial	9,531	6,434	4,837
Total net sales and revenue	166,380	152,356	155,929
Costs and expenses			
Automotive cost of sales	136,333	128,321	138,082
GM Financial interest, operating and other expenses	8,792	5,733	4,039
Automotive selling, general and administrative expense	11,710	13,405	12,158
Goodwill impairment charges	—	—	120
Total costs and expenses	156,835	147,459	154,399
Operating income	9,545	4,897	1,530
Automotive interest expense	572	443	403
Interest income and other non-operating income, net	429	621	823
Gain on extinguishment of debt	—	449	202
Equity income	2,282	2,194	2,094
Income before income taxes	11,684	7,718	4,246
Income tax expense (benefit)	2,416	(1,897)	228
Net income	9,268	9,615	4,018

Source: GM 10-K Report.

	December 31, 2016	December 31, 2015
ASSETS		
Current Assets		
Cash and cash equivalents	$ 12,960	$ 15,238
Marketable securities	11,841	8,163
Accounts and notes receivable (net of allowance of $303 and $327)	9,638	8,337
GM Financial receivables, net	22,065	18,051
Inventories	13,788	13,764
Equipment on operating leases, net	1,896	2,783
Other current assets	4,015	3,072
Total current assets	76,203	69,408

EXHIBIT 2

Consolidated Balance Sheets (in millions of dollars)

continued

EXHIBIT 2
continued

	December 31, 2016	December 31, 2015
Non-current Assets		
GM Financial receivables, net	20,724	18,500
Equity in net assets of nonconsolidated affiliates	8,996	9,201
Property, net	35,820	31,229
Goodwill and intangible assets, net	6,259	5,947
GM Financial equipment on operating leases, net	34,526	20,172
Deferred income taxes	35,092	36,860
Other assets	4,070	3,021
Total non-current assets	145,487	124,930
Total Assets	$ 221,690	$ 194,338
LIABILITIES AND EQUITY		
Current Liabilities		
Accounts payable (principally trade)	$ 26,961	$ 24,062
Short-term debt and current portion of long-term debt		
Automotive	1,167	817
GM Financial	27,861	18,745
Accrued liabilities	29,192	27,593
Total current liabilities	85,181	71,217
Non-current Liabilities		
Long-term debt		
Automotive	9,585	7,948
GM Financial	46,015	35,601
Postretirement benefits other than pensions	5,803	5,685
Pensions	17,951	20,911
Other liabilities	13,080	12,653
Total non-current liabilities	92,434	82,798
Total Liabilities	177,615	154,015
Commitments and contingencies		
Equity		
Common stock, $0.01 par value	15	15
Additional paid-in capital	26,983	27,607
Retained earnings	26,168	20,285
Accumulated other comprehensive loss	(9,330)	(8,036)
Total stockholders' equity	43,836	39,871
Noncontrolling interests	239	452
Total Equity	44,075	40,323
Total Liabilities and Equity	$ 221,690	$ 194,338

Source: GM 10-K report.

EXHIBIT 3 Market Shares

	Years Ended December 31,								
	2016			2015			2014		
	Industry	GM	Market Share	Industry	GM	Market Share	Industry	GM	Market Share
North America									
United States	17,882	3,043	17.0%	17,854	3,082	17.3%	16,859	2,935	17.4%
Other	3,989	587	14.7%	3,650	531	14.5%	3,375	478	14.2%
Total North America	21,871	3,630	16.6%	21,504	3,613	16.8%	20,234	3,413	16.9%
Europe									
United Kingdom	3,121	289	9.3%	3,063	312	10.2%	2,845	305	10.7%
Germany	3,709	260	7.0%	3,540	244	6.9%	3,357	237	7.1%
Other	13,379	658	4.9%	12,704	620	4.9%	12,503	719	5.7%
Total Europe(a)	20,209	1,207	6.0%	19,307	1,176	6.1%	18,705	1,261	6.7%
Asia/Pacific, Middle East, and Africa									
China(b)	28,270	3,914	13.8%	25,050	3,730	14.9%	24,035	3,540	14.7%
Other	18,905	673	3.6%	19,527	795	4.1%	19,722	840	4.3%
Total Asia/Pacific, Middle East, and Africa	47,175	4,587	9.7%	44,577	4,525	10.2%	43,757	4,380	10.0%
South America									
Brazil	2,048	346	16.9%	2,568	388	15.1%	3,498	579	16.6%
Other	1,623	238	14.6%	1,616	257	15.9%	1,815	299	16.5%
Total South America	3,671	584	15.9%	4,184	645	15.4%	5,313	878	16.5%
Total Worldwide	92,926	10,008	10.8%	89,572	9,959	11.1%	88,009	9,932	11.3%
United States									
Cars	6,895	890	12.9%	7,483	931	12.4%	7,617	1,085	14.2%
Trucks	5,464	1,325	24.2%	5,181	1,274	24.6%	4,754	1,113	23.4%
Crossovers	5,523	828	15.0%	5,190	877	16.9%	4,488	737	16.4%
Total United States	17,882	3,043	17.0%	17,854	3,082	17.3%	16,859	2,935	17.4%
China(b)									
SGMS		1,806			1,711			1,710	
SGMW and FAW-GM		2,108			2,019			1,830	
Total China	28,270	3,914	13.8%	25,050	3,730	14.9%	24,035	3,540	14.7%

(a) Our Europe sales include Opel and Vauxhall sales of 1,159, 1,113 and 1,078, and market share of 5.7%, 5.8% and 5.8% in the years ending December 31, 2016, 2015 and 2014.

(b) Our China sales include the Automotive China JVs SAIC General Motors Sales Co., Ltd. (SGMS), SAIC GM Wuling Automobile Co., Ltd. (SGMW) and FAW-GM Light Duty Commercial Vehicle Co., Ltd. (FAW-GM). Wholesale volumes were used for Industry, GM and Market Share. Our retail sales in China were 3,871, 3,613 and 3,435 in the years ended December 31, 2016, 2015 and 2014. In 2017, we will begin using vehicle registrations data as the basis for calculating industry volume and market share in China on a prospective basis.

Source: GM 10-K report.

astonished by the emphasis on past glories and the commitment to the status quo they had found to be quite widespread among the firm's management ranks. "Those values were driven from the top on down," said Rob Kleinbaum, a former GM executive and consultant. "And anybody inside who protested that attitude was buried."[2]

Over the following year, GM was led by two different board members. Edward E. Whitacre, Jr., ran the firm for about a year before being replaced by Dan Ackerson. Ackerson had been appointed by the U.S. government as a board member during GM's bankruptcy. A no-nonsense former navy officer, Ackerson began to address the various problems that continued to plague the firm. There was a strong consensus among the executives that the company was beginning to change its approach to its business. Shortly after he took over, Ackerson wrote in an internal memo: "Our results show that we are changing the company so we never go down that path again."[3]

In January 2014, GM was finally able to move past the bankruptcy. The government-appointed Ackerson was replaced by Barra, who had worked her way up within the firm, and became the first woman to ever run a big automobile company. She had been a rank-and-file engineer, a plant manager, the head of corporate human resources and most recently, the senior executive overseeing all of GM's global product development. Barra's appointment came on the heels of the sale of the last shares that the U.S. government held in the firm, finally making it free of its bankruptcy obligations. "This is truly the next chapter in GM's recovery and turnaround history," Barra told employees upon her appointment. "And I am proud to be a part of it."[4]

Focusing on Fewer Brands

One of the issues that GM had wrestled with for years was the number of brands of vehicles that it offered. For years, the firm had built its position of dominance by offering cars that were designed for different customers by separate divisions. Each of these divisions came to represent a distinct nameplate or brand. Its extensive brand lineup had long been GM's primary weapon in beating back both domestic and foreign rivals. But as the firm's market share began to decline, it became difficult to design and market cars under several brands. In order to cut costs, GM began to share designs and parts across divisions, leading to some loss of distinctiveness among the different brands.

Analysts had been questioning for many years GM's decision to stick with as many as eight U.S. brands, with the recent addition of Hummer. The decision to carry so many brands placed considerable strain on GM's efforts to revamp its product line on a regular basis. The firm agreed to cut out four of its brands, Pontiac, Saturn, Saab, and Hummer, when it was forced to turn to the U.S. government for funding to stay afloat. A. Andrew Shapiro, an analyst, believes that GM should have started to think seriously about cutting back on its car divisions during the 1980s. "There are always short-term reasons for not doing something," commented Shapiro.[5]

Since it has cut down on its brands, GM has been working on revamping its remaining lineup of cars. The firm has been able to successfully reinvent Chevrolet as a global mass-market brand, with over 60 percent of its sales now coming from outside the U.S. Recent sales have been driven by the new Cruze and the plug-in hybrid-Volt. The Volt family of vehicles now ranks as one of the world's leading hybrids. GM is expecting to build upon this success with the new Bolt all-electric subcompact car, which can run for almost 230 miles on a single charge. An executive explained the motivation behind pushing to develop cars that move away from a reliance on fuel: "We wanted to prove we could do it."[6]

GM has also been focusing on strengthening its more upscale brands such as Buick and Cadillac. Buick, the oldest active automobile brand in the U.S., caters to a shrinking population of people over 65. Over the last couple of years, the firm has worked on updating the brand by sticking to its image of "refined luxury" but moving away from being regarded as a living room on wheels. GM has tried to accomplish this by adding new models such as the Casada and the Envision designed to attract a younger, performance-oriented customer. In spite of these efforts, China has become the major market for Buick, which contributes as much as 80 percent of its sales. Buick is no longer offered in most other markets other than the U.S., Canada, and Mexico (see Exhibits 4 to 6).

Finally, GM has separated its Cadillac luxury brand from the others and relocated its headquarters to the trendy SoHo area of New York City. The firm hired Johan de Nysschen away from Audi to manage the brand. De Nysschen pushed for the change, as he believed that the marketing and sales departments will be more in touch with their target customers in super-fashionable SoHo rather than in Detroit. GM earmarked roughly $12 million for developing new Cadillac models in order to compete with the elite class of top-level luxury cars. "It's going to take tremendous time and money," said Uwe Ellinghaus, Cadillac's energetic chief marketing officer. "There's a lot of cultural inertia behind Cadillac, and there's a huge amount of competition coming from a German auto industry that's getting even more aggressive."[7]

Revamping Product Development

GM is trying to get all of the functional areas to work together more closely throughout the product development process. In the past, even if a bold design made it off the drawing board, it had little chance of surviving as it was handed over to marketing, then passed to engineering, and finally sent to manufacturing. In a concentrated effort to wean the GM culture away from a focus on engineering processes, the firm is pushing for designers to get more involved with the development process and for engineers to find ways to stick with the original car design.

Another problem that has plagued GM's product development process has been the lack of standardization of

EXHIBIT 4

Vehicle Sales
(deliveries in
thousands)

	Years Ended	
	December 31, 2016	December 31, 2015
United States		
Chevrolet - Cars	736	767
Chevrolet - Trucks	915	888
Chevrolet - Crossovers	445	471
Cadillac	170	175
Buick	230	223
GMC	547	558
Total United States	3,043	3,082
Canada, Mexico, and Other	587	531
Total North America	3,630	3,613
Europe		
Opel/Vauxhall	1,159	1,113
Chevrolet(a)	48	63
Total Europe	1.207	1,176
Asia/Pacific, Middle East, and Africa(b)		
Chevrolet	987	1,174
Wuling	1,352	1,519
Buick	1,183	1,035
Baojun	755	499
Cadillac	124	87
Other	186	211
Total Asia/Pacific, Middle East, and Africa(b)	4,587	4,525
South America(c)	584	645
Total Worldwide	10,008	9,959

Source: General Motors.

"platforms" on which the firm has built its cars. A platform is the basic underpinnings of a vehicle, and building multiple vehicles on a single platform reduces development and production costs. In India, for example, GM has been producing seven car models using as many as six different underlying platforms, resulting in considerable inefficiencies. Executives admit that the firm has lagged behind its rivals and is only now trying to cut the number of platforms down to 14 by 2018, compared to 30 in 2010. It is also planning to cut down to 12 engine families and eventually just 10, compared to 20 a few years ago.

The firm has assigned engineers to work in car dealerships to learn more about what customers want and need in their cars and trucks. And it has encouraged everyone involved with the design of new vehicles to raise concerns during the development process and to take steps to hold back a new model in order to make changes to improve its chances of success. Since the bankruptcy, GM has been trying to reduce their reliance on sales incentives to sell cars.

At the same time, GM has also been attempting to roll out new models faster by making changes to its cumbersome decision-making process. Under the old system, any

EXHIBIT 5
Income by Operating
Regions ($ millions)

	Years Ended	
	December 31, 2016	December 31, 2015
Operating segments		
GM North America (GMNA)	$ 12,047	$ 11,026
GM Europe (GME)	(257)	(813)
GM International Operations (GMIO)	1,135	1,397
GM South America (GMSA)	(374)	(622)
General Motors Financial Company, Inc. (GM Financial)(a)	913	837
Total operating segments(b)	13,464	11,825
Corporate and eliminations	(934)	(1,011)
EBIT-adjusted	12,530	10,814

Source: General Motors.

EXHIBIT 6
GM Global and Regional
Market Share

	Years Ended	
	December 31, 2016	December 31, 2015
Market Share		
United States - Cars	12.9%	12.4%
United States - Trucks	24.2%	24.6%
United States - Crossovers	15.0%	16.9%
Total United States	17.0%	17.3%
Total North America	16.6%	16.8%
Total Europe	6.0%	6.1%
Total Asia/Pacific, Middle East, and Africa	9.7%	10.2%
Total South America	15.9%	15.4%
Total Worldwide	10.8%	11.1%

Source: General Motors.

product decisions would be reviewed by as many as 70 executives, often taking months for a decision to wind its way through a series of committees. The firm has reduced the number of executives overseeing a vehicle program and come up with a new system where all product decisions are made in a single weekly meeting that is run by the top management team. This has led to much faster decisions.

Responding to Safety Concerns

Even as Barra was working on making GM more efficient, GM executives decided that a recall of the 619,000 Chevrolet Cobalts and Pontiac G5s was necessary.

Questions were being raised about the delay of several years in recalling these vehicles in spite of knowledge of a faulty ignition switch that could cause these cars to shut off and disable the airbags. In 2004, engineers had suggested a fix, but executives decided against it because of potential delays and cost overruns in production. GM finally decided to move only after the reports of accidents that had led to deaths and injuries could no longer be ignored. This was particularly embarrassing for the firm as GM had developed the Cobalt to show that it was no longer cutting corners and was capable of making competitive small cars.

In testimony before a subcommittee of the House Committee on Energy and Commerce, Barra acknowledged that the safety problems resulted from deep underlying problems with the GM culture. A report was released by Anthony R. Valukas, a former U.S. attorney whom the firm hired to conduct a three-month investigation of the decision to ignore the problems with the ignition switch. The findings indicated that all the issues that arose were passed through a number of committees without being resolved. This was typical of the organization. Furthermore, no minutes were taken of any of the meetings to indicate who was responsible or accountable for any decisions that were taken.

Valukas concluded that shifting responsibility for problems back and forth was deep in the firm's DNA. He referred to a GM salute that involved a crossing of arms and pointing outward toward others, indicating that responsibility always belongs to someone else. In particular, Valukas found that employees at GM were actually given formal training about how to avoid accountability in documenting any safety issues. They were told to avoid using words such as "problem" or "defect" and replacing them with softer words such as "safety" or "condition." "The story of the Cobalt is one of a series of individual and organizational failures that led to devastating consequences," Valukas stated to a committee hearing.[8]

Under Barra, GM executives have moved more quickly to respond to the safety problems. The firm dismissed 15 employees, including a vice president for regulatory affairs and several corporate lawyers, and disciplined others. GM has appointed a new global head of vehicle safety and named a new vice president in charge of global product integrity. The company has more than doubled to 55 a team of safety investigators that work within engineering. Finally, it hired a compensation expert to examine claims and make cash settlements for those that either died or were injured as a result of accidents caused by the defective ignition switch. "We are a good company," Barra insisted. "But we can and must be much better."[9]

Firing on All Cylinders?

Barra feels confident that the investments GM has been making will yield results in the future. Not only is the Bolt the first inexpensive long-range electric car on the road, it is also expected to function as the firm's platform for testing new models for ride-sharing and autonomous driving. Soon after GM made an investment in Lyft, it also announced that it would launch a proprietary car-sharing service called Maven. A Zipcar-like offering, Maven taps into another possible future of mobility: replacing ownership with sharing. This start-up within GM, which has features that are not available on Zipcar, lays the groundwork for a possible future when GM owns and operates a fleet of its own autonomous cars that could be tapped for ride-sharing.

Product chief Mark Reuss believes that with its acquisition of Cruise, GM is well positioned to integrate self-driving technology into its cars. Over the last couple of years, GM has already begun to incorporate aspects of self-driving technology into a few of its models, including software that alerts drivers if they veer out of their lane or stops the car if it detects an imminent collision. Talking about the challenges of this technology in cars, Reuss said: "The piece that is not well understood outside of the automotive industry is how hard it is to take technology and integrate it into a car. It seems like you should be able to layer it in and have it work and that would be great."[10]

Barra is aware that none of these moves will matter unless GM continues to make changes in its culture. She has launched initiatives across the firm to push GM in a new direction. These range from a program called GM 2020 which builds cross-functional "co-labs" to address all kinds to problems to a year-long "transformational leadership" course for development of senior executives. With her vision of GM's revved-up culture, Barra tells everyone at GM that best efforts alone will not be enough. "Are you doing what you can?" she asks. "Or are you doing what it takes to win?"[11]

ENDNOTES

1. Rick Tetzeli. The Accelerators. *Fast Company,* November 2016, p. 72.
2. Bill Vlasic. Culture Shock: G.M. Struggles to Shed a Legendry Bureaucracy. *New York Times,* November 13, 2009, p. B4.
3. Michael J. De La Merced & Bill Vlasic. U.S. to Shed Its Stake in General Motors. *New York Times,* December 21, 2012, p. B3.
4. Bill Vlasic. Company Woman Becomes New G.M. Chief. *International New York Times,* December 12, 2013, p. 1.
5. Micheline Maynard. A Painful Departure for Some G.M. Brands. *New York Times,* February 18, 2009, p. B4.
6. Bill Vlasic. To Make Tiny American Car, G.M. Also Shrinks Plant and Wages. *New York Times,* July 13, 2011, p. A19.
7. James B. Stewart. A Bid to Bring Back That Cadillac Swagger. *New York Times,* April 3, 2015, p. B2.
8. Bill Vlasic & Danielle Ivory. G.M. Vows to Address "Cultural Problems" That Led to Deadly Recall Delays. *International New York Times,* June 19, 2014, p. 18.
9. Ibid.
10. *Fast Company,* November 2016, p. 74.
11. Ibid., p. 100.

CASE 19

JOHNSON & JOHNSON[*]

On January 26, 2017, Johnson & Johnson, the world's largest health care company, bolstered its roster of treatments for rare diseases by announcing a $30 billion deal to acquire Actelion, a Swiss biotechnology firm. The deal expanded its portfolio of leading medicines and promising late stage products. "We believe this transaction offers compelling value to both Johnson & Johnson and Actelion shareholders" Alex Gorsky, the chairman and chief executive of J&J, stated in a news release.[1]

With 250 companies in virtually every country, J&J has under its banner the world's largest medical device business, an even bigger pharmaceutical business, and a consumer products division with a dozen megabrands, from Neutrogena to Tylenol. Although the firm is best known for its common consumer products, its biggest recent growth has come from its vast range of pharmaceuticals. J&J has advantages from its diversified businesses such as greater financial stability, a wider range of expertise, and a customer base that spans consumers to hospitals to governments.

Financial stability has been J&J's calling card for decades. Its sales have risen on a regular basis, with profits showing an annualized growth rate of over 12 percent over the three years 2014–2016 (see Exhibits 1 and 2). The firm has consistently raised its dividend for well over 50 years and it remains one of only two U.S. companies with an AAA credit rating from Standard and Poor. "They're in a great position," said Kristen Stewart, an analyst at Deutsche Bank. "They have the luxury of time and the ability to look at different opportunities across different business units. That is what a diversified business platform affords them."[2]

---

[*] Case prepared by Jamal Shamsie, Michigan State University, with the assistance of Professor Alan B. Eisner, Pace University. Material has been drawn from published sources to be used for purposes of class discussion. Copyright © 2017 Jamal Shamsie and Alan B. Eisner.

EXHIBIT 1 Income Statement (in $ millions)

	Year Ending		
	2016	2015	2014
Total Revenue	$71,890	$70,074	$74,331
Gross Profit	21,685	21,536	51,585
Operating Income	20,645	17,556	20,959
Net Income	16,540	15,409	16,323

Source: Johnson & Johnson.

EXHIBIT 2 Balance Sheet (in $ millions)

	Year Ending		
	2016	2015	2014
Current Assets	$ 65,032	$ 60,210	$ 55,744
Total Assets	141,208	133,411	130,358
Current Liabilities	26,287	27,747	25,031
Total Liabilities	70,790	62,261	60,606
Stockholder Equity	70,418	71,150	69,752

Source: Johnson & Johnson.

However, even as it has grown and become more diversified, J&J has struggled to extract the greatest value from its vast portfolio of diversified businesses. Much of its growth has come from acquisitions, and it has developed a culture of granting considerable autonomy to each of the firms that it has absorbed. Although this was intended to cultivate an entrepreneurial attitude among each of its units, it has probably prevented the firm from pursuing opportunities that would result from closer collaboration among the units. Because the units fiercely guard their independence, they have rarely searched for opportunities on which they could combine their different areas of expertise.

William C. Weldon, who spearheaded a period of dramatic growth at J&J, began to direct efforts at trying to get the business units to work with each other on a more regular basis. After Gorsky took over as CEO in 2012, he pushed harder to weave together the operations of the different units. The need for greater oversight became more urgent after the firm ran into quality issues in two of its three divisions, with some consumer products being recalled. At the same time, Gorsky realized that J&J must preserve its entrepreneurial culture.

Cultivating Entrepreneurship

Johnson & Johnson was founded in 1886 by three Johnson brothers. The company grew slowly for a generation before Robert Wood Johnson II decided reluctantly to take the family business public. He fretted about the effects that market pressures would have on the company's practices and values, which led him to write a 307-word statement of corporate principles. This spelled out that J&J's primary responsibility was to patients and physicians, followed by employees, and then by communities. Shareholders were placed last on the list. This credo is inscribed in stone at the entrance of the firm's headquarters and is routinely invoked at the company.

Over the years, as J&J has grown by acquisitions of firms engaged in some aspect of health care, it has been guided by its original credo. The task has become more challenging as J&J has developed into an astonishingly complex enterprise, made up of over 250 different subsidiaries broken into three divisions. The most widely known of these is the division that makes consumer products such as Johnson & Johnson baby care products, Band-Aid adhesive strips, and Visine eye drops. Its pharmaceuticals division sells several blockbuster drugs such as anemia drug Procit and schizophrenia drug Risperdal. Its medical devices division is responsible for best selling products such as Depuy orthopedic joint replacements and Cyper coronary stents.

J&J's credo has kept the firm focused on quality of health care, even as it has expanded into several different business segments and adopted a decentralized approach in managing its different businesses. Most of its far-flung subsidiaries across its three divisions were acquired because of potential demonstrated by promising new products in their pipeline. Each of these units was granted near-total autonomy to develop and expand upon their best selling products in order to better serve their patients (see Exhibit 3).

EXHIBIT 3 Segment Information

Johnson & Johnson is made up of over 250 different companies, many of which it has acquired over the years. These individual companies have been assigned to three different divisions.

Geographic Areas			
		Sales to Customers	
(Dollars in Millions)	2016	2015	2014
Consumer —			
United States	$ 5,420	5,222	5,096
International	7,887	8,285	9,400
Total	13,307	13,507	14,496
Pharmaceutical —			
United States	20,125	18,333	17,432
International	13,339	13,097	14,881
Total	33,464	31,430	32,313
Medical Devices —			
United States	12,266	12,132	12,254
International	12,853	13,005	15,268
Total	25,119	25,137	27,522
Worldwide total	$71,890	70,074	74,331

Business Segments					
	Income Before Tax			Identifiable Assets	
(Dollars in Millions)	2016	2015	2014	2016	2015
Consumer	$ 2,441	1,787	1,941	$ 23,971	20,772
Pharmaceutical	12,827	11,734	11,696	27,477	26,144
Medical Devices	5,578	6,826	7,953	39,773	40,979
Total	20,846	20,347	21,590	91,221	87,895
Less: Expense not allocated to segments	1,043	1,151	1,027		
General corporate				49,987	45,516
Worldwide total	$19,803	19,196	20,563	$141,208	133,411

Source: J&J.

It is widely believed that this independence has fostered an entrepreneurial attitude that has kept J&J intensely competitive. The relative autonomy that is accorded to the business units has provided the firm with the ability to respond swiftly to emerging opportunities. A commitment from everyone throughout these units to the principles that had been laid out in the famous credo was considered to be sufficient to provide the necessary direction.

J&J is proud of the considerable freedom that it gives to its different subsidiaries to develop and execute their own strategies. Besides developing their strategies, these units have also been allowed to work with their own resources. Many of them have been able to operate their own finance and human resources departments. While this degree of decentralization led to relatively high overhead costs, none of the executives that have run J&J, Weldon included, have ever thought that this was too high a price to pay. "J&J is a huge company, but you didn't feel like you were in a big company," recalled a scientist who used to work there.[3]

Pushing for More Collaboration

The entrepreneurial culture at Johnson & Johnson has consistently developed top-notch products in each of the areas in which it operates. It spends heavily on research and development (see Exhibit 4), currently about 12 percent of its sales on about 9,000 scientists working in research laboratories around the world. The three divisions continually introduce promising new products.

In spite of the benefits that J&J has derived from giving its various enterprises considerable autonomy, however, there have been growing concerns that they can no longer be allowed to operate in near isolation. Weldon soon realized that J&J was in a strong position to exploit new opportunities by drawing on the diverse skills across the three divisions. The firm might derive more benefits from combining its knowledge in drugs, devices, and diagnostics, since few companies matched its reach and strength in these basic areas. This led Weldon to seek ways to make its fiercely independent units work together. In his words: "There is a convergence that will allow us to do things we haven't done before."[4] Through pushing the various far-flung units of the firm to pool their resources, Weldon believed they could deliver real synergy. Accordingly, he created a corporate office that would get business units to work together on promising new opportunities. "It's a recognition that there's a way to treat disease that's not in silos," Weldon stated, referring to collaboration between J&J's largely independent businesses.[5]

For the most part, however, Weldon confined himself to taking steps to foster better communication and more frequent collaboration among J&J's disparate operations. He was convinced that such a push for communication and coordination would allow the firm to develop the synergy that he was seeking. But any effort to get the different business units to collaborate must not quash the entrepreneurial spirit that has always spearheaded most of the growth of the firm. Jerry Caccott, managing director of consulting firm Strategic Decisions Group, emphasized that cultivating those alliances "would be challenging in any organization, but particularly in an organization that has been so successful because of its decentralized culture."[6]

These collaborative efforts did lead to the introduction of some highly successful new products (see Exhibit 5). Even the company's fabled consumer brands have started

EXHIBIT 4 Research Expenditures (in $ millions)

2016	$9,095
2015	9,046
2014	8,494
2013	8,183
2012	7,665
2011	7,548
2010	6,864
2009	6,986
2008	7,577
2007	7,680
2006	7,125
2005	6,462

Source: J&J.

EXHIBIT 5 Significant Innovations

Antiseptic Surgery (1888)

Three brothers start up a firm based on antiseptics designed for modern surgical practices.

Band-Aids (1921)

Debuts the first commercial bandages that can be applied at home without oversight by a professional.

No More Tears (1954)

Introduces a soap-free shampoo that is gentle enough to clean babies' hair without irritating their eyes.

Acuvue Contact Lenses (1987)

Offers the first-ever disposable lenses that can be worn for up to a week and then thrown away.

Sirturo (2012)

Gets approval to launch a much-needed treatment for drug-resistant tuberculosis, the first new medication to fight this disease in more than 40 years.

Source: *Fast Company,* March 2014.

to show growth as a result of increased collaboration between the consumer products and pharmaceutical divisions. Its new liquid Band-Aid is based on a material used in a wound-closing product sold by one of J&J's hospital-supply businesses. And J&J has used its prescription antifungal treatment, Nizoral, to develop a dandruff shampoo. By now, products that have developed in large part out of such cross-fertilization have allowed the firm's consumer business to experience considerable internal growth.

Making a Difficult Transition

As Johnson & Johnson sought more interaction among its business units, it ran into problems with quality control with two of its divisions. Its medical devices division ran into problems with its newest artificial hip. It recalled the device, amidst rumors that company executives may have concealed information out of concern for firm profits. These problems were compounded by serious issues that arose with the consumer products division, which led to the biggest children's drug recall of all time.

Quality problems had arisen before, but they were usually fixed in a routine manner inside the units. Analysts suggest that problems at subsidiary McNeil may have been exacerbated in 2006 when J&J decided to combine it with the newly acquired consumer health care unit from Pfizer. The firm believed that it could achieve $500 to $600 million in annual savings by merging the two units together. After the merger, McNeil was also transferred from the heavily regulated pharmaceutical division to the marketing driven consumer products division, which was not subjected to the same level of quality control.

Much of the blame for such stumbles fell on Weldon, who stepped down as CEO in April 2012 after presiding over one of the most tumultuous decades in the firm's history. Critics said the company's once vaunted attention to quality had slipped under his watch. Weldon, who had started out as sales representative at the firm, was believed to have been obsessed with meeting tough performance targets, even by cutting costs that might affect quality. Erik Gordon, who teaches business at the University of Michigan, elaborated on this cost-cutting philosophy: "We will make our numbers for the analysts, period."[7]

In April 2012, J&J appointed Gorsky to lead the way out of the difficulties. Gorsky had been with the firm since 1988, holding positions in its pharmaceutical businesses across Europe, Africa, and the Middle East before leaving for a few years to work at Novartis. Shortly after his return to J&J in 2008, he took over its medical devices unit that was being investigated about its faulty hip replacements. Because of his extensive background with the firm, Gorsky was regarded as the ideal person to take the job.

When Gorksy took over as CEO, it was expected that he would sort out the quality problems that had recently surfaced at the firm. But because he was a consummate insider, having run the two biggest of its three divisions, it was assumed he would do it without major changes.

However, shortly after he settled into his job as CEO, Gorsky began to challenge the firm's once-sacrosant principle of giving complete autonomy to its 250-odd units. In his view, decentralization that fostered creativity should not allow these different units to be completely disconnected. Gorksy wanted to push further than Weldon had to get the various units of the firm to work together to find synergies, to cross-fertilize ideas, and to reap cost savings that could be reinvested in the business.

Pushing for Tighter Integration

In order to tie the units more closely together, Gorsky lured Sandi Peterson from Bayer and gave her the position of group worldwide chairman. The newly created position gave Peterson sweeping responsibly to oversee technology across the entire firm. Gorsky believed that the very nature of the job required him to hire an outsider who had not had much exposure to J&J's existing culture. Because decentralization had allowed the business units to make all of their own decisions, there had been no consistency in their different practices. Gorsky wanted to bring order to this unwieldy machine. "Sometimes a customer doesn't want to deal with 250 J&J's," he said.[8]

Peterson began feverishly working to align everything from HR policy to procurement processes from the 250 business units, which had been making their own decisions independently. She covered everything from the timing of financial forecasts to employee car policies, consolidating all of the firm's data, such as about all of its 120,000 employees, to a single HR database. Peterson claimed that her efforts would allow the company to save about $1 billion. She processed as much data per day as eBay, warehousing about 500 terabytes of data. According to Peterson, this represented "2.5 times as much data as resides in the IRS data warehouse."[9]

An even more significant effort had already been initiated by Paul Stoffels three years earlier when he was appointed J&J's global head of pharmaceuticals. All of the units that operated within the pharmaceutical division had also operated with complete autonomy. J&J's seven different drug R&D organizations had operated in completely siloed fashion. In some cases, multiple companies pursued the development of the same drugs and each had its own system for handling clinical or regulatory development. Stoffels began to merge all of the units under his purview into one group and organized it to target 11 diseases. In the process, 12 of the division's 25 facilities were shuttered and nearly 200 projects were slashed.

This new integrated unit developed a streamlined development process, a highly coordinated system that Stoffels calls Accererando. Under this model, global teams—statisticians in China, data managers in India, regulatory folks in Europe—work 24/7 to speed drugs to market. The assembly-line approach has cut months, and in some cases years, off development time. Seventeen drug approvals in 10 years put J&J in a league of its own. "No other company has come close to that," said Bernard Munos, a pharmaceutical innovation consultant.[10]

Stoffels has accomplished more than just reduce the time needed to bring drugs to market. He has begun to look for ideas from all sources, whether it is from any of J&J's own business units or from entrepreneurs or scientists outside the firm. He has set up four innovation centers in biotech clusters in Cambridge, MA; Menlo Park, CA; London; and Shanghai, where scientific entrepreneurs can interact with J&J's own drug and technology scouts. His flexible approach with these outsiders lets J&J work with them more casually and helps build stronger relationships. Since 2013, the firm has reviewed more than 3,400 opportunities through these centers, leading to 200 partnerships.

Is There a Cure Ahead?

Gorsky's biggest challenge came from a demand that Johnson & Johnson might be better off if it was broken off into smaller companies, perhaps along the lines of its different divisions. There were growing concerns about the ability of the conglomerate to provide sufficient supervision to all of its subsidiaries that were spread all over the globe. Gorsky dismissed the proposal, claiming that J&J drew substantial benefits from the diversified nature of its businesses. Given the enormous shifts in the health care industry and the large number of government and institutional customers and partners involved, he believed that the firm's huge scale could be a rare asset for negotiating deals.

Gorsky did concede, however, that the firm will have to be more selective, careful, and decisive about the products that it pursues. Since he took over, J&J has begun to divest some of its lower growth businesses and reduce annual costs by $1 billion. The firm had just completed the sale of Cordis, which makes medical devices such as stents and catheters. J&J, which helped to develop the roughly $5 billion global market for cardiac stents, announced that it was shifting its focus to other medical technologies that showed more potential for growth.

As he plotted a future course for Johnson & Johnson, Gorsky realized that although much of the firm's success had always resulted from the relative autonomy granted to each of its businesses, he must continue to emphasize ongoing collaboration among them to pursue emerging opportunities. As recent problems had demonstrated, it was also critical for J&J to maintain and develop sufficient quality control across its vast business. The health care giant must manage its diversified portfolio of companies to keep growing without creating issues that could pose any further threats to its reputation. "This is a company that was purer than Caesar's wife, this was the gold standard, and all of a sudden it just seems like things are breaking down," said William Trombetta, a professor of pharmaceutical marketing at Saint Joseph's University in Philadephia.[11]

ENDNOTES

1. Chad Bray. Johnson & Johnson Says It Will Acquire Actelion. *New York Times,* January 27, 2017, p. B5.
2. Erika Fry. Can Big Still Be Beautiful? *Fortune,* August 1, 2016, p. 84.
3. Katie Thomas & Reed Abelson. J&J Chief to Resign One Role. *New York Times,* February 22, 2012, p. B8.
4. Katie Thomas. J&J's Next Chief Is Steeped in Sales Culture. *New York Times,* February 24, 2012, p. B8.
5. Peter Loftus & Shirley S. Wang. J&J Sales Show Health Care Feels the Pinch. *Wall Street Journal,* January 21, 2009, p. B1.
6. Avery Johnson. J&J's Consumer Play Paces Growth. *Wall Street Journal,* January 24, 2007, p. A3.
7. *New York Times,* February 24, 2012, p. B.6.
8. *Fortune,* August 1, 2016, p. 86.
9. Ibid., p. 87.
10. Ibid., p. 88.
11. Natasha Singer. Hip Implants Are Recalled by J&J Unit. *New York Times,* August 27, 2010, p. B1.

CASE 20

AVON: A NEW ERA?*

"If we stop and look over the past and then into the future, we can see that the possibilities are growing greater and greater every day; that we have scarcely begun to reach the proper results from the field we have before us."

—David McConnell, Avon Founder, late 19th century[1]

Overcoming the Challenges

The year of Avon Products' 131th anniversary, 2017, brought numerous challenges for CEO Sheri McCoy. For the first time since David McConnell had founded Avon in 1886, his vision of endless possibilities and growth for Avon had begun to seem unattainable. Could McCoy prove the naysayers wrong and return the iconic, direct-selling company to profitable growth? Or was it time to wake up and sell the company to an interested bidder?

CEO McCoy had recently taken some promised steps to turn around the company. To combat their continuous financial deficit, Avon had made a strategic partnership deal with Cerberus Capital Management, a prominent financial institution based in New York City. Avon Products sold 80 percent of its North American business to Cerberus Capital Management for $170 million, forming a separate private entity called New Avon LLC. Cerberus had also bought

* This case was developed by graduate students Saad Nazir, Dev Das, and Professor Alan B. Eisner, Pace University. Material has been drawn from published sources to be used for class discussion. Copyright © 2017 Alan B. Eisner.

approximately 16.6 percent of Avon Products Inc.'s international business, investing an additional $435 million.[2] New Avon LLC appointed former president of Abbot Laboratories Scott White as its CEO on April 25, 2016. White had a proven record of delivering consistent revenue growth at Abbott Laboratories.[3] The formation of New Avon LLC was expected to take advantage of significant operational expertise from Cerberus Capital. Having thus split Avon Product's North American business with Cerberus Capital, CEO Sheri McCoy expected that additional capital and suspension of dividend payouts would enable the company to achieve some operational efficiency and financial flexibility.

Ms. McCoy had laid out a three-year transformation plan for Avon starting 2016 through 2018 to improve the declining revenues and to achieve cost efficiency. The transformation plan had three key objectives: driving out cost, improving financial resilience, and investing in growth.[4] First, in order to drive out cost by about $350 million by the end of 2018, the company would move Avon Products' headquarters from New York to the United Kingdom and cut about 2,500 jobs. Despite the Brexit vote, the decision to relocate the company headquarters to the U.K. was expected to save about $70 million by 2017. It also put the company closer to its lucrative European customers.[5] Second, to improve financial resilience, the company suspended dividend payouts and divested its Liz Earle business, in addition to making the promising Cerberus deal. Third, the company would invest in growth by increasing digital media spending to expand their product presence in the market. (See Exhibit 1.)

EXHIBIT 1
Avon's Three-Year Transformation Plan

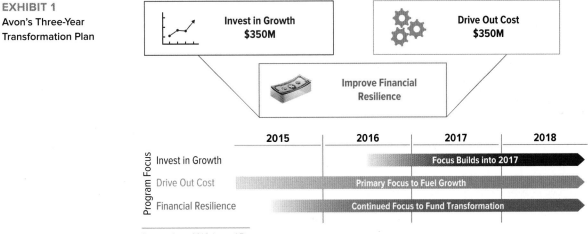

Source: Avon 2015 Annual Report.

CEO McCoy stated that the execution of the transformation plan would be evolutionary over at least three years and must reflect the direct-selling representative perspective. Improving growth of their direct-selling representatives in the most promising markets was another significant priority for the company. In the past, radical changes to selling approaches had been unsuccessful (e.g., selling Avon products in retail locations) because they had attempted to do too much too fast and did not involve the critical direct-selling representatives in the planning process.

There were other challenges. In several emerging markets within the Latin America, EMEA,[6] and Asia-Pacific regions, intense competition and price discounting threatened to erode market share and profitability. On the other hand, the company's attempted price increases in these markets had only hurt its cause further. Last but not least, Avon had agreed to a $135 million settlement to address charges that it had violated the Foreign Corrupt Practices Act (FCPA) in China. This fine was nearly 10 times higher than its original settlement offer to the Securities and Exchange Commission (SEC).

Avon Background—First 100 Years Marked by Opportunity and Growth[7]

Unique Opportunity for Women

In 1886, David H. McConnell, a book salesman from rural New York, created a novel opportunity for women—a chance to become financially independent by selling perfumes. This was at a time when only one-fifth of women in the United States were working outside the home and for wages that were a fraction of what men earned. Most of these working women were employed in agriculture, domestic service, and manufacturing jobs, which did not always provide safe environments.

As a book salesman, McConnell had noticed that his women customers were far more interested in free perfume samples than in the books he sold. He had started using these samples as "door openers" when visiting the homes of potential customers. But McConnell had also noticed one more need that, if effectively tapped, could provide tremendous growth potential for both him and his women customers. Women were looking for ways to supplement their household incomes, and he believed many would make the perfect perfume salespersons for other women customers. McConnell could offer women the opportunity to create and manage their own perfume businesses using a unique direct-selling approach. Earning a commission for selling perfumes to other women like themselves could create an exciting and glamorous solution for an existing need.

McConnell's first recruit for Avon, or the California Perfume Company as it was known then, was Mrs. P. F. E. Albee of New Hampshire. He provided Albee and other early sales representatives with an earnings opportunity within a supportive, family-like environment. The attractiveness of the offering was tremendous, and the army of

representatives rose to 5,000 within only 13 years. With the seed of an idea, McConnell had created a "company for women," which would eventually become the slogan for the company a century later.

Pioneering Direct-Selling Model

The company had thus pioneered a new direct-selling model. Company representatives sold products directly to the end users, bypassing any go-between distribution channels. The model generated efficiencies by eliminating the need for a middleman. In addition it made for direct and regular contact with consumers.

In the late 19th century, direct selling at Avon connected women, who were otherwise isolated and immersed in domestic life, through what the company called "the original social network." An intimate, personal selling approach allowed many women to bond over beauty products. Many women no longer had to travel to the closest department store or drugstore to purchase beauty products or seek beauty advice. The Avon Ladies (as the sales representatives came to be known) brought the store to them. Decades of success followed, and Avon and its direct-selling approach became famous.

In the 1970s and 1980s, when the company's core customer base of stay-at-home women began to shrink, the company adapted its direct-selling approach to keep up with the times. Avon Ladies began to leave samples and call-back brochures on front doorknobs, and with more women entering the workforce, even began offering the opportunity to buy products at the workplace.

Direct selling continued to evolve over the years as needs and technologies evolved. The advent of the Internet prompted the company to engage in online promotion and to offer online selling options. In 2017, realizing the growing importance of e-commerce, CEO McCoy decided to further increase spending on digital media sources.

The Power of Partnerships

Fragrances were the first products Avon (then known as the California Perfume Company) sold, and they became an integral part of the company product line. Avon relied on partnerships to market its fragrance products. Celebrities from the movie and music industries were often used in advertising and created excitement for new fragrance launches. In addition, partnerships with fashion designers were established for enhanced image and efficiency.

New Century Brings Many Changes

Evolution of the Direct-Selling Model

Throughout the long history of the company, representatives could earn money only on commissions by selling to customers. With the launch of Avon's Sales Leadership program in the 1990s, representatives could now also earn money by recruiting and training others. This new earnings avenue exponentially increased the amount of money an individual representative could generate.

With the advent of the Internet, Avon created a collection of digital tools that enabled representatives to use the technology in their businesses. Online ordering, an e-brochure, and customized online communities allowed Avon Ladies to contemporize their offerings and image.

"The relevance of direct selling has to do with what the consumer expects from service," said Angie Rossi, group vice president of North America Sales. "There will always be a space for relationship-based service to the consumer." So, while the media and tools might change with time, the company believed the relevance of direct selling as a strategy would never diminish.

In the 21st century, Avon was producing and selling its products worldwide through its direct-selling, boutique store, and online channels.

Launch of New Products and Partnerships[8]

The first product that Avon sold was the Little Dot Perfume Set. Over time, Avon product sales expanded to a wide range of color cosmetics, as well as skin care, fragrance, fashion, and home products. Some of its more established brand names were Avon Color, ANEW, Skin-So-Soft, Advance Techniques, and *mark*. Revenues came from three main categories:

- *Beauty* (73 percent of net sales): cosmetics, fragrances, and personal care products.
- *Fashion* (17 percent of net sales): jewelry, watches, apparel and accessories.
- *Home* (10 percent of net sales): home products and decorative products.

The company continued to rely on celebrity partnerships to launch and market its new (mainly fragrance) products. These included Uninhibited by Cher (1988) and Undeniable by Billy Dee Williams (1990). Outspoken by Fergie (2010) was the most successful fragrance launch in the company's history. The company then teamed up with the popular singer to offer a follow-up fragrance, Outspoken Intense (2011). American Ballet Theatre, was the new face of Avon Prima that highlighted creative confidence among women (2016).

Avon also established partnerships with international design houses Christian Lacroix, Herve Leger, and Ungaro, which allowed the company to offer premium products at affordable prices for its mainstream customer base. On the fashion apparel front, it teamed up with designer Diane von Furstenberg to create a customized line for Avon called The Color Authority.

Expansion into Emerging Markets

The 20th century had seen expansion into neighboring markets in Canada and Latin America. As the 21st century approached, Avon was rapidly expanding into additional emerging markets.[9]

The company started selling its products in China in 1990. However, a direct-selling ban in China forced the company to open brick-and-mortar retail locations (Beauty Boutiques) within the Chinese market. The ban was lifted in 2006, and the company then started to sell via both direct-selling and retail routes in China. Avon also expanded into Russia in 1993 with retail stores, and it started direct selling its products there in 1995.

By 2016, Avon products were sold in over 100 countries (sold through subsidiaries in 63 and through distributors in an additional 41). Operations were managed over four regions: North America, Latin America, EMEA (Europe, Middle East, Africa), Asia-Pacific. Latin America now accounted for nearly half of total company revenues, with Brazil being the largest market (see Exhibit 2).

Global and Regional Competition

On a broader level, Avon's beauty products faced competition from international cosmetics companies (e.g., Procter & Gamble, L'Oreal, Estee Lauder, Revlon, and Mary Kay) as well as regional players (e.g., Natura in Brazil).

In the direct-selling space, the company primarily competed with Mary Kay, which had a similar product lineup. Mary Kay Inc. was created in 1963 by Mary Kay Ash, direct-selling sales director, who believed women needed more opportunities in business.[10] Mary Kay and Avon used slightly different approaches to reimbursing their representatives:

- Avon representatives (Avon Ladies) bought their products on credit without paying for anything up front. After completing product sales, they reimbursed the company for the products and pocketed a 20 percent margin.
- Mary Kay representatives considered themselves "skin care consultants" and were required to invest $100 up front to buy a demo kit to provide skin care and makeup training to customers. To maintain the position, consultants had to buy at least $200 worth of Mary Kay products at 50 percent wholesale discount offered by the company.

By the beginning of 2017, Avon was one of the biggest direct-selling enterprises globally, with over 6 million active sales representatives. Between 2006 and 2011, this selling route had grown by an impressive 30 percent into a $136 billion global market. Unlike traditional retailers, which used a pull strategy to get customers into the store, direct selling was a push business.[11]

Direct selling also presented a tremendous entrepreneurship opportunity in emerging markets like Brazil, Russia, China, and India. Avon faced intense competition from Mary Kay in recruiting representatives in these markets.[12] In Brazil, Avon also faced intense competition from a regional direct-selling player, Natura. Direct selling accounted for nearly one-third of the sales of beauty products in the country, due to an underdeveloped retail sector.

Avon's remaining beauty competitors distributed their products to retail resellers such as department

EXHIBIT 2 Business by Region

Total Revenue	2016	2015	2014
Europe, Middle East, and Africa	$2,138.2	$2,229.2	$2,614.1
South Latin America	2,145.9	2,309.6	3,028.9
North Latin America	829.9	901.0	1,003.6
Asia Pacific	556.0	626.0	700.9
Total segment revenue	5,670.0	6,065.8	7,347.5
Other operating segments and business activities	47.7	94.7	300.5
Total revenue	$5,717.7	$6,160.5	$7,648.0
Operating Profit	**2016**	**2015**	**2014**
Segment Profit			
Europe, Middle East, and Africa	$ 329.9	$ 311.2	$ 432.3
South Latin America	200.5	238.9	466.0
North Latin America	114.4	107.2	128.3
Asia Pacific	59.9	68.6	59.0
Total segment profit	704.7	725.9	1,085.6

Source: Avon 2016 annual report.

stores, drugstores, or cosmetic stores. In recent years more of these competitors and channels had begun offering discounted products that encroached on Avon's traditional value-shopping customer base. Many international competitors like L'Oreal had also made major strides in growing the retail channel within emerging markets like Brazil.

In the fashion and home categories, Avon had competitors in the jewelry, accessories, apparel, housewares, and gift and decorative products industries globally, including retail establishments (principally department stores, gift shops and specialty retailers, and mass merchandisers) and direct-sales companies specializing in these products.

Management Changes[13]

The 1990s ushered in a period of management change and the first woman CEO in the company's history. Andrea Jung arrived at the company in 1993 with a background in high-end retail (i.e., Neiman Marcus, I. Magnin, and Bloomingdale's). She was appointed by then-CEO Jim Preston to look into the feasibility of selling Avon products in retail outlets. Jung quickly assessed that Avon didn't have the right packaging or positioning to compete in that arena. Impressed by her work, Preston invited her to join the company full-time in 1994 as president of the product marketing group for Avon U.S., a newly created position.

When Preston retired in 1998 after nine years with the company, Charles Perrin (Avon board member and former head of Duracell) became the new CEO. Jung rose to the prominent role of president and chief operating officer. Perrin had planned on staying for about five years but remained for less than two. Jung then took over in November 1999, becoming the first woman to ever lead the company.

Focus Shifts from Direct Selling to Retailing and Marketing

In 1998, Avon opened the Avon Center, with a store, spa, and salon, in Trump Tower on Fifth Avenue. When Jung became CEO in 1999, Avon adopted the slogan "the company for women," moving away from its long-time ad campaign "Ding Dong, Avon Calling." The change was meant to modernize Avon, but it also paralleled a shift in focus within the company. The old tagline emphasized the direct-selling side of the business; now the priority was retail.

A year later, Jung launched the "Let's Talk" global advertising initiative, with Venus and Serena Williams as spokespersons. Advertising spending jumped from $63 million in 1999 to a high point of $400 million in 2010. "Mark," a hipper, trendier product line, was launched to attract a younger demographic and contemporize the company's image.

Business Slows Down Due to Competition and Execution Issues

In 2005, earnings flattened for the first time due to competitive encroachments in key markets. Avon completed a major restructuring, cutting 30 percent of managers and chopping its 15 layers down to 8. Consultants were hired and acquisitions explored to achieve growth. Senior managers were brought in from top-tier companies that Avon wanted to emulate. Liz Smith, who joined as president of global brand marketing in 2005 after working for Kraft, tried to bring a new kind of discipline to Avon. New rigor was infused into the marketing evaluation and execution process. The changes created some friction with existing managers. "Avon's an iconic brand," said one former marketing executive in the U.S. business. "It's not the same as macaroni and cheese."

Another restructuring began in 2009 and left employees demoralized and uncertain about the leadership and future of the company. Rather than working toward a long-term vision, employees often felt as though they were patching up problems for the short term. "At Avon, when something doesn't go right, just put some concealer on it," said a former communications manager. A major gap appeared to exist between what the company wanted to accomplish and what it was capable of executing:

Also in 2010, Avon announced an ambitious five-year plan called the "Road to $20 billion." Less than a year later, the company cut off funding for most of the initiatives in this plan. Executives then communicated a new directive that Avon would eventually hit $20 billion but not by 2017. Avon had revenues of only $5.57 billion by 2016 (see Exhibits 3 and 4).

Problems in Emerging Markets

Avon pursued an ambitious global growth strategy by expanding its presence in Brazil and China. Unfortunately, there were several hiccups in this ambitious effort.

Brazil Brazil was the third-largest beauty market, behind the United States and Japan. Importantly, direct selling accounted for almost 30 percent of the booming market. Vivienne Rudd, head of beauty research at Mintel, explained: "The retail structure in Brazil isn't sufficiently developed yet for the beauty industry, so direct selling is a much more valuable model." Brazil surpassed the U.S. in 2010 to become the biggest market for Avon in terms of sales, but managing operations there proved to be a major challenge.

When the government required electronic invoicing for tax purposes in June 2010, Avon's computer systems were not prepared to handle the additional load. The change created service issues for representatives, forecasting problems, and product shortages.

A year later the company went ahead with implementing a new information-management system in Brazil, one it had been planning for nearly two years. However, when the new

system went live, there were additional execution problems. Orders were missed, and shipments to representatives got delayed. The service problems dragged down sales, with nearly half of the decrease coming from lost sales due to a problem with representatives. Unlike the case in the U.S. direct-sales market, representatives in Brazil often sold for multiple companies, and Avon lost many of them to its regional competitor, Natura.

China In China, Avon's problems were more pronounced. Avon opened for business there in 1990 amid press reports that the company had sold out six months' worth of inventory in just four weeks. However, a direct-selling ban by the Chinese government in 1998 forced Avon to seek alternate approaches to selling and eventually open brick-and-mortar locations called Beauty Boutiques. Avon received the first license to resume direct selling in China in 2006.

Despite these efforts, in 2008 Avon received a whistleblower letter with allegations of bribery and possible violations of the Foreign Corrupt Practices Act. Avon began an internal investigation, which subsequently led to the departure of six employees. The highest-level dismissal took place in January 2012, when Avon reported that Charles Cramb, the former CFO, was no longer with the company. In October 2012, Avon disclosed that the SEC had opened a formal investigation. (The company finally settled for a whopping $135 million with the agency.)[14]

New CEO Seeks New Solutions

Faced with Avon's soft performance and also its legal issues, the board decided the company needed a change of leadership. Jung resigned as CEO in 2011, and the search for a new CEO began.

In April 2012, Sheri McCoy was appointed CEO of the company. She came with a proven track record at the Johnson & Johnson (J&J) Company, where she was responsible for the global pharmaceutical and consumer businesses. The consumer business included well-known skin care brands like Neutrogena. She had a good pedigree, with a master's in chemical engineering from Princeton and broad experience in a number of roles of increasing responsibility at J&J. Despite the impressive background, McCoy had no prior experience in direct selling. In some ways, her profile matched that of Jung when Jung took the reins of the company.

Shortly after becoming Avon CEO in 2012, McCoy sought the input of current and former sales representatives to hear firsthand what the company could do better. She then used the information to develop a plan for the future, and she laid out how this plan would be different from things the company had tried in the past.

As she prepared to lead the transformation of the company, she made some critical changes to her executive team:[15]

EXHIBIT 3 Avon Products, Inc., Consolidated Income Statements ($ millions, except per-share data)

	Years Ended December 31		
	2016	2015	2014
Net sales	$5,578.8	$ 6,076.5	$7,472.5
Other revenue	138.9	84.0	175.5
Total revenue	5,717.7	6,160.5	7,648.0
Costs, expenses and other:			
Cost of sales	2,257.0	2,445.4	3,006.9
Selling, general and administrative expenses	3,138.8	3,543.2	4,206.8
Impairment of goodwill	—	6.9	—
Operating prolit	321.9	165.0	434.3
Interest expense	136.6	120.5	108.8
(Gain) loss on extinguishment of debt	(1.1)	5.5	—
Interest income	(15.8)	(12.5)	(14.8)
Other expense, net	171.0	73.7	139.5
Gain on sale of business	—	(44.9)	—
Total other expenses	290.7	142.3	233.5
Income from continuing operations, before taxes	31.2	22.7	200.8
Income taxes	(124.6)	(819.2)	(545.3)
Loss from continuing operations, net of tax	(93.4)	(796.5)	(344.5)
Loss from discontinued operations, net of tax	(14.0)	(349.1)	(40.4)
Net loss	(107.4)	(1,145.6)	(384.9)
Net income attributable to nonconlrolling interests	(0.2)	(3.3)	(3.7)
Net loss attributable to Avon	$ (107.6)	$(1,148.9)	$ (388.6)
Loss per share:			
Basic from continuing operations	$ (0.25)	$ (1.81)	$ (0.79)
Basic from discontinued operations	(0.03)	(0.79)	(0.09)
Basic attributable to Avon	(0.29)	(2.60)	(0.88)
Diluted from continuing operations	$ (0.25)	$ (1.81)	$ (0.79)
Diluted from discontinued operations	(0.03)	(0.79)	(0.09)
Diluted attributable to Avon	(0.29)	(2.60)	(0.88)
Weighted-average shares outstanding:			
Basic	437.0	435.2	434.5
Diluted	437.0	435.2	434.5

Source: Avon 2016 annual report.

	December 31	
	2016	2015
Assets		
Current Assets		
Cash, including cash equivalents of $79.4 and $123.2	$ 654.4	$ 686.9
Accounts receivable (less allowances of $131.1 and $86.7)	458.9	443.0
Inventories	586.4	624.0
Prepaid expenses and other	291.3	296.1
Current assets of discontinued operations	1.3	291.1
Total current assets	1,992.3	2,341,1
Property, plant and equipment, at cost		
Land	29.5	32.2
Buildings and improvements	621.5	665.8
Equipment	773.1	797.7
	1,424.1	1,495.7
Less accumulated depreciation	(712.8)	(728.8)
Property, plant and equipment, net	711.3	766.9
Goodwill	93.6	92.3
Other assets	621.7	490.0
Noncurrent assets of discontinued operations	—	180.1
Total assets	$3,418.9	$3,870.4
Liabilities and Shareholders' (Deficit) Equity		
Current Liabilities		
Debt maturing within one year	$18.1	$ 55.2
Accounts payable	768.1	774.2
Accrued compensation	129.2	157.6
Other accrued liabilities	401.9	419.6
Sales and taxes other than income	147.0	174.9
Income taxes	10.7	23.9
Payable to discontinued operations	—	100.0
Current liabilities of discontinued operations	10.7	489.7
Total current liabilities	1,485.7	2,195.1
Long-term debt	1,875.8	2,150.5
Employee benefit plans	164.5	177.5

continued

EXHIBIT 4 *Continued*

	December 31	
	2016	2015
Long-term income taxes	78.6	65.1
Other liabilities	205.8	78.4
Noncurrent liabilities of discontinued operations	—	260.2
Total liabilities	3,810.4	4,926.8
Commitments and contingencies (Notes 14 and 17)		
Series C convertible preferred stock	444.7	—
Shareholders' Deficit		
Common stock, par value $.25 - authorized 1,500 shares; issued 754.9 and 751.4 shares	188.8	187.9
Additional paid-in capital	2,273.9	2,254.0
Retained earnings	2,322.2	2,448.1
Accumulated other comprehensive loss	(1,033.2)	(1,366.2)
Treasury stock, at cost (317.3 and 315.9 shares)	(4,599.7)	(4,594.1)
Total Avon shareholders' deficit	(848.0)	(1,070.3)
Nocontrolling interests	11.8	13.9
Total shareholders' deficit	(836.2)	(1,056.4)
Total liabilities, series C convertible preferred stock and shareholders' deficit	$3,418.9	$3,870.4

Source: Avon 2016 Annual Report.

- In August 2012, McCoy made her first C-level appointment: PR expert Cheryl Heinonen was recruited as chief communications officer and senior vice president of Corporate Relations. The company could clearly benefit from an image makeover.
- Soon after, McCoy appointed Jeff Benjamin and Scott Crum to lead the Legal and Human Resource departments, signaling the importance of legal compliance and personnel development in the new company environment.
- In December 2012, she appointed P&G veteran Patricia Perez-Ayala as chief marketing officer. Perez-Ayala had started her career with P&G in Venezuela and was an expert on Latin America.
- In 2013, more critical additions were made to the leadership team. Experienced transformation guru David Powell joined as senior vice president of Business Transformation and Supply Chain. Tupperware executive Pablo Munoz, who had a successful track record of direct selling and turning around businesses, was brought in to lead the ailing North American business. Brian Salsberg, an Asia-Pacific market expert from McKinsey, was recruited to head up Strategy.
- In 2015, James Scully joined the firm as its new CFO after 9 years at J.Crew, a multichannel apparel retailer. He replaced company veteran Kimberly Ross, who had resigned to pursue an external opportunity.

McCoy believed the company needed to evolve by focusing on three critical areas: executing growth platforms, driving simplification and efficiency, and improving organizational effectiveness. She indicated that the company was making progress in these three areas and the new turnaround would increase the prospects of future success:

- In the area of growth platforms, the company had begun refining its consumer value proposition. This involved clearly defining product categories and developing fully integrated marketing plans. It also included a renewed organizational focus on improving all aspects of the representative experience and achieving geographic optimization. An important priority was given to expand the company's presence through digital media and advertising.

- In the area of simplification and efficiency, the company was streamlining complex processes and trying to create a mind-set of cost management. To improve the cost efficiency, the company divested its low performing segment Liz Earle in 2015.
- In the area of organizational effectiveness, a new culture of discipline and accountability was being implemented.

Soon after taking charge, McCoy pushed the adoption of technology at all levels, including mobile applications and online brochures. The company invested nearly $200 million in expanding its information technology systems and in updating and repositioning brands.

Unlike past changes, however, these changes were implemented with the direct-selling representative at the center of the planning effort. In the past, some of the changes that had been implemented without active involvement of the sales representatives had failed due to lack of relevance and inconvenience for the representatives.

As mentioned at the start of this case, McCoy's new three-year transformational plan cut about 2,500 jobs, announced Avon's exit from unprofitable markets, and sold off 80 percent of the North American business as part of a plan to save $350 million by the end of 2018. Previously, in July 2013, Avon had sold its Silpada jewelry unit to Rhinestone Holdings (original owner of Silpada) for $85 million.

McCoy believed marketing would play a critical role during the transformation. "We have to continue to look at how we make direct selling more modern in some ways," including using technology and social media to amplify the social connections forged by the reps, she said. "You see this blurring of the channels, and that's why the brand is so important because in the end, the consumer is going to buy on the brand."

If CEO McCoy was unable to turn the company with the new three-year transformational plan, there would continue to be takeover bids that investors would expect the board to consider for the remaining international and North America business.

The Rocky Road Ahead

High Tab of Litigation[16]

According to company releases, an internal investigation was being conducted and covered a broad range of areas: travel, entertainment, gifts, use of third-party vendors and consultants, joint ventures and acquisitions, and payments to third-party agents and others. The legal fees and costs for the outside counsel conducting the internal investigation totaled $59 million in 2009 and $95 million in 2010. In December 2014, the company revealed it had settled with the SEC for $135 million.

Women-Centric Philanthropic Efforts

The "company for women" had a rich history and mission of supporting women-centric causes (see Exhibit 5). However, its 2015 balance sheet (see again Exhibit 4) showed a drop from $249 million to $92 million in assets relating to goodwill. The company had lost the majority of its goodwill value after Egypt business accounting signified that carried business was considerably overvalued relative to its fair price. Similarly, revenue decline in China indicated loss of goodwill in the Chinese market as well, shrinking the company's intangible assets.[17] Will the company be able to continue to fund these causes in the future? Could these commitments eventually become a financial liability for the company?

Breast Cancer

- Avon's Breast Cancer Crusade was launched in the United Kingdom in 1992. Through Avon's sales channel, an army of Avon Ladies was mobilized to raise awareness and funds for the cause. In 1998, the Avon Foundation was named the beneficiary of the first long-distance walk series for breast cancer. Five years later, the foundation launched its current highly successful event model in the United States: the Avon Walk for Breast Cancer, a marathon-and-a-half walk (39.3 miles) over two days.
- In 2005, the company started the Avon Walk Around the World for Breast Cancer series, bringing grassroots activism to a global scale. Walk Around the World mobilized a quarter of a million people each year for the breast cancer cause. This "walk" sometimes included runs, concerts, and educational seminars. World walkers trekked past historic sites, including the Great Wall of China and the Kremlin, and through diverse locales such as Kuala Lumpur, and Prague.
- In 2007, popular actress Reese Witherspoon was appointed as Avon's global ambassador and as honorary chairperson of the Avon Foundation for Women.
- By 2017, the Avon Breast Cancer Crusade had become a powerful global force, and Avon was the leading corporate supporter of the breast cancer cause worldwide. The crusade had donated more than $800 million to accelerate research progress and improve access to care.

Domestic Violence

- The Avon Foundation supported efforts to build awareness of domestic violence as a problem. By 2017, Avon and Avon Foundation had contributed approximately $60 million to the cause.

EXHIBIT 5 Avon Values and Principles

Avon's Vision

- To be the company that best understands and satisfies the product, service, and self-fulfillment needs of women globally.

Avon's Mission

Avon's mission is focused on six core aspirations the company continually strives to achieve:

- **Leader in global beauty:** Build a unique portfolio of beauty and related brands, striving to surpass competitors in quality, innovation, and value, and elevating Avon's image to become the world's most trusted beauty company.
- **Women's choice for buying:** Become the shopping destination for women, providing a personal, high-touch experience that helps create lifelong customer relationships.
- **Premier direct-selling company:** Expand Avon's presence in direct selling, empowering women to achieve economic independence by offering a superior earnings opportunity as well as recognition, service and support, making it easy and rewarding to be affiliated with Avon.
- **Most admired company:** Deliver superior returns to shareholders by pursuing new growth opportunities while maintaining a commitment to be a responsible, ethical company and a global corporate citizen that is held as a model of success.
- **Best place to work:** Elevate the company's leadership, including its high standards, respect for diversity, and commitment to helping Associates achieve their highest potential in a positive work environment.
- **To have the largest foundation dedicated to women's causes:** Be a committed global champion for the health and well-being of women through philanthropic efforts, with a focus on breast cancer, domestic violence, and women's empowerment.

The Avon Values

- **Trust** means we want to live and work in an environment where communications are open—where people feel free to take risks, to share their points of view and to speak the truth as they see it. Trust people to do the right thing—and help them to understand your underlying reasoning and philosophy—and they won't disappoint.
- **Respect** helps us to value differences, to appreciate each person for her or his unique qualities. Through respect, we help bring out the full potential of each person.
- **Belief** is the cornerstone of empowering Associates to assume responsibilities and be the very best they can be. Believe in someone—and show it—and that person will move mountains to prove you're right.
- **Humility** simply means we're not always right—we don't have all the answers—and we know it. We're no less human than the people who work for us, and we're not afraid to ask for help.
- **Integrity** should be the hallmark of every Avon Associate. In setting and observing the highest ethical standards and doing the right thing, we fulfill a duty of care, not only to our Representatives and customers in the communities we serve, but to our colleagues and ourselves.

Principles That Guide Avon

- To provide individuals an **opportunity to earn** in support of their well-being and happiness.
- To serve families throughout the world with **products of the highest quality** backed by a guarantee of satisfaction.
- To render a **service to customers** that is outstanding in its helpfulness and courtesy.
- To give full **recognition to employees and Representatives,** on whose contributions Avon depends.
- To **share with others,** the rewards of growth and success.
- To meet fully the obligations of **corporate citizenship** by contributing to the well-being of society and the environment in which it functions.
- To maintain and cherish the **friendly spirit** of Avon.

Source: *www.avoncompany.com.*

The Future—A Fix or Sell Proposition

By 2017, CEO McCoy had a big challenge and opportunity ahead of her. She had developed and articulated her ambitious three-year transformation plan, and sold off a large part of the company. However, she would quickly need to prove to shareholders that the plan was working and that the company was returning to growth and profitability. Shareholders were getting increasingly impatient and wanted to see their stocks appreciate again. If a turnaround was not the answer, they would expect the CEO and board to seek value by selling rest of the company as well.

ENDNOTES

1. Avon company website, www.avoncompany.com.
2. http://www.marketwatch.com/story/
   avons-stock-soars-after-cerberus-buys-80-stake-2015-12-17.
3. http://about.avon.com/media/04182016New-Avon-LLC-Appoints-Scott-
   White-CEO.html.
4. Avon 2015 annual report.
5. https://www.bloomberg.com/news/articles/2016-06-24/
   avon-will-go-ahead-with-move-to-the-u-k-despite-brexit-vote.
6. Europe, Middle East, and Africa.
7. Avon company website, www.avoncompany.com.
8. Avon 2014 annual report.
9. Avon 2015 annual report.
10. Mary Kay company website, www.marykay.com.
11. Coleman-Lochner, L. 2013. Avon CEO embraces technology to reverse
    profit slump. *Bloomberg News,* February 22.
12. Stanley, A. 1996. Avon and Mary Kay create opportunities for women.
    www.nytimes.com, August 14.
13. Kowitt, B. 2012. Avon: The rise and fall of a beauty icon. *Fortune,* April
    30.
14. Areddy, James T., & Wang, F. 2014. Avon aims to wash off China mud
    with $135 million graft settlement. *Wall Street Journal,* December 18.
15. Company press releases in 2012 and 2013.
16. Hennings, Peter J. 2011. The high price of internal inquiries. *New York
    Times,* May 6.
17. Avon 2015 Annual Report (page 112).

CASE 21

THE BOSTON BEER COMPANY: POISED FOR GROWTH*

The Boston Beer Company, well known for its Samuel Adams brand, is the largest craft brewery in the United States. The beer industry as a whole has been declining, and in 2016 so did Boston Beer's revenues. Jim Koch, the company's founder and chairman, stated, "We are disappointed with our depletion trends in 2016, which have remained weak so far in 2017. These trends are affected by the general softening of the craft-beer category and cider category and a more challenging retail environment with a lot of new options for our drinkers. New craft brewers continue to enter the market, and existing craft brewers are expanding their distribution and tap rooms, with the result that drinkers are seeing more choices, including a wave of new beers in all markets."[1]

On February 2, 2017, Martin Roper, the second CEO of Boston Beer, and successor of the founder, announced his upcoming retirement in 2018, saying, "I remain fully engaged and committed to leading the business as CEO until a successor is found and a seamless transition is completed. I am incredibly proud of everything that the employees of Boston Beer have accomplished and believe our future is very bright."[2] Boston Beer's revenues had experienced a rough year as the company's revenue declined 14 percent according to the third quarter financial results of 2016. Mr. Roper's retirement announcement came about 20 days before the company released its 2016 yearly financial report. On Wednesday, February 22, 2017, shares fell 7 percent after the company released its annual report. Several management changes had been made during 2016 including hiring a new Chief Financial Officer, Chief Marketing Officer, and senior supply chain executive. The departure of the main leadership of the company diminished confidence of shareholders and investors about future of the company.

In January 2017, Boston Beer launched two new beers—Samuel Adams Hopscape and Samuel Adams Fresh. Neither of the new beers achieved the expected response from consumers. Disappointed by the market response, Koch said that its first spring brew of the season, Samuel Adams Hopscape, had flopped—and "it's not even spring yet."[3]

In 2016, Boston Beer sold approximately four million barrels of over 60 types of beers under the brand name of Samuel Adams.[4] In 2017, the biggest challenge for Boston Beer remained increasing competition as consumers had more variety of craft beers to choose from in the market.

In recent years Boston Beer had focused on improving its supply chain and distribution, while new entrants in craft beer industry kept challenging the brand name. Along with the substantial competition from small brewers, the company faced immense competition from its four largest competitors, MillerCoors, AB Inbev, Heineken, and Constellation. These competitors aggressively acquired small and medium-sized brewers and launched new domestic specialty brands to compete with the domestic market in various regions. Boston Beer's focus remained on enhancing distribution, which perhaps cost the company missed acquisition opportunities taken by its competitors. The question remained that if customers had so many options to choose from, why should they buy Boston Beer? What was so special about it?

The Boston Beer Company, with its Samuel Adams brand, was the largest craft brewery in the U.S., holding a 1 percent stake in the overall beer market.[5] In the past several years, the beer industry had declined, while sales of wines and spirits had increased. The Boston Beer Company competed within the premium-beer industry, which included craft beer and premium imported beers like Heineken and Corona. Although the beer industry had been on a decline, the premium-beer industry had seen a small amount of growth and the craft-beer industry had seen a surge in popularity. Because of the success of the craft breweries in particular, the major breweries had taken notice and many new craft breweries had sprung up.

Anheuser-Busch Inbev and MillerCoors, LLC, accounted for over 80 percent of the beer market in the United States.[6] They had caught on to the current trend in the beer industry toward higher-quality beers and started releasing their own. For example, Anheuser-Busch Inbev released Bud Light Wheat and Bud Light Platinum in an effort to provide quality beers to its loyal customers. MillerCoors introduced Blue Moon beer, and Anheuser-Busch Inbev released ShockTop to combat the popularity of Blue Moon. These companies also began to purchase smaller craft breweries, whose products had been rising in popularity. Anheuser-Busch Inbev purchased Goose Island Brewing Company in March 2011. MillerCoors started a group within the Tenth and Blake Beer Company for the purpose of creating and purchasing craft breweries. According to MillerCoors CEO Tom Lang, the plan was to grow Tenth and Blake Beer Company considerably in the coming years.[7] The two major companies used their massive marketing budgets to tell people about their craft beers.

According to the Brewers Association, 1,940 craft breweries and 1,989 total breweries operated in the United States. While craft breweries accounted for over 97 percent of

---

*This case was developed by graduate students Peter J. Courtney, Eric S. Engelson, Dev Das, and Saad Nazir and Professor Alan B. Eisner, Pace University. Material has been drawn from published sources to be used for class discussion. Copyright © 2017 Alan B. Eisner.

all the breweries in the United States, they produced only approximately 25 percent of all beer sold.[8] However, with the rise in popularity of premium beers, the craft breweries were expected to continue to grab more of the market. As the country's largest craft brewery, the Boston Beer Company had revenue of over $900 million in 2016 and sold over 4 million barrels of beer. Other large craft breweries included New Belgium Brewing Company and Sierra Nevada Brewing Company.[9] In addition, some smaller breweries had been merging to take advantage of economies of scale and enhance their competitive position. (See Exhibit 1.)

According to the Boston Beer Company, there were approximately 770 craft breweries that shipped their product domestically, up from only 420 a decade earlier. There were also an estimated 800 craft breweries in the planning stage, expecting to be operational within the next two to three years. Boston Beer Company assumed that 300 of those 800 would be shipping breweries (i.e., breweries that sell their product beyond their local market). Thus, within the next few years, Samuel Adams beer would be competing with over 1,000 other craft breweries around the country.

The Boston Beer Company competed not only with domestic craft breweries but also with premium-beer imports, such as Heineken and Corona, which sold beer in a similar price range. Like Anheuser-Busch Inbev and MillerCoors, Heineken and Corona had large financial resources and could influence the market. It was projected that the craft beer category would grow by approximately 7 percent. However the total beer category volume would remain essentially flat over the next five years.

The Brewers Association defined a craft brewery as brewing less than 6 million barrels per year and being less than 25 percent owned or controlled by another economic interest. Maintaining status as a craft brewery could be important for image and, therefore, sales. Thus, MillerCoors purchased less than a 25 percent stake in Terrapin Beer, still allowing it to maintain its craft brewery status.[10] The size of the Boston Beer Company, however, was an issue. With continued growth, the brewery could potentially increase its volume output to more than 6 million barrels per year, thus losing its craft brewery status. Furthermore, with the size of the company and its ability to market nationwide, the company ran the risk of alienating itself from fans of craft brews that could come to believe Samuel Adams no longer fit the profile.

Many such aficionados of craft breweries already believed that the company, which had been public since 1995, was more concerned with making money than with providing quality beer and educating the public on craft beers.

Size did have advantages, of course, providing more money for marketing and, especially in the beer business, facilitating distribution. A complaint heard from all craft breweries was the difficulty they had distributing their product in the current three-tier system (discussed in a later section). The large breweries had power over the independent distributors because they accounted for most of their business. Thus, they could influence the distributors and make it difficult for craft breweries to sell their product. Because of its size, the Boston Beer Company had fewer problems with distributors than its smaller competitors did. Consequently, the company had less in common with other craft breweries and more in common with the major breweries in regard to distribution. This was good for Boston Beer Company's distribution but maybe bad for its image. One brewer from the Defiant Brewing Company in Pearl River, New York, said that the Boston Beer Company was becoming too large to be considered a craft brewery and that its substantial connections with distributors proved it.[11]

Clearly, the Boston Beer Company was facing a difficult competitive environment. It faced direct competition from both larger and smaller breweries and from premium imported beers. Some of the smaller craft breweries were growing quickly and wanted to be larger than the Boston Beer Company. Other craft breweries felt that the Boston Beer Company was too large already. Thus, while further growth would be beneficial in terms of revenue, growing too large could negatively affect the company's status as a craft brewery and the perceptions of its customers. The company had to pay close attention to maintaining its image among the growing customer base of premium-beer drinkers.

Company Background

Jim Koch started the Boston Beer Company in 1984 along with fellow Harvard MBA graduates Harry Rubin and Lorenzo Lamadrid. The company began with the sale of the now popular Samuel Adams Boston Lager, named after the famous American patriot who was known to have been a brewer himself. The recipe for the lager had actually been passed down from generation to generation in Koch's family, dating back to the 1860s. Koch began home brewing the beer in his own

EXHIBIT 1 Historical U.S. Brewery Count

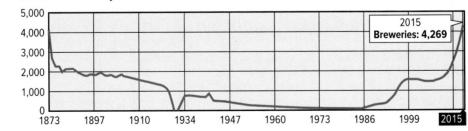

Source: Brewers Association, 2017.

kitchen and soliciting local establishments in Boston to purchase and sell it. Just one year after its initial sales, Samuel Adams Boston Lager was voted "Best Beer in America" at the Great American Beer Festival in Denver, Colorado. In 1985 Samuel Adams grew immensely and sold 500 barrels of beer in Massachusetts, Connecticut, and West Germany.[12]

To avoid the high up-front capital costs of starting a brewery, Koch contracted with several existing breweries to make his beer. This allowed the production of the Boston Lager to grow quickly from the relatively small quantities Koch could brew himself. Growth continued after that, and in 1988 the Boston Beer Company opened a brewery in Boston. By 1989 the Boston Beer Company produced 63,000 barrels of Samuel Adams beer annually.

The company went public in 1995, selling Class A common stock to potential investors. The stock was sold at two different prices, $15 to loyal customers and $20 through an IPO run by Goldman-Sachs. Koch decided to reward his loyal customers by advertising the stock offering on the packages of his six-packs, estimating that 30,000 buyers would be interested. He believed that those who enjoyed the beer and supported it should be the ones to have a stake in the company. After 100,000 potential investors sent checks in, Koch randomly chose 30,000.[13] Managers from Goldman-Sachs were upset that they did not receive the lowest-price offering. Koch owns 100 percent of the Class B common stock, which confers the right to make all major decisions for the company. This was seen as a risk to potential investors because Koch could make important decisions on the strategy of the company without receiving approval from them.

Continued success for the business led to the purchase of a large brewery in Cincinnati in 1997. Since 2000, Samuel Adams has won more awards in international beer-tasting competitions than any other brewery in the world. In 2008 the Boston Beer Company purchased a world-class brewery in Lehigh, Pennsylvania, to support growth.

As of 2016, in the craft brewery category, the Boston Beer Company was the second largest in craft brewery, after D. G. Yuengling and Son, in the United States. Boston Beer, brewing over 2 million barrels of Samuel Adams beer, still served only a fraction of the total U.S. beer market.[14] The company had expanded its selections to over 50 beer flavors, including seasonal and other flavorful beers, such as Samuel Adams Summer Ale, Samuel Adams Cherry Wheat, and Samuel Adams Octoberfest, as well as the nonbeer brands Twisted Tea and HardCore Cider. The Boston Beer Company planned to use the profits gained from its nonbeer brands to invest in Samuel Adams and build a stronger portfolio. Revenue for the company shrank from $1.02 billion in 2015 to $969 million in 2016, while operating costs reduced from $804 million to $769 million. Net income decreased from $98 million to $87 million in the same period (see Exhibits 2 and 3). In March 2017, the company stock was selling at $149, nearly $171 below its peak of $320 in January 2015.

EXHIBIT 2 Boston Beer Co., Inc., Income Statements ($ millions, except per-share and net-revenue-per-barrel data)

	Year Ended:		
	Dec. 31, 2016	Dec. 26, 2015	Dec. 27, 2014
Income Statement Data:			
Revenue	$968.99	$1,024.04	$966.48
Less excise taxes	62.55	64.11	63.47
Net revenue	906.45	959.93	903.01
Cost of goods sold	446.78	458.32	438.00
Gross profit	459.67	501.62	465.01
Operating expenses:			
Selling / General and administrative expenses	322.25	345.19	316.67
Impairment assets held for use	−0.24	0.26	1.78
Total operating expenses	768.79	803.76	756.44
Operating income	137.66	156.17	146.57
Other (expense) income, net	(0.54)	(1.16)	(0.97)
Income before provision for income taxes	137.12	155.01	145.59
Provision for income taxes	49.77	56.60	54.85
Net income	$ 87.35	$ 98.41	$ 90.74

Source: Boston Beer Company.

EXHIBIT 3
Boston Beer Co., Inc.,
Balance Sheets

	Dec. 31, 2016	Dec. 26, 2015
Assets		
Current Assets:		
Cash and cash equivalents	$ 91.04	$ 94.19
Total Account receivables	41.62	53.91
Inventories	52.50	56.46
Prepaid expenses	6.95	9.84
Deferred income tax	7.35	6.98
Other current assets	1.78	2.22
Total current assets	201.24	223.60
Property, plant and equipment, net	408.41	409.93
Other long term assets	9.97	8.19
Goodwill	3.68	3.68
Total assets	$623.30	$645.40
Liabilities and Stockholders Equity		
Current Liabilities:		
Accounts payable	$ 40.59	$ 42.72
Current portion of debt and capital lease obligations	0.06	0.06
Accrued expenses and other current liabilities	60.88	68.38
Total current liabilities	101.52	111.16
Deferred income taxes	64.61	56.00
Debt and capital lease obligations, less current portion	0.47	0.53
Other liabilities	10.17	16.55
Total liabilities	176.72	184.18
Total liabilities and stockholder's equity	$623.30	$645.40

Source: Boston Beer Company.

The goal of the Boston Beer Company was to become the leading brewer in the premium-beer market. As of 2015, it was the largest craft brewery, but it trailed Crown Imports, LLC, and Heineken USA in the premium-beer market. The company planned to surpass the large importers by increasing brand availability and awareness through advertising, drinker education, and the support of its over 300-member sales force. The salespeople for the company had a high level of product knowledge about beer and the brewing process and used this to educate distributors and the public on the benefits of Samuel Adams. The Boston Beer Company had formed a subsidiary called Alchemy & Science to seize new opportunities in the craft brewing industry. The purpose of this group was to identify better beer ingredients, methods for better brewing, and opportunities to purchase breweries that would help the business grow. One such opportunity, for instance, led to the group's purchase of Southern California Brewing.

Over the years, the company had continued to invest in efficiency initiatives to lower costs within its breweries and increase margins. One large program in late 2010 was its Freshest Beer Program. Typically, bottled and canned beer sat in a distributor's warehouse for three to five weeks, while kegs sat for three to four weeks. In an effort to reduce storage time in the distributor warehouses by approximately two weeks and consequently increase freshness of the beer at retailers, the company focused not only on better on-time service, forecasting, and production planning but also on great coordination and cooperation with distributors. By 2017, the company had 159 distributers participating in the Freshest Beer program, which accounted for 77 percent of its beer volume in the Freshest Beer Program, with the goal of expanding that number in the future.[15]

While expansion and growth are commonly deemed positive attributes, the Boston Beer Company was aware of the many other possible risks in the growth of its business, beyond the issue of being a "craft" beer or not. With the acquisition of the Lehigh brewery, the Boston Beer Company now brewed over 90 percent of its beer at its own breweries. With capital tied up in large investments, there was a potential for the business to falter if an unexpected event affected one of the breweries and halted production at that facility. The company had also put forth a sizable investment to increase product offerings and another to keep its beer fresh during distribution. However, with its reliance on independent distributors, a mishap in its relationship with major distributors could lead to complications within its supply chain. The Boston Beer Company also depended on foreign suppliers of raw ingredients for its beer. An unexpected shortage of a crop might lead to a drop in production volume. In short, the company was still not large enough to be shielded from such risk and to be able to lean on suppliers and distributors like the largest breweries could. The image of the company would suffer if its products were not available to loyal fans whose enjoyment of the brand relied on the wide accessibility of its craft beer. Finally, with the surge of an enormous number of other craft-beer choices, customers increasingly had many options to choose from.

Industry

Among the top 15 alcohol growth segments in the United States, craft beer remained on top with a 9.4 percent increase in dollar sales, followed by table wine and import beer (see Exhibit 4).

Although Samuel Adams was sold in other countries, the United States was where 95 percent of the company's beer was sold and where the brand held the most prominence in the beer market.[16] Within the beer industry, Samuel Adams fell into the craft-beer category, and in terms of volume of beer sold, the Boston Beer Company was the second largest craft brewery in the country. Samuel Adams brand beers were more costly than standard lagers and were counted with the premium beers; it ranked fifth in terms of dollar sales (see Exhibit 5).

As seen in the exhibit, Boston Beer accounted for over $162 million worth of craft beer sold in the United States. In overall beer sales, Anheuser-Busch Inbev dominated the domestic beer industry, totaling over 35 percent of the market. MillerCoors also had a large share of the market at just over 22 percent. Together these two companies sold approximately 8 out of every 10 beers purchased in the United States.

The third-largest brewer in terms of volume of beer sold was Constellation Beer, LLC, which accounted for about 9.14 percent of the market (see Exhibit 5). As the fifth-largest brewery in the country by dollar sales in

EXHIBIT 4 Top 15 Alcohol Growth Segments

Change vs Year Ago

Segment	Change vs Year Ago	% Change vs Year Ago	Dollar Sales
CRAFT - BEER	$120,783,939	9.4%	$1,406,884,139
($11.00 - $14.99) TABLE WINE	$103,876,505	14.7%	$809,390,823
IMPORT - BEER	$88,323,613	5.8%	$1,620,390,500
FMB - BEER	$81,227,527	18.6%	$518,354,008
WHISKEY	$54,814,471	6.4%	$911,347,229
($8.00 - $10.99) TABLE WINE	$49,816,304	4.2%	$1,229,647,595
SUPER PERMIUM - BEER	$40,733,056	8.0%	$548,201,950
VODKA	$36,541,372	4.6%	$834,239,219
($4.50 +) BOX TABLE WINE	$36,166,326	22.5%	$196,745,741
PREMIUM - BEER	$32,832,622	1.2%	$2,839,600,874
($20.00 - $24.99) TABLE WINE	$29,975,539	27.1%	$140,407,729
($8.00 - $12.99) SPARKLING WINE	$27,391,062	13.9%	$224,167,437
($15.00 - $19.99) TABLE WINE	$25,782,926	10.3%	$274,906,187
($13.00 - $17.99) SPARKLING WINE	$19,009,671	27.7%	$96,032,618
TEQUILA	$15,685,139	8.3%	$204,170,844

Legend:
- Beer
- Alcohol but not beer

Source: Information Resources Inc. 2016.

	Dollar Sales	Dollar Sales % Chg Year Ago	Dollar Share	Dollar Share Chg Year Ago	
ANHEUSER-BUSCH INBEV*	$1,951,436,712	2.1%	35.21	−0.70	**EXHIBIT 5**
MILLERCOORS BREWING	$1,254,472,257	1.2%	22.63	−0.66	Top Beer
CONSTELLATION BRANDS	$506,408,977	10.7%	9.14	0.55	Companies in
HEINEKEN USA INC	$301,991,386	−2.7%	5.45	−0.38	the U.S., by
BOSTON BEER CO	$162,449,756	−7.8%	2.93	−0.38	Dollar Sales
PABST BREWING CO	$128,538,282	17.0%	2.32	0.25	
DIAGEO GUINNESS USA	$101,628,137	2.8%	1.83	−0.02	
MARK ANTHONY BRANDS INC	$82,283,582	7.2%	1.48	0.04	
SIERRA NEVADA BREWING CO	$81,318,157	−0.4%	1.47	−0.07	
D.G. YUENGLING & SON INC	$76,107,341	3.3%	1.37	−0.01	
NEW BELGIUM BREWING COMPANY	$65,809,941	4.6%	1.19	0.01	
NORTH AMERICAN BREWERIES	$52,234,002	−2.6%	0.94	−0.07	
CRAFT BREW ALLIANCE INC	$51,176,170	−2.2%	0.92	−0.06	
THE LAGUNITAS BREWING COMPANY	$48,861,570	14.2%	0.88	0.08	
THE GAMBRINUS COMPANY	$35,546,909	−6.0%	0.64	−0.07	

*Anheuser-Busch InBev data includes Four Peaks and Breckenridge

Source: Information Resources Inc. 2016.

2016, the Boston Beer Company had a 2.93 percent share of the market, which was down from 3.6 percent in the previous year.

The Three-Tier System

Seventy-five percent of the volume of beer sold in the U.S. was sold at off-trade value in supermarkets, beer distributors, and such, while the other 25 percent was sold in bars and restaurants. Despite the vast difference in the volumes sold, the values of beer sold at off-trade and on-trade sites were equal because of the premium charged for beer at a bar or a restaurant.

Breweries were not permitted to own either off-trade or on-trade establishments, so their beer had to be distributed. Before Prohibition, however, beer was sold in tavern-like establishments called "tied houses," which supplied and sold their own beer. There were no regulations regarding brewing companies owning all of the retail tied houses and

	Dollar Sales	Dollar Sales % Chg Year Ago	Dollar Share	Dollar Share Chg Year Ago	
BUD LIGHT	$649,171,043	1.1%	11.71	−0.36	**EXHIBIT 6**
COORS LIGHT	$356,878,081	2.6%	6.44	−0.09	Top Beer Brands
MILLER LITE	$308,708,380	3.0%	5.57	−0.06	in the U.S., by
BUDWEISER	$240,945,777	0.6%	4.35	−0.15	Individual Brand
CORONA EXTRA	$229,286,804	3.0%	4.14	−0.04	
MICHELOB ULTRA LIGHT	$191,889,027	20.1%	3.46	0.46	
MODELO ESPECIAL	$128,746,884	20.6%	2.32	0.32	
HEINEKEN	$112,113,195	−2.2%	2.02	−0.13	
NATURAL LIGHT	$105,926,920	−1.2%	1.91	−0.10	
BUSCH LIGHT	$98,419,779	0.3%	1.78	−0.07	
STELLA ARTOIS LAGER	$83,357,643	14.4%	1.50	0.13	
CORONA LIGHT	$77,884,905	6.1%	1.41	0.03	
MILLER HIGH LIFE	$68,255,517	−1.2%	1.23	−0.07	
BUSCH	$61,007,443	−0.5%	1.10	−0.05	
BLUE MOON BELGIAN WHITE ALE	$60,746,494	3.2%	1.10	−0.01	

Source: Information Resources Inc. 2016.

selling only their own beer. After Prohibition, a system was put in place to discourage monopolies in the supply and sale of beer. This system was called the Three-Tier System, and it divided the beer industry into suppliers, distributors, and retailers, all independent of each other. Aside from the brew-pub, breweries could not own retailers or distributors, thus ensuring a level of competition in the brewing industry.[17]

Although the three categories of the industry were separate, they had a large influence on one another. For instance, Anheuser-Busch Inbev and MillerCoors sold 80 percent of the beer in the country. That meant that 80 percent of distributors' volume, and consequently revenue, was from these two companies. Hence, the distributors valued the business of Anheuser-Busch Inbev and MillerCoors to a higher degree, in fear of losing their business. In an effort to maintain its dominant position in the industry, Anheuser-Busch Inbev had contracted with several distributors on the condition that they would not work with any other breweries. Likewise, the other large breweries imposed restrictions on their distributors regarding which other breweries they could work with.

The distributors acted as the intermediary in the beer industry, providing the beer to retailers. The beer that was available from retailers was a result of the products that their distributors carried. The distributors were major decision makers for what beer taps would be available in bars, as well as the location of beer selections in supermarkets. Small breweries did not like the system because the distributors were heavily influenced by the major breweries. Since distributors had little incentive to treat them as equal business partners, small breweries found it difficult to compete and achieve growth. Consequently, it was a challenge for a small brewery to gain widespread recognition in the industry. Despite this challenge, the Boston Beer Company had made a name for itself and sold its beer to a network of approximately 350 distributors by 2017.

Competition

The Boston Beer Company mainly competed with other beers sold in the United States. The company faced competition from other craft brewers, premium import brewers, and the two major domestic breweries, Anheuser-Busch Inbev and MillerCoors.

The U.S. Open Beer Championship was a highly recognized nationwide beer competition that included professional breweries as well as home brewers. In 2016 more than 5,000 beers in 90 different categories were submitted. The top 10 brewers were chosen on the basis of receiving the highest overall grade in the most categories collectively. The Boston Beer Company was named as 'Cidery of the Year' and received the fourth-place ribbon, an impressive feat with so many breweries participating in 2014. However, the company fell of the U.S. Open Beer Championship list in 2016 (See Exhibit 7).

Home brewing had become an extremely popular hobby, and in many instances it led home brewers to pursue their passion in the form of an actual brewery. The Homebrewers

EXHIBIT 7 Top 10 Brewers, U.S. Open Beer Championship, 2016

Top 10 Breweries 2016
1. Firestone Walker Brewing - California
2. Melvin Brewing(Jackson) - Wyoming
3. Cigar City Brewing - Florida
4. Red Hare Brewing - Georgia
5. Cherry Street Brewing Cooprative - Georgia
6. Brew Bus Brewing - Florida
7. Track 7 Brewing - California
8. Guadalupe Brewing - Texas
9. Latitude 42 Brewing - Michigan
10. Elm City Brewing - New Hampshire
10. Rahr & Sons Brewing - Texas

Source: U.S. Open Beer Championship 2016.

Association was founded in 1978 and now includes more than 30,000 beer-enthusiasts as members. Its rankings of the top 10 beers, top 10 breweries, and top 10 most diverse breweries are shown in Exhibit 8.[18]

Sierra Nevada Brewing Company

Ken Grossman and Paul Camusi started the Sierra Nevada Brewing Company in 1980. It was the largest private craft

EXHIBIT 8 Top 10 Home-Brewed Beers and Breweries, 2017

	Top Ranked Beers
Rank	**Beer**
1.	Russian River Pliny the Elder
2.	Bell's Two Hearted Ale
3.	The Alchemist Heady Topper
4.	Ballast Point Sculpin IPA
5.	Ballast Point Grapefruit Sculpin IPA
6.	Founders Breakfast Stout
7.	Three Floyds Zombie Dust
8.	Bell's Hopslam Ale
9.	Goose Island Bourbon County Brand Stout
T10.	Deschutes Fresh Squeezed IPA
T10.	Stone Enjoy By IPA

Source: Homebrewers Association.

brewery behind the publicly traded Boston Beer Company. Sierra Nevada made the highest-selling pale ale in the United States. Sierra Nevada was one of the earliest craft breweries, and its founders were consequently referred to as pioneers in the craft brewing industry. The company planned to open another brewing facility within the next few years to continue growth of the business. Sierra Nevada created goodwill by promoting the craft-beer industry and by striving to be environmentally friendly in its beer's production. One of Sierra Nevada Brewing's goals was to overtake the Boston Beer Company as the largest craft brewery in the country.[19]

New Belgium Brewing Company

Jeff Lebesch founded the New Belgium Brewing Company in Fort Collins, Colorado, in 1991. New Belgium Brewing was the third-largest craft brewery in the United States, behind the Boston Beer Company and Sierra Nevada. The company's flagship beer was an amber ale called Fat Tire, but it had over 25 different beers in production. In recent years the company had sold over 800,000 barrels of beer, which were distributed in 29 states. Over the last several years, the company had growth of approximately 15 percent. In 2014, New Belgium started building a $100 million brewery in North Carolina that was completed in May 2016 with capacity of brewing around 500,000 barrels per year. Like Sierra Nevada, New Belgium focused on energy-efficient practices. The company also hoped to become the largest craft brewery in the country.[20] According to the Brewers association, New Belgium was the fourth-largest craft brewery as of 2015, whereas overall it was the eighth-largest brewery in the United States.

Crown Imports, LLC

Crown Imports, LLC, was a joint venture between Grupo Modelo and Constellation Brands. Crown Imports had a portfolio of beers that included Corona Extra, Corona Light, Modelo Especial, Pacifico, and others. Crown Imports had market share of approximately 9.97 percent, and its Corona Extra was the top imported beer in the United States.[21] Constellation owned over 200 brands of beer, wine, and spirits and had sales of above $6 billion as of 2017. With a large financial backing, Crown Imports wanted to remain the number-one import in the country and close the gap in market share between the company and the top two breweries in the U.S. market. Due to its large amount of capital, Crown Imports was able to advertise its brands nationally. Crown also hosted several charitable events.[22] Crown recently started a campaign to make Corona Extra "the most liked beer" in America.

Heineken

Heineken was the second-largest import brewing company and the fourth-largest brewing company in the United States. As of 2016, the company had a market share of 12.3 percent in the United States.[23] The company was founded in 1873, and its beers were sold in 71 countries worldwide. Heineken imported popular brands such as Heineken, Amstel Light,

Sol, Dos Equis, and Newcastle. The company had a revenue of about $22.5 billion in 2016.[24] With Heineken's large size and excellent reputation, it had the ability to advertise its products nationally. The Dos Equis brand had grown by over 10 percent since the popular "Most Interesting Man in the World" commercials began airing. Most of the brands offered by Heineken were in the price range of Samuel Adams, making them a close competitor.[25]

Anheuser-Busch Inbev NV

Anheuser-Busch Inbev was one of the largest beer companies in the world, with roughly $45.5 billion in revenue in 2016. The brewing portion of the company remained the largest brewery in the United States and had an approximately 45 percent stake in the U.S. beer industry.[26] It had the two best-selling beers in the country, Bud Light and Budweiser, and the fifth-best-selling beer, Natural Light. However, the company had seen the sale of its products decline over the last several years. In an effort to combat the lower volume of sales, it had raised the prices of its beer products.

Additionally, the company had witnessed the explosive growth of the craft-beer industry. Although it could never be considered a craft brewery because of its size, Anheuser-Busch planned to make more craftlike beers, as it had done with its brand Shock Top. The company also planned to invest in and purchase small craft breweries, like Goose Island, which made the popular beer 312. Anheuser-Busch was not opposed to merging with other large breweries, and closed a merger deal of over $100 billion with SABMiller in 2016, creating the largest beer company in the world.[27] The company was reported to be in talks with the maker of Corona to purchase that company. The size and influence of the Anheuser-Busch and SABMiller merger posed a threat to the Boston Beer Company because of its substantial lead in available capital and market share.

MillerCoors, LLC

MillerCoors, LLC, was the second-largest brewing company in the country, a joint venture between the Miller and Coors brands, accounting for approximately 30 percent of the market. It had two of the top five most popular beers, Miller Lite and Coors Light, and wanted to catch up with Anheuser-Busch Inbev. The company traded publicly as Molson Coors Brewing Company and SAB Miller, which closed a merger deal with Anheuser-Busch Inbev in 2016. As a result of the merger the combined company has become the largest brewery in the world. Prior to the merger, MillerCoors wanted to push its craft beers after witnessing the growth in the market. It had a popular craftlike beer called Blue Moon Belgian White. The company's group Tenth and Blake focused on the craft-beer industry and premium imports, and it planned to expand the group by 60 percent over the next few years. Some of its premium beers were Leinenkugel's Honey Weiss, George Killian's Irish Red, Batch 19, Henry Weinhard's IPA, Colorado Native, Pilsner Urquell, Peroni Nastro Azzurro, and Grolsch.[28]

Thinking about the Future for Beer

The Boston Beer Company created high-quality craft beers and sold them at higher prices than standard and economy lagers. It was the second-largest craft brewery in the United States and the fifth-largest overall brewery in terms of dollar sales (See Exhibit 5). Boston Beer's goal was to become the third-largest overall brewery in the country in terms of dollar sales. Brand recognition is key to any business, and this is especially obvious in the beer industry. Anheuser-Busch Inbev and MillerCoors spent enormous amounts of capital each year to advertise their products and the new merger would result in a substantial increase in competition for Boston Beer. Due in large part to Anheuser-Busch Inbev and MillerCoors, beer has become synonymous with sports, and nowhere is this more apparent than the Super Bowl. Anheuser-Busch Inbev was one of the main sponsors of the Super Bowl in 2016, and beer commercials were apparent throughout the game, as usual. The challenge for craft brewers is that they need to gain a bigger share of the attention of potential customers, while the large brewers have a great deal of money to spend vying for the same consumers. One might argue that the larger brewers' beers do not taste as good as the craft beers, but it is hard to be heard in a crowded space.

Jim Koch and the Samuel Adams team emphasized the number of hops and flavors that their products had, and they wanted to get "better beer" to potential customers. Boston Beer even tried to help the craft-beer movement as a whole, with the potential of hurting its own Samuel Adams line of business. For instance, the company sold excess hops to small brewers that were struggling to pay for the rising cost. Boston Beer also partnered with Accion to provide microloans to small businesses trying to start up breweries and to help small breweries in distress.[29]

Over the last several years, the craft brewing industry has grown at the expense of standard and economy lagers. The major breweries have taken notice, and they've started to build up their craft-style beer portfolios. In the past, the Boston Beer Company had the advantage of being one of the only craft breweries that was nationally recognized. With other craft breweries on a steady rise, the Boston Beer Company has to position itself to remain in front. Exhibit 9 shows the pricing and alcohol by volume for popular U.S. beers.

EXHIBIT 9 Comparison of Domestic Beer Brands

Domestic Beers	Alcohol by Volume (%)	Average Price (six-pack)	Market Share (%)
Bud Light	4.20	$7.00	18.8
Coors Light	4.20	7.99	9.7
Miller Light	4.20	6.99	8.2
Budweiser	5.00	6.99	6.6
Michelob Ultra Light	4.60	6.99	4.7
Natural Light	4.20	3.49	3.1
Busch Light	4.10	7.99	2.9
Miller High Life	4.60	4.70	1.8
Busch	4.70	6.99	1.7
Keystone Light	4.13	5.99	1.5
Blue Moon Belgian White	5.36	8.49	1.5
Yuengling Traditional Lager	5.00	5.99	1.3
Bud Light Lime	4.90	8.49	1.2
Pabst Blue Ribbon	5.20	8.49	1.2
Coors	5.60	8.49	1.1
Natural Ice	5.20	8.99	0.9
Bud Light Platinum Lager	4.40	6.49	0.9
Samuel Adams Seasonal	5.00	8.99	0.9
Sierra Nevada Pale Ale	5.20	7.99	0.7
Leinenkugels Shandy	4.20	8.75	0.7

Source: Statistica 2017.

The Boston Beer Company made an effort to move away from contract brewing and toward brewing its own beer with the purchase of the large brewery in Pennsylvania. However, the effort had not achieved results by 2017. The company mentioned in their annual report that it might be difficult for Boston Beer to increase production to meet the expected demand in 2017 because of the company's reliance on contract brewing.

The company has put a focus on growing the brand in countries outside the United States. For example, Boston Beer established a relationship with Moosehead Breweries in Canada to expand the Samuel Adams brand presence there. In addition, with the increased popularity of alcoholic beverages besides beer, Boston Beer has positioned its Twisted Teas and HardCore Cider products to be recognized nationwide.

Boston Beer Company is in a tough position, as both the smaller craft breweries and the larger breweries want to compete with it. The year 2017 began with the departure of many key executives including the 16-year CEO of the company. Lately it has faced shrinking profit. Only time will tell whether Boston Beer will continue to brew flavorful beers that people enjoy, and maintain a loyal customer base in the future.

ENDNOTES

1. https://www.fool.com/investing/2017/02/22/boston-beer-finds-growth-the-hard-way.aspx.
2. https://www.brewbound.com/news/martin-roper-retire-ceo-boston-beer-company-2018.
3. http://www.barrons.com/articles/boston-beer-leaking-after-weak-projection-1487803302.
4. The Boston Beer Company Annual Report 2016.
5. Global Market Information Database. 2012. The Boston Beer Company, in alcoholic drinks (USA). February.
6. Global Market Information Database. 2012. Beer in the U.S. February.
7. *Los Angeles Times.* 2011. MillerCoors CEO Tom Long seeks growth with craft beers. August.
8. www.brewersassociation.org.
9. *Washington Times.* 2012. Top ten: Craft beers of 2011. January.
10. Rotunno, Tom. 2011. MillerCoors crafts small beer strategy. *CNBC.com*, October 31, www.cnbc.com/id/45079554.
11. Personal interview with Woody from Defiant Brewery in Pearl River, NY, June 2012.
12. www.bostonbeer.com.
13. *New York Times.* 2012. An IPO that is customer-friendly. February.
14. http://www.cnbc.com/2015/03/31/yuengling-tops-boston-beer-as-largest-craft-brewer.html.
15. The Boston Beer Company Annual Report 2016.
16. Ibid.
17. www.abdi.org.
18. The Homebrewers Association.
19. www.sierranevada.com; and Solomon, B. 2014. King of craft beer: How Sierra Nevada rules the hops world. *Forbes,* March 3.
20. www.newbelgium.com.
21. http://csimarket.com/stocks/compet_glance.php?code=STZ.
22. www.crownimportsllc.com.
23. https://www.statista.com/statistics/586521/market-share-imported-beer-brands-in-the-united-states/.
24. http://www.theheinekencompany.com/media/media-releases/press-releases/2017/02/2078667.
25. www.heineken.com.
26. https://www.forbes.com/sites/greatspeculations/2017/01/26/the-year-that-was-anheuser-busch-inbev/#a3cfb0115585.
27. https://www.forbes.com/sites/taranurin/2016/10/10/its-final-ab-inbev-closes-on-deal-to-buy-sabmiller/#7ddeae98432c.
28. www.millercoors.com.
29. Anonymous. 2008. Sharing beers: Largest craft brewer offers scarce hops to rivals. Associated Press, April 6, www.pantagraph.com/business/article_3f06ff0a-44a8-53c2-bd18-52b5e6e25977.html.

CASE 22

NINTENDO'S SWITCH*

Did Nintendo's Switch Have the Flair to Turn On the Gamers?

On March 3, 2017, Nintendo launched its latest gaming console called Nintendo Switch. It was their ninth-generation portable gaming platform, initially launched with 58 compatible games. Nintendo Switch came with a pair of new and innovative controllers called Joy-Con Controllers, a hybrid of an attachable game pad and a controller that could be used separately for multiplayer game play. A pair of Joy-Cons was included in the $299.99 price tag of the Switch console. The Joy-Con came in two color options for customers to choose from, one grey and red/blue and the other grey and black. A more innovative feature in the new gaming console was that it could be transformed into a 6.2-inch high-definition on-the-go gaming screen if a user decided to move away from the TV. The new Switch console also marked the release of Nintendo Switch's very first epic game called "The Legend of Zelda: Breadth of the Wild," which could be played both on Switch and Wii U consoles for a price of $59.99. Nintendo of America's COO and president, Reggie Fils-Aime, said, "Nintendo Switch makes it easy for anyone to enjoy their games in the living room and then quickly take them on the go."[1] The new gaming console design meant that console-gaming was not only limited to one stationary TV anymore and could be experienced anywhere anytime.

The launch of Nintendo's Switch caught the attention of consumers and mostly received a positive response, but apparently the news did not impress the investors, leaving the company's stock tumbling. This may have reflected concerns regarding the battery life of the portable console, its price, and third-party support. Nevertheless, a flood of customer orders led to stock shortages in stores like GameStop and Toys R Us, among others. Addressing the stock shortage, Reggie Fils-Aime said, "Our focus is making sure that the consumer who wants to buy a Nintendo Switch can buy a Nintendo Switch." The initial plan had been to ship 2 million consoles. Nintendo decided to double the production to deal with the shortage and meet the strong demand.

To meet demand for one year out, ending April 2018, according to *The Wall Street Journal,* the company's management decided to manufacture 16 million Switch consoles, which was double the yearly quantity of 8 million, Nintendo's traditional production target. Company management was highly optimistic about the Switch, and Nintendo believed that it could sell about 10 million units of Switch consoles within a year after the launch.[2]

One of the key topics of discussion in the popular press was whether or not the Switch console defined the "next generation" of gaming. This echoed similar press concerns after the launch of Nintendo's previous console, the Wii U. Prior to the launch of the Switch, its predecessor the Nintendo Wii U console had been on the market for only a short while, with the addition of innovative controls and new game titles. Then there had been uncertainty among industry experts, such as Gabrielle Shrager of Ubisoft and Mikael Haveri of Frozenbyte, as to whether or not the improved power and new controller interface justified that system's being considered a "new" generation.[3]

The Wii U initially was launched with 50 available games and a new controller interface, termed the GamePad. While the GamePad offered a new take on the Wii's controls, the new console was still compatible with the same motion-sensing controllers of the original Wii. However, the Wii U console was not sold with these controllers included. Instead, it came with just one of the new GamePads. Incorporating traits from tablet devices, the GamePad integrated both traditional input methods—such as buttons, dual analog sticks, and a D-pad (directional pad)—and a touchscreen. The touchscreen could be used to supplement a game by providing alternative functionality or an alternative view of a scenario in a game. With the Off TV Play function, the screen could also be used to play a game strictly on the GamePad screen, without the use of a television display at all. With the Wii U console turned on, the GamePad could be used to display the same picture on its screen as would be seen using a TV display. There were also nongaming functions, such as the ability to use the GamePad as a television remote. While Nintendo was the first of the competitors to release its new gaming console, there was no doubt that both Sony's PlayStation and Microsoft's Xbox would be close behind in releasing their own upgraded systems.

Nintendo's inability to leap ahead of its competition could be seen clearly in its financial figures. As of 2017, Nintendo's income was off from previous years (see Exhibits 1 and 2).

Background

Although Nintendo dated back to 1889 as a playing-card maker, Nintendo's first video-game systems were developed

---

* This case was prepared by Professor Alan B. Eisner and graduate students Saad Nazir, Eshai J. Gorshein, and Eric S. Engelson of Pace University. This case is based solely on library research and was developed for class discussion rather than to illustrate either effective or ineffective handling of an administrative situation. Copyright © 2017 Alan B. Eisner.

EXHIBIT 1 Income Statement (1 USD = 112.3095 JPY as of March 31, 2016)

| | Year Ended March 31 | | |
| | Previous fiscal year (From April 1, 2014 to March 31, 2015) | Current fiscal year (From April 1, 2015 to March 31, 2016) | |
	(Millions of yen)	(Millions of yen)	(Millions of dollars)
Net sales	549,780	504,459	4,464
Cost of sales	335,194	283,494	2,508
Gross profit	214,584	220,965	1,955
Selling, general and administrative expenses	189,814	188,083	1,644
Operating income	24,770	32,881	290
Non-operating income			
Interest income	4,018	4,693	41
Foreign exchange gains	34,051	–	–
Gain on redemption of securities	5,233	6,801	60
Share of profit of entities accounted for using equity method	952	1,887	16
Other	1,788	1,168	10
Total non-operating income	46,043	14,550	128
Non-operating expenses			
Sales discounts	205	106	0
Foreign exchange losses	–	18,356	162
Other	77	178	1
Total non-operating expenses	283	18,641	164
Ordinary income	70,530	28,790	254
Extraordinary income			
Gain on sales of non-current assets	47	9	0
Gain on sales of investment securities	–	398	3
Gain on sales of shares of subsidiaries	3,689	–	–
Total extraordinary income	3,737	407	3
Extraordinary losses			
Loss on disposal of non-current assets	446	351	3
Restructuring loss	1,729	1,130	10
Total extraordinary losses	2,176	1,482	13
Profit before income taxes	72,091	27,715	245
Income taxes - current	25,922	2,482	21
Income taxes - deferred	4,306	8,714	77
Total income taxes	30,228	11,197	99
Profit	41,862	16,518	146
Profit attributable to non-controlling interests	18	13	0
Profit attributable to owners of parent	41,843	16,505	146

Source: http://financials.morningstar.com/income-statement/.

EXHIBIT 2 Balance Sheet (1 USD = 112.3095 JPY as of March 31, 2016)

	Year Ended March 31		
	Previous fiscal year (As of March 31, 2015)	Current fiscal year (As of March 31, 2016)	
	(Millions of yen)	(Millions of yen)	(Millions of dollars)
Assets			
Current assets			
Cash and deposits	534,706	570,448	5,048
Notes and accounts receivable - trade	55,794	38,731	342
Securities	380,587	338,892	2,999
Inventories	76,897	40,433	357
Deferred tax assets	15,597	6,597	58
Other	34,466	26,401	233
Allowance for doubtful accounts	(451)	(369)	(3)
Total current assets	1,097,597	1,021,135	9,036
Non-current assets			
Property, plant and equipment			
Buildings and structures, net	42,447	39,977	353
Machinery, equipment and vehicles, net	1,330	1,120	9
Tools, furniture and fixtures, net	4,770	3,791	33
Land	42,925	42,553	376
Construction in progress	14	309	2
Total property, plant and equipment	91,488	87,752	776
Intangible assets			
Software	11,190	9,408	83
Other	1,240	568	5
Total intangible assets	12,430	9,977	88
Investments and other assets			
Investment securities	96,294	125,774	1,113
Deferred tax assets	30,558	32,195	284
Net defined benefit asset	9,174	7,092	62
Other	15,399	12,974	114
Total investments and other assets	151,426	178,037	1,575
Total non-current assets	255,346	275,766	2,440
Total assets	1,352,944	1,296,902	11,477
Liabilities			
Current liabilities			
Notes and accounts payable - trade	58,464	31,857	281
Income taxes payable	16,529	1,878	16
Provision for bonuses	2,220	2,294	20
Other	67,018	62,407	552

continued

EXHIBIT 2 *Continued*

	Year Ended March 31		
	Previous fiscal year (As of March 31, 2015)	Current fiscal year (As of March 31, 2016)	
	(Millions of yen)	(Millions of yen)	(Millions of dollars)
Total current liabilities	144,232	98,437	871
Non-current liabilities			
Net defined benefit liability	25,416	23,546	208
Other	15,739	14,017	124
Total non-current liabilities	41,155	37,563	332
Total liabilities	185,387	136,001	1,203
Net assets			
Shareholders' equity			
Capital stock	10,065	10,065	89
Capital surplus	11,734	13,256	117
Retained earnings	1,409,764	1,401,359	12,401
Treasury shares	(270,986)	(250,563)	(2,217)
Total shareholders' equity	1,160,578	1,174,118	10,390
Accumulated other comprehensive income			
Valuation difference on available-for-sale securities	16,671	11,909	105
Foreign currency translation adjustment	(9,804)	(25,250)	(223)
Total accumulated other comprehensive income	6,866	(13,341)	(118)
Non-controlling interests	110	124	1
Total net assets	1,167,556	1,160,901	10,273
Total liabilities and net assets	1,352,944	1,296,902	11,477

Source: http://financials.morningstar.com.

in 1979 and known as TV Game 15 and TV Game 6.[4] In 1980 Nintendo developed the first portable LCD video game with a microprocessor. In 1985 Nintendo created the Nintendo Entertainment System (NES), an 8-bit video game console. The original NES was very successful, as its graphics were superior to any home-based console available at the time. As a result, more than 60 million units were sold worldwide.[5] The NES set the bar for subsequent consoles in platform design, as well as for accepting games that were manufactured by third-party developers.

When competitors began developing 16-bit devices, such as Sega's Genesis system and NEC's PC Engine, Nintendo responded with its own 16-bit system, the Super Nintendo Entertainment System (SNES). The Super Nintendo was released in 1991 and, when purchased, came with one game—Super Mario World. In 1996 Nintendo released Nintendo 64. The Nintendo 64 was the company's third-generation video game console and was named after the 64-bit processor. During its product lifetime, more than 30 million Nintendo 64 units were sold worldwide.[6]

The Nintendo 64, like its predecessors, used cartridges to play its games, but at the time the competing Sony and Sega systems were using CDs for game storage. Cartridges could store 64 megabytes of data, while CDs could store around 700 megabytes. Also, CDs were much cheaper to manufacture, distribute, and create; the average cost of producing a Nintendo 64 cartridge was $25, compared to 10 cents to produce a CD. Game producers passed the higher expense to the consumer, which explained why Nintendo 64 games tended to sell for higher prices than Sony PlayStation games. While most Sony PlayStation games rarely exceeded $50, Nintendo 64 titles could reach $70. To increase profits and to take advantage of the programming possibilities of the larger storage space, many third-party game developers that had traditionally supported Nintendo platforms began creating games for systems that used a CD platform (such as the PlayStation).[7]

In 2001 Nintendo released its GameCube, which was part of the sixth-generation era of video game systems. These systems included Sony's PlayStation 2, Microsoft's

Xbox, and Sega's Dreamcast. Although the GameCube did not use cartridges, Nintendo began producing its games using a proprietary optical-disk technology. This technology, while similar in appearance to CDs, was actually smaller in diameter and could not be played using a standard CD player.

Genyo Takeda, general manager of Integrated Research and Development for Nintendo, explained that innovation and creativity were fostered by giving several different development teams "free rein to couple a dedicated controller or peripheral with a GameCube title and then seeing whether or not the end result was marketable. This project gave rise not only to the Donkey Kong Bongos and the Dancing Stage Mario Mix Action Pad, but also to a number of ideas and designs that would find their way into the Wii Remote."[8]

When Nintendo released the Wii video game console in 2006, it was already in the midst of a very competitive market. The previous generation of video game consoles consisted of the Sega Dreamcast, Sony PlayStation 2, Nintendo GameCube, and Microsoft Xbox. These systems were all released between 1999 and 2001 in the United States, and although the GameCube sold more systems than did the Sega Dreamcast, it fell into third place behind the PlayStation 2 and the Xbox. The PlayStation 2 sold more than 115 million units worldwide, more than twice the combined unit sales of the GameCube and Xbox (21 million and 24 million, respectively).

The Term *Wii*

In 2006 Nintendo released its direct successor to the GameCube, the Wii (pronounced "we"). There were many reasons cited as to why the name *Wii* was chosen, but perhaps the most compelling reason was that "'Wii' sounded like 'we,' which emphasized that the console was for everyone. Wii could be remembered easily by people around the world, no matter what language they spoke. No confusion."[9] Initially the system was known by its code name, Revolution, but later the name was changed to Wii. Nintendo stated that it wanted to make the Wii a system that would make anyone who tried it talk to his or her friends and neighbors about it.[10]

The Making of the Remote

The original Wii was created to establish a new standard in game control, using an innovative and unprecedented interface, the Wii Remote.[11] The Wii Remote was what made the Wii unique. The remote acted as the primary controller for the Wii. Its motion-sensor capabilities allowed the user to interact with and manipulate objects on the screen by moving and pointing the remote in various directions. The Wii Remote was the size of a traditional remote control, and it was "limited only by the game designer's imagination."[12] For example, in a game of tennis it served as the racket when the user swung his or her arm, while in a shooting game it served as the user's gun. Not only did the remote

serve as a controller, but it also had a built-in speaker and a rumble feature for even greater tactile feedback and game involvement. Exhibit 3 shows the Wii and Wii Remote.

The second part of the Wii Remote innovation was the Wii Nunchuk. The Nunchuk was designed to perfectly fit the user's hand, and it connected to the remote at its expansion port. The Nunchuk had the same motion-sensing capabilities that the remote had, but it also had an analog stick to help the user move his or her characters. The ambidextrous nature of the Wii controllers was something seldom seen in other game controllers; the Wii controllers permitted the user to hold the remote and Nunchuk whichever way felt most comfortable.[13] In addition to the analog stick, the Nunchuk had two buttons that gave the user quick access to other game functions. Thus, the Nunchuk offered some of the benefits of a standard game controller coupled with the high-technology motion sensors of the remote. Users could hold a Nunchuk in one hand and the Wii Remote in the other while playing the Wii Sports boxing game and be transported into the boxing ring with on-screen opponents. The game controls were intuitive for jabs and punches. (However, a missed block did not hurt as much as if one were really in the boxing ring.)

While the Wii U was still compatible with the original Wii controllers, Nintendo revamped the controller usability when designing the Wii U. The new GamePad sold with the Wii U allowed the user to be more in touch with the game and provided more depth by offering multi-perspective capabilities on the Pad's screen. While using the TV display, players could now multitask within a game by using a variety of functions on their controller and could even play using solely the GamePad, with no TV display necessary. With the game console turned on, players had the option of using the GamePad as their main viewing screen, without the need for a TV monitor display (see Exhibit 4).

Nintendo Switch Features

Nintendo Switch came with a portable game console with a built-in screen, a pair of Joy-Con controllers, Joy-Con

EXHIBIT 3 Wii Console and Remote

©McGraw-Hill Education/Jill Braaten, photographer

EXHIBIT 4 Wii U GamePad Controller

©Robin Van Lonkhuisen/epa/Newscom

Straps, a Joy-Con grip, and a Nintendo Switch dock. The controllers' straps were detachable from the grip to be used with the portable screen to turn the Switch into a portable video game. The 6.2-inch detachable screen console came with a standard USB c plug for charging. Along with the traditional method of playing games by using buttons, the Joy-Cons could also be used for motion-sensitive games just like their predecessors. Nintendo also offered an additional controller called Nintendo Switch ProController, which could be bought separately at a price of $69.99, had the same features as Joy-Con, but looked like a traditional gaming controller. This was not the first time Nintendo had surprised the market with such a new design. For instance, the company had done it in the past when it introduced motion-sensitive controllers. However, this time, in a way, Nintendo had combined the GamePad controller with the Wii U console to design the Switch. Gamers could play games by attaching the Nintendo Switch dock with the TV or could convert it into a portable handheld game by attaching the controller straps with the 6.2-inch high-definition screen (720p), which also included a kick-stand to be placed on a flat surface and multi-touch features for various compatible games to enhance the gaming experience. The gamers could also take a screenshot of the game they played using a capture button on the left Joy-Con, which then users could share with their friends or put on the social media. Similar to the past Nintendo controllers, both Joy-Cons included the motion controls. (See Exhibit 5.)

Switch supported the Nintendo eShop, an online game store that could be used to download games from different publishers and developers. Switch also supported the games by third-party publishers including Electronic Arts, Activision, and Ubisoft, among others. The user interface of the Switch software was a UI design. The home screen displayed several different icons, including icons for featured games, settings, controllers, albums (screenshots, videos), Nintendo eShop, and options. Users could make different player profiles to sign in to maintain exclusive game progress similar to what most people do using their personal computers. The top right corner of the screen showed battery status along with the time.

Prior to Nintendo Switch, the company had introduced Amiibo figurines that depicted popular Nintendo characters, and each contained a wireless antenna and flash memory. They allowed consumers to include digital versions of their favorite characters in compatible video games. The "toys to life" segment had been created in 2011 when Activision Blizzard launched the hugely successful Skylanders line of games and figures. (Disney subsequently jumped into the ring by launching a competing product, Disney Infinity, in August 2013.) Nintendo's first round of Amiibo characters were Mario, Peach, Yoshi, Donkey Kong, Link, Fox, Samus, Wii Fit Trainer, Villager, Pikachu, Kirby, and Marth. Accompanying the launch of Nintendo Switch on March 3, 2017, the company introduced a new game called "The Legend of Zelda: Breadth of the Wild" that hosted Nintendo's most popular character Zelda.

In the past, Nintendo had hoped to penetrate the segment and boost sales of its Wii U console and 3DS handheld in the process. However, in 2017, the company combined both Wii U console and 3DS into a single gaming platform that was Nintendo Switch.

Demographics

According to Nintendo, one of the key differences between the Switch and competitors' systems was the broad audience that the Switch targeted. Many of the Switch games could be played by people of all ages and experience, and the Switch's Joy-Cons were easier to use than the complicated controllers of the Sony PlayStation 4 or Microsoft Xbox One. Nintendo's TV commercials for the Switch showed people playing the Switch at home by connecting the game console to TV and outdoors by connecting the Joy-Cons with the portable screen. The Switch offered something for

EXHIBIT 5 Switch Console and Joy-Con Controller

©Dmitry Loshkin/123RF

both the advanced gamer and the person who had never played a video game before, according to the company. The advanced gamer would enjoy the remote's unique features, whereas the novice gamer could use the remote as his or her hand and wouldn't need elaborate instructions on how to play a new game straight out of the box.

Although the Nintendo games were easily played by a greater range of ages and featured improved graphics, the company's competitors Xbox and Sony were offering 4K resolutions, best in the market at the time. While Nintendo hoped to target people of all ages, it had long been seen as a system that made video games for children, as evident from its Mario, Zelda, and Donkey Kong series. However, despite the limitation of this reputation, the innovation and uniqueness of its game play were enough to lure the masses, and sales were excellent.

Success, of course, bred competition. Upon seeing the success of the movement-sensing Switch, Microsoft and Sony moved quickly to release competing systems. Microsoft released its Kinect for the Xbox, while Sony released the Move for the PlayStation. Both the Move and Kinect used camera systems for their motion detectors, but in different ways. Move's camera sensed the movement of the light-up Move controller, whereas Microsoft's Kinect sensor tracked skeletal motion, eliminating the need for a controller.[14] While it was inevitable that gamers would have their favorite of the bunch, the relevant point was that it didn't take long for Microsoft and Sony to catch up to Nintendo. They moved forward to the new generation(s) of gaming quickly, maintaining an even playing field among competitors for gamer interaction and motion detection.

Gaining the Interest of Game Developers

As evident from the history of game consoles, game developers had tried to make games more and more complex with each new generation of systems. This meant that more money was invested in the production of each subsequent generation of games. Because game developers were spending more money on developing games, they were at great financial risk if games did not succeed. Thus, many developers felt more secure in simply creating sequels to existing games, which restrained innovation. The Switch's innovative controller, the Joy-Cons, now required a rethinking and reengineering of the human interface by game developers and programmers. Another issue with developing games for the Switch was that its graphics were not quite as good as those of the PlayStation 4 and Xbox One, and therefore game developers had to be more creative and develop special Switch editions of their games.

Many game developers used virtual-machine software in developing new games. It was believed that game developers could develop games for the Switch and then make them for other platforms on the basis of the same programming, thereby reducing production costs. However, while

the Joy-Con distinguished itself from its competitors, it created a hurdle for developers. When developers created a game for the PlayStation, they could create the same game for the Xbox and vice versa. When developers created a game for the Switch, however, it required significant rework to deploy the title for the other platforms. Converting a title from the Xbox or PlayStation also required significant work to modify the game to incorporate code for the Joy-Con's special features.

While this uniqueness had served Nintendo well in the past, the Joy-Con's incompatibility with the likes of Microsoft and Sony limited the selection of games immediately available to the Nintendo Switch's audience. The selection of games had to be fulfilling enough to keep Nintendo's audience happy, without leaving them feeling that they were missing out on games available only on the other platforms.

The Competition

If the launch of Nintendo's Switch was a foray into the fierce competition among such existing models as Xbox One and PS4, Switch's competitors were offering many features that Nintendo didn't offer. The price of $299 for the basic Switch included a portable game console with a built-in screen, a pair of Joy-Con controllers, Joy-Con Straps, a Joy-Con grip, and a Nintendo Switch dock. The price of the PlayStation 4 was also $299 (500 GB edition), and the new Xbox One was $229, as well. At a base price of $299 the Switch was intended to compete with the upper echelon of the next generation of gaming consoles—unlike the low-cost position of the original Wii. Apart from pricing, there were many differences among the performance specifications of Switch in comparison to its fiercest competitors (for examples, see Exhibits 6 and 7).

Xbox One

The Xbox One by Microsoft was released in November 2013. While the configurations were changed several times, the Xbox One was available at two different prices: $299 for the 500-GB model and $349 for the 1-TB model, as of 2017. However, although its higher-end model was pricier than the Switch, Microsoft was in fact losing money on every Xbox sale, due to costs of production and manufacturing.

One of the important features of the Xbox One was Xbox Live. This feature allowed individuals to play online against other users around the world. Thus, Microsoft had created a community of individuals who were able to communicate with one another by voice chats and play against each other in a video game. Another service offered by Xbox Live was the Xbox Live Marketplace, which enabled users to download movies, game trailers, game demos, and arcade games. It was estimated that more than 70 percent of connected Xbox users were downloading content from the Xbox Live Marketplace, totaling more than 8 million

EXHIBIT 6 Game Systems Comparison, 2017

Featurs	Switch	Xbox One	P54
CPU: Cores	4x ARM Cortex A57	8x AMD Jaguar	8x AMD Jaguar
CPU: Clock speed	1,020MHz	1,750MHz	1,600MHz
CPU: Cores	256 Nvidia CUDA	768x AMD Shaders	1152 AMD shaders
CPU: Docked speed	768MHz	853MHz	800MHz
CPU: Undocked speed	307.2MHz	N/A	N/A
HDR	No?	Yes (One S)	Yes
Memory	4GB	8GB	8GB
Storage	32GB flash (microSD-expandable)	500GB HDD	500GB HDD
Physical game formats	Game Card	Disc	Disc
USB ports	2x USB2, 1x USB3.0	3x USB 3.0	2x USB 3.1 (gen1)
Video output	HDMI	HDMI	HDMI (HDR supported)
Audio ports	None	Optical	Optical
Networking ports	None	Gigabit Ethernet	Gigabit Ethernet
Power consumption	Unknown	~125W	~140W

Source: Trusted Reviews, http://www.trustedreviews.com/opinions/nintendo-switch-vs-ps4-and-xbox-one.

EXHIBIT 7 Game Controllers Comparison, 2017

Feature	Joy-Con pair	Switch Pro	Xbox One	P54	P54 Move pair
Control buttons	18 touchscreen	18	17	17 touch	18
Analogue sticks	2	2	2	2	2
Vibration	Yes	Yes	Yes	Yes	Yes
Wireless	Yes	Yes	Yes	Yes	Yes
Battery capacity	525mAh (each)	1300mAh	N/A	l000mAh	1520mAh (each)
Battery life	20h (official)	40h (official)	Variable	~7h	~10h
Motion controls	Yes	Yes	No	Yes	Yes
IR camera	Yes	No	No	No	No
Removable batteries	No	No	Yes	No	No
Play and charge	Yes	Yes	Yes	Yes	Yes
Headphone jack	No	No	Yes	Yes	No

Source: Trusted Reviews, http://www.trustedreviews.com/opinions/nintendo-switch-vs-ps4-and-xbox-one.

members. According to Microsoft, there were more than 12 million downloads in less than a year, and because of this popularity, major publishers and other independent gamers had submitted more than 1,000 Xbox Live games.[15]

Kinect for Xbox One

In October 2014 Microsoft introduced Kinect for Xbox One, which was based around a webcam-style add-on peripheral for the Xbox One console. It enabled users to control and interact with the Xbox One using gestures and spoken commands, without the need to touch a game controller. Kinect allowed the Xbox One to "see" the user and act according to the user's motions and gestures. This took the concept of the Wii and pursued it to its natural culmination, making the user the game controller. Kinect used software technology that enabled advanced gesture recognition, facial recognition, and voice recognition. Some critics believed that the concept used by Kinect had potential far beyond games and might even become a new way of controlling computers of all kinds. It automatically identified who one player was and paused when the player left its vicinity, so it was not hard to imagine this ingenuity controlling all kinds of devices, such as a PC, smartphone, or tablet.[16] Microsoft also released Xbox One S following the release of Xbox One. The Xbox One S was more compact in design, lighter in weight, had slight performance and graphic improvement, and supported better HDMI connectivity options. However, these changes were not so significant that critics would count Xbox One S as a next generation Xbox.

Sony PlayStation 4

Sony PlayStation 4 was released in November 2013. It was available at two different prices in two variations: PlayStation 4 Pro was priced at $400 with 4K resolution, and PlayStation 4 was priced at $300 with Blu-ray video quality. The PS4 included 8 GB of GDDR5 memory, which enabled rapid performance. Also, a player could use the loading power of this memory to power down the PS4 mid-game and then later turn it back on and within seconds be playing again right where he or she left off. The PS4 supported Blu-ray discs, DVDs, and HDMI output, as well as analog and optical digital output. The included controller was the DualShock 4 pad. Its design and function were similar to that of the PS3 controller, but it offered upgraded vibrations, enhanced motion sensors, and a Vita-like touchpad. PS4 also launched with the ability to stream games directly to the PS Vita, Sony's handheld gaming device. As with the Switch, this allowed users to play on the tablet controller through a wireless connection, without the use of a TV display. A number games were released for the PS4 including Horizon Zero Dawn, Unchartered 4: A Thief's End, Over Watch, Mass Effect: Endormeda, and Battlefield One, among others. Part of the PlayStation Network's success was the ability to play games online. This allowed

individuals to play with other players located in other parts of the world. The PlayStation Network allowed users to download games, view movie and game trailers, send text messages, and chat with friends, and these capabilities were sure to continue. As of February 19, 2017, Sony had sold about 53.4 million units of PS4 worldwide, which evidently made PS4 the most successful video game console in the gaming industry.[17]

PlayStation Move

In September 2010, Sony released the PlayStation Move, which basically copied the Wii's wand-like controller but with more accuracy. As with the Wii, users could wave the Move's controller around and swing it like a bat and hit the ball on the screen. The PlayStation Move combined a video camera with a physical controller packed with motion-sensing electronics, making it a technological cross between the Kinect and the Nintendo Wii. The Move Motion Controller, or "wand," combined a gyroscope, accelerometer, and magnetic sensor to track the controller in three dimensions, while the glowing ball at the end gave the PlayStation Eye camera a visual reference for handling aiming, cursor movement, and other motion.[18] While Switch's graphics were of low resolution and inferior detail, PS4 was a high-definition powerhouse. Moreover, the PS4 played Blu-ray movie discs and could display 3-D images, two things the Switch could not do. Also, the PS4 had a full lineup of great traditional games. Sony had shipped 4.1 million units of PlayStation Move worldwide in the first two months after its release. Although Sony was criticized for merely imitating Wii's technology, it turned out to be a successful imitation.[19] However, Nintendo's new controllers, Joy-Cons, priced at $80 were still less pricey as compared to PS4's Move priced at $100. The least expensive version of the PlayStation 4, which did not include Move, cost $300. Thus, Nintendo and Sony offered comparable controllers rigged to machines with very different technical power and with fairly close prices. Move was a successful product offering for Sony. While the 4 Eye was introduced with the PS4 soon after, Sony still intended to include and utilize the Move as well, but to what degree was uncertain.

PlayStation 4 Eye

This device was a newly developed camera system that was introduced for the first time with the release of the PlayStation 4 in 2013. It utilized two high-sensitivity cameras equipped with wide-angle lenses and 85-degree diagonal angle views. Sony claimed that the cameras could cut out the image of a player from the background or differentiate between players in the background and foreground, enhancing game play. In 2016, PS4 released an upgraded version of PS4 Eye that had better resolution and performance.

PlayStation VR

In October 2016, Sony launched the PlayStation Virtual Reality headset that was developed by Sony Interactive Entertainment. Although PlayStation VR had a price tag of $400, it was the one of its kind at the time of release, hence the company was able to charge the high price. It was a step up in gaming technology as PlayStation VR could be used with PS4 console that could mirror the television screen in a virtual reality view for the user. PlayStation VR could be used with PS4 DualShock controllers as well as with the PlayStation Move. PlayStation VR had an OLED panel that supported a 5.7-inch display with a full high-definition resolution of 1080p. As of February 19, 2017, PlayStation had sold about 915,000 units of PlayStation VR.[20]

Mobile Gaming

Recently, another form of competition in the gaming industry had become widely available. Mobile devices such as smartphones and tablets allowed casual gamers to have the ability to download and play a wide variety of free or low-priced games. The games could be seamlessly downloaded to the handheld device. While the interactivity on these devices was limited by a lack of controls and features, the convenience and price were something that console makers were starting to notice. Convenience made mobile gaming a $100 billion industry by 2016, a trend which is expected to increase steadily in coming years.[21]

Mobile gaming companies like Super Cell and Machine Zone have crossed the billion-dollar threshold in annual revenues. Although these companies charge little per purchase, the huge number of worldwide users enables them to collect enormous total revenues. The number of smartphone users has grown dramatically during last decade, which automatically grows the potential users for mobile gaming companies, without having to sell game consoles. Just having a smartphone opens the option of thousands of games for mobile gamers at a single platform for a minimal price. The growing trend and popularity of mobile gaming is definitely posing competition for gaming companies like Nintendo, among others.

The Future of Switch

While Sony and Microsoft envision long-term profits on software sales for PlayStation 4 and Xbox One, both companies experience losses producing their consoles. Among the three rivals, Nintendo is the only one earning a significant profit margin on each Switch unit sold. According to David Gibson at Macquarie Securities and *Bloomberg*'s Yuji Nakamura, Nintendo Switch has sold at a profit from day one.[22] Sony's and Microsoft's gaming consoles are commonly thought of as superior to Nintendo's, perhaps the Switch's smaller processing unit and hardware, but simplicity and family-friendly appeal, have assisted it to

become profitable. These traits attract not only end users but game developers as well, allowing the Nintendo to have the largest selection of games compared with its competitors. Although there was not enough data about the number of games for Switch at the time of writing this case, historically, the number of its games indicated that Switch's predecessor Wii was obviously a successful system—one that has drawn a good amount of interest from game developers and gamers around the world.

Microsoft and Sony have started to invade the casual family-user market, a key market for Nintendo, expanding beyond their former customer base of mainly hard-core gamers. The Xbox and PS4 are becoming more like entertainment hubs for families. Now, with the Switch on the market, and introductions from ninth-generation competitors expected soon, the competition seems to be better positioned to combat Nintendo. As motion-sensing gaming—the undisputed "next best thing" to come out of the gaming industry—is a capability that all competitors now possess, it is a matter of whose system is most desirable to the gaming population, and whether or not sales volume solely will determine which system comes out on top. With similar technology being widespread across the industry, it may prove to be more difficult for Nintendo to set itself apart and portray itself as the "family favorite," as it did in its early days of the Wii.

To keep winning over the gaming population, will Nintendo rely on its price and its quantity of games, or will it have to find a new leg to stand on? With both of its competitors yet to release their next-generation consoles, perhaps the Switch will keep its lead simply by having been first to the market. Could the new Amiibo figures be the key to Nintendo's regaining its position as the pre-eminent player in the interactive gaming industry?

ENDNOTES

1. http://www.nintendo.com/whatsnew/detail/nintendo-switch-ushers-in-a-new-era-of-console-gaming-on-the-go.
2. http://www.digitaltrends.com/gaming/nintendo-reportedly-doubles-switch-production/.
3. Ba-Oh, Jorge. 2013. Industry folk comment on Nintendo Wii U potential—new or next generation? January 1, www.cubed3.com/news/17809/1/industry-folk-comment-on-wii-u-potential.html.
4. Nintendo. 2008. Annual report, March 31.
5. Nintendo. urlwww.nintendo.com/systemsclassic?type5nes.
6. Nintendo, 2008, op. cit.
7. Bacani, C., & Mutsuko, M. 1997. Nintendo's new 64-bit platform sets off a scramble for market share. *AsiaWeek,* April 18, www.asiaweek.com/asiaweek/97/0418/cs1.html; GamePro. 2005. Biggest blunders. May: 45.
8. Nintendo. wii.nintendo.com/iwata_asks_vol2_p1.jsp.
9. Morris, C. 2006. Nintendo goes "Wii" . . . . *CNNMoney.com,* April 27, money.cnn.com/2006/04/27/commentary/game_over/nintendo/index.htm.
10. Surette, T. 2006. Nintendo exec talks Wii online, marketing. *GameSpot.com,* August 17, www.cnet.com.au/games/wii/0,239036428,240091920,00.htm.
11. Nintendo. 2006. Annual report.

12. Nintendo. wii.nintendo.com/controller.jsp.

13. Ibid.

14. PlayStation Move vs. Xbox 360 Kinect. *cnet,* http://reviews.cnet.com/2722-9020_7-1079.html.

15. Microsoft. 2007. As Xbox LIVE turns five, Microsoft announces next wave of social fun. November 13, www.microsoft.com/Presspass/press/2007/nov07/11-13XboxLIVEFivePR.mspx.

16. Boehret, K. 2010. Xbox Kinect: Just how controlling can a body be? *Wall Street Journal,* November 24, online.wsj.com/article/SB10001424052748704369304575632723525779384.html.

17. http://www.sie.com/en/corporate/release/2017/170227.html.

18. Greenwald, W. 2010. Kinect vs. PlayStation Move vs. Wii: Motion-control showdown. *PC Magazine,* November 6, www.pcmag.com/article2/0,2817,2372244,00.asp.

19. Schiesel, S. 2010. A real threat now faces the Nintendo Wii. *New York Times,* December 2, www.nytimes.com/2010/12/03/technology/personaltech/03KINECT.html.

20. http://www.sie.com/en/corporate/release/2017/170227.html.

21. https://newzoo.com/insights/articles/global-games-market-reaches-99-6-billion-2016-mobile-generating-37/.

22. https://www.technobuffalo.com/2017/01/31/nintendo-switch-sold-at-profit/.

CASE 23

TATA STARBUCKS: HOW TO BREW A SUSTAINABLE BLEND FOR INDIA[*]

Tata Starbucks Pvt. Ltd in India is a joint venture of U.S. beverage company Starbucks and Tata Global Beverages, begun in October 2012. At first Tata Starbucks, under CEO Avani Davda, offered the usual Starbucks coffee menu in India, which was not successful. By early 2017, Tata Starbucks had adopted an India-specific strategy, as a more promising path for future growth and success among Indian customers. One of the first things they did was to introduce Starbucks Teavana with 18 diverse varieties of tea to serve the Indian market.[1]

On January 1, 2016, Sumi Ghosh succeeded Avani Davda. From the start Ghosh replaced the menu-as-usual approach with his India-specific strategic vision.[2] As a result, Tata Starbucks narrowed its ongoing losses from above Rs. 50 crores to Rs. 40 crores,[a] increasing sales by 39 percent. Ghosh said, "We are focused on a long-term, disciplined and focused approach to building our brand in this dynamic market, earning the trust and respect of Indian consumers."[3]

The start of the venture had been disastrous, and the financial press reported that the Tata Starbucks joint venture had incurred major losses in its first full year in the Indian market, 2012–13. However, the company remained committed to making the venture a success over the long term.[4] Starbucks had had its eye on the large Indian market for some time before the joint venture was initiated. An attempt to enter the market several years earlier had failed due to complications with the Indian government and foreign direct investment (FDI) restrictions.[b] The company had withdrawn its application then, but when India's esteemed Tata Group knocked on its door with a partnership opportunity, Starbucks eagerly responded. A 50-50 joint venture was formed, and Starbucks coffee was introduced to the Indian market in October 2012 with a generous initial investment of $80 million.[5] The Tata Global Beverages board of directors expressed excitement about the potential of the newly formed joint venture between the company and Starbucks.[c] "Through Tata Starbucks, your company offers the legendary Starbucks coffee experience, backed by the trust of the Tata name, to the Indian consumer," announced Cyrus P. Mistry, chairman of Tata Global Beverages.[6]

The Indian café market certainly seemed to offer a lot of potential for the new Tata Starbucks alliance. While India was a nation known for tea drinkers, sipping coffee and socializing at coffee shops was becoming increasingly popular. Domestic consumption of coffee had risen 80 percent in the past decade. Given these encouraging trends, Starbucks CEO Howard Schultz believed that India could one day rival the company's successful venture in China.

In 2017, the Tata Starbucks joint venture had clearly come a long way since it was kicked off in 2012, but it was much too early to celebrate, since the company was still incurring losses. Success in the Indian café market would require overcoming the usual two key challenges— competition and profitability.

The market in India is intensely competitive, with multiple domestic and foreign players. The most formidable competitor of the Tata Starbucks venture is domestic giant Café Coffee Day (CCD), with its strategy of flooding the market with its cafés, closely mimicking what Starbucks has done in the United States. At the same time, high real estate costs and rental rates, along with competitive pricing pressures and India-specific cultural preferences, make it extremely difficult for new coffee companies in India to recover their initial investments.

Former Tata Starbucks CEO Avani Davda admits that the initial consumer experience was a humbling one. Tata Starbucks opened its first store with a lot of fanfare in the trendy Horniman Circle area of Mumbai. Despite having a high-profile local partner, Starbucks was unable to use its name to secure any discounted rates in renting real estate. The first store was located in a Tata Group–owned 4,000-square-foot site that had been vacant for a while.

By 2017, Tata Starbucks had expanded to over 80 locations across the country in major metropolises such as Mumbai, Delhi, Pune, and Bengaluru.[7] Yet this was still well short of initial expectations. Clearly, something had changed in management's expectations of the size and pace of the venture's growth. Quarterly earnings presentations boasted of robust store profitability, but with no numbers provided, possibly pointing to a slower and more selective approach to expansion.[8] In its first full year in the Indian market (12 months ending March 2014), Tata Starbucks reported losses of Rs 51.87 crores,[d] more than half its total sales of 95.42 crores during the same period.[9]

---

[*] This case was developed by graduate students Dev Das and Saad Nazir, and Professor Alan B. Eisner, Pace University. Material has been drawn from published sources to be used for class discussion. Copyright © 2017 Alan B. Eisner.

[a] 1 crore = 10 million Exchange Rate: $1 USD = Rs. 64.92 as of April, 2017

[b] The Government of India at the time permitted foreign retailers a maximum ownership stake of only 51 percent.

[c] Tata Global Beverages is the Tata Group subsidiary that manages coffee and tea sales.

[d] 1 crore = 10 million Exchange Rate: $1 USD = Rs. 64.92 as of April, 2017

The joint venture appeared to be at the crossroads of an important strategic decision. It could revert to a plan to grow its store count aggressively, much like Starbucks did in the U.S. It is possible that this was the original intent. After all, the initial launch pricing had been set to be competitive with CCD's pricing (coffee drinks available for as low as Rs 100). This approach would have put it in direct price competition with CCD, the domestic café market leader.

Gaining market share among the youth of the country was critical for Tata Starbucks to tap into a large demographic segment. India's population showed a pronounced skew to younger age brackets (see Exhibit 1) and lower incomes when compared to countries like Japan and the United States. Building a presence within these segments as CCD had done was critical for success in the long term.

Alternatively, instead of trying to saturate the country with stores at once, the venture could choose a premium-priced, niche approach similar to the one Starbucks had used successfully in other Asian countries, like Japan and China. The premium offering would cater to an older business elite with higher spending power. This would result in less rapid growth, with a cherry-picked list of high-profile, business-friendly locations, allowing the venture to build a premium brand with premium pricing.

Would Starbucks and Tata under Ghosh's leadership be able to crack the code for sustained success in the competitive and complex Indian market? While in 2017 Ghosh appeared optimistic about the success of Teavana as the company focused on offering products exclusively according to the taste of Indian customer, some critical strategic choices would need to be made to ensure the long-term success of Starbucks in India.

Schultz and Starbucks—Cultivating a Company from an Idea

Starbucks started out in 1971 with a single coffee roaster and retail store in the Pike Place Market in Seattle. Since then the company had expanded its global footprint mightily, with over 17,000 coffee stores in more than 50 countries.[10] The visionary behind this international success story was CEO Howard Schultz.

Schultz joined the company in 1981 and quickly assessed its growth potential after visiting coffeehouses in Italy. He envisioned his coffeehouses offering much more than just a cup of coffee. They were to become a third place, in addition to home and work, for people to meet and socialize. In addition to serving coffee, the coffeehouses would help people connect with other people and their local communities. Employees would be trained on coffee, company products, and customer service to deliver a positive "Starbucks Experience" to each and every customer.

Starbucks quickly acquired a reputation for being an employer of choice and a socially responsible player:

- When the company went public in 1992, all employees were made "partners" in the company and given a share of Starbucks equity (commonly known as "bean stock"). Comprehensive health care coverage was also provided to both full-time and part-time employees.

- Efforts were made to ethically source products and establish strong relationships with coffee-producing farmers all over the world. In later years, the company began to utilize reusable and recyclable cups in its stores. Its employee partners contributed many hours of volunteer work to help with community causes.

- After the 2008–2009 recession and the introduction of the Affordable Care Act in 2010, several companies began to cut employee benefits to manage costs. Schultz refused to reduce benefits for his partners, arguing that this was a short-term reaction and not in the interests of a company in the long term.

- In early 2017, to help provide employment opportunities for refugees and military veterans in the United States, Starbucks announced a goal to hire 10,000 refugees by 2022, and 25,000 military veterans by 2025.

EXHIBIT 1

Age Distribution by Country, 2016

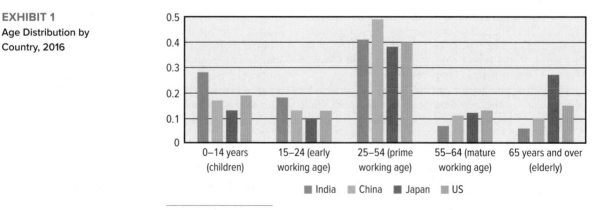

Source: CIA World Factbook.

The company's mission was to inspire and nurture the human spirit, one person, one cup, and one neighborhood at a time. The company planned on doing this not just in the U.S. but across the globe. The Starbucks name had been taken from a character in Herman Melville's classic adventure novel *Moby Dick*. It was felt that the history of the coffee trade and Seattle had a strong association with the sea. In keeping with the sea theme, the image of a Norse twin-tailed siren was adopted as the company logo.[11]

The company under Schultz's leadership performed remarkably well financially over time. Performance in 2016 showed total revenues up 11 percent to $21.3 billion, and $2.8 billion in cash flow. Operating income, however, was back on progressive track after a one-time litigation charge with Kraft Foods Global, which resulted in a pretax charge of $2.8 billion in fiscal 2013 operating results. Excluding this one-time charge, operating income would have grown 23 percent to $2.5 billion in 2013.[12] Net income was on a rising track, increasing from $2 billion in 2015 to $2.8 billion in 2016. On April 3, 2017, former Chief Operating Officer and member of Starbucks board of directors Kevin Johnson became the successor of Howard Schultz as the new CEO, with a vision similar to Schultz's.

Initial Expansion into Asia—Targeting the Westernized and the Wealthy

The first Starbucks store outside North America opened in the fashionable Ginza district in Japan in 1996. Within the next few years, Starbucks became a well-known brand name in Japan. Like Starbucks shops in the United States, those in Japan featured comfy sofas with American music playing in the background. Unlike most Japanese *kisaten,* or local coffee shops, Starbucks did not allow smoking. The policy proved popular with women, who didn't smoke as much as men in Japan. Men eventually followed the women to Starbucks locations, and business started humming. Given the strong performance, the stock of Starbucks Coffee Japan Ltd. made its debut on the NASDAQ Japan exchange and performed strongly. "Any way you measure it, we've exceeded our wildest expectations," CEO Howard Schultz announced jubilantly at the initial public offering in Tokyo, October 2001.

Tea-drinking Japan was not a total stranger to coffee. Dutch traders first brought coffee to Japan in the 17th century, but the shogun prohibited them from traveling freely in Japan, so very few Japanese were exposed to coffee and those who were lived mainly in port cities like Nagasaki. Coffee penetrated Japan further in the 1850s with the arrival of American ships. Soon after, Japanese started to travel overseas and brought back elements of the European coffee culture.

The first coffee shop opened in the1880s in Tokyo's Ueno district, and drinking the brew became associated with the wealthy classes. Over the next few decades, coffee increased in popularity within Japan, and a number of coffee chains entered the market. As business flourished between the United States and Japan, many Japanese traveled to the United States. West Coast cities like Seattle were popular destinations. So when Starbucks finally entered Japan in 1996, many Japanese were already familiar with the brand. Starbucks soon cultivated a loyal clientele of wealthy Japanese, who considered it to be the original gourmet coffee shop and aspired to emulate the Western lifestyle.

Starbucks Coffee Japan turned its first profit in 2000, nearly four years after its initial launch. Clearly, Starbucks entered markets with a commitment to win them over the long haul. Starbucks grew to over 1,000 stores in the country. For a while, sales volume per store in Japan was twice as high as that in the United States.[13]

Between 1996 and 1999, Starbucks expanded to additional markets in other countries that had a high number of international travelers and a growing segment of westernized and wealthy locals. These were countries with high or growing per capita incomes (see Exhibit 2).

- Starbucks Singapore opened its first store in December 1996 at Liat Towers, strategically located along the nation's renowned Orchard Road shopping belt.
- Starbucks then entered the Philippines (1997), Taiwan, Thailand, and Malaysia (1998), and South Korea (1999), once again selecting premium locations frequented by the country's growing westernized, affluent classes and international travelers.[14]

Happy with its initial successes, Starbucks began planning expansions into countries with more entrenched cultures and large, diverse populations.

Next Expansion Wave—Cracking the Cultural Codes

Unlike Japan, tea-drinking China had little prior experience with coffee. In addition, the emerging superpower had deeply entrenched cultural traditions with regard to food and drink. Succeeding in China would be a critical challenge and opportunity for Starbucks. Cracking the cultural code there could facilitate conquering other emerging markets—like India.

Starbucks opened its first store in Beijing in 1999. The company recognized there was a universal need among individuals to be respected for their differences and to feel connected with others. Starbucks catered to this need by applying its own culture and values in a way that was yet conducive to local values and tastes.

In China, instant coffee accounted for upward of 80 percent of all coffee consumption. Given the average Chinese consumer's limited prior exposure to coffee, instant coffee had proved to be a highly effective and affordable way of expanding consumption. Starbucks took a different approach and targeted affluent Chinese consumers with beverages priced up to 50 percent higher than the prices at its U.S. stores. Most Starbucks beverages in China cost

EXHIBIT 2 Annual per Capita Income (in $USD)

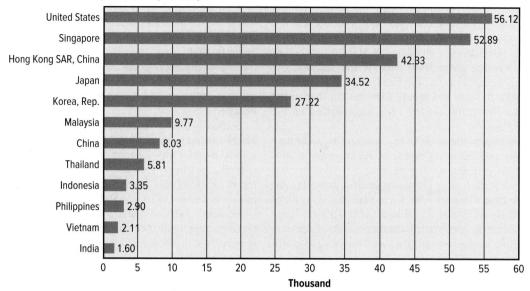

Country	Thousand
United States	56.12
Singapore	52.89
Hong Kong SAR, China	42.33
Japan	34.52
Korea, Rep.	27.22
Malaysia	9.77
China	8.03
Thailand	5.81
Indonesia	3.35
Philippines	2.90
Vietnam	2.11
India	1.60

Source: World Bank.

upward of 30 renminbi (RMB), or about US$5. In contrast, Nestlé's Nescafé instant coffee could cost as little as RMB1.5 (US$0.10) per packet.

Fueled—caffeinated—by Starbucks, the wealthy commercial capital Shanghai quickly became the coffee culture capital of China. The owner of Shanghai-based Café del Volcán, one of Shanghai's popular coffee retail outlets, had noticed an interesting phenomenon in the initial days after opening his café. The prices had not yet been displayed, yet most customers ordered their beverages without inquiring about prices. Clearly, the Shanghai elite were not price-sensitive. Much like Starbucks, the café then began to focus primarily on achieving the highest level of quality and service.

In 2016, Starbucks generated an annual revenue of $2.94 billion from its business in China. Starbucks' Chinese outlets had become more profitable than those in the U.S. market. To capitalize further on the Chinese market, Starbucks announced 1,400 additional stores in China to be built by 2019, bringing the total store count in China to 3,400. In December 2016, Starbucks CEO Howard Schultz stated that he expected profits in China to exceed those in the United States eventually.[15]

While Nestlé and Starbucks had radically different methods for getting the Chinese to drink coffee, both succeeded. This success in part can be attributed to segmenting the market and recognizing the Chinese as unique consumers with different tastes and habits than those of American consumers. For instance, Chinese consumers do not like the bitter taste associated with black coffee or espresso, so both players tailored their beverages accordingly. Nestlé's Nescafé packets included sugar and powdered milk, while

Starbucks emphasized milk-based drinks like frappuccinos, lattes, and mochas in its stores. Starbucks' Chinese menus also added some local flavor, with customized choices like green tea tiramisu and Chinese moon cakes.

In addition, Starbucks localized its outlets by offering large seating areas, since Chinese tend not to like to take their drinks off-site. Local Chinese customers began to enjoy the "Starbucks Experience" while sitting with friends and having something to munch on along with their coffee. Further, "family forums" were introduced to explain to parents the merits of having their children work at Starbucks. Large lounges with couches were provided at stores to accommodate working customers' need to relax for a bit during afternoons. Menus were modified to include foods that were tailored to local tastes, for example, a Hainan Chicken sandwich and a Thai-style Prawn wrap.[16]

By the end of 2017, Starbucks had opened about 2,500 stores in China and expected to take the total store count in China to 5,000 by 2021. In terms of Starbucks' expansion in China, it meant opening more than one store per day.[17] It was this success in China that made Schultz particularly eager to venture into India. Like China, India was another large market with culturally entrenched tastes.[18]

In a press interview, CEO Howard Schultz later reminisced:

> Our stores, domestically and around the world, have become the third place for customers between home and work. The environment, the store design, the free Wi-Fi — everything we've been able to do has created this primary destination. That is the same in Honshu (China), in Beijing, in Shanghai, in Spain, in Tokyo or in New York City. We've cracked the code on universal relevance.[19]

Conquering Unfamiliar Markets—Seeking the Magic Formula

With Starbucks' stellar performance in its initial expansion into Asia, numerous industry analysts speculated on the best practices that could be used by the company to penetrate other markets, or that could be emulated by other companies.[20] Three key themes emerged:

1. *Be tactful in marketing the brand:*

   - Once Starbucks decided to enter China, it implemented a smart market-entry strategy. It did not use any advertising and promotions that could be perceived by the Chinese as an American intrusion into the local tea-drinking culture. It just quietly focused on carefully selecting premium locations to build its brand image.

   - Starbucks capitalized on the tea-drinking culture of Chinese consumers by introducing beverages using popular local ingredients such as green tea. It also added more milk-based beverages, such as frappuccinos, since the Chinese did not like the taste of bitter coffee.

2. *Find a good local partner:*

   - Working with the right partners could be an effective way to reach local customers and expand quickly without going through a significant learning curve.

   - China was not one homogeneous market. There were many Chinas. The culture of northern China was very different from that of the east. Consumer spending power inland was not on par with that in coastal cities. To address this complexity of the Chinese market, Starbucks collaborated with three regional partners as part of its expansion plans.

   - In the north, Starbucks entered a joint venture with Beijing Mei Da coffee company. In the east, Starbucks collaborated with the Taiwan-based Uni-President. In the south, Starbucks worked with Hong Kong–based Maxim's Caterers. Each partner brought different strengths and local expertise that helped Starbucks gain insights into the tastes and preferences of local Chinese consumers.

3. *Make a long-term commitment:*

   - Long-term commitment required patience. It took Starbucks time to educate the market and gain customer loyalty. Starbucks also did an excellent job in recruiting and training its employees. This turned out to be a win-win strategy because employees were, after all, the face of the Starbucks brand and were at the heart of delivering the "Starbucks Experience" to customers.

This knowledge armed Starbucks as it prepared to penetrate an even more complex and competitive market—India.

Passage to India—Tata Group a Worthy Partner

Founded by Jamsetji Tata in 1868, Tata's early years were inspired by the spirit of nationalism. Tata pioneered several industries of national importance in India: steel, power, hospitality, and airlines. In more recent times, its pioneering spirit was showcased by companies such as TCS, India's first software company, and Tata Motors, which made India's first indigenously developed car, the Tata Indica, and the world's most affordable car, the Tata Nano.

The Tata Group comprised over 100 operating companies in seven business sectors: communications and information technology, engineering, materials, services, energy, consumer products, and chemicals. The group had operations in more than 100 countries across six continents, and its companies exported products and services to 150 countries.

Along with the increasing global footprint of Tata companies, the Tata brand was also gaining international recognition. Tata ranked 278th among *Forbes'* list of the World's Biggest Public Companies, as of 2017. Brand Finance, a U.K.-based consultancy firm, valued the Tata brand at $13.7 billion and ranked it 89th among the top 500 most valuable global brands in its Brand Finance Global 500 2016 report.

Like Starbucks, Tata had a strong belief in social responsibility. The company created national institutions for science and technology, medical research, social studies, and the performing arts. Its trusts provided aid and assistance to nongovernment organizations (NGOs) working in the areas of education, health care, and livelihoods. Individual Tata companies were known to extend social welfare activities to communities around their industrial units. The Tata name had been respected in India for more than 140 years because of the company's adherence to strong values and business ethics.

The total revenue of Tata companies was $103 billion in 2016, with nearly two-thirds coming from business outside India. Tata companies employed over half a million people worldwide. Every Tata company or enterprise operated independently. Each of these companies had its own board of directors and shareholders. The major Tata companies were Tata Steel, Tata Motors, Tata Consultancy Services (TCS), Tata Power, Tata Chemicals, Tata Teleservices, Titan Watches, Tata Communications, Indian Hotels, and Tata Global Beverages.

Much like Starbucks, the Tata Global Beverages unit was looking for a retail partner to sell its coffee products. Its broad product portfolio also included tea and bottled water. As with its Tata Group parents and Starbucks, Tata Global Beverages was proud of having strong values and purpose as a company. Thus, a promising partnership was formed, and Starbucks was ready to make a grand entry into the market.[21]

Coffee in India—An Existing but Lesser-Known Tradition

Unlike China, tea-drinking parts of south India did have some historical experience with coffee. The crop was first cultivated in Ethiopia, and by the 1600s, it was hugely popular throughout the Ottoman Empire. According to coffee historian and author Mark Pendergrast, the Turks boiled or roasted coffee beans before they left the Yemeni port of Mocha to keep them from being grown elsewhere. That is why, according to legend, a 17th-century Muslim pilgrim named Baba Budan taped seven coffee beans to his stomach and smuggled them to India. The hills where he planted those beans are now known as the Bababudan Giris.

When the British arrived in the 1600s, intending to break a Dutch monopoly on the spice trade, tea and coffee were "backyard crops" in India. Over the centuries, the British installed plantations and established more organized production processes. Tea, which was a much larger crop than coffee, was grown mostly in the north, while coffee was grown mostly in the south.

For decades, the Coorg (also called Kodavu) region in south India had been home to coffee plantations. The British began planting coffee there in the 19th century. When India gained independence in 1947, the original British planters sold their estates to the locals (known as Kodavas) and other southern Indians. Since the mid-1990s, when the Indian government changed its policies and allowed farmers to take control of their own sales, India's coffee industry has experienced a boost in quality and profits and taken a seat in gourmet coffee circles.[22]

With the Tata alliance, Starbucks gained access to locally produced premium-quality beans from Tata-owned plantations in the Coorg region. Tata Coffee, a unit of Tata Global Beverages, produced more than 10,000 metric tons of shade-grown Arabica and Robusta coffees at its 19 estates in south India.[23] This was a strategic asset for Starbucks as it prepared to do battle with the domestic giant, Café Coffee Day.

Indian Café Market—Dominated by Café Coffee Day

The Indian coffeehouse market was strong and growing at a robust rate of above 11 percent. While the market was crowded with international and domestic players, Starbucks' main competition came from a domestic giant, Café Coffee Day (CCD). The presence of international coffee chains was significant, but the combined number of their outlets was only about one-third of the 1,600 outlets operated by home-grown CCD.[24]

CCD had been the market leader since its beginnings as a "cyber café" in 1996. As the retailing arm of the nearly 150-year-old Amalgamated Bean Coffee Trading Company Limited (ABCTCL), it had the benefit of sourcing its coffee locally from a network of ABCTCL-owned coffee plantations and using ABCTCL-manufactured coffee-roasting machines. This allowed CCD to insulate itself from global price fluctuations and serve coffee at lower prices than the competition. Most of the foreign competitors relied on imported coffee and foreign roasting machines.[25]

ABCTCL's charismatic CEO, V. G. Siddhartha, had rapidly expanded CCD stores across the country. The mission of the company was to provide a world-class coffeehouse experience at affordable prices. This made the stores ubiquitous, much like Starbucks stores in the U.S. It also made CCD the destination of choice for the youth in the country who had limited money to spend and were looking for socially acceptable places to socialize. The majority of India still disapproved of socializing at bars, and cafés offered a respectable alternative. An industry study showed that the CCD brand was synonymous with coffee for most coffee drinkers in India.[26]

After CCD, the next-biggest player was the Barista chain, which started in 2000. In 2001–2004, Tata Global Beverages explored the option of partnering with Barista to sell its coffees but eventually sold its stake. In keeping with Barista's premium positioning, most of the company's products were imports and its coffee was roasted in Venice, Italy. In 2007, Barista was acquired by Italian coffee company Lavazza. However, profits proved elusive despite several years on the market and heavy investments. In 2014, Lavazza sold the Barista business to Carnation Hospitality Pvt. Ltd for an undisclosed amount.

Industry watchers said that the coffee business in India was becoming a difficult one to turn profitable even after years of operations. High rental expenses and intense competition had left most foreign players struggling to achieve profitability despite years of trying. According to industry estimates, rentals could account for 15 to 25 percent of the cost of running a café chain. Typical monthly rental market rates were 200 to 300 rupees (Rs) per square foot of real estate.[27] Then, there was the investment in making the stores appealing to customers, finding people to run them, and building a food and beverage menu that was hip enough to keep 18- to 24-year-olds—the target market for many coffee chains—coming back for more. CCD had found a way around this problem by entering into a revenue-sharing deal, paying 10 to 20 percent of a unit's proceeds as a fee. Coffee bars were a sit-in concept in India, where consumers generally hung around such outlets for hours, unlike the global phenomenon of grabbing coffee on the go from generally tiny outlets and kiosks.[28]

Industry experts argued that coffee chains in India had to maintain elaborate and plush outlets—not kiosks—to give Indian consumers what they were looking for from a coffee chain even if the proposition turned out to be very expensive, and this concept made it difficult for many companies to stay in the business and made it hard to scale up. Unlike countries such as the United States, where purchasing coffee was often a quick transaction at a counter or kiosk for customers on the go, the culture in India was to sit down and socialize for hours over coffee or tea.[29] Some frustrated customers stopped frequenting stores because it was so hard to find a free table.[30] This made it much harder for coffee retailers to turn a profit. According to Manmeet Vohra, Tata Starbucks marketing and category chief, peak hours in India were 2 p.m. to 6 p.m. (compared to 5 a.m. to 11 a.m. in the U.S.) and takeout orders accounted for barely 20 percent of the business in India (compared to 80 percent in the U.S.).[31]

Other international entrants like the U.K.'s Costa Coffee, the U.S.-based Coffee Bean and Tea Leaf Company, and Australia's Gloria Jean's Coffee experienced similar profitability challenges.[32] Costa Coffee entered the market in 2005 and soon found its stores were too small to handle the peak-time crowds. The Coffee Bean and Tea Leaf Company started out in 2007 and tried to entice customers by offering new menu items each month. Gloria Jean's Coffee entered the market in 2008 hoping it could crack the profitability code by serving coffee in more kiosks, which required a lower capital investment. However, achieving profitability continued to remain elusive for most international players.

Starbucks appeared to be doing well in its initial stores. As mentioned previously, in quarterly investor presentations, Tata Global Beverages reported robust profitability in its stores. While the company shared no numbers, industry experts corroborated the information. The 4,000-square-foot Horniman Circle store was estimated to be generating 8.5 lakh[e] in daily sales, which compared to 1 lakh rupees generated by the 400-square-foot CCD store at the Mumbai airport. Top Indian store revenues in U.S. dollars were comparable to those generated by the stores in China (about $600,000 per year). Since the real estate for the first store was obtained from the Tata Group, certainly that store, at least, was brewing a healthy profit.

Quick-Service Restaurant Chains— A Looming Threat

In addition to traditional coffee chains, the Indian café market was being encroached upon by other quick-service restaurant (QSR) options like McDonald's and Dunkin' Donuts. These players threatened to steal market share with lower-priced options for drinking coffee at existing quick-service establishments.

One of the major advantages for these chains over Starbucks and other competitors was the already-existing network of locations in the country that allowed ready access and brought down establishment costs. Further, this ubiquity and lower pricing would enable these players to tap into the larger demographic segments that made up a large section of the Indian population.

Amit Jatia, vice chairman and CEO of Hardcastle Restaurants, which is the McDonald's franchise for South Indian operations, stated: "McDonald's has the advantage

as their ability to expand is better, considering that they have a larger footprint now."

Price was another factor by which McDonald's McCafe expected to hold an edge over Starbucks. Getting a cappuccino for 90 rupees for a global brand like McCafe sounded more appealing than spending more than 110 rupees for the same drink at Starbucks. Like Starbucks, McCafe was sourcing its coffee locally from Chikmagalur in Karnataka.[33]

Tata Starbucks—Challenging Decisions Ahead

In the words of John Culver, president of Starbucks Coffee China and Asia Pacific:

> We have studied and evaluated the market carefully to ensure we are entering India the most respectful way. We believe the size of the economy, the rising spending power and the growth of café culture hold strong potential for our growth and we are thrilled to be here and extend our high-quality coffee, handcrafted beverages, locally relevant food, legendary service and the unique Starbucks Experience to customers here.[34]

The business looked simple—have a standardized decor, choose a suitable location, and offer good coffee and food—but ensuring that a customer's cappuccino tasted the same as it did yesterday and that the service did justice to the iconic Starbucks brand name every single day was far more complex. Doing so required carefully selected partners (store managers and stewards who went through intensive training) and an incredibly complex planning effort. For that reason, Starbucks had avoided the franchisee route, which could have seemed like the obvious choice for rapid expansion.

In addition, Starbucks had to meet the expectations of its world-traveled customers, who were aware of the "Starbucks Experience." Many of these customers would check whether the coffee tasted the same as it did abroad and whether the store ambience was equally comfortable. If the experiences matched up, they would become regulars.

Nevertheless, for sustained success, Starbucks needed to penetrate the domestic young and middle-income markets. Starbucks laid out plans for different formats, such as "abbreviated stores" that would be smaller in size and stores at college and school campuses. The stores in India began experimenting with their food menu. While Starbucks globally offered blueberry and chocolate muffins, it wanted to serve local innovations at its Indian locations. Coinciding with its first anniversary in India, the company launched a new, local India Estates blend. This blend was Tata Starbucks' special country-specific coffee, developed thoughtfully with Tata for the Indian market, and it reflected the high-quality Arabica coffee available in India. The company also launched the Indian Espresso Roast, which was sourced locally through a coffee sourcing and roasting agreement between Starbucks and Tata. It was felt that the coffees captured the essence and rich heritage

---

[e] 1 lakh rupees = 100,000 rupees

of the Indian coffee history. As already mentioned, to enrich the experience of Indian customers, Starbucks now unveiled a modern tea experience with 18 different varieties of premium tea in its stores.

The challenge facing CEO Ghosh and Tata Starbucks was a difficult one. How could the company maximize the long-term success of the venture in India? Doing so would mean going beyond "the westernized and the wealthy" targeting that had worked so well in relatively older and more affluent Asian markets. Ghosh also emphasized positioning the company to be socially responsible by promoting worker rights in India, saying, "We are proud to be a progressive workplace in India and will continue to engage in discussions with our partners to determine how to make their experience better and more valuable in line with the mission and values of both Tata Global Beverages and Starbucks"[35] While the partnership with Tata was occasionally helping in negotiating for good real estate, Starbucks still needed to figure out how to leverage the partnership to win over the larger young and middle-income demographic segments. Store financials needed to be managed to maintain profitability.

Going into the future, all these issues will need to be addressed quickly by Tata Starbucks as the company prepares to expand into the next tier of Indian cities. "As they move from high traffic and high spends locations, revenues or productivity of the stores will come down. Hence, per store sales might come down over the years once they open stores in smaller locations," says Devangshu Dutta, chief executive at the Indian retail consultancy Third Eyesight.[36]

ENDNOTES

1. Tata Starbucks introduces Teavana to serve tea in India. Special Correspondent, http://www.thehindu.com/business/Tata-Starbucks-introduces-Teavana-to-serve-tea-in-India/article17055965.ece.
2. Tata Starbucks' CEO Avani Davda quits, replaced by Sumi Ghosh. Sagar Malviya, http://economictimes.indiatimes.com/industry/services/retail/tata-starbucks-ceo-avani-davda-quits-replaced-by-sumi-ghosh/articleshow/50217972.cms.
3. Starbucks Sales Jump 39 percent in FY 2016. Sagar Malvia, http://economictimes.indiatimes.com/industry/services/retail/starbucks-sales-jump-39-per-cent-in-fy16/articleshow/55301130.cms.
4. Vijayaraghavan, K. 2015. Growth for now, but profits still need to come in, says Starbucks CEO Avani Saglani Davda. *Economic Times.*
5. Bahree, M. 2012. Starbucks will open cafes in India. *Wall Street Journal.*
6. Tata. 2012. Annual report.
7. Tata Starbucks introduces Teavana to serve tea in India. Special Correspondent, http://www.thehindu.com/business/Tata-Starbucks-introduces-Teavana-to-serve-tea-in-India/article17055965.ece.
8. Tata. 2014. Company website.
9. Tata Starbucks introduces Teavana to serve tea in India. Special Correspondent, http://www.thehindu.com/business/Tata-Starbucks-introduces-Teavana-to-serve-tea-in-India/article17055965.ece.
10. Starbucks. 2014. Company website.
11. Tata. 2012. Annual report.
12. Starbucks. 2013. Annual report.
13. Belson, K. 2001. As Starbucks grows, Japan too is awash. *New York Times.*
14. Tata. 2012. Annual report.
15. Starbucks will be bigger in China than in the U.S. Adam Levy, https://www.fool.com/investing/2016/12/31/starbucks-will-be-bigger-in-china-than-the-us.aspx.
16. Burkitt, L. 2012. Starbucks plays to local Chinese tastes. *Wall Street Journal.*
17. Starbucks will be bigger in China than in the U.S. Adam Levy, https://www.fool.com/investing/2016/12/31/starbucks-will-be-bigger-in-china-than-the-us.aspx.
18. Barlow, N. 2013. China's coffee industry is booming. *China Briefing.*
19. Bartiromo, M. 2013. Starbucks' Schultz eyes global growth. *USA Today.*
20. Wang, H. 2012. Five things Starbucks did to get China right. *Forbes.*
21. Bahree, M. 2012. Starbucks will open cafes in India. *Wall Street Journal.*
22. Allison, M. 2010. As India gains strength, so does its coffee. *Seattle Times.*
23. Tata Coffee. Corporate company profile. https://www.tatacoffee.com/corporate/company_profile.htm.
24. The massive gap between Cafe Coffee Day and other coffee shops in India, charted. Madhura Karnik, https://qz.com/377135/the-massive-gap-between-cafe-coffee-day-and-other-coffee-shops-in-india-charted.
25. CCD. 2014. Company website.
26. Kaushik, M. 2011. A stronger caffeine kick. *Business Today.*
27. Srivastava, S. 2012. Starbucks India isn't celebrating yet. *Forbes.*
28. Sachitanand, R. 2014. How Starbucks and Cafe Coffee Day are squaring up for control of India's coffee retailing market. *Economic Times.*
29. Bailay, R. 2014. Coffee chain Starbucks expanding aggressively in India. *Economic Times.*
30. Wang, H. 2012. Five things Starbucks did to get China right. *Forbes.*
31. Tata Coffee. Corporate company profile. https://www.tatacoffee.com/corporate/company_profile.htm.
32. The massive gap between Cafe Coffee Day and other coffee shops in India, charted. Madhura Karnik, https://qz.com/377135/the-massive-gap-between-cafe-coffee-day-and-other-coffee-shops-in-india-charted.
33. Anonymous. 2013. Coffee war: McDonald's McCafe set to make its Indian debut, aims to "wipe out" Starbucks. *Daily Bhaskar.*
34. Bhattacharya, A. 2013. Pour out the coffee. *Financial Express.*
35. Tata Starbucks to focus on progressive workplace in India, http://www.franchiseindia.com/restaurant/Tata-Starbucks-to-focus-on-progressive-workplace-in-India.8258.
36. Malviya, S. 2014. Starbucks outshines coffee chain rivals in first full year in India. *Economic Times.*

CASE 24

WEIGHT WATCHERS INTERNATIONAL INC.[*]

In early 2017, Weight Watchers initiated a new "Beyond the Scale" advertising campaign that featured the entrepreneur and talk show host, Oprah Winfrey, claiming that she had lost 40 pounds by using the Weight Watchers program. Winfrey concluded her weight loss experience by emphasizing "It Works!"[1]

As it happens, this was not the first time Winfrey lost weight with Weight Watchers. Winfrey started investing in Weight Watchers in October 2015 and obtained an approximately 10 percent stake in the company by paying about $43 million. Three months later, in January 2016, she said that she was able to lose 26 pounds with the help of Weight Watchers' program. Winfrey's continual endorsements and investment had changed the direction of the company over the past two years as it had increased the number of subscriptions by 10 percent to about 2.8 million. It was believed her stake in the company could be worth $27.3 million more than her original investment, or $682,000 per pound lost.[2]

The company was in search of a new CEO after James Chambers resigned in September 2016.[3] As a company running without a CEO, Weight Watchers had a good start for the New Year of 2017, expecting that Winfrey's contribution could be sufficient to turn around the company. Furthermore, to boost membership, Weight Watchers was offering a "Lose 10 lbs on us" incentive: Anyone joining the program by Valentine's Day, February 14, 2017, who lost at least 10 pounds within two months, would receive a $100 prepaid card or subscription credit toward their membership fee.[4] Would this new campaign work to further boost the company's weight-loss business? Would Oprah Winfrey's support continue to boost the stock price and sales?

Winfrey's involvement, corresponding boosts in stock prices, the advertising campaigns, and discount offers in 2016 were all part of a rebranding effort that ultimately had failed to impress investors. The price of Weight Watchers shares (ticker symbol: WTW) had been tumbling through 2016 into 2017, just when most might expect New Year's resolutions to kick in and bolster the weight-loss stock. This price decline echoed the financial reality: seven straight quarters of declining sales.[5] Although Weight Watchers had been working to update its image and offerings and was

still able to boast a high gross profit margin. However, revenue and cash generation as well as the firm's growth were significantly lower than the industry's average. During the year 2016, Weight Watchers stock's high volatility considerably impacted its overall valuation and reflected the altering market sentiment for the company.[6] Clearly, Weight Watchers was in trouble.[7]

Weight Watchers had recently celebrated 50 years of success in helping people lose weight, and this celebration had come after some significant financial gains as well. In 2011 Weight Watchers had hit a new revenue record of $1.8 billion.[8] In 2012 the company saw a slight reduction in revenue but still beat all pre-2011 numbers; however, by 2013 things started to slide. Weight Watchers, while still the undeniable industry standard bearer, had lost some of its luster.

Originally started in 1963 by Jean Nidetch as a women's support group in her home, Weight Watchers International Inc. grew into a multibillion-dollar weight-loss goliath in four decades' time. In December 2015 Weight Watchers launched a new food plan called the SmartPoints system. SmartPoints' unique feature was that it was a scale for food management introduced to work along with a new weight management program "Beyond the Scale," which emphasized weight loss by taking a holistic approach to a fit and healthy life style. Customers could make their personal SmartPoints budget according to their fitness goals and eat any type of food as long as it was within the consumption or calories limit allowed by their SmartPoints budget. Food with higher calories had lower SmartPoints value as compared to the food with lower calories. Previously, Weight Watchers had introduced the PointsPlus system, which replaced an even older calorie-counting system. Even though calories still counted, PointsPlus encouraged people to eat a wide variety of healthy foods—split between three meals plus snacks within an individualized calorie level. With a counting system based on dietary guidelines, dieters were encouraged to maximize their PointsPlus allowance by choosing more "Power Foods"—the healthiest, most filling foods, such as whole grains, lean meats, low-fat dairy, and unlimited quantities of fresh fruit and non-starchy vegetables.

Although doctors and nutritionists gave the Points program (the original program) and the subsequent PointsPlus version a thumbs up,[9] Weight Watchers' then-CEO David Kirchhoff felt it wasn't enough. Citing evidence from behavioral scientists, in 2012 Kirchhoff said he "realized that Weight Watchers needed to take into account social, environmental, and behavioral factors that led members to fail."[10] Weight Watchers had always believed in behavior change, encouraging people to be

* This case was developed by Professor Alan B. Eisner, Pace University; Professor Helaine J. Korn, Baruch College–City University of New York; Associate Professor Pauline Assenza, Western Connecticut State University; and graduate students Saad Nazir and Jennifer M. DiChiara, Pace University. Material has been drawn from published sources to be used for class discussion. Copyright © 2017 Alan B. Eisner.

mindful of what they ate, and just counting calories, as the PointsPlus system did, was not enough.

In 2013, Weight Watchers created the "360-degree Program"—the "Points Plus program with a 21st-century makeover." By monitoring the amount of carbohydrates, fats, fiber, and proteins in the food choices people made on a daily basis, and using current scientific research on why people eat what they eat, Weight Watchers could help guide members toward making healthier eating decisions in all sorts of situations.[11] The 360-degree Program added two new components to tracking caloric intake: "spaces," which included tips for how to handle eating situations in the different environments members might encounter, and "routines," which encouraged members to create new habits for themselves—for instance, changing just three small behaviors a day, such as walking an extra five minutes, eating lunch at the same time, and drinking an additional glass of water. These 360-degree components—tracking, spaces, and routines—were even available as apps on the Weight Watchers website as well as on Apple and Android mobile devices. By adding the mobile apps and other online social networking support to the direct face-to-face support of the weekly meetings, Kirchhoff believed that Weight Watchers finally had a program that tied everything together and that people would be willing to pay for.[12]

However, in August 2013, Kirchhoff resigned in order to "pursue other opportunities." This left the company floundering to reinvent itself in the Internet age, a time when community social support for weight loss could be provided virtually rather than at a physical weekly meeting. Also, the next generation of diet programs and online apps, like MyFitnessPal and the FitBit activity monitor, were providing this support basically for free, since the companies offering them didn't need to charge meeting fees or employ trained support staff.[13] In January 2014, new CEO Jim Chambers admitted, "The consumer has changed and we haven't kept pace. We need to turn this company inside out."[14]

The market for weight-loss products was growing, as obesity levels were on the rise in more and more parts of the world, and this made weight management an attractive industry for firms, especially deeply entrenched firms such as Weight Watchers. However, faced with increased competition from traditional rivals Nutrisystem and Medifast and other weight-loss programs such as Jenny Craig and the Biggest Loser franchise, Weight Watchers had to increase customer value and seek new target segments to preempt the competition and stay on top of its industry. In the highly competitive weight-management industry, Weight Watchers International had to remain cognizant of the major trends that had the potential to adversely affect industry and firm profitability and revenues. Those trends, as they related to Weight Watchers and the weight-loss industry as a whole, included the temporary emergence of fad diets; decreased effectiveness of marketing and advertising programs; the need for developing new and innovative products and services, many of which had to be delivered via online or mobile apps; the

development of more favorably perceived or more effective weight-management methods (e.g., pharmaceuticals and surgical options such as the Lap-Band); and the threat of impairment of the Weight Watchers brand itself.[15] The challenge for Weight Watchers was repositioning itself and creating a forward-focused diet plan for the 21st century while staying true to the mission initially established by Jean Nidetch, its founder. The brand needed to remain relevant and, at the same time, pursue additional medium- to long-term initiatives, such as reaching out to new market segments.[16]

History and Expansion

Jean Nidetch began Weight Watchers in an unlikely, and unintended, way. The origins of the company started when Jean invited six women into her home to help both herself and her neighbors and friends lose weight by communally discussing their weight-loss issues. Nidetch's belief, which became the core of the Weight Watchers philosophy, was that anyone could be given a "diet" but the group and social setting of "talk therapy" was the true component not only to losing weight but also *to keeping it off.* She believed in fostering success through group support, and she created a simple reward system that included pins and tie bars to reward increments of weight loss. The idea was simple, yet very effective.[17]

The basic concept of the Weight Watchers plan consisted of two components: the Weight Watchers program and the group support. The program was essentially a food plan and an activity plan. The food plan was intended to provide people with the educational tools they needed for weight loss as well as to provide control mechanisms so that individuals could find their way to healthier food choices. The company radically simplified the food selection process involved in dieting by assigning each food a corresponding point value, which eliminated the need to tally calories.[18]

Nidetch accomplished what she set out to do and much more. Weight Watchers, originally targeting primarily women, ages 25 to 55, experienced a rapid expansion. Of the behemoth that Weight Watchers came to be, Nidetch said, "My little group became an industry. I really didn't mean it to—it was really just a club for me and my fat friends." She continued by commenting on something a lecturer once said: "It's a place where you walk in fat and hope nobody notices you, and four or five months later you walk out thin and hope that everyone sees you." Nidetch believed that the love, information, companionship, and commiseration of fellow overweight individuals were the key components in an effective formula many people needed to succeed at weight loss.[19]

What Weight Watchers evolved into was a globally branded company providing weight-management services worldwide. By 2017, the company had about 1 million members who attended above 32,000 Weight Watchers meetings around the world organized by more than 9,000 leaders who had successfully lost weight using Weight Watcher programs.[20] Expansion and the onset of the dot-com era had inevitably led to the creation of WeightWatchers.com, an Internet-based version of the Weight Watchers plan. Weight Watchers was selling a wide range of branded products and services, including meetings conducted by Weight Watchers International and its franchisees (and the products sold at the meetings), subscriptions to WeightWatchers.com, licensed products sold by retailers, magazine subscriptions, and various publications.[21] In addition, the company had put its name and point values on a variety of food products sold in supermarkets, such as Progresso soups,[22] and it had created a separate Weight Watchers menu for certain restaurants.[23]

Reflecting the growing popularity of online apps and activity monitors for weight control, at the end of 2014 Weight Watchers announced that its members could sync with third-party open APIs such as Fitbit and Jawbone for a more complete and integrated weight-loss experience. Also in 2014, as part of a new technology strategy, Weight Watchers acquired Silicon Valley–based weight-loss start-up Wello, an app that enabled people to attend fitness classes or one-on-one fitness training through any Internet or webcam-enabled device. This acquisition was part of Weight Watchers' strategy to compete in "an increasingly digital weight loss market." As explained by CTO Dan Crowe:

> [Weight Watchers will] become a 21st-century technology organization, engineered for the digital era, whose innovative technology fundamentally improves the way people manage their weight, health and wellness. We will be agile service-oriented, data-driven, cloud-enabled and efficient. We will be a model for digital technology in the markets in which we compete and we will be a magnet for talented innovators both inside and outside the company.[24]

Supporting the long-term strength of the brand, in 2017 Weight Watchers was ranked at the top for "Best Weight-Loss Diet," "Best Commercial Diet Plan," and "Easiest Diet to Follow," and number four for "Best Diet Overall" by *U.S. News & World Report.*[25]

Industry and Competitive Environment

Weight Watchers International had experienced stock price volatility in the past, as had the majority of its competitors, because of rival weight-management options—such as the over-the-counter weight-loss drug Alli, launched by GlaxoSmithKline in June 2006, and the development of Allergan's Lap-Band device. However, there had yet to be a widely supported "magic pill" or surgical option to weight management. In the absence of a safe and effective pharmaceutical or surgical alternative for weight loss, Weight Watchers and its competitors faced a weight-management industry characterized not only by competition and threats, but by opportunity as well.

Obesity was on the rise in the developed countries, especially in North America, and by 2014 weight loss, including the overall health and fitness industry, constituted a $64 billion-a-year industry in the United States alone.[26] Although Americans' dieting had dropped from 31 percent at the peak in 1991 to only 19 percent in 2014,[27,28] this did not mean there were no profits to be made. In part due to an improving economy and a growing awareness of men as a target group, the weight-loss industry alone was projected to grow from $2.4 billion in 2013 to over $2.7 billion by 2018.[28] In addition, the obesity problem was not confined to the United States, and this made geographic expansion a possibility for weight-loss firms. Worldwide, the World Health Organization estimated 2.3 billion people to be overweight by 2015 and more than 700 million obese.[29] Overall, the statistics proved there were still opportunities, and therefore competition, in the weight-loss industry.

Weight Watchers was attempting to reinvent itself while still paying close attention to the moves of its weight-loss rivals. Competition for Weight Watchers International included both price competition and competition from self-help, pharmaceutical, surgical, dietary supplement, and meal-replacement products, as well as other weight-management brands, diets, programs, and products.[30] The main competitors for Weight Watchers had traditionally included Jenny Craig, Slim-Fast, NutriSystem (NASDAQ: NTRI), and Medifast, as well as programs from fitness gurus such as *The Biggest Loser* star Jillian Michaels.[31]

Over the years, among the commercial plans, Weight Watchers had consistently earned the highest overall rating, according to various surveys, because of its nutritionally based diet, weekly meetings, and weigh-ins for behavioral support. In 2017, according to *U.S. News & World Report,* Jenny Craig's prepackaged-food diet plan came in second with its rapid weight loss and easy-to-follow features, followed by the HMR Program. Other traditional competitors, Nutrisystem and Medifast, came in much further down the list. Going into 2015, competitors included those listed in Exhibit 1.

One important factor in all these diets was the extent to which they were do-it-yourself efforts. Many of the successful diets, including the DASH and Mayo Clinic diets, required consistent self-control without any external support system. Obviously, Weight Watchers was different in this respect, as were Jenny Craig and Nutrisystem.

Another differentiating factor was cost. The cost of plans in which people bought their own food depended, of course, on each person's food choices. The cost of the commercial plans also varied widely. Weight Watchers' cost depended on whether the member chose to attend weekly in-person meetings or use only the online tools. A monthly pass to unlimited in-person meetings could cost up to $39.95, which also included access to eTools. Or members could pay per meeting; meetings were $10 to $15 per week. For new online members, a per-month plan was $19.95 plus a one-time registration fee of $29.95. None of the costs included food. With Jenny Craig, the initial registration fee could exceed $400, and a week's worth of Jenny's Cuisine might cost at least $100. Nutrisystem, which had basically fallen off the survey charts due to complaints about costs and the poor taste of the food, had a 28-day Select Plan, which included 10 days of frozen meals and 18 days of pantry food, and generally cost between $240 and

EXHIBIT 1 Competitors for Weight Watchers

Diet Plan	Diet Type	Good For	Ratings*	Price	Comments
The DASH Diet	Government-developed suggested eating plan	Heart health, diabetes	First for heart health and diabetes control; best do-it-yourself diet	Buy-it-yourself food	Stands for "Dietary Approaches to Stop Hypertension"
The Mediterranean Diet	Developed by Harvard School of Public Health	Overall healthy eating	Third-best diet overall (tie)	Buy-it-yourself food; fresh produce, olive oil, and nuts are expensive	Plant based, do it yourself, easy to follow
MIND Diet	Commercial diet	Enhances Brain Function	Third-best commercial diet plan	$10 for a pack	Contains 10 good for brain health foods
The TLC Diet	Developed by National Institutes of Health	Heart health	One of the best do-it-yourself diets overall	Buy-it-yourself food	Stands for "Therapeutic Lifestyle Changes"
Weight Watchers	Commercial diet	Weight loss, heart health	First for weight loss; tied for third as best diet overall	Membership costs less than $40/mo.; buy-it-yourself food is extra	Rated easiest to follow
Mayo Clinic Diet	Nutritionist-developed, do-it-yourself plan	Diabetes	Third-best for diabetes control	Buy-it-yourself food	Best for health, not necessarily weight control
Flexitarian Diet	Developed by dietitian Dawn Jackson Blatner	Heart health, diabetes	Fourth-best diabetes diet	Buy-it-yourself food	Consists of plants, good for vegetarians
The Fertility Diet	Nutritionist-developed, do-it-yourself plan	Boost ovulation and improve fertility	Fourth-best diabetes diet	Buy-it-yourself food	Need to supplement with your own food
Volumetrics Diet	Developed by Penn State University	Weight loss	Second-best weight loss diet	Buy-it-yourself food	Need to supplement with your own food
The Ornish Diet	Developed by Dr. Ornish for overall nutrition	Heart health, diabetes	Third for heart health and diabetes control	Buy-it-yourself food	Plant based, from book by Dean Ornish
Jenny Craig	Commercial diet	Weight loss	Second-best commercial diet plan	Membership and food can run as high as $400/mo.	Customized meal plan plus weekly one-on-one counseling
Vegetarian Diet	Harvard School of Public Health	Weight loss	Third-best vegetarian diet	Buy-it-yourself food	Lacto-ovo approach to healthy eating habits

*Ratings are from *U.S. News & World Report,* Best diets methodology: How we rated 38 eating plans, January 4, 2017.[32]

$300. Packaged diets such as Slim-Fast didn't have a personal support system, but food supplements could be customized to achieve a "satisfied feeling" that reduced regular food intake. An 8-pack of shakes cost about $20.54, and 24 snack bars cost about $17.

One major advantage Weight Watchers had was the extent of research done on its results. Two studies published in 2012 found that Weight Watchers was just as good as clinical weight-loss programs under a physician's control and that some Weight Watchers participants lost more than twice as much weight as individuals following clinical advice.[33] A physician from the Mayo Clinic said, "It's only natural that the weekly weigh-ins and 'group spirit' of programs such as Weight Watchers would prove more effective

EXHIBIT 2
Weight Watchers'
Revenue Sources
($ millions)

	2016	2015	2014
Service revenues	$ 949.1	$ 937.4	$1,181.9
In-meeting product sales	125.5	127.3	169.1
Licensing, franchise royalties, and others	90.3	99.7	128.9
Total	$1,164.9	$1,164.4	$1,479.9

Go to library tab in Connect to access Case Financials.

Source: Weight Watchers 10K filings.

than occasional guidance from a doctor or nurse, since research has shown that dieters are more likely to stick with weight-loss programs that stress accountability."[34]

Business Model

Revenues for Weight Watchers International Inc., as shown in Exhibit 2, were principally gained from meeting fees (members paid to attend weekly meetings), product sales (bars, cookbooks, and the like, sold as complements to weight-management plans), online revenues (from Internet subscription products), and revenues gained from licensing (the placement of the Weight Watchers logo on certain foods and other products) and franchising (franchisees typically paid a royalty fee of 10 percent of their meeting fee).[35] The costs of running meetings were low, with part-time class instructors paid on a commission basis, and many meeting locations were rented hourly in inexpensive local facilities such as churches. This lean organizational structure allowed wide profit margins.[36] Meeting fees were paid up front or at the time of the meeting by attendees, resulting in net negative working capital for Weight Watchers—an indication of cash-flow efficiency.[37]

What was perhaps most important about Weight Watchers' business model was its flexibility. The number of meetings could be adjusted according to demand and seasonal fluctuations. The business model's reliance on a variable cost structure had enabled the company to maintain high margins even as the number of meetings over the same time period was expanded. When attendance growth outpaced meeting growth, the gross margins of Weight Watchers typically improved. Since fiscal year 2005, Weight Watchers International had maintained an annual gross margin in the operating segment of 50 percent or more.[38] Weight Watchers' business model yielded high profit margins as a result of the company's low variable expenses and low capital expenditure requirements. By allowing its meetings to be held anywhere, Weight Watchers kept its capital costs low—unlike Jenny Craig, which maintained its own centers with food inventories. This model also allowed Weight Watchers to gain entry into the workplace at wellness-minded companies via its Weight Watchers at Work Program.[39] Exhibits 3 to 5 show financial statements of the firm.

EXHIBIT 3
Income Statements
($ millions)

	2016	2015	2014
Total revenue	**1,165**	**1,164**	**1,480**
Cost of Goods Sold	579	590	677
Gross profit	**586**	**574**	**803**
Operating expenses:	385	406	529
Operating income	**201**	**168**	**273**
Interest Expense	115	122	123
Other income/expenses net	(2)	9	7
Income before taxes	84	56	158
Provision for income taxes	17	23	59
Net income from continuing operations	67	33	99
Net income	**68**	**33**	**99**
Earnings per share	1.06	0.56	1.74

Go to library tab in Connect to access Case Financials.

Source: Weight Watchers 10K filings.

EXHIBIT 4
Balance Sheets
($ thousands)

Go to library tab in Connect
to access Case Financials.

	2016	2015	2014
Assets			
Current assets:			
Cash and cash equivalents	109	242	301
Net receivables	28	29	32
Inventory	33	28	32
Deferred income taxes	--	8	24
Prepaid expenses	66	53	38
Total current assets	**235**	**359**	**428**
Gross property plant and equipment	205	202	204
Accumulated Depreciation	(155)	(144)	(130)
Net property, plant and equipment	50	58	75
Goodwill	166	159	107
Intangible assets	807	814	868
Other long-term assets	13	32	38
Total non-current assets	1,036	1,063	1,087
Total assets	**1,271**	**1,422**	**1,515**
Current liabilities:			
Short-term debt	21	213	24
Accounts payable	41	38	54
Accrued liabilities	136	146	125
Deferred revenue	63	62	66
Other current liabilities	32	44	107
Total current liabilities	**292**	**503**	**377**
Long-term debt	1,981	2,021	2,334
Deferred taxes	175	160	172
Other long-term liabilities	30	28	22
Total liabilities	**2,479**	**2,712**	**2,905**
Stockholders' equity:			
Retained earnings	2,057	1,995	1,883
Treasury stock	(3,237)	(3,247)	(3,254)
Other comprehensive income	(27)	(37)	(20)
Total shareholder's equity	**(1,208)**	**(1,290)**	**(1,390)**
Total Liabilities & Deficit	**1,271**	**$1,422**	**$1,515**

Source: Weight Watchers 10K filings.

	2016	2015	2014
Net income	67	33	$99
Depreciation	53	53	49
Amortization deferred financing costs	6	7	9
Impairment of assets	1	2	27
Share-based compensation expense	7	25	11
Deferred tax provision	–	–	22
Inventory	(10)	(3)	(3)
Prepaid expenses	(15)	(18)	(1)
Accounts payable	0	14	(10)
Accrued Liabilities	9	31	10
Income taxes payable	–	–	1
Other working capital	0	(7)	(4)
Other non-cash items	18	8	(4)
Net cash provided by operating activities	**119**	**55**	**323**
Investment in property, equipment and plan	(34)	(36)	(52)
Acquisitions	(3)	(3)	(17)
Other investing activities	0	(1)	(1)
Net cash provided by investment activities	**(38)**	**(40)**	**(38)**
Debt issued	–	48	–
Debt repayment	(165)	(158)	(30)
Common stock issued	–	41	–
Common stock repurchased	–	–	–
Dividend paid	(0)	(0)	(0)
Other, financing activities	(47)	0	1
Net cash provided by financing activities	**(212)**	**(69)**	**(29)**
Effects of exchange rate	–	(6)	(7)
Net change in cash	(131)	(60)	127
Cash at beginning of period	242	301	175
Cash at end of period	**111**	**242**	**301**
Operating cash flow	119	55	232
Capital expenditure	(34)	(36)	(52)
Free cash flow	**85**	**19**	**180**

EXHIBIT 5
Cash Flow Statements
($ millions)

Go to library tab in Connect
to access Case Financials.

Source: Weight Watchers 10K filings.

Innovation

Domestically and abroad, Weight Watchers was fortunate enough to build on a foundation of five decades of weight-management expertise that had allowed the company to become one of the most recognized and trusted brand names among weight-conscious consumers worldwide.[40] The innovation initiatives at Weight Watchers were focused on three main objectives: (1) rejuvenating the brand through more effective marketing, (2) providing more customer value by introducing new products, and (3) broadening the customer mix by targeting new customer segments.

The Brand

With regard to its brand, Weight Watchers was fortunate that consumers considered its brand credible and effective. The brand image was reinforced by involvement of Oprah Winfrey advocating the effectiveness of Weight Watchers diet programs by sharing her personal experience over several months. However, the company needed to more adequately differentiate its lifestyle-based approach from the strictly dieting orientation utilized by many of its competitors. In a focus group for Weight Watchers, a woman who had considered joining expressed concern that her weight would be called out in public and that she would have to tell her whole weight-loss struggle as if she were at an Alcoholics Anonymous meeting. Thus, one of the primary challenges for Weight Watchers was to correct such misperceptions as to what Weight Watchers actually was.[41] Weight Watchers had the challenge of dispelling concerns that the meeting experience was something akin to a *Biggest Loser* weigh-in and competition.

The second thing that Weight Watchers was trying to do was to reenergize the brand with more effective and differentiated marketing. Weight Watchers believed that its advertising needed to accomplish three basic tasks. First, it had to be noticed when it was seen. Second, on noticing it, people had to associate the advertising with the Weight Watchers brand. Third, it had to accomplish both the first and the second aims while communicating something new about Weight Watchers that would cause consumers to reconsider Weight Watchers as *their solution*—a plan at which they could be successful.[42] Though the company had experienced success in the first two tasks, communicating something new to consumers still seemed like a long shot. Weight Watchers had to actively emphasize the innovative things that it was doing in order to overcome consumers' preconceived notions. The company needed to show its consumers that its approach was different from the other diets out there to unleash the power that Weight Watchers believed had become a little dormant in its brand. Weight Watchers also had to consider the potential of marketing to relay relevant information that would appeal to a wider net of demographic groups.

The Program

To increase customer value, Weight Watchers had introduced programs that provided members with more flexibility and satisfaction. One innovation was a Monthly Pass payment option. When a member became a Monthly Pass subscriber, he or she participated in an eight-month recurring billing commitment in exchange for complete access to the full range of product offerings. So the underlying benefit was customization—members could utilize the different options as they saw fit in meeting their weight-loss needs. And it seemed to work. People on the Monthly Pass were losing 30 percent more weight since the pass's implementation. Further, there was a higher attendance intensity for Monthly Pass holders than for those who paid per meeting.[43] If members canceled their Monthly Pass because of not reaching the goal weight, and then later regained weight, they knew that they could always return to Weight Watchers because the plan had worked in the past.

PointsPlus, introduced at the end of 2010, was a revision of the traditional Points program. The revised program was designed to educate and encourage people to make choices that favored foods the body worked harder to convert into energy, resulting in fewer net calories absorbed. Users were encouraged to focus on foods that created a sense of fullness and satisfaction and were more healthful; they were nudged toward natural foods, rather than foods with excess added sugars and fats, but were allowed flexibility for indulgences, special occasions, and eating out. While calorie counting had been the foundation of many weight-loss programs, including the Weight Watchers' original Points system, the new PointsPlus program went beyond just calories to help people make healthful and satisfying choices. It took into account the energy contained in each of the components that made up calories—protein, carbohydrates, fat, and fiber—and it also factored in how hard the body worked to process them (conversion cost) as well their respective eating satisfaction (satiety).[44]

The next program innovation, introduced in December 2012, was the 360-degree plan. This plan built on the PointsPlus program, with members still encouraged to track their food intake with numbers based on the content of protein, fiber, carbohydrates, and fat. In addition, however, the program helped participants make better food-related decisions and did more to incorporate physical activity. For instance, an optional physical activity monitor, called Active Link, could track physical movements. This monitor, costing $40 plus a $5 monthly charge, measured all activity and converted it into PointsPlus values. Also, members were encouraged to use more of the Weight Watchers smartphone apps and website tools during the meetings while participating in hands-on demonstrations such as learning to estimate portion sizes. Other new tips included teaching people to better manage food environments at home, at work, on their travels, or at restaurants. According to Karen Miller-Kovach, chief scientific officer for the company, the emphasis on controlling food in the spaces where people live and work was based on research on "hedonic hunger—the desire to seek out high-sugar, high-fat foods that bring pleasure . . . you have to control your environment to avoid that drive."[45]

Furthermore, Weight Watchers Personal Coaching included on-demand 24/7 Expert Chat with Weight Watchers–certified coaches to "Help with the Hard Part" of managing weight loss. Supporting this program was a new ad campaign that dropped the celebrity spokesperson, formerly Jessica Simpson or Jennifer Hudson, in favor of showing regular people dealing with difficult food choices. The point was "not to pass judgment on anyone eating in an unhealthy way, but rather to demonstrate that Weight Watchers understands that eating can be emotionally charged . . . that at the end of the day, we get it and we're here to help." One former Biggest Loser contestant felt that Weight Watchers' new approach could "cause a stir in the category" and agreed that celebrity before-and-after pictures aren't realistic, while using real people shows "what it's really like for the millions with weight issues."[46]

As mentioned earlier in this case, in December 2015, Weight Watchers launched its newest food plan, called the SmartPoints system. Customers could make their personal SmartPoints budget according to their fitness goals and eat any type of food as long as it was within the consumption or calories limit allowed by their SmartPoints budget. Food with higher calories had lower SmartPoints value as compared to the food with lower calories.[47] Customers could set daily or weekly targets using the SmartPoints system to set and achieve personal dietary goals.

Again, as mentioned earlier, in 2017 the company started a new weight management program called "Beyond the Scale" for its North American customers. This new program was advertised by Oprah Winfrey, who claimed the effectiveness of the program based on personal experience, saying "It Works." The new Beyond the Scale weight management program went beyond the emphasis on weight loss by taking a holistic approach to a fit and healthy life style. The focus was more toward living a happier and healthier life by staying more active.

The Customer

Innovation at Weight Watchers also involved broadening the customer mix and targeting new customer segments. Weight Watchers was expanding beyond its target consumer market of women, ages 25 to 55.[48] In an attempt to appeal to other demographic groups, such as men and the Hispanic community in the United States, Weight Watchers retooled its offerings and approach to appear more relevant to weight-loss consumers who sought different methods of weight management.

The company was committed to work to better serve the growing Hispanic population. For example, it had improved its Spanish-language meeting materials and increased the number of Spanish meetings offered.[49] Men, another attractive market segment, appeared to be more the self-help type and were not as much in favor of a group-support experience.[50] Weight Watchers meetings had been attended mostly by women, with men making up only 5 percent of members. Morgan Stanley analyst Catherine Lewis said,

"Weight Watchers has a pipeline of unpenetrated and underpenetrated markets," and thus was testing home weight-loss services for men.[51]

To attract this segment, Weight Watchers Online, the step-by-step online guide to following the Weight Watchers plan, was intentionally customized for men and their unique set of weight-loss challenges.[52] The WeightWatchers.com for Men customization was born of the realization that Weight Watchers needed to be more culturally relevant to more groups of people who wanted different things.[53] For instance, a research study showed that about 70 percent of men were overweight and about 30 percent of men were obese. Yet, according to the study, only 28 percent of men were actively engaged in weight loss. Weight Watchers sought to provide the weight-loss answer for men by applying its 40 years of experience to its customized Internet offerings for men.

While the fundamental concepts of weight loss—eat less and exercise more—were the same for both genders, the approach to weight loss for each gender was different. As Chief Scientific Officer Miller-Kovach noted, "Men and women are biologically and emotionally different, and multiple variables factor into how each loses weight." However, the same underlying motivators for weight loss were shared between the genders: "appearance and health."[54] Thus, while the preferred means might be different, the desired end was the same. Weight Watchers Online for Men allowed men to follow the Weight Watchers plan and get food and fitness ideas, as well as other content and resources, tailored specifically to them. These products afforded Weight Watchers a new opportunity to appeal to a large market segment that might not have otherwise considered giving the program a try.[55] The percentage of men as a percentage of the Weight Watchers' total market had been on the rise. Weight Watchers was pleased with the results of the male-focused products and continued working to identify the proper levers for building that part of the business.[56] One of those levers was spokesman–sports legend Charles Barkley, whose humorous approach was intended to appeal to the everyday man.

Questions Remain

Following the onslaught and subsequent demise of fad diets such as the low-carbohydrate-focused Atkins Challenge and South Beach Diet, Weight Watchers had attempted to reinvent itself in several ways. It began to look beyond its core market of women to include men, and it expanded its business model to include not only in-person meetings but also online weight-management tools. Weight Watchers also was transitioning into a business-to-business model by partnering with major health care plans and large self-insured corporations, which offered subsidized Weight Watchers memberships to eligible members and employees. Weight Watchers was actively promoting its larger health message. Colin Watts, senior vice president of health solutions and global innovation, pointed out:

The *American Journal of Preventive Medicine* indicates that obesity has become an equal, if not greater, contributor to the burden of disease than smoking, and with alarming predictions for 2030, it's more important than ever to provide practical solutions that are not only proven effective, but that are also accessible and scalable.[57]

Weight Watchers intended to be that provider.

The question remains, will Weight Watchers be effective in staying true to the core of Jean Nidetch's goals, while still expanding to different target groups, different dieting platforms, and different means of offering them? Only time will tell, but one thing is certain: The weight-loss industry is not going away, and members of Weight Watchers' senior management continue to have many tough decisions to make.

ENDNOTES

1. http://www.marketwatch.com/story/oprah-winfrey-is-8-million-richer-after-saying-she-was-40-pounds-lighter-2016-12-22.

2. http://www.marketwatch.com/story/5-people-getting-even-richer-off-your-new-years-resolutions-2016-12-27.

3. https://www.wsj.com/articles/AP95bb977b105c4787b7e6aa85a18d6603.

4. https://www.weightwatchers.com/us/?cid=sem_ggl_rlsa_all_brand_core_main_exweight-watchers.

5. Rupp, L., Coleman-Lochner, L., & Hwang, I. 2015. Weight Watchers tumbles as rebranding fails to wow investors. *BloombergBusiness,* January 2, www.bloomberg.com/news/articles/2015-01-02/weight-watchers-tumbles-as-rebranding-fails-to-impress-investors?cmpid=yhoo.

6. http://www.marketwatch.com/story/oprah-winfrey-is-8-million-richer-after-saying-she-was-40-pounds-lighter-2016-12-22.

7. Ingram, S. 2015. There's a reason why Weight Watchers (WTW) stock is falling today. *The Street,* January 2, www.thestreet.com/story/12998430/1/weight-watchers-wtw-stock-is-falling-today-after-magazine-redesign.html?puc=yahoo&cm_ven=YAHOO.

8. Weight Watchers International Inc. (Weight Watchers). 2012. Form 10-K, 2011 annual report, April 9, www.weightwatchersinternational.com/phoenix.zhtml?c=130178&p=irol-reportsAnnual.

9. Zelman, K. M. Undated. Weight Watchers diet. *WebMD Expert Review,* www.webmd.com/diet/features/weight-watchers-diet.

10. Kosner, A. W. 2012. Weight Watchers 360: Mobile apps can break hard habits with easy-to-follow steps. *Forbes,* December 17, www.forbes.com/sites/anthonykosner/2012/12/17/weight-watchers-360-mobile-apps-can-break-hard-habits-with-easy-to-follow-steps/.

11. Lane, C. 2013. Weight Watchers: 50 years of losing. *TimesUnion,* January 11, www.timesunion.com/living/article/Weight-Watchers-50-years-of-losing-4187277.php#page-1.

12. Ibid.

13. DePillis, L. 2013. Internet killed the dieting star: Why Weight Watchers is floundering. *Washington Post,* August 4, www.washingtonpost.com/blogs/wonkblog/wp/2013/08/04/internet-killed-the-dieting-star-why-weight-watchers-is-floundering/.

14. Berr, J. 2014. The Flabby business of shrinking waistlines. *The Fiscal Times,* February 3, www.thefiscaltimes.com/Articles/2014/02/03/Weight-Watchers-and-Flabby-Business-Shrinking-Waistlines.

15. Weight Watchers. 2011. Form 10-K, 2010 annual report.

16. Ibid.

17. Nidetch, J. T., & Rattner, J. 1979. *The Story of Weight Watchers.* New York: Penguin.

18. Weight Watchers. 2010. Weight Watchers introduces revolutionary new program to help Americans improve their eating habits and successfully lose weight. November

19. Weight Watchers. 2011. Form 10-K, 2010 annual report.

20. Weight Watchers. 2015 annual report.

21. Ibid.

22. Let the countdown to soup begin! 2007. *Business Wire,* August 14.

23. Perrenot, G., & Durnan, K. 2005. Lunch ladies: Applebee's Weight Watchers menu. *Dallas Morning News,* April 11.

24. Dolan, B. 2014. Weight Watchers confirms Wello acquisition, plans API-enabled fitness platform. *MobileHealthNews,* May 6, http://mobihealthnews.com/32838/weight-watchers-confirms-wello-acquisition-plans-api-enabled-fitness-platform/.

25. http://health.usnews.com/best-diet/weight-watchers-diet.

26. http://fortune.com/2015/05/22/lean-times-for-the-diet-industry/.

27. https://www.franchisehelp.com/industry-reports/weight-loss-industry-report/.

28. Hill, C. 2014. 10 things the weight-loss industry won't tell you. *MarketWatch,* January 14, http://www.marketwatch.com/story/10-things-the-weight-loss-industry-wont-tell-you-2014-01-10?page=7.

29. Weight Watchers. 2010. Tackling the growing obesity epidemic: New research shows Weight Watchers works globally. July 13, www.weightwatchersinternational.com/phoenix.zhtml?c=130178&p=irol-newsArticle&ID=1446897.

30. Weight Watchers. 2011. Form 10-K, 2010 annual report.

31. Lee, J. 2010. Diet plan review: Best ways to lose 20 pounds. *MoneyWatch,* January 4, moneywatch.bnet.com/saving-money/article/diet-plan-review-best-ways-to-lose-weight/377880/.

32. http://health.usnews.com/wellness/food/articles/2017-01-04/us-news-best-diets-how-we-rated-38-eating-plans.

33. Salahi, L. 2012. Study: Weight Watchers as successful as clinical weight-loss programs. ABC News, October 9, abcnews.go.com/Health/w_DietAndFitness/study-weight-watchers-successful-clinical-weight-loss-programs/story?id=17424647#.UOeEE6zNl8E.

34. MacMillan, A. 2012. Dieters in Weight Watchers study drop up to 15 pounds in a year. *Health.com,* January 4, www.cnn.com/2011/09/07/health/weight-watchers-lancet/index.html.

35. Weight Watchers. Form 10-K, annual reports.

36. Florian, E. 2002. When it comes to fat, they're huge. *Fortune,* October 14: 54.

37. Choe. 2004. Weight Watchers' attractive figures.

38. Weight Watchers. Form 10-K, annual reports.

39. Serafin. 2006. The fat of the land.

40. Weight Watchers. Form 10-K, annual reports.

41. Weight Watchers. 2007. Event brief of Q2 2007 Weight Watchers International, Inc. earnings conference call—final.

42. Weight Watchers. 2007. Event brief of Q1 2007 Weight Watchers International, Inc. earnings conference call.

43. Ibid.

44. Weight Watchers. 2010. Weight Watchers introduces revolutionary new program to help Americans improve their eating habits and successfully lose weight. November 29, www.weightwatchersinternational.com/phoenix.zhtml?c=130178&p=irol-newsArticle&ID=1500758.

45. Hellmich, N. 2012. New Weight Watchers 360 plan unveiled. *USA Today,* December 2, www.usatoday.com/story/news/nation/2012/12/02/weight-watchers-new-program/1732297/.

46. Newman, A. A. 2014. Weight Watchers serving up understanding to those who eat their feelings. *New York Times,* November 24, www.nytimes.com/2014/11/25/business/media/weight-watchers-serving-up-understanding-to-those-who-eat-their-feelings.html?_r=0.

47. Weight Watchers annual report 2015.

48. Sunoo, B. P. 1997. Changing behavior at Weight Watchers. *Workforce,* July: 27–29.

49. Weight Watchers. 2006. Event brief of Q4 2006 Weight Watchers International, Inc. earnings conference call.

50. Ibid.

51. Marcial, G. G. 2002. Hefty gains for Weight Watchers? *BusinessWeek,* October 21: 168.

52. Weight Watchers. 2007. Weight loss: Announcing the launch of Weight Watchers Online for Men and Weight Watchers eTools for Men. *Women's Health Law Weekly,* April 22: 251.

53. Weight Watchers. Form 10-K, annual reports.

54. Weight Watchers. 2007. Weight loss: Announcing the launch of Weight Watchers Online for Men.

55. Weight Watchers. 2007. Event brief of Q1 2007 Weight Watchers International, Inc. earnings conference call—final. *Fair Disclosure Wire,* May 3.

56. Weight Watchers. 2007. Event brief of Q2 2007 Weight Watchers International, Inc. earnings conference call—final. *Fair Disclosure Wire,* August 1.

57. Weight Watchers. 2012. Weight Watchers and WellCare join forces to support better health for Georgians. *PRNewswire,* December 6, www.weightwatchersinternational.com/phoenix. zhtml?c=130178&p=irol-newsArticle&ID=1765083&highlight=.

CASE 25

SAMSUNG ELECTRONICS 2017[*]

On February 17, 2017, Lee Jae-yong, the vice chairman of Samsung, was arrested on bribery charges. This drew considerable attention since the conglomerate is one of the most formidable in South Korea with Samsung Electronics alone accounting for 20 percent of the country's exports. Lee has been the de facto leader of Samsung since his father, Lee Kun-hee, became incapacitated after suffering a heart attack in 2014. The son was charged with paying $36 million to a secret confidante of the South Korean president in return for government support for a series of internal moves that would allow Lee Jae-yong to inherit control of the firm from his father.

The charges came at a tough time for the firm, which has been struggling to break from its past and forge changes to its top-down rigid management approach that pushes its employees to meet demanding goals fast—some say too fast (see Exhibits 1 and 2). "In the Samsung culture, managers

* Case prepared by Jamal Shamsie, Michigan State University, with the assistance of Professor Alan B. Eisner, Pace University. Material has been drawn from published sources to be used for purposes of class discussion. Copyright © 2017 Jamal Shamsie and Alan B. Eisner.

constantly feel pressured to prove themselves with short-term achievements," said Kim Jin-baek, who worked at the firm until 2010.[1] Lee Jae-yong had been trying to change this highly goal-driven culture. But he could not help rushing to launch the Samsung Note 7.

Driven by the need to prove that it was more than a fast follower of Apple, Samsung pushed the Note 7 to market ahead of Apple's anticipated iPhone 7 (see Exhibit 3). One of the firm's most ambitious efforts, the latest Samsung smartphone was packed with new features, like a super-high-resolution camera, waterproof technology, and iris-scanning for added security. It apparently also came with some problems. Experts claimed that the battery was packed too tightly, in order to keep the phone relatively thin. This was borne out when the Note 7 revealed a tendency to burst into flames. Subsequently Samsung engaged in one of its most extensive and costly recalls and eventually had to kill the new product.

The highly publicized debacle of the Note 7 suggested to some observers that Samsung has problems that may stem from its basic culture. Critics claim that the firm maintains an atmosphere of constant crisis, which drives employees to work incredibly hard to the point of overly speeding

EXHIBIT 1 Income Statement (billions of KRW)

	Years Ending December 31			
	2016	**2015**	**2014**	**2013**
Net Sales	201,866	200,653	206,206	228,693
Gross Profit	79,983	74,920	77,927	90,996
Pretax Income	30,694	24,859	27,532	37,860
Net Income	22,415	18,694	23,082	39,821

Source: Samsung.

EXHIBIT 2 Balance Sheet (billions of KRW)

	Years Ending December 31			
	2016	**2015**	**2014**	**2013**
Total Assets	262,174	242,179	230,422	214,075
Total Liabilities	69,211	63,119	62,334	64,059
Total Shareholders Equity	186,424	172,876	162,181	144,442

Source: Samsung.

EXHIBIT 3 Smartphone Sales Worldwide

2016 Market Shares	
Samsung	18.1%
Apple	18.3%
Huawei	10.6%
OPPO	7.3%
Vivo	5.8%
Others	40.0%

Source: Statistica, 2017.

EXHIBIT 4 Global Market Ranking, 2016

Product Category	Market Rank
Mobile Phones	1
Memory Chips	1
Digital Televisions	1
DVD Players	2
Washers & Dryers	2
Camcorders	3
Digital Cameras	3

Source: Samsung.

to market. Further, analysts suggest that a related problem lies with the heavy reliance of Samsung on competing with its hardware, while other providers, ranging from Apple to Xiaomi, offer software and Internet services that set their products apart because they run only on their devices. Samsung has introduced its own operating system, Tizen, which is unlikely to challenge existing systems though, such as Google's Android.

Executives at Samsung claim the firm's strength lies in the diverse line of its products that includes televisions, cameras, laptops, and even washing machines (see Exhibit 4). Although smartphones account for as much as two-thirds of Samsung's profits, revenues are diversified from their other offerings. Furthermore, unlike their rivals, Samsung makes most of its own components allowing it to offer better products with lower costs. The firm can generate profits even if profit margins on some of these products continue to decline.

Discarding a Failing Strategy

Yun Jong Yong was appointed to the position of president and CEO in 1996. When Yun took charge, Samsung was still making most of its profits from lower-priced appliances

that consumers were likely to pick up if they could not afford a higher-priced brand such as Sony or Mitsubishi. Samsung was an established low-cost supplier of various components to larger and better-known manufacturers around the world. Samsung chairman Lee Kun-hee had called for a shift in the firm's strategy; the transformation could not have been possible without the ceaseless efforts of Yun Jong Yong.

Although the firm was making profits, Lee Kun-hee and Yun Jong Yong were concerned about the future prospects of a firm that was relying on a strategy of competing on low price with products based on technologies that had been developed by other firms. The success of this strategy was tied to the ability of Samsung to continually scout for locations that would allow it to keep its manufacturing costs down. At the same time, it would need to keep generating sufficient orders to maintain a high volume of production. The firm was likely to face growing competition from the many low-cost producers that were springing up in countries such as China.

These concerns were well founded. Within a year of Yun's takeover, Samsung was facing serious financial problems that threatened its very survival. The company was left with huge debt as an economic crisis engulfed most of Asia in 1997, leading to a drop in demand and a crash in the prices of many electronic goods. In the face of such a deteriorating environment, Samsung continued to push for maintaining its production and sales quotas even as much of its output was ending up unsold in warehouses.

By July 1998, Samsung Electronics was losing millions of dollars each month. "If we continued, we would have gone belly-up within three or four years," Yun recalled.[2] He knew that he had to make some drastic moves in order to turn things around. Yun locked himself in a hotel room for a whole day with nine other senior managers to try to find a way out. They all wrote resignation letters and pledged to resign if they failed.

After much deliberation, Yun and his management team decided to take several steps to push Samsung out of its precarious financial position. To begin with, they decided to lay off about 30,000 employees, representing well over a third of its entire workforce. They also closed down many of Samsung's factories for two months so that they could get rid of its large inventory. Finally, they sold off about $2 billion worth of businesses such as pagers and electric coffeemakers that were perceived to be of marginal significance for the firm's future.

Developing a Premium Brand

Having managed to stem the losses, Yun decided to move Samsung away from its strategy of competition based largely on the lower price of its products. He began to push the firm to develop its own unique products rather than to copy those that other firms had developed. In particular, Yun placed considerable emphasis on the development of products that would impress consumers with their attractive designs and their advanced technology. By focusing on such products, Yun hoped that he could develop Samsung into a premium brand that could charge higher prices.

In order to achieve all this, Yun had to reorient the firm and help it to develop new capabilities. He recruited new managers and engineers, many of whom had developed considerable experience in the U.S. Once they had been recruited, Yun got them into shape by putting them through a four-week boot camp that consisted of martial drills at the crack of dawn and mountain hikes that would last all day. To create incentives for this new talent, Yun discarded Samsung's rigid seniority-based system and replaced it with a merit-based system for advancement.

As a result of these efforts, Samsung began launching an array of products designed to make a big, and new, impression on consumers: the largest flat-panel televisions, cell phones with a variety of features such as cameras and PDAs, ever-thinner notebook computers, and speedier and richer semiconductors. The firm called them "wow products," designed to elevate Samsung in the same way the Triniton television and the Walkman had helped to plant Sony in the minds of consumers

Finally, to help Samsung change its image among consumers, Yun hired a marketing whiz, Eric Kim, who worked hard to create a more upscale image of the firm and its products. Kim moved Samsung's advertising away from 55 different advertising agencies around the world and placed it with one firm, Madison Avenues's Foote, Cone & Belding Worldwide in order to create a consistent global brand image for Samsung products. Yun pulled Samsung out of big discount chains like Walmart and Kmart and placed more of its products in more upscale specialty stores such as Best Buy and Circuit City.

Yun also began a practice of working closely with retailers to get more information about the specific needs of prospective consumers. Since then, unlike Apple, Samsung has focused heavily on studying existing markets and innovating inside them. "We get most of our ideas from the market," said Kim Hyun-suk, an executive vice president at Samsung.[3] The firm has been able to develop strong relationships with retailers because of this practice. Over the years, Samsung has also worked successfully with wireless carriers, because of their willingness to work with them in figuring out what to offer in their smartphones and tablets.

Speeding Up New Product Development

Yun also took many steps to speed up Samsung's new product development process, well aware that higher margins depended on introducing new products to the market well ahead of rivals. Samsung managers who have worked for big competitors say they have to go through far fewer layers of bureaucracy than they had to in the past to win approval for new products, budgets, and marketing plans, speeding up their ability to seize opportunities.

Apart from reducing bureaucratic obstacles, Yun was able to take advantage of the emerging shift to digital technologies. He made heavy investments into key technologies ranging from semiconductors to LCD displays that could allow it to push out a wide variety of revolutionary digital products. Samsung has continuously invested more than any of its rivals on its research and development, rising to almost $12 billion by 2014. The firm's large force of designers and engineers work in several research centers that are spread all around the world (see Exhibit 5).

Yun forced Samsung's own internal production units to compete with outside suppliers in order to speed up the process of developing innovative new products. In the liquid-crystal-display business, for example, Samsung bought half of its color filters from Sumitomo Chemical Company of Japan and sourced the other half internally, pitting the two teams against each other. "They really press these departments to compete," said Sumitomo President Hiromasa Yonekura.[4] As a result, Samsung claims that it has been able to reduce the time it takes to go from new product concept to rollout to as little as five months, compared to over a year that it used to take the firm in 2000.

The firm's top managers, engineers, and designers work relentlessly in the five-story VIP center nestled amid the firm's industrial complex in Suwon. They work day and night in the center, which has dormitories and showers for brief rests during work sprints to sort out any problems that may hold back a product launch. The teams that pursue new product design in the VIP center strive to reduce complexity in the early stages of the design cycle. This allows the firm to get its products to move quickly to manufacturing with minimal problems and at the lowest possible cost. Kyunghan Jung, a senior manager of the center, explained: "Seventy to eighty percent of quality, cost and delivery time is determined in the initial stages of product development."[5]

The speedier development process has allowed Samsung to introduce the first voice-activated phones, handsets with MP3 players, and digital camera phones that send photos over global mobile communications networks. As an example

EXHIBIT 5 Designers Employed

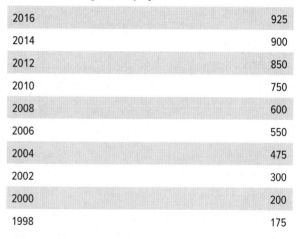

2016	925
2014	900
2012	850
2010	750
2008	600
2006	550
2004	475
2002	300
2000	200
1998	175

Source: Samsung.

of the firm's speed and agility, Charles Golvin of Forrester Research talked about Samsung's having created four different industrial designs of its Galaxy S smartphone for four different wireless network types around the world and delivered them simultaneously. "They've had a long history of responding to market trends with a lot of alacrity," he remarked.[6]

Perfecting a Design Process

As Yun was building up the Samsung brand, he was already positioning the firm to compete on the basis of the "irresistible" design of its wide range of products from home appliances to handheld computers to flat-screen televisions that would all be eventually linked to each other. In fact, the firm does seem to be well placed to develop attractive gadgets that straddle traditional technology categories. "We have to combine computers, consumer electronics and communications as Koreans mix their rice with vegetables and meats," said Dae Je Chin, the head of Samsung's digital media division.[7]

As Samsung tries to pack its products with various attractive features, it draws on the knowledge of some 900 designers with backgrounds in disciplines as diverse as psychology, sociology, economics, and engineering. These designers absorb information collected by over 60,000 staff members working in 24 research centers across the globe in San Francisco, London, Tokyo, Mumbai, and Shanghai. The researchers observe the way that consumers actually use various products. The wide Galaxy Note phone, for example, resulted from the responses of focus groups who wanted a device that was good for handwriting, drawing, and sharing notes. Asian consumers said that they found it easier to write characters on a device using a pen than to type on a keyboard.

"The research process is unimaginable," says Chang Donghoon, an executive vice president of Samsung who has led the company's design efforts. "We go through all avenues to make sure we read the trends correctly."[8] Samsung sends its growing group of designers to various locations to spend a few months at fashion houses, furniture designers, and cosmetic specialists to stay current with trends in other industries. Designers of the latest Galaxy smartphone have said that they drew inspiration from trips to ruins in Cambodia, vistas in Helinski, a Salvador Dali art exhibit in London, and even a balloon ride in Africa.

Further, Samsung has appointed designers to executive positions in order to make sure that they can get their ideas to top managers. In 2015, the firm managed to recruit Lee Don-tae, who had been a top executive at a leading UK design agency. He joined Chang Don-hoon, who had been given charge of the firm's design strategy team, which oversees the design of products across all of the product lines. In the fall of 2014, Samsung unveiled a slick design website to shore up its self-proclaimed status as a design powerhouse. As a result of these efforts, Samsung has earned a total of well over 200 design awards since 2006 at contests in the U.S., Europe, and Asia. After winning awards at a recent U.S. consumer electronics show, an executive said: "Samsung strives to consistently lead the consumer electronics industry in product design and engineering innovation."[9]

Samsung's ambition is to leverage the attractiveness of its products to make them the center piece of a digital home. In a showroom in the lobby of its headquarters in Seoul, the firm shows off many of its latest offerings ranging from tablet computers to digital cameras. Visitors can put on goggles to watch characters jump out on 3-D televisions or shuffle their feet on an interactive LED floor. Roger Entner, a wireless industry analyst at Neilson, said about Samsung's efforts: "With its resources and experience, it's trying to capitalize on the emergence of smart connected devices. The question is, 'Can they be a cutting-edge trendsetter like Apple?'"[10]

Creating a Sustainable Model?

Samsung Electronics has been managed since 2012 by Kwon Oh-hyun, who helped the firm to become a leader in memory and semiconductor operations. As chip technology improves more incrementally, Samsung is one of the few companies left that can make the investments into new generations of semiconductors. As a result, it could become one of the biggest suppliers to other smartphone manufacturers. It is already one of the major suppliers of chips, among other components, for firms such as Apple, Sony, and Hewlett-Packard. "Then Samsung will have greater control over the whole ecosystem," said Sundeep Bajikar, a securities analyst. "The benefits of that can be enormous."[11]

At the same time, Samsung has been pushing to make its products more accessible to end customers. It has teamed up with Best Buy to create the Samsung Experience Shop, a store-within-a-store which allows customers to test the company's newest products as well as get training in mobile products they already own. By the end of 2015, these Experience Shops had expanded to over 2,000 Best Buy locations across the U.S.

Samsung has acknowledged that Lee's arrest poses a setback to its reputation. It hopes the more internal-to-the-business nature of the problem will allow it to fade and that the usefulness and attractiveness of its products will remain uppermost in the mind of the buying public. It seems to have gotten past the recent problem with the battery of its smartphone.

Aware that it must continue to search for new opportunities, in a marked shift from its past strategy, the firm has made several acquisitions. It bought start-ups SmartThings, a platform for connected devices, and Viv, a digital assistant that can compete with Apple's Siri. Its most aggressive move has been into development of connected, driverless vehicles via investments in Vinli and nuTonomy, two start-ups that make software for connected cars. It followed these up with an $8 billion acquisition of U.S.-based Harman International in November 2016, which is also expanding into similar services for automobiles.

"We think technology is more critical than being in the metal-bending business," said Young Sohn, a strategist at Samsung.[12] The firm is hoping to sell more of its semiconductors, display panels, and mobile services to manufacturers of the new generation of driverless cars. The firm faces competition from several existing and potential entrants into this new area. Analysts believe that Samsung's success with these recent moves is likely to depend on its ability to transfer its expertise in one sort of mobile technology to others.

Change everything except your wife and children.

—Address to employees from Samsung chairman Lee Kun-hee to push for its transformation to a leading electronics brand

ENDNOTES

1. Choe Sang-Hun & Paul Mozur. A top-down breakdown. *New York Times,* January 24, 2017, p. B5.

2. Frank Gibney, Jr. Samsung moves upmarket. *Time.* March 25, 2002, p. 49.

3. Brian X. Chen. Samsung's strategy to brake Apple juggernaut. *New York Times,* February 11, 2013, p. B1.

4. Peter Lewis. A perpetual crisis machine. *Fortune,* September 19, 2005, p. 65.

5. Cliff Edwards, Moon Ihlwan & Pete Engardio. The Samsung way. *BusinessWeek,* June 16, 2003, p. 61.

6. Roger Yu. Samsung cranks up creativity. *USA Today,* November 16, 2010, p. 4B.

7. David Rocks & Moon Ihlwan. Samsung design. *BusinessWeek,* December 6, 2004, p. 90.

8. *New York Times,* February 11, 2013, p. B1.

9. Anonymous. Samsung Electronics gets 46 CES innovations awards for 2009. *Wireless News,* November 24, 2008.

10. *USA Today,* November 16, 2010, p. 4B.

11. Eric Pfanner. Chip profits help soften other losses at Samsung. *New York Times,* January 25, 2014, p. B 2.

12. Jonathan Cheng. Samsung seeks auto expansion. *Wall Street Journal,* November 15, 2016, p. A10.

CASE 26

PROCTER & GAMBLE*

On February 14, 2017, The Wall Street Journal reported that Trian Fund Management, one of the biggest activist investors has built up a more than $3 billion stake in Procter & Gamble, a leading global consumer products firm. The move added urgency to P&G's efforts to turn around its business and boost its stock price. The firm's closely watched organic sales growth, which excludes acquisitions or divestments as well as currency swings, has been stuck between 1% and 3% in recent years (see Exhibits 1 and 2). It has struggled to boost sales growth as it has confronted a sluggish global economy and competition from global competitors and Internet upstarts.

Since its founding 175 years ago, P&G had risen to the status of an American icon with well-known consumer products such as *Pampers, Tide, Downy* and *Crest* (see Exhibit 3).

* Case prepared by Jamal Shamsie, Michigan State University, with the assistance of Professor Alan B. Eisner, Pace University. Material has been drawn from published sources to be used for purposes of class discussion. Copyright © 2017 Jamal Shamsie and Alan B. Eisner.

In fact, the firm has long been admired for its superior products, its marketing brilliance, and the intense loyalty of its employees who have respectfully come to be known as Proctoids. But a downward spiral in the 1990's led the firm to turn to Alan G. Lafley to try and turn things around. He spent $70 billion over his tenure scooping up brands such as *Gillette* razors, *Clairol* cosmetics and *Iams* pet food. With 25 brands that generated more than $1 billion in sales, P&G became the largest consumer products company in the world.

Under Lafley's chosen successor, Bob McDonald, however, P&G's growth stalled as recession-battered consumers abandoned the firm's premium-priced products for cheaper alternatives. More significantly, the firm's vaunted innovation machine stalled with no major product success during his tenure. P&G's decline eroded morale among employees, with many managers taking early retirement or bolting to competitors. Says Ed Artzt, who was CEO from 1990 to 1995: "The most unfortunate aspect of this whole thing is the brain drain. The loss of good people is almost irreparable when you depend on promotion from within to continue building the company."[1]

EXHIBIT 1
Income Statement
(in millions of $)

	Year Ending		
	June 30, 2017	June 30, 2016	June 30, 2015
Total Revenue	65,058	65,299	70,749
Operating Income	13,955	13,441	11,049
EBIT	13,257	13,369	11,012
Net Income	15,411	10,604	7,144

Source: P&G.

EXHIBT 2
Balance Sheet
(in millions of $)

	Year Ending		
	June 30, 2017	June 30, 2016	June 30, 2015
Current Assets	26,494	33,782	29,646
Total Assets	120,406	127,136	129,495
Current Liabilities	30,210	30,770	29,790
Total Liabilities	64,628	69,153	66,445
Stockholder Equity	55,778	57,983	63,050

Source: P&G.

EXHIBIT 3
Significant Innovations

- Tide was the first heavy-duty laundry detergent
- Crest was the first fluoride toothpaste clinically proven to prevent tooth decay
- Downy was the first ultra-concentrated rinse-add fabric softener
- Pert Plus was the first 2-in-1 shampoo and conditioner
- Head & Shoulders was the first pleasant-to-use shampoo effective against dandruff
- Pampers was the first affordable, mass-marketed disposable diaper
- Bounty was the first three-dimensional paper towel
- Always was the first feminine protection pad with an innovative, dry-weave topsheet
- Febreze was the first fabric and air care product that actually remove odors from fabrics and the air
- Crest White Strips was the first patented in-home teeth whitening technology

Source: P&G.

Pressure from the board forced Lafley to back come out of retirement in May 2013 to make another attempt to pull P&G out of its doldrums. Soon after he took back the helm of the firm, Lafley announced that he would get rid of more than half of its brands. Over the next three years, the firm sold off many of the brands that it had acquired, capped by the $11.6 billion sale of dozens of beauty brands to Coty. He announced that the company would narrow its focus to 65 or 70 of its biggest brands such as *Tide, Crest*, and *Pampers*. "Less will be more," Lafley told analysts. "The objective is growth and much more reliable generation of cash and profit."[2]

David S. Taylor, who had spent years managing P&G's businesses finally took over as chairman and CEO of the firm in November 2015. He has been confident that he can resurrect the firm but has opted against launching new brands or making new acquisitions. "I understand the desire for faster growth and for a single-minded short-term objective, but we've seen this movie before" he said at a meeting with analysts last November.[3]

Fighting off a Decline

For most of its long history, P&G has been one of America's preeminent companies. The firm has developed several well-known brands such as *Tide,* one of the pioneers in laundry detergents, which was launched in 1946 and *Pampers,* the first disposable diaper, which was introduced in 1961. P&G also built its brands through its innovative marketing techniques. Nevertheless, by the 1990s, P&G was in danger of becoming another Eastman Kodak or Xerox, a once-great company that might have lost its way. Sales on most of its eighteen top brands were slowing as it was being outhustled by more focused rivals such as Kimberly-Clark and Colgate-Palmolive.

In 1999, P&G decided to bring in Durk I. Jaeger to try and make the big changes that were obviously needed to get P&G back on track. However, the moves that he made generally misfired, sinking the firm into deeper trouble. He introduced expensive new products that never caught on while letting existing brands drift.

He also put in place a company-wide reorganization that left many employees perplexed and preoccupied. During the fiscal year when he was in charge, earnings per share showed an anemic rise of just 3.5%, much lower than in previous years. In addition, during that time, the share price slid 52%, cutting P&G's total market capitalization by $85 billion.

In 2000, the board of P&G asked Lafley to take charge of the troubled firm. He began his tenure by breaking down the walls between management and the employees. Since the 1950s, all of the senior executives at P&G used to be located on the eleventh floor at the firm's corporate headquarters. Lafley changed this setup, moving all five division presidents to the same floors as their staff. He replaced more than half of the company's top 30 managers, more than any P&G boss in memory, and trimmed its work force by as many as 9,600 jobs. Moreover, he moved more women into senior positions. In fact, Lafley skipped over 78 general managers with more seniority to name 42-year-old Deborah A. Henretta to head P&G's then-troubled North American baby-care division.

In fact, Lafley was simply acknowledging the importance of developing people, particularly those in managerial roles at P&G. For years, the firm has been known to dispatch line managers rather than human resource staffers to do much of its recruiting. For the few that get hired, their work life becomes a career long development process. At every level, P&G has a different 'college' to train individuals and every department has its own 'university.' The general manager's college holds a weeklong school term once a year when there are a handful of newly promoted managers.

Under Lafley, P&G also continued with its efforts to maintain a comprehensive database of all of its more than 130,000 employees, each of which is tracked carefully through monthly and annual talent reviews. All managers are reviewed not only by their bosses but also by lateral managers who have worked with them, as well as on their own direct reports. Every February, one entire board meeting is devoted to reviewing the high-level executives, with the goal of coming up with at least three potential candidates for each of the 35 to 40 jobs at the top of the firm.

Gambling on its Brands

Above all, however, Lafley had been intent on shifting the focus of P&G back to its consumers. At every opportunity that he got, he tried to drill his managers and employees not to lose sight of the consumer. He felt that P&G has often let technology dictate its new products rather than consumer needs. He wanted to see the firm work more closely with retailers, the place where consumers first see the product on the shelf. In addition, he placed a lot of emphasis on getting a better sense of the consumer's experience with P&G products when they actually use them at home.

Over the decade of Lafley's leadership, P&G managed to update all of its 200 brands by adding innovative new products. It begun to offer devices that build on its core brands, such as *Tide StainBrush,* a battery-powered brush for removing stains and *Mr. Clean AutoDry,* a water pressure powered car-cleaning system that dries without streaking. P&G also begun to approach its brands more creatively. *Crest,* for example, which used to be marketed as a toothpaste brand, was redefined an oral care brand. The firm now sells *Crest*-branded toothbrushes and tooth whiteners.

In order to ensure that P&G continues to come up with innovative ideas, Lafley had also confronted head-on the stubbornly held notion that everything must be invented within P&G, asserting that half of its new products should come from the outside. Under the new 'Connect and Develop' model of innovation, the firm pushed to get almost 50% of its new product ideas from outside the firm. This could be compared to the 10% figure that existed at P&G when Lafley had taken charge.

A key element of P&G's strategy, however, was to move the firm away from basic consumer products such as laundry detergents, which can be knocked off by private labels, to higher-margin products. Under Lafley, P&G made costly acquisitions of Clairol and Wella to complement its *Cover Girl* and *Oil of Olay* brands. The firm had even moved into prestige fragrances through licenses with Hugo Boss, Gucci and Dolce & Gabbana. When he stepped down, beauty products had risen to account for about a quarter of the firm's total revenues.

But P&G's riskiest moves had been its expansion into services, starting with car washes and dry cleaning. The car washes build on *Mr. Clean,* P&G's popular cleaning product. In expanding the brand to car washes, the firm expected to distinguish its outlets from others by offering additional services such as *Febreze* odor eliminators, lounges with Wi-Fi and big screen televisions and spray guns that children can aim at cars passing through the wash. Similarly, P&G's dry cleaning outlets are named after *Tide,* its bestselling laundry detergent. The stores will include drive-through services, 24-hour pickup and environmentally benign cleaning methods.

Losing the Momentum

On July 1, 2009, Lafley passed the leadership of P&G to McDonald, who had joined the firm in 1980 and worked his way up through posts in Canada, Japan, the Philippines and Belgium to become chief operating officer. McDonald took over after the start of a calamitous recession, and had to deal with various emerging problems. Even as consumers in U.S. and Europe were not willing to pay premium prices, the firm's push to expand in emerging markets was also yielding few results in the face of stiff competition from Unilever and Colgate-Palmolive, who already had a strong presence. Furthermore, commodity prices were surging, even as P&G's products were already too expensive for the struggling middle-class that it was targeting everywhere.

In order to deal with all of these challenges, McDonald replaced Lafley's clear motto of "the consumer is boss" with his own slogan of "purpose-inspired growth." In his own words, this meant that P&G was "touching and improving more consumers' lives, in more parts of the world, more completely." "Purpose" was an undeniably laudable ambition, but many employees simply could not fathom how to translate this rhetoric into action. Dick Antoine, P&G's head of HR from 1998 to 2008 commented: "'Purpose-inspired growth' is a wonderful slogan, but it doesn't help allocate assets."[4]

The new focus seemed to fit well with McDonald, who seemed more comfortable with the details of P&G's operations. Even when McDonald tried to broaden his scope, McDonald found it difficult to establishing priorities for P&G. Given the wide range of problems that he faced, in terms of pushing for growth across several different businesses across many markets, he made some effort to try and address all of them at the same time. Ali Dibadj, a senior analyst at Sanford Bernstein commented on this multi-pronged effort by P&G: "The strategic problem was that they decided to go after everything. But they ran out of ammo too quickly."[5]

By the middle of 2012, it was becoming obvious that P&G was struggling under McDonald's leadership. Known for its reliable performance, the firm was forced to lower its profit guidelines three times in six months frustrating analysts and investors alike. Even within the firm, many executives realized that McDonald would not be able to take the bold moves that may allow the firm to recover from its slump. Activist investor Bill Ackerman commented: "We're delighted to see the company's made some progress. But P&G deserves to be led by one of the best CEO's in the world."[6]

Striving for Agility

Shareholder dissatisfaction with lack of improvement in performance led P&G to push McDonald out and bring back Lafley in May 2013. As soon as he stepped back in,

EXHIBIT 4 Business Segments, 2016

Reportable Segments	% of Net Sales	% of Net Earnings	Product Categories (Sub-Categories)	Major Brands
Beauty	18%	20%	Hair Care (*Conditioner, Shampoo, Styling Aids, Treatments*)	Head & Shoulders, Pantene, Rejoice
			Skin and Personal Care (*Antiperspirant and Deodorant, Personal Cleansing, Skin Care*)	Olay, Old Spice, Safeguard, SK-II
Grooming	11%	15%	Grooming (Shave Care - *Female Blades & Razors, Male Blades & Razors, Pre- and Post-Shave Products, Other Shave Care;* Appliances)	Braun, Fusion, Gillette, Mach3, Prestobarba, Venus
Health Care	11%	12%	Oral Care (*Toothbrushes, Toothpaste, Other Oral Care*)	Crest, Oral-B
			Personal Health Care (*Gastrointestinal, Rapid Diagnostics, Respiratory, Vitamins/Minerals/ Supplements, Other Personal Health Care*)	Prilosec, Vicks
Fabric & Home Care	32%	27%	Fabric Care (*Fabric Enhancers, Laundry Additives, Laundry Detergents*)	Ariel, Downy, Gain, Tide
			Home Care (*Air Care, Dish Care, P&G Professional, Surface Care*)	Cascade, Dawn, Febreze, Mr. Clean, Swiffer
Baby, Feminine & Family Care	28%	26%	Baby Care (*Baby Wipes, Diapers, and Pants*)	Luvs, Pampers
			Feminine Care (*Adult Incontinence, Feminine Care*)	Always, Tampax
			Family Care (*Paper Towels, Tissues, Toilet Paper*)	Bounty, Charmin

Source: P&G Annual Report 2016.

Lafley was under pressure to respond to investor concerns that P&G had become too large and bloated to respond quickly to changing consumer demands. In April 2014, he began the process of streamlining the firm by selling of most of its pet food brands—including *Iams* and *Eukanuba*— to Mars for $2.9 billion. A few months later, in August 2014, Lafley took a bolder step. He announced that the firm would unload as many as 100 of its brands in order to better focus on 60 to 70 of its biggest ones—such as *Tide* detergent and *Pampers* diapers—that generate about 90% of its $83 billion in annual sales and over 95% of its profit (see Exhibits 4 and 5). Lafley did not specify which ones would be sold off or shut down, but the company owns scores of lesser brands such as *Cheer* laundry detergent and *Metamucil* laxatives.

Lafley insisted that sales would not be the only criteria for shedding brands. He stated that some large brands would be jettisoned if they didn't fit with the firm's core business: "If it's not a core brand—I don't care whether it's a $2 billion brand—it will be divested."[7] He demonstrated this by the decision to spin off its Duracell into a stand-alone company. Although batteries have been generating $2.2 billion annually in sales, their sluggish growth did not fit with Lafley's push for a more focused company.

Although analysts have been receptive to the reduction of brands, they have pointed out that P&G has already sold off more than 30 established brands over the past 15 years which were supposedly hindering growth. Many of these sold off brands have been performing well with other firms. J.M. Smucker, for example, that brought *Crisco* shortening, *Folgers* coffee and *Jif* peanut butter, has had 50 percent sales growth since 2009. Some critics charge that P&G, which was once was most successful in building and managing brands, has lost its touch.

In large part, the focus is on the cumbersome centralized and bureaucratic structure that has developed at P&G. Unlike many of its newer competitors, the firm still tends to rely less on working with outside partners. The 'Connect and Develop' program that had been started by Lafley to bring in new ideas from outsiders has led to 50 percent of its new technologies coming from outside, but these are then reworked or modified by P&G's internal R&D group. This has stifled innovation, with most of the firm's growth coming from line extensions of existing brands or from costly acquisitions.

On November 1, 2015, Lafley stepped down, passing the reins to David Taylor, who had built his career at P&G. He had most recently been assigned to take over the firm's

EXHIBIT 5 Financial Breakdown 2016

Global Segment Results		Net Sales	Earnings/(Loss) from Continuing Operations Before Income Taxes	Net Earnings/(Loss) from Continuing Operations	Depreciation and Amortization	Total Assets	Capital Expenditures
BEAUTY	2016	$11,477	$ 2,636	$ 1,975	$ 218	$ 3,888	$ 435
	2015	12,608	2,895	2,181	247	4,004	411
	2014	13,401	3,020	2,300	256	4,564	376
GROOMING	2016	6,815	2,009	1,548	451	22,819	383
	2015	7,441	2,374	1,787	540	23,090	372
	2014	8,009	2,589	1,954	576	23,767	369
HEALTH CARE	2016	7,350	1,812	1,250	204	5,139	240
	2015	7,713	1,700	1,167	202	5,212	218
	2014	7,798	1,597	1,083	199	5,879	253
FABRIC & HOME CARE	2016	20,730	4,249	2,778	531	6,919	672
	2015	22,274	4,059	2,634	547	7,155	986
	2014	23,506	4,264	2,770	539	7,938	1,057
BABY, FEMININE & FAMILY CARE	2016	18,505	4,042	2,650	886	9,863	1,261
	2015	20,247	4,317	2,938	924	10,109	1,337
	2014	20,950	4,310	2,940	908	10,946	1,317
CORPORATE	2016	422	(1,379)	(174)	788	78,508	323
	2015	466	(4,333)	(2,420)	674	79,925	412
	2014	737	(2,271)	(389)	663	91,172	476
TOTAL COMPANY	2016	$65,299	$13,369	$10,027	$3,078	$127,136	$3,314
	2015	70,749	11,012	8,287	3,134	129,495	3,736
	2014	74,401	13,509	10,658	3,141	144,266	3,848

Source: P&G Annual Report 2016.

struggling beauty unit. Taylor continued with Lafley's strategy of cutting back on P&G's brands. The sale of 43 of the firm's beauty brands to Coty in a $12 billion deal was completed in October 2016. A few months earlier, P&G had completed the transfer of Duracell to Berkshire Hathaway through an exchange of shares.

Fighting for Its Iconic Status

For years, P&G had spent heavily to build on its success with legacy soap and detergent brands to acquire hundreds of additional brands in new businesses that it hoped could also become part of consumers' daily routines. The latest effort to jettison over half of its brands indicated that the strategy was not working anymore. In particular, P&G has been struggling with its push to place more emphasis on products that carry higher margins in order to move it away from its dependence on household staples.

The firm's aggressive push into beauty, for example, has struggled to show much growth. Lafley had tried to build the firm's presence in this business for years, regarding it as a high margin, faster growing complement to the firm's core household products. The firm has struggled to show growth in this business and it has been generating the lowest profit margins. Sales of *Olay* skin care products and *Pantene* hair care products have mostly sagged in recent years. Its efforts to build a line of perfumes around licenses with Dolce & Gabbana, Gucci and Hugo Boss were also running into problems.

Having discarded more than half of its brands over the past two years, P&G was optimistic that its turnaround efforts were starting to show results. On January 20, 2017, the firm offered a more upbeat outlook for sales growth in the coming year. "We are essentially on track with where we hoped we would be," finance chief Jon Moeller said in a call with analysts.[8] Yet a half-dozen analysts have cut their downgraded P&G's stock over the past month. "Cosmetics, household and personal care stocks are no longer in vogue," wrote Barclays analyst Lauren Lieberman in a recent report.[9]

ENDNOTES

1 Jennifer Reingold & Doris Burke. Can P&G's CEO hang on? Fortune, February 25, 2013, p. 69.

2 Alex Coolridge. P&G plans to unload more than its brands. Cincinnati Enquirer, August 2, 2014, p. 1.

3 David Benoit & Sharon Terlep. Activist Builds $3 Billion Stake in P&G. Wall Street Journal, February 15, 2017, p. A1.

4 Fortune, February 25, 2013, p. 70.

5 Fortune, February 25, 2013, p. 70.

6 Fortune, February 25, 2013, p. 75.

7 Cincinnati Enquirer, August 2, 2014, p. 1.

8 Sharon Terlep. Procter & Gamble's Outlook Improves. Wall Street Journal, January 21, 2017, p. B3.

9 Alexander Coolridge. 4 Things That Could Sink P&G in 2017. Cincinnati Enquirer, January 15, 2017, p. G2.

CASE 27

APPLE INC.:IS THE INNOVATION OVER?*

In April 2017 Apple formally opened its second corporate campus, Apple Park, a ring-shaped 2.8-million-square-foot building with walls of curved glass surrounding an inner greenspace courtyard. Part of a 175-acre campus, the facility would ultimately house more than 12,000 employees and was said to be one of the most energy-efficient buildings in the world. It was also the most recent and possibly the last evidence of the direct vision and innovation of Apple co-founder Steve Jobs. Originally envisioned by Jobs in 2011 as a center for creativity and collaboration, the building honors his legacy, his memory, and enduring influence on Apple and the world: The 1,000-seat auditorium that overlooks meadows and the main building is named the Steve Jobs Theater. Jobs, who died in 2011, would have turned 62 in February 2017. As Apple's current CEO Tim Cook said, "Steve's vision for Apple stretched far beyond his time with us. He intended Apple Park to be the home of innovation for generations to come."[1]

Yet the pace of innovation at Apple has slowed considerably. Since Steve Jobs's death, the only new products launched have been the Apple Watch and Apple Pay in 2014, and the Apple Music streaming service in 2015. The iconic iPhone, in FY2016 representing 64 percent of total revenues, is over 10 years old, and even though upgrades keep customers coming back, competition has eroded Apple's smartphone market share such that 2016 iPhone revenues declined in three consecutive quarters, year over year. Mac computer and iPad sales have declined as well, with iPad revenues falling continuously since 2013: Apple's FY2016 revenues were down by about 8 percent overall, gross profit fell by 10 percent, and net income was off by 15 percent, making 2016 the first financial setback for Apple since 2008.

In this environment, a new campus that was reported to cost over $5B was considered by many to be a "huge investment of time and energy" and perhaps a distraction, keeping "management from running the business and innovating."[2] In addition, there was some concern that although research and development spending was up in FY2016, research output had not produced any recent meaningful breakthroughs. Speculation was that perhaps this new campus, with its emphasis on amenities such as a fitness center and movie theater, might have been designed to attract new engineering talent, something badly needed by companies seeking innovative growth. This posed yet again the unavoidable question that looms large over the 41-year-old Apple: What happens to a modern company whose innovations and inspirations are so closely tied to the vision of one leader when that leader's influence is no longer present?[3]

Tim Cook is considered a highly effective leader, yet has been criticized for "lack of ambition and vigor," for being perhaps too cautious about entering new product categories, pursuing acquisitions, or driving employees to achieve almost impossible stretch goals.[4] On the other hand, investors have been mostly very pleased with the stock performance; under Cook, since he was named CEO in August 2011, Apple share price has risen more than 175 percent, and the company's market capitalization of over $750 billion makes it the most valuable company in the world. Cook instituted Apple's first dividend since 1995 in 2012, and bought back more than $200 billion of shares, producing strong free cash flows and an "impressive" balance sheet.[5] Cook has done what CEOs of public companies are supposed to do—drive up value. But something major would have to happen in order for Apple to grow even more (see Exhibits 1 and 2). As one analyst said, it is hard to find "ways to make the world's most valuable company even more valuable when it's already so big that conventional growth strategies—extending product lines, moving into new territories—would barely move the needle."[6]

Apple, *Fortune Magazine*'s "world's most admired company" since 2008,[7] has distinguished itself by excelling over the years not only in product innovation but also in revenue and margins (since 2006 Apple has consistently reported gross margins of over 30 percent). Founded as a computer company in 1976 and known early on for its intuitive adaptation of the "graphical user interface" or GUI (via the first mouse and the first on-screen "windows"),[8] Apple dropped the word *computer* from its corporate name in 2007. By 2017, Apple Inc. was known for having top-selling products not only in desktop (iMac) and notebook (MacBook) personal computers but also in online music and "app" services (iTunes and App Store), mobile communication devices (iPhone), digital consumer entertainment (Apple TV), tablet computers (iPad), and online services (iCloud), as well as wearable technology (Apple Watch), mobile payment systems (Apple Pay), and a subscription-based music streaming service (Apple Music) (see Exhibit 3).

Most of those innovations occurred after 1998, when Apple was under Steve Jobs's leadership. However, there was also a 12-year period in which Jobs was not in charge.

*This case was prepared by Professor Alan B. Eisner of Pace University and Associate Professor Pauline Assenza, Western Connecticut State University. This case is based solely on library research and was developed for class discussion rather than to illustrate either effective or ineffective handling of an administrative situation. Copyright © 2017 Alan B. Eisner.

EXHIBIT 1 Apple Sales

	2016	Change	2015	Change	2014
Net Sales by Operating Segment:					
Americas	$ 86,613	(8)%	$ 93,864	17%	$ 80,095
Europe	49,952	(1)	50,337	14	44,285
Greater China	48,492	(17)	58,715	84	31,853
Japan	16,928	8	15,706	3	15,314
Rest of Asia Pacific	13,654	(10)	15,093	34	11,248
Total net sales	$215,639	(8)%	$233,715	28%	$ 182,795
Net Sales by Product:					
iPhone (1)	$136,700	(12)%	$155,041	52%	$ 101,991
iPad (1)	20,628	(11)	23,227	(23)	30,283
Mac (1)	22,831	(10)	25,471	6	24,079
Services (2)	24,348	22	19,909	10	18,063
Other Products (1)(3)	11,132	11	10,067	20	8,379
Total net sales	$215,639	(8)%	$233,715	28%	$ 182,795
Unit Sales by Product:					
iPhone	211,884	(8)%	231,218	37%	169,219
iPad	45,590	(17)	54,856	(19)	67,977
Mac	18,484	(10)	20,587	9	18,906

(1) Includes deferrals and amortization of related software upgrade rights and non-software services.

(2) Includes revenue from Internet Services, AppleCare ®, Apple Pay, licensing and other services.

(3) Includes sales of Apple TV, Apple Watch, Beats ® products, iPod and Apple-branded and third-party accessories.

Source: Apple 10K SEC filing, 2016.

The company's ongoing stated strategy was to leverage "its unique ability to design and develop its own operations systems, hardware, application software, and services to provide its customers new products and solutions with superior ease-of-use, seamless integration and innovative industrial design."[9] This strategy required not only product design and marketing expertise but also scrupulous attention to operational details. Given Apple's global growth in multiple product categories, and the associated complexity in strategic execution, CEO Tim Cook was challenged to be able to sustain the level of innovation the company had been known for.

Company Background

Founder Steve Jobs

Apple Computer was founded in Mountain View, California, on April 1, 1976, by Steve Jobs and Steve Wozniak. Jobs was the visionary and marketer, Wozniak was the technical genius, and A. C. "Mike" Markkula Jr., who had joined the team several months earlier, was the businessman. Jobs set the mission of empowering individuals, one person–one computer, and doing so with elegance of design and fierce attention to detail. In 1977 the first version of the Apple II became the first computer ordinary people could use right out of the box, and its instant success in the home market caused a computing revolution, essentially creating the personal computer industry. By 1980, Apple was the industry leader and went public in December of that year.

In 1983, Wozniak left the firm and Jobs hired John Sculley away from PepsiCo to take the role of CEO at Apple, citing the need for someone to spearhead marketing and operations while Jobs worked on technology. The result of Jobs's creative focus on personal computing was the Macintosh. Introduced in 1984, with the now-famous Super Bowl television ad based on George Orwell's novel *Nineteen Eighty-Four*,[10] the Macintosh was a breakthrough

EXHIBIT 2
Apple First Quarter
2017 Sales

	1st Quarter 2017 (in millions)	1st Quarter 2016 (in millions)	Percentage Change
Product Net Sales			
iPhone*	$ 54,378	$ 51,635	5%
iPad*	5,533	7,084	(22)%
Mac*	7,244	6,746	7%
Services**	7,172	6,056	18%
Other Products***	4,024	4,351	(8)%
Total net sales	**$ 78,351**	**$ 75,872**	**3%**
Region Net Sales			
Americas	$ 31,968	$ 29,325	9%
Europe	18,521	17,932	3%
Greater China	16,233	18,373	(12)%
Japan	5,766	4,794	20%
Rest of Asia-Pacific	5,863	5,448	8%

*Includes deferrals and amortization of related non-software services and software upgrade rights.

**Includes revenue from Digital Content and Services, AppleCare, Apple Pay, licensing, and other services.

***Includes sales of Apple TV, Apple Watch, Beats products, iPod, and Apple-branded and third-party accessories.

Source: Apple 10Q SEC filing, 2017.

EXHIBIT 3 Apple Innovation Time Line

Date	Product	Events
1976	Apple I	Steve Jobs, Steve Wozniak, and Ronald Wayne found Apple Computer.
1977	Apple II	Apple logo first used.
1979	Apple II1	Apple employs 250 people; the first personal computer spreadsheet software, *VisiCalc*, is written by Dan Bricklin on an Apple II.
1980	Apple III	Apple goes public with 4.6 million shares; IBM personal computer announced.
1983	Lisa	John Sculley becomes CEO.
1984	Mac 128K, Apple IIc	Super Bowl ad introduces the Mac desktop computer.
1985		**Jobs resigns** and forms NeXT Software; Windows 1.01 released.
1986	Mac Plus	Jobs establishes Pixar.
1987	Mac II, Mac SE	Apple sues Microsoft over GUI.
1989	Mac Portable	Apple sued by Xerox over GUI.
1990	Mac LC	Apple listed on Tokyo Stock Exchange.
1991	PowerBook 100, System 7	System 7 operating-system upgrade released, the first Mac OS to support PowerPC-based computers.
1993	Newton Message Pad (one of the first PDAs)	Sculley resigns; Spindler becomes CEO; PowerBook sales reach 1 million units.

continued

EXHIBIT 3 *Continued*

Date	Product	Events
1996		Spindler is out; Amelio becomes CEO; Apple acquires NeXT Software, with Jobs as adviser.
1997		Amelio is out; **Jobs returns** as interim CEO; online retail Apple Store opened.
1998	iMac	iMac colorful design introduced, including USB interface; Newton scrapped.
1999	iMovie, Final Cut Pro (video editing software)	iBook (part of PowerBook line) becomes best-selling retail notebook in October; Apple has 11% share of notebook market.
2000	G4Cube	**Jobs becomes permanent CEO.**
2001	iPod, OS X	First retail store opens, in Virginia.
2002	iMac G4	Apple releases iLife software suite.
2003	iTunes	Apple reaches 25 million iTunes downloads.
2004	iMac G5	**Jobs undergoes successful surgery for pancreatic cancer.**
2005	iPod Nano, iPod Shuffle, Mac Mini	First video iPod released; video downloads available from iTunes.
2006	MacBook Pro	Apple computers use Intel's Core Duo CPU and can run Windows software; iWork software competes with Microsoft Office.
2007	iPhone, Apple TV, iPod Touch	Apple Computer changes name to Apple Inc.; Microsoft Vista released.
2008	iPhone 3G, MacBook Air, App Store	App Store launched for third-party applications for iPhone and iPod Touch and brings in $1million in one day.
2009	17-inch MacBook Pro, iLife, iWork '09	iTunes Plus provides DRM-free music, with variable pricing; **Jobs takes medical leave.**
2010	iPad, iPhone 4, Mac App Store	iPhone 4 provides FaceTime feature; iTunes reaches 10 billion songs sold.
2011	iPad2, iPhone 4S, iCloud	iPhone available on Verizon Wireless; **Jobs resigns as CEO, dies on October 5th. Tim Cook becomes CEO.**
2012	iBook Author, iPhone5, iPad Mini	iBook supports textbook creation on iPad. Apple becomes world's most valuable company (market cap). Mac Retina displays, skinny Macs.
2013	Mega Mac, iPad Air	Workstation in a small aluminum cylinder.
2014	iPhone 6 Plus, Apple Watch, Apple Pay	Biggest iPhone yet, Apple Watch = computer on your wrist introduced in 2014, actual delivery in 2015, Apple Pay mobile payment service, acquisition of Beats Electronic for streaming digital content.
2015	Apple Music	Streaming music subscription service, including Internet radio station Beats 1, blog platform Connect.
2016	iPhone 7, iPhone 7 Plus	Seventh generation iPhone.
2017	iPhone 8, iPhone X	Fall 2017 release.

Source: http://en.wikipedia.org/wiki/Timeline_of_Apple_Inc._products; Editor, "Apple: The first 30 years," *Macworld*, March 30, 2006: https://www.macworld.com/article/1050115/macs/30timeline.html; author estimates.

in terms of elegant design and ease of use. Its ability to handle large graphic files quickly made it a favorite with graphic designers, but it had slow performance and limited compatible software was available. That meant the product as designed at the time was unable to help significantly Apple's failing bottom line. In addition, Jobs had given Bill Gates at Microsoft some Macintosh prototypes to use to develop software, and in 1985, Microsoft subsequently came out with the Windows operating system, a version of GUI for use on IBM PCs.

Steve Jobs's famous volatility led to his resignation from Apple in 1985. Jobs then founded NeXT Computer. The NeXT Cube computer proved too costly for the business to become commercially profitable, but its technological contributions could not be ignored. In 1997 then Apple CEO Gilbert Amelio bought out NeXT, hoping to use its Rhapsody, a version of the NeXTStep operating system, to jump-start the Mac OS development, and Jobs was brought back as a part-time adviser.

Under CEOs Sculley, Spindler, and Amelio

John Sculley tried to take advantage of Apple's unique capabilities. Because of this, Macintosh computers became easy to use, with seamless integration (the original plug-and-play) and reliable performance. This premium performance meant Apple could charge a premium price. However, with the price of IBM compatibles dropping, and Apple's costs, especially R&D, way above industry averages, this was not a sustainable scenario.

Sculley's innovative efforts were not enough to substantially improve Apple's bottom line, and he was replaced as CEO in 1993 by company president Michael Spindler. Spindler continued the focus on innovation, producing the PowerMac in 1994. Even though this combination produced a significant price-performance edge over both previous Macs and Intel-based machines, the IBM clones continued to undercut Apple's prices. Spindler's response was to allow other companies to manufacture Mac clones, a strategy that ultimately led to clones stealing 20 percent of Macintosh unit sales.

Gilbert Amelio, an Apple director and former semiconductor turnaround expert, was asked to reverse the company's financial direction. Amelio intended to reposition Apple as a premium brand, but his extensive reorganizations and cost-cutting strategies couldn't prevent Apple's stock price from slipping to a new low. However, Amelio's decision to stop work on a brand-new operating system and jump-start development by using NeXTStep brought Steve Jobs back to Apple in 1997.

Steve Jobs's Return

One of Jobs's first strategies on his return was to strengthen Apple's relationships with third-party software developers, including Microsoft. In 1997 Jobs announced an alliance with Microsoft that would allow for the creation of a Mac version of the popular Microsoft Office software. He also made a concerted effort to woo other developers, such as Adobe, to continue to produce Mac-compatible programs.

In late October 2001, Apple released its first major noncomputer product, the iPod. This device was an MP3 music player that packed up to 1,000 CD-quality songs into an ultraportable, 6.5-ounce design: "With iPod, Apple has invented a whole new category of digital music player that lets you put your entire music collection in your pocket and listen to it wherever you go," said Steve Jobs. "With iPod, listening to music will never be the same again."[11] This prediction became even truer in 2002, when Apple introduced an iPod that would download from Windows—its first product that didn't require a Macintosh computer and thus opened up the Apple "magic" to everyone. In 2003 all iPod products were sold with a Windows version of iTunes, making it even easier to use the device regardless of computer platform.

In April 2003, Apple opened the online iTunes Music Store to everyone. This software, downloadable on any computer platform, sold individual songs through the iTunes application for 99 cents each. When announced, the iTunes Music Store already had the backing of five major record labels and a catalog of 200,000 songs. Later that year, the iTunes Music Store was selling roughly 500,000 songs a day. In 2003 the iPod was the only portable digital player that could play music purchased from iTunes, and this intended exclusivity helped both products become dominant.

After 30 years of carving a niche for itself as the premier provider of technology solutions for graphic artists, Web designers, and educators, Apple was reinventing itself as a digital entertainment company, moving beyond the personal computer industry. The announcement in 2007 of the iPhone, a product incorporating a wireless phone, a music and video player, and a mobile Internet browsing device, meant Apple was also competing in the cell phone/smartphone industry.

Also introduced in 2007, the iPod Touch incorporated Wi-Fi connectivity, allowing users to purchase and download music directly from iTunes without a computer. Then, in 2008 Apple opened the App Store. Users could now purchase applications written by third-party developers specifically for the iPhone and iPod Touch.

In 2010 Apple launched the large-screen touch-based tablet called the iPad and sold over 2 million of these devices in the first two months.[12] That same year, Apple's stock value increased to the extent that the company's market cap exceeded Microsoft's, making it the biggest tech company in the world.[13] In 2011 Steve Jobs made his last product launch appearance to introduce iCloud, an online storage and syncing service. On October 4, 2011, Apple announced the iPhone 4S, which included "Siri," the "intelligent software assistant." The next day, on October 5, came the announcement that Steve Jobs had died.

Apple continued to innovate, however, and on September 21, 2012, Apple had its biggest iPhone launch ever, with the iPhone 5.[14] On September 19, 2012, Apple stock reached $702.10, its highest level to date, which made Apple the most valuable company in the world. 2013 saw the iPhone5C and the high-range iPhone5S, which introduced the Touch ID fingerprint recognition system. The iPhone 6 and 6 Plus, with larger displays, faster processors and support for mobile payments, were released in September 2014.[15] The prototype of the Apple Watch was unveiled in 2014, and production began in 2015. Also introduced in 2014 was Apple Pay, a mobile payment system meant to augment all Apple mobile products. February 2015 saw Apple reach the highest market cap of any U.S.-traded company. During 2016 Apple introduced Apple Music, a streaming music service meant to take advantage of its already strong relationship with artists and music publishers, and therefore positioned to successfully compete with Pandora and Spotify. In addition, iPhone 7 and 7 Plus and the Apple Watch Series 2 all had a positive response from customers. Reporting on the first quarter 2017 results, CEO Cook pointed to "all-time revenue records for iPhone, Services, Mac and Apple Watch."[16]

Apple has become a diversified digital entertainment corporation. All the way back in 2005 analysts believed Apple had "changed the rules of the game for three industries—PCs, consumer electronics, and music and appears to have nothing to fear from major rivals."[17] On top of steady sales increases of its computers, of the iPod, and of iTunes, the added categories of iPhone and iPad had shown substantial growth, but by 2013, Samsung had outperformed Apple in worldwide smartphone sales,[18] and Google's Android had captured the largest market share of cell phone operating systems. At the same time, both the Amazon Kindle Fire HD and Microsoft's Surface tablet were nipping at the iPad's heels. 2015 was marked by competition in the wearable tech space, and 2017 saw Windows 10 operating system become four times more popular than the macOS, the Microsoft Surface defeating iPad in user satisfaction, and customers frustrated that the MacPro had not yet been redesigned to recover from the 2013 design misstep. Can Apple continue to grow, and, if so, in what categories?

Apple's Operations

Maintaining a competitive edge requires more than innovative product design. Operational execution is also important. For instance, while trying to market its increasingly diverse product line, Apple believes that its own retail stores can serve customers better than can third-party retailers. By the beginning of 2017, Apple had 494 stores open, including 224 international locations. Some of these stores worldwide are considered architectural wonders, including the iconic Fifth Avenue glass cube in New York City. Apple has even received trademark protection for its retail stores' "distinctive design and layout."[19] Partly due to the appealing design of both the shopping experience and the products being sold within, Apple retail stores generate more sales per square foot than any other U.S. retailer, including its closest luxury rival Tiffany & Co.[20]

To solidify its supply chain, Apple has entered into multiyear agreements with suppliers of key components. Apple has had historically excellent margins, partly because of its simpler product line, leading to lower manufacturing costs.[21] Apple has outsourced almost all manufacturing and final assembly to its Asian partners, paying close attention to scheduling and quality issues. Outsourcing to Asian manufacturers is not without its problems, however. In 2012, headlines worldwide exposed China's Foxconn manufacturing facility for labor abuses that led to worker suicide threats. Apple, as well as most other technology companies, used Foxconn facilities to assemble products, including the iPad and iPhone. After the story broke, Apple CEO Tim Cook visited the Foxconn plant and reviewed an audit of working conditions that found violations in wages, overtime, and environmental standards. Apple stated that it remained "committed to the highest standards of social responsibility across our worldwide supply chain,"[22] and Cook announced that Apple might be bringing some of the production of Mac computers back to the U.S., starting in 2013. They could do this without affecting the company's profitability, because of automation cost savings.[23]

Apple has also historically paid attention to research and development, increasing its R&D investment year after year. In the first quarter of 2017, Apple spent $2.9 billion on R&D, an increase of 4 percent from the previous year. As one of Steve Jobs's legacies, Apple has traditionally kept the specifics of its research and development a closely guarded secret and fiercely protected its innovative patents. A well-publicized series of lawsuits in 2012 highlighted rifts between Apple and Samsung, both a rival and supplier. Samsung smartphones had captured more market share than Apple's iPhones in the beginning of 2012, and Apple argued that Samsung had succeeded with both its phones and tablets only by copying Apple's designs. Samsung replied by claiming that Apple had infringed on Samsung's patents.[24] U.S. intellectual property courts found in favor of Apple, but Japanese courts found in favor of Samsung. The ongoing battle meant Apple needed to look for other suppliers of chips and displays. Supply chain watchers pointed out that Apple still had a major challenge finding reliable suppliers for increasingly scarce components, and that the continued reliance on Foxconn as the sole manufacturer of the iPhone meant that any disruption there could have major consequences for delivery.[25]

Status of Apple's Business Units in 2017

The Apple Computer Business

In the computer market, Apple has always refused to compete on price, relying instead on its reliability, design elegance, ease of use, and integrated features to win customers. An opportunity for increased market share was realized when Apple began using Intel processors in the iMac desktop and the MacBook portables, which allowed them to run Microsoft Office and other business software.

However, in FY2016 Apple's worldwide Mac computer sales decreased 10 percent over the previous year, continuing to signal the decline of this category since the introduction of the iPad in 2010. Overall it appeared that sales of desktop computers, especially, were slowing worldwide as the tablet and smartphone markets grew, and this was evident in the worldwide PC market share data from 2016, where only HP and Dell saw any growth (see Exhibit 4). Apple saw the greatest decline amongst its rivals, a decline also evident in its own revenue profile, which had seen the Mac's share of Apple overall revenue drop from more than 40 percent in 2007 to just 11 percent in 2016, and slipping further to 9 percent in the first quarter of 2017.[26]

In 2017, Apple was planning to refresh the iMac, and completely revamp the Mac Pro. Targeting professional users, and very expensive at around $3,000, the Mac Pro

EXHIBIT 4 Worldwide PC Market Share, Calendar Year 2016, units in thousands

Vendor	2016 Shipments	2016 Market Share	2015 Shipments	2015 Market Share	2016/2015 Growth
Lenovo	55,502	21.3%	57,233	20.8%	−3.0%
HP Inc	54,290	20.9%	53,587	19.4%	1.3%
Dell Technologies	40,731	15.7%	39,049	14.2%	4.3%
ASUS	19,203	7.4%	19,360	7.0%	−0.8%
Apple	18,446	7.1%	20,452	7.4%	−9.8%
Others	72,012	27.7%	86,110	31.2%	−16.4%
Total	260,183	100.0%	275,790	100.0%	−5.7%

Source: IDC Worldwide Quarterly Personal Computing Device Tracker, January 11, 2017, http://www.businessinsider.com/apple-mac-lost-most-pc-market-share-in-2016-chart-2017-1.

product had never had a large market share, but the creative professionals, the videographers, designers and photographers who embraced the original product were still waiting for a delayed redesign that was scheduled for 2018.[27]

In contrast, even though the iMac and MacBook products are targeted at the consumer and education market, Apple's share of the computer business and enterprise market has grown such that 74 percent of organizations had seen in increase in Mac adoption during 2016, with 91 percent of enterprise organizations allowing employees to use the Mac. Interestingly, this growth has been explained not in terms of the Apple machines themselves, but in the shift toward the "consumerization of IT," where companies allow employees to use devices of their choice: "Apple devices are overwhelmingly the devices that employees choose when given the chance to bring their own devices to the office."[28]

Personal Digital Entertainment Devices: iPod

Although many analysts at the time felt the MP3 player market was oversaturated, Apple introduced the iPod Touch in 2007, intending it to be an iPhone without the phone, a portable media player, and Wi-Fi Internet device without the

AT&T phone bill. The iPod Touch borrowed most of its features from the iPhone, including the finger-touch interface, but it remained mainly an iPod, with a larger viewing area for videos. Apple released the fifth-generation iPod Touch in September 2012, and a new version debuted in 2015. It was possible a seventh-generation might still be released in 2017. The device was still a cheap way to get entertainment, and used for portable gaming, this device plus a cheap phone for calling and texting was still less expensive than an iPhone.[29]

Mobile Communication Devices: iPhone

In 2007 Apple's iPhone combined an Internet-enabled smartphone and video iPod. The iPhone allowed users to access all iPod content and play music and video content purchased from iTunes. Subsequent smartphone models increased the quality of the photo and video components to make even the digital camera or camcorder appear obsolete. By the fourth quarter of 2015 Apple had achieved almost 19 percent market share, in a close tie with Samsung (see Exhibit 5), and in July 2016 it sold over one billion units, becoming "one of the most important, world-changing and successful products in history."[30]

EXHIBIT 5 Worldwide Market Share—Smartphones, 3rd Quarter 2016

Period	Samsung	Apple	Huawei	OPPO	vivo	Others
2015Q4	20.4%	18.7%	8.2%	3.6%	3.0%	46.2%
2016Q1	23.7%	15.4%	8.4%	5.9%	4.4%	42.2%
2016Q2	22.8%	11.7%	9.3%	6.6%	4.8%	44.9%
2016Q3	21%	12.5%	9.3%	7.1%	5.9%	44.2%

Source: IDC Smartphone Vendor Market Share 2016 Q3: http://www.idc.com/promo/smartphone-market-share/vendor.

EXHIBIT 6 Smartphone Operating System Market Share Q3 2016

Period	Android	iOS	Windows Phone	Others
2015Q4	79.6%	18.7%	1.2%	0.5%
2016Q1	83.5%	15.4%	0.8%	0.4%
2016Q2	87.6%	11.7%	0.4%	0.3%
2016Q3	86.8%	12.5%	0.3%	0.4%

Source: IDC, Smartphone OS Market Share, Q3 2016, http://www.idc.com/promo/smartphone-market-share/os.

However, the smartphone market was increasingly turning into a battle between mobile operating systems. Apple's iPhone, running on iOS, had considerable competition from Samsung's line of smartphones. This was partly due to Samsung's use of Google's Android operating system. Historical worldwide leader Nokia stumbled badly with its outdated Symbian operating system and had to partner with Microsoft, using the Windows Phone operating system. By 2017 the operating system map had Android devices capturing the majority of market share (see Exhibit 6).[31]

In recent years it has appeared some of the "cool" factor has disappeared from the iPhone. In Asian markets, especially, Apple's shares of mobile devices has fallen sharply, losing considerable ground to Samsung, HTC, and other smartphones produced by Asian manufacturers. Younger users, the 20-something college students and fresh graduates, look for the next new thing, and that is increasingly an Android-driven device.[32]

Going into 2017, overall iPhone first quarter sales were up 4.5 percent from the previous year, but this may have been due more to Samsung's Galaxy Note 7 exploding battery problems than to anything Apple did. The overall smartphone market was slowing down as mature markets were increasingly dependent on replacement purchases, and emerging markets appeared more interested in low-cost devices. Other than the removal of the headphone port in the iPhone 7, Apple had been unable to innovate the iPhone design or features in any major way, so if Apple wanted to address its declining market share, it might have to lower prices, which, given the iPhone's major contribution to Apple's bottom line ($215B or 64 percent of total sales in 2016), would make it difficult for the company to grow net income going forward.

Tablet Computer: iPad

In April 2010 Apple released the iPad, a tablet computer, as a platform for audio-visual media, including books, periodicals, movies, music, games, and web content. More than 300,000 iPads were scooped up by eager tech consumers during the device's first day on store shelves. Weighing only 1.5 pounds, this lightweight, portable, and touch-screen device was seen as a gigantic iPod Touch.[33] Features like the sleek design, touch screen, multiple apps, and fast

and easy-to-navigate software made the iPad popular in business, education, and the entertainment industry. The iPad was selected by *Time* magazine as one of the 50 Best Inventions of the Year 2010.[34]

Up until September 2010, Apple iPads accounted for 95 percent of tablet computer sales,[35] but by the end of 2012, that figure had fallen to 78.9 percent, and by the end of 2016 Apple held only 21.5 percent of the market. The loss of share was partly due to tablet devices, such as Samsung's Galaxy, that were based on Google's open-source Android system. Other platforms and devices had also appeared, including Google's Nexus, Amazon's Kindle Fire, and Microsoft Windows' Surface tablet.[36] Going into 2017 there were signs that the iPad models' sales, as well as the entire tablet industry were "going downhill," partly due to the "jumbo" phones coming from the likes of Samsung (and Apple), and low-cost Google-based Chromebook laptops (Exhibit 7).[37]

Once again, as with the Mac computer lineup and the iPhone, Apple had not introduced any major redesign or refresh to the iPad since the iPad Air in 2013, so even within the category Apple was losing respect. In 2017 consumer research firm J.D. Power announced that Microsoft's Surface tablets ranked higher than the iPad in customer satisfaction. Citing the Surface's versatility and "original approach," the research also pointed out that "when Apple released the iPad Pro in 2015, with a keyboard and stylus option, it was essentially a copy of the Surface."[38]

The Software Market

Although Apple has always created innovative hardware, software development also has been an important goal. Software has been Apple's core strength, especially in its computers, due to its reliability and resistance to virus infections and resulting crashes.[39] The premier piece of Apple software is the operating system. The iOS allows Apple to develop software applications such as Final Cut Pro, a video-editing program for professionals' digital camcorders; GarageBand, for making and mixing personally created music; the iTunes digital music jukebox; and iWork, containing a PowerPoint-type program called Keynote and a word-processor/page-layout program called Pages.

EXHIBIT 7 Worldwide Quarterly Tablet Market Share Q3 2016

Vendor	Top Five Tablet Vendors, Shipments, Market Share, and Growth, Third Quarter 2016 (Preliminary results, shipments in millions)				
	3Q16 Unit Shipments	3Q16 Market Share	3Q15 Unit Shipments	3Q15 Market Share	Year-Over-Year Growth
Apple	9.3	21.5%	9.9	19.6%	−6.2%
Samsung	6.5	15.1%	8.1	16.0%	−19.3%
Amazon.com	3.1	7.3%	0.8	1.5%	319.9%
Lenovo	2.7	6.3%	3.1	6.0%	−10.8%
Huawei	2.4	5.6%	1.9	3.7%	28.4%
Others	19.0	44.2%	26.9	53.2%	−29.2%
Total	43.0	100.0%	50.5	100.0%	−14.7%

Source: IDC Worldwide Quarterly Tablet Tracker, October 31, 2016, https://www.idc.com/getdoc.jsp?containerId=prUS41885416.

Apple's Web browser, Safari, was upgraded in 2009 to compete with Windows Internet Explorer, Mozilla Firefox, and the new entrant, Chrome from Google. Apple announced, "Safari 4 is the world's fastest and most innovative browser,"[40] but analysts were quick to point out that Google's Chrome, which debuted six months earlier, was perhaps the first to take the browser interface in a new direction. One commentator called Chrome "a wake-up call for the Safari UI guys."[41] Browser market share data in 2017 showed Chrome in the top spot, with its various versions grabbing almost 48 percent of global market share. Recent versions of Microsoft Internet Explorer and Edge held second place with 23 percent, and Firefox had 7.57 percent. Safari had 2 percent share.[42]

iCloud was introduced in 2011 during one of Steve Jobs's last public appearances. The web-based storage service initially struggled to get traction, but in 2014 was upgraded to iCloud Drive, allowing users to interoperate with Windows and connect all iOS devices. As an alternative to Google Drive and Dropbox, this gave Apple an intro into the enterprise/corporate user space, a market CEO Tim Cook had begun to target.[43]

In other software development areas, Apple has not been that successful. In 2012 Apple stumbled badly with its Maps software. Released in iOS6, Apple Maps was meant to replace Google Maps on the iPhone, but instead produced distorted images and gave really bad directions. CEO Tim Cook had to apologize that Apple had fallen short of its commitment to making "world-class products," and suggested customers go back to using its competitor's mapping software.[44]

iTunes

Arguably, Apple's most innovative software product is iTunes, a free downloadable software program for consumers running on either Mac or Windows operating systems.

It is bundled with all Mac computers and iPods and connected with the iTunes Music Store for purchasing digital music and movie files that can be downloaded and played by iPods, iPads, and the iPhone, and by iTunes on PCs.

Although the volume is there, iTunes has not necessarily been a profitable venture. Traditionally, out of the 99 cents Apple charges for a song, about 65 cents goes to the music label; 25 cents for distribution costs, including credit card charges, servers, and bandwidth; and the balance to marketing, promotion, and the amortized cost of developing the iTunes software.[45] However, if not wildly profitable, iTunes is still considered a media giant, especially with its over 35 million songs, 2.2 million apps, 25,000 TV shows and 65,000 films available in its database as of 2017.[46]

In 2013, iTunes accounted for over 60 percent of all digital music sales. In second place was Amazon's MP3 store with 16 percent market share. Google Play, eMusic, Zune Music Pass, Rhapsody, and a few others each captured 5 percent or less of the remaining sales. Growth, however, was occurring in the streaming service market, especially with the rising popularity of online radio and Internet streaming providers Pandora and Spotify, and by 2015, music sales on iTunes had fallen by over 14 percent worldwide. This trend helped explain why Apple acquired the monthly subscription streaming service Beats Music in 2014. The $3 billion acquisition included headphone maker Beats Electronics,[47] and ultimately led to the development of Apple Music.

The App Store

In March 2008, Apple announced that it was releasing the iPhone software development kit (SDK), allowing developers to create applications for the iPhone and iPod Touch and sell these third-party applications via the Apple App Store. The App Store was made available on iTunes, and it was directly available from the iPhone, iPad, and iPod

Touch products. This opened the window for another group of Apple customers, the application developers, to collaborate with Apple. Developers could purchase the iPhone Developer Program from Apple for $99, create either free or commercial applications for the iPhone and iPod Touch, and then submit these applications to be sold in the App Store. Developers would be paid 70 percent of the download fee iPhone or iPod Touch customers paid to the App Store, and Apple would get 30 percent of the revenue.

In September 2016, over 140 billion apps were downloaded from Apple's App Store,[48] but Google Play, the app store for Android users, was gaining ground, with 65 billion downloads in May 2016, indicating that Google might be attracting top-tier developers and quality titles to its marketplace.[49]

Apple Pay

Introduced in late 2014, Apple Pay allowed iPhone 6 and 6 Plus users in the U.S. to make secure payments for goods and services using their phones. With over 1 million credit and debit card activations within the first 72 hours of its release, Apple Pay was intended to replace the user's wallet, and, according to CEO Tim Cook, would "forever change the way all of us buy things," primarily because the process was more secure than a traditional card-based transaction. Major retailers such as Macy's, Walgreens, McDonald's, Whole Foods, and Disney had all agreed to accept Apple Pay. Apple reportedly received 0.15 percent of each purchase, making the service a potentially lucrative venture. Competition was coming from Google Wallet, especially given Google's 2015 acquisition of technology from Softcard.[50] Google Wallet had also seen an increase in usage as the Apple Pay system was launched,[51] but usage of these payment forms appeared to have peaked in 2015, such that by 2017 nearly 49 percent of Apple Pay users reported that they didn't use the service anymore because they were happy with existing payment methods; they believed plastic cards were just fine.[52]

Other Products: Apple Watch, Apple TV and Apple Music

Apple Watch was the first all-new product since the iPad, and therefore CEO Tim Cook's most ambitious gamble. Once again, Apple was not the first company to enter the wearable tech space, following the lead of Samsung, Sony, and Motorola, and competing against fitness trackers produced by Nike, FitBit and others. However, Apple's pre-orders for the launch in 2015 indicated demand would run to a combined five to six million units of the three watch models.[53] This category was a bit of a departure for Apple as it had positioned the Watch as a personalized device, with the market segmented between mass market and luxury.[54] In 2017, the Apple Watch was the number 1 smartwatch, and the third largest maker of wearable devices behind Fitbit and China's Xiaomi,[55] but overall sales appear to be disappointing (Apple did not disclose the exact number, burying

Watch activity under the "Other Products" category), and the updated Series 2 watch wasn't that innovative, with the only notable improvement the ability to spit out water after being dunked.

Apple TV, around since 2007, has undergone four upgrades, and in 2017, was partnering with NBC Universal to offer users access to seven of its networks' most popular series. Similar to rivals Roku, Amazon Fire, and Chromecast, Apple TV is a digital media player that can stream content to a compatible television. Unlike its rivals, Apple TV can play all the content from iTunes, apps and games from the iPhone, and use Siri voice recognition software to search and recognize viewer choices. However, it is more expensive, and does not provide easy access to Amazon Prime content, a popular destination for many viewers.

Apple Music, a music streaming subscription service, was launched in 2015, and by the end of 2016, had over 20 million subscribers. Working closely with Beats, this service takes advantage of the growing popularity of music streaming. Assuming a subscription price of $10 per month, it is estimated that Apple Music generates about $7 billion in yearly revenue (financials for Apple Music, like Apple Watch and AppleTV, are reported in the "Other Products" category). Among the major competitors, Pandora, YouTube, Spotify, iHeart Radio, and Amazon Prime Music, only Apple Music and Spotify have the support of the overall music industry, because of how well they treat their artists.[56]

Product Extensions, Growth of Services, Mergers and Acquisitions

Rumors in 2015 surfaced that Apple had acquired resources, primarily engineers and related technology, that would enable it to develop an automobile, ready for market by 2020. Speculation was that the Apple would not do the actual assembly, but as with its other products, would use its sophisticated supply chain expertise to outsource manufacturing, focusing its considerable innovation skills on the design and sales of a product that incorporates Apple technology in multiple configurations.[57] By 2017, rumors had spread that Apple would not pursue the actual automobile, but instead was investigating the development of self-driving car software, using its "heavy investment in machine learning and autonomous systems."[58]

With the existing hardware products all appearing to languish, analysts are looking to Apple's services and "other products" for growth opportunities. This category, which includes Apple Pay, Apple Music, iCloud, iTunes, and the App Store, grew 24 percent as of FY2016 to a fourth quarter record of $6.3 billion, and in the first quarter of 2017 accounted for 9 percent of all revenues. In addition, making this sector more attractive, profit margin estimates average almost 39 percent, ranging from a low of 15 percent for Apple Music to a high of 85 percent for the App Store.[59] In particular, the App Store, having tripled revenue between

2013 and 2016, is projected to produce about two-thirds of Apple's growth target for 2020.[60] Analysts point out that services demand grew out of hardware sales such as the iPhone, and that the high margins for services could "represent an opportunity for Apple to juice the profitability of each of those hardware sales. That way, Apple can grow net income even if total revenue stays relatively flat."[61]

One final opportunity for Apple in coming years comes from the company's positive cash flow. Accumulating cash over the years from 2012, Tim Cook has positioned the company to be able to bid for acquisitions in related industries or spend to develop vertically within the Apple ecosystem. Apple has not made any significant acquisitions since Beats in 2014, but speculation has been growing, with analysts supposing targets such as Tesla, Pandora, or even Disney.[62] In addition, Apple has been internalizing supplier components, especially semiconductors, in search of performance and power consumption advantages. This means Apple might eventually ditch current highly integrated suppliers such as Intel and Qualcomm in favor of in-house solutions.[63] This would increase Apple's ability to move in new directions, and truly be innovative in hardware and component design.

The Future of Apple

Under Cook, Apple has transitioned itself "from being a hypergrowth company to being a premium, branded consumer company."[64] Apple is a truly vertically integrated designer and marketer of products that increasingly inhabits a world "dominated by the Internet of Things." Apple just loves "designing great stuff," and can use its current products as "building blocks and core components of future, more important products."[65] Some of those future products might include enterprise software, augmented reality glasses, automobile on-board navigation systems, solar power systems, and anything else that takes advantage of the Apple ecosystem.[66] Why not?

However, going into 2017 there was no doubt in some analysts' minds that Apple was no longer the growth engine of innovation it once was, instead becoming "a value company with lots of hungry competitors seeking to eat away at its market share."[67] Tim Cook was entering his seventh year as Apple's CEO, and although acknowledged as "a significant leader in his own right," he has yet to be identified as one to infuse new energy and emerge with a major breakthrough product. One analyst said, "the creative legacy and marketing savvy of Steve Jobs will be forever in the background of Apple, even as Cook and future company leaders seek to continue Apple's innovations and industry disruptions."[68]

ENDNOTES

1. Apple Press Release. 2017. Apple Park opens to employees in April. *Apple Newsroom,* February 22, http://www.apple.com/newsroom/2017/02/apple-park-opens-to-employees-in-april.html.

2. The Frugal Prof. 2017. Why isn't Apple doing better? *Seeking Alpha,* March 16, https://seekingalpha.com/article/4055719-apple-better?app=1&auth_param=70583:1ccl155:9b22d5200e30f0a38718f77ff85b4289&uprof=14#alt1.

3. Stone, B., & Burrows, P. 2011. The essence of Apple. *Bloomberg Businessweek,* January 24–30.

4. Dudovskiy, John. 2017. Apple leadership–an effective leadership by Tim Cook that is difficult to sustain. *Research Methodology,* March 2, http://research-methodology.net/apple-leadership-and-apple-organizational-structure/.

5. Sure Dividend. 2017. Will Apple be the next AAA-rated company? *Seeking Alpha,* March 21, https://seekingalpha.com/article/4056857-will-apple-next-aaa-rated-company?app=1&auth_param=70583:1cd2qfc:b996ecb86441181f700647f3f12dfd52&uprof=14.

6. Colvin, Geoff. 2016. Tim Cook's epic growth challenge at Apple. *Fortune,* January 7, http://fortune.com/2016/01/07/tim-cook-apple-growth-challenge/.

7. World's most admired companies. 2015. *Fortune,* http://fortune.com/worlds-most-admired-companies/.

8. Apple was the first firm to have commercial success selling GUI systems, but Xerox developed the first systems in 1973. Xerox PARC researchers built a single-user computer called the Alto that featured a bit-mapped display and a mouse and the world's first what-you-see-is-what-you-get (WYSIWYG) editor. From www.parc.xerox.com/about/history/default.html.

9. Apple Inc. 2012. 2012 annual report, 10-K filing. Available at www.apple.com/investor.

10. January 24, 2009, was the 25th anniversary of the Macintosh, unveiled by Apple in the "Big Brother" Super Bowl ad in 1984. Watch via YouTube: www.youtube.com/watch?v5OYecfV3ubP8. See also the 1983 Apple keynote speech by a young Steve Jobs, introducing this ad: www.youtube.com/watch?v5lSiQA6KKyJo.

11. Apple Inc. 2001. Ultra-portable MP3 music player puts 1,000 songs in your pocket. October 23, www.apple.com/pr/library/2001/oct/23ipod.html.

12. Apple Inc. 2010. Apple sells two million iPads in less than 60 days. Press release. May 31, www.apple.com/pr/library/2010/05/31Apple-Sells-Two-Million-iPads-in-Less-Than-60-Days.html.

13. BBC News. 2010. Apple passes Microsoft to be biggest tech company. BBC News, May 27, www.bbc.co.uk/news/10168684.

14. Keizer, G. 2012. Apple drains iPhone5 pre-order supplies in an hour. *Computerworld,* September 14, www.computerworld.com/s/article/9231285/Apple_drains_iPhone_5_pre_order_supplies_in_an_hour.

15. IDC. 2015. In a near tie, Apple closes the gap on Samsung in the fourth quarter as worldwide smartphone shipments top 1.3 billion for 2014, according to IDC. *IDC,* January 29, http://www.idc.com/getdoc.jsp?containerId=prUS25407215.

16. Apple Newsroom. 2017. Apple reports record first quarter results. January 31, http://www.apple.com/newsroom/2017/01/apple-reports-record-first-quarter-results.html.

17. Schlender, B. 2005. How big can Apple get? *Fortune,* February 21, money.cnn.com/magazines/fortune/-fortune_archive/2005/02/21/8251769/index.htm.

18. Tofel, K. C. 2012. Why only Samsung builds phones that outsell iPhones. *GigaOM,* November 9, www.businessweek.com/articles/2012-11-09/why-only-samsung-builds-phones-that-outsell-iphones.

19. Apple Inc. 2012. 2012 Annual Report; Palladino, V. 2013. Apple Store receives trademark for "distinctive design and layout." *Wired,* January 30, www.wired.com/design/2013/01/apple-store-trademark/.

20. Wahba, Phil. 2015. Apple extends lead in U.S. top 10 retailers by sales per square foot. *Fortune,* March 13, http://fortune.com/2015/03/13/apples-holiday-top-10-retailers-iphone/.

21. Fox, F. 2008. Mac Pro beats HP and Dell at their own game: Price. *LowEndMac.com,* May 16, lowendmac.com/ed/fox/08ff/mac-pro-vs-dell-hp.html.

22. Lowensohn, J. 2012. Lingering issues found at Foxconn's iPhone factory. *CNET,* December 14, news.cnet.com/8301-13579_3-57559327-37/lingering-issues-found-at-foxconns-iphone-factory/.

23. Bennett, D. 2012. Apple's Cook says more Macs will be born in the U.S.A. *Bloomberg Businessweek,* December 10, www.businessweek.com/articles/2012-12-10/apples-cook-says-more-macs-will-be-born-in-the-u.dot-s-dot-a-dot.

24. Jones, A., & Vascellaro, J. E. 2012. Apple v. Samsung: The patent trial of the century. *Wall Street Journal,* July 24, online.wsj.com/article/SB10000872396390443295404577543221814648592.html?mod5wsj_streaming_apple-v-samsung-trial-over-patents.

25. Noel, P. 2014. iProblems: Learning from Apple's strained supply chain. *MBTMag,* November 11, http://www.mbtmag.com/articles/2014/11/iproblems-learning-apple%E2%80%99s-strained-supply-chain.

26. Rexaline, Shanthi. 2017. Amid reports of a revamp how much does the Mac mean to Apple? *Yahoo Finance,* April 7, https://finance.yahoo.com/news/amid-reports-revamp-much-does-180029678.html.

27. Haslam, Karen. 2017. New Mac Pro 2018 latest rumours: Release date, UK price, features & specs. *Mac World,* April 10, http://www.macworld.co.uk/news/mac/new-mac-pro-2018-latest-rumours-release-date-uk-price-features-specs-3536364/.

28. Ogg, Erica. Analyst Report: Why the Mac is infiltrating the enterprise. *Gigaom,* https://gigaom.com/report/why-the-mac-is-infiltrating-the-enterprise/; Kahn, Jordan. 2017. Report highlights growth for Apple devices in enterprise: 91% now using Mac, 99% iPhone and iPad. *9to5 Mac,* March 7, https://9to5mac.com/2017/03/07/apple-enterprise-data-mac-ios-jamf/.

29. Sudhakar. 2016. Apple iPod Touch 7: Will we see it in 2017. *Tech and Us,* October 28, http://techandus.com/2016/10/28/apple-ipod-touch-7-2017/.

30. Apple Newsroom. 2016. Apple celebrates one billion iPhones. July 27, https://www.apple.com/newsroom/2016/07/apple-celebrates-one-billion-iphones.html.

31. IDC. 2012. Worldwide mobile phone growth expected to drop to 1.4% in 2012 despite continued growth of smartphones, according to IDC. *IDC,* December 4, www.idc.com/getdoc.jsp?containerId5prUS23818212#.UQSn-_J5V8E.

32. Wagstaff, J. 2012. In Asia's trend-setting cities, iPhone fatigue sets in. Reuters, January 27, news.yahoo.com/asias-trend-setting-cities-iphone-fatigue-sets-212849658–finance.html.

33. Pogue, D. 2010. Looking at the iPad from two angles. *New York Times,* March 31, www.nytimes.com/2010/04/01/technology/personaltech/01pogue.html?_r51&pagewanted5all&partner5rss&emc5rss.

34. McCracken, H. 2010. iPad. *Time,* November 11, www.time.com/time/specials/packages/article/0,28804,2029497_2030652,00.html.

35. Cellan-Jones, R. 2011. iPad 2 tablet launched by Apple's Steve Jobs. BBC News, March 2, www.bbc.co.uk/news/technology-12620077.

36. Johnson, J. 2013. Kindle Fire, Android tablets chip away at iPad marketshare. *Inquisitr,* January 2, www.inquisitr.com/465784/kindle-fire-android-tablets-chip-away-at-ipad-marketshare/#Q2bAVTfXbEpu72tB.99.

37. Inquisitr. 2015. Galaxy Tab S2 tries to kill Apple's 'already dying' iPad Air. *Inquisitr,* February 18, http://www.inquisitr.com/1853887/samsung-galaxy-tab-s2-tries-to-kill-apples-already-dying-ipad-air/.

38. Eule, Alex. 2017. iPad or Surface? Consumers make surprising choice. *Barrons,* April 7, http://www.barrons.com/articles/ipad-or-surface-consumers-make-surprising-choice-1491582428?mod=yahoobarrons&ru=yahoo&yptr=yahoo.

39. Schlender. 2005. How big can Apple get?

40. Apple Inc. 2009. Apple announces Safari 4—the world's fastest and most innovative browser. Press release. February 24, www.apple.com/pr/library/2009/02/24safari.html.

41. Siracusa, J. 2008. Straight out of Compton: Google Chrome as a paragon of ambition, if not necessarily execution. *ars technica,* September 2, arstechnica.com/staff/fatbits/2008/09/straight-out-of-compton.ars.

42. Widder, B. 2014. Battle of the best browsers. *Digital Trends,* November 25, http://www.digitaltrends.com/computing/the-best-browser-internet-explorer-vs-chrome-vs-firefox-vs-safari/; NetMarketShare data,

March 2017, https://www.netmarketshare.com/browser-market-share.aspx?qprid=2&qpcustomd=0.

43. Sanders, J. 2014. iCloud Drive: Apple's appealing recipe for cloud storage. *TechRepublic,* June 5, http://www.techrepublic.com/article/icloud-drive-apples-appealing-recipe-for-cloud-storage/.

44. Cheng, R. 2012. Apple CEO: We are "extremely sorry" for Maps flap. CNET, September 28, news.cnet.com/8301-13579_3-57522196-37/apple-ceo-we-are-extremely-sorry-for-maps-flap/.

45. Cherry, S. 2004. Selling music for a song. *Spectrum Online,* December, www.spectrum.ieee.org/dec04/3857.

46. https://www.apple.com/itunes/music/.

47. Karp, H. 2014. Apple iTunes sees big drop in music sales. *Wall Street Journal,* October 24, http://www.wsj.com/articles/itunes-music-sales-down-more-than-13-this-year-1414166672.

48. https://www.statista.com/statistics/263794/number-of-downloads-from-the-apple-app-store/.

49. https://www.statista.com/statistics/281106/number-of-android-app-downloads-from-google-play/.

50. Hibben, M. 2015. Apple Pay vs. Google Wallet: The rematch. *SeekingAlpha,* February 25, http://seekingalpha.com/article/2948836-apple-pay-vs-google-wallet-the-rematch?auth_param=70583:1aernv3:56a2cade662c710219a5a9ca9968ad60&uprof=14.

51. MacRumors, 2015. Apple Pay overview, http://www.macrumors.com/roundup/apple-pay/.

52. Webster, Karen. 2017. An inconvenient Apple Pay truth. *Seeking Alpha,* April 10, https://seekingalpha.com/article/4061585-inconvenient-apple-pay-truth?app=1&auth_param=70583:1ceo200:e4485021eb4a508529c7e2cd5ef51905&uprof=14.

53. Luk, L. & Wakabayashi, D. 2015. Apple orders more than 5 million Watches for initial run. *Wall Street Journal,* February 17, http://blogs.wsj.com/digits/2015/02/17/apple-orders-more-than-5-million-watches-for-initial-run/?mod=rss_Technology.

54. Cybart, N. 2015. Don't focus on Apple Watch edition pricing. *SeekingAlpha,* February 25, http://seekingalpha.com/article/2950516-dont-focus-on-apple-watch-edition-pricing.

55. Deagon, Brian. 2017. Best opportunity for Apple Watch still ahead as wearables market evolves. *Investors.com,* April 7, http://www.investors.com/news/technology/best-opportunity-for-apple-watch-still-ahead-as-wearable-market-evolves/?src=A00220A&yptr=yahoo.

56. Greve, Max. 2017. Apple Music is successful, but limited: Pandora retains large opening. *Seeking Alpha,* April 13, https://seekingalpha.com/article/4062243-apple-music-successful-limited-pandora-retains-large-opening?app=1&auth_param=70583:1cev3dh:cf65d2c062bb39b259d22eca1afd81dc&uprof=14; Hibben, Mark. 2017. Apple: A power in streaming music. *Seeking Alpha,* March 31, https://seekingalpha.com/article/4059382-apple-power-streaming-music?app=1&auth_param=70583:1cdsfs6:e9fc79c4ef8c9d4c4055614308f26e86&uprof=14.

57. DoctoRx. 2015. The real importance of the Apple car project. *SeekingAlpha,* February 20, http://seekingalpha.com/article/2935276-the-real-importance-of-the-apple-car-project?auth_param=70583:1aeel0c:036a6dfaf470ca644123bac661ffb276&uprof=14.

58. Painter, Lewis. 2017. iCar release date rumours, features and images–Apple Car rumours. *MacWorld,* March 3, http://www.macworld.co.uk/news/apple/icar-apple-car-release-date-rumours-news-caros-evidence-patents-march-2017-3425394/.

59. Cho, Alex. 2017. Can Apple double its service business by 2020? *Seeking Alpha,* April 7, https://seekingalpha.com/article/4061015-can-apple-double-service-business-2020?app=1&auth_param=70583:1cef0vr:aa847ec68d336116b79be86fe3aa64b4&uprof=14.

60. D.M.Martins Research. 2017. App store: key to apple's growth target. *Seeking Alpha,* March 29, https://seekingalpha.com/article/4058813-app-store-key-apples-growth-target?app=1&auth_param=70583:1cdnih0:243d936e23ab6d685e106ccb80db6615&uprof=14.

61. Levy, Adam. 2017. Apple's app store sales could double in 5 years. *Motley Fool,* April 6, https://www.fool.com/investing/2017/04/06/apples-app-store-sales-could-double-in-5-years.aspx?yptr=yahoo.

62. D.M.Martins Research. 2017. How would an Apple-Disney merger make any sense? *Seeking Alpha,* April 14, https://seekingalpha.com/article/4062472-apple-disney-merger-make-sense?app=1&auth_param=70583:1cf1puf:19c3dab0ebc344639142e842c72fa5e1&uprof=14.

63. Santos, Paulo. 2017. Who will Apple come for next? *Seeking Alpha,* April 13, https://seekingalpha.com/article/4062308-will-apple-come-next?app=1&auth_param=70583:1cevdgo:79501019595ffd8c4c821268800f710f&uprof=14.

64. Russolillo, S. 2013. Apple losing luster: Is it now a value stock? *Wall Street Journal,* January 14, blogs.wsj.com/marketbeat/2013/01/14/apple-growth-or-value-stock/.

65. DoctoRx. 2015.

66. Ibid.

67. Dergunov, Victor. 2017. Apple's shrinking share of the smartphone market. *Seeking Alpha,* April 4, https://seekingalpha.com/article/4060160-apples-shrinking-share-smartphone-market?app=1&auth_param=70583:1ce7gvo:25cccc03232b7cf629a98b819a7d2744&uprof=14.

68. Dividend Sleuth. 2017. Apple is a top 5 holding. *Seeking Alpha,* March 20, https://seekingalpha.com/article/4056614-apple-top-5-holding.

CASE 28

JETBLUE AIRWAYS CORPORATION: GETTING OVER THE "BLUES"?

In 2017 JetBlue faced challenges that included rising fuel prices, troubling technical disruptions, and declining quality of the flying experience. Since the beginning of 2016, JetBlue had enjoyed low fuel prices that helped increase their earnings about 18 percent during the second quarter of 2016,[1] but the company experienced technical issues that caused booking problems and resulted in delays, as well as bad publicity. In order to cope with the likelihood of a rise in future fuel prices, JetBlue undertook massive cost reductions by investing in cabin restyling, for instance, adding more seats to JetBlue's A320 airplanes. However, the shrinking legroom that accompanied the cabin restyling was despised by passengers, which posed a problem for an airline that had once offered customers a captivating (as opposed to a captive) flying experience.

* This case study was prepared by Professor Naga Lakshmi Damaraju of the Indian School of Business, Professor Alan B. Eisner at Pace University, Professor Gregory G. Dess at the University of Texas at Dallas, and graduate student Saad Nazir of Pace University. The purpose of the case is to stimulate class discussion rather than to illustrate effective or ineffective handling of a business situation. The authors thank Ms. Parul Agarwal, Indian School of Business, for her research assistance and Professor Michael Oliff at the University of Texas at Dallas for his valuable comments on an earlier version of this case. Copyright © 2017 Damaraju, Eisner, and Dess.

To meet the challenges, new CEO Robin Hayes orchestrated various initiatives that the company planned to take through 2017. Those initiatives included wider fare options, enhanced Mint services, cabin restyling, new lines of JetBlue credit cards, and partnerships with other airlines.[2]

The founding CEO of JetBlue, David Neeleman, had been ousted by the board of directors after a notorious event when an ice storm severely disrupted the airline's operations.[3] In 2007, Dave Barger, an employee since the inception of JetBlue in 1998, became the second CEO of the company. Ultimately Barger was pressured to step down amid constantly depressed stock prices. In February 2015, Robin Hayes took charge of the company as its third chief executive. Hayes was the executive vice president of British Airways for the Americas before joining JetBlue in August 2008. Having worked for about 25 years and having extensive experience in the airline industry, Hayes was considered an optimal choice to become the third chief executive of JetBlue.

In promoting Robin Hayes to be the airline's new CEO, JetBlue's board signaled its readiness to focus on investor-friendly changes. With news of his selection, the share price immediately soared by 5 percent. But JetBlue loyalists who loved the company for its customers-first policies were getting more and more uncomfortable (see Exhibit 1).[4] Would JetBlue soar into clearer skies, or would it sink into the "blues" again?

EXHIBIT 1 JetBlue's Stock Performance versus S&P 500

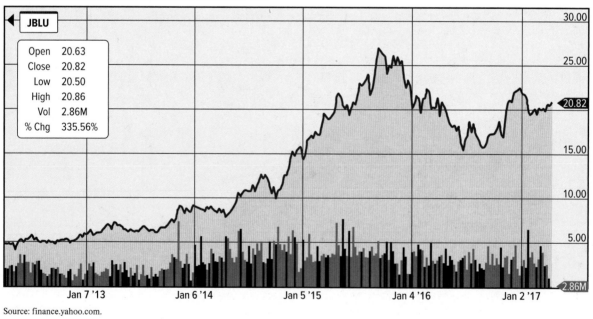

Source: finance.yahoo.com.

The U.S. Airline Industry[5]

The U.S. airline industry consists of three primary segments: major airlines, regional airlines, and low-fare airlines. Major U.S. airlines, as defined by the Department of Transportation, are those with annual revenues of over $1 billion. Most major airlines utilize the hub-and-spoke route system. In this system, the operations are concentrated in a limited number of hub cities, while other destinations are served by providing one-stop or connecting service through the hub. Scheduled flights serve most large cities within the United States and abroad and also serve numerous smaller cities.

Regional airlines typically operate smaller aircraft on lower-volume routes than do major airlines. They typically enter into relationships with major airlines and carry their passengers on the "spoke"—that is, between a hub or larger city and a smaller city. Unlike the low-fare airlines, the regional airlines do not have an independent route system.

Deregulation of the U.S. airline industry in 1978 ushered in competition in the previously protected industry. Several low-cost, low-fare operators entered the competitive landscape that Southwest had pioneered in 1971. The low-fare airlines operate from point to point with their own route systems. The target segment of low-fare airlines is fare-conscious leisure and business travelers who might otherwise use alternative forms of transportation or not travel at all. Low-fare airlines have stimulated demand in this segment and been successful in weaning business travelers from the major airlines. Southwest is the outstanding example; however, Southwest has become a major airline, having crossed the $1 billion mark in 1990.[6]

The main bases of competition in the airline industry are fare pricing, customer service, routes, flight schedules, types of aircraft, safety record and reputation, code-sharing relationships, in-flight entertainment systems, and frequent-flier programs. The economic downturn in the late 1990s and the terrorist attacks on the World Trade Center and the Pentagon on September 11, 2001, severely affected the airline industry and changed the competitive relationships among carriers. The demand for air travel dropped significantly, leading to a reduction in traffic and revenue. Security concerns, security costs, and liquidity concerns increased. Lower fares and the increased capacity of the low-cost airlines created a very unprofitable environment for traditional networks. Since 2011 most of the traditional network, hub-and-spoke airlines have filed for bankruptcy or undergone financial restructuring, mergers, or consolidations.[7] With these restructurings, many of them have been able to significantly reduce labor costs, restructure debt, and generally gain a more competitive cost structure. This has enabled the major airlines to provide innovative offerings similar to those of low-cost airlines while still maintaining their alliances, frequent-flier programs, and expansive route networks. The gap between low-cost airlines and traditional network airlines has diminished drastically.

JetBlue: The Humble Beginnings and the Great Rise[8]

Born in São Paulo, Brazil, and brought up in Salt Lake City, David Neeleman, along with June Morris, launched Utah-based Morris Air, a charter operation, in 1984. Morris Air was closely modeled after Southwest Airlines, the legendary discount airline. Neeleman considered Herb Kelleher, Southwest's founder, his idol.

While following the Southwest model, Neeleman brought his own innovations into the business. He pioneered the use of at-home reservation agents, routing calls to agents' homes to save money on office rent and infrastructure expense. He also developed the first electronic ticketing system in the airline industry. Impressed by Morris's low costs and high revenue, Southwest bought the company for $129 million in 1992. Neeleman became an executive vice president of Southwest. However, he could not adjust to Southwest's pace of doing things. By 1994, he was at odds with top executives, and he left after signing a five-year noncompete agreement.

After the noncompete agreement with Southwest Airlines ended in 1999, Neeleman launched his own airline. He raised about $130 million of capital in two weeks.[9] With such strong support from venture capitalists, JetBlue began as the highest-funded start-up airline in U.S. aviation history. JetBlue commenced operations in August 2000, with John F. Kennedy International Airport (JFK) as its primary base of operations. In 2001, JetBlue extended its operations to the West Coast with its base at Long Beach Municipal Airport, which served the Los Angeles area. In 2002, the company went public and was listed on NASDAQ as JBLU. JetBlue's stock offering was one of the hottest IPOs of the year.[10]

JetBlue had been established with the goal of being a leading low-fare passenger airline that offered customers a differentiated product and high-quality customer service on point-to-point routes. JetBlue had a geographically diversified flight schedule that included both short-haul and long-haul routes. The mission of the company, according to Neeleman, was "to bring humanity back to air travel." To stimulate demand, the airline focused on underserved markets and large metropolitan areas that had high average fares.

JetBlue was committed to keeping its costs low. To achieve this objective, the company originally operated a single-type aircraft fleet comprising Airbus A320 planes as opposed to the more popular but costly Boeing 737. The A320s had 162 seats, compared to 132 seats in the Boeing 737. According to JetBlue, the A320 was less expensive to maintain and more fuel-efficient. Since all of JetBlue's planes were new, the maintenance costs were also lower. In addition, the single type of aircraft kept training costs low and increased personnel utilization. JetBlue was the first to introduce the "paperless cockpit," in which pilots, equipped with laptops, had ready access to flight manuals that were constantly updated at headquarters. As a result, pilots could quickly calculate the weight, balance, and takeoff performance of the aircraft instead of having to download and print the manuals to make the calculations. The paperless cockpit ensured faster takeoffs by reducing paperwork and thus helped the airline achieve quicker turnarounds and higher aircraft utilization.[11] No meals were served on the planes, and pilots even had to be ready, if need be, to do cleanup work on the plane to minimize the time the aircraft was on the ground. Turnaround time was also reduced by the airline's choice of less congested airports.[12] Innovation was everywhere. For example, there were no paper tickets to lose and no mileage statements to mail to frequent fliers.

With friendly, customer service–oriented employees; new aircraft; roomy leather seats with 36 channels of free LiveTV, 100 channels of free XM satellite radio, and movie channel offerings from FOXInflight; and more legroom (one row of seats was removed to create additional space), JetBlue promised its customers a distinctive flying experience, the "JetBlue experience." With virtually no incidents of passengers being denied boarding; high completion factors (99.6 percent as compared to 98.3 percent at other major airlines); the lowest incidence of delayed, mishandled, or lost bags; and the third-lowest number of customer complaints, the company was indeed setting standards for low-cost operations in the industry. JetBlue was voted the best domestic airline in the *Conde Nast Traveler*'s Readers' Choice Awards for five consecutive years. Readers of *Travel + Leisure* magazine also rated it the World's Best Domestic Airline in 2006. In addition, it earned the Passenger Service Award from *Air Transport World.*[13]

Hitting Bumpy Air

Nevertheless, high fuel prices, the competitive pricing environment, and other cost increases made it increasingly difficult to keep JetBlue growing and profitable. The airline suffered its first-ever losses after its IPO in 2005. It posted net losses of $20 million and $1 million for 2005 and 2006, respectively.[14]

The ice storm on Valentine's Day 2007 that cost Neeleman his job was a nightmare in JetBlue's hitherto high-flying history for more than one reason. Not only did the event destroy JetBlue's reputation for customer friendliness, but it also exposed critical weaknesses in the systems that had kept the airline's operations going. The airline's reputation hit rock bottom. To limit the damage, JetBlue announced huge compensations to customers—refunds and future flights—which were to cost the airline about $30 million. Neeleman quickly followed up with a new Customer Bill of Rights. The Customer Bill of Rights outlined self-imposed penalties for JetBlue and major rewards for its passengers if the airline experienced operational problems and could not adjust to weather-related cancelations within a "reasonable" amount of time. All these announcements and even a public apology could not restore things to normalcy. Neeleman was pushed out as CEO on May 10, 2007. Dave Barger, the president, assumed the position of chief executive officer.

Restoring JetBlue's Luster?

Under the second CEO, Dave Barger, JetBlue added several new services and embarked on capacity expansion to give the airline a new boost. In July 2007, it became the first U.S. carrier to let passengers send free email and text messages from wireless handheld devices, a technology developed through its LiveTV LLC subsidiary.[15] Later, in September 2007, it expanded to smaller cities that did not have sufficient demand for the larger planes flown by Southwest, Virgin America, and Skybus Airlines. It also introduced Embraer jets to its fleet.[16]

In 2007, JetBlue had its first full-year profit in three years as an increase in traffic and operational improvements helped compensate for skyrocketing fuel costs. However, as a result of global financial turmoil and skyrocketing fuel prices, JetBlue's profits tanked again in 2008, and the company reported a net loss of $85 million.[17] Nevertheless, the company returned to profitability in 2009. In April 2010, JetBlue successfully completed the International Air Transport Association's (IATA's) Operational Safety Audit (IOSA) and achieved IOSA registration, meeting the same highest industry benchmarks as other world-class airlines.[18]

Dave Barger was known for "being overly concerned" with customer service and comfort.[19] During Barger's tenure, JetBlue earned tributes for its customer service. However, its low-fare business model was being threatened as its costs kept going up. In April 2014, its pilots, long nonunion, voted to join the Air Line Pilots Association.[20] In the wintertime the airline was again racked by weather-driven flight cancelations. JetBlue's stock under Barger's leadership lagged behind big legacy carriers Delta Air Lines and fellow discounter Southwest Airlines. The shares were up just 9 percent since Barger became CEO.[21] In the same period, Southwest's shares gained more than 140 percent and the overall Bloomberg U.S. Airline index gained 49 percent.[22]

Current Leadership

The new CEO, Robin Hayes, unveiled a new pricing model that included four different pricing categories (see Exhibit 2). Under the new fare structure, passengers were able to choose which features they did or didn't want included in the ticket price. At the low end of the pricing spectrum, tickets did not include a checked bag. Passengers who paid higher fares were entitled to checked bags (one bag at Blue-Plus level, two at the Blue-Flex and Mint levels) and got bonus loyalty points. At the high end of the pricing, the "Even More" seating option offered extra legroom (38 inches of pitch), expedited security clearance, and priority access to overhead bin space. With this fare structure, seats were subject to variable pricing not only by flight but also by their specific position in the aircraft. Hayes said that the airline was committed to delivering "the best travel experience for our customers. . . . JetBlue's core mission to Inspire Humanity and its differentiated model of serving underserved customers remain unchanged."[23]

The substantial challenge regarding a trade-off between travel experience and profit margins remained. The question was, would JetBlue be able to hold onto its core mission and still be able to make its stakeholders happy? Investors wondered if JetBlue really had a strong and clear strategic position

EXHIBIT 2 JetBlue Fare Options

	BLUE	BLUE PLUS	BLUE FLEX	MINT
CHECKED BAGS INCLUDED[1]	0	1	2	2
CARRY-ON (1 BAG + PERSONAL ITEM) INCLUDED	✓	✓	✓	✓
BASE TRUEBLUE POINTS (PER DOLLAR)[2]	3	3	3	3
TRUEBLUE ONLINE BOOKING BONUS (PER DOLLAR)[3]	3	4	5	3
CANCELLATIONS OR CHANGES (PLUS ANY FARE DIFFERENCE)[4]	$75 (FARES UP TO $99) $100 (FARES UP TO $149) $150 (FARES $150+)	$75 (FARES UP TO $99) $100 (FARES UP TO $149) $150 (FARES $150+)	0	$75 (60+ DAYS FROM DEPARTURE; FARES < $950) $150 (WITHIN 60 DAYS FROM DEPARTURE, FARES < $950)
SAME DAY CHANGES	$50	$50	✓	$50
EVEN MORE®SPEED (EXPENDED SECURITY)[5]	$10/$15	$10/$15	✓	✓
MOST LEGROOM IN COACH[6]	✓	✓	✓	N/A
FREE SNACKS & SOFT DRINKS	✓	✓	✓	✓
EATUP® & EATUP®CAFÉ[7]	$3 – $12	$3 – $12	$3 – $12	✓
FLY-FI® (HIGH-SPEED INTERNET)[8]	✓	✓	✓	✓
DIRECTTV®[9]	✓	✓	✓	✓
SIRIUS XM RADIO®[10]	✓	✓	✓	✓
MOVIES[11]	✓	✓	✓	✓
LIE-FLAT SEAT, EARLY BOARDING, ARTISANAL DINING, DEDICATED CHECK-IN & MORE!	N/A	N/A	N/A	✓

Source: JetBlue official website.

and coherent business model to support it. Were too many complexities being introduced into its simple model of success?

The "Interline" Model

Unlike many other carriers around the world, JetBlue chose to stay independent. The carrier relied on signing a series of "interline" agreements instead of joining an airline alliance. While the interline agreements do not fit into a strict hub-and-spoke model, they nearly amount to the same thing, allowing JetBlue passengers in New York, Boston, and San Juan to connect to destinations around the world.

In February 2007, under the leadership of Barger, JetBlue had announced its first code-share agreement, with Cape Air. Under this agreement, JetBlue passengers from Boston's Logan Airport were carried to Cape Air's destinations throughout Cape Cod and the surrounding islands, and customers were able to purchase seats on both airlines under one reservation.[24] While Lufthansa's January 2008 acquisition of a minority equity stake (42.6 million shares of common stock) in JetBlue did not automatically lead to any code-share agreements, Lufthansa expected to have "operational cooperation" with JetBlue.[25]

JetBlue continued on the path of signing more interline agreements. In March 2011, it announced an interline

agreement with Virgin Atlantic. Virgin Atlantic and Virgin America have some shared ownership, with Virgin Group owning 25 percent of Virgin America. Virgin America is a major competitor of JetBlue.[26] In March 2013, JetBlue entered its 22nd code-share agreement, with Qatar Airways, which followed its partnerships with the UAE-based Emirates airline, Korean Air, Air China, and the Indian carrier Jet Airways, allowing JetBlue to expand its reach far beyond the Americas, into India, China, the Middle East, and other parts of Asia.[27] Etihad Airways and El Al Israel joined this list in January 2014 and November 2014, respectively.[28] After replacing the second CEO, Hayes continued expanding the partnership and codeshare agreements throughout 2016. JetBlue signed codeshare agreements with Seaborne Airlines and Azul Brazilian Airlines, and expanded the existing codeshare agreements with many airlines including Hawaiian Airlines, Cape Air, and Icelandair Airlines, among others. In response to growing competition, JetBlue's expansion of codeshare agreements marked a departure from the company's initial strategy to stay independent.

More Goodies for Customers

Over the years, JetBlue has constantly tried to maintain its customer-first attitude. It introduced its "Go Places" application on Facebook, which rewarded customers with TrueBlue points and special discounts so they could earn free trips faster. The "Even More" suite of products and services—including early boarding, early access, expedited security experience, and extra legroom—has been an interesting innovation. JetBlue has added more benefits for its frequent fliers through its "TrueBlue Mosaic" loyalty program. The services include a free second checked bag, a dedicated 24-hour customer service line, and bonus points, among many other offers.[29]

JetBlue became the first Federal Aviation Administration-certified carrier in the U.S. to utilize the new satellite-based Special Required Navigation Performance Authorization Required (RNP AR) approaches at its home base at New York's JFK airport. These unique procedures have resulted in stabilized approach paths, shorter flight times, and reduced noise levels and greenhouse gas emissions, and they have increased fuel savings by as much as 18 gallons per flight.[30] In 2017, with an operating margin of 19.65 percent, JetBlue was doing better than in previous years as compared to its close competitors (see Exhibit 3).

Nevertheless, in October 2013, amid cost cutting, JetBlue had announced a fleet modernization program that included deferral of 24 Embraer aircraft from 2014–2018 to 2020–2022 so that capital expenditures could be reduced over the near term (see Exhibits 4 and 5). It also converted 18 orders with Airbus from A320 to A321 aircraft. It said its future focus would be on adding aircraft with more fuel-efficient engines. JetBlue also shrank legroom, adding 15 more seats to its Airbus A320 planes.[31]

Reinventing JetBlue

Under Hayes's leadership, JetBlue has gone through many changes to "reinvent" the company, including new interline agreements, new codesharing agreements, various strategic partnerships with other commercial airlines, launch of JetBlue credit cards, and creation of JetBlue Technology Ventures LLC to invest in emerging technologies related to the travel and hospitality industry.[32] However, the company has also faced challenges, including technical problems when customers were unable to book or modify their existing reservations amid an outage in computer systems.[33] In May 2016, eight passengers were injured amid heavy turbulence on a JetBlue flight from San Juan to Orlando.[34] In August 2016, heavy turbulence on another JetBlue flight from Boston to Sacramento put 24 people in the hospital, including two crew members and 22 passengers.[35]

Numerous factors will determine the future of JetBlue under Hayes's leadership. Will the company be able to maintain high operating margins if the fuel price starts to go up after the oil supply glut evaporates? At the same time will the company be able to provide its customers a great travel experience by keeping low fares?

EXHIBIT 3 Operating Margins of Major U.S. Airlines

Airline	Operating Margin, 2016
Southwest Airlines	23.17%
JetBlue	19.65
Delta Air Lines	18.39
American Airlines	14.95
United Continental	14.10

Source: *Wall Street Journal.*

EXHIBIT 4 Income Statement of JetBlue

Fiscal year is January–December. All values USD millions.	2016	2015	2014	2013	2012
Sales/Revenue	6,632	6,416	5,817	5,441	4,982
Sales Growth	3.37%	10.30%	6.91%	9.21%	–
Cost of Goods Sold (COGS) incl. D&A	5,070	4,831	5,048	4,789	4,412
COGS excluding D&A	4,677	4,486	4,728	4,499	4,154
Depreciation & Amortization Expense	393	345	320	290	258
Depreciation	337	288	263	258	230
Amortization of Intangibles	56	57	57	32	28
COGS Growth	4.95%	−4.30%	5.41%	8.54%	–
Gross Income	1,562	1,585	769	652	570
Gross Income Growth	−1.45%	106.11%	17.94%	14.39%	–

Fiscal year is January–December. All values USD millions.	2016	2015	2014	2013	2012
SG&A Expense	259	264	231	223	204
Other SG&A	259	264	231	223	204
SGA Growth	−1.89%	14.29%	3.59%	9.31%	–
EBIT	1,303	1,321	538	429	366
Unusual Expense	(1)	(13)	16	11	1
Non Operating Income/Expense	16	(118)	234	1	–
Interest Expense	104	119	133	140	157
Interest Expense Growth	−12.61%	−10.53%	−5.00%	−10.83%	–
Gross Interest Expense	112	127	147	153	165
Interest Capitalized	8	8	14	13	8
Pretax Income	1,216	1,097	623	279	209
Pretax Income Growth	10.85%	76.08%	123.30%	33.49%	–
Income Tax	457	420	222	111	81
Income Tax – Current Domestic	155	43	10	4	5
Income Tax – Current Foreign	32	–	–	–	–
Income Tax – Deferred Domestic	270	377	212	107	76
Consolidated Net Income	759	677	401	168	128
Net Income	759	677	401	168	128
Net Income Growth	12.11%	68.83%	138.69%	31.25%	–
Net Income After Extraordinaries	759	677	401	168	128
Net Income Available to Common	759	677	401	168	128
EPS (Basic)	2.22	1.98	1.19	0.52	0.40
EPS (Basic) Growth	12.12%	66.39%	128.85%	30.62%	–
Basic Shares Outstanding	327	315	295	283	282
EPS (Diluted)	2.22	1.98	1.19	0.52	0.40
EPS (Diluted) Growth	12.60%	66.19%	130.59%	29.46%	–
Diluted Shares Outstanding	342	345	343	343	344
EBITDA	1,696	1,666	858	719	624
EBITDA Growth	1.80%	94.17%	19.33%	15.22%	–
EBIT	1,303	1,321	538	429	366

Source: JetBlue Annual Report, 2016.

EXHIBIT 5 Balance Sheet of JetBlue

Fiscal year is January–December. All values USD millions.	2016	2015	2014	2013	2012
Cash & Short-Term Investments	971	876	708	627	731
Cash Only	433	318	341	225	182
Short-Term Investments	538	558	367	402	549
Cash & Short-Term Investments Growth	10.84%	23.73%	12.92%	−14.23%	–
Cash & ST Investments / Total Assets	10.24%	10.12%	9.03%	8.53%	10.34%
Total Accounts Receivable	172	136	136	129	106
Accounts Receivables, Net	172	136	136	129	106
Accounts Receivables, Gross	177	142	142	135	113
Bad Debt/Doubtful Accounts	(5)	(6)	(6)	(6)	(7)
Acounts Receivable Growth	26.47%	0.00%	5.43%	21.70%	–
Accounts Receivable Turnover	38.56	47.18	42.77	42.18	47.00
Inventories	47	44	46	48	36
Raw Materials	–	–	46	48	–
Other Current Assets	377	317	310	252	227
Prepaid Expenses	–	172	135	126	119
Miscellaneous Current Assets	377	145	175	126	108
Total Current Assets	1,567	1,373	1,200	1,056	1,100
Net Property, Plant & Equipment	7,271	6,652	6,072	5,656	5,343
Property, Plant & Equipment – Gross	9,624	8,679	7,817	7,208	6,652
Machinery & Equipment	8,091	7,250	6,440	5,959	5,506
Construction in Progress	561	561	561	561	561
Other Property, Plant & Equipment	972	868	816	688	585
Accumulated Depreciation	2,353	2,027	1,745	1,552	1,309
Machinery & Equipment	1,823	1,573	1,354	1,185	995
Construction in Progress	185	161	139	116	93
Other Property, Plant & Equipment	345	293	252	251	221
Total Investments and Advances	152	112	121	171	187
Other Long-Term Investments	152	112	121	171	187
Intangible Assets	97	93	73	70	129
Other Assets	400	430	373	397	311
Tangible Other Assets	400	430	373	397	311
Total Assets	9,487	8,660	7,839	7,350	7,070
Assets – Total – Growth	9.55%	10.47%	6.65%	3.96%	–

Fiscal year is January–December. All values USD millions.	2016	2015	2014	2013	2012
ST Debt & Current Portion LT Debt	189	448	265	469	394
Current Portion of Long-Term Debt	189	448	265	469	394
Accounts Payable	242	205	208	180	846
Accounts Payable Growth	18.05%	−1.44%	15.56%	−78.72%	–
Other Current Liabilities	1,792	1,622	1,463	1,225	368
Accrued Payroll	342	302	203	171	172
Miscellaneous Current Liabilities	1,450	1,320	1,260	1,054	196
Total Current Liabilities	2,223	2,275	1,936	1,874	1,608
Current Ratio	0.70	0.60	0.62	0.56	0.68
Quick Ratio	0.68	0.58	0.60	0.54	0.66
Cash Ratio	0.44	0.39	0.37	0.33	0.45
Long-Term Debt	1,652	1,867	2,455	2,590	2,457
Long-Term Debt excl. Capitalized Leases	1,528	1,727	2,300	2,493	2,457
Non–Convertible Debt	1,528	1,727	2,300	2,493	2,457
Capitalized Lease Obligations	124	140	155	97	–
Deferred Taxes	1,509	1,218	832	605	481
Deferred Taxes – Credit	1,509	1,218	832	605	481
Other Liabilities	90	90	87	147	636
Other Liabilities (excl. Deferred Income)	90	90	87	147	636
Total Liabilities	5,474	5,450	5,310	5,216	5,182
Total Liabilities / Total Assets	57.70%	62.93%	67.74%	70.97%	73.30%
Common Equity (Total)	4,013	3,210	2,529	2,134	1,888
Common Stock Par/Carry Value	4	4	4	3	3
Additional Paid–In Capital/Capital Surplus	2,050	1,896	1,711	1,573	1,495
Retained Earnings	2,446	1,679	1,002	601	433
Other Appropriated Reserves	13	(3)	(63)	–	(8)
Treasury Stock	(500)	(366)	(125)	(43)	(35)
Common Equity / Total Assets	42.30%	37.07%	32.26%	29.03%	26.70%
Total Shareholders' Equity	4,013	3,210	2,529	2,134	1,888
Total Shareholders' Equity / Total Assets	42.30%	37.07%	32.26%	29.03%	26.70%
Total Equity	4,013	3,210	2,529	2,134	1,888
Liabilities & Shareholders' Equity	9,487	8,660	7,839	7,350	7,070

Source: JetBlue Annual Report, 2016.

ENDNOTES

1. Stynes, T. 2016. Low fuel costs help JetBlue's profit rise. July 26. Retrieved January 9, 2017, from www.wsj.com/articles/low-fuel-costs-help-jetblues-profit-rise-1469545330.

2. http://blueir.investproductions.com/~ /media/Files/J/Jetblue-IR-V2/reports-and-presentations/2016-investor-day-12-12-2016.pdf. Retrieved January 9, 2017.

3. Airways, J. 2016. Leadership. Retrieved January 3, 2017, www.blueir.investproductions.com/investor-relations/corporate-governance/leadership.

4. Tuttle, B. 2014. A new era has begun for JetBlue, and travelers will hate it. *Time,* November 19, www.time.com/money/3595360/jetblue-fees-legroom-hates/.

5. This section draws heavily on the SEC filings of JetBlue for the years 2008 and 2009. Other sources include Zellner, W. 2003. Look who's buzzing the discounters. *BusinessWeek,* November 24; Zellner, W. 2004. Folks are finally packing their bags. *BusinessWeek,* January 12; and a joint study by A. T. Kearney and the Society of British Aerospace Companies, www.atkearney.com/shared_res/pdf/Emerging_Airline_Industry_S.pdf.6.

6. Serwer, A., & Bonamici, K. 2004. Southwest Airlines: The hottest thing in the sky; through change at the top, through 9/11, in a lousy industry, it keeps winning most admired kudos. How? *Fortune,* March 8: 88–106, money.cnn.com/magazines/fortune/fortune_archive/2004/03/08/363700/index.htm.

7. Peterson, K., and Daily, M. 2011. American Airlines files for bankruptcy. Reuters, November 29, www.reuters.com/article/2011/11/29/us-americanairlines-idUSTRE7AS0T220111129.

8. This section draws heavily on Gajilan, A. T. 2004. The amazing JetBlue. *Fortune Small Business,* www.fortune/smallbusiness/articles/0.15114,444298-2,00.html.

9. Gale/Cengage Learning. Undated. JetBlue Airways Corporation. In International directory of company histories, galenet.galegroup.com.

10. *CNNMoney.* 2002. JetBlue IPO soars. April 12, money.cnn.com/2002/04/12/markets/ipo/jetblue.

11. *BusinessWeek.* 2003. WEBSMART50. November 24: 92.

12. Bay, W., & Neeleman, D. 2002. JetBlue reaches new heights in airline industry (interview with David Neeleman by Willow Bay of *CNN Business Unusual*). Aired June 23, www.cnn.com/TRANSCRIPTS/0206/23/bun.00.html.

13. JetBlue. SEC filings, 2006.

14. JetBlue. SEC filings, 2007 and 2008.

15. Associated Press. 2007. N.Y. discount carrier JetBlue to detail wireless email plans. *Toronto Star,* July 6.

16. Ray, S. 2007. Repaired planes boost JetBlue expansion plan. *Bloomberg News,* September 1.

17. JetBlue. SEC filings, 2008–2010.

18. From company press releases, 2010. JetBlue completes top international safety audit. April 19, www.jetblue.com.

19. Tuttle, B. 2014. A new era has begun for JetBlue, and travelers will hate it. *Time,* November 19, www.time.com/money/3595360/jetblue-fees-legroom-hates/.

20. Nicas, J. 2014. Jetblue's pilots vote to unionize. *Wall Street Journal,* April 22, www.wsj.com/articles/SB10001424052702304049904579517911131169286.

21. Carey, S. 2014. JetBlue CEO Barger to retire in February. *Wall Street Journal,* September 18, www.wsj.com/articles/jetblue-ceo-barger-to-retire-in-february-1411072958.

22. Schlangenstein & Sasso, op. cit.

23. Schaal, D. 2014. The new JetBlue will have more bag fees and less legroom. November 19, http://skift.com/2015/01/29/jetblue-to-unveil-bag-fees-and-new-types-of-fares-in-the-second-quarter/.

24. Compart, A. 2007. JetBlue's pact with Cape Air is airline's first codeshare deal. February 19, www.travelweekly.com/Travel-News/Airline-News/JetBlue-s-pact-with-Cape-Air-is-airline-s-first-codeshare-deal/.

25. Associated Press. 2007. Lufthansa pays $300 million for JetBlue stake.

26. Associated Press. 2011. JetBlue partners with Virgin Atlantic; and Blank, D. 2011. JetBlue and Virgin Atlantic (finally) announce interline agreement. *Online Travel Review,* March 22, www.onlinetravelreview.com/2011/03/22/jetblue-and-virgin-atlantic-finally-announce-interline-agreement/.

27. Unnikrishnan, M. 2012. JetBlue signs codeshare agreement with Air China. *Aviation Week,* June 12, www.aviationweek.com/Article.aspx?id=/article-xml/awx_06_12_2012_p0-467058.xml.

28. Associated Press. 2014. JetBlue, Etihad Airlines announce partnership. *New Zealand Herald,* January 22; and JetBlue Airways and El Al Israel Airlines sign codeshare agreement, November 21, 2014, www.heritagefl.com/story/2014/11/21/features/jetblue-airways-and-el-al-israel-airlines-sign-codeshare-agreement/3600.html.

29. JetBlue. Press releases.

30. Drum, B. 2012. JetBlue Airways becomes first FAA-certified carrier to fly special (non-public) RNP AR approaches with Airbus A320s at New York's JFK Airport. June 20, http://worldairlinenews.com/2012/06/20/jetblue-airways-becomes-first-faa-certified-carrier-to-fly-special-non-public-rnp-ar-approaches-with-airbus-a320s-at-new-yorks-jfk-airport/.

31. Tuttle, B. 2014. A new era has begun for JetBlue, and travelers will hate it. *Time,* No-vember 19, www.time.com/money/3595360/jetblue-fees-legroom-hates/.

32. JetBlue Annual Report, 2015.

33. http://fortune.com/2016/10/17/southwest-jetblue-booking-system/?iid=sr-link7.

34. http://fortune.com/2016/08/12/jetblue-turbulence-injuries/?iid=sr-link5.

35. http://fortune.com/2016/08/12/jetblue-turbulence-injuries/?iid=sr-link5.

APPENDIX A

GLOSSARY OF KEY TERMS USED*

aircraft utilization The average number of block hours operated per day per aircraft for the total fleet of aircraft.

available seat-miles The number of seats available for passengers multiplied by the number of miles the seats are flown.

average fare The average one-way fare paid per flight segment by a revenue passenger.

average stage length The average number of miles flown per flight.

break-even load factor The passenger load factor that will result in operating revenues being equal to operating expenses, assuming constant revenue per passenger-mile and expenses.

*From JetBlue SEC filings.

load factor The percentage of aircraft seating capacity that is actually utilized (revenue passenger-miles divided by available seat-miles).

operating expense per available seat-mile Operating expenses divided by available seat-miles.

operating revenue per available seat-mile Operating revenues divided by available seat-miles.

passenger revenue per available seat-mile Passenger revenue divided by available seat-miles.

revenue passenger-miles The number of miles flown by revenue passengers.

revenue passengers The total number of paying passengers flown on all flight segments.

yield per passenger-mile The average amount one passenger pays to fly 1 mile.

CASE 29

UNITED WAY WORLDWIDE*

In 2017, United Way Worldwide remained America's largest charity organization. However, the organization had experienced a decline in total funds received over the past few years. The total funds collected dropped about 4 percent to $3.71 billion by the beginning of 2016, and the organization sought a change to its strategic direction.[1] In April 2017, Mary Sellers, the president of United Way of Central Iowa, became the U.S. President of United Way Worldwide, along with many other new appointments in United Way's leadership. Sellers was expected to lead the new strategic direction of the organization. With more than 20 years of leadership experience at various nonprofit organizations, Sellers had achieved remarkable success as the president of United Way of Central Iowa, which the most successful of the United Ways in the country.[2]

In March 2017, the organization had launched its Join the Fight campaign, which marked a distinct approach to United Way's mission. The focus of the campaign was to bring attention to the challenges faced by communities around the world, most importantly lack of education, unemployment, poor health care, and homelessness. "By putting a human face to the extreme educational, financial and health challenges that our communities are facing, United Way shines a spotlight on these issues in a way that cannot be ignored. The imagery is intentionally jarring and meant to serve as a wakeup call to get people off the sidelines and involved with their local United Way in solving these issues. The message is ultimately one of hope, however, as the viewer sees how United Way is tackling these issues every day," said Lisa Bowman, Chief Marketing Officer, United Way Worldwide.[3]

In the past, the organization had been hit particularly hard during economic downturns, and contributions were always slow to pick up after economists announced a rebound. Charitable giving usually rose about one-third as fast as the stock market.[4] In 2014 United Way Missouri chapter executive director Tim Rich mourned the fact that a perfect storm of factors was causing a surge in need. "We're seeing stagnated wages, jobs with fewer hours and less pay, church giving is down," Rich said. "It's just harder to write a check right now." This challenging situation was faced by United Way chapters all around the country.[5]

* By Professor Alan B. Eisner of Pace University, Associate Professor Pauline Assenza of Western Connecticut State University, and graduate students Luz Barrera, Dev Das, and Saad Nazir of Pace University. This case is based upon public documents and was developed for class discussion rather than to illustrate either effective or ineffective handling of the situation. This research was supported in part by the Wilson Center for Social Entrepreneurship, Pace University. Copyright © 2017 Alan B. Eisner.

The continuing trend—reduction in giving, increase in need—had earlier prompted United Way to change its strategy.[6] On July 1, 2009, United Way of America (UWA) changed its name to United Way Worldwide (UWW) and merged with United Way International (UWI). UWW initiated a 10-year program, "Live United," focused less on distribution of funds and more on advancing the common good by addressing underlying causes of problems in the core areas of education, financial stability, and health. Yet positive financial results were slow in coming. The question remained, would donors finally become reenergized and create real change in the communities United Way served? Or had universal struggles weakened the ability and eagerness to donate of even those most able to do so?

United Ways worldwide are part of a federation of nonprofits formed by caring people to serve the needs of their communities. UWW provides support for over 1,800 local United Way member organizations or affiliates operating in 41 countries.[7] These local organizations rely on their respective parents for resources such as leadership education, public policy advocacy, marketing support, and standards for ethical governance and financial reporting. According to UWW's website, "We advance the common good by focusing on improving education, helping people achieve financial stability, and promoting healthy lives, and by mobilizing millions of people to give, advocate, and volunteer to improve the conditions in which they live." United Way raises funds and distributes them to the most effective local service providers; builds alliances and coordinated volunteer support among charities, businesses, and other entities; and supposedly acts as a best-practice model of management and financial accountability. This last item had become a problem. With three high-profile ethical scandals since 1995 at both the national and local levels, the United Way brand had to combat an erosion of trust at the same time that it was dealing with an increasingly competitive and changing environment for charitable contributors.

After over 120 years of solid financial performance and steady growth, by the year 2000 United Way seemingly had reached a plateau of fund raising in the United States (see Exhibit 1). Certainly, there were opportunities for growth from international members, and from the energy and direction of nationwide objectives as stated by United Way of America. These objectives included education about and implementation of the national 2-1-1 phone network; the early childhood educational initiatives Success by 6 and Born Learning; encouragement of nationwide voluntarism through the Lend a Hand public service announcements funded by a donation from the NFL; and the Assets for Family Success economic self-sufficiency program for working families. Yet charitable donations had declined from the inflation-adjusted peak-year campaign of the late 1980s.[8]

Veteran fund raisers on all fronts were citing challenges, such as competition for donations, difficulty recruiting and keeping qualified fund raisers, difficulty raising money for general operating costs, and a growing focus on large gifts from very wealthy individuals, which, when publicized, could reduce the motivation for smaller donors to contribute. Small donors might think, "If someone like Bill Gates is providing funds, why do they need my dollars?"[9] Additionally, from the donors' perspective, the opportunities for both individuals and businesses to engage in charitable giving had expanded, with over 40 percent of new nonprofits having appeared since 2000.[10] Many of these, such as those supporting disaster relief in the wake of 9/11, Hurricane Katrina, and Hurricane Sandy, had a single-issue focus that had the potential for creating a close bond with the donor. This meant that some individuals might bypass organizations such as the United Way, believing that the United Way had support targets that were too broad, and preferring, instead, to specify exactly where donations should go. Such a donor might think, "If I'm giving, I want to make sure my money is going exactly where I want it to go, to the cause I want to support."

Even prior to 9/11, American donors had expressed concern about their ability to access information regarding how their donations were going to be used, what percentage of the charity's spending went toward actual current programs, how their privacy was going to be protected when giving via the Internet, and whether the charity met voluntary standards of conduct.[11] It didn't help that many nonprofits, including United Way of America, had suffered widely publicized scandals over misappropriation of funds. Organizations that serve community or broader social needs must continually be perceived as legitimate, as acting in an appropriate and desirable way within "some socially constructed set of norms, values, beliefs and definitions" in order to receive needed donations.[12] It is especially difficult for nonprofits such as United Way to maintain trust, because their products and services do not easily lend themselves to traditional quality assessment and performance review; and once trust is broken, it is difficult to get it back.

Responding to all the challenges, United Way Worldwide's CEO, Brian Gallagher, formally initiated a shift in strategy. He established new membership standards to enhance the level of accountability and transparency in United Way affiliates' operations. He rebranded United Way as doing "what matters" in the communities it serves. Finally, he updated the "standards of excellence," providing a description of benchmark standards and best practices to better reflect the organization's strategic shift from its traditional role as strictly a fund raiser to a new mission focused on identifying and addressing the long-term needs of communities.

These initiatives require that United Way affiliates buy into the change effort, because the power of the parent organization is limited to removing an affiliate from United Way membership if it doesn't comply. As a nonprofit organization, it is imperative for United Way Worldwide to get the necessary support at the local level in order to achieve its stated organizational goals. Will Gallagher's various strategies be successfully implemented? Will the shift in strategy be sufficient to ensure the continued viability of United Way, or is its very mission perhaps no longer relevant?

Overview and History of the United Way of America

United Way was founded in 1887 as the Charity Organizations Society of Denver, raising $21,700 for 22 local agencies in its second year of operation. In 1913 this model was expanded to become a "Community Chest" in Cleveland, and in 1918 a dozen fund-raising federations met in Chicago to form the American Association for Community Organizations. From 1919 to 1929, over 350 Community Chests were created, and by 1948 more than 1,000 communities had United Way Community Chests in operation. In 1973 the partnership between United Way and the National Football League began, with the goal to increase public awareness of social-service issues facing the country. Through the partnership, United Way public service announcements featured volunteer NFL players, coaches, and owners, and NFL players supported their local United Ways through personal appearances, special programs, and membership on United Way governing boards.

In 1974 United Ways in America and Canada raised $1,038,995,000, marking the first time in history that an annual campaign of a single organization raised more than $1 billion. In the same year, United Way International was formed to help nations around the world create United Way–type organizations. The 1981–1985 and 1997–1998 campaigns generated the greatest percentage increase in revenues, possibly driven by economic trends. Amounts raised since 2000 have generally failed to keep up with the rate of inflation (see Exhibit 1).[13]

The United Way is essentially a financial intermediary, providing fund-raising activities, primarily through donor organizations' employee payroll deductions, and then distributing those funds to agencies that can actually deliver services to clients in the target community. The parent organization, United Way Worldwide, services the local United Way chapters, which perform the bulk of the fund raising. Although there are other sources of revenue, including individual donations and government grants, around 70 percent of donations come from employees in local businesses; of the employee contributions, 75 percent are considered unrestricted dollars that the local United Ways put to use to address critical needs in their respective communities.

The parent organization, United Way Worldwide (UWW), is supported primarily by local United Way member

EXHIBIT 1 United Way Campaign History

Year	Amount Raised ($ billions)	Change ($ billions)	%	CPI (1982–1984, 100)*	Inflation Rate (%)	Amount Raised in Constant Dollars	Change ($ billions)	%
2000	3.912	0.14	3.8	172.2	3.4	2.272	0.095	0.4
2001	3.949	0.37	0.9	177.1	2.8	2.230	−0.042	−1.8
2002	3.709	−0.24	−6.1	179.9	1.6	2.062	−0.168	−7.5
2003	3.591	−0.11	−3.2	184.0	2.3	1.952	−0.110	−5.3
2004	3.606	0.15	0.4	188.9	2.7	1.909	−0.043	−2.2
2005	4.048	0.44	12.3	195.3	3.4	2.054	0.145	7.6
2006	4.143	0.95	2.3	201.6	3.2	2.043	−0.011	−0.5
2007	4.236	0.93	2.2	207.3	2.8	2.007	−0.036	−1.8
2008	4.023	−0.21	−5.0	215.3	3.8	1.919	−0.088	−4.4
2009	3.84	−0.18	−4.5	214.5	−0.4	1.795	−0.124	−6.5
2010	3.912	0.72	1.9	218.1	1.6	1.794	−0.001	−0.1
2011	3.927	0.15	0.4	224.9	3.2	1.746	−0.048	−2.7
2012	3.97	0.43	1.1	229.6	2.1	1.729	−0.017	−1.0
2013	3.939	−0.31	−0.8	233.0	1.5	1.691	−0.038	−2.2
2014	3.87	−0.69	−1.75	236.7	1.6	1.717	0.026	1.5
2015	3.71	−0.16	−4.13	237.0	0.1	1.719	−0.002	0.1
2016	3.87	0.16	4.13	240.0	1.3	1.741	0.002	1.3

*CPI is the annualized rate for a calendar year.

Source: United Way of America research services and author estimates.

organizations that pay annual membership fees based on an agreed-on formula, 1 percent of their communitywide campaign contributions. Trademark members, United Way member organizations raising less than $100,000, pay a fee of 0.3 percent of their total contributions. In addition to membership support, individual and corporate sponsorship, and federal grants, other sources for funds for the national umbrella organization are conferences, program service fees, promotional material sales, investment income, rental income, and service income (see Exhibits 2 and 3).

United Way is a system that operates as a federation—a network of local affiliates that share a mission, a brand, and a program model but are legally independent from one another and from the national office. Historically, United Way has been the loosest of federations, with almost all power residing at the local level. Each United Way chapter member is not only independent but also separately incorporated and governed by a local volunteer board. Through communitywide campaigns, each local United Way utilizes a network of local volunteers for raising funds to support a great variety of health and human services organizations.

Over the years, as United Way's local chapters grew bigger and more prosperous, they began to consider themselves more autonomous—gatekeepers, allocators, and managers of the local public trust—and began to question whether the seal of approval bestowed by United Way affiliation was worth it in light of the declining financial rewards. Therefore, some United Way agencies have considered forming their own member-oriented, self-governing federations.

Current Competition and Challenges

By 2017, the charitable-giving industry had fragmented into tiny, single-focus agencies (some of them probably fraudulent) that could be both competitors and recipients of United Way programs. In addition, because United Way's traditional function had been to parcel out the contributions it received to local charities, donors had begun to question the need for an organization that essentially just processed money. (A donor might ask, "Why not just give

Governance
Chief Executive: Brian A. Gallagher, President and CEO
Total Compensation: $1,236,611
Chair of the Board: James Bullard
Board Size: 18   Paid Staff Size: 220

EXHIBIT 2
Charity Report for United Way America, 2015

Uses of Funds as Percentage of Total Expenses for Year Ended December 31, 2016

Fund-Raising: 2.01%   General and Administrative: 4.37%   Programs: 93.62%

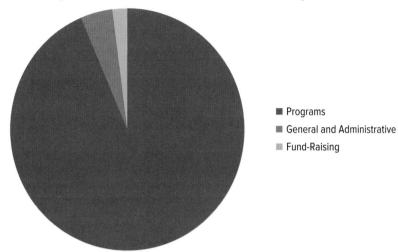

■ Programs
■ General and Administrative
▩ Fund-Raising

EXHIBIT 3 United Way of America Consolidated Financial Statements ($ thousands)

	Dec. 31, 2016	Dec. 31, 2015	Dec. 31, 2014	Dec. 31, 2013	Dec. 31, 2012	Dec. 31, 2011
Source of Funds						
Contributions	$67,729	$63,510	$53,599	$48,634	$49,932	$ 50,481
Membership support (net)	31,391	28,484	28,647	28,869	28,608	28,379
Campaign efforts (net)	—	—	(1,121)	(4,625)	7,507	44,757
Promotional material sales	489	608	725	694	2,995	3,364
Conferences	2,502	3,009	2,590	2,708	2,639	2,061
Program service fees	5,321	2,074	2,487	2,238	2,212	3,276
Investment return, net	681	190	610	1,099	745	161
Miscellaneous and other	1,413	1,124	983	1,044	895	870
Total Revenue	**109,526**	**98,999**	**88,521**	**80,661**	**95,532**	**$96,808**
Program Expenses						
Brand strategy and marketing	9,800	7,164	5,376	6,929	8,499	9,701
Impact, strategy and innovation	14,199	10,702	9,170	8,757	14,840	23,331
Campaign and public relations	164	316	1,249	5,739	4,888	4,183
Other expenses, e.g., investor relations, international expenses	86,128	63,794	57,268	60,312	59,708	46,553
Total Program Expenses	**110,291**	**81,976**	**73,063**	**81,737**	**87,935**	**$83,768**

continued

EXHIBIT 3 *Continued*

	Dec. 31, 2016	Dec. 31, 2015	Dec. 31, 2014	Dec. 31, 2013	Dec. 31, 2012	Dec. 31, 2011
Total Revenue	109,526	98,999	88,521	80,661	95,532	96,808
Program expenses	110,291	81,976	73,063	81,737	87,935	83,768
Fund-raising expenses	2,368	3,265	2,641	2,392	2,973	2,084
Administrative expenses	5,149	4,367	4,526	5,791	6,448	7,767
Total expenses	117,808	89,608	80,230	89,919	97,356	93,619
Income in excess of expenses	(8,282)	9,391	8,480	(9,258)	(1,824)	3,189
Beginning net assets	46,815	38,723	36,845	39,501	38,607	42,239
Changes in net assets	(6,131)	8,091	1,878	(2,656)	894	−3,631
Ending net assets	40,684	46,815	38,724	36,845	39,501	38,607
Total liabilities	35,986	37,599	37,455	29,859	42,076	64,861
Total liabilities and net assets	76,670	84,414	76,178	66,704	81,577	103,468

directly to the charity of my choice?") The perception was that the administrative function of United Way and other blanket charities just added an additional level of overhead to organizational costs, with a smaller portion of the original donation actually reaching the intended target.

Donors were increasingly supporting specific causes and therefore were more attracted to alternative recipient organizations, those possibly more responsive to the idea of community based on gender, race, or sexual orientation, among other socially driven issues.[14] A spokesperson for the American Cancer Society remarked, "Today a person might have an interest in prostate cancer, because his father died of it, or breast cancer, because it is a social issue as well as a health issue. We have to remember that an organization's mission is at least as important to supporters as its integrity." This meant that "donor-advised funds, which allow people to create grant-making accounts and recommend which charities get the money," were becoming increasingly popular.[15] This did not mean that traditional and venerable organizations like United Way, the Red Cross, the Salvation Army, and the American Cancer Society were necessarily in trouble; it just meant that they were perhaps in need of some strategic adjustment (see Exhibit 4).

The partnership between United Way and the disaster relief organizations, such as the Red Cross, the Salvation Army, Boys & Girls Clubs, and Catholic Charities, was still a strong and viable one, but increasingly all these national charities needed to understand the need for a diversified revenue stream. In a video interview with UWW's Brian Gallagher, *Forbes* asked about what had changed. Gallagher acknowledged that 55 percent of donations still came from employees in the workplace and corporate contributions from companies such as UPS, Microsoft, and IBM and that the relationship with the NFL was still a powerful one,

with 50 percent of volunteers being recruited through the NFL campaign. He mentioned that online participation was growing and that individual donations averaged $200 per year per individual. These donations included contributions coming increasingly from women and people of color, accounting for $75 million from all United Way chapters.[16]

Entering 2017, with the donor community becoming increasingly diverse and societal problems increasingly challenging, charitable nonprofits needed to engage in ongoing assessment of the relevance of their respective missions. This was not a new problem. In 1999 Michael Porter and Mark Kramer considered the strategic challenges facing nonprofits. Noting that the number of charitable foundations in the United States had doubled in the two decades after the 1970s, they believed that these philanthropic organizations were not devoting enough effort to measuring their results and to figuring out how to create the most value for society with the resources they had at their disposal. This value could be created by selecting the appropriate grantees, signaling other donors of appropriately chosen charities, improving the performance of grant recipients, and advancing the state of knowledge and practice. However, many philanthropic organizations lacked such a strategic focus: Their resources were scattered across too many fields, and their staffs were spread too thin, servicing too many small grants. One suggestion was that they engage in more performance assessment and unique positioning, with unique activities aimed specifically at creating value. This would require most nonprofits to also assess the effectiveness of their governance systems.[17]

Scandals and Governance

As if the plateau in donations by the charitable-giving community were not enough, the year 2002 was bad for corporate

EXHIBIT 4 Top 10 U.S. Charities, 2016

Rank	Name	Private Support ($ millions)	Total Revenue ($ millions)	Fund-Raising Efficiency (%)	Charitable Commitment (%)	Donor Dependency (%)
1	United Way	3,708	3,867	92	86	100
2	Task Force for Global Health	3,154	3,176	100	100	100
3	Feeding America	2,150	2,200	99	99	99
4	Salvation Army	1,904	2,927	88	82	86
5	YMCA of the USA	1,202	7,284	89	85	56
6	St. Jude Children's Research Hospital	1,181	1,382	83	71	83
7	Food for The Poor	1,156	1,158	97	96	100
8	Boys & Girls Club of America	923	1,805	89	81	81
9	Catholic Charities USA	921	3,887	92	88	77
10	Goodwill Industries International	902	5,600	97	88	82

Note: For Catholic Charities and AmeriCares, the contributions were mostly donated goods, food, and medicine, not money.

Source: https://www.forbes.com/top-charities/list/2016.

scandals: Enron, ImClone, WorldCom, and Tyco all hit the headlines with examples of corporate greed and misappropriation of both funds and public trust. Given such egregious wrongdoing in publicly held organizations, the tolerance of the general population for similar activities in nonprofits was increasingly approaching zero, especially given the nature of the relationship—one based on donor trust.

The first major scandal at United Way had occurred 10 years earlier, in 1992, when William Aramony, president and CEO of United Way of America, and two other UWA executives, were convicted of fraud, conspiracy, and money laundering in a scheme that siphoned around $1 million from the organization. This event was perceived as a turning point in public perceptions of charitable organizations and was blamed for the first drop in United Way donations since World War II.[18]

In 2001 the United Way of the National Capital Area—the Washington, D.C., chapter and the second-largest local United Way member in the country in donations—was in the news because of fraud. CEO Oral Suer had taken more than $500,000 from the charity to pay for personal expenses, annual leave, and an early pension payout he was not entitled to. Other employees had taken additional money for personal use, with the total fraud amounting to $1.6 million.

Then, in 2002, new United Way National Capital Area CEO Norman O. Taylor was asked to resign over misstated revenues and questionable overhead and credit card charges. In 2003 the CFO of the Michigan Capital Area United Way, Jacqueline Allen-MacGregor, was imprisoned for the theft of $1.9 million from the charity, which she had used to purchase racehorses for her personal farm. Also in 2003, Pipeline Inc., a spin-off from the California Bay Area United Way that was created to collect contributions, was investigated for losing $18 million when the financial records did not accurately reflect the amount owed by the charity.[19] In 2006 a former CEO of the United Way of New York City was investigated for diverting organizational assets valued at $227,000 for his own personal use.[20]

To be fair, United Way was not the only high-profile charity to experience these kinds of problems. After 9/11, Katrina, and Hurricane Sandy, the American Red Cross came under scrutiny for misdirection of disaster funds. In addition, the bookkeeper at Easter Seals of Iowa stole $230,000, the former president and seven others at Goodwill Industries of California embezzled $26 million, the financial administrator of the American Heart Association of New Jersey was convicted of theft of $186,000, and an executive at Goodwill Industries of Michigan was found guilty of stealing $750,000 from the agency over a 23-year period.[21]

The problem of official misconduct and lax oversight among the charitable organizations had reached alarming proportions. The picture it painted for the charitable giving community was not a cheerful one. What could be done to curtail this extremely disturbing trend?

The United Way of America's board during the Aramony scandal had consisted of many Fortune 500 CEOs who were, according to Aramony, fully informed about his compensation and perquisites.[22] Yet it appeared they still failed to exercise appropriate oversight, as did the boards at the D.C. and Michigan chapters. Finding committed and knowledgeable board members was critical to United Way's continued success. Given the federation model, each local chapter had its own board, recruited from community members who had not only fund-raising skills but also relationships with local leaders, politicians, and even regulators. Many local United Ways wanted to distance themselves from the scandals at UWA and high-profile chapters, and therefore they tried to stress local leadership and board autonomy. Serving on such a board required a commitment to the community and to the goals of the local United Way.

However, regardless of the degree of well-intentioned communication and disclosure, sometimes the goals of board members were in conflict. A 2004 survey by McKinsey & Company of executives and directors at 32 of *Worth* magazine's top 100 nonprofit performers found that many nonprofit boards had recurring problems, one of which was consensus over mission and goals: "Only 46 percent of the directors we surveyed thought that other directors on their boards could both summarize the mission of the organizations they serve and present a vision of where those organizations hope to be in five years' time." In addition, for an organization such as United Way, the goals of the diverse stakeholders, both donors and recipients, might differ widely. This lack of consensus, coupled with the difficulty of measuring and evaluating performance, meant that nonprofit boards in general needed to practice serious self-scrutiny: "The time when nonprofit boards were populated by wealthy do-gooders who just raised money, hired CEOs, and reaffirmed board policy is over."[23]

Given the degree to which the public trust had been violated by nonprofits that were found to be acting irresponsibly, the U.S. Senate Finance Committee was considering "tax-exempt reform containing provisions similar to those found in the Sarbanes-Oxley Act."[24] The 2008 scandal involving the Association of Community Organizations for Reform Now (ACORN), although focused on voter registration fraud, brought attention in Washington once again to the question of nonprofit legitimacy.[25]

This demand for greater accountability was not new. Nonprofits had sometimes been notoriously ineffective at accomplishing their social missions, inefficient at getting maximum return on the money they raised due to high administration costs, and willing to take on too much risk, either through inexperience or ignorance. Sometimes because of lax oversight procedures, individuals in control of the nonprofits were willing to engage in outright fraud, acquiring excessive benefits for themselves. These problems were enhanced by nonprofits' failure to provide extensive analysis, disclosure, and dissemination of relevant performance information and the lack of sanctions.[26] If nonprofit organizations would not police themselves, watchdog agencies would create external standards and provide public feedback, sometimes to the detriment of the organizations under scrutiny (see Exhibit 5).[27]

Gallagher's Response

In 2006 United Way of America CEO Brian Gallagher was invited by the U.S. Senate Finance Committee to participate in a roundtable discussion on needed reforms in nonprofit boards and governance. He was prepared to provide specific commentary. Since accepting the CEO position in 2001, Gallagher had been working to promote a change in the United Way strategy, including a change in mission, the creation of standards of performance excellence, and a

EXHIBIT 5 Watchdog Agencies—Information Resources for Nonprofits

- American Institute of Philanthropy
  www.charitywatch.org
- Better Business Bureau Wise Giving Alliance
  www.give.org
- Board Source
  www.boardsource.org
- Charity Navigator
  www.charitynavigator.org
- Governance Matters
  www.governancematters.com
- Guidestar
  www.guidestar.org
- Independent Sector
  www.independentsector.org
- Internet Nonprofit Center
  www.nonprofits.org
- IRS Exempt Organizations
  www.irs.gov/charities
- National Association of Attorneys General
  www.naag.org
- National Association of State Charity Officials
  www.nasconet.org
- National Council of Nonprofits
  www.councilofnonprofits.org
- Network for Good
  www1.networkforgood.org
- New York State Attorney General
  www.charitiesnys.com
- OMB Watch
  www.ombwatch.org
- Standards for Excellence Institute
  www.standardsforexcellenceinstitute.org

requirement that local members certify their adherence to the membership standards.

Regarding the mission of United Way, Gallagher had worked to change the focus from fund raising to community impact-from "How much money did we raise?" to "How much impact did we have on our community?" In his initial statement to the Senate committee, Gallagher said:

> The ultimate measure of success is whether family violence rates have gone down and whether there is more affordable housing. And fund-raising is [just] part of making that happen. When you are asking people to contribute, you're asking for an investment in your mission. And like a for-profit business, you are then accountable to your investors, not just for keeping good books, but for creating value and offering a concrete return. For those of us in human development, that means efforts that lead to measurable improvements in people's lives. In other words, the organizations that produce the greatest results should grow and be rewarded. Those that do not should be forced to change or go out of business. The American public doesn't give us money just because our operations are clean. Why they really give us money is because they want to make a difference.[28]

As a result of the new mission, UWW required local affiliates to provide the national headquarters with annual financial reports with greater transparency and to embrace the revised standards of excellence developed by more than 200 United Way employees, volunteers, and consultants. Of interest is the fact that these standards were not mandatory but were presented as guidelines, giving chapters' suggestions for how they might revise their local strategies. The standards urged the affiliates to identify community problems, raise money to solve them, and demonstrate measurable progress toward their goals by adopting a code of ethics that included an annual independent financial audit. The hope was that by adopting these guidelines, the chapters would be able to provide tangible proof to donors, especially wealthy contributors, that the United Way chapters and the charities they support were making a difference (see Exhibit 6).[29]

Local United Ways faced a continual challenge, with inevitable tension between the diverse constituencies they served: Were their primary "customers" the donors who contributed needed funds or the agencies that received these charitable donations? Or should the local United Way act as a networking institution, providing mechanisms for discussion of local problems and community-service needs? Or, going even further, should it act as an activist organization, leading the way with comprehensive community planning, advocating major public policy, and redistributing resources as needed? Kirsten Gronbjerg of the Center on Philanthropy, Indiana University, stated, "The activist role is very difficult for United Ways to play, because they need to satisfy diverse constituency groups and therefore avoid conflict. As they become more donor-driven institutions, they will be less able to take an activist approach just when such an approach is sorely needed."[30]

In addition, the local United Ways needed to maintain their internal consensus, providing a coherent and inspiring vision for their mainly volunteer workforce while managing potential conflicts and sharing resources with other United Way chapters in their geographic areas. The problem of potentially scarce resources and the fact that

EXHIBIT 6 United Way New Standards of Excellence

Standards of Excellence, a comprehensive description of benchmark standards and best practices: Developed in conjunction with United Way executives, staff, and volunteers throughout the country, the standards are designed to enhance the effectiveness of the 1,350 United Way affiliates.

- **Introduction to the Standards of Excellence.** Spanning more than 100 pages, the new standards provide highly detailed descriptions regarding five key areas of operation.

- **Community Engagement and Vision.** Working with formal and informal leaders to develop a shared vision and goals for a community, including the identification of priority issues affecting the overall well-being of its citizens.

- **Impact Strategies, Resources, and Results.** Creating "impact strategies" that address the root causes and barriers of a community's priority issues; mobilizing essential assets such as people, knowledge, relationships, technology, and money; effectively implementing impact strategies; and evaluating the effectiveness of impact strategies in fostering continuous improvement.

- **Relationship Building and Brand Management.** Developing, maintaining, and growing relationships with individuals and organizations in order to attract and sustain essential assets.

- **Organizational Leadership and Governance.** Garnering trust, legitimacy, and support of the United Way in local communities through leadership and overall management.

- **Operations.** Providing efficient and cost-effective systems, policies, and processes that enable the fulfillment of the United Way's mission, while ensuring the highest levels of transparency and accountability.

Source: United Way of America, http://liveunited.org/.

traditional donor organizations were either consolidating their physical operations or leaving an area meant that the traditional broad base of business and industry was shrinking. This and other factors prompted the consolidation of several United Ways into more regional organizations. This movement meant potential savings and operational efficiencies from sharing marketing, financial management, and information technology functions.[31] However, it also meant a possible diffusion of mission over a larger community, with a potential loss of focus, and more challenges in communicating this mission and marketing services to a more diverse donor and recipient base. In 2009, 21 nonprofit groups in the Washington, D.C., area suspended their memberships in United Way and joined a new organization, Community1st. These groups were lured away from United Way by a promise of "lower overhead costs, easily customized fund-raising campaigns, and fewer restrictions on where donors' money is directed."[30]

In essence, the ongoing issues faced by United Way in its more than 120-year history have remained constant. Consider this: During the holiday season, "when local United Way drives take place almost everywhere, likely as not questions will arise about what United Way is up to, how well it is doing what it claims to do, and for that matter, whether United Way is the best way for you to do your charitable giving." This statement was written in 1977, yet it could still apply in 2017. Concerns about United Way apparently are timeless, and Brian Gallagher is only one in a long line of CEOs determined to answer the critics once and for all.

ENDNOTES

1. William Barrett. The largest U.S. charities for 2016. https://www.forbes.com/sites/williampbarrett/2016/12/14/the-largest-u-s-charities-for-2016/#52878d8d4abb.

2. Sellers will lead U.S. operations of United Way Worldwide; Buck will take the helm of United Way of Central Iowa. http://www.businessrecord.com/Content/Culture/Culture/Article/Sellers-will-lead-U-S-operations-of-United-Way-Worldwide-Buck-will-take-the-helm-of-United-Way-of-Central-Iowa/170/832/77269.

3. United Worldwide. United Way Worldwide and BVK premiere new public service announcement: "Join the Fight." http://www.prnewswire.com/news-releases/united-way-worldwide-and-bvk-premiere-new-public-service-announcement-join-the-fight-300429180.html.

4. National Philanthropic Trust. Undated. Charitable giving statistics. www.nptrust.org/philanthropic-resources/charitable-giving-statistics/.

5. Rich, Tim. 2014. *Columbia Daily Tribune,* December 2.

6. Riley, C. 2011. America's wealthy turn less charitable. *CNN Money,* February 6, money.cnn.com/2011/02/06/news/economy/charity_gifts/index.htm; and Zongker, B. 2010. Top charities see decrease in donations. Associated Press, October 18, www.tulsaworld.com.

7. United Way. 2012 annual report.

8. Barrett, W. P. 2006. United Way's new way. *Forbes.com,* January 16, www.forbes.com.

9. Barton, N., & Hall, H. 2006. A year of big gains. *Chronicle of Philanthropy,* October 26, philanthropy.com/article/A-Year-of-Big-Gains/54908/.

10. Barrett, op. cit.

11. Princeton Survey Research Associates. 2001. Executive summary of the Donor Expectations Survey, conducted in the spring of 2001. As reported by Give.org BBB Wise Giving Alliance, www.give.org.

12. Suchman, M. 1995. Managing legitimacy: Strategic and institutional approaches. *Academy of Management Review,* 20: 571–610.

13. From the United Way website, liveunited.org.

14. Graddy-Gamel, A. 2007. Review of *Contesting Community: The Transformation of Workplace Charity,* by Emily Barman (2006: Stanford University Press). *Philanthropy News Digest,* February 27, foundationcenter.org/pnd/offtheshelf/ots_print.jhtml?id5171600045.

15. Barton & Hall, op. cit.

16. Charitable giving diversifies. 2006. *Forbes* (video report), December 13, www.forbes.com.

17. Porter, M. E., & Kramer, M. R. 1999. Philanthropy's new agenda: Creating value. *Harvard Business Review,* 77(6): 121–130.

18. United Way ex-head sentenced to 7 years in prison for fraud. 1995. *New York Times,* June 23: B2.

19. Gibelman, M., & Gelman, S. R. 2004. A loss of credibility: Patterns of wrongdoing among nongovernmental organizations. *International Journal of Voluntary and Nonprofit Organizations,* 15(4): 355–381. This article provides a content analysis of worldwide NGO scandals from 2001 to 2004. Although the United States is overrepresented, it is certainly not alone in the world for incidents of wrongdoing.

20. Investigation finds former United Way of NYC CEO improperly diverted funds. 2006. *Philanthropy News Digest,* April 17, foundationcenter.org/pnd/news/story_print.jhtml?id5140000004.

21. Gibelman & Gelman, op. cit.

22. Sinclair, M. 2002. William Aramony is back on the streets. *NonProfit Times,* March 1.

23. Jansen, P., & Kilpatrick, A. 2004. The dynamic nonprofit board. *McKinsey Quarterly,* 2: 72–81.

24. Kelley, C., & Anderson, S. 2006. Advising nonprofit organizations. *CPA Journal,* 76(8): 20–26.

25. McRay, G. 2009. Bad seeds—Why the ACORN scandal matters to other nonprofits. *Foundation Group,* September 16, www.501c3.org/blog/acorn-scandel-matters-to-nonprofits/.

26. Herzlinger, R. 1996. Can public trust in nonprofits and governments be restored? *Harvard Business Review,* March–April: 97–107.

27. Gibelman & Gelman, op. cit.

28. Gallagher, B. 2005. Statement of Brian A. Gallagher, president and CEO United Way of America, before United States Senate Committee on Finance. *liveunited.org,* April 5:1.

29. Blum, D. E. 2005. Held to a new standard. *Chronicle of Philanthropy,* 17(13).

30. The Aspen Institute. 2002. United Way system at the crossroads: Valuable lessons from the United Way of Chicago. *Snapshots: Research Highlights from the Nonprofit Sector Research Fund,* November/December, no. 26.

31. Gosier, C. 2007. 3 chapters of United Way to combine. *Knight Ridder Tribune Business News,* February 23.

32. Greenwell, M. 2009. 21 regional nonprofits withdraw from United Way. *Washington Post,* April 29, www.washingtonpost.com/wp-dyn/content/article/2009/04/28/ar2009042803701.html.

33. United Way: Are the criticisms fair? 1977. *Changing Times,* October: 29.

CASE 30

eBAY*

In 2017, eBay CEO Devin Wenig said, "Online commerce is a dynamic and exciting space, and we believe that eBay is poised to benefit from massive changes that are occurring across the retail landscape. We also believe that technology is the most important factor that will separate winners from losers in this rapidly changing environment. This is a world in which eBay can thrive."[1]

Wenig's optimism had its limitations, as eBay was facing various new and existing challenges, especially in terms of vigorous competition. eBay competes primarily on the basis of differentiating services and product selection it offers. Consumers can buy from or sell using a vast variety of online retailers around the globe.

The past few years were difficult for eBay's Marketplaces. A security-related password reset and web search engine optimization (SEO) changes heavily impacted customer traffic. The company publicly admitted that "criminals were able to penetrate and steal certain data, including user names, encrypted user passwords and other non-financial user data. We require all buyers and sellers on our platform to reset their passwords in order to log into their account."[2] eBay's loyal customers returned following the password changes, but the more occasional customers did not return as quickly as expected. Further, the SEO changes significantly diminished eBay's presence in natural search results, which impacted new-user growth.

A stronger dollar impacted eBay's cross-border trade, depressing U.S. exports and affecting the financial results for North America. With traffic and sales slowing over the years, eBay had tried to reposition its well-known auction site from being an online yard sale to being a trendy e-retailer. But the company faced intense competition from online giants like Amazon and Google and relative newcomers like Etsy, as well as traditional brick-and-mortar retailers like Walmart, Staples, and Home Depot, which were now aggressively promoting their online retail sites.

eBay's fierce competition was not limited only to the U.S. market. In April 2017, the company announced that it was selling its India business to Flipkart in exchange for a $500 million equity stake in the Indian e-commerce start-up. India was projected to be one of the most lucrative markets in coming years, with an e-commerce market of about $16 billion

in 2016 that was expected to grow to $48 billion by 2021.[3] Nonetheless, Wenig showed optimism, saying, "The combination of eBay's position as a leading global e-commerce company and Flipkart's market stature will allow us to accelerate and maximize the opportunity for both companies in India."[4] As eBay sold its India business, however, the company's competitors such as Amazon and Alibaba Group heavily invested in India. Along with eBay's debacle in China in the past, a major question seemed to loom, whether the company really had the potential to maintain a sustainable competitive position in the e-commerce market.

Nonetheless, eBay was taking many initiatives to innovate and improve its offered services to combat the increasing competition. In March 2017, eBay announced an exclusive partnership between its StubHub ticketing service and Visa, which would enable the StubHub customers to make additional modifications to their purchases if they paid using a Visa checkout.[5] Additionally, the company announced a new advertising strategy that would focus on first party data and help boost trade activity through the company's website.[6] eBay claimed that its new advertising strategy would increase the brand awareness of the products for many renowned companies as well as enhance the consumer's online shopping experience. Moreover, in order to compete with popular two-day delivery services offered by many online retailers including Amazon and Walmart, eBay introduced a guaranteed rapid delivery service in summer 2017.[7] Guaranteed delivery service will enable the customers to buy more than 20 million eligible items with guaranteed delivery within 2 days. If a guaranteed-item arrives later than 2 days, the company will refund the shipping cost to the customer in the form of store credit that can be used for future purchases. Brett Thome, Vice President of Business Development at Spreetail (eBay store: VMInnovations), said, "We're very excited about eBay's Guaranteed Delivery. There are so many great sellers on eBay delivering an incredible shipping experience where they deliver in 2 days, and even next day, so the ability to highlight Guaranteed Delivery will further increase customer confidence and satisfaction."[8]

The past few years had brought considerable pressure from Carl Icahn, an activist investor. Icahn had challenged the board by increasing his stake in the company and pressuring it to spin off its noncore businesses. The company finally agreed to spin off its PayPal and Enterprise businesses. At the same time, it applied time and resources to repurchasing shares to counter Icahn's influence. An agreement was reached to allow one of Icahn's representatives to join the board of directors. As eBay prepared itself for

---

* This case was prepared by Professor Alan B. Eisner and graduate students Dev Das, David J. Morates, Shruti Shrestha, and Saad Nazir of Pace University. This case was solely based on library research and was developed for class discussion rather than to illustrate either effective or ineffective handling of an administrative situation. Copyright ©2017 Alan B. Eisner.

the split with PayPal, it announced that it was laying off 7 percent of its workforce, with many of the cuts coming from its legacy Marketplaces business. The upcoming split would provide PayPal with $5 billion in cash and no debt, but would leave eBay with $7.6 billion in debt and only $2 billion in net cash.

Clearly, by taking new initiatives and announcing new partnerships in just the first quarter of 2017, eBay anticipated a tough year ahead. Only time would tell which moves would prove right for the company and increase shareholder value over the long term. Or would eBay be better off offering itself for sale to a potential bidder?

A Successful Past

Since its inception in 1995, eBay had enjoyed strong revenue growth and been a dominant player in the online auction industry. Within two decades, the company had grown considerably, and it had a net revenue of about $9 billion and an operating income of $2.3 billion in 2016 (see Exhibits 1 and 2).

eBay's founder, Pierre Omidyar, had envisioned a community built on commerce, sustained by trust, and inspired by opportunity. The company's mission was to "enable individual self-empowerment on a global scale" and employ "business as a tool for social good." Omidyar cited "trust between strangers" as the social impact tied to eBay's ability to remain profitable.

The company's unique business model united buyers and sellers in an online marketplace. eBay enabled e-commerce at multiple levels (local, national, and international) through an array of websites, including eBay Marketplaces, PayPal, Rent.com, Shopping.com, and eBay Style. The company's range of products and services evolved from collectibles to household products, customer services, automobiles, and the mobile industry. The variety of products attracted a range of users that included students, small businesses, independent sellers, major corporations, and government agencies.

Despite eBay's outstanding growth performance, the company faced a number of challenges in both domestic and international markets. The low entry barriers in the online marketplace attracted a number of large dot-com competitors, including Amazon, Yahoo/Taobao, Google/Overstock, and Etsy. Historically, eBay had acquired other online competitors, such as StubHub (tickets), but established players such as Yahoo, Google, and Amazon posed a major threat to eBay's market share and ability to sustain profitability. Still, eBay's top management felt that the company would end up as a specialty business, an idea suggesting that it would face little threat from these major competitors. The company had no plans for further big acquisitions but intended to expand and identify synergies within existing business lines.

eBay acknowledged its inability to grow and compete in certain international markets. The company had created localized sites in 30 countries and established a presence in Latin America through its investment in Mercado Libre, a Latin American e-commerce company.[9] However, eBay sold a majority stake of the Latin American platform in 2016. eBay's numerous attempts to penetrate the Asia-Pacific market, specifically China and Japan, ended in failure, with the company pulling out of Japan and buying out Chinese start-up Eachnet, essentially canceling years of invested work. According to many analysts, the company's recent interest in its South Korean rival Gmarket Inc. and its joint venture with Beijing-based Tom Online were further indications that eBay couldn't compete in Asia-Pacific countries. eBay enjoyed financial benefits as a result of a tax provision in 2016 that considerably improved the company's cash flow (see Exhibit 3). However, in order to remain successful and enjoy the same financial performance as it had in the past, eBay needed to develop an effective strategy to compete in major Asian markets and to mitigate the risk of existing local competitors.

eBay's overall strategy had traditionally comprised three primary components: products, sense of community, and aggressive expansion. All three components evolved around the various geographic and specialty platforms the company introduced.

Product Categories

eBay had an array of product categories and trading platforms that offered a range of pricing formats, such as fixed pricing. Relatively new for the company, the fixed-price format allowed eBay to compete directly with major competitors such as Amazon and penetrate new market space. Before fixed pricing, selling prices were solely determined by the highest auction bid, and this took days or weeks, depending on the length of the auction. eBay's different trading platforms also offered distinct services and target-specific market niches, which allowed eBay to broaden its customer base. The platforms included:

- *PayPal:* Founded in 1998 and acquired by eBay in 2002, PayPal enabled individuals to securely send payments quickly and easily online. PayPal was considered the global leader in online payments, with tens of millions of registered users. In 2011 PayPal's president, Scott Thompson, expected revenue to double, reaching $6 billion to $7 billion, by 2013. He also predicted that 75 to 80 percent of eBay transactions would be done through PayPal by 2013, up from 69 percent in 2010.[10] However, in 2014, the company decided it was more prudent to spin off its PayPal business as a separate company. The spin-off was being contemplated for the end of 2015.[11]

- *Online classifieds:* By 2009, eBay had the world's leading portfolio of online classified sites, including Kijiji, Intoko, Gumtree, LoQUo.com, Marktplaats.nl, and mobile.de. CEO John Donahoe said, "We are the global leader in classifieds, with top positions in Canada, Australia, Germany, Japan and the United Kingdom, and sites in more than 1,000 cities across 20 countries."[12]

- *Shopping.com:* With thousands of merchants and millions of products and reviews, Shopping.com

EXHIBIT 1 Income Statement ($ millions)

eBay Inc. CONSOLIDATED STATEMENT OF INCOME			
	Year Ended December 31,		
	2016	**2015**	**2014**
	(In millions, except per share amounts)		
Net revenues	$8,979	$8,592	$8,790
Cost of net revenues	2,007	1,771	1,663
Gross profit	6,972	6,821	7,127
Operating expenses:			
Sales and marketing	2,368	2,267	2,442
Product development	1,114	923	983
General and administrative	900	1,122	889
Provision for transaction losses	231	271	262
Amortization of acquired intangible assets	34	41	75
Total operating expenses	4,647	4,624	4,651
Income from operations	2,325	2,197	2,476
Interest and other, net	1,326	209	39
Income from continuing operations before income taxes	3,651	2,406	2,515
Income tax benefit (provision)	3,634	(459)	(3,380)
Income (loss) from continuing operations	$7,285	$1,947	$ (865)
Income (loss) from discontinued operations, net of income taxes	(19)	(222)	911
Net income	$7,266	$1,725	$ 46
Income (loss) per share–basic:			
Continuing operations	$ 6.43	$ 1.61	$ (0.69)
Discontinued operations	(0.02)	(0.18)	0.73
Net income per share–basic	$ 6.41	$ 1.43	$ 0.04
Income (loss) per share–diluted:			
Continuing operations	$ 6.37	$ 1.60	$ (0.69)
Discontinued operations	(0.02)	(0.18)	0.73
Net income per share–diluted	$ 6.35	$ 1.42	$ 0.04
Weighted average shares:			
Basic	1,133	1,208	1,251
Diluted	1,144	1,220	1,251

Source: eBay SEC filings.

EXHIBIT 2 Balance Sheet ($ millions)

	December 31,	
eBay Inc. CONSOLIDATED BALANCE SHEETS	2016	2015
	(In millions, except per value)	
Assets		
Current assets:		
Cash and cash equivalents	$ 1,816	$ 1,832
Short-term investments	5,333	4,299
Accounts receivable, net	592	619
Other current assets	1,134	1,154
Total current assets	8,875	7,904
Long-term investments	3,969	3,391
Property and equipment, net	1,516	1,554
Goodwill	4,501	4,451
Intangible assets, net	102	90
Deferred tax asset, non-current	4,608	–
Other assets	276	365
Total assets	$23,847	$17,755
Liabilities and Stockholders' Equity		
Current liabilities:		
Short-term debt	$ 1,451	$ –
Accounts payable	283	349
Accrued expenses and other current liabilities	1,893	1,736
Deferred revenue	110	106
Income taxes payable	110	72
Total current liabilities	3,847	2,263
Deferred and other tax liabilities, net	1,888	2,092
Long-term debt	7,509	6,749
Other liabilities	64	75
Total liabilities	13,308	11,179
Commitments and contingencies		
Stockholders' equity:		
Common stock, $0.001 par value; 3,580 shares authorized; 1,087 and 1,184 shares outstanding	2	2
Additional paid-in capital	14,907	14,538
Treasury stock at cost, 557 and 443 shares	(19,205)	(16,203)
Retained earnings	14,959	7,713
Accumulated other comprehensive income	(124)	526
Total stockholders' equity	10,539	6,576
Total liabilities and stockholders' equity	$23,847	$17,755

Source: eBay SEC filings.

EXHIBIT 3 Cash Flow Statement ($ millions)

	2016	2015	2014
eBay Inc. CONSOLIDATED STATEMENT OF CASH FLOWS			
	Year Ended December 31,		
	(In millions)		
Cash flows from operating activities:			
Net income	$7,266	$1,725	$ 46
(Income) loss from discontinued operations, net of income taxes	19	222	(911)
Adjustments:			
Provision for transaction losses	231	271	262
Depreciation and amortization	682	687	682
Stock-based compensation	416	379	344
Gain on sale of investments and other, net	(1,236)	(195)	(12)
Deferred income taxes	(4,556)	(32)	2,744
Excess tax benefits from stock-based compensation	(15)	(74)	(75)
Changes in assets and liabilities, net of acquisition effects			
Accounts receivable	(48)	(105)	51
Other current assets	23	(143)	(36)
Other non-current assets	94	143	(3)
Accounts payable	(28)	226	81
Accrued expenses and other liabilities	(130)	(202)	(81)
Deferred revenue	4	9	4
Income taxes payable and other tax liabilities	105	(34)	132
Net cash provided by continuing operating activities	2,827	2,877	3,228
Net cash provided by (used in) discontinued operating activities	(1)	1,156	2,449
Net cash provided by operating activities	2,826	4,033	5,677
Cash flows from investing activities:			
Purchases of property and equipment	(626)	(668)	(622)
Purchases of investments	(11,212)	(6,744)	(8,752)
Maturities and sales of investments	10,063	6,781	8,115
Acquisitions, net of cash acquired	(212)	(24)	(55)
Other	(21)	(18)	(11)
Net cash used in continuing investing activities	(2,008)	(673)	(1,325)
Net cash used in discontinued investing activities	—	(2,938)	(1,348)
Net cash used in investing activities	(2,008)	(3,611)	(2,673)

continued

EXHIBIT 3 *Continued*

		eBay Inc.		
		CONSOLIDATED STATEMENT OF CASH FLOWS		
			Year Ended December 31,	
		2016	**2015**	**2014**
			(In millions)	
Cash flows from financing activities:				
Proceeds from issuance of common stock		102	221	300
Repurchases of common stock		(2,943)	(2,149)	(4,658)
Excess tax benefits from stock-based compensation		15	74	75
Tax withholdings related to net share settlements of restricted stock awards and units		(121)	(245)	(252)
Proceeds from issuance of long-term debt, net		2,216	—	3,482
Repayment of debt		(20)	(850)	—
Other		7	(11)	6
Net cash used in continuing financing activities		(744)	(2,960)	(1,047)
Net cash provided by (used in) discontinued financing activities		—	(1,594)	25
Net cash used in financing activities		(744)	(4,554)	(1,022)
Effect of exchange rate changes on cash and cash equivalents		(90)	(364)	(148)
Net increase (decrease) in cash and cash equivalents		(16)	(4,496)	1,834
Cash and cash equivalents at beginning of period		1,832	6,328	4,494
Cash and cash equivalents at end of period		$1,816	$1,832	$6,328
Less: Cash and cash equivalents of discontinued operations–Enterprise		—	—	29
Less: Cash and cash equivalents of discontinued operations–PayPal		—	—	2,194
Cash and cash equivalents of continuing operations at end of period		$1,816	$1,832	$4,105
Supplemental cash flow disclosures:				
Cash paid for interest		$ 220	$ 175	$ 99
Cash paid for income taxes		$ 492	$ 256	$ 343

Source: eBay SEC filings.

empowered consumers to make informed choices, which drove value for merchants. In 2013, it was rebranded as the eBay Commerce Network.

- *Stubhub.com:* StubHub was an online marketplace for selling and purchasing tickets for sports events, concerts, and other live entertainment events.
- *eBay Express:* eBay Express behaved like a standard Internet shopping site but gave sellers access to over 200 million buyers worldwide. Sellers could design product categories within minutes, and buyers could purchase from multiple sellers by using a single shopping cart.
- *eBay Motors:* This specialty site was considered the largest marketplace for automobile buyers and sellers. Buyers could purchase anything from automobile parts to new or antique vehicles.

- *Skype:* Acquired by eBay in October 2005, Skype was the world's fastest-growing online communication solution, allowing free video and audio communication between users of Skype software. By November 2009, Skype connected more than 480 million registered users.[13] eBay's acquisition of Skype was expected to enhance the customer experience by improving communication between buyers and sellers. In November 2009, however, eBay sold Skype to a group led by Silver Lake Partners, a private equity firm in Silicon Valley, which eventually sold the entity to Microsoft.

Sense of Community

The underlying key to all eBay sites and trading platforms was creating trust between sellers and buyers. The company created "community values," and this was why eBay users were willing to send money to strangers across the country. The Feedback Forum was created in February 1996 and encouraged users to post comments about trading partners. Originally, Omidyar had handled disputes between buyers and sellers via email by putting the disputing parties in touch with each other to resolve the issue themselves. He soon realized that an open forum in which users could post opinions and feedback about one another would create the trust and sense of community the site required. Buyers and sellers were encouraged to post comments (positive, negative, or neutral) about each other at the completion of each transaction. The individual feedback was recorded and amended to a user profile, which ultimately established a rating and reputation for each buyer and seller. eBay users could view this information before engaging in a transaction. The company believed that the Feedback Forum was critical for creating initial user acceptance for purchasing and selling over the Internet and that it contributed more than anything else to eBay's success.

Aggressive Expansion

To compete effectively and create a global trading platform, eBay continued to develop in U.S. and international markets that utilized the Internet. With intense competition in the online auction industry, eBay aimed to increase its market share and revenue through acquisitions and partnerships in related and unrelated businesses. For example:

- In June 2000 eBay acquired Half.com for $318 million.
- In August 2001 eBay acquired MercadoLibre, Lokau, and iBazar, Latin American auction sites.
- On August 13, 2004, eBay took a 25 percent stake in Craigslist, an online network of urban communities.
- In September 2005 eBay invested $2 million in the Meetup social networking site.
- In August 2006 eBay announced international cooperation with Google.
- In January 2007 eBay acquired online ticket marketplace StubHub for $310 million.
- In June 2010 eBay acquired RedLaser, a mobile application that let customers scan bar codes to list items faster on its online auction site and to compare prices.[14]
- In December 2010 eBay acquired Milo, a leading local shopping engine that provided consumers access to accurate, real-time, local-store inventory and pricing, giving them even more choices and flexibility when shopping online.[15]
- In December 2010 eBay acquired Critical Path Software Inc., a developer of smartphone applications, to accelerate its lead in mobile commerce.[16]
- In 2014 eBay announced its agreement to acquire Shutl, a U.K.-based marketplace that used a network of couriers to deliver local goods the same day.
- In July 2016 eBay completed the acquisition of SalesPredict, an artificial intelligence system that would help the company to effectively predict customer buying behavior, preferences, and machine learning.[17]
- In August 2016 eBay acquired Ticket Utils that became part of StubHub platform. Ticket Utils was a New Jersey–based software company that helped large ticket sellers organize and manage their tickets and distribution.[18]
- In February 2017 eBay announced its partnership agreement with Snupps, a social organizing app used to buy and sell online.[19]
- In March 2017 eBay announced an exclusive partnership with Flipkart, a popular e-commerce platform in India. eBay acquired a $500 million equity stake in exchange for eBay's India business.[20]

Evolution of the Auction Market

Traditional Auctions

According to Greek scribes, the first known auctions occurred in Babylon in 500 BC. At that time, women were sold on the condition of marriage, and it was considered illegal for daughters to be sold outside auctions. Auctions evolved during the French Revolution and throughout the American Civil War, where colonels auctioned goods that had been seized by armies.[21] Although there were various types of auctions, they all provided a forum at which sellers could find buyers. Auctions were considered one of the purest markets because buyers paid what they were willing to spend for an item, thereby determining the true market value of the item. Over time, auction formats evolved, and through technological advances and improved communication, they found a new home—the Internet.

Online Auctions

The primary difference between traditional and online auctions is that the online auction process occurs over the Internet rather than at a specific location where both buyers and sellers are present. Online auctions offer strategic advantages to both parties not typically available in traditional auctions. Buyers select from millions of products and engage in multiple auctions simultaneously. Given the massive inventory of an online auction market, items are usually available in multiple auctions, allowing buyers to compare starting-bid prices and search for better prices. Sellers are exposed to millions of buyers, since more buyers have access to the Internet and feel comfortable making purchases online. Thus, the Internet gives buyers and sellers access to a marketplace that spans the world.

Online auctions also offer the following strategic advantages:

1. *No time constraints:* A bid can be placed at any time.
2. *No geographic constraints:* Sellers and buyers can participate from any location with Internet access.
3. *Network economies:* The large number of bidders attracts more sellers, which attracts more bidders, and so on.

This creates a large system that has more value for both parties. Online auctions also allow businesses to easily sell off excess inventory or discontinued items. This is done through either business-to-business (B2B) or business-to-consumer (B2C) auctions. Offering products and services in an online auction helps small businesses build their brand and reputation by establishing a devoted customer base. Finally, some businesses use the online marketplace as an inexpensive yet effective way to test-market upcoming products.

World of E-Commerce

Although Vannevar Bush originally conceived the idea of the Internet in 1945, it wasn't until the 1990s that the Internet became overwhelmingly popular. According to Internet World Stats, as of March 2017 there were about 3.7 billion Internet users in over 150 countries. Exhibit 4 shows world Internet usage and population as of March 31, 2017, and Internet usage growth between 2000 and 2017.

As of 2017, North America was the region most penetrated by the Internet, with approximately 88 percent of the population online. However, Internet usage growth between 2000 and 2017 was considerably less in North America than in other regions. Internet usage growth was highest in developing regions, such as Africa, the Middle East, Latin America, and Asia, where penetration was low. Considering that close to 80 percent of the world's population resides in these areas, it was inevitable that Internet usage growth would continue to increase dramatically in these regions.

Although Asia constituted approximately 55 percent of the world's population, its penetration rate was only 45.2 percent.

Compared to other regions with high usage growth rates, such as Africa and the Middle East, Asia invested more in its technology infrastructure and contained by far the most current Internet users, making it a more attractive market.

As the usage growth of the Internet increased, so did the popularity of e-commerce. E-commerce, or electronic commerce, was the concept of conducting business transactions over the Internet. Like online auctions, e-commerce eliminated boundaries such as time and geography, allowing businesses and customers to interact with one another constantly. As more users were exposed to the Internet, they became comfortable with the idea of conducting transactions online. In correlation with Internet growth usage, revenue generated through e-commerce increased dramatically after the 1990s.

In Asia, e-commerce had grown rapidly since China's admission into the World Trade Organization (WTO) on December 11, 2001. Induction into the WTO allowed China to conduct business with other nations more freely by reducing tariffs and eliminating market and government impediments.

Track Record of Proven Leadership

Computer programmer Pierre Omidyar founded the online auction website in San Jose, California, on September 3, 1995. Omidyar was born in Paris, France, and moved to Maryland with his family when his father took up a residency at Johns Hopkins University Medical Center. Omidyar became fascinated with computers and later graduated from Tufts University with a degree in computer science. While living and working in the San Francisco Bay area, he met his current wife, Pamela Wesley, a management consultant, who later became a driving force in launching the auction website. The couple's vision was to establish an online

EXHIBIT 4 World Internet Usage and Population Statistics, 2017

World Regions	Population (2017 Est.)	Population % of World	Internet Users June 30, 2017	Penetration Rate (% Pop.)	Growth 2000–2017	Users % Table
Africa	1,246,504,865	16.6	345,676,501	27.7	7,557.2	9.3
Asia	4,148,177,672	55.2	1,873,856,654	45.2	1,539.4	50.2
Europe	822,710,362	10.9	636,671,824	77.4	506.1	17.1
Latin America / Caribbean	647,604,645	8.6	385,919,382	59.6	2,035.8	10.3
Middle East	250,327,574	3.3	141,931,765	56.7	4,220.9	3.8
North America	363,224,006	4.8	320,068,243	88.1	196.1	8.6
Oceania / Australia	40,479,846	0.5	27,549,054	68.1	261.5	0.7
WORLD TOTAL	7,519,028,970	100.0	3,731,973,423	49.6	933.8	100.0

NOTES: (1) Internet Usage and World Population Statistics updated as of June 30, 2017. (2) Demographic (Population) numbers are based on data from the United Nations Population Division. (3) Internet usage information comes from data published by Nielsen Online, by ITU, the International Telecommunications Union, by GfK, by local ICT Regulators and other reliable sources.

Source: Internet World Stats 2017. Usage and Population Statistics, http://www.internetworldstats.com/stats.htm.

marketplace at which people could share the same passion and interest as Pamela had for her hobby of collecting and trading Pez candy dispensers.[22] Omidyar also envisioned an online auction format that would create a fair and open marketplace, where the market truly determined an item's value. To ensure trust in the open forum, Omidyar based the site on five main values:

1. People are basically good.
2. Everyone has something to contribute.
3. An honest, open environment can bring out the best in people.
4. Everyone deserves recognition and respect as a unique individual.
5. You should treat others the way you want to be treated.

On Labor Day weekend in 1995, Omidyar launched Auction Web, an online trading platform. After the business exploded, Omidyar decided to dedicate more attention to his new enterprise and work as a consultant under the name Echo Bay Technology Group. When he tried to register a website for his company, Omidyar discovered the name Echo Bay was unavailable, so he decided to use the abbreviated version eBay, which also stood for "electronic bay area." The company's name was also selected to attract San Francisco residents to the site and prompt them to buy and sell items.

Initially, the company did not charge fees to either buyers or sellers, but as traffic grew rapidly, Omidyar was forced to charge buyers a listing fee to cover Internet service provider costs. When Omidyar noticed that the fees had no effect on the level of bids, he realized the potential for profitability of his business. To handle and manage the company's day-to-day operations, Omidyar hired Jeffrey Skoll (BASc from University of Toronto and MBA from Stanford University). Skoll was hired as the company's first president, and he wrote the business plan that eBay later followed from its emergence as a start-up to its maturity as a financial success. The two worked out of Skoll's living room and various Silicon Valley facilities until they eventually settled in the company's current location in San Jose, California.

By the middle of 1997, after less than a year under the name eBay, the company was hosting nearly 800,000 auctions a day.[23] Although the rapid expansion of eBay's traffic caused the company to suffer a number of service interruptions, the site remained successful and continued to gain the confidence of its strong customer base. Skoll remained president until early 1998, when the company hired Meg Whitman as president and CEO. At the time, the company had only 30 employees and was solely located in the United States; in a decade the number of employees went up to over 15,000. In September 1998 eBay launched a successful public offering, making both Omidyar and Skoll instant billionaires. By the time eBay went public, less than three years after Omidyar had created the company, the site had more than 1 million registered users. The company grew exponentially in the late 1990s and, based on its 2013 performance, indicated no sign of stopping. Exhibit 5 highlights the company's recent growth performance in terms of active user accounts, in millions.

Whitman stepped down as the president and CEO of the company on March 31, 2008, but remained on the board of

EXHIBIT 5 Number of eBay Active Users from 2010 to 2017 (in millions)

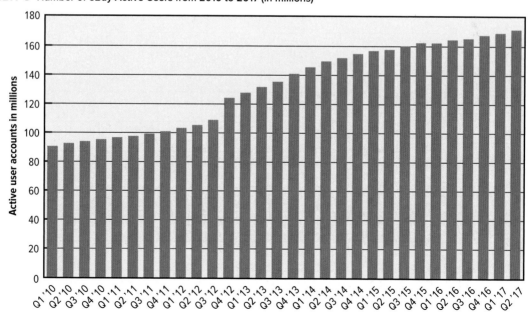

Source: Statistica 2017, https://www.statista.com/statistics/242235/number-of-ebays-total-active-users/.

directors. Omidyar, the chairman of the board, said this about Whitman: "With humor, smarts and unflappable determination, Meg took a small, barely known online auction site and helped it become an integral part of our lives."[24] Both Omidyar and Whitman were confident that the new CEO, John Donahoe, was a good choice to lead eBay. Donahoe had joined the company in 2005 as president of eBay's largest division, Marketplaces, and within three years managed to double the revenues and profits for this business unit. Before joining eBay, Donahoe served as the CEO of Bain & Company, an international consulting firm based in Boston.[25] "I'm extremely confident in John's skills and the abilities of John's veteran management team," Meg Whitman commented on the transition.[26]

Whitman's confidence appears to have been well founded. New CEO Donahoe helped eBay make impressive progress. Although eBay's financial outlook was not dreadful when Donahoe took over in March 2008, there was a growing perception that its growth was beginning to decline and that its run as the leader of the e-commerce industry was behind it, as Amazon began to make strides toward becoming the next best thing. "What John Donahoe has accomplished over the past few years is one of the most remarkable feats in the valley's history," said Gil Luria, an analyst at Wedbush Securities. So what had the new CEO done to spur this turnaround? Luria noted that eBay began investing more in technology and was willing to take risks regarding altering the look and feel of the platform's shopping experience.[27] However, Donahoe stepped down from his role as CEO after the announcement of eBay's PayPal spinoff in 2015. Devin Wenig, the president of the eBay

marketplace since 2011, took charge of the company as its new CEO in July of 2015. eBay's stock price took a hit after the departure of Donahoe, perhaps because of investors' lack of confidence regarding changing leadership of eBay; however, the stock price rebounded after the third quarter of 2015. eBay's stock price surged in the following years, and it was trading at about $32 per share by April 2017 (see Exhibit 6).

Board of Directors versus Activist Investor

During the previous few years, activist investor Carl Icahn had put together a 0.8 percent ownership stake in eBay and started pushing for strategy changes. The company refused to take his advice, so Icahn bought more shares and tried again. eBay had already decided to spin off its PayPal online payments service, but Icahn owned 2.5 percent of the company and insisted that management think about selling that operation to a cash-rich tech giant instead. eBay management still preferred the PayPal spin-off idea, much to Icahn's chagrin. Eventually, Ichan's eBay ownership expanded to 3.7 percent, and the company was pretty much doing what he wanted, or close to it.

eBay announced that it had reached a standstill agreement with Carl Icahn. The activist investor would not buy any more eBay stock in return for some concessions from eBay's active leadership. The concessions included adding an Icahn-selected individual to eBay's board of directors and accepting "certain corporate governance provisions" to PayPal's starting papers.

EXHIBIT 6 eBay Stock Performance

EBAY	
Open	25.61
High	26.74
Low	24.76
Close	26.43
Volume	57.18M
% Change	18.87%

Source: Yahoo Finance.

Icahn picked Icahn Capital hedge fund manager Jonathan Christodoro, who was a merger analyst and already served on four boards under Icahn's influence. eBay also gave Icahn the option of placing his candidate on either eBay's or PayPal's board when the two companies split later in the year. Given Christodoro's field of expertise, industry circles expected him to move on with PayPal and continue looking for buyout-style exit strategies.

Icahn, of course, was expected to use his large stock ownership and board representation to explore his favorite options for using surplus cash. He was known to like selling operations that no longer made sense, but he was not a big supporter of making acquisitions himself. Instead, he preferred enormous share buyback and dividend programs.

eBay had become a high-stakes games of chess. Icahn and his team wanted to monetize PayPal to the hilt before the service peaked, while eBay would rather hold on a little tighter and see where this train was headed. Industry analysts concluded that the arguments on both sides had merit but that the uncertainty of squabbling over the long-term strategy would hurt the company overall. Finally, eBay and PayPal split in July 2015 and PayPal's market value scaled around $49 billion as an independent publicly traded company, which had secured to achieve a bigger market cap than eBay.[28]

Company Business Model

eBay's business model is based on a person-to-person marketplace on the Internet, where sellers conveniently list items for sale and interested buyers bid on those items. The objective is to create a forum that allows buyers and sellers to come together in an efficient and effective manner. The business model overcame the inefficiencies of traditional fragmented marketplaces, which tended to offer a limited variety of goods. According to former CEO Meg Whitman, the company started with commerce and what grew out of that was a community, essentially creating a community-commerce model.[29] The company's success relied primarily on establishing a trustworthy environment that attracted a large number of buyers and sellers. As eBay's reputation grew, so did the number of buyers and sellers, keeping the company in line with Omidyar's original vision. However, as new competitors entered the online auction business and the popularity of the Internet increased, eBay tweaked its business model to accommodate changes in the fast-paced environment.

The company was aggressively expanding globally and looking for new products and services to offer to customers. It was also looking closely at the kind of merchants who sold on eBay. In the beginning, eBay focused on a consumer-to-consumer business model, but since some of the individuals became small dealers, the model changed to a mix of consumer-to-consumer and business-to-consumer. The sellers wanted to maintain their business on eBay, since it was their most profitable distribution channel. eBay wanted new ways to generate revenue as a result of more small dealers and businesses selling their products through the company's website.

In addition to the primary revenue sources, there were specific elements of eBay's business model that made the company a success (see Exhibit 7). eBay's dominance of the online auction market and the large number of buyers, sellers, and listed items were primary reasons for eBay's tremendous growth. The trust and safety programs, such as the Feedback Forum, continued to attract and retain new and current eBay users. The cost-effective and convenient trading, coupled with the strong sense of community, added further value to the company's business model. However, as the company continued to grow and new trends evolved, eBay had to continue to adjust its model to remain competitive.

International Expansion

As competition intensified in the online auction industry, eBay expanded its international presence in an effort to create an online global marketplace. Gradually, eBay localized sites in the following countries:[30]

- *Asia Pacific:* Australia, China, Hong Kong, Japan, India, Malaysia, New Zealand, Philippines, Singapore, South Korea, Taiwan, Thailand and Vietnam.
- *Europe:* Austria, Belgium, Denmark, France, Germany, Ireland, Italy, Netherlands, Poland, Spain, Sweden, Switzerland, United Kingdom and Turkey.
- *North America:* Canada and United States.
- *Latin America:* Argentina, Brazil, Mexico.

Intense Competitive Environment

As eBay's product offerings and pricing formats evolved, so did its range of competitors. Originally, the company faced competition from alternative auctions or other venues for collectors, such as flea markets and garage sales. However, as the company grew and introduced fixed pricing, the range of competitors included large retailers like Walmart and Kmart that also had online selling websites. eBay faced the harshest competition from major online companies, including Yahoo, Etsy, and Amazon, which also had online auctions that rivaled eBay's.

Yahoo!

eBay's largest online competitor was Yahoo, which had a strong global presence, particularly in Asian markets. Yahoo originally started as a search engine and quickly evolved to include additional products and services, such as Yahoo! Mail, Yahoo! Maps, and Yahoo! Messenger. The company also offered e-commerce services through Yahoo! Shopping, Yahoo! Autos, Yahoo! Auctions, and Yahoo! Travel. As with eBay, Yahoo's e-commerce sites allowed users to obtain relevant information and make transactions and purchases online. However, Yahoo's business model primarily focused on generating revenue through search advertising. In the United States, in response to potential threats from web giant Google, Yahoo and eBay formed an alliance in which Yahoo utilized eBay's

EXHIBIT 7 Net Revenues by Type ($ millions, except percentage changes)

	2016	% Change	2015	% Change	2014
			Year Ended December 31,		
Net Revenues by Type:					
Net transaction revenues:					
Marketplace	$6,107	–%	$6,103	(4)%	$6,351
StubHub	937	29%	725	15%	629
Total net transaction revenues	7,044	3%	6,828	(2)%	6,980
Marketing services and other revenues:					
Marketplace	1,137	6%	1,078	(2)%	1,103
Classifieds	791	13%	703	(2)%	716
StubHub, Corporate and other	7	**	(17)	**	9
Total marketing services and other revenues	1,935	10%	1,764	(3)%	1,810
Total net revenues	$8,979	5%	$8,592	(2)%	$8,790
Net Revenues by Geography:					
U.S.	$3,866	7%	$3,624	3%	$3,525
International	5,113	3%	4,968	(6)%	5,265
Total net revenues	$8,979	5%	$8,592	(2)%	$8,790

Source: eBay SEC filings.

payment system, PayPal, and eBay gained additional advertising through Yahoo searches. Still, Yahoo posed a major competitive threat in foreign markets, particularly the Asia-Pacific area, through its partnerships with Gmarket and Taobao.

Amazon

Despite not having a huge presence in the online auction industry, Amazon was still considered a fierce online global competitor. Amazon started as Earth's biggest bookstore and rapidly evolved to selling everything, including toys, electronics, home furnishings, apparel, health and beauty aids, groceries, and so on. Although Amazon had a large international presence, the company's linkage to brick-and-mortar shops in the United States made it a greater threat in local markets than in foreign markets. Amazon's international sites were in Canada, the United Kingdom, Germany, Japan, France, and China. Despite its large online presence, Amazon scaled back its online auction business, cutting staff and shutting down Livebid, as part of an overall corporate restructuring.

Google

Google started out as a browser much like Yahoo but ventured into the e-commerce space by acquiring Overstock.com.

While it did not compete directly with eBay in the online auction market, it did compete with eBay in online retailing.

Etsy

As eBay tried to position itself as a trendy e-retailer, it directly competed with the trendy Etsy.com retailing site. The site was managed from an office in Brooklyn and had a strong and growing user base. Much like the customers of eBay, Etsy's customers went to its site for quaint collectible items.

Traditional Retailers

Given the trend toward e-commerce, many traditional brick-and-mortar companies like Walmart, Staples, and Home Depot were investing heavily in developing their online retail sites.

Taobao

eBay faced unyielding competition in China from Alibaba Group's Taobao.com, the largest Chinese online retailer. Like eBay, Taobao strove to implement a more interactive and user-friendly customer service initiative. Taobao began using an instant communication tool called Aliwangwang to help buyers and sellers interact with one another. Alipay, an online payment system, was started soon after.

Interestingly, Taobao's parent company, Alibaba, seemed to be exploring expansion opportunities in the United States. It had a record-breaking IPO in the New York Stock Exchange in September 2014 and raised about $25 billion. U.S. retailers and industry analysts expected Alibaba would soon launch a service targeted at American consumers. Alibaba sold to American consumers through its global retail service AliExpress. But its core Taobao service, often likened to eBay's Marketplaces, was not yet available to U.S. customers in English.

Jack Ma, chairman of Alibaba, had apparently learned from the eBay playbook. At the IPO he repeatedly stressed the importance of trust in an e-commerce venture. "Today what we got is not money. What we got is the trust from the people," Ma said. This had also been the mantra of Pierre Omidyar, founder of eBay.

The Future of eBay

Interested Bidders

As eBay prepares to hold a progressive position in a fiercely competitive market, the industry is rife with rumors about potential acquisitions of the remaining online auction business. "It would give a player like Alibaba a legitimate foothold into the American market," predicted Sean Udall, CIO of Quantum Trading Strategies and author of *The TechStrat Report.*

Who exactly might acquire any of eBay's units, or the company itself someday, remains the speculation of analysts and the media. Amazon, Google, and Alibaba are each occasionally mentioned by Wall Street analysts.

Unhappy Customers

eBay's handling of the hacking incident created a number of disgruntled customers. The company had reset all customer passwords and adversely affected Internet browser search results. Further, a revision to the fee structure displeased a number of small business owners. Fleur Filmer, a customer who ran a picnic gear business called Hanging Rock Picnics, was frustrated with the way changes were introduced at eBay:

> Any fee increases are buried deep within policy updates and the level of fine print is staggering. My store has fared quite well but I must admit that fee increases from three per cent to four per cent [of gross sales value] up to nine per cent are very hard to absorb. . . . A lot of investment and resources have gone to their promotion of the majors online. They have actively gone after the big brands to establish eBay stores and haven't offered any new resources or assistance to small store owners.

New Competitors

eBay was once the go-to site for selling unwanted secondhand goods, but Facebook has now entered the fray. Millions of people have already conveniently bought and sold items using "For Sale" groups, and the social network is rolling out tools to make the process even easier. The new features are designed to regulate the process so buyers know exactly what is for sale, how much it costs, and where it is going to be sourced from. Users have said they prefer to trade on Facebook because the accounts show the names and details of the persons buying and selling. On sites such as eBay and Craigslist, members have a certain level of anonymity, and this makes resolving problems with transactions more difficult.

Moreover, smartphone apps like Offer-up are also posing additional competition for eBay in local neighborhoods. According to the founder of Offer-up, millions of Americans replace the old items with new ones that require a free or additional space. Offer-up provides a solution that frees up the space for new products by selling or tossing the used items through its platform. Offer-up provides an online platform for customers to buy and sell used items through a mobile app and a website. A customer can find used items for sale sorted by the zip code and specific neighborhoods. According to Offer-up, "The idea was a new kind of local marketplace to bring people together to get more value out of their used stuff that could start with something as simple as a photo from a smartphone."[31]

The years ahead are going to be challenging for eBay. Although the company has announced many initiatives that include exclusive partnerships and acquisitions, investors and shareholders will be watching keenly to see if management and the board can really fix things and chart a new course for the future. With senior management, an expanded board of directors, an activist investor, and potential acquirers in the mix, gaining alignment on the path forward will not be an easy task. Only time will tell which option proves right for the company to increase shareholder value over the long term. And the question remains, might eBay be better off offering itself for sale to a bidder?

ENDNOTES

1. eBay Inc. Annual Report 2016.
2. Ibid.
3. Purnell, Newley. Microsoft, eBay, Tencent Invest $1.4 Billion in Amazon's India Rival, https://www.wsj.com/articles/microsoft-ebay-tencent-invest-1-4-billion-in-indias-flipkart-1491819470.
4. eBay and Flipkart Sign Exclusive Agreement to Jointly Address the eCommerce Market Opportunity in India, https://www.wsj.com/articles/PR-CO-20170410-902304.
5. Visa & StubHub Achieve Perfect Harmony in Austin, https://www.wsj.com/articles/PR-CO-20170313-910141.
6. eBay Announces New Advertising Strategy, https://www.wsj.com/articles/PR-CO-20170316-907625.
7. eBay to Roll Out Guaranteed Delivery for 20 Million Items, https://www.wsj.com/articles/PR-CO-20170320-905880.
8. Ibid.
9. ThaiPortal. eBay Regional Sites, https://thaiportal.ru/en/ebay-regional-sites.
10. Galante, J. 2011. PayPal's Revenue Will Double by 2013, Thompson Says. *Bloomberg News,* February 10, www.businessweek.com/news/2011-02-10/paypal-s-revenue-will-double-by-2013-thompson-says.html.
11. Bensinger, G. 2014. eBay to Split as Apple, Others Prepare to Challenge PayPal. *Wall Street Journal,* September 30.
12. eBay Inc. 2008. eBay Inc. Buys Leading Payments and Classifieds Businesses, Streamlines Existing Organization to Improve

Growth. Press release, October 6, www.ebayinc.com/content/press_release/20081006005605.

13. eBay Inc. 2009. Annual report.

14. MacMillan, D. 2010. eBay Buys Bar-Code App. *Bloomberg Businessweek,* June 23, www.businessweek.com/technology/content/jun2010/tc20100623_901174.htm.

15. eBay Inc. 2010. eBay Acquires Milo, a Leading Local Shopping Engine. Press release, December 2, www.ebayinc.com/content/press_release/20101202006358.

16. eBay Inc. 2010. eBay Acquires Industry Leading Mobile Application Developer. Press release, December 15, www.ebayinc.com/content/press_release/20101215006520.

17. eBay Completes the Acquisition of SalesPredict, https://www.ebayinc.com/stories/news/ebay-acquires-salespredict/.

18. eBay Completes the Acquisition of Ticket Utils, https://www.ebayinc.com/stories/news/ebay-completes-the-acquisition-of-ticket-utils/.

19. eBay Partners with Snupps, A Social Organizing App, for Seamless Selling, https://www.ebayinc.com/stories/news/ebay-partners-with-snupps-a-social-organizing-app-for-seamless-selling/.

20. eBay and Flipkart Sign Exclusive Agreement to Jointly Address the eCommerce Market Opportunity in India, https://www.ebayinc.com/stories/news/ebay-and-flipkart-sign-exclusive-agreement-to-jointly-address-the-ecommerce-market-opportunity-in-india/.

21. Doyle, R. A. 2002. The History of Auctions. *Auctioneer,* November 1, www.absoluteauctionrealty.com/history_detail.php?id=5094.

22. Internet Based Moms. 2007. Pierre Omidyar—The Man Behind eBay. April.

23. Academy of Achievement. 2005. Biography—Pierre Omidyar. www.achievement.org, November 9.

24. eBay Inc. 2008. Meg Whitman to Step Down.

25. eBay corporate website, ebayinc.com.

26. eBay Inc. 2008. Meg Whitman to Step Down.

27. O'Brien, Chris. 2012. Is eBay's John Donahoe the best CEO in Silicon Valley? *Mercurynews.com,* November 4, www.mercurynews.com/chris-obrien/ci_21908264/obrien-is-ebays-john-donahoe-best-ceo-silicon.

28. Rao, Leena. PayPal Makes Big Splash on First Day of Trading After eBay Spinoff, http://fortune.com/2015/07/20/paypal-ebay-split-valuation/.

29. Himelstein, L., & Whitman, M. 1999. Q&A with eBay's Meg Whitman. *BusinessWeek Online,* May 31, www.businessweek.com/1999/99_22/b3631008.htm.

30. ThaiPortal. eBay Regional Sites, https://thaiportal.ru/en/ebay-regional-sites/.

31. Offer-up website, https://offerup.com/about/.

CASE 31

JAMBA JUICE: MIXING IT UP & STARTING AFRESH*

On January 3, 2017, Dave Pace, CEO of Jamba Juice, rang the Opening Bell of the Nasdaq MarketSite in Times Square. As part of what Nasdaq had done for the last six years during its annual "Fit Week," Jamba Juice's appearance was meant to focus attention on those companies that helped individuals lead healthier lifestyles. It was especially appropriate for Jamba Juice, because the lifestyle brand with a passion for making healthy living fun was undergoing a refresh of its own. To be announced in March 2017, preliminary financial results for fiscal 2016 had indicated a decrease in revenue and a loss for the year. Although the company had tried to explain this by pointing to the non-recurring expenses of business model adjustment and corporate relocation, investors were wary as the stock price continued to slide.[1] The largest shareholder and activist investor, Engaged Capital, had called on the company to "slash costs and close unprofitable stores"[2] which CEO Pace was in the process of doing.

In May 2016 Pace had announced that Jamba would move its headquarters from California to a less expensive location in Texas, restructure the overall organization, and make changes to the leadership team to ensure support for the transition from company-owned stores to a full franchise model. Commenting on this decision, Pace said, "Jamba has pursued our vision to inspire and simplify healthy living for 26 years, starting with a single juice shop in San Luis Obispo, but as we continue to spread our healthy living mission globally, it has become increasingly clear that a relocation of our support center will better position the company to extend our brand and continue to support our franchise partners for the long term."[3]

In January 2017 Jamba Juice announced the launch of its ReSet Super Blends, a protein smoothie line developed in collaboration with celebrity fitness trainer Harley Pasternak.[4] The new line of protein smoothies included real fruit fortified with calcium, riboflavin, and phosphorus, making for an ideal pre- or post-workout snack or midday "pick-me-up."

But the question remained, would these ongoing initiatives, mixing up the product line and starting afresh with franchise partners, be enough to keep Jamba Juice top-of-mind with its current customers and attractive to new consumers, especially given the increased competition from smoothies served at the likes of McDonald's, Burger King, and Dairy Queen?[5]

Company Background

Juice Club was founded by Kirk Perron and opened its first store in San Luis Obispo, California, in April 1990.[6] While many small health-food stores had juice bars offering fresh carrot juice, wheat germ, and protein powder, dedicated juice and smoothie bars were sparse in 1990 and didn't gain widespread popularity until the mid- to late 1990s.

Juice Club began with a franchise strategy and opened its second and third stores in northern and southern California in 1993. In 1994 management decided that an expansion strategy focusing on company stores would provide a greater degree of quality and operating control. In 1995 the company changed its name to Jamba Juice Company to provide a point of differentiation as competitors began offering similar healthy juices and smoothies in the marketplace.

In March 1999 Jamba Juice Company merged with Zuka Juice Inc., a smoothie retail chain with 98 smoothie retail units in the western United States. On March 13, 2006, Jamba Juice Company agreed to be acquired by Services Acquisition Corp. International (headed by Steven Berrard, former CEO of Blockbuster Inc.) for $265 million.[7] The company went public in November 2006 as Nasdaq-traded JMBA. Jamba Juice stores were owned and franchised by Jamba Juice Company, which was a wholly owned subsidiary of Jamba Inc.

In August 2008 Jamba Juice faced significant leadership changes. Steven Berrard agreed to assume the responsibilities of interim CEO.[8] In December 2008, James D. White was named CEO and president, while Berrard remained chairman of the board of directors. Prior to joining Jamba Juice, White had been senior vice president of consumer brands at Safeway, a publicly traded Fortune 100 food and drug retailer. During what CEO White called the turn-around years from 2009 to 2011, he worked to eliminate short-term debt, innovate, expand the menu, and change the business model by refranchising stores, growing internationally, and commercializing product lines.

Ongoing Strategic Initiatives

Jamba pursued elusive financial health during James D. White's tenure as CEO. Although revenue had been down, the company was profitable, and things appeared to be back on track in 2015 as White moved forward with

---

* This case was developed by Professor Alan B. Eisner, Pace University; associate Professor Pauline Assenza, Western Connecticut State University; Professor Jerome C. Kuperman, Minnesota State University–Moorhead; and Professor James Gould, Pace University. Material has been drawn from published sources to be used for class discussion. Copyright © 2017 Alan B. Eisner.

his "BLEND 2.0" strategic priorities. This BLEND strategy was part of a business redirection that included shifting from a company ownership to a franchise ownership model, refreshing the product line, and accelerating global retail growth through new and existing formats. When he retired in 2015, White had been partly successful, growing revenue and returning the company to profitability in fiscal 2012, only to see a loss in 2014. (See Exhibits 1 and 2.)

When White announced his retirement in October 2015, he felt the accelerated refranchising initiative was virtually complete, and that the company would benefit from a "new generation" of leadership.[9] Nearly two years earlier, Jamba Juice CEO White had also rung the opening bell at Nasdaq in New York City. Headlines had announced "Jamba Juice Rings in the New Year with the Unveiling of Brand-New Jamba Kids™ Meals." This new menu targeting Jamba's newest and youngest customers involved smaller 9.5-ounce sizes of fruit smoothies—Strawberries Gone Bananas, Blueberry Strawberry Blast-off, Popp'in Peach Mango, and Berry Beet It—plus two new food items: a Pizza Swirl with

EXHIBIT 1 Income Statements

(Dollars in thousands, except share and per share amounts)	December 29, 2016	December 29, 2015	December 30, 2014
Revenue:			
Company stores	$134,285	$137,025	$198,737
Franchise and other revenue	23,739	24,651	19,311
Tolal revenue	158,024	161,676	218,048
Costs and operating expenses (income):			
Cost of sales	30,586	33,737	52,236
Labor	41,484	44,732	61,749
Occupancy	16,855	18,951	27,630
Store operating	22,882	25,152	33,089
Depreciation and amortization	5,925	6,569	10,084
General and administrative	36,347	36,872	37,278
Gain on disposal of assets	(2,785)	(21,609)	(2,957)
Store pre-opening	924	1,031	763
Impairment of long-lived assets	345	2,523	175
Store lease termination and closure	1,283	1,669	575
Other operating, net	1,143	1,795	726
Total costs, operating expenses, and gain	154,989	151,422	221,348
Income (loss) from operations	3,035	10,254	(3,300)
Other income (expense):			
Interest income	140	137	74
Interest expense	(235)	(220)	(195)
Total other expense, net	(95)	(83)	(121)
Income (loss) before income taxes	2,940	10,171	(3,421)
Income tax expense	(203)	(701)	(168)
Net income (loss)	2,737	9,470	(3,589)
Redeemable preferred stock dividends and deemed dividends	–	–	–
Less: Net income attributable to noncontrolling interest	48	52	43
Net income (loss) attributable to Jamba, Inc.	$ 2,689	$ 9,418	$ (3,632)

(Dollars in thousands, except share and per share amounts)	December 29, 2016		December 29, 2015		December 30, 2014
Weighted-average shares used in the computation of earnings (loss) per share attributable to Jamba, Inc.:					
Basic	n/a		15,787,806		17,197,904
Diluted	n/a		16,228,033		17,197,904
Earnings (loss) per share attributable to Jamba, Inc. common stockholders:					
Basic	$ n/a	$	0.60	$	(0.21)
Tainted	$ n/a	$	0.58	$	(0.21)

Source: Jamba 10-K reports.

EXHIBIT 2 Balance Sheets (in thousands of dollars)

JAMBA, INC. CONSOLIDATED BALANCE SHEETS			
(Dollars in thousands, except share and per share amounts)	December 29, 2016	December 29, 2015	December 30, 2011
Assets			
Current assets:			
Cash and cash equivalents	$ 11,900	$ 19,730	$ 17,750
Receivables, net of allowances of $618 and $280	13,451	16,932	16,977
Inventories	750	818	2,300
Prepaid and refundable taxes	195	356	474
Prepaid rent	1,458	1,682	504
Assets held for sale	–	–	22,845
Prepaid expenses and other current assets	3,865	4,495	8,105
Total current assets	31,619	44,013	68,955
Property, fixtures and equipment, net	20,400	18,744	17,988
Goodwill	1,260	1,184	945
Trademarks and other intangible assets, net	1,675	1,464	2,360
Notes receivable and other long-term assets	3,813	4,211	2,241
Total assets	$ 58,767	$ 69,616	$ 92,489
Liabilities and stockholders' equity			
Current liabilities:			
Accounts payable	$ 4,225	$ 3,815	$ 3,926
Accrued compensation and benefits	3,554	3,788	6,325
Workers' compensation and health insurance reserves	1,268	633	1,311
Accrued jambacard liability	24,184	29,306	38,184
Other current liabilities	15,667	18,093	16,454
Total current liabilities	58,898	55,635	66,200

continued

EXHIBIT 2 *Continued*

JAMBA, INC. CONSOLIDATED BALANCE SHEETS			
(Dollars in thousands, except share and per share amounts)	December 29, 2016	December 29, 2015	December 30, 2011
Deterred rent and other long-term liabilities	7,099	8,990	9,544
Total liabilities	55,997	64,625	75,744
Commitments and contingencies (Notes 8 and 17)			
Stockholders' equity:			
Common stock, $.001 par value, 30,000,000 shares authorized; 17,938,820 and 17,478,616 shares issued, respectively	16	18	17
Additional paid-in capital	401,346	403,605	396,629
Treasury shares, at cost, 1,948,004 and 910,813, respectively	(35,749)	(40,009)	(11,991)
Accumulated deficit	(362,843)	(358,623)	(368,041)
Total equity attributable to Jamba, Inc.	2,770	4,991	16,614
Noncontrolling interest	–	–	131
Total stockholders' equity	2,770	4,991	16,745
Total liabilities and stockholders' equity	$ 58,767	$ 69,616	$ 92,489

Source: Jamba 10-K reports.

Turkey and a Cheesy Stuffed Pretzel. The idea for this kid's menu came from listening to customers, who had struggled to share the larger smoothie drinks with their young children. It also meshed with Jamba's overall strategy: to create "good-for-you food that tastes good" and to continue to add more full-meal options to the menu for both kids and adults.[10] The Jamba Juice Company had been expanding its product line over the years to offer Jamba products that pleased a broader palate. In addition, Jamba had been pursuing an aggressive expansion program, evolving from a made-to-order smoothie company into a healthy, active-lifestyle company.

Just after his arrival as the new Jamba Juice CEO in 2008, White had instituted a set of strategic priorities. Believing it was necessary to revitalize the company, White had outlined the following goals:[11]

- Transform the chain through refranchising existing stores.
- Initiate international growth.
- Build a retail presence with branded consumer packaged goods and licensing.
- Bring more food offerings to the menu across all dayparts—breakfast, lunch, afternoon, dinner.
- Implement a disciplined expense-reduction plan and improve comparable sales.

In 2012, Jamba Juice had pronounced this turnaround complete and begun to focus on achieving a second phase of growth. CEO White had called this next set of initiatives an accelerated growth BLEND Plan 2.0. By 2016 this plan had evolved into BLEND 3.0 and included the following:

- Become a top-of-mind brand by simplifying and sharpening Jamba's healthy food and beverage marketing message to better clarify value and make the brand more relevant through brand activation and leadership.
- Create new products, provide category leadership in smoothies, juices and bowls.
- Accelerate global retail growth through new and existing formats.
- Drive the asset-light business model to enhance shareholder value, continuing to reduce operational costs, driving store-level productivity and profitability, and improving efficiency in the supply, sourcing, and distribution process.[12]

According to White, these strategic priorities supported the company's mission to "accelerate growth and development of Jamba as a globally recognized healthy, active lifestyle brand."[13]

Top-of-Mind Brand

By 2017 Jamba Juice was the smoothie brand leader and #1 retailer for fresh squeezed made-to-order juices. Jamba also boasted over 1.8 million Facebook fans and over 100 million annual visits to its stores. The consumer messaging was centered around the theme "Blend In The Good," centered on "Whole Food Nutrition," designed to focus consumers on the benefits of the fresh fruits and vegetables that were used to make Jamba's smoothies, juices, and bowls. This campaign was executed over multiple media sources, including digital, social, public relations, TV, radio and print. The campaign reached millions of Millennials through the power of social media in partnership with DanceOn, the number one ranked YouTube channel, and with Pharrell Williams. Jamba also entered into or expanded programs with strategic partners including with Spendgo, Google, Twitter, SoftCard, and Groupon, incorporating the Jamba Juice mobile application, helping customers locate stores, order ahead, speed up transactions, and improve the online and in-store experience.

In 2017 the Jamba Insider Rewards ("JJR") e-mail marketing program had 2 million loyalty members who were rewarded with promotional offers such as discounts, free products, and advance notice of in-store events. Franchisees were provided with tools and technologies that targeted their customers through e-mail, social media, radio and out-of-home advertising, and in late 2015 Jamba piloted a first-ever television ad campaign in key markets.

Regarding its marketing efforts, historically, Jamba had not engaged in any mass-media promotional programs, relying instead on word of mouth and in-store promotions to increase customer awareness. However, Jamba was featured in stories appearing in the *Wall Street Journal, New York Times, USA Today,* and a host of local newspapers and magazines, as well as profiled spots on TV news shows such as *Good Morning America.* Jamba had also run an "Ambassadors of WOW" contest nationwide, encouraging fans to nominate themselves or worthy friends or family members to be the new faces of Jamba Juice, creating "wow" through support and involvement within their communities. These ambassadors would have the opportunity to appear in Jamba Juice advertisements and promotional campaigns.[14]

Jamba also capitalized on the openings of new sites as opportunities to reach out to the media and secure live local television coverage, radio broadcasts, and articles in local print media. Openings were also frequently associated with a charitable event, thus serving to reinforce Jamba Juice Company's strong commitment to its communities. In addition, Jamba aligned itself with "active living" spokespeople, such as tennis star Venus Williams, who had partnered with Jamba to open two stores in the Maryland–Washington, D.C., area.[15]

Jamba also re-launched its corporate social responsibility initiatives under the banner of "Team Up For a Healthy Whirl'd," a platform that encouraged consumers, partners, and employees to join in the company's efforts to inspire healthy people, products, planet, and community. Through Team Up For a Healthy Whirl'd Jamba led sustainability initiatives, programs to inspire healthier employees, and a number of community engagement activities in the markets it served. Continuing on its mission to serve the community, Jamba launched a grant program, partnering with the National Gardening Association and their Kid's Gardening program, continuing to drive awareness of the need to encourage better dietary and fitness habits in kids through the Team Up For a Healthy America program and through partnerships with the American heart Association, National Gardening Association, and the GenYouth Foundation.

New Products, Category Leadership

Jamba sought "top-of-mind" leadership by creating innovative and "craveable" menu items they could offer throughout the day—for breakfast, lunch, afternoon, and dinner. Jamba Juice stores offered customers a range of fresh squeezed fruit juices, blended beverages, baked goods and meals, nutritional supplements, and healthy snacks. Jamba smoothie and juice options were made with real fruit and 100 percent fruit juices. Jamba smoothies were rich in vitamins, minerals, proteins, and fiber, were blended to order, and provided four to six servings of fruits and vegetables. In addition to the natural nutrients in Jamba smoothies, Jamba offered supplements in the form of Boosts and Shots. Boosts included 10 combinations of vitamins, minerals, proteins, and extracts designed to give the mind and body a nutritious boost. Shots included three combinations of wheatgrass, green tea, orange juice, and soymilk designed to give customers a natural concentrate of vitamins, minerals, and antioxidants.

As complements to its smoothie and boost offerings, Jamba also offered baked goods and other meal items. Called "tasty bites," each of these items was made with natural ingredients and was high in protein and fiber. One popular item was steel cut hot oatmeal with fruit, a low-calorie organic product that captured a "best of" rating by nutritionists when compared against offerings from McDonald's, Starbucks, Au Bon Pain, and Cosi.[16] Jamba also offered a variety of grab-and-go wraps, sandwiches, and California flatbread food offerings, as well as "energy bowls" that incorporated whole fruit, fresh Greek yogurt and/or soy milk, and an assortment of dry toppings.

Jamba featured an organic brew-by-the-cup coffee service and a line of Whirl'ns frozen yogurt and sorbet bar treats, with probiotic fruit and yogurt blends. In 2012 Jamba added to the hot beverage category by acquiring premium tea blender Talbott Teas. This acquisition was championed by ABC TV's *Shark Tank* venture capitalists Kevin O'Leary, Daymond John, and Barbara Corcoran, who convinced Jamba CEO James White that this acquisition would be a good fit for Jamba's strategy to "accelerate growth through the acquisition of specialty lifestyle brands that support the company's expansion into new and relevant product categories."[17]

Jamba also transitioned existing stores in selected markets to a fresh-squeezed juice emphasis. This addressed competition from both Juice It Up! and Starbucks, who were expanding their premium juice bar businesses. But the big announcement was when Jamba introduced its Kids Meals.

This new menu was targeted toward children ages 4 to 8, with a complete meal—a smoothie plus a food item—containing fewer than 500 calories. The items included whole grains, 2.5 servings of fruit or vegetables, and no added sugar.

One of the key objectives of Jamba's growth strategy was to market itself in a way to increase sales year-round and significantly decrease weather and seasonal vulnerabilities. Seasonal issues were serious, since the traditional driver of Jamba's revenue and profit was the sale of smoothies during hot weather. In southern states (e.g., California), where the weather remained warm year-round, Jamba experienced fairly steady sales. However, in the northern states (e.g., New York), where there was a cold and fairly lengthy winter season, Jamba experienced severe seasonal variability. To counter the seasonal slump, Jamba pushed to increase the presence of nontraditional stores inside existing venues.

Nontraditional Locations

Jamba had generally characterized its stores as either traditional or nontraditional. Traditional locations included suburban strip malls and various retail locations in urban centers. Traditional stores averaged approximately 1,400 square feet in size and were designed to be fun, friendly, energetic, and colorful to represent the active, healthy lifestyle that Jamba Juice promoted.

Nontraditional stores were considered those located in areas that allowed Jamba to generate awareness and try out new products to fuel the core business. Jamba's nontraditional opportunities included store-within-a-store locations, airports, shopping malls, and colleges and universities.

Store-within-a-store: Jamba Juice had developed franchise partner relationships with major grocers and retailers to develop store-within-a-store concepts. The franchise partnerships provided it with the opportunity to reach new customers and enhance the brand without making significant capital investments. An example of this was the 2016 opening of a combination Timothy's World Coffee and Jamba Juice franchise location within a Stop & Shop store in Long Island, New York.[18]

Airports: Jamba operated several airport locations and had the opportunity to develop stores in numerous additional airports. Jamba Juice Company's highly portable product appealed to travelers on the go and provided them with an energizing boost.

Shopping malls: Jamba had opportunistically established stores in shopping malls that presented attractive expansion opportunities. In addition, as with the airport locations, the indoor setting helped to alleviate weather and seasonal vulnerabilities that challenged traditional locations.

Colleges and universities: The Jamba brand was appealing to the average college student's active, on-the-go lifestyle, and Jamba had developed multiple on-campus locations across the United States.

Other potential nontraditional store locations: Additional high-traffic, nontraditional locations existed. Many large health clubs included a juice and smoothie bar within their buildings. Jamba could partner with a major gym chain or individual private gyms with high membership rates. Another possibility was to partner with a large school district. Schools across the country were under increasing scrutiny to offer healthy alternatives to the traditional fat-, carbohydrate-, and preservative-rich foods served in cafeterias, especially as a number of states were prohibiting the sale of junk food on K–12 campuses.

Jamba had introduced self-service JambaGO automated drink stations in nontraditional locations, including schools. Taking roughly the space of a soda fountain beverage dispenser, the JambaGo format, which CEO White called a wellness center, included the chain's branded packaged products, as well as the option of several preblended smoothies. The JambaGO concept was a way to reinforce Jamba as a healthy, active lifestyle brand that was also convenient and portable. This licensed concept represented no capital investment for Jamba and used the razor/razor blade net profit model. White was hoping Jamba would become "the go-to resource for healthy solutions for school foodservice directors."[19] However, current CEO Dave Pace announced plans to exit the JambaGo platform in 2017, stating "the Jamba team has committed to strengthening its core retail business, improving franchise profitability, accelerating ongoing global development, and updating the Jamba Juice brand position. After a detailed review, the Company determined that the JambaGo platform does not align with these objectives and is not a viable option through which to drive long-term profitability and shareholder value."[20] Interestingly, customer feedback had indicated that the quality of the JambaGo product was not up the standards that consumers expected from Jamba; therefore Jamba management felt JambaGo would degrade the brand and impact the company's opportunity to grow the core business and brand over the long term.

Building a Global Consumer Packaged Goods Platform

Jamba Inc. was also aggressively pursuing licensing agreements for commercialized product lines in the areas of Jamba-branded make-at-home frozen smoothie kits, frozen yogurt novelty bars, all-natural energy drinks, coconut water fruit juice beverages, Brazilian super fruit shots, trail mixes, and fruit cups. The objective was to reinforce the Jamba better-for-you message with convenient and portable products available at multiple consumer locations.

In aggressive moves, Jamba had expanded licensing agreements to include a line of fruit-infused coconut water, to be distributed through the Pepsi Beverage Company, Brazilian super fruit shots, and all-natural fruit cups to be produced in partnership with Zola and Sundia Corporation.

Other Jamba-branded consumer products included yogurt and sorbet frozen novelty items manufactured under license by Oregon Ice Cream LLC out of Eugene, Oregon, and Jamba-branded apparel, including cotton T-shirts, beanies, and a canvas tote bag, developed in partnership with licensee Headline Entertainment.

Jamba also promoted "At Home Smoothies," a kit containing fruit and yogurt with a healthy antioxidant boost, one full serving of fruit, and 100% daily value of vitamin C. Available in the local grocer's fruit aisle, the package made two eight-ounce servings by adding juice and blending. The blending was facilitated by Jamba's new appliance line, offering a juice extractor, manual juicer, professional blender, and a "quiet blend" blender for quick midnight meals.

Transition from Company-Owned to Franchise "Asset-light" Format

Originally, Jamba Juice Company had followed a strategy of expanding its store locations in existing markets and only opening stores in select new markets. Jamba soon began acquiring the assets of Jamba Juice franchised stores in an attempt to gain more control over growth direction. Under CEO Paul E. Clayton, Jamba acquired several franchise stores and expected to continue making additional franchise acquisitions as part of its ongoing growth strategy. However, the company-owned franchises were not as productive and accounted for a disproportionately low portion of company revenues.[21]

Clayton stepped down after eight years, and was ultimately replaced by James White. White reversed the trajectory of the company-owned growth strategy, focusing on the acceleration of franchise and nontraditional store growth. The more heavily franchised business model tended to require less capital investment and reduced the volatility of cash flow performance over time. However, revenue sources then came more from royalties and franchise fees rather than retail sales. This plan, set into motion by CEO White in December 2008, saw the percentage of Jamba's stores that are franchised increase from 30 percent to nearly 90 percent. Jamba Juice was recognized by *Forbes* in 2014 as one of the Top 10 Best Franchises in America.

Current CEO Dave Pace planned to oversee the continuing transition. The "asset-light" franchise model had several efficiencies that translated to increased profitability. When a company placed most of the risk for running a business in the hands of a franchisee, the franchisor, Jamba Juice in this case, did not have to pay for employees, rent, or upkeep on the store assets. The franchisee was expected to put his or her capital to work, running the business. In this case, store management was "more likely to act in the best interest of shareholders because the franchisee's net worth is more often directly correlated with the outcome" of his or her store.[22] The incentives were clear. The franchisee took the risk and earned the profits, while the franchisor made 7.5 to 10 percent royalty on all sales, and collected a marketing fee.

Going into 2017, Jamba Juice had 896 locations, consisting of 69 company-owned and -operated stores and 759 franchise stores, with 68 licensed sites overseas. (See Exhibit 3.)

International growth was also a priority. Starting with the first South Korean location in January 2011, Jamba Juice had grown to 68 stores internationally by 2017, with outlets in Indonesia, South Korea, the Philippines, Taiwan, United Arab Emirates, Mexico, and Canada, with additional franchisees to open in Thailand. International stores were located in prominent locations like the Mall of Asia, the largest integrated shopping, dining, and leisure destination in the Philippines.[23]

Competition

Jamba was the smoothie industry leader and initially had several competitors with similar health and fitness focuses, such as Juice It Up!, Planet Smoothie, and Smoothie King, but over time that had changed. Starbucks and Panera Bread had entered the smoothie market, and McDonald's brought its marketing machine into the frozen drink category, launching its line of smoothies with a value pitch. When McDonald's introduced a 12-ounce smoothie for $2.29, Jamba Juice's berry smoothies started at $3.55 for 16 ounces. When asked about the McDonald's push into its competitive space, Jamba Juice's CEO White said, "We view the entry of McDonald's into the smoothie category as an overall validation of the potential of smoothies. Their advertising will expand interest in the category." Burger King had also entered the smoothie market, and Starbucks, with its smoothies already in place, had acquired both Evolution Fresh, the premium juice bar operator, and Teavana Teas. This positioned Starbucks as a head-to-head competitor to Jamba Juice.

Jamba Juice Company's desire to grow by expanding its selection of nonjuice menu items seemed to follow the Starbucks model. Although originally just a coffeehouse, by 2012 most Starbucks stores offered a variety of muffins, fruit plates, sandwiches, quiches, and desserts. And with the 2012 acquisition of juice bar operator Evolution Fresh and premium loose tea purveyor Teavana, Starbucks had pushed boundaries even further. This menu expansion helped Starbucks attract customers who were looking for a light meal or dessert to go with their coffee and also attracted non-coffee drinkers who just came in for the food, tea, and juice beverages. Offering iced coffees, teas, and juices helped Starbucks overcome some of its seasonal variability, giving customers a cool-drink offering during hot-weather months. Offering ready-to-go-drinks in grocery and convenience stores also enabled Starbucks to get its products to a wider customer base.

Likewise, Jamba had set out to strengthen its customer reach by offering ready-to-drink products, and hot food and drink items to attract customers during the cold-weather months, plus a range of breakfast and lunch food items to

EXHIBIT 3 Store Types and Locations

	Fiscal Year Ended			
	December 29, 2016	December 29, 2015	December 30, 2014	December 31, 2013
Company Stores:				
Beginning of year	70	263	268	301
Company Stores opened	–	–	–	2
Company Stores acquired from franchisees	–	2	26	–
Company Stores closed	(1)	(16)	(13)	(4)
Company Stores sold to franchisees	–	(179)	(18)	(31)
Total Company Stores	69	70	263	268
	Fiscal Year Ended			
	December 29, 2016	December 29, 2015	December 30, 2014	December 31, 2013
Franchise Stores – Domestic:				
Beginning of year	748	543	535	473
Franchise Stores opened	8	51	43	52
Franchise Stores purchased by Company	–	(2)	(26)	–
Franchise Stores closed	(34)	(23)	(27)	(21)
Franchise Stores purchased from Company	–	179	18	31
Total Franchise Stores – Domestic	722	748	543	535
	Fiscal Year Ended			
	December 29, 2016	December 29, 2015	December 30, 2014	December 31, 2013
International Stores:				
Beginning of year	75	62	48	35
International Stores opened	1	22	24	15
International Stores closed	(8)	(9)	(10)	(2)
Total International Stores	68	75	62	48

Source: Jamba 10-K reports.

complement its juice-based offerings and satisfy customer desires all day and all year-round. Could Jamba continue to follow Starbucks' path of broadening its menu base but still maintaining its brand identity?

One of the issues with growth is how to manage the pace of innovation—by choosing a direction that capitalizes on the organization's core competencies and then validating new ideas by testing them in the marketplace—and then making sure the financial and human assets are available to invest in sustaining needed operational components. Consultant Robert Sher advises CEOs of mid-market companies who are trying to plan for growth. He pointed to Jamba CEO James White as one who seemed to get it, explaining that White's team uses "a well-disciplined 'stage-gate' process to de-risk each idea, from conception through testing." As an example, Sher pointed to Jamba's launch of its steel-cut oatmeal, a product that took two years of field testing but ended up a winner.[24]

The juice and smoothie bar industry had seen a reduction in growth since 2012 as competition increased from fast-food chains and yogurt shops. The category of smoothies and juices had seen increasing consumer acceptance as health claims become more commonplace, especially as the "cold press" juice option, yielding highly nutritious juice from chopped spinach, kale and ginger, gained in popularity. However, the juice category was still relatively expensive compared with other refreshment options, and more informed consumers became concerned about the high sugar content from natural fructose. This, combined with the fact that the regular quick-serve restaurants such as McDonald's and Burger King were reported to make up nearly 40 percent of the juice and smoothie bar market, meant that the pure juice and smoothie providers such as Jamba Juice, Planet Smoothie, and Smoothie King were facing difficult growth options.[25] Clearly international growth was possible, and there was always the additional possibility of consolidation through merger, acquisition or other co-branded partnerships. What would the future look like?

CEO Dave Pace's remarks during the third quarter earning call in 2016 restated the challenge: "I'd just like to reiterate the importance of the work being done by the new team in 2016 to eliminate distractions, tightening refocus of the portfolio, and thus allow us to direct our energy to reigniting core sales, and sales and profit growth in 2017 and beyond. You'll see us continue to implement disciplined processes including deeper consumer insights and analytical vigor into all of our decision making. . . . 2016 is obviously a year of significant transition for Jamba. But as I hope you can see, we're developing the organization, executing the strategy, and building the environment that we need to successfully deliver value to our shareholders over the short, medium, and long term."[26] Would Pace and Jamba be successful?

ENDNOTES

1. Pines, L. 2016. Jamba Juice Stock: 4 things to watch. *Investopedia*, August 31, http://www.investopedia.com/articles/company-insights/083116/jamba-juice-stock-4-things-watch-jmba.asp.

2. Bennett, J. 2016. Jamba Juice feels investors' heavy hand. *FranchiseTimes*, September 21, http://www.franchisetimes.com/October-2016/Jamba-Juice-feels-investors-heavy-hand/.

3. Bay City News Service. 2016. Jamba Juice announces that it will move to Texas. *SFGate*, May 5, http://www.sfgate.com/news/bayarea/article/Jamba-Juice-Announces-That-It-Will-Move-To-Texas-7396715.php#photo-9377710.

4. Business Wire. 2017. Jamba introduces Super Blend Smoothies created with celebrity trainer Harley Pasternak. *Business Wire,* January 4, https://finance.yahoo.com/news/jamba-introduces-super-blend-smoothies-140000541.html.

5. Wolf, B. 2013. Bringing the juice. *QSR Magazine,* February, https://www.qsrmagazine.com/consumer-trends/bringing-juice.

6. *FundingUniverse.com.* n.d. Jamba Juice Company (company history), www.fundinguniverse.com/company-histories/Jamba-Juice-Company-Company-History.html.

7. Jamba Juice Company. 2006. Jamba Juice Company and Services Acquisition Corp. International announce merger. March 13, www.sec.gov/Archives/edgar/data/1316898/000110465906015960/a06-6826_1ex99d1.htm.

8. Jamba Inc. 2008. Jamba, Inc. announces changes to its senior management team. *Business Wire,* August 6, ir.jambajuice.com/phoenix.zhtml?c=192409&p=irol-newsArticle&ID=1189166.

9. Jargon, J. 2015. Jamba launches search for CEO. *Wall Street Journal,* Eastern edition, October 2, 2015, B5.

10. Dostal, E. 2013. Jamba Juice introduces kids' meals. *Nation's Restaurant News,* January 4, http://nrn.com/latest-headlines/jamba-juice-introduces-kids-meal.

11. Jamba Inc. 2010. Jamba Inc. Form 10K annual report, for period ending December 29, 2009. Available at http://ir.jambajuice.com/phoenix.zhtml?c=192409&p=irol-sec.

12. Jamba Inc. 2015. Jamba Inc. Form 10K annual report for the fiscal year ended December 29, 2015. Available at http://ir.jambajuice.com/phoenix.zhtml?c=192409&p=irol-sec.

13. Ibid.

14. Jamba Inc. 2011. Jamba Juice announces two new "Ambassadors of WOW." *PRNewswire,* May 9, ir.jambajuice.com/phoenix.zhtml?c=192409&p=irol-newsArticle&id=1561602.

15. Jamba Inc. 2012. Jamba Juice growth continues: New stores open in Washington D.C. with tennis-great Venus Williams. *Business Wire,* July 9, ir.jambajuice.com/phoenix.zhtml?c=192409&p=irol-newsArticle&ID=1712664.

16. Jamba Inc. 2011. Jamba Juice oatmeal favorite pick on Good Morning America today. ABC News, February 8, ir.jambajuice.com/phoenix.zhtml?c=192409&p=irol-news&nyo=0; video clip available at abcnews.go.com/GMA/video/fast-food-oatmeal-how-healthy-is-it-12865436.

17. *QSR Magazine.* 2012. Jamba Juice acquires premium tea company, Talbott Teas. February 21, www.qsrmagazine.com/news/jamba-juice-acquires-premium-tea-company-talbott-teas.

18. Industry News. 2016. Timothy's World Coffee and Jamba Juice team up, https://www.qsrmagazine.com/news/.

19. Jennings, L. 2012. Jamba Juice launches next phase of growth. *Nation's Restaurant News,* January 10, nrn.com/archive/jamba-juice-launches-next-phase-growth.

20. *Business Wire.* 2016. Jamba, Inc. announces strategic exit from JambaGo Platform. *PR Newswire,* October 5. http://ir.jambajuice.com/phoenix.zhtml?c=192409&p=irol-newsArticle&ID=2209604.

21. Lee, L. 2007. A smoothie you can chew on: To appeal to diners as well as drinkers, Jamba Juice is adding heft to its concoctions. *BusinessWeek,* June 11: 64.

22. Clayton, N. 2016. Jamba Juice's business transformation 7 years in the making is nearly complete. *Seeking Alpha,* March 8, http://seekingalpha.com/article/3956540-jamba-juice-business-transformation-7-years-making-nearly-complete.

23. Jamba Inc. 2012. Jamba announces significant progress in international expansion. *Business Wire,* July 17, ir.jambajuice.com/phoenix.zhtml?c=192409&p=irol-newsArticle&ID=1715180.

24. Sher, R. 2012. Google can survive too much innovation. You can't. *Forbes,* May 15, www.forbes.com/sites/forbesleadershipforum/2012/05/15/google-can-survive-too-much-innovation-you-cant/.

25. Wolf, B. 2013. Bringing the Juice. *QSR Magazin,.* February, https://www.qsrmagazine.com/consumer-trends/bringing-juice.

26. Jamba Juice. 2016. Q3 2016 Earnings Call Transcript, http://seekingalpha.com/article/4019663-jambas-jmba-ceo-dave-pace-q3-2016-results-earnings-call-transcript.

CASE 32

BLACKBERRY LIMITED: IS THERE A PATH TO RECOVERY?*

In mid-2017, the once high-flying Blackberry stock was trading for less than $7 a share. Remarkably, that was a drop of more than 94 percent from $139 in 2008.[1] The competitive landscape had shifted in recent years, and BlackBerry had lost its strong position in the industry. The company faced a severe reduction in hardware revenues and mobile subscribers.[2] BlackBerry Limited hired John Chen, a turnaround specialist, as its new CEO to get the former dominant smartphone producer back to profitability.[3] Soon after joining the company, Chen formulated a turnaround plan that emphasized corporate and government enterprises. This new plan significantly reduced the company's operating costs.[4] After Chen started turning the steering wheel, BlackBerry appeared to be stabilizing, but the sustainability of his strategy was still a big unknown. There have been rumors regarding a potential sale of the company to Samsung Group, privatization of operations to reduce the risk of shareholder activism, hostile takeovers, and a move to focus only on software and licensing agreements.[5] Each of these would be a very different scenario from what the Canadian tech giant faced just a few years ago. Industry experts speculate on what lies ahead, but new CEO John Chen seems to be optimistic about the future of Blackberry.

The return to success of Blackberry in the smartphone industry might sound farfetched but it was not impossible. Once Blackberry had held significant market share in the smartphone space. It remained a question of what strategy the company should adopt to revive the admiration it once enjoyed and re-boot demand for Blackberry smartphones. The smartphone industry had become immensely competitive with giants Apple Inc. and Samsung Group the two companies that held most of the market share in the industry. With Blackberry's specialization in data and mobile security there seemed to be potential in Blackberry's software security enterprise division, which had not received as much attention and resources as the smartphone division.

Research in Motion

Milhal "Mike" Lazaridis and his childhood friend Doug Freign founded Research in Motion (RIM) in 1984. Lazaridis was born in Istanbul in 1960 and came from a Greek working-class family. His father's aspirations to become a tool-and-die maker led the family to relocate to Ontario, Canada. Lazaridis displayed remarkable intelligence at an early age and excelled in both reading and science. Lazaridis was frequently exposed to electrical engineering and sharpened his intuitive understanding of the basic science behind every electrical innovation.[3] After graduating from high school, Lazaridis attended the University of Waterloo. However, he dropped out before graduation and decided to try his luck in business at the age of 23. The Canadian government enabled the formation of RIM by granting Lazaridis and Freign a $15,000 loan. The duo set up RIM headquarters in Waterloo, Canada, as an electronics and computer science consulting company. According to Lazaridis, the name Research in Motion meant, "we never stop, we never end,"[3] signaling innovation that would drive RIM forward.

During the company's early years, Lazaridis accepted all sorts of contracts, most of which entailed writing code or making small insignificant technological gadgets. None of the early projects proved to be a commercial success, but they generated enough revenue to keep the company viable for more than a decade.

The company's game changer was introduction of e-mail and data devices. Lazaridis had been exposed to e-mail while in college, at a time when only professors and scientists were using the service. Lazaridis was convinced that data would become extremely important in the near future, but it was hard to find the funding for a project involving e-mail, because the early 1990s was a time when major mobile carriers were interested in devices with voice capabilities and in selling as much as possible until the market became saturated. Reading e-mails on a handheld device was unheard of. A nonexistent demand for devices with e-mail support did not weaken Lazaridis's determination; he developed initial prototypes by writing gateway codes hooked up to an HP Palmtop, the company's first device with "e-mail on a belt." Although the device was not commercially applicable, it became extremely popular with RIM employees. Lazaridis recalls that "employees started taking these things home, and they wouldn't return them."[3] What he then understood was that the idea of "e-mail on a belt" had the potential to generate high demand, but the challenge lay in making such a product practical enough for consumers to use on a daily basis.

The business aspect of RIM was made easier by the emergence of Harvard graduate Jim Balsillie. In the 1990s, Balsillie was an employee of a small technology company

* This case was prepared by Professor Alan B. Eisner and graduate student Saad Nazir of Pace University, and Professor Helaine J. Korn of Baruch College, City University of New York. This case was solely based on library research and was developed for class discussion rather than to illustrate either effective or ineffective handling of an administrative situation. Copyright © 2017 Alan B. Eisner.

called Sutherland and Schultz, which would become one of RIM's clients. Lazaridis and Balsillie first crossed paths when Sutherland and Schultz tried to acquire RIM. Lazaridis passed on the offer, but he got a chance to see Balsillie in action and was impressed. Lazaridis wanted someone to help out with the business aspect of his company. When a company from the Netherlands bought Sutherland and Schultz in 1992, Balsillie was left without a job. Lazaridis was quick to pick up the phone and invite Balsillie to join his company.[3] Due to RIM's small size and limited resources, Balsillie had to accept a severe salary reduction and to spend $250,000 to acquire 33 percent of RIM. Balsillie believed in Lazaridis's abilities and the potential for the company, so he agreed to the terms.[3] The two shared duties as co-CEOs and formed a powerful leadership team in which Lazaridis focused on product development, and Balsillie took responsibility for the business part of the company. Balsillie was clear about different responsibilities and said, "My job is to raise money, and Mike's job is to spend it."[3]

With limited success up until 1992, RIM made a conscious decision to leave its comfort zone and pursue home-run products such as wireless data. Balsillie truly believed that the future could be great for RIM, and according to former Senior VP Patrick Spence, "Balsillie was really strategic in terms of how he was thinking and really ambitious in terms of what he wanted to do."[5] Introduced in 1996, the Interactive Pager 900 contained peer-to-peer messaging and also an e-mail gateway. Unfortunately, the device had several deficiencies and operating errors. It was also too big and bulky to gain commercial acceptance.[3] Thinking of its size, Lazaridis nicknamed it "the Bullfrog."

Following "the Bullfrog" came "the Leapfrog." The revolutionary component of "the Leapfrog" was its ability to send e-mails at any time from any place. This product set the stage for the eventually hugely popular signature product we know today as BlackBerry. The product was a success: BellSouth, which had spent over $300 million in building its mobile "Mobitex" network, ordered Leapfrogs worth $60 million in 1997.[3] In order to get the necessary funds to continue its product development, RIM went public at the Toronto Stock Exchange in 1997, and the IPO raised more than $115 million.[6]

The Blackberry and Its Success

Lazaridis was responsible for developing RIM's next version of a wireless data device that would have better parts, longer battery power, and a bigger screen. RIM hired Lexicon, the company that was credited for naming Apple's PowerBook and Intel's Premium brands, to come up with a name for the device. The buttons on the new device looked like tiny seeds. Lexicon played around with different fruit names such as strawberry and melon, before it eventually settled on BlackBerry.[3] Thus, RIM had a great product with a catchy name, and it became Balsillie's responsibility to spread the word on the new offering.

The BlackBerry 850 hit the market in 1999, with wireless data, e-mail, and a tiny QWERTY keyboard.[6,7] Initially, the Leapfrog and the early BlackBerry device were mostly used by law enforcement, firefighters, and ambulance workers. One of the things that this niche group greatly valued was the product's extreme reliability and security features. Balsillie thought this would resonate well with corporations on Wall Street. He knew that corporate IT departments often made decisions regarding companywide hardware and purchased the same devices for all their employees. RIM next resorted to a guerilla marketing strategy, in which hundreds of devices were given away to ground-level employees on Wall Street. The strategy became an instant success as Wall Street employees got hooked on the device and subsequently pressured IT departments to make BlackBerry the official device for their companies. Big corporations like Credit Suisse and Merrill Lynch gave in to this pressure and ordered BlackBerrys by the thousands.[3] The success led RIM to go public on the NASDAQ in 1999, and RIM raised an additional $250 million to invest in the development of its technology.[8] Revenues increased from $47.34 million in 1999 to $84.96 million in 2000, with BlackBerry accounting for 41 percent of the revenues.[9] Balsillie, along with his management team, utilized the same guerilla tactic at the Capitol, where security and reliability are perhaps even more desired features than they are in corporate world. Soon, a large number of politicians and congressional staffers were ordering BlackBerrys.

RIM's reputation was seriously enhanced during the tragic events that transpired on September 11, 2001. Instead of relying on cellular telephone systems Blackberry functioned on data systems that held up extraordinarily well. Data systems could be used exclusively to communicate data in the form of text messages or e-mails by using dedicated data networks which were abundant in lower Manhattan. Almost all cellular networks shut down during the terrorist attacks, which disabled both incoming and outgoing telephone calls. However, the BlackBerry and its network remained operational, enabling victims to call loved ones and keeping vital communication lines between law enforcement and rescue workers open. One of the victims of 9/11, a Ms. Federman, recalled, "I had my cellphone in one hand, and it was useless, and my BlackBerry in the other, and it was my lifeline that day."[10] In the eyes of the government there was no doubt that BlackBerry's features were important for public servants. Almost directly after the events on 9/11, the American government ordered 3,000 BlackBerrys for representatives, staffers, and senators.[3]

This initial success meant that growth was rapid at RIM in this period, and it was enhanced by something that the company did not anticipate. All of a sudden, actors, athletes, and other high profile individuals were spotted using BlackBerrys. Among other organizations, the BlackBerry was standardized for 31 out of 32 teams in the NFL.[5] This created a demand among the general public, who wanted to use the same device they saw their favorite celebrities using.

The increase in demand resulted in rapidly expanding sales and market share; RIM had more than 2 million users in 2004 and sold devices in 40 countries through 80 carriers.[5] The massive popularity in the 2000s saw RIM emerge as a dominant producer of smartphones, and at its peak in 2009 it had acquired 20.1 percent market share (see Exhibit 1) and sold nearly 15 million devices per quarter.[3,11]

According to former account and carrier manager Chris Key, the BlackBerry became so popular with major companies that CTOs often referred to it as "digital heroin,"[5] and many started calling it "CrackBerry." With competition from Google, Samsung, and Apple mounting in the mid-2000s, however, RIM decided to focus on its core competencies in security and reliability. Lazaridis and Balsillie were convinced that enterprises would continue to drive the market, and therefore RIM continued to create devices that primarily appealed to professionals.[3]

Patent Trolls

Despite RIM's success, all was not rosy because its management failed to keep an efficiency check on product and service development, which led the company into trouble with patent trolls. A critical component of the tech industry is the presence of companies called patent trolls. These are companies that do not manufacture anything or provide services but instead seek to make money on patent infringement claims. These companies often have no other assets than a portfolio of patents, and the patents are usually purchased from others. RIM got tangled up with one of such patent trolls, NTP Inc., a company with a portfolio of 50 patents, one of which was in the field of mobile e-mails. NTP took the Canadian tech giant to court, where RIM successfully proved that its e-mail system was invented before the patent in question.[3] However, NTP's attorneys persisted and uncovered that an enhanced version of SAM software being used by RIM was launched after NTP's invention patent. The judge subsequently disregarded RIM's initial explanation. The case was long and complicated, and it consumed a considerable amount of RIM's energy and resources. Consequently, Lazaridis and Balsillie accepted a $600 million settlement to close the case in 2006.[3] This was a huge financial setback to the company. As RIM was experiencing exponential growth after the success of Blackberry, the company needed all its funds and resources to keep pace with the growth. This setback formed a managerial and financial obstacle for the company in the long run.

Industry Landscape

Apple Inc. entered the smartphone industry in 2007 when its CEO, Steve Jobs, introduced the world to the company's newest innovation, the iPhone. Apple had a completely different strategy from that of BlackBerry. Apple's strategy was to cater to all the smartphone customers and not just the corporations. Steve Jobs and management at Apple believed that the individual consumer would drive the next surge in the market.[3] Clearly, RIM's management did not believe that the market was

EXHIBIT 1 RIM (BlackBerry) Revenue 2004–2017

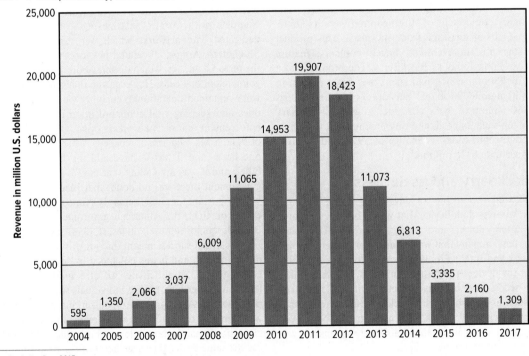

Source: Statistica Inc. 2017.

shifting, and BlackBerry continued to enhance what it thought made its product great—battery life, security, and e-mail. In 2006, corporations accounted for the majority of RIM revenues, and the company intended to keep enterprises as its main target market.[3] Lazaridis believed that the iPhone would be a fad and could not understand why anyone would want an iPhone, given its poor battery life and capacity. He was also extremely skeptical of the touchscreen keyboard. In an interview in 2007, Lazaridis said, "As nice as the Apple iPhone is, it poses a real challenge to its users. Try typing a web key on a touchscreen on an Apple iPhone, that's a real challenge. You cannot see what you type."[12] BlackBerry's inventor believed that consumers preferred typing e-mails and messages using a physical keyboard rather than using a touchscreen. Co-CEO Balsillie declared that the iPhone was "not a sea-changer for BlackBerry."[11]

With further developments in touchscreen phones, consumers cared more about iPhone and Android phones' access to applications rather than battery life, security features, and QWERTY keyboards. The touchscreen smartphones also gained traction among suppliers. Software developers found it easier to work with Android and iPhone systems as compared to Blackberry's complex Java-based system.[3] Consequently, iPhone and Android phones experienced rapid growth and market acceptance, which created internal tensions within RIM. There were those who thought that the company should change its strategy, but the co-CEOs unanimously rejected that notion.

The competitive landscape changed further when the "Bring Your Own Device" (BYOD) trend emerged in 2009, when consumers started to take their personal devices to the workplace.[13] The BYOD trend had been directly related to the BlackBerry and the way the device became popular in the first place. It was the pressure from ground-level employees that led IT departments to adopt the BlackBerry—a bottom up rather than a top down process. All of a sudden those same employees started bringing iOS and Android devices to work. Consumers valued the additional features in iPhone and Android phones, such as cameras, games, and Internet browsing.[3,5]

In several instances, corporations abandoned BlackBerry as the company phone, because products like the iPhone also had e-mail capabilities. Over past years, Android-based smartphones overtook RIM (shown among others in the graph) in terms of market share followed by the iPhone's iOS (see Exhibit 2).

When it was unable to acquire a license to sell iPhones, Verizon contacted RIM with an offer to collaborate on developing an "iPhone killer," which meant a smartphone with touchscreen capabilities and no QWERTY keyboard. The result of this partnership was the "BlackBerry Storm," which unfortunately did not gain popularity among consumers because the Storm's touchscreen was not easy to use, and the device was slow and full of bugs.[3] Verizon subsequently shifted its focus toward Google and its Android operating system, and launched a gigantic marketing campaign for Motorola's Droid smartphone that operated on Google's Android platform. The new campaign called "iDont" highlighted the iPhone's shortcomings.[3] However, instead of hurting Apple, the campaign enabled Android phones to steal market share from companies like Palm, Microsoft, and eventually RIM. The Blackberry Storm debacle ended up hurting the company considerably.

EXHIBIT 2 Global Smartphone Market Shares, 2014–2017

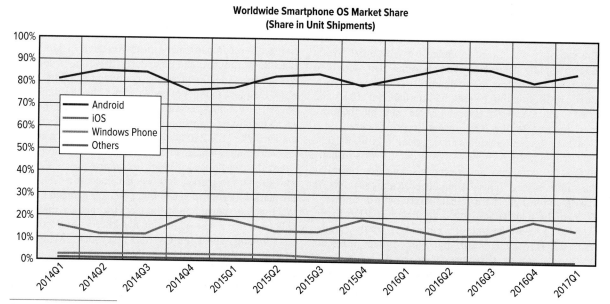

Source: International Data Corporation 2017.

RIM tried its luck with a touchscreen phone once again in 2010, when AT&T contracted with the company to make a competitor to the iPhone. This could help AT&T to differentiate itself from Verizon, which now had obtained licenses for the sale of the iPhone. The result was the "Blackberry Torch," but this too was not a commercial success.

Even though iPhone and Android phones were gaining market share rapidly, Lazaridis remained optimistic about the BlackBerry's sustainable advantage. He warned his fellow RIM directors in a board meeting that trying to sell all-touch smartphones in a crowded market would be a huge mistake.[14] Lazaridis maintained full of confidence that RIM would catch up to Apple and Google (Android) with their newest device, the BlackBerry 10. While developing the BlackBerry 10, Lazaridis decided to acquire QNX Software, a leading-edge software maker. QNX had the technology that the BlackBerry 10 operating system needed.

Tensions were now growing between Balsillie and Lazaridis. Lazaridis was certain that the BlackBerry 10 would resurrect the company, while Balsillie was doubtful.[14] One of the keys to the company's early success had been the co-CEO structure, where Lazaridis was responsible for engineering, product management, and supply chain, while Balsillie focused on sales, finance, and other corporate functions.[3] This complementary leadership structure was successful for a long time, as Lazaridis and Balsillie worked well together. However, the growing tension between the two led to a breakdown of communication, and RIM missed internal deadlines for launch dates as confusion and doubt spread among the company's employees.[3]

In order to fix the problem, Lazaridis decided that for their turnaround project, the BlackBerry 10, the development team would report directly to him and circumvent other top executives like Balsillie. The breakdown of communication and friction between management led to a disastrous 2011 for the company, where RIM's network experienced tremendous difficulties for the first time, and the company was forced to undertake substantial layoffs due to rapidly decreasing sales. Balsillie also started to separate himself from the company. He established an academic institution that focused on international affairs and tried to buy a National Hockey League team, but the move was opposed by the NHL. At an icebreaker event at a weeklong seminar regarding arctic issues in 2010, Balsillie said that BlackBerry's success was due to extraordinary luck at key moments and voiced his concerns regarding the future, saying, "This is a rapidly expanding market. We have a diminishing share of that market, but who knows?"[6] To end the managerial issues, the board at RIM finally decided to relieve Balsillie and Lazaridis from their duties as co-CEOs in January 2012 but allowed them to remain on the Board of Directors. Thorsten Heins replaced Lazaridis and Balsillie as CEO in 2007. Mr. Heins had previously held an executive position at Siemens before joining RIM.[14]

The BBM Messaging Service

To generate revenue for RIM, former co-CEO Balsillie saw great potential with the BBM messaging service. The BBM messenger was developed as an application for the BlackBerry in 2005, and it enabled users to communicate by using their devices' PIN numbers. The BBM was innovative and is credited with being the first instant messaging service on wireless devices.[14] Among the BBM's key strengths were its reliability and the fact that users could send an unlimited number of messages without any extra cost, unlike standard SMS text messaging. Further, the messaging service was very secure and gave users the privacy they sought.

With increasing competition and the decreasing sales and market share of Blackberry, Balsillie wanted to make the BBM platform available on all devices. He envisioned that telecom carriers could integrate BBM as their own enhanced version of SMS text messaging. This could generate additional sales for the carriers, which would get RIM a percentage of the carriers' revenues.[14]

Balsillie's plan created a divide within RIM's management, particularly because BBM was still a key driver of sales of BlackBerry devices. Making the BBM service available to competitors could lead to market cannibalization. As Balsillie continued his push for the BBM strategy, the new CEO squashed it a few weeks after taking office. Lazaridis showed full support for the CEO's decision, and Balsillie subsequently resigned from the Board of Directors in March 2012 and sold all the stock of the company that he possessed.[14] In a statement to Canadian newspaper *Globe and Mail*, Balsillie left no doubt as to why he left: "My reason for leaving the RIM board in March 2012, was due to the company's decision to cancel the BBM cross-platform strategy."[15]

The Blackberry 10

During Heins's tenure as CEO, BlackBerry finally released the BlackBerry 10 in the market in January 2013 and changed the company name from Research in Motion to BlackBerry Limited. The BlackBerry 10 was not a commercial success, and the company continued spiraling downward. Despite a number of good reviews, the new phone did not sell very well. Afterward, Blackberry launched the Z10, an all-touchscreen version to compete in the smartphone market. When the Z10 launched, BlackBerry had a confusing marketing campaign and was unsuccessful in communicating the new device's distinctive competencies.[14] The Z10 was also late to market and was launched at a time when the market was crowded and there was low demand for new touchscreen smartphones. In fact, the people that were willing to buy a new edition of BlackBerrys were consumers who still valued the QWERTY keyboard. Many loyal BlackBerry customers thought that the new system was far too different from the classic BlackBerry design, and that the new phones seemed to have relinquished all ties to old BlackBerry devices. The company incurred a quarterly loss of $965 million in the second quarter of 2013, mostly due to a huge number of BlackBerry Z10 phones that were not sold.[14] As a result of the company's underperformance, Toronto-based investment company Fairfax Financial Holdings Ltd tried to take over Blackberry Limited, offering $4.7 billion, but the deal did not materialize.[16]

Despite RIM's diminishing position in the industry, its management continued to remain optimistic. Former managing director for the U.S. and Canada, Andrew MacLeod, stated, "I am heartened by the fact that we have tons of assets–IP assets, technology assets. We have a culture that at its core is about innovation and are in an industry that moves incredibly fast."[5] This signaled that there was a belief internally at BlackBerry that its core competencies could redefine the industry with new innovations. Lazaridis solidified this notion in an interview to the *Globe and Mail:* "Many companies go through cycles. Intel experienced it, IBM experienced it, and Apple experienced it." He went on to say, "People counted IBM, Apple, and other companies out only to be proven wrong. I am rooting that they are wrong on BlackBerry as well."[14]

In order to prove naysayers wrong, BlackBerry needed to address the immense reduction in sales that it had experienced since FY 2011. The company sold $1.431 billion worth of hardware in FY 2015 (see Exhibit 3), a reduction of 91 percent since FY 2011. Further, the sale of services lost 49 percent, while software performed better with a reduction of 20 percent for the same period.[17, 18, 19, 20]

Future of the Smartphone Industry

The smartphone industry had been experiencing rapid development and high growth during the past decade. There were over a billion units of smartphones shipped worldwide, which constituted more than half of total mobile phone shipments. The industry was a large one, with total industry sales revenue reaching $429 billion in 2016. Although that was a remarkable number, new trends showed that the smartphone industry growth rate had started declining. Growth in smartphone shipments was 40 percent in 2014, down from 46 percent in 2013.[21] This trend was expected to increase in future, as growth in smartphone shipments was forecast at a 9.8 percent compounded annual growth rate for the period 2014–2018, which constituted 1.9 billion units in 2018.[22] The primary culprit for this decrease was the low growth in North American and Western European markets. Most individuals in these countries already had smartphones, so growth was driven by replacement sales due to a low number of first-time buyers. Research showed that as much as 60 percent of sales were expected to be replacements in North America and 40 percent in Western Europe. Along with the increase in reliability and lifespan for smartphones, such replacement sales put a downward pressure on the growth rate. More importantly, only 25 percent of smartphone shipments would go to mature or developed markets by 2018.[21] As a rational response to the conditions in developed markets, smartphone manufacturers were shifting their focus toward emerging markets, for instance, China and India, which were the most lucrative of the emerging markets.[21]

Recent developments had made the industry much more complex and competitive. The most significant development had been the vast reduction in entry barriers, enabling emerging manufacturers to collectively become a significant force in the industry. Low entry barriers were propelled by two trends that were expected to continue. First, Google's Android operating system was open source software that allowed mass adoption and customization. Secondly, turnkey reference designs from chipset companies like Qualcomm and MediaTek were shortening the design and manufacturing process.[21] This was due to the expertise of such tech companies to provide fully packaged solutions with certified and tested components that were ready to go.

Most emerging manufacturers originated out of Shenzhen, China, and they took advantage of the low-cost supply chain of their home market and expanding sales beyond their borders. In December 2014, Chinese smartphone producer Xiaomi cemented its position as the world's most valuable tech start-up, with value exceeding $46 billion.[23] The emergence of low-cost Chinese manufacturers had segmented the market into a two-tier pricing strategy. Xiaomi, Vivo, Huawei, and countless other Chinese no-name brands were making very affordable products with attributes that were good enough for most consumers. Apple had branded its iPhone as a luxury good, where a huge selection of well-implemented apps and other services went a long way to differentiating the iPhone from other smartphones. Because of these features,

EXHIBIT 3 BlackBerry Revenue Mix by Segments, in Millions USD 2015–2017

Segments	FY 2015	FY 2016	FY 2017
Software & Services	249	530	652
Mobility Solutions	1,480	884	409
SAF (System Access Fees)	1,606	779	313
Segment Totals	**3,335**	**2,193**	**1,374**

Source: BlackBerry (RIM) annual reports.

EXHIBIT 4 The Stratagem of Value versus Volume in Smartphone Industry

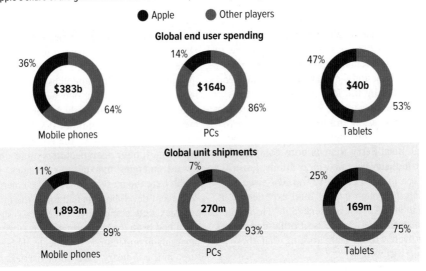

Apple's Strength is in Value Not in Volume
Apple's share of the global device market in 2016 (end user spending and unit shipments)

● Apple   ● Other players

Global end user spending

Mobile phones	PCs	Tablets
36% $383b 64%	14% $164b 86%	47% $40b 53%

Global unit shipments

Mobile phones	PCs	Tablets
11% 1,893m 89%	7% 270m 93%	25% 169m 75%

Source: Statistica Inc. 2017.

Apple was charging a premium for its product, which resulted in high operating margins. Just 11% of the Apple's global market share grabbed 36% of the global end user spending on smartphones (see Exhibit 4).[21] The emergence of Chinese players had put everybody else virtually in a "no-man's land" between Apple and low-cost providers. As a result, average prices on Android phones had dropped, a trend that was likely to continue. Industry forecasts projected smartphones to have an average selling price of $241 worldwide by 2018.

In many respects, the smartphone industry resembled a duopoly. Apple and Samsung accounted for the vast majority of industry sales and for most of the profits generated by the top 10 manufacturers.[21] Nonetheless, Apple and Samsung's dominance and profit margins would be challenged in the future, primarily because of the competition emerging from China. Chinese manufacturers were expected to ship more than 350 million smartphones in 2018. The increase in competition was squeezing industry incumbents such as Motorola, Nokia, and Blackberry, and such competition was vigorously pressuring their profit margins.

Most existing smartphones were similar in design, and had touchscreen capabilities, ranging from four to seven inches. The similarity in design meant that innovation in hardware was at a historic low, because new hardware had to fit existing design models.[21] Curtailed difference in hardware had increased the importance of marketing expenditures, and leading industry incumbents in Western markets were allocating more and more resources to brand building and advertising. Another critical success factor in the industry was intellectual property. IP strength not only protected against infringement claims, but also constituted a significant source of revenue owing to licensing agreements.

By 2017, in operating systems, Android dominated with 81.7 percent market share. Apple's iOS ranked at number 2, with 17.9 percent market share.[24] The main difference between iOS and Android operating systems was that Android was spread across a broad range of manufacturers and prices, while iOS was Apple's exclusive operating system designed only for Apple products. Windows phones were also generating some momentum and had a market share of 0.3 percent in 2017 and ranked number 3 in the industry.[25] Mobile network carriers functioned either with or without subsidies. It was a norm for mobile network operators (such as AT&T and Verizon) to subsidize, or pay, the manufacturer of smartphones to carry their products. In unsubsidized markets, the competition was higher, and the markets were characterized by a more open supply profile in which manufacturers had the incentive to sell directly to the end consumer and circumvent network operators. It might have been beneficial for the market if carriers committed to offering many operating platforms, because doing so would increase competition and reduce the duopoly features of Android and iOS. However, having iOS and Android in their portfolio was ultimately beneficial for carriers because it meant that they distributed the vast majority of products among manufacturers.[21]

Smart Phone Industry Competitor Analysis

Apple Inc.

A major player in the smartphone industry is iPhone by Apple Inc. The company has a core competence in product design, software development, application development, and hardware. Apple Inc. not only targets corporations and

EXHIBIT 5 Selected Information on Apple iPhones (without carrier contract)

Model	iPhone X	iPhone 8 Plus	iPhone 8	iPhone 7 Plus	iPhone 7
Price	$999	$799	$699	$749	$649
Capacity	64 or 256 GB	64 or 256 GB	64 or 256 GB	32, 128, or 256 GB	32, 128, or 256 GB
Display	5.8" Super Retina HD	5.5" Retina HD	4.7" Retina HD	5.5" Retina HD	4.7" Retina HD
Talk time	Up to 21 hours	Up to 21 hours	Up to 14 hours	Up to 21 hours	Up to 14 hours
Intelligent assistant	Siri	Siri	Siri	Siri	Siri

Source: Company websites.

governments as potential customers but also targets general consumers, academic institutions, and SMEs. Most of the Apple products are sold through Apple's own retail and online stores; however, the company also utilizes indirect distribution channels such as telecom carriers, wholesalers, retailers, and value-added resellers. Another core competence for Apple is a continuous focus on R&D, in order to keep up with and lead technological advancements. Apple Inc.'s R&D expenditure was about $10 billion by 2017[25] which is more than most smartphone companies were worth. A significant source of Apple's competitive strength is its ecosystem.[26] Apple's iCloud service enables users to sync a particular file or data on all Apple devices, so if one edits a photo on iPhone, the changes show up automatically on all other devices.[27] These features give Apple users an incentive to purchase other Apple products, because benefits and convenience of use bring value to the consumer. (See Exhibit 5 for information on the most popular iPhone models that are on the market.)

Samsung Electronics Co.

The other major player in the smartphone industry is the South Korean tech giant Samsung Electronics Co. Samsung maintains its leadership status across multiple sectors by investing heavily in R&D. In recent years, Samsung has invested $13 billion in R&D, which has led to 4,676 new patents in the United States alone.[27] Samsung has strategic resources that competitors find hard to replicate, such as substantial economies of scale, which drive down per-unit cost. The company has a very favorable cost structure because of its great efforts in vertical integration. Samsung has an aggressive pricing strategy and allocates a large amount of resources toward marketing expenditures.[28] The company is a dominant force in the Android operating system. With Android, consumers purchase and download multiple applications, similar to Apple's app store. Samsung sells products to authorized distributors, mainly through mobile network carriers or large electronic outlets like Best Buy. Samsung offers a wide range of smartphones with low, medium, and high price points. (See Exhibit 6 for information on the four most popular Samsung smartphones that are competitors of iPhone.)

Restructuring and Future Operations of Blackberry

In March 2013, BlackBerry announced the retirement of Lazaridis as Vice Chair.[29] After the board at BlackBerry abandoned the buyout deal from Fairfax Financial Holdings,

EXHIBIT 6 Information on Selected Samsung Smartphones (by Verizon)

Model	Galaxy S8 plus	Galaxy S8	Galaxy S7 Edge	Galaxy S7
Price	$840	$756	$670	$570
Capacity	64 GB	64 GB	32 GB	32 GB
Display	6.2" Quad HD + & Dual Edged Superv AMOLED	5.8" Quad HD + & Dual Edged Superv AMOLED	5.5" Quad HD SupervAMOLED	5.1" Quad HD SupervAMOLED
Talk time	Up to 34 hours	Up to 30 hours	Up to 28 hours	Up to 28 hours
Intelligent assistant	S Voice	S Voice	S Voice	S Voice

Source: Samsung.[28]

Model	Passport	Leap	DTEK 60	KEYone
Price	$549	$218	$440	$225
Capacity	32 GB	16 GB	32 GB	32 GB
Display	4.5" Square touch display	5" Touch Display	5.2" or 5.5" Fully Touch Display	4.5" Partially Touch Display with Key Hard Board
Talk time	Up to 14 hours	Up to 12 hours	Up to 26 hours	N/A
Operating system	BlackBerry 10 OS	BlackBerry 10 OS	Fully Android	Fully Android

Source: BlackBerry.

Mr. Heins was also ousted, and Mr. John S. Chen was brought in as CEO. Mr. Chen was previously the chairman and CEO of Sybase Inc., and his background also included executive positions at Siemens AG, Pyramid Technology Corp. and Burroughs Corp.[1] In 2014, the company announced a joint venture with Foxconn to develop a consumer smartphone tailored for Indonesia and other growth markets.[30] By 2017, the company carried six different versions of BlackBerry smartphones. Three out of the six smartphones were Android operated while the other half supported BlackBerry's operating system. BlackBerry's recent smartphone models that supported company software had the ability to download apps, through the company's own app store "BlackBerry World," or through the Amazon Android app store[31] (see Exhibit 7 for information regarding BlackBerry smartphones).

According to Chen, the company was in a far better position than industry experts claimed. Under his leadership, BlackBerry intended to return to its core strengths that catered to enterprises with security and efficiencies. Chen's first task as CEO was to restructure the operating units. By 2017, the company had four distinct operating units: Enterprise Software, Secure Communications, Technology Solutions, and Secure Smartphones.[32] Chen believed this structure would lead BlackBerry to an increased focus on software services and would make the smartphones unit more efficient. The company was still the leader when it came to enterprises, with a customer base exceeding 80,000. BlackBerry also continued to remain popular with governments; seven out of the seven G7 countries' governments were BlackBerry customers. Furthermore, the company's BBM messaging service was released for Android and iOS users through their respective app stores. BBM had generated more than 40 million users on Android and iOS devices.[33] Chen saw great potential with BBM, and BlackBerry was expected to continue reinvesting in this technology to update features and channels.

Looking at the revenue trajectory of BlackBerry over past few years, a dramatic drop in the company's revenues couldn't be ignored. Company revenues dropped from $19.9 billion in FY 2011 to $935 million in FY 2017

(see Exhibits 8 and 9 for detailed information regarding BlackBerry's financial situation). Nonetheless, in April 2017, BlackBerry's shareholders received momentous news when the company was awarded $815 million in an arbitration against Qualcomm, which boosted the company's share price more than 18 percent.[34]

Software Security Competitor Analysis

Blackberry's software security division has limited competition in the software security industry as compared to the competition that the company faces in the smartphone (hardware) industry. There is a long list of companies providing a wide range of different types of enterprise security. However, Blackberry Limited specializes in Mobile and Data Security for Enterprises. A few of Blackberry Limited's close competitors in the mobile and data security industry are Symantec, Verizon Enterprise Solutions, and Imperva.

Symantec (Mobile Security)

Symantec is a California-based public limited company founded in April 1982 that offers a variety of mobile security solutions, and its security software is most popularly known as Norton.[35] Symantec specializes in mobile (software) security, and its information security revenue was about $3.77 billion by 2017. Symantec is a large company and employs about 11,000 people around the world.[36] Symantec is a tough competitor for Blackberry. Nevertheless, by maximizing the allocation of resources to its software business, Blackberry might be able to do better than it was doing by the second quarter of 2017.

Verizon Enterprise Solutions (Data Security)

Verizon Enterprise Solutions is a unit of New Jersey–based Verizon Communications that offers mobility and data security solutions. It was founded in 2006 and renamed Verizon Enterprise Solutions in 2012.[37] Verizon Communications is a big player in its competitive market of wireless networks. But Verizon Enterprise Solutions is relatively new in the software security industry. No doubt a company backed by such a giant market player is a challenge for Blackberry

EXHIBIT 8 Blackberry Consolidated Statement of Operations, 2017

BlackBerry Limited **(United States dollars, in millions, except per share data)** **Consolidated Statements of Operations**			
	For the Years Ended		
	February 28, 2017	**February 29, 2016**	**February 28, 2015**
Revenue			
Software, services and service access fees	$ 935	$1,276	$1,854
Hardware and other	374	884	1,481
	1,309	2,160	3,335
Cost of sales			
Software, services and service access fees	109	247	287
Hardware and other	433	936	1,349
Inventory write-down	150	36	95
	692	1,219	1,731
Gross margin	617	941	1,604
Operating expenses			
Research and development	306	469	711
Selling, marketing and administration	553	653	769
Amortization	186	277	298
Impairment of goodwill	57	—	—
Impairment of long-lived assets	501	—	—
Loss on sale, disposal and abandonment of long-lived assets	171	195	169
Debentures fair value adjustment	24	(430)	80
	1,798	1,164	2,027
Operating loss	(1,181)	(223)	(423)
Investment income (loss), net	(27)	(59)	38
Loss before income taxes	(1,208)	(282)	(385)
Recovery of income taxes	(2)	(74)	(81)
Net loss	$(1,206)	$ (208)	$ (304)
Loss per share			
Basic	$ (2.30)	$ (0.40)	$ (0.58)
Diluted	$ (2.30)	$ (0.86)	$ (0.58)

Source: Blackberry Financial Documents, Blackberry Inc., 2017.

EXHIBIT 9 Blackberry Balance Sheet, 2017

BlackBerry Limited
Incorporated under the Laws of Ontario
(United States dollars, in millions)
Consolidated Balance Sheets

	As at	
	February 28, 2017	February 29, 2016
Assets		
Current		
Cash and cash equivalents	$ 734	$ 957
Short-term investments	644	1,420
Accounts receivable, net	181	338
Other receivables	34	51
Inventories	26	143
Income taxes receivable	17	—
Other current assets	55	102
	1,691	3,011
Long-term investments	269	197
Restricted cash and cash equivalents	51	50
Property plant and equipment, net	91	412
Goodwill	559	618
Intangible assets, net	602	1,213
Deferred income tax asset	—	33
	$3,263	$5,534
Liabilities		
Current		
Accounts payable	$ 103	$ 270
Accrued liabilities	258	368
Income taxes payable	—	9
Deferred revenue	245	392
	606	1,039
Long-term debt	591	1,277
Deferred income tax liability	9	10
	1,206	2,326
Shareholders' equity		
Capital stock and additional paid-in capital		
Issued - 530,497,193 voting common shares (February 29, 2016 - 521,172,271)	2,512	2,448
Retained earnings (deficit)	(438)	768
Accumulated other comprehensive loss	(17)	(8)
	2,057	3,208
	$3,263	$5,534

Source: Blackberry Financial Documents, Blackberry Inc., 2017.

Limited, yet a well-thought-out Blackberry strategy might turn out to be a success in the long run.

Imperva (Data Security)

Imperva is a California-based public limited company that provides a variety of data security solutions. It was founded in 2002.[38] It employs almost 1,000 people and operates in approximately 100 countries. Imperva's revenue for fiscal year 2017 was about $264 million. Imperva has also experienced financial difficulties as its stock performance has been volatile over the past years.[39] Hence, Blackberry certainly might successfully compete against Imperva.

Future of Blackberry

Industry experts believe BlackBerry's sales are yet to bottom out, putting a strain on the company's cost structure. In a very crowded and highly competitive industry, the road to profitability will not come easy for Blackberry and will certainly test the company's managerial skills as well as strategic thinking at higher levels. With rumors and speculations surrounding the Canadian tech giant's future running rampant, Chen released an open letter to BlackBerry users, highlighting the company's strengths, commitment to innovation, and dedication to "earning your business—or earning it back."[40] The letter diminished speculations regarding a potential sale of the company, but a profitable future is still uncertain. Chen has difficult strategic choices to make. Nonetheless, on December 20, 2016, Blackberry reported a GAAP gross margin of 67 percent driven by tremendous growth in software and service revenue.[41] Looking at the changing momentum of BlackBerry's leadership as well as financial inflow, an objective observer might perhaps be optimistic that BlackBerry can make a big comeback.

ENDNOTES

1. *Bloomberg Business.* "BBRY:US." Bloomberg LP, September 22, 2016. From the web: http://www.bloomberg.com/quote/BBRY:US.

2. Tsai, Allan. "The True Story Behind the Rise and Fall of BlackBerry." 2machines Corp., 2013. From the web: http://2machines.com/184127/.

3. Silcoff, Sean, McNish, Jacquie, and Erman, Boyd. "BlackBerry Financing Aims for a New Lease of Life." *The Globe and Mail,* November 4, 2013. From the web: http://www.theglobeandmail.com/report-on-business/blackberry-fairfax-deal-dies-thorsten-heins-out/article15240310/.

4. CBC News. "BlackBerry CEO Chen on His Turnaround Strategy." *CBC/Radio-Canada,* March 28, 2014. From the web: http://www.cbc.ca/news/business/blackberry-ceo-john-chen-on-his-turnaround-strategy-1.2590576.

5. Gillette, Felix; Brady, Diane; and Winter, Caroline. "The Rise and Fall of BlackBerry: An Oral History." December 5, 2013. From the web: http://www.bloomberg.com/bw/articles/2013-12-05/the-rise-and-fall-of-blackberry-an-oral-history#p3.

6. CBC News. "BlackBerry Timeline: A Tech Titans Roller Coaster Ride." *CBC/Radio-Canada,* March 17, 2014. From the web: http://www.cbc.ca/news2/interactives/timeline-rim/.

7. Global News Staff, "BlackBerry Timeline: A Look Back at The Tech Company's History." September 24, 2013. From the web: http://globalnews.ca/news/860689/blackberry-timeline-a-look-back-at-the-tech-companys-history/

8. *The Telegraph.* "BlackBerrys Timeline: From RIM to RIP?" August 12, 2013. From the web: http://www.telegraph.co.uk/technology/blackberry/10237847/BlackBerry-timeline-from-RIM-to-RIP.html.

9. Research in Motion. "Annual Report Fiscal 2000." Research in Motion. From the web: http://us.blackberry.com/content/dam/bbCompany/Desktop/Global/PDF/Investors/Documents/2000/2000rim_ar.pdf.

10. http://www.nytimes.com/2001/09/20/technology/the-right-connections-the-simple-blackberry-allowed-contact-when-phones-failed.html.

11. *TheAtlas.* "Global Smartphone Market Share Held by RIM (BlackBerry) from 2007 to 2015." *TheAtlas,* September 27, 2016. From the web: https://www.theatlas.com/charts/4kkGhxGWx.

12. Arthur, Charles. "RIM Chiefs Mike Lazaridis and Jim Balsillie's Best Quotes." *Guardian News and Media Limited,* June 29, 2012. From the web: http://www.theguardian.com/technology/2012/jun/29/rim-chiefs-best-quotes.

13. Information Security Media Group Corp. "Mobile: Learn from Intel's CISO on Securing Employee-Owned Devices." May 10, 2015. From the web: http://www.govinfosecurity.com/webinars/mobile-learn-from-intels-ciso-on-securing-employee-owned-devices-w-264.

14. Silcoff, Sean; McNish, Jacquie; and Laudrantaye, Steve. "Inside the BlackBerry: How the Smartphone Inventor Failed to Adapt." *The Globe and Mail,* September 27, 2013. From the web: http://www.theglobeandmail.com/report-on-business/the-inside-story-of-why-blackberry-is-failing/article14563602/

15. CBC News. "Balsillie Quit BlackBerry over Mixed BBM Plan." *CBC/Radio-Canada,* September 30, 2013. From the web: http://www.cbc.ca/news/canada/kitchener-waterloo/balsillie-quit-blackberry-over-nixed-bbm-plan-report-1.1872572

16. Zettel, Jonathan. "BlackBerry Links US$4.7 Billion Deal with Toronto-based Fairfax." Bell Media, September 23, 2013. From the web: http://www.ctvnews.ca/business/blackberry-inks-us-4-7-billion-deal-with-toronto-based-fairfax-1.1466420.

17. BlackBerry Limited. "Form 40-F Fiscal 2015." BlackBerry Limited. From the web: http://us.blackberry.com/content/dam/bbCompany/Desktop/Global/PDF/Investors/Documents/2014/Q4_FY14_Filing.pdf.

18. BlackBerry Limited. "Form 40-F Fiscal 2014." BlackBerry Limited. From the web: http://us.blackberry.com/content/dam/bbCompany/Desktop/Global/PDF/Investors/Documents/2014/Q4_FY14_Filing.pdf.

19. Research in Motion. "Form 40-F Fiscal 2013." Research in Motion. From the web: http://press.blackberry.com/content/dam/rim/press/PDF/Financial/FY2013/Q4FY13_final_filing.pdf.

20. Research in Motion. "Form 40-F Fiscal 2012." Research in Motion. From the web: http://us.blackberry.com/content/dam/bbCompany/Desktop/Global/PDF/Investors/Documents/2012/2012rim_ar_40F.pdf.

21. CCS Insight. "Global Smartphone Market Analysis and Outlook: Disruption in Changing Market." *CCS Insight,* July 2014. From the web: http://www.lenovo.com/transactions/pdf/CCS-Insight-Smartphone-Market-Analysis-Full-Report-07-2014.pdf.

22. Llamas, Ramon; Chau, Melissa; and Shirer, Michael. "Worldwide Smartphone Growth Forecast to Slow from a Boil to a Simmer as Prices Drop and Markets Mature." *IDC Corporate USA.* From the web: http://www.idc.com/getdoc.jsp?containerId=prUS25282214.

23. Mims, Christopher. "In Smartphone Market, It's Luxury or Rock Bottom." *The Wall Street Journal,* February 1, 2015. From the web: http://www.wsj.com/articles/in-smartphone-market-its-luxury-or-rock-bottom-1422842032.

24. https://www.statista.com/statistics/266136/global-market-share-held-by-smartphone-operating-systems.

25. http://www.businessinsider.com/apples-cfo-explains-the-companys-10-billion-rd-budget-2017-2.

26. Jackson, Eric. "Apple Isn't a Hardware or Software Company—It's an Ecosystem Company." *Forbes.com,* June 3, 2014. From the web: http://www.forbes.com/sites/ericjackson/2014/06/03/apple-isnt-a-hardware-or-software-company-its-an-ecosystem-company/2/.

27. Samsung. "About Samsung—The Way Forward." Samsung Group. From the web: http://www.samsung.com/us/aboutsamsung/samsung_group/download/2014-aboutsamsung-eng.pdf.

28. Samsung Electronics. "Cell Phones." Samsung Group. From the web: http://www.samsung.com/us/mobile/phones/galaxy-s/galaxy-s8-plus-64gb–verizon–midnight-black-sm-g955uzkavzw/#specs.

29. Tibken, Share. "BlackBerry Co-founder Lazaridis to Retire May 1st." CBS Interactive Inc., March 28, 2013. From the web: http://www.samsung.com/us/mobile/cell-phones.

30. Cochrane, Joe, and Austen, Ian. "BlackBerry's Partnership with Foxconn Signals Shifting Priorities." *The New York Times,* May 18, 2014. From the web: http://www.nytimes.com/2014/05/19/technology/blackberrys-partnership-with-foxconn-signals-a-shift.html?_r=0.

31. BlackBerry. "Smartphones." BlackBerry Limited. From the web: https://us.blackberry.com/smartphones.

32. Chen, John. "BlackBerry: The Way Forward." CNBC LLC. December 30, 2013. From the web: http://www.cnbc.com/id/101300396.

33. Symantec Company Profile. From the web: https://www.symantec.com/about/corporate-profile.

34. http://www.cnbc.com/2017/04/12/blackberry-awarded-815-million-in-arbitration-case-against-qualcomm.html.

35. Symantec Company Profile. From the web: https://www.symantec.com/about/corporate-profile.

36. See https://www.symantec.com/content/dam/symantec/docs/data-sheets/corporate-fact-sheet-en.pdf.

37. Verizon Enterprise website. "Solutions," http://www.verizonenterprise.com/solutions.

38. See https://www.imperva.com/docs/Imperva_Company_Overview.pdf.

39. See https://finance.yahoo.com/quote/impv/financials?ltr=1.

40. Chen, John. "An Open Letter from John Chen." September 29, 2014. BlackBerry Inc. From the web: http://blogs.blackberry.com/2014/10/classic-john-chen/.

41. https://us.blackberry.com/company/newsroom/press.

CASE 33

ASCENA: ODDS OF SURVIVAL IN SPECIALTY RETAIL?*

In the first quarter of 2017 ten retailers filed for bankruptcy, with nineteen others teetering on a "distressed" list,[1] giving 2017 the dubious distinction of being the worst year for retailing since 2009 when eighteen entities closed shop.[2] Names of shuttered and at-risk stores in 2017 included footwear and apparel retailers BCBG Max Azria, Eastern Outfitters, Wet Seal, Limited Stores, Payless, Bon-Ton, Claire's Stores, rue21, Gymboree, and Toms Shoes. Other chains such as the department stores Macy's, J.C. Penney, Sears, and Kmart, and smaller specialty retailers Aeropostale, Abercrombie & Fitch, and Sports Authority were closing stores, consolidating operations, and trying to figure out what to do when top-line growth inevitably slowed.

Customers need a reason to shop. Whether it be in a physical location or online, the shopping experience needs to be appealing, not only in quality and assortment of merchandise, but also in customer service and personalization options, including how browsing, ordering, and payment systems are integrated seamlessly across channels. Although analysts expected 2017 to be no worse for apparel retailers than 2016, and even expected single digit growth in some venues, the opinion was that the apparel sector would "struggle to remain a priority spend . . . as younger consumers seek and spend on services and experiences more than ever." There was a need for innovative concepts in both the shopping experience and back-end operations, and those retailers who didn't embrace change would suffer: "it will be mission-critical for brands to converge all their channels and touchpoints into single, seamless, branded shopping experiences."[3] Commenting on the closing of Ralph Lauren's New York City flagship store, one researcher noted, "at the end of the day, there is no natural law that suggests that an iconic brand, as iconic as his has been, is guaranteed to be successful forever and always."[4] This comment could also apply to other iconic retailers. Just having a powerful brand strategy might not be enough. There was a paradigm shift under way, and only those with results-oriented operations might be able to survive and thrive.

Going into 2017, Ascena Retail Group, Inc. (NASDAQ: ASNA), owners of a well-rounded portfolio of brands providing women's and girl's specialty apparel, was trying to digest recent acquisitions and position itself for this challenge. The biggest and most recent news concerned Ascena's acquisition of ANN INC., iconic specialty retailer of women's apparel provided under its Ann Taylor, LOFT, and Lou & Grey brands. Since 2014 ANN had seen poor product performance in its core Ann Taylor brand, forcing it to engage in widespread discounting in order to move product.[5] Although this discounting activity was not an unusual strategy employed by retailers facing declining traffic, ANN had other problems. ANN's missed earning projections, stagnant same-store sales, slow inventory turnover, and significant margin compression had activist investors demanding additional changes. These realities led to the announcement, in August 2015, that ANN INC. had been acquired by Ascena.

With the acquisition of ANN, Ascena Retail Group became the largest U.S. specialty retailer focused exclusively on women and girls. Only exceeded in net sales by L Brands, the owner of Victoria's Secret and Bath & Body Works, and by The Gap, Inc., Ascena offered apparel, shoes, and accessories for women and girls. Ascena operated four focused, branded retail options: the "Premium Fashion" segment with brands Ann Taylor, LOFT, and Lou & Grey; the "Value Fashion" segment, represented by the brands Maurices and Dressbarn; its "Plus Fashion" segment with Lane Bryant and Catherine's stores; and merchandise for tween girls via the Justice brand, under the "Kids Fashion" segment. Ascena also offered intimate apparel via Cacique and Catherine's Intimates. The ANN acquisition meant Ascena had expanded its brand profile even further across multiple segments, and would operate over 4,900 stores with annual projected sales of more than $7 billion.

Ascena Retail Group acquired ANN INC. in 2015 for $47 per share in an accretive transaction where ANN stockholders received $37.34 in cash and 0.68 of a share of Ascena common stock in exchange for each share of ANN. After the closing, ANN stockholders ended up owning approximately 16 percent of Ascena. As a result of the acquisition, Ascena not only gained a presence in the premium women's fashion market, but also hoped to realize $150 million in annualized run rate synergies through the integration of ANN's sourcing, procurement, distribution, and logistics operations. This anticipated synergy was a potential lifeline for ANN, but what might it mean for Ascena? Ascena had had disappointing same-store sales in its previous portfolio for several years, and had boosted overall revenue primarily through acquisitions. Industrywide

* This case was prepared by Associate Professor Pauline Assenza, Western Connecticut State University, and Professor Alan B. Eisner of Pace University. Special acknowledgment to Janelle T. Bennett, graduate student at Pace University, for research assistance. This case is solely based on library research and was developed for class discussion of strategies rather than to illustrate either effective or ineffective handling of the situation. Copyright © 2017 Pauline Assenza and Alan B. Eisner.

retail sales projections continued to be on the soft side, and many analysts worried that the increased debt Ascena now carried into 2017 would need positive cash flow in order to provide adequate coverage. Given the uncertainty, analysts wondered if Ascena had pursued a growth strategy at the wrong time, asking, "did Ascena overplay its hand and is ANN's acquisition a threat for the company?"[6]

Ascena Retail Group Background

In 1962 there were few wear-to-work dresses and other clothing options for women entering the workforce, so Roslyn Jaffe and her husband Eliot opened the first Dress Barn in Stanford, Connecticut. By 1982 the company had become successful enough to go public as NASDAQ:DBRN and by 1985 they were operating 200 stores through the U.S. Their vision of working women ages 35 to 55 expanded in 1989 with the opening of Dress Barn Woman, targeting plus-size individuals.

In the 1990s trends in workplace fashion for women had shifted to a more casual look, and the company began to offer more sportswear, and expanded into shoes, petites, and jewelry. In 2002, Eliot and Roslyn's son David succeeded Eliot as CEO, while the elder Jaffe remained as chairman. Then, following the diversification trend, in 2005 Dress Barn Inc. acquired Maurices, a clothing chain from Duluth, Minnesota, that catered to women ages 17 to 34 who shopped primarily in the small-town strip malls of mid-America. Maurices was known for having sizing from 0–26 and employing "stylists" who could outfit customers for a reasonable price. In 2009, Dress Barn acquired Justice, the tween brand chain from New Albany, Ohio, that offered reasonably priced clothing and accessories to girls aged 7 to 14. Justice was formerly owned by Tween Brands, originally a subsidiary of The Limited.

In 2011 Dress Barn reorganized as Ascena Retail Group and changed its stock symbol to NASDAQ:ASNA. The following year Ascena acquired Charming Shoppes, adding the Land Bryant and Catherine's plus-size brands to its portfolio. The Cacique line of intimates, sleepwear, and swimwear and Catherine's Intimates were added later to round out the offerings for full-sized women. The acquisition of ANN with its brands Ann Taylor, LOFT, and Lou & Grey in 2015 meant Ascena had ten brands across four segments, a portfolio meant to serve the many wardrobing needs of women and tween girls, in all different ages, sizes, and demographics.

The New Acquisition: ANN Brands

Founded in 1954, Ann Taylor had been the traditional wardrobe source for busy, socially upscale women, and the classic basic black dress and woman's power suit with pearls were Ann Taylor staples. The Ann Taylor client base consisted of fashion-conscious women from age 25 to 55. The overall Ann Taylor concept was designed to appeal to professional women who had limited time to shop and who were attracted to Ann Taylor stores by their total wardrobing strategy, personalized client service, efficient store layouts, and continual flow of new merchandise.

ANN had regularly appeared in the *Women's Wear Daily* Top 10 list of firms selling dresses, suits, and evening wear and the Top 20 list of publicly traded women's specialty retailers, and had three branded divisions focused on different segments of its customer base:

- Ann Taylor (AT), the company's original brand, provided sophisticated, versatile, and high-quality updated classics.
- Ann Taylor LOFT (LOFT), launched in 1998, was a newer brand concept that appealed to women who had a more relaxed lifestyle and work environment and who appreciated the more casual LOFT style and compelling value. Certain clients of Ann Taylor and LOFT cross-shopped both brands.
- Lou & Grey had evolved from the LOFT lounge collection in 2014 as a full lifestyle brand. Incorporating easygoing, texture-rich clothing with a selection of accessories and more, handcrafted by independent U.S. makers, Lou & Grey was for the woman on the go who didn't want to have to choose between style and comfort.

Additional Ascena Portfolio Brands

In addition to the Premium Fashion ANN brands Ann Taylor, LOFT, and Lou & Grey, the Ascena portfolio included the following:

Total Value Fashion

- Dressbarn—over 800 store locations throughout the U.S. with private label and contemporary fashions at great value to women in their mid-30s to mid-50s, including women's career, special occasion, casual, activewear, accessories, and footwear.
- Maurices—up-to-date casual, career/dressy, and athleisure fashion designed to appeal to middle-income females in their 20s and 30s in core and plus sizes who preferred a "hometown retailer." Over 40 percent of the almost 1,000 stores were in the Midwest, with 37 stores in Canada.

Total Plus Fashion

- Lane Bryant—with over 770 locations, this was the most widely recognized brand name in plus-size fashion, catering to middle-income, female customers aged 25 to 45 in sizes 12–28 through private labels Lane Bryant, Cacique, and Livi Active. Products included intimate apparel, wear-to-work, casual sportswear, activewear, accessories, select footwear, and social occasion apparel.
- Catherine's—catered to women in U.S. sizes 16W–34W and 0X–5X. With over 370 stores nationwide, Catherine's had a competitive advantage with female consumers looking for hard-to-find extended sizes in clothing and intimates.

Total Kids Fashion

- Justice—offering fashionable apparel to 6 to 12-year-old tween girls in an energetic environment. In over 930 locations, products included apparel, activewear, footwear, intimates, accessories, and lifestyle products. The brand was positioned at the mid- to upper-end of pricing.

In 2017, with this portfolio, Ascena appeared solidly positioned to serve the specialty apparel needs of women and girls from multiple consumer sectors. However, there were some significant challenges.

Apparel Retail Industry

Industry Sectors

To better appreciate the issues facing Ascena, it's helpful to understand the apparel retail industry. Several industry publications report data within the clothing sector. In addition to industry associations such as the National Retail Federation (NRF), the *Daily News Record* (DNR) reports on men's fashion news and business strategies, while *Women's Wear Daily* (WWD) reports on women's fashions and the apparel business. Practically speaking, industry watchers tend to recognize three categories of clothing retailers:

- *Discount mass merchandisers:* Chains such as Target, Walmart, TJX (T.J. Maxx, Marshall's, HomeGoods), and Costco.
- *Multitier department stores:* Those offering a large variety of goods, including clothing (e.g., full price examples Macy's and JCPenney, lower price options Ross Stores and Kohls), and the more luxury-goods-focused stores (e.g., Nordstrom and Neiman Marcus).
- *Specialty store chains:* Those catering to a certain type of customer or carrying a certain type of goods, for example, Abercrombie & Fitch for casual apparel.

More specifically in the case of specialty retail, many broadly recognized primary categories exist, such as women's, men's, and children's clothing stores (e.g., Victoria's Secret for women's undergarments,[7] Men's Wearhouse for men's suits, Abercrombie Kids for children ages 7 to 14[8]). Women's specialty stores are "establishments primarily engaged in retailing a specialized line of women's, juniors' and misses' clothing."[9]

Specialty Retailer Growth: Branding Challenges

Unlike department stores that sell many different types of products for many types of customers, specialty retailers focus on one type of product item and offer many varieties of that item. However, this single-product focus increases risk, as lost sales in one area cannot be recouped by a shift of interest to another, entirely different product area. Therefore, many specialty retailers constantly seek new market segments (i.e., niches) that they can serve. However, this strategy creates potential problems for branding.[10]

The Gap Inc. is an example of a specialty retailer that added several brand extensions to appeal to different customer segments. In addition to the original Gap line of casual clothing, the company offered the following: Old Navy with casual fashions at low prices, Banana Republic for more high-end casual items, and Athleta with performance apparel and gear for active women. Regarding other brand extensions, Gap spent $40 million to open a chain for upscale women's clothing called Forth & Towne, which closed after only 18 months. The store was supposed to appeal to upscale women over 35—the baby-boomer or "misses" segment—but, instead, the designers seemed "too focused on reproducing youthful fashions with a more generous cut" instead of finding an "interesting, affordable way" for middle-aged women to "dress like themselves."[11] Gap also acquired Intermix, providing curated designer fashions in upscale boutiques, and Weddington Way, a virtual showroom for bridesmaid dresses: customers would view the items online, discuss using social media, and then visit one of The Gap's other stores to try on and purchase their choices. These acquisitions were attempts to adapt to the new retail business models, providing personalization and the ability for younger customers to browse, order and shop across what should be seamlessly integrated channels. As of 2017, The Gap was the industry's leading specialty retailer.

Chico's FAS Inc. is another specialty retailer that tried brand expansions. Chico's focused on private-label, casual-to-dressy clothing for women age 35 and older, with relaxed, figure-flattering styles constructed out of easy-care fabrics. An outgrowth of a Mexican folk art boutique, Chico's was originally a stand-alone entity, but made the decision to promote two new brands: White House/Black Market (WH/BM) and Soma by Chico's (Soma). Chico's WH/BM brand was based on the acquisition of an existing store chain, and it focused on women age 25 and older, offering fashion and merchandise in black-and-white and related shades. Soma was a brand offering intimate apparel, sleepwear, and active wear. Each brand had its own storefront, mainly in shopping malls, and was augmented by both mail-order catalog and Internet sales.

Similar to other women's specialty retailers, Chico's had seen increasing competition for its baby-boomer customers, and at one time had lost momentum, partly because of "fashion missteps" and lack of sufficiently new product designs. The company's response was to create brand presidents for the different divisions to create more "excitement and differentiation."[12] Subsequently, Chico's FAS had been able to manage its market well, and by 2017, with its strong balance sheet and little debt, was a leading omni-channel specialty retailer of private branded, sophisticated, casual-to-dressy clothing, intimates, and complementary accessories for women aged 35 and older.

In an attempt to better manage the proliferation of brands, many firms, similar to Chico's, created an organizational structure in which brands had their own dedicated managers, with titles such as executive vice president (EVP), general merchandise manager, chief merchandising officer, or outright "brand president."[13] With each brand supposedly unique, companies felt the person responsible for a brand's creative vision should be unique as well. Ascena is an example of how this structure worked: each of the segments was led by a CEO, CFO or President with expertise in that area. For instance, the Premium Fashion segment, containing the ANN brands, was run by Gary Muto, previously President of all ANN's brands, throughout all channels.

An alternative to brand extension is the divestiture of brands, and here's where history might be informative— Ascena might want to take note. In 1988, Limited Brands acquired Abercrombie and Fitch (A&F) and rebuilt A&F into what would become its current iconic representation of the "preppy" lifestyle of teenagers and college students ages 18 to 22. In 1996, Limited Brands spun A&F off as a separate public company, and by 2017 A&F was facing declining revenues, closing stores, and looking for a buyer.[14] Limited Brands had continued divesting:

- Teenage clothing and accessories brand The Limited TOO was divested in 1999, eventually became Justice, and was acquired by Ascena in 2009.
- Plus-size women's clothing brand Lane Bryant was sold to Charming Shoppes in 2001 and subsequently bought by Ascena in 2012.
- Professional women's clothing brand Lerner New York was divested in 2002, and in 2007 the casual women's clothing brands Express and The Limited were sold to Sun Capital Partners. Sun Capital ran these stores under The Limited brand until it filed for bankruptcy on January 7, 2017.

In 2013 Limited Brands renamed itself L Brands. Paring down in order to focus mostly on its key assets, Victoria's Secret and Bath & Body Works, the corporation had made a clear strategic decision to limit its exposure to changing clothing trends.[15] This strategy was successful. In 2017, L Brands, at $12 billion net sales, with Pink, La Senza and Henri Bendel in addition to its other two iconic brands, was the second largest specialty apparel retailer in the U.S. L Brands secured the spot behind Gap and just ahead of Ascena. Gap had five brands, L Brands had five, and Ascena had ten.

Women's Specialty Retail: Competitors and the Challenge of the "Misses" Segment

The National Retail Federation, a trade group based in Washington, DC, had proposed that the retail niches anticipating the greatest growth were department stores, stores catering to the teenage children of baby boomers, and apparel chains aimed at women over 35.[16] This group of older women was part of the baby-boomer demographic, born between 1946 and 1964, and retailers had been eager to tap this segment's purchasing power.[17] The four major women's specialty retailers that had tried to target these older upscale shoppers were Ann Taylor, Chico's FAS, Coldwater Creek, and Talbots. Ann Taylor was the only one

of these with a significant brand extension for the younger professional, but all four had tried to pursue a shopping environment and merchandise clearly focused on the "misses" segment. Although it seemed the rewards were there if a retailer could figure it out, this had been difficult to do.

Women's specialty retailer Talbots Inc., a stalwart destination for mature upscale women since 1948, had acquired catalog and mail order company J.Jill Group in an attempt to offer casual fashion through multichannel mail order, Internet, and in-store venues. J.Jill targeted women ages 35 to 55, while Talbots focused on the 45 to 65 age group. Although the acquisition had supposedly positioned Talbots as a "leading apparel retailer for the highly coveted age 35+ female population,"[18] Talbots subsequently decided to sell off this division, and by 2013 Talbots had shut dozens of stores and been bought out by a private equity firm for less than $3 per share.[19]

Coldwater Creek, with its large jewelry, accessory, and gift assortment in addition to apparel, described itself as "the fashion informed advocate for the 50 year old woman."[20] The company had begun in 1984 by appealing with a Northwest/Southwest lifestyle approach and subsequently included a group of spa locations. The company was unable to successfully weather economic fluctuations, and consistently had to close stores and reconsider merchandise decisions. In 2014, Coldwater Creek filed for bankruptcy, and was subsequently purchased by the same private equity group that previously acquired Talbots.[21] Although both companies were still operating in 2017, the stories of Talbots and Coldwater Creek illustrate how hard it can be for retailers to try to appeal to niche customer segments.[22]

Chico's FAS was one of the first to introduce the concept of apparel designed for the lifestyle of dynamic mature women who were at the higher-age end of the boomer demographic.[23] Of the four retailers targeting the "mature women" segment, Chico's was the only one successful with inventory control, supply-chain management, and a strategy for reducing reliance on China's manufacturing power, and therefore was considered the winner of the group.[24] In 2017 Chico's FAS was still a solidly focused niche performer.

ANN had also considered creating a new chain of stores targeting this "older-women" segment. However, noting The Gap's experience with Forth & Towne, research showed it was not feasible. Instead, ANN made the decision to sell clothes to more affluent women in general, regardless of age range. By the time of the Ascena acquisition, ANN had over twice as many LOFT stores as Ann Taylor stores, and the LOFT customer was normally a younger woman.

Further differentiating within the LOFT space, LOFT Lounge was created to highlight a more relaxed, casual style. This store-in-store venue allowed for the testing of a new brand concept under the Lou & Grey name. Lou & Grey was a move into the active-wear fashion space, and included lace sweat pants, knit moto jackets and linen T-shirts. The intent was to pull in "a younger clientele, while not alienating 40- and 50-year-olds."[25] In 2014 the first free-standing Lou & Grey store opened in Westport, CT. This portfolio, with Ann Taylor, LOFT, and Lou & Grey combining to address the shopping preferences of women of all ages and lifestyles, was what Ascena acquired in 2015 and was positioning for success in all segments in 2017. This history of the pursuit of the "misses" segment demonstrates once again how difficult it is to define a consistently profitable niche strategy in specialty retail. Would Ascena be able to do this with its decision to provide a broad range of brand offerings?

Ascena Retail Group Operations

According to Ascena's CEO David Jaffe, in 2017 Ascena was the largest specialty retailer focused exclusively on women and girls, and had a well-diversified portfolio of brands, covering multiple customer segments. Ascena had a revenue base spread across multiple real estate formats, and an efficient, scalable shared services platform. A $300[+] million investment from FY13 to FY16 had consolidated corporate functions and created a global sourcing capability. An efficient distribution and fulfillment network fully supported an omni-channel platform, both online and in store. In 2017 Ascena's strong cash flow and liquidity was also positioned to navigate industry change.

Ascena intended to evolve from the original seven $1 billion companies into ONE $7 billion powerhouse, using that "combined strength, expertise and scale to exceed our customers' expectations and become a leader in specialty retail."[26] Ascena planned to do this via "centers of excellence" in procurement, global sourcing, real estate expertise, digital/customer platforms, supply chain optimization, and advanced analytics, with corporate oversight for human resources and finance. Refining the capabilities it had acquired with ANN, this would transform the enterprise through centralization, standardization, and using better methodologies and best practices. Through efficiency (reducing costs) and effectiveness (increasing capabilities) Ascena hoped to drive top line sales at profitable margins.

At the end of FY2016 Ascena had over 4,900 stores located throughout the U.S. in various real estate configurations. The majority of stores were located in strip malls, but the ANN properties were in downtown locations that attracted more affluent lifestyle customers. (See Exhibit 1.) Acknowledging the challenges of 2017, Ascena had agreed it "probably" had too many stores, and was developing a "fleet optimization project" that would reduce the physical footprint as it transferred more business either to nearby stores or online.[27]

In addition to physical shopping locations, Ascena was investing in technology platforms to support the growth of its omni-channel strategy. ANN, Justice, and Maurices all had e-commerce platforms, with the other brands scheduled to roll out in FY2017. Retailers in 2017 had to have an omni-channel strategy in order to compete. ANN had already brought Ascena the capability to ship from store, use an iPad app to shop an "endless aisle," do cross-channel returns, and use an "online find" app in the store. Upcoming, ANN and other Ascena brands would add the capability to buy online and pick up in the store, provide for alternative payments using a 1-click checkout, and allow enhanced site reviews.[28]

Ascena Retail Group Financial Profile

Sales at the Ascena Retail Group were now at almost $7.0 billion. Growth had been the result of acquisitions and the expansion of technology platforms to augment e-commerce. Exhibit 2 represents a detailed income statement by segment for the last three fiscal years. Indicating the role of acquisitions, without ANN, FY2016 sales would have been $3,562 million versus $4,802.9 in FY2015. Of note was the FY2015 loss of $308 million for impairment of Lane Bryant's goodwill and intangible assets incurred during its 2012 acquisition, and a $62.8 million loss due partly to the settlement of a class action regarding falsely advertised pricing at Justice. Going forward, it was expected that the synergies resulting from these acquisitions would reduce costs of sales.

However, results from the second quarter of 2017 showed a decline in comparable sales in all segments, and a reduction in net numbers across the board. (See Exhibits 3 to 6.)

EXHIBIT 1 Ascena Shopping Facilities as of July 30, 2016

Type of Facility	ANN	Justice	Lane Bryant	maurices	dressbarn	Catherines	Total
Strip Shopping Centers	56	209	383	568	600	362	2,178
Enclosed Malls	348	518	190	349	52	6	1,463
Outlet Malls and Outlet Strip Centers	265	113	115	56	157	2	708
Lifestyle Centers and Downtown Locations	353	97	84	20	—	3	557
Total	1,022	937	772	993	809	373	4,906

EXHIBIT 2 Net Sales & Operating Income Fiscal Year 2014–2016

	Fiscal 2016	Fiscal 2015	Fiscal 2014
Net sales:		(millions)	
ANN[a]	$2,330.9	$ —	$ —
Justice	1,106.3	1,276.8	1,384.3
Lane Bryant	1,130.3	1,095.9	1,080.0
maurices	1,101.3	1,060.6	971.4
dressbarn	993.3	1,023.6	1,022.5
Catherines	333.3	346.0	332.4
Total net sales	$6,995.4	$4,802.9	$4,790.6

	Fiscal 2016	Fiscal 2015	Fiscal 2014
Operating income (loss):		(millions)	
ANN[a]	$ 13.3	$ —	$ —
Justice	29.0	(62.8)	99.3
Lane Bryant	20.6	(308.0)	(4.3)
maurices	105.6	125.9	86.0
dressbarn	(13.6)	10.7	39.4
Catherines	16.3	31.0	24.4
Unallocated acquisition and integration expenses	(77.4)	(31.7)	(34.0)
Total operating income (loss)	$ 93.8	$ (234.9)	$ 210.8

[a] The results of ANN for the post-acquisition period from August 22, 2015 to July 30, 2016 are included within the company's consolidated results of operations for Fiscal 2016.

Source: Ascena 10K for the fiscal year ended July 30, 2016.

EXHIBIT 3 Ascena Comparable Sales by Segment–Q2 Fiscal Year 2017

		Net Sales (millions) Three Months Ended	
	Comparable Sales	January 28, 2017	January 23, 2016
Ann Taylor	(9)%	$ 206.6	$ 227.8
LOFT	(2)%	401.6	409.7
Total Premium Fashion	(5)%	608.2	637.5
maurices	(8)%	274.5	291.6
dressbarn	(3)%	207.1	221.6
Total Value Fashion	(6)%	481.6	513.2
Lane Bryant	(5)%	269.8	282.3
Catherines	flat	77.5	81.3
Total Plus Fashion	(4)%	347.3	363.6
Justice	(1)%	311.1	327.5
Total Kids Fashion	(1)%	311.1	327.5
Total Company	(4)%	$ 1,748.2	$ 1,841.8

Ascena Retail Group, Inc.
Condensed Consolidated Statements of Operations (Unaudited)
(millions, except per share data)

| | Three Months Ended | | | |
	January 28, 2017	% of Net sales	January 23, 2016	% of Net sales
Net sales	$ 1,748.2	100.0%	$ 1,841.8	100.0%
Cost of goods sold	(802.4)	(45.9)%	(873.8	(47.4)%
Gross margin	945.8	54.1%	968.0	52.6%
Other costs and expenses:				
Buying, distribution and occupancy expenses	(320.1)	(18.3)%	(329.9)	(17.9)%
Selling, general and administrative expenses	(538.1)	(30.8)%	(549.5)	(29.8)%
Acquisition and integration expenses	(15.8)	(0.9)%	(16.0)	(0.9)%
Restructuring and other related charges	(20.2)	(1.2)%	—	—%
Depreciation and amortization expense	(96.3)	(5.5)%	(89.4)	(4.9)%
Operating loss	(44.7)	(2.6)%	(16.8)	(0.9)%
Interest expense	(25.0)	(1.4)%	(27.8)	(1.5)%
Interest income and other income (expense), net	0.4	—%	(0.8)	—%
Gain on extinguishment of debt	—	—%	0.8	—%
Loss before benefit for income taxes	(69.3)	(4.0)%	(44.6)	(2.4)%
Benefit for income taxes	34.1	2.0%	22.0	1.2%
Net loss	$ (35.2)	(2.0)%	$ (22.6)	(1.2)%
Net loss per common share:				
Basic	$ (0.18)		$ (0.12)	
Diluted	$ (0.18)		$ (0.12)	
Weighted average common shares outstanding:				
Basic	194.8		195.8	
Diluted	194.8		195.8	

Ascena Retail Group, Inc.
Condensed Consolidated Statements of Operations (Unaudited)
(millions, except per share data)

| | Six Months Ended | | | |
	January 28, 2017	% of Net Sales	January 23, 2016	% of Net Sales
Net sales	$ 3,426.6	100.0%	$ 3,513.8	100.0%
Cost of goods sold	(1,466.8)	(42.8)%	(1,643.1)	(46.8)%
Gross margin	1,959.8	57.2%	1,870.7	53.2%

continued

EXHIBIT 4 *Continued*

Ascena Retail Group, Inc. Condensed Consolidated Statements of Operations (Unaudited) (millions, except per share data)				
	Six Months Ended			
	January 28, 2017	% of Net sales	January 23, 2016	% of Net sales
Other costs and expenses:				
Buying, distribution and occupancy expenses	(640.7)	(18.7)%	(632.9)	(18.0)%
Selling, general and administrative expenses	(1,062.5)	(31.0)%	(1,036.2)	(29.5)%
Acquisition and integration expenses	(27.8)	(0.8)%	(58.5)	(1.7)%
Restructuring and other related charges	(32.1)	(0.9)%	—	—%
Depreciation and amortization expense	(190.2)	(5.6)%	(171.9)	(4.9)%
Operating income (loss)	6.5	0.2%	(28.8)	(0.8)%
Interest expense	(50.3)	(1.5)%	(48.3)	(1.4)%
Interest income and other income (expense), net	0.3	—%	(0.2)	—%
Gain on extinguishment of debt	—	—%	0.8	—%
Loss before benefit for income taxes	(43.5)	(1.3)%	(76.5)	(2.2)%
Benefit for income taxes	22.7	0.7%	35.8	1.0%
Net loss	$ (20.8)	(0.6)%	$ (40.7)	(1.2)%
Net loss per common share:				
Basic	$ (0.11)		$ (0.21)	
Diluted	$ (0.11)		$ (0.21)	
Weighted average common shares outstanding:				
Basic	194.6		190.3	
Diluted	194.6		190.3	

See accompanying notes: Results for the six months ended January 23, 2016 include the post-acquisition results of **ANN,** which was acquired on August 21, 2015. Accordingly, **ANN**'s results for the first two quarters of Fiscal 2016 have been included herein for the post-acquisition period from August 22, 2015 to January 30, 2016. The remainder of the Company's businesses ended the second quarter of Fiscal 2016 on January 23, 2016. The effect of **ANN**'s one-week reporting period difference is not material. All segments of the Company are on the same fiscal calendar as of the end of Fiscal 2016.

EXHIBIT 5 Consolidated Balance Sheets

Ascena Retail Group, Inc. Condensed Consolidated Balance Sheets (Unaudited) (millions)		
	January 28, 2017	July 30, 2016
ASSETS		
Current assets:		
Cash and cash equivalents	$ 299.5	$ 371.8
Inventories	676.1	649.3
Prepaid expenses and other current assets	192.8	218.9
Total current assets	1,168.4	1,240.0
Property and equipment, net	1,545.3	1,630.1
Goodwill	1,279.3	1,279.3

Ascena Retail Group, Inc.
Condensed Consolidated Balance Sheets (Unaudited) (millions)

	January 28, 2017	July 30, 2016
Other intangible assets, net	1,270.0	1,268.7
Other assets	96.2	88.2
Total assets	**$ 5,359.2**	**$ 5,506.3**
LIABILITIES AND EQUITY		
Current liabilities:		
Accounts payable	$ 464.0	$ 429.4
Accrued expenses and other current liabilities	354.4	420.3
Deferred income	141.6	110.0
Current portion of long term debt	—	54.0
Total current liabilities	960.0	1,013.7
Long-term debt, less current portion	1,532.0	1,594.5
Lease-related liabilities	369.2	387.1
Deferred income taxes	442.1	442.2
Other non-current liabilities	196.4	205.5
Total liabilities	3,499.7	3,643.0
Equity	1,859.5	1,863.3
Total liabilities and equity	**$ 5,359.2**	**$ 5,506.3**

See accompanying notes: Includes the impact of non-cash expenses associated with the purchase accounting adjustments of ANN's assets and liabilities to fair market value. For the three months and six months ended January 28, 2017, adjustments of $11.5 million and $22.5 million, respectively, primarily consist of depreciation and amortization associated with the write-up of ANN's customer relationships and property and equipment and other purchase accounting adjustments, which are primarily lease-related. For the three and six months ended January 23, 2016, adjustments of $29.9 million and $140.6 million, respectively, primarily consist of the impact of non-cash inventory expense associated with the purchase accounting adjustment of ANN's inventory to fair market value, and depreciation and amortization expense associated with the write-up of ANN's customer relationships and property and equipment. Reference is made to Note 2 of the unaudited condensed consolidated financial information included herein for a reconciliation of operating income on a GAAP basis to adjusted operating income.

EXHIBIT 6 Segment Information

Ascena Retail Group, Inc.
Segment Information (Unaudited)
(millions)

	Three Months Ended		Six Months Ended	
	January 28, 2017	January 23, 2016	January 28, 2017	January 23, 2016
Net sales:				
Premium Fashion	$ 608.2	$ 637.5	$ 1,187.4	$ 1,138.7
Value Fashion	481.6	513.2	985.7	1,043.3
Plus Fashion	347.3	363.6	665.0	698.9
Kids Fashion	311.1	327.5	588.5	632.9
Total net sales	$ 1,748.2	$ 1,841.8	$ 3,426.6	$ 3,513.8

continued

EXHIBIT 6 *Continued*

Ascena Retail Group, Inc. Segment Information (Unaudited) (millions)				
	Three Months Ended		Six Months Ended	
	January 28, 2017	January 23, 2016	January 28, 2017	January 23, 2016
Operating (loss) income:				
Premium Fashion	$ 22.7	$ (5.8)	$ 66.3	$ (53.9)
Value Fashion	(19.8)	(1.3)	(7.7)	33.7
Plus Fashion	(10.0)	(6.9)	(3.8)	(3.5)
Kids Fashion	(1.6)	13.2	11.6	53.4
Unallocated acquisition and integration expenses	(15.8)	(16.0)	(27.8)	(58.5)
Unallocated restructuring and other charges	(20.2)	—	(32.1)	—
Total operating (loss) income	$ (44.7)	$ (16.8)	$ 6.5	$ (28.8)
	Three Months Ended		Six Months Ended	
	January 28, 2017	January 23, 2016	January 28, 2017	January 23, 2016
Non-GAAP adjusted operating income:				
Premium Fashion	$ 34.2	$ 24.1	$ 88.8	$ 88.0
Value Fashion	(19.8)	(1.3)	(7.7)	33.7
Plus Fashion	(10.0)	(6.9)	(3.8)	(3.5)
Kids Fashion	(1.6)	13.2	11.6	53.4
Total adjusted operating income	$ 2.8	$ 29.1	$ 88.9	$ 171.6

Source: Ascena Second Quarter Report FY2017, http://www.businesswire.com/news/home/20170306006212/en/.

Commentary on the FY2017 financials so far had analysts noting the following: "Unfortunately, the company needs much of the cash flow to pay down the debt and the balance sheet is too levered to provide the margin of safety."[29]

Odds of Survival in Specialty Retail?

At the conference call for the second quarter results in 2017, Ascena COO Brian Lynch said

We really are seeing a paradigm shift in retail and the operational changes necessary to reposition for success are complex and comprehensive. . . . Over multiple years Ascena has made significant investments in acquisitions, in capital equipment and in operational realignment. As a result of that strategy, we've achieved a number of cornerstones. We certainly have built scale. We're the third-largest specialty retailer and the largest women's specialty retailer.

Importantly, despite that focus, we're relatively a diverse brand portfolio. Our shared services model enables our merchandising organizations to really focus on the front end of omni-channel and the customers they serve. . . . In short, we're working to deliver capabilities for our brands that are better, faster and more cost-efficient than our competitors . . . we're working hard to adopt a mindset of continuous improvement across the business, across all of our functions at all levels of responsibilities. I certainly believe that's the kind of results-oriented operational culture necessary for sustainable success.[30]

However, as all specialty retail industry watchers note, "earnings are soft, traffic is soft, and customers are cautious."[31] Ascena may have made an expensive, risky acquisition at the wrong time. The increased debt it now has to carry might make it a takeover target itself as a larger competitor would gain a large store count and additional synergies, which would allow for the repayment or replacement of debt with better terms over time.[32] It appears the odds of survival in specialty retail are not favorable, even for top companies.

ENDNOTES

1. Gustafson, Krystina. 2017. Retail bankruptcies march toward post-recession high. *CNBC.com*, March 31, http://www.cnbc.com/2017/03/31/retail-bankruptcies-march-toward-post-recession-high.html.

2. Fader, Peter, and Cohen, Mark A. 2017. Are retailers facing a coming "tsunami"? *Knowledge @ Wharton,* April 6, http://knowledge.wharton.upenn.edu/article/are-retailers-facing-a-coming-tsunami/.

3. Ewen, Lara. 2017. The 7 trends that will shape apparel retail in 2017. *RetailDive.com,* January 4, http://www.retaildive.com/news/the-7-trends-that-will-shape-apparel-retail-in-2017/433249/.

4. Fader and Cohen, 2017.

5. Zacks Equity Research, 2015. ANN Inc. (ANN) stands on the back foot as 2015 unveils. *Zacks,* January 6, http://www.zacks.com/stock/news/159433/ann-inc-ann-stands-on-the-back-foot-as-2015-unveils?source=sa.

6. The Frugal Prof. 2017. Ascena: No end in sight for shareholder pain. *SeekingAlpha,* March 23, https://seekingalpha.com/article/4057390-ascena-end-sight-shareholder-pain; Longauer, Peter, 2017. Retail discount: Ascena. *SeekingAlpha,* February 13, https://seekingalpha.com/article/4045321-retail-discount-ascena; Arnold, Josh. 2016. Ascena retail group is an unmitigated disaster, *SeekingAlpha,* December 27, https://seekingalpha.com/article/4032967-ascena-retail-group-unmitigated-disaster.

7. Victoria's Secret is a division of L Brands (formerly Limited Brands), which also operates Pink (a subbrand of Victoria's Secret focused on sleepwear and intimate apparel for high school and college students), Bath & Body Works, C.O. Bigelow (personal beauty, body, and hair products), The White Barn Candle Co. (candles and home fragrances), Henri Bendel (high-fashion women's clothing), and La Senza (lingerie sold in Canada and worldwide).

8. Abercrombie & Fitch, as of 2015, had three brand divisions in addition to the flagship Abercrombie & Fitch stores: abercrombie (the brand name is purposely lowercase) for kids ages 7 to 14; Hollister Co. for southern California surf-lifestyle teens; and Gilly Hicks: Sydney, launched in 2008, specializing in women's intimate apparel. RUEHL No. 925, launched in 2004 with more sophisticated apparel for ages 22 to 35, closed in 2010.

9. U.S. Census Bureau. Monthly Retail Trade and Food Services NAICS Codes, Titles, and Descriptions, www.census.gov/svsd/www/artsnaics.html.

10. According to the American Marketing Association (AMA), a brand is a "name, term, sign, symbol or design, or a combination of them intended to identify the goods and services of one seller or group of sellers and to differentiate them from those of other sellers. . . . Branding is not about getting your target market to choose you over the competition, but it is about getting your prospects to see you as the only one that provides a solution to their problem." A good brand will communicate this message clearly and with credibility, motivating the buyer by eliciting some emotion that inspires future loyalty. From marketing.about.com/cs/brandmktg/a/whatisbranding.htm.

11. Turner, J. 2007. Go forth and go out of business. *Slate,* February 26, www.slate.com/id/2160668.

12. Lee, G. 2007. Chico's outlines plan to improve results. *Women's Wear Daily,* March 8: 5.

13. The responsibilities of these positions include "creative vision" for the brand: marketing materials, store design, and overall merchandising (developing product, ensuring production efficiency, monitoring store inventory turnover, and adjusting price points as needed).

14. LaMonica, P. R. 2017. Abercrombie & Fitch's latest sale may be itself. *Money.com,* May 10, http://money.cnn.com/2017/05/10/investing/abercrombie-fitch-takeover-rumors/index.html.

15. *Columbus Business First.* 2007. Limited Brands cutting 530 jobs. June 22, columbus.bizjournals.com/columbus/stories/2007/06/18/daily26.html.

16. Jones, S. M. 2007. Sweetest spots in retail. *Knight Ridder Tribune Business News,* July 31: 1.

17. See, for instance, the website www.aginghipsters.com, a "source for trends, research, comment and discussion" about this group.

18. Talbots Inc. 2006. Talbots completes the acquisition of the J.Jill Group. *Business Wire,* May 3, phx.corporate-ir.net/phoenix.zhtml?c565681&p5irol-newsArticle&ID5851481.

19. Protess. B. 2012. After rejecting higher offers, Talbots agrees to $369 million buyout. *New York Times Dealbook,* May 31, dealbook.nytimes.com/2012/05/31/after-rejecting-higher-offer-talbots-agrees-to-369-million-buyout/.

20. Lomax, A. 2013. Chilly post-holiday news from Coldwater Creek. *Motley Fool,* January 15, www.fool.com/investing/general/2013/01/15/chilly-post-holiday-news-from-coldwater-creek.aspx.

21. Palank, J. 2014. Coldwater Creek creditors group settle payment plan dispute. *Wall Street Journal,* July 11, http://www.wsj.com/articles/coldwater-creek-creditors-group-settle-payment-plan-dispute-1405098894.

22. Lutz, A. 2011. How Talbots grew—and lost—its customers. *Bloomberg Businessweek,* June 16, www.businessweek.com/magazine/content/11_26/b4234025390837.htm.

23. Some marketers believe that the boomers are a bifurcated demographic. Although the boomer market encompasses those born from 1946 to 1964, boomers born between 1946 and 1954 have slightly different life experiences than those born between 1955 and 1964 have.

24. Caplinger, D. 2012. Was 2012 Coldwater Creek's turning point? *Motley Fool,* December 14, www.fool.com/investing/general/2012/12/24/was-coldwater-creeks-2012-turning-point.aspx; Caplinger, D. 2013. Can Coldwater Creek stay hot in 2013? *Motley Fool,* January 7, www.fool.com/investing/general/2013/01/07/can-coldwater-creek-stay-hot-in.aspx; Lomax, A. 2013. Chilly post-holiday news from Coldwater Creek. *Motley Fool,* January 15, www.fool.com/investing/general/2013/01/15/chilly-post-holiday-news-from-coldwater-creek.aspx.

25. Moore, B. 2014. New Ann Taylor brand Lou & Grey taps into active-wear fashion trend. *LA Times,* April 29, http://www.latimes.com/fashion/alltherage/la-ar-new-ann-taylor-brand-lou-grey-taps-into-active-wear-fashion-trend-20140428-story.html\#page=1.

26. See Slideshow Investor Presentation, January 18, 2017, https://seekingalpha.com/article/4038010-ascena-retail-group-asna-investor-presentation-slideshow.

27. Ascena Retail Group's Q2 2017 Results–Earnings Call Transcript, March 6, 2017, https://seekingalpha.com/article/4052526-ascena-retail-groups-asna-ceo-david-jaffe-q2-2017-results-earnings-call-transcript?part=single.

28. Slideshow Investor Presentation, January 18, 2017.

29. The Frugal Prof, 2017.

30. Ascena Retail Group's Q2 2017 Results.

31. The Frugal Prof, 2017.

32. Longauer, Peter. 2017.

Competitors
  hardball attack methods, 255
  intensity of rivalry among, 54–55, 56, 58–59
Complements, 60–61
  conflicts among, 60
  defined, 60
Compliance-based ethics programs, 350–351
Conflict-inducing techniques, 407–411
  devil's advocacy, 410
  dialectical inquiry, 411
  groupthink and its prevention, 123–124, 407–410
  to improve decision making, 410
Conflict minerals, 46, 290
Conflict resolution, 324
Conglomerate structure. *See* Business groups; Holding company structure
Consolidation strategy, 163–164
Contracts, cultural differences in negotiating, 221
Co-opetition, 259–260
Coordination
  in boundaryless organizational design, 322
  of extended value chain, 153–154
Core competencies, 175–178
  Amazon, 177–178
  defined, 176
  Fujifilm, 177
  IBM Watson Health, 177
  leveraging, 175–178
Corporate Citizenship poll, 19
Corporate credos, 352
Corporate culture. *See* Organizational culture
Corporate entrepreneurship (CE), 13, 373–385
  in case analysis, 415
  defined, 373
  dispersed approaches, 374, 375–377
  diversification in, 186, 193–194
  focused approaches, 373–375
  measuring success of, 377–378
  real options analysis (ROA), 378–381
Corporate gadflies, 292
Corporate governance, 13, 278–292. *See also* Board of directors (BOD); Chief executive officers (CEOs); Strategic control
  aligning interests of owners and managers, 280–285
  aspect of strategic control, 268
  cynicism regarding, 16–17
  defined, 16, 278
  external control mechanisms, 286–290
    auditors, 287–288
    banks and stock analysts, 288
    defined, 286
    market for corporate control, 287
    media, 290

public activists, 290
    regulatory bodies, 288–289, 430
  international perspective, 290–292
    business groups, 291–292, 309
    expropriation of minority shareholders, 291
    governance reform in Japan, 289
    Japanese governance reform, 289
    principal-principal (PP) conflicts, 290–291
  key elements, 16
  problems, 278–279
  separation of owners and management, 279–280
  Tesco, 267
  United Way Worldwide (UWW), C218, C219, C223–C224
Corporate-level strategy, 12–13, 172–201
  in case analysis, 413–414
  defined, 174
  diversification. *See* Diversification
  mergers and acquisitions. *See* Acquisitions; Mergers and acquisitions
Corporate social responsibility (CSR). *See* Social responsibility
Corporations. *See also entries beginning with* "Corporate"
  CEO compensation, 17, 89–90, 280, 285
  defining, 279
Cost focus strategy
  defined, 150
  erosion of cost advantage, 151–152
Cost reduction
  versus adaptation, 216–217
  as motive for international expansion, 209
  through relational systems, 323
Cost surgery, 164
Counterfeiting
  counterfeit drugs, 212, 213
  defined, 212
Country Risk Rating, 211
Creativity
  and learning organizations, 347–348
  Pixar, C87–C88
Cross-functional skills, 319
Cross-functional teams, 325
Crossing the Chasm (Moore), 383
Crowdfunding
  defined, 243
  Kickstarter, C68–C74
  lax rules for, 244
  potential downsides, 243–244
Crowdsourcing
  Apple in retail rental market, 53
  for differentiation ideas, 148
  examples, 79
  nature of, 79
  perils of, 79–80
CSR (corporate social responsibility). *See* Social responsibility
Culture. *See* Organizational culture
Culture of dissent, 347–348

Currency risk, 212–213
Current ratio, 91, 399, 421–422, 427
Customer perspective
  in balanced scorecard, 93
  defined, 93
Customers
  and corporate social responsibility (CSR), 19–20
  innovation from interactions with, 147
  integrated into value chain, 78–80
Customer service organizations, 147

D

Data analytics, 47–49
  Caterpillar Inc., 153
  defined, 47
  in differentiation strategy, 148
  to enhance organizational control, 277
  IBM, 177
  to increase employee retention, 116
  monitoring government expenditures, 49
Days' sales in inventory, 91, 399, 424, 427
Days' sales in receivables, 91, 399, 424, 427
Debt-equity ratio, 91, 399, 423, 427
Decision making, 404–411
  analysis-decision-action cycle, 411–415
  conflict-inducing techniques, 407–411
  heretical questions in, 406–407
  integrative thinking in, 404–406
  intended *vs.* realized strategy, 10–11
Decline stage
  defined, 163
  examples, 164
  and new technology, 164
  strategic options, 163–164
Demand conditions
  defined, 205
  in diamond of national advantage, 205–206, 207
  in India, 207
Demographic segment of the general environment
  defined, 43
  impact on industries, 48
  key trends and events, 42
  Millennials, 107, 109–110, 118
  older workers, 43, 44–45
Designing the organization, 335. *See also* Organizational design
Developing human capital, 107–108. *See also* Human capital
  evaluating, 113–114
  mentoring, 112
  monitoring progress, 112–113
  widespread involvement, 110–112
Devil's advocacy, 410
Devil's Dictionary (Bierce), 279
Dialectical inquiry, 411
Diamond of national advantage, 205–208
  conclusions on, 206–208
  defined, 205

Human capital—*Cont.*
  technology for leveraging, 124–128
    codifying knowledge, 126–128
    electronic teams, 125–126
    networks for information sharing, 124–125
  value creation through, 128
Human Equation, The (Pfeffer), 314
Human resource management
  in boundaryless organizations, 323
  defined, 76
  in differentiation strategy, 146
  examples, 76–77
  in overall cost leadership, 142

I

Imitation
  causal ambiguity, 86–87
  in differentiation strategy, 149
  difficult for competitors, 84–87, 88
  of focus strategy, 152
  path dependency, 85–86
  physical uniqueness, 85
  social complexity, 87
Imitative new entry, 248–249
Inbound logistics
  defined, 73
  in differentiation strategy, 146
  just-in-time systems, 73
  in overall cost leadership, 142
Incentives, 271–273
  CEO compensation, 17, 89–90, 280, 285
  creating effective programs, 273
  in employee retention, 115, 130
  financial and nonfinancial, 115, 130
  for managers, 285
  motivating with, 271–273
  potential downsides, 272–273
Income share agreements, 63
Incremental innovations
  continuum, 364
  defined, 363
India
  business groups in, 309
  diamond of national advantage for software, 207–208
  Dream Mall, 203
  location of employee learning and financial performance, 317
  Tata Starbucks Pvt. Ltd., C165–C172
Industry, defined, 50
Industry analysis
  caveats on using, 59–61
  complements concept, 60–61
  effect of Internet on five forces, 55–59
  financial ratios, 92–93
  five-forces model, 50–59
  global casino industry, C3–C6
  industry, defined, 50
  industry information sources, 429, 432–433

  intensity of rivalry among competitors, 54–55, 56, 58–59, 255
  and low-profit industries, 59, 61
  static analysis problem, 60
  strategic groups, 61–64
  time horizon, 61
  zero-sum game assumption, 59–60
Industry life cycle, 159–166
  decline stage, 163–164
  defined, 159
  growth stage, 161
  importance of, 159–160
  introduction stage, 161
  maturity stage, 162
  overview, 160
  and turnaround strategies, 164–165
Informational control
  aspect of strategic control, 268
  defined, 269
  in traditional approach to strategic control, 268
Information power, 340
Information technology (IT)
  in boundaryless organizations, 322–323
  for extended value chain, 153–154
  role in enhancing value, 77–78
Initial public offerings (IPOs), 288, C25
Innovation, 360–373
  adapting to loss of star employee, 371
  Apple Inc., 4–5, 41, 129, 130, 275, 365, 369, C195–C200
  Avon Products, C135
  in balanced scorecard, 94
  Blackberry Limited, C251–C252, C254–C255
  Boston Beer Company, C144, C145–C146, C153
  challenges of, 364–365
  collaboration in, 370
  cultivating skills for, 365–367
  customer service interactions and, 147
  defined, 362
  defining scope of, 368
  Dippin' Dots, C58, C59–C60
  eBay, C227, C233–C234
  as entrepreneurial strategy, 382–383
  Fair Oaks Farms, 368
  Ford Motor Company, C107–C109, C114–C118
  General Electric (GE), 375
  General Motors (GM), C120, C124–C126
  Google Inc., 361, 365
  innovator's DNA, 367
  Jamba Juice, C245–C246, C248
  JetBlue Airways Corporation, C209–C212
  Johnson & Johnson, C130
  Kraft Heinz, 362, 363
  managing pace of, 369
  McDonald's Corporation, C7–C8, C10–C12

  Procter & Gamble (P&G), 18, 365, 366, C189–C190, C191
  real options analysis (ROA), 378–381
  Samsung Electronics Co., C185–C187
  staffing to capture value from, 369–370
  Tesla, 385
  types, 362–364
  United Way Worldwide (UWW), C218, C219, C224–C226
  unsuccessful, value of, 370–373
  Weight Watchers International Inc., C173–C175, C180–C181
Innovation and learning perspective
  in balanced scorecard, 94
  defined, 94
Innovation paradox, 8
Innovativeness, 382–383
Inputs, increased cost of, 144
Intangible resources, 82–83. *See also* Intellectual assets
  defined, 82
  types, 82
Integrative thinking
  in case analysis, 394, 404–406
  defined, 404
  Red Hat, Inc., 406
  stages of, 405
Integrity-based ethics programs, 350–351
Intellectual assets, 102–136
  analysis of, 12
  Apple Inc., 129
  in case analysis, 413
  development costs, 129
  Dippin' Dots, C64–C67
  knowledge economy and, 104–106, 124–128
  legal battles over, 129
  Microsoft Corporation, 212
  protecting, 128–130
    dynamic capabilities, 129–130
    intellectual property rights, 129
  Samsung Electronics Co., 129
  technology in leveraging, 124–128. *See also* Technology
  Zynga, C17–C18
Intellectual capital. *See also* Intellectual assets
  defined, 106
  explicit knowledge, 106
  human capital as foundation of, 107–118
  and market *vs.* book value, 105–106
  social capital, 106, 118–124
  tacit knowledge, 106
  technology to leverage, 124–128
Intellectual property rights, 129
Intended strategy, 10
Intensity of rivalry among competitors in an industry
  competitive analysis checklist, 56
  defined, 54

for enhancing revenue and differentiation, 178–179

examples, 176

for market power, 176, 179–182

pooled negotiating power, 176, 179

vertical integration, 176, 179–182

Relational approach. *See* Boundaryless organizational designs; Emotional intelligence (EI)

Rents, 88–89

Replacement cost, employee, 89

Research and development, 159–160

Research insights

boomerang employees, 111

employee learning and financial performance, 317

innovation and customer insights, 147

myths about older workers, 44–45

passion and motivation process, 274

Resource-based view (RBV) of the firm, 81–90

Blockbuster bankruptcy, 88

defined, 81

overview, 82

profit generation and distribution, 88–90

sustainable competitive advantage, 83–88

availability of substitutes, 84, 87–88

inimitability, 84–87, 88

rarity, 84, 88

value, 83–84, 88

types of resources, 81–83

Resource similarity, 254–255

Restructuring

defined, 182

in unrelated diversification, 176, 182–183

Retailers and retailing

buying power for retail space, 53

differentiation strategy, 252

Dream Mall (India), 203

online retailers opening stores, 95–96

Return on assets (ROA), 91, 399, 425, 427

Return on book assets, 426

Return on book equity, 426

Return on equity (ROE), 91, 399, 425–426, 427

Revenue

diversification to enhance, 178–179

in growth stage, 161

miscalcultating sources of, 154

Reverse innovation

defined, 210

as motive for international expansion, 210

Reverse positioning, 162

Reward power, 340

Reward systems, 271–273

CEO compensation, 17, 89–90, 280, 285

creating effective programs, 273

defined, 271

in employee retention, 115, 130

in ethical organizations, 352–353

evolving from boundaries, 277–278

for managers, 285

motivating with, 271–273

potential downsides, 272–273

Risk reduction

through diversification, 185–186

as motive for international expansion, 210

Risk-sharing problem, 280

Risk taking, 382, 384–385

ROA (return on assets), 91, 399, 425, 427

ROE (return on equity), 91, 399, 425–426, 427

Role models, 351–352

Role playing, in case analysis, 395–396

Romantic view of leadership, 4–5

Rule of law, 211–212

Russia

Campbell Soup Company, C92–C93

Country Risk Rating, 211

S

Sales. *See* Marketing and sales

Sarbanes-Oxley Act of 2002, 42, 45, 353

SBU structure. *See* Strategic business unit (SBU) structure

Scenario analysis

defined, 40

PPG Industries, 40

Scent of a Mystery (film), 248

Self-awareness, 342

Self-regulation, 342–343

Sell-offs, 191n

Service representatives, 147

Services

complements, 60–61

defined, 75

in differentiation strategy, 146

in overall cost leadership, 142

substitute. *See* Substitute products and services

value-chain analysis, 80–81

Setting a direction, 335

Shareholder activism, 283–285

defined, 283

eBay, C227–C228, C236–C237

institutional investor, 283–285

Procter & Gamble (P&G), C189

rise of privately owned firm, 288

shareholder proposals, 292

Shareholders

activism. *See* Shareholder activism

alignment with management, 280–285, 292

and balanced scorecard, 93–95

expropriation of minority, 291

of privately owned firms, 288

separation from management in corporate governance, 279–280

stakeholders *vs.*, 8–9, 17–18

Shareholder value, in acquisitions, 190

Sharing activities

cost savings, 178

defined, 178

in related diversification, 176, 178

Shirking, 287

Short-term perspective, 7–8

Short-term solvency ratios

cash ratio, 91, 399, 422, 427

current ratio, 91, 399, 421–422, 427

quick ratio, 91, 399, 422, 427

Simple organizational structure, 302–303

advantages and disadvantages, 304

defined, 304

Social capital, 118–124

to attract and retain talent, 119

in boundaryless organizations, 324

bridging relationships, 121, 122, 124

career success and, 122–123

closure relationships, 121, 122, 124

defined, 106

for new ventures, 245

potential downsides, 123–124

and social networks, 119–123

value creation through, 128

Social complexity, 87

Social network analysis, 120–122

Social networks, 119–123

benefits for firms, 123

bridging relationships, 121, 122, 124

closure relationships, 121, 122, 124

implications for careers, 122–123

potential downside, 123–124

Social responsibility, 19–20. *See also* Environmental sustainability; Ethical organizations; Ethics; Sustainable competitive advantage

defined, 19

theaters of practice, 19

Social skill, 342, 343

Sociocultural segment of the general environment

defined, 43

educational attainment of women, 43

impact on industries, 48

key trends and events, 42

Spec. Ops (McRaven), 14

Speculation, in case analysis, 394

Spin-off, 191n

Split-ups, 191n

Stakeholder management. *See also* Environmental sustainability; Social responsibility

alternative perspectives, 17–18

defined, 17

obligation paradox, 8–9, 17–18

zero-sum game thinking, 17–18

Stakeholders

and balanced scorecard, 93–95

defined, 7

generation and distribution of profits, 88–90

key groups, 18

shareholders *vs.*, 8–9, 17–18

in strategic management process, 7

Standard financial statements, 418

Standard & Poor's 500 Index, 17, 20–21, 105, 285

Venture capitalists, 242–243
Vertical integration, 176, 179–182
  benefits and risks, 179–181
  defined, 179
  examples, 180–181, 182
  Tesla, 180
  transaction cost perspective, 181–182
Vested interest in the status quo, 338
Virtual organizations, 314, 320–321
  challenges and risks, 321
  defined, 320
  pros and cons, 321
Vision, 24–25
  defined, 24
  entrepreneurial, 246
  organizational, 24–25
Vision statement, 24–25
  compared to mission statement, 25
  examples, 24–25
  problems, 25

W

Wall Street Journal, 47, 119, 256, 290
Weight loss
  employer incentives for, 130
  Weight Watchers International Inc.,
    C173–C183
Wholly owned subsidiaries
  benefits, 229
  defined, 229
  risks and limitations, 229
Win-lose solutions, 323
Win-win solutions, 323
Wisdom of Teams, The (Smith), 322
Women
  Avon Products woman-centered causes,
    C141, C142
  beer marketing and, 166
  on boards of directors, 283, 284
  educational attainment, 43

Working Knowledge, 352
World Economic Forum Global Report, 212
World Trade Organization (WTO)
  China becomes member, C234
  report on production, 214–215
Worldwide functional structure, 303, 312
Worldwide holding company structure, 303
Worldwide matrix structure, 303, 312
Worldwide product division structure,
    303, 312
Written case analysis, 404

Z

Zero-sum game, 59–60
  defined, 59
  threat of substitutes, 307